Race Law

Race Law

Cases, Commentary, and Questions

FIFTH EDITION

F. Michael Higginbotham

Dean Joseph Curtis Professor of Law
University of Baltimore School of Law

CAROLINA ACADEMIC PRESS

Durham, North Carolina

ISBN   978-1-5310-1863-4
e-ISBN   978-1-5310-1864-1
LCCN   2020937876

Carolina Academic Press
700 Kent Street
Durham, NC 27701
Telephone (919) 489-7486
Fax (919) 493-5668
www.caplaw.com

Printed in the United States of America

Dedication

This book is dedicated to the memory of Judge A. Leon Higginbotham, Jr.,[1] "Uncle Leon" as I called him,[2] whose life and work represent a commitment to racial justice for all. During his professional career as a lawyer, teacher, and judge, Leon Higginbotham often spoke for those who needed it most—the poor, the powerless, and the hopeless. As a result, he provided inspiration to many and the belief in a better tomorrow. In recognition of Leon Higginbotham's values and steadfastness, many referred to him as the conscience of the American judiciary on issues relating to race.

Preparation for this book began in 1995 as a joint project between Leon Higginbotham and me. It was a project we discussed for more than a decade but one that had been delayed due to job demands and time constraints. After Leon Higginbotham retired from the federal bench in 1993, I was determined to go forward with this project. This co-authorship was an outgrowth of our close personal and professional relationship. Leon Higginbotham served as a second father to me providing guidance, support, and love. Our working relationship began in 1974 and included my service as a research assistant on Shades of Freedom: Racial Politics and Presumptions of the American Legal Process, co-author of three law review articles, and co-teacher of Race and the Law classes at the University of Pennsylvania and

---

1. For articles honoring the work of A. Leon Higginbotham, Jr., *see* Gates, *Remembering Leon*, VI Harv. J. Afr. Am. Pol. 1 (2000); Nye, *Harvard Farewell*, VI Harv. J. Afr. Am. Pol. 5 (2000); Sellers, *Working With the Judge*, VI Harv. J. Afr. Am. Pol. 7 (2000); Higginbotham, *Promises Kept*, VI Harv. J. Afr. Am. Pol. 11 (2000); Chon, *The Mentor and His Message*, 33 Loy. L.A. L. Rev. 973 (2000); Adams, Sinins & Yueh, *A Life Well Lived: Remembrances of Judge A. Leon Higginbotham, Jr.—His Days, His Jurisprudence, and His Legacy*, 33 Loy. L.A. L. Rev. 987 (2000); Higginbotham & Anderson, *Who Will Carry the Baton?*, 33 Loy. L.A. L. Rev. 1015 (2000); Costilo, *An Unforgettable Year Clerking For Judge Higginbotham*, 33 Loy. L.A. L. Rev. 1009 (2000); Higginbotham, *A Man for All Seasons*, 16 Harv. B.L. L.J. 7 (2000); Fitts, *The Complicated Ingredients of Wisdom and Leadership*, 16 Harv. B.L. L.J. 17 (2000); Green & Franklin-Suber, *Keeping Thurgood Marshall's Promise—A Venerable Voice For Equal Justice*, 16 Harv. B.L. L.J. 27 (2000); Higginbotham, *Saving the Dream for All*, 26 Hum. Rights 23 (1999); Becker, *In Memoriam: A. Leon Higginbotham, Jr.*, 112 Harv. L. Rev. 1813 (1999); Ogletree, *In Memoriam: A. Leon Higginbotham, Jr.*, 112 Harv. L. Rev. 1818 (1999); N. Jones, *In Memoriam: A Leon Higginbotham, Jr.*, 112 Harv. L. Rev. 1818 (1999); E. Jones, *In Memoriam: A. Leon Higginbotham, Jr.*, 112 Harv. L. Rev. 1823 (1999); Norton, *In Memoriam: A. Leon Higginbotham, Jr.*, 112 Harv. L. Rev. 1829 (1999); Hocker, *A. Leon Higginbotham: A Legal Giant*, 13 Nat. Bar Assoc. Mag. 16 (1999); and Brennan, *Tribute to Judge A. Leon Higginbotham, Jr.*, 9 Law & Ineq. 383 (1991).

2. Although Leon Higginbotham has no brothers or sisters, I always refer to him as my Uncle even though he and my Dad are cousins. In the Higginbotham Family, it is customary to refer to cousins of one's parents who are from the same generation as Uncle or Aunt, consistent with a tradition followed by some black families with southern roots.

New York University. Some of the original material contained in this book was initially drafted or edited by Leon Higginbotham.

Upon Leon Higginbotham's death in 1998, I decided to complete the project we started together. While my name appears as the sole author, the idea for this book and its earlier development represent a collaborative effort of Higginbotham and Higginbotham.

Summary of Contents

Table of Contents	xvii
Table of Cases	xli
Table of Authorities	li
Foreword	lvii
Preface	lxxi
Acknowledgments	lxxiii

Part One • Analysis and Framework

I.	Introduction	3
II.	The Racial Prejudices That Judges Share	4
	A. Introduction	4
	B. Background on *Mann*	4
	C. *State v. Mann*, 13 N.C. 263 (1829)	5
	D. Commentary on *Mann*	8
	E. Explaining Judge Thomas Ruffin	17
	F. Judge Thomas Ruffin's Rough Drafts of Mann	25
	G. Questions and Notes	30
	H. Point/Counterpoint	30
III.	Race Classification	30
	A. Introduction	30
	B. The Nature of Race	36
	C. Definitions of Race	44
	D. Preserving the Myth of White Racial Purity	55
	E. Background on *Hall*	59
	F. *People v. Hall*, 4 Cal. 399 (1854)	63
	G. Commentary on *Hall*	67
	H. Questions and Notes	68
	I. Point/Counterpoint	69

Part Two • Slavery

IV.	Slavery, Free Blacks, and the Constitution	79
	A. Introduction	79
	B. Race, Values, and the Constitution	80

C.	The 1787 Compromise on Slavery	92
D.	Questions and Notes	94
E.	Point/Counterpoint	94
V.	The Northern Approach to Free Blacks	95
A.	Introduction	95
B.	Background on *Crandall*	96
C.	*Crandall v. The State of Connecticut*, 10 Conn. Rep. 339 (1834)	96
D.	Commentary on *Crandall*	111
E.	Background on *Roberts*	111
F.	*Roberts v. The City of Boston*, 59 Mass. 198 (1850)	112
G.	Commentary on *Roberts*	118
H.	Questions and Notes	119
I.	Point/Counterpoint	119
VI.	The Southern Approach to Slavery and Free Blacks	119
A.	Introduction	119
B.	Background on *Hudgins*	120
C.	*Hudgins v. Wrights*, 11 Va. 134 (1806)	120
D.	Commentary on *Hudgins*	124
E.	Background on *Souther*	125
F.	*Souther v. The Commonwealth*, 48 Va. 673 (1851)	126
G.	Commentary on *Souther*	128
H.	Explaining Thomas Jefferson	129
I.	Explaining Judges St. George Tucker and George Wythe	131
J.	Questions and Notes	131
K.	Point/Counterpoint	133
VII.	Slavery, Free Blacks, and the United States Supreme Court	133
A.	Introduction	133
B.	Background on *Amistad*	138
C.	*The United States v. The Libellants and Claimants of the Schooner Amistad*, 40 U.S. 518 (1841)	140
D.	Commentary on *Amistad*	143
E.	Background on *Prigg*	144
F.	*Prigg v. The Commonwealth of Pennsylvania*, 41 U.S. 539 (1842)	148
G.	Commentary on *Prigg*	153
H.	Background on *Scott*	165
I.	*Scott v. Sandford*, 60 U.S. 393 (1857)	169
J.	Commentary on *Scott*	192
K.	Background on Justice Joseph Story	196
L.	Explaining Chief Justice Roger Taney	198
M.	Questions and Notes	198
N.	Point/Counterpoint	202

VIII. The Beginning of the End of Slavery   203
    A. Introduction   203
    B. The Life of John Brown   203
    C. Summary   204
    D. Questions and Notes   204
    E. Point/Counterpoint   204

Part Three • Reconstruction, Citizenship, and Sovereignty

IX. The Supreme Court's Betrayal of Reconstruction   213
    A. Introduction   213
    B. Background on *The Slaughterhouse Cases*   229
    C. *The Slaughterhouse Cases*, 16 Wall. 36 (1873)   238
    D. Commentary on *The Slaughterhouse Cases*   249
    E. Background on *Cruikshank*   254
    F. *United States v. Cruikshank*, 92 U.S. 542 (1875)   275
    G. Commentary on *Cruikshank*   279
    H. Background on *The Civil Rights Cases*   280
    I. *The Civil Rights Cases*, 109 U.S. 3 (1883)   281
    J. Commentary on *The Civil Rights Cases*   297
    K. Background on Justice Joseph Bradley   300
    L. Questions and Notes   301
X. Race and Citizenship   301
    A. Introduction   301
    B. Background on *Ozawa*   307
    C. *Ozawa v. United States*, 260 U.S. 178 (1922)   307
    D. Commentary on *Ozawa*   311
    E. Background on *Thind*   312
    F. *United States v. Thind*, 261 U.S. 204 (1923)   312
    G. Commentary on *Thind*   317
    H. Background on *De La Guerra*   318
    I. *People v. De La Guerra*, 40 Cal. 311 (1870)   320
    J. Commentary on *De La Guerra*   321
    K. Background on *Ping*   322
    L. *Ping v. United States*, 130 U.S. 581 (1889)   322
    M. Commentary on *Ping*   326
    N. Background on *Ark*   327
    O. *United States v. Ark*, 169 U.S. 649 (1898)   327
    P. Commentary on *Ark*   331
    Q. Background on *Korematsu*   332
    R. *Korematsu v. United States*, 323 U.S. 214 (1944)   332
    S. Commentary on *Korematsu*   342

T. Background on *Trump* 342

U. *Trump v. Hawaii*, 138 S. Ct. 2392 (2018) 343

V. Commentary on *Trump* 348

W. Questions and Notes 348

X. Point/Counterpoint 349

XI. Race, American Indians, and Sovereignty 360

A. Introduction 360

B. Background on *Johnson* 362

C. *Johnson v. McIntosh*, 21 U.S. 543 (1823) 362

D. Commentary on *Johnson* 368

E. Background on *Cherokee Nation* 369

F. *Cherokee Nation v. The State of Georgia*, 30 U.S. 1 (1831) 369

G. Commentary on *Cherokee Nation* 375

H. Background on *Elk* 388

I. *Elk v. Wilkins*, 112 U.S. 94 (1884) 388

J. Commentary on *Elk* 399

K. Background on Chief Justice John Marshall 401

L. Questions and Notes 402

M. Point/Counterpoint 402

Part Four • Segregation

XII. The Separate but Equal Doctrine 407

A. Introduction 407

B. Background on *Strauder* 407

C. *Strauder v. West Virginia*, 100 U.S. 303 (1880) 407

D. Commentary on *Strauder* 412

E. Background on *Plessy* 414

F. *Plessy v. Ferguson*, 163 U.S. 537 (1896) 417

G. Commentary on *Plessy* 429

H. Background on Justice Henry Billings Brown 431

I. Questions and Notes 431

J. Point/Counterpoint 432

XIII. Expanding the Separate but Equal Doctrine 432

A. Introduction 432

B. Background on *Berea College* 433

C. *Berea College v. The Commonwealth of Kentucky*, 211 U.S. 45 (1908) ... 435

D. Commentary on *Berea College* 439

E. Explaining Justice David Brewer 441

F. Questions and Notes 451

XIV. Racial Segregation and Housing 451

A. Introduction 451

B. Background on *Buchanan*   456

C. *Buchanan v. Warley*, 245 U.S. 60 (1917)   459

D. Commentary on *Buchanan*   464

E. Questions and Notes   466

XV. Racial Segregation and Interstate Commerce   467

A. Introduction   467

B. Background on *Morgan*   467

C. *Morgan v. Commonwealth of Virginia*, 328 U.S. 373 (1946)   467

D. Commentary on *Morgan*   478

E. Questions and Notes   478

XVI. Racial Segregation and State Action   478

A. Introduction   478

B. Background on *Shelley*   479

C. *Shelley v. Kraemer*, 334 U.S. 1 (1948)   479

D. Commentary on *Shelley*   486

E. Questions and Notes   487

XVII. Interpreting the Separate but Equal Doctrine   487

A. Introduction   487

B. Background on *Cumming*   488

C. *Cumming v. County Board of Education*, 175 U.S. 528 (1899)   492

D. Commentary on *Cumming*   496

E. Background on *Lum*   502

F. *Lum v. Rice*, 275 U.S. 78 (1927)   502

G. Commentary on *Lum*   508

H. Background on *Hernández*   508

I. *Hernández v. Texas*, 347 U.S. 475 (1954)   509

J. Commentary on *Hernández*   511

K. Background on Chief Justice William Howard Taft   511

L. Explaining Justice John Harlan   512

M. Questions and Notes   525

XVIII. Applying the Separate but Equal Doctrine   525

A. Introduction   525

B. Background on *Gaines*   530

C. *Gaines v. Canada*, 305 U.S. 337 (1938)   531

D. Commentary on *Gaines*   536

E. Background on Justice James McReynolds   538

F. Background on *McLaurin*   538

G. *McLaurin v. Oklahoma State Regents for Higher Education*,
    339 U.S. 637 (1950)   539

H. Commentary on *McLaurin*   541

I. Background on *Sweatt*   542

J. *Sweatt v. Painter*, 339 U.S. 629 (1950) 542

K. Commentary on *Sweatt* 544

L. Questions and Notes 545

XIX. Ending State-Mandated Segregation 545

A. Introduction 545

B. Background on *Brown I* 545

C. *Brown v. Board of Education (Brown I)*, 347 U.S. 483 (1954) 548

D. Commentary on *Brown I* 554

E. Background on Chief Justice Earl Warren 555

F. Questions and Notes 556

G. Point/Counterpoint 556

XX. Applying the *Brown* Rationale 559

A. Introduction 559

B. Background on *Loving* 560

C. Loving v. Virginia, 388 U.S. 1 (1966) 560

D. Commentary on *Loving* 566

E. Questions and Notes 569

Part Five • Attempted Eradication of Inequality

XXI. Race Conscious Remedies 571

A. Introduction 571

B. Background on *Brown II* 571

C. *Brown v. Board of Education (Brown II)*, 349 U.S. 294 (1955) 571

D. Commentary on *Brown II* 575

E. Background on *Milliken* 578

F. *Milliken v. Bradley*, 418 U.S. 717 (1974) 582

G. Commentary on *Milliken* 593

H. Background on *Adarand* 598

I. *Adarand Constructors, Inc. v. Peña*, 515 U.S. 200 (1995) 603

J. Commentary on *Adarand* 612

K. Background on *Grutter* 613

L. *Grutter v. Bollinger*, 539 U.S. 306 (2003) 613

M. Commentary on *Grutter* 633

N. Background on *Parents Involved* 636

O. *Parents Involved in Community Schools v. Seattle School District No. 1* (2007) 636

P. Commentary on *Parents Involved* 649

Q. Background on *Fisher* 652

R. *Fisher v. University of Texas*, 133 S.Ct. 2411 (2013) 653

S. Commentary on *Fisher* 660

T. Background on *Schuette* 661

U. *Schuette v. Coalition To Defend Affirmative Action*, 134 S.Ct.
   1623 (2014)   661
V. Commentary on *Schuette*   675
W. Background on Justice Ruth Bader Ginsburg   677
X. Background on Justice Sandra Day O'Connor   678
Y. Questions and Notes   679
Z. Point/Counterpoint   679

XXII. Maintaining Racial Inequity   689
A. Introduction   689
B. Background on *Washington*   690
C. *Washington v. Davis*, 426 U.S. 229 (1976)   690
D. Commentary on *Washington*   692
E. Background on *Batson*   695
F. *Batson v. Kentucky*, 476 U.S. 79 (1986)   696
G. Commentary on *Batson*   702
H. Background on *McCleskey*   703
I. *McCleskey v. Kemp*, 481 U.S. 279 (1987)   703
J. Commentary on *McCleskey*   720
K. Background on *Shaw*   722
L. *Shaw v. Reno*, 509 U.S. 630 (1993)   723
M. Commentary on *Shaw*   731
N. Background on *Shelby*   733
O. *Shelby County v. Holder*, 133 S. Ct. 2612 (2013)   735
P. Commentary on *Shelby*   755
Q. Background on *Ricci*   757
R. *Ricci v. DeStefano*, 129 S. Ct. 2658 (2009)   758
S. Commentary on *Ricci*   770
T. Background on Justice Thurgood Marshall   770
U. Questions and Notes   771
V. Point/Counterpoint   772

Part Six • Supreme Court Confirmation Racial Controversies

XXIII. Race, Values, and Justice Thomas   783
A. Introduction   783
B. Pre-Supreme Court Jurisprudence   784
C. Supreme Court Jurisprudence   802
D. Race, Gender, and the Thomas Confirmation Process   815
E. Background on Justice Clarence Thomas   817
F. Questions and Notes   818

XXIV. Race, Values, and Justice Alito   818
A. Introduction   818

B. Pre-Supreme Court and Supreme Court Jurisprudence   819
C. Background on Justice Samuel Alito   829
D. Questions and Notes   829

XXV. Race, Values, and Justice Sotomayor   829
A. Introduction   829
B. Pre-Supreme Court Jurisprudence   830
C. Background on Justice Sonia Sotomayor   832
D. Questions and Notes   833

Part Seven • Ongoing Racial Controversies

XXVI. Race and the Administration of Justice   835
A. Introduction   835
B. Race, Arrest, and Henry Louis Gates   835
C. Race and the O.J. Simpson Trial   837
D. Race and the Rodney King Beating   845
E. Race and the Death of Trayvon Martin   847
F. Race and the Death of Jordan Davis   853
G. Questions and Notes   855
H. Point/Counterpoint   855

XXVII. Race and Immigration   855
A. Introduction   855
B. History of Race and Immigration   856
C. Current Approach to Race and Immigration   863
D. Questions and Notes   867
E. Point/Counterpoint   867

XXVIII. Race and Politics   868
A. Introduction   868
B. History of Race and Politics   868
C. Current Approach to Race and Politics   872
D. Questions and Notes   876

Part Eight • Appendix

XXIX. Conclusion   877
XXX. Documents   883
A. The Constitution of the United States   883
B. The Earliest Protest against Slavery (February 18, 1688) 900
C. Declaration of the Causes and Necessity of Taking
    Up Arms (July 6, 1775)   901
D. The Declaration of Independence (July 4, 1776)   903
E. The Articles of Confederation (March 1, 1781)   907
F. The Northwest Ordinance (July 13, 1787)   908

G. The Fugitive Slave Act (1793)   910

H. The Missouri Compromise (1820)   911

I. The Fugitive Slave Act (1850)   912

J. The Emancipation Proclamation (January 1, 1863)   913

K. The Freedmen's Bureau (March 3, 1865)   915

L. Black Code of Mississippi (1865)   916

M. Indian Removal Act (May 28, 1830)   919

N. Executive Order 8802 (June 25, 1941)   920

O. Executive Order 9981 (July 26, 1948)   921

P. Southern Manifesto (March 1956)   922

Q. § 2000a of the Civil Rights Act of 1964
    (Public Accommodations)   922

R. § 2000d of Title VI of the Civil Rights Act of 1964
    (Federally Assisted Programs)   922

S. § 2000e-2 of Title VII of the Civil Rights Act of 1964
    (Employment)   922

T. Voting Rights Act of 1965   923

U. § 3601 of the Fair Housing Act of 1968 (Housing)   925

V. Restitution for World War II Internment of Japanese
    Americans and Aleuts (August 10, 1988)   926

W. Senate Resolution Apologizing for the Enslavement and
    Racial Segregation of African Americans (June 11, 2009)   926

XXXI. History Timeline   929

Index   943

Contents

Table of Cases   xli

Table of Authorities   li

Foreword   lvii

Preface   lxxi

Acknowledgments   lxxiii

Part One • Analysis and Framework

I. Introduction   3

II. The Racial Prejudices That Judges Share   4

    A. Introduction   4

    B. Background on *Mann*   4

    C. *State v. Mann*, 13 N.C. 263 (1829)   5

        1. Facts   5

        2. Opinion   6

        3. Holding   8

    D. Commentary on *Mann*   8

        1. *State v. Mann*: An "Objective" Legal Analysis or an Expression of Individual Whim and Social and Economic Bias?   8

        2. The Ruling of the Trial Court: Special Property versus Absolute Property in the Slave   10

        3. Precedent and Analogies: The Choices the Court Had   11

        4. The Role of the Court versus the Role of the Legislature   14

        5. Is There a Universal View of Slavery on Which Ruffin Could Rely?   14

        6. Remedies and Change through the Judicial Process   16

    E. Explaining Judge Thomas Ruffin   17

        1. Ruffin's Biography   17

        2. Ruffin's Petition for a Pardon   18

        3. Letter from His Father   20

        4. Ruffin's Treatment of His Slaves   21

            Paul Lawrence Dunbar, *We Wear the Mask*   22

            Martin H. Brinkley, *Judge Thomas Ruffin*   23

        5. Ruffin's Place in History   24

F. Judge Thomas Ruffin's Rough Drafts of Mann   25
    1. First Draft   25
    2. Second Draft   28
G. Questions and Notes   30
H. Point/Counterpoint   30
III. Race Classification   30
A. Introduction   30
        Michael J. Bamshad and Steve E. Olson, *Does Race Exist?*   31
B. The Nature of Race   36
        Charles R. Lawrence III, *The Id, The Ego, and Equal
        Protection: Reckoning with Unconscious Racism*   36
        Peggy McIntosh, *White Privilege: Unpacking the Invisible
        Knapsack*   39
        F. Michael Higginbotham, *Racism Less Pervasive, More
        Complex*   43
C. Definitions of Race   44
        A. Leon Higginbotham, Jr. and Barbara Kopytoff,
        *Racial Purity and Interracial Sex in the Law of Colonial
        and Antebellum Virginia*   44
D. Preserving the Myth of White Racial Purity   55
        A. Leon Higginbotham, Jr. and Barbara Kopytoff,
        *Racial Purity and Interracial Sex in the Law of Colonial
        and Antebellum Virginia*   55
E. Background on *Hall*   59
        D. Wendy Greene, *Title VII: What's Hair (and Other
        Race-Based Characteristics) Got to Do with It?*   59
        Ariela J. Gross, *Litigating Whiteness: Trials of Racial
        Determination in the Nineteenth-Century South*   61
F. *People v. Hall*, 4 Cal. 399 (1854)   63
    1. Facts   63
    2. Opinion   63
    3. Holding   67
G. Commentary on *Hall*   67
H. Questions and Notes   68
I. Point/Counterpoint   69
        Langston Hughes, *Cross*   69
        Kamaria A. Kruckenberg, *Multi-Hued America:
        The Case for the Recognition of a Multiethnic Identity in
        US Data Collection*   69
        Tanya Katerí Hernández, *"Multiracial" Discourse: Racial
        Classifications in an Era of Color-blind Jurisprudence*   72
        Roderick Harrison, *The Multiracial Responses on the Census Pose
        Unforeseen Risks to Civil Rights Enforcement and Monitoring*   72

Tseming Yang, *Choice and Fraud in Racial Identification;*
The Dilemma of Policing Race in Affirmative Action,
the Census, and a Color-Blind Society   73

Part Two • Slavery

IV. Slavery, Free Blacks, and the Constitution   79
  A. Introduction   79
  B. Race, Values, and the Constitution   80
    A. Leon Higginbotham, Jr., *The Bicentennial of the*
    Constitution: A Racial Perspective   80
  C. The 1787 Compromise on Slavery   92
  D. Questions and Notes   94
  E. Point/Counterpoint   94

V. The Northern Approach to Free Blacks   95
  A. Introduction   95
  B. Background on *Crandall*   96
  C. *Crandall v. The State of Connecticut*, 10 Conn. Rep. 339 (1834)   96
    1. Facts   96
    2. Trial Court Opinion   97
    3. Arguments on Appeal   102
    4. Opinion of Connecticut Supreme Court   108
    5. Holding   110
    6. Judge Daggett Dissenting   110
  D. Commentary on *Crandall*   111
  E. Background on *Roberts*   111
  F. *Roberts v. The City of Boston*, 59 Mass. 198 (1850)   112
    1. Facts   112
    2. Opinion of Massachusetts Supreme Court   115
    3. Holding   117
  G. Commentary on *Roberts*   118
    Leonard Levy and Harlan Phillips, *The Roberts Case: Source*
    of the Separate But Equal Doctrine   118
  H. Questions and Notes   119
  I. Point/Counterpoint   119

VI. The Southern Approach to Slavery and Free Blacks   119
  A. Introduction   119
  B. Background on *Hudgins*   120
  C. *Hudgins v. Wrights*, 11 Va. 134 (1806)   120
    1. Facts   120
    2. Trial Court Opinion   121
    3. Opinion of Virginia Court of Appeals   121

        4. Holding   124

   D. Commentary on *Hudgins*   124

        A. Leon Higginbotham, Jr. and F. Michael Higginbotham,
           "Yearning to Breathe Free": Legal Barriers Against and
           Options in Favor of Liberty in Antebellum Virginia   124

   E. Background on *Souther*   125

   F. *Souther v. The Commonwealth*, 48 Va. 673 (1851)   126

      1. Facts   126

      2. Trial Court Opinion   126

      3. Opinion of Virginia Court of Appeals   126

      4. Holding   128

   G. Commentary on *Souther*   128

        A. Leon Higginbotham, Jr. and Anne Jacobs,
           "The Law Only As An Enemy": The Legitimization of
           Racial Powerlessness Through the Colonial and Antebellum
           Criminal Laws of Virginia   128

   H. Explaining Thomas Jefferson   129

        William Jefferson Harrison, *The Ambivalent Statesman:*
           Did Thomas Jefferson Find Slavery Abhorrent   129

   I. Explaining Judges St. George Tucker and George Wythe   131

        A. Leon Higginbotham, Jr. and F. Michael Higginbotham,
           "Yearning to Breathe Free": Legal Barriers Against and
           Options in Favor of Liberty in Antebellum Virginia   131

   J. Questions and Notes   131

        Louis D. De Saussure, *Ryan's Mart Slave Auction Handbill*   132

   K. Point/Counterpoint   133

VII. Slavery, Free Blacks, and the United States Supreme Court   133

   A. Introduction   133

        Don Fehrenbacher, *Slavery, the Framers, and the Living*
           Constitution in Slavery and Its Consequences: The Constitution,
           Equality, and Race (Edited by Goldwin and Kaufman)   133

   B. Background on *Amistad*   138

        John T. Noonan, Jr., *The Antelope: the Ordeal of the*
           Recaptured Africans in the Administrations of James Monroe
           and John Quincy Adams   138

   C. *The United States v. The Libellants and Claimants of the*
     Schooner Amistad, 40 U.S. 518 (1841)   140

      1. Facts   140

      2. Opinion   140

      3. Holding   143

   D. Commentary on *Amistad*   143

   E. Background on *Prigg*   144

       Donald E. Lively, *The Constitution and Race* 144

  F. *Prigg v. The Commonwealth of Pennsylvania*, 41 U.S. 539 (1842) 148

    1. Facts 148

    2. Opinion 149

    3. Holding 152

  G. Commentary on *Prigg* 153

       William D. Green, *The Summer Christmas Came to*
         Minnesota: The Case of Eliza Winston, A Slave 153

       Donald E. Lively, *The Constitution and Race* 154

       John Hope Franklin, *From Slavery to Freedom:*
         A History of Negro Americans (Fifth Edition) 161

  H. Background on *Scott* 165

    1. Introduction 165

    2. Dred Scott's Travels 167

       Don Fehrenbacher, *The* Dred Scott *Case: Its Significance*
         in American Law 167

    3. *The* Dred Scott *Cases in the State Courts of Missouri* 167

       Don Fehrenbacher, *The* Dred Scott *Case: Its Significance*
         in American Law 167

  I. *Scott v. Sandford*, 60 U.S. 393 (1857) 169

    1. Facts 169

    2. Opinion 169

      a. Plea of Abatement 169

      b. Blacks and Citizenship 170

    3. Holding 183

    4. Additional Issues 184

    5. Justice McLean Dissenting 186

    6. Justice Curtis Dissenting 191

  J. Commentary on *Scott* 192

       G. Hudson, *Black Americans vs. Citizenship:*
         The Dred Scott *Decision* 192

       F. Michael Higginbotham, *After 150 Years, Worst Supreme*
         Court Decision Ever Continues to Haunt 194

  K. Background on Justice Joseph Story 196

       Geoffrey Stone, et al., *Justice Joseph Story* 196

       A. Leon Higginbotham, Jr., *The Life of the Law: Values,*
         Commitment, and Craftsmanship 197

  L. Explaining Chief Justice Roger Taney 198

  M. Questions and Notes 198

  N. Point/Counterpoint 202

VIII. The Beginning of the End of Slavery 203

  A. Introduction 203

B. The Life of John Brown   203

C. Summary   204

D. Questions and Notes   204

E. Point/Counterpoint   204

    John Hope Franklin, *From Slavery to Freedom: A History
        of Negro Americans* (5th Edition)   204

    Derrick Bell, *Race, Racism and American Law* (4th Edition)   207

Part Three • Reconstruction, Citizenship, and Sovereignty

IX. The Supreme Court's Betrayal of Reconstruction   213

A. Introduction   213

    John Hope Franklin, *From Slavery to Freedom: A History
        of Negro Americans* (5th Edition)   214

    1. Apology   216

    Associated Press, *Clinton to Think about Apology*   216

    2. Point/Counterpoint   217

    F. Michael Higginbotham, *"A Dream Deferred":
    Comparative and Practical Considerations for the
    Black Reparations Movement*   218

    Peter Flaherty, *Reparation Issue Is a Smoke Screen
    and a Shakedown*   221

    Stanley Crouch, *Money Isn't Cure for Blacks' Problems*   222

    Randall Robinson, *The Debt: What America Owes to Blacks*   223

    Michael Fletcher, *Reparations for Slavery Is No Laughing
    Matter*   226

    Adrienne Davis, *The Case for United States Reparations
    to African Americans*   228

B. Background on *The Slaughterhouse Cases*   229

    John Hope Franklin, *From Slavery to Freedom: A History
        of Negro Americans* (5th Edition)   229

    Thomas Brook, *Plessy v. Ferguson: A Brief History with
    Documents*   233

    Geoffrey Stone, et al., *Constitutional Law*   236

C. *The Slaughterhouse Cases*, 16 Wall. 36 (1873)   238

    1. Facts   238

    2. Opinion   238

      a. The Constitutional Issues   238

      b. The Thirteenth Amendment   240

      c. The Fourteenth Amendment   242

      d. Citizenship   243

      e. The Privileges and Immunities Clause   243

      f. The Property Clause   246

g. The Equal Protection Clause 246

h. State/Federal Relations 246

3. Holding 247

4. Justice Field Dissenting 247

a. The Thirteenth Amendment 247

b. The Fourteenth Amendment 248

5. Justice Bradley Dissenting 248

D. Commentary on *The Slaughterhouse Cases* 249

D. Marvin Jones, *No Time for Trumpets: Title VII, Equality, and the Fin de Siecle* 249

Charles Warren, *The Supreme Court in United States History* 250

David S. Bogen, *Slaughter-House Five: Views of the Case* 251

E. Background on *Cruikshank* 254

Peggy Cooper Davis, *Introducing Robert Smalls* 254

W. David Wiseman, Jr., *White Crimes: American History and the Case for African-American Reparations* 257

Lewis Allan, *Strange Fruit* 259

Charles Lane, *The Day Freedom Died: The Colfax Massacre, the Supreme Court, and the Betrayal of Reconstruction* 259

F. *United States v. Cruikshank*, 92 U.S. 542 (1875) 275

1. Facts 275

2. Opinion 276

3. Holding 279

G. Commentary on *Cruikshank* 279

Derrick Bell, *Race, Racism and American Law* (5th Edition) 279

H. Background on *The Civil Rights Cases* 280

I. *The Civil Rights Cases*, 109 U.S. 3 (1883) 281

1. Facts 281

2. Opinion 281

a. Prohibiting State Laws 281

b. State Law and State Action 283

c. Scope and Impact of the 1875 Civil Rights Act 283

d. Private Action 285

e. Exceptions and Limitations 285

f. The Thirteenth Amendment 286

3. Holding 290

4. Justice Harlan Dissenting 290

a. Constitutional Precedent 291

b. The Thirteenth Amendment 293

c. The Social Rights Issue 295

d. Other Constitutional Grounds 296

e. The Favoritism Issue 296

J. Commentary on *The Civil Rights Cases*   297

    Peggy Cooper Davis, *Introducing Robert Smalls*   297

    Thomas Brook, *Plessy v. Ferguson: A Brief History with Documents*   300

K. Background on Justice Joseph Bradley   300

    Geoffrey Stone, et al., *Justice Joseph Bradley*   300

L. Questions and Notes   301

X. Race and Citizenship   301

A. Introduction   301

    Juan F. Perea, *Ethnicity and the Constitution: Beyond the Black and White Binary Constitution*   302

    Ian F. Haney Lopez, *White by Law: The Legal Construction of Race*   303

B. Background on *Ozawa*   307

C. *Ozawa v. United States*, 260 U.S. 178 (1922)   307

    1. Facts   307

    2. Opinion   308

    3. Holding   311

D. Commentary on *Ozawa*   311

E. Background on *Thind*   312

    Vinay Harpalani, *Memorandum on United States v. Thind*   312

F. *United States v. Thind*, 261 U.S. 204 (1923)   312

    1. Facts   312

    2. Opinion   313

    3. Holding   316

G. Commentary on *Thind*   317

    Vinay Harpalani, *Memorandum on United States v. Thind*   317

H. Background on *De La Guerra*   318

I. *People v. De La Guerra*, 40 Cal. 311 (1870)   320

    1. Facts   320

    2. Opinion   320

    3. Holding   321

J. Commentary on *De La Guerra*   321

K. Background on *Ping*   322

L. *Ping v. United States*, 130 U.S. 581 (1889)   322

    1. Facts   322

    2. Opinion   323

      a. Treaties and Legislation   323

      b. Powers of Congress   324

    3. Holding   326

M. Commentary on *Ping* 326

N. Background on *Ark* 327

O. *United States v. Ark*, 169 U.S. 649 (1898) 327

    1. Facts 327

    2. Opinion 327

    3. Holding 330

    4. Chief Justice Fuller and Justice Harlan Dissenting 330

P. Commentary on *Ark* 331

Q. Background on *Korematsu* 332

    Tseming Yang, *Choice and Fraud in Racial Identification:
The Dilemma of Policing Race in Affirmative Action,
the Census, and a Color-Blind Society* 332

R. *Korematsu v. United States*, 323 U.S. 214 (1944) 332

    1. Facts 333

    2. Opinion 333

        a. Level of Scrutiny 333

        b. Power of the Federal Government 333

        c. Rationale 336

    3. Holding 336

    4. Justice Murphy Dissenting 336

        a. Presence of Racism 336

        b. No Real Military Threat 340

S. Commentary on *Korematsu* 342

T. Background on *Trump* 342

U. *Trump v. Hawaii*, 138 S. Ct. 2392 (2018) 343

    1. Facts 343

    2. Opinion 344

    3. Holding 346

    4. Justice Sotomayor, with whom Justice Ginsburg joins dissenting ... 347

V. Commentary on *Trump* 348

W. Questions and Notes 348

X. Point/Counterpoint 349

    Leticia Saucedo, *Mexicans, Immigrants, Cultural Narratives
and National Origin* 349

XI. Race, American Indians, and Sovereignty 360

A. Introduction 360

    Andrew Jackson, *Excerpt from the Fifth Annual Message
to Congress, December 3, 1833* 360

    Bethany Berger, *After Pocahontas: Indian Women and
the Law 1830–1934* 361

B. Background on *Johnson* 362

C. *Johnson v. McIntosh*, 21 U.S. 543 (1823)   362
    1. Facts   362
    2. Opinion   363
        a. Principle of Discovery   363
        b. Justification for Principle of Discovery   365
        c. Application of the Principle of Discovery   366
    3. Holding   368
D. Commentary on *Johnson*   368
E. Background on *Cherokee Nation*   369
F. *Cherokee Nation v. The State of Georgia*, 30 U.S. 1 (1831)   369
    1. Facts   369
    2. Opinion   370
        a. Jurisdiction   370
        b. Foreign State   370
    3. Holding   373
    4. Justice Johnson Concurring   373
    5. Justice Thompson Dissenting   374
G. Commentary on *Cherokee Nation*   375
        Stephen Breyer, *Making Our Democracy Work*   375
        William Bradford, *"With a Very Great Blame on our Hearts":*
            Reparations, Reconciliation, and an American Indian Plea
            for Peace with Justice   381
H. Background on *Elk*   388
I. *Elk v. Wilkins*, 112 U.S. 94 (1884)   388
    1. Facts   389
    2. Opinion   390
        a. The Original Constitution   390
        b. The Reconstruction Amendments   392
        c. Citizenship by Birth   392
        d. Citizenship by Naturalization   393
    3. Holding   395
    4. Justice Harlan and Justice Woods Dissenting   396
J. Commentary on *Elk*   399
        Rennard Strickland, *Tonto's Revenge*   399
K. Background on Chief Justice John Marshall   401
        Geoffrey Stone, et al., *Chief Justice John Marshall*   401
L. Questions and Notes   402
M. Point/Counterpoint   402
        Alfred S. Chavez Jr., *What's in a Name?*   402
        Scot P. Hillier, *Race and the Redskins*   403
        Barbara Munson, *Not for Sport*   403

Part Four • Segregation

XII. The Separate but Equal Doctrine 407
    A. Introduction 407
    B. Background on *Strauder* 407
    C. *Strauder v. West Virginia*, 100 U.S. 303 (1880) 407
        1. Facts 407
        2. Opinion 408
        3. Holding 412
    D. Commentary on *Strauder* 412
        Donald E. Lively, *The Constitution and Race* 412
    E. Background on *Plessy* 414
        Thomas Brook, *Plessy v. Ferguson: A Brief History
        with Documents* 414
    F. *Plessy v. Ferguson*, 163 U.S. 537 (1896) 417
        1. Facts 417
        2. Opinion 418
          a. The Thirteenth Amendment 418
          b. The Fourteenth Amendment 419
            1. Equal Protection 419
            2. Property 421
            3. Police Powers 421
        3. Holding 423
        4. Justice Harlan Dissenting 423
          a. The Thirteenth and Fourteenth Amendments 423
          b. The Meaning of Liberty 425
          c. Harlan's Vision of American Justice 425
    G. Commentary on *Plessy* 429
        A. Leon Higginbotham, Jr., *The Life of the Law:
        Values, Commitment, and Craftsmanship* 429
    H. Background on Justice Henry Billings Brown 431
    I. Questions and Notes 431
    J. Point/Counterpoint 432
XIII. Expanding the Separate but Equal Doctrine 432
    A. Introduction 432
    B. Background on *Berea College* 433
        Richard Epstein, *Race and the Police Power: 1890 to 1937* 433
    C. *Berea College v. The Commonwealth of Kentucky*, 211 U.S. 45 (1908) 435
        1. Facts 435
        2. Opinion 436
        3. Holding 437
        4. Justice Harlan Dissenting 437

D. Commentary on *Berea College*   439
     A. Leon Higginbotham, Jr., *Book Review: Race, Racism,*
       and American Law   439
     Donald E. Lively, *The Constitution and Race*   440
E. Explaining Justice David Brewer   441
     G. Hylton, *The Judge Who Abstained in Plessy v. Ferguson:*
       Justice David Brewer and the Problem of Race   441
F. Questions and Notes   451

XIV. Racial Segregation and Housing   451
   A. Introduction   451
      Peggy Cooper Davis, *Introducing Robert Smalls*   451
      James Weldon Johnson, *Lift Every Voice and Sing*   455
   B. Background on *Buchanan*   456
      Malaika Adero, *Up South*   456
      Chicago Defender, *Laborers Going North*
       Chicago Defender *News Service*   456
      Opportunity Magazine, *October 1923 Why They Come North*   457
      Augusta Georgia, *May 12, 1917*   457
      A. Leon Higginbotham, Jr., F. Michael Higginbotham,
       and S. Sandile Ngcobo, De Jure *Housing Segregation*
       in the United States and South Africa: The Difficult
       Pursuit for Racial Justice   458
   C. *Buchanan v. Warley*, 245 U.S. 60 (1917)   459
     1. Facts   459
     2. Opinion   461
       a. Standing   461
       b. Police Powers   461
       c. Denial of Property   462
     3. Holding   464
   D. Commentary on *Buchanan*   464
      Donald E. Lively, *The Constitution and Race*   464
   E. Questions and Notes   466

XV. Racial Segregation and Interstate Commerce   467
   A. Introduction   467
   B. Background on *Morgan*   467
   C. *Morgan v. Commonwealth of Virginia*, 328 U.S. 373 (1946)   467
     1. Facts   468
     2. Opinion   469
       a. Undue Burden   469
       b. Race and Interstate Travel   471
     3. Holding   474
     4. Justice Burton Dissenting   474

D.	Commentary on *Morgan*	478
E.	Questions and Notes	478
XVI.	Racial Segregation and State Action	478
A.	Introduction	478
B.	Background on *Shelley*	479
C.	*Shelley v. Kraemer*, 334 U.S. 1 (1948)	479
	1. Facts	479
	2. Opinion	481
	a. Precedent	481
	b. State Action and Judicial Enforcement	482
	c. The Meaning of Equal Protection	484
	3. Holding	486
D.	Commentary on *Shelley*	486
	A. Leon Higginbotham, Jr., *Race, Sex, Education, and Missouri Jurisprudence*	486
E.	Questions and Notes	487
XVII.	Interpreting the Separate but Equal Doctrine	487
A.	Introduction	487
B.	Background on *Cumming*	488
	C. Ellen Connally, *Justice Harlan's "Great Betrayal?" A Reconsideration of Cumming v. Richmond County Board of Education*	488
C.	*Cumming v. County Board of Education*, 175 U.S. 528 (1899)	492
	1. Facts	492
	C. Ellen Connally, *Justice Harlan's "Great Betrayal"? A Reconsideration of Cumming v. Richmond County Board of Education*	492
	2. Opinion	494
	3. Holding	496
D.	Commentary on *Cumming*	496
	C. Ellen Connally, *Justice Harlan's "Great Betrayal"? A Reconsideration of Cumming v. Richmond County Board of Education*	497
E.	Background on *Lum*	502
F.	*Lum v. Rice*, 275 U.S. 78 (1927)	502
	1. Facts	502
	2. Arguments on Appeal	504
	3. Mississippi Supreme Court Opinion	504
	4. Opinion	505
	5. Holding	507
G.	Commentary on *Lum*	508

Jonathan Entin, Sweatt v. Painter: *The End of Segregation
and the Transformation of Education Law*   508

H. Background on *Hernández*   508
I. *Hernández v. Texas*, 347 U.S. 475 (1954)   509
    1. Facts   509
    2. Opinion   509
    3. Holding   511
J. Commentary on *Hernández*   511
K. Background on Chief Justice William Howard Taft   511
    Geoffrey Stone, et al., *Justice William Howard Taft*   511
L. Explaining Justice John Harlan   512
    1. Harlan's Background   512
    Geoffrey Stone, et al., *Justice John Harlan*   512
    2. The Brilliance of Harlan   512
    3. Shattering the Harlan Myth   512
        Gabriel Chin, *The Plessy Myth: Justice Harlan and the
        Chinese Cases*   512
        C. Ellen Connally, *Justice Harlan's "Great Betrayal"?
        A Reconsideration of* Cumming v. Richmond County
        Board of Education   514
    4. Harlan's Black Brother   517
        J. Gordon, *Did the First Justice Harlan Have a Black Brother?* 517
    5. The Amazing Grace Syndrome   524
M. Questions and Notes   525

XVIII. Applying the Separate but Equal Doctrine   525
A. Introduction   525
    A. Leon Higginbotham, Jr., *A Tribute to Justice
    Thurgood Marshall*   525
    F. Michael Higginbotham, *Soldiers for Justice: the Role
    of the Tuskegee Airmen in the Desegregation of the
    American Armed Forces*   526
    Jonathan Entin, Sweatt v. Painter: *The End of Segregation
    and the Transformation of Education Law*   529
B. Background on *Gaines*   530
    F. Michael Higginbotham and José F. Anderson,
    Drum Majors for Justice   530
C. *Gaines v. Canada*, 305 U.S. 337 (1938)   531
    1. Facts   532
    2. Opinion   533
        a. Obligations of the State   533
        b. Group Rights or Personal Rights   534

       c. Appropriate Remedies 534

      3. Holding 535

      4. Justice McReynolds Dissenting 535

  D.   Commentary on *Gaines* 536

      Donald E. Lively, *The Constitution and Race* 536

      A. Leon Higginbotham, Jr., *Race, Sex, Education, and*

      Missouri Jurisprudence 537

  E.   Background on Justice James McReynolds 538

      Geoffrey Stone, et al., *Justice James McReynolds* 538

  F.   Background on *McLaurin* 538

  G.   *McLaurin v. Oklahoma State Regents for Higher Education,*

      339 U.S. 637 (1950) 539

      1. Facts 539

      2. Opinion 540

      3. Holding 541

  H.   Commentary on *McLaurin* 541

  I.   Background on *Sweatt* 542

  J.   *Sweatt v. Painter*, 339 U.S. 629 (1950) 542

      1. Facts 542

      2. Opinion 543

      a. Defining Equality 543

      b. Applying *Plessy* 544

      3. Holding 544

  K.   Commentary on *Sweatt* 544

  L.   Questions and Notes 545

XIX. Ending State-Mandated Segregation 545

  A.   Introduction 545

  B.   Background on *Brown I* 545

      Donald E. Lively, *The Constitution and Race* 545

  C.   *Brown v. Board of Education (Brown I)*, 347 U.S. 483 (1954) 548

      1. Facts 548

      2. Opinion 550

      a. History of the Fourteenth Amendment 550

      b. Value of Public Education 552

      c. Effect of Segregation 553

      3. Holding 554

  D.   Commentary on *Brown I* 554

  E.   Background on Chief Justice Earl Warren 555

      Geoffrey Stone, et al., *Justice Earl Warren* 555

  F.   Questions and Notes 556

G. Point/Counterpoint   556
    Richard Delgado, *Explaining the Rise and Fall
        of African American Fortunes:Interest Convergence
        and Civil Rights Gains*   556
    Derrick A. Bell, Jr., *Brown v. Board of Education
        and the Interest-Convergence Dilemma*   557

XX. Applying the *Brown* Rationale   559
    A. Introduction   559
    B. Background on *Loving*   560
    C. Loving v. Virginia, 388 U.S. 1 (1966)   560
        1. Facts   560
        2. Opinion   563
        3. Holding   566
    D. Commentary on *Loving*   566
        A. Leon Higginbotham, Jr. and Barbara Kopytoff,
            *Racial Purity and Interracial Sex in the Law of
            Colonial and Antebellum Virginia*   566
    E. Questions and Notes   569

Part Five • Attempted Eradication of Inequality

XXI. Race Conscious Remedies   571
    A. Introduction   571
    B. Background on *Brown II*   571
    C. *Brown v. Board of Education (Brown II)*, 349 U.S. 294 (1955)   571
        1. Facts   573
        2. Opinion   574
            a. Authorities Responsible for Implementation   574
            b. Guiding Principles   574
        3. Holding   575
    D. Commentary on *Brown II*   575
        Newsreel Incorporated, *Negroes with Guns:
            Rob Williams and Black Power*   576
        John Hope Franklin, *From Slavery to Freedom: A History
            of Negro Americans* (Fifth Edition)   576
    E. Background on *Milliken*   578
        Donald E. Lively, *The Constitution and Race*   579
    F. *Milliken v. Bradley*, 418 U.S. 717 (1974)   582
        1. Facts   582
        2. Trial Court Opinion   583
        3. Court of Appeals Opinion   585
        4. Opinion   587
        5. Holding   590

6. Justice White Dissenting 591

7. Justice Marshall Dissenting 592

G. Commentary on *Milliken* 593

José Felipe Anderson, *Perspectives on* Missouri v. Jenkins 593

Donald E. Lively, *The Constitution and Race* 595

H. Background on *Adarand* 598

Leslie Yalof Garfield, *The Glass Half Full: Envisioning the Future of Race Preference Policies* 599

I. *Adarand Constructors, Inc. v. Peña*, 515 U.S. 200 (1995) 603

1. Facts 603

2. Opinion 604

a. Equal Protection Case Law 604

b. *Adarand* Rationale 606

3. Holding 608

4. Meaning of Strict Scrutiny 608

5. Justice Scalia Concurring 609

6. Justice Stevens Dissenting 609

7. Justice Ginsburg Dissenting 611

J. Commentary on *Adarand* 612

F. Michael Higginbotham, *Affirmative Action, Selective Memory Loss, and the Mistakes of Adarand* 612

K. Background on *Grutter* 613

L. *Grutter v. Bollinger*, 539 U.S. 306 (2003) 613

1. Facts 613

2. Opinion 616

a. *Bakke* Decision 616

b. Equal Protection Rationale 618

c. Compelling State Interest 619

d. Narrowly Tailored 623

3. Holding 629

4. Chief Justice Rehnquist Dissenting 630

M. Commentary on *Grutter* 633

Leslie Yalof Garfield, *The Glass Half Full: Envisioning The Future of Race Preference Policies* 634

N. Background on *Parents Involved* 636

O. *Parents Involved in Community Schools v. Seattle School District No. 1* (2007) 636

1. Facts 636

2. Opinion 637

3. Holding 642

4. Justice Stevens Dissenting 643

5. Justice Breyer Dissenting 643

P. Commentary on *Parents Involved*   649

       Leonard M. Baynes, *Perspectives: Abandoning Brown
and '[Race]ing' Backwards on K–12 Education*   649

       Leslie Yalof Garfield, *The Glass Half Full: Envisioning
the Future of Race Preference Policies*   651

Q. Background on *Fisher*   652

R. *Fisher v. University of Texas*, 133 S.Ct. 2411 (2013)   653

    1. Facts   653

    2. Opinion   655

    3. Holding   660

S. Commentary on *Fisher*   660

T. Background on *Schuette*   661

U. *Schuette v. Coalition To Defend Affirmative Action*, 134 S.Ct.
1623 (2014)   661

    1. Facts   661

    2. Opinion   663

    3. Holding   671

    4. Justice Sotomayor Dissenting   672

V. Commentary on *Schuette*   675

W. Background on Justice Ruth Bader Ginsburg   677

       Geoffrey Stone, et al., *Justice Ruth Bader Ginsburg*   677

X. Background on Justice Sandra Day O'Connor   678

       Geoffrey Stone, et al., *Justice Sandra Day O'Connor*   678

Y. Questions and Notes   679

Z. Point/Counterpoint   679

       The Chronicle Review/The Chronicle of Higher Education,
May It Please the Court . . .   679

       A. Lee Parks, Jr., *Racial Diversity's Effect on Education
Is a Myth*   680

       F. Michael Higginbotham and Kathleen Bergin,
The Court Has Granted Wide Deference to Colleges   684

XXII. Maintaining Racial Inequity   689

A. Introduction   689

B. Background on *Washington*   690

C. *Washington v. Davis*, 426 U.S. 229 (1976)   690

    1. Facts   690

    2. Opinion   690

    3. Holding   692

D. Commentary on *Washington*   692

       Bradford C. Mank, *Are Title VI's Disparate Impact
Regulations Valid?*   692

E. Background on *Batson*   695

Kim Taylor-Thompson, *Empty Votes in Jury Deliberations*   695
F. *Batson v. Kentucky*, 476 U.S. 79 (1986)   696
    1. Facts   696
    2. Opinion   696
      a. Case Law   696
      b. Rationale   697
    3. Holding   701
    4. Justice Marshall Concurring   701
G. Commentary on *Batson*   702
H. Background on *McCleskey*   703
I. *McCleskey v. Kemp*, 481 U.S. 279 (1987)   703
    1. Facts   703
    2. Opinion   705
      a. Argument   705
      b. Rationale   706
    3. Holding   713
    4. Justice Brennan Dissenting   713
J. Commentary on *McCleskey*   720
    Charles R. Lawrence III, *The Id, The Ego, and Equal
      Protection: Reckoning with Unconscious Racism*   720
K. Background on *Shaw*   722
    José Felipe Anderson, *History Says That Blacks Should Vote*   722
L. *Shaw v. Reno*, 509 U.S. 630 (1993)   723
    1. Facts   723
    2. Opinion   725
    3. Holding   728
    4. Justice White Dissenting   728
    5. Justice Souter Dissenting   729
M. Commentary on *Shaw*   731
    A. Leon Higginbotham, Jr., Gregory Clarick, and
      Marcella David, *Shaw v. Reno: A Mirage of Good
      Intentions with Devastating Racial Consequences*   731
N. Background on *Shelby*   733
    David Crump et al., *Cases and Materials on
      Constitutional Law* (Fifth Edition)   734
O. *Shelby County v. Holder*, 133 S. Ct. 2612 (2013)   735
    1. Facts   735
    2. Opinion   739
    3. Holding   746
    4. Justice Ginsburg Dissenting   747
P. Commentary on *Shelby*   755

F. Michael Higginbotham, *Keynote Speech: A Letter
From The Original Cause Lawyer* 755
F. Michael Higginbotham, *Congress must act to guard
our most important right* 756

Q. Background on *Ricci* 757
R. *Ricci v. DeStefano*, 129 S. Ct. 2658 (2009) 758
   1. Facts 758
   2. Opinion 759
   3. Holding 769
   4. Justice Ginsburg Dissenting 769
S. Commentary on *Ricci* 770
T. Background on Justice Thurgood Marshall 770
   Geoffrey Stone, et al., *Justice Thurgood Marshall* 770
U. Questions and Notes 771
V. Point/Counterpoint 772
   Darren Lenard Hutchinson, *Progressive Race Blindness?:
Individual Identity, Group Politics, and Reform* 772
   Derrick Bell, *Color-Blind Constitutionalism:
A Rediscovered Rationale* 773
   Charles R. Lawrence III, *The Id, The Ego, and
Equal Protection: Reckoning with Unconscious Racism* 778
   Barbara J. Flagg, *"Was Blind, But Now I See":
White Race Consciousness and the Requirement of
Discriminatory Intent* 779

Part Six • Supreme Court Confirmation Racial Controversies

XXIII. Race, Values, and Justice Thomas 783
A. Introduction 783
B. Pre-Supreme Court Jurisprudence 784
   A. Leon Higginbotham, Jr., *An Open Letter to Justice
Clarence Thomas from a Federal Judicial Colleague* 784
C. Supreme Court Jurisprudence 802
   1. Letter to National Bar Association 802
   A. Leon Higginbotham, Jr., *Letter to Judicial Council
May 27, 1998* 802
   2. Editorial on Thomas's Speech to the National Bar Association 812
   F. Michael Higginbotham, *Bar Group Rolls
Up Welcome Mat* 812
D. Race, Gender, and the Thomas Confirmation Process 815
   A. Leon Higginbotham, Jr., *The Hill-Thomas
Hearings — What Took Place and What Happened:
White Male Domination, Black Male Domination,*

and the Denigration of Black Women, in Race,
Gender, and Power in America: The Legacy of the
Hill-Thomas Hearing (edited by Anita Faye Hill &
Emma Coleman Jordan) 815

   E. Background on Justice Clarence Thomas 817

      Geoffrey Stone, et al., *Justice Clarence Thomas* 817

   F. Questions and Notes 818

XXIV. Race, Values, and Justice Alito 818

   A. Introduction 818

   B. Pre-Supreme Court and Supreme Court Jurisprudence 819

      F. Michael Higginbotham, *An Open Letter from Heaven*
to Justice Samuel Alito 819

   C. Background on Justice Samuel Alito 829

      Geoffrey Stone, et al., *Justice Samuel Alito* 829

   D. Questions and Notes 829

XXV. Race, Values, and Justice Sotomayor 829

   A. Introduction 829

   B. Pre-Supreme Court Jurisprudence 830

      Richard Lacayo, *A Justice Like No Other* 830

   C. Background on Justice Sonia Sotomayor 832

      Richard Lacayo, *A Justice Like No Other* 832

   D. Questions and Notes 833

Part Seven • Ongoing Racial Controversies

XXVI. Race and the Administration of Justice 835

   A. Introduction 835

   B. Race, Arrest, and Henry Louis Gates 835

   C. Race and the O.J. Simpson Trial 837

      A. Leon Higginbotham, Jr., Aderson Francois, and
Linda Yueh, *The O.J. Simpson Trial: Who Was*
Improperly Playing the Race Card, in Birth of a Nationhood:
Gaze, Script, and Spectacle in the O.J. Simpson Case
(edited by Toni Morrison and Claudia Brodsky Lacour) 837

   D. Race and the Rodney King Beating 845

      A. Leon Higginbotham, Jr. and Aderson Francois,
Looking for God and Racism in All the Wrong Places 845

   E. Race and the Death of Trayvon Martin 847

      Cynthia Lee, *(E)Racing Trayvon Martin* 847

   F. Race and the Death of Jordan Davis 853

      F. Michael Higginbotham, *Valuing Black Life* 853

   G. Questions and Notes 855

   H. Point/Counterpoint 855

XXVII. Race and Immigration   855
    A. Introduction   855
    B. History of Race and Immigration   856
        Lisa Sandoval, *Race and Immigration Law: A Troubling
          Marriage*   856
    C. Current Approach to Race and Immigration   863
        Lisa Sandoval, *Race and Immigration Law: A Troubling
          Marriage*   863
    D. Questions and Notes   867
    E. Point/Counterpoint   867
XXVIII. Race and Politics   868
    A. Introduction   868
    B. History of Race and Politics   868
        Leland Ware and David Wilson, *Jim Crow on the
          "Down Low": Subtle Racial Appeals in Presidential
          Campaigns*   868
    C. Current Approach to Race and Politics   872
        F. Michael Higginbotham, *Bush and the Black Vote*   872
        F. Michael Higginbotham, *The Case of the Missing
          Post-Racial Election*   874
        F. Michael Higginbotham, *America's Racial Soul*   875
    D. Questions and Notes   876

Part Eight • Appendix

XXIX. Conclusion   877
        F. Michael Higginbotham, *A Request from Heaven to
          President Obama: Don't Forget the Race Issue*   878
        F. Michael Higginbotham, *Keynote Speech: A Letter From
          The Original Cause Lawyer*   880
        A. Leon Higginbotham, Jr., *Book Review: Race, Racism,
          and American Law*   881
        Langston Hughes, *Dream of Freedom*   883
XXX. Documents   883
    A. The Constitution of the United States   883
    B. The Earliest Protest against Slavery (February 18, 1688)   900
    C. Declaration of the Causes and Necessity of Taking
        Up Arms (July 6, 1775)   901
    D. The Declaration of Independence (July 4, 1776)   903
    E. The Articles of Confederation (March 1, 1781)   907
    F. The Northwest Ordinance (July 13, 1787)   908
    G. The Fugitive Slave Act (1793)   910
    H. The Missouri Compromise (1820)   911

I. The Fugitive Slave Act (1850) 912

J. The Emancipation Proclamation (January 1, 1863) 913

K. The Freedmen's Bureau (March 3, 1865) 915

L. Black Code of Mississippi (1865) 916

    1. Civil Rights of Freedmen in Mississippi 916

    2. Mississippi Apprentice Law 917

    3. Mississippi Vagrant Law 918

    4. Penal Laws of Mississippi 918

M. Indian Removal Act (May 28, 1830) 919

N. Executive Order 8802 (June 25, 1941) 920

O. Executive Order 9981 (July 26, 1948) 921

P. Southern Manifesto (March 1956) 922

Q. § 2000a of the Civil Rights Act of 1964
(Public Accommodations) 922

R. § 2000d of Title VI of the Civil Rights Act of 1964
(Federally Assisted Programs) 922

S. § 2000e-2 of Title VII of the Civil Rights Act of 1964
(Employment) 922

T. Voting Rights Act of 1965 923

U. § 3601 of the Fair Housing Act of 1968 (Housing) 925

V. Restitution for World War II Internment of Japanese
Americans and Aleuts (August 10, 1988) 926

W. Senate Resolution Apologizing for the Enslavement and
Racial Segregation of African Americans (June 11, 2009) 926

XXXI. History Timeline 929

Index 943

Table of Cases

The principal cases appear in bold; all other listed cases appear in the text or the footnotes of the principal cases, articles, commentary, or documents.

Ableman v. Booth, 248
Adair v. United States, 361, 369
Adarand Constructors, Inc. v. Peña, 187, 546, 670, 777
Adarand Constructors, Inc. v. Skinner, 500
Ah How v. United States, 365
Ah Sin v. Wittman, 365
Akins v. Texas, 578
Al-Khazraji v. Saint Francis College, 590
Albemarle Paper Co. v. Moody, 630
Alexander v. Choate, 575
Alexander v. Hillman, 475
Alexander v. Louisiana, 578–580
Alexander v. Sandoval, 574
Allen v. State Bd. of Elections, 621
Allgeyer v. Louisiana, 359, 361, 369, 383
Allied Stores of Ohio, Inc. v. Bowers, 467
Allied-Bruce Terminix Cos. v. Dobson, 568
American Ry. Exp. Co. v. Kentucky, 398
Anderson v. Bessemer City, 580
Andrews v. Swartz, 367
Arizona v. Inter Tribal Council of Ariz., Inc., 614
Arlington Heights v. Metropolitan Housing Development Corp., 501, 578, 579, 602

Associated General Contractors v. Coalition for Economic Equity, 507
Associated General Contractors of Cal., Inc. v. San Francisco, 506
Atkins v. Parker, 629
Atlantic Coast Line Co. v. Wharton, 388
Atlantic Coast Line R. Co. v. Georgia, 387
Atlantic Coast Line R. Co. v. North Carolina Corp. Comm., 387
AT&T Corp. v. Hulteen, 633
Avery v. Georgia, 579

Bailey v. Alabama, 367, 368, 419
Bailey v. Bowman, 368
Baker v. Carr, 661
BAMN v. Regents of Univ. of Mich., 549
Bank of Columbia v. Okely, 236
Barron v. The City of Baltimore, 235
Batson v. Kentucky, 577, 593, 594, 777
Bazemore v. Friday, 587
Beer v. United States, 605
Berea College v. Kentucky, 359, 362, 363, 367–369, 411, 416, 456, 775
Bertonneau v. Board, 418
Bertonneau v. Directors of City Schools, 346
Block v. Hirsh, 283
Blodgett v. Holden, 619

Bolling v. Sharpe, 495, 502

Bond v. United States, 549, 613

Booker v. Jabe, 580, 581

Bordenkircher v. Hayes, 589

Boyd v. Nebraska ex rel. Thayer, 614

Bradley v. School Board of the City of Richmond, 486

Bray v. Marriott Hotels, 681

Briggs v. Elliott, 453, 475

Brown v. Board of Education (Brown I), 453, 491, 776

Brown v. Board of Education (Brown II), 473, 487, 776

Brownfield v. South Carolina, 367

Buchanan v. Warley, 377, 378, 662, 775

Buckley v. Valeo, 502

Burton v. Wilmington Parking Authority, 468

Bush v. Kentucky, 350

Bush v. Com., 346

Capen v. Foster, 347

Carey v. City of Atlanta, 382

Carrington v. Rash, 614

Carter v. Texas, 367, 398

Case of the Cherokee Tobacco, 321

Case of the Kansas Indians, 321

Case of the New York Indians, 321

Cassell v. Texas, 578

Castaneda v. Partida, 578, 579, 587

Castledine v. Mundy, 94

Celotex Corp. v. Catrett, 634

Chambers v. Florida, 663

Charles River Bridge v. Warren Bridge, 168

Charley Smith v. Mississippi, 367

Chastleton Corporation v. Sinclair, 283

Cherokee Nation v. Georgia, 306, 311, 315, 321, 327, 772

Chesapeake & Ohio Ry. v. Kentucky, 367

Chicago, B. & O.R. Co. v. Babcock, 588

Chicago, B. & O.R. Co. v. Chicago, 388, 398, 588

Chicago, B. & O.R. Co. v. Railroad Comm. of Wisconsin, 388

Chicago Firefighters Local 2 v. Chicago, 636

Chicago, R.I. & P.R. Co. v. Arkansas, 387

Chin Bak Kan v. United States, 365

Chin Yow v. United States, 365

Chinese Cases, 365, 423, 586, 710

Chirac v. Chirac, 325

Chirre v. Chirre, 159

City of Boerne v. Flores, 623

City of New York v. Miln, 235

City of Rome v. United States, 611, 621

Civil Rights Cases, 207, 216, 237, 238, 251, 253, 345, 356, 367–369, 397, 398, 405, 450, 471, 495, 507, 560, 567, 642, 656, 658, 675, 721, 774

Cleburne v. Cleburne Living Center, Inc., 506

Cleveland Bd. of Ed. v. Lafleur, 586

Cleveland R. Co. v. Illinois, 388

Close v. Glenwood Cemetery, 360

Clyatt v. United States, 367, 368

Coalition for Economic Equity v. Wilson, 549

Coker v. Georgia, 592, 593

Commissioners on Inland Fisheries v. Holyoke Water Power Co., 360

Commonwealth v. Jones, 772

Commonwealth v. Maxwell, 93

Commonwealth of Virginia v. Rives, 398

Commonwealth v. Robinson, 581

Cooper v. Aaron, 476, 491

Connecticut v. Teal, 634

Coral Constr., Inc. v. City and County of San Francisco, 554

Corfield v. Coryell, 87, 90, 207

Corrigan v. Buckley, 397

Cory v. Carter, 346, 418
Coyle v. Smith, 614
Crandall v. Connecticut, 81, 772
Crandall v. Nevada, 208
Creek Nation v. United States, 312
Crow Dog's Case, 321
Cumming v. Board of Education, 403, 406, 410, 418, 425, 442, 456, 775

Daggett v. Hudson, 347
Dameron v. Bayless, 418
Davis v. County School Board, 454
Dawson v. Lee, 346
Dean v. Commonwealth, 46
Defunis v. Odegaard, 540
Donnelly v. DeChristoforo, 593

Eddings v. Oklahoma, 587
Edmonson v. Leesville Concrete Co., 556, 603, 605
Edwards v. Elliott, 235
Elk v. Wilkins, 319, 774
Erb v. Morasch, 387
Erie R.R. Co. v. Tompkins, 170
Escambia County v. McMillan, 612, 629
Ex parte Kawato, 283
Ex parte Virginia, 240, 340, 350, 398, 456, 467, 624

Federated Publications, Inc. v. Board of Trustees of Mich. State Univ., 550
Fellows v. Blacksmith, 325
Firefighters v. Cleveland, 631
Fisher v. University of Texas, 541, 547, 549
Fletcher v. Peck, 168, 304
Fok Yung Yo v. United States, 365
Fong Yue Ting v. United States, 365
Fox v. Ohio, 235
Fullilove v. Klutznick, 500, 544, 569, 605, 643, 653

Gaines v. Canada, 400, 439, 443, 446, 456, 651, 775
Gebhart v. Belton, 454
George v. State, 75, 773
Georgia v. Ashcroft, 612
Georgia v. United States, 306, 321, 564, 593, 611
Gibbons v. Ogden, 234
Gibson v. Mississippi, 346
Gibson v. State, 346, 350
Giles v. Harris, 367, 368, 620
Giles v. Teasley, 367, 368
Gladson v. Minnesota, 387
Gomillion v. Lightfoot, 513, 586, 587, 602, 606
Goon Shung v. United States, 365
Graham v. Richardson, 499
Grant v. Shalala, 680
Gratz v. Bollinger, 525, 527, 542, 548, 563
Gray v. Coffman, 321
Gray v. State, 348
Green v. County School Board, 486, 489, 492
Gregg v. Georgia, 588, 589, 595
Gregory v. Ashcroft, 549, 613
Gregory v. Baugh, 42
Griffin v. Prince Edward County Board of Education, 477
Griggs v. Duke Power Co., 630, 638
Grutter v. Bollinger, 508, 525, 527, 541, 542, 548, 557, 559, 563, 624, 638, 687, 778
Gue Lin, 365
Guinn v. United States, 602
Gwinn v. Bugg, 50

H.K. Porter Co. v. Metropolitan Dade County, 502
Hall v. DeCuir, 393
Hansberry v. Lee, 398
Harriet v. Emerson, 142, 143

Hastings v. Farmer, 321

Hecht Co. v. Bowles, 475

Henry v. Bollar, 42

Hepburn v. Griswold, 254

Hernández v. Texas, 420, 578, 581, 590, 776

Herndon v. Chicago, Rock Island & P.R. Co., 388

Hicks v. Butrick, 321

Hirabayashi v. United States, 282, 468, 602

Hitchcock v. Dugger, 587

Ho v. San Francisco Unified School Dist., 553

Hodges v. United States, 367, 368

Holden v. Hardy, 381

Holland v. Illinois, 602

Holyoke Co. v. Lyman, 360

Holmes v. South Carolina, 686

Home Telephone and Telegraph Co. v. Los Angeles, 398

Hopkins v. City of Richmond, 661

Hopwood v. Texas, 508, 511, 512, 541, 564, 565, 668, 682

Hovey v. Elliott, 398

Hudgins v. Wrights, 43, 102, 771

Hudson v. McMillan, 675

Hulseman v. Rems, 347

Hunter v. Erickson, 550, 558

Hunter v. Underwood, 589

Illinois Central Railroad Co. v. Illinois, 388

Imbler v. Pachtman, 588

In re Lau Ow Bew, 365

In re Shibuya Jugiro, 367

In re Wood, 367

James v. Alabama, 367, 368

James v. Bowman, 367, 368

Johnson v. California, 556

Johnson v. De Grandy, 610

Johnson v. McIntosh, 300, 315, 772

Jones v. Alfred H. Mayer Co., 662

Jones v. Com., 348

Jones v. Georgia, 578

Jones v. Montague, 367, 368

Karrahoo v. Adams, 321

Katzenbach v. Morgan, 623

Kelly v. Board of Education, 476

Kelly v. New Haven, 636

King v. County of Nassau, 582

Kinney v. Commonwealth of Virginia, 469

Kies v. Lowrey, 484

Korematsu v. United States, 280, 452, 459, 468, 590, 775

Kraemer v. Shelley, 395, 396, 447, 468, 503, 662, 776

Kramer v. Union Free School District, 488

Kromnick v. School Dist. of Philadelphia, 501

Lake Shore & M.S. Railway Co. v. Ohio, 387

Lane v. Wilson, 602

Lau Ow Bew v. United States, 365

League of United Latin American Citizens v. Perry, 625, 684

League of United Latin American Citizens v. Texas, 625

Lee Lung v. Patterson, 365

Legal Tender Cases, 254

Legrand v. Darnall, 155, 171

Lehew v. Brummel, 416

Lem Wong King Ark, 365

Lessee of Livingston v. Moore, 235

Lessee of Pollard v. Hagan, 614

Li Sing v. United States, 365

Liu Hop Fong v. United States, 365

Lochner v. New York, 384

Lockett v. Ohio, 587, 589, 594

Lopez v. Monterey County, 611, 624

Lone Wolf v. Hitchcock, 312

Louisville & N.R. Co. v. Kentucky, 347

Louisville, New Orleans & Texas Ry. v. Mississippi, 367, 368

Louisville Railway Co. v. Mississippi, 390

Loving v. Virginia, 38, 452, 463, 468–471, 512, 544, 586, 602, 662, 777

Lum v. Rice, 415, 416, 419, 442, 456, 775

Mann v. City of Albany, 502

Marbles v. Creecy, 367

Marbury v. Madison, 330

Marks v. United States, 510

Martin v. Hunter's Lessee, 168

Martin v. Texas, 367, 398

Matsushita Elec. Industrial Co. v. Zenith Radio Corp., 634

Maurer v. Hamilton, 387

Maxwell v. Bishop, 592

Maynard v. Hill, 466

McCabe v. Atchison, T. & S. F. Ry. Co., 400, 441

McCleskey v. Kemp, 583, 777

McCray v. Abrams, 580

McCray v. New York, 579

McCulloch v. Maryland, 618, 623

McDonald v. Pless, 588

McDonnell Douglas Corp. v. Green, 588

McFarland v. Jefferson County Public Schools, 539

McGowan v. Maryland, 586

McLaughlin v. Florida, 467, 468, 470, 544, 602

McLaurin v. Oklahoma State Regents, 445, 456, 457, 776

McMillan v. School Committee, 418

Metro Broadcasting v. FCC, 500, 502, 503, 520, 553, 565, 570, 653

Meyer v. State of Nebraska, 466

Milliken v. Bradley, 462, 482, 492, 493, 777

Mills v. Green, 367

Mississippi R. Comm. v. Illinois Cent. R. Co., 388

Mississippi University for Women v. Hogan, 562

Missouri, K. & T.R. Co. v. Texas, 388

Missouri Pac. R. Co. v. Kansas, 387

Mitchell v. Harmony, 284

Mitchell v. United States, 284, 385

Monroe v. Board of Comm'rs, 490

Monroe v. Collins, 347, 348

Mooney v. Holohan, 398

Morgan v. Virginia, 385, 394, 775

Morris v. Duby, 387

Muller v. Oregon, 365

Murray v. Louisiana, 367

Murray v. Pearson, 657

Murray v. The Charming Betsey, 86

Naim v. Naim, 466, 469, 471

Neal v. Delaware, 346, 350, 398

New York Trust Co. v. Eisner, 582

Nishimura Ekiu v. United States, 365

Nixon v. Herndon, 620

Norris v. Alabama, 421, 580

Northwest Austin Municipal Utility District No. 1 v. Holder, 609

Osborn v. United States, 277

Osborn v. United States Bank, 277

Osman v. Riley, 347

Ow Bew v. United States, 365

Oyama v. California, 400

Oyler v. Boles, 586

Ozawa v. United States, 260, 264, 268, 775

Pace v. Alabama, 452, 467

Parents Involved In Community Schools v. Seattle School District No. 1, 527, 778

Parker v. Brown, 393

Pasadena City Board of Education v. Spangler, 494

Patton v. Mississippi, 581

Pease v. Peck, 162

Pennock v. Commissioners, 321

People v. De La Guerra, 270

People v. Dean, 348

People v. Gallagher, 346, 348, 418

People v. Hall, 53, 582, 773

People v. Rousseau, 581

People ex rel. Cisco v. School Board, 418

People v. Orenthal James Simpson, 695

Perez v. Sharp, 465

Perry v. Perez, 614

Personnel Administrator of Massachusetts v. Feeney, 588

Pervear v. The Commonwealth, 235

Peter v. Hargrave, 10

Ping v. United States, 272, 710, 711, 774

Planned Parenthood v. Casey, 568

Plessy v. Ferguson, 79, 100, 178, 198, 253, 341–343, 363, 367–369, 382, 405, 416, 418, 429, 430, 432, 434, 450, 454, 456, 457, 596, 601, 644, 653, 671, 721, 774

Poafpybitty v. Skeely Oil Company, 312

Presley v. Etowah County Comm'n, 615

Prigg v. Pennsylvania, 126, 130, 131, 169, 772

Prudential Ins. Co. v. Cheek, 398

Pulley v. Harris, 589

Quock Ting v. United States, 365

Quock Walker, 171

Railway Express Agency, Inc. v. People of State of New York, 467

Railroad Co. v. Brown, 347

Railroad Co. v. Husen, 347

Raney v. Board of Education, 486

Raymond v. Chicago Union Traction Co., 398

Raymond v. Thomas, 284

Regents of the University of California v. Bakke, 590, 606, 654, 669

Reitman v. Mulkey, 550

Reno v. Bossier Parish School Bd., 611

Reynolds v. Board of Education, 418

Reynolds v. Sims, 621

Ricci v. DeStefano, 628, 688, 778

Rice v. Cayetano, 544, 617

Rice v. Gong Lum, 416, 419, 442, 456, 775

Richmond v. J.A. Croson Co., 501, 505, 513, 514, 516, 517, 519, 521, 544, 602, 605, 632, 643

Riggins v. United States, 367

Riley v. Taylor, 681

Ristaino v. Ross, 593

Roberts v. City of Boston, 96, 346, 354, 418, 419, 456, 657, 772

Robinson v. Memphis & C.R. Co., 250

Roe v. Wade, 562, 568

Rogers v. Alabama, 367

Rogers v. Paul, 492

Rose v. Mitchell, 582, 593

Sailors v. Board of Ed. of County of Kent, 556

San Antonio Independent School District v. Rodriguez, 495

Schuette v. Coalition To Defend Affirmative Action, 548, 559, 778

Scott v. Emerson, 142, 143, 163

Scott v. Harris, 634

Scott v. McNeal, 398

Scott v. Sandford, 124, 131, 144, 278, 321, 322, 596, 710, 711, 773

Seaboard Air Line R. Co. v. Blackwell, 388

Shaare Tefila Congregation v. Cobb, 590

Shaw v. Barr, 600

Shaw v. Reno, 553, 599, 606, 607, 621, 640, 672, 777

Sheet Metal Workers v. EEOC, 501, 517

Shelby County v. Holder, 609, 627, 778

Shelley v. Kraemer, 395, 396, 447, 468, 503, 662, 776

Shurberg Broadcasting v. FCC, 502

Silverman v. United States, 555

Singer v. United States, 589

Sipuel v. Board of Regents, 446, 456

Skinner v. State of Oklahoma, 466

Slaughterhouse Cases, 195, 201, 202, 211, 212, 221, 237, 249, 253, 254, 279, 322, 335, 345, 401, 455, 607, 774

Smith v. Alabama, 387

Smith v. Allright, 660

Smith v. Goodell, 86, 88

Smith v. Maryland, 235

Smith v. Mississippi, 367

Smith v. Morse, 93

Solem v. Helm, 590

Sommersett v. Stuart, 106

South Carolina v. Katzenbach, 609, 611, 619, 624

South Carolina State Hwy. Dept. v. Barnwell Bros., 387

South Covington & C. St. R. Co. v. Covington, 387, 390

South Covington & C. Street R. Co. v. Commonwealth, 391

South Covington R. Co. v. Kentucky, 390

South Florida Chapter of Associated General Contractors of America, Inc. v. Metropolitan Dade County, 501

Souther v. The Commonwealth, 107, 772

Southern Pacific Co. v. Arizona, 388, 392, 393

Southern Railway Co. v. King, 388

Spieres v. Parker, 93

Sproles v. Binford, 387

St. Louis I.M. & S.R. Co. v. Arkansas, 387

St. Louis S.W.R. Co. v. Arkansas, 388

St. Louis-San Francisco R. Co. v. Public Serv. Comm., 388

State v. Baker, 347, 661

State v. Boon, 75, 771

State v. Cantey, 51

State v. Chavers, 348

State v. Gibson, 346, 350

State v. Hale, 10

State v. Mann, 4, 5, 8, 11, 12, 15, 19, 21, 113, 772

State v. McCann, 346, 418

State v. Treadway, 416

State ex rel. Stoutmeyer v. Duffy, 418

State of Virginia v. Rives, 456

Sterling v. Constantin, 284

Strauder v. West Virginia, 187, 248, 255, 279, 322, 335, 346, 350, 399, 401, 416, 455, 467, 576, 590, 774

Sturgis v. Crowninshield, 129

Sugarman v. Dougall, 613

Swain v. Alabama, 577, 581

Sweatt v. Painter, 419, 437, 445, 447, 448, 456, 457, 515, 682, 776

Sweezy v. New Hampshire, 514, 543, 568

Swift v. Tyson, 168

Talbot v. Janson, 86

Tang Tun v. Edsell, 365

Tarrance v. Florida, 367, 368, 578

Teamsters v. United States, 630

Tennessee v. Garner, 681

Terry v. Adams, 620

Texas v. Inclusive Communities
  Project, 778

Texas v. Johnson, 555, 565

Texas v. White, 547, 614, 668

Texas Dept. of Community Affairs v.
  Burdine, 578, 588

The Exchange, 75, 122, 270, 274, 291,
  301, 316, 317, 333, 435, 449, 512, 514,
  566, 570, 764, 765, 772

The Japanese Immigrant Case, 365

The Santissima Trinidad, 86

Thomas v. Texas, 367, 668

Thompson v. United States, 580

Thornburg v. Gingles, 605

Tom Hong v. United States, 365

Truax v. Raich, 380, 590

Trump v. Hawaii, 343

Trustees of Dartmouth College v.
  Woodward, 368

Tucker v. Blease, 416

Turner v. Fouche, 587

Turner v. Murray, 593

Turner's Case, 108

Twining v. New Jersey, 398

Twitchell v. The Commonwealth,
  235

United Jewish Organizations of
  Williamsburgh, Inc. v. Carey, 604,
  605

United States v. Ark, 365, 774

United States v. Atlantic Research
  Corp., 631

United States v. Buntin, 418

United States v. Carolene Products
  Co., 419, 452

United States v. Cruikshank, 221, 233,
  236, 271, 397, 405, 774

United States v. Falso, 691

United States v. Gue Lim, 365

United States v. Harris, 216, 397, 620

United States v. Holliday, 321, 325

United States v. Joseph, 221, 325

United States v. Ju Toy, 365

United States v. Kagama, 311

United States v. Lee Yen Tai, 365

United States v. The Libellants
  and Claimants of the Schooner
  Amistad, 119

United States v. Lopez, 521, 549, 611

United States v. Louisiana, 221, 361,
  369, 614

United States v. Newman, 581

United States v. Paradise, 499, 501, 504

United States v. Price, 616

United States v. Robinson, 581

United States v. Rogers, 321, 327, 367

United States v. Russell, 284

United States v. Shipp (I), 367

United States v. Shipp (II), 367

United States v. Sing Tuck, 365

United States v. Thind, 263, 264, 268,
  713

United States v. Whiskey, 321

United States v. Williams, 86

United States Postal Service Board of
  Governors v. Aikens, 578

University of Maryland v. Murray, 440,
  442

Vasquez v. Hillery, 582, 593

Virginia v. Rivers, 346

Virginia v. Rives, 240, 350, 398, 456

Wan Shing v. United States, 365

Wang Wing v. United States, 365

Ward v. Flood, 346, 418

Wards Cove Packing Co. v. Antonio,
  663

Washington v. Davis, 501, 505, 572,
  577–579, 597, 601, 644, 645

Washington v. Seattle School Dist. No. 1, 549, 558, 601

Watson v. Fort Worth Bank & Trust, 630

Wayte v. United States, 586, 593

Weinberger v. Wiesenfeld, 502

West Chester & Philadelphia Railroad Co. v. Miles, 354, 416

Whitcomb v. Chavis, 606

Whitus v. Georgia, 578, 581, 586–588, 593

Williams v. Mississippi, 367, 405

Williams v. New Orleans, 501

Wilson v. Wall, 321

Winter Park Communications, Inc. v. FCC, 502

Withers v. Buckley, 235

Wong Him v. Callahan, 418

Woodson v. North Carolina, 594

Worcester v. Georgia, 316 , 321

Wright v. Council of the City of Emporia, 487, 489

Wright v. Rockefeller, 603

Wygant v. Jackson Bd. of Ed., 519, 546, 602, 604, 605, 631

Wysinger v. Crookshank, 418

Yick Wo v. Hopkins, 347, 441, 586, 590, 602, 623, 774

Zant v. Stephens, 589

Table of Authorities

Adero, Malaika, Up South: Stories, Studies, and Letters of this Century's African American Migrations, 17–18, 59, 112–14 (1993).

Allan, L., Strange Fruit, originally performed by Billie Holiday on Delco Records (1939).

Anderson, Jose, Perspectives on *Missouri v. Jenkins*: Abandoning the Unfinished Business of Public School Desegregation "With All Deliberate Speed," 39 How. L.J. 693, 701–4 (1996).

Anderson, Jose, History Says that Blacks Should Vote, The Baltimore Sun, 25A, October 25, 2000.

Associated Press, Clinton To Think About Apology, The Baltimore Sun, June 17, 1997, at 3A.

Bamsham, M. and Steve Olson, Does Race Exist?, December 2003 Biology 1, 1–9 (2003).

Baynes, Leonard M., Perspectives: Abandoning *Brown* and '[Race]ing' Backwards on K–12 Education 1–2 (2005).

Bell, Derrick, *Brown v. Board of Education* and the Interest-Convergence Dilemma, 93 Harvard L. Rev. 518, 524–28 (1980).

Bell, Derrick, Race, Racism and American Law, Fourth Ed., 131–39, 653–58 (2000).

Berger, Bethany, After Pocahontas: Indian Women and the Law 1830–1934, 21 American Indian L. Rev. 1, 6–8 (1997).

Bogen, David S., Slaughter-House Five: Views of the Case, 55 Hastings Law Journal 333, 337–41 (2003).

Breyer, Stephen, Making Our Democracy Work 26-31 (2010).

Brinkley, M., Memorandum Prepared on Judge Thomas Ruffin 2–4 (1997).

Brook, T., *Plessy v. Ferguson*, A Brief History with Documents in the Bedford Series in History and Culture 1–10 (1997).

Calleros, Charles, Paternalism, Counterspeech, and Campus Hate-Speech Codes: A Reply to Delgado and Yun, 27 Ariz. St. L.J. 1249, 1255–63 (1995).

Chavez Jr., Alfred, What's in a Name?, The Washington Post, A22, October 29, 1991.

Chin, G., The *Plessy* Myth: Justice Harlan and the Chinese Cases, 82 Iowa L. Rev. 151, 171–74 (1996).

Connally, C., Justice Harlan's Great Betrayal? A Reconsideration of *Cummings v. Richmond County Board of Education*, Journal of Supreme Court History 72, 73–87 (1998).

Crouch, Stanley, Money Isn't Cure for Blacks' Problems, The Baltimore Sun, 15A, February 27, 2001.

Davis, A., The Case for United States Reparations to African-Americans, 7 Human Rights Brief 1, 2–4 (2000).

Davis, Peggy Cooper, Introducing Robert Smalls, 69 Fordham L. Rev. 1695, 1702–4, 1708–16 (2001).

De Saussure, L., Ryan's Mart Slave Auction Handbill (1852).

Delgado, Richard, Explaining the Rise and Fall of African American Fortunes — Interest Convergence and Civil Rights Gains, 37 Harv. Civ. rights-Civ. Liberties L. Rev. 369, 370–71 (2002).

Dunbar, P., We Wear The Mask in The Collected Poetry of Paul Lawrence Dunbar 71 (1989).

Entin, J., *Sweatt v. Painter*, The End of Segregation and the Transformation of Education Law, 5 Rev. Litig. 1, 13–17 (1986).

Epstein, R., Race and the Police Power, 46 Wash. & Lee L. Rev. 741, 750–52 (1989).

Fehrenbacher, D., Slavery and Its Consequences: The Constitution, Equality, and Race, 11–18 (1988).

Fehrenbacher, D., The *Dred Scott* Case: Its Significance in American Law and Politics, 264–66 (1978).

Flaherty, Peter, Reparation Issue Is a Smoke Screen and a Shakedown, The Los Angeles Times, April 22, 2002, at Part 2, p. 11.

Fletcher, M., Reparations For Slavery Is No Laughing Matter, The Baltimore Sun, May 16, 1997, at A16.

Franklin, J., From Slavery to Freedom: A History of Negro Americans, 180–86, 189–94, 204–07, 234–37 (1980).

Garfield, Leslie Yalof, The Glass Half Full: Envisioning The Future Of Race Preference Policies, 63 N.Y.U. Ann. Surv. Am. L. 385, 385–401 (2008).

Gordon, J., Did the First Justice Harlan Have a Black Brother?, 15 W. New Eng. L. Rev. 119, 122–24, 131–32, 134–39 (1993).

Green, W., The Summer Christmas Came to Minnesota: The Case of *Eliza Winston, A Slave*, 8 Law & Ineq. 151, 156–58 (1989).

Gross, Ariela J., Litigating Whiteness: Trials of Racial Determination in the Nineteenth-Century South, 108 Yale Law Journal 109, 111–12, 120–22 (1998).

Haney Lopez, I., White by Law: The Legal Construction of Race, 37–46 (1996).

Harpalani, Vinay, Memorandum on *Bhagat Singh Thind*, 2–3 (2008).

Harrison, Roderick, The Multiracial Responses on the Census Pose Unforeseen Risks to Civil Rights Enforcement and Monitoring, Focus Magazine, 5–6 (April 2001).

Harrison, W., The Ambivalent Statesman: Did Thomas Jefferson Find Slavery Abhorrent Because It Was Immoral or Because It Was Inconvenient?, 4 Emerge 50–52 (May 1993).

Hernández, Tanya Katerí, Multiracial Discourse: Racial Classifications in an Era of Color-blind Jurisprudence, 57 Maryland Law Rev. 97, 98–103, 107–12 (1998).

Higginbotham, A. and A. Jacobs, The "Law Only as an Enemy": The Legitimization of Racial Powerlessness Through the Colonial and Antebellum Criminal Laws of Virginia, 70 N.C. L. Rev. 1035–36 (1992).

Higginbotham, A., A Tribute to Justice Thurgood Marshall, 105 Harv. L. Rev. 55, 56–57 (1991).

Higginbotham, A., An Open Letter to Justice Clarence Thomas from a Federal Judicial Colleague, 140 U. Pa. L. Rev. 1005, 1005–28 (1992).

Higginbotham, A., and A. Francois, Looking for God and Racism in All The Wrong Places, 70 Den. L. Rev. 191, 192–93 (1993).

Higginbotham, A., and B. Kopytoff, Racial Purity and Interracial Sex in the Law of Colonial and Antebellum Virginia, 77 Geo. L.J. 1967, 1969–2007 (1989).

Higginbotham, A., and F. Higginbotham, "Yearning to Breathe Free": Legal Barriers Against and Options in Favor of Liberty In Antebellum Virginia, 68 N.Y.U. L. Rev. 1213, 1239–41, 1242, 1271 (1993).

Higginbotham, A., et al., De Jure Housing Segregation in the United States and South Africa: The Difficult Pursuit for Racial Justice, 1990 U. Ill. L. Rev. 763, 848–51 (1990).

Higginbotham, A., et al., The O.J. Simpson Trial: Who Was Improperly Playing the Race Card, in Birth of a Nationhood 31–44 (Toni Morrison, ed., 1997).

Higginbotham, A., et. al., Shaw v. Reno: A Mirage of Good Intentions with Devastating Racial Consequences, 62 Fordham L. Rev. 1593, 1644–46 (1994).

Higginbotham, A., Letter To Judicial Council, Unpublished (1997).

Higginbotham, A., Race, Racism, and American Law, 122 U. Pa. L. Rev. 1044, 1044–45, 1051–52, 1057–58 (1974).

Higginbotham, A., Race, Sex, Education, and Missouri Jurisprudence: Shelley v. Kramer in Historical Perspective, 67 Wash. U.L.Q. 701, 737–38 (1989).

Higginbotham, A., The Bicentennial of the Constitution: A Racial Perspective, 22 Stan. Law. 8–13, 52–53 (Fall 1987).

Higginbotham, A., The Hill-Thomas Hearings — What Took Place and What Happened: White Male Domination, Black Male Domination, and the Denigration of Black Women in Race, Gender, and the Power in America 33–35 (Anita Hill and Emma Jordan, eds., 1997).

Higginbotham, A., The Life of the Law: Values, Commitment, and Craftsmanship, 100 Harv. L. Rev. 795, 804–6 (1987).

Higginbotham, F. and Anderson, Jose, Drum Majors for Justice, The Sun, A17 (Feb. 18, 1999).

Higginbotham, F. and Bergin, Kathleen, The Court has Granted Wide Deference to Colleges, The Chronicle Review, B14–B17, March 28, 2003.

Higginbotham, F., A Dream Deferred: Comparative and Practical Considerations for the Black Reparations Movement, 58 N.Y.U. Ann. Surv. Am. L. 447, 447–50 (2003).

Higginbotham, F., A Request From Heaven To President Obama: Don't Forget The Race Issue, The Daily News, A19 (January 26, 2010).

Higginbotham, F., Affirmative Action, Selective Memory Loss, and the Mistakes of *Adarand*, 1995 Annual Survey 415, 418–20 (1995).

Higginbotham, F., After 150 Years, Worst Supreme Court Decision Ever Continues to Haunt, The Washington Afro-American, A8 (March 9, 2007).

Higginbotham, F., America's Racial Soul, The Sun, A15 (June 9, 2016).

Higginbotham, F., Bar Group Rolls Up Welcome Mat, 105 The Crisis 12 (1998).

Higginbotham, F., Bush and the Black Vote, Washington Afro-American, A13 (October 30, 2004).

Higginbotham, F., The Case of the Missing Post-Racial Election, Baltimore Afro-American, A7 (November 6, 2012).

Higginbotham, F., Congress Must Act to Guard Our Most Important Right, Orlando Sentinel, A14 (August 16, 2013).

Higginbotham, F., Keynote Speech: A Letter From The Original Cause Lawyer, 35 LaVerne L. Rev. 205, 211–215 (2014).

Higginbotham, F., Racism Less Pervasive More Complex, The Sun, A21 (April 4, 2008).

Higginbotham, F., Soldiers for Justice: The Role of the Tuskegee Airmen in the Desegregation of the American Armed Forces, 8 Wm. & Mary Bill Rights J. 273, 300–2 (2000).

Higginbotham, F., Valuing Black Life, Baltimore Afro-American, A7 (February 26, 2014).

Hillier, Scot, Race and the Redskins, The Washington Post, A14, August 10, 1993.

Hudson, G., Black Americans vs. Citizenship: The *Dred Scott* Decision, 36 Negro Hist. Bull. 26, 27–29 (1983).

Hughes, L., Dream of Freedom in The Collected Poems of Langston Hughes 542 (1994).

Hutchinson, Darren, Progressive Race Blindness?: Individual Identity, Group Politics, and Reform, 49 U.C.L.A. L. Rev. 1455, 1456–57 (2002).

Hylton, G., The Judge Who Abstained in *Plessy v. Ferguson*: Justice David Brewer and the Problem of Race, 61 Miss. L.J. 315, 316–22, 357–62 (1991).

Jones, D., No Time For Trumpets: Title VII, Equality, and the *Fin de Siecle*, 92 Mich. L. Rev. 2311, 2325–26 (1994).

Kruckenberg, K., Multi-Hued America: The Case For The Recognition Of A Multiethnic Identity In US Data Collection, 4 The Modern American 50–55 (2008).

Lane, Charles, The Day Freedom Died: The Colfax Massacre, The Supreme Court, and the Betrayal of Reconstruction, xv–xviii, 1–23 (2008).

Lawrence III, Charles R., The Id, The Ego, and Equal Protection: Reckoning with Unconscious Racism, 39 Stan. L. Rev. 317–18, 327, 330–45 (1987).

Lee, C., (E) Racing Trayvon Martin, 12 Ohio St. J. C. L. 91, 100–113 (2014).

Levy, L., and H. Phillips, The *Roberts* Case: Source of the Separate But Equal Doctrine, American Historical Rev. 517, 517–18 (1950).

Lively, Donald E., The Constitution and Race, 11–17, 20–26, 75–77, 94–96, 98–99, 102–4, 119–22, 123–25 (1992).

Mank, Bradford, Are Title VI's Disparate Impact Regulations Valid?, 71 Cincinnati L. Rev. 517, 517–20 (2002).

McIntosh, Peggy, White Privilege: Unpacking the Invisible Knapsack, White Privilege and Male Privilege: A Personal Account of Coming to See Correspondences through Work in Women's Studies, Working Paper 189 (2001).

Munson, Barbara, Not for Sport, Teaching Tolerance, 40–42 (Spring 1999).

Newsreel Incorporated, Negroes With Guns: Rob Williams and Black Power (2005).

Newton, J., Amazing Grace (T. Nelson, 1859).

Noonan, Jr., John T., The Antelope: The Ordeal of the Recaptured Africans in the Administrations of James Monroe and John Quincy Adams, The Antelope, 17–19 (1977).

Parks, Jr., A., Racial Diversity's Effect on Education is a Myth, The Chronicle Review, B11–B14 (March 28, 2003).

Robinson, R., The Debt: What America Owes To Blacks, 201–5 (2000).

Sandoval, L., Race and Immigration Law: A Troubled Marriage, 7 Mod. Am. 42, 43–51 (2011).

Saucedo, L., Mexicans, Immigrants, Cultural Narratives, and National Origin, 44 Ariz. St. L. J. 305, 314–331 (2012).

Stone, G., et al., Constitutional Law lxxviii, lxxxvii, lxxxiii, xcii, xciii–xciv (3rd ed. 1996).

Strickland, Rennard, Tonto's Revenge, 48–49, 52–54, 110–11 (1997).

Taylor-Thompson, K., Empty Votes In Jury Deliberations, 113 Harv. L. Rev. 1261, 1279–81 (2000).

Ware, L. and Wilson, D., Jim Crow on the "Down Low": Subtle Racial Appeals in Presidential Campaigns, 24 St. John's J.L.Comm. 299, 307–314 (2009).

Warren, Charles, The Supreme Court in United States History, 539–50 (1932).

Wisemen, W., White Crimes: American History and the Case for African-American Reparations, 1–4 (Unpublished manuscript 2004).

Yang, Tseming, Choice and Fraud In Racial Identification: The Dilemma of Policing Race In Affirmative Action, the Census, and a Color-Blind Society, 11 Mich. J. Race & Law 357, 368–377, 383–387, 416 (2006).

Foreword

F. Michael Higginbotham*

Speaking Truth to Power:
*A Tribute to A. Leon Higginbotham, Jr.***

It has been several years since that November day when A. Leon Higginbotham, Jr.[1] made his last public appearance, testifying before the House Judiciary Committee considering the impeachment of President William Jefferson Clinton.

---

* (footnote omitted).

** The phrase "speaking truth to power" is taken from Anita Hill's wonderful book of the same name examining the 1991 Anita Hill-Clarence Thomas hearings before the Senate Judiciary Committee. ANITA HILL: SPEAKING TRUTH TO POWER (1997). To speak truth to power is to maintain the truthfulness of one's speech or actions in the face of a powerful and potentially hostile audience.

As will be indicated in footnotes throughout this Tribute, portions of this Tribute are reprinted with permission from F. Michael Higginbotham, A Man for All Seasons, 16 HARV. BLACKLETTER L.J. 7, 13–14 (2000) [hereinafter Higginbotham, A Man for All Seasons]; F. Michael Higginbotham & Jose Felipe Anderson, A. Leon Higginbotham, Jr.: Who Will Carry the Baton?, 33 LOY. L.A. L. REV. 1015 (2000); and F. Michael Higginbotham, Saving the Dream for All, HUMAN RTS., Summer 1999, at 23 (Reprinted by Permission: Copyright © 1999 by the American Bar Association; F. Michael Higginbotham) [hereinafter Higginbotham, Saving the Dream].

1. Aloyisus Leon Higginbotham, Jr. was born the only child of Aloyisus Leon Higginbotham, Sr. And Emma Douglas Higginbotham in Trenton, New Jersey. He graduated from Ewing Park High School in Trenton at the age of sixteen and went on to Purdue University, but transferred to Antioch College in Ohio, from which he graduated in 1949. He graduated at the top of his class from Yale Law School in 1952 and was admitted to the Pennsylvania Bar in 1953. In the years following, Judge Higginbotham served as President of the Philadelphia branch of the NAACP, a commissioner of the Pennsylvania Human Relations Commission, and a special deputy attorney general.

In 1962, after a successful private practice, Judge Higginbotham was appointed by President John F. Kennedy to the Federal Trade Commission. In 1964, President Lyndon B. Johnson appointed him a federal district court judge, and in 1977, President Jimmy Carter appointed him to the United States Court of Appeals for the Third Circuit. Judge Higginbotham served as Chief Judge of that court from 1989 to 1991, and as a senior judge from 1991 until his retirement in 1993.

During his judicial service, Chief Justices Warren, Burger, and Rehnquist appointed Judge Higginbotham to a variety of judicial conference committees and other related responsibilities. Judge Higginbotham also found time to teach at the law schools of Harvard University, University of Michigan, New York University, University of Pennsylvania, Stanford University, and Yale University.

By appointment of President Johnson, Judge Higginbotham also served as Vice Chairman of the National Commission on the Causes and Prevention of Violence. In November 1995, he was appointed to the United States Commission on Civil Rights. Also in 1995, he received the Presidential Medal of Freedom, the nation's highest civilian award.

His candid, objective, and scholarly testimony before the Committee helped to convince many members of Congress that the impeachment of Clinton was inconsistent with constitutional provisions, unsupported by legal history, and intellectually dishonest. As he did so many times throughout his professional career, Leon spoke truth to power.[2] Sometimes, power acceded to his truth, but more often only history proved him right. Nonetheless, Leon had the courage to speak the truth no matter how strong the opposition or controversial the issue.

Leon's position regarding impeachment was that, while Congress certainly has the power to remove the President from office when an impeachable offense has been committed, President Clinton's alleged act of perjury was not such an offense.[3] In Leon's view, not all illegal acts, not even all felonies, rise to the level justifying Congress's removal of the President. Leon posed the following hypothetical question: Would the Judiciary Committee have proposed impeaching President Clinton had he been cited for driving at a speed of fifty-five miles per hour in a fifty mile-per-hour speed zone, yet later falsely testified, under oath, that he had been driving only forty-nine miles per hour?[4] He then stated:

> I submit that as to impeachment purposes, there is not a significant substantive difference between the hypothetical traffic offense and the actual sexual incident in this matter. The alleged perjurious statements denying a sexual relationship between the President of the United States and another consenting adult do not rise to the level of constitutional egregiousness that triggers the impeachment clause of Article II.[5]

As Leon intimated, yes, it was true that President Clinton may have lied under oath. Yes, it was true that President Clinton's behavior with Monica Lewinsky may have been unwise. Yes, it was true that some of these activities could reasonably be characterized as felony offenses. Yet, as Leon so persuasively argued, it was also true that not all felonious conduct would or should lead to impeachment. The Senate's subsequent refusal to convict President Clinton and remove him from office suggests its recognition of Leon's truth.

---

2. *See supra* note **. Perhaps Leon's most famous "truth to power" was the letter he sent to Justice Clarence Thomas in 1992 after Thomas's confirmation as an Associate Justice of the United States Supreme Court. A. Leon Higginbotham, *An Open Letter to Justice Clarence Thomas from a Federal Judicial Colleague*, 140 U.PA. L. REV. 1005 (1992). Much has been written about this letter, but a further examination of it and the circumstances surrounding its writing are beyond the scope of this article.

3. Portions of the following anecdote are reprinted with permission from Higginbotham, *A Man for All Seasons, supra* note **, at 13–14.

4. *Consequences of Perjury and Related Crimes Before the House Comm. on the Judiciary*, 105th Cong. 67 (1998), *available at* http://www.house.gov/judiciary/full.htm (statement of A. Leon Higgin-botham, Jr.).

5. *Id.*

A. Leon Higginbotham, Jr. began speaking truth to power in 1944 when he was a sixteen-year-old freshman at Purdue University. In the preface to his first book, *In the Matter of Color*,[6] Leon wrote about his first experience speaking truth to power:

> I was . . . one of twelve black civilian students. If we wanted to live in West Lafayette, Indiana, where the university was located, solely because of our color the twelve of us at Purdue were forced to live in a crowded private house rather than, as did most of our white classmates, in the university campus dormitories. We slept barracks-style in an unheated attic.
>
> One night, as the temperature was close to zero, I felt that I could suffer the personal indignities and denigration no longer. The United States was more than two years into the Second World War, a war our government had promised would "make the world safe for democracy." Surely there was room enough in that world, I told myself that night, for twelve black students in a northern university in the United States to be given a small corner of the on-campus heated dormitories for their quarters. Perhaps all that was needed was for one of us to speak up, to make sure the administration knew exactly how a small group of its students had been treated by those charged with assigning student housing.
>
> The next morning, I went to the office of Edward Charles Elliot, president of Purdue University, and asked to see him. I was given an appointment.
>
> At the scheduled time I arrived at President Elliot's office, neatly (but not elegantly) dressed, shoes polished, fingernails clean, hair cut short. Why was it, I asked him, that blacks—and blacks alone—had been subjected to this special ignominy? Though there were larger issues I might have raised with the president of an American university (this was but ten years before *Brown v. Board of Education*) I had not come that morning to move mountains, only to get myself and eleven friends out of the cold. Forcefully, but nonetheless deferentially, I put forth my modest request: That the black students of Purdue be allowed to stay in some section of the state-owned dormitories; segregated, if necessary, but at least not humiliated.
>
> Perhaps if President Elliot had talked with me sympathetically that morning, explaining his own impotence to change things but his willingness to take up the problem with those who could, I might not have felt as I did. Perhaps if he had communicated with some word or gesture, or even a sigh, that I had caused him to review his own commitment to things as they were, I might have felt I had won a small victory. But President Elliot, with

---

6. A. LEON HIGGINBOTHAM, JR., IN THE MATTER OF COLOR: RACE IN THE AMERICAN LEGAL PROCESS, THE COLONIAL PERIOD (1978). The book has been cited by federal and state courts as a reliable source of the legal history of the American colonial period. *E.g.*, *McCleskey v. Kemp*, 481 U.S. 279, 329 (1987) (Brennan, J., dissenting); *United States v. Long*, 935 F.2d 1207, 1211 (11th Cir. 1991); *Commonwealth v. Rogers*, 393 A.2d 876, 880 (Pa. Super. Ct. 1978).

directness and with no apparent qualms, answered, "Higginbotham, the law doesn't require us to let colored students in the dorm, and you either accept things as they are or leave the University immediately."

As I walked back to the house that afternoon, I reflected on the ambiguity of the day's events. I had heard, on that morning, an eloquent lecture on the history of the Declaration of Independence, and of the genius of the founding fathers. That afternoon I had been told that under the law the black civilian students at Purdue University could be treated differently from their 6,000 white classmates. Yet I knew that by nightfall hundreds of black soldiers would be injured, maimed, and some even killed on far flung battlefields to make the world safe for democracy. Almost like a mystical experience, a thousand thoughts raced through my mind as I walked across campus. I knew then I had been touched in a way I had never been touched before, and that one day I would have to return to the most disturbing element in this incident—how a legal system that proclaims "equal justice for all" could simultaneously deny even a semblance of dignity to a 16-year-old boy who had committed no wrong.[7]

Leon explained the simple facts to the most powerful person at Purdue University. It was true that the attic was cold. It was true that the attic was overcrowded. Unfortunately, as Leon found out that day, it was also true that those in power at Purdue University would not remedy this injustice. In this initial experience, Leon began to display the commitment, leadership, dedication, sacrifice, honesty, directness, and courage that would guide him throughout his life.

Some of Leon's most powerful truth was reserved for the leaders of the National Party, the ruling political party in South Africa from 1948 until 1994 and the creator of apartheid.[8] In 1986, on one of his six trips to South Africa, Leon and a group of American business and academic leaders[9] visited during a period of "reform" of the apartheid system.[10] While the National Party had instituted apartheid in 1948 and had vigorously defended it for forty years, due to some recent newspaper

---

7. HIGGINBOTHAM, *supra* note 7, at vii–ix.

8. After winning its first national election in 1948, the National Party began to implement a variety of racial segregation laws and policies that collectively became known as apartheid. *See* A. Leon Higginbotham, Jr. et al., *De Jure Housing Segregation in the United States and South Africa: The Difficult Pursuit for Racial Justice*, 1990 U. ILL. L. REV. 763; A. Leon Higginbotham, Jr., *Racism in American and South African Courts: Similarities and Differences*, 65 N.Y.U. L. REV. 479 (1990) [hereinafter *American Experience and the South African Challenge*, 42 DUKE L.J. 1028 (1993) [hereinafter Higginbotham, *Seeking Pluralism*]. The following anecdote is in large part reprinted with permission from Higginbotham, *A Man for All Seasons, supra* note **, at 9–10.

9. The group included W. Michael Reisman, Professor of Law at Yale University, James Laney, President of Emory University and member of the board of directors of Coca Cola, and Robert Rotberg, President of the World Peace Foundation.

10. For improved domestic and international relations, on several occasions, the National Party made minor or cosmetic changes to the racial laws of South Africa. *See* TOM LODGE, BLACK POLITICS IN SOUTH AFRICA SINCE 1945 (1985).

accounts, there was some sense among members of the American delegation that the Party might be willing to reevaluate its position. Upon arrival at the impressive government building in Capetown, however, the American delegates were roundly informed that the National Party remained enthusiastically committed to racial segregation and discrimination. Several National Party members of Parliament explained that blacks and whites had vastly different cultures, resulting in constant conflict between the races. Consequently, they said, it was necessary to separate the races in order to protect each from the other and to create an atmosphere where each culture could thrive. These lawmakers were adamant that the races must remain separated, and throughout their presentation, they appeared to ignore Leon, the only black person in the delegation.

Most of the Americans seemed stunned that the National Party officials had reiterated their commitment to racial separation so enthusiastically, had been so dogmatic in their presentation, and had displayed such rudeness to Leon. When the Americans were asked to respond, they all looked to Leon to articulate their collective feelings.[11]

Leon addressed the Party officials without fear or hesitation. He began by talking about how much all human beings have in common. They all need food, shelter, and clothing. They all desire love and happiness. And they all are able to benefit from education, scientific discoveries, and health care. He kept reiterating the theme that we are all part of the human family, and that when we work together we are able to accomplish so much more. Leon then discussed the infamous atrocities that human beings had committed against one another over the years and how the perpetrators of such oppression had been judged in the corridors of history. He talked about how wrongs would not go unpunished much longer. In conclusion, Leon quoted the character Shylock from William Shakespeare's play "The Merchant of Venice." Shylock said to his adversaries:

> He hath disgraced me . . . scorned my nation . . . cooled my friends, heated mine enemies, and what's his reason? . . . If you prick us do we not bleed? If you tickle us do we not laugh? If you poison us do we not die? And if you wrong us shall we not revenge? If we are like you in the rest, we will resemble you in that. . . . The villainy you teach me I will execute, and it shall go hard but I will better the instruction.[12]

Leon then added a final, stinging observation. He stated that based upon the substance and behavior of the speakers, he could no longer, in good conscience, consider them part of the human family.[13]

---

11. *Id.* at 9.

12. WILLIAM SHAKESPEARE, THE MERCHANT OF VENICE, *in* THE COMPLETE WORKS, act 3, sc. 1, 11, 50–68 (Stanley Wells & Gary Taylor eds., Clarendon Press 1986).

13. Leon often quoted Shakespeare in responding to comments made in support of apartheid. *Cf.* Higginbotham, *Seeking Pluralism, supra* note 9, at 1061–63.

As Leon knew so well, Shakespeare's expression captures the hidden fears of all persons who are or have been oppressors. While none of the Americans were deluded into thinking that any racist attitudes had been changed that day by Leon's truth, there was a great sense of satisfaction in knowing that these race supremacists had been made to understand that they, not black South Africans, were the real outcasts, and that sooner or later there would be a high price to pay for their continued oppression. As each American delegate stood, indicating unanimous agreement with Leon's response, the powerful members of Parliament were made to consider the truth of those statements. The National Party's subsequent negotiation with the African National Congress to end apartheid suggests their recognition of Leon's truth.

Leon had a special gift for helping decision-makers in positions of authority realize the error of their thinking and to open up their hearts' compassion.[14] He could criticize without being offensive, prod without being irritating, and motivate without being preachy. One of his favorite stories involved his alma mater, Yale University, and its decision to make its undergraduate program coeducational. Leon was the first African American to serve on Yale's board of directors,[15] and he was a vigorous advocate for the admission of women into Yale College. Leon often reminded listeners of the vast contributions of both America's forefathers and foremothers, and how Americans should recognize the significant involvement of women in the abolition of slavery and in the Civil Rights Movement.[16] More specifically, Leon spoke at several board meetings about how to measure the quality of a university. He talked about the extent of the resources, the quality of the faculty, but, most significantly, the contribution of its students. He then began to identify the many contributions to the life of the university made by female graduate students at Yale, and how those contributions had benefited the entire school. After an historic meeting where, at the urging of Leon and others, the board of directors decided to admit women to its undergraduate ranks,[17] one of the directors opposed to such admission remarked to Leon that it was a sad day in Yale's great history and one that they all would come to regret. Several years later that same director told Leon at a Yale graduation ceremony how happy he was and what a great day it was for him because his daughter was in Yale College's graduating class.

It was true that Yale College would admit women for the first time. It was true that such admittance would help to create gender equality, which would fundamentally change Yale forever. History has proven Leon's assertion that this fundamental change would be good for far more than just those women admitted. It was also

---

14. Some portions of the following anecdote are reprinted with permission from Higginbotham, *A Man for All Seasons, supra* note **, at 10.

15. Samuel M. Hughes, *Summing Up Leon Higginbotham*, Pa. Gazette, Feb. 1993, at 18, 20.

16. *See* A. Leon Higginbotham, Jr., *Rosa Parks: Foremother & Heroine Teaching Civility & Offering a Vision for a Better Tomorrow*, 22 Fla. St. U. L. Rev. 899, 900–8 (1995).

17. The Yale Law School had begun admitting women in 1884. A. Leon Higginbotham, Jr., *The Life of the Law: Values, Commitment, and Craftsmanship*, 100 Harv. L. Rev. 795, 796 n. 2 (1987).

good for those men who would be their classmates, and for the university. It was good for those who lacked the foresight to perceive the long-term common benefit, for those who lacked the compassion to see the unfairness of such exclusion, and for those who possessed the selfishness to want to keep the greatness of Yale all to themselves.

As an enthusiastic supporter of the Civil Rights Movement, Leon often spoke to conservatives who had unsuccessfully opposed the movement and subsequently attempted to reverse its accomplishments. In an eye-opening 1992 editorial entitled "The Case of the Missing Black Judges,"[18] Leon examined the impact and meaning of the judicial appointments of President Reagan and the first President Bush, concluding that their desire to create a more "conservative" federal court system resulted in few judicial appointments of African Americans. He explained:

> [T]o the extent that the appointment of judges is a barometer of a President's feelings about placing historically excluded groups in positions of power, Jimmy Carter showed that he had complete confidence in African Americans.

President Reagan apparently felt otherwise and President Bush apparently does, too. On taking office, they both asserted that they wanted a far more "conservative" Federal court system. In that, they have succeeded admirably. But in the process they have turned the Courts of Appeals into what Judge Stephen Reinhardt of the Court of Appeals for the Ninth Circuit has called "a symbol of white power."

In eight years of office, out of a total of 83 appellate appointments, Ronald Reagan found only one African American whom he deemed worthy of appointment, Lawrence W. Pierce. President Bush's record is just as abysmal. Of his 32 appointments to the Courts of Appeals, he also has been able to locate only one African American he considered qualified to serve: Justice Clarence Thomas. . . .

By 1993, six of the 10 African Americans sitting on the Courts of Appeals will be eligible for retirement. As the African-American judges appointed by President Carter have retired, Presidents Reagan and Bush have replaced them largely with white judges in their 30s and early 40s. . . .

I am forced to conclude that the record of appointments of African Americans to the Courts of Appeals during the past 12 years demonstrates that, by intentional Presidential action, African-American judges have been turned into an endangered species, soon to become extinct.[19]

Shortly after publication of this editorial, the first President George Bush was defeated by Bill Clinton, whose judicial appointments were much more racially diverse than his immediate predecessors. In seven years, Clinton appointed 52

---

18. A. Leon Higginbotham, Jr., *The Case of the Missing Black Judges*, N.Y. TIMES, July 29, 1992, at A15.

19. *Id.*

African-American judges out of a total of 296, including five to the courts of appeals.[20] Thanks to a concerted effort to reverse political conservatism in the courts, which was initially identified and enthusiastically supported by Leon, it seems that President Clinton was able to recognize the truth of Presidents Reagan and Bush's judicial appointments records and to solve "the case of the missing black judges."

Leon served as a judge on the federal bench for twenty-nine years.[21] In one of his most powerful opinions, *Commonwealth v. Local 542, International Union of Operating Engineers*,[22] Leon responded to a motion asking that he recuse himself because he was black. This case was a civil rights employment action brought by black construction workers against the construction industry. The defendants moved for Judge Higginbotham to recuse himself because of comments the Judge had made while speaking to a luncheon organized by the Association for the Study of Afro-American Life and History. At the luncheon, Leon stated that African Americans could no longer rely exclusively on the Supreme Court as an instrument for social change. In responding to this recusal motion, Leon explained that the presence of bias, not skin color, should be the determining factor in a recusal decision.[23] He explained:

> I concede that I am black. I do not apologize for that obvious fact. I take rational pride in my heritage, just like most other ethnics take pride in theirs. However, that one is black does not mean, ipso facto, that he is anti-white; no more than being Jewish implies being anti-Catholic, or being Catholic implies being anti-Protestant.[24]

Again, Leon spoke truth to power. It was true, he was a proud black man understanding and appreciating the obstacles, sacrifices, and accomplishments of those African Americans who had fought and, in some cases died, for freedom and equality. It was true that he was not consequently anti-white. Leon spent his entire professional career writing, speaking, and treating all individuals, irrespective of race, as equal and respected members of the human family.[25] But as Leon so truthfully pointed out, he was not going to allow wealthy and powerful white litigants to characterize him as less objective than white judges just because he happened to be black.

Leon saved his most frequent criticism, however, for those who refused to acknowledge the continued presence of racism in America. He frequently reminded

20. Sheldon Goldman & Elliot Slotnick, *Clinton's Second Term Judiciary: Picking Judges Under Fire*, 82 JUDICATURE 264, 275, 280 (1999).
21. Leon was appointed to the United States District Court for the Eastern District of Pennsylvania in 1964 by President Lyndon Johnson. He was elevated to the United States Court of Appeals for the Third Circuit in 1977 by President Jimmy Carter. He became Chief Judge of the Third Circuit in 1989. The following story is reprinted with permission from Higginbotham, *A Man for All Seasons, supra* note **, at 11.
22. 388 F. Supp. 155 (E.D. Pa. 1974).
23. *See id*. At 159–60.
24. *Id*. at 163.
25. (footnote omitted).

listeners of Justice Roger Brooke Taney's[26] 1857 opinion in *Dred Scott v. Sandford*,[27] where Taney reasoned that blacks were "beings of an inferior order, and altogether unfit to associate with the white race . . . and so far inferior, that they had no rights which the white man was bound to respect; and that the Negro might justly and lawfully be reduced to slavery for his [own] benefit."[28] Leon reminded listeners that the *Dred Scott* opinion will be remembered as the legal decision that paved the way for the Civil War.[29]

Leon also recognized that *Dred Scott* will be remembered as the case that most clearly demonstrates that many white Americans embraced the notion of black inferiority. Justice Taney explained that the assumed inferiority of blacks at the time the country was founded was "fixed and universal in the civilized portion of the white race. It was regarded as an axiom in morals as well as in politics, which no one thought of disputing, or supposed to be open to dispute."[30] This view was shared by writers of the time[31] and endured after the Civil War into the early 1900s.[32]

Leon observed that this belief that "African Americans are of an 'inferior order' is an idea some find difficult to abandon."[33] Although he recognized that many people would challenge this notion and even more would find the suggestion that they harbor such feelings "downright insulting,"[34] he nevertheless was adamant in opposing the notion that the Civil War had a cleansing effect on the wrongness and impact of slavery.[35] He spoke truth in the face of an unreceptive white majority. He began by identifying the problem that the majority of white Americans believe "that they personally have nothing whatsoever to do with slavery, segregation, or racial oppression because neither they nor—as far as they know—their ancestors ever enslaved anyone, ever burned a cross in the night in front of anyone's house, or

---

26. Taney served as Chief Justice of the United States Supreme Court from 1836–1864. "Taney brought infamy upon himself because he viewed the alleged inferiority of blacks as an axiom of both law and the Constitution, a legal discrimination that he saw sanctioned even in the Declaration of Independence." THE OXFORD COMPANION TO THE SUPREME COURT OF THE UNITED STATES 859 (Kermit L. Hall ed., 1992).

27. 60 U.S. 393 (1857).

28. *Id.* at 407.

29. Professor Derrick Bell points out that "the very excessiveness of the decision's language likely spurred those opposed to slavery to redouble their efforts to abolish [slavery]." DERRICK BELL, RACE, RACISM, AND AMERICAN LAW 25–26 (3d ed. 1992). Portions of the following discussion are reprinted with permission from Higginbotham & Anderson, *supra* note **, at 1027.

30. *Dred Scott*, 60 U.S. at 407.

31. For an interesting collection of pro-slavery writings produced in the decades prior to the Civil War, see SLAVERY DEFENDED: THE VIEWS OF THE OLD SOUTH (Eric L. McKitrick ed., 1963).

32. After the Civil War, attitudes about racial inferiority were sometimes presented as being supported by dubious scientific research. *See* HARVARD SITKOFF, A NEW DEAL FOR BLACKS: THE EMERGENCE OF CIVIL RIGHTS AS A NATIONAL ISSUE 5–6 (1978) (summarizing research at the turn of the century alleging that black inferiority was a hereditary characteristic).

33. A. LEON HIGGINBOTHAM, JR.: SHADES OF FREEDOM 7 (1996).

34. *Id.*

35. *See id.* at 29.

ever denied anyone a seat at the front of the bus."[36] This "self-absolving denial," Leon maintained, made it "nearly impossible to have an honest discussion about what used to be called 'the Negro Problem.'"[37] In Leon's view, this explains why it is so difficult to remove racial oppression from our society even though *de jure* segregation and discrimination have been eliminated in the law. He would ask rhetorically, why are so many statistical,[38] economic,[39] and educational[40] disparities attributed to racism by most blacks, but dismissed as mere coincidence by many whites? Leon's explanation for this dichotomy was that the effects of dormant or even unconscious racism emerge through the application of law, but cannot be directly traced to the law itself.

As Leon pointed out in his book *Shades of Freedom*, the statistical disparities continue to be overwhelming, and as Leon also highlighted, these disparities began and were exacerbated by slavery, segregation, and discrimination. Leon wrote volumes on the connection between past discrimination and present inequities,[41] but when reason failed he always seemed to return to the one simple axiom "we should not be ignorant as judges of what we know to be true as men."[42]

Leon refused to accept any award, no matter how prestigious, from organizations that did not reflect racial, ethnic, religious, and gender pluralism.[43] I will never forget the time he rejected the University of Chicago Law School's invitation to judge their prestigious moot court competition because they had no black faculty at the law school and had not for many years.[44]

Speaking so much truth to power did have its benefits. Throughout his professional career and particularly during the last ten years of his life, Leon received numerous awards, including the Lifetime Achievement Award from the National Bar Association, the NAACP's Spingarn Medal, and the nation's highest civilian honor — the Presidential Medal of Freedom. He was the first member of a minority group and the youngest person ever appointed to be a federal commissioner of the

---

36. HIGGINBOTHAM, *supra* note 34, at 7. This belief was articulated by Justice Scalia. *See* Antonin Scalia, *The Disease As Cure: "In Order To Get Beyond Racism, We Must First Take Account of Race,"* 1979 WASH. U. L.Q. 147, 152.

37. *Id.* at 7–8.

38. Blacks have been over-represented in the criminal justice system compared to their relative numbers in the population. *See* JAMES Q. WILSON & RICHARD J. HERRNSTEIN, CRIME AND HUMAN NATURE 461 (1985).

39. *See* HIGGINBOTHAM, *supra* note 34, at 7.

40. *See* BELL, *supra* note 29, at 611 (discussing the lower quality of education in predominantly black schools).

41. *See* HIGGINBOTHAM, *supra* note 34, at 207–12.

42. Justice Frankfurter used these words in *Watts v. Indiana*, 338 U.S. 49, 52 (1949) (citing *Bailey v. Drexel Furniture Co.* (The Child Labor Tax Case), 259 U.S. 20, 37 (1922)).

43. Much of the following discussion is Reprinted by Permission. It is taken from Higginbotham, *Saving the Dream*, *supra* note **, at 24.

44. Letter from A. Leon Higginbotham, Jr., Judge of the United States Court of Appeals for the Third Circuit, to Geoffrey Stone, Dean, University of Chicago Law School (Mar. 12, 1987) (on file with Yale Law and Policy Review).

Federal Trade Commission. At the age of thirty-six, he was the youngest African American appointed to the federal bench. At the time of his death, Leon held more than sixty honorary degrees.

While no stranger to criticism from conservatives[45] and never hesitant to refute their constant policy attacks,[46] Leon's primary concern was to continue the progress begun by the Civil Rights Movement.[47] He recognized that the civil rights tradition that he was fighting to preserve was much more important than his own popularity. Personal attacks, no matter how unfounded, would not dissuade him from this focus. Leon expressed specific concerns about several recent decisions of federal circuit courts of appeals that attacked traditional civil rights doctrine. He critiqued the Fifth Circuit's affirmative action decisions[48] and the Fourth Circuit's approaches to accused criminals' procedural rights[49] that represented what he called a "substantial threat to what [he] thought was well-settled legal doctrine."[50]

In one of the last conversations I had with Leon during Thanksgiving weekend of 1997, he suggested that some legal scholars needed to get together and "do the difficult work of reviewing every reported civil rights decision of the circuit courts and attack those decisions which would serve as precedent to turn back the civil rights clock." He lamented that he did not have time to do it himself, saying that such an effort done properly would require thousands of hours by many diligent academics. Nevertheless, he considered such an effort to be the single most important scholarly project one could imagine.

Leon concluded the conversation with the hope that sometime soon he could sponsor a conference in order to discuss some of these ideas with the many supporters of civil rights throughout the country. He thought that such a gathering could be

---

45. Al Knight, *New Racial Stereotypes Are Replacing the Old*, Denver Post, Aug. 2, 1998, at G3; Jeffrey Rosen, *The Bloods and the Crits*, New Republic Dec. 9, 1996, at 27–28; Tony Snow, *Thomasphobes Are Unremitting; Clarence Thomas Is Hate Target*, Cincinnati Enquirer, June 22, 1998, at A6.

46. *See* A. Leon Higginbotham Jr., *Blacks Remember Other Contracts Put Out on Them*, Phila. Inquirer, May 11, 1995, at A19; A. Leon Higginbotham Jr., *Breaking Thurgood Marshall's Promise*, N.Y. Times, Jan. 18, 1998, Magazine, at 28; Higginbotham, *supra* note 19, at A21; A. Leon Higginbotham, Jr., *Dear Mr. Speaker: An Open Letter to Newt Gingrich*, Nat'l L.J., June 5, 1995, at A19.

47. This discussion is reprinted with permission from Higginbotham & Anderson, *supra* note **, at 1029–30.

48. In 1996, the United States Court of Appeals for the Fifth Circuit held that "the use of race to achieve a diverse student body . . . simply cannot be a state interest compelling enough to meet the steep standard of strict scrutiny." *Hopwood v. Texas*, 78 F.3d 932, 948 (5th Cir. 1996).

49. The Fourth Circuit had been described as "by far the most restrictive appeals court in the nation granting new hearings in death penalty cases, according to statistical studies." Recently the Fourth Circuit issued an opinion that directly challenged the validity of the Supreme Court's precedent in *Miranda v. Arizona*, 384 U.S. 436 (1966), which provided that criminal defendants be advised of their rights upon arrest. *United States v. Dickerson*, 166 F.3d 667 (4th Cir. 1999) *See* Neil A. Lewis, *A Court Becoming a Model of Conservative Pursuits*, N.Y. Times, May 24, 1999, at A1.

50. This quotation and the following story (including the footnotes) are reprinted with permission from Higginbotham & Anderson, *supra* note **, at 1030.

the touchstone for new strategies and initiatives to create equal opportunity in the new millennium. He imagined a conference similar to the legendary Niagara Project, which served as a catalyst for the important work of the NAACP.[51]

Soon thereafter, Leon passed away. But his idea for a second Niagara Conference is alive and well today at Yale. As we go forward to discuss the issues that meant so much to A. Leon Higginbotham, Jr., remember his life, his dedication, his compassion, but most importantly his belief that speaking the truth about injustice, no matter how powerful the recipient or unwelcomed the message, will one day set us all free.

20 *Yale Law & Policy Review* 341, 341–51.
Copyright © (2002) *Yale Law & Policy Review.*
Reprinted with permission of *Yale Law & Policy Review* and
F. Michael Higginbotham.

---

51. The NAACP was started when a distinguished group of blacks and whites convened a conference on the Canadian side of Niagara Falls in early 1905 to discuss ways to reduce racial discrimination in the United States. A location in Canada was chosen to avoid racial segregation laws in the United States. *See* John Hope Franklin & Alfred A. Moss, Jr., From Slavery to Freedom: A History of Negro Americans 318–20 (7th ed. 1994).

Gift Chapel—Fort Sam Houston. Houston, Texas. November 1, 1917. Largest murder trial in American history. Negro Almanac Collection, Amistad Research Center at Tulane University. Copyright © (1966) Amistad Research Center. Reprinted with permission of the Amistad Research Center. For background information on the trial, see text accompanying the Preface.

Preface

F. Michael Higginbotham

*Soldiers for Justice: The Role of the Tuskegee Airmen in the
Desegregation of the American Armed Forces*

Perhaps because of the symbolic nature of military service or of the fear of blacks who were organized, disciplined, and trained in the use of firearms and explosives, black military personnel paid a high price for opposing racially discriminatory treatment and policies. Two famous incidents involving black protests and self-defense demonstrate the high price many blacks paid for their patriotism.

The first incident occurred in Brownsville, Texas, in 1906. Soldiers of the Twenty-Fifth Infantry were accused of rioting against white residents of Brownsville who were discriminating against black soldiers. Incidents of discrimination were widespread including refusals of service at stores open to the public, verbal and physical assaults, and false arrests. White residents reported that in the early morning hours of August 14, a group of six to twenty black soldiers fired hundreds of shots into several buildings within a three block radius. One white civilian was killed and a police officer was injured. An investigation failed to identify the soldiers involved in the incident, yet President Theodore Roosevelt imposed a never before utilized group punishment approach and dishonorably discharged three entire companies, totaling 167 men. Some of these men had twenty-seven years of service and six of them were recipients of the Medal of Honor, the Nation's highest military award.

A second incident occurred in Houston, Texas, in 1917. Black soldiers were subjected to the scorn of certain racist civilians and police officers living near the military base, just like those at Brownsville. Not only were they segregated on trolleys, black soldiers were spat upon, called derogatory names, assaulted, and incarcerated in the city jail. After one particularly brutal arrest involving threats of lynching, soldiers of the Twenty-Fourth Infantry broke into the base armory, seized weapons, and attacked some of the townspeople involved in the incident including several of the racist police officers. Seventeen people were killed. In response to the deaths, the military indicted 118 soldiers. Again, military justice was swift, deadly, and severely prejudiced. Thirteen soldiers were tried, convicted, and executed for murder and mutiny before their appeal could be heard. Six additional soldiers were hung at a later date. Moreover, approximately sixty-three soldiers received sentences of life imprisonment.

While duty, honor, and country were values universally embraced by the United States armed forces, when it came to black soldiers, such values were minimized or completely ignored. The values of duty, honor, and country were subordinated to the notion of white supremacy. Despite a legal system based on the premise of individual guilt and responsibility, African-American soldiers were collectively blamed for the alleged criminal activity of fellow black soldiers. Despite a legal system based on due process of law, African-American soldiers on trial were rushed to judgment and punishment. Finally, despite a legal system based on the notion that the punishment should fit the crime, African-American soldiers were given the harshest sanctions available even in the presence of numerous mitigating circumstances.

These two incidents exemplify the military's notion of race law prior to its desegregation in 1948. As the picture accompanying the preface so starkly portrays, race law often involved white prosecutors, white judges, and white jurors interpreting and enforcing racially discriminatory laws and choosing the harshest options available for non-whites in order to maintain and strengthen the notion of white racial superiority.

8 *William & Mary Bill of Rights Journal* 273, 300–2 (2000).
Copyright © (2000) F. Michael Higginbotham.
Reprinted with permission of F. Michael Higginbotham.

Acknowledgments

5th Edition

The author wishes to thank the following students for invaluable research and editorial assistance: Olivia Gordon, Dionne Hopkins, Ricardo Murga, and Rena Neuman. The author also wishes to thank Gloria Joy for secretarial support. Suggestions from students, teachers, or scholars are welcome.

4th Edition

The author wishes to thank the following students for invaluable research and editorial assistance: Matthew Osei-Bonsu and Matthew Bradford. The author also wishes to thank Shavaun O'Brien and Rose McMunn for secretarial support. Suggestions from students, teachers, or scholars are welcome.

3rd Edition

The author wishes to thank the following students for invaluable research and editorial assistance: Anastasia Albright, Paul Chandler, Danielle Grilli, Felise Kelly, Andrew Moss and Jonathan Singer. The author also wishes to thank Barbara Coyle and Martha Kahlert for secretarial support. A special debt of gratitude is owed to Professor Gloria Wittico for suggested revisions to the second edition. Further suggestions from students, teachers, or scholars are welcome.

2nd Edition

The author wishes to thank the following students for invaluable research and editorial assistance: Nadia Firozvi, David Krum, Grace McBride, Mark Monson, Alicia Ritchie, David Wiseman, and Andre Wynn. The author also wishes to thank Donna Frank and Barbara Jones for secretarial support, and Bob Pool for assistance with citations. A special debt of gratitude is owed to Professor Carla Pratt for suggested revisions to the first edition.

1st Edition

The author wishes to thank the following students for invaluable research and editorial assistance: Dave Armitage, Cheryl Brown, Sean Brown, Miatta Dabo, Kay Diaz, Brenda Holley, Danni Jahn, Dawn Landon, Lisa Lawler, Sondra Martin,

Donna McElroy, Melissa McNair, Cynthia Norris, Tracey Parker, Mike Settles, Eric Williams, Karen Williams, and Allison Villafane. The author also wishes to thank Martha Kahlert and Barbara Jones for secretarial support. A special debt of gratitude is owed to Kathleen Bergin for reviewing earlier drafts of the book and to Suzette Malveaux and Michael Meyerson for reviewing a final draft of the book. Finally, I am grateful to the many Race and the Law students who provided insightful suggestions over the years.

Race Law

Part One

Analysis and Framework

I. Introduction

From my experience in teaching Race and the Law for a period of thirty-five years, I have concluded that it is advantageous for the student to have a textbook-type analysis consisting of historical background, commentary, biographical information, and questions, as well as original materials such as cases, statutes, and executive orders. Though textbook-type analysis offers the professor's focus and evaluation of the materials and the era, it is essential that students become proficient with the skill of critically reading cases, statutes, and related historical and legal documents. Accordingly, most of the information contained in this book has been collected from original source materials related to the federal legal process. It is contemplated that in addition to this book, the student will read textbook-type analysis in other sources including, *In The Matter of Color: Race and the American Legal Process, The Colonial Period (In the Matter of Color); Shades of Freedom: Racial Politics and Presumptions of the American Legal Process (Shades of Freedom)*, both authored by A. Leon Higginbotham, Jr.; and, *Ghosts of Jim Crow: Ending Racism in Post-Racial America (Ghosts of Jim Crow)*, my recent book on racial inequality in the twenty-first century. Analysis of race in connection to the American legal process will always be subject to the criticism that a focus primarily from the legal perspective fails to deal in detail with the additional economic, sociological, historical, and anthropological factors that surround the complex subject matter. In his introduction to *In The Matter of Color,* Leon Higginbotham identifies the benefits of focusing primarily on the legal aspects of this analysis rather than a multiple disciplinary approach. In addition to the time limitations inherent in a semester course, the effort to include all of the other disciplines often results in a blurring of the impact and manipulation of the legal process. The strength and weakness of my approach is that it requires a focus primarily on legal aspects, which were the mechanism of systematic deprivations, and simultaneously serve as a measure of the other societal factors. Accordingly, I suggest that you reflect upon William Goodell's admonition:

No people were ever yet found who were better than their laws, though many have been known to be worse.[1]

---

1. WILLIAM GOODELL, THE AMERICAN SLAVE CODE IN THEORY AND IN PRACTICE 17 (1853). Goodell attributes this statement to Dr. Priestly.

The foci of *Race Law: Cases, Commentary, and Questions* (*Race Law*), however, are not limited merely to the rules of law adopted. The book explores the values of the individuals who held power in the past or who currently hold power, and it probes how their personal values affected the choices they made within their available options. In this way, *Race Law* provides an important link between the traditional approach to case study which emphasizes substantive rules, and the more modern approach of critical race theory which emphasizes techniques, strategies, and practices. For those with limited previous exposure to the history of American race relations law, this book provides a unique introductory learning experience.

Race Law is divided into eight parts: Analysis and Framework; Slavery; Reconstruction, Citizenship, and Sovereignty; Segregation; Attempted Eradication of Inequality; Supreme Court Confirmation Controversies; Ongoing Controversies; and Appendix. While the material is presented primarily in chronological order, a few cases are strategically placed for pedagogical reasons consistent with the book's focus on the values held by the decision-makers, and how those values influenced their actions. In addition, all original source materials have been lightly edited and structured for easier reading and understanding. References reflecting the values of the authors of the original source materials, however, remain intact, consistent with the book's theme.

II. The Racial Prejudices That Judges Share

A. Introduction

> The life of the law has not been logic; it has been experience. The felt necessities of the time, the prevalent moral and political theories, intuitions of public policy, avowed or unconscious, even the prejudices which judges share with their fellowmen, have had a good deal more to do than the syllogism in determining the rules by which men should be governed.[2]

Justice Holmes' analysis deserves careful examination. At the very least, judges are expected to follow the law. However, if Holmes is correct, it is critical not only to identify the rules of law enunciated by the decision-makers but also to uncover the values that those decision-makers embrace. What exactly is the relationship between the values held by decision-makers and the rules they promulgate in court decisions and enact in legislation?

B. Background on *Mann*

More than any other case on slavery, *State v. Mann* (13 N.C. 263), an 1829 North Carolina Supreme Court case, exemplifies the preferences and indeed the

---

2. Oliver Wendell Holmes, The Common Law 1 (1881).

"prejudices which judges share[d] with their fellow" plantation owners. In order for society to execute a race-based system of rights and privileges, there must be a socially accepted or legally sanctioned scheme in place. In order for this race-based system to be maintained over time, the decisions that implement it, and keep it in place, must reflect the social values in which the system is based. The *State v. Mann* decision is an example of just such implementation. When reading this case, ask whether Judge Ruffin was making his judgment on indisputable legal doctrines, sound principles of logic, and historical precedent, or simply on the security and profit of the slaveowner. Did he have any humanitarian concern for the slaves' welfare? Applying Justice Holmes's analysis of the judicial process, one should ask which conclusions were based on long standing precedential law or *stare decisis,* and which were based on previous "moral and political theories." Is it possible for a judge to have a "neutral" view which has not been shaped and influenced by contemporaneous economic concerns or racial biases? Which concepts were more an exemplification of the prejudices which some judges shared with their fellow plantation owners and which doctrines, if any, were devoid of economic preferences or racial "prejudices"? Finally, one must ask whether there were any other options that Judge Ruffin could have followed under the rule of law. Did an application of available common law to the existing facts support any other possible outcome for the plaintiff, the slave Lydia, here represented by the State? If several outcomes were possible, what does Ruffin's conclusion reveal about his personal values?

C. *State v. Mann,* 13 N.C. 263 (1829)

1. Facts

Judge RUFFIN delivered the opinion of the court.

The Defendant was indicted for an assault and battery upon *Lydia*, the slave of one *Elizabeth Jones*. On the trial it appeared that the Defendant had hired the slave for a year—that during the term, the slave had committed some small offence, for which the Defendant undertook to chastise her—that while in the act of so doing, the slave ran off, whereupon the Defendant called upon her to stop, which being refused, he shot at and wounded her. His honor, Judge Daniel, charged the Jury that if they believed the punishment inflicted by the Defendant was cruel and unwarrantable, and disproportionate to the offense committed by the slave, that in law the Defendant was guilty, as he had only a special property in the slave.

A verdict was returned for the State, and the Defendant appealed. No Counsel appeared for the Defendant. The Attorney General contended that no difference existed between this case and that of the *State v. Hall* (2 Hawks 562). In this case, the weapon used was one calculated to produce death. He assimilated the relation between a master and a slave to those existing between parents and children, masters and apprentices, and tutors and scholars, and upon the limitations to the right of the Superiors in these relations, he cited *Russell on Crimes,* 866.

2. Opinion

A judge cannot but lament, when such cases as the present are brought into judgment. It is impossible that the reasons on which they go can be appreciated, but where institutions similar to our own, exist and are thoroughly understood. The struggle, too, in the Judge's own breast between the feelings of the man, and the duty of the magistrate is a severe one, presenting strong temptation to put aside such questions, if it be possible. It is useless however to complain of things inherent in our political state. And it is criminal in a Court to avoid any responsibility which the laws impose. With whatever reluctance therefore it is done the Court is compelled to express an opinion upon the extent of the dominion of the master over the slave in North Carolina.

The indictment charges a battery on *Lydia*, a slave of *Elizabeth Jones*. Upon the face of the indictment, the case is the same as the *State v. Hall* (2 Hawks 582) — no fault is found with the rule then adopted; nor would be, if it were now open. But it is not open; for the question, as it relates to a battery on a slave by a stranger, is considered as settled by that case. But the evidence makes this a different case. Here the slave had been hired by the Defendant, and was in his possession; and the battery was committed during the period of hiring. With the liabilities of the hirer to the general owner, for an injury permanently impairing the value of the slave, no rule now laid down is intended to interfere. That is left upon the general doctrine of bailment. The inquiry here is whether a cruel and unreasonable battery on a slave, by the hirer is indictable. The Judge below instructed the Jury that it is. He seems to have put it on the ground that the Defendant had but a special property. Our laws uniformly treat the master or other person having the possession and command of the slave as entitled to the same extent of authority. The object is the same — the services of the slave; and the same powers must be confided. In a criminal proceeding, and indeed in reference to all other persons but the general owner, the hirer and possessor of a slave, in relation to both rights and duties, is, for the time being, the owner.

This opinion would perhaps dispose of this particular case; because the indictment, which charges a battery upon the slave of *Elizabeth Jones*, is not supported by proof of a battery upon Defendant's own slave; since different justifications may be applicable to the two cases. But upon the general question, whether the owner is answerable *criminalizer*, for a battery upon his own slave, or other exercise of authority or force, not forbidden by statute, the Court entertains but little doubt. That he is so liable, has never yet been decided; nor, as far as is known, been hitherto contended. There have been no prosecutions of the sort. The established habits and uniform practice of the country in this respect, is the best evidence of the portion of power, deemed by the whole community, requisite to the preservation of the master's dominion. If we thought differently, we could not set our notions in array against the judgment of everybody else, and say that this, or that authority, may be safely lopped off. This has indeed been assimilated at the bar to the other domestic relations; and arguments drawn from the well established principles which confer and restrain the authority of the parent over the child, the tutor over the pupil, the master over the apprentice, have been pressed on us. The Court does not recognize their application. There is no likeness between the cases. They are in opposition to each other and there is an impassable gulf between them. The difference is that which exists between freedom and slavery—and a greater cannot be imagined. In the one, the end in view is the happiness of the youth, born to equal rights with that governor, on whom the duty devolves of training the young to usefulness, in a station which he is afterwards to assume among freemen. To such an end, and with such a subject, moral and intellectual instruction seem the natural means; and for the most part, they are found to suffice. Moderate force is superadded only to make the others effectual. If that fail, it is better to leave the party to his own headstrong passions, and the ultimate correction of the law, than to allow it to be immoderately inflicted by a private person. With slavery it is far otherwise. The end is the profit of the master, his security and the public safety; the subject, one doomed in his own person, and his posterity, to live without knowledge, and without the capacity to make anything his own, and to toil that another may reap the fruits. What moral considerations shall be addressed to such a being to convince him what, it is impossible but that the most stupid must feel and know can never be true—that he is thus to labor upon a principle of natural duty, or for the sake of his own personal happiness, such services can only be expected from one who has no will of his own; who surrenders his will in implicit obedience to that of another. Such obedience is the consequence only of uncontrolled authority over the body. There is nothing else which can operate to produce the effect. The power of the master must be absolute to render the submission of the slave perfect. I most freely confess my sense of the harshness of this proposition, I feel it as deeply as any man can. And as a principle of moral right every person in his retirement must repudiate it. But in the actual condition of things, it must be so. There is no remedy. This discipline belongs to the state of slavery. They cannot be disunited without abrogating at once the rights of the master and absolving the slave from his subjection. It constitutes the curse of slavery to both the bond and free portions of our population. But it is inherent in the relation of master and slave.

That there may be particular instances of cruelty and deliberate barbarity, where, in conscience the law might properly interfere, is most probable. The difficulty is to determine where a Court may properly begin. Merely in the abstract it may well be asked which power of the master accords with right. The answer will probably sweep away all of them. But we cannot look at the matter in that light. The truth is that we are forbidden to enter upon a train of general reasoning on the subject. We cannot allow the right of the master to be brought into discussion in the Courts of Justice. The slave, to remain a slave, must be made sensible that there is no appeal from his master; that his power is in no instance usurped; but is conferred by the laws of man at least if not by the law of God. The danger would be great indeed, if the tribunals of justice should be called on to graduate the punishment appropriate to every temper, and every dereliction of menial duty. No man can anticipate the many and aggravated provocations of the master, which the slave would be constantly stimulated by his own passions, or the instigation of others to give; or the consequent wrath of the master prompting him to bloody vengeance upon the turbulent traitor—a vengeance generally practiced with impunity by reason of its privacy. The Court therefore disclaims the power of changing the relation in which these parts of our people stand to each other.

We are happy to see that there is daily less and less occasion for the interposition of the Courts. The protection already afforded by several statutes, that all powerful motive the private interest of the owner, the benevolence towards each other seated in the hearts of those who have been born and bred together, the frowns and deep execrations of the community upon the barbarian who is guilty of excessive and brutal cruelty to his unprotected slave, all combined, have produced a mildness of treatment and attention to the comforts of the unfortunate class of slaves, greatly mitigating the rigors of servitude and ameliorating the condition of the slaves. The same causes are operating and will continue to operate with increased action, until the disparity in numbers between the whites and blacks shall have rendered the latter in no degree dangerous to the former, and when the policy now existing may be further relaxed. This result, greatly to be desired, may be much more rationally expected from the events above alluded to and now in progress, than from any rash expositions of abstract truths by a Judiciary tainted with a false and fanatical philanthropy seeking to redress an acknowledged evil by means still more wicked and appalling than even that evil.

3. Holding

I repeat that I would gladly have avoided this ungrateful question. But being brought to it the Court is compelled to declare that while slavery exists amongst us in its present state, or until it shall seem fit to the Legislature to interpose express enactments to the contrary, it will be the imperative duty of the Judges to recognize the full dominion of the owner over the slave except where the exercise of it is forbidden by statute. And this we do upon the ground that this dominion is essential to the value of slaves as property, to the security of the master, and the public tranquility greatly dependent upon their subordination; and in fine, as most effectually securing the general protection and comfort of the slaves themselves.

Let the judgment below be reversed and judgment entered for the Defendant.

D. Commentary on *Mann*

1. State v. Mann: *An "Objective" Legal Analysis or an Expression of Individual Whim and Social and Economic Bias?*

Although this book is organized generally in chronological historical sequence, this chapter departs from such a pattern. *State v. Mann*, decided in 1829, is set within the context of a highly structured and developed agricultural system of plantation slavery in the nineteenth-century American South. At that point in time, slavery was deeply ingrained in the social structure of the colonies and was the basis of their economic growth. This case is included at the outset to raise basic questions concerning race and the law that will be relevant to the analysis of each historical period in subsequent chapters.

Without great exaggeration, it may be said that an entire course on the relationship of the American legal system to the development of slavery and the status of black Americans might be taught from *State v. Mann*. Certainly the problems presented by the facts of this case and the court's response raise many of the questions that will be considered throughout this book. For example, what was the logic, clarity, forthrightness, and moral sensitivity of the court's opinion and what was the impact of contemporary values, racial attitudes, and legal traditions in affecting the status of blacks?

Legal opinions cannot be read as abstract syllogisms unrelated to the current and past historical events from which the opinion evolves. Without an understanding of these events, an opinion such as *State v. Mann* can be deceptive.

In the beginning it must be emphasized that, like all of the court opinions reprinted in this book, *State v. Mann* should be slowly and carefully read several times. For only then does one recognize that the legal judgment made by Judge Ruffin was not as self-evident or necessary as he implied. Only after careful analysis does one recognize that Ruffin's opinion raises more questions than it provides answers. Even more importantly, there was just as compelling an argument for the court to have reached a completely opposite result and holding, had the rationale been rooted in both law and history.

In North Carolina in 1830, there were 245,601 slaves, 19,543 free blacks, and 472,823 whites. All plantation owners recognized that their economic success was dependent upon the maintenance of the slavery system. When speaking to the State Agricultural Society of North Carolina in 1855, Ruffin expressed his views on slavery as follows:

> Then let me say once more to you, men of North Carolina, stick to her, and make her what she can and ought to be. For you and your sons she will yield a rich harvest; to some thirtyfold, some sixtyfold, and some hundredfold, according to the skill and diligence with which the tillage of the good ground is done.

> The nature of the labor employed in our agriculture is the next subject for our consideration. It is a most important element in the cost, amount, and value of production. I very frankly avow the opinion that our mixed labor of free white men of European origin and of slaves of the African race is as well adapted to the public and private ends of our agriculture as any other could be—making our cultivation not less thorough, cheap, and productive than it would be, if carried on by the whites alone, and far more so than the blacks by themselves would make it; and therefore, that it has a

beneficial influence on the prosperity of the country, and the physical and moral state of both races, rendering both better and happier than either would be here, without the other.[3]

Though in the above comments Ruffin was speaking solely as a plantation owner to an agricultural group in 1855, he may have had those same economic views when authoring *State v. Mann* 26 years earlier, in 1829. Yet, if he had included in *State v. Mann* the more precise economic preferences and social biases that he expressed when speaking to the State Agricultural Society, his opinion in *State v. Mann* might be regarded as "less objective." For then, on its face, the opinion would be more vulnerable to criticism, leaving some to have questioned whether Ruffin was relying on legal precedent or merely on his individual whim. Thus, we see in *State v. Mann* that Ruffin could mask his economic philosophy through use of legal nomenclature and legal doctrines; the way he expresses his views changes but not the result. Ruffin's economic philosophy, personal racial biases, and preferences obviously carried more weight in determining the result than any "legal precedent" he cited or legal analysis he used. Notwithstanding, Ruffin still expressed his biases, political and economic views, and values more candidly and precisely than most jurists of the era. Thus, from a sociological and historical standpoint, *State v. Mann* is still a significant opinion. Indeed, it is not that others were more objective in their ultimate findings and holdings; it is just that they were not as brutally candid about the factors that motivated their findings.

Professor Vilhelm Aubert has said "[B]eneath the veneer of consensus on legal principles, *a struggle of interest is going on, and the law is seen as a weapon in the hands of those who possess the power to use it for their own ends.*"[4] Thus, law is seen both as a cohesive force and as an instrument that maintains and confirms basic cleavages in a society. Was Ruffin as a judge, in the words of Professor Aubert, involved in a "struggle of interest" and using the law "as a weapon in the hands of those who possess the power to use it for their own ends?"

2. The Ruling of the Trial Court: Special Property versus Absolute Property in the Slave

In the lower trial court, Judge Daniel did not accept the concept that the hirer had absolute property in the slave. Obviously, Judge Daniel felt that there was some limitation on the hirer's property interest and some restraint on the brutality which the hirer could impose on his slaves. Thus, Judge Daniel instructed the jury that Mann could be guilty of assault and battery upon Lydia because Mann had only a "special property" interest in Lydia. Judge Daniel charged the jury that if they believed "the punishment inflicted by the defendant was *cruel and unwarrantable*

---

3. *Publications of the North Carolina Historical Commission*, Volume 6, Part 4, "The Papers of Thomas Ruffin," IV, pp. 329–37.

4. Vilhelm Aubert, Sociology of Law 11 (1972).

and *disproportionate* to the offense committed by the slave, that in law the defendant was guilty as he had only a *special property* in the slave." (13 N.C. at 265)

The issue of special property goes to the core of a longstanding debate as to whether slaves were persons having rights of their own. Did slaves have a soul, a personality, or any human rights recognized by the law? Were there any limitations in terms of the abuse that a hirer or an owner could impose upon slaves?

The view that slaves were like animals with no rights of their own was often expressed. For example, Judge Baldwin explained:

> [P]ersons in the *status* of slavery have no civil rights, save that of suing for freedom when entitled to it: they can make no contracts, nor acquire any property: they can obtain no redress by action against their masters or others, for personal injuries: they are in truth *civiliter mortuus*, and without protection of public authority, except that of the criminal law.[5]

Ruffin, who was aligned with these sentiments, rejected Judge Daniel's view that the hirer had merely a special property right, instead of an absolute total property right in the slave. Did Ruffin choose to support an absolute property right because he sought to make the power of the hirer, as well as the master, absolute "to render submission of the slave perfect"? On what precedent did Ruffin rely?

3. Precedent and Analogies: The Choices the Court Had

In his opinion, Ruffin cites only one case, *State v. Hall* (2 Hawks 582). This opinion in the official volumes is cited as *State v. Hale*, 9 N.C. 582 (1823). Ruffin distinguishes *State v. Hall* because it involved "a battery on a slave by a stranger." The Supreme Court of North Carolina held that it was an indictable crime to assault, beat, and wound a slave. Ironically, in *State v. Hall*, Judge Daniel in the lower court, had ruled that it was not a crime to beat a slave even without provocation because neither the common law nor statute specified that such attacks were criminally indictable offenses. In an appeal from Judge Daniel's dismissal of the case at the trial court level, the Supreme Court of North Carolina held, in a plurality opinion, that such an attack was a criminal offense. Chief Justice Taylor acknowledged that there was "no positive law decisive to the question. A solution of it must be deduced from general principles, from reasonings founded on the common law adapted to the existing conditions and circumstances of our society, and indicating that result which is best adapted to general expedience." (13 N.C. at 266).

Chief Justice Taylor wrote:

> It would be a subject of regret to every thinking person, if Courts of Justice were restrained, by any austere rule of judicature, from keeping pace with march of benignant policy, and provident humanity, which for many years, has characterized every Legislative act, relative to the protection of

---

5. *Peter v. Hargrave*, 46 Va. (5 Gratt.) 12, 17 (1848).

slaves, and which Christianity, by the mild diffusion of its light and influence, has contributed to promote; and even domestic safety and interest equally enjoin. The wisdom of this course of legislation, has not exhausted itself on the specific objects to which it was directed, but has produced wider and happier consequences, in securing to this class of persons, milder treatment and more attention to their safety; for the very circumstance of their being brought within the pale of legal protection, has had a corresponding influence upon the tone of public feeling towards them; has rendered them of more value to their masters, and suppressed many outrages, which were, before, but too frequent. It is, however, objected in this case, that no offense has been committed, and the indictment is not sustainable, because the person assaulted is a slave, who is not protected by the general criminal law of the State; but that, as the property of an individual, the owner may be redressed by a civil action. But though neither the common law, nor any other code yet devised by man, could foresee and specify every case that might arise, and thus supersede the use of reason in the ordinary affairs of life, yet it furnishes the principles of justice adapted to every state and condition of society. It contains general rules, fitted to meet the diversified relations, and various conditions of social man. Many of the most important of these rules are not set down in any statute or ordinance, but depend upon common law for their support. . . . The common law has often been called into efficient operation, for the punishment of public cruelty inflicted upon animals, for needless and wanton barbarity exercised even by masters upon their slaves, and for various violations of decency, morals and comfort. Reason and analogy seem to require that a human being, although the subject of property, should be so far protected as the public might be injured through him. . . . Mitigated as slavery is by the humanity of our laws, the refinement of manners, and by public opinion, which revolts at every instance of cruelty towards them, it would be an anomaly in the system of police which affects them, if the offence stated in the verdict were not indictable. At the same time it is undeniable, that such offence must be considered with a view to the actual condition of society, and the difference between a white man and a slave, securing the first from injury and insult, and the other from needless violence and outrage. From this difference it arises, that many circumstances which would not constitute a legal provocation for a battery committed by one white man on another, would justify it, if committed on a slave, provided the battery were not excessive. It is impossible to draw the line with precision, or lay down the rule in the abstract; but . . . , the circumstances must be judged by the Court and Jury, with a due regard to the habits and feelings of society. But where no justification is shown, as in this case, I am of opinion the indictment is maintainable. [6]

------

6. 2 N.C. 582, 583–86 (1823).

The other two judges concurred in the result. Judge Hall noted:

> I concur in the opinion given. I think it would be highly improper that
> every assault and battery upon a slave should be considered an indictable
> offence; because the person making it, might have matter of excuse or justi-
> fication on his side, which could not be used as a defense for committing an
> assault and battery upon a free person. But where an assault and battery is
> committed upon a slave without cause, lawful excuse, or without sufficient
> provocation, I think it amounts to an indictable offence. Much depends
> upon the circumstances of the case when it happens; these circumstances
> are not set forth in this case, and I think it material that they should appear.
> I therefore think the judgment of the Court below should be reversed, and
> a new trial granted for that purpose.[7]

State v. Hall is cited in such detail to show that, even under North Carolina law in
1823 (six years before *Mann*), the North Carolina Supreme Court did recognize that
it had some options in defining which acts constituted a criminal offense—even if a
particular act had not been previously categorized as a crime by statute or the common law. Thus, *State v. Hall* was good precedent, and demonstrates that the court
in *State v. Mann* in 1829 could have held that an unprovoked[8] attack on a slave by her
hirer constituted a criminal offense.

The Attorney General also argued by analogy that Lydia could be protected
because her situation was similar to the "well established principles which confer authority of restraint of the parent over the child, the tutor over the pupil, the
master over the apprentice."[9] Ruffin summarily dismissed these analogies by saying
"the Court does not recognize their application. There is no likeness between the
cases. They are in opposition to each other, and there is an impassable gulf between
them."[10] From the standpoint of legal analysis, what was the criteria Ruffin used to
conclude that there is no likeness between the two situations? Does he announce
any criteria leading to his conclusion? You will note that Ruffin cites no cases where
courts have rejected these analogies; apparently, even from Ruffin's view, no courts
had ever considered these analogies. Since there were no cases or statutes that controlled, Ruffin indeed had an option either to provide some semblance of protection for the slave or to sanction repressing all rights for slaves. Did Ruffin object to
the analogies for any compelling legal reasons that he sought but failed to note in
his opinion? Or was the decisive factor that Ruffin feared his wealth and property
would suffer some diminution of value if the doctrines of Judge Daniel in the court
below were sustained? Did Ruffin fear that extending to slaves some protection
under the law would or could lessen the value of slaves or contribute to the gradual

---

7. 2 N.C. 582, 586–87 (1823).
8. The attack is considered "unprovoked" because Lydia had done nothing to Mann.
9. 13 N.C. 263, 265 (1829).
10. *Id.*

abolition of slavery?[11] Was the profitability of slavery the most significant factor in his judgment in finding no likeness between the analogies?

Consider the relevance of the Attorney General's analogies concerning the relation between master and slave and those existing between "parent and children, masters and apprentices, and tutors and scholars . . . and the limitations to the right of the superiors" in these latter relations. Without assuming that these analogies are sufficient authority to support the intervention of courts in the relationship between master and slave, do they not at least suggest that courts have been authorized and competent to make some judgments about the appropriate degree of punishment a social superior may inflict on a person who is his social inferior?

4. The Role of the Court versus the Role of the Legislature

Is there any basis for Ruffin's conclusion other than his judicial perception of the social and moral nature of slavery? Do any facts in the record of the case developed in the trial court concern these questions? Generally, legislatures make the laws, executives implement the laws, and courts interpret the laws. Ruffin, however, appears to be doing two tasks. Is this form of historical, social, and ultimately moral perception and judgment a function which one would expect courts to perform? Are there any qualities of the judicial process that give courts a particular competence to engage in this form of historical and psychological judgment concerning the nature of slavery, which Judge Ruffin finds necessary to define the limits of criminal responsibility for the violent discipline of slaves? Are there aspects of the legislative process, on the other hand, that might make representative assemblies more qualified than courts to make these ultimate judgments about the nature and goals of slavery? In what ways might the legislative process be ineffective in resolving the problems presented by *State v. Mann*? In his holding, Ruffin indicates that an express statute to the contrary could prevent a judge from recognizing the "full dominion of the owner over the slave."

5. Is There a Universal View of Slavery on Which Ruffin Could Rely?

In his opinion, Ruffin asserts that "the established habits and uniform practice of the country in this respect, is the best evidence of the portion of power, deemed by the whole community, requisite to the preservation of the master's dominion." (13 N.C. at 265). Ruffin also says:

> The end is the profit of the master, his security and the public safety; the subject, one doomed in his own person, and his posterity, to live without knowledge, and without the capacity to make anything his own, and to toil that another may reap the fruits. What moral considerations shall be addressed to such a being, to convince him what, it is impossible but that the most stupid must feel and know can never be true—that he is thus to

---

11. See Ruffin's second rough draft of the opinion in *State v. Mann*, especially the first paragraph.

labor upon a principle of natural duty, or for the sake of his own personal happiness, such services can only be expected from one who has no will of his own; who surrenders his will in implicit obedience to that of another. Such obedience is the consequence only of uncontrolled authority over the body. There is nothing else which can operate to produce the effect. The power of the master must be absolute, to render the submission of the slave perfect.[12]

What is the historical and social validity of Judge Ruffin's conclusions concerning the nature of slavery, its ends, and the necessary means of enforcing discipline over slaves? In reaching these conclusions, does Judge Ruffin consider the historical origin of slavery in the United States? Would this history be relevant to his judgment concerning the nature of slavery in North Carolina at the time and his legal conclusions concerning the limits of a master's right to discipline his slaves? If slavery in the United States evolved in part from lesser forms of servitude, such as apprenticeship and indentured servitude, would this history be relevant to Judge Ruffin's view of what he considers the natural, if not inevitable, nature of slavery?

Does Judge Ruffin conclude, or at least assume, that the relationship of master and slave is essentially the same for all times and places where slavery has existed? Does he consider the possibility that different legal restrictions on the authority of the master, and consequently greater legal protection of the slave, might exist under other legal and social systems? Would it be relevant to his opinion to seek out and consider such evidence? According to Frank Tannenbaum, during the time that *Mann* was decided, if a slave in Brazil considered himself mistreated by his owner, he had the right to be sold to another, more humane, owner.[13] Would the existence of this legal possibility in another society undermine the force of Judge Ruffin's reasoning against limiting the authority of the master over the slave? Would the Brazilian practice most strongly support the adoption of a similar right for slaves in North Carolina at that time?

What is the relevance of the court's conclusion concerning the nature and end result of slavery to its conclusion concerning the need for uncontrolled authority over the body of the slave? If the end result of slavery includes the profit of the master and the public safety, how can the shooting of a slave under the facts of the present case be justified as serving either interest? Does the court consider whether the doctrine of uncontrolled authority contributes to either of these ends? Assuming the importance of slavery to the economy and society of North Carolina at the time, does not the decision of the court restrict the protection of slaves; an interest that if only on grounds of expedience, a slaveholding society would be expected to protect? Consider also the end of public safety. How does the exposure of slaves to shooting under these circumstances contribute to the advancement of public safety? Would

---

12. 13 N.C. 263, 266 (1829).
13. F. Tannenbaum, Slave and Citizen: The Negro in the Americas 54 (1967).

not such brutality create greater risk of provoking slaves and creating increased instability in the slave society?[14]

6. Remedies and Change through the Judicial Process

Ruffin seemed to concede that in some instances there were grave abuses, but he believed that the courts could not deal with those injustices because the courts would be "seeking to redress and acknowledge evil by means still more wicked and appalling than that evil."[15] Was he suggesting that the courts were incapable of differentiating abuses from appropriate treatment? Or was he suggesting that some white masters were such villains that any legal interventions would be to the ultimate detriment of the slaves? Did Ruffin rely on any legal basis when he sought to limit the court's judicial scope to some injustices but not others?

If redress were possible, would blacks feel that such means would be "more wicked and appalling" than no redress at all? Would non-slaveholding whites consider redress for slaves to be evil? In other words, what competence does the judge have to conclude that such means would be "more wicked and appalling" than a battery without legal remedy?

What factors, other than its judgment of the nature of slavery and the discipline necessary to this system, contribute to the court's refusal to uphold criminal liability under the facts of this case? Consider how the court is affected by its estimate of the probable impact of a decision upholding criminal liability in this case. Note Judge Ruffin's declaration that "the court disclaims the power of changing the relation, in which these parts [master and slave] of our people stand to each other."[16] Do you agree with the court that the imposition of criminal responsibility on a master or hirer for the shooting of a slave under the circumstances of this case (or in any circumstances other than actual self-defense) would seriously change the relationship between master and slave? Is there any indication in the opinion that the shooting of a slave under these circumstances was either frequent or in any way condoned by the community? If such brutality was not frequent or necessary or acceptable, how would the imposition of criminal liability under these circumstances "change the relation" between master and slave?

If one concludes that a finding of criminal liability under the facts of this case would not greatly change the "established habits and uniform practices"[17] of the community, what other consequences of the decision may trouble the court? Note the following comment: "[t]he danger would be great indeed if the tribunals of justice should be called on to graduate the punishment appropriate to every temper,

---

14. On these questions of the psychological and social structure of slavery, *see generally* JOHN BLASSINGAME, THE SLAVE COMMUNITY (1979).

15. 13 N.C. 263, 268 (1829).

16. *Id.* at 267.

17. *Id.* at 265.

and every dereliction of menial duty."[18] Consider again the holding of the trial court. Do you agree with the appellate court that a finding of criminal liability in this case would necessarily serve as precedent for the court's future involvement, through the criminal law, in graduating "the punishment appropriate to every temper, and every dereliction of menial duty"?[19]

For example, would a holding sustaining criminal liability under the facts of this case serve as precedent for a finding of criminal liability in the case of an owner, who without justification, struck a slave with a piece of wood, a whip, or with his fists? Would not Judge Ruffin be equally justified in anticipating that a decision in favor of the State in *State v. Mann* would serve as precedent for judging similar punishment "appropriate to *every* temper, and *every* dereliction of duty between master and slave"? What principle of decision would justify a finding of criminal liability for an unreasonable battery in the present case, but which would not require the court to become involved extensively in administering the relationship between master and slave? Could you argue convincingly that the shooting for any unprovoked act of any person by another (except in legitimate self-defense) is always unreasonable and that the adoption of this *per se* rule need not compel the court to become involved in evaluating the propriety of every form of discipline administered by masters to slaves, or of tutors to scholars, or masters to apprentices?

E. Explaining Judge Thomas Ruffin

1. Ruffin's Biography

1787	
Nov. 17	Born at "Newington," King and Queen County, Va.
1801–03	Student at Warrenton Academy, Warrenton, N.C.
1803	Entered Junior Class at Nassau Hall, Princeton, N.J.
1805	
Sept. 26	Received degree of A.B. from Princeton
1806–07	Law student at Petersburg, Va., under David Robertson
1807	Moved to "Oakland," Rockingham County, N.C.
1807–08	Law student under Archibald D. Murphey.
1808	Admitted to the bar.
1809	
June 9	Moved to Hillsboro, N.C.
Dec. 9	Married to Anne Kirkland of Hillsboro.
1813	Member of the House of Commons for the borough of Hillsboro.
1815	Member of the House of Commons for the borough of Hillsboro.

---

18. *Id.* at 267.
19. *Id.*

1816	Presidential elector on the Monroe ticket. Member of the House of Commons for the borough of Hillsboro. Speaker of the House of Commons.
Dec. 16 1813	Elected judge of the Superior Court.
Dec. 23	Resigned from the bench to engage in the practice of law.
1820–22	Reporter of the Supreme Court of North Carolina.
1824	Candidate for presidential elector on the Crawford ticket.
1825	Elected judge of the Superior Court.
1828	Resigned from the bench to become president of the State Bank of North Carolina.
1829	Elected judge of the Supreme Court of North Carolina. Authored the decision in *State v. Mann*.
1830	Moved to "Haw River."
1833	Became Chief Justice of the Supreme Court.
1834	Received degree of Doctor of Laws from the University of North Carolina.
1835	Delivered address before the Dialectic and Philanthropic Societies at the University of North Carolina.
1852	Resigned from the Bench.
1853	Delegate to the General Convention of the Protestant Episcopal Church in New York City.
1854–60	President of the North Carolina Agricultural Society.
1858	Elected judge of the Supreme Court of North Carolina.
1861	Delegate to the Peace Conference. Delegate from Alamance to the Convention of 1861.
1866	Moved to Hillsboro.
1870 Jan.15	Died at his home in Hillsboro.

2. Ruffin's Petition for a Pardon

On August 19, 1865 Judge Ruffin petitioned President Andrew Johnson for a "full and free pardon" as to his own acts on behalf of the Confederacy during the Civil War. In 1861 he had been a member of a North Carolina Convention that supported the ordinances of secession and confederation, and he had supported military and financial measures on behalf of North Carolina's secession. Now he wanted a Presidential pardon for his former misdeeds.

In his petition Ruffin pled:

> It is here submitted, whether for such acts the People, who made him their organ, or he, as their representative, ought under our form of Government, to be subject to the pains and penalties of *Treason*, either in person or property; and whether, if legally liable thereto, it be not true, as well as the benignant policy of the Government, not to bring that point to Judicial

decision before a Jury and Judge, but rather by a general amnesty bring back a conciliated People with such small means of livelihood as a protracted and most wasting war has left them, with renewed citizenship in this great country, with a patient submission to the losses they have incurred and quiet acquiescence in the laws under which they may have to live—

He further pledged:

That for his own part he purposes to pass the short remnant of his days in unbroken retirement and certainly without any resistance in any form to the National authorities, and has attested to that purpose by having taken the Oath prescribed by your Proclamation . . .

He asked that his property not be "liable to the confiscation" or any other penalty or forfeiture. Ruffin emphasized his economic losses:

He further represents, that he was during and up to the close of the war the owner of more than one hundred Slaves, nearly all of whom were born his and raised by him; and furthermore had investments in corporate and public stocks to a considerable amount which are now of little or no value in the market; so that his losses from the war will, directly or indirectly, amount probably to the sum of Two hundred and Fifty Thousand dollars or more and the residue of property still held by him has been so reduced in value as to render it at least doubtful, whether it could be fairly assessed for taxation to $20,000 . . .

In his last paragraph, he requested a maximum compassion for himself. Ruffin said:

In conclusion then, he submits, that, considering the course of his life as herein set forth, his age, the motives for his actions, the condition of his family, his pecuniary losses already incurred, the state of the Country and the propriety of healing our political troubles by acts of Pardon and Oblivion, his be not a proper case for Executive interposition under the powers vested in the President by the Act of Congress: and therefore if any of his acts herein mentioned can be construed to amount to Treason, he asks for a full and free pardon therefore, or one on such other terms as may seem right and proper—and he will ever pray, etc.—[20]

Thus, in 1865, there was Judge Ruffin, a former owner of slaves and a harsh judge, pleading for a liberality from the legal process; yet in *State v. Mann* in 1829 he could not find that liberality or compassion in himself to aid a slave woman, Lydia, who had been shot without legal provocation.

---

20. *Publications of the North Carolina Historical Commission*, Volume 8, Part 4, The Papers of Thomas Ruffin, IV, pp. 16–21 (emphasis added). (Collected and Edited by J.G. De Roulhac Hamilton, 1918).

3. Letter from His Father

Judge Ruffin received the following letter from his father, Sterling Ruffin, who wrote:

> I have no apology to offer for not complying with the promise made in my last, of writing again, in a few days, except that I wished to have forwarded you a small B. Note, for fear, from some unforeseen event, it might be serviceable to you; as yet, I have not been able to procure one; and as I find from your last which has come to hand, you are anxious to receive the promis'd one, I now do myself the pleasure of gratifying your wishes.
>
> I was not surpris'd at reading your sentiments on Slavery, as I was well aware of the impressions which a different mode of treatment than that pursued in Virginia, would make on a Heart, which I hop'd was capable at all times of sympathizing in the misfortunes of a fellow mortal; and would as the mind matur'd, and contemplated the miserable situation of those unhappy beings, feel most sensibly for them; but alas! Like all others who are not entirely void of every spark of Sensibility, you feel for them, lament, greatly lament their uncommon hard fate, without being able to devise any means by which it may be ameliorated! That they are a great civil, political, and moral evil no Person will deny, but how to get rid of them, is a question which has imploy'd many much more expansive minds than mine, without fixing on any rational, or probable means to make their situations more comfortable, without endangering the political safety of the State, and perhaps Jeopardizing the lives, property, and everything sacred and dear of the Whites. You will not pretend to throw blame on the present generation for the situation of these unhappy domestics, for as they are impos'd on us, and not with our consent, the thing is unavoidable. You will perhaps ask why we do not treat them with more humanity? the answer is obvious: the fewer there are of this description intermix'd with the Whites, the more they are under our immediate eye, and the more they partake of the manners and habits of the whites, and thereby require less rigidness of treatment to get from them, those services which are absolutely necessary for their support and very existence. Unhappily for us and them, there are too many with us to render a tolerably free intercourse of sentiment possible, and of course their minds have degenerated into as abject slavery as their persons; and as there is no gratitude or affection on their parts towards their masters, nothing is to be expected from them, but as fear, servile fear operates on them, which produces a sluggishness of action, which must be increased momentarily by a greater degree of fear, with a greater degree of personal attention on our parts. It has been one of many benefits which has resulted to Society from the Christian Religion to expose the impropriety of keeping our Brothers in bondage, and however we may at present justify ourselves from the peculiar situation of our Country consider'd politically; I cannot but look forward with pleasure to the time, when an All wise, and Merciful!

Creator will by a more universal revival of his blessed Religion prepare the Hearts of all men to consider each other as Brothers, and put us more on an equality even in temporal things—When this much to be wished for period will arrive, or what will be the means adopted for a general emancipation, I do not pretend to divine; but that such a time will be, I have little doubt.

Tom you cannot conceive the happiness that I receive in believing from your letters that you begin to see the necessity and reality of Religion; believe me my Son, who have had a fair opportunity of contimating the pleasure of Sin, (by enjoying all the comforts that independence and the things of this world could bestow unconnected with a Spiritual love for the giver of these blessings) that there is no comparison between the real solid happiness of a life spent in faith, bringing forth the fruits of the Spirit, and a hope growing therefrom that [Rest of letter missing.][21]

4. Ruffin's Treatment of His Slaves

Ruffin felt confident that he had an accurate perception of the slave personality; he never doubted his belief that slavery was beneficial to the slave. He also thought well of the property class, particularly the slave-owners. In his famous 1855 speech he said, "[W]e, like every other people, have the idle and the vicious amongst us. But they are chiefly those who have the least connection with slaves, and particularly those employed in agriculture, and are to be found, without means, lounging about cities and villages."[22] He favored religion for slaves, so "[t]he comfort, cheerfulness, and happiness of the slave should be, and generally is the study of the master; and every Christian master rejoices over the soul of his slave saved, as of a brother, and allows of his attendance on the ministry of God's word and sacraments, in any church of his choice in his vicinity."[23] But he was quick to add that "[t]he condition of a slave denies to him, indeed, opportunities of education sufficient for searching the Scriptures for himself, and working there out his own conversion; but God forbid that should be necessary to salvation . . . among the slaves of this country there are many exemplary Christians. Indeed, slavery in America has not only done more than the civilization and enjoyments of the African race than all other causes, but it has brought more of them into the Christian fold than all the missions to that benighted continent from the Advent to this day."[24]

Ruffin was confident that slaves were inherently docile. He said:

---

21. *Letter to Judge Thomas Ruffin from His Father, Sterling Ruffin* written from Brunswick in June of 1804. Taken from THE PAPERS OF THOMAS RUFFIN, Vol. I, pp. 54–55 (Collected & Edited by J.G. De Roulhac Hamilton, 1918).

22. *Publications of the North Carolina Historical Commission*, Volume 6, Part 4, THE PAPERS OF THOMAS RUFFIN, Vol. IV, pp. 335–36.

23. *Id.*

24. *Id.*

We know that our slaves are generally humble, obedient, quiet and a con-
tented and cheerful race of laborers. Scattered over the plantations in rural
occupations, they are never riotous or dangerous, as the same number of
uneducated working men have often been in other parts of our country.
Slaves are no part of this State, with no political power, and seek no violent
or sudden changes in the law or policy of the country; and where slavery
exists labor and capital never come in conflict, because they are in the same
hands, and operate in harmony. It is not, then, a blot upon our laws, nor a
stain on our morals, nor a blight upon our land.[25]

Between Ruffin and Paul Lawrence Dunbar, who most accurately captures the
inner mood and tension of the slave? In his writings, Ruffin expressed his belief that
slaves were "content" and "cheerful." Dunbar wrote in 1896 of the "mask" worn to
cover the reality of suffering:

Paul Lawrence Dunbar

We Wear the Mask

We wear the mask
That grins and lies,
It hides our cheeks and shades our eyes,—
This debt we pay to human guile;
with torn and bleeding hearts we smile,
And mouth with myriad subtleties.
Why should the word be over-wise,
In counting all our tears and sighs?
Nay, let them only see us,
While we wear the mask.
We smile, but, O Great Christ, our cries
To thee from tortured souls arise.
We sing, but O, the clay is vile.
Beneath our feet and along the mile;
To let the world think otherwise
We wear the mask!

The Collected Poetry of Paul Lawrence Dunbar 71 (1993).
Copyright © 1993 The University Press of Virginia.
Reprinted with permission of The University Press of Virginia.

Ruffin's private actions toward the blacks on his own plantation at the Hawfields (Alamance County, N.C.) and at his homes in Hillsborough and Raleigh mirrored the harsh philosophy he displayed in *State v. Mann*. He had little compassion
for slaves' human condition. This lack of compassion is also evident from letters

---

25. *Id.*

which were written to Judge Ruffin by those who witnessed his mistreatment of his own slaves.

Martin H. Brinkley
Judge Thomas Ruffin

a. Archibald DeBow Murphey to TCR,[26] June 3, 1824 (Archibald DeBow Murphey Papers, SHC): Murphey writes Ruffin, his former law student and the purchaser of his Hawfields plantation, a carefully worded and tactful, but clearly urgent, letter about the treatment of Ruffin's slaves by his overseer, Cephus Hudson. Murphey told Ruffin that his character was at stake; all his neighbors were complaining. To convince Ruffin that the allegations of cruelty were true, Murphey added that he had seen the slaves' backs himself. Murphey wrote: "I know nothing myself, except that the Negroes have often applied to me and begged me to let them strip and show me their Backs. We are all the more astonished at what is going on, from the fact that your overseer is a mild, placid, Man in his social Intercourse and a good, kind neighbor. Messrs. Albright, Wm. Rogers, Jo. Russell and Wm. Faucette are witnesses." *Cf.* Herbet Snipes Turner, *The Dreamer: Archibald DeBow Murphey, 1777–1832* 26 (1971) ("In after years when the farm passed into the hands of Thomas Ruffin, he was determined to make it financially profitable. Under a new overseer all the leisurely way of life which the slaves had known under Murphey was changed and they were driven to their work under the lash. Reluctantly, Murphey interceded on their behalf.").

b. Dr. John Webb to TCR, Jan. 16, 1823 (SHC): Dr. Webb, a Hillsborough physician, wrote of a Ruffin slave who complained to him of Ruffin's treatment; even Anne K. Ruffin, who seldom wrote letters, even to her husband, wrote to him of a woman and child who could no longer endure their treatment and were planning to leave. Not surprisingly, Ruffin was plagued with cases of runaway slaves.

c. TCR to Anne K. Ruffin (wife), Jan. 3, 1852: Patty Ruffin (dau. of TCR) to TCR, Jan. 11, 1852 (Thomas Ruffin Papers, SHC): A neighbor, General Allison, inquired whether Ruffin would be willing to sell Noah, a long-time Ruffin slave, for $150. The price was high for a slave past his working days. Ruffin told his daughter to consult Noah about his wishes in the matter. Although he learned from his daughter that Noah was anxious to spend the "remnant of his pilgrimage here on earth on the society of his beloved better half," Ruffin was unmoved and took the $150. "Old Uncle Noah," Sally Ruffin wrote her father, "left here this morning according to your directions; he disliked parting very much." *Sally Ruffin to TCR, Jan. 17, 1852; Peter Browne Ruffin (son of TCR) to TCR, Jan. 29, 1852* (Thomas Ruffin Papers, SHC).

---

26. SHC denotes the Southern Historical Collection, Wilson Library, University of North Carolina. TCR denotes Thomas Carter Ruffin.

d. Given the above facts, it is hardly surprising that Anne K. Ruffin privately feared her slaves or that in 1835 the Ruffin house was twice set on fire by an unhappy house servant.

e. TCR's participation in Slave Trading; TCR Partnership with Benjamin Chambers, Oct. 26, 1821, June 15, 1825: In 1821, when his affairs were in precarious shape, Ruffin resorted to a solution that most men of his standing would have found repugnant—slave trading. He formed a partnership with Benjamin Chambers "to carry on together and as copartners the purchasing of slaves and the selling the same." Chambers would do the actual dirty work while Ruffin would put up the initial $4,000 to get the operation started. When their original contract expired, it was renewed, presumably because it had proved profitable. It was terminated only by Chambers's death in 1826.

f. TCR's Willingness to Sell Slaves at a Moment's Notice: In 1811 Ruffin purchased forty-three acres on the eastern boundary of Hillsborough and set up housekeeping with his new wife, Anne K. Ruffin. The same year Sterling Ruffin, TCR's father, gave him seven slaves, two of whom TCR immediately sold (he kept Cupid, Henry, Molly, Parmy, and Dick). TCR's father-in-law, William Kirkland, also helped with a gift of a woman Milly and her two children, all of whom TCR sold within a year or so. Gifts of slaves, Aug. 1, 26, 1811; Anne K. Ruffin to TCR, Nov. 29, 1815; John MacRae to Ruffin, July 29, 1859 (Thomas Ruffin Papers, SHC).

> *Unpublished manuscript* (1997).
> Reprinted with permission of Martin H. Brinkley.

5. Ruffin's Place in History

State v. Mann is the focus of this introductory chapter because in many ways it typifies the judicial process of the South in the early 1800s. The case illustrates the judicial atmosphere of that time because Ruffin was regarded by many commentators as an exemplary judge. He was no anti-black fanatic; he cannot claim to be uneducated or unaware of the principles of liberty and justice that were being demanded by people of good will, both throughout the nation and the world. He was not uninformed about the persuasive arguments which had been made in condemnation of racial slavery. Rather, he was a product of a superior education— Princeton University, class of 1805, well aware of the disparities within society, and a member of the property class, with at least second-generation wealth. His father was an Episcopalian minister, and so his upbringing was likely steeped in moral and religious values.

In 1938 Roscoe Pound listed Judge Ruffin as one of the ten great state judges who "must be ranked first in American judicial history in shaping the peculiar contours of American history during the century after the American Revolution."[27] Harvard's

---

27. ROSCOE POUND, THE FORMATIVE ERA OF AMERICAN LAW 4 (1938) as quoted in 31 S. L. Rev. 144 by Nash.

esteemed James Bradley Thayer in 1895 in his famous casebook, *Cases on Constitutional Law*—the first casebook on constitutional law—compares Ruffin with men like Chief Justice John Marshall and Judge Lemuel Shaw of the Massachusetts Supreme Court. Thayer says, "[I]n this wide and novel field of . . . [constitutional law] our judges have been pioneers. There have been men among them, like Marshall, Shaw, and Ruffin,[28] who were sensible of the true nature of their work and of the large method of treatment which it required, who perceived that our constitutions had made them, in a limited and secondary way, but yet a real one, coadjutors with the other departments in the business of government; but many have fallen short of the requirements of so great a function."[29]

How then is a study of Ruffin relevant to an understanding of race and the law? Examining Ruffin helps focus on what factor has been most important in determining the rules of American law. While precedent, analogies, facts, and statutory construction are significant, a decision-maker's personal values most accurately reflect how the rules of law will be formulated or interpreted. While no direct legal precedent existed, Ruffin had several viable options grounded in general principles of common law, statutory interpretation, and analogy. At the least, Ruffin could have ruled that Lydia was entitled to some minimal legal protection. Instead, he chose the harshest option available for Lydia, one giving her no rights whatsoever. The reason for this choice was not a legal justification but a personal one, based entirely on the profit and safety of the slave-owner.

F. Judge Thomas Ruffin's Rough Drafts of Mann[30]

1. First Draft

The Indictment charges a battery by the defendant on *Lydia*, the slave of E. Jones. Upon the face of the indictment, the case is the same as the *State v. Hall*, 2 Hawks, 382.—That case is considered as settling this question, as it relates to a stranger. The Court finds no fault with the rule then adopted, even if it were now open. But it is then put to rest. The evidence makes this a different case. Here the slave had been hired by the defendant and was in his possession, and the battery was committed during the period of hiring. With the liabilities of the hirer the general owner for an injury to the slave permanently impairing the value, no rule now to be adopted can

---

28. Note that, in many ways, Thayer's selection of these three jurists as particularly great men reflects the perception of the unimportance of the rights of blacks under the legal process, even in 1895. Marshall and Shaw had each written several opinions adverse to blacks while on the bench.

29. J. Thayer, Cases on Constitutional Law 178 (1895).

30. Three drafts of Judge Ruffin's decision in this famous case were found among his papers written in his own handwriting, and present a most interesting illustration of his method of developing an opinion. The last draft is identical to the printed opinion of the Supreme Court as found in 13 N.C. 263 and, therefore, has been omitted from this section. *See* The Papers of Thomas Ruffin, Vol. IV, pp. 251–54 (Collected and edited by J.G. De Roulhac Hamilton, 1918).

interfere. The common doctrine of bailment would, no doubt, apply to that state of facts, modified to the emergency. The enquiry is, whether a cruel and unreasonable battery on a slave, by the hirer, is indictable. The Judge below instructed the Jury, that it is. It seems in the charge, to be put upon the ground, that the defendant had but a special property.

Our laws uniformly treat the master, overseer or other person having the possession and command of the slave, as entitled to the same authority. The object is the same—the services of the slave: And the same powers must be confided. In a criminal proceeding and in reference to all other persons but the general owner, the hirer and possessor of a slave in relation to both rights and duties, is, for the time being, the owner. This opinion would dispose of the particular case before us; because this indictment, which charges a battery upon the slave of E. Jones, is not supported by proof of a battery upon the defendant's own slave, since, certainly, different kinds of justification are applicable to the two cases. But upon the general question, whether the owner is answerable criminaliter for a battery upon his own slave or other exercise of authority or force on him, not forbidden by Statute, the Court entertains as little doubt. That he is so liable has never yet been decided: nor even, as far as is known, has been before contended. There have been no prosecutions of the sort. The established habits and uniform practice of the Country, in this respect, is the best evidence of the portion of Power deemed by the whole Community, requisite to the preservation of the Master's dominion. We cannot set our notions in array against the judgment of everybody else and say that this or that authority may be safely topped off. This has, indeed, been assimilated: the Bar to the other domestic relations; and arguments drawn from the well-established principles which confer and restrain the authority of the Parent over the child, the Tutor over the Pupil, and the Master over the Apprentice have been pressed on us. The Court does not recognize their application. There is no likeness between the cases. They are in opposition to each other and there is an impassable gulf between them. The difference is that, which exists between Freedom and Slavery—and a greater cannot be imagined. In the one, the end in view is the happiness of the youth, born to equal rights with that governor, on whom the duty devolves of training the young to usefulness in that Station which he is afterwards to assume among free men. To such an end and with such a subject moral and intellectual instruction seem the natural means; and for the most part, they are found to suffice. Force is suppurated, only to make the others effectual. With slavery it is far otherwise. The end is, the profit of the Master, his security, and the public safety: The subject, one deemed in his own person and his posterity to live without knowledge and without capacity to make anything his own and to toil, that another may reap the fruits. What moral consideration shall be addressed to such a being, to convince him what it is impossible but that the most stupid must know can never be true,—that he is thus to labor upon a principle of natural duty or for the sake of his personal happiness? Surely such services can be expected only from one, who has no will of his own; who surrenders his will, in implicit obedience to that of another. Such obedience is the consequence only of uncontrolled authority over the Body. The power of the master must be absolute to render the submission of the slave perfect. I most freely and fully confess my sense of the harshness of this position. I feel it as deeply as any man can, and as a principle of moral right everyone in his retirement must repudiate and condemn it. But in the actual conditions of things, there is no remedy. This discipline belongs to the State of Slavery. They cannot be disunited without abrogating at once the rights of the Master and destroying the subjugation of the slave. It constitutes the curse of slavery to both the bond and free portions of our population. But it is inherent in the relation of Master and Slave.

That there may be particular cases of cruelty and deliberate barbarity where, in conscience, the law might properly interfere is most probable. The difficulty is to determine, which is the proper case. Merely in the abstract, it may be asked, what power of the master accords with right? The answer will probably be found to sweep away all. The truth is that every consideration forbids their being brought into discussion before Courts of justice. The Slave, to remain a slave, must be made sensible that there is no appeal from his master and that his power is, in no instance usurped but is conferred by the laws of man at least, if not the law of God. The danger would be great indeed, if the tribunals of justice should be called on to graduate the punishment appropriate to every temper and dereliction of menial duty. We are happy to see, that there is daily less and less occasion for their interposition. The protection already afforded by sundry statutes, the private interest of the owner, the benevolence towards each other seated in the hearts of those who have been born and bred together, the frowns and deep execrations of the Community upon the barbarian who is guilty of excessive and brutal cruelty to his unprotected slave, all combined, have produced a mildness of treatment and an attention to the comforts of that unfortunate class, greatly mitigating the rigors of slavery and ameliorating the condition of the slaves. The same causes will continue to produce and enlarge the same effects, until the disparity between the numbers of the whites and blacks shall leave the latter without power dangerous to the others, when the police now existing may be further relaxed. This result, much to be desired, may be much more rationally expected from the events above alluded to and now in progress than from any rash expositions of abstract truths by a Judiciary tainted with a fanatical philosophy and philanthropy.

I repeat therefore, that we would gladly have avoided this ungrateful question, but Courts are often compelled to set on principles, which outrage individual feeling. This is one instance of it. We are obliged therefore to declare, that, until the Legislature shall otherwise order the Courts must recognize the rights of the owner to full dominion over the person of the Slave, unless restrained in particular instances by Statute. And this we do upon the ground, that such dominion is essential to their value as property and to the public peace, greatly dependent upon their subordination: and while slavery shall continue to exist in its present form as most effectually securing the general protection and comfort of the Slave — Let there be a new trial.

2. Second Draft

This is one of those cases which a Court will always regret being brought into judgment—One in which principles of policy urge the Judge to a decision in discord with the feelings of the man. But until the condition of our population be much changed or it shall seem fit to the Legislature to alter the rule, Courts are obliged, however reluctantly, to recognize the rights of the owner to full dominion over the *Slave*, as essential to their value as property, to the public peace as dependent upon their subordination and, indeed, while slavery in its present form shall continue to exist, as most effectually securing the general protection and comfort of the slave himself.

The Indictment charges the defendant with an assault and battery on Lydia, a slave, the property of Elizabeth Jones. This brings the case within the rule established in the *State vs. Hall*, 2 Hawks, 532. It is not intended to question what is there decided even if it were an open question and had not been decided. But it is not considered open. It is settled by that case. The question, here, is altogether different, upon the evidence. The slave had been hired by the defendant for the year 1825 from E. Jones; and the battery complained of was committed during that year. The liability of the defendant to the general owner for a permanent injury, impairing the value of the slave, caused by the excessive and wanton battery on her or other fault of the hirer is a distinct matter of consideration. There can be no doubt, that the common doctrines of bailments are applicable to such a study of facts. But in a criminal proceeding and in reference to all other persons but the owner, the hirer and possessor of a slave in relation to his rights and duties, is, for the time being, the owner. The case therefore presents the general question, whether the owner of a slave is responsible criminaliter for a battery upon his own slave or other exercise of authority or force over him, not expressly forbidden by statute. Such a rule has not yet been established. This Court disclaims the power to lay down such a rule, or to enforce it, without it be first prescribed by the Legislature. The province of interposing between Master and Slave is too delicate, in our State of Society, to be assumed by Courts without the positive injunction of the lawmaker. This has been assimilated to the other domestic relations; and arguments drawn from the well established principles, which confer and restrain the authority of the Parent over the child, the Master over the apprentice and the tutor over the pupil, have pressed on us with seal and ability. The Court cannot recognize their application. There is no likeness between the Cases. They are separated from each other by an impassable gulf. Without enlarging on the subject, it is enough to say that the difference between them is that, which exists between Freedom and Slavery. A contrast greater than that cannot be imagined. In the one case the subject of government is one born to equal rights with the governor, his offspring or his ward, young, helpless or inexperienced, the object of affection or benevolence, confided by providence or the law to the charge of another to be trained for usefulness in a station among freemen—the end in view, the happiness of the youth, the means, morals and intellectual instruction which, for the most part, are found to suffice. Force is suppurated, only to make the former effectual in cases of intractability. In the other, the end is the profit of the master and the security of his person, and the public safety. And who is the subject of this authority? One who has only intelligence and moral feeling enough to make his service reluctant to enable him to understand that the laws, which condemn him to toil for another is unjust, to condemn that injustice and abhor the master who avails himself of it. Can he who has these consciousness be prevailed on by moral considerations to perform the functions of servitude? What moral consideration can be presented to him? Is it that there is to be no end to the degradation of himself and his descendants — that, thro' time, his offspring as well as himself are to have no will of their own and that their exertions are never to yield fruit but for a master? Surely every passion, good or bad, of the human heart combine to rebuke the folly of him, who advises or expects the Slave to serve his master upon a principle of natural duty. A submissive and entire obedience to the will of the Master can alone be expected to produce that subordination and those efforts of labor exacted from the slave. That submission of will can only follow from the power of the Master over the Body — a power which the Slave must be made sensible is not usurped, but conferred at least by the law of man, if not of God. Restraint, therefore, constant, vigilant, not infrequently severe and exemplary and painful punishments of the slave is the unwelcome, and the necessary task of the Master. This discipline belongs to the state of slavery. They cannot be disunited without abrogating all the rights of the master and annulling the duties of the slave. It makes the curse of slavery both to the bond and the free portion of our population. But in the actual condition of things, there is no remedy. The power of the master must be as strong and as absolute as the submission of the Slave must be unconditional and implicit. It is inherent in the relation of Master and Slave.

It is with pride as Citizens and sincere joy as men, that we observe every day improvements in the condition of slaves. The Legislature compels the owner to provide a comfortable subsistence for them, and gives him the same security of life which belongs to a free man: The Courts protect him from the cruelty and abuse of a stranger. Public opinion, in accordance with the humanity of the laws, demands a mitigation of the rigors of slavery, which has not been without the happiest effects upon the feelings of Masters, who now, generally, practice towards the blacks more mildness than formerly and as much indulgence as is consistent with the true interests of both classes and the common safety.

It is to be lamented when such cases as the present are brought into judgment. It is impossible that the reasons on which they go can be appreciated, but when institutions similar to our own exist and are thoroughly understood. Besides, the struggle in the Judge's own breast between the feelings of the man and the convictions of the Magistrate is a severe one — presenting a strong temptation to put aside such questions if it be possible. It is useless however to complain of things inherent in our political State. And it is criminal in a Court to avoid any duty which the laws impose. While therefore Slavery exists among men or until it shall seem fit to the Legislature to interpose express enactments to the contrary, it will be the imperative duty of the Judges to refrain from laying down any rule, which can diminish that dominion of the Master, which is necessary to enforce the obedience and exact the services of the Slave accorded by our law to the owner.

G. Questions and Notes

The two drafts and the opinion in *State v. Mann* reveal much about Judge Ruffin's methods and values. Can you identify and describe these methods and values? In any of his drafts did he explore the possibility that Lydia had any rights at all?

Lydia, as did most slaves in North Carolina in 1829, suffered immense physical and emotional cruelty at the hands of evil overseers. Was there any direct cause or catalyst for such cruelty? Whom do you blame for such cruelty?

H. Point/Counterpoint

Abolitionist and former slave Frederick Douglass described the risk to white society of relinquishing firm control and domination of slaves:

> Beat and cuff the slave, keep him hungry and spiritless, and he will follow the chain of his master like a dog, but feed and clothe him well, work him moderately and surround him with physical comfort, and dreams of freedom will intrude. . . . You may hurl a man so low beneath the level of his kind that he loses all just ideas of his natural position, but elevate him a little, and the clear conception of rights rises to life and power, and leads him onward.

Do you agree or disagree with the theory of Frederick Douglass?

III. Race Classification

A. Introduction

Race consciousness is primarily a modern development. As Professor Roger Sanjek explains:

> [I]n the ancient world, human rank ordering was largely a product of ethnocentrism or caste consciousness. In large part, this organization stemmed from the arrangement of primitive communities in close proximity to one another where, among the peoples of these communities, gradations in physical characteristics were not very marked. The contemporary social hierarchy, on the other hand, particularly in the United States, is largely a function of race consciousness. It was only after the global expansion undertaken by western Europeans in the fifteenth century had led to the colonization of the new world and the discovery of new sea passages to Asia that "race" assumed social significance. Western Europeans sought to maintain

and rationalize their economic and political dominance by demonstrating that their subjugation of newly encountered and physically distinct peoples was natural, inevitable, and divinely predetermined.[31]

Recent scientific advances have shed new light on genetic bases for legal definitions of race. While research has revealed that there are genetic codes that cause blue eyes or dark skin, there are no genetic codes by which we can group people according to race. Consequently, it would appear that race is a socio-legal construction rather than a genetic one. The formation of race classifications, therefore, evolved through a series of choices and practices within societies, not from a genetic basis. Race classifications are a social construct, sustained by the legal system, not by science. As a result, the primary focus of this chapter is law instead of science.

Michael J. Bamshad and Steve E. Olson

Does Race Exist?

Look around on the streets of any major city, and you will see a sampling of the outward variety of humanity: skin tones ranging from milk-white to dark brown; hair textures running the gamut from fine and stick-straight to thick and wiry. People often use physical characteristics such as these—along with area of geographic origin and shared culture—to group themselves and others into "races." But how valid is the concept of race from a biological standpoint? Do physical features reliably say anything informative about a person's genetic makeup beyond indicating that the individual has genes for blue eyes or curly hair?

The problem is hard in part because the implicit definition of what makes a person a member of a particular race differs from region to region across the globe. Someone classified as "black" in the U.S., for instance, might be considered "white" in Brazil and "colored" (a category distinguished from both "black" and "white") in South Africa.

Yet common definitions of race do sometimes work well to divide groups according to genetically determined propensities for certain diseases. Sickle cell disease is usually found among people of largely African or Mediterranean descent, for instance, whereas cystic fibrosis is far more common among those of European ancestry. In addition, although the results have been controversial, a handful of studies have suggested that African Americans are more likely to respond poorly to some drugs for cardiac disease than are members of other groups.

Individuals from different populations are, on average, just slightly more different from one another than are individuals from the same population. In general, we would answer the first question yes, the second no, and offer a qualified yes to the third. Our answers rest on several generalizations about race and genetics. Some

---

31. *See* Roger Sanjek, *The Enduring Inequalities of Race*, in Race 2–4 (Steven Gregory and Roger Sanjek eds. 1994). *See generally* Michael Omi and Howard Winant, Racial Formation in the United States from the 1960s to 1980s (1986).

groups do differ genetically from others, but how groups are divided depends on which genes are examined; simplistically put, you might fit into one group based on your skin-color genes but another based on a different characteristic. Many studies have demonstrated that roughly 90 percent of human genetic variation occurs within a population living on a given continent, whereas about 10 percent of the variation distinguishes continental populations. In other words, individuals from different populations are, on average, just slightly more different from one another than are individuals from the same population. Human populations are very similar, but they often can be distinguished.

As a first step to identifying links between social definitions of race and genetic heritage, scientists need a way to divide groups reliably according to their ancestry. Over the past 100,000 years or so, anatomically modern humans have migrated from Africa to other parts of the world, and members of our species have increased dramatically in number. This spread has left a distinct signature in our DNA.

To determine the degree of relatedness among groups, geneticists rely on tiny variations, or polymorphisms, in the DNA—specifically in the sequence of base pairs, the building blocks of DNA. Most of these polymorphisms do not occur within genes, the stretches of DNA that encode the information for making proteins (the molecules that constitute much of our bodies and carry out the chemical reactions of life). Accordingly, these common variations are neutral, in that they do not directly affect a particular trait. Some polymorphisms do occur in genes; however, these can contribute to individual variation in traits and to genetic diseases.

Given that people can be sorted broadly into groups using genetic data, do common notions of race correspond to underlying genetic differences among populations? In some cases they do, but often they do not. For instance, skin color or facial features—traits influenced by natural selection—are routinely used to divide people into races. But groups with similar physical characteristics as a result of selection can be quite different genetically. Individuals from sub-Saharan Africa and Australian Aborigines might have similar skin pigmentation (because of adapting to strong sun), but genetically they are quite dissimilar.

In contrast, two groups that are genetically similar to each other might be exposed to different selective forces. In this case, natural selection can exaggerate some of the differences between groups, making them appear more dissimilar on the surface than they are underneath. Because traits such as skin color have been strongly affected by natural selection, they do not necessarily reflect the population processes that have shaped the distribution of neutral polymorphisms affected by natural selection may be poor predictors of group membership and may imply genetic relatedness where, in fact, little exists.

Another example of how difficult it is to categorize people involves populations in the U.S. Most people who describe themselves as African American have relatively recent ancestors from West Africa, and West Africans generally have polymorphism frequencies that can be distinguished from those of Europeans, Asians and Native Americans. The fraction of gene variations that African Americans share with West Africans, however, is far from uniform, because over the centuries African Americans have mixed extensively with groups originating from elsewhere in Africa and beyond.

Over the past several years, Mark D. Shriver of Pennsylvania State University and Rick A. Kittles of Howard University have defined a set of polymorphisms that they have used to estimate the fraction of a person's genes originating from each continental region. They found that the West African contribution to the genes of individual African-Americans averages about 80 percent, although it ranges from 20 to 100 percent. Mixing of groups is also apparent in many individuals who believe they have only European ancestors. According to Shriver's analyses, approximately 30 percent of Americans who consider themselves "white" have less than 90 percent European ancestry. Thus, self-reported ancestry is not necessarily a good predictor of the genetic composition of a large number of Americans. Accordingly, common notions of race do not always reflect a person's genetic background.

Understanding the relation between race and genetic variation has important practical implications. Several of the polymorphisms that differ in frequency practical implications. Several of the polymorphisms that differ in frequency from group to group have specific effects on health. The mutations responsible for sickle cell disease and some cases of cystic fibrosis, for instance, result from genetic changes that appear to have risen in frequency because they were protective against diseases prevalent in Africa and Europe, respectively. People who inherit one copy of the sickle cell polymorphism show some resistance to malaria; those with one copy of the cystic fibrosis trait may be less prone to the dehydration resulting from cholera. The symptoms of these diseases arise only in the unfortunate individuals who inherit two copies of the mutations.

Genetic variation also plays a role in individual susceptibility to one of the worst scourges of our age: AIDS. Some people have a small deletion in both their copies of a gene that encodes a particular cell-surface receptor called chemokine receptor 5 (CCR5). As a result, these individuals fail to produce CCR5 receptors on the surface of their cells. Most strains of HIV-1, the virus that causes AIDS, bind to the CCR5 receptor to gain entry to cells, so people who lack CCR5 receptors are resistant to HIV-1 infection. This polymorphism in the CCR5 receptor gene is found almost exclusively in groups from northeastern Europe.

Several polymorphisms in CCR5 do not prevent infection but instead influence the rate at which HIV-1 infection leads to AIDS and death. Some of these polymorphisms have similar effects in different populations; others only alter the speed of disease progression in selected groups. One polymorphism, for example, is associated with delayed disease progression in European Americans but accelerated disease in African Americans. Researchers can only study such population-specific effects—and use that knowledge to direct therapy—if they can sort people into groups.

In these examples—and others like them—a polymorphism has a relatively large effect in a given disease. If genetic screening were inexpensive and efficient, all individuals could be screened for all such disease-related gene variants. But genetic testing remains costly. Perhaps more significantly, genetic screening raises concerns about privacy and consent: some people might not want to know about genetic factors that could increase their risk of developing a particular disease. Until these issues are resolved further, self-reported ancestry will continue to be a potentially useful diagnostic tool for physicians.

Ancestry may also be relevant for some diseases that are widespread in particular populations. Most common diseases, such as hypertension and diabetes, are the cumulative results of polymorphisms in several genes, each of which has a small influence on its own. Recent research suggests that polymorphisms that have a particular effect in one group may have a different effect in another group. This kind of complexity would make it much more difficult to use detected polymorphisms as a guide to therapy. Until further studies are done on the genetic and environmental contributions to complex diseases, physicians may have to rely on information about an individual's ancestry to know how best to great some diseases.

But the importance of group membership as it relates to health care has been especially controversial in recent years. Last January the U.S. Food and Drug Administration (FDA) issued guidelines advocating the collection of race and ethnicity data in all clinical trials. Some investigators contend that the differences between groups are so small and the historical abuses associated with categorizing people by race so extreme that group membership should play little if any role in genetic and medical studies. They assert that the FDA should abandon its recommendation and instead ask researchers conducting clinical trials to collect genomic data on each individual. Others suggest that only by using group membership, including common definitions of race based on skin color, can we understand how genetic and environmental differences among groups contribute to disease. This debate will be settled only by further research on the validity of race as a scientific variable.

A set of articles in the March 20 issue of the *New England Journal of Medicine* debated both sides of the medical implications of race. The authors of one article— Richard S. Cooper of the Loyola Stritch School of Medicine, Jay S. Kaufman of the University of North Carolina at Chapel Hill and Ryk Ward of the University of Oxford—argued that race is not an adequate criterion for physicians to use in choosing a particular drug for a given patient. They pointed out two findings of racial differences that are both now considered questionable: that a combination of certain blood vessel-dilating drugs was more effective in treating heart failure in people of African ancestry and that specific enzyme inhibitors (angiotensin converting enzyme, or ACE, inhibitors) have little efficacy in such individuals. In the second article, a group led by Neil Risch of Stanford University countered that racial or ethnic groups can differ from one another genetically and that the differences can have medical importance. They cited a study showing that the rate of complications from type 2 diabetes varies according to race, even after adjusting for such factors as disparities in education and income.

The intensity of these arguments reflects both scientific and social factors. Many biomedical studies have not rigorously defined group membership, relying instead on inferred relationships based on racial categories. The dispute over the importance of group membership also illustrates how strongly the perception of race is shaped by different social and political perspectives.

In cases where membership in a geographically or culturally defined group has been correlated with health-related genetic traits, knowing something about an individual's group membership could be important for a physician. And to the extent that human groups live in different environments or have different experiences that affect health, group membership could also reflect nongenetic factors that are medically relevant.

Regardless of the medical implications of the genetics of race, the research findings are inherently exciting. For hundreds of years, people have wondered where various human groups came from and how those groups are related to one another. They have speculated about why human populations have different physical appearances and about whether the biological differences between groups are more than skin deep. New genetic data and new methods of analysis are finally allowing us to approach these questions. The result will be a much deeper understanding of both our biological nature and our human interconnectedness.

The study of DNA, and specifically polymorphisms, indicates there is extremely low variation between the genetic sequencing found in distinct populations or different geographic regions. A system of race-based classifications is not supported by the science of DNA. The science of DNA reveals that humans all over the world have more characteristics in common than in contrast.

For many Americans race may exist biologically (which differs from genetically due to the development of illnesses reflective of a particular group), visually, culturally, socially, psychologically, or geographically; however, race does not exist genetically. Genetically speaking, all human beings are the same, yet the social constructs of racial differentiation continue.

This chapter examines the nature of race in America today, definitions of race, the laws maintaining racial purity and barring interracial marriage, and the meaning of the term "black" in American race-classification law. It explores problems in defining racial discrimination, identifies difficulties in delineating racial categories, reveals the myth of white racial purity, discusses the contribution of this body of law to the development and maintenance of racial classification systems throughout the country, and analyses cases interpreting race-classification schemes.

B. The Nature of Race

Charles R. Lawrence III

*The Id, The Ego, and Equal Protection: Reckoning with Unconscious Racism**

Much of one's inability to know racial discrimination when one sees it results from a failure to recognize that racism is both a crime and a disease. This failure is compounded by a reluctance to admit that the illness of racism infects almost everyone. Acknowledging and understanding the malignancy are prerequisites to the discovery of an appropriate cure. But the diagnosis is difficult, because our own contamination with the very illness for which a cure is sought impairs our comprehension of the disorder.

Scholarly and judicial efforts to explain the constitutional significance of disproportionate impact and governmental motive in cases alleging racial discrimination treat these two categories as mutually exclusive. That is, while disproportionate impact may be evidence of racially discriminatory motive, whether impact or motive is the appropriate focus is normally posed in the alternative: Should racially disproportionate impact, standing alone, trigger a heightened level of judicial scrutiny? Or, should the judiciary apply a deferential standard to legislative and administrative decisions absent proof that the decisionmakers intended a racial consequence? Put another way, the Court thinks of facially neutral actions as either intentionally and unconstitutionally or unintentionally and constitutionally discriminatory.

I argue that this is a false dichotomy. Traditional notions of intent do not reflect the fact that decisions about racial matters are influenced in large part by factors that can be characterized as neither intentional—in the sense that certain outcomes are self-consciously sought—nor unintentional—in the sense that the outcomes are random, fortuitous, and uninfluenced by the decisionmaker's beliefs, desires, and wishes.

Americans share a common historical and cultural heritage in which racism has played and still plays a dominant role. Because of this shared experience, we also inevitably share many ideas, attitudes, and beliefs that attach significance to an individual's race and induce negative feelings and opinions about nonwhites. To the extent that this cultural belief system has influenced all of us, we are all racists. At the same time, most of us are unaware of our racism. We do not recognize the ways in which our cultural experience has influenced our beliefs about race or the occasions on which those beliefs affect our actions. In other words, a large part of the behavior that produces racial discrimination is influenced by unconscious racial motivation.

There are two explanations for the unconscious nature of our racially discriminatory beliefs and ideas. First, Freudian theory states that the human mind defends itself against the discomfort of guilt by denying or refusing to recognize those ideas,

* (footnotes and chapter headings omitted).

wishes, and beliefs that conflict with what the individual has learned is good or right. While our historical experience has made racism an integral part of our culture, our society has more recently embraced an ideal that rejects racism as immoral. When an individual experiences conflict between racist ideas and the societal ethic that condemns those ideas, the mind excludes his racism from consciousness.

Second, the theory of cognitive psychology states that the culture—including, for example, the media and an individual's parents, peers, and authority figures—transmits certain beliefs and preferences. Because these beliefs are so much a part of the culture, they are not experienced as explicit lessons. Instead, they seem part of the individual's rational ordering of her perceptions of the world. The individual is unaware, for example, that the ubiquitous presence of a cultural stereotype has influenced her perception that blacks are lazy or unintelligent. Because racism is so deeply ingrained in our culture, it is likely to be transmitted by tacit understandings: Even if a child is not told that blacks are inferior, he learns that lesson by observing the behavior of others. These tacit understandings, because they have never been articulated, are less likely to be experienced at a conscious level.

In short, requiring proof of conscious or intentional motivation as a prerequisite to constitutional recognition that a decision is race-dependent ignores much of what we understand about how the human mind works. It also disregards both the irrationality of racism and the profound effect that the history of American race relations has had on the individual and collective unconscious . . .

Racism is in large part a product of the unconscious. It is a set of beliefs whereby we irrationally attach significance to something called race. I do not mean to imply that racism does not have its origins in the rational and premeditated acts of those who sought and seek property and power. But racism in America is much more complex than either the conscious conspiracy of a power elite or the simple delusion of a few ignorant bigots. It is a part of our common historical experience and, therefore, a part of our culture. It arises from the assumptions we have learned to make about the world, ourselves, and others as well as from the patterns of our fundamental social activities . . .

Whatever our preferred theoretical analysis, there is considerable commonsense evidence from our everyday experience to confirm that we all harbor prejudiced attitudes that are kept from our consciousness.

When, for example, a well-known sports broadcaster is carried away by the excitement of a brilliant play by an Afro-American professional football player and refers to the player as a 'little monkey' during a nationally televised broadcast, we have witnessed the prototypical parapraxes, or unintentional slip of the tongue. This sportscaster views himself as progressive on issues of race. Many of his most important professional associates are black, and he would no doubt profess that more than a few are close friends. After the incident, he initially claimed no memory of it and then, when confronted with videotaped evidence, apologized and said that no racial slur was intended. There is no reason to doubt the sincerity of his assertion. Why would he intentionally risk antagonizing his audience and damaging his reputation and career? But his inadvertent slip of the tongue was not random. It is evidence of the continuing presence of a derogatory racial stereotype that he has repressed from consciousness and that has momentarily slipped past his ego's censors. Likewise, when Nancy Reagan appeared before a public gathering of then-presidential-candidate Ronald Reagan's political supporters and said that she wished he could be there to "see all these beautiful white people," one can hardly imagine that it was her self-conscious intent to proclaim publicly her preference for the company of Caucasians.

Incidents of this kind are not uncommon, even if only the miscues of the powerful and famous are likely to come to the attention of the press. But because the unconscious also influences selective perceptions, whites are unlikely to hear many of the inadvertent racial slights that are made daily in their presence.

Another manifestation of unconscious racism is akin to the slip of the tongue. One might call it a slip of the mind: While one says what one intends, one fails to grasp the racist implications of one's benignly motivated words or behavior. For example, in the late 1950s and early 1960s, when integration and assimilation were unquestioned ideals among those who consciously rejected the ideology of racism, white liberals often expressed their acceptance of and friendship with blacks by telling them that they 'did not think of them as Negroes.' Their conscious intent was complimentary. The speaker was saying, "I think of you as normal human beings, just like me." But he was not conscious of the underlying implication of his words. What did this mean about most Negroes? Were they not normal human beings? If the white liberal were asked if this was his inference, he would doubtless have protested that his words were being misconstrued and that he only intended to state that he did not think of anyone in racial terms. But to say that one does not think of a Negro as a Negro is to say that one thinks of him as something else. The statement is made in the context of the real world, and implicit in it is a comparison to some norm. In this case the norm is whiteness. The white liberal's unconscious thought, his slip of the mind, is, "I think of you as different from other Negroes, as more like white people." . . .

A crucial factor in the process that produces unconscious racism is the tacitly transmitted cultural stereotype. If an individual has never known a black doctor or lawyer or is exposed to blacks only through a mass media where they are portrayed in the stereotyped roles of comedian, criminal, musician, or athlete, he is likely to deduce that blacks as a group are naturally inclined toward certain behavior and unfit for certain roles. But the lesson is not explicit: It is learned, internalized, and used without an awareness of its source. Thus, an individual may select a white job applicant over an equally qualified black and honestly believe that this decision was based on observed intangibles unrelated to race. The employer perceives the white candidate as "more articulate," "more collegial," "more thoughtful," or "more charismatic." He is unaware of the learned stereotype that influenced his decision. Moreover, he has probably also learned an explicit lesson of which he is very much aware: Good, law-abiding people do not judge others on the basis of race. Even the most thorough investigation of conscious motive will not uncover the race-based stereotype that has influenced his decision.

This same process operates in the case of more far-reaching policy decisions that come to judicial attention because of their discriminatory impact. For example, when an employer or academic administrator discovers that a written examination rejects blacks at a disproportionate rate, she can draw several possible conclusions: that blacks are less qualified than others; that the test is an inaccurate measure of ability; or that the testers have chosen the wrong skills or attributes to measure. When decisionmakers reach the first conclusion, a predisposition to select those data that conform with a racial stereotype may well have influenced them. Because this stereotype has been tacitly transmitted and unconsciously learned, they will be unaware of its influence on their decision.

Peggy McIntosh

White Privilege: Unpacking the Invisible Knapsack

"I was taught to see racism only in individual acts of meanness, not in invisible systems conferring dominance on my group."

Through work to bring materials from women's studies into the rest of the curriculum, I have often noticed men's unwillingness to grant that they are overprivileged, even though they may grant that women are disadvantaged. They may say they will work to improve women's status, in the society, the university, or the curriculum, but they can't or won't support the idea of lessening men's. Denials that amount to taboos surround the subject of advantages that men gain from women's disadvantages. These denials protect male privilege from being fully acknowledged, lessened, or ended.

Thinking through unacknowledged male privilege as a phenomenon, I realized that, since hierarchies in our society are interlocking, there was most likely a phenomenon of white privilege that was similarly denied and protected. As a white person, I realized I had been taught about racism as something that puts others at a disadvantage, but had been taught not to see one of its corollary aspects, white privilege, which puts me at an advantage.

I think whites are carefully taught not to recognize white privilege, as males are taught not to recognize male privilege. So I have begun in an untutored way to ask what it is like to have white privilege. I have come to see white privilege as an invisible package of unearned assets that I can count on cashing in each day, but about which I was "meant" to remain oblivious. White privilege is like an invisible weightless knapsack of special provisions, maps, passports, codebooks, visas, clothes, tools, and blank checks . . .

I decided to try to work on myself at least by identifying some of the daily effects of white privilege in my life. I have chosen those conditions that I think in my case attach somewhat more to skin-color privilege than to class, religion, ethnic status, or geographic location, though of course all these other factors are intricately intertwined. As far as I can tell, my African-American coworkers, friends, and acquaintances with whom I come into daily or frequent contact in this particular time, place, and line of work cannot count on most of these conditions.

1. I can, if I wish, arrange to be in the company of people of my race most of the time.

2. I can avoid spending time with people whom I was trained to mistrust and who have learned to mistrust my kind to me.

3. If I should need to move, I can be pretty sure of renting or purchasing housing in an area which I can afford and in which I would want to live.

4. I can be reasonably sure that my neighbors in such a location will be neutral or pleasant to me.

5. I can go shopping alone most of the time, fairly well assured that I will not be followed or harassed by store detectives.

6. I can turn on the television or open to the front page of the newspaper and see people of my race widely and positively represented.

7. When I am told about our national heritage or about "civilization," I am shown that people of my color made it what it is.

8. I can be sure that my children will be given curricular materials that testify to the existence of their race.

9. If I want to, I can be pretty sure of finding a publisher for this piece on white privilege.

10. I can be fairly sure of having my voice heard in a group in which I am the only member of my race.

11. I can be casual about whether or not to listen to another woman's voice in a group in which she is the only member of her race.

12. I can go into a book store and count on finding the writing of my race, represented, into a supermarket and find the staple foods that fit with my cultural traditions, into a hairdresser's shop and find someone who can deal with my hair.

13. Whether I use checks, credit cards, or cash, I can count on my skin color not to work against the appearance that I am financially reliable.

14. I could arrange to protect our young children most of the time from people who might not like them.

15. I did not have to educate our children to be aware of systemic racism for their own daily physical protection.

16. I can be pretty sure that my children's teachers and employers will tolerate them if they fit school and workplace norms; my chief worries about them do not concern others' attitudes toward their race.

17. I can talk with my mouth full and not have people put this down to my color.

18. I can swear, or dress in secondhand clothes, or not answer letters, without having people attribute these choices to the bad morals, the poverty, or the illiteracy of my race.

19. I can speak in public to a powerful male group without putting my race on trial.

20. I can do well in a challenging situation without being called a credit to my race.

21. I am never asked to speak for all the people of my racial group.

22. I can remain oblivious to the language and customs of persons of color who constitute the world's majority without feeling in my culture any penalty to such oblivion.

23. I can criticize our government and talk about how much I fear its policies and behavior without being seen as a cultural outsider.

24. I can be reasonably sure that if I ask to talk to "the person in charge," I will be facing a person of my race.

25. If a traffic cop pulls me over or if the IRS audits my tax return, I can be sure I haven't been singled out because of my race.

26. I can easily buy posters, postcards, picture books, greeting cards, dolls, toys, and children's magazines featuring people of my race.

27. I can go home from most meetings of organizations I belong to feeling somewhat tied in, rather than isolated, out of place, outnumbered, unheard, held at a distance, or feared.

28. I can be pretty sure that an argument with a colleague of another race is more likely to jeopardize her chances for advancement than to jeopardize mine.

29. I can be fairly sure that if I argue for the promotion of a person of another race, or a program centering on race, this is not likely to cost me heavily within my present setting, even if my colleagues disagree with me.

30. If I declare there is a racial issue at hand, or there isn't a racial issue at hand, my race will lend me more credibility for either position than a person of color will have.

31. I can choose to ignore developments in minority writing and minority activist programs, or disparage them, or learn from them, but in any case, I can find ways to be more or less protected from negative consequences of any of these choices.

32. My culture gives me little fear about ignoring the perspectives and powers of people of other races.

33. I am not made acutely aware that my shape, bearing, or body odor will be taken as a reflection of my race.

34. I can worry about racism without being seen as self-interested or self-seeking.

35. I can take a job with an affirmative action employer without having my co-workers on the job suspect that I got it because of my race.

36. If my day, week, or year is going badly, I need not ask of each negative episode or situation whether it has racial overtones.

37. I can be pretty sure of finding people who would be willing to talk with me and advise me about my next steps, professionally.

38. I can think over many options, social, political, imaginative, or professional, without asking whether a person of my race would be accepted or allowed to do what I want to do.

39. I can be late to a meeting without having the lateness reflect on my race.

40. I can choose public accommodation without fearing that people of my race cannot get in or will be mistreated in the places I have chosen.

41. I can be sure that if I need legal or medical help, my race will not work against me.

42. I can arrange my activities so that I will never have to experience feelings of rejection owing to my race.

43. If I have low credibility as a leader, I can be sure that my race is not the problem.

44. I can easily find academic courses and institutions that give attention only to people of my race.

45. I can expect figurative language and imagery in all of the arts to testify to experiences of my race.

46. I can choose blemish cover or bandages in "flesh" color and have them more or less match my skin . . .

Disapproving of the systems won't be enough to change them. I was taught to think that racism could end if white individuals changed their attitudes. But a "white" skin in the United States opens many doors for whites whether or not we approve of the way dominance has been conferred on us. Individual acts can palliate, but cannot end, these problems . . .

Excerpted from Working Paper 189,
"White Privilege and Male Privilege: A Personal Account of Coming to See Correspondences through Work in Women's Studies."
Copyright © (1988) Peggy McIntosh.
Reprinted with permission of Peggy McIntosh.

F. Michael Higginbotham

Racism Less Pervasive, More Complex

Forty years ago today, the Rev. Martin Luther King Jr. was murdered. The night before he died, the Nobel Peace Prize winner delivered a speech predicting the nation's future and his own demise. Dr. King prophesied that, while he likely would not live to see the day, he had no doubts that all Americans, including blacks, would someday "get to the promised land" of racial equality.

Four decades after Dr. King's death, Barack Obama, the U.S. Senate's only black member, may become America's first black president. This stirs powerful emotions. In a country with a long history of slavery and segregation, what a monumental moment in the American story.

That is why the cover of many major magazines feature variations on the question, "Does Barack Obama's Rise Mean the End of Racism?" The answer is not a short yes or no, but rather a long maybe. Whether racism ends in America depends upon what Americans do with this latest opportunity.

Many say Mr. Obama's success is insignificant. Some even suggest that his popularity with whites is a cynical ploy on their part to end, once and forever, any discussion of current racism. They are wrong. Mr. Obama's multiracial coalition demonstrates an eagerness for dialogue, a desire for change, and a sense of the possibilities of this moment.

Progress and setbacks in racial equality have occurred in a cyclical nature in American history. Three major opportunities for change presented themselves: the founding, Reconstruction, and the civil rights movement. In each, racial progress was made, but setbacks followed due to continuing notions of white superiority. Mr. Obama's achievement, whether or not he wins the presidency in 2008, signifies a fourth era of opportunity.

This is not to suggest that Mr. Obama's success indicates the end of racism. Those who believe that are as wrong as those who say racism today is as bad as it was under Jim Crow. It does, however, indicate an opportunity to take the final step in a long journey. As Mr. Obama recognized in his momentous speech last month on America's racial divide, now is the time for the real conversation to begin.

No doubt, for many Americans the conversation will be uncomfortable. It must, however, take place if we are ever to realize those "self-evident truths" of equality identified more than 200 years ago by the Founding Fathers and reiterated in 1963 in Dr. King's "I Have a Dream" speech.

Racial inequality today is much more complex than it was when Dr. King led protests against Jim Crow. Forty years ago, laws enshrined discrimination, and violence was used to maintain the divide. Today, what I call the ghosts of Jim Crow are caused by choices that result in housing isolation, inequitable school funding, criminal justice stereotyping, and health care service inadequacy that maintain inequality.

One ghost of Jim Crow is exemplified in the story of Tim Carter and Richard Thomas, arrested in 2004 in separate incidents three months apart in nearly the same location in St. Petersburg, Fla. Police found one rock of cocaine on Mr. Carter, who is white, and a crack pipe with cocaine residue on Mr. Thomas, who is black.

Both men claimed drug additions, neither had any prior felony arrests or convictions, and both men potentially faced five years in prison. Mr. Carter had his prosecution withheld, and the judge sent him to drug rehabilitation. Mr. Thomas was prosecuted, convicted and went to prison. Their only apparent difference was race.

Harsher punishment for blacks is common, even today. Statistics indicate that nationally blacks are prosecuted and imprisoned at a rate more than five times that of whites.

Equally reflective of current racial disparities is the pattern of property ownership, and the fact that whites continue to embrace the "tipping point" notion in housing integration.

"Tipping point" bigotry inspired Jeremy Parady, who pleaded guilty in 2005 to conspiracy to commit arson in a series of fires in a new housing development in Southern Maryland. Mr. Parady admitted that he set fire to this development because many of the buyers were blacks and the surrounding neighborhood was mostly white.

Much progress toward equality has been made; official government discrimination is rare, and blatant bigotry has been substantially reduced.

But racial disparities continue to haunt us decades after Dr. King's assassination, and racist choices continue to influence those disparities. These ghosts of Jim Crow must be eradicated if Dr. King's "Promised Land" prediction is ever to come true.

C. Definitions of Race

A. Leon Higginbotham, Jr. and Barbara Kopytoff

*Racial Purity and Interracial Sex in the Law of Colonial and Antebellum Virginia**

In order to separate by race you must first define race. There is probably no better place than Virginia to examine the origins of the American doctrine of racial purity and its maintenance through prohibitions on interracial sex and interracial marriage. Many people applaud Virginia as the "mother of Presidents" (four of the

---

* (some footnotes omitted).

first five Presidents were Virginians)[3] and the "mother of revolutionaries," such as Thomas Jefferson, George Washington, and Patrick Henry. Yet few stress that colonial Virginia was also the "mother" of American slavery and a leader in the gradual debasement of blacks[4] through its institution of slavery. Virginia was also one of the first colonies to formulate a legal definition of race[5] which it enforced through prohibitions against interracial marriage and interracial sex. For more than three centuries,[6] the Virginia courts and legislatures advocated and endorsed concepts of racial purity that most Americans today would call racist.

While Virginia was a pioneer in these areas of law both before and after the Civil War, the pre-Civil War law differed significantly from that of the early twentieth century. The law of racial purity in the eighteenth and nineteenth centuries defined "white" as a less exclusive term than did the law of the twentieth century: People with some ancestors known to be African could be legally white. The laws banning interracial sex and marriage were less harsh on blacks before the Civil War than they were afterwards: blacks were not punished at all for marrying or for engaging in voluntary sexual relations with whites.

This is not to say that Virginia was less racist and oppressive to blacks before the Civil War than it was in the late nineteenth and twentieth centuries, but merely that the legal mechanisms of oppression were somewhat different. Slavery had its own mechanisms for legal control. When it was abolished, white Virginians devised other mechanisms to preserve the racial hierarchy of the slave era, such as the laws regarding racial purity and interracial sex.

The laws regarding racial purity and interracial sex and marriage in pre-Civil War Virginia sprang from two concerns. The first concern was with the maintenance of clear racial boundaries in a society that came to be based on racial slavery. Starting in the late seventeenth century, white Virginia legislators enacted statutes to discourage racial intermingling. Later, they enacted statutes to racially classify the mixed-race children born when the earlier statutes were ineffective. The statutes

---

3. These were Presidents Washington, Jefferson, Madison, and Monroe.

4. The term "black" is used to include all those who, during the pre-Civil War period, were classified by law as Negroes or mulattoes. The two comprised a single legal category, but a single term was not generally used in legal writing of the time. After the Civil War, the term "colored" was used for both, which term has recently been replaced by "black" or African American. *See* 1888 CODE OF VIRGINIA tit. 4, ch. VI, §49 (defining "colored" persons and Indians).

5. *See* Ch. IV, 3 LAWS OF VA. 250, 252 (Hening 1823) (enacted 1705) (mulatto defined as child, grandchild, or great-grandchild of Negro (and presumably a white) or child of Indian (and presumably a white)).

6. The first prohibition against interracial sex came in a 1662 statute; Act XII, 2 LAWS OF VA. 170, 170 (Hening 1823) (enacted 1662). Virginia's prohibition on interracial marriage was declared unconstitutional in 1967. *Loving v. Virginia*, 388 U.S. 1, 12 (1967) (prohibition violated equal protection and due process clauses of the fourteenth amendment).

punishing voluntary interracial sex and marriage were directed only at whites; they alone were charged with the responsibility of maintaining racial purity.[7]

When Europeans, sub-Saharan Africans, and Native Americans first encountered one another in large numbers during the seventeenth century, the three populations had effectively been separated for thousands of years and each had developed distinctive physical characteristics. The visible differences, especially between Africans and Europeans, were so striking that travelers usually commented on them: "indeed when describing Negroes they frequently began with complexion and then moved on to dress (or rather lack of it) and manners." The causes of the physical variations were open to question, and theories to explain them abounded. But the more important issue in the Americas became the consequence of racial difference rather than its causes: that is, the legal and social significance of race.

In practical terms, the fact that the differences between Africans and Europeans were so visible made it particularly easy to operate a racially based system of slavery. In theoretical terms, when people bothered to ponder the question, they often saw the differences among races as part of a "natural ordering of creatures by Providence into a Great Chain of Being, from the highest to the lowest." Clearly, such a conception of a hierarchical ordering of races need not imply slavery; the English thought that the Irish were an inferior "race" but did not advocate denying them all basic human rights. Yet just as clearly, the idea of racial hierarchy could be, and came to be, used as a justification for slavery.

In a 1772 suit in Virginia brought by a group of Native Americans who claimed they had been unjustly enslaved, Colonel Bland, the lawyer for the slave owner, argued:

> That societies of men could not subsist unless there were a subordination of one to another, and that from the highest to the lowest degree. That this was conformable with the general scheme of the Creator, observable in other parts of his great work, where no chasm was to be discovered, but the several links run imperceptibly into one another. That in this subordination the department of slaves must be filled by some, or there would be a defect in the scale of order.

In Colonel Bland's notion of the "Great Chain of Being," Native Americans and blacks were created inferior and were meant to be subservient to whites. Although seldom expressed clearly and explicitly in eighteenth-century Virginia, the view was implicitly held throughout Virginia society, especially with regard to blacks.

Since the racially-based systems of slavery that developed in the New World were premised on the concept of the racial inferiority of the enslaved, it would have been

---

7. The second concern was with involuntary interracial sex—that is, rape. This was seen primarily as an aspect of power relations between the races. Virginia applied the early law of rape more harshly to blacks than to whites: it punished only black men for interracial rape and, in the nineteenth century, the state formulated anti-rape statutes directed specifically at blacks.

far simpler to maintain that system had there been no intermingling of races, no anomalous offspring, and no confusion of the "natural order" by beings who did not clearly belong to one rather than another of the three populations of Indians, Africans, and Europeans. But human sexual behavior did not respect the "natural order," and mixed-race children invariably sprang up wherever the races had contact. Many white Virginians were disturbed by racial intermingling, especially white-black mixtures, and introduced laws penalizing whites who engaged in interracial sex in order to prevent what they saw as the "abominable mixture and spurious issue." When that failed, they turned to drawing strict racial boundary lines, defining some mixed-race children as white and others as mulatto. They also devised a separate rule to settle the status of mixed-race children as slave or free, depending on the status of the mother. This rule applied generally to all children born in Virginia, whether of mixed race or not.

Virginia did not create a perfect social system in which black equaled slave and white equaled free with no confusing middle ground. Virginia's racially-based system of slavery was created in the context of continuous racial mixing, legal anomalies, and recurring attempts to patch holes in the fabric of the system. Looking at the system in terms of its anomalies and patches helps bring into focus some of the central concepts of race in pre-Civil War Virginia.

The Law of Slave Status

Part of the reason there was no complete correlation of race with slave status in pre-Civil War Virginia was that the rule for the inheritance of slave status was, as written, technically independent of race. While white Virginians seemed increasingly to want blacks to be slaves, the statutes avoided a direct and explicit statement equating race and status. In 1662, the House of Burgesses set down the law on the inheritance of slave status, and it remained virtually unchanged throughout the slave period in Virginia. It was devised to settle the status of the mulatto children of free white fathers and black slave mothers. The act read:

> Whereas some doubts have arisen whether children got by any Englishman upon a negro woman should be slave or free. Be it therefore enacted and declared by this present grand assembly, that all children borne in this country shall be held bond or free only according to the condition of the mother. . . .

There was an implicit confounding of "black" and "slave" in this early statute. It stated that the problem was the doubtful status of the mulatto children of "Negro" women; yet "Negro" must have meant "slave" or there would have been no question of the slave or free status of the children. In a world in which whites were assumed to be free and blacks were increasingly assumed to be slaves, a decision had to be made about the status of individuals who did not clearly belong to one race or the other: children whose parents represented two distinct races and two extreme statuses.

The statute did not say that all children of black men or of black women were to be slaves, probably because not all blacks were then slaves. It would have seemed extreme, no doubt, even to white Virginians of that time, to enslave the child of two free people just because one or both of them were black. Some blacks were landowners and held slaves themselves. The statute said, rather, that all children would be "bond or free" according to the status of the mother.[8] The rule embodied in the statute was thus phrased only in terms of status, not in terms of race.

Nonetheless, a rough correlation of race and status was assumed; even though the two categories did not correspond entirely then and they diverged over time, partly as a result of the 1662 statute. Consider, for example, the status of free blacks. Some blacks imported into Virginia before 1662 had never been slaves, and others who had been born slaves were later emancipated. The children of free black women were free under the statute, as were mulatto children born to white women. Free mulattoes were classified with free blacks in terms of race and position in society.[9] They also failed to correspond because white men mated with mulatto slave women producing a class of very light-skinned slaves. Some individuals were slaves because they were remotely descended in the maternal line from a black slave woman, but

8. It was contrary to English tradition for children to inherit the status of their mothers, but since the children who posed the problem were almost certainly illegitimate, it may also have been contrary to English tradition for them to inherit a position or status from their fathers. Indeed, the inheritance of slave status was itself anomalous in English law of that era. Villeinage had died out in England and all English men and women of the 17th century were free born, whether legitimate or not. When it existed, villeinage had been heritable in the male line. *See* Morris, *"Villeinage . . . as it existed in England, Reflects but little light on our subject": The Problem of the "Sources" of Southern Slave Law*, 32 Am. J. Leg. Hist. 95, 105–7 (1988) (concluding common law of property rather than villeinage source of slave law). The decision to make slave status heritable in the female line marked a departure. The rule of having children take their mother's status is known in Civil Law as *partus sequitor venturm*. Exactly how the doctrine came into use in Virginia is unclear. It is not known whether it came with slaves brought from Civil Law countries, or was borrowed by the legislators from Roman Law, or was independently invented by Virginians. It is clear that the legislators did not in 1662 invent the idea that the progeny of female slaves were also to serve for life; there is evidence for that practice as early as the 1640s. *See* Jordan, *Modern Tensions and the Origins of American Slavery*, 28 J.S. Hist. 18, 23–24 (1962) (sales of Negroes for life and of Negro women with future progeny recorded in 1640s).

9. While one can sort out the legal categories of race, the numbers in each are uncertain. The population figures on which estimates are based are incomplete, especially for the early period, and they do not distinguish Negroes and mulattoes and sometimes do not distinguish slave and free blacks. Edmund Morgan has given population estimates for 17th-century Virginia in the appendix to American Slavery, American Freedom: The Ordeal of Colonial Virginia 404 (1975). He also has estimated the number of blacks, but he says those figures are largely conjectural. In 1964, by his estimates, Virginia had 1,000 to 3,000 blacks out of a total population of 13,392. By the end of the century, in 1699, he suggests, Virginia's population included 6,000 to 10,000 blacks out of 58,040. *Id.* at 423. There is even less idea how many of those blacks were free.

The first U.S. census reports, from 1790, show that during the 18th century the free and slave black population increased at a far greater rate than the white. In 1790, the total black population was 305,493 — of whom 12,866 were free — and the white population was 442,117. By 1860, the last U.S. census under slavery, the total black population was 548,907 — of whom 58,042 were free — and the white population was 1,047,299. U.S. Bureau of the Census, Negro Population in the United States 1790–1915, at 57 (W. Katz ed. 1968) [hereinafter Negro Population 1790–1915] (figures for black population); *id.* at 44–45 (figures for white population).

had such a high proportion of European ancestry that they looked white.[10] Some would even have qualified as legally white under eighteenth and nineteenth-century Virginia statutes that defined race in terms of a specific proportion of white and non-white ancestry. Yet, legally, they were also slaves.[11] Being legally white did not make one free if one's mother was a slave; being black or mulatto did not make one a slave if one's mother was free.[12] The law of the inheritance of slave status was technically independent of race. As a result, many people obtained a social status considered inappropriate for their race in the white Virginians' ideal conception of their slave society.

To say that a person could legally be a slave if he or she were descended in the maternal line from a slave raises the question of whether the first woman in the line had been legally enslaved. It seems clear from the early documents that Virginians gradually made what Winthrop Jordan has called an "unthinking decision" to enslave blacks, and they did so in the absence of any specific legal sanction for the practice. It was only after the practice was well established that it was reinforced by positive law. Thus the first statute on the legality of enslavement came in 1670, eight years after the statute on the inheritance of slave status.

The stated purpose of the 1670 statute was to settle the question of whether Native Americans who were bought as war captives from other American Indians could be

---

10. There are a number of references to slaves who looked white. *See J.* JOHNSTON, RACE RELATIONS IN VIRGINIA & MISCEGENATION IN THE SOUTH, 1776–1860, at 209–14 (1970) (contemporary accounts of fair-skinned slaves). The numbers of fair-skinned slaves increased over time, as the slave population "lightened."

[T]he glaring fact is that throughout the South, Mulatto slavery was on the rise in the decade before the Civil War. Slavery as an institution was becoming whiter and whiter, a direct contradiction to the fundamental white notion that slavery was meant for black people. In 1835, Chancellor Harper of South Carolina had declared that it was "hardly necessary to say that a slave cannot be a white man," but by the end of the ante-bellum period the facts said otherwise. Growing number of persons with predominantly white blood were being held as slaves.

J. MENCKE, MULATTOES AND RACE MIXTURE 20 (1979).

11. No case held that a slave was free solely on the ground that he or she was legally white. The point was raised in *Henry v. Bollar*, 34 Va. (7 Leigh) 552 (1836), in which the plaintiffs alleged, among other things, "that they were in fact white persons, and therefore could never have been lawfully held in slavery." *Id.* at 556. The defendants in the case claimed that those suing for their freedom were mulattoes. *Id.* at 557. The court did not address the interesting question of whether persons who had so small a proportion of black ancestry that they were legally white could, in fact, be slaves. It found the plaintiffs free on other grounds, namely, that their owner, who had tried to free them both by will and by deed of emancipation, had been mentally competent to do so. *Id.*

12. For a brief period of fifteen years, starting in 1676, some Native Americans also could be legally enslaved, and a female ancestor from that period could produce a line of descendants who were legally slaves. Act I, 2 LAWS OF VA. 341, 346 (Hening 1823) (enacted 1676) (Native-Americans taken during war held as slaves for life); Act I, 2 LAWS OF VA. 401, 404 (Hening 1823) (enacted 1676) (same); Act I, 2 LAWS OF VA. 433, 440 (Hening 1823) (enacted 1679) (same); Act IX, 3 LAWS OF VA. 69, 69 (Hening 1823) (enacted 1691) (abolition of all trade restrictions with Native Americans). The 1691 statute was later interpreted as having made enslavement of Native Americans illegal. *See Gregory v. Baugh*, 25 Va. (4 Rand.) 246, 252 (1827) (Green, J.) (discussion of these and other statutes regarding enslavement of Native Americans).

slaves. Blacks were not mentioned explicitly, but by curiously circumspect language the legislature indicated that imported blacks were to be slaves. The act as published was captioned "what tyme Indians to serve." It read, in its entirety:

> Whereas some dispute have [sic] arisen whither Indians taken in warr by any other nation . . . that taketh them sold to the English, are servants for life or terms of years, It is resolved and enacted that all servants not being Christians imported into this colony by shipping shalbe slaves for their lives; but what shall come by land shall serve, if boyes or girles, untill thirty years of age, if men or women twelve years and no longer.[13]

Why was enslavement made to depend on manner of importation? If the legislators wanted to enslave blacks but not American Indians, why did they not say so? There seems to have been a curious avoidance of any mention of blacks in the statute. In 1682, the statute was revised to eliminate the distinction based on the manner of importation, for the legislature had, in the interim, approved the enslavement of Indians. This time the legislators offered explicit examples of the people whom they contemplated enslaving: "all [imported] servants except Turkes whilest in amity with his majesty, . . . whether Negroes, Moors, Mullattoes or Indians." The list of likely slave peoples was dropped from the act in the 1705 revision; the revised act noted only which imported servants could not be enslaved, not which could be.

Thus, the rule of enslavement, like the rule of the inheritance of slave status, was technically independent of race. However, even a superficial familiarity with the history of the era would indicate that white Virginians did not truly intend that slave status and race be independent. As the 1682 statute shows, they saw slaves as "Negroes, Moors, Mullatoes or Indians."[14] Yet, for the most part, they avoided racial designations in their laws, making enslavement depend on other characteristics instead. Were white Virginians of the mid-seventeenth century reluctant to admit, even to themselves, what they were doing: establishing a slave society based on race?

Statutory Definitions of Race in Virginia

There existed the anomaly of people whose status in Virginia society was not entirely dependent on their race. There were also racial anomalies: people whose race was in itself ambiguous, who did not fit into one or another of the set categories of race that comprised the white Virginian's view of nature.

When Europeans, Native Americans, and Africans first came into contact with each other in Virginia, there was no question or problem as to which race

---

13. Id. at 283 (italics omitted). The treatment of Native Americans by the Virginia legislature and courts is an area which goes far beyond the coverage of this Chapter. However, even within the context of racial purity and interracial sex, the Virginia legal process demonstrated a hostility to Native Americans because they were nonwhite.

14. Act I, 2 Laws of Va. 490, 491 (Hening 1823) (enacted 1682). The Moors that the Virginians meant to enslave were most likely blacks while those "in amity with his majesty" who were not to be enslaved were most likely lighter-skinned people from North Africa.

an individual belonged. It was evident at first glance. As Judge Roane observed in *Hudgins v. Wrights:*

> The distinguishing characteristics of the different species of the human race are so visibly marked, that those species may be readily discriminated from each other by mere inspection only. This, at least, is emphatically true in relation to the negroes, to the Indians of North America, and the European white people.

Thus, there was no need to establish an immediate statutory definition of race and there were no problems of racial identity to be solved by legislative fiat. However, as soon as the races began to mingle and reproduce, problems of racial identity arose. How should mixed-race offspring be classified?

Strictly in terms of genetic contribution, the child of one white parent and one black parent had the same claim to being classified as white as he or she did to being classified as black. The child was neither, or either, or both. One could decide to call such half/half mixtures mulattoes, but that merely raised the question of classification again in the next generation. Was the child of a mulatto and a white to be deemed a mulatto or a white? Or should another name, like quadroon, be devised for such a person?

Of course, the important point was not the classification itself but the set of rights and privileges that accompanied that classification. In Virginia, there were only three racial classifications of any legal significance, though there were far more combinations and permutations of racial mixture. Those three were "white," "Indian," and "Negro and mulatto."[15] Mulattoes of mixed African and European ancestry had the same legal position as blacks, although their social position may have been somewhat different. These legal classifications gave rise to the need for a legal definition of race. As Winthrop Jordan notes, "if mulattoes were to be considered Negroes, logic required some definition of mulattoes, some demarcation between them and white men." Virginia was one of only two colonies to bow to the demands of logic by creating a precise statutory definition in the colonial period.

As noted above, slave status was legally independent of race. Slaves who looked white had no special legal privileges until the nineteenth century, and then their only advantage was that they were relieved of the burden of proof in freedom suits. Race did, however, make a considerable difference for free people. Thus, the first legal definition of "mulatto" appeared in a statute dealing with the rights of free persons.

---

15. Other aspects of an individual's heritage might, of course, determine important legal rights. For example, whether his mother was a slave or freewoman, or whether his mother was an unwed indentured white servant or a free white woman. *See* Act XII, 2 Laws of Va. 170, 170 (Hening 1823) (enacted 1662) (whether children bound or free depends solely on condition of mother); Act C, 2 Laws of Va. 114, 114–15 (Hening 1823) (enacted 1661) (birth of bastard child by servant extends term of indenture or subjects servant to fine).

In 1705, the Virginia legislature barred mulattoes, along with blacks, Native Americans, and criminals, from holding "any office, ecclesiastical, civil or military, or be[ing] in any place of public trust or power." The mixed-race individuals defined as mulatto under the statute were "the child of an Indian, or the child, grandchild, or great grandchild of a Negro." Whites had distinct legal advantages, but mulattoes had no greater rights than blacks. Thus, the important dividing line was the white/ mulatto boundary, not the mulatto/black boundary. The fact that some people were classified as mulatto rather than as black seems to have been simply a recognition of their visible differences.

One notes in the statute's definition of "mulatto" the different treatment of those whose non-white ancestors were American Indians as opposed to blacks. A person with one Native American parent and one white parent was a mulatto. Someone with one Native American grandparent and three white grandparents was, by implication, legally white and not barred from public office under the statute. For black-white mixtures, it took two additional generations to "wash out the taint" of Negro blood to the point that it was legally insignificant. A person with a single black grandparent or even a single black great-grandparent was still considered a mulatto.

This 1705 statute represents the beginning of racial hierarchy in American race classification law. The black, Native American, and mulatto classifications were inferior to the white classification, at least for purposes of holding a high government job. In addition, the black classification was inferior to the Native American classification.

Why was there a difference in the legal treatment of white Native American mixtures and white-black mixtures? Perhaps it was related to the degree to which a mixed-race individual looked white to eighteenth-century white Virginians. Perhaps it was also because Europeans tended to see Native Americans as higher on the scale of creation than blacks, though still lower than themselves.[16]

Though these definitions of race state the rule in theory, they were not rigidly followed in practice. There is no case from this period in which a claim to being legally white was based on the exact proportion of white blood. At the time of the statute in 1705, some eighty-five years after the first blacks had arrived in Virginia, there would barely have been time for the four generations of offspring necessary to

---

16. The favored treatment of Indians was still present in 1924 as indicated by an act of the Virginia legislature that made it unlawful for a white person to marry anyone but another white. A white was defined as someone with "no trace whatsoever of any blood other than Caucasian" or someone with no admixture of blood other than white and a small proportion of Native American blood. 1924 Va. Acts ch. 371, § 5, at 535. This provision was the so-called "Pocahontas exception," designed to protect descendants of John Rolfe and Pocahontas, who were by then considered part of the white race. However, in 1924, John Rolfe could not have married Pocahontas. Under the most likely interpretation of the statute, he would have been limited to whites or those who were no more than 1/ 16 Native American. Wadlington, *The Loving Case: Virginia's Anti-Miscegenation Statute in Historical Perspective*, 52 Va. L. Rev. 1189, 1202–3 (1966).

"dilute the taint" of black blood to the point that it did not count under law. Thus, few if any white-black mixtures would have qualified as white, though there were likely some white Native American mixtures who did.

The Virginia legislature, meeting in 1785, changed the legal definition of mulatto to those with "one-fourth part or more of negro blood."[17] Thus, by implication, those of one-eighth black ancestry (one black great-grandparent), who by the 1705 statute had been mulattoes, were now legally white. There is no mention in the statute of Native American ancestry. Interestingly, while the definition of mulatto in 1705 excluded from the category of white virtually all of those with any black ancestry at the time, the 1785 definition, some four generations later, did not attempt to do the same. Instead, under the 1785 act, a number of mixed-race people who previously would have been classified as mulatto could be considered white. This was the only time Virginia law was changed to allow persons with a greater proportion of black ancestry to be deemed white. All subsequent changes were in the opposite direction—making a smaller proportion of black blood bar one from being considered white.

Was this statute, as James Hugo Johnston suggests, an effort to bring the law into line with social practice? He says, "[i]t would appear that the lawmakers of the early national period feared that a declaration to the effect that the possession of any black ancestry, however remote, made a man a mulatto might bring embarrassment on certain supposedly white citizens." He notes that before the Civil War, in no state did the law provide that a person having less than one-eighth black blood should be deemed a mulatto.

Johnston also says that it was no doubt believed to be exceedingly difficult, if not impossible, to enforce a more drastic law of racial identity. Yet, in fact, Virginia did enact more drastic laws in the twentieth century. Under a 1910 statute, as small a proportion as one-sixteenth African ancestry made one "colored." Then, in 1924 and 1930, any African ancestry at all, no matter how small a proportion, meant that one was not legally white.

Another possible explanation for the 1785 statute is that it reflected strategic considerations. If supposedly white men of power and position were declared to be mulatto and thus deprived of civil and political rights, they might have formed a dangerous alliance with other "less white" free mulattoes and blacks whose rights were similarly denied. Their combined forces would have threatened the social control over the society of the remaining smaller number still classified as white. For

---

17. The statute was entitled "An Act declaring what persons shall be deemed mulattoes," and it stated:

[E]very person whose grandfathers or grandmothers any one is, or shall have been a negro, although all his other progenitors, except that descending from the negro, shall have been white persons, shall be deemed a mulatto; and so every person who shall have one-fourth part or more of negro blood, shall, in like manner, be deemed a mulatto.

Ch. LXXVIII, 12 Laws of Va. 184, 184 (Hening 1823) (enacted 1785; effective 1787).

example, at that time, Georgia legislators were apparently more concerned about hostile Native Americans on their southern border than they were about the racial makeup of the colony's white population. To encourage the immigration of free mixed-race persons into the colony, the Georgia legislature provided in 1765 that free mulatto and "mustee"[18] immigrants might be declared "whites," with "all the Rights, Privileges, Powers and Immunities whatsoever which any person born of British parents" would have, except the right to vote and to sit in the Assembly.

These explanations are merely suggestions. There is no satisfactory answer as to why the 1785 Virginia statute redefined racially mixed persons who formerly were classified as mulatto as legally white. The Act itself does not articulate a reason for the change. The percentage of allowable African ancestry in a legally white person was not changed again until the twentieth century, and Native American mulattoes were reintroduced in an 1866 statute making a person who was one-quarter Native American a mulatto, if he or she was not otherwise "colored."

Objectively, the effect of statutes defining a mulatto as someone with a certain proportion of African or Native American ancestry, and implying that someone with a smaller proportion of nonwhite ancestry was legally white, was to make "white" into a mixed-race category. By the early twentieth century, when those classified as white had to have "no trace whatsoever"[19] of black "blood," there was indeed a great deal of untraced (and, in some cases, untraceable) "black blood" in the white population.

One can see the notion that African ancestry can be gradually diluted into legal insignificance in the case of *Dean v. Commonwealth*. There, a criminal defendant claimed that two witnesses were incompetent to testify against him because they were mulattoes and mulattoes could not testify against whites. The court found the witnesses competent, since they had less than one-fourth black blood, the legal dividing line under the statute then in force. The description of legal "lightening" over the generations in the reporting of the case is telling:

"... [F]rom the testimony it appeared certainly, that they had less than one fourth of negro blood. Their grandfather, David Ross, who was spoken of as a respectable man, though probably a mulatto, was a soldier in the revolution and died in the service. The evidence as to the grandmother was contradictory; though

---

18. "Mustee" was a term used in Georgia and the Carolinas to describe a person who was part Indian, "usually Indian-Negro but occasionally Indian-white."

19. Ch. 371, §5, 1924 Va. Acts 534–35. All of the acts setting out racial definitions, with the exception of the 1924 "Act to Preserve [white] Racial Integrity" defined "mulatto" or "colored" rather than "white." White is defined by implication. In the 1924 act, "white" is given an explicit definition for the first time in the statute which sets out whom whites could marry. It is the most restrictive of the racial definitions. It defines a white person as one "who has no trace whatsoever of any blood other than Caucasian; but persons who have [only] one-sixteenth or less of the blood of the American Indian ... shall be deemed to be white persons." Ch. 371, 1924 Va. Acts 535. The 1930 statute defining as colored anyone "in whom there is ascertainable any Negro blood" is only slightly less restrictive. Ch. 85, 1930 Va. Acts 97.

she was probably white, the mother was so certainly." The grandfather would have been incompetent to testify because he was a mulatto, but the grandchildren were not. Thus, in mid-nineteenth century Virginia, mulatto parents and grandparents could have children and grandchildren who were legally white. That became legally impossible only in the twentieth century, when any trace of African ancestry would disqualify a person from being considered white under the law.

Whites in pre-Civil War Virginia paid a strategic price to maintain their ideal of white racial purity. Had they declared, for example, that anyone with more than fifty percent white blood was legally white, they would have had less to fear from an alliance of free mulattoes and slaves. Then, however, their racial rationale for slavery would have been undermined because the number of legally white slaves would have increased greatly. It would have been hard to maintain that slavery was justified by the inferiority of blacks if large numbers of slaves were classified as white under Virginia law. The white population was in fact racially mixed, but the proportion of non-white ancestry allowable in a white person was so small that it was not very visible. It was so small that, as we shall see, white Virginians could maintain the myth that it was not there at all.

In nineteenth-century Virginia, the concept of a "pure white race" as a category of nature was a myth. It was a powerful myth, however, one used to support social and legal action, as in the *Kinney* decision, and to justify the oppression of non-whites. Pure white race as a legal concept was a vigorous and powerful cultural construct. It gained force in the late nineteenth and early twentieth centuries and was called on to justify an ever harsher set of repressive legal measures against blacks.

D. Preserving the Myth of White Racial Purity

A. Leon Higginbotham, Jr. and Barbara Kopytoff

*Racial Purity and Interracial Sex in the Law of Colonial
and Antebellum Virginia**

Concern over the Production of Mulatto Children

A special group of cases concerned white women who produced mulatto children while being married to white men. Several of these men applied to the House of Burgesses for a special act granting them a divorce. The question of whether a white woman was to be divorced or punished under the criminal code, or both, for producing a mulatto child outside of marriage was sometimes complicated by

---

* (some footnotes omitted).

uncertainty as to whether the child was a mulatto. It seems that this question may have been at issue in the case of Peggy and Richard Jones.[25] In that case, a divorce was granted provisionally, pending the outcome of a jury trial deciding the husband's claim. The divorce would take effect, "provided that it shall be found by the verdict of a jury, upon . . . trial . . . that the child of said Peggy Jones is not the child of said Richard Jones, but is the offspring of some man of colour."[26] In other cases no reference was made to a trial.[27] The Jones child probably looked white enough so that there was some question as to whether Richard Jones might not be the father after all, and Peggy Jones may have contested the accusation of adultery.

It is interesting to note that when a couple classified as white produced a child whose racial identity was uncertain, the wife was suspected of having committed adultery with a black or mulatto man. Another possible explanation was that either the husband or the wife or both were in fact of mixed black-white ancestry, though legally white (if the proportion of black ancestry were small enough), or passing as white. Mixed-race parents would, on occasion, produce a child whose complexion was darker than either of theirs, a child who looked mulatto when they did not. That possibility was not explored. It may not have occurred to white Virginians, or it may have been suppressed. It may have been more disturbing to them than the attribution of adultery to the women, for it called into question the idea of clear racial classifications, an idea that was central to the maintenance of slave society in Virginia.

Offspring of Interracial Unions

Virginians from an early date lashed out at interracial sex in language "dripping with distaste and indignation." The distaste turned to revulsion when they spoke of the resulting mulatto children, especially those with white mothers, as an "abominable mixture and spurious issue."

---

25. Act of Nov. 25, 1814, divorcing Richard Jones from his wife Peggy, Ch. XCVIII, 1814 Acts of Va. 145.

26. *Id.* at 145.

27. Act of Jan 4, 1803, dissolving a marriage between Dabney Pettus and his wife Elizabeth, Ch. LXIV, 1802 Acts of Va. 46, 47 (divorce granted without trial when wife publicly acknowledged mulatto child as son of black slave); Act of Dec. 20, 1803, dissolving a marriage between Benjamin Butt, Jr. and Lydia his wife, Ch. VI, 1803 Acts of Va. 20, 20–21 (same); Ch. LIX, 1806 Acts of Va. 26, 26 (divorce granted without trial when 'reasons to believe' that child born to white woman was fathered by black slave and not her white husband); Act of Jan. 10, 1817, divorcing Abraham Newton from his wife Nancy, Ch. 120, 1817 Va. Acts 176, 176 (divorce granted without trial when white woman gave birth to mulatto child five months after marriage to white man). In the case of Hezekiah Mosby and his wife Betsy, a trial was also ordered to determine the facts. Act of Jan. 25, 1816, authorizing the divorce of Hezekiah Mosby from his wife Betsy, Ch. CXXXV, 1816 Acts of Va. 246, 246–47. The fate of these women after the divorce is unknown, though they were subject to the act penalizing white women who had mulatto bastards with a heavy fine or five years of servitude. Act XVI, 3 Laws of Va. 86, 87 (Hening 1823) (enacted 1691); Ch. XLIV, 3 Laws of Va. 447, 453 (Hening 1823) (enacted 1705).

Mixed-race offspring were disturbing to white Virginians for several reasons. First, they were anomalies. They simply did not fit into the whites' vision of the natural order of things: a great chain of being comprised of fixed links, not of infinite gradations. Things which do not fit into the perceived natural order are seen as unnatural and often as dangerous and "abominable." The term "spurious," used by the Virginia legislature for the children of marriages between whites and blacks, shows a fundamental uneasiness and aversion to the idea of racial mixture, an aversion that is not entirely explainable by practical considerations. The aversion was greatest toward the mulatto children of white women. Since mulattoes were classified with blacks, the prospect of a mulatto child of a black mother was not as disturbing as that of a mulatto child of a white mother. It seemed less anomalous. Second, the idea of a racially based system of slavery depended on a clear separation of the races. Mulattoes challenged that idea. Winthrop Jordan suggests that the psychological problem was handled in part by categorizing mixed-blood offspring as belonging to the lower caste, thus, in effect, denying their existence:

> The colonist . . . remained firm in his rejection of the mulatto, in his categorization of mixed-bloods as belonging to the lower caste. It was an unconscious decision dictated perhaps in large part by the weight of blacks on his community, heavy enough to be a burden, yet not so heavy as to make him abandon all hope of maintaining his own identity, physically and culturally. Interracial propagation was a constant reproach that he was failing to be true to himself. Sexual intimacy strikingly symbolized a union he wished to avoid. If he could not restrain his sexual nature, he could at least reject its fruits and thus solace himself that he had done no harm. Perhaps he sensed as well that continued racial intermixture would eventually undermine the logic of the racial slavery upon which his society was based. For the separation of slaves from free men depended on a clear demarcation of the races, and the presence of mulattoes blurred this essential distinction. Accordingly, he made every effort to nullify the effects of racial intermixture. By classifying the mulatto as a black he was in effect denying that intermixture had occurred at all.

Third, mulattoes created a practical problem for a racially based system of slavery. They had to be classified in terms of status as well as in terms of race, and as discussed earlier, race did not automatically determine one's status as slave or free. The law of the inheritance of slave status was a response to the question of how to classify the children of white men and slave women, and the 1662 statute gave them the status of their mothers.

It has been suggested that, rather than having been dictated solely by racism, this policy might have reflected, among other things, the "prudential considerations of keeping a child with its mother and reimbursing the mother's master for its support." However, keeping a child with its slave mother hardly required such a drastic measure as making the child a slave. Many free white children were raised from infancy by slave women. If mulatto children by white fathers had been declared free, the slave mothers would probably have continued to raise them. Furthermore, masters could have been reimbursed by making the child serve an indenture as well as by making it a slave. Whatever the precise combination of motives behind the rule of the inheritance of slave status, it had two notable practical effects: first, it separated the large majority of the children of interracial unions from whites by assigning them the status of slave; second, it provided slave owners with easy and cheap ways to increase the number of slaves they held. In the psychological terms suggested by Jordan, it also allowed white men to deny their responsibility for racial intermixture far more effectively than they could have done had the child inherited its status from the father.

The rule that children were to take the status of their mothers meant that some mulattoes (the great majority) were slave and some were free. Free mulattoes fell into two categories that were treated very differently. Under a 1691 statute, a mulatto child born out of wedlock to a white woman was to be bound out as a servant by the church wardens until the age of thirty. The statute prescribed no similar fate for the legitimate mulatto children of white mothers or the legitimate or illegitimate mulatto children of free black mothers. The same statute prescribed banishment within three months for white women who married black, mulatto, or Native-American men, so that the mother, and any legitimate mulatto children who went with her, were removed from local society anyway. When, however, in 1705, the penalty was changed to six months in prison and a fine, white women who served their time presumably were able to raise families of free legitimate mulatto children. These children were not to be sold into service for the benefit of the parish for that provision applied only to bastard children. While the products of the mixed marriages might have been "spurious and abominable" to the white Virginians, they were not illegitimate. The sacrament of marriage was effective even in the case of interracial marriage until 1849.

Just as the legislators were much harder on white women who produced free mulatto bastards than they were on free black women who also produced free mulatto bastards, the legislators were also much harder on the free mulatto bastards descended from white women than they were on other free mulattoes.[33] What was

---

33. When female mulatto bastards of white women who were bound out as servants had children during their service, those children served the mother's master until they reached the age their mother was when she completed her service. Ch. IV, 4 Laws of Va. 126, 133 (Hening 1820) (enacted 1723). It was left to the courts to decide the fate of the third generation of children born to such mulatto women servants, and the courts did so. In *Gwinn v. Bugg*, 1 Va. (Jeff.) 48 (1769), the General Court interpreted the statute prescribing indenture for the mulatto bastards of white women to apply to the bastard children of females so indentured whether such children had been formally bonded out by the church wardens or had simply stayed on with the master of their mother. *Id.* at 48–49.

Despite the revulsion the legislators seemed to feel toward mulattoes, and especially toward free mulattoes with white mothers, the one 'solution' they would not tolerate was for the mothers quietly to kill their children at birth. To discourage free women wishing to avoid penalties for producing bastards from killing their infants, the legislators prescribed the death penalty for any

the difference between the free mulattoes of white mothers and the others that the former should be treated more harshly? Perhaps it was an extension of the outrage the legislators felt toward the mothers of such children. Perhaps it was that they were evidence of the corruption of the white race in a way that the mulatto children of black mothers were not. Once Virginians had made the decision to classify mulattoes with blacks, the mulatto child of a white mother was an assault on racial purity. The mulatto child of a black mother merely exhibited a lighter shade within the range of skin color of the lower racial caste.

E. Background on *Hall*

D. Wendy Greene

Title VII: What's Hair (and Other Race-Based Characteristics)
Got to Do with It?

"Race must be understood as a sui generis social phenomenon in which contested systems of meaning serve as the connections between physical features, faces and personal characteristics . . . social meanings connect our faces to our souls."

Throughout American history, skin color has been used to determine an individual's race, but it has not served as the sole marker of one's race. Distinguishable physical markers signifying "whiteness" and "non-whiteness" generated the creation of a hierarchical social system based on race and color, whereby whiteness represented the superior status and non-whiteness the inferior. Accordingly, philosophers and scientists promulgated hierarchical racial nomenclatures based upon discernible corporal traits. These racial classification systems gained credence throughout the seventeenth and eighteenth centuries. For example, in 1797, George Léopold Cuvier theorized that the "Ethiopian" or "negro race" was

> marked by a black complexion, crisped or woolly hair, compressed cranium, and a flat nose. The projection of the lower parts of the face, and the thick lips, evidently approximate it to the monkey tribe; the hordes of which it consists have always remained in the most complete state of utter barbarism.

Whereas the "Caucasion" or "white race" was

---

non-slave woman who killed her bastard child to conceal it. Ch. XII, 3 Laws of Va. 516, 516 (Hening 1823) (enacted 1710). Presumably, a mother who killed her child might always face the death penalty, but the legislators felt the practice in this case warranted a special statute.

distinguished by the beauty of the oval formed by its head, varying in complexion and the colour of the hair. To this variety, the most highly civilized nations, and those which have generally held all others in subjection, are indebted for their origin.

And, though Cuvier declared that Native Americans could not be classified within a particular race, he did propound an essentialist portrayal of Native Americans comprising of a "copper-coloured complexion[,] . . . generally black hair . . . defined features, projecting nose, large and open eye."

. . . However, it was not the physical markers alone that engendered the relative subordination and empowerment of racial groups; it was the meaning that society attached to these physical markers. These physical markers—skin color, hair texture, the shape of one's lips, nose, eyes and head—fostered notions about the individual's intellectual ability, morality, and humanity. Consequently, society's interpretation of these physical markers, in other words "race," determined the individual's participation and status in society socially, politically, legally, and economically. Whiteness signified positive attributes such as freedom, respectability, civilization; non-whiteness represented the inferior opposite.

Race provided the basis for American slavery, racial segregation, and the attainment or denial of political, social, legal and economic privileges and rights, including voting, owning property, traveling freely, receiving an education, and even becoming a citizen. Because of interracial unions which produced offspring who destabilized predetermined and (presumably permanent) racial constructs based on physical characteristics, early American courts concluded that "biological" or "immutable characteristics" were not reliable determiners of one's "race." In addition to miscegenation, emancipation threatened the foundations of American slavery: the putative natural inferiority of Blacks and superiority of whites. The independence free Blacks exhibited by establishing schools, churches, and communities, for example, contravened the notions that Blacks were subordinate to whites and the agency of whites was critical to Blacks' survival, and thereby undermined core justifications for the perpetual enslavement of Blacks. In order to retain the privileges restricted to whites, the purity of the white race and, thus, white supremacy, courts promulgated a more "absolute" and "consistent" test to determine one's race by examining one's behavior in relation to other members of society. As a result, daily actions and interactions became racialized and an individual's performance or non-performance of certain behaviors could signify one's race.

In its 1835 decision in *State v. Cantey*, the South Carolina Court of Appeals illustrated this shift from appropriating a "biological" definition of race to determining race based on an individual's "performance" in society through its explicit rejection of a biological construct of race. The *Cantey* court held that an individual's race was not determined by the degree of white or colored "blood" a person possessed but

> by [his] reputation, by his reception into society, and his having commonly exercised the privileges of a white man. But his admission to these

privileges, regulated by the public opinion of the community in which he lives, will very much depend on his own character and conduct; and it may be well and proper, that a man of worth, honesty, industry and respectability, should have the rank of a white man, while a vagabond of the same degree of blood should be confined to the inferior caste.

In 1866, the Michigan Supreme Court in *People v. Dean* expressed similar sentiments depicting a naturally autonomous and universally accepted method of determining an individual's Blackness (or whiteness) by his or her social behaviors. According to the *Dean* court,

> it is very well known that the associations of persons having visible portions of African blood, have generally been closer with each other than with those acknowledged as white. They consider themselves as of one race, and live and act together. This mutual recognition, coupled as it undoubtedly is with a general disposition on the part of white persons to avoid social relations with the mass of mixed, as well as unmixed, races of African descent, furnishes a commentary on the terms *white* and *colored*, which can hardly be resisted.

As the courts in *Cantey* and *Dean* reveal, genetic inheritance or physical appearance did not simply determine one's race. Conformity with race-based stereotypes and behaviors, which were constructed through group-based social relations as well as the law, also determined one's race.

79 Colorado L. Rev. 1355, 1365–1369.
Copyright © (2008) Colorado Law Review.
Reprinted with permission of Colorado Law Review and D. Wendy Greene.

Ariela J. Gross

*Litigating Whiteness: Trials of Racial Determination in the Nineteenth-Century South**

In April of 1855, Abby Guy sued William Daniel in the Circuit Court for Ashley County, Arkansas, complaining that he held her and her children unfairly in slavery despite the fact that she was white. The trial was held in the small town of Hamburg's brand-new courthouse, no doubt drawing spectators from all over the county to witness the dramatic determination of Guy's racial status. After Guy won her case, William Daniel appealed it to the state supreme court, and it was tried again in a neighboring county before she finally prevailed in the Arkansas Supreme Court on the eve of the Civil War. At the two trials, jurors watched Guy and her children display themselves for inspection, read documents of sale and a will, and listened to the opinions and descriptions of medical experts and witnesses from several counties. Witnesses testified about Guy's appearance, her reception in

---

* (footnotes omitted).

society, her conduct, her self-presentation, and her inherited status. In each case, the judge left the question of "race" for the jury to decide, because the jury represented the community consensus.

Trials like Abby Guy's, at which the central issue became the determination of a person's racial identity, were a regular occurrence in Southern county courts in the nineteenth century. While nineteenth-century white Southerners may have believed in a racial "essence" inhering in one's blood, there was no agreement about how to discover it. Legal determinations of race could not simply reflect community consensus, because there was no consensus to reflect. Despite the efforts of legislatures to reduce racial identities to a binary system, and of judges to insist that determining race was a matter of common sense, Southern communities harbored disagreement, suspicion, and conflict—not only over who was black and who was white, but over how to make such determinations at all . . .

This Article is based on a reading of all of the surviving trial records that I have been able to locate for the sixty-eight cases of racial determination appealed to state supreme courts in the nineteenth-century South. More than half of these (thirty-six) took place in the last years of slavery—between 1845 and 1861—and the majority involved men. These cases arose from a variety of circumstances. Certain criminal statutes specified that a crime was particular to persons of color or "Negroes," so that one might raise the defense of whiteness to an indictment. Nearly all of these cases involved men. In inheritance disputes, one claimant to the estate sometimes claimed that another claimant, or the testator himself, was black and therefore could not inherit or devise property. In other inheritance disputes, racial determination often arose in litigating questions of legitimacy: one party might attempt to overcome the presumption of paternity with evidence that the child was mulatto. In the only kind of case in which women were disproportionately the subject of racial determination, slaves sued for their freedom by claiming whiteness. In suits for slander, a man who held himself out as white sued for lost status or property because another person impugned his whiteness. The circumstances of these cases included scuttled weddings, economic disputes between neighboring grocers, and blackballing from clubs or militia units. There were also a few criminal cases in which defendants sought to disqualify witnesses by claiming that they had "colored" blood. Finally, slaveholders sued steamboats and railroad companies that carried runaway slaves "passing" as white; the transportation companies usually defended by arguing that the slaves were, for all intents and purposes, white.

Of course, courtroom battles were not the routine mechanism for knowing a person's racial status in Southern society. For Southerners whose appearance seemed clearly to mark them as "black," the vast majority of whom were enslaved before 1863 or 1864, racial status was over-determined. The confluence of dark skin, degraded status, reputation, and ancestry rendered the possibility of litigation over racial identity impossible for those African Americans. Yet litigated cases of racial determination are important to the understanding of the creation of racial meanings for a number of reasons. First, there was a substantial and growing number of people of mixed racial ancestry for whom racial presumptions based on appearance could not settle the question of identity. Second, the presence of Indians in the population complicated the equation of dark skin with "Negro" identity or slave status. Even dark skin and curly hair did not automatically consign one to the "Negro" race if one could trace one's color to "Indian blood." But even more importantly, the possibility of ambiguity created by people of contested racial identity was a source of great anxiety to white Southerners, who expended a great deal of energy trying to foreclose the possibility of white slaves, "passing" blacks, and the interracial sex that lay behind both. If we take their anxiety seriously as a clue to what mattered to white Southerners in their struggle to define racial categories, we cannot simply dismiss the litigated cases as odd or freakish.

108 *Yale Law Journal* 109, 111–12, 120–22.
Copyright © (1998) *Yale Law Journal*.
Reprinted with permission of *Yale Law Journal* and Ariela Gross.

While blackness was certainly the mark of slavery, being classified as nonwhite was the mark of a degraded caste. As the slave cases indicate, Asian or Indian ancestry through the maternal line may legally justify freedom, but such non-African ancestry would not alleviate the burdens of state-imposed racial discrimination.

F. *People v. Hall*, 4 Cal. 399 (1854)

1. Facts

Chief Justice MURRAY delivered the opinion of the Court.

The appellant, a free white citizen of this State, was convicted of murder upon the testimony of Chinese witnesses.

The point involved in this case, is the admissibility of such evidence.

2. Opinion

The 394th section of the Act Concerning Civil Cases, provides that no Indian or Negro shall be allowed to testify as a witness in any action or proceeding in which a White person is a party.

The 14th section of the Act of April 16th, 1850, regulating Criminal Proceedings, provides that "No Black, or Mulatto person, or Indian, shall be allowed to give evidence in favor of, or against a white man."

The true point at which we are anxious to arrive, is the legal signification of the words, "Black, Mulatto, Indian and White person," and whether the Legislature adopted them as generic terms, or intended to limit their application to specific types of the human species.

Before considering this question, it is proper to remark the difference between the two sections of our Statute, already quoted, the latter being more broad and comprehensive in its exclusion, by use of the word "Black," instead of Negro.

Conceding, however, for the present, that the word "Black," as used in the 14th section, and "Negro," in 394th, are convertible terms, and that the former was intended to include the latter, let us proceed to inquire who are excluded from testifying as witnesses under the term "Indian."

When Columbus first landed upon the shores of this continent, in his attempt to discover a western passage to the Indies, he imagined that he had accomplished the object of his expedition, and that the Island of San Salvador was one of those Islands of the Chinese sea, lying near the extremity of India, which had been described by navigators.

Acting upon this hypothesis, and also perhaps from the similarity of features and physical conformation, he gave to the Islanders the name of Indians, which appellation was universally adopted, and extended to the aboriginals of the New World, as well as of Asia.

From that time, down to a very recent period, the American Indians and the Mongolian, or Asiatic, were regarded as the same type of the human species.

In order to arrive at a correct understanding of the intention of our Legislature, it will be necessary to go back to the early history of legislation on this subject, our Statute being only a transcript of those of older States.

At the period from which this legislation dates, those portions of Asia which include India proper, the Eastern Archipelago, and the countries washed by the Chinese waters, as far as then known, were denominated the Indies, from which the inhabitants had derived the generic name of Indians.

Ethnology, at that time, was unknown as a distinct science, or if known, had not reached that high point of perfection which it has since attained by the scientific inquiries and discoveries of the master minds of the last half century. Few speculations had been made with regard to the moral or physical differences between the different races of mankind. These were general in their character, and limited to those visible and palpable variations which could not escape the attention of the most common observer.

The general, or perhaps universal opinion of that day was, that there were but three distinct types of the human species, which, in their turn, were subdivided into varieties or tribes. This opinion is still held by many scientific writers, and is supported by Cuvier, one of the most eminent naturalists of modern times.

Many ingenious speculations have been resorted to for the purpose of sustaining this opinion. It has been supposed, and not without plausibility, that this continent was first peopled by Asiatics, who crossed Behring's Straits, and from thence found their way down to the more fruitful climates of Mexico and South America. Almost every tribe has some tradition of coming from the North, and many of them, that their ancestors came from some remote country beyond the ocean. . . .

The similarity of the skull and pelvis, and the general configuration of the two races; the remarkable resemblance in eyes, beard, hair, and other peculiarities, together with the contiguity of the two continents, might well have led to the belief that this country was first peopled by the Asiatics, and that the difference between the different tribes and the parent stock was such as would necessarily arise from the circumstances of climate, pursuits, and other physical causes, and was no greater than that existing between the Arab and the European, both of whom were supposed to belong to the Caucasian race.

Although the discoveries of eminent archeologists, and the researches of modern geologists, have given to this continent an antiquity of thousands of years anterior to the evidence of man's existence, and the light of modern science may have shown conclusively that it was not peopled by the inhabitants of Asia, but that the Aborigines are a distinct type, and as such claim a distinct origin, still, this would not, in any degree, alter the meaning of the term, and render that specific which was before generic.

We have adverted to these speculations for the purpose of showing that the name of Indian, from the time of Columbus to the present day, has been used to designate, not alone the North American Indian, but the whole of the Mongolian race, and that the name, though first applied probably through mistake, was afterwards continued as appropriate on account of the supposed common origin.

That this was the common opinion in the early history of American legislation, cannot be disputed, and, therefore, all legislation upon the subject must have borne relation to that opinion.

Can, then, the use of the word "Indian," because at the present day it may be sometimes regarded as a specific, and not as a generic term, alter this conclusion? We think not; because at the origin of the legislation we are considering, it was used and admitted in its common and ordinary acceptation, as a generic term, distinguishing the great Mongolian race, and as such, its meaning then became fixed by law, and in construing Statutes the legal meaning of words must be preserved.

Again: the words of the Act must be construed in *pari materia*. It will not be disputed that "White" and "Negro," are generic terms, and refer to two of the great types of mankind. If these, as well as the word "Indian," are not to be regarded as generic terms, including the two great races which they were intended to designate, but only specific, and applying to those Whites and Negroes who were inhabitants of this Continent at the time of the passage of the Act, the most anomalous consequences would ensue. The European white man who comes here would not be shielded from the testimony of the degraded and demoralized caste, while the Negro, fresh from the coast of Africa, or the Indian of Patagonia, the Kanaka, South Sea Islander, or New Hollander, would be admitted, upon their arrival, to testify against white citizens in our courts of law.

To argue such a proposition would be an insult to the good sense of the Legislature.

The evident intention of the Act was to throw around the citizen a protection for life and property, which could only be secured by removing him above the corrupting influences of degraded castes.

It can hardly be supposed that any Legislature would attempt this by excluding domestic Negroes and Indians, who not unfrequently have correct notions of their obligations to society, and turning loose upon the community the more degraded tribes of the same species, who have nothing in common with us, in language, country or laws.

We have, thus far, considered this subject on the hypothesis that the 14th section of the Act Regulating Criminal Proceedings, and the 394th section of the Practice Act, were the same.

As before remarked, there is a wide difference between the two. The word "black" may include all Negroes, but the term "Negro" does not include all black persons.

By the use of this term in this connection, we understand it to mean the opposite of "white," and that it should be taken as contradistinguished from all white persons.

In using the words, "No black, or mulatto person, or Indian shall be allowed to give evidence for or against a white person," the Legislature, if any intention can be ascribed to it, adopted the most comprehensive terms to embrace every known class or shade of color, as the apparent design was to protect the white person from the influence of all testimony other than that of persons of the same caste. The use of these terms must, by every sound rule of construction, exclude everyone who is not of white blood.

The Act of Congress in defining what description of aliens may become naturalized citizens, uses the phrase "free white citizen." In speaking of this subject, Chancellor Kent says, that "the Act confines the description to "white" citizens, and that it is a matter of doubt, whether, under this provision, any of the tawny races of Asia can be admitted to the privileges of citizenship." 2 Kent's Com. 72.

We are not disposed to leave this question in any doubt. The word "white" has a distinct signification, which *ex vi termini,* excludes black, yellow, and all other colors. It will be observed, by reference to the first section of the second article of the Constitution of this State, that none but white males can become electors, except in the case of Indians, who may be admitted by special Act of the Legislature. On examination of the constitutional debates, it will be found that not a little difficulty existed in selecting these precise words, which were finally agreed upon as the most comprehensive that could be suggested to exclude all inferior races.

If the term "White," as used in the Constitution, was not understood in its generic sense as including the Caucasian race, and necessarily excluding all others, where was the necessity of providing for the admission of Indians to the privilege of voting, by special legislation?

We are of the opinion that the words "white," "Negro," "Mulatto," "Indian," and "black person," wherever they occur in our Constitution and laws, must be taken in their generic sense, and that, even admitting the Indian of this Continent is not of the Mongolian type, that the words "black person," in the 14th section must be taken as contradistinguished from white, and necessarily excludes all races other than the Caucasian.

We have carefully considered all the consequences resulting from a different rule of construction, and are satisfied that even in a doubtful case we would be impelled to this decision on grounds of public policy.

The same rule which would admit them to testify, would admit them to all the equal rights of citizenship, and we might soon see them at the polls, in the jury box, upon the bench, and in our legislative halls.

This is not a speculation which exists in the excited and over-heated imagination of the patriot and statesman, but it is an actual and present danger.

The anomalous spectacle of a distinct people, living in our community, recognizing no laws of this State except through necessity, bringing with them their prejudices and national feuds, in which they indulge in open violation of law; whose mendacity is proverbial; a race of people whom nature has marked as inferior, and who are incapable of progress or intellectual development beyond a certain point, as their history has shown; differing in language, opinions, color, and physical conformation; between whom and ourselves nature has placed an impassable difference, is now presented, and for them is claimed, not only the right to swear away the life of a citizen, but the further privilege of participating with us in administering the affairs of our Government.

3. Holding

These facts were before the Legislature that framed this Act, and have been known as matters of public history to every subsequent Legislature.

There can be no doubt as to the intention of the Legislature, and that if it had ever been anticipated that this class of people were not embraced in the prohibition, then such specific words would have been employed as would have put the matter beyond any possible controversy.

For these reasons, we are of opinion that the testimony was inadmissible.

The judgment is reversed and the cause remanded.

G. Commentary on *Hall*

Before emancipation, oppression had operated largely through the institution of slavery, but, as noted above, slave status was technically independent of race. There were the anomalies of free blacks and of slaves who, based on appearance of their skin alone, were considered to be white. These "anomalies" interfered with a perfect correlation of race and status. Oppression thus operated partly in terms of race and partly in terms of slave status. Mistreatment could be based on former status, even if a racial classification could not be made.

After emancipation, the special, precise status of slave ceased to exist. Racial oppression then became entirely based on the notion of white supremacy. Thus, as indicated in *Hall*, all those identified as black, mulatto, or Indian had a special low status and were subject to discrimination. Unless expressly stated otherwise, the term "black" used in the context of a white/black divide would include all other racial minorities. The classification "black" became ever more expansive. Moreover, as race became the sole means of identifying those who belonged to the lower caste, the legal definition of white became more exclusive, and the maintenance of the myth of white racial purity became more important.

As Professor Derrick Bell has noted:

> Race, racialization, and racism are largely modern-day concepts. The three concepts, although distinct in meaning, necessarily developed in tandem. Whereas the concept of "race" implies "the framework of ranked categories segmenting the human population,[34] racialization denotes the process by which individuals are assigned membership in those categories. Racism is a product of the two: the assignment of negative value to the traits commonly associated with a particular race and the subordinate ranking of that race on the social hierarchy.[35]

In order for a race-based system of rights and privileges to function, there must be an articulable, identifiable race-classification. In order for this system to be maintained continuously, the decisions implementing it must reflect the values held by the society in which the system is based, and it must be sustained by ongoing political and legal support.

While the basis for white supremacy has varied over the years from biological to sociological to historical or a combination thereof, one constant is the use of race classification as the critical factor in determining and limiting legal status and privilege. Definitions of racial categories and exceptions to these categories were created and manipulated by those who held positions of power: elected officials, legislators, and judges. The ongoing manipulation of race classification schemes over time demonstrates that race was an indeterminate social concept, continually altered and revised in order to maintain domination by those classified as white.

H. Questions and Notes

This chapter traced the roots of the law of racial purity and related prohibitions on interracial sex and marriage that arose during the era of slavery, and discussed the role played by such laws in maintaining the slave society. Unfortunately, those

---

34. *See* Roger Sanjek, *The Enduring Inequalities of Race*, in RACE 1 (Steven Gregory and Roger Sanjek eds., 1994).

35. D. BELL, RACE, RACISM AND AMERICAN LAW 1–2 (4th ed. 2000). *See generally,* MICHAEL OMI AND HOWARD WINANT, RACIAL FORMATION IN THE UNITED STATES FROM THE 1960s TO 1980s (1986).

laws did not end with slavery. Northern states, as well as Southern states, were determined to uphold the racially based social, economic, and political hierarchy of their slave society, even after the institution of slavery had been outlawed.

If you had to classify yourself based upon race, what category would you place yourself in, and on what basis would you make that determination? What factors and elements comprise your notion of race classification? What is the source and basis of your perception?

I. Point/Counterpoint

The subject of race and the Census has been extremely controversial in recent years. Do you support a multiracial category on the census form on which respondents must check one box and only one? Does the merger of several racial categories lead to benefits or setbacks for minorities?

Langston Hughes

Cross

My old man's a white old man / And my old mother's black. / If ever I cursed my white old man/ I take my curses back. / If ever I cursed my black old mother / And wished she were in hell, / I'm sorry for that evil wish / And now I wish her well. / My old man died in a fine big house. / My ma died in a shack. / I wonder where I'm gonna die, / Being neither white nor black?

Collected Poems by Langston Hughes 58–59.
Copyright © (1994) by the Estate of Langston Hughes.
Reprinted with permission of Alfred A. Knopf,
a Division of Random House, Inc.

Kamaria A. Kruckenberg

*Multi-Hued America: The Case for the Recognition of
a Multiethnic Identity in US Data Collection**

My little girl in her multi-hued skin
When asked what she is, replies with a grin
I am a sweet cuddlebums,
A honey and a snugglebums:
Far truer labels than those which are in.

The above poem resonates deeply with me, and it should: my mother wrote it about me. She recited its lines to me during my childhood more times than I can count. It was a reminder that I, daughter of a woman whom the world saw as a white and a man whom the world called black, could not be summed up into any neat

---

* (footnotes and chapter headings omitted).

ethnic category. The poem told me that, though my skin reflected the tones of a variety of cultures, I was more than the sum of my multiple ethnic identities. Over my lifetime, I have recalled this message each time someone asked, "What are you?" and every time I checked "other" in response to the familiar form demand that I mark one box to describe my race.

The classification of multiethnic individuals like myself recently has been the focus of many heated debates. The Office of Management and Budget ("OMB") sets the racial categories used on numerous forms, including the census. In 1997, the OMB revised Statistical Policy Directive 15, its rule for racial data classification, requiring all federal agencies to allow individuals to mark multiple races on all federal forms. Because the implications of the classification of multiethnic individuals in federal racial data collection are potentially far reaching, this change has been surrounded by controversy. The census tracks the numbers and races of Americans for legislative and administrative purposes. This information is particularly important for this country's enforcement of civil rights laws.

Numerous authors argue that the recognition of multiethnic identity will hamper traditional civil rights efforts. They claim that policies that maintain civil rights must win out over the individual caprice of those who advocate for multiethnic recognition. On the other hand, many argue that the recognition of the personal meaning of multiethnic identity is important and does not hamper the traditional goals of civil rights groups.

Civil rights advocates ought to support and encourage multiethnic people as they struggle for governmental recognition. The experience of multiethnic individuals is descriptively different than that of their monoethnic peers and ethnic self-identification is a basic right that once was championed by civil rights groups. Both civil rights and multiethnic activists stand to benefit from such a partnership.

While some writers argue that because it crosses culture, heritage, and physical biology, multiethnic status is different from other ethnic categories, multiethnic people share certain characteristics. The socioeconomic status of bi-ethnic people, for instance, consistently falls between that of the lower and higher status parent. Additionally, multiethnic people frequently report prejudice based on having varied heritages. Finally, there is a growing sense of multiethnic community, which will further develop as multiethnicity becomes more prevalent and accepted. Perhaps the demand for a multiethnic identity is reflective of a new understanding of race, one that recognizes that the lines that divide us by race or ethnic status are actually quite blurry.

Perhaps the strongest reason to recognize multiethnicity is that self-definition ought to be encouraged. The individual and collective right of ethnic self-identification has been recognized and exercised by other racial and ethnic advocates as they redefined themselves with new terms like *Chicano, Xicano, Latino, Asian American, Black, African American,* or *Native American.* Multiethnic people are similarly looking for a way to turn experiences of alienation, racism, and marginalization into positive experiences of shared cultural identity. Giving an official label to those who identify as multiethnic creates a forum in which to discuss the discrimination and marginalization of those experiences. Recognition is the first step toward securing rights.

Self-definition allows people to express an ethnic identity that causes less cognitive dissonance with their experience than being forced to choose between ethnicities. The recognition of multiethnic identity marks a shift to an understanding of race that is more fluid and multi-faceted than before.

Of course, some multiethnic people will not want such a label, but for those who do, the classification system ought to be flexible. Recognizing that racial identification is not a simple process in which any given person can correctly categorize any other is beneficial to all. Internal perspective ought not be the only factor in determining someone's ethnicity, but individuals deserve as much freedom as reasonably possible to engage in good-faith self-definition. While a multiple race box may not make sense for data collection given its potential negative impact on civil rights enforcement, the ability of multiethnic people to list multiple identities provides room for the growth of a concept of multiethnic identity. It seems the least society can offer.

The growth in the numbers of multiethnic people has forced America to ask what race means today. While multiethnic advocates have noted the point so often that it is almost cliché, a recognized multiethnic identity will benefit society if only by raising the question. Civil rights advocates now must consider whether they are more concerned with the principles they have espoused, including self-identification and multicultural pride and acceptance, or in maintaining the system as it is. Multiethnic identity is a double-edged sword because it begs the question of how we can move to a world in which our historical race categories to not limit us without risking the accomplishments that civil rights advocates struggled so hard and long to achieve.

If civil rights comes to encompass multiethnic rights, civil rights groups are likely to gain members who currently may feel unrepresented. This is especially true given the concern that multiethnic advocates have been willing to work with conservatives to accomplish their goals. If more established civil rights leaders step forward, the multiethnic agenda and the civil rights agenda can be framed hand in hand, rather than in potential conflict. Additionally, multiethnic individuals ought to be free to be members of ethnic groups without feeling required to check their multiethnic identity at the door. In a world increasingly aware of multiculturalism, the framing of fluid identities, including multiple identities, ought to be a priority.

Tanya Katerí Hernández

"Multiracial" Discourse: Racial Classifications in
an Era of Color-blind Jurisprudence*

For the past several years, there has been a Multiracial Category Movement (MCM) promoted by some biracial persons and their parents for the addition of a "multiracial" race category on the decennial census. The stated aim of such a new category is to obtain a more specific count of the number of mixed-race persons in the United States and to have that tallying of mixed-race persons act as a barometer and promoter of racial harmony. As proposed, a respondent could choose the "multiracial" box in lieu of the presently listed racial classifications of American Indian or Alaskan Native, Asian or Pacific Islander, black, white, or other. The census schedule also includes a separate Hispanic Origin ethnicity question. On October 29, 1997, the U.S. Office of Management and Budget (OMB) adopted a Federal Interagency Committee recommendation to reject the multiracial category in favor of allowing individuals to check more than one racial category. Some MCM proponents are not satisfied with the OMB's decision, because multiple box checking does not directly promote a distinct multiracial identity. These MCM proponents are committed to continue lobbying for a multiracial category on the 2010 census . . .

Roderick Harrison

The Multiracial Responses on the Census Pose Unforeseen Risks
to Civil Rights Enforcement and Monitoring

For the first time in the nation's history, the 2000 Census allowed respondents to check more than one race. Although the great majority of Americans—98 percent—selected a single race, more than 6.8 million people took the opportunity to declare a mixed racial heritage. This number represents a small portion of the total population—2.4 percent—but the impact could be substantial as we try to figure how to count these numbers. Brought to the forefront again is the age-old American question of race, as the multiracial responses on the census compel us to ask what it means to be white, African American, American Indian, Asian American, or other minority. Our answer to this question will have enormous ramifications for the future of the nation's efforts to meet civil rights goals, to allocate funding equitably, and to produce reliable, useful data for a variety of purposes.

The great majority of the nation's 281.4 million people (98 percent) still chose one race in identifying themselves. Of those, 75.1 percent were white, 12.3 percent were African American, 0.9 percent were American Indian, 3.6 percent were Asian

---

* (footnotes omitted).

American, 0.1 percent were native Hawaiians or Pacific Islanders, an 5.5 percent (mostly Hispanics) chose the designation "Some other race."

The official count of the African-American population will be the 34,658,190 who reported their race as black or African American alone. However, another 1,761,244 people reported black or African American in combination with one or more other races. Almost half (44.6 percent) of those who marked another race along with black or African American reported that they were also white. Nearly another quarter (23.7 percent) gave "Some other race" as their second race. The majority of these are likely black Hispanics since about 60 percent of those reporting "Some other race" were Hispanic. A little over 10 percent (10.4 percent) of the multiple responses involving African Americans gave American Indian or Alaska Native as the second race, and 6.4 percent listed Asian American.

So how many African Americans were there in the United States in 2000? How many American Indians and Alaska Natives? How many Asian American? What are their poverty and birth rates? The answer is: It depends on how you do the counting.

There were at least 34.7 million blacks in the United States in April 2000. If the 1.76 million who checked "black or African American" together with other races were added to the number who reported black as a single race, the total would be 36,419,434. This "all-inclusive" figure is about 5 percent higher than the single race count and would represent 12.9 percent of the nation's population.

Although some might be happy to use the higher, all-inclusive number for their own group, the result is that people who reported two races are counted twice, those who reported three are counted three times, and so forth. If this is done for all groups, the total counted becomes larger than the actual population by 2.6 percent. The all-inclusive numbers are, therefore, of little use in the major applications that require data on race, including monitoring and enforcing civil rights and tracking trends in education, employment, health, housing and other sectors of society. As the data from the 2000 Census roll out, a question likely to be asked with increasing frequency and urgency is: How should the multiple responses be tabulated for these important purposes?

Tseming Yang

*Choice and Fraud in Racial Identification; The Dilemma of Policing
Race in Affirmative Action, the Census, and a Color-Blind Society**

In 1989, the case of the Malone brothers triggered a well-publicized inquiry into the racial and ethnic backgrounds of a number of Boston firefighters. The Malones,

---

* (footnotes and chapter headings omitted).

two fair-haired and fair-skinned identical twins, had claimed in their job applications over twelve years earlier that they were Black for affirmative action hiring purposes. During a job promotion review, the fire commissioner was startled to learn that the brothers' names appeared on a list of Black firefighters. Their justification was that in 1976, after they had been passed over for jobs in the fire department and before they applied a second time, their mother had informed them about a Black maternal great grandmother. The Malones were eventually fired and their dismissals affirmed by the Massachusetts Supreme Judicial Court. Further investigations within the Boston fire department and at fire and police departments in several other cities revealed similar troubling claims about racial identity.

In early 2005, Ward Churchill, ethnic studies chair and tenured professor at the University of Colorado, was charged with ethnic fraud. Churchill was an expert on indigenous issues and, according to the Denver Post, had "described himself as an Indian." His opponents, however, pointed out that he was not a regularly enrolled member in the tribe he claimed, but rather only an "associate" member. Moreover, U.S. Census records showed an ancestor whom Churchill had claimed as an American Indian listed as White. While Churchill has continued to assert "that he is an Indian," a claim that he has maintained since his high school days, political pressures associated with Churchill's controversial views on the 9/11 terrorist attacks triggered a university investigation into Churchill's scholarship and other aspects of his past. A preliminary review suggested that fraud in "misrepresenting himself as a Native American in order either to gain an employment-related benefit or to add credibility and public acceptance to his scholarship" could be sanctionable conduct. He was later cleared of those charges.

In recent years, the practice of "box-checking," and the abuse of affirmative action programs has increasingly become a concern. In such instances, applicants for university admission and affirmative action programs "check" ethnic and racial heritage boxes indicating minority status even if the actual personal connection is remote, tenuous, or even non-existent. There have even been reports of systematic efforts to find such connections via genetic analysis. It appears to be most prevalent with respect to American Indian and Hispanic/Latino identities. While it is unclear how often such incidents occur, they do not appear to be rare. There seem to be no formal mechanisms to challenge or check abuses and opportunism.

In a color-blind society, under the premise that race or skin color are no different from personal physical attributes like hair or eye color, alteration or misrepresentation ought to be irrelevant or of minimal consequence. Accurate racial identification and classification, however, remain crucial to the effective implementation of racial affirmative action programs and the administration of anti-discrimination laws more generally. It remains important to the federal government's decennial census and has continuing salience in many areas of life, such as health care.

The historical role of race in maintaining systems of slavery, segregation, and racial caste has shaped the meaning of race and methods of racial classification. Criticism of contemporary uses of racial classification have either denied their necessity wholesale or focused on the substantive "accuracy" of classifications and designations. Largely ignored has been the question of process in the assignment of racial identity—*who* should determine racial identity and the meaning of the chosen process. Who should control the construction of the concept central to anti-discrimination law in the present?

The acts and circumstances of individuals like the Malone brothers, Churchill, and Korematsu raise important questions about the nature of racial identification and its determinants. When individual choice does not conform with community perception, which prevails and what are the consequences? How should be understand such contradictions? To leave such questions unresolved leaves the racial identification process open to opportunistic manipulation by the unscrupulous. Alternatively, a rigid system of racial classification raises the specter of South African Apartheid or the Jim Crow Deep South. In times when society seeks to erase racial lines and redress racial inequality, how do we manage the dilemma of contradictory efforts by individuals to shape and manage racial identity?

Efforts to cross color and race lines have traditionally manifested themselves in two ways: racial passing and formal efforts to gain legal recognition of a particular racial identity, usually Whiteness.

In the past, racial passing referred to the efforts of an individual with non-White ancestry to hold themselves out as White when "prevailing social standards" (or legal ones) would bar that identification. It was most often, but not always, associated with individuals of mixed-race ancestry who had "White" physical features—primarily fair skinned individuals of African and White backgrounds.

Prior to the Civil War, being able to pass as White facilitated the escape of light-skinned slaves. For example, a racial deception enabled Ellen Craft to flee from slavery in Georgia to freedom in Philadelphia in 1848. She disguised herself for four days as a White man and had her husband pretend to be her servant. In later times, being "mistaken" as White allowed some African Americans also to avoid some of the burdens of segregation, social stigma, and racial violence. One of the most prominent examples includes Walter White, an active member of the NAACP during the first half of the 20th century. He was a "fair-skinned, blue-eyed, and blond-haired . . . son of light-complexioned Negroes who were stalwarts of Atlanta's black middle class." Using his ability to pass as White, he investigated lynchings for the NAACP during Jim Crow times.

Passing has not disappeared in modern day times. Prominent author and critic Anatole Broyard, a daily book reviewer for the New York Times for over a decade, was born to Negro parents in 1920s New Orleans; he passed as White for most of his adult life until his death in the early 1990s. Racial passing has not been unique to African Americans. Among Asian Americans, Fred Korematsu's cosmetic surgery and pretense of being Spanish-Hawaiian may be seen as an exemplar. Erika Lee has also described the attempts by some sojourner Chinese to disguise themselves as American Indian or Mexican in the late 19th and early 20th century. During the period of Chinese Exclusion, it was one of the only means available to enter the United States via Mexico or Canada. Thus,

> [I]t was not uncommon for White "smugglers" to disguise Chinese as Native Americans crossing from Canada to the United States in pursuit of trade. They would be dressed in "Indian garb," given a basket of sassafras, and rowed across the border in a boat. . . . [For crossings to the United states from Mexico,] Chinese [immigrants] cut their queues and exchanged their "blue jeans and felt slippers" for "the most picturesque Mexican dress." They received fraudulent a Mexican citizenship papers, and they also learned to say a few words of Spanish, in particular 'Yo soy Mexicano' ('I am Mexican').

A U.S. immigration inspector who examined fake Mexican citizenship papers of such Chinese immigrants in 1907 "expressed with some amazement that it was 'exceedingly difficult to distinguish these Chinamen from Mexicans.'"

Racial passing by individuals with Native American and Latino ancestry has had additional wrinkles. For Native Americans, centuries of forced assimilation and intermarriage with Whites has resulted in many mixed-race individuals with a White phenotype. Like African American families who have permanently passed into Whiteness, many such individuals no longer have any knowledge of their Native American ancestry. They simply consider themselves, and may be considered by prevailing social standards, as White. Such individuals arguably are not engaged in any deliberate "deception" about their racial identity. In fact, even during colonial times, some states considered such mixed-race individuals to be legally White if the blood quantum of American-Indian ancestry was sufficiently small.

For individuals of Latino, and in particular Mexican, ancestry, lineage has always been multi-racial by definition. As descendants of Latin American indigenous people and Spanish colonizers, attempts at passing as White were often facilitated by innate physical characteristics. It may have been as simple as denying one's indigenous ancestry and holding oneself out as Spanish.

Racial line crossing has not only occurred in the direction of Whiteness. With respect to Asian Americans, for example, the on-screen roles of actors Lou Diamond Philips and Tommy Chong have led them to be commonly perceived as Latino. Tiger Woods is predominantly and primarily perceived as African American, even though his mother is Thai. During World War II, some Japanese Americans claimed to be Chinese in order to avoid war-time internment. In Louisiana, individuals with both African American and American Indian ancestry frequently choose to assert their Native American identity rather than their African American identity.

There have been some well-known instances of White individuals passing as Native Americans. Passing as African American, however, has generally been rare. Some instances when Whites did attempt to do so have been described by Rachel Moran; it usually occurred when interracial couples sought advantage or to avoid embarrassment. An unusual, but well-known instance involved John Howard

Griffin. Seeking to explore the experience of being Black in America, Griffin, a White journalist, chemically darkened his skin to journey through the South in 1959.

A less obvious effort in crossing racial lines has had little equivalent to passing in other contexts: seeking legal recognition of a different racial identity, primarily Whiteness. Until 1954, federal naturalization statutes restricted U.S. citizenship to free White persons. Before the Supreme Court authoritatively held in 1922 and 1923 that Asians were not White, hundreds of Chinese and Japanese were able to persuade the federal courts that they were White, enabling them to become naturalized U.S. citizens. In doing so, they crossed the color line within the eyes of the law, even if their social status and standing within the community may have remained unchanged.

Similar efforts are exemplified by lawsuits filed by slaves seeking judicial declarations that they were White. For example, in ante-bellum Alabama, Abby Guy contested her status as a slave by asserting and litigating her Whiteness. At trial, her purported owner submitted documentary evidence supporting her status as a slave, and hence Black. The judge found in her favor. The court's judgment not only set her free but also determined as a judicial matter that she was White.

Contemporary litigation-driven efforts to acquire a White racial identity have become less significant with the end of legal segregation. The continuing significance of racial identity in individual self-conception and everyday social interactions have not made such efforts irrelevant, however. Some contemporary cases have focused on government practices of collecting and maintaining racial identity information. In Louisiana, the acts of Naomi Drake, supervisor and deputy registrar of the Louisiana Bureau of Vital Statistics, led to a series of cases beginning in the 1950s and up until the 1980s that challenged racial identity designations on birth certificates. Most of the lawsuits were unsuccessful.

One particularly well-publicized case involved Suzie Phipps. Phipps found out late in life that she was classified as Black in her birth records; all her life she had believed herself to be white. When the registrar refused to change the racial designation on her birth certificate, she sued. The courts acknowledged the arbitrariness of the racial designations. Unfortunately, they also found that such designations were "correct" according to the standards of the times when they were made. Hence, the registrar could not be legally required to change the designation.

Legal recognition of non-White identity has remained significant, primarily in three contexts: race discrimination claims, affirmative action, and federal programs for members of federally recognized Indian tribes. In race discrimination cases, the plaintiff's membership in a legally protected class — usually a racial minority — is a threshold question for any discrimination claim. In the tribal programs and affirmative action context, racial identity is a pre-requisite for program eligibility.

The Census adopts a system of self-identification as opposed to classification by some set of "objective" criteria, or by a disinterested third-party. Its position reflects the view that race is a social and political construct rather than a fixed attribute dependent only on physical, phenotypic appearance (or genetic make-up, for that matter). Arguably, the most important reason for doing so is the history of government-sponsored classification. The racial caste systems of segregation and slavery were vitally dependent on government sponsorship of rigid racial classification criteria. Explicit choice of a self-recognition approach as the primary and conclusive method openly rejects the past. The Census position also supports the strong popular sentiment that racial identity is a matter of individual autonomy and self-determination.

Self-identification is usually also most accurate. Racial identity is not only a function of physical characteristics and appearances, but also of an individual's social interactions and relationships. The full spectrum of social perceptions and interactions with others is known most completely only to the census respondent him or herself.

Finally, the most powerful reason for self-identification is the common wisdom that our society now lives in, or at least is striving to create, a color-blind society. In a color-blind society, racial designation is relevant only as a vital statistic, like hair or eye color, and ought not have any social or legal significance. As a corollary, an individual's choice of racial identity presumably would have no social or legal significance either. Governmental regulation would not only be unnecessary but also non-sensical—just like the regulation of ice cream flavor preference.

Sole reliance on a system of self-identification encounters problems, however. It leaves unaddressed concerns about manipulation, administrative workability, and fairness. After all, a color-blind society still remains (and may forever be) more a great sounding slogan than an existing reality. Race is still a salient personal characteristic in social interactions. It continues to be relevant in legal contexts such as anti-discrimination laws and affirmative action programs.

How can one "check" opportunistic manipulation of the system, as in the case of the Malone brothers? If classification is solely a function of an individual's choice with no constraints and criteria ensuring consistency, how can the designation be useful for any systematic regulatory use? Is it possible to maintain public confidence and support for governmental programs that rely on such classifications if there is no assurance that such programs are being fairly and effectively applied?

11 Mich. J. Race & Law 367, 368–377, 383–387, 416.
Copyright © 2006 Mich. J. Race & Law.
Reprinted with permission of Mich. J. Race & Law and Tseming Yang.

The 2010 Census form continues the self-identification option of choosing more than one racial category for an individual's race classification. Question number 8 asks about ethnicity as to whether one is of "Hispanic, Latino, or Spanish origin." Question number 9 asks about race regardless of whether the person is of "Hispanic, Latino, or Spanish origin" and permits more than one racial category to be identified. The race and ethnicity definitions and approach of the 2020 Census remain consistent with the 2010 Census.

Part Two

Slavery

IV. Slavery, Free Blacks, and the Constitution

A. Introduction

The Preamble of the United States Constitution invokes lofty principles stating:

> We the people of the United States, in order to form a more perfect union, establish justice, insure domestic tranquility, provide for the common defense, promote the general welfare, and secure the blessings of liberty to ourselves and our posterity, do ordain and establish this Constitution of the United States of America.[1]

The first two stated goals at the outset of this identity-defining, foundational document were "to form a more perfect union," and "to establish justice." Yet, for blacks and abolitionists, the union could be neither "more perfect" nor "just" unless it made domestic slavery illegal, or at least lay the groundwork for a gradual abolition of slavery. The original Constitution, therefore, encompassed a paradox: it sought to establish justice, and yet it recognized no rights for a segment of the population; it sought to insure tranquility, and yet it preserved slavery. Viewed from a perspective denying the reality of slavery, the Constitution could be considered, as literally suggested in the Preamble, a document designed to insure justice, domestic tranquility, and to "secure the blessings of liberty to ourselves and our posterity." (Preamble, United States Constitution). Nevertheless, these venerable aspirations were then meaningless to the blacks who knew that for them and their posterity, the Constitution neither eradicated nor lessened the harshness of domestic slavery. Thus, while viewing the same document, abolitionist William Lloyd Garrison would call it a "covenant with Hell," while its Framers would call it a compact to "establish justice." At a time when our national identity was being articulated, your position within society determined whether the Constitution delineated your rights or completely denied them.

The materials in this chapter demonstrate that the Constitutional Convention of 1787 produced a document that on its face gave no promise of immediate justice for blacks. In fact, the Constitution did not provide even a ray of hope that blacks could secure justice through the federal legal system. In the legal system at that time, blacks could not bring a cause of action in an attempt to secure justice. These

---

1. U.S. CONST. pmbl. (1789).

basic rights and securities were not attained until the nation became embroiled in a devastating war sixty-four years after the Constitution was adopted.

One could debate endlessly the theoretical options that were available for consideration by the Framers during the Constitutional Convention in 1787 for improving the plight of blacks. As a matter of theory, the Framers could have required the immediate abolition of all slavery, or they could have provided for a system of gradual abolishment of slavery similar to a plan that was subsequently adopted by Pennsylvania in 1780. Furthermore, even if they did not take a forthright position on recognizing the inhumanity and immorality of slavery, they could have inserted some ancillary type of "bill of rights" for slaves. For example, the Framers could have provided that slaves had the right to marry, or that slave families could not be broken up, or that, without provocation, owners or others could not assault slaves, or that slaves could under some circumstances purchase their freedom. All of these individual provisions were in fact adopted by various jurisdictions at different times in subsequent decades. The possibility of enacting provisions to abolish slavery or to limit its cruelty would be contingent upon whether the Founding Fathers held such goals with any sense of priority. However, justice for blacks was not the Framers' predominant concern.

For even though a few of the founding fathers were sympathetic to the plight of slaves, their concern was offset by opposing issues: what protection or assistance could be given to blacks without endangering the Union's protection of whites, including the economic prosperity enjoyed by whites? In making judgments on what was theoretically possible or pragmatically feasible, one must first understand and evaluate those decisive non-racial and non-slavery components that concerned the Framers as they sat down in Philadelphia to prepare the document. Several key provisions in the Constitution reveal the priorities held by the Framers, and set in place absolute constraints on freedom for the people who were enslaved within the colonies.

B. Race, Values, and the Constitution

A. Leon Higginbotham, Jr.

The Bicentennial of the Constitution: A Racial Perspective

The meeting at the Annapolis Convention of the Continental Congress on February 21, 1787, adopted a resolution that "it is expedient that on the second Monday of May next, a convention of delegates who shall have been appointed by the several states be held at Philadelphia for the sole and express purpose of revising the Articles of Confederation." The revision was necessary because of the critical lack of power and authority in the national government. The government had been unable to enforce its laws or exercise control over the states in the important functions of taxation, regulation of trade, protection of commerce, security, and the enforcement of treaty obligations.

New England's main incentive toward a stronger union was commercial. It was the hope that a united nation could enter into, enforce better commercial arrangements with foreign nations, and among the states, than any single state could by itself. The northeastern states had no motive to unite but a commercial one. They were able to protect themselves, were not afraid of external danger, and did not need the aid of the southern states. Conversely, the southern states were interested in mutual defense, protection against external threats, and strengthening the institution of slavery.

The Key Racist Provisions in the Constitution

Despite their seeming innocuousness, there were four key provisions included to assure each state the option to perpetuate slavery and these provisions ultimately maximized political power for southern slaveholders: Article 1, § 2, Clause 3, the "three-fifths of all other persons" standard for representation and direct taxes; Article 1, § 9, Clause 1, the guarantee that "[t]he migration or importation of such persons . . . shall not be prohibited by the Congress prior to . . . 1808"; Article 4, § 2, Clause 3, "No person held to service or labor in one state, . . . escaping into another, shall . . . be discharged from such service or labor, but shall be delivered up on claim of the party to whom such service or labor may be due"; and Article 5, which prohibits the amendment of the Constitution prior to 1808 as to the Article 1, § 9 provision. In each of these clauses "persons" meant slaves, but the drafting was such that only the most sophisticated would know that "persons" had such a malevolent meaning.

The Three-Fifths Clause

Initially, there were two different approaches at the Constitutional Convention which partially reflected the demographic differences in the slave population of various states. If federal taxation was to be based solely on property value, it was in the interest of the North (and against that of the South) for slaves to be considered as property in making tax assessments. In contrast, on the issue of political representation, it was in the interest of the South to have slaves counted as a portion of the census base from which political representation would be determined; and of course the inclusion of slaves on any formula on which political representation was based would be ultimately disadvantageous to the Northern states.

After the competing positions and theories had been argued in detail, the delegates agreed upon a compromise. As it turned out, this settlement was a major triumph for the South since under this provision the States were never taxed or assessed to finance the federal government.

Direct taxes were not levied, and the three-fifths rule in representation gave the slave states a voting power in the House of Representatives and in the Electoral College far beyond that to which their free population entitled them. With this extra representation made possible by the three-fifths compromise, the South was always able to have a disproportionately larger number of congressmen than northern states. This is largely because the predominant base of the census for northern congressmen was free persons, while the base for southern congressional representation included free persons plus a substantial slave population. Thus, in effect, on every major issue in the House of Representatives the South always had some extra votes over Northern congressmen; that is, they had more congressmen than they would have had if representation was based solely on free persons. Note that in many instances this extra disproportionate representation may have changed the course of history. For example, it enabled Thomas Jefferson, a slaveholder, to defeat John Adams, an opponent of slavery, for the Presidency in 1800.

The Importation Clause

Opposition to the international slave trade was not strictly along sectional lines for there were definite advantages to certain southern and northern states in the continuance of this traffic. The South was sharply divided on this issue.

South Carolina and Georgia opposed restrictions on the importation of slaves. Mr. Rutledge of South Carolina warned that "[i]f the Convention thinks that North Carolina, South Carolina, and Georgia will ever agree to the plan, unless their right to import slaves be untouched, the expectation is [in] vain."

These southernmost states were supported to some extent by Massachusetts and Rhode Island, which while purportedly anti-slavery in their moral outlook were economically involved in the African slave trade as financiers, merchants, shipbuilders, captains and seamen.

In contrast, states of the upper South wanted the international slave trade stopped as soon as possible. In 1790 there were 293,000 slaves in Virginia, 103,000 in Maryland, 107,000 in South Carolina, and 29,000 in Georgia. With their depleted tobacco lands and their overstock of slaves, Maryland and Virginia were interested in the highest prices for the sale of their slaves. These areas could serve as breeding places which would export their surplus blacks to the newer and more fertile slave-operated agricultural areas south and west of their frontiers.

The Fugitive Slave Clause

Though it gave the Southern slave holders an extraordinary power which they had never possessed under the Articles of Confederation, the proposal was accepted without debate or dissent and was substantially the clause that finally appeared in Section 2 of Article IV after being submitted to the Committee of Style for a few minor changes. The fugitive slave clause was of profound importance because as a matter of federal law it extended a constitutional obligation to each state to honor and approve some aspects of slavery—at least as to fugitive slaves. Prior to this provision even under the Articles of Confederation, states were not obligated to recognize the slave laws of sister states and were not obligated to aid in the assistance of fugitive slaves. Under the normal conflict of law or choice of law doctrines, if a slave escaped from a state or nation which recognized slavery, the free state might consider slavery to be such an abhorrent condition and so repugnant to its public policy that it would not honor the slave owner's demand for return of the slave.

This possibility was feared greatly by Southern slave owners for it was this doctrine which Lord Mansfield announced in the *Sommersett* case. It was a particularly apt precedent because Sommersett had been a slave under Virginia law, but the English court held that it need not and should not enforce the Virginia law when the slave was in England because "so high an act of dominion was to be recognized by the law of the country" where the slave is found. Mansfield emphasized that "the state of slavery is of such a nature, that it is incapable of being introduced on any reasons, moral or political, but only by positive law . . . it is so odious that nothing can be suffered to support it, but positive law." Since Massachusetts did not recognize slavery under its positive law, and since many of the other Northern states would probably soon not recognize slavery under their positive law, the normal conflict of law doctrines would mean that such states would not have to recognize the Virginia slave laws as to any slaves found in these Northern jurisdictions. To preclude this *Sommersett*-type problem the fugitive slave clause was written to assure slave owners a federal constitutional right to retrieve their slaves regardless of whether other states recognized slavery.

Who Were the Delegates

In Washington's letter to Lafayette, and Madison's letter to Thomas Jefferson, they had described the Constitutional Convention as a "Miracle at Philadelphia" in the year 1787. Yet Thomas Jefferson, writing from Paris to John Adams in London, had called them an "assembly of demi-gods". The delegates were appointed by their state legislatures, and Patrick Henry refused to accept an appointment as a delegate to the Convention because he "smelt a rat." As former Chief Justice Warren E. Burger has said,

> the "rat" he smelled was the replacement of the Articles of the Confederation with a Constitution creating a strong national government. In his view, we had not fought a revolution to rid ourselves of one distant despot only to set up a domestic version of the same—more republican in form, perhaps, but nevertheless a despotism of centralized power.

I will not enter the debate as to whether they were miracle men or demi-gods. From my perspective, the true "miracle" is that such an unrepresentative group of representatives could create a document that would one day secure liberty and the promise of true equality for all Americans, not just wealthy, white, American men.

Of the 55 delegates to the Constitution, only two—Daniel Carroll of Maryland and Thomas Fitzsimons of Pennsylvania—were Catholic. There were no Jews. There were, of course, no blacks, Indians or women. It is not without significance that I speak of the drafters solely as my forefathers—because with the minuscule status of women in America's public life, there were no foremothers of our American Constitution. Some of the states at that time had provisions prohibiting Jews, blacks and Catholics from holding public offices.

These delegates represented the privileged members of society—most were wealthy, some exceedingly wealthy.[2] One of them, Robert Morris of Pennsylvania, was considered the wealthiest and most powerful man of his time. Known to both friends and foes as "the Great Man," he has been compared to J. P. Morgan. It is estimated that he exercised some amount of control over property totaling approximately two million dollars. Morris, like some of the other delegates, later went bankrupt and even spent time in debtor's prison, but at the time of the Convention, he was a man of phenomenal wealth. John Langdon of New Hampshire was one of the richest in his state. John Lansing of New York was perhaps the wealthiest man in his political party—the Clinton anti-Federalist faction. Even those of "modest means" came from well-to-do families. They had either squandered their wealth, lost their money on risky investments, or in some instances held public positions yielding modest salaries. Thirteen of the "miracle men" were at one time or another debtors for significant amounts of money; several died poor or insolvent.

Many of the delegates were from the leading families in their respective states. Approximately one half were college educated and received their educations from the finest schools: Four were from Harvard, ten from Princeton, four from Yale, two from Columbia, two from the University of Pennsylvania, four from William and Mary, and a few were educated either in London or at the Scottish universities.

Many of the delegates had more than one occupation. Thirty-four were lawyers, at least eight of whom were judges. Some of the lawyers derived major portions of their income from other commercial ventures and agriculture. A few of the delegates ultimately went on to become President or Justices on the United States Supreme Court. Three were governors, five served as state attorney general, three were surgeons, two were professors, two were ministers, a few were speculators, and one (Benjamin Franklin, then 81 years old) was a printer/publisher, educator, inventor, philosopher, and, above all, a wise pragmatist. Fifteen of the delegates were engaged in or associated with mercantile activities. A few owned ships.

The most significant group of men for purposes here were the farmers and planters. Eighteen of the delegates were farmers, sixteen of whom conducted large-scale agricultural operations—i.e., plantations. All but two of them—John Lansing of New York and Richard Bassett of Delaware—owned slaves. In addition Luther Martin, James Madison, John Blair, George Wythe, James McClurg, and John Rutledge owned slaves. Hence, 20 of the delegates (over one-third) were slaveowners. Those with the most significant slave holdings included: George Mason of Virginia, with 300 slaves; John Rutledge of South Carolina, who owned 243 slaves; Charles Cotesworth Pinckney of South Carolina, with 200 slaves at the beginning of the Revolutionary War; his cousin, Charles Pinckney, of the same state, who in 1790 owned 111 slaves; Pierce Butler of South Carolina, who owned 143 slaves; and

---

2. The author has relied heavily on the classic study by FORREST MCDONALD, entitled WE THE PEOPLE (1958), and have thus paraphrased his penetrating analysis in this section.

George Washington, the father of our country, who had a tremendous fortune in land and slaves, and at times owned more than 200 slaves.

Forrest McDonald's description of the delegates' wealth in his magnificent book, *We the People,* is itself quite telling. James Madison, "a delegate of comparatively modest means, owned six adult slaves, and three slave children, and five horses." Slaves and horses were lumped in the same category as chattel. Edmund Randolph was from one of Virginia's leading families but was always plagued with financial difficulties. He once complained to Madison of his regret that his father had not "hand[ed] down a fortune" to him. The land that Randolph did inherit from his uncle in 1784 was burdened with debts: "Randolph derived little benefit from his uncle's bequest; the produce of the land scarcely sufficed to support the increasing number of negroes."

In sum, the most common and most valuable holdings of the 55 delegates were farmland and slaves.[3] As McDonald observes:

> The 569 slaves owned by the four delegates from South Carolina were prob-ably worth half[,] again as much as the total public security holdings of all other members. [Thirty of the delegates held securities in various amounts.] The slaves and farmlands owned by the delegates from Virginia and Mary-land were worth far more than the mercantile, banking, and manufactur-ing property owned by all the other delegates.

These were the interests that were represented at the Constitutional Convention—men who rose to, or were born into, wealth and power, many serv-ing in public office. These were the elite, the aristocracy of America, who assumed the awesome and solemn responsibility of speaking for "We the People." Yet by their document they did not mean to include *all* of the people. Blacks, who were 19 percent of the population, were not included.

---

3. The primary commercial interests of the delegates were as follows:

Including lawyers whose practice was primarily or exclusively concerned with farming or other realty interests, twenty derived all or almost all of their income from the soil; that is to say, their interests were primarily realty-agrarian, as opposed to personalty. . . .

Including lawyers whose incomes were derived largely or exclusively from mercantile clients, thirteen had interests that were primarily mercantile—that is, in personal property as opposed to real property. . . .

Two derived their incomes almost equally from agricultural pursuits and the practice of law with mercantile clients. . . .

Twelve derived all or the greater part of their income from salaries in public offices.

Two derived all or almost all of their income from their practice as physicians. . . .

Three had retired from active economic pursuits with substantial fortunes. . . . The estates of all three men consisted primarily of realty, but . . . two had made their fortunes in mercantile pursuits.

Three are loosely classifiable as pensioners. . . .

All three men were in rather trying economic circumstances.

FORREST McDONALD, WE THE PEOPLE 80 (1958).

We the Other People

Despite the almost universal admiration most Americans have today for our current Constitution, at the time of its ratification, people held different visions of the original Constitution. The images one sees and the perspectives one takes are determined by the lens through which one views the document. One's view of the Constitution will depend on whether one identifies primarily with the plantation owners and those (55) powerful persons who met in Philadelphia to form a more perfect union for whites, or whether one identifies with what Professor Philip Foner calls "We the *Other* people."[4] The *other* people were the Native Americans, the blacks—particularly the slaves—the indentured servants, the white unpropertied poor, and women regardless of their status. These "the other people" were not the *immediate* beneficiaries of the "more perfect union" formed in 1787.

The Original Constitution from a Racial Perspective

Even today the debate continues as to how the accomplishments of the Founding Fathers should be evaluated. At one end of the spectrum are the views articulated by former Chief Justice Warren Burger, former President Ronald Reagan and Senator Strom Thurmond, and at the other end of the spectrum are the very different views of former Justice Thurgood Marshall and Professor Leon Litwack, former president of the Organization of American Historians.

Chief Justice Warren Burger has said that the Constitution of 1787 gave to all Americans "a new kind of freedom," and people everywhere hoped for a better life. President Reagan said to the Congress: "In this two-hundredth year of our Constitution, you and I stand on the shoulders of giants, men whose words and deeds put wind in the sails of freedom." Senator Strom Thurmond of South Carolina asserted that no document in history did more "to give people freedom and opportunity."

Justice Marshall rejected the view that "the vision of those who debated and compromised in Philadelphia yielded the 'more perfect union.'" He went on to assert:

> I do not believe that the meaning of the Constitution was forever 'fixed' at the Philadelphia convention. Nor do I find the wisdom, foresight and sense of justice exhibited by the framers particularly profound. To the contrary, the government they devised was defective from the start, requiring several amendments, a Civil War, a momentous social transformation to attain the system of constitutional government and its respect for the individual freedoms and human rights we hold as fundamental today. When contemporary Americans cite 'the Constitution,' they invoke a concept that is vastly different from what the framers barely began to construct two centuries ago.

Professor Litwack, in his Presidential Address before America's most distinguished group of historians, has said that to take the Burger, Reagan and Thurmond position is to read:

---

4. Philip S. Foner, We The Other People 1–3 (1976).

American history without the presence of black men and women, to define them out of American identity, to exclude a people who enjoyed neither liberty, impartial government, nor the equal protection of the law. It is to read out of American history a long legacy of slavery and segregation. The same "wind in the sails of freedom" perceived by the President condemned some 700,000 black men and women to nearly three-quarters of a century of unfreedom. The same nation that boasted of its dedication to the proposition that "all men are created equal" was based on the most enormous of human inequalities.

What are the facts? Which of these distinguished Americans has the more accurate historical perception of the Constitution as it pertained to blacks during the nation's first seventy-eight years? What 'blessings of liberty,' as that phrase is used in the Preamble, did blacks receive?

The scholars differ. In his published book, *The Making of America: The Substance and Meaning of the Constitution*, which reflected the views of several scholars and was initially promoted by the California Bicentennial Commission, Professor W. Cleon Skousen minimizes the disadvantages of slavery and seemingly lauds the institution of slavery.[5] His historical analysis paints a picture of what I call the "Happy, Docile Negro" who actually enjoyed the deprivations of slavery. Professor Skousen writes:

> The gang in transit were usually a cheerful lot, though the presence of a number of the more vicious type sometimes made it necessary for them all to go in chains.[6]

He goes on to argue that,

> . . . If the pickaninnies ran naked it was generally from choice, and when the white boys had to put on shoes and go away to school they were likely to envy the freedom of their colored playmates. The color line began to appear at about that time. . . .[7]

Despite Professor Skousen's adulation of the joys of slaves, I cannot believe that George Washington, Thomas Jefferson, James Madison, Patrick Henry or James

---

5. Professor W. Cleon Skousen begins the preface of his book by stating:

This book was written to fill a special need. For many years in the United States there has been a gradual drifting away from the Founding Fathers' original success formula. This has resulted in some of their most unique contributions for a free and prosperous society becoming lost or misunderstood. Therefore, there has been a need to review the history and development of the making of America in order to recapture the brilliant precepts which made Americans the first free people in modern times.

As to the extent that Skousen's themes are a mere repetition of the articles of other scholars, *see* S. SHANNON, ECONOMIC HISTORY OF THE PEOPLE OF THE UNITED STATES. pp. 317–30 (1982).

6. W. SKOUSEN, THE MAKING OF AMERICA: THE SUBSTANCE AND MEANING OF THE CONSTITUTION 731 (1986).

7. *Id.*

Monroe envied the "pickaninnies" who were enslaved in Virginia where statutes made it a crime even to teach blacks how to read and write. Would any sane white person have wanted to change places with a slave child who could be sold from his mother as if he were cattle? As a partial rebuttal to this portrayal, we suggest that one consider actual slave advertisements, to determine how happy blacks really were.

> One hundred and twenty Negroes for sale — The subscriber has just arrived from Petersburg, Virginia, with one hundred and twenty likely young Negroes of both sexes and every description, which he offers for sale on the most reasonable terms. The lot now on hand consists of plough-boys, several likely and well-qualified house servants of both sexes, several women and children, small girls suitable for nurses, and several small boys without their mothers. Planters and traders are earnestly requested to give the subscriber a call previously to making purchase elsewhere, as he is enabled to sell as cheap or cheaper than can be sold by any person in the trade.
>
> — Hamburg, South Carolina, Benjamin Davis

Benjamin Davis' advertisement was not unique; it was typical of thousands of advertisements posted in newspapers and on bulletin boards throughout our land. In the *New Orleans Bee*, an advertisement noted:

> Negroes for sale — a Negro woman 24 years of age, and her two children, one eight and the other three years old. Said Negroes will be sold separately or together, as desired. The woman is a good seamstress. She will be sold low for cash, or exchange for groceries. For terms apply to Matthew Bliss and Company, 1 Front Levee.[8]

It is important to distinguish facts from myths; hopefully we will not remain uncritical of a legal system that encouraged and sanctioned such cruelty — cruelty that permitted the sale, as Benjamin Davis advertised, of "several small boys without their mothers." How happy was the mother, twenty four years of age, who could be sold in exchange for groceries and separated from her children, only eight and three years old? Looking past the commercial facade, one sees the advertisement as stating that American laws, under our then Constitution, encouraged the destruction of black families and the selling of human beings. The only limitation was the demand of the marketplace.

In response to the theory about these "happy pickaninnies," I ask, would any white in America have wanted to exchange places with any slave in antebellum America? Would any white female have wanted to change places with a black female in Mississippi, a state whose highest court said it was not a crime to rape a slave woman? *George v. State*, 37 Miss. 316 (1859). Would any white male have wanted to exchange places with the slave victim in *State v. Boon*, a case in which the lauded

---

8. *See* A. Leon Higginbotham, Jr., In the Matter of Color 12 (1978).

and purportedly liberal North Carolina Supreme Court held in 1801 that it was not a crime for a white person to kill a slave?[9]

The delegates to the Constitutional Convention of 1787 produced a document providing no substance of justice for blacks. In fact, the Constitution did not provide even a ray of hope that blacks could secure justice through the federal legal system. The Constitution's eloquent references to justice, welfare, and liberty were mocked by the treatment meted out daily to blacks through the courts, in legislative statutes, and in those provisions of the Constitution itself that sanctioned slavery for the majority of black Americans and provided no rights for those few blacks legally "free."

The Absence of Religion and Humanity

Most Americans would like to believe that the Founding Fathers in 1787 had some serious concerns about the inhumanity of slavery, and that on the floor of the convention they addressed these concerns with compassion and condemnation. Yet, if we had to identify the primary racial theme of the founding fathers during the constitutional debates, it would be that slaves were to be viewed primarily as property—as subhuman—and that their degraded status should not be improved by the law if it would cause plantation owners to sustain any diminution of their economic power.

For those who wish to remain blind to the Founding Fathers' inhumane position regarding blacks, I suggest they read the heated debate on the floor of the convention over whether the Constitution should prohibit the international slave trade and the importation of slaves into the states from foreign countries. South Carolina's delegate John Rutledge, who had studied law in London, rose to his feet to state the position of South Carolina and Georgia. He declared that:

> Religion and humanity have nothing to do with this question—interest alone is the governing principle with nations—the true question at present is whether the southern states shall or shall not be parties to the Union. If the northern states consult their interest, they will not oppose the increase of slaves which will increase the commodities of which they will become the carriers.

When debating the representation issue on July 11, George Mason of Virginia referred to slaves as that "peculiar species of property" that the "southern states have . . . over and above the other species of property common to all the [other] states." When speaking of the compromise reached on the representation issue, General Charles Cotesworth Pinckney asserted proudly that "we thus obtained a representation for our property; and I confess I did not expect that we had conceded too much to the eastern states, when they allowed us a representation for a species

---

9. 11 N.C. (Taylor) 246 (1801).

of property which they have not among them." His cousin, Mr. Pinckney, followed him and said:

> South Carolina can never receive the plan [of a United States] if it prohibits the slave trade.

Later, when writing to James Madison, Thomas Jefferson stressed:

> The result is seen in the Constitution. South Carolina and Georgia were inflexible on the point of slaves.

The Intentional Non-Disclosure of Slavery

An intriguing paradox is that although there were hundreds, if not thousands, of hours of discussion and debate about slavery, there was no direct mention of the words "slave" or "slavery" in the Constitution until it was abolished in December 1865 by the 13th Amendment. The original Constitution was an exercise in non-disclosure, an intentional sanctioning of slavery while studiously excluding the word "slavery" from the document. To assure creation of a national union, there was an overwhelming consensus that the new federal government would sanction slavery as it had in the past. However, the framers were seeking the most artful method of not publicly disclosing on the face of the document their maintenance of the perfidious institution of slavery. They were concerned that the face of the document not patently reveal their sanctioning of an institution the morality of which was being increasingly questioned throughout the world.

The words of Dr. Samuel Johnson in 1775 in response to the resolution and address of the American colonists still rang in their ears. Dr. Samuel Johnson said:

> If slavery be thus fatally contagious, how is it that we hear the loudest yelps for liberty among the drivers of Negroes.

Johnson summed up the colonists' arguments as "too foolish for buffoonery [and] too wild for madness." In 1841, John Quincy Adams, a former president of the United States, when arguing before the United States Supreme Court on behalf of a slave in the *Amistad* case, said:

> The words slave and slavery are studiously excluded from the Constitution. Circumlocutions are the fig leaves under which these parts of the body politic are decently concealed.

Justice McLean, dissenting in *Dred Scott*, explained the constitutional terminology:

> [W]e know as a historical fact that James Madison, that great and good man, a leading member in the federal convention, was solicitous to guard the language of that instrument so as not to convey the idea that there could be property in man.

In his message to the Maryland legislature, Luther Martin commented that the word "slaves" was struck out of the migration and importation clause because "they anxiously sought to avoid the admission of expressions of [slavery] which might be odious in the ears of Americans, although they were willing to admit into their system those things which the expressions signified." Twenty-one years after the Constitutional Convention, delegate Abraham Baldwin of Georgia said to the House of Representatives that "it was found expedient" to avoid the word "slavery" in the Constitution and instead use the term "person" in Article I, Section 9, allowing the international slave trade until 1808. Some delegates objected "to the use of the word slaves, as Congress by none of their acts had ever acknowledged the existence of such a condition." In 1819, James Madison commented on the Constitutional Convention as follows:

> They had scruples against admitting the term "slaves" into the instrument because some persons were scrupulous of acknowledging expressly a property in human beings, some might have had an eye to the case of freed blacks, as well as malefactors.

One could argue that Madison guarded the language not for humanitarian purposes but solely for the sake of politics and linguistic sensitivity to the larger moral problem. As Justice Story noted in his classic *Commentaries*, the Constitution referred to servitude and the slave trade only in vague terms as "things the existence of which under a free constitution was to be overlooked rather than recognized." Yet others—though probably the minority—thought, as did delegate John Ellsworth of Connecticut, that slavery would gradually come to a halt—without violence or even the need for federal governmental pressures.

Professor Kelly Miller suggests:

> [S]omehow, the fathers and fashioners of this basic document of liberty hoped that the reprobated institution would in time pass away when there should be no verbal survival as a memorial of its previous existence.

Thus, unlike the prior Articles of Confederation which had phrases which clearly implied that blacks were excluded from the protection of that document (the Articles of Confederation used the terms "free inhabitants" and "white inhabitants" in articles 4 and 9), the Constitution of 1787 had no such recognizable phrases. It was not until 1865 with the passage of the 13th amendment for the abolition of slavery, that the word "slavery" was mentioned in the Constitution. "To hide the evil, one may hide its name. To expunge it, brings its name to light."

As noted, there were several key provisions that did not mention "slavery", but were included in the Constitution to assure each state the option to perpetuate slavery. Those clauses ultimately maximized political power for southern slaveholders.

The first, the "three-fifths clause," was included in Article 1, Section 2, Clause 3. It set forth the method by which representatives and direct taxes were to be apportioned among the states, specifying that "the whole number of free persons" was to be added to "three fifths of all other persons." "All other persons," of course, was a euphemism for slaves.

The second, the "international slave trade clause," was found in Article 1, Section 9, Clause 1. It provided that the "migration or importation of such Persons as any of the States ... shall think proper to admit" could not be prohibited before 1808. Despite its euphemistic reference to "such Persons," we know that clause was nothing more than a grant of permission to the states to continue the international slave trade.

Yet another obfuscation is found in Article 4, Section 2, Clause 3, which provided:

> No person held to service or labor in one state under the laws therof, escaping into another, shall in consequence of any law or regulation therein be discharged from such service or labor, but shall be delivered up on the claim of the *party* to whom such service or labor may be due.

As we know, this clause was an assurance that slaveholders would be guaranteed the right of capturing fugitive slaves even in states such as Massachusetts where slavery had been abolished.

Fall 1987 *Stanford Law Magazine* 8.
Copyright © 1987 Stanford University.
Reprinted with permission of the *Stanford Lawyer.*

C. The 1787 Compromise on Slavery

The ultimate eradication of slavery was significantly aided by the abolitionists' persistent attacks on the inhumaneness of a Constitution that sanctioned slavery. Most of the abolitionists' moral arguments were unassailable. Yet, it is intriguing to speculate what would have been the nation's race relations history if in 1787 the Founding Fathers had split the United States into two separate regional sovereignties because of irreconcilable disputes over the slavery issues. Was it better that abolitionists, though opposed to slavery, conceded to the pro-slavery interests which resulted in the "three-fifths" compromise, the international slave trade provision (until at least 1808), and the fugitive slave clause? Or, would it have been better for them to have refused to be parties to a document that tolerated a system wherein some human beings, solely because of their race, could be owned by others?

If in 1787 the nation had been divided into two separate sovereignties—one the northern states and the other the southern states—the ultimate abolishment of slavery in the North would probably not have occurred any sooner than that which actually resulted under the gradual emancipation statutes in states such as Pennsylvania, Connecticut, New York, and New Jersey. Southern states had relatively little influence on debates over abolishment in northern states. But, as to the South, the ultimate emancipation process would have been far slower if in 1787 two separate sovereignties had been created. Most of the pressure for abolishment in southern states came from actions of individuals in northern states and pressure from northern states within the federal system. The North's ability to influence the South would have been less, had they been two separate sovereigns. By the 1860 census, there were 3,368,765 slaves in the southern states, while there were no slaves in either the New England states or in the northeast region, and only a few in the middle Atlantic states.

With such an economic interest in slavery in the southern states, there is no reason to assume that by 1863 the South would have been more receptive to an Emancipation Proclamation. The Emancipation Proclamation of 1863 issued by President Abraham Lincoln was directly related to the issue of secession—for if the South had not seceded, Lincoln would not have issued it. Of course, if the South had originally been created as a separate sovereignty in 1787, there would have been no necessity for secession and hence no southern Emancipation Proclamation in 1863. Consider as an example Brazil, which in many respects was purportedly far more liberal on race and slavery issues than any of the southern states, yet did not abolish slavery until 1888. Generally, milder forms of slavery were not subjected to the same degree of opposition as more harsh systems of bondage. Finally, if there had been a separate southern sovereignty, ultimately abolishing slavery at some date subsequent to 1863, the South would have operated more similar to the apartheid practices of South Africa than to the mandate of the Constitution of the United States, which it tried to circumvent anyway.

Because the abolitionists made a moral and political compromise of their position in 1787 by refusing to run the risk of creating two separate sovereigns, the slavery problem was partially solved on the battlefields of the 1860s. By abolitionists making this compromise in 1787, it was possible to have both North and South become subject to the subsequently enacted Thirteenth, Fourteenth and Fifteenth Amendments, which Justice Harlan suggested in his moving dissent in *Plessy v. Ferguson* was intended to make certain that:

> [I]n view of the Constitution, the eye of the law, there is in this country no superior, dominant, ruling class of citizens. There is no caste here. Our Constitution is color blind, and neither knows or tolerates classes among citizens. In respect of civil rights, all citizens are equal before the law. The humblest is the peer of the most powerful. The law regards man as man, and takes no account of his surroundings or of his color when his civil rights is guaranteed by the supreme law of the land.[10]

To repeat the intriguing philosophical question: are Americans—both black and white—as a nation, better off because of a 1787 compromise, which William Lloyd Garrison appropriately termed as a "covenant with death and an agreement with hell"?[11] By raising this question I am not lauding those slavemasters who insisted that the Constitution should give them the right to own others. To the contrary, I believe it is clear that the immediate consequences of a federal process sanctioning

---

10. *Plessy v. Ferguson*, 163 U.S. 537, 559 (J. Harlan dissenting) (1896).
11. William L. Garrison, Selections from the Writings and Speeches of William Lloyd Garrison 140–41 (1852).

and in many respects encouraging domestic slavery worked to the great detriment of slaves and free blacks.

D. Questions and Notes

Mounting agitation against slavery finally led Pennsylvania to become the first state to abolish slavery in the eighteenth century by *legislative* enactment when, in 1780, it passed "An Act for the Gradual Abolition of Slavery." "Gradual" was the key word in the Act, if one were asked to describe its effect on the majority of black people in the state. Those who were already slaves when the statute was passed were not freed by its enactment; only the black and mulatto children born *after* the passage of the law were to be freed and those only after serving their mothers' masters for twenty-eight years. Freedom was thus conferred upon a generation yet unborn, and "the living [slaves] were given merely the consolation of a free posterity."

As a state legislator morally opposed to slavery whose electoral district is equally divided on the issue and the statute, would you vote for or against the 1780 Pennsylvania Gradual Abolition Act? Would your answer change if you were a legislator in 1944 Nazi Germany and the statute under consideration was a "gradual protection of human life" act?

The most powerful words in the Constitution, "We the People," were the subject of much debate over the years. Whom do you think they meant to include when the drafters of the Constitution used those words? Currently, in the context of the immigration debate, the Constitution's use of the term "people" is used to show that it provides broad protections; in contrast, did the Founding Fathers have a narrow scope in mind?

The drafters of the Constitution used many equalitarian terms within the document, many of which they may not have actually meant. How would you characterize "the Founding Fathers?" Were they hypocrites and racists, realistic pragmatists, or both?

In 1987, during the bicentennial celebration of the creation of the Constitution, President Ronald Reagan reflected that the words of the Constitution "put wind in the sails of freedom."[12] Do you agree or disagree with this characterization?

E. Point/Counterpoint

In hindsight, if you were one of the members of the Constitutional Convention who was opposed to slavery, would you have signed the final document?

---

12. D. HOUCK AND A. KIEWE, ACTOR, IDEOLOGUE, POLITICIAN 299 (1993).

V. The Northern Approach to Free Blacks

A. Introduction

The words immortalized in the Declaration of Independence seem to embrace the principle of equal rights for all: "We hold these truths to be self-evident that all men are created equal." For blacks during the eighteenth and nineteenth centuries, however, the Constitution did not afford such protection. The law denied those few blacks not enslaved, most of the rights and privileges enjoyed by other Americans. Even in Northern states where slavery had been abolished, a careful distinction existed between granting African Americans liberty and providing them with political and social equality. That delineation was defined and maintained throughout the wide sweep of the legal system, from our most fundamental documents to state and local laws.

Free blacks were treated little better than slaves. They were denied political, economic, and social rights under the law and, in most instances, were prohibited from voting or participating in the political process. Even in the most progressive states, some free blacks who attempted to vote were beaten or killed. They were prohibited from obtaining an education, from engaging in certain types of employment, and from enjoying certain kinds of property ownership. Their travel was restricted, and they were required to pay extra taxes. Finally, schools, churches, and public accommodations were subject to *de jure* racial segregation. Flagrant segregation, as a matter of law, was widely practiced and unreservedly upheld. Despite such discriminatory treatment, a few free blacks were able to achieve some degree of economic and political success.

Paul Cuffe was born in 1759 as a free child. His father, Kofi, was an Ashanti in West Africa who was captured at the age ten and brought to the colonies as a slave, where he became the property of the Slocum family. Kofi spent his entire young life as a slave, taught himself the trade of carpentry, and gradually earned enough money to buy his freedom. Kofi was freed in the early 1740s and married Ruth Moses, a Wampanoag American Indian, in 1745. Becoming members of the Quaker church, Kofi and Ruth moved to Cuttyhunk Island in Massachusetts. Paul Cuffe was the seventh of their ten children. Kofi educated himself and he received an income for copying letters as well as being a carpenter. He eventually purchased a 166-acre farm in Dartmouth.

After his father's death in 1772, Cuffe became a "Marineer" at the age of sixteen. He traveled on cargo ships as well as whaling vessels where he acquired navigational skills. In 1779, Paul Cuffe and his brother David started a costal trade business where they transported cargo. The Cuffe brothers' business ventures also allowed them to act as blockade-runners for the Colonials during the Revolutionary War. They sailed with a crew that consisted primarily of African Americans and American Indians. Ultimately, Cuffe's business proved highly successful and lucrative as a result of the booming codfish industry in the Northeast further enabling him to expand his cargo business.

Cuffe later married Alice Pequit, a woman of Wampanoag heritage, like his mother. In 1799, Cuffe purchased 140 acres in Westport, Connecticut.

James Forten was born free in Philadelphia in 1766. He attended a Quaker school and at the age of 14 joined the colonial navy. When his navy service concluded, Forten returned to Philadelphia where he secured employment as a sail-maker. Several years later at the age of 20, Forten was promoted to foreman; and he took over the business when the owner retired in 1798. Forten invented several sail-handling devices that earned him over $100,000. Forten put his money to good use funding abolitionist newspapers. In 1833, he helped to start the American Anti-Slavery Society. Staying true to his beliefs, James Forten's company refused to rig any ship that participated in the slave trade.

The original Constitution did not expressly prohibit racial discrimination. The provisions that sustained slavery and laid a basis for discrimination were subtly meshed within several Clauses. Thus, between 1789 and 1857, the Supreme Court did not consider any direct challenges to racially discriminatory practices. Several state courts, however, contemplated such cases, but brazenly continued to uphold discriminatory treatment against blacks.

B. Background on *Crandall*

Like most other northern states, Connecticut had been a state where educating free blacks was controversial. In 1831, several abolitionists, including Arthur Tappan and William Lloyd Garrison, had unsuccessfully supported the idea of starting a black college located in New Haven near Yale University. Due to opposition by local community leaders, the idea was abandoned.

C. *Crandall v. The State of Connecticut*, 10 Conn. Rep. 339 (1834)

Goddard and *W.W. Ellsworth* for the plaintiff. *Judson* and *C.F. Cleaveland* for the state.

1. Facts

Judge WILLIAMS delivered the opinion of the Court.

This was an information, filed by the prosecuting attorney for the county of Windham, for a violation of the statute of 1833, regarding the instruction of coloured persons not inhabitants of this state. The information alleged, That at Canterbury, in said county, on the 24th of September, 1833, for the purpose of attending and being taught and instructed in a certain school, which before that time had been and then was set up, in said town of Canterbury, for the instruction and education of coloured persons, not inhabitants of this State, Prudence Crandall, of said Canterbury, with force and arms, willfully and knowingly did harbour and board certain coloured persons, to wit, Ann Eliza Hammond, and others, whose names are to the attorney aforesaid unknown, and who, when so harboured and boarded, were not inhabitants of any town in this state; all which acts and doings of the said Prudence Crandall were done and committed without the consent in writing first obtained of a majority of the civil authority and also of the select-men of said town of Canterbury, where said school was then situated; against the peace of this state, and contrary to the form and effect of the statute law of this state in such case made and provided.

2. Trial Court Opinion

Judge DAGGETT delivered the opinion of the Trial Court.

The preamble and first section of that act, are in the following words:

> Whereas, attempts have been made to establish literary institutions in this state, for the instruction of coloured persons belonging to other states and countries, which would tend to the great increase of the coloured population of the state, and thereby to the injury of the people: Therefore, be it erected by the Senate and House of Representatives, in General Assembly convened, That no person shall set up or establish in this state or harbour or board, for the purpose of attending or being taught or instructed in any such school, academy, or literary institution, any coloured person who is not an inhabitant of any town in this state, without the consent, in writing, first obtained of a majority of the civil authority, and also of the select men of the town in which such school, or literary institution is situated; and each and every person who shall knowingly do any act forbidden as aforesaid, or shall forfeit and pay a fine of one hundred dollars, and for the second offence, shall forfeit and pay a fine of two hundred dollars and so double for every offense of which he or she shall be convicted. And all informing officers are required to make due presentment of all breaches of this act. Provided, That nothing in this act shall extend to any district school established in any school society under the laws of this state, or to any incorporated academy or incorporated school for instruction in this state.

The attorney for the state claimed to have proved the defendant had harboured and boarded coloured persons for the purpose of attending the school mentioned in the information; and that such coloured persons were not inhabitants of this state, when so harboured and boarded, but that they belonged to the state of Rhode Island, Pennsylvania, and New York, and were born in those states respectively, of coloured parents there belonging and had continued to reside in the places of their birth until the Spring of the year 1833, when they came to Canterbury to attend said school, for the purpose of being instructed in the ordinary branches of school education. Upon these facts being proved, the attorney claimed that the defendant had incurred the penalty provided by the act; no claim being made that a license had been granted for the school. The defendant claimed, and prayed the court to instruct the jury, that if they should find these facts proved, such coloured persons were to be regarded as citizens of the states where they respectively belonged and were born; and that they were entitled to the privileges and immunities secured by the 2nd section of the 4th article of the Constitution of the United States and void. The court instructed the jury as follows:

> Many things said upon this trial, may be laid out of the case. The consideration of slavery, with all its overlays and degrading evil. The benefits, blessings and advantages of instruction and education, may also cease to claim your attention, except you may well consider that education is a 'fundamental privilege,' for this is the basis of all free government.

> Having read this law, the question comes to us with peculiar force, does it clearly violate the constitution of the United States? The section claimed to have been violated, reads as follows, to wit: *Art. 4. sec. 2.* The citizens of each state shall be entitled to all privileges and immunities of citizens in the several states. It has been urged, that this section was made to direct, exclusively, the action of the general government, and therefore, can never be applied to state laws. This is not the opinion of the court. The plain and obvious meaning of this provision, is, to secure to the citizens of all the states, the same privileges as are secured to our own, by our own state laws. Should a citizen of Connecticut purchase a farm in Massachusetts, and the legislature of Massachusetts tax the owner of that farm, four times as much as they would tax a citizen of Massachusetts, because the one reside in Connecticut and the other in Massachusetts, or should a law be passed, by either of those states, that no citizen of the other, should reside or trade in that other, this would, undoubtedly, be an unconstitutional law, and should be so declared.

> The act in question provides, that coloured persons, who are not inhabitants of this State, shall not be harboured and boarded for the purposes therein mentioned, within this state, without the consent of the civil authority and select-men of the town. We are, then, brought to the great question, are they citizens within the provisions of this section of the constitution? The law extends to all persons of colour not inhabitants of this state, whether they live in the state of New York, or in the West Indies, or in any other foreign country.

> In deciding this question, I am happy that my opinion can be revised, by the supreme court of this state and of the United States, should you return a verdict against the defendant.

> The persons contemplated in this act are not citizens within the obvious meaning of that section of the constitution of the United States, which I have just read. Let me begin, by putting this plain question. Are slaves citizens?

At the adoption of the constitution of the United States, every state was a slave state. Massachusetts had begun the work of emancipation within her own borders. And Connecticut, as early as 1784, had also enacted laws making all those free at the age of 25, who might be born within the State, after that time. We all know, that slavery is recognized in that constitution; and it is the duty of this court to take that constitution as it is, for we have sworn to support it. Although the term "slavery" cannot be found written out in the constitution, yet no one can mistake the object of the 3d section of the 4th article: "No person held to service or labour in one state, under the laws thereof, escaping into another, shall, in consequences of any law or regulation therein, be discharged from such service or labour, but shall be delivered, upon claim of the party to whom such service or labour may be due."

The 2d section of the 1st article, reads as follows:—"Representatives and direct taxes, shall be apportioned among the several states which may be included in this Union, according to their respective numbers, which shall be determined by adding to the whole number of free persons, including those bound to service for a term of years, and excluding Indians not taxed, three fifths of all other persons." The "other persons" are slaves, and they became the basis of representation, by adding them to the white population in that proportion. Then slaves were not considered citizens by the framers of the constitution.

A citizen means a freeman. By referring to Dr. Webster, one of the most learned men of this or any other country, we have the following definition of the term—Citizen: 1. A native of a city, or an inhabitant who enjoys the freedom and privileges of the city in which he resides. 2. A townsman, a man of trade, not a gentleman. 3. An inhabitant; a dweller; a dweller in any city, town or country. 5. In the United States, it means a person, native or naturalized, who has the privilege of exercising the elective franchise, and of purchasing and holding real estate.

Are Indians citizens? It is admitted in the argument, that they are not; but it is said, they belong to distinct tribes. This cannot be true; because all Indians do not belong to a tribe. It may be now added, that by the declared law of New York, Indians are not citizens; and the learned Chancellor Kent, says 'they never can be made citizens.' Indians were literally natives of our soil; they were born here; and yet they are not citizens.

The Mohegans were once a mighty tribe, powerful and valiant; and who among us ever saw one of them performing military duty, or exercising, with the white men, the privilege of the elective franchise, or holding an office? And what is the reason? I answer, they are not citizens, according to the acceptation of the term in the United States.

Are free blacks, citizens? It has been ingeniously said, that vessels may be owned and navigated, by free blacks, and the American flag will protect them; but you will remember, that the statute which makes that provision, is an act of Congress, and not the constitution. Admit, if you please, that Mr. Cuffee, a respectable merchant, has owned vessels, and sailed them under the American flag; yet this does not prove him to be such a citizen as the constitution contemplates. But that question stands undecided, by any legal tribunal within my knowledge. For the purposes of this case, it is not necessary to determine that question.

It has been also urged, that as coloured persons may commit treason, they must be considered citizens. Every person born in the United States, as well as every person who may reside here, owes allegiance, of some sort, to the government, because the government affords him protection. Treason against this government, consists in levying war against the government of the United States, or aiding its enemy in time of war. Treason may be committed, by persons who are not entitled to the elective franchise. For if they reside under the protection of the government, as much as if they were citizens.

I think Chancellor Kent, whose authority it gives me pleasure to quote, determines this question, by fair implication. Had this authority considered free blacks citizens, he had an ample opportunity to say so. But what he has said excludes that idea: 'In most of the United States, there is a distinction in respect to political privileges, between free white persons and free coloured persons of African blood; and in no part of the country do the latter, in point of fact, participate equally with the whites, in the exercise of civil and political rights. The African race are essentially a degraded caste, of inferior rank and condition in society. Marriages are forbidden between them and whites, in some of the states, and when not absolutely contrary to law, they are revolting, and regarded as an offence against public decorum. By the revised statutes of Illinois, published in 1820, marriages between whites and negroes, or mulattos, are declared void, and the persons so married are liable to be whipped, fined and imprisoned. By an old statute of Massachusetts, of 1705, such marriages were declared void, and are so still. A similar statute provision exists in Virginia and North Carolina. Such connexions in France and Germany, constitute the degraded state of concubinage, which is known in the civil law. But they are not legal marriages, because the parties want the contract. 2 Kent's Comm. 258.

I go further back still. When the constitution of the United States was adopted, every state (Massachusetts excepted,) tolerated slavery. And in some of the states, down to a late period, severe laws have been kept in force regarding slaves. With respect to New York, at that time, here laws and penalties were severe indeed; and it was not until July 4th, 1827, that this great state was ranked among the free states.

To my mind, it would be a perversion of terms, and the well known rule of construction, to say, that slaves, free blacks, or Indians, were citizens, within the meaning of that term, as used in the constitution. God forbid that I should add to the degradation of this race of men; but I am bound, by my duty, to say, they are not citizens.

I have thus shown you that this law is not contrary to the 2d section of the 4th art. of the constitution of the United States; for that embraces only citizens.

But there is still another consideration. If they were citizens, I am not sure this law would then be unconstitutional. The legislature may regulate schools. I am free to say, that education is a fundamental privilege; but this law does not prohibit schools. It places them under the care of the civil authority and select men; and why is not this a very suitable regulation? I am not sure but the legislature might make a law like this, extending to the white inhabitants of other states, who are unquestionably citizens, placing all schools for them under suitable boards of examination, for the public good; and I can see no objection to the board created by this act.

What can the legislature of this state do? It can make any law, which any legislature can make, unless it shall violate the constitution of the United States, or the constitution of its own state; and in my opinion, this law is not inconsistent with either.

The jury have nothing to do with the popularity or unpopularity of this or any other law, which may come before them for adjudication. They have nothing to do with its policy or impolicy. Your only enquiry is, whether it is constitutional.

I may say with truth, that there is no disposition in the judicial tribunals of this state, nor among the people, to nullify the laws of the state, but if constitutional, to submit to them and carry them into full effect, as good citizens. If individuals do not like the laws enacted by one legislature, their remedy is at the ballot boxes. It often occurs, on subjects of taxation, that laws are supposed, by some, to be unjust and oppressive. Nearly every session of the Assembly, attempts have been made to alter and change such laws; but as long as they exist, they must have effect.

You will now take this case into your consideration, and notwithstanding my opinion of the law, you will return your verdict according to law and evidence. I have done my duty, and you will do yours.

The jury returned a verdict against the defendant; and she thereupon filed a motion in arrest of judgment, on two grounds; first, that the superior court had not jurisdiction of the offence charged; and secondly, that the information was insufficient. The court overruled the motion and rendered judgment against the defendant to pay a fine of 100 dollars and costs. The defendant thereupon filed exceptions to the charge, and a motion in error, containing the following assignment of errors:

That the superior court, in the opinions expressed and intimations given to the jury in the cause, and in deciding that the superior court had jurisdiction of the same, and that said information and the matters therein contained were sufficient, manifestly erred and mistook the law; for that the court should have informed the jury, that said coloured persons were to be regarded as citizens of the states to which they respectively belonged and of the United States, and were entitled to the privileges and immunities secured by the 4th article of the constitution of the United States; and that said law of the state of Connecticut was repugnant to the constitution of the United States and void; and said court should have decided, that it had no jurisdiction of the cause, and that said information was insufficient.

3. Arguments on Appeal

Goddard and *W. W. Ellsworth*, for the plaintiff in error, contended, that the act of the General Assembly, on which this prosecution is founded, is unconstitutional and void. In support of this proposition, they insisted:

First, that the coloured persons mentioned in the information, are citizens of their respective states. If they were white, it is conceded they would be. The point turns, then, upon a distinction in colour only. This distinction, as the basis of fundamental rights, is, in the first place, novel. It is not recognized; by the common law of England, or the principles of the British constitution; by our own declaration of independence; or by the constitution of Connecticut.

Secondly, it would be extremely inconvenient, if not impracticable, in its application. Who can tell the proportions and trace the mixtures of blood? What shall be the scale for the ascertainment of citizenship? Shall one half, one quarter, one twentieth, or the least possible taint of Negro blood, be sufficient to take from its possessor the citizen character?

Thirdly, the persons in question are human beings, born in these states, and owe the same obligation to the state and to its government as white citizens. In all the writers on public law there is one ancient and universal classification of the people of a country: all who are born within the jurisdiction of a state are natives, and all others are aliens. This classification grows out of the doctrine of natural allegiance, a tie created by birth. All writers agree in the foundation of allegiance, and in its obligations, while it exists; some holding that it can never be thrown off, and some that it may be, under legislative enactments; but all agreeing that while the residence of the citizen continues in the state of his birth, allegiance demands obedience from the citizen and protection from the government. Allegiance is not peculiar to any one government or country; but it is held to exist in every country and every government where there are pretensions to social order and civil institutions. It reaches the man of one complexion as much as that of another. . . . The doctrine of natural allegiance was recognized in *Talbot v. Janson*, 3 Dal. 133. *The United States v. Williams*, in 1799, before Ellsworth, Ch. J. and Law, Dist. J. cited 2 Cranch 82. *Murray v. The Charming Betsey*, 2 Cranch 64. The case of *The Santissima Trinidad*, 7 Wheat. 283. *Jackson D. Smith v. Goodell*, 20 Johns. Rep. 188.

Fourthly, there is nothing in the constitutions of the native states of these persons, or in the Constitution of the United States, depriving them of fundamental rights on the ground of colour. [Here the counsel went into an examination of all the provisions bearing on this subject in the constitution or charter of Rhode Island, the constitutions of Pennsylvania and New York, the articles of confederation, the Constitution of the United States and the acts of Congress.]

Fifthly, by the free and excellent form of civil government, adopted by the people of this state, and secured by the charter of Charles II, as well as by the constitution of 1818, the privileges of the *habeus corpus* act, which, in Great Britain, made coloured people freeman, are adopted and established as fundamental principles. Stat. Conn. 5.22. ed. 1808. Const. Conn. art. 1. sec. 1. 5. 14. 16. 17. art. 6.

2. That as citizens, the constitution of the United States secures to the persons in question the right of residing in Connecticut, and pursuing the acquisition of knowledge, as people of colour may do, who are settled here.

In the first place, the language of the constitution (art. 4. sec. 2.) is universal and unqualified; it says, "every citizen."

Secondly, a citizen of another state may come here to reside, without being fined, or laid under any peculiar exactions. He must have a right to do what our citizens may do, under like circumstances.

Thirdly, he may come here to be educated. The right of education is a fundamental right. It is the main pillar of our free institutions. *Corfield v. Coryell*, 4 Wash. C. C. Rep. 850. 3 Story's Com. 674. 2 Kent's Com. 61.

The law under consideration forbids a citizen of another state to come here to pursue education, as all others may do, because he has not a legal settlement in the state. It is a crime to feed him, to teach him or entertain him.

The principal objections against these positions, are, first, that men of colour cannot *vote* in Connecticut; and therefore, they are not citizens of Connecticut.

The first answer to this objection is, that in Pennsylvania and New York, (as well as in Maine, New Hampshire, Massachusetts, Vermont, New Jersey, Delaware, Maryland, North Carolina and Tennessee,) they *can* vote; and if voting is the criterion of citizenship, they are citizens there.

But secondly, the right of voting is not the criterion of citizenship: the one has no natural or necessary connexion with the other. Cases may exist where persons vote who are not citizens, and where persons are citizens and do not vote. The right of suffrage is no where universal and absolute. It is founded in notions of internal police, varying frequently, even in the same government; whereas citizenship grows out of allegiance, which is every where the same, and is unchanging. Persons sometimes vote for one branch of the government only, as was lately the case in New York. How much of a citizen was such a voter? Formerly, property was a necessary qualification in Connecticut. Were none but persons of property citizens? Suppose a voter in Connecticut should lose his right of suffrage, by reason of criminal conduct, as by law he may do, does he cease to be a citizen? Does he become an alien? No female can vote, nor any minor; but are not females and minors citizens? . . .

Another objection is, that Indians are not citizens; and hence it is inferred, that these pupils are not. In the first place, these pupils are not Indians. But secondly, Indians have hitherto been treated as members of national tribes, in alliance with the United States, according to treaty stipulations and the intercourse law. They have been held to be without the practical jurisdiction of the states. But since Congress has withdrawn its ancient jurisdiction, the states have extended theirs over these tribes, it is not certain what is the exact political character of an Indian born in these states. Even in New York, before the late change in our Indian affairs, they were there decided to be citizens, by a unanimous opinion of the supreme court, on the ground of the state's having jurisdiction and the Indians owing allegiance. *Jackson D. Smith v. Goodell*, 20 Johns. Rep. 188. 191, 2, 3.

Again, it is objected, that slaves are not citizens. But these pupils are not slaves. The reason why slaves are not citizens, is, because they are held to be property, and not men, and hence have not freedom of choice or action. The reason does not reach these pupils.

It is further objected, that the legislature may, as it has often done, superintend and regulate schools; and that the act in question is only an exercise of that power. The fact asserted here is not true. The power in question is not one of mere supervision and regulation, but it is a power of exclusion on the ground of alienage. Such it is in effect; and so it was designed to be. . . .

The legislature may, undoubtedly, superintend public schools; for they are instituted by the legislature, and sustained by public money. Nor is it doubted that the legislature may superintend and regulate private schools, as it does trades, professions, taverns, sales at auction, peddling, etc. It may superintend and regulate all the pursuits of the citizens; but then this must be done, by a general and equal law. Mere birth in another state cannot be seized upon as ground of distinction and consequent privation. This is not consistent with the paramount authority of the constitution, that "the citizens of each state shall be entitled to all the privileges and immunities of citizens in the several states. . . ."

But it is asked, may we not keep out of Connecticut paupers and vagabonds; and have not such laws been of long standing? Stat. 281, 2. tit. 51. s. 6. 7. 8. This ancient statute was enacted before the adoption of the articles of confederation, or the present constitution of the United States, when this state had a right to exclude the citizens of other states or colonies; for they then stood in no other light than aliens. But this law is now contrary to the constitution of the United States, and cannot be sustained. If the 2nd section of the 4th article means any thing, it secures to a citizen of New York a right to come here, and remain here, if he offends against no general law. . . . So the state may guard itself against thieves from without or within, by punishing them for crimes committed in our territory, or by enacting general laws of prevention; but it cannot prohibit a citizen of the United States from entering this state and remaining in it, because he has offended elsewhere, or may offend again.

Judson and *C. F. Cleaveland*, for the state, (defendant in error,) after remarking upon the magnitude of the question, as affecting not the town of Canterbury alone, but every town in the state and every state in the Union; as the principles urged by the counsel for the plaintiff in error, if established, would, in their consequences, destroy the government itself and this American nation—blotting out this nation of white men and substituting one from the African race—thus involving the honour of the state, the dignity of the people and the preservation of its name—contended,

1. That the state does possess the power to regulate its own schools, and pursue its own systems of education, in its own chosen way, independently of the question of citizenship. The matter of education was never given up to the general government; because the structure, object, and end of that government were of a different character. The government has never attempted any control over education, in any one state in the Union, but only in the *District of Columbia*. The state governments have uninterruptedly exercised this power; and their capacity to do so will be found much more congenial, than that of the general government. We ought to be satisfied that the state sovereignties maintain their internal police—their domestic arrangements, while the general government moves on in its elevated sphere of action. . . .

It is incident to all these literary corporations, that students may be admitted or excluded at pleasure. Suppose the corporation of Yale College should, by solemn vote, prohibit students from South Carolina, would any constitutional question arise on that prohibition, or could they claim admission, as matter of right under the constitution? The answer is obvious. The corporation has that right of exclusion; and so has the state. Should the trustees of the Plainfield Academy pass an order that in future, no student from the state of Rhode Island should be admitted, is that a violation of the constitution of the United States? Surely not. The state created these corporations, and could not impart to them power it did not itself possess.

2. That these pupils are not "citizens" within the 2nd sect. of the 4th art. of the constitution of the United States, and as such entitled to all the privileges and immunities of citizens of the several states.

In deciding this question, every thing must depend upon the rules of construction, established by the common law. These rules are well understood, and as established in ages gone by, they will now be of infinite service in guiding to a correct result.

1st. The intention of the enacting power is to be sought for.

2d. The whole instrument or act must be taken together, so that its parts may be consistent with the whole. And

3d. The period of time when the enactment was made, embracing the language then in use, and the circumstances of the country, enter into the construction of the instrument and indicate its meaning. . . .

What was the intention of those who framed the constitution? Did they mean to place persons of colour on the footing of equality with themselves, and did they mean to make them citizens?

In answering this question, it matters little what may be the opinion of a few madmen or enthusiasts now, but what was the intention of the people of the United States, at the time when the constitution was adopted. . . . We must now advert to the condition of the country, and the circumstances of the human race, then upon the face of this country. The white men and the coloured men composed the grand divisions of the human family. The white men then were entitled to partic-ular privileges, above the coloured men: civil and political rights belonged, by the laws of all the states, to the former, but not to the latter. . . . Go back to the time when the constitution was made, and enquire after the condition of the country, and take into consideration all its circumstances, and all difficulties will be out of the way. Then it was not immoral to hold slaves. The best men bought and sold negroes, without a scruple. This impulse is of modern date; and however credit-able to the heart, cannot alter the constitution. The immortal Washington, who presided at the convention, and who subscribed the instrument, under the laws of Virginia held more than one hundred slaves, as his property, on that day; and he was not thus inconsistent. He never intended to have you say, that the portion of the human race which were held in bondage were slaves, and the residue of that same colour were citizens.

The distinction of colour, so far from being novel, is marked, in numerous ways, in our political system.

The first Congress after the constitution was adopted, was composed of many of those distinguished patriots, who framed the constitution, and from that circum-stance would be supposed to know what its spirit was. Some of the earliest work they performed for the country, was to establish by law a uniform rule of naturalization. The first law regarding naturalization was passed by Congress in 1790, and in it this precise and technical language is used: "Any alien, being a free white person, may become a citizen, by complying with the requisites hereinafter named." Chancel-lor Kent settles this question . . . : "The act of Congress confines the description of aliens capable of naturalization to 'free white persons.' I presume that this excludes the inhabitants of Africa and their descendants; and it may become a question, to what extent persons of mixed flood, as mulattoes, are excluded, and what shades or degrees of mixture of colour disqualify an alien from application for the benefits of the act of naturalization. Perhaps there might be difficulties as to the copper-coloured natives of America, or the yellow or tawny race of Asiatics, though I should doubt whether any of those were 'white persons,' within the purview of the law." 2 Kent's Com. 72.2nd ed.

Again: "In most of the United States, there is a distinction, in respect to political privileges, between free white persons and free coloured persons of African blood; and in no part of the country do the latter, in point of fact, participate equally with the whites, in the exercise of civil and political rights. The African race are essentially a degraded caste, of inferior rank and condition in society. Marriages are forbidden between them and whites, in some of the states, and when not absolutely contrary to law, they are revolting, and regarded as an offence against public decorum."

There is another part of their argument, which may require an answer. It is claimed, that all such state laws as may authorize the removal of paupers from one state, to that to which they belong, is an infringement of the constitution. A citizen of one state, although a pauper, may come here, and it is not in our power to remove him to his home. This doctrine, if true, would overturn half our state legislation. It would put down, as unconstitutional, our statute, which directs that persons coming from another state, may be warned out, and if they refuse, may be removed. Other states have a deep interest in this question. There is not a state in New England, nor in the Union, but have laws of this character. These laws are made in self defence—to preserve the state from the overwhelming effects of a bad population and from pauperism.

In relation to these various restrictions, we have a judicial decision of high authority, the case before referred to, of *Corfield v. Coryell*, 4 Wash. C.C. Rep. 371. It is in principle exactly similar to the one on trial. The counsel in that case, made the same argument that is here made—they urged an infringement of the 4th article; but the learned Judge denied that claim. Judge Washington lived when the constitution was adopted—he had imbibed its true spirit; and when called upon to construe its provisions, he gave harmony to the whole, while at the same time he preserves the state governments. His language is emphatic: "These fundamental rights are secured to the citizens, subject, nevertheless, to such restraints as the government may justly prescribe for the general good of the whole."

So we may say with equal propriety, and equal force, in this case, that the "privileges and immunities" of education shall be subject to such restraints as the government may justly prescribe, for the general good of the whole. And who will not say it is for the general good of the whole, to have all schools, academies and colleges, under the superintendence of some board of visitors, that the good ends of education may not be lost? Who will not say, that these states must regulate education, or it never can be regulated? Who will not say, that the whole system of education does not rest with the states? Who will not say, that a state police, and the whole system of pauper laws, do not remain with the state governments? Who will say, that Judge Washington was wrong in declaring that these fundamental privileges, whatever they may be, must be subject to restraints for the general good of the whole? May we not, under this wise decision, preserve our constitutions—our pauper laws—our police laws, and our school laws? Yes, we may exclude from our state a bad population;—we may provide that pauperism shall not overwhelm the state; and we may provide for its safety, in doing so.

4. Opinion of Connecticut Supreme Court

The first question has not been argued.

The other point presented, is, that the information is insufficient; and this has been argued on the ground, that this law is contrary to the Constitution of the United States.

That question is one of the deepest interest to this community, involving the rights of a large and increasing population, and the correct construction of a clause in the constitution as to the privilege of citizens of the several states in other states, and who compose that class called citizens.

When the nature and importance of these questions are considered, the difficulties actually attending the construction of this clause of the constitution, the magnitude of the interests at stake, the excitement which always attends the agitation of questions connected with the interests of one class, and the liberties of another, more particularly at the present time; the jealousies existing on the one hand, and the expectations excited on the other; no desire is felt to agitate the subject unnecessarily. In addition to which, the respect that is due from one branch of the government of this state to another, while it would never deter me from expressing, when necessary, an opinion against the constitutionality of a law, would always lead me to decline an expression on the subject, in a case not requiring such a decision. If then it appears, that the same result must follow, if we do not examine at all this constitutional question, which has been argued with so much ability, as if it was decided, for one, I feel no disposition to volunteer an opinion on that subject.

And on examination of this information, it seems to me, that no crime is charged upon this defendant, even if this law is constitutional.

The act provides:

> That no person shall set up or establish any school, academy or literary institution for the instruction and education of coloured persons, who are not inhabitants of this state; nor instruct or teach in any school, academy or literary institution whatsoever, within this state; or harbour or board, for the purpose of attending or being taught or instructed in any such school, academy or literary institution, any coloured person, who is not an inhabitant of any town in this state, without consent in writing first obtained of a majority of the civil authority, and also of the selectmen of the town in which such school, academy or literary institution is situated: Provided that nothing therein shall extend to any district school, incorporated academy, etc.

This information charges Prudence Crandall with harbouring and boarding certain coloured persons, not inhabitants of any town in this state, for the purpose of attending and being taught and instructed in a school, set up and established in said town of Canterbury, for the instruction and education of certain coloured persons, not inhabitants of this state.

She is not charged with setting up a school contrary to law, not with teaching a school contrary to law; but with harbouring and boarding coloured persons, not inhabitants of this state, without license, for the purpose of being instructed in such school.

It is, however, no where alleged, that the school was set up without license, or that the scholars were instructed by those who had no license.

If it is an offence within the statute to harbour or board such persons without license, under all circumstances, then this information is correct. But if the act, in the description of the offence itself, shows, that under some circumstances, it is no offence, then this information is defective.

The object in view of the legislature, as disclosed by the preamble, is to prevent injurious consequences resulting from the increase of the coloured population, by means of literary institutions, attempted to be established for the instruction of that class of inhabitants of other states.

Such institutions and instructors teaching such scholars are prohibited, unless licensed, as are also persons from harbouring or boarding scholars of that description, without license . . .

This information charges, that this school was set up in Canterbury, for the purpose of educating these persons of colour, not inhabitants of this state, that they might be instructed and educated; but omits to state, that it was not licensed. This omission is a fatal defect; as in an information on a penal statute, the prosecutor must set forth every fact that is necessary to bring the case within the statute; and every exception within enacting clause of the act, descriptive of the offense, must negated . . .

Being of opinion that the information is insufficient on this ground, it would seem that the judgment must of course be reversed. But as it is a rule of this court, that in every writ or motion in error, there shall be a special assignment of errors, and the court will hear no other; (6 Conn. Rep. 427) and as this writ, though it avers that this information is insufficient, points out only two causes of error, of which this is not one, it becomes important to enquire, what is the construction of that rule? Is this an error assigned within that rule? The object of this rule was to apprize the opposite party of the particular questions intended to be raised upon the writ of error; not of the arguments, but of the points to be argued.

The benefit of this would be almost lost, if under a general assignment of insufficiency of the declaration, the plaintiff in error might assign particular causes, and then rely upon other exceptions; it would rather tend to lead the opposite party from the real point of difficulty to examine other questions, as the case might be, of less difficulty. The rule might thus be made use of as a means to divert the defendant in error, rather than to present to him the real objection. Such a construction is not admissible.

This is not, then, so assigned, that the plaintiff in error can be heard upon it. What then shall be done? Shall the court render judgment, and that too in a criminal case, that the information is sufficient, when, upon inspection, they are clearly of opinion that it is insufficient? If the rule require this, it ought to be abolished without delay, as tending to place the court in a position which might be most embarrassing.

Suppose in a capital case, a writ of error was brought, alleging that the indictment was insufficient; and the court found it sufficient; but on looking at the record, discovered some other fatal defect: could it be their duty to affirm that judgment, and send the prisoner to execution? The rule admits of a construction which will effectuate its object, and yet not cripple the court. The plaintiff shall not be heard to allege any cause he has not assigned. This will be a sufficient inducement for him to point out every cause on which he relies. At the same time, if the court should see or believe, that some other defect existed, the rule would not prevent them from calling on the defendant in error to remove the objection, which had occurred to them, nor the court from deciding upon the objection, if it could not be obviated.

Such a construction of the rule, is entirely analogous to that which has long been adopted in the superior court, and has been found perfectly satisfactory. There is a rule, that no motion in arrest shall be allowed, (or heard) unless made within twenty-four hours after verdict. But if no such motion is made, did the court ever hesitate to arrest a judgment, if they discovered that the declaration was insufficient, or the record was so fatally defective, that any judgment upon it must be reversed?

If this practice is correct, it seems to me more important to adopt it in this court, from which there cannot (except in a particular case) be any appeal.

Such a construction is also supported, by the principles of a case recently decided in the court of King's Bench; where a writ of error was brought for error in fact. On the trial errors in law were discovered; and although it is a well settled rule, that errors in law and fact cannot be united in one writ, yet the court held, that it was their duty, *ex officio*, to look through the record, and to reverse the judgment, for those errors which could not, by the settled rules of proceedings, be assigned in that writ as a ground of error. *Castledine v. Mundy*, 4 Barn & Adol. 90 (24 Serg. & Lowb. 30)

5. Holding

The result, therefore, to which I have arrived, is, that there is error in the judgment complained of.

Judges BISSELL and CHURCH concurred in the judgment.

6. Judge Daggett Dissenting

Daggett had no doubt that the information was insufficient, for want of an averment that the school was not licensed; but as this had not been assigned as cause of error, he was of opinion, that the Court was precluded, by the rule of 1826, from regarding it as such; and consequently, that the judgment could not be reversed on that ground.

D. Commentary on *Crandall*

On appeal, the Connecticut Supreme Court dismissed the case on a technicality without reversing the trial court's ruling that free blacks were not citizens of the United States. This dismissal enabled the United States Supreme Court twenty-three years later to rely on *Crandall* in declaring that blacks, whether slave or free, were not citizens of the United States.

After the dismissal of the case, Prudence Crandall returned to her teaching duties. Crandall's victory, however, was short-lived. Soon after her return, the building where Crandall's school was located was destroyed by a fire started under suspicious circumstances. In response to the destruction of the school building, Crandall decided to leave Connecticut. With her departure, the school ceased operation.

E. Background on *Roberts*

Although most people look back to the famous 1896 United States Supreme Court case of *Plessy v. Ferguson* as the first legal challenge to racial segregation and discrimination in the United States, blacks challenged such racial practices long before *Plessy* and long before the passage of the Thirteenth and Fourteenth Amendments, which guaranteed the equal protection of the laws. In Pennsylvania, for example, blacks chose to form their own churches rather than worship in racially segregated arrangements.[13] In Massachusetts, protests led to the eradication of segregated seating on trains,[14] and, in the area of education, blacks resorted to state courts for relief against a segregated public school system.

By law, students in Massachusetts attended the school nearest their home without regard to race. By 1787, however, all but a handful of black students had withdrawn from public school because threats, harassment, and bullying from white classmates made their experience intolerable. That year, Revolutionary War hero Prince Hall organized efforts to petition the state legislature to open a school just for blacks. Lawmakers rejected the request, but 11 years later, Hall and his supporters began make-shift classes in the basement of his son's Beacon Hill home, charging 12 and a half cents per week for three and a half months of lessons a year. Enrollment expanded over the next 20 years, and the school moved to Beacon Hill's African Meeting House in 1808.

---

13. J. FRANKLIN, FROM SLAVERY TO FREEDOM 111–12 (1980).

14. LEONARD LEVY AND HARLAN PHILLIPS, THE ROBERTS CASE: SOURCE OF THE SEPARATE BUT EQUAL DOCTRINE, THE AMERICAN HISTORICAL REVIEW 517 (1950).

In 1815, Abiel Smith, a wealthy white businessman, bequeathed $2,000 upon his death to the City of Boston for the education of black children. Influenced by Thomas Jefferson's *Notes on Virginia*, Smith believed in colonizing blacks back to Africa to solve the nation's race "problem." Education was a way to prepare black children to establish independence from America's shores. Boston school officials used the gift to establish the Abiel Smith School and assumed responsibility for its operations. They also limited admission to blacks. The Smith School thus became America's first formally segregated black educational institution. Hall was its first teacher.

The School Committee joined with blacks to support the Smith School, but for very different reasons. The School Committee supported segregation. Blacks supported educational opportunity.

Over-crowded, under-funded, and unable to recruit enough qualified teachers, the quality of education at the Smith School began to suffer. A group of abolitionist reformers organized opposition to the school around the premise that segregation was a holdover from slavery meant to degrade and demean blacks. William Cooper Nell, head of Boston's Equal School Association, rallied concerned parents to demand that the Smith School be closed. Among them was a printer from Beacon Hill named Benjamin Roberts.

Roberts sued the City of Boston on his daughter's behalf, arguing for her right to attend the school closest to their home. A first grader when the suit began, five-year-old Sarah walked past five white schools each morning on her way to the Smith School for blacks. Robert Morris, a 27-year-old black lawyer, took up the cause. Prominent abolitionist and future senator Charles Sumner soon joined him, making them what is presumed to be the first mixed-race legal team in the country. Their partnership put their personal conviction against segregation on display. So did Sumner's argument before the Massachusetts Supreme Court.

Sumner argued not only against the "practical inconvenience" of barring Sarah from neighborhood white schools, but in favor of Massachusetts' constitutional commitment that "all men, without distinction of color or race, are equal before the law." Sumner also emphasized the social and emotional toll of segregation: "The separation of the schools, so far from being for the benefit of both races, is an injury to both. It tends to create a feeling of degradation in the blacks, and of prejudice and uncharitableness in the whites."

F. *Roberts v. The City of Boston*, 59 Mass. 198 (1850)

C. Sumner and R. Morris, Jr., for the plaintiff.

1. Facts

Justice SHAW delivered the opinion of the Court.

This was an action on the case, brought by Sarah C. Roberts, an infant, who sued by Benjamin F. Roberts, her father and next friend, against the city of Boston, under the statute of 1845, c. 214. which provides that any child, unlawfully excluded from public school instruction in this commonwealth, shall recover damages therefor against the city or town by which such public instruction is supported.

The case was submitted to the court of common pleas, from whence it came to this court by appeal, upon the following statement of facts:

Under the system of public schools established in the city of Boston, primary schools are supported by the city, for the instruction of all children residing therein between the ages of four and seven years. For this purpose, the city is divided for convenience, but not by geographical lines, into twenty-one districts, in each of which are several primary schools making the whole number of primary schools in the city of Boston one hundred and sixty-one. These schools are under the immediate management and superintendence of the primary school committee, so far as that committee has authority, by virtue of the powers conferred by votes of the general school committee.

At a meeting of the general school committee, held on the 12th of January, 1848, the following vote was passed:—

> Resolved, that the primary school committee be, and they hereby are, authorized to organize their body and regulate their proceedings as they may deem most convenient; and to fill all vacancies occurring in the same, and to remove any of their members at their discretion during the ensuing year; and that this board will cheerfully receive from said committee such communications as they may have occasion to make.

The city of Boston is not divided into territorial school districts; and the general school committee; by the city charter, have the care and superintendence of the public schools. In the various grammar and primary schools, white children do not always or necessarily go to the schools nearest their residences; and in the case of the Latin and English high schools (one of each of which is established in the city) most of the children are obliged to go beyond the school houses nearest their residences.

The regulations of the primary school committee contain the following provisions:—

> ADMISSIONS. No pupil shall be admitted into a primary school, without a ticket of admission from a member of the district committee.

> ADMISSIONS OF APPLICANTS. Every member of the committee shall admit to his school, all applicants, of suitable age and qualifications, residing nearest to the school under his charge, (excepting those for whom special provision has been made,) provided the member in his school will warrant the admission.

> SCHOLARS TO GO TO SCHOOLS NEAREST THEIR RESIDENCES. Applicants for admission to the schools, (with the exception and provision referred to in the preceding rule,) are especially entitled to enter the schools nearest to their places of residence.

At the time of the plaintiff's application, as hereinafter mentioned, for admission to the primary school, the city of Boston had established, for the exclusive use of colored children, two primary schools, one in Belknap street, in the eight school district, and one in Sun Court street, in the second school district.

The colored population of Boston constitute less than one sixty-second part of the entire population of the city. For half a century, separate schools have been kept in Boston for colored children, and the primary school for colored children in Belknap street was established in 1820, and has been kept there ever since. The teachers of this school have the same compensation and qualifications as in other like schools in the city. Schools for colored children were originally established at the request of colored citizens, whose children could not attend the public schools, on account of the prejudice then existing against them.

The plaintiff is a colored child, of five years of age, a resident of Boston, and living with her father, since the month of March, 1847, in Andover street, in the sixth primary school district. In the month of April, 1847, she being of suitable age and qualifications, (unless her color was a disqualification,) applied to a member of the district primary school committee, having under his charge the primary school nearest to her place of residence, for a ticket of admission to that school, the number of scholars therein warranting her admission, and no special provision having been made for her, unless the establishment of the two schools for colored children exclusively, is to be so considered. . . .

The member of the school committee, to whom the plaintiff applied, refused her application, on the ground of her being a colored person, and of the special provision made as aforesaid. The plaintiff thereupon applied to the primary school committee of the district, for admission to one of their schools, and was in like manner refused admission, on the ground of her color and the provision aforesaid. . . . She thereupon petitioned the general primary school committee, for leave to enter one of the schools nearest her residence. That committee referred the subject to the committee of the district, with full powers, and the committee of the district thereupon again refused the plaintiff's application, on the sole ground of color and the special provision aforesaid, and the plaintiff has not since attended any school in Boston. Afterwards, on the 15th of February, 1848, the plaintiff went into the primary school nearest her residence, but without any ticket of admission or other leave granted, and was on that day ejected from the school by the teacher.

The school established in Belknap street is twenty-one hundred feet distant from the residence of the plaintiff, measuring through the streets; and in passing from the plaintiff's residence to the Belknap street school, the direct route passes the ends of two streets in which there are five primary schools. The distance to the school in Sun Court street is much greater. The distance from the plaintiff's residence to the nearest primary school is nine hundred feet. The plaintiff might have attended the school in Belknap street, at any time, and her father was so informed, but he refused to have her attend there.

In 1846, George Putnam and other colored citizens of Boston petitioned the primary school committee, that exclusive schools for colored children might be abolished, and the committee, on the 22nd of June, 1846, adopted the report of a sub-committee, and a resolution appended thereto, which was in the following words:

> Revised, that in the opinion of this board, the continuance of the separate schools for colored children, and the regular attendance of all such children upon the schools, is not only legal and just but is best adapted to promote the education of that class of our population.

The court was to draw such inferences from the foregoing facts as a jury would be authorized to draw; and the parties agreed that if the plaintiff was entitled to recover, the case should be sent to a jury to assess damages; otherwise the plaintiff was to become nonsuit.

2. Opinion of Massachusetts Supreme Court

The present case does not involve any question in regard to the legality of the Smith school, which is a school of another class, designed for colored children more advanced in age and proficiency; though much of the argument, affecting the legality of the separate primary schools, affects in like manner that school. But the question here is confined to the primary schools alone. The plaintiff had access to a school, set apart for colored children, as well conducted in all respects, and as well fitted, in point of capacity and qualification of the instructors, to advance the education of children under seven years old, as the other primary schools; the objection is, that the schools thus open to the plaintiff are exclusively appropriated to colored children, and are at a greater distance from her home. Under these circumstances, has the plaintiff been unlawfully excluded from public school instruction? Upon the best consideration we have been able to give the subject, the court are all of opinion that she has not.

It will be considered, that this is a question of power, or of the legal authority of the committee entrusted by the city with this department of public instruction; because, if they have the legal authority, the expediency of exercising it in any particular way is exclusively with them.

The great principle, advanced by the learned and eloquent advocate of the plaintiff, is, that by the constitution and laws of Massachusetts, all persons without distinction of age or sex, birth or color, origin or condition, are equal before the law. This, as a broad general principle, such as ought to appear in a declaration of rights, is perfectly sound; it is not only expressed in terms, but pervades and animates the whole spirit of our constitution of free government. But, when this great principle comes to be applied to the actual and various conditions of persons in society, it will not warrant the assertion, that men and women are legally clothed with the same civil and political powers, and that children and adults are legally to have the same functions and be subject to the same treatment; but only that the rights of all, as they are settled and regulated by law, are equally entitled to the paternal consideration and protection of the law, for their maintenance and security. What those rights are, to which individuals, in the infinite variety of circumstances by which they are surrounded in society, are entitled, must depend on laws adapted to their respective relations and conditions.

Conceding, therefore, in the fullest manner, that colored persons, the descendants of Africans, are entitled by law, in this commonwealth, to equal rights, constitutional and political, civil and social, the question then arises, whether the regulation in question, which provides separate schools for colored children, is a violation of any of these rights.

The statute, after directing what length of time schools shall be kept in towns of different numbers of inhabitants and families, provides (§ 10) that the inhabitants shall annually choose, by ballot, a school committee, who shall have the general charge and superintendence of all the public schools in such towns. There being no specific direction how schools shall be organized; how many schools shall be kept; what shall be the qualifications for admission to the schools; the age at which children may enter; the age to which they may continue; these must all be regulated by the committee, under their power of general superintendence.

There is, indeed, a provision (§§ 5 and 6) that towns may and in some cases must provide a high school and classical school, for the benefit of all the inhabitants. It is obvious how this clause was introduced; it was to distinguish such classical and high schools, in towns districted, from the district schools. These schools being of a higher character, and designed for pupils of more advanced age and greater proficiency, were intended for the benefit of the whole of the town, and not of particular districts. Still it depends upon the committee, to prescribe the qualifications, and make all the reasonable rules, for organizing such schools and regulating and conducting them.

The power of general superintendence vests a plenary authority in the committee to arrange, classify, and distribute pupils, in such a manner as they think best adapted to their general proficiency and welfare. If it is thought expedient to provide for very young children, it may be, that such schools may be kept exclusively by female teachers, quite adequate to their instruction, and yet whose services may be obtained at a cost much lower than that of more highly qualified male instructors. So if they should judge it expedient to have a grade of schools for children from seven to ten, and another for those from ten to fourteen, it would seem to be within their authority to establish such schools. So too it would seem to be within their authority to separate male and female pupils into different schools. It has been found necessary, that is to say, highly expedient, at times, to establish special schools for poor and neglected children, who have passed the age of seven, and have become too old to attend the primary school, and yet have not acquired the rudiments of learning, to enable them to enter the ordinary schools. If a class of youth, of one or both sexes, is found in that condition, and it is expedient to organize them into a separate school, to receive the special training, adapted to their condition, it seems to be within the power of the superintending committee, to provide for the organization of such special school.

A somewhat more specific rule, perhaps, on these subjects, might be beneficially provided by the legislature; but yet, it would probably be quite impracticable to make full and precise laws for this purpose, on account of the different condition of society in different towns. In towns of a large territory, over which the inhabitants are thinly settled, an arrangement or classification going far into detail, providing different schools for pupils of different ages, of each sex, and the like, would require the pupils to go such long distances from their homes to the schools, that it would be quite unreasonable. But in Boston, where more than one hundred thousand inhabitants live within a space so small, that it would be scarcely an inconvenience to require a boy of good health to traverse daily the whole extent of it, a system of distribution and classification may be adopted and carried into effect, which may be useful and beneficial in its influence on the character of the schools, and in its adaptation to the improvement and advancement of the great purpose of education, and at the same time practicable and reasonable in its operation.

In the absence of special legislation on this subject, the law has vested the power in the committee to regulate the system of distribution and classification; and when this power is reasonably exercised, without being abused or perverted by colorable pretenses, the decision of the committee must be deemed conclusive. The committee, apparently upon great deliberation, have come to the conclusion, that the good of both classes of schools will be best promoted, by maintaining the separate primary schools for colored and for white children, and we can perceive no ground to doubt, that this is the honest result of their experience and judgment.

It is urged, that this maintenance of separate schools tends to deepen and perpetuate the odious distinction of caste, founded in a deep-rooted prejudice in public opinion. This prejudice, if it exists, is not created by law, and probably cannot be changed by law. Whether this distinction and prejudice, existing in the opinion and feelings of the community, would not be as effectually fostered by compelling colored and white children to associate together in the same schools, may well be doubted; at all events, it is a fair and proper question for the committee to consider and decide upon, having in view the best interests of both classes of children placed under their superintendence, and we cannot say, that their decision upon it is not founded on just grounds of reason and experience, and in the results of a discriminating and honest judgment.

3. Holding

The increased distance, to which the plaintiff was obliged to go to school from her father's house, is not such, in our opinion, as to render the regulation in question unreasonable, still less illegal.

On the whole the court are of opinion, that upon the facts stated, the action cannot be maintained.

G. Commentary on *Roberts*

Leonard Levy and Harlan Phillips

The Roberts Case: Source of the Separate But Equal Doctrine*

By 1855 the unceasing efforts of the abolitionists and free blacks proved to be of greater weight in Massachusetts than the opinion of its distinguished chief justice. A new statute was enacted which rooted out the last legal refuge of discrimination. Nevertheless, courts throughout the nation continued to play the Shaw record of "separate but equal" long after it had worn out its validity as law in the state of its origin.

In constitutional history, however, Shaw's opinion has had a continuing vitality. It was initially cited with approval by the high court of the Territory of Nevada in 1872. Two years later the California Supreme Court endorsed the doctrine by quoting most of Shaw's opinion, and concluded: "We concur in these views and they are decisive." The courts of New York, Arkansas, Missouri, Louisiana, West Virginia, Kansas, Oklahoma, South Carolina, and Oregon have also relied upon the *Roberts* case as a precedent for upholding segregated education. It has been mentioned by lower federal courts twice in recent years, as well as on earlier occasions. In the United States Supreme Court, the *Roberts* case was first discussed by Justice Clifford in *Hall v. De Cuir* as an authority for the rule that "equality does not mean identity." In *Plessy v. Ferguson*, the court turned to Shaw's opinion as a leading precedent for the validity of state legislation which required segregation of the white and colored races "in places where they are liable to be brought into contact. . . ." When it is considered that the *Plessy* case itself is deemed the leading authority on the constitutionality of the "separate but equal" doctrine, and is universally cited in all segregation cases, the influence of the *Roberts* case has been immeasurable.

The American Historical Review 517 (1950).
Copyright © 1950 *The American Historical Review.*
Reprinted with permission of The American Historical Society.

In ruling against Roberts, the Massachusetts Supreme Court concluded that neither state law nor the Constitution prohibited segregation as long as such segregation was reasonable in light of the circumstances. In the court's view, the only applicable limitations were procedural ones. Absent fraud or coercion in government deliberations, racial segregation of blacks, unlike segregation based on hair color, was not prohibited by state constitutional language requiring racial equality. In Chief Justice Shaw's view, public school officials were free to conclude that it was as American as apple pie to separate blacks from whites in public schools.

---

* (footnotes omitted).

H. Questions and Notes

Judges are more responsive than legislators to the prevailing sentiment and prejudice of the electorate. Do you agree or disagree with this statement? Do the decisions in *Crandall* and *Roberts* support or refute your position?

While *Crandall* and *Roberts* were state court decisions, the Supreme Court would later rely upon them. What major Supreme Court cases cite *Crandall* and *Roberts*?

I. Point/Counterpoint

In authoring the opinion in *Roberts*, Chief Justice Shaw explained the relationship between racial prejudice and the law. Justice Shaw reasoned:

> It is urged, that this maintenance of separate schools tends to deepen and perpetuate the odious distinction of caste, founded in a deep-rooted prejudice in public opinion. This prejudice, if it exists, is not created by law, and probably cannot be changed by law.

Do you agree or disagree with Chief Justice Shaw? What led Shaw to resign any hope that the system of justice could be used to combat deeply entrenched discriminatory ideologies? If changing a "deep-rooted prejudice" cannot be facilitated through the legal system, what other approaches are available?

VI. The Southern Approach to Slavery and Free Blacks

A. Introduction

> Not like the brazen giant of Greek fame,
> With conquering limbs astride from land to land;
> Here at our sea-washed, sunset gates shall stand
> A mighty woman with a torch, whose flame
> Is the imprisoned lightning, and her name
> Mother of Exiles. From her beacon-hand
> Glows world-wide welcome; her mild eyes command
> The air-bridged harbor that twin cities frame,
> "Keep ancient lands, your storied pomp!" cries she
> With silent lips. "Give me your tired, your poor,
> Your huddled masses *yearning to breathe free*,
> The wretched refuse from your teeming shore.
> Send these, the homeless, tempest-tost to me,
> I lift my lamp beside the *golden door*!"[15]

---

15. Emma Lazarus, "The New Colossus," reprinted in THE WORLD OF EMMA LAZARUS 178–79 (H.E. Jacob ed., 1949) (emphasis added). "The New Colossus," Emma Lazarus's sonnet to the

Emma Lazarus' poem, inscribed on the pedestal of the Statue of Liberty, captures the spirit of millions of immigrants who "yearned to breathe free" and who found freedom upon American shores. Those eloquent words also stand as a stark reminder that, for more than two centuries, American law denied Africans any "golden door" of welcome when they entered the United States as slaves.

Since the arrival of the first Africans in North America in 1619, the legal system sanctioned oppression and discrimination against blacks. American law condoned the enslavement of blacks and upheld such abhorrent practices as the kidnapping, torture, and forced labor of blacks as part of the institution of American slavery. Moreover, the law in most states made it a crime for a slave to obtain an education, to own property, or to participate in the political process. Slaves were deemed under the law to be property possessing no personal rights or legal protections.

B. Background on *Hudgins*

While most blacks were slaves, the Constitution did not require their enslavement. Rather, bondage based upon color was a product of state law. In Virginia, for example, all whites were presumed to be free while all blacks were presumed to be slaves. By denying blacks the "presumption in favor of liberty" contained in the 1776 Virginia Bill of Rights and assigning blacks the burden of proof in freedom suits, Virginia institutionalized black enslavement.

C. *Hudgins v. Wrights*, 11 Va. 134 (1806)

1. Facts

Judge TUCKER delivered a concurring opinion of the Court.

In this case, the paupers claim their freedom as being descended from Indians entitled to their freedom. They have set forth their pedigree in the bill, which the evidence proves to be fallacious. But as there is no Herald's Office in this country, nor even a Register of births for any but white persons, and those Registers are either all lost, or of all records probably the most imperfect, our Legislature, even in a writ of *praecipequod reddat*, has very justly dispensed with the old common law precision required in a writ of right, and the reason for dispensing with it in

---

Statue of Liberty, was inscribed on a bronze plaque on the statue's pedestal in 1903.

The Statue of Liberty was originally the model of a black woman holding chains. French historian Edourd de Laboulaye, Chairman of the French anti-slavery society, and sculptor Frederic Auguste Bartholdi, proposed to the government of France the idea of the Statue of Liberty. The statue would be a gift in recognition of the role of black soldiers in winning the Civil War and ending slavery. In 1884, when the model of the statue was presented to the U.S. Minister to France, he felt that the dominant view of the broken chains would be offensive to former supporters of the Confederacy because it would be a reminder to the defeated South that blacks had participated in winning their freedom. Bartholdi was encouraged to alter the image and change the model.

the present case, is a thousand times strong. In a claim for freedom, like a claim for money had any received, the plaintiff may well be permitted to make out his case on the trial according to the evidence.

What then is the evidence in this case. Unequivocal proof adduced perhaps by the defendant, that the plaintiffs are in the maternal line descended from Butterwood Nan, an old Indian woman;—that she was 60 years old, or upwards, in the year 1755;—that it was always understood, as the witness Robert Temple says, that her father was an Indian, though he cautiously avoids saying he knew, or ever heard, who, or what, her mother was. The other witness Mary Wilkinson, the only one except Robert Temple who had ever seen her, describes her as an old Indian: and her testimony is strengthened by that of the other witnesses, who depose that her daughter Hannah had long black hair, was of a copper complexion, and generally called an Indian among the neighbours;—a circumstance which could not well have happened, if her mother had not had an equal, or perhaps a larger portion of Indian blood in her veins. As the rule partus sequitur ventrem obtains in this country, the deposition of Robert Temple as to who was reputed to be the father of Butterwood Nan, without noticing her mother, is totally irrelevant to the cause. It could not serve the complainant, a fortiori it shall not prejudice her. It was, perhaps, intended as a sort of negative pregnant. But it has not even the tithe of that importance in my estimation.

In aid of the other evidence, the Chancellor decided upon his own view. This, with the principles laid down in the decree, had been loudly complained of.

2. Trial Court Opinion

On the hearing, the late chancellor, perceiving from his own view, that the youngest of the appellees was perfectly white, and that there were gradual shades of difference in colour between the grand-mother, mother and grand-daughter, (all of whom were before the court) and considering the evidence in the cause, determined that the appellees were entitled to their freedom; and, moreover, on the ground that freedom is the birthright of every human being, which sentiment is strongly inculcated by the first article of our "political catechism," the bill of rights—he laid it down as a general position, that whenever one person claims to hold another in slavery, the onus probandi lies on the claimant.

3. Opinion of Virginia Court of Appeals

As a preliminary to my opinion upon this subject, I shall make a few observations upon the laws of our country, as connected with natural history.

From the first settlement of the colony of Virginia to the year 1778 (Oct. Sess.) all negroes, Moors, and mulattoes, except Turks and Moors in amity with Great Britain, brought into this country by sea, or by land, were slaves. And by the uniform declarations of our laws, the descendants of the females remain slaves, to this day, unless they can prove a right to freedom, by actual emancipation, or by descent in the maternal line from an emancipated female.

By the adjudication of the General Court, in the case of Hannah and others against Davis, April term, 1777, all American Indians brought into this country since the year 1705, and their descendants in the maternal line, are free. Similar judgments have been rendered in this court. But I carry the period further back, *viz.* to the 16th day of April, 1691, the commencement of a session of the General Assembly at which an act passed, entitled "An Act for a free trade with Indians," the title of which (chap. 9,) will be found in the edition of 1733, p. 94: And the enacting clause of which, I have reason to believe, is in the very words of the act of 1705, upon which this Court have pronounced judgment in the cases referred to.

I will here mention those reasons. On the trial of a similar question on the Eastern Shore, two copies of Purvis's edition of the laws of Virginia, were produced. At the end of both was added a manuscript transcript of all the acts of Assembly subsequently passed for a series of years; the titles, number of chapters, &c. perfectly agreeing with the titles, number and order in which they are printed in the edition of 1733. In one of these copies, (both evidently of ancient date, and as I think both attested by the secretary of the colony, (1) I found the enacting clause in the same precise words, as they stand in the act of 1705.(2) In the other copy, the leaf on which the act must have been transcribed, was with one, or at most two others, evidently torn out: probably with a view to hide the act from the scrutinizing eye of a Court. I think it highly probable, that at that period, the County Courts were furnished with the laws of the colony in this mode; there being at that time no printing presses in Virginia, Purvis's collection being printed in England. I have myself a mutilated copy of the same character and description; but those in whose possession it had been, had torn out almost a hundred pages at the beginning, and so many at the end as not to leave the act in question, before I became possessed of it. These are my reasons for referring the commencement of the law in question to so remote a period; for the acts of 1705, were like those of 1792, a digest of the former laws of the colony, rather than a new code. — By an act passed in the year 1679, it was, for the better encouragement of soldiers, declared that what Indian prisoners should be taken in a war in which the colony was then engaged should be free purchase to the soldier taking them. In 1682, it was declared that all servants brought into this country, by sea or land, not being Christians, whether negroes, Moors, mulattoes, or Indians, except Turks and Moors in amity with Great Britain; and all Indians which should thereafter be sold by neighboring Indians, or any others trafficking with us, as slaves, should be slaves to all intents and purposes. The General Court held, (and I presume this Court, consisting nearly of the same judges, have done the same,) that passing the act authorizing a free and open trade for all persons, at all times, and at all places, with all Indians whatsoever, did repeal the acts of 1679 and 1682. I concur most heartily in that opinion; referring the commencement of that act to 1691 instead of 1705, for the reasons mentioned. Consequently I draw this conclusion, that all American Indians are prima facie free: and that where the fact of their nativity and descent, in a maternal line, is satisfactorily established, the burthen of proof thereafter lies upon the party claiming to hold them as slaves. To effect which, according to my opinion, he must prove the progenitrix of the party claiming to be free, to have been brought into Virginia, and made a slave between the passage of the act of 1679, and its repeal in 1691.

All white persons are and ever have been free in this country. If one evidently white, be notwithstanding claimed as a slave, the proof lies on the party claiming to make the other his slave.

Though I profess not an intimate acquaintance with the natural history of the human species, I shall add a few words on the subject as connected with the preceding laws.

Nature has stampt upon the African and his descendants two characteristic marks, besides the difference of complexion, which often remain visible long after the characteristic distinction of colour either disappears or becomes doubtful; a flat nose and woolly head of hair. The latter of these characteristics disappears the last of all: and so strong an ingredient in the African constitution is this latter character, that it predominates uniformly where the party is in equal degree descended from parents of different complexions, whether white or Indians; giving to the jet black lank hair of the Indian a degree of flexure, which never fails to betray that the party distinguished by it, cannot trace his lineage purely from the race of Native Americans. Its operation is still more powerful where the mixture happens between persons descended equally from European and African parents. So pointed is this distinction between the natives of Africa and the aborigines of America, that a man might as easily mistake the glossy, jetty clothing of an American bear for the wool of a black sheep, as the hair of an American Indian for that of an African, or the descendant of an African. Upon these distinctions as connected with our laws, the burthen of proof depends. Upon these distinctions not unfrequently does the evidence given upon trials of such questions depend; as in the present case, where the witnesses concur in assigning to the hair of Hannah, the daughter of Butterwood Nan, the long, straight, black hair of the native aborigines of this country. That such evidence is both admissible and proper, I cannot doubt. That it may at sometimes be necessary for a Judge to decide upon his own view, I think the following case will evince.

Suppose three persons, a black or mulatto man or woman with a flat nose and wooly head; a copper-colored person with long jetty black, straight hair; and one with a fair complexion, brown hair, not wooly nor inclining thereto, with a prominent Roman nose, were brought together before a Judge upon a writ of Habeas Corpus, on the ground of false imprisonment and detention in slavery: that the only evidence which the person detaining them in his custody could produce was an authenticated bill of sale from another person, and that the parties themselves were unable to produce any evidence concerning themselves, or whence they came. How must a judge act in such a case? I answer he must judge from his own view. He must discharge the white person and the Indian out of custody, taking surety, if the circumstances of the case should appear to authorize it, that they should not depart the state within a reasonable time, that the holder may have an opportunity of asserting and proving them to be lineally descended in the maternal line from a female African slave; and he must redeliver the black or mulatto person, with the flat nose and wooly hair to the person claiming to hold him or her as a slave, unless the black person or mulatto could procure some person to be bound for him, to produce proof of his descent, in the maternal line, from a free female ancestor. But if no such caution should be required on either side, but the whole case be left with the Judge, he must deliver the former out of custody, and permit the latter to remain in slavery, until he could produce proofs of his right to freedom. This case shows my interpretation how far the *onus probandi* may be shifted from one party to the other: and is, I trust, a sufficient comment upon the case to shew that I do not concur with the Chancellor in his reasoning on the operation of the first clause of the Bill of Rights, which was notoriously framed with a cautious eye to this subject, and was meant to embrace the case of free citizens, or aliens only; and not by a side wind to overturn the rights of property, and give freedom to those very people whom we have been compelled from imperious circumstances to retain, generally, in the same state of bondage that they were in at the revolution, in which they had no concern, agency or interest.

4. Holding

But notwithstanding this difference of opinion from the Chancellor, I heartily concur with him in pronouncing the appellees absolutely free; and am therefore of opinion that the decree be affirmed.

D. Commentary on *Hudgins*

A. Leon Higginbotham, Jr. and F. Michael Higginbotham

"Yearning to Breathe Free": Legal Barriers Against and Options in Favor of Liberty in Antebellum Virginia

The effect of the opinion in *Hudgins* was to impose upon all black people a heavier burden in freedom suits on account of their "woolier hair, their flatter noses, or their darker skin." As did many white Virginians, Judge Tucker equated slavery with blackness almost as if there were no free blacks in Virginia. As of 1800, however, over 20,000 free blacks resided in the state. More than thirty years earlier in England, Francis Hargrave, counsel in *Sommersett v. Stuart*, had successfully argued for the application of the common law doctrine of *in favoram liberatis* in British courts hearing similar freedom suits. In *Hudgins*, the Virginia Supreme Court of Appeals implicitly rejected this traditional presumption in favor of liberty for all persons, replacing it with a presumption in favor of slavery for those with African features. Whites or "copper-colored person[s] with long jetty black, straight hair" referring to Native-Americans were presumed to be free. Accordingly, the burden always fell upon the black person to disprove the claim of an owner's right to enslave. Such a burden was impossible for most blacks with legitimate freedom claims because of the difficulty of acquiring the documentation and testimony necessary to defeat this presumption.

Since Virginia was a leading slave state, its type of laws were adopted in many other jurisdictions; laws which provided that white and light-skinned people would be presumptively free while black people would be presumptively slaves. Consequently, the color of a slave was the single most important factor in determining the outcome of a freedom suit.

For the vast majority of slaves, the only realistic means of release from life in bondage were extralegal. A few slaves, like Nat Turner and Gabriel Prosser, attempted to organize slaves in rebellion. Others, like Harriet Tubman and Frederick Douglass, were able to escape to states where slavery had been abolished.

68 *New York University Law Review* 1213, 1242, 1271.
Copyright © (1993) *New York University Law Review*.
Reprinted with permission of the *New York University Law Review*.

E. Background on *Souther*

Life was mercilessly harsh for slaves. Unlike other societies throughout history that accorded slaves varying degrees of rights, under American law, slaves had no personal rights. The slave owner possessed complete dominion over the slave and was free to engage in any measure of oppressive practice against those held in bondage. For most slaves that meant long hours of arduous labor, minimal food and shelter, separation from parents or children, and physical beatings. In addition, male owners often raped their female slaves.

In June of 1855, an African-American woman named Celia killed a man for whom she worked as a slave and with whom she had been forced to have a sexual relationship for several years. Celia killed him because, despite her numerous attempts to dissuade him, slave-owner Robert Newsom forcibly and repeatedly sought to have sexual intercourse with her. Celia was convicted of murder in a Missouri trial court and subsequently hanged; her defense of justification, based on the fact that she was resisting an attempted rape, was rejected by the trial court. The judge ruled that Celia was not entitled to resist the sexual advances of her owner due to her status as a slave. As property of her slave-owner, she had no rights of her own, including no right to defend her own well-being.

The 1851 case of *Souther v. The Commonwealth* reveals the same legal framework in which slaves have no rights, and they are valued only as property. Souther, a slave-owner, severely tortured and whipped one of his slaves, named Sam, who died as a result. The Virginia courts debated whether this act counted as first or second-degree murder or mere manslaughter; ultimately, Souther received only a five-year sentence. The court noted that a slave-owner cannot be indicted or even prosecuted for "cruel and excessive whipping of his own slave." If death resulted, even if intended, it would not be characterized as first degree murder. Though the courts and slave-owners had several options, their choices reveal they had no regard for the humanity of slaves.

F. *Souther v. The Commonwealth,* 48 Va. 673 (1851)

1. Facts

Justice FIELD delivered the opinion of the Court.

Simeon Souther was indicted at the October term for 1850, of the Circuit court for the county of Hanover, for the murder of his own slave.

2. Trial Court Opinion

The prisoner's trial came on at the April term 1851, when the jury found him guilty, and fixed the term of his imprisonment in the penitentiary at five years. Whereupon the prisoner moved the Court to set aside the verdict, and grant him a new trial; but the Court overruled the motion, and entered a judgment according to the verdict. The prisoner again excepted, . . . and applied to this Court for a writ of error.

3. Opinion of Virginia Court of Appeals

The prisoner was indicted and convicted of murder in the second degree in the Circuit court of Hanover, at its April term last past, and was sentenced to the penitentiary for five years, the period of time ascertained by the jury. The murder consisted in the killing of a negro man slave by the name of Sam, the property of the prisoner, by cruel and excessive whipping and torture, inflicted by Souther, aided by two of his other slaves, on the 1st day of September 1849. The prisoner moved for a new trial, upon the ground that the offence, if any, amounted only to manslaughter. The motion for a new trial was overruled, and a bill of exceptions taken to the opinion of the Court, setting forth the facts proved, or as many of them as were deemed material for the consideration of the application for a new trial. The bill of exceptions states: "That the slave Sam in the indictment mentioned, was the slave and property of the prisoner. That for the purpose of chastising the slave for the offence of getting drunk, and dealing as the slave confessed and alleged, with Henry and Stone, two of the witnesses for the Commonwealth, he caused him to be tied and punished in the presence of the said witnesses, with the exception of slight whipping with peach or apple tree switches, before the said witnesses' arrival at the scene after they were sent for by the prisoner, (who were present by request from the defendant,) and of several slaves of the prisoner, in the manner and by the means charged in the indictment; and the said slave died under and from the infliction of the said punishment, in the presence of the prisoner, one of his slaves, and one of the witnesses for the Commonwealth. But it did not appear that it was the design of the prisoner to kill the said slave, unless such design be properly inferrible from the manner, means and duration of the punishment. And on the contrary, it did appear that the prisoner frequently declared while the said slave was undergoing the punishment, that he believed the said slave was feigning and pretending to be suffering and injured, when he was not." The Judge certifies that the slave was punished in the *manner and by the means charged in the indictment.* The indictment contains fifteen counts, and sets forth a case of the most cruel and excessive whipping and torture. The negro was tied to a tree and whipped with switches. When Souther became fatigued with the labour of whipping, he called upon a Negro man of his, and made him cob Sam with a shingle. He also made a Negro woman of his help to cob him. And after cobbing and whipping, he applied fire to the body of the slave; about his back, belly and private parts. He then caused him to be washed down with hot water, in which pods of red pepper had been steeped. The Negro was also tied to a log and to the bed post with ropes, which choked him, and he was kicked and stamped by Souther. This sort of punishment was continued and repeated until the Negro died under its infliction. It is believed that the records of criminal jurisprudence do not contain a case of more atrocious and wicked cruelty than was presented upon the trial of Souther; and yet it has been gravely and earnestly contended here by his counsel, that his offence amounts to manslaughter only.

It has been contended by the counsel of the prisoner, that a man cannot be indicted and prosecuted for the cruel and excessive whipping of his own slave. That it is lawful for the master to chastise his slave; and that if death ensues from such chastisement, unless it was intended to produce death, it is like the case of homicide, which is committed by a man in the performance of a lawful act, which is manslaughter only. It has been decided by this Court, in *Turner's* Case 5 Rand., that the owner of a slave, for the malicious, cruel and excessive beating of his own slave, cannot be indicted; yet it by no means follows when such malicious, cruel and excessive beating results in death, though not intended and premeditated, that the beating is to be regarded as lawful, for the purpose of reducing the crime to manslaughter, when the whipping is inflicted for the sole purpose of chastisement. It is the policy of the law in respect to the relation of master and slave, and for the sake of securing proper subordination and obedience on the part of the slave, to protect the master from prosecution in all such cases, even if the whipping and punishment be malicious, cruel and excessive. But in so inflicting punishment for the sake of punishment, the owner of the slave acts at his peril; and if death ensues in consequence of such punishment, the relation of master and slave affords no ground of excuse or palliation. The principles of the common law in relation to homicide, apply to his case, without qualification or exception; and according to those principles, the act of the prisoner, in the case under consideration, amounted to murder. Upon this point we are unanimous.

But what was the law in respect to felonious homicide on the 1st day of September 1849, when the offence was committed. It is to be found in the Sessions Acts of 1847–48, p. 95. By that act it is declared "that unlawful homicide shall be murder of the first degree, murder of the second degree, or manslaughter."

"Murder committed by poison, lying in wait, duress of imprisonment, starving, *wilful* and *excessive whipping, cruel treatment,* or any kind (not any other kind as the law theretofore was) 'of wilful,' deliberate and premeditated killing, or in the attempt to commit any arson, rape, robbery, or burglary, shall be murder in the first degree, and all other murder shall be murder in the second degree." "Murder in the first degree shall be punished with death." The Judge certifies in his bill of exceptions, as a fact proved in the case, that "the slave died under and from the infliction of the said punishment." Apply the words of the act of Assembly to this case, and it clearly appears that the crime of the prisoner is not manslaughter, but murder in the first degree.

Judge Leigh does not concur in this last view, namely, that homicide committed by excessive whipping, must be necessarily murder in the first degree, without regard to the intention of the offender. He is of opinion that to constitute murder in the first degree, there must be an intention to kill.

4. Holding

Upon the whole we are clearly of opinion that there is no error in the record of which the prisoner can complain, and the writ of error is refused.

G. Commentary on *Souther*

A. Leon Higginbotham, Jr. and Anne Jacobs

"The Law Only As An Enemy": The Legitimization of Racial Powerlessness Through the Colonial and Antebellum Criminal Laws of Virginia

While the *Souther* court was unanimous in holding that under certain circumstances a slaveowner could be convicted for murdering his slave, the judges disagreed as to whether the defendant was guilty of first- or second-degree murder. Judge Field, delivering the opinion of the court, referred to the Sessions Acts of 1847–48, which provided that murder committed by "wilful and *excessive whipping* [or] *cruel treatment*" was murder in the first degree, which was to be punished with *death*. Hence, it was obvious to Judge Field that Souther was guilty of first-degree murder, not manslaughter. Judge Leigh, on the other hand, believed that excessive whipping of a slave did not necessarily constitute first-degree murder; in order to be so characterized, there must have been an intent to kill.

The opinion does not indicate whether the court ultimately ruled that Souther was guilty of first- or second-degree murder. The court upheld the five-year sentence which the jury imposed, however, which indicates that Souther was found to have committed second-degree murder, since the 1847–48 statute made first-degree murder punishable with death.

Souther was an important ruling because the court refused to give slaveowners total immunity from the laws punishing the murder of slaves. Nevertheless, the disparity in legal treatment when blacks were the victims is revealed when one considers the sentence Souther received. Regardless of whether he committed first- or second-degree murder, he received only a five-year sentence. That a man could receive so inconsequential a sentence for such a brutal crime indicates how little value was placed on the humanity of slaves. Had the defendant tortured, whipped, beaten, choked, and killed a white person the way he did his slave, it is inconceivable that a jury would have imposed, and the court would have accepted, a mere five-year term of incarceration for such a killing.

It also is important to emphasize that if by some twist of fate a slave managed to survive such a ferocious attack, the master was *completely immune* from prosecution. He could beat his slave with impunity and without limits so long as the slave did not die from the assault.

"The numerous civil suits that masters brought against overseers and hirers for severely wounding or killing slaves indicated that gross abuse was all too common." By law an owner could bring an action to recover against another for killing or dismembering his slave. In effect, slaveowners had a choice of remedies—they could collect a fine or press criminal charges—which depended on the ability of the defendant to pay the fine, as well as his social and economic status.

70 *North Carolina Law Review* 969, 1035–36.
Copyright © (1991) A. Leon Higginbotham, Jr.
Reprinted with permission of Evelyn Brooks Higginbotham.

H. Explaining Thomas Jefferson

Author of the Declaration of Independence, Ambassador to France during the French Revolution, and the third President of the United States, Thomas Jefferson is a monumental figure in American history. Yet, his acknowledgment of the immorality of slavery while continuing to own slaves personally and his long-term involvement with one of his slaves, Sally Hemings, continues to keep Jefferson at the center of controversy.

William Jefferson Harrison

The Ambivalent Statesman: Did Thomas Jefferson Find Slavery Abhorrent

Despite his professed desire for an end to slavery, Jefferson's stated abhorrence of it was unmatched by positive action. He acted, in part, to slow the spread of slavery but did nothing to abolish it, not even in his own household. If read out of context, Jefferson's statements place him not only out of step but in conflict with slavery and the racial practices of the era. Yet at each juncture, when he could have lived by his professed concerns about slavery, he declined to do so. Jefferson continued to his death—in some ways, after it—his unwillingness or inability to show by example that he stood by his stated beliefs about slavery's evils.

Jefferson shared not only the prevailing economic and social views of 18th-century America, but also its racism and established racial stereotypes. Like many of his contemporaries, he thought African Americans were mentally inferior and had excessive sexual appetites.

"To our reproach it must be said, that though for a century and a half we have had under our eyes the race of black and of red men, they have never yet been viewed by us as subjects of natural history," Jefferson wrote, "I advance it therefore as a suspicion only, that the blacks whether originally a distinct race, or made them distinct by time and circumstances, are inferior to the whites in the endowments both of body and mind."

He professed to have reconsidered some of his racial "suspicions" after learning about Benjamin Banneker, a black inventor, scientist and surveyor. Banneker might have impressed Jefferson, but not enough to inspire him to dispense with his slaves. Jefferson, George Washington, and James Madison were, indeed, representative of their times—leaders of a white America whose freedom was bought with slave labor, who fought for that freedom while denying it to Africans transplanted from their homeland. . . .

One can only speculate on whether it was Jefferson's suspicions about black intelligence or sexuality that attracted him to Sally Hemings. History describes her as an attractive and intelligent mulatto slave who was his wife's half sister. That his relationship with her lasted more than 39 years would seem to indicate that he was fond of her. Though many historians over several generations have frenetically denied Jefferson's liaison with Hemings, Jefferson himself never disavowed it.

His lack of denial may help explain why even at his death, Jefferson provided for freeing only five of his 200 slaves. (Fellow revolutionaries and slaveholders Washington and John Randolph, who had not spent as much time as Jefferson lamenting the evils, at their deaths freed all their slaves.)

Closer examination provides some explanation of why Jefferson finally, in death, released his grip on a handful of the slaves he owned. These five shared familial relationships with him. Two, Burwell and Joe Fosset, were sons of Sally Hemings' sisters. Another, John Hemings, was Sally Hemings' half brother. The remaining two, Madison and Easton Hemings, were sons of Jefferson and Hemings. Sally was not set free. Instead, she was listed on the slave roster as worth $50 and willed to Jefferson's daughter, Martha. This was probably meant as an act of kindness because as a free person Hemings would have had to leave Virginia. The Monticello plantation was Hemings' home; she had no other. Martha Jefferson freed her two years later.

The 1830 census listed Easton Hemings, who lived near Monticello, as white. Sally Hemings, as an older woman living with him, was also listed as white. Neither Sally Hemings nor her son Easton could legally have remained in Virginia as blacks after they were freed.

I. Explaining Judges St. George Tucker and George Wythe

A. Leon Higginbotham, Jr. and F. Michael Higginbotham

"Yearning to Breathe Free": Legal Barriers Against and
Options in Favor of Liberty in Antebellum Virginia

St. George Tucker, author of the opinion in *Hudgins*, was one of the most respected jurists of his time. He became a professor of law at William and Mary in 1792, and in 1796 published a paper on the policy implications of slavery, focusing primarily on proposals for emancipation in Virginia. Tucker examined prior Pennsylvania and Massachusetts plans to formulate his own proposal, which the Virginia legislature eventually tabled without formal rejection. Subsequently, Tucker was appointed to the Virginia Supreme Court of Appeals and in his new capacity authored a number of opinions favorable to slavery. While a Professor at William and Mary, however, Tucker wrote that:

> [O]ur bill of rights, declares, "that all men, are, by nature *equally free,* . . ." This is, indeed, no more than a recognition of the first principles of the law of nature. . . . It would be hard to reconcile reducing the Negroes to a state of slavery to these principles, unless we first degrade them below the rank of human beings . . . but surely it is time we should admit the evidence of moral truth, and learn to regard them as our fellowmen.

George Wythe emancipated all of the slaves he inherited including one of his slaves to the guardianship of his friend Thomas Jefferson. Wythe died in 1806 after being poisoned.

The preliminary hearings of the case strongly suggested that Wythe's grand-nephew, George Wythe Sweeney, had administered the poison. Sweeney had amassed considerable gambling debts, had forged six bank checks in his grand-uncle's name, and, along with Brown and Wythe's other servants, was the main beneficiary of George Wythe's will. Arsenic powder was found in the jail where Sweeney had been detained, and arsenic-blotted papers were found in Sweeney's room and in the Wythe outhouses. Nevertheless, Sweeney was found not guilty of the poisoning at trial, primarily because the most damning evidence against him "was gleaned from Negroes, which is not permitted by our laws to go against a white man."

J. Questions and Notes

With the end of the legal authorization for the international slave trade, whereby no new slaves could be brought into the U.S. legally, the domestic slave trade of existing slaves and their descendants, became more profitable. Slaves who were imported illegally, in violation of law and international commerce, were still enslaved in many states. Slaves were the most valuable property in the southern states, and auctions were the method in which this property was bought and sold. Many businesses that supplied farm equipment and animals also supplied slaves. Farmers who were selling their lands, abandoning their farms, or had an overabundance of slaves needed an efficient way to sell or exchange slaves. Both of these groups, farmers and farm-supply businesses, looked to auction houses as a way to facilitate slave sales and purchases. As a result of these developments, auctioneers, who handled real estate and personal property, sold slaves along with other items.

While the institution of slavery was harsh and oppressive, it was also a business motivated by economic concerns. Perhaps more than any other aspect of slavery, slave auction advertisements captured the horrific, yet profitable, reality of this institution.

Louis D. De Saussure

Ryan's Mart Slave Auction Handbill

Gang of 25 Sea Island Cotton and Rice Negroes,

On THURSDAY the 25th Sept., 1852, at 11 o'clock, A.M., will be sold at RYAN'S MART, in Chalmers Street, in the City of Charleston, *A prime gang of 25 Negroes, accustomed to the culture of Sea Island Cotton and Rice.*

CONDITIONS. — One-half Cash, balance by Bond, bearing interest from day of sale, payable in one and two years, to be secured by a mortgage of the Negroes and approved personal security. Purchasers to pay for papers.

No.	Age	Capacity	
1	Aleck,	33	Carpenter
2	Mary Ann,	31	Field hand, prime
3-3	Louisa,	10	
4	Abram,	25	Prime field hand
5	Judy,	24	Prime field hand,
6	Carolina,	5	
7	Simon,	1-1/2	
5-8	Daphne,	infant	
9	Daniel,	45	Field hand, not prime
10	Phillis,	32	Field hand
11	Will,	9	
12	Daniel,	6	
13	Margaret,	4	
24	Delia,	2	
7-15	Hannah,	2 months	
16	Hannah,	60	Cook
17	Cudjoe,	22	Prime field hand.

3-18	Nancy,	20	Prime field hand, sister of Cudjoe.
19	Hannah,	34	Prime field hand.
20	James,	13	Slight defect in knee from a broken leg.
21	Richard,	9	
22	Thomas,	6	
5-23	John,	3	
1-24	Squash,	40	Prime field hand.
1-25	Thomas,	28	Prime field hand.

Unpublished.
Copyright © Old Slave Mart Museum.

K. Point/Counterpoint

Anti-colonialist and non-violent freedom fighter Mohandas Gandhi described how individuals remain in bondage:

> The moment the slave resolves that he will no longer be a slave, his fetters fall.

> He frees himself and shows the way to others. Freedom and slavery are mental states.[16]

Do you agree or disagree with the theory of Mohandas Gandhi? Would this theory have helped Lydia resolve her problem in *State v. Mann*?

VII. Slavery, Free Blacks, and the United States Supreme Court

A. Introduction

Don Fehrenbacher

Slavery, the Framers, and the Living Constitution in Slavery and Its Consequences: The Constitution, Equality, and Race (Edited by Goldwin and Kaufman)*

The three-fifths clause and the slave-trade clause were side effects of the Convention's progress toward a new constitutional design. One resulted from the introduction of proportional representation at the national level; the other, from the empowering of Congress to regulate foreign commerce; and both were highly controversial. The fugitive-slave clause, in contrast, had no such connections and

---

16. T. AUGARDE, THE OXFORD DICTIONARY OF MODERN QUOTATIONS 88 (1991).

* (footnotes omitted).

provoked little argument. Presented late in the Convention by two South Carolina delegates, but certainly not as a sine quo non, it received unanimous approval. The fact that a similar provision had already been incorporated in the Northwest Ordinance no doubt encouraged its ready acceptance. Again the framers chose not to name the thing they were talking about: "No person held to service or labour in one state, under the laws thereof, escaping into another, shall, in consequence of any law or regulation therein, be discharged from such service or labour, but shall be delivered up on claim of the party to whom such service or labour may be due."

The fugitive-slave clause was not placed in Article I with the enumerated powers of Congress but appears instead in Article IV, section 2. That whole article is about states and statehood, and the second section is about interstate comity. Of the three other sections in the article, two expressly confer power on Congress, and the other vests power more generally in the "United States"—meaning, presumably, all three branches of the federal government. There is no such conferral of power in section 2, which lends credence to the view of the fugitive-slave clause as nothing more than a declaratory limitation on state authority. That view, if accurate, goes a long way toward explaining the absence of controversy in the genesis of a clause that became the basis for some of the most controversial legislation ever passed by Congress.

The three-fifths, slave-trade, and fugitive-slave clauses, together with the double lock put on the slave-trade clause, were the only parts of the Constitution written with slavery primarily in mind, and none of them called the institution by its name. Without a doubt, the three-fifths clause, or some equivalent, was essential for the success of the Constitution as we know it. The slave-trade clause may have been a necessary concession to the lower South—one that proved, however, to be antislavery rather than proslavery in its ultimate effect. The fugitive-slave clause was a more gratuitous addition to the Constitution, and it alone provided slaveholders with some measure of protection, though only in vague and passive terms. Each of the three clauses dealt with a marginal feature of slavery that had some claim on national attention. None of the three recognized slavery as having any legitimacy in federal law. On the contrary, the framers were doubly careful to treat it explicitly as a state institution. Most revealing in this respect was a last-minute change in the fugitive-slave clause whereby the phrase "legally held to service or labour in one state" was changed to read: "held to service or labour in one state, under the laws thereof." The revision made it impossible to infer from the passage that the Constitution itself legally sanctioned slavery.

Other parts of the Constitution have sometimes been labeled proslavery, most notably the clauses providing for suppression of insurrections and for protection of the states against domestic violence. Both clauses obviously covered various kinds of resistance to civil authority, including servile rebellion, but the 1780s were not a period of serious disturbances among the slave population. What the framers did have in mind was the alarming series of events in Massachusetts known as Shays's Rebellion, which had come to an end just a few months before the opening of the

Convention. Wendell Phillips, writing in the 1840s, conceded that the two clauses were "perfectly innocent in themselves." Furthermore, neither was ever invoked to deal with a slave uprising. Phillips nevertheless insisted that since they were potentially usable for that purpose, the clauses implicated all Americans in "the guilt of sustaining slavery." Perhaps the best way to comment on such reasoning is to ask what alternatives were available to the framers. Should they have excepted slave revolts from the insurrections to be suppressed and from the domestic violence to be guarded against? Any such proposal would have been dismissed as absurd and outrageous. But then the only other option, one that likewise would have received little support in the Convention, was omission or deletion of the two clauses from the text of the Constitution. That would have deprived the federal government of needed authority—authority used as early as 1794 in the Whisky Rebellion and invoked by Lincoln in 1861 to suppress an insurrection, not of slaves, but of slaveholders.

Slavery had a stronger influence on the deliberations of the Convention than on the text of the Constitution. The few concessions to slavery in the text were, as Gerrit Smith maintained, more like eddies in a stream than part of the current. Moreover, the concessions were offset by a stylistic tone of repugnance for the institution and by indications that it could be regarded as something less than permanent in American life. In short, the Constitution as it came from the hands of the framers dealt only minimally and peripherally with slavery and was essentially open-ended on the subject. Nevertheless, because it substantially increased the power of the national government, the Constitution had greater proslavery potential and greater antislavery potential than the Articles of Confederation. Its meaning with respect to slavery would depend heavily upon how it was implemented.

Antislavery implementation was confined largely to two categories, involving three provisions of the Constitution—the Territory Clause and the Commerce Clause, reinforced after 1807 by the slave-trade clause. Beginning with reenactment of the Northwest Ordinance in 1789, Congress used its control over federal territories to prohibit slavery in the northern part of the country from the western boundary of Pennsylvania to the Mississippi River, then to the Rocky Mountains, and finally to the Pacific Ocean. Beginning in 1794, Congress prohibited American participation in the foreign slave-trade, and in 1807 it passed the first of several laws forbidding the importation of slaves from abroad. Both of these categories of antislavery achievement were plainly within the purview of the Constitution and the expectations of the framers, but each in its own way came to suffer from erosion. Enforcement of the slave-trade law was chronically inadequate, and American complicity in the traffic remained an international issue right up to the Civil War. As for federal exclusion of slavery from the territories, all attempts to extend the ban into southern parts of the country were unsuccessful. Then in the Kansas-Nebraska Act of 1854, Congress virtually repudiated the whole idea, and in the *Dred Scott* decision three years later, the Supreme Court held such legislation to be unconstitutional.

The extraordinary amount of historical attention given to the sectional conflict over slavery in the territories—a conflict in which the antislavery forces managed at least to hold their own—has obscured the fact that an often tacit proslavery interpretation of the Constitution was predominant in the operation of the federal government from 1789 to 1861. A striking case in point is the implementation of the clause empowering Congress "to exercise exclusive legislation in all cases whatsoever, over such district (not exceeding ten miles square) as may, by cession of particular states, and the acceptance of Congress, become the seat of the government of the United States." In 1790, after a long legislative battle, Congress voted in favor of a site on the Potomac River, to be donated jointly by Virginia and Maryland. The decision was made without a word being said about slavery and apparently without any reflection on the possible consequences of locating the national capital within a slaveholding region. Then, when the time came a decade later to provide a system of government for the federal district, Congress avoided a lot of hard work by directing that the laws of Virginia and Maryland should continue in force. Thus, silently and almost casually, in actions a decade apart, slavery was legalized as a federal institution in Washington, D.C. More than that, the city soon became a major center of the domestic slave trade. At the very center of national power, the United States presented itself to foreign visitors and its own citizens as a slaveholding republic.

At the same time, a body of historical and constitutional myth was being fashioned to justify and guarantee slaveholding in the District of Columbia as an inalienable right. Even though the words "exclusive legislation in all cases whatsoever" would seem to have given Congress full power over slavery in the District, abolitionist petitions on the subject were met with emphatic southern denials of such power and, indeed, with much insistence that Congress did not even have the authority to receive such petitions, let alone give them serious consideration. It was asserted, furthermore, that any abridgment of slaveholders' rights in the District would be a breach of faith because the inviolability of slavery had been an implicit condition of the transfer of land from Virginia and Maryland to the United States. The assertion was wholly without foundation, but reiteration made it credible even to many northerners. One finds the argument embraced, for example, in a joint resolution of the New Hampshire legislature, passed in 1839 by a vote of 124 to 21. The southern point of view prevailed throughout the antebellum period.

Congress did outlaw the slave trade as part of the Compromise of 1850, but not until a year after the firing on Fort Sumter was slavery itself abolished in the national capital.

Not even Wendel Phillips blamed the framers of the Constitution for the entrenchment of slavery in the District of Columbia. Neither did Phillips attach the label "proslavery" to any of the clauses defining the role of the president in foreign affairs, and yet the actual conduct of foreign relations from 1789 to 1861 could scarcely have been more proslavery if there had been nothing but slaveholding states in the Union. Although the question of whether slaves were property under federal law remained a controversial and unsettled issue in Congress, the Department of State treated them as property from the beginning. One American minister lectured the British foreign secretary at length on the subject in his official correspondence. Under the Constitution, he declared, slaves were fully protected as property and there was "no distinction in principle between property in persons and property in things." Domestic slavery, he added, was "infused" into the laws of the United States and mixed itself "with all the sources of their authority."

The facilities of the State Department were used habitually and assiduously in behalf of slave owners, such as those seeking recovery of slaves who had escaped to Canada and those seeking restitution for slaves liberated in the British West Indies. During the presidency of John Quincy Adams, who later became an antislavery terror in the House of Representatives, the United States made strenuous though unsuccessful efforts to arrange by treaty for the return of fugitive slaves from Mexico and Canada. The government also followed a consistent proslavery policy in refusing for more than fifty years to recognize the black republic of Haiti, which, by the very example of its revolutionary origins and continued existence, posed a threat to every slaveholding society. The South, as Senator Thomas Hart Benton of Missouri frankly explained, could not permit "black Consuls and Ambassadors to establish themselves in our cities, and to parade through our country, and give their fellow blacks in the United States, proof in hand of the honors which await them, for a like successful effort on their part."

The implication of the federal government with slavery extended to all departments. For example, slave labor was often used on federal construction projects, such as military installations and the national Capitol itself. Army troops on the southern frontier frequently lent assistance in the recovery of fugitive slaves. Southern postmasters, with the approval of their superiors in Washington, excluded antislavery literature from the mails. High federal offices were often occupied by proslavery zealots like John C. Calhoun, Roger Taney, and Jefferson Davis, whereas no vigorous critic of slavery had the slightest chance of receiving such an appointment. Furthermore, the Supreme Court, with its southern majority reinforced by northern doughfaces, became ever more obviously proslavery in the 1840s and 1850s—until at last it virtually proclaimed that slavery was fully entitled to federal protection and wholly immune from federal restraint.

While the Constitution did not prohibit slavery, for economic and moral reasons, many individual states had contemporaneous laws and policies seeking to restrict or abolish it. Pennsylvania led the anti-slavery movement when it passed the first abolition legislation in 1780. As many states followed Pennsylvania's lead throughout the first half of the nineteenth century, the conflict between slave states and free states was heightened. Slave states were particularly disturbed by the degree to which free states provided protection to runaway slaves and free blacks. By the late 1850s, however, the Supreme Court would severely curtail the power of states to contest or abolish slavery within their borders. Three Supreme Court cases contributed to the nationalization of slavery and indirectly limited a state's power to make its own laws to abolish slavery. These three cases, reinforcing slavery, were the *Amistad*, *Prigg*, and *Dred Scott*.

B. Background on *Amistad*

John T. Noonan, Jr.

The Antelope: the Ordeal of the Recaptured Africans in the Administrations of James Monroe and John Quincy Adams

Under Article II of the Constitution, Congress was denied power before January 1, 1808, to prevent "the Migration or Importation of Such Persons as any of the States now existing shall think proper to admit." The Constitution's authors deliberately did not mention slaves or slavery. In John Quincy Adams' ambivalent sexual metaphor, they had used "fig leaves under which these parts of the body politic are decently concealed." After this twenty-year period of grace for the slave traders, it became by act of Congress a crime to import slaves anywhere in the United States. It also became a federal crime to equip ships as slavers.

What Congress did not decide for ten years was what should be done with persons who were being illegally brought in as slaves when the slaver carrying them was captured. In the face of congressional silence, each state applied its own law. If illegally smuggled slaves were found in a slave state, they were auctioned by the state for its own benefit. What else, Attorney General Wirt asked rhetorically, could be done? "Should they have been turned loose as free men in the State? The impolicy of such a course is too palpable to find an advocate in anyone who is acquainted with the condition of the slave-holding States." The Attorney General did not suppose that any state would at its own expense return the slaves to their own country.

These Africans who were transported to the United States against the law, who were rescued from the criminals who has held them captive, and who nonetheless were finally made American slaves, were objects on whom the Colonization Society could exercise its benevolence. The irony of the federal government, in the course of suppressing the slave trade, becoming a supplier of slaves was evident. The society had a solution which tied together its long-run and immediate objectives and gained a base inside the government which could in time be expanded. The rescued slaves, it proposed, should be sent back to Africa. They could not be sent whence they had come, because they would only be enslaved again. They should not be cast on the shores of Africa at random. But they should be returned to their own continent, and the only way of assuring their safe re-establishment there was to establish American jurisdiction over an area to which they could be brought. The Society's plan for a colony was the only feasible response to the plight of the criminally enslaved and federally liberated Africans.

The Colonization Society turned with confidence to Congress and was not disappointed. Speaker Clay assigned its petition to a Special Committee, appointed by the Speaker. The Special Committee recommended that the suppression of the slave trade be more justly carried out by establishing a colony of the United States in Africa. The "iniquity" of federal participation in the selling of rescued slaves must be ended.

The bill the Special Committee actually drafted was more circumspect than its report. The possibly controversial term "colony" did not appear. A thrust in the direction of an African outpost could be found only by a benevolent reading. There was some debate in the House, little in the Senate, and no record vote. On March 2, 1819, "The Act in Addition to the Acts prohibiting the slave trade" was passed by Congress. In the opinion of Mason, Jones and Key, its enactment shed "a ray of light dear to humanity on the expiring moments of the Fifteenth Congress and elevated the American character in the estimation of the world."

The aim of the Society had been to avoid controversy in Congress and rely on a sympathetic Administration. The Act left every detail to the President, and what he did with the details would determine what the Act became. He was given authority to use the Navy or other armed ships wherever the slave trade was conducted and, on capture of a slaver, to take charge of the Africans aboard and assure their "safe-keeping, support, and removal beyond the United States." How the President was to safekeep and support his charges, the Act did not say. Nor did it say how he was to remove them from the United States. But it gave the President all power "to make such regulations and arrangements as he may deem expedient." The not remarkably generous sum of one hundred thousand dollars, four-tenths of one percent of the federal budget, was appropriated for the execution of the Act.

The Antelope 17–19 (1977).
Copyright © (1977) The Regents of the University of California.
Reprinted with permission of The Regents of the University of California.

The *Amistad* case became a battleground between the leading supporters of slavery and abolitionists. President Martin Van Buren, who was counting on strong support from slaveholding states in the upcoming presidential election of 1840, was anxious to appease slave states and avoid any ruling that might call into question the fundamental legality of slavery. Those opposed to slavery, on the other hand, including former President John Quincy Adams, believed the case presented an opportunity to reveal the violence and cruelty of the international slave trade. Both Martin Van Buren and John Quincy Adams, however, would be overshadowed by Cinque, the leader of the slave revolt and the center of attention during the *Amistad* litigation, whose courage against oppression and commitment to family and freedom were steadfast.

C. *The United States v. The Libellants and Claimants of the Schooner Amistad,* 40 U.S. 518 (1841)

1. Facts

Justice STORY delivered the opinion of the Court.

The leading facts, as they appear upon the transcript of the proceedings, are as follows: On the 27th of June, 1839, the schooner L'Amistad, being the property of Spanish subjects, cleared out from the port of Havana, in the island of Cuba, for Puerto Principe, in the same island. On board of the schooner were the captain, Ransom Ferrer, and Jose Ruiz, and Pedro Montez, all Spanish subjects. The former had with him a Negro boy, named Antonio, claimed to be his slave. Jose Ruiz had with him forty-nine Negroes, claimed by him as his slaves, and stated to be his property, in a certain pass or document, signed by the Governor General of Cuba. Pedro Montez had with him four other negroes, also claimed by him as his slaves, and stated to be his property, in a similar pass or document, also signed by the Governor General of Cuba. On the voyage, and before the arrival of the vessel at her port of destination, the Negroes rose, killed the captain, and took possession of her.

On the 26th of August, the vessel was discovered by Lieutenant Gedney, of the United States Brig Washington, at anchor on the high seas, at the distance of half a mile from the shore of Long Island. A part of the Negroes were then on shore at Culloden Point, Long Island; who were seized by Lieutenant Gedney, and brought on board. The vessel, with the Negroes and other persons on board, was brought by Lieutenant Gedney into the district of Connecticut, and there libelled for salvage in the District Court of the United States. A libel for salvage was also filed by Henry Green and Pelatiah Fordham, of Sag Harbour, Long Island. On the 18th of September, Ruiz and Montez filed claims and libels, in which they asserted their ownership of the Negroes as their slaves, and of certain parts of the cargo, and prayed that the same might be "delivered to them, or to the representatives of her Catholic majesty, as might be most proper. . . ."

2. Opinion

. . . Before entering upon the discussion of the main points involved in this interesting and important controversy, it may be necessary to say a few words as to the actual posture of the case as it now stands before us. In the first place, then, the only parties now before the Court on one side, are the United States, intervening for the sole purpose of procuring restitution of the property as Spanish property, pursuant to the treaty, upon the grounds stated by the other parties claiming the property in their respective libels. The United States do not assert any property in themselves, or any violation of their own rights, or sovereignty, or laws, by the acts complained of. They do not insist that these negroes have been imported into the United States, in contravention of our own slave trade acts. They do not seek to have these negroes delivered up for the purpose of being transported to Cuba as pirates or robbers, or as fugitive criminals found within our territories, who have been guilty of offences against the laws of Spain. They do not assert that the seizure, and bringing the vessel, and cargo, and negroes into port, by Lieutenant Gedney, for the purpose of adjudication, is a tortious act. They simply confine themselves to the right of the Spanish claimants to the restitution of their property, upon the facts asserted in their respective allegations.

In the next place, the parties before the Court on the other side as appellees, are Lieutenant Gedney, on his libel for salvage, and the Negroes, (Cinque, and others,) asserting themselves, in their answer, not to be slaves, but free native Africans, kidnapped in their own country, and illegally transported by force from that country; and now entitled to maintain their freedom. . . .

If, then, these negroes are not slaves, but are kidnapped Africans, who, by the laws of Spain itself, are entitled to their freedom, and were kidnapped and illegally carried to Cuba, and illegally detained and restrained on board of the Amistad; there is no pretence to say, that they are pirates or robbers. We may lament the dreadful acts, by which they asserted their liberty, and took possession of the Amistad, and endeavoured to regain their native country; but they cannot be deemed pirates or robbers in the sense of the law of nations, or the treaty with Spain, or the laws of Spain itself; at least so far as those laws have been brought to our knowledge. Nor do the libels of Ruiz or Montez assert them to be such.

This posture of the facts would seem, of itself, to put an end to the whole inquiry upon the merits. But it is argued, on behalf of the United States, that the ship, and cargo, and negroes were duly documented as belonging to Spanish subjects, and this Court have no right to look behind these documents; that full faith and credit is to be given to them; and that they are to be held conclusive evidence in this cause, even although it should be established by the most satisfactory proofs, that they have been obtained by the grossest frauds and impositions upon the constituted authorities of Spain. To this argument we can, in no wise, assent. There is nothing in the treaty which justifies or sustains the argument. We do not here meddle with the point, whether there has been any connivance in this illegal traffic, on the part of any of the colonial authorities or subordinate officers of Cuba; because, in our view, such an examination is unnecessary, and ought not to be pursued, unless it were indispensable to public justice, although it has been strongly pressed at the bar. What we proceed upon is this, that although public documents of the government, accompanying property found on board of the private ships of a foreign nation, certainly are to be deemed prima facie evidence of the facts which they purport to state, yet they are always open to be impugned for fraud; and whether that fraud be in the original obtaining of these documents, or in the subsequent fraudulent and illegal use of them, when once it is satisfactorily established, it overthrows all their sanctity, and destroys them as proof. Fraud will vitiate any, even the most solemn transactions; and an asserted title to property, founded upon it, is utterly void. The very language of the ninth article of the treaty of 1795, requires the proprietor to make due and sufficient proof of his property. And how can that proof be deemed either due or sufficient, which is but a connected, and stained tissue of fraud? This is not a mere rule of municipal jurisprudence. Nothing is more clear in the law of nations, as an established rule to regulate their rights, and duties, and intercourse, than the doctrine, that the ship's papers are but prima facie evidence, and that, if they are shown to be fraudulent, they are not to be held proof of any valid title. . . .

It is also a most important consideration in the present case, which ought not to be lost sight of, that, supposing these African Negroes not to be slaves, but kidnapped, and free Negroes, the treaty with Spain cannot be obligatory upon them; and the United States are bound to respect their rights as much as those of Spanish subjects. The conflict of rights between the parties under such circumstances, becomes positive and inevitable, and must be decided upon the eternal principles of justice and international law. If the contest were about any goods on board of this ship, to which American citizens asserted a title, which was denied by the Spanish claimants, there could be no doubt of the right of such American citizens to litigate their claims before any competent American tribunal, notwithstanding the treaty with Spain. A fortiori, the doctrine must apply where human life and human liberty are in issue; and constitute the very essence of the controversy. The treaty with Spain never could have intended to take away the equal rights of all foreigners, who should contest their claims before any of our Courts, to equal justice; or to deprive such foreigners of the protection given them by other treaties, or by the general law of nations. Upon the merits of the case, then, there does not seem to us to be any ground for doubt, that these Negroes ought to be deemed free; and that the Spanish treaty interposes no obstacle to the just assertion of their rights.

There is another consideration growing out of this part of the case, which necessarily arises in judgment. It is observable, that the United States, in their original claim, filed it in the alternative, to have the Negroes, if slaves and Spanish property, restored to the proprietors; or, if not slaves, but Negroes who had been transported from Africa, in violation of the laws of the United States, and brought into the United States contrary to the same laws, then the court to pass an order to enable the United States to remove such persons to the coast of Africa, to be delivered there to such agent as may be authorized to receive and provide for them. At a subsequent period, this last alternative claim was not insisted on, and another claim was interposed, omitting it; from which the conclusion naturally arises that it was abandoned. The decree of the District court, however, contained an order for the delivery of the Negroes to the United States to be transported to the coast of Africa, under the act of the 3d of March, 1819, ch. 224. The United States do not now insist upon any affirmance of this part of the decree; and, in our judgment, upon the admitted facts, there is no ground to assert that the case comes within the purview of the act of 1819, or of any other of our prohibitory slave trade acts. These Negroes were never taken from Africa, or brought to the United states in contravention of those acts. When the Amistad arrived she was in possession of the Negroes, asserting their freedom; and in no sense could they possibly intend to import themselves here as slaves, or for sale as slaves. In this view of the matter, that part of the decree of the District court is unmaintainable, and must be reversed.

The view which has been thus taken of this case, upon the merits, under the first point, renders it wholly unnecessary for us to give any opinion upon the other point, as to the right of the United States to intervene in this case in the manner already stated. We dismiss this, therefore, as well as several minor points made at the argument.

As to the claim of Lieutenant Gedney for the salvage service, it is understood that the United States do not now desire to interpose any obstacle to the allowance of it, if it is deemed reasonable by the Court. It was a highly meritorious and useful service to the proprietors of the ship and cargo; and such as, by the general principles of maritime law, is always deemed a just foundation for salvage. The rate allowed by the Court, does not seem to us to have been beyond the exercise of a sound discretion, under the very peculiar and embarrassing circumstances of the case.

3. Holding

Upon the whole, our opinion is, that the decree of the Circuit Court, affirming that of the District Court, ought to be affirmed, except so far as it directs the Negroes to be delivered to the President, to be transported to Africa, in pursuance of the act of the 3d of March, 1819; and, as to this, it ought to be reversed; and that the said Negroes be declared to be free, and be dismissed from the custody of the Court, and go without delay.

D. Commentary on *Amistad*

The declaration of freedom for the slaves in the *Amistad* case represented the first shot fired in the Civil War. The case had helped galvanize the proslavery and antislavery forces, pitting them against one another in the first direct legal confrontation over slavery before the Supreme Court. Although it came thirty years before the official outbreak of the war, the abolitionist victory in *Amistad* was a precursor to the North's ultimate victory over southern pro-slavery forces. Despite the bravery, courage, and character of Cinque and the other freedom fighters, most Africans already enslaved in the United States would remain in bondage until the end of the Civil War in 1865. The *Amistad* was the first in a series of abolitionist cases. It was, to some extent, a pyrrhic victory, given that six million slaves still suffered throughout the colonies, with many casualties in the coming years of continued slavery and through the civil war.

Given that Cinque was taken captive after the ban on the international slave trade, and he fought against his kidnappers for his own freedom, how would you characterize his actions? Was he a criminal or a freedom fighter? How do Cinque and his freedom fighters differ from the slave Celia, who defended herself against her owner when he repeatedly attacked her and forced himself upon her?

E. Background on *Prigg*

Donald E. Lively

*The Constitution and Race**

The finessing of slavery at the republic's inception effectively accommodated the institution, albeit in terms that obscured the Constitution's connection to it. The calculated bypass, however, deferred rather than avoided eventual reckoning. Despite Congress's explicit power to terminate the import of slaves beginning in 1808, the decision to allow or prohibit the institution itself was left to each state. Even before the ink had dried in Philadelphia, problematic questions pertaining to slavery had materialized. As the nation evolved over the next several decades, effective answers would be increasingly scarce. Original expectations that slavery would die of its own accord, or be satisfactorily reckoned with by the political process, were miscalculated or misplaced. Society instead became ever more deeply immersed in and confounded by the slavery issue.

In 1787, the Congress under the Articles of Confederation passed the Northwest Ordinance, which precluded "slavery . . . in the said territory, otherwise than in the punishment of crimes, whereof the party shall have been duly convicted." Competing sentiment exists as to whether the enactment represented "a symbol of the [American] Revolution's liberalism" or was "part of a larger, and insidious bargain" constituting "the first and last antislavery achievement by the central government." On its face, and despite inclusion of a fugitive slave clause, the Northwest Ordinance may seem consonant with a sense that slavery was a terminal institution. Some historians, noting that the ordinance was enacted by a southern dominated Congress one day after the three-fifths compromise on appointment, suggest that the prohibition was an exercise in calculated cynicism. They propose that support for the territorial proscription was offered in exchange for constitutional concessions on slavery, to secure political debts that would translate into support of the South's agenda in Congress, and to establish a tacit understanding that slavery was permissible in the Southwest.

Two years after the Northwest Ordinance was passed, the Southwest Territory, comprising the future states of Kentucky and Tennessee, was created in almost identical terms. The key difference in the new enactment was a provision to the effect that the federal government would not interfere with or prohibit slavery. A like restriction conditioned establishment of the Mississippi Territory. As the nineteenth century began to unfold, the Louisiana and Missouri territories elicited more extensive debate over slavery, and antislavery amendments to the respective enactments were defeated. Pertinent legislation eventually was structured without any explicit provisions for or against slavery. Congress, however, did prohibit slavery in Illinois, Indiana, and Michigan territories. By the early Nineteenth Century, slavery

---

* (footnotes omitted).

had become an increasingly complicating factor in the process of establishing new territories and expanding the union. Over the next few decades, what commenced as a thorny issue hardened into an intractable problem and national crisis.

An especially portentous confrontation between North and South on the issue of slavery occurred in 1819, as Congress considered proposals to grant Missouri statehood and to create an Arkansas territory. An initial House bill that would have banned slavery in Missouri, where it already was well established, provoked a profoundly negative southern response. Arkansas's territorial candidacy was advanced without restrictions on slavery, and southern representatives coalesced to block Maine's simultaneous application for admission to the union. With Maine's statehood held hostage by the South, the House eventually approved a Senate amendment that allowed Missouri to become a state without slavery restrictions and admitted Maine as a free state. The resultant Missouri compromise provided that slavery would be forever forbidden in the remaining Louisiana Territory north of a line etched at 36° 30' North. The Maine and Missouri controversy, although eventually settled, disclosed that the slavery debate was ratcheting in the direction of increasing sectional rancor. Despite persisting expressions that slavery was a dying institution and individual decisions by such luminaries as Madison, Taney and others to liberate their slaves, the issue was enlarging rather than vanishing.

Early decades of territorial expansion indicate a general assumption that Congress possessed the power to determine slavery's permissibility in the territories and to condition statehood accordingly. That sense originally was disclosed by the South's endorsement of the Northwest Ordinance in antislavery terms. It persisted, despite sectional antagonism manifested by the Missouri and Maine controversy. Evolving political thought, increasingly acrimonious debates over new territories and states, northern recognition of slavery's actual reach, and southern perceptions of vulnerability, however, eventually destabilized initial assumptions. Further challenging the basic premise of federal neutrality and the models of compromise and accommodation was the emergence of radical abolitionism.

During the 1830s, abolitionism burst into American thinking with new arguments about what the Constitution required or prohibited. The South's intolerant response to the promulgation of abolitionist views evidenced not only the region's heightened sense of imperilment but also its evolving sense that the issue was no longer debatable. Southern prohibition of antislavery literature would have presented in later times a First Amendment crisis. Asserting that Congress had no power over slavery, southern representatives maintained also that abolitionists had no freedom to petition for antislavery legislation. Southern political assumptions, previously consonant with the exercise of federal power on questions of slavery, began to challenge the legitimacy of such authority. Debates concerning slavery in the District of Columbia and Texas further evidenced the hardening of proslavery sentiment. Although Congress possessed authority "[t]o exercise exclusive Legislation in all Cases whatsoever" in the District of Columbia, southern influence assured the vitality of slavery there.

As perceived threats to slavery had magnified and the stakes accordingly had increased, southern strategists searched for more secure doctrinal footing. A key reference was the Constitution itself, which, although originally avoiding outright endorsement or repudiation of slavery, was increasingly the object of revisionist interpretive notions. Abolitionist thinking would divide over whether the Constitution was an anti-slavery document that should be so animated or a pro-slavery charter that should be structurally overhauled. The South, meanwhile, turned toward doctrinal formulations that would not just accommodate but support slavery. In championing slavery in the District of Columbia, southern legislators asserted that the federal government was an agent of the several states with the affirmative obligation of supporting their various institutions, including slavery. Presaging a significant premise in *Scott v. Sandford*, they also argued that slaves were property protected by the Fifth Amendment.

The issue of Texas annexation, which Congress faced in the 1840s, disclosed further how constitutional thought was coursing beyond premises of a neutral federal role to competition over whether the document required an affirmative position for or against slavery. The Wilmot Proviso, which would have prohibited slavery in all territory acquired from Mexico, ultimately failed but not without sharpening sectional divisions. The proviso was significant, even if not enacted, insofar as it contemplated a deviation from the lines drawn and the sectional balance struck by the Missouri Compromise. Its mere proposal suggested a movement in the North and South away from accommodation and toward confrontation.

Such events were the backdrop against which consensus was fragmenting. Pro-slavery sentiment, as noted previously, progressed toward an assertive interpretation of the Constitution as prohibiting interference with the institution. Antislavery thinking, which never merged into a unified front, presented a variety of sometimes conflicting positions. The perspective of William Lloyd Garrison was that the Constitution endorsed slavery. For him, the deficiency could be accounted for only by dissolving the union. Competing with Garrison's analysis was the notion that the federal government had no power over slavery in the state and must dissociate itself from any support for the institution. Other theorists, described as "constitutional utopians," considered the due process and privileges and immunities clauses, notwithstanding their operation against federal power, as potential reference points for an antislavery charter or at least a theory of review favoring liberation.

Multiplying perspectives of what the Constitution did or did not require were consistent with the expanding contours of debate beyond the original question of whether Congress had the authority to ban slavery in territories. Congress's territorial powers, if analyzed without the distorting frictions of the time, may not have presented such difficult questions or have been so susceptible to competing interpretation. The exercise of such power during and after the Constitution's drafting, with southern participation and support, suggests that the federal interest and role were apt and initially uncontroversial. This impression is reinforced by review of congressional power in circumstances unrelated to slavery. In *American Insurance*

Co. v. Canter, the Supreme Court had determined that "[i]n legislating for the territories, Congress exercises the combined powers of the general, and of a state government." Despite recognition of broad federal power over the territories, reflected by jurisprudence and by actual practice, arguments for slavery sought to redefine congressional authority. The debate thus reflected movement beyond original considerations of state determination and federal neutrality and toward an eventual constitutional showdown.

Attention to the Constitution's meaning for slavery was renewed and revised as a function not merely of the nation's expansion but of other realities and perceptions as well. Like territorial governance, the question of fugitive slaves originally presented no significant controversy. The fugitive slave clause of the Constitution was not a subject of significant attention or debate when framed. Soon after ratification, Congress enacted a fugitive slave law which also was notable for its immediate uncontroversiality. As the nation's attention became more focused on slavery in subsequent decades, however, the fugitive slave clause would move from the margins to the center of debate. Even if the actual number of slave renditions was relatively few, fugitive slave legislation, more discernibly than territorial compromise, manifested congressional aiding and abetting of the institution. The fugitive slave controversy effectively heightened northern awareness of the reality that slavery implicated the entire nation rather than just a region. Even if a slave was apprehended and returned, his or her economic value was diminished by the act of running away and the consequently disclosed risk of future escape. The fugitive slave issue nonetheless acquired significant political meaning. For the South, it represented a test of the federal government's willingness to accommodate and later support slavery. For the North, it clarified how entangled the entire society was in the institution.

Fugitive slave legislation, more visibly than its constitutional predicate, directly implicated the federal government in the cause of slavery. The Constitution's fugitive slave clause provided that

> [n]o person held to Service or Labour in one State, under the Laws thereof, escaping into another, shall, in Consequence of any Law or Regulation therein, be discharged from such Service or Labour, but shall be delivered up on Claim of the Party to whom such Service or Labour may be due.

The provision was housed in Article IV, which concerns interstate relations, rather than in Article I, which delineates the powers of Congress. Because it also did not have an explicit implementation provision, like the Full Faith and Credit clause in the same article, a credible argument existed that it provided no authority for a congressional enactment. Although the clause eventually elicited intense constitutional controversy, its original purpose is uncertain. The provision was drafted and adopted without debate or formal vote as the convention was winding down. Not surprisingly, given its vagueness and relative inattention afforded it, the fugitive slave clause was a source of diverging interpretations ranging from the sense that it established a right of recovery anywhere in the nation to the perception that it simply precluded another state's emancipation of runaway slaves. The observation has been made that, during the framing process, no one "could foresee a federally regulated Fugitive Slave Law with marshals and special commissioners." Soon after ratification, however, Congress enacted legislation that enshrined the clause as a predicate for affirmative federal support of slavery.

Congress initially accounted for the fugitive slave problem by passing the Fugitive Slave Act of 1793. The act (1) imposed on a state the duty to return fugitives upon official demand, and (2) enabled a slave owner to cross state lines, apprehend the alleged fugitive, and, upon proof of ownership to a judicial officer, reclaim and remove the person. Although the act itself provided no incidents of due process, such as the right to a hearing, several states enacted laws prohibiting the kidnaping of blacks or at least providing opportunities to contest the claims of slave owners or their agents.

Fugitive slave legislation represented an early paradox in the federal system. Slavery had been constitutionally accommodated pursuant to the premise of federal neutrality and individual state determination. Imposition of universal obligations to account for fugitive slaves constituted an early exercise in the expansion of federal power. The constitutional predicate for the policy, as previously noted, was dubious but originally uncontroverted. Reaction to and debate over the fugitive slave clause and federal legislation, therefore, was effective in illuminating sectional incompatibility and enhancing mutual disaffection.

The Constitution and Race 11–17.
Copyright © (1992) Donald E. Lively.
Reprinted with Permission of Donald E. Lively.

Less than a year after *Amistad*, the Supreme Court would strengthen the chains of bondage for enslaved blacks by making it easier to capture and return runaway slaves. As northern states outlawed slavery, some became more tolerant of and receptive to runaway slaves. Safe havens for runaway slaves began to develop gradually in some northern states. This development created legal and political conflict between slave states and free states.

F. *Prigg v. The Commonwealth of Pennsylvania,* 41 U.S. 539 (1842)

1. Facts

Justice STORY delivered the opinion of the Court.

The plaintiff in error was indicted in the Court of Oyer and Terminer for York county, for having, with force and violence, taken and carried away from that county to the state of Maryland, a certain negro woman, named Margaret Morgan, with a design and intention of selling and disposing of, and keeping her as a slave or servant for life, contrary to a statute of Pennsylvania, passed on the 26th of March, 1826. That statute in the first section, in substance, provides, that if any person or persons shall from and after the passing of the act, by force and violence take and carry away, or cause to be taken and carried away, and shall by fraud or false pretense, seduce, or cause to be seduced, or shall attempt to take, carry away, or seduce any negro or mulatto from any part of that commonwealth, with a design and intention of selling and disposing of, or causing to be sold, or of keeping and detaining, or of causing to be kept and detained, such Negro or mulatto as a slave or servant for life, or for any term whatsoever; every such person or persons, his or their aiders or abettors, shall, on conviction thereof, be deemed guilty of a felony, and shall forfeit and pay a sum not less than five hundred, nor more than one thousand dollars; and moreover, shall be sentenced to undergo a servitude for any term or terms of years, not less than seven years nor exceeding twenty-one years; and shall be confined and kept to hard labour. There are many other provisions in the statute which is recited at large in the record, but to which it is in our view unnecessary to advert upon the present occasion.

The plaintiff in error pleaded not guilty to the indictment; and at the trial the jury found a special verdict, which, in substance, states, that the Negro woman, Margaret Morgan, was a slave for life, and held to labour and service under and according to the laws of Maryland, to a certain Margaret Ashmore, a citizen of Maryland; that the slave escaped and fled from Maryland into Pennsylvania in 1832; that the plaintiff in error, being legally constituted the agent and attorney of the said Margaret Ashmore, in 1837, caused the said Negro woman to be taken and apprehended as a fugitive from labour by a state constable, under a warrant from a Pennsylvania magistrate; that the said Negro woman was thereupon brought before the said magistrate, who refused to take further cognisance of the case; and thereupon the plaintiff in error did remove, take, and carry away the said Negro woman and her children out of Pennsylvania into Maryland, and did deliver the said Negro woman and her children into the custody and possession of the said Margaret Ashmore. The special verdict further finds, that one of the children was born in Pennsylvania, more than a year after the said Negro woman had fled and escaped from Maryland.

Upon this special verdict, the Court of Oyer and Terminer of York county, adjudged that the plaintiff in error was guilty of the offence charged in the indictment. A writ of error was brought from that judgment to the Supreme Court of Pennsylvania, where the judgment was, pro forma, affirmed. From this latter judgment, the present writ of error has been brought to this Court. . . .

2. Opinion

There are two clauses in the Constitution upon the subject of fugitives, which stand in juxtaposition with each other, and have been thought mutually to illustrate each other. They are both contained in the second section of the fourth article, and are in the following words: "A person charged in any state with treason, felony, or other crime, who shall flee from justice, and be found in another state, shall, on demand of the executive authority of the state from which he fled, be delivered up, to be removed to the state having jurisdiction of the crime."

"No person held to service or labour in one state under the laws thereof, escaping into another, shall in consequence of any law or regulation therein, be discharged from such service or labour; but shall be delivered up, on claim of the party to whom such service or labour may be due."

The last clause is that, the true interpretation whereof is directly in judgment before us. Historically, it is well known, that the object of this clause was to secure to the citizens of the slaveholding states the complete right and title of ownership in their slaves, as property, in every state in the Union into which they might escape from the state where they were held in servitude. The full recognition of this right and title was indispensable to the security of this species of property in all the slave-holding states; and, indeed, was so vital to the preservation of their domestic interests and institutions, that it cannot be doubted that it constituted a fundamental article, without the adoption of which the Union could not have been formed. Its true design was to guard against the doctrines and principles prevalent in the non-slaveholding states, by preventing them from intermeddling with, or obstructing, or abolishing the rights of the owners of slaves. . . .

The clause manifestly contemplates the existence of a positive, unqualified right on the part of the owner of the slave, which no state law or regulation can in any way qualify, regulate, control, or restrain. The slave is not to be discharged from service or labour, in consequence of any state law or regulation. Now, certainly, without indulging in any nicety of criticism upon words, it may fairly and reasonably be said, that any state law or state regulation, which interrupts, limits, delays, or postpones the right of the owner to the immediate possession of the slave, and the immediate command of his service and labour, operates, pro tanto, a discharge of the slave therefrom. The question can never be, how much the slave is discharged from; but whether he is discharged from any, by the natural or necessary operation of state laws or state regulations. The question is not one of quantity or degree, but of withholding, or controlling the incidents of a positive and absolute right. . . .

And this leads us to the consideration of the other part of the clause, which implies at once a guaranty and duty. It says, "But he (the slave) shall be delivered up on claim of the party to whom such service or labour may be due." Now, we think it exceedingly difficult, if not impracticable, to read this language and not to feel that it contemplated some farther remedial redress than that which might be administered at the hands of the owner himself. A claim is to be made. What is a claim? It is, in a just juridical sense, a demand of some matter as of right made by one person upon another, to do or to forbear to do some act or thing as a matter of duty . . .

It is plain, then, that where a claim is made by the owner, out of possession, for the delivery of a slave, it must be made, if at all, against some other person; and inasmuch as the right is a right of property capable of being recognised and asserted by proceedings before a Court of justice, between parties adverse to each other, it constitutes, in the strictest sense, a controversy between the parties, and a case "arising under the Constitution" of the United States; within the express delegation of judicial power given by that instrument. Congress, then, may call that power into

activity for the very purpose of giving effect to that right; and if so, then it may prescribe the mode and extent in which it shall be applied, and how, and under what
circumstances the proceedings shall afford a complete protection and guaranty to
the right.

Congress has taken this very view of the power and duty of the national government. As early as the year 1791, the attention of Congress was drawn to it, (as we
shall hereafter more fully see) in consequence of some practical difficulties arising
under the other clause, respecting fugitives from justice escaping into other states.
The result of their deliberations, was the passage of the act of the 12th of February,
1793, ch. 51,(7), which, after having, in the first and second sections, provided for
the case of fugitives from justice by a demand to be made of the delivery through
the executive authority of the state where they are found. . . .

But it has been argued, that the act of Congress is unconstitutional, because it
does not fall within the scope of any of the enumerated powers of legislation confided to that body; and therefore it is void. Stripped of its artificial and technical
structure, the argument comes to this, that although rights are exclusively secured
by, or duties are exclusively imposed upon the national government, yet, unless the
power to enforce these rights, or to execute these duties can be found among the
express powers of legislation enumerated in the Constitution, they remain without
any means of giving them effect by any act of Congress; and they must operate
solely proprio vigore, however defective may be their operation; nay, even although,
in a practical sense, they may become a nullity from the want of a proper remedy to
enforce them, or to provide against their violation. If this be the true interpretation
of the Constitution, it must, in a great measure, fail to attain many of its avowed and
positive objects as a security of rights, and a recognition of duties. Such a limited
construction of the Constitution has never yet been adopted as correct, either in
theory or practice. No one has ever supposed that congress could, constitutionally,
by its legislation, exercise powers, or enact laws beyond the powers delegated to it
by the Constitution; but it has, on various exercised powers which were necessary
and proper as means to carry into effect rights expressly given, and duties expressly
enjoined thereby. The end being required, it has been deemed a just and necessary
implication, that the means to accomplish it are given also; or, in other words, that
the power flows as a necessary means to accomplish the end. . . .

It is scarcely conceivable that the slaveholding states would have been satisfied
with leaving to the legislation of the non-slaveholding states, a power of regulation,
in the absence of that of Congress, which would or might practically amount to a
power to destroy the rights of the owner. If the argument, therefore, of a concurrent power in the states to act upon the subject-matter in the absence of legislation
by Congress, be well founded; then, if Congress had never acted at all; or if the act
of Congress should be repealed without providing a substitute, there would be a
resulting authority in each of the states to regulate the whole subject at its pleasure;
and to dole out its own remedial justice, or withhold it at its pleasure and according
to its own views of policy and expediency. Surely such a state of things never could

have been intended, under such a solemn guarantee of right and duty. On the other hand, construe the right of legislation as exclusive in Congress, and every evil, and every danger vanishes. The right and the duty are then co-extensive and uniform in remedy and operation throughout the whole Union. The owner has the same security, and the same remedial justice, and the same exemption from state regulation and control, through however many states he may pass with his fugitive slave in his possession, in transitu, to his own domicile. But, upon the other supposition, the moment he passes the state line, he becomes amenable to the laws of another sovereignty, whose regulations may greatly embarrass or delay the exercise of his rights; and even be repugnant to those of the state where he first arrested the fugitive. Consequences like these show that the nature and objects of the provision imperiously require, that, to make it effectual, it should be construed to be exclusive of state authority. We adopt the language of this Court in *Sturgis v. Crowninshield*, 4 Wheat, Rep. 193, and say, that "it has never been supposed that the concurrent power of legislation extended to every possible case in which its exercise by the states has not been expressly prohibited. The confusion of such a practice would be endless." And we know no case in which the confusion and public inconvenience and mischiefs thereof, could be more completely exemplified than the present.

These are some of the reasons, but by no means all, upon which we hold the power of legislation on this subject to be exclusive in Congress. To guard, however, against any possible misconstruction of our views, it is proper to state, that we are by no means to be understood in any manner whatsoever to doubt or to interfere with the police power belonging to the states in virtue of their general sovereignty. That police power extends over all subjects within the territorial limits of the states; and has never been conceded to the United States. It is wholly distinguishable from the right and duty secured by the provision now under consideration; which is exclusively derived from and secured by the Constitution of the United States, and owes its whole efficacy thereto. We entertain no doubt whatsoever, that the states, in virtue of their general police power, possess full jurisdiction to arrest and restrain runaway slaves, and remove them from their borders, and otherwise to secure themselves against their depredations and evil example, as they certainly may do in cases of idlers, vagabonds, and paupers. The rights of the owners of fugitive slaves are in no just sense interfered with, or regulated by such a course; and in many cases, the operations of this police power, although designed essentially for other purposes, for the protection, safety, and peace of the state, may essentially promote and aid the interests of the owners. But such regulations can never be permitted to interfere with or to obstruct the just rights of the owner to reclaim his slave, derived from the Constitution of the United States; or with the remedies prescribed by Congress to aid and enforce the same.

3. Holding

Upon these grounds, we are of opinion that the act of Pennsylvania upon which this indictment is founded, is unconstitutional and void. It purports to punish as a public offence against that state, the very act of seizing and removing a slave by his master, which the Constitution of the United States was designed to justify and uphold. The special verdict finds this fact, and the State Courts have rendered judgment against the plaintiff in error upon that verdict. That judgment must, therefore, be reversed, and the cause remanded to the Supreme Court of Pennsylvania; with directions to carry into effect the judgment of this Court rendered upon the special verdict in favour of the plaintiff in error.

G. Commentary on *Prigg*

William D. Green

The Summer Christmas Came to Minnesota:
*The Case of Eliza Winston, A Slave**

The question of fugitive slaves was volatile: what duty did northern state and local officials have to return them to their masters? The United States Supreme Court, in the 1842 case of *Prigg v. Pennsylvania*, provided no guidance, holding that state and local officials were not required to assist in the return of fugitive slaves. Rather, the decision to return slaves to their owners was left to the officials' discretion. Moreover, Justice Story, writing for the Court, held that claimants of fugitive slaves had a right of self-help—they could forcibly take the slave—provided the action in no way breached the peace of the community. Indeed, "Story admitted that free states had the power to prohibit their officials from enforcing a federal law. After *Prigg*, many states passed legislation barring the use of state facilities for fugitive rendition and prohibiting state officials from participating in the rendition process." Abolitionists could use the courts to frustrate slaveholders. Another effective means of frustrating slaveowners' legal right to self-help was to threaten violence, sometimes to the consternation of the community at large. To stall slave owners from reclaiming fugitive slaves, abolitionists needed only to resist those owners by force of arms. For example, in Salem, Iowa, in 1848, nineteen abolitionists forced slave catchers who had captured nine slaves to bring the fugitives before the justice of the peace. The slaves were released. Outnumbered, and threatened with violence, the slave catchers returned to Missouri empty-handed. After *Prigg*, the institution of slavery was shaken and violence was inevitable. The opinion came to be used as a weapon against slavery. Even Chief Justice Taney, who agreed with the majority, nevertheless bitterly attacked Justice Story for what he "perceived (correctly as it turned out) to be the antislavery implications of the opinion."

Eight years later when southern states threatened to leave the Union, thereby forcing the ratification of the Missouri Compromise, Congress mollified the South with assurances that *Prigg* would be mitigated by strict enforcement of the Fugitive

* (footnotes omitted).

Slave Act of 1850. In practical terms, the new law was unenforceable where the community sentiment was virulently antislavery.

8 *Law and Inequality* 151, 156–58.
Copyright © (1989) *Law and Inequality Review*.
Reprinted with permission of the *Law and Inequality Review*.

Donald E. Lively

*The Constitution and Race**

The implications of fugitive slave arrangements could not be permanently avoided or downplayed, however, given a system in which sectional competition over slavery in general was enlarging and deepening. Many northern states, responding to Congress's failure to afford basic legal process or to deter disregard of even pro forma legal procedure, enacted personal liberty laws. Legislation in some instances provided for writs of habeas corpus or like devices and prohibited the kidnapping of blacks. During the 1820s, Pennsylvania authorized detention of alleged fugitives only by judicial officers, required more extensive proof of ownership, and criminalized private seizure of a black person. The legislation endeavored to balance the state's obligation under the 1793 act with due process concerns, especially for free blacks who otherwise were vulnerable to mistaken identification or exploitation. It also resulted in comprehensive judicial review of the fugitive slave law. The consequent decision, in *Prigg v. Pennsylvania*, has been described as "rival[ing] *Dred Scott v. Sandford* in historical importance."

The circumstances of the *Prigg* decision illuminated precisely the concerns that prompted enactment of the Pennsylvania law. At issue was the status of a Maryland slave couple's daughter, never herself previously claimed as a slave, and her children. The woman had married a free man and moved to Pennsylvania where some of her children were born. After she had resided in Pennsylvania for five years, descendants of her parents' owner sought to have her and the children returned to Maryland. Although the offsprings' agent Edward Prigg obtained a warrant for arrest, the Pennsylvania court refused to provide a certificate for removal. Prigg nonetheless took the woman and her children in violation of the state law. Maryland initially refused to extradite Prigg, but the Pennsylvania legislature enacted a law providing him with special procedural consideration and safeguards so that the constitutionality of the state law could be assessed. Prigg was convicted and, within a year, had appealed to the U.S. Supreme Court.

The *Prigg* decision was authored by Justice Story who had been a longtime critic of slavery. Story nonetheless rendered a decision that invalidated the Pennsylvania law on the grounds it conflicted with the Fugitive Slave Act of 1793 and the Constitution. In sum, he determined that the federal law was constitutional, a state law at

---

* (footnotes omitted).

odds with the statute was impermissible, and slave owners could recapture fugitive slaves on their own initiative and by their own devices.

Determination that the federal law of 1793 was constitutional, although perhaps unsettling to Story's moral precepts, was consistent with a jurisprudential style characterized by a nationalist ideology and a commitment to judicial restraint. He discerned that congressional power to enact the Fugitive Slave Act of 1793 was reasonably inferred from the fugitive slave clause of the Constitution. Simple as the premise was, the Court's analysis was not airtight. Because the fugitive slave clause is set forth in Article IV, as noted previously, a credible argument existed that it spoke to relations among the states instead of providing a basis for congressional action. The Court itself avoided meaningful inquiry into whether the act was at odds with specific constitutional guarantees. The federal law denied even the rudimentary incidents of due process to free blacks who might be wrongly or mistakenly apprehended. As a consequence, Congress and the Court permitted a deprivation of fundamental liberty that they almost certainly would have repaired if white persons had been similarly slighted. The enactment and Story's response to it suggest that Taney's subsequent blurring of legal distinctions between free blacks and slaves was neither aberrational nor unique.

A critical aspect of the Court's decision was the determination that fugitive slaves were within the federal government's exclusive jurisdiction. This finding was consistent with jurisprudence that, in the time between *Marbury v. Madison* and *Scott v. Sandford*, had invalidated no federal statute. The grounding of the Fugitive Slave Act in Article IV at least offered an eminent point for distinguishing *Prigg* from otherwise expansive readings of national power. The Court, however, bypassed any such analysis.

The *Prigg* decision warned against state legislation that would "interfere with or . . . obstruct the just rights of the owner to reclaim his slave." Favorable as the ruling was to the immediate interests of slavery, it nonetheless communicated a mixed message to the South. Although resolving the fugitive slave question in terms favorable to southern interests, the decision introduced the unsettling prospect that slavery itself was a federal rather than a state concern. Chief Justice Taney sensed the possibility that if the federal government could provide for slavery, it also could operate against it. He thus wrote separately to make the point that states were not only prohibited from interfering with a slave owner's rights but also obligated to protect them.

The Court's decision, if examined solely within the context of its four corners, would seem to have an undeniably proslavery cast. Endorsement of a virtually unqualified right to recapture a slave, pursuant to a slave owner's own methodology, effectively extended the law of southern states into the North. Despite constitutional and statutory intimations of at least minimal procedural protection, the only limitation on recapturing a slave or kidnapping a free black was that it be effected "without any breach of the peace, or illegal violence." Demands of the South, at least for fugitive slave purposes, thus became requirements of the nation.

The *Prigg* ruling, however, enhanced rather than terminated the controversy. By illustrating how inextricably the whole nation was bound up in slavery, it compounded anti-slavery sentiment and destabilized rather than secured the institution. For radical abolitionists, the *Prigg* ruling further validated their view of the Constitution as a proslavery document. The manifest implication of the entire nation in slavery defeated imagery of a wall between northern and southern custom and enhanced the conviction that the Constitution should be resisted even at the cost of disunion. In his abolitionist publication *The Liberator*, William Lloyd Garrison observed that allowing a slave owner to claim his property in any state "establish[ed] the constitutionality of slavery in every State in the Union."

Despite the criticism it engendered, the decision soon became a source for undermining the interests it supposedly had secured. Story had determined that Congress could authorize state courts to enforce the law but could not, without abridging state powers, require them to do so. He further ventured that "it might well be deemed an unconstitutional exercise of power of interpretation, to insist that the states are bound to carry into effect the duties of the national government, nowhere delegated or instructed to them by the Constitution." Story also noted that state judges, although not obligated to enforce federal law, nonetheless could do so "unless prohibited by state legislation." Such observations restated common understandings of the imperatives and incidents of federalism. Offered in the context of a profoundly divisive ideological conflict, however, effect proved disproportionate to purpose. As Chief Justice Taney accurately forecast, these statements, although not part of the Court's holding and thus not binding, became a departure point for neutralizing the otherwise proslavery cast of the *Prigg* decision. Noting the scarcity of federal judges in many states, he warned that "if the state authorities are absolved from all obligation to protect this right, and may stand by and see it violated without an effort to defend it, the act of Congress of 1793 scarcely deserves the name of a remedy."

Taney's worst fears promptly were confirmed, as many northern legislatures and courts, respectively, enacted laws and rendered decisions transforming a principle favorable to slavery into one antagonistic to the institution. Several states prohibited their judges from enforcing the federal law. Even without legislation, courts cited to *Prigg* itself for purposes of disclaiming authority to hear fugitive slave actions. Five years after the decision, Pennsylvania enacted a law precluding jurisdiction in all fugitive slave cases. Instead of settling an account in favor of slavery, therefore, the ruling actually advanced the antislavery cause. Having been sensitized to their nexus with the institution they condemned, northern states responded in terms and deeds calculated to sever their linkage. Ambivalence that could accommodate slavery thus became increasingly susceptible to displacement by cognition of the institution's real and broad demands.

By enhancing northern awareness of slavery's national significance, the *Prigg* decision quickened and deepened societal antagonisms. Prior to *Prigg*, the law had accommodated slavery while largely avoiding the imagery of real involvement with the institution. Evidencing how effectively that illusion was pierced, northern participation in rendering fugitive slaves actually diminished after *Prigg*. Despite pervasive racism in the North, conversion of an essentially proslavery decision into an antislavery principle disclosed an enhanced sense of how slavery infected the entire nation and consequent effort to minimize its reach.

So extensively and effectively was *Prigg* repudiated and offset in the following decade that Congress enacted a new fugitive slave law. Central to the legislation was neutralization of the dicta that had become the basis for northern resistance to rather than cooperation in recaption and rendition. To compensate for state reluctance to effectuate the law, a federal bureau was established and vested with enforcement power. Fortification of the fugitive slave law was part of a broad congressional effort to resolve several thorny problems associated with the general question of slavery. Not only did the resultant Compromise of 1850 codify new fugitive slave legislation, it also provided for California's admission to the union as a free state, organized the Utah and New Mexico territories as slave jurisdictions, and prohibited the slave trade in the District of Columbia. Architects and supporters of the compromise envisioned it as a final resolution of the slavery issue. The legislative premises, however, were grounds in the problem-solving model of the past when the South perceived less peril to slavery and the North was less conscious of its connection to the institution. Given the significantly altered operational circumstances, it is not surprising that the Compromise of 1850 proved to be a temporary rather than a permanent melioration.

Just how unsettled pertinent norms and practices had become was evinced shortly after the Compromise of 1850 was enacted. Southern opposition to the creation of Nebraska as a free territory challenged the long-established dividing line etched by the Missouri Compromise. Instead of maintaining a geographical bright line Congress considered more complex premises for determining how territories were to be established and states admitted to the union. Competing for acceptance were Democratic Party concepts of popular sovereignty and competing notions of free soil. Experience in Kansas and Nebraska was defined by the Democratic principle of allowing a territory's populace to determine its institutions. The result was unbridled turmoil, chicanery, and violence. The Democratic consensus itself would soon subdivide into competing northern and southern positions respectively staked to readings of the Constitution as neutral but accommodating slavery and actually supporting and protecting it.

Having wrestled with slavery for more than half a century, and having crafted policy yielding ever-diminishing returns, Congress appeared increasingly incapable of formulating a durable solution. Hardened differences between northern and southern legislators of different parties, compounded by the split between northern and southern Democrats, augured unfavorably for a consensus on federal policy. In its representative capacity, Congress was a microcosm of the profound sectional antagonism and mutual distrust that had come to define the nation. Increasing attention to constitutional imperatives, although a competitive exercise among slavery's supporters and detractors, pointed toward the judiciary as a possible forum for resolving the issue. What the framers had avoided and Congress could not successfully compromise thus eventually was reckoned with by means of litigation.

Constitutional jurisprudence by the midpoint of the century already had established a favorable disposition toward the South at least in terms of accommodating slavery. Dominated by southern jurists, the Court in the 1850s enhanced that tradition. Decisions preceding *Scott v. Sandford* revealed an enthusiasm for the southern position that at times was excessive. In *Strader v. Graham*, the Court dismissed a case on procedural grounds but proceeded to decide substantive questions anyway. The action originated in Kentucky, where a slave owner sued a party who helped his slaves escape to Canada. The defense was premised on the argument that upon setting foot in Ohio the slaves were free. The Kentucky court rejected the proposition, and the Supreme Court dismissed the case for lack of jurisdiction. Normative principle of review precluded the Court from resolving issues unnecessary for disposition of a case. Despite that basic premise, the Court gratuitously observed that the law of a slave state applied in determining the issue of freedom. Although the principle was not essential to the action's resolution, the Court in 1852 asserted the primacy of the slave state's interest.

A decade after *Prigg*, the Court revisited fugitive slave questions. In *Moore v. Illinois*, it upheld a state law punishing individuals who aided fugitive slaves. The decision was an extension of *Prigg* insofar as the Court earlier had suggested that state police power could be used to promote and aid but not interfere with the interest of slave owners. Unlike *Prigg*, the ruling was an unequivocal reminder of the North's unwanted obligations to the South. Northern understanding of slavery as a national rather than regional phenomenon accordingly was further enhanced.

By 1850, the debate between North and South was notable for how it had been redefined. With respect to slavery, original thinking had contemplated a neutral federal role and individual state determination. Over the course of several decades, that premise was unsettled by fugitive slave experience and territorial expansion. Congress effectively extended the reach of slavery nationwide in 1793 when it enacted legislation protecting slaveowner interests in runaways. Despite jurisprudential efforts to effectuate the act and legislative attempts to enhance it, southern attitudes increasingly and accurately assumed that the North wished to distance itself from and minimize the operation of slavery. The refusal of free states to turn over fugitive slaves, contrary to the Supreme Court's delineation of duty, represented an exercise in detachment. Refusal to respect the claims and interests of slave owners, which the South had secured through the legislative and judicial processes, revealed that a final and comprehensive decision on the institution itself could not be avoided forever.

Intense competition between North and South already was manifesting itself in efforts to define policy in the remaining territories. The admission of California as a free state denoted the South's failure to extend the Missouri Compromise line to the Pacific. Southern legislators responded by defeating a bill for the Nebraska Territory, which was introduced on the premise that slavery was prohibited north of the latitude of compromise. The Kansas-Nebraska Act, passed the following year, divided what originally was one territory into two and provided that eventual admission of each as a free or a slave state would depend on what their respective constitutions resolved. Implicit in the act was the possibility that the proposition of slavery might be resolved according to the concept of popular sovereignty. Subsequent political events and violence in Kansas over the content of the state's constitution indicated the high stakes involved for North and South.

Dispute over the status of Kansas and Nebraska revealed compounding fractures in the body politic and a further diminished congressional capacity. The Republican party emerged from the Kansas-Nebraska episode as a national force and primary exponent of free soil principles. The Democratic party split into northern and southern wings, divided by subtle but significant distinctions over the meaning of popular sovereignty. At issue was not the general question of territorial or state status but when and by whom the decision would be made. For southern Democrats, popular sovereignty enabled the people of a territory to permit or prohibit slavery when framing the constitution for statehood. Northern Democrats maintained that territorial legislatures could determine whether slavery should be permitted or prohibited. Both shared the view that the Constitution's territory clause did not vest the federal government with power to provide for or against slavery. The northern position, expounded most notably by Senator Stephen A. Douglas of Illinois, differed from the southern view in that territories were regarded as incipient states with full sovereignty. Such a perspective was inimical to southerners, concerned that if Congress could delegate power to prohibit slavery in the territories, it could pass judgment on the institution in general. The Douglas formula, which has been referred to as territorial rather than popular sovereignty, represented an effort to bridge the widening gap between North and South. Its failure demonstrated the profundity and insurmountability of sectional differences.

The Kansas-Nebraska controversy and contemporary political developments disclosed how vexing and convoluted the slavery problem had become for representative governance. The Kansas-Nebraska Act advanced a notion of popular sovereignty that, although subject to varying interpretations, added a new wrinkle to the traditional federal policy of neutrality. Self-determination in the new jurisdictions was made "subject only to the constitution." Given the manifest division over constitutional meaning and requirements, such direction was at least imprecise. It also was superfluous because judicial review is appropriate for any legislative action alleges to be unconstitutional. Even if unintended, passage of the act symbolized a timely invitation for judicial attention to an otherwise intractable problem. The Court, although having rendered several decisions concerning slavery, had yet to confront the territorial question. Judicial review thus loomed as an option for an effectively stalemated legislative process and the nations interest in a final constitutional resolution of a seemingly interminable problem.

The Constitution and Race 20–26.
Copyright © (1992) Donald E. Lively.
Reprinted with permission of Donald E. Lively.

In spite of the apparent loopholes for abolitionists, *Prigg* was for the most part a proslavery decision. In reversing Prigg's criminal conviction, the Supreme Court declared that the Pennsylvania law prohibiting the forcible removal of escaped slaves from the state violated the fugitive slave clause of the Constitution. According to the Justices, the clause prohibited any state provision that impaired the apprehending of fugitive slaves. *Prigg*, therefore, effectively prevented free states from lawfully providing any assistance or protection to runaway slaves. The fugitive slave clause appears in Article IV of the Constitution, under the power of the states. The clause recognizes slavery as a state institution, and recognizes that states have police powers to regulate themselves. The Supreme Court, therefore, erred in finding the fugitive slave clause an exclusive empowerment to Congress.

Most harmful to the protection of blacks, however, was the Supreme Court's support in *Prigg* of the presumption that all blacks, even those found in free states, had the status of slaves. The holding in *Prigg* provided a basis whereby blacks found by slave catchers in slave states were presumed to be slaves, and blacks found by slave catchers in free states also were presumed to be slaves. As a result, free blacks were constantly in jeopardy of being kidnapped by slave catchers and sold into slavery.[16] For the thousands of free blacks in Pennsylvania and other northern states, *Prigg* represented a clear denial of the due process of law guaranteed by the Constitution to all American citizens.

The life of Solomon Northrup provides a frightening example. Northrup was a free black man from New York who was kidnapped in 1841 and enslaved in Louisiana for twelve years. He was one of many victims to a system, supported by the Supreme Court decision in *Prigg*, that re-enslaved free blacks. After enduring twelve years of labor as a slave, Northrup finally regained his freedom by a New York State Supreme Court order in 1853.

Supreme Court decisions like *Prigg* helped to persuade abolitionists of the increased need for private initiatives. One of the most successful such initiatives was the "Underground Railroad,"[17] which involved organizing escapes and assisting runaway slaves' travel to freedom in Canada. Thousands of slaves secured their freedom in this way. Harriet Tubman, known as Black Moses, a runaway slave herself,

---

16. *See* OLAUDAH EQUIANO, THE INTERESTING NARRATIVE OF THE LIFE OF OLAUDAH EQUIANO (1814) reprinted in THE CLASSIC SLAVE NARRATIVES 3, 118 (Henry Louis Gates, Jr. ed., 1987); SOLOMON NORTHRUP, TWELVE YEARS A SLAVE, IN PUTTIN' ON OLE MASSA: THE SLAVE NARRATIVES OF HENRY BIBB, WILLIAM WELLS BROWN AND SOLOMON NORTHRUP (Gilbert Osofsky ed., 1969).

17. For a detailed description of the "Underground Railroad," *see* J. FRANKLIN, FROM SLAVERY TO FREEDOM: A HISTORY OF NEGRO AMERICANS 189–94 (5th ed. 1980).

personally led over nineteen separate missions.[18] With a five hundred dollar reward for her capture, dead or alive,[19] Tubman's exploits became a symbol of courage and defiance.

John Hope Franklin

From Slavery to Freedom: A History of Negro Americans (Fifth Edition)

Perhaps nothing did more to intensify the strife between North and South, and to emphasize in a most dramatic way the determination of abolitionists to destroy slavery, than the Underground Railroad. Slaves who ran away were irritating and troublesome enough, and the South had been plagued with them from the earliest days of slavery. But when free blacks and whites, fired with an almost fanatical zeal, undertook systematically to wreak havoc on an institution that meant so much to the South, it was almost too much to bear. It was this organized effort to undermine slavery, this manifestation of the workings of a presumably higher law, that put such a strain on intersectional relations and sent antagonists and protagonists of slavery scurrying headlong into the 1850s determined to have their uncompromising way.

The origin of the Underground Railroad goes back to the eighteenth century. Perhaps there were people to help fugitives as early as there were runaway slaves. By the end of the War for Independence, however, organized resistance seemed to be taking shape. At least George Washington thought so when he complained in 1786 of a slave, escaping from Alexandria to Philadelphia, "whom a society of Quakers, formed for such purposes, have attempted to liberate." By the following year Isaac T. Hopper had settled in Philadelphia, and though still in his teens he began to develop a program for the systematic assistance of slaves escaping from the South. Within a few years they were being helped in a number of towns in Pennsylvania and New Jersey. Slowly these antislavery operations spread in various directions.

Henrietta Buckmaster gives 1804 as the year of "incorporation" of the Underground Railroad. It was then that Gen. Thomas Boude, an officer during the Revolution, purchased a slave, Stephen Smith, and brought him home to Columbia, Pennsylvania, followed by Smith's mother, who had escaped to find her son. The Boudes took her in. Within a few weeks the woman who owned Smith's mother arrived and demanded her property. Not only did the Boudes refuse to surrender the slave, but the town supported them. The people of Columbia resolved to champion the cause of fugitives. By 1815 this sentiment was expressed in Ohio. And by 1819 underground methods were used to spirit slaves out of North Carolina. Even before the period of militant abolitionism, the movement that was to be known as the Underground Railroad had grown into a widespread institution.

The name "Underground Railroad" was probably coined shortly after 1831 when steam railroads became popular. There are several versions of how the movement

---

18. *Id.* at 194.
19. *Id.*

got its name. A plausible one concerns a slave, Tice Davids, who escaped from his Kentucky master in 1831 and got across the Ohio River. Although the master was in hot pursuit, he lost all trace of the slave after crossing the river, and was so confounded that he declared the slave must have "gone off on an underground road." That was entirely possible, for by 1831 there were plenty of "underground" roads on the Ohio River, and they had stations, conductors, and means of conveyance. From that time, which coincided exactly with the emergence of Garrison and his militant followers, down to the outbreak of the Civil War, the Underground Railroad operated in flagrant violation of the federal fugitive slave laws. It was the most eloquent defiance of slaveholders that abolitionists could make.

In the case of anything as full of adventure and danger as the Underground Railroad, it is difficult to separate fiction from fact. There are stories of breathtaking escapes and exciting experiences that would be quite incredible save for unquestionable verification by reliable sources. After the Railroad had developed an efficient organization, there was a generality of practice that makes possible a brief description of its operation. All, or almost all, of the operations took place a night, for that was the only time when the fugitive and his helpers felt even partially secure. Slaves prepared to make their escape by taking supplies from their masters and, if necessary, by disguising themselves. Those of fair complexion frequently passed as white persons and sometimes posed as their own masters. Darker ones posed as servants on their way to meet their owners. There are several cases on record where fugitives were provided at crucial moments with white babies in order to make their claims of being nurses appear more convincing. At times men posed as women and women as men.

In the early days of the Underground Railroad most of the fugitives were men and they usually traveled on foot. Later, when the traffic was heavy and women and children were fleeing, escorts and vehicles were provided. The conductors carried their human cargo in covered wagons, closed carriages, and farm wagons specially equipped with closed compartments. Negroes were sometimes but in boxes and shipped as freight by rail or boat. Thus Henry Box Brown was shipped from Richmond to Philadelphia by the Adams Express Company. When traveling by land—and at night—conductors and fugitives were guided by the North Star, by tributaries of the Ohio or other rivers, and by mountain chains. On cloudy nights, when there were no other means of finding directions, they even resorted to feeling the moss on tree trunks and moving north upon discovering it.

Since travel was almost exclusively at night, it was necessary to have stations rather close together, from ten to twenty miles apart, where fugitives could rest, eat, and wait for the next night's journey. During the day they were hidden in barns, in the attics of homes, and in other out-of-the-way places. Meanwhile, the word was passed to succeeding stations, by what was called "the grape vine telegraph," that fugitives were on their way. One ambiguous message mailed by a conductor to the next stationmaster in 1859 gave much more information than a casual glance revealed. It read, "By tomorrow evening's mail, you will receive two volumes of "The Irrepressible Conflict" bound in black. After perusal, please forward and oblige."

All Underground Railroad lines led north. They began on various plantations in the South and ran vaguely — and dangerously — up rivers and valleys, and across mountains to some point on the Ohio or upper Mississippi River in the West, and to points in Pennsylvania and New Jersey in the East. Once the North had been reached the route was much clearer, though traversed with only slightly less danger, for planters, traders, and sheriffs pursued fugitives relentlessly and resorted to the most desperate means to recover them.

Even if the Underground Railroad did not need papers of incorporation, it needed capital. The fugitives required food and clothing, and frequently there were unexpected expenses such as boarding a train in order to evade a pursuing owner, or displaying affluence to convey the impression that one had been free long enough to accumulate wealth. Quakers and similar groups raised funds to carry on the work. The vigilance committees of Philadelphia and New York solicited money. Philanthropists contributed, as did the conductors and other "officials" of the Railroad. Harriet Tubman, one of the greatest of all conductors, would take several months off whenever she was running low in funds and hire herself out as a domestic servant in order to raise money for conveying slaves to freedom.

The Underground Railroad did not seem to suffer for want of operators. Wilbur H. Siebert has catalogued more than thirty-two hundred active workers; and there is every reason to believe that there were many more who will remain forever anonymous. Outstanding among the white workers was Levi Coffin, a Quaker and so-called president of the Underground Railroad. His strategic location in southern Indiana as well as his remarkable zeal made it possible for him to help more than three thousand slaves escape. Calvin Fairbanks, who had learned to hate slavery as a student at Oberlin College, began to travel in the South in 1837 on the dangerous business of freeing slaves. In Kentucky he engaged in a regular business of transporting slaves across the Ohio River. On one occasion, with a teacher from Vermont known as Miss Webster, he helped three salves escape by their posing as her servants. It was said that not one of his fugitives was ever recaptured, though he spent many years in jail for his work.

In many respects the most daring white conductor on the Underground Railroad was John Fairfield. Son of a Virginia slaveholding family, he would have nothing to do with the institution and decided to live in a free state. Before going north, he helped a slave who was his friend escape to Canada. News of his exploit spread: not only did the whites of his community seek to find and arrest him, but the slaves of his community also sought his aid to escape. He could not refuse to help, and thus began his career as a conductor on the Underground Railroad. He delivered slaves "on order." Negroes in the North and Canada would give him money and a description of their friends or relatives and he would deliver them. At times he conveyed as many as fifteen. He posed as a slaveholder, a Negro trader, or a peddler of eggs and poultry in Louisiana, Alabama, Mississippi, Tennessee, and Kentucky in order to gain the confidence of slaveholders. He was so convincing in each role that he was seldom suspected of being implicated in a slave's escape. Negroes he did not take to Canada he delivered to Levi Coffin, who arranged the rest of their journey. His greatest triumph was in conveying twenty-eight slaves to freedom by organizing them into a funeral procession. He suffered in his work from privations and exposure, and one time he was shot, but he persevered in his missions of freedom until his death in 1860, when he was believed to have been killed in an insurrection of slaves in Tennessee. John Brown, dashing from Missouri with twelve slaves and later attacking Harpers Ferry in an attempt at insurrection, has received more notice from historians, but Fairfield was as effective a fighter of slavery as any man who lived before the Civil War.

There were many Negro officials on the Underground Railroad. Jane Lewis of New Lebanon, Ohio, rowed fugitives regularly across the Ohio River. John Parker, who purchased himself for two thousand dollars, was in league with John Rankin and other white workers on the Railroad. Josiah Henson, born a slave, escaped with his wife and two children to Canada, learned to read and write, and returned south often to assist slaves in their escape. Once he went to Kentucky by a circuitous route through New York, Pennsylvania, and Ohio in order to avoid suspicion. He took 30 refugees out of Kentucky and led them to Toledo within a period of two weeks. Elijah Anderson has been called the general superintendent of the Underground Railroad in northwestern Ohio. From 1850 until his death seven years later in the Kentucky state prison, he worked arduously on behalf of fugitive slaves. By 1855 he had led more than 1,000 to freedom. John Mason, himself a fugitive slave from Kentucky, was one of the most astute conductors. According to William Mitchell, a Negro missionary in Canada, Mason brought 265 slaves to his home in the course of nineteen months. On one occasion he was captured and sold back into slavery, but again he made good his escape. In all he delivered about 1,300 slaves into free territory.

Easily the most outstanding Negro conductor on the Underground Railroad was Harriet Tubman. Although frail of body and suffering from recurrent spells of dizziness, she not only escaped from slavery herself, but conveyed many others to freedom, including her sister, her two children, and her aged mother and father. She is said to have gone south nineteen times and to have emancipated more than three hundred slaves. Unable to read or write, she nevertheless displayed remarkable ingenuity in the management of her runaway caravans. She preferred to start the journey on Saturday night, so that she could be well on her way before the owners had an opportunity the following Monday to advertise the escape of their slaves. She tolerated no cowardice and threatened to kill any slave who wished to turn back. Well known in Philadelphia, New York, and Boston, where she frequently delivered the escaped slaves, she preferred to lead them all the way to Canada after the passage of the Fugitive Slave Law in 1850, explaining that she could not trust Uncle Sam with her people any longer.

The very nature of the institution prevents any accurate estimate of the number of salves who found freedom by the Underground Railroad. Governor Quitman of Mississippi declared that between 1810 and 1850 the South lost 100,000 slaves valued at more than $30 million. This is a much larger figure than the census gives for Negroes in the North who were born in slaveholding states, but Wilbur H. Siebert believes that it is fairly accurate. He is certain, for example, that approximately 40,000 passed through Ohio alone.

The Underground Railroad intensified the resentment that the South felt toward outside interference. It was not realized that the Railroad ran inside the South. Not only Northerners participated in its management, but Southern whites and blacks were among its most valuable engineers and conductors, and all the passengers were Negroes desperately anxious to get away from the peculiar institution of the South.

> *From Slavery to Freedom: A History of Negro Americans* 189–94.
> Copyright © (1980) McGraw-Hill, Inc.
> Reprinted with permission of McGraw-Hill, Inc.

In 1850, Congress passed the Fugitive Slave Act. The Act provided that anyone who helped a slave become free or hid a slave could be fined $1,000 or jailed for six months. Suddenly at risk of a return to bondage, thousands of slaves who had escaped to Northern states fled a second time to Canada. All slaves in Southern states now made Canada, a much longer journey, their ultimate and final destination.

The journey on the "Underground Railroad" was often difficult. Runaway slaves faced many risks, including starvation, exposure to severe climate conditions, and slave patrols, which were authorized to shoot, maim, and torture captured runaways. Nevertheless, slavery was so oppressive that oftentimes slaves determined that freedom was worth the myriad risks and, occasionally, runaway slaves about to be caught would kill themselves rather than suffer a return to slavery.[20]

H. Background on *Scott*

1. Introduction

Through the nineteenth century, several legislative compromises attempted to define the balance between slavery and freedom in the states and territories. The Missouri Compromise of 1820 prohibited the introduction of slavery in the Louisiana territory above the line of latitude of 36 degrees, 30 minutes, while admitting Missouri as a slave state. From the year 1820 on, in spite of the Missouri Compromise, slave states in the South vigorously attempted to secure new land and to expand the economic and political power of slavery. At the same time, the opposition to the expansion of slavery by the manufacturing and commercial North and agricultural West increased in scope and intensity. The development of antislavery as a political movement was marked by the emergence of the Republican Party in the 1840s and 1850s.

---

20. *See* PHILLIP SCHWARTZ, TWICE CONDEMNED: SLAVES AND THE CRIMINAL LAWS OF VIRGINIA 1705–1865, 252 n. 33 (1988).

Opposition to the expansion of slavery, particularly among western settlers, was not founded on moral objections to slavery; rather, early settlers opposed competition with slave labor and held contempt for blacks, whether free or slave.[21] Republicans considered that the institution of slavery itself, not the race of the slave, posed a threat to society. More often, however, Republicans indicated that they made little distinction between free blacks and slaves, and felt that association with any blacks degraded the white race.[22]

In this light, the increasingly intense conflict in the United States in the decades before the Civil War—though it ultimately centered on slavery—was not based primarily on moral opposition to slavery or on a political struggle for the abolition of slavery where it already existed. Radical elements of the Republican Party were, in fact, concerned with the morality of slavery, its abolishment wherever it existed, and the granting of some form of legal equality and political rights to blacks. Abolitionists and political radicals, however, represented a distinct minority, both in numbers and in popular acceptance of their goals. In the western regions, where opposition to the expansion of slavery was particularly vehement, the abolitionists were generally held in equally low esteem.

Prior to the Civil War, especially in the Southern states, whites maintained absolute control over all social, political, and legal aspects of society. With the partial exception of the New England states, evidence indicates that up to the outbreak of the Civil War, and in fact through the outbreak of World War II, the dominant theme of American history, North and South, was that this nation should be under the absolute control and dominance of whites—a government of white men in which blacks would occupy an inferior and subjugated position. In the South, slavery ensured dominance by whites. Conversely, in the Western states, the prohibition of slavery was viewed as the best means of preserving white dominance. Limited legal equality for blacks was successful only along the eastern seaboard, where slavery had gradually dissipated and the black population remained constant and small.

Against the pervasive reality of white dominance, throughout the country, in which blacks were viewed fit only for slavery in the South,[23] the Supreme Court considered the questions presented by the *Dred Scott* case concerning the status of blacks and the expansion of slavery. A century of nationwide disdain for the rights of blacks set the stage for Chief Justice Taney's infamous statement that they were "so far inferior, that they had no rights which the white man was bound to respect." Under *Dred Scott*, even if blacks were free, they had no means to become citizens, and no constitutionally protected rights.

---

21. *See* generally Eric Foner, Reconstruction: America's Unfinished Revolution, 1863–1877 (1988).

22. *Id.*

23. *See* generally G. Frederickson, The Black Image in the White Mind (1971).

2. Dred Scott's Travels

Don Fehrenbacher

The Dred Scott Case: Its Significance in American Law

December 1833: Illinois: Dr. John Emerson goes to Fort Armstrong in Illinois. Dred Scott, his slave, accompanies him. (Emerson bought Scott from the Blow family in St. Louis, Missouri. Peter Blow later helps Scott sue for freedom.)

—Illinois is FREE STATE. (Ordinance of 1787 and state law)

1836: Emerson transferred to Fort Snelling in the free part of the Louisiana Purchase. (The Army vacated Fort Armstrong). (That area was part of Wisconsin Territory until 1838 when part of Iowa Territory.)

—Slavery was forbidden in that area by the Missouri Compromise

—While there, Scott "marries" (his wife is sold to Emerson).

February 1838: Emerson marries Eliza Irene Sanford. They live at Fort Jesup in western Louisiana.

Spring 1838: The Scotts, who had been hired out at Fort Snelling, join the Emersons in Louisiana at Fort Jesup.

Fall 1838: The Emersons (and Scotts) return to Fort Snelling (Louisiana Purchase).

—Scott's daughter, Eliza (named after Mrs. Emerson), born on a Mississippi River boat in Missouri (FREE) Territory, north of Missouri border.

Spring 1840: Dr. Emerson transferred to Florida. Mrs. Emerson and Scott family live on Mrs. Emerson's father's estate (Sanford Estate) in St. Louis.

December 1843: Emerson, who was living in Iowa, dies, leaving his estate to his wife and then to their child.

June 1846: Mrs. Emerson hired the Scotts out to Samuel Russell.

The Dred Scott Case 264.
Copyright © 1978 Oxford University Press.
Reprinted with permission of Oxford University Press.

3. The Dred Scott *Cases in the State Courts of Missouri*

Don Fehrenbacher

The Dred Scott Case: Its Significance in American Law

Prior to 1846:

Scott tries to buy his and his family's freedom from Mrs. Emerson. She refuses. (This was Scott's report to a newspaper reporter years later.)

1846: First Suit Filed. Against Mrs. Emerson.

Scott v. Emerson and *Harriet v. Emerson* filed in Missouri Circuit Court. (For Scott and his wife's freedom.)

(a) Allege assault and false imprisonment (the required allegations for a suit for freedom in Missouri.)

(b) Mrs. Emerson pleads not guilty.

(c) *Trial.* Jury verdict for Mrs. Emerson (1847).

—Judge Alexander Hamilton

—Had to prove 1) Scotts had resided on free soil.

2) Mrs. Emerson now holds as slaves.

—Scott's attorney failed to prove the second fact.

(d) Scott asks for NEW TRIAL.

1847: Simultaneously with request for new trial, Scotts file new suits against Sanford, Russell and Mrs. Emerson—everyone involved in holding the Scotts as slaves.

—Court requires Scotts to choose one set of suits (those filed in 1846 or those filed in 1847).

November 1847. New Trial Ordered on first suit and new suits withdrawn.

1848: To *Missouri Supreme Court* because Mrs. Emerson challenges retrial. Scott "wins" right to have a retrial of the first suits.

1850: Retrial (second trial *Scott Wins.* He is nominally free. (Since 1847, the Scotts had been taken charge of by the sheriff and hired out.)

March 1850. Mrs. Emerson appeals the result of the retrial to the Missouri Supreme Court.

June 22, 1852. Missouri Supreme Court Decision: *Mrs. Emerson Wins.* Scott is still a slave.

—Decision turns not on whether Scotts became free while in free territory, but that Missouri need not give effect to those laws. "Extending comity was optional."

—2–1 decision (reversing Missouri's own precedent).

1854. Suit initiated in U.S. Courts.

I. *Scott v. Sandford*, 60 U.S. 393 (1857)

1. Facts

Chief Justice TANEY delivered the opinion of the Court.

Dred Scott, a Negro, brought an action in the Federal Circuit Court for the district of Missouri against Sandford, asserting his right to freedom under State and Federal law.

From 1834 to 1836, Scott had been in service to his owner, a Dr. Emerson, in the state of Illinois, a state which prohibited slavery and where slavery had been prohibited by the Northwest Ordinance of 1787. From 1836 to 1838 Emerson, with Scott as his slave, lived in the territory of the Louisiana Purchase and north of the latitude of 36 degrees 30 minutes. In that region, slavery and the taking of slaves to this part of the Louisiana Purchase had been prohibited by Act of Congress in 1820, 3 Stat. 544 (The "Missouri Compromise"). In 1838 Scott and his family moved with Emerson to Missouri, a state which permitted slavery. Emerson died in 1843 and Sandford was the executor of Emerson's estate, and by the will, Mrs. Emerson purportedly had a "life estate" interest in the Scotts and their two children. It was out of Sandford's attempts and/or Mrs. Emerson's efforts to exercise what they thought were their rights of ownership over Scott and his family that caused the initiation of the litigation.

2. Opinion

There are two leading questions presented by the record:

1. Had the Circuit Court of the United States jurisdiction to hear and determine the case between these parties? And

2. If it had jurisdiction, is the judgment it has given erroneous or not?

The plaintiff in error, who was also the plaintiff in the court below, was, with his wife and children, held as slaves by the defendant, in the State of Missouri; and he brought this action in the Circuit Court of the United States for that district, to assert the title of himself and his family to freedom. . . .

a. Plea of Abatement

Before we speak of the pleas in bar, it will be proper to dispose of the questions which have arisen on the plea in abatement.

That plea denies the right of the plaintiff to sue in a court of the United States, for the reasons therein stated.

If the question raised by it is legally before us, and the court should be of opinion that the facts stated in it disqualify the plaintiff from becoming a citizen, in the sense in which that word is used in the Constitution of the United States, then the judgment of the Circuit Court is erroneous, and must be reversed.

It is suggested, however, that this plea is not before us; and that as the judgment in the court below on this plea was in favor of the plaintiff; he does not seek to reverse it, or bring it before the court for revision by his writ of error; and also that the defendant waived this defence by pleading over, and thereby admitted the jurisdiction of the court.

(Justice Taney concluded that the right of Dred Scott to sue in the Federal Courts was properly before the Court.)

b. Blacks and Citizenship

This is certainly a very serious question, and one that now for the first time has been brought for decision before this court. But it is brought here by those who have a right to bring it, and it is our duty to meet it and decide it.

The question is simply this: Can a Negro, whose ancestors were imported into this country, and sold as slaves, become a member of the political community formed and brought into existence by the Constitution of the United States, and as such become entitled to all the rights, and privileges, and immunities, guaranteed by that instrument to the citizen? One of which rights is the privilege of suing in a court of the United States in the cases specified in the Constitution.

It will be observed, that the plea applies to that class of persons only whose ancestors were Negroes of the African race, and imported into this country, and sold and held as slaves. The only matter in issue before the court, therefore, is, whether the descendants of such slaves, when they shall be emancipated, or who are born of parents who had become free before their birth, are citizens of a State, in the sense in which the word citizen is used in the Constitution of the United States. And this being the only matter in dispute on the pleadings, the court must be understood as speaking in this opinion of that class only, that is, of those persons who are the descendants of Africans who were imported into this country, and sold as slaves.

The situation of this population was altogether unlike that of the Indian race. The latter, it is true, formed no part of the colonial communities, and never amalgamated with them in social connections or in government. But although they were uncivilized, they were yet a free and independent people, associated together in nations or tribes, and governed by their own laws. Many of these political communities were situated in territories to which the white race claimed the ultimate right of dominion. But that claim was acknowledged to be subject to the right of the Indians to occupy it as long as they thought proper, and neither the English nor colonial Governments claimed or exercised any dominion over the tribe or nation by whom it was occupied, nor claimed the right to the possession of the territory, until the tribe or nation consented to cede it. These Indian Governments were regarded and treated as foreign Governments, as much so as if an ocean had separated the red man from the white; and their freedom has constantly been acknowledged, from the time of the first emigration to the English colonies to the present day, by the different Governments which succeeded each other. Treaties have been negotiated with them, and their alliance sought for in war; and the people who compose these Indian political communities have always been treated as foreigners not living under our Government. It is true that the course of events has brought the Indian tribes within the limits of the United States under subjection to the white race; and it has been found necessary, for their sake as well as our own, to regard them as in a state of pupilage, and to legislate to a certain extent over them and the territory they occupy. But they may, without doubt, like the subjects of any other foreign Government, be naturalized by the authority of Congress, and become citizens of a State, and of the United States; and if an individual should leave his nation or tribe, and take up his abode among the white population, he would be entitled to all the rights and privileges which would belong to an emigrant from any other foreign people.

We proceed to examine the case as presented by the pleadings.

The words "people of the United States" and "citizens" are synonymous terms, and mean the same thing. They both describe the political body who, according to our republican institutions, form the sovereignty, and who hold the power and conduct the Government through their representatives. They are what we familiarly call the "sovereign people," and every citizen is one of this people, and a constituent member of this sovereignty. The question before us is, whether the class of persons described in the plea in abatement compose a portion of this people, and are constituent members of this sovereignty?

We think they are not . . .

It is not the province of the court to decide upon the justice or injustice, the policy or impolicy, of these laws. The decision of that question belonged to the political or law making power; to those who formed the sovereignty and framed the Constitution. The duty of the court is, to interpret the instrument they have framed, with the best lights we can obtain on the subject, and to administer it as we find it, according to its true intent and meaning when it was adopted.

In discussing this question, we must not confound the rights of citizenship which a State may confer within its own limits, and the rights of citizenship as a member of the Union. It does not by any means follow, because he has all the rights and privileges of a citizen of a State, that he must be a citizen of the United States. He may have all of the rights and privileges of the citizen of a State, and yet not be entitled to the rights and privileges of a citizen in any other State. For, previous to the adoption of the Constitution of the United States, every state had the undoubted right to confer on whomsoever it pleased the character of citizen, and to endow him with all its rights. But this character of course was confined to the boundaries of the State, and gave him no rights or privileges in other States beyond those secured to him by the laws of nations and the comity of States. Nor have the several States surrendered the power of conferring these rights and privileges by adopting the Constitution of the United States. Each State may still confer them upon an alien, or any one it thinks proper, or upon any class or description of persons; yet he would not be a citizen in the sense in which that word is used in the Constitution of the United States, nor entitled to sue as such in one of its courts, nor to the privileges and immunities of a citizen in the other States. The rights which he would acquire would be restricted to the State which gave them. The Constitution has conferred on Congress the right to establish an uniform rule of naturalization, and this right is evidently exclusive, and has always been held by this court to be so. Consequently, no State, since the adoption of the Constitution, can by naturalizing an alien invest him with the rights and privileges secured to a citizen of a State under the Federal Government, although, so far as the State alone was concerned, he would undoubtedly be entitled to the rights of a citizen, and clothed with all the rights and immunities which the Constitution and laws of the State attached to that character.

It is very clear, therefore, that no State can, by any act or law of its own, passed since the adoption of the Constitution, introduce a new member into the political community created by the Constitution of the United States. It cannot make him a member of this community by making him a member of its own. And for the same reason it cannot introduce any person, or description of persons, who were not intended to be embraced in this new political family, which the Constitution brought into existence, but were intended to be excluded from it.

The question then arises, whether the provisions of the Constitution, in relation to the personal rights and privileges to which the citizen of a State should be entitled, embraced the Negro race, at that time in this country, or who might afterwards be imported, who had then or should afterwards be made free in any State; and to put it in the power of a single State to make him a citizen of the United States, and endue him with the full rights of citizenship in every other State without their consent? Does the Constitution of the United States act upon him whenever he shall be made free under the laws of a State, and raised there to the rank of a citizen, and immediately clothe him with all the privileges of a citizen in every other State, and in its own courts?

The court think the affirmative of these propositions cannot be maintained. And if it cannot, the plaintiff in error could not be a citizen of the State of Missouri, within the meaning of the Constitution of the United States, and, consequently, was not entitled to sue in its courts.

It is true, every person, and every class and description of persons, who were at the time of the adoption of the Constitution recognized as citizens in the several States, became also citizens of this new political body; but none other; it was formed by them, and for them and their posterity, but for no one else. And the personal rights and privileges guarantied to citizens of this new sovereignty were intended to embrace those only who were then members of the several State communities, or who should afterwards by birthright or otherwise become members, according to the provisions of the Constitution and the principles on which it was founded. It was the union of those who were at that time members of distinct and separate political communities into one political family, whose power, for certain specified purposes, was to extend over the whole territory of the United States. And it gave to each citizen rights and privileges outside of his State which he did not before possess, and placed him in every other State upon a perfect equality with its own citizens as to rights of person and rights of property; it made him a citizen of the United States.

It becomes necessary, therefore, to determine who were citizens of the several States when the Constitution was adopted. . . .

In the opinion of the court, the legislation and histories of the times, and the language used in the Declaration of Independence, show, that neither the class of persons who had been imported as slaves, nor their descendants, whether they had become free or not, were then acknowledged as a part of the people, nor intended to be included in the general words used in that memorable instrument.

It is difficult at this day to realize the state of public opinion in relation to that unfortunate race, which prevailed in the civilized and enlightened portions of the world at the time of the Declaration of Independence, and when the Constitution of the United States was framed and adopted. But the public history of every European nation displays it in a manner too plain to be mistaken.

They had for more than a century before been regarded as beings of an inferior order, and altogether unfit to associate with the white race, either in social or political relations; and so far inferior, that they had no rights which the white man was bound to respect; and that the Negro might justly and lawfully be reduced to slavery for his benefit. He was bought and sold, and treated as an ordinary article of merchandise and traffic, whenever a profit could be made by it. This opinion was at that time fixed and universal in the civilized portion of the white race. It was regarded as an axiom in morals as well as in politics, which no one thought of disputing, or supposed to be open to dispute; and men in every grade and position in society daily and habitually acted upon it in their private pursuits, as well as in matters of public concern, without doubting for a moment the correctness of this opinion.

And in no nation was this opinion more firmly fixed or more uniformly acted upon than by the English Government and English people. They not only seized them on the coast of Africa, and sold them or held them in slavery for their own use; but they took them as ordinary articles of merchandise to every country where they could make a profit on them, and were far more extensively engaged in this commerce than any other nation in the world.

The opinion thus entertained and acted upon in England was naturally impressed upon the colonies they founded on this side of the Atlantic. And, accordingly, a Negro of the African race was regarded by them as an article of property, and held, and bought and sold as such, in every one of the thirteen colonies which united in the Declaration of Independence, and afterwards formed the Constitution of the United States. The slaves were more or less numerous in the different colonies, as slave labor was found more or less profitable. But no one seems to have doubted the correctness of the prevailing opinion of the time.

The legislation of the different colonies furnishes positive and indisputable proof of this fact. . . .

The language of the Declaration of Independence is equally conclusive:

"We hold these truths to be self-evident: that all men are created equal; that they are endowed by their Creator with certain unalienable rights; that among them is life, liberty, and the pursuit of happiness; that to secure these rights, Governments are instituted, deriving their just powers from the consent of the governed."

The general words above quoted would seem to embrace the whole human family, and if they were used in a similar instrument at this day would be so understood. But it is too clear for dispute, that the enslaved African race were not intended to be included, and formed no part of the people who framed and adopted this declaration; for if the language, as understood in that day, would embrace them, the conduct of the distinguished men who framed the Declaration of Independence would have been utterly and vagrantly inconsistent with the principles they asserted; and instead of the sympathy of mankind, to which they so confidently appealed, they would have deserved and received universal rebuke and reprobation.

Yet the men who framed this declaration were great men—high in literary acquirements—high in their sense of honor, and incapable of asserting principles inconsistent with those on which they were acting. They perfectly understood the meaning of the language they used, and how it would be understood by others; and they knew that it would not in any part of the civilized world be supposed to embrace the Negro race, which, by common consent, had been excluded from civilized Governments and the family of nations, and doomed to slavery. They spoke and acted according to the then established doctrines and principles, and in the ordinary language of the day, and no one misunderstood them. The unhappy black race were separated from the white by indelible marks, and laws long before established, and were never thought of or spoken of except as property, and when the claims of the owner or the profit of the trader were supposed to need protection.

This state of public opinion had undergone no change when the Constitution was adopted, as is equally evident from its provisions and language.

The brief preamble sets forth by whom it was formed, for what purposes, and for whose benefit and protection. It declares that it is formed by the *people* of the United States: that is to say, by those who were members of the different political communities in the several States; and its great object is declared to be to secure the blessings of liberty to themselves and their posterity. It speaks in general terms of the *people* of the United States, and of *citizens* of the several States, when it is providing for the exercise of the powers granted or the privileges secured to the citizen. It does not define what description of persons are intended to be included under these terms, or who shall be regarded as a citizen and one of the people. It uses them as terms so well understood, that no further description or definition was necessary.

But there are two clauses in the Constitution which point directly and specifically to the Negro race as a separate class of persons, and show clearly that they were not regarded as a portion of the people or citizens of the Government then former.

One of these clauses reserves to each of the thirteen States the right to import slaves until the year 1808, if it thinks proper. And the importation which it thus sanctions was unquestionably of persons of the race of which we are speaking, as the traffic in slaves in the United States had always been confined to them. And by the other provision the States pledge themselves to each other to maintain the right of property of the master, by delivering up to him any slave who may have escaped from his service, and be found within their respective territories. By the first above mentioned clause, therefore, the right to purchase and hold this property is directly sanctioned and authorized for twenty years by the people who framed the Constitution. And by the second, they pledge themselves to maintain and uphold the right of the master in the manner specified, as long as the Government they then formed should endure. And these two provisions show, conclusively, that neither the description of persons therein referred to, nor their descendants, were embraced in any of the other provisions of the Constitution; for certainly these two clauses were not intended to confer on them or their posterity the blessings of liberty, or any of the personal rights so carefully provided for the citizen.

No one of that race had ever migrated to the United States voluntarily; all of them had been brought here as articles of merchandise. The number that had been emancipated at that time were but few in comparison with those held in slavery; and they were identified in the public mind with the race to which they belonged, and regarded as a part of the slave population rather than the free. It is obvious that they were not even in the minds of the framers of the Constitution when they were conferring special rights and privileges upon the citizens of a state in every other part of the Union.

Indeed, when we look to the condition of this race in the several States at the time, it is impossible to believe that these rights and privileges were intended to be extended to them. . . .

We need not refer, on this point, particularly to the laws of the present slaveholding States. Their statute books are full of provisions in relation to this class, in the same spirit with the Maryland law which we have before quoted. They have continued to treat them as an inferior class, and to subject them to strict police regulations, drawing a broad line of distinction between the citizen and the slave races, and legislating in relation to them upon the same principle which prevailed at the time of the Declaration of Independence. As relates to these States, it is too plain for argument, that they have never been regarded as a part of the people or citizens of the State, nor supposed to possess any political rights which the dominant race might not withhold or grant at their pleasure. And as long ago as 1822, the Court of Appeals of Kentucky decided that free Negroes and mulattoes were not citizens within the meaning of the Constitution of the United States; and the correctness of this decision is recognized, and the same doctrine affirmed, in 1 Meigs's Tenn. Reports, 331.

And if we turn to the legislation of the States where slavery had worn out, or measures taken for its speedy abolition, we shall find the same opinions and principles equally fixed and equally acted upon.

Thus, Massachusetts, in 1786, passed a law similar to the colonial one of which we have spoken. The law of 1786, like the law of 1705, forbids the marriage of any white person with any Negro, Indian, or mulatto, and inflicts a penalty of fifty pounds upon any one who shall join them in marriage; and declares all such marriages absolutely null and void, and degrades thus the unhappy issue of the marriage by fixing upon it the stain of bastard. . . .

So, too, in Connecticut. We refer more particularly to the legislation of this State, because it was not only among the first to put an end to slavery within its own territory, but was the first to fix a mark of reprobation upon the African slave trade. The law last mentioned was passed in October, 1788, about nine months after the State had ratified and adopted the present Constitution of the United States; and by that law it prohibited its own citizens, under severe penalties, from engaging in the trade, and declared all policies of insurance on the vessel or cargo made in the State to be null and void. But, up to the time of the adoption of the Constitution, there is nothing in the legislation of the State indicating any change of opinion as to the relative rights and position of the white and black races in this country, or indicating that it meant to place the latter, when free, upon a level with its citizens. And certainly nothing which would have led the slaveholding States to suppose, that Connecticut designed to claim for them, under the new constitution, the equal rights and privileges and rank of citizens in every other State.

The first step taken by Connecticut upon this subject was as early as 1774, when it passed an act forbidding the further importation of slaves into the State. But the section containing the prohibition is introduced by the following preamble:

"And whereas the increase of slaves in this State is injurious to the poor, and inconvenient."

This recital would appear to have been carefully introduced, in order to prevent any misunderstanding of the motive which induced the Legislature to pass the law, and places it distinctly upon the interest and convenience of the white population — excluding the inference that it might have been intended in any degree for the benefit of the other. . . .

And still further pursuing its legislation, we find that in the same statute passed in 1774, which prohibited the further importation of slaves into the State, there is also a provision by which any Negro, Indian, or mulatto servant, who was found wandering out of the town or place to which he belonged, without a written pass such as is therein described, was made liable to be seized by any one, and taken before the next authority to be examined and delivered up to his master — who was required to pay the charge which had accrued thereby. And a subsequent section of the same law provides, that if any free Negro shall travel without such pass, and shall be stopped, seized, or taken up, he shall pay all charges arising thereby. And this law was in full operation when the Constitution of the United States was adopted, and was not repealed till 1797. So that up to that time free negroes and mulattoes were associated with servants and slaves in the police regulations established by the laws of the State.

And again, in 1833, Connecticut passed another law, which made it penal to set up or establish any school in that State for the instruction of persons of the African race not inhabitants of the State, or to instruct or teach in any such school or institution, or board or harbor for that purpose, any such person, without the previous consent in writing of the civil authority of the town in which such school or institution might be.

And it appears by the case of *Crandall v. The State*, reported in 10 Conn. Rep., 340, that upon an information filed against Prudence Crandall for a violation of this law, one of the points raised in the defense was, that the law was a violation of the Constitution of the United States; and that the persons instructed, although of the African race, were citizens of other States, and therefore entitled to the rights and privileges of citizens in the State of Connecticut. But Chief Justice Daggett, before whom the case was tried, held, that persons of that description were not citizens of a State, within the meaning of the word citizen in the Constitution of the United States, and were not therefore entitled to the privileges and immunities of citizens in other States.

The case was carried up to the Supreme Court of Errors of the State, and the question fully argued there. But the case went off upon another point, and no opinion was expressed on this question.

We have made this particular examination into the legislative and judicial action of Connecticut, because, from the early hostility it displayed to the slave trade on the coast of Africa, we may expect to find the laws of that State as lenient and favorable to the subject race as those of any other State in the Union; and if we find that at the time the Constitution was adopted, they were not even there raised to the rank of citizens, but were still held and treated as property, and the laws relating to them passed with reference altogether to the interest and convenience of the white race, we shall hardly find them elevated to a higher rank anywhere else. . . .

It would be impossible to enumerate and compress in the space usually allotted to an opinion of a court, the various laws, marking the condition of this race, which were passed from time to time after the Revolution, and before and since the adoption of the Constitution of the United States. In addition to those already referred to, it is sufficient to say, that Chancellor Kent, whose accuracy and research no one will question, states in the sixth edition of his Commentaries, (published in 1848, 2 vol., 258, note b,) that in no part of the country except Maine, did the African race, in point of fact, participate equally with the whites in the exercise of civil and political rights.

The legislation of the States therefore shows, in a manner not to be mistaken, the inferior and subject condition of that race at the time the Constitution was adopted, and long afterwards, throughout the thirteen States by which that instrument was framed; and it is hardly consistent with the respect due to these States, to suppose that they regarded at that time, as fellow citizens and members of the sovereignty, a class of beings whom they had thus stigmatized; whom, as we are bound, out of respect to the State sovereignties, to assume they had deemed it just and necessary thus to stigmatize, and upon whom they had impressed such deep and enduring marks of inferiority and degradation; or, that when they met in convention to form the Constitution, they looked upon them as a portion of their constituents, or designed to include them in the provisions so carefully inserted for the security and protection of the liberties and rights of their citizens. It cannot be supposed that they intended to secure to them rights, and privileges, and rank, in the new political body throughout the Union, which every one of them denied within the limits of its own dominion. More especially, it cannot be believed that the large slaveholding States regarded them as included in the word citizens, or would have consented to a Constitution which might compel them to receive them in that character from another State. For if they were so received, and entitled to the privileges and immunities of citizens, it would exempt them from the operation of the special laws and from the police regulations which they considered to be necessary for their own safety. It would give to persons of the Negro race, who were recognized as citizens in any one State of the Union, the right to enter every other State whenever they pleased, singly or in companies, without pass or passport, and without obstruction, to sojourn there as long as they pleased, to go where they pleased at every hour of the day or night without molestation, unless they committed some violation of law for which a white man would be punished; and it would give them the full liberty of speech in public and in private upon all subjects upon which its own citizens might speak; to hold public meetings upon political affairs, and to keep and carry arms wherever they went. And all of this would be done in the face of the subject race of the same color, both free and slaves, and inevitably producing discontent and insubordination among them, and endangering the peace and safety of the State.

It is impossible, it would seem, to believe that the great men of the slaveholding States, who took so large a share in framing the Constitution of the United States, and exercised so much influence in procuring its adoption, could have been so forgetful or regardless of their own safety and the safety of those who trusted and confided in them.

Besides, this want of foresight and care would have been utterly inconsistent with the caution displayed in providing for the admission of new members into this political family. For, when they gave to the citizens of each State the privileges and immunities of citizens in the several States, they at the same time took from the several States the power of naturalization, and confined that power exclusively to the Federal Government. No State was willing to permit another State to determine who should or should not be admitted as one of its citizens, and entitled to demand equal rights and privileges with their own people, within their own territories. The right of naturalization was therefore, with one accord, surrendered by the States, and confided to the Federal Government. And this power granted to

Congress to establish an uniform rule of *naturalization* is, by the well understood meaning of the word, confined to persons born in a foreign country, under a foreign Government. It is not a power to raise to the rank of a citizen any one born in the United States, who, from birth or parentage, by the laws of the country, belongs to an inferior and subordinate class. And when we find the States guarding themselves from the indiscreet or improper admission by other States of emigrants from other countries, by giving the power exclusively to Congress, we cannot fail to see that they could never have left with the states a much more important power—that is, the power of transforming into citizens a numerous class of persons, who in that character would be much more dangerous to the peace and safety of a large portion of the Union, than the few foreigners one of the States might improperly naturalize. The Constitution upon its adoption obviously took from the States all power by any subsequent legislation to introduce as a citizen into the political family of the United States any one, no matter where he was born, or what might be his character or condition; and it gave to Congress the power to confer this character upon those only who were born outside of the dominions of the United States. And no law of a State, therefore, passed since the Constitution was adopted, can give any right of citizenship outside of its own territory.

A clause similar to the one in the Constitution, in relation to the rights and immunities of citizens of one State in the other States, was contained in the Articles of Confederation. But there is a difference of language, which is worthy of note. The provision in the Articles of Confederation was, "that the *free inhabitants* of each of the States, paupers, vagabonds, and fugitives from justice, excepted, should be entitled to all the privileges and immunities of free citizens in the several States."

It will be observed, that under this Confederation, each State had the right to decide for itself, and in its own tribunals, whom it would acknowledge as a free inhabitant of another State. The term *free inhabitant*, in the generality of its terms, would certainly include one of the African race who had been manumitted. But no example, we think, can be found of his admission to all the privileges of citizenship in any State of the Union after these Articles were formed, and while they continued in force. And, notwithstanding the generality of the words "free inhabitants," it is very clear that, according to their accepted meaning in that day, they did not include the African race, whether free or not: for the fifth section of the ninth article provides that congress should have the power "to agree upon the number of land forces to be raised, and to make requisitions from each State for its quota in proportion to the number of *white* inhabitants in such State, which requisition should be binding."

Words could hardly have been used which more strongly mark the line of distinction between the citizen and the subject; the free and the subjugated races. The latter were not even counted when the inhabitants of a State were to be embodied in proportion to its numbers for the general defence. And it cannot for a moment be supposed, that a class of persons thus separated and rejected from those who formed the sovereignty of the States, were yet intended to be included under the words "free inhabitants," in the preceding article, to whom privileges and immunities were so carefully secured in every State.

But although this clause of the Articles of Confederation is the same in principle with that inserted in the Constitution, yet the comprehensive word *inhabitant*, which might be construed to include an emancipated slave, is omitted; and the privilege is confined to *citizens* of the State. And this alteration in words would hardly have been made, unless a different meaning was intended to be conveyed, or a possible doubt removed. The just and fair inference is, that as this privilege was about to be placed under the protection of the General Government, and the words expounded by its tribunals, and all power in relation to it taken from the State and its courts, it was deemed prudent to describe with precision and caution the persons to whom this high privilege was given — and the word *citizen* was on that account substituted for the words *free inhabitant*. The word citizen excluded, and no doubt intended to exclude, foreigners who had not become citizens of some one of the States when the Constitution was adopted; and also every description of persons who were not fully recognized as citizens in the several States. This, upon any fair construction of the instruments to which we have referred, was evidently the object and purpose of this change of words.

To all this mass of proof we have still to add, that Congress has repeatedly legislated upon the same construction of the Constitution that we have given. Three laws, two of which were passed almost immediately after the Government went into operation, will be abundantly sufficient to show this. The two first are particularly worthy of notice, because many of the men who assisted in framing the Constitution, and took an active part in procuring its adoption, were then in the halls of legislation, and certainly understood what they meant when they used the words "people of the United States" and "citizen" in that well considered instrument.

The first of these acts is the naturalization law, which was passed at the second session of the first Congress, March 26, 1790, and confines the right of becoming citizens "*to aliens being free white persons.*"

Now, the Constitution does not limit the power of Congress in this respect to white persons. And they may, if they think proper, authorize the naturalization of any one, of any color, who was born under allegiance to another Government. But the language of the law above quoted, shows that citizenship at that time was perfectly understood to be confined to the white race; and that they alone constituted the sovereignty in the Government.

Congress might, as we before said, have authorized the naturalization of Indians, because they were aliens and foreigners. But, in their then untutored and savage state, no one would have thought of admitting them as citizens in a civilized community. And, moreover, the atrocities they had but recently committed, when they were the allies of Great Britain in the Revolutionary war, were yet fresh in the recollection of the people of the United States, and they were even then guarding themselves against the threatened renewal of Indian hostilities. No one supposed then that any Indian would ask for, or was capable of enjoying, the privileges of an American citizen, and the word white was not used with any particular reference to them.

Neither was it used with any reference to the African race imported into or born in this country; because Congress had no power to naturalize them, and therefore there was no necessity for using particular words to exclude them.

It would seem to have been used merely because it followed out the line of division which the Constitution has drawn between the citizen race, who formed and held the Government, and the African race, which they held in subjection and slavery, and governed at their own pleasure.

Another of the early laws of which we have spoken, is the first militia law, which was passed in 1792, at the first session of the second Congress. The language of this law is equally plain and significant with the one just mentioned. It directs that every "free able bodied white male citizen" shall be enrolled in the militia. The word *white* is evidently used to exclude unnaturalized foreigners; the latter forming no part of the sovereignty, owing it no allegiance, and therefore under no obligation to defend it. The African race, however, born in the country, did owe allegiance to the Government, whether they were slave or free; but it is repudiated, and rejected from the duties and obligations of citizenship in marked language.

The third act to which we have alluded is even still more decisive; it was passed as late as 1813, (2 Stat., 800,) and it provides: "That from and after the termination of the war in which the United States are now engaged with Great Britain, it shall not be lawful to employ, on board of any public or private vessels of the United States, any person or persons except citizens of the United States, or persons of color, native of the United States."

Here the line of distinction is drawn in express words persons of color, in the judgment of Congress, were not included in the word citizens, and they are described as another and different class of persons, and authorized to be employed, if born in the United States. . . .

But it is said that a person may be a citizen, and entitled to that character, although he does not possess all the rights which may belong to other citizens; as, for example, the right to vote, or to hold particular offices; and that yet, when he goes into another State, he is entitled to be recognized there as a citizen, although the State may measure his rights by the rights which it allows to persons of a like character or class resident in the State, and refuse to him the full rights of citizenship.

This argument overlooks the language of the provision in the Constitution of which we are speaking.

Undoubtedly, a person may be a citizen, that is, a member of the community who form the sovereignty, although he exercises no share of the political power, and is incapacitated from holding particular offices. Women and minors, who form a part of the political family, cannot vote; and when a property qualification is required to vote or hold a particular office, those who have not the necessary qualification cannot vote or hold the office, yet they are citizens.

So, too, a person may be entitled to vote by the law of the State, who is not a citizen even of the State itself. And in some of the States of the Union foreigners not naturalized are allowed to vote. And the State may give the right to free Negroes and mulattoes, but that does not make them citizens of the State, and still less of the United States. And the provision in the Constitution giving privileges and immunities in other States, does not apply to them. . . .

The case of *Legrand v. Darnall* (2 Peters, 664) has been referred to for the purpose of showing that this court has decided that the descendant of a slave may sue as a citizen in a court of the United States; but the case itself shows that the question did not arise and could not have arisen in the case.

It appears from the report, that Darnall was born in Maryland, and was the son of a white man by one of his slaves, and his father executed certain instruments to manumit him, and devised to him some landed property in the State. This property Darnall afterwards sold to Legrand, the appellant, who gave his notes for the purchase money. But becoming afterwards apprehensive that the appellee had not been emancipated according to the laws of Maryland, he refused to pay the notes until he could be better satisfied as to Darnall's right to convey. Darnall, in the mean time had taken up his residence in Pennsylvania, and brought suit on the notes, and recovered judgment in the Circuit Court for the District of Maryland.

The whole proceeding, as appears by the report, was an amicable one; Legrand being perfectly willing to pay the money, if he could obtain a title, and Darnall not wishing him to pay unless he could make him a good one. In point of fact, the whole proceeding was under the direction of the counsel who argued the case for the appellee, who was the mutual friend of the parties, and confided in by both of them, and whose only object was to have the rights of both parties established by judicial decision in the most speedy and least expensive manner.

Legrand, therefore, raised no objection to the jurisdiction of the court in the suit at law, because he was himself anxious to obtain the judgment of the court upon his title. Consequently, there was nothing in the record before the court to show that Darnall was of African descent, and the usual judgment and award of execution was entered. . . .

Besides, we are by no means prepared to say that there are not many cases, civil as well as criminal, in which a Circuit Court of the United States may exercise jurisdiction, although one of the African race is a party; that broad question is not before the court. The question with which we are now dealing is, whether a person of the African race can be a citizen of the United States, and become thereby entitled to a special privilege, by virtue of his title to that character, and which, under the Constitution, no one but a citizen can claim. It is manifest that the case of Legrand and Darnall has no bearing on that question, and can have no application to the case now before the court.

This case, however, strikingly illustrates the consequences that would follow the construction of the Constitution which would give the power contended for to a State. It would in effect give it also to an individual. For if the father of young Darnall had manumitted him in his lifetime, and sent him to reside in a State which recognized him as a citizen, he might have visited and sojourned in Maryland when he pleased, and as long as he pleased, as a citizen of the United States; and the State officers and tribunals would be compelled, by the paramount authority of the Constitution, to receive him and treat him as one of its citizens, exempt from the laws and police of the State in relation to a person of that description, and allow him to enjoy all the rights and privileges of citizenship, without respect to the laws of Maryland, although such laws were deemed by it absolutely essential to its own safety.

The only two provisions which point to them and include them, treat them as property, and make it the duty of the Government to protect it; no other power, in relation to this race, is to be found in the Constitution; and as it is a Government of special, delegated, powers, no authority beyond these two provisions can be constitutionally exercised. The Government of the United States had no right to interfere for any other purpose but that of protecting the rights of the owner, leaving it altogether with the several States to deal with this race, whether emancipated or not, as each State may think justice, humanity, and the interests and safety of society, require. The States evidently intended to reserve this power exclusively to themselves.

No one, we presume, supposes that any change in public opinion or feeling, in relation to this unfortunate race, in the civilized nations of Europe or in this country, should induce the court to give to the words of the Constitution a more liberal construction in their favor than they were intended to bear when the instrument was framed and adopted. Such an argument would be altogether inadmissible in any tribunal called on to interpret it. If any of its provisions are deemed unjust, there is a mode prescribed in the instrument itself by which it may be amended; but while it remains unaltered, it must be construed now as it was understood at the time of its adoption. . . .

What the construction was at that time, we think can hardly admit of doubt. We have the language of the Declaration of Independence and of the Articles of Confederation, in addition to the plain words of the Constitution itself; we have the legislation of the different States, before, about the time, and since, the Constitution was adopted; we have the legislation of Congress, from the time of its adoption to a recent period; and we have the constant and uniform action of the Executive Department, all concurring together, and leading to the same result. And if anything in relation to the construction of the Constitution can be regarded as settled, it is that which we now give to the word "citizen" and the word "people."

3. Holding

And upon a full and careful consideration of the subject, the court is of opinion, that, upon the facts stated in the plea in abatement, Dred Scott was not a citizen of Missouri within the meaning of the Constitution of the United States, and not entitled as such to sue in its courts; and, consequently, that the Circuit court had no jurisdiction of the case, and that the judgment on the plea in abatement is erroneous. . . .

4. Additional Issues

The correction of one error in the court below does not deprive the appellate court of the power of examining further into the record, and correcting any other material errors which may have been committed by the inferior court. There is certainly no rule of law—nor any practice—nor any decision of a court—which even questions this power in the appellate tribunal. On the contrary, it is the daily practice of this court, and of all appellate courts where they reverse the judgment of an inferior court for error, to correct by its opinions whatever errors may appear on the record material to the case; and they have always held it to be their duty to do so where the silence of the court might lead to misconstruction or future controversy, and the point has been relied on by either side, and argued before the court. . . .

It is true that the result either way, by dismissal or by a judgment for the defendant, makes very little, if any, difference in a pecuniary or personal point of view to either party. But the fact that the result would be very nearly the same to the parties in either form of judgment, would not justify this court in sanctioning an error in the judgment which is patent on the record, and which, if sanctioned, might be drawn into precedent, and lead to serious mischief and injustice in some future suit.

We proceed, therefore, to inquire whether the facts relied on by the plaintiff entitled him to his freedom. . . .

In considering this part of the controversy, two questions arise: 1. Was he, together with his family, free in Missouri by reason of the stay in the territory of the United States herein before mentioned? And 2. If they were not, is Scott himself free by reason of his removal to Rock Island, in the state of Illinois, as stated in the above admissions?

We proceed to examine the first question.

The act of Congress, upon which the plaintiff relies, declares that slavery and involuntary servitude, except as a punishment for crime, shall be forever prohibited in all that part of the territory ceded by France, under the name of Louisiana, which lies north of thirty-six degrees thirty minutes north latitude, and not included within the limits of Missouri. And the difficulty which meets us at the threshold of this part of the inquiry is, whether congress was authorized to pass this law under any of the powers granted to it by the Constitution; for if the authority is not given by that instrument, it is the duty of this court to declare it void and inoperative, and incapable of conferring freedom upon any one who is held as a slave under the laws of any one of the States. . . .

Whether, therefore, we take the particular clause in question, by itself, or in connection with the other provisions of the Constitution, we think it clear, that it applies only to the particular territory of which we have spoken, and cannot, by any just rule of interpretation, be extended to territory which the new Government might afterwards obtain from a foreign nation. Consequently, the power which Congress may have lawfully exercised in this Territory, while it remained under a Territorial Government, and which may have been sanctioned by judicial decision, can furnish no justification and no argument to support a similar exercise of power over territory afterwards acquired by the Federal Government. . . .

This brings us to examine by what provision of the Constitution the present Federal Government, under its delegated and restricted powers, is authorized to acquire territory outside of the original limits of the United States, and what powers it may exercise therein over the person or property of a citizen of the United States, while it remains a Territory, and until it shall be admitted as one of the States of the Union.

There is certainly no power given by the Constitution to the Federal Government to establish or maintain colonies borging on the United States or at a distance, to be ruled and governed at its own pleasure; nor to enlarge its territorial limits in any way, except by the admission of new States. . . .

Taking this rule to guide us, it may be safely assumed that citizens of the United States who migrate to a Territory belonging to the people of the United States, cannot be ruled as mere colonists, dependent upon the will of the General Government, and to be governed by any laws it may think proper to impose. The principle upon which our Governments rest, and upon which alone they continue to exist, is the union of States, sovereign and independent within their own limits in their internal and domestic concerns, and bound together as one people by a General Government, possessing certain enumerated and restricted powers, delegated to it by the people of the several States, and exercising supreme authority within the scope of the powers granted to it, throughout the dominion of the United States. A power, therefore, in the General Government to obtain and hold colonies and dependent territories, over which they might legislate without restriction, would be inconsistent with its own existence in its present form. Whatever it acquires, it acquires for the benefit of the people of the several States who created it. It is their trustee acting for them, and charged with the duty of promoting the interests of the whole people of the Union in the exercise of the powers specifically granted. . . .

These powers, and others, in relation to rights of person, which it is not necessary here to enumerate, are, in express and positive terms, denied to the General Government; and the rights of private property have been guarded with equal care. Thus the rights of property are united with the rights of person, and placed on the same ground by the fifth amendment to the Constitution, which provides that no person shall be deprived of life, liberty, and property, without due process of law. And an act of Congress which deprives a citizen of the United States of his liberty or property, merely because he came himself or brought his property into a particular Territory of the United States, and who had committed no offence against the laws, could hardly be dignified with the name of due process of law. . . .

But in considering the question before us, it must be borne in mind that there is no law of nations standing between the people of the United States and their Government, and interfering with their relation to each other. The powers of the Government, and the rights of the citizen under it, are positive and practical regulations plainly written down. The people of the United States have delegated to it certain enumerated powers, and forbidden it to exercise others. It has no power over the person or property of a citizen but what the citizens of the United States have granted. And no laws or usages of other nations, or reasoning of statesmen or jurists upon the relations of master and slave, can enlarge the powers of the Government, or take from the citizens the rights they have reserved. And if the Constitution recognizes the right of property of the master in a slave, and makes no distinction between that description of property and other property owned by a citizen, no tribunal, acting under the authority of the United States, whether it be legislative, executive, or judicial, has a right to draw such a distinction, or deny to it the benefit of the provisions and guarantees which have been provided for the protection of private property against the encroachments of the Government. . . .

Upon these considerations, it is the opinion of the court that the act of Congress which prohibited a citizen from holding and owning property of this kind in the territory of the United States north of the line therein mentioned, is not warranted by the Constitution, and is therefore void; and that neither Dred Scott himself, nor any of his family, were made free by being carried into this territory; even if they had been carried there by the owner, with the intention of becoming a permanent resident. . . .

5. Justice McLean Dissenting

. . . There is no averment in this plea which shows or conduces to show an inability in the plaintiff to sue in the Circuit Court. It does not allege that the plaintiff had his domicil in any other State, nor that he is not a free man in Missouri. He is averred to have had a Negro ancestry, but this does not show that he is not a citizen of Missouri, within the meaning of the act of Congress authorizing him to sue in the Circuit Court. It has never been held necessary, to constitute a citizen within the act, that he should have the qualifications of an elector. Females and minors may sue in the Federal courts, and so may any individual who has a permanent domicil in the State under whose laws his rights are protected, and to which he owes allegiance.

Being born under our Constitution and laws, no naturalization is required, as one of foreign birth, to make him a citizen. The most general and appropriate definition of the term citizen is "a freeman." Being a freeman, and having his domicil in a State different from that of the defendant, he is a citizen within the act of Congress, and the courts of the Union are open to him. . . .

It has been argued that, if a colored person be made a citizen of a State, he cannot sue in the Federal court. The Constitution declares that Federal jurisdiction "may be exercised between citizens of different States," and the same is provided in the act of 1789. The above argument is properly met by saying that the Constitution was "intended to be a practical instrument; and where its language is too plain to be misunderstood, the argument ends."

In *Chirre v. Chirre*, (2 Wheat, 261; 4 Curtis, 99,) this court says: "That the power of naturalization is exclusively in Congress does not seem to be, and certainly ought not to be, controverted." No person can legally be made a citizen of a State, and consequently a citizen of the United States, of foreign birth, unless he be naturalized under the acts of Congress. Congress has power "to establish a uniform rule of naturalization."

It is a power which belongs exclusively to Congress, as intimately connected with our Federal relations. A State may authorize foreigners to hold real estate within its jurisdiction, but it has no power to naturalize foreigners, and give them the rights of citizens. Such a right is opposed to the acts of Congress on the subject of naturalization, and subversive of the Federal powers. I regret that any countenance should be given from this bench to a practice like this in some of the States, which has no warrant in the Constitution.

In the argument, it was said that a colored citizen would not be an agreeable member of society. This is more a matter of taste than of law. Several of the States have admitted persons of color to the right of suffrage, and in this view have recognized them as citizens; and this has been done in the slave as well as the free States. On the question of citizenship, it must be admitted that we have not been very fastidious. Under the late treaty with Mexico, we have made citizens of all grades, combinations, and colors. The same was done in the admission of Louisiana and Florida. No one ever doubted, and no court ever held, that the people of these Territories did not become citizens under the treaty. They have exercised all the rights of citizens, without being naturalized under the acts of Congress.

There are several important principles involved in this case, which have been argued, and which may be considered under the following heads:

1. The locality of slavery, as settled by this court and the courts of the States.

2. The relation which the Federal Government bears to slavery in the States.

3. The power of Congress to establish Territorial Governments, and to prohibit the introduction of slavery therein.

4. The effect of taking slaves into a new State or Territory, and so holding them, where slavery is prohibited.

5. Whether the return of a slave under the control of his master, after being entitled to his freedom, reduces him to his former condition.

6. Are the decisions of the Supreme Court of Missouri, on the questions before us, binding on this court, within the rule adopted.

In the course of my judicial duties, I have had occasion to consider and decide several of the above points.

1. As to the locality of slavery. The civil law throughout the Continent of Europe, it is believed, without an exception, is, that slavery can exist only within the territory where it is established; and that if a slave escapes, or is carried beyond such territory, his master cannot reclaim him, unless by virtue of some express stipulation. (Grotius, lib. 2, chap. 15, 5, 1; lib. 10, chap. 10, 2, 1; Wicqueposts Ambassador, lib. 1, p. 418; 4 Martin, 385; Case of the Creole in the House of Lords, 1842; 1 Phillimore on International Law, 316, 335.)

I will now consider the relation which the Federal Government bears to slavery in the States:

Slavery is emphatically a State institution. In the ninth section of the first article of the Constitution, it is provided "that the migration or importation of such persons as any of the States now existing shall think proper to admit, shall not be prohibited by the Congress prior to the year 1808, but a tax or duty may be imposed on such importation, not exceeding ten dollars for each person. . . ."

The only connection which the Federal Government holds with slaves in a State, arises from that provision of the constitution which declares that "No person held to service or labor in one State, under the laws thereof, escaping into another, shall, in consequence of any law or regulation therein, be discharged from such service or labor, but shall be delivered up, on claim of the party to whom such service or labor may be due."

This being a fundamental law of the Federal Government, it rests mainly for its execution, as has been held, on the judicial power of the Union; and so far as the rendition of fugitives from labor has become a subject of judicial action, the Federal obligation has been faithfully discharged.

In the formation of the Federal Constitution, care was taken to confer no power on the Federal Government to interfere with this institution in the States. In the provision respecting the slave trade, in fixing the ration of representation, and providing for the reclamation of fugitives from labor, slaves were referred to as persons, and in no other respect are they considered in the Constitution.

We need not refer to the mercenary spirit which introduced the infamous traffic in slaves, to show the degradation of Negro slavery in our country. This system was imposed upon our colonial settlements by the mother country, and it is due to truth to say that the commercial colonies and States were chiefly engaged in the traffic. But we know as a historical fact, that James Madison, that great and good man, a leading member in the Federal Convention, was solicitous to guard the language of that instrument so as not to convey the idea that there could be property in man.

I prefer the lights of Madison, Hamilton, and Jay, as a means of construing the Constitution in all its bearings, rather than to look behind that period, into a traffic which is now declared to be piracy, and punished with death by Christian nations. I do not like to draw the sources of our domestic relations from so dark a ground. Our independence was a great epoch in the history of freedom; and while I admit the Government was not made especially for the colored race, yet many of them were citizens of the New England States, and exercised the rights of suffrage when the Constitution was adopted, and it was not doubted by any intelligent person that its tendencies would greatly ameliorate their condition.

Many of the States, on the adoption of the constitution, or shortly afterward, took measures to abolish slavery within their respective jurisdictions; and it is a well-known fact that a belief was cherished by the leading men, South as well as North, that the institution of slavery would gradually decline, until it would become extinct. The increased value of slave labor, in the culture of cotton and sugar, prevented the realization of this expectation. Like all other communities and States, the South were influenced by what they considered to be their own interests.

But if we are to turn our attention to the dark ages of the world, why confine our view to colored slavery? On the same principles, white men were made slaves. All slavery has its origin in power, and is against right. . . .

I will now consider the fourth head, which is: "The effect of taking slaves into a State or Territory, and so holding them, where slavery is prohibited."

If the principle laid down in the case of *Prigg v. The State of Pennsylvania* is to be maintained, and it is certainly to be maintained until overruled, as the law of this court, there can be no difficulty on this point. In that case, the court says: "The state of slavery is deemed to be a mere municipal regulation, founded upon and limited to the range of the territorial laws." If this be so, slavery can exist nowhere except under the authority of law, founded on usage having the force of law, or by statutory recognition. And the court further says: "It is manifest, from this consideration, that if the Constitution had not contained the clause requiring the rendition of fugitives from labor, every non-slaveholding State in the Union would have been at liberty to have declared free all runaway slaves coming within its limits, and to have given them entire immunity and protection against the claims of their masters."

Now, if a slave abscond, he may be reclaimed; but if he accompany his master into a State or Territory where slavery is prohibited, such slave cannot be said to have left the service of his master where his services were legalized. And if slavery be limited to the range of the territorial laws, how can the slave be coerced to serve in a State or Territory, not only without the authority of law, but against its express provisions? What gives the master the right to control the will of his slave? The local law, which exists in some form. But where there is no such law, can the master control the will of the slave by force? Where no slavery exists, the presumption, without regard to color, is in favor of freedom. Under such a jurisdiction, may the colored man be levied on as the property of his master by a creditor? On the decease of the master, does the slave descend to his heirs as property? Can the master sell him? Any one or all of these acts may be done to the slave, where he is legally held to service. But where the law does not confer this power, it cannot be exercised. . . .

The slave States have generally adopted the rule, that where the master, by a residence with his slave in a State or Territory where slavery is prohibited, the slave was entitled to his freedom everywhere. This was the settled doctrine of the Supreme

Court of Missouri. It has been so held in Mississippi, in Virginia, in Louisiana, formerly in Kentucky, Maryland, and in other States.

The law, where a contract is made and is to be execute, governs it. This does not depend upon comity, but upon the law of the contract. And if, in the language of the Supreme Court of Missouri, the master, by taking his slave to Illinois, and employing him there as a slave, emancipates him as effectually as by a deed of emancipation, is it possible that such an act is not matter for adjudication in any slave State where the master may take him? Does not the master assent to the law, when he places himself under it in a free State?

The States of Missouri and Illinois are bounded by a common line. The one prohibits slavery, the other admits it. This has been done by the exercise of that sovereign power which appertains to each. We are bound to respect the institutions of each, as emanating from the voluntary action of the people. Have the people of either any right to disturb the relations of the other? Each State rests upon the basis of its own sovereignty, protected by the Constitution. Our Union has been the foundation of our prosperity and national glory. Shall we not cherish and maintain it? This can only be done by respecting the legal rights of each State.

If a citizen of a free State shall entice or enable a slave to escape from the service of his master, the law holds him responsible, not only for the loss of the slave, but he is liable to be indicted and fined for the misdemeanor. And I am bound here to say, that I have never found a jury in the four States which constitute my circuit, which have not sustained this law, where the evidence required them to sustain it. And it is proper that I should also say, that more cases have arisen in my circuit, by reason of its extent and locality, than in all other parts of the Union. This has been done to vindicate the sovereign rights of the Southern States, and protect the legal interests of our brethren of the South.

Let these facts be contrasted with the case now before the court. Illinois has declared in the most solemn and impressive form that there shall be neither slavery nor involuntary servitude in that State, and that any slave brought into it, with a view of becoming a resident, shall be emancipated. And effect has been given to this provision of the Constitution by the decision of the Supreme Court of that State. With a full knowledge of these facts, a slave is brought from Missouri to Rock Island, in the State of Illinois, and is retained there as a slave for two years, and then taken to Fort Snelling, where slavery is prohibited by the Missouri Compromise Act, and there he is detained two years longer in a state of slavery. Harriet, his wife, was also kept at the same place four years as a slave, having been purchased in Missouri. They were then removed to the State of Missouri, and sold as slaves, and in the action before us they are not only claimed as slaves, but a majority of my brethren have held that on their being returned to Missouri the status of slavery attached to them.

I am not able to reconcile this result with the respect due to the State of Illinois. Having the same rights of sovereignty as the State of Missouri in adopting a Constitution, I can perceive no reason why the institutions of Illinois should not receive the same consideration as those of Missouri. Allowing to my brethren the same right of judgment that I exercise myself, I must be permitted to say that it seems to me the principle laid down will enable the people of a slave State to introduce slavery into a free State, for a longer or shorter time, as may suit their convenience; and by returning the slave to the State whence he was brought, by force or otherwise, the status of slavery attaches, and protects the rights of the master, and defies the sovereignty of the free State . . .

I think the judgment of the court below should be reversed.

6. Justice Curtis Dissenting

On the 25th of June, 1778, the Articles of Confederation being under consideration by the Congress, the delegates from South Carolina moved to amend this fourth article, by inserting after the word "free," and before the word "inhabitants," the word "white," so that the privileges and immunities of general citizenship would be secured only to white persons. Two States voted for the amendment, eight States against it, and the vote of one State was divided. The language of the article stood unchanged, and both by its terms of inclusion, "free inhabitants," and the strong implication from its terms of exclusion, "paupers, vagabonds, and fugitives from justice," who alone were excepted, it is clear, that under the Confederation, and at the time of the adoption of the constitution, free colored persons of African descent might be, and, by reason of their citizenship in certain States, were entitled to the privileges and immunities of general citizenship of the United States.

It has been often asserted that the Constitution was made exclusively by and for the white race. It has already been shown that in five of the thirteen original States, colored persons then possessed the elective franchise, and were among those by whom the Constitution was ordained and established. If so, it is not true, in point of fact, that the constitution was made exclusively by the white race. And that it was made exclusively for the white race is, in my opinion, not only an assumption not warranted by anything in the constitution, but contradicted by its opening declaration, that it was ordained and established by the people of the United States, for themselves and their posterity. And as free colored persons were then citizens of at least five States, and so in every sense part of the people of the United States, they were among those for whom and whose posterity the Constitution was ordained and established.

Again, it has been objected, that if the constitution has left to the several States the rightful power to determine who of their inhabitants shall be citizens of the United States, the States may make aliens citizens.

The answer is obvious. The Constitution has left to the States the determination what persons, born within their respective limits, shall acquire by birth citizenship of the United States; it has not left to them any power to prescribe any rule for the removal of the disabilities of alienage. This power is exclusively in Congress.

A naturalized citizen cannot be President of the United States, nor a Senator till after the lapse of nine years, nor a Representative till after the lapse of seven years, from his naturalization. Yet, as soon as naturalized, he is certainly a citizen of the United States.

The conclusions at which I have arrived on this part of the case are:

First. That the free native born citizens of each State are citizens of the United States.

Second. That as free colored persons born within some of the States are citizens of those States, such persons are also citizens of the United States.

Third. That every such citizen, residing in any State, has the right to sue and is liable to be sued in the Federal courts, as a citizen of that State in which he resides.

Fourth. That as the plea to the jurisdiction in this case shows no facts, except that the plaintiff was of African descent, and his ancestors were sold as slaves, and as these facts are not inconsistent with his citizenship of the United States, and his residence in the State of Missouri, the plea to the jurisdiction was bad, and the judgment of the Circuit Court overruling it was correct.

I dissent, therefore, from that part of the opinion of the majority of the court, in which it is held that a person of African descent cannot be a citizen of the United States; and I regret I must go further, and dissent both from what I deem their assumption of authority to examine the constitutionality of the act of Congress commonly called the Missouri Compromise Act, and the grounds and conclusions announced in their opinion.

J. Commentary on *Scott*

G. Hudson

Black Americans vs. Citizenship: The Dred Scott *Decision*

The prime mover and spokesman in the case was Chief Justice Roger Brooke Taney, a Maryland slaveholder. Taney, third Chief Justice of the United States, graduated from Dickinson College in 1795. He drafted that part of Andrew Jackson's bankcharter veto message of July 10, 1832, which stipulated that the President was not bound by the interpretation placed upon the Constitution by the Supreme Court. On Chief Justice John Marshall's death on July 6, 1835, the president appointed Taney, Chief Justice of the United States Supreme Court over bitter Whig opposition. Reversing the Court's nationalist trend, Taney's most notable decision was the Charles River Bridge case in 1837 which curtailed the scope of the Dartmouth College Case and curbed the growth of monopolies.

Taney's most fateful decision, however, was the *Dred Scott* Case of 1857. Under cover of a discussion of jurisdiction, Taney declared invalid the Missouri Compromise and the Compromise of 1850. Although the federal Courts never made a final disposition of the same, the *Dred Scott* case, after eleven years of litigation (April 6,

1846 to March 18, 1957) was terminated in the court where it had originated leaving Dred Scott in slavery. Soon therefore, ownership of the Scotts was transferred to Taylor Blow, the third son of Dred's original owner, Peter Blow, for a nominal sum. On May 26, 1857, Blow manumitted the Scott family. After a year of freedom, Dred Scott, on September 17, 1858, succumbed to rapid consumption and was buried in the Wesleyan Cemetery. Mrs. Scott and Harriet Scott followed soon after.

In the mind of Chief Justice Taney the question was simply this: "Can a Negro [sic], whose ancestors were imported into this country, and sold as slaves, become a member of the political community formed and brought into existence by the Constitution of the United States and as such become entitled to all the rights, and privileges, and immunities, guaranteed by that instrument to the citizen? One of which rights is the privilege of suing in a court of the United States in the cases specified in the Constitution. "It will be observed", Taney contended:

> That the plea applies to that class of persons only whose ancestors were Negroes [sic] of the African race, and imported into this country and sold as slaves . . . this being the only matter on dispute . . . the court must be understood as speaking . . . of those persons who are descendants of Africans who were imported into this country, and sold as slaves.

Taney's statement on black American citizenship, far from instituting a new policy, was but a ratification of the second-class legal status of free blacks in most states, North as well as South.

Only New England's tiny black population enjoyed anything approaching equal citizenship, and even there black's suffered considerable discrimination.

Justice Benjamin Curtis pointed out the weakness of Taney's argument. Justice Curtis, in his dissenting opinion, pointed out that free blacks were citizens in New Hampshire, Massachusetts, New Jersey, New York, and North Carolina before the Constitution was adopted. He added that nothing in the Constitution denied citizenship to blacks. In fact, the Constitution contained no definition of United States citizenship.

The dissenting opinion of Justice John McClean and Curtis, both of whom are generally held responsible for introducing the thorny issue of the Missouri Compromise, maintained that free Negroes were citizens of the United States and that Congress was constitutionally empowered (Art. IV., Sect. 3) to regulate slavery in the territories. Curtis' opinion was subsequently used by republican and abolitionist elements as one of their chief grounds for attacking the Court's decision.

Even more interesting were some of the other opinions relating to the merits of the case. All nine Justices discussed the merits in one way or another—some very fully, and others, like James N. Wayne and Robert C. Grier, merely expressed their concurrences with the opinions expressed by another Justice. Seven of the nine— all but Curtis and McLean—upheld the decision of the lower court that Dred Scott was a slave by virtue of the laws of Missouri as construed by the Missouri Supreme Court. Six—Taney, James M. Peter, Wayne Daniel, Grier, John Catron and John

Campbell—declared that Dred Scott should be remanded to slavery because the slavery prohibition of the Missouri Compromise Act of March 6, 1820, was unconstitutional.

To blacks the *Dred Scott* decision, the Kansas-Nebraska Act and the Fugitive Slave Law of the 1850s seemed to foreshadow a determined movement to rob free blacks of the free right that they possessed, and impose the peculiar institution on all of the new territories. Seemingly, the only recognized relationship the federal government had with black Americans was in the enforcement of the fugitive slave law. As a Columbus, Ohio newspaper editor observed, the United States Government was now dedicated to the principle of "Life, Liberty, and the Pursuit of the Nigger."

36 *Negro History Bulletin* 26, 27.
Copyright © (1973) Association for the Study of Afro-American Life.
Reprinted with permission of the Association for the
Study of Afro-American Life.

F. Michael Higginbotham

After 150 Years, Worst Supreme Court Decision Ever Continues to Haunt

On March 6, 1857, Chief Justice Roger Taney of Maryland authored the United States Supreme Court's *Dred Scott v. Sandford* opinion, declaring that it had no jurisdiction to hear Dred Scott's claim to freedom because he was black and, therefore, not a citizen of the United States. The case had been set in motion almost 25 years earlier when Dr. John Emerson, a physician in the United States Army, voluntarily took his slave, Dred Scott, from Missouri, a slave state, to the free state of Illinois. After returning to Missouri, Scott filed suit claiming that by virtue of his time in Illinois, he became a free person consistent with Illinois law. In holding against Scott, Taney reasoned that residence in a free state did not automatically eliminate slave status. That determination was left to the state having jurisdiction over the trial, and Missouri had already determined that, despite his stay in Illinois, Scott was still a slave.

Dred Scott's legacy lies in the Supreme Court's determination that blacks, whether slave or free, were not citizens and therefore were not entitled to Constitutional protection. Despite being born in the United States, possessing citizenship in a free state, or having served in the United States Armed Forces, blacks were viewed by the majority of justices as belonging to "an unfortunate race." Unfortunate, because Justice Taney reasoned that blacks were viewed by the founding fathers as socially and legally inferior to whites. Accordingly, Scott's color, not his free status, determined his rights under the law. Whether slave or free, Taney declared blacks to be "so far inferior, that they had no rights which the white man was bound to respect." With these words, the confusion surrounding constitutional rights held by free blacks was clarified. While slavery was a despicable institution that should have been eradicated, the truth of the matter is that the original constitution permitted its existence. The real tragedy of *Dred Scott* is that the Supreme Court went well beyond the Founding Fathers' express direction by denying rights to free blacks as if they were slaves.

The fundamental flaw in the *Dred Scott* decision was the courts lumping of free blacks and slaves together. Scott did not argue that slaves had rights. He argued that free blacks had rights and that he was free by virtue of having been brought voluntarily by his owner to a free state. Scott viewed his transportation to a free state as an act of manumission since Dr. Emerson had knowledge of Illinois law prohibiting slavery when he brought Scott to Illinois. The court ignored this argument claiming that it did not matter whether Scott was slave or free because he was black. Blackness, not slave status, was the mark of inferiority thus making Scott unprotected by the Constitution. Without providing any data, Taney concluded that it was universally recognized among civilized men that blacks were inferior.

Taney said blacks were inferior because they were discriminated against under various state laws. While certainly such discrimination existed, in nine of the 13 original states, including two slave states, free black men were permitted to vote.

The *Dred Scott* case is the worst ever because it is immoral in that it sanctioned slavery and impractical because it exacerbated political divisions by preventing compromises on abolition favored by congress. The decision was especially antagonizing to abolitionists because it meant that even if they somehow managed to prevail politically, the constitution absolutely prevented both the abolition of slavery and elevation of free blacks to citizenship. One consequence of *Dred Scott* is that those who were not abolitionists, but were either sympathetic to, or members of antislavery groups, were deprived of the hope of a political solution, and became increasingly radicalized.

Most significantly, however, Taney got the law wrong. Taney had no textual support for lumping free blacks and slaves together. Taney's basis for doing so was his interpretation of the original intent of the Founding Fathers. Yet, Taney appears to have exaggerated, mischaracterized, utilized inconsistent reasoning, and made up evidence to support his view. . . .

The Baltimore Afro-American, March 9, 2007, p. A8.
Copyright © (2007) F. Michael Higginbotham.
Reprinted with permission of F. Michael Higginbotham.

The *Dred Scott* holding was unquestionably racist. Chief Justice Taney's opinion constitutionally doomed blacks to the status of mere property, whether they were born in this country or not, whether they were "free" or slaves. The forceful dissents by Justices McLean and Curtis[24] emphasized that "[a] slave is not a mere chattel. He bears the impress of his Maker, and is amenable to the laws of God and man; and he is destined to an endless existence."[25] However, the dissenters could

---

24. 60 U.S. (19 How.) at 529 (McLean, J., dissenting), 564 (Curtis, J., dissenting).
25. *Id.* at 550 (McLean, J., dissenting).

not sway a majority of the Court. Others have suggested that Taney's decision was nothing more than a political maneuver to aid President James Buchanan, who was seeking reelection. Abraham Lincoln, who was a Presidential candidate at the time of the ruling, said that the *Dred Scott* opinion made it seem that "all the powers of the earth" were combining against the black person, and "now they have him, as it were, bolted in with a lock of a hundred keys, which can never be unlocked without the concurrence of a hundred men, and they scattered to a hundred different and distant places."[26]

K. Background on Justice Joseph Story

Geoffrey Stone, et al.

Justice Joseph Story

Joseph Story was only thirty-two years old and had no judicial experience when James Madison appointed him to the Court in 1811. Although not a Federalist, Story had strong nationalist sympathies and sided with John Marshall throughout much of his judicial career. His opinion in *Martin v. Hunter's Lessee*, 14 U.S. (1 Wheat.) 304 (1816), established the finality of the Court's constitutional authority against the states. His nationalist inclinations were also reflected in *Swift v. Tyson*, 41 U.S. (16 Pet.) 1 (1842), which upheld the power of federal courts to create a national commercial law. As a circuit justice, Story was said to absorb "jurisdiction as a sponge took up water," and some claimed that, "if a bucket of water were brought into his court with a corn cob floating in it, he would at once extend the admiralty jurisdiction of the United States over it." A serious scholar, Story was elected to the Harvard Board of Overseers and played a key role in the founding of the Harvard Law School. His Commentaries on the Constitution, published in 1833, was a classic of its time. On Marshall's death in 1835, Story hoped to be nominated chief justice, but Andrew Jackson, who had called him "the most dangerous man in America," named Roger Taney instead. Story was frequently in dissent during the nine years he sat on the Taney Court. *See, Charles River Bridge v. Warren Bridge*, 36 U.S. (11 Pet.) 420 (1837). Frustrated by the direction of the Court, which he saw as undermining the Marshall Court's conception of the Constitution, he planned to resign in 1845, but fell ill and died before he could complete his unfinished business.

Constitutional Law xci (3rd edition).
Copyright © (1996) Stone, et al.
Reprinted with permission of Aspen Law & Business.

---

26. *See* DON FEHRENBACHER, THE DRED SCOTT CASE: ITS SIGNIFICANCE IN AMERICAN LAW 241 (1978).

A. Leon Higginbotham, Jr.

The Life of the Law: Values, Commitment, and Craftsmanship

Justice Joseph Story,[27] was the first recipient of the Dane Professorship at Harvard.[28] While sitting as a Circuit Justice in Massachusetts, he authored the seminal 1822 opinion in *United States v. La Jeune Eugenie*.[29] His moving opinion in that case declared that the international slave trade violated the law of nations.[30] Later, Justice

---

27. Born in 1779, the son of a physician and Revolutionary War hero, Joseph Story was the youngest person ever appointed to the United States Supreme Court "and one of the great jurists of the western world." He graduated from Harvard in 1798, second in his class. In his short political career, he served in both the Massachusetts legislature and the United States House of Representatives, making a name for himself as a supporter of free trade practices. *See generally* G. DUNNE, JUSTICE JOSEPH STORY AND THE RISE OF THE SUPREME COURT 60–70 (1970).

In his professional life, Story established a successful commercial practice, gaining national prominence by successfully pleading before the Supreme Court a case involving a claim to the famous "Yazoo" lands. *See Fletcher v. Peck*, 10 U.S. (6 Cranch) 87 (1810). "He wrote nine important treatises, taught at—virtually created—Harvard Law School. . . ." R. COVER, JUSTICE ACCUSED: ANTISLAVERY AND THE JUDICIAL PROCESS 238 (1975).

Story was a strong abolitionist who struggled with his hatred of slavery and the Constitution's sanction of it. Story perhaps "attempted the impossible—to resolve disputed points within a libertarian framework while giving effect to the basic constitutional design and making the Court a composing rather than a disruptive element in the irrepressible conflict."

28. The Dane Professorship was established in 1829 by Nathan Dane, whose $10,000 contribution allowed Harvard Law School to hire then-Supreme Court Justice Story to lecture whenever his official duties permitted. *See* J. SELIGMAN, THE HIGH CITADEL 23 (1978).

29. 26 F. Cas. 832 (C.C.D. Mass. 1822).

30. In *La Jeune*, Justice Story expressed his belief that slavery, because it "involve[d] the enslavement of human beings," was "a breach of all the moral duties, of all the maxims of justice, mercy and humanity, and of the admitted rights, which independent Christian nations now hold sacred in their intercourse with each other." *Id.* at 845. Justice Story went on to detail the evils that arise and flourish because of slavery:

It begins in corruption, and plunder, and kidnapping. It creates and stimulates unholy wars for the purpose of making captives. It desolates whole villages and provinces for the purpose of seizing the young, the feeble, the defenceless, and the innocent. It breaks down all the ties of parent, and children, and family, and country. It shuts up all sympathy for human suffering and sorrows. It manacles the inoffensive females and the starving infants. It forces the brave to untimely death in defence of their humble homes and firesides, or drives them to despair and self-immolation. It stirs up the worst passions of the human soul, darkening the spirit of revenge, sharpening the greediness of avarice, brutalizing the selfish, envenoming the cruel, famishing the weak, and crushing to death the broken-hearted. This is but the beginning of the evils.

Id.

The significance of the opinion is that it is a contemporary page of history describing the events of the slavery era. Story's opinion recounted the tragedies suffered by millions of innocent black slaves. He established that at least one-fourth of the slaves transported perished in cold blood due to the inhumane and thoughtless treatment that they received from their oppressors. The question before the *LaJeune* Court was whether the international slave trade could be a violation of international law. Justice Story noted:

All the wars, that have desolated Africa for the last three centuries, have had their origin in the slave trade. The blood of thousands of her miserable children has stained her shores, or quenched the dying embers of her desolated towns, to glut the appetite of slave dealers. The ocean has

Story wrote the Supreme Court opinion in *United States v. The Schooner Amistad* and *Prigg v. The Commonwealth of Pennsylvania*.

100 *Harvard Law Review*, 795, 797–98.
Copyright © (1987) The Harvard Law Review Association.
Reprinted with permission of The Harvard Law Review Association and
Evelyn Brooks Higginbotham.

L. Explaining Chief Justice Roger Taney

On the issue of slavery and free blacks, Chief Justice Roger Taney appears to have had mixed emotions. Taney came from a slaveholding family in Maryland. He freed most of the slaves he inherited, and as a practicing attorney, he successfully represented a free black man in an estate dispute against some white relatives, and he also represented a white preacher indicted for encouraging slave revolts through anti-slavery sermons. Nevertheless, Taney's opinion in *Scott* is clearly one-sided in its support for the institution of slavery and the oppression of blacks. The opinion clearly demonstrates that despite all of Justice Taney's conflicting concerns, the protection of the institution of slavery and the maintenance of white supremacy were the principles he valued most.

M. Questions and Notes

While some claim that slavery is a distant memory, there are numerous links to slavery in aspects of modern culture, including language. A vast array of modern sayings emanate from slavery. For example, small fried balls of cornmeal dough are referred to in most southern states as "hushpuppies" because slave mothers would use this food to quiet crying babies. Fried dough possessed a powerful scent that would attract the attention of babies and would act as a soothing and calming remedy.[31] The phrase "sold down the river" relates to the threat of enslavement in increasingly harsh conditions as one goes farther south. Can you identify any other sayings?

The Court considers two major problems in the *Dred Scott* case: first, whether a black person, whose ancestors were brought to the United States as slaves, could be considered a citizen under the Constitution of the United States; and second, whether Congress has the constitutional authority to prohibit owners from taking slaves into territories administered by the United States.

As to the first problem, consider the following specific questions:

---

received in its deep and silent bosum thousands more, who have perished from disease and want during their passage from their native homes to the foreign colonies.
Id.
31. *See* W. MORRIS & M. MORRIS, DICTIONARY OF WORD AND PHRASE ORIGIN 187 (1962). Used by slave mothers to quiet crying babies.

Why was it necessary for Dred Scott to establish his citizenship in order to bring his lawsuit in federal court? What specific provision defined the citizenship necessary for Dred Scott to assert his freedom in federal court? Is it state citizenship or national citizenship that the Court finds is required by the provision in question? Justice Taney noted that the plaintiffs claimed the federal court had jurisdiction to hear their lawsuit "under that provision of the Constitution which gives jurisdiction in controversies between citizens of different states." (Article 3, Section 2, United States Constitution). Article 3, Section 2 provides "[t]he Judicial Power of the United States shall extend to all Cases . . . between Citizens of different States. . . ." For what reason might this power to hear suits between citizens of different states have been provided? Writing for the Court in *Erie R.R. Co. v. Tompkins*,[32] Justice Brandeis asserted that "[d]iversity of citizenship jurisdiction was conferred in order to prevent apprehended discrimination in state courts against those not citizens of the state." (304 U.S. at 71). Does Justice Taney's opinion consider the reasons for diversity of citizenship jurisdiction in assessing whether such diversified jurisdiction was available to the plaintiff Dred Scott? If Justice Brandeis' interpretation of the original rationale for diversity jurisdiction is correct, what would be the relevance of this original purpose in determining the right of a black person to bring a suit in federal court founded on "diversity of citizenship" jurisdiction? In the text of the clause in the Constitution, or in the reasons for the inclusion of this power, is there a basis to doubt Justice Taney's construction that the citizenship referred to must be United States citizenship? Remember that Dred Scott in this case sought the aid of the federal court to establish his entitlement to freedom. Should not Justice Taney be concerned that an impartial federal forum be available for a person claiming he is being held illegally as a slave? Can a consistent argument be made that a person asserting a claim to freedom should be entitled under the Constitution at least to raise this claim in federal court — and, if successful, be considered a citizen at least for the purpose of vindicating this claim?

Review the evidence and reasoning of Justice Taney in support of his conclusion that black people were not intended to be citizens of the United States. Refer to the earlier sections of the materials on slavery and free blacks. Do you find Taney's conclusion supported by the weight of historical evidence? Even if you might find that the preponderance of evidence is in favor of Taney's position, note the difficulties in reasoning and treatment of evidence that undermine the certainty of his conclusions. For example, Justice McLean notes that although "the Government was not made especially for the colored race, [sic] many of them were citizens of the New England states, and exercised the rights of suffrage when the Constitution was adopted."[33] Justice Taney might also have noted that free blacks voted in North Carolina until 1835, a much longer period than blacks who enjoyed the franchise in many northern states before the Civil War.

---

32. 304 U.S. 64 (1938).
33. 60 U.S. (19 How.) at 529 (McLean, J., dissenting).

Note two logical difficulties undermining Taney's conclusions concerning the exclusion of blacks from national citizenship under the Constitution. First, consider his inductive reasoning from particular instances to general principle, to support the view that blacks were not fully citizens. For example, he notes that marriage between whites and blacks was prohibited by Maryland in 1717 and by Massachusetts in 1704–1705 and again in 1786. What is the relevance of this particular discrimination to the political and legal issue of citizenship? Does Justice Taney assume that the desire of a community to prevent social relationships, and particularly marriage between whites and blacks necessarily implies the exclusion of blacks from political and economic participation in the society? What is the validity of this assumption? Is not the decision in *Quock Walker* significant in recognizing the inconsistency of slavery with the doctrine of natural rights embodied in the Massachusetts Bill of Rights?[34] Why is the prohibition of interracial marriage relevant to the question of citizenship, but the adoption of prohibition of slavery through the affirmation of a doctrine of natural rights ignored (and to Taney, presumably irrelevant) in determining the legal status of blacks at the time of the adoption of the Constitution?

Consider Justice Taney's discussion of *Legrand v. Darnall*. Darnall, who was a slave, was the son of a white man and was eventually freed by his father. Justice Taney is apparently shocked by the fact that Darnall, following his manumission, might become entitled to the privileges of national citizenship. Is it not unusual that the acknowledged son of a citizen would not be admitted to the political community and granted the privileges of his parents? If Darnall's mother had been white and his father black, would his status as a citizen have been different according to the principle that a person follows the condition of his mother? If this were the rule, what should be the relevance of race to the capacity of a person to become a citizen upon his release from slavery? If, on the other hand, a person could only become a citizen when both of his parents were citizens, how can this illogical, as well as pernicious, view be explained? Does Taney recognize any obligation to explain why the Constitution should be interpreted to prohibit a process where interracial children at least are brought into the political and legal community when such a desire is manifested by the parent?

Compare the great fluidity and openness in Latin American society in this regard where manumission and acceptance into the social community were far more available to blacks and particularly to mulattos. In *Neither Black nor White*,[35] Carl Degler has argued that the central difference in race relations of the United States and Brazil may be traced to the availability in Brazil of what he terms the "mulatto escape hatch," and its absence in the United States. Because of economic, demographic, and

---

34. For a detailed examination of the *Quock Walker* case, *see* A. Higginbotham, In the Matter of Color 91–98 (1978).

35. C. Degler, Neither Black Nor White: Slavery and Race Relations in Brazil and in the United States 219(1971).

cultural patterns in Brazil that have not been present in the United States, Degler finds that in Brazil persons of mixed blood and lighter skin have been accepted without a stigma attached to the slave status or darker skin of one parent. In the United States, this process, as evidenced by the hostility of Justice Taney toward Darnall's becoming a citizen, did not exist. One should consider why this process did not occur and the consequences for our society due to the absence of such a gradual and evolutionary process. Is this an area where courts and the legal system generally could have made an important contribution?

A second logical problem in the structure of Taney's argument is his duplicitous treatment of the implications of denying certain civil or political rights to other groups in society, such as women and minors. Taney notes that women and minors were denied the right to vote and subjected to other legal disadvantages. If blacks were denied citizenship because of these legal disadvantages, why does this reasoning not lead to the same conclusion for women and minors? How can the same set of legal disadvantages lead to a denial of citizenship for one group, but not for another? How convincing is Taney's treatment of this logical difficulty?

Taney's analysis of the reasons for the decline of slavery at the time of the American Revolution raises important questions of historical judgment as well as those pertaining to the role of courts in the articulation and support of moral values. Taney notes that "when the Constitution was adopted, [slavery] had entirely worn out in one of [the Northern states] and measures had been taken for its abolition in several others."[36] Taney goes on to note that this restriction of slavery "had not been produced by any change of opinion in relation to this race; but because it was discovered, from experience, that slave labor was unsuited to the climate and production of these States."[37]

According to Taney's analysis, one might imagine that there were no principles or moral values—particularly principles and values of universal application—that were involved in the American Revolution and the formation of a national government in the Constitution. On this point, refer to the segment from Bernard Bailyn's *The Ideological Origins of the American Revolution*.[38] In terms of historical causation, Taney explains the abolishment and decline of slavery entirely in terms of economic causes and disregards—either on principle or on the basis of ignorance—the moral, intellectual, and ideological forces that were brought to bear against slavery during the period of the American Revolution and the writing of the Constitution.

Beyond this mistaken historical judgment, Taney's analysis has important implications concerning the role of courts in affirming and transmitting moral values. Does not Taney's history and sociology, summed up in his interpretation of the Declaration of Independence, implicitly deny the role of courts in affirming the

36. 60 U.S. 393, 398 (1857).
37. *Id.*
38. B. Bailyn, The Ideological Origins of the American Revolution 22–54, 230–319 (1967).

ideals of society even when, or especially when, these ideals have not been carried into full effect? Taney's analysis and conclusions raise the important question of whether courts should simply be a mouthpiece for the expediency and prejudice of society, or whether the courts should seek to contribute a distinct element to democratic society by articulating and supporting the presence and force of ideals and moral values? Perhaps Justice Taney's restrictive view of the Court's role, and his related amoral reading of history, is connected to his conception of the limits of the formal power of the Court in overriding the decisions of other institutions of government. According to Justice Taney, "[i]t is not the province of the court to decide upon the justice or injustice, the policy or impolicy of these laws [relating to the subjugation of blacks by the 'dominant' white race]."[39] That decision "belonged to the political or law-making power; to those who formed the sovereignty and framed the Constitution. The duty of the court is to interpret the instrument they have framed with the best lights we can obtain on the subject, and to administer it as we find it, according to its true intent and meaning when it was adopted."[40] This formulation might be unexceptional enough if it related only to the power of the Court to overturn or alter the provisions of the Constitution and the legislation of Congress according to some personal standard of judges concerning the "justice or injustice, the policy or impolicy" of these measures. But this formulation is clearly objectionable if it is conceived as a rationale for precluding judges from considering the justice or injustice of the measures brought before them, in light of the totality of the moral experience and ideals of the society, or ultimately the "moral universe" in which they find themselves.

It is certainly the responsibility of courts to comprehend and articulate the injustice of measures brought before them and to consider this injustice in determining the proper exercise of their power. Where the court has a principled basis for overturning a ruling inconsistent with the Constitution and has the power to do so, it should exercise its authority accordingly. Where a principled basis for overturning an unjust measure does not exist, the court should use its creativity and power to avoid legitimizing the measure or practice in question. This zealous affirmation of the place and legitimacy of slavery in the United States—an affirmation in no way tempered by the moral traditions and ideals of the country—is the fundamental basis for indicting the role of Justice Taney and his majority brethren in the *Dred Scott* decision.

N. Point/Counterpoint

Is *Prigg v. Pennsylvania* a proslavery or antislavery decision?

---

39. 60 U.S. 393, 401 (1857).
40. *Id.*

VIII. The Beginning of the End of Slavery

A. Introduction

The decision by the Supreme Court in *Dred Scott* restricted Congress's power to limit the expansion of slavery into new states and territories and ruled that the Constitution did not protect slaves and free blacks. Abolitionists viewed the decision as a severe blow to the efforts to end slavery. Some abolitionists began to believe that slavery could not be ended within the existing constitutional framework.

B. The Life of John Brown

In the Kansas territory during the 1850s, armed conflicts between abolitionists and slave owners occurred frequently. This is the land that eventually would become the state of Kansas, a territory that both abolitionists and slave owners wanted to claim exclusively for themselves. In the spring of 1856, two abolitionists were murdered by a group of proslavery supporters. Several days later, the free-state city of Lawrence was attacked by proslavery supporters. During this attack, several people were injured and a number of buildings were destroyed. In retaliation for these and other similar acts, John Brown, a dedicated white abolitionist who believed that slavery violated God's will, led an attack on a proslavery settlement in which five proslavery supporters were killed.

Based on his leadership in Kansas, Brown became a national symbol of forceful resistance to slavery. In 1857, Brown received financial assistance from wealthy abolitionists for an invasion of the South. As a military operation, however, Brown's attack was illogical.

On the night of October 16, 1859, Brown led an armed group of twenty-two men into Harper's Ferry, where they seized the armory and announced they had come to free the slaves of Virginia. Brown hoped the slaves in the area would join him, and he would then arm them with weapons in the arsenal and with provisions stored nearby. He then planned to lead a large uprising of slaves throughout the South.

Brown, however, disregarded the advice of the famous abolitionist and former slave, Frederick Douglass, who warned him that slaves would not know of the raid and even if they did, most would be unable to join him. Although Brown had seized the armory and could flee with its weapons, he refused to leave Harper's Ferry because he was waiting for the slaves to join him. He mercifully released some hostages, and thus word of the raid spread.

The following evening, federal troops arrived under the command of Colonel Robert E. Lee.[41] The next day, the troops captured Brown and his remaining force. Of the twenty-two men in Brown's group, including several free blacks, five escaped,

---

41. Lee would later serve as the Commander of the Confederate Army.

ten were killed (including two of Brown's sons) and seven were captured. His son Watson Brown and several others were killed while attempting to surrender.

Brown was injured during the fighting but lived to stand trial. He was indicted a week after his capture and was placed on trial the same day. Six days later, he was found guilty of committing murder and treason. John Brown was sentenced to death and hung on December 2, 1859. Brown's raid ended in defeat; however, he inspired many, as the ongoing bitter dispute over slavery gradually crystallized into war.

C. Summary

Less than a year after John Brown's execution, the Civil War began. Millions of American lives would be lost before slavery would be brought to an end.

D. Questions and Notes

In his speech before a joint session of Congress in 1990, Nelson Mandela spoke about those Americans throughout history he recognized and admired. Mandela explained:

> We could not have heard of and admired John Brown, Sojourner Truth, Frederick Douglass, W.E.B. DuBois, Marcus Garvey, Martin Luther King, Jr., and others — we could not have heard of these and not be moved to act as they were moved to act.

Do you have the same level of admiration for John Brown as Mandela describes?

E. Point/Counterpoint

Responses to racial oppression have varied over the years. In 1858, which approach would you support in order to end slavery: litigation, legislation, non-violent protest, violent resistance, or any others? Did the severe nature of slavery's oppression justify any means that would bring it to an end?

John Hope Franklin

From Slavery to Freedom: A History of Negro Americans (5th Edition)

The antislavery sentiment generated by the humanitarian philosophy of the eighteenth century never completely died out in America. To be sure, there was a period of quiescence as the South found new opportunities for the profitable employment of slaves and as the North became concerned with her own economic and political problems. But some people continued to oppose slavery as an institution, and long before militant abolitionists appeared on the scene around 1830 the most convincing arguments against slavery had already been developed. Soon after the War of 1812 sectionalism was apparent as the North swung to manufacturing; and the

South, still wedded to an agrarian civilization, came to see clearly that the interests of the two sections were becoming antagonistic. Indeed, the industrial development of the North changed the point of view of this section; as people there were brought closer together, they sought to solve their pressing problems through cooperation. In the South, however, the plantation system tended to preserve frontier independence: there was little communal life, only slight civic responsibility, and little interest in various program for the improvement of mankind. The contest over Missouri, moreover, crystallized the sectional conflict and emphasized the importance of slavery as a national issue.

Antislavery sentiment in the North increased steadily after 1815, as more ministers, editors, and other leaders of public opinion spoke out against the evils of the institution. Several years passed before almost all these critics were confined to the North. In 1817 Charles Osborn published the *Philanthropist*, an antislavery paper, in Ohio, but two years later he moved to Tennessee and published the *Manumission Intelligencer*. In 1820 Elihu Embree was publishing the *Emancipator* in Jonesboro, Tennessee, while William Swaim was expressing the opposition of Quakers to slavery in his *Patriot*, published at Greensboro, North Carolina. In 1821 the itinerant Benjamin Lundy began editing the *Genius of Universal Emancipation*, in which he set forth a complete program for the emancipation and colonization of Negroes. Although he lacked the emotional fervor of later abolitionists, he was not without courage and devotion to the cause of freeing the slaves.

Within ten years after the beginning of Lundy's work, three events indicated that the age of the militant abolitionists had arrived. These events were the publication of David Walker's *Appeal*, the appearance of William Lloyd Garrison's the *Liberator*, and the insurrection of Nat Turner, which many incorrectly thought was inspired by the activities of men like Garrison (see chapter X). David Walker was a North Carolina free Negro who had moved to Boston, where he engaged in selling secondhand clothes. His bitter hatred for slavery was not diminished by his leaving the South. If anything, it was increased. In September 1829 his essay appeared: "Walker's Appeal in Four Articles Together with a Preamble to the Colored Citizens of the World But in Particular and very Expressly to those of the United States of America." It was one of the most vigorous denunciations of slavery ever printed in the United States. In unmistakable language he called upon Negroes to rise up and throw off the yoke of slavery.

> Are we men!! I ask you . . . are we MEN? Did our creator make us to be slaves to dust and ashes like ourselves? Are they not dying worms as well as we? . . . How we could be so *submissive* to a gang of men, whom we cannot tell whether they are as good as ourselves or not, I never conceive. . . . America is more our country than it is the whites—we have enriched it with our *blood and tears*. The greatest riches in all America have arisen from our blood and tears: And they will drive us from our property and homes, which we have earned with our blood.

Walker closed his appeal by quoting the Declaration of Independence to show that blacks were justified in resisting, with force if necessary, the oppression of white masters. A startled country read the words of this Negro who called for militant action.

In January 1831 the first issue of Garrison's *Liberator* appeared. Garrison had served his novitiate as Lundy's assistant on the *Genius of Universal Emancipation* and in jail for libelous words against a ship captain who had transported slaves to New Orleans. He was done with gradualism; he had shifted from supporting colonization to opposing it. In the first issue of his newspaper he also invoked the Declaration of Independence, claiming that the black man was as much entitled to "life, liberty and the pursuit of happiness" as the white man. Immediate and unconditional abolition of slavery was, from his point of view, the only solution. He laid down his challenge to slavery in most dramatic language when he said:

> I *will* be as harsh as truth, and as uncompromising as justice. On this subject, I do not wish to think, to speak, or write, with moderation. . . . I am in earnest—I will not equivocate—I will not excuse—I will not retreat a single inch—AND I WILL BE HEARD.

Thus Garrison became the most articulate spokesman of nonviolent militant abolition. For a whole generation he was one of the most important forces working for the freedom of slaves. It was an auspicious beginning for an exciting career. Small wonder that people in the South connected the so-called incendiary writings of Walker and Garrison with the insurrections of Nat Turner and of others; but Garrison always followed a policy of nonviolent, passive resistance . . .

It was the countenancing of violence by abolitionists that caused many law-abiding citizens to oppose them and rendered utterly hopeless their schemes to obtain government support. Convinced that slave-holders had the law of the land on their side, the abolitionists resorted to the principle of a higher law, which they felt justified their circumventing or breaking the law. Garrison and his followers, although nonviolent, pointed out the inevitability of violence of the Nat Turner insurrection. In 1839 Jabez Hammond of New York said that only force would end slavery and that Negro military schools should be set up in Canada and Mexico. When slaves revolted aboard the *Creole* on its voyage from Hampton Roads to New Orleans, Representative Joshua Giddings not only opposed treating the slaves as common criminals but even praised them for seeking freedom. The House of Representatives, shocked by his open defiance of the law, censured Giddings. Forthwith he resigned, went home to Ohio, and was immediately returned to Congress by his antislavery constituency. The redoubtable Giddings later praised other blacks and whites for seeking to abolish slavery, and finally the House became accustomed to his tirades against the institution. By 1850 the philosophy of force was so integral a part of abolitionist doctrine that many viewed it as a movement toward anarchy.

The whites were not alone in their opposition to slavery. From the beginning, Negroes, who suffered most from the subjugation of their race, gave enthusiastic support to abolition. Indeed, strong abolitionist doctrine was preached by Negroes long before Garrison was born. Before the War for Independence, slaves in Massachusetts brought actions against their masters for the freedom that they regarded as their inalienable right. During and after the Revolutionary War, Negroes sought the abolition of slavery by petitioning the state and federal governments to outlaw the slave trade and to embark upon a program of general emancipation. Prince Hall, Benjamin Banneker, Absolom Jones, and Richard Allen issued strong denunciations of slavery before 1800, and organizations like the Free African Society of Philadelphia passed resolutions calling for its abolition. In the nineteenth century Negroes organized antislavery societies. By 1830 they had fifty groups, one that was very active in New Haven, and several in Boston, New York, and Philadelphia.

Derrick Bell

Race, Racism and American Law (4th Edition)

Blacks and other minority groups in this country, though, lacking economic and political power, and subject to continuing—if increasingly subtle—racial discrimination, have often relied heavily on protests in one form or another as the only available mechanism for airing their grievances. And during each "direct action" campaign, civil rights leaders have wrestled with the dilemma of how to structure demonstrations that will dramatize their plight to the majority community so as to spur action that will improve rather than worsen conditions for the black community. Protest actions clearly entitled to protection, such as a non-disruptive speech at an appropriate time and place, a petition properly filed with a governmental body, or a parade that conforms with all rules and regulations, are likely to gain little attention when they are not entirely ignored. On the other hand, more vigorous protests—those that cannot be ignored—are likely to contravene either existing laws or laws that are promptly enacted to transform what was arguably legal protest into criminal activity. In addition to this risk, there is general uncertainty as to whether or not protest activity actually helps to bring about racial reform. Indeed, there is a tendency by those in policymaking positions to separate reform from protest activity even when the latter was fairly clearly the major motivation for the former. Thus, university officials have seen nothing inconsistent in proceeding with disciplinary action against student protesters at the same time as steps are taken to reform the conditions about which the protest was mounted.

One would have thought that when Federal Judge A. Leon Higginbotham, serving as a member of the National Commission on the Causes and Prevention of Violence in 1969, indicated that the sit-ins and other nonviolent protests paved the way for the elimination of Jim Crow practices throughout the South, he would have been stating no more than the obvious. But he was speaking as one of the minority in a 7–6 decision by the Commission when he wrote:

Recent advances in the field of civil rights have not come about and could never have come about solely through judicial tests "by one individual" while all others in the silent black majority waited for the ultimate constitutional determination.

Rather, the majority impetus for the Civil Rights Acts of 1957, 1960, 1964 and 1965, which promised more equal access to the opportunities of our society, resulted from the determination, the spirit and the nonviolent commitment of the many who continually challenge the constitutionality of racial discrimination and awakened the national conscience.[42]

The Commission majority had expressed the view that the constitutionality of a law could be effectively challenged in a test case brought by one individual or a small group. "While the judicial test is in progress," the majority urged, "all other dissenters should abide by the law involved until it is declared unconstitutional." There are, however, a whole host of civil rights activists who would urge that without the drama and confrontation of direct action protest, the basic mandate of *Brown*, ending the "separate but equal" doctrine of *Plessy v. Ferguson*, might never have been implemented. Certainly, there had been little voluntary compliance from 1954 until the sit-in era in the early 1960s. So, while the majority of the President's Commission on the Causes and Prevention of Violence was not ready, even in 1969, to accept Judge Higginbotham's assessment of the limitations of litigation as an effective challenge to racial discrimination, thousands of blacks had reached Higginbotham's conclusion that the long awaited promise of *Brown v. Board of Education* would not be self-executing.

It is not clear why the President's Commission in 1969 was unable to acknowledge what a President had recognized seven years earlier. John F. Kennedy admitted to civil rights leaders privately in June 1963 "that the demonstrations in the streets had brought results, they had made the executive branch act faster and were forcing Congress to entertain legislation which a few weeks before would have had no chance."[43] It should be noted that Kennedy's statement was "off the record." Violence, as H. Rap Brown once said, may be as American as cherry pie, but few boast of the centrality of violence in American history. Coercive tactics, even peaceful

---

42. Additional Statement of Judge Higginbotham, Commission Statement on Civil Disobedience, Natl. Commn. on the Causes & Prevention of Violence 16 (Dec. 1969).

43. A. Schlesinger, A Thousand Days 970 (1965). Kennedy was not the first president who "got religion" on racial issues in the face of a massive civil rights protest in the nation's capital. In 1941, Franklin D. Roosevelt feared his effort to gear up the nation for war would be disrupted by a march on Washington by 100,000 blacks under the leadership of A. Philip Randolph, head of the Brotherhood of Pullman Car Porters. To get the march called off, Roosevelt agreed to issue an Executive Order barring discrimination in war industries and apprenticeship programs. Using similar tactics, Randolph later pressured President Truman to issue two Executive Orders. One provided for "equal treatment and equal opportunity" in the armed services and the other sought to abolish "racial discrimination in federal employment." L. Bennet, Before the Mayflower 366–70 (5th ed. 1982).

ones for the most justifiable cause, are deplored. The absence of an effective alternative gains only minimum sympathy for protests with disruptive potential, particularly if they are mounted by blacks.

A politics of dissimulation seems involved here. The tenor of the legal institution's opposition to protests and boycotts suggests that more is at stake than just the weighing of First Amendment rights and limits. Also at stake could be the status of protesting as a form of political expression (opposition to which would contradict a fundamental element of Americans' self-image, given that it was often violent protest against England that led to the American Revolution), or perhaps an unconscious rejection of the potential inherent in protests and boycotts. At some level, protest actions place in issue the relationship of "the law" to peace and social order. Legal analysis of protests would have to change if the law were recognized as a king of violence rather than as the antithesis of violence.

Thus, it should not surprise us that the rhetorical definition of certain protest traditions as "coercive" both casts them as "violent" or potentially "violent" and insulates state institutions in general and the judiciary in particular from interrogation. May of the protests discussed in this chapter were aimed at challenging state racism and state-sanctioned racism. To call these protests "coercive" is to simultaneously (albeit, implicitly) position the state practices being challenged, if not the state itself, as the "coerced."

Martin Luther King, in his famous "Letter from Birmingham City Jail,"[44] tried to address this issue by distinguishing between just and unjust laws. He would obey the former because they square with moral law or the law of God, but he would disobey the latter because they are out of harmony with moral law. In King's view, segregation laws are immoral for they distort the soul and damage the personality of both the segregator and the segregated. Segregation laws are also evil, King said, because the majority inflicts on a minority standards it would not impose on itself. Dr. King provided additional examples, but his key distinction was made at that point where he said:

> In no sense do I advocate evading or defying the law as the rabid segregationist would do. This would lead to anarchy. One who breaks an unjust law must do it openly, lovingly (not hatefully as the white mothers did in New Orleans when they were seen on television screaming "nigger, nigger, nigger") and with a willingness to accept the penalty. I submit that an individual who breaks a law that conscience tells him is unjust, and willingly accepts the penalty by staying in jail to arouse the conscience of the community over its injustice, is in reality expressing the very highest respect for law.[45]

44. M. KING, WHY WE CAN'T WAIT (1963).
45. *Id.* at 84–86. The famous Montgomery bus boycott, which brought Dr. King national prominence, provided a definitive model for combining a committed community protest action with effective litigation. According to Dr. King, the months of walking and the constant harassment of

Impressive, but many legal commentators remained troubled by Dr. King's philosophy. Professor Charles Fried expressed concern that the protestors expected others to abide by the law but were unwilling to contribute like sacrifice by abiding by the principle of "institutional settlement" of claims determined against them by some fair procedure.[46] Moreover, Professor Fried claims, if the demonstrators get the law changed to suit them, their tactics would enable those who think the former law justified to resist the "remedial" laws. Standing ready to pay the penalty for civil disobedience does, he concedes, evidence an affirmation of law in general, and he emphasized his belief that the law protested against is not simply disadvantageous, but wrong. "This is a gamble," he concludes, "but civil disobedience is a risky, maybe a desperate course."[47]

Professor Fried speaks of the resolution of differences by a *fair procedure*. This hardly fits the history of segregation laws enacted at a time when most blacks were disenfranchised, and enforced by a legal structure from which blacks were almost entirely excluded. And yet the law, at least at the Supreme Court level, did provide crucial support to the racial reforms achieved during the 1960s. This support, however, tended to reinforce the characterization of the protests as "coercive." While reversing convictions of protesters arrested during clearly nonviolent protests, the Court seemed to adopt Fried's position that the law should be *beyond* coercion, that is, the law should be absolute and transcendentally present. By Fried's account, the law should not countenance any violence. This position casts law as the antithesis of violence. Robert Cover, however, suggests that law operates in a field of violence. In particular, he refers to the law in the following terms:

> I believe the more general term "legal interpretation" is warranted for it is my position that the violence which judges deploy as instruments of a modern nation-state necessarily engages anyone who interprets the law in

local officials had taken their toll, and the boycott was about to collapse. M. King, Strike Toward Freedom 151–53, 157–60 (1958). The Supreme Court then affirmed a three-judge court order that voided the state and local laws requiring segregation on Montgomery's motor buses. *Browder v. Gayle*, 142 F. Supp. 707 (N.D. Ala. 1956), *aff'd per curiam*, 352 U.S. 903 (1956). The Supreme court's decision came on the same day that an Alabama judge enjoined the protestors from operating an alternative car pool system to replace bus services—a ruling which may have marked the end of the boycott. For an extensive discussion of the Montgomery bus boycott, *see* R. Kennedy, *Martin Luther King's Constitution: A Legal History of the Montgomery Bus Boycott*, 98 Yale L.J. 999 (1989). And even after the decision, Alabama officials continued vehemently to enforce segregation. Mayor Gayle's response to the decision that carried his name was typical of this reaction: "The recent Supreme Court decisions . . . have seriously lowered the dignified relations which did exist between the races in our city and in our state. . . . The difficulties [which the segregation laws were] meant to prevent and the dignities which they guard are not changed here in Alabama by decisions of the Supreme Court. . . . To insure public safety, to protect people of both races, and to promote order in our city we shall continue to enforce segregation." Quoted in Kennedy, *supra*, at 1056–57.

46. Fried, *Moral Causation*, 77 Harv. L. Rev. 1258, 1268–69 (1964).

47. Id. at 1269.

a course of conduct that entails either the perpetration or the suffering of this violence.[48]

Jacques Derrida goes even farther in asserting that the law *is* violence. It is through the imposition of "order" that law functions as authority. Derrida writes that "law is always an authorized force, a force that justifies itself or is justified in applying itself, even if this justification may be judged from elsewhere to be unjust or unjustifiable."[49] "Enforceability," Derrida indicates, is not a second order condition; it structures the very possibility of law. We are trained to think about law as referencing itself for authority (precedent, and so on). Initially, however, law had to install itself without its own prior approval. Derrida refers to this installation as an "originary violence."[50] This "originary" violence replays itself over and over. Thus, according to Derrida, to categorically equate law with justice is to participate in the elaboration of a fiction that posits the law as the dyadic opposite of violence. It is a fiction to which the courts are committed. To quote Montaigne, who referred to this phenomenon as the "mystical foundation" of the authority of laws, "[L]aws keep up their good standing, not because they are just, but because they are laws: that is the mystical foundation of their authority, they have no other."

Race, Racism and American Law 654–58.

Copyright © (2000) Aspen Publishers.

Reprinted with permission of Aspen Publishers and Derrick A. Bell.

---

48. Robert M. Cover, Violence and the Word, 95 Yale L.J. 1601 n.1 (1986).

49. Jacques Derrida, Force of Law: The "Mystical Foundation of Authority" in Deconstruction and the Possibility of Justice 5 (Drucilla Cornell, Michel Rosenfeld, David Gray Carlson, eds. 1992).

50. *Id.* at 6.

Part Three

Reconstruction, Citizenship, and Sovereignty

IX. The Supreme Court's Betrayal of Reconstruction

A. Introduction

A series of Supreme Court decisions through the nineteenth century and into the twentieth century restricted freedom for blacks. The justices of the Supreme Court affirmatively denied rights and limited freedom, in areas of housing, education, and legal recourse. Through a number of its decisions, particularly the opinion in the *Dred Scott* case, the Supreme Court prevented blacks from pursuing freedom through the federal system. When Chief Justice Roger Taney said that under the United States Constitution, a black man "had no rights which the white man was bound to respect,"[1] it became "self-evident" that the federal system under the Constitution could not protect the rights, hopes, and aspirations of persons who recognized that the chains of slavery were incongruous with religious precepts and civilized government.

The Supreme Court's constriction of freedom, however, was removed through the Emancipation Proclamation of 1863, the defeat of the Confederacy in the Civil War in 1865, the Thirteenth Amendment in 1865, the Freedmen's Bureau Legislation in 1865, the Military Reconstruction Act in 1867, the Fourteenth Amendment in 1868, the Fifteenth Amendment in 1870, and the Civil Rights Acts of 1866 and 1875. Through these turbulent years, other branches of government, the Presidency and Congress, mollified and neutralized some of the limitations imposed by the Judiciary.

Freedom was also constrained by forces within society and the media. President Abraham Lincoln signed the Emancipation Proclamation on January 1, 1863, but it was not until mid-June 1865, some two and a half years later that most slaves in the Deep South began to receive the news. When slaves in Galveston, Texas on June 19 heard word of their freedom, they poured into the streets by the thousands to celebrate. Ever since that date, "Juneteenth" has existed as the oldest and longest running celebration in honor of slavery's demise in the United States.

---

1. 60 U.S. (19 How.) 393, 407 (1857).

John Hope Franklin

From Slavery to Freedom: A History of Negro Americans (5th Edition)

In the closing months of the war and afterward, the South suffered acutely. The abandoned lands, the want of food and clothing, the thousands of displaced persons, and the absence of organized civil authority to cope with the emergency merely suggest the nature of the disorder and suffering. A most interesting and poignant feature of the time was freedmen searching for husbands, wives, or children who years earlier had been separated by sale or other transactions. Negroes were distressed, moreover, not only because they lacked the necessaries of life but also because they genuinely feared, especially after the death of President Lincoln, that they would gradually slip back into a condition hardly better than that of slaves. In the summer and fall of 1865 they held several conventions, all looking toward an improvement of their conditions. A Negro convention in Nashville protested seating the Tennessee delegation to Congress because the legislature had not passed just laws for Negroes. It also demanded that Congress recognize Negro citizenship. A group of 120, meeting in Raleigh, North Carolina, declared that they wanted fair wages, education for their children, and repeal of the discriminatory laws passed by the state legislature. Mississippi Negroes protested against reactionary policies in their state and asked Congress to extend the franchise to Negroes. It was the same thing in Charleston and Mobile: Negroes were demanding suffrage, the abolition of Black Codes, and measures for the relief of suffering.

While the pleas of Negroes were largely ignored in the South, there were Northerners who worked to relieve their distress. Private organizations had taken up this work during the war, and considerable pressure was applied to Congress as early as 1863 to assume responsibility for the welfare of needy whites and blacks in the South. Military commanders did whatever they could or wanted to do with regard to relief.

The need, however, was for a comprehensive and unified service for freedmen. It was not until March 1865 that the Bureau of Refugees, Freedman, and Abandoned Lands, better known as the Freedmen's Bureau, was established. With officials in each of the Southern states, the bureau aided refugees and freedmen by furnishing supplies and medical services, establishing schools, supervising contracts between freedmen and their employers, and managing confiscated or abandoned lands, leasing and selling some of them to freedmen.

The atmosphere in which the Freedmen's Bureau worked was one of hostility. Many Northerners looked upon it as an expensive agency, the existence of which could not be justified in time of peace. In the South the opposition to the bureau was vehement. There was serious objection to federal interference with the relations between the worker and his employer. It was believed, moreover, that the bureau had a political program for enfranchising the Negro and establishing a strong Republican party in the South.

There can be no doubt that the Freedmen's Bureau relieved much suffering among blacks and whites. Between 1865 and 1869, for example, the bureau issued 21 million rations, approximately 5 million going to whites and 15 million to blacks. By 1867 there were forty-six hospitals under the bureau staffed with physicians, surgeons, and nurses. The medical department spent over $2 million to improve the health of freedmen, and treated more than 450,000 cases of illness. The death rate among freedmen was reduced, and sanitary conditions were improved.

The bureau undertook to resettle many people who had been displaced during the war. Because of the urgent need for labor to cultivate the land, free transportation was furnished freedmen to leave congested areas and to become self-supporting. By 1870 more than thirty thousand persons had been moved. Although abandoned and confiscated lands were generally restored to their owners under the amnesty proclamations of Lincoln and Johnson, the bureau distributed some land to freedmen. Colonies of infirm, destitute, and vagrant Negroes were set up in several states. Small parcels of land were first allotted and then leased to them for management and cultivation.

The bureau sought to protect the Negro in his freedom to choose his own employer and to work at a fair wage. Both parties were required to live up to their contract. Agents of the bureau consulted with planters and freedmen, urging the former to be fair in their dealings, and instructing the latter in the necessity of working to provide for their families and to achieve independence and security. Thousands of Negroes returned to work under conditions more satisfactory than those that had existed before the bureau supervised their relations with employers. General Oliver Otis Howard, the bureau's commissioner, reported that "in a single state not less than fifty thousand [labor] contracts were drawn." Paul S. Peirce has estimated that in the South as a whole there must have been several hundred thousand contracts.

When it was felt that the interest of Negroes could not be safely entrusted to local courts, the bureau organized freedmen's courts and boards of arbitration. They had civil and criminal jurisdiction over minor cases where one or both parties were freedmen. Frequently an expression of the bureau's interest was sufficient to secure justice for freedmen in the regular courts. In Maryland, for example, the case of a white physician who assaulted a Negro without provocation was carried by the bureau agent to the state supreme court, which admitted the Negro's testimony and convicted the physician.

The bureau achieved its greatest successes in education. It set up or supervised all kinds of schools: day, night, Sunday, and industrial schools, as well as colleges. It cooperated closely with philanthropic and religious organizations in the North in the establishment of many institutions. Among the schools founded in this period that received aid from the bureau were Howard University, Hampton Institute, St. Augustine's College, Atlanta University, Fisk University, Storer College, and Biddle Memorial Institute (now Johnson C. Smith University). The American Missionary Association, the Baptists, Methodists, Presbyterians, and Episcopalians were all active in establishing schools. Education was promoted so vigorously that by 1867 schools had been set up in "the remotest counties of each of the confederate states."

Teachers came down from the North in large numbers. Besides Edmund Ware at Atlanta, Samuel C. Armstrong at Hampton, and Erastus M. Cravath at Fisk, there were hundreds whose services were not as widely known. In 1869 there were 9,503 teachers in the freedmen's schools of the South. Although some of the white teachers were Southerners, a majority of the whites came from the North. The number of Negro teachers was growing; and gradually they took over supervision of some schools.

By 1870, when educational work of the bureau stopped, there were 247,333 pupils in 4,329 schools. Reports from all quarters "showed a marked increase in attendance, and advance in scholarship, and a record of punctuality and regularity which compared favorably with the schools in the north." The bureau had spent more than $5 million in schooling Negroes. The shortcomings in the education of blacks arose not for a want of zeal on the part of teachers but from ignorance of the needs of Negroes and from the necessary preoccupation of students with the problem of survival in a hostile world.

Despite Southern hostility to the bureau, and the inefficiency of many officials, it performed a vastly important task. As a relief agency it deserves to be ranked with the great efforts of recent depressions and wars. It demonstrated that the government could administer an extensive program of relief and rehabilitation, and suggested a way in which the nation could grapple with its pressing social problems. To be sure, there was corruption and inefficiency, but not enough to prevent the bureau from achieving a notable success in ministering to human welfare.

From Slavery to Freedom: A History of Negro Americans 234–37.
Copyright © (1980) McGraw-Hill, Inc.
Reprinted with permission of McGraw-Hill, Inc.

For five years, from 1865 to 1870, programs supported by the Freedmen's Bureau Act provided much needed economic, medical, and educational assistance. However, given the duration and degree of oppression suffered by blacks as a result of slavery for two and a half centuries, should more have been done?

1. Apology

Associated Press

Clinton to Think about Apology

President Clinton says he will consider extending a national apology to black Americans for slavery—but not compensation for their ancestors' suffering. "It's been so long and we're so many generations removed," he says.

The idea of an apology came from Democratic Rep. Tony P. Hall of Ohio, a white lawmaker who introduced apology legislation in Congress last week (June 10, 1997), just as Clinton was preparing to unveil his national initiative on race in a speech in San Diego. In a radio interview broadcast yesterday, Clinton said the apology proposal caught him off guard. He said he would think about it because "there's still some unfinished business out there among black and white Americans."

"I think it has to be dealt with," Clinton told the American Urban Radio network. "I think this would be a helpful debate."

Last month, he apologized for the nation to the black men who were unwitting subjects in the government's Tuskegee Syphilis Study, and in January he awarded— 50 years late—the Medal of Honor to seven black World War II soldiers for valor in combat. But Clinton said he disagrees with the idea of paying reparations to descendants of slaves, something many black activists have said is needed to begin rectifying centuries of inequality that blacks have experienced.

"What I think we ought to do instead of reparations is to be repairing," he said. "That is why I don't want to abandon affirmative action without an effective alternative when there's still so many people living at least with the aftermath of discrimination."

Of his apology proposal, Hall said, "To me, it's a moral issue. We used to count African Americans as three-fifths of a person. They were not treated as people."

"When you've hurt somebody, nothing solves the problem at first like a good, old-fashioned apology," Hall said. "Then we can begin to heal. If you don't say that, the whole issue lingers and lingers."

Hall ran his idea past the Congressional Black Caucus, which cheered it. He began seeking co-sponsors and immediately found eleven, all of them white. Four more lawmakers signed on yesterday, Hall said.

The bill has been sent to the House Judiciary Committee.

But Hall, too, has declined to embrace reparations, saying that issue has nothing to do with the apology he is seeking. "This has to do with something basic and important," Hall said. Rep. John Conyers, Jr., a Michigan Democrat, has introduced legislation on reparations in every session of Congress since 1989. Each time his proposal, which would create a commission to study the feasibility, has died in committee.

"I don't know what the problem is," Conyers told CNN yesterday. "I think it's time we should be able to talk about this subject without going ballistic."

The Baltimore Sun, June 17, 1997, p. 3A.
Copyright © (1997) The Associated Press.
Reprinted with permission of The Associated Press.

2. Point/Counterpoint

Discussions and debates over race and reparations continue to be contentious to the present day. Most recently, Ta-Nehisi Coates revived the debate with an article (The Case for Reparations) in the June 2014 edition of the Atlantic Magazine where he provided a comprehensive argument in support of reparations. Do you support reparations for slavery and, if so, what form should those reparations take?

F. Michael Higginbotham

"A Dream Deferred": Comparative and Practical Considerations for the Black Reparations Movement*

It has been said that a dream deferred will eventually just shrivel up "like a raisin in the sun."[2] But thanks to the black reparations movement, the dream of compensation and restitution for enslavement is still very much alive. Begun during the Civil War, the black reparations movement ceased to command serious attention from political leaders between the end of Reconstruction in 1876 and the rise of the modern civil rights movement during the 1960s, though several other substantial reparations movements developed during the late 1800s and early 20th century.[3] In recent years, the drive for black reparations has gained widespread support and media attention.[4]

Like an idea whose time has come, reparations, compensation or restitution to African Americans for years of enslavement, is a subject worthy of careful consideration. American slavery was sanctioned, albeit by implication, by the United States Constitution,[5] and both the federal government and many state governments, actively or passively, participated in and benefited from the institution of slavery.[6] Pursuant to such authorization, African Americans suffered unimaginable cruelty and hardship which lasted through two centuries. While monetary compensation

---

* (footnote omitted).

2. This statement refers to Langston Hughes's famous poem, "Harlem," which begins:
What happens to a dream deferred?
Does it dry up
Like a raisin in the sun?
Langston Hughes, Collected Poems of Langston Hughes 363 (Arnold Rampersad and David Roessel eds., Vintage Classics 1995).

3. *See* Adjoa A. Aiyetoro, *Formulating Reparations Litigation Through the Eyes of the Movement*, 58 N.Y.U. Ann. Surv. Am. L. 457 (2003) (discussing the history of post-Reconstruction reparations movements).

4. *See id.* (discussing recent support from political and popular leaders for reparations).

5. *See* U.S. Const. art. I, §2, cl. 3 (counting slaves as three-fifths of "free Persons" in determining the apportionment of representatives); U.S. Const. art. I, §9, cl. 1 (prohibiting Congressional prohibition of importation of slaves prior to 1808); U.S. Const. art. IV, §2, cl. 3 (requiring all states to return fugitive slaves).

6. Slavery was an integral part of the economics of most southern states. See A. Leon Higginbotham & F. Michael Higginbotham, *"Yearning to Breathe Free": Legal Barriers Against and Options in Favor of Liberty in Antebellum Virginia*, 68 N.Y.U. L. Rev. 1213, 1223–27 (1993). Some northern states where slavery had been abolished, such as Massachusetts and Rhode Island, also benefited economically from its continuance. See F. Michael Higginbotham, Race Law: Cases, Commentary, and Questions 64–66 (2001) (excerpting commentary by A. Leon Higginbotham, Jr., *The Bicentennial of the Constitution: A Racial Perspective*). Even the federal government was heavily invested in the institution of slavery. *See id.* at 114–16.

and other forms of assistance have been provided by the United States government to other groups who have been the victims of discriminatory treatment and internment,[7] none has yet been provided to African Americans for the legacy of slavery.

The first slaves arrived in Jamestown, Virginia, in 1619.[8] They were characterized as property and afforded no personal rights. They were prohibited from education, entering contracts, or holding property. They were kidnapped, whipped, beaten, and chained, and forced to labor under harsh conditions.[9]

All slaves were freed from actual slavery by the Emancipation Proclamation issued by President Abraham Lincoln in 1863 or by the 13th Amendment to the United States Constitution passed two years later.[10] No mandatory compensation or other form of assistance, however, was provided by either provision.

Freed slaves were subjected to widespread racial discrimination and intimidation. From lynchings, cross burnings, and night raids destroying their homes, to black codes that subjected them to convict labor farms and prisons, freed slaves experienced onerous burdens that other Americans did not. Often times, American law sanctioned such practices. At other times, laws were ignored or circumscribed. As a result, economic opportunities for African Americans were drastically limited.[11]

Reparations have been provided by the United States government, and by foreign governments and corporations, on several previous occasions. While some reparations were provided by legislative order, others were generated by court order when inadequate compensation or restitution had been provided for injuries suffered or for appropriations of labor or assets owned by those harmed.[12]

The issue of reparations has been raised since the beginning of the Civil War in 1860. Calls for reparations came from abolitionists, freed slaves, and Republican

---

7. *See, e.g.,* Brophy, *supra* note 1 (discussing provision of reparations to Native Americans and interned Japanese Americans).

8. A. Leon Higginbotham, In the Matter of Color 20 (1978).

9. *See* Robinson, *supra* note 1, at 208.

10. *See* U.S. Const. amend. XIII; Abraham Lincoln, The Emancipation Proclamation (Jan. 1, 1863), *reprinted in* 12 Stat. 1268 (1863).

11. *See, e.g.,* Emma Coleman Jordan, *A History Lesson: Reparations for What?*, 58 N.Y.U. Ann. Surv. Am. L. 557 (2003) (discussing the racial violence, some state-sanctioned, that pervaded post-Civil War American life and oppressed African Americans); John Hope Franklin, From Slavery to Freedom: A History of Negro Americans 238–42 (5th ed. 1980); Derrick Bell, Race, Racism, and American Law § 2.13, at 58–63 (4th ed. 2000). *See generally* Rayford W. Logan, The Betrayal of the Negro (2d ed. 1997).

12. *See, e.g.,* Burt Neuborne, *Holocaust Reparations Litigation: Lessons for the Slavery Reparations Movement*, 58 N.Y.U. Ann. Surv. Am. L. 615 (2003) (discussing recent successfully-settled litigation for restitution to victims of the Holocaust who lost property to, and worked as slave laborers for, Swiss and German entities); Brophy, *supra* note 1 (discussing recent successful domestic and foreign reparations movements).

party leaders.[13] Despite these widespread calls of support, reparations bills during Reconstruction were vetoed by President Andrew Johnson.[14]

The movement for reparations is not a recent phenomenon. It has its roots in the immediate post-Civil War period. Yet, as the articles contained in this issue suggest, the debate has not subsided. In fact, the debate seems just as intense today as it was when Thaddeus Stevens stood on the floor of the House of Representatives in 1866 and unsuccessfully called for the United States government to provide "40 acres and a mule" for every freedman.[15]

Much has changed as to racial justice in America since 1866. First, state-imposed racial segregation and discrimination have been outlawed. Second, lynchings and other bias crimes have been substantially reduced and most perpetrators are now prosecuted and convicted. Moreover, some discrimination in the private sector, particularly in areas of employment and education, has been diminished. As a result, educational and employment opportunities for African Americans are greater today than ever before. Yet, even with all the changes, widespread socio-economic inequities between blacks and other Americans continue to exist. Incidents of discrimination, both public and private, blatant and subtle, continue to occur.[16] In recognition of these continuing inequities and incidents, the movement for black reparations continues its mission.

58 *N.Y.U. Ann. Surv. Am. L.* 447, 447–50.
Copyright © (2003) *Annual Survey of American Law.*
Reprinted with permission of *Annual Survey of American Law* and
F. Michael Higginbotham.

---

13. Abolitionist and author David Walker protested the lack of compensation for the labor of slaves as early as 1829. *See* Bell, *supra* note 11, at 72 n.11. Former slave Henry McNeal Turner made numerous speeches in support of reparations during the Reconstruction period. *See id.* Thaddeus Stevens, a leader of the Republican party and member of the United States House of Representatives from Pennsylvania, requested support for a reparations bill before Congress which failed in 1866. *See id.* at §2.13, at 58–59. Charles Sumner, another leader of the Republican party and a member of the United States Senate from Massachusetts, spoke in Congress in support of a reparations bill. *See id.* at §2.13, at 59 n.1 (quoting Lerone Bennett, Before the Mayflower 189 (1961)).

14. John Hope Franklin, From Slavery to Freedom: A History of Negro Americans 233 (5th ed. 1980).

15. Robinson, *supra* note 1, at 204 (quoting Derrick A. Bell, *Dissection of a Dream*, 9 Harv. C.R.-C.L. L. Rev. 156 (1974) (book review)).

16. *See Strauder v. West Virginia*, 100 U.S. 303 (1880) (declaring unconstitutional a West Virginia statute prohibiting African Americans from serving on juries); *Brown v. Bd. of Educ.*, 347 U.S. 483 (1954) (declaring unconstitutional state-imposed racial segregation in primary schools); *Adarand Constructors, Inc. v. Pena*, 515 U.S. 200 (1995) (Ginsburg, J., dissenting) (describing the continuing existence of racial discrimination in employment, housing, and government contracts); *see also* A. Leon Higginbotham, Jr., Shades of Freedom 152–68 (1996) (describing Supreme Court decisions between 1930 and 1941 reducing racial discrimination in education, voting, and criminal justice system); F. Michael Higginbotham, Race Law: Cases, Commentary, and Questions 394–430 (2001) (describing Supreme Court decisions since 1976 permitting vast racial inequities to continue in employment, criminal justice, and voting).

Peter Flaherty

Reparation Issue Is a Smoke Screen and a Shakedown

Imagine getting sued for what your great-great grandfather did—legally—a century and a half ago. That is the predicament of Aetna Inc., which now faces a lawsuit demanding reparations because the company insured slaves in the 1850s.

Other firms that did not even exist during the time of slavery, such as CSX Corp. And FleetBoston Financial Corp., are named in the same suit. CSX was formed in 1980, the end product of numerous railroad mergers and acquisitions. FleetBoston can be traced to hundreds of predecessor banks, only one of which the plaintiffs can single out for its links to slavery.

The suit, filed in federal court in Brooklyn, N.Y., by a 36-year-old black activist named Deadria Farmer-Paellmann, puts the value of slave labor at $1.4 trillion-almost as much as the federal government collects in individual and corporate income taxes each year.

Those seeking reparations have their eyes on other potential targets, which could include some of the nation's oldest newspapers and universities. The Hartford Courant, Baltimore Sun and the forerunner of the New Orleans Times-Picayune "profited" from slavery by printing runaway slave notices during the 1800s. Harvard, Yale and other universities were built on the backs of slave labor, it could be argued, because their early benefactors profited from the institution of slavery.

Don't assume that the reparations lawsuits are destined to fail. During the past few decades, it has become possible to win meritless lawsuits, especially against corporations. A big impetus for that was the $246-billion tobacco settlement. The prospect of billions of dollars in tobacco money prompted state governments to abandon legal precedent and rewrite statutes to make it easier to sue. In asbestos litigation as well, companies with only the most tenuous links to the substance are now being bankrupted.

Forum shopping—the practice of finding sympathetic judges—also has become easier, as has the practice of lawyers suing with no real clients. In the slave reparations case, neither Farmer-Paellmann nor the millions of blacks she claims to represent were ever slaves.

Even if Farmer-Paellmann loses in court, she knows that because of negative publicity generated against the targeted companies they will be under pressure to make massive payouts to African-American interest groups.

This is a manifestation of the new form of corporate shakedown. Activists and trial lawyers work the media to demonize certain companies, often prompting the latter to hand over fistfuls of cash to make them go away.

The master of the craft is Jesse Jackson, who extracts billions out of corporations fearful of being branded racist if they do not pay up.

Last year, Toyota caved in to Jackson's threat of a boycott by pledging to spend a whopping $7.8 billion on a "diversity" plan, even though the company already had an excellent record of hiring and awarding dealerships to blacks.

Other scam artists are promoting a nonexistent reparations tax credit among African Americans. The IRS recently revealed that it had paid out as much as $30 million to taxpayers, including four or more current or former IRS employees, who had claimed such a credit in 2000 and part of 2001. One woman received a $500,000 payment.

The reparations issue is a smoke screen for those unwilling to tackle the real problems affecting blacks, such as failing schools, crumbling inner cities and family disunity. It is an attempt at easy money, either by litigation or by shakedown. The companies involved must not give in to such legalized extortion. If they do, it will never end.

The Los Angeles Times, April 22, 2002, California Metro Section, Part 2, p. 11.

Copyright © (2002) Times Mirror, Inc.

Reprinted with permission of the Times Mirror, Inc.

Stanley Crouch

Money Isn't Cure for Blacks' Problems

New York—A public debate is brewing over the idea that America owes black people reparations for 246 years of chattel slavery.

The idea is that slaves sweated behind the building of this country and the making of many fortunes and that compensation for all that labor is overdue.

The reparations theory says further that slavery and the various forms of discrimination that followed it are the reasons so many blacks have trailed so far behind in the American race for success, why black wealth is no more than about 1 percent of the nation's wealth, why black young people are often such poor students and why there is an unemployment problem among black people.

Randall Robinson of TransAfrica is a driving force for reparations, as are Rep. John Conyers, D-Mich., Harvard's Charles Ogletree and a growing number of others.

But resistance is starting to grow.

Jeff Jacob of the *Boston Globe* recently wrote two op-ed page columns on the subject. The first column took the position that blacks were actually lucky to have been brought to this nation, even in chains, because they were able to take advantage of things that would never have been theirs in Africa.

Mr. Jacob argued in his second column that the Civil War itself was reparations that the more than 300,000 Union troops who died were sacrifice enough, not to mention the impact that the war had on American society for decades after the South surrendered.

I, for one, have neither great love nor great hatred for Africa, but I do not believe that there is any more advanced or influential group of black people on the face of this earth than African Americans.

In fact, one of the marvels of the 20th century was the emergence of the modern black American.

I have no sentimental feeling of lost heritage because I feel connected to the African, Asian, European and Choctaw heritage of my family line, which makes me, like so many black Americans, quite different from Africans.

In fact, knowing who they are and where they came from and the languages of their various ethnic groups hasn't helped Africans run their own countries any better or taught them how to fight indigenous diseases or shown them how to stop their own slave trades, some of which are still thriving.

What's more, if some dollar figures were actually attached to reparations, all hell would break loose. As with affirmative action, all kinds of black people—not just African Americans—would try to figure out how to get their slice of the payback pie.

Eventually, descendants of Mexicans would realize that they could make the case that since their people once owned the Southwest and the West, they, too, should receive reparations for the land they lost as America pushed its imperial chest from the Atlantic to the Pacific.

It would be a mess, but, then, America has always been a mess, either a beautiful or an ugly one or some combination of both.

What we truly need, whatever we call it, is serious focus on the problems of black America, which, we should understand, almost always foreshadow those of the nation at large.

If we can begin to truly win against those problems, we will be prepared to fight them if and when they spread to the rest of the country.

The Baltimore Sun, February 27, 2001, p. 15A.
Copyright © (2001) The Associated Press.
Reprinted with permission of The Associated Press.

Randall Robinson

The Debt: What America Owes to Blacks

On January 5, 1993, Congressman John Conyers, a black Democrat from Detroit, introduced in Congress a bill to "acknowledge the fundamental injustice, cruelty, brutality, and inhumanity of slavery in the United States and the 13 American colonies between 1619 and 1865 and to establish a commission to examine the institution of slavery, subsequent *de jure* and *de facto* racial and economic discrimination against African Americans, and the impact of these forces on living African Americans, to make recommendations to the Congress on appropriate remedies, and for other purposes."

The bill, which did not ask for reparations for the descendants of slaves but merely a commission to study the effects of slavery, won from the 435-member U.S. House of Representatives only 28 cosponsors, 18 of whom were black.

The measure was referred to the House Committee on the Judiciary and from there to the House Subcommittee on Civil and Constitutional Rights. The bill has never made it out of committee.

More than twenty years ago, black activist James Foreman interrupted the Sunday morning worship service of the largely white Riverside Church in New York City and read a *Black Manifesto* which called upon American churches and synagogues to pay $500 million as "a beginning of the reparations due to us as people who have been exploited and degraded, brutalized, killed and persecuted." Foreman followed by promising to penalize poor response with disruptions of the churches' program agency operations. Though Foreman's tactics were broadly criticized in the mainstream press, the issue of reparations itself elicited almost no thoughtful response. This had been the case by then for nearly a century, during which divergent strains of black thought had offered a variety of reparations proposals. The American white community had turned a deaf ear almost uniformly.

Gunnar Myrdal, a widely respected thinker, wrote of dividing up plantations into small parcels for sale to ex-slaves on long-term installment plans. He theorized that American society's failure to secure ex-slaves with an agrarian economic base had led ultimately to an entrenched segregated society, a racial caste system. But while Myrdal had seen white landowners being compensated for their land, he never once proposed recompense of any kind for the ex-slave he saw as in need of an economic base. In fact, in his book on the subject, *An American Dilemma*, Myrdal never once uses the words: reparation, restitution, indemnity, or compensation.

In the early 1970s Boris Bittker, a Yale Law School professor, wrote a book, *The Case for Black Reparations*, which made the argument that slavery, Jim Crow, and a general climate of race-based discrimination in America had combined to do grievous social and economic injury to African Americans. He further argued that sustained government-sponsored violations had rendered distinctions between *de jure* and *de facto* segregation meaningless for all practical purposes. Damages, in his view, were indicated in the form of an allocation of resources to some program that could be crafted for black reparations. The book evoked little in the way of scholarly response or follow-up.

The slim volume was sent to me by an old friend who once worked for me at TransAfrica, Ibrahim Gassama, now a law professor at the University of Oregon. I had called Ibrahim in Eugene to talk over the legal landscape for crafting arguments for a claim upon the federal and state governments for restitution or reparations to the derivative victims of slavery and the racial abuse that followed in its wake.

"It's the strangest thing," Ibrahim had said to me. "We law professors talk about every imaginable subject, but when the issue of reparations is raised among white professors, many of whom are otherwise liberal, it is met with silence. Clearly, there is a case to be made for this as unpaid debt. Our claim may not be enforceable in the courts because the federal government has to agree to allow itself to be sued. In fact, this will probably have to come out of the Congress as other American reparations have. Nonetheless, there is clearly a strong case to be made. But, I tell you, the mere raising of the subject produces a deathly silence, not unlike the silence that greeted the book I'm sending you."

Derrick Bell, who was teaching at Harvard Law School while I was a student there in the late 1960s, concluded his review of Bittker's book in a way that may explain the reaction Ibrahim got from his colleagues. Bell explained:

> Short of a revolution, the likelihood that blacks today will obtain direct payments in compensation for their subjugation as slaves before the Emancipation Proclamation, and their exploitation as quasi-citizens since, is no better than it was in 1866, when Thaddeus Stevens recognized that his bright hope of "forty acres and a mule" for every freedman had vanished "like the baseless fabric of a vision."

If Bell is right that African Americans will not be compensated for the massive wrongs and social injuries inflicted upon them by their government, during and after slavery, then there is *no* chance that America can solve its racial problems—if solving these problems mean, as I believe it must, closing the yawning economic gap between blacks and whites in this country. The gap was opened by the 246-year practice of slavery. It has been resolutely nurtured since in law and public behavior. It has now ossified. It is structural. Its framing beams are disguised only by the counterfeit manners of a hypocritical governing class.

For twelve years Nazi Germany inflicted horrors upon European Jews. And Germany paid. It paid Jews individually. It paid the state of Israel. For two and a half centuries, Europe and America inflicted unimaginable horrors upon Africa and its people. Europe not only paid nothing to Africa in compensation, but followed the slave trade with the remapping of Africa for further European economic exploitation. (European governments have yet even to accede to Africa's request for the return of Africa's art treasures looted along with its natural resources during the century-long colonial era.)

While President Lincoln supported a plan during the Civil War to compensate slave owners for their loss of "property," his successor, Andrew Johnson, vetoed legislation that would have provided compensation to ex-slaves.

Under the Southern Homestead Act, ex-slaves were given six months to purchase land at reasonably low rates without competition from white southerners and northern investors. But, owing to their destitution, few ex-slaves were able to take advantage of the homesteading program. The largest number that did were concentrated in Florida, numbering little more than three thousand. The soil was generally poor and unsuitable for farming purposes. In any case, the ex-slaves had no money on which to subsist for months while waiting for crops, or the scantiest wherewithal to purchase the most elementary farming implements. The program failed. In sum, the United States government provided no compensation to the victims of slavery.

Michael Fletcher

Reparations for Slavery Is No Laughing Matter

Does the second-class social and economic status of many African Americans today have any connection to the brutal and dehumanizing system of slavery?

Is segregation in any way to blame? What about the myriad other forms of discrimination once sanctioned by our government?

My answer is yes, on all counts. But until recently, I mostly ignored those who want to press the U.S. government to pay compensation to the victims of those injustices. The whole notion struck me as laughable, a waste of valuable energy and, more to the point, unrealistic.

"I don't believe that this issue has passed the political laugh test," agreed Wade Henderson, the NAACP's chief Washington lobbyist. "There are many people who do not believe the reparations movement has credibility."

Not that Mr. Henderson doesn't think that can change. He is part of a small but growing movement vying to move the discussion of reparations for African Americans out of the domain of militants and nationalists and into the mainstream of political debate.

The Rev. Jesse L. Jackson, the NAACP, Coretta Scott King, and several members of the Congressional Black Caucus support the idea of compensating African Americans for past, government-sanctioned injustices.

And after really listening to the argument for the first time at last month's black caucus conference in Washington, I think there is a strong case to be made for reparations.

But in a political environment where social programs aimed at preventing crime are derided as "pork," and where even modest attempts to address past discrimination—such as affirmative action—are attacked, it seems clear to me a reparations bill has little chance of winning approval in Washington.

But reparations proponents press against the odds. In Detroit last summer, black activists from around the country gathered for the fifth annual convention of the National Coalition of Blacks for Reparations in America. And a forum on the subject is now a fixture at the black caucus' annual legislative conference.

Reparations is a long-held concept that has been upheld by international courts. For example, Jews collected reparations from Germany for the Holocaust. Japan has compensated several of its neighbors for its transgressions in that war. In 1988,

Congress passed a bill authorizing payments of $20,000 each to surviving Japanese Americans who had been held in detention camps in the United States during World War II. Several Native-American groups have been paid for land snatched from their ancestors.

"Reparations really grow out of a very simple concept in the law," Mr. Henderson said. "For every wrong, every injustice, there should be a way to be made whole."

Few would question that African Americans have been wronged in this society. Still, the idea of reparations being paid to the descendants of slaves usually brings rolled eyes, pained expressions or, as Mr. Henderson points out, laughs.

"People say, 'why don't you just let bygones be bygones?'" said Adjoa Aiyetoro, executive director of the National Conference of Black Lawyers and a reparations proponent.

The problem, of course, is that the damage wrought by slavery and the systems that followed have very real consequences, even today. If nothing else, a full-blown discussion of reparations would give Americans—many of whom are baffled by the hopelessness engendered by segments of the African-American community—a fuller appreciation of the centuries of wide-ranging oppression directed at blacks.

But many African Americans do not want to be associated with a movement that threatens to underscore the stereotype that blacks only want a handout. Many think reparations is just a far-fetched distraction. They believe blacks would do better to emphasize more realistic avenues for improving their lot—thrift, hard work and family and community cooperation, values that have already lifted so many out of poverty.

There also is the question of what would constitute adequate payment to America's more than 30 million blacks. Tax amnesty? Free college tuitions? Or some derivative of the 40 acres and a mule passed by Congress and vetoed after the Civil War by President Andrew Johnson?

Since 1989, Rep. John Conyers, a Michigan Democrat, has been pushing a measure that would establish a national commission to study reparations. But the legislation has never gotten a hearing in Congress and probably never will.

"Opponents of this commission argue that the transgressions of slavery took place 150 years ago and we owe nothing to victims' descendants," Mr. Conyers said. "[But] African Americans are still victims of slavery as surely as those who lived under its confinement. Just as white Americans have benefitted from education, life experiences and wealth that was handed down to them by their ancestors, so too have African Americans been harmed by the institution of slavery."

Despite the multitude of blacks who are successful nowadays—two-thirds of blacks are not poor—a disproportionate share are mired in poverty and despair, a condition reparations proponents attribute to slavery and its equally crippling successors that for generations excluded many blacks from jobs, educational opportunities, and full citizenship.

And while there has been undeniable improvement, blacks continue to lag far behind whites socially and economically, a fact documented by many economic indicators.

Disproportionate numbers of blacks drop out of school, go to prison, and end up on welfare. Black median income of $21,500 a year was 57 percent of the white median of $38,000 in 1991. Similarly, unemployment was 14.1 percent for blacks and 6.5 percent for whites in 1992.

Reparations proponents say they know where to place the blame for that gap and that only government acknowledgment — and payment — would repair the damage. It is an argument that should not be laughed off.

The Baltimore Sun, May 16, 1997, p. 17A.
Copyright © (1997) The Associated Press.
Reprinted with permission of The Associated Press.

Adrienne Davis

The Case for United States Reparations to African Americans

The political and juridical viability of reparations for descendants of enslaved black people is emerging as a highly contested concept in U.S. debates about justice and law. For decades, reparations have been an essential part of the international discourses of war and human rights. Even the United States has paid some reparations awards to Native nations. Today, Korean women seek reparations from the Japanese government as recompense for what amounted to sexual enslavement during World War II. And, in addition to on-going suits against the German state, Holocaust survivors seek damages awards from corporations who enslaved them, banks who appropriated their funds, and insurance companies that refused to pay the life insurance claims of those murdered. Among the political mainstream in the United States, there is support for all of these reparations efforts. From newspaper op-eds to legislation, Americans have expressed their outrage about these immoral practices. California State Senator Tom Hayden wrote a law giving the state jurisdiction over claims stemming from World War II slave labor issues, and extending the statute of limitations for filing such claims until 2010. Also, California, the sixth largest economy in the world, bars insurance companies who refused to pay or work to settle claims from doing business in the state. Within U.S. legal culture, the language of economic rights and justice is persuasive and remedies seem natural.

Yet the U.S. government has refused to consider the need for domestic reparations to be paid for the labor and sexual slavery enforced in the United States for over two centuries. In contrast to Hayden's legislation, U.S. Representative John Conyers's bill, H.R. 40, Commission to Study Reparation Proposals for African Americans Act, introduced in 1993 to study the economic effects of slavery on black Americans has not made it out of the House of Representatives Subcommittee on Civil and Constitutional Rights. At its initial vote, the bill received 28 cosponsors out of 435 members in the House of Representations. Only ten of those co-sponsors were not black. Even as the United States demands other nations make moral and economic recompense for their actions, it declines to consider even the possibility of repairing its own history.

But what are reparations? What support do they find in law? How are they different from ordinary civil lawsuits and other civil rights remedies? Who awards them and who gets them? The framework of reparations is the duty to repair injury imposed on another. Unlike tort law, which addresses individual injury, in their conceptualization, reparations suits frame harm as group-based, even when the plaintiffs are individuals. Unlike criminal law, the harm is explicitly conceived of as against the group, not the state. Therefore, unlike criminal cases, the decision for bringing and shaping reparations lawsuits should lie with the victims, not with the state. In this sense, these suits should be organized at the grass-roots level and should be designed to recompense the harm as understood by communities, not decided by lawyers.

Another distinction is that the explicit function of reparations would be national atonement for the moral wrong and financial injuries of enslavement to black Americans. The primacy of atonement and morality differentiates such suits from ordinary civil suits that do not rest on these principles.

Finally, such suits emphasize the economic damage of enslavement to black Americans as serious and in need of national recognition and compensation. In this sense, they depart from other civil rights remedies that address post-slavery racial harms or rest on political or criminal remedies. Affirmative action, for instance, was a remedy to combat existing racism against blacks and the on-going effects of post-slavery racial apartheid. It did not compensate black people for slave labor, nor did it seek to. The point of reparations is not to "make blacks equal" or to ensure racial opportunities, like affirmative action. These are necessary and important goals, but other causes of action and frameworks of analysis address them better. Instead, the theory of domestic reparations is to identify and atone for economic injuries and harms that blacks as a group suffered under enslavement.

Human Rights Brief, Volume 7, Issue 3, pp. 2–4.
Copyright © (2000) Adrienne Davis.
Reprinted with permission of Adrienne Davis.

B. Background on *The Slaughterhouse Cases*

John Hope Franklin

From Slavery to Freedom: A History of Negro Americans (5th Edition)

Lincoln early saw the need for a policy of dealing with the states of the South as they capitulated to the Union army and handling the large number of Negroes who came under the control of the United States before the end of the war. Since he had insisted that the war was a rebellion of Southern citizens rather than a revolt of the states, he could deal with citizens of the Confederacy on the assumption that they had misled their state governments. It was the function of the president, he believed, to undertake whatever measures were necessary to reorganize the states in the South. As states collapsed, Lincoln appointed military governors who had complete power until civil authority could be established. In December 1863 he outlined to congress his comprehensive plan for Reconstruction and issued a proclamation containing its essential features.

Acting on the assumption that Reconstruction was an executive problem, President Lincoln extended general amnesty to the people of the South, except for certain high Confederate civil and military officials, and called on them to swear allegiance to the United States. When as many as one-tenth of the people of a state as had cast votes in the election of 1860 complied with the proclamation, a government could be established that would be recognized by the president. Although his proclamation was generally well received and the Southern states proceeded to reconstruct themselves under its provisions, some members of Congress were of the opinion that the president was too lenient, and that Reconstruction was a matter to be handled by Congress. They enacted their own measure, the Wade-Davis bill, which disfranchised a larger number of ex-Confederates, delayed action until a majority of the whites had qualified as loyal voters, and required greater assurances of loyalty from the reconstructed governments. The president refused to sign the bill, but granted that it provided one way for a state to reorganize if it chose to do so.

As far as the freedmen were concerned, Lincoln realized that there must be a satisfactory settlement of their status if peace was to be secured in the South. All during the war Lincoln had entertained the hope that a substantial number of Negroes would choose to emigrate from the United States, and he had tried to secure congressional cooperation in encouraging them to do so. It must have become obvious to him that the problem could not be solved in this way, and he was faced with having to reach some solution based on the Negro's continued presence in the United States and in the South. He permitted the establishment of a number of departments of Negro affairs, which assumed responsibility for administering to the needs of Negroes in the early years of the war. Gradually, the work of these departments was taken over by the Freedmen's Bureau.

Concerning the recognition of the Negro's citizenship, Lincoln was of the opinion that with education the Negro would qualify for it, at least on a restricted basis. In 1864 he wrote to Governor Georg M. Han of Louisiana asking "whether some of the colored people may not be let in [to the elective franchise] as, for instance, the very intelligent, and especially those who have fought gallantly in our ranks." Doubtless he was disappointed when the new legislature met in the fall of 1864 and failed to extend the franchise to any of the Negroes of Louisiana, despite the fact that many of them were persons of considerable intellectual and economic achievement.

There was some evidence of a conflict between the president and Congress over the policy of reconstructing the South before the death of Lincoln in April 1865. Shortly after Andrew Johnson took office as president, he made it clear that he would follow essentially the plan of Reconstruction outlined by Lincoln. There were some signs that he might go beyond it. When Charles Sumner, the ardent protagonist of Negro rights, conferred with Johnson shortly after he became president, Johnson assured him that they were agreed on Negro suffrage. In his proclamation of May 1865, he called for complete abolition of slavery, repudiation of the Confederate war debts, nullification of the ordinances of secession, and the disqualification of the people Lincoln had disfranchised as well as all Southerners worth $20,000 or more. He appointed provisional governors in the Southern states; and legislatures, based on white suffrage, were called to modify their constitutions in harmony with that of the United States.

Through 1865 and 1866 the whites of the South gradually assumed the responsibility of governing their people. The greatest concern of Southerners was the problem of controlling the Negro. There were all sorts of ugly rumors of a general uprising in which Negroes would take vengeance on whites and dispossess them of their property. Most Southern whites, although willing to concede the end of slavery even to the point of voting for the adoption of the Thirteenth Amendment, were convinced that laws should be speedily enacted to curb the Negroes and to insure their role as a laboring force in the South. These laws, called Black Codes, bore a remarkable resemblance to the antebellum Slave Codes (see Chapter VIII) and can hardly be described as measures that respected the rights of Negroes as free persons. Several of them undertook to limit the areas in which Negroes could purchase or rent property. Vagrancy laws imposed heavy penalties that were designed to force all Negroes to work whether they wanted to or not. The control of blacks by white employers was about as great as that which slaveholders had exercised. Negroes who quit their jobs could be arrested and imprisoned for breach of contract. Negroes were not allowed to testify in court except in cases involving members of their race. Numerous fines were imposed for seditious speeches, insulting gestures or acts, absence from work, violating curfew, and the possession of firearms. There was, of course, no enfranchisement of blacks and no indication that in the future they could look forward to full citizenship and participation in a democracy.

As it became clear to Northern protagonists of the Negro that the Reconstruction policy of President Johnson sanctioned white home rule in the South in ways strikingly similar to those existing before the Civil War, they became furious. Friends of the Negro refused to tolerate a policy that would nullify the gains made during the war. Abolitionists, roused again to their crusade, demanded that Negroes be enfranchised and a harsher policy adopted toward the South. Practical Republicans, fearful of the political consequences of a South dominated by Democrats, became convinced that Negro suffrage in the South would aid in the continued growth of the Republican Party. Industrialists with an eye on markets and cheap labor in the South, were fearful that the old agrarian system would be resurrected by the Democrats. These groups began to pool their interests in order to modify substantially the Johnson policy of Reconstruction.

When Congress met in December 1865, it was determined to take charge of Reconstruction. If there had been any doubt as to the direction the South was moving, it was dispelled by the character of the representatives sent to Congress. One had been vice president of the confederacy, and there were four Confederate generals, five Confederate colonels, six Confederate cabinet officers, and fifty-eight members of the Confederate Congress. Although none could take the oath of office, their election indicated that the South stood solidly behind its defeated leaders. Thaddeus Stevens, a wily Republican leader and vigorous supporter of a stern policy toward the South, was exasperated. He proposed that Congress assume control of Reconstruction, asserting that the president's policy had been essentially provisional. Congress adopted a Stevens resolution creating the Joint Committee on Reconstruction to inquire into the condition of the Southern states and to make recommendations for a new policy.

In two bills, one to strengthen the Freedmen's Bureau and extend its life and the other to guarantee civil rights to Negroes, Congress sought to exercise its influence in behalf of blacks. President Johnson vetoed the Freedmen's Bureau bill on the grounds that it was unconstitutional and proposed to do more for blacks than had ever been done for whites. The attempt to override the veto failed. He likewise vetoed the civil rights bill and declared that blacks were not yet ready for the privileges and equalities of citizens. Johnson's veto of these two bills, his condemnation of the proposed Fourteenth Amendment, and his attack on Stevens, Sumner, and other Northern leaders, put Congress in an angry mood. Consequently, on April 9, 1866, it passed the civil rights bill over his veto.

The fight between the President and Congress was now in the open. Both believed that they could muster enough strength to have their way. Johnson was so confident that he decided to carry the fight to the people and call on them to return men to Congress in the fall of 1866 who would support his program. His conduct during the well-known "swing around the circle" was so unbecoming and his utterances so indiscreet that the entire country was outraged. He was soundly repudiated at the polls when the nation elected to Congress an overwhelming majority to oppose him and his Reconstruction program.

The rejection of the Fourteenth Amendment by the Southern states, their enactment of Black Codes, the widespread disorder in the South, and President Johnson's growing obstinacy persuaded many people that the South had to be dealt with harshly. Consequently, the Joint Committee presented to Congress a measure that ultimately was the basis of the principal Reconstruction Act of 1867. Through this measure the ex-Confederate states except Tennessee, where Reconstruction was moving satisfactorily, were divided into five military districts in which martial law was to prevail. On the basis of universal suffrage a convention in each state was to draw up a new constitution acceptable to Congress. No state was to be admitted until it ratified the Fourteenth Amendment. The former rebels who could not take the ironclad oath were of course disfranchised. President Johnson vetoed the bill, contending that it was unconstitutional, unfair to the states that had been reorganized, and that the Negroes, not having asked to vote, did not even understand what the franchise was. Congress overrode the veto and proceeded to enact other measures in the new program of Reconstruction.

The victory of Congress over the president was complete. It had enfranchised blacks in the District of Columbia, put the Freedmen's Bureau on a firm footing, carried forward its program of reconstructing the South through stern and severe treatment, and laid plans for subordination of the presidency by removal of its incumbent. The victory of Congress marked not only the beginning of a harsh policy toward the South; it also signified the triumph of a coalition of interests—crusaders, politicians, and industrialists—all of whom hoped to gain something substantial through congressional reconstruction. It produced new conflicts, more bitter than preceding ones, and created so much confusion and chaos in almost every aspect of life that many of the problems would persist for more than a century.

Thomas Brook

*Plessy v. Ferguson: A Brief History with Documents**

There were two stages of Reconstruction: presidential and radical or congressional. The first was led by Andrew Johnson, who assumed the presidency after the assassination of Abraham Lincoln in 1865, toward the end of the war. This stage was relatively uncontroversial and consisted mainly in using the federal government's power to enforce the Thirteenth Amendment, passed in 1865, which abolished slavery. Abolishing slavery, however, did not eliminate racial hierarchy. Most southern states passed "Black Codes," which, although they granted African Americans the right to own property and bring suits in court, still forbade them from serving on juries, testifying against whites, or voting. Some Black Codes also kept former slaves, or freedmen, in a subservient economic position by requiring that they sign yearly labor contracts. Those who did not were subject to arrest and imprisonment as vagrants. Since in many states prisoners could in turn be leased out at minimal costs as laborers, the Black Codes allowed a form of disguised slavery.

This repression of freedmen sparked new efforts at reform from members of Congress, and in 1866 a Civil Rights Act was passed, effectively voiding practices mandated by Black Codes by making African Americans full United States citizens and guaranteeing certain rights of citizenship. To ensure the constitutionality of this act, Congress also passed the Fourteenth Amendment, which was ratified by the states in 1868. The passage of the 1866 Civil Rights Act and the Fourteenth Amendment marked the move toward Radical Reconstruction, which was extremely controversial. Shortly we will come to a more detailed explanation of the Civil Rights

---

* (footnotes omitted).

Act and the Fourteenth Amendment, but first we need to examine the controversy over the attempt to use them to expand the goals of Reconstruction.

A member of the 1866 Congress, future president James A. Garfield proclaimed that with the passage of both measures, "personal liberty and personal rights are placed in the keeping of the nation. . . . We must make American citizenship the shield that protects every citizen, on every foot of American soil." But President Johnson and most Southerners strongly disagreed with the wisdom of such action. Indeed, it violated two of their most sacred beliefs: white supremacy and states' rights. For them, African Americans were unworthy of United States citizenship. Furthermore, they resisted the federal government's intrusion into the internal affairs of the states. In heated and partisan debates they opposed both the Civil Rights Act and the Fourteenth Amendment.

Supporters of both countered by pointing out a historical inconsistency in their opponents' arguments against federal control. Recalling how the federal government had enforced a law passed in 1850 requiring the return to the South of slaves who had escaped to freedom in the North, Senator Lyman Trumbull of Illinois noted, "Surely we have the authority to enact a law as efficient in the interests of freedom, now that freedom prevails throughout the country, as we had in the interest of slavery when it prevailed in a portion of the country." Another senator found "poetic justice" in using constitutional powers previously used to support slavery to support the rights of freedmen. But there was a danger in remedying past injustices by using the means of the past. When the federal government used its power to return fugitive slaves in the 1850s, many people evoked higher authority to disobey the law. Similarly, white southerners were prepared to appeal to higher law to resist what they felt were revengeful federal laws designed to punish the South for its rebellion. The Ku Klux Klan, for instance, claimed to serve the dictates of divine justice.

The white South felt particularly abused in 1867 when Congress passed the Reconstruction Act, which expanded the federal government's control by dividing the South into military zones and giving federal troops power to enforce regulations emanating from Washington. Johnson promptly vetoed this and other Reconstruction legislation. In response, the House voted to impeach Johnson for what it considered treasonable offenses. As provided in the Constitution, the Senate then tried Johnson, but its vote of thirty-five to nineteen fell one short of the two-thirds majority required to remove him from office. The first president ever to be impeached, Johnson remained in office, but he was virtually powerless for the remainder of his term. Congress continually overrode his vetoes, thus closing out the state of presidential Reconstruction and instituting the second phase, of Radical Reconstruction.

Radical Reconstruction was implemented by a group of Republicans known as Radical Republicans, who controlled Congress in the period right after the Civil War. Radical Republicans passed laws designed to bring about a second American revolution, in which all citizens, including blacks, would enjoy equal civil and political rights. The presidential election of 1868 was in effect a referendum on their legislation. Democrats, who primarily supported the interests of white southerners and those white laborers in the North who feared competition from African-American labor, nominated Horatio Seymour, the governor of New York. Republicans nominated Ulysses S. Grant, the hero of the North's military victory in the Civil War. The campaign produced vicious and simplistic attacks. Republicans frequently identified Democrats with secession and treason, while Democrats had but one issue: opposition to Reconstruction. That opposition appealed to the racist sentiment of some white voters. For instance, Francis P. Blair, Seymour's vice presidential candidate, accused the Republicans of allowing the South to be controlled by a "semi-barbarous race of blacks who are worshippers of fetishes and poligamists" intent on subjecting "white women to their unbridled lust."

Democrats also warned that the new rights granted to African Americans would force states in the North and the South to rescind antimiscegenation laws that prohibited marriages between whites and people from other races. In fact, debates over the Civil Rights Act indicate that few Republicans were egalitarian enough to support interracial marriage. Furthermore, as Tourgée pointed out, it was hypocritical to worry so much about interracial marriage when illicit sexual contact between the races, which had been widespread under slavery, continued in the South. Nonetheless, irrational fears of racial intermixture continued to capture the imaginations of a number of voters.

In the end, however, the Democrats' racist campaign did not succeed, and Grant won an overwhelming victory that he repeated in 1872. Radical Reconstruction was in effect during his two administrations. As many historians have pointed out, this stage of Reconstruction was not quite as radical as its name implies. The Fifteenth Amendment, the third and last of the Civil War amendments to the Constitution, removed race and color as barriers to the vote for male citizens. But most supporters of Radical Reconstruction did not envision total social equality for African Americans. Furthermore, whereas its supporters tried to bring about a new social order in the South, they did not aim for a truly egalitarian society. Granted, freedmen were given political power and were provided economic and educational opportunities unimaginable a generation earlier. Nonetheless, the model for the new order was small-scale competitive capitalism in the North that celebrated the moral superiority of free labor. In that order African Americans were not treated as equals, and laborers were often exploited.

A new social order did arise in the South. But it was neither egalitarian nor a reflection of northern society. Instead, it was one in which the "color line" separating the races was honored as much as, if not more than, it had been under slavery. It was also one bound together by the resentful belief of most white southerners that the North had used military rule during Reconstruction to allow freedmen to lord over their former masters.

Geoffrey Stone, et al.

Constitutional Law

Congress attempted to make the Thirteenth Amendment effective against the challenge posed by the Black Codes through enactment of the Civil Rights Act of 1866. Passed over President Johnson's veto, the act declared that "all persons born in the United States and not subject to any foreign power, excluding Indians not taxed," were citizens of the United States. Such citizens were granted the same right to make and enforce contracts, sue, give evidence, acquire property and "to full and equal benefit of all laws and proceedings for the security of person and property as is enjoyed by white citizens." Moreover, all citizens were to be "subject to like punishment, pains, and penalties, and to none other, any law, statute, ordinance, regulation or custom to the contrary notwithstanding."

Even before the civil rights bill was passed, doubt arose about Congress's power to enact such a law. Thus, on February 13 and 26, 1866, Congressman Bingham introduced the first version of what was to become the Fourteenth Amendment. It stated that "[t]he Congress shall have the power to make all laws which shall be necessary and proper to secure to the citizens of each State all privileged and immunities of citizens in the several States, and to all persons in the several States equal protection in the rights of life, liberty, and property." Cong. Globe, 39th Cong., 1st Sess. 813, 1034 (1866).

On April 30, 1866, after extensive debate, the Joint Committee on Reconstruction reported a new proposal that provided that "[n]o state shall make or enforce any law which shall abridge the privileges or immunities of citizens of the United States, nor shall any State deprive any person of life, liberty, or property without due process of law; nor deny any person within its jurisdiction the equal protection of the laws." These substantive prohibitions were coupled with another grant of power to Congress to enforce them "by appropriate legislation." The amendment was adopted by the House in this form. When the amendment reached the Senate, the first sentence of section 1 — making all persons born or naturalized in the United States and subject to the jurisdiction thereof citizens of the United States and of the state wherein they reside — was added. The amendment was ratified on July 28, 1868.

Two years later, on March 30, 1870, Congress added the last of the Reconstruction amendments, which prohibited both the United States and any state from denying or abridging the right to vote on account of race, color, or previous condition of servitude. The amendment granted Congress the power to enforce this provision by appropriate legislation.

Invoking this new constitutional authority, the Reconstruction Congress enacted an extensive legislative program. In 1870, Congress reenacted the 1866 Civil Rights Act and added criminal penalties for deprivation of rights under the law. In the same year, Congress passed the Enforcement Act, which attached criminal penalties to interference with the right to vote and made it a felony to conspire to injure, oppress, threaten, or intimidate any citizen with the intent to prevent or hinder the free exercise of any right granted by the Constitution or laws of the United States. One year later Congress enacted the Ku Klux Klan Act, which criminally punished conspiracies to deprive a class of persons of equal protection of the laws and created civil liability for state officials who deprived persons of federal rights under the color of state laws. Finally in 1875 Congress enacted a sweeping public accommodations law requiring all inns, public conveyances, theaters, and other places of public amusement to admit all persons regardless of race, color, or previous condition of servitude.

Did this flurry of legislative activity fundamentally alter the constitutional structure that existed before the Civil War? This question has two dimensions. First, how did the Reconstruction Congress alter the power balance between the federal and state government? No doubt the Reconstruction amendments were intended to provide a new source of federal power to protect the newly freed slaves. But were they also a more general rejection of the traditional theory that state governments would serve to protect individual liberties? Or was the federal government to intervene only interstitially when the states were unwilling or unable to provide protection? Second, how did the amendments alter the balance of power between the judiciary and the political branches? As noted above, the primary impetus for passage of the fourteenth amendment was the need to provide a basis for federal *legislative* action against the states. But was the amendment intended as well to be a basis for federal *judicial* power?

> *Constitutional Law* 507–8 (3rd edition).
> Copyright © (1996) Stone, et al.
> Reprinted with permission of Aspen Law & Business.

In a republican form of government with a Constitution of enumerated powers, the federal government's effectiveness in eradicating racial injustices will seldom exceed the Supreme Court's definition of the limitations of federal power to intervene in such matters. As seen in the latter half of the nineteenth century, judicial decisions could be used to limit reconstructive efforts by the President and Congress. Going beyond checks and balances, these decisions by the Supreme Court systematically constrained freedom. Most often, the federal law's actual impact in racial spheres is considerably less than the theoretical or potential power of the federal government to intervene. Additionally, definitive rulings in Supreme Court cases that do not directly involve the issue of race frequently dilute the federal racial remedies or options. *The Slaughterhouse Cases* are a prime example of such factors operating adversely on blacks. It was not until 1870, when the *Slaughterhouse Cases* were filed, that the groundwork was set for the Court to articulate the scope or breadth of the Thirteenth, Fourteenth and Fifteenth Amendments, which were primarily intended to protect blacks. These cases, however, did not facially involve blacks directly — in that the record does not indicate that any of the primary parties were black. Presumably the butchers seeking to preserve their livelihood were white, but the holdings in the *Slaughterhouse Cases* are of profound significance in that they showcase the Supreme Court's view of the scope of the Thirteenth, Fourteenth and Fifteenth Amendments and the rights, privileges, immunities and definitions of United States citizenship. These cases were so complex that they remained before the Supreme Court for twenty-eight months before the final decisions were released. To the same extent that the Supreme Court could constrain freedom, they could also enforce justice and uphold Congressional efforts toward Reconstruction. For example, the Fourteenth Amendment nullified the denial of citizenship in *Scott*, but in *Slaughterhouse*, the Supreme Court severely constricted the effectiveness of the amendment.

C. *The Slaughterhouse Cases*, 16 Wall. 36 (1873)

1. Facts

Justice MILLER delivered the opinion of the Court.

Petitioners were challenging the constitutionality of a March 8, 1869 Louisiana statute which granted to one statutorily created private corporation the "sole and exclusive privilege" of conducting the "livestock landings" and slaughterhouses in the city of New Orleans. Purportedly passed to "protect the health of the city of New Orleans," the statute required construction of one grand slaughterhouse with sufficient capacity for slaughtering 500 animals per day. After construction of the new corporation's facilities all other stock landings and slaughterhouses were required to close, but the new statutorily created slaughterhouse corporation was required to permit any person to slaughter animals in the new facilities and there was a statutory limit to the charges which could be made for each animal slaughtered. There was required an inspection of all animals intended to be slaughtered by an officer appointed by the Governor of Louisiana. The Supreme Court of Louisiana had upheld the validity of the statute upon both federal and state constitutional grounds.

2. Opinion

a. The Constitutional Issues

The act divides itself into two main grants of privilege—the one in reference to stocklandings and stockyards, and the other to slaughter-houses. That the landing of livestock in large droves, from steamboats on the bank of the river, and from railroad trains, should, for the safety and comfort of the people and the care of the animals, be limited to proper places, and those not numerous, it needs no argument to prove. Nor can it be injurious to the general community that while the duty of making ample preparation for this is imposed upon a few men, or a corporation, they should, to enable them to do it successfully, have the exclusive right of providing such landing-places, and receiving a fair compensation for the service.

It is, however, the slaughter-house privilege, which is mainly relied on to justify the charges of gross injustice to the public, and invasion of private right.

It is not, and cannot be successfully controverted, that it is both the right and the duty of the legislative body—the supreme power of the State or municipality—to prescribe and determine the localities where the business of slaughtering for a great city may be conducted. To do this effectively it is indispensable that all persons who slaughter animals for food shall do it is those places *and nowhere else.*

The statute under consideration defines these localities and forbids slaughtering in any other. It does not, as has been asserted, prevent the butcher from doing his own slaughtering. On the contrary, the Slaughter-House Company is required, under a heavy penalty, to permit any person who wishes to do so, to slaughter in their houses; and they are bound to make ample provision for the convenience of all the slaughtering for the entire city. The butcher then is still permitted to slaughter, to prepare, and to sell his own meats; but he is required to slaughter at a specified place and to pay a reasonable compensation for the use of the accommodations furnished him at that place.

The wisdom of the monopoly granted by the legislature may be open to question, but it is difficult to see a justification for the assertion that the butchers are deprived of the right to labor in their occupation, or the people of their daily service in preparing food, or how this statute, with the duties and guards imposed upon the company, can be said to destroy the business of the butcher, or seriously interfere with its pursuit.

The power here exercised by the legislature of Louisiana is, in its essential nature, one which has been, up to the present period in the constitutional history of this country, always conceded to belong to the States, however it may *now* be questioned in some of its details.

'Unwholesome trades, slaughter-houses, operations offensive to the senses, the deposit of powder, the application of steam power to propel cars, the building with combustible materials, and the burial of the dead, may all,' says Chancellor Kent, 'be interdicted by law, in the midst of dense masses of population, on the general and rational principle, that every person ought so to use his property as not to injure his neighbors; and that private interests must be made subservient to the general interests of the community.' This is called the police power; and it is declared by Chief Justice Shaw that it is much easier to perceive and realize the existence and sources of it than to mark its boundaries, or prescribe limits to its exercise.

This power is, and must be from its very nature, incapable of any very exact definition or limitation. Upon it depends the security of social order, the life and health of the citizen, the comfort of an existence in a thickly populated community, the enjoyment of private and social life, and the beneficial use of property. 'It extends,' says another eminent judge, 'to the protection of the lives, limbs, health, comfort, and quiet of all persons, and the protection of all property within the State; . . . and persons and property are subject to all kinds of restraints and burdens in order to secure the general comfort, health, and prosperity of the State. Of the perfect right of the legislature to do this no question ever was, or, upon acknowledged general principles, ever can be made, so far as natural persons are concerned.'

The regulation of the place and manner of conducting the slaughtering of animals, and the business of butchering within a city, and the inspection of the animals to be killed for meat, and of the meat afterwards, are among the most necessary and frequent exercises of this power. It is not, therefore, needed that we should seek for a comprehensive definition, but rather look for the proper source of its exercise.

In *Gibbons* v. *Ogden*, Chief Justice Marshall, speaking of inspection laws passed by the States, says: 'They form a portion of that immense mass of legislation which controls everything within the territory of a State not surrendered to the General Government—all which can be most advantageously administered by the States themselves, . . .'

It may, therefore, be considered as established, that the authority of the legislature of Louisiana to pass the present statute is ample, unless some restraint in the exercise of that power be found in the constitution of that State or in the amendments to the Constitution of the United States, adopted since the date of the decisions we have already cited.

The plaintiffs in error accepting this issue, allege that the statute is a violation of the Constitution of the United States in these several particulars: that it creates an involuntary servitude forbidden by the thirteenth article of amendment; that it abridges the privileges and immunities of citizens of the United States; that it denies to the plaintiffs the equal protection of the laws; and, that it deprives them of their property without due process of law contrary to the provisions of the first section of the fourteenth article of amendment. This court is thus called upon for the first time to give construction to these articles.

We do not conceal from ourselves the great responsibility which this duty devolves upon us. No questions so far-reaching and pervading in their consequences, so profoundly interesting to the people of this country, and so important in their bearing upon the relations of the United States, and of the several States to each other and to the citizens of the States and of the United States, have been before this court during the official life of any of its present members. We have given every opportunity for a full hearing at the bar; we have discussed it freely and compared views among ourselves; we have taken ample time for careful deliberation, and we now propose to announce the judgments which we have formed in the construction of those articles, so far as we have found them necessary to the decision of the cases before us, and beyond that we have neither the inclination nor the right to.

b. The Thirteenth Amendment

The institution of African slavery, as it existed in about half the States of the Union, and the contests pervading the public mind for many years, between those who desired its curtailment and ultimate extinction and those who desired additional safeguards for its security and perpetuation, culminated in the effort, on the part of most of the States in which slavery existed, to separate from the Federal government, and to resist its authority. This constituted the war of the rebellion, and whatever auxiliary causes may have contributed to bring about this war, undoubtedly the overshadowing and efficient cause was African slavery.

In that struggle slavery, as a legalized social relation, perished. It perished as a necessity of the bitterness and force of the conflict. When the armies of freedom found themselves upon the soil of slavery they could do nothing less than free the poor victims whose enforced servitude was the foundation of the quarrel. And when hard pressed in the contest these men (for they proved themselves men in that terrible crisis) offered their services and were accepted by thousands to aid in suppressing the unlawful rebellion, slavery was at an end wherever the Federal government succeeded in that purpose. The proclamation of President Lincoln expressed an accomplished fact as to a large portion of the insurrectionary districts, when he declared slavery abolished in them all. But the war being over, those who had succeeded in re-establishing the authority of the Federal government were not content to permit this great act of emancipation to rest on the actual results of the contest or the proclamation of the Executive, both of which might have been questioned in after times, and they determined to place this main and most valuable result in the Constitution of the restored Union as one of its fundamental articles. Hence the thirteenth article of amendment of that instrument. Its two short sections seem hardly to admit of construction, so vigorous is their expression and so appropriate to the purpose we have indicated.

"1. Neither slavery nor involuntary servitude, except as a punishment for crime, whereof the party shall have been duly convicted, shall exist within the United States or any place subject to their jurisdiction. 2. Congress shall have power to enforce this article by appropriate legislation."

To withdraw the mind from the contemplation of this grand yet simple declaration of the personal freedom of all the human race within the jurisdiction of this government—a declaration designed to establish the freedom of four millions of slaves—and with a microscopic search endeavor to find in it a reference to servitudes, which may have been attached to property in certain localities, requires an effort, to say the least of it.

That a personal servitude was meant is proved by the use of the word "involuntary," which can only apply to human beings. The exception of servitude as a punishment for crime gives an idea of the class of servitude that is meant. The word servitude is of larger meaning than slavery, as the latter is popularly understood in this country, and the obvious purpose was to forbid all shades and conditions of African slavery. It was very well understood that in the form of apprenticeship for long terms, as it had been practiced in the West India Islands, on the abolition of slavery by the English government, or by reducing the slaves to the condition of serfs attached to the plantation, the purpose of the article might have been evaded, if only the word slavery had been used. The case of the apprentice slave, held under a law of Maryland, liberated by Chief Justice Chase, on a writ of habeas corpus under this article, illustrates this course of observation. And it is all that we deem necessary to say on the application of that article to the statute of Louisiana, now under consideration.

c. The Fourteenth Amendment

The process of restoring to their proper relations with the Federal government and with the other States those which had sided with the rebellion, undertaken under the proclamation of President Johnson in 1865, and before the assembling of Congress, developed the fact that, notwithstanding the formal recognition by those States of the abolition of slavery, the condition of the slave race would, without further protection of the Federal government, be almost as bad as it was before. Among the first acts of legislation adopted by several of the States in the legislative bodies which claimed to be in their normal relations with the Federal government, were laws which imposed upon the colored race onerous disabilities and burdens, and curtailed their rights in the pursuit of life, liberty, and property to such an extent that their freedom was of little value, while they had lost the protection which they had received from their former owners from motives both of interest and humanity.

They were in some States forbidden to appear in the towns in any other character than menial servants. They were required to reside on and cultivate the soil without the right to purchase or own it. They were excluded from many occupations of gain, and were not permitted to give testimony in the courts in any case where a white man was a party. It was said that their lives were at the mercy of bad men, either because the laws for their protection were insufficient or were not enforced.

These circumstances, whatever of falsehood or misconception may have been mingled with their presentation, forced upon the statesmen who had conducted the Federal government in safety through the crisis of the rebellion, and who supposed that by the thirteenth article of amendment they had secured the result of their labors, the conviction that something more was necessary in the way of constitutional protection to the unfortunate race who had suffered so much. They accordingly passed through Congress the proposition for the Fourteenth Amendment, and they declined to treat as restored to their full participation in the government of the Union the States which had been in insurrection, until they ratified that article by a formal vote of their legislative bodies. . . .

We repeat, then, in the light of this recapitulation of events, almost too recent to be called history, but which are familiar to us all; and on the most casual examination of the language of these amendments, no one can fail to be impressed with the one pervading purpose found in them all, lying at the foundation of each, and without which none of them would have been even suggested; we mean the freedom of the slave race, the security and firm establishment of that freedom, and the protection of the newly-made freeman and citizen from the oppressions of those who had formerly exercised unlimited dominion over him. It is true that only the Fifteenth Amendment, in terms, mentions the negro by speaking of his color and his slavery.

But it is just as true that each of the other articles was addressed to the grievances of that race, and designed to remedy them as the Fifteenth Amendment.

We do not say that no one else but the negro can share in this protection. Both the language and spirit of these articles are to have their fair and just weight in any question of construction. Undoubtedly while negro slavery alone was in the mind of the Congress which proposed the thirteenth article, it forbids any other kind of slavery, now or hereafter. If Mexican peonage or the Chinese coolie labor system shall develop slavery of the Mexican or Chinese race within our territory, this amendment may safely be trusted to make it void. And so if other rights are assailed by the States which properly and necessarily fall within the protection of these articles, that protection will apply, though the party interested may not be of African descent. But what we do say, and what we wish to be understood is, that in any fair and just construction of any section or phrase of these amendments, it is necessary to look to the purpose which we have said was the pervading spirit of them all, the evil which they were designed to remedy, and the process of continued addition to the Constitution, until that purpose was supposed to be accomplished, as far as constitutional law can accomplish it. . . .

d. Citizenship

"All persons born or naturalized in the United States, and subject to the jurisdiction thereof, are citizens of the United States and of the State wherein they reside." The first observation we have to make on this clause is, that it puts at rest both the questions which we stated to have been the subject of differences of opinion. It declares that persons may be citizens of the United States without regard to their citizenship of a particular State, and it overturns the *Dred Scott* decision by making *all persons* born within the United States and subject to its jurisdiction citizens of the United States. . . .

e. The Privileges and Immunities Clause

The language is, "No State shall make or enforce any law which shall abridge the privileges or immunities of citizens of *the United States*." It is a little remarkable, if this clause was intended as a protection to the citizen of a State against the legislative power of his own State, that the word citizen of the State should be left out when it is so carefully used, and used in contradistinction to citizens of the United States, in the very sentence which precedes it. It is too clear for argument that the change in phraseology was adopted understandingly and with a purpose.

Of the privileges and immunities of the citizen of the United States, and of the privileges and immunities of the citizen of the State, and why they respectively are, we will presently consider; but we wish to state here that it is only the former which are placed by this clause under the protection of the Federal Constitution, and that the latter, whatever they may be, are not intended to have any additional protection by this paragraph of the amendment.

If, then, there is a difference between the privileges and immunities belonging to a citizen of the United States as such, and those belonging to the citizen of the State as such the latter must rest for their security and protection where they have heretofore rested; for they are not embraced by this paragraph of the amendment. . . .

Fortunately we are not without judicial construction of this clause of the Constitution. The first and the leading case on the subject is that of *Corfield v. Coryell*, decided by Justice Washington in the Circuit Court for the district of Pennsylvania in 1823.

> The inquiry is what are the privileges and immunities of citizens of the several States? We feel no hesitation in confining these expressions to those privileges and immunities which are *fundamental*; which belong of right to the citizens of all free governments, and which have at all times been enjoyed by citizens of the several States which compose this Union, from the time of their becoming free, independent, and sovereign. What these fundamental principles are, it would be more tedious than difficult to enumerate. They may all, however, be comprehended under the following general heads: protection by the government, with the right to acquire and possess property of every kind, and to pursue and obtain happiness and safety, subject, nevertheless, to such restraints as the government may prescribe for the general good of the whole.

It would be the vainest show of learning to attempt to prove by citations of authority, that up to the adoption of the recent amendments, no claim or pretense was set up that those rights depended on the Federal government for their existence or protection, beyond the very few express limitations which the Federal Constitution imposed upon the States—such, for instance, as the prohibition against *ex post facto* laws, bills of attainder, and laws impairing the obligation of contracts. But with the exception of these and a few other restrictions, the entire domain of the privileges and immunities of citizens of the States, as above defined, lay within the constitutional and legislative power of the States, and without that of the Federal government. Was it the purpose of the Fourteenth Amendment, by the simple declaration that no State should make or enforce any law which shall abridge the privileges and immunities of *citizens of the United States*, to transfer the security and protection of all the civil rights which we have mentioned, from the states to the Federal government? And where it is declared that Congress shall have the power to enforce that article, was it intended to bring within the power of Congress the entire domain of civil rights heretofore belonging exclusively to the States?

All this and more must follow, if the proposition of the plaintiffs in error be sound. For not only are these rights subject to the control of Congress whenever in its discretion any of them are supposed to be abridged by State legislation, but that body may also pass laws in advance, limiting and restricting the exercise of legislative power by the States, in their most ordinary and usual functions, as in its judgment it may think proper on all such subjects. And still further, such a construction followed by the reversal of the judgments of the Supreme Court of Louisiana in these cases, would constitute this court a perpetual censor upon all legislation of the States, on the civil rights of their own citizens, with authority to nullify such as it did not approve as consistent with those rights, as they existed at the time of the adoption of this amendment. The argument we admit is not always the most conclusive which is drawn from the consequences urged against the adoption of a particular construction of an instrument. But when, as in the case before us, these consequences are so serious, so far-reaching and pervading, so great a departure from the structure and spirit of our institutions; when the effect is to fetter and degrade the State governments by subjecting them to the control of Congress, in the exercise of powers heretofore universally conceded to them of the most ordinary and fundamental character; when in fact it radically changes the whole theory of the relations of the State and Federal governments to each other and of both these governments to the people; the argument has a force that is irresistible, in the absence of language which expresses such a purpose too clearly to admit of doubt.

We are convinced that no such results were intended by the Congress which proposed these amendments, nor by the legislatures of the States which ratified them.

But lest it should be said that no such privileges and immunities are to be found if those we have been considering are excluded, we venture to suggest some which owe their existence to the Federal government, its National character, its Constitution, or its laws.

One of these is well described in the case of *Crandall v. Nevada*. It is said to be the right of the citizen of this great country, protected by implied guarantees of its Constitution, "to come to the seat of government to assert any claim he may have upon that government, to transact any business he may have with it, to seek its protection, to share its offices, to engage in administering its functions. He has the right of free access to its seaports, through which all operations of foreign commerce are conducted, to the subtreasuries, land offices, and courts of justice in the several States." And quoting from the language of Chief Justice Taney in another case, it is said "that *for all the great purposes for which the Federal government* was established, we are one people, with one common country, *we are all citizens of the United States;*" and it is, as such citizens, that their rights are supported in this court in *Crandall v. Nevada*.

Another privilege of a citizen of the United States is to demand the care and protection of the Federal government over his life, liberty, and property when on the high seas or within the jurisdiction of a foreign government. Of this there can be no doubt, nor that the right depends upon his character as a citizen of the United States. The right to peaceably assemble and petition for redress of grievances, the privilege of the writ of *habeas corpus*, are rights of the citizen guaranteed by the Federal Constitution. The right to use the navigable waters of the United States, however they may penetrate the territory of the several States, all rights secured to our citizens by treaties with foreign nations, are dependent upon citizenship of the United States, and not citizenship of a State. One of these privileges is conferred by the very article under consideration. It is that a citizen of the United States can, of his own volition, become a citizen of any State of the Union by a *bona fide* residence therein, with the same rights as other citizens of that State. To these may be added the rights secured by the Thirteenth and Fifteenth Articles of Amendment, and by the other clause of the Fourteenth, next to be considered.

But it is useless to pursue this branch of the inquiry, since we are of opinion that the rights claimed by these plaintiffs in error, if they have any existence, are not privileges and immunities of citizens of the United States within the meaning of the clause of the Fourteenth Amendment under consideration. . . .

f. The Property Clause

We are not without judicial interpretation, therefore, both State and National, of the meaning of this clause. And it is sufficient to say that under no construction of that provision that we have ever seen, or any that we deem admissible, can the restraint imposed by the State of Louisiana upon the exercise of their trade by the butchers of New Orleans be held to be a deprivation of property within the meaning of that provision.

g. The Equal Protection Clause

"Nor shall any State deny to any person within its jurisdiction the equal protection of the laws." In the light of the history of these amendments, and the pervading purpose of them, which we have already discussed, it is not difficult to give a meaning to this clause. The existence of laws in the States where the newly emancipated negroes resided, which discriminated with gross injustice and hardship against them as a class, was the evil to be remedied by this clause, and by it such laws are forbidden.

If, however, the States did not conform their laws to its requirements, then by the fifth section of the article of amendment Congress was authorized to enforce it by suitable legislation. We doubt very much whether any action of a State not directed by way of discrimination against the negroes as a class, or on account of their race, will ever be held to come within the purview of this provision. It is so clearly a provision for that race and that emergency, that a strong case would be necessary for its application to any other. But as it is a State that is to be dealt with, and not alone the validity of its laws, we may safely leave that matter until Congress shall have exercised its power, or some case of State oppression, by denial of equal justice in its courts, shall have claimed a decision at our hands. We find no such case in the one before us, and do not deem it necessary to go over the argument again, as it may have relation to this particular clause of the amendment. . . .

h. State/Federal Relations

The adoption of the first eleven amendments to the Constitution so soon after the original instrument was accepted, shows a prevailing sense of danger at that time from the Federal power. And it cannot be denied that such a jealousy continued to exist with many patriotic men until the breaking out of the late civil war. It was then discovered that the true danger to the perpetuity of the Union was in the capacity of the State organizations to combine and concentrate all the powers of the State, and of contiguous States, for a determined resistance to the General Government. Unquestionably this has given great force to the argument, and added largely to the number of those who believe in the necessity of a strong National government.

But, however pervading this sentiment, and however it may have contributed to the adoption of the amendments we have been considering, we do not see in those amendments any purpose to destroy the main features of the general system. Under the pressure of all the excited feeling growing out of the war, our statesmen have still believed that the existence of the States with powers for domestic and local government, including the regulation of civil rights — the rights of person and of property — was essential to the perfect working of our complex form of government, though they have thought proper to impose additional limitations on the States, and to confer additional power on that of the Nation.

But whatever fluctuations may be seen in the history of public opinion on this subject during the period of our national existence, we think it will be found that this court, so far as its functions required, has always held with a steady and an even hand the balance between State and Federal power, and we trust that such may continue to be the history of its relation to that subject so long as it shall have duties to perform which demand of it a construction of the Constitution, or of any of its parts.

3. Holding

The judgments of the Supreme Court of Louisiana in these cases are affirmed.

4. Justice Field Dissenting

I am unable to agree with the majority of the court in these cases, and will proceed to state the reasons of my dissent from their judgment.

a. The Thirteenth Amendment

Still it is evident that the language of the amendment is not used in a restrictive sense. It is not confined to African slavery alone. It is general and universal in its application. Slavery of white men as well as of black men is prohibited, and not merely slavery in the strict sense of the term, but involuntary servitude in every form.

The words "involuntary servitude" have not been the subject of any judicial or legislative exposition, that I am aware of, in this country, except that which is found in the Civil Rights Act, which will be hereafter noticed. It is, however, clear that they include something more than slavery in the strict sense of the term; they include also serfage, vassalage, villenage, peonage, and all other forms of compulsory service for the mere benefit or pleasure of others. Nor is this the full import of the terms. The abolition of slavery and involuntary servitude was intended to make every one born in this country a freeman, and as such to give to him the right to pursue the ordinary avocations of life without other restraint than such as affects all others, and to enjoy equally with them the fruits of his labor. A prohibition to him to pursue certain callings, open to others of the same age, condition, and sex, or to reside in places where others are permitted to live, would so far deprive him of the rights of a freeman, and would place him, as respects others, in a condition of servitude. A person allowed to pursue only one trade or calling, and only in one locality of the country, would not be, in the strict sense of the term, in a condition of slavery, but probably none would deny that he would be in a condition of servitude. He certainly would not possess the liberties nor enjoy the privileges of a freeman. The compulsion which would force him to labor even for his own benefit only in one direction, or in one place, would be almost as oppressive and nearly as great an invasion of his liberty as the compulsion which would force him to labor for the benefit or pleasure of another, and would equally constitute an element of servitude. The counsel of the plaintiffs in error therefore contend that "wherever a law of a State, or a law of the United States, makes a discrimination between classes of persons, which deprives the one class of their freedom or their property, or which makes a caste of them to subserve the power, pride, avarice, vanity, or vengeance of others," there involuntary servitude exists within the meaning of the Thirteenth Amendment. . . .

b. The Fourteenth Amendment

The Fourteenth Amendment, in my judgment, makes it essential to the validity of the legislation of every State that this equality of right should be respected. How widely this equality has been departed from, how entirely rejected and trampled upon by the act of Louisiana, I have already shown. And it is to me a matter of profound regret that its validity is recognized by a majority of this court, for by it the right of free labor, one of the most sacred and imprescriptible rights of man, is violated. As stated by the Supreme Court of Connecticut, in the case cited, grants of exclusive privileges, such as is made by the act in question, are opposed to the whole theory of free government, and it requires no aid from any bill of rights to render them void. That only is a free government, in the American sense of the term, under which the inalienable right of every citizen to pursue his happiness is unrestrained, except by just, equal, and impartial laws.

Chief Justice SWAYNE and Justice BRADLEY concur in this dissent.

5. Justice Bradley Dissenting

I concur in the dissent which has just been read by Justice Field; but desire to add a few observations for the purpose of more fully illustrating my views on the important question decided in these cases, and the special grounds on which they rest. . . . Every citizen, then, being primarily a citizen of the United States, and, secondarily, a citizen of the State where he resides, what, in general, are the privileges and immunities of a citizen of the United States? Is the right, liberty, or privilege of choosing any lawful employment one of them? . . . I think sufficient has been said to show that citizenship is not an empty name, but that, in this country at least, it has connected with it certain incidental rights, privileges, and immunities of the greatest importance. And to say that these rights and immunities attach only to State citizenship, and not to citizenship of the United States, appears to me to evince a very narrow and insufficient estimate of constitutional history and the rights of men, not to say the rights of the American people.

D. Commentary on *The Slaughterhouse Cases*

D. Marvin Jones

No Time for Trumpets: Title VII, Equality, and the Fin de Siecle

In *Slaughterhouse* the Louisiana state legislature gave a twenty-five year monopoly to a particular slaughterhouse company to land and slaughter livestock. This cramped the ability of previous slaughterhouse owners and butchers to practice their trade and profession. The plaintiffs seized upon the Privileges or Immunities Clause as a possible source of protection of the fundamental civil rights associated with natural law: "[t]he right to oneself, to one's own faculties, physical and intellectual." These fundamental rights, in the plaintiffs' view, extended to the right to practice one's profession. The Supreme Court accepted that these fundamental rights existed but suggested that the state, not the federal government, was the guarantor of basic civil rights generally. The Court adopted a structural reading of the Constitution, emphasizing that the first eleven amendments were directed at confining federal power and inferring that the core danger with which the Constitution concerned itself was the danger posed by federal power. As a result, the *Slaughterhouse Cases* severely circumscribed the Privileges or Immunities Clause and emptied it of natural law norms. The *Slaughterhouse* Court reduced the command of the Privileges or Immunities Clause to a procedural rule that rights be allocated evenhandedly with respect to citizens of different states.

92 *Michigan Law Review* 2311, 2325–26 (footnotes omitted).
Copyright © (1994) *Michigan Law Review.*
Reprinted with permission of the *Michigan Law Review.*

In his dissent in the *Slaughterhouse Cases*, note Justice Bradley's broad interpretation of the purposes of the Thirteenth, Fourteenth, and Fifteenth Amendments where white citizens complained of impingement on their butcher and slaughterhouse activities in contrast to his more narrow interpretation where blacks complained of their civil rights being violated in the *Civil Rights Cases* in 1883. Justice Bradley was the Circuit Justice who heard one of the first challenges to the 1869 Louisiana statute. On appeal, the Supreme Court reversed his position and thus he dissented.

Charles Warren

The Supreme Court in United States History

It was with the decision of the famous *Slaughterhouse Cases*, 16 Wall. 36, in 1878, however, that the change in the attitude of the Court became most marked. In these cases, the Court, in construing for the first time the scope of the Fourteenth Amendment, rendered a decision which profoundly affected the course of the future history of the country. To the Radical Republicans the decision came as a tremendous shock and disappointment, for their intent in framing the language of the Amendment was directly contrary to the narrow construction now placed upon it by the Court. Though the country at large may not have understood at the time of the passage of the Fourteenth Amendment, the Radical leaders in Congress had very definite ideas in drafting and submitting the Amendment to the people, despite its general phraseology. Not only did they desire punishment of the South (to be achieved through the second, third and fourth sections, which were easily understood by the people) and the elevation of the negro to the plane of equality with the white man (which was to be achieved by section five, as well as by the Thirteenth and Fifteenth Amendments), but they also intended by section one to centralize in the hands of the Federal Government large powers, hitherto exercised by the States. The interval between the adoption of the Thirteenth Amendment and the proposal of the Fourteenth had been marked by legislation in the Southern States, designed under the guise of repressing vagrancy and regulating contracts of employment, to keep blacks in a state of subjugation; and in order to gain control over the race problem in the South, wide extension of Federal power, and withdrawal of power previously vested in the States, were deemed necessary.

Opinions of this nature, however, were not generally shared; for it was seen by most of the press and by the Bar that "... Nothing is clearer than that the new Amendments, fairly interpreted, leave all the broader relations between the States and the Federal Government unchanged and untouched...." "The principal value of this decision grows out of the fact that it clearly and unmistakably defines the province of the constitutional Amendments, and will hereafter put a quietus upon the thousand and one follies seeking to be legalized by hanging on to the Fourteenth Amendment...." "The decision has long been needed, as a check upon the centralizing tendencies of the Government and upon the determination of the Administration to enforce its policy and to maintain its power, even at the expense of the constitutional prerogatives of the States. The Supreme Court has not spoken a moment too soon or any too boldly on this subject."

Sentiments like these, widely expressed in the North, the East and the West, illustrate how far the pendulum had swung away from centralization and toward the most extreme states' rights views held by the Democratic Party before the war. In the view of state rights advocates, the development of the law since the date of this great decision has, on the whole, justified its wisdom, and Judge Miller's opinion has justly been regarded as one of the glorious landmarks of American law.

The defeated counsel, John A. Campbell admitted that it was "probably best for the country that the case so turned out"; and another Southerner, John S. Wise, said at the celebration of the Centennial of the Court: "That decision did more than all the battles of the Union to bring order out of chaos. . . . When war had ceased, when blood was stanched, when the victor stood above his vanquished foe with drawn sword, the Supreme Court of this Nation planted its foot and said: This victory is not an annihilation of State Sovereignty but a just interpretation of Federal power."

No criticism, however, could be based on the political or sectional attitude of the judges. The Democrat, Judge Field, and the Republican, Chief Justice Chase, both of whom were of the moderate State-Rights school, were joined by the pronouncedly Nationalistic Republican Judges, Bradley and Swayne, in delivering the minority opinion directed against the power of the State; while in favor of the State authority were three Republicans, including Judges Miller and Hunt, in addition to Judge Clifford, a Democrat, and Judge Davis whose political views were tending towards the Democracy.

The Supreme Court in United States History 539–50.
Copyright © (1932) The President and Fellows of Harvard University.

David S. Bogen

*Slaughter-House Five: Views of the Case**

The Fourteenth Amendment to the Constitution was adopted to deal with the aftermath of slavery and the racial discrimination that prevailed after the Civil War. The first sentence asserts that "All persons born or naturalized in the United States, and subject to the jurisdiction thereof, are citizens of the United States and of the State wherein they reside." This repudiated Taney's *Dred Scott* opinion on African-American citizenship. The framers wished to secure for all citizens the privileges and immunities of citizens to which Article IV of the Constitution referred when it said that "The Citizens of each State shall be entitled to all Privileges and Immunities of Citizens in the several States." Supporters of the new Amendment intended to make a constitutional principle of the Civil Rights Act of 1866, which stated that citizens

> shall have the same right . . . to make and enforce contracts, to sue, be parties and give evidence, to inherit, purchase, lease, sell, hold, and convey real and personal property, and to [have] full and equal benefit of all laws and proceedings for the security of person and property, as is enjoyed by white citizens, and shall be subject to like punishment, pains, and penalties, and to none other. . . .

Every speaker in Congress who touched on the issue during the discussion of the adoption of the Privileges or Immunities Clause of the Fourteenth Amendment

---

* (footnotes and chapter headings omitted).

either stated that it was derived from the Privileges and Immunities Clause of Article IV or that it made the Civil Rights Act into a constitutional command, or both. Thus, "privileges or immunities" referred to the fundamental rights that citizens ought to enjoy in any society, because congressmen understood that the term meant fundamental rights in Article IV and because the prohibition of racial discrimination in fundamental rights was the basic principle of the Civil Rights Act of 1866.

The privileges and immunities of citizens that Article IV protected against discrimination based on state citizenship were never completely defined, but congressmen and judges generally described them as fundamental rights prior to passage of the Fourteenth Amendment. They included rights to acquire and possess property. Northern republicans also claimed that southern states violated Article IV when they denied free African Americans and northern whites entrance into the state, rights of speech within the state, and the ability to sue for their rights in the state courts. Thus, fundamental rights included affirmative benefits from the state (e.g., suit in court, enforceable property and contract rights) and negative rights against state interference (e.g., interstate movement, free speech).

The Civil Rights Act of 1866 was the epitome of fundamental rights. Its principle was that racial discrimination in contract, property, access to and testimony in courts, in laws for the security of person and property, or in punishments, deprived citizens of fundamental rights that were privileges or immunities of citizenship. Republican supporters argued that the law was a valid exercise of congressional power to enforce the Thirteenth Amendment, because the failure to treat the individual as a citizen was a badge or incident of slavery.

Although congressmen voting on the Fourteenth Amendment believed that "privileges or immunities" referred to fundamental rights, the *Slaughter-House* Cases rejected a fundamental rights interpretation of the clause only five years after the Amendment's ratification. The *Slaughter-House* Cases arose from a monopoly to operate a slaughterhouse in New Orleans that the Louisiana legislature granted the Crescent City Livestock Company. The justification for regulating slaughterhouses may have been the stench and pollution produced by massive slaughtering, but those emissions were a pale reflection of the corruption of the political process that secured the monopoly. Nevertheless, bribery was not the basis for challenging the grant.

In the *Slaughter-House* Cases, the plaintiff butchers claimed that the monopoly violated the Fourteenth Amendment primarily because it deprived them of the privilege and immunity of pursuing a trade on terms applicable to everyone. Counsel for the defendant slaughterhouse company accepted the proposition that the privileges and immunities specified in the Fourteenth Amendment were the fundamental rights of citizens, including the right to pursue a trade, but argued that the Amendment protected those rights only against discrimination based on race.

Justice Samuel Miller wrote the majority opinion, in which he was joined by Justices Nathan Clifford, David Davis, William Strong, and Ward Hunt. He rejected the fundamental rights views of the Privileges or Immunities Clause held by counsel on both sides of the case. Mixing text and policy analysis, Miller concluded that the privileges and immunities of citizens of the United States were distinct from the fundamental rights of citizens. The Fourteenth Amendment's text makes citizenship in the United States depend on place of birth, and state citizenship depend on place of residence. Noting that citizenship in the United States and citizenship in a state are different matters that depend on different characteristics, Miller said:

> It is a little remarkable, if this clause was intended as a protection to the citizen of a State against the legislative power of his own State, that the word citizen of the State should be left out when it is so carefully used, and used in contradistinction to citizens of the United States in the very sentence which precedes it. It is too clear for argument that the change in phraseology was adopted understandingly and with a purpose.

Justice Miller said that the privileges and immunities protected by Article IV were those of state citizens. Those rights embrace "nearly every civil right for the establishment and protection of which organized government is instituted. They are ... those rights which are fundamental[,]" and they encompass "the class of rights which the State governments were created to establish and secure." But those privileges were secured only against discrimination based on state of citizenship. If a state denied a fundamental right to its own citizens, it could deny it to others. Miller argued these privileges and immunities in Article IV were quite distinct from the privileges and immunities of citizens of the United States protected by the Fourteenth Amendment. The right to pursue a trade was a fundamental right of citizenship within Article IV's protection against discrimination based on state residence. It was not, however, a privilege or immunity of United States citizenship. An interpretation of the Fourteenth Amendment's Privileges or Immunities Clause that gave Congress power to legislate on the rights of person and property protected under Article IV would vastly expand Congressional power, and Miller argued that the clause should not have that effect.

According to Justice Miller, a fundamental rights construction of the Fourteenth Amendment "radically changes the whole theory of the relations of the State and Federal governments to each other and of both these governments to the people," and it should not be adopted unless the language was clear. Fundamental rights, such as the right to pursue an occupation, belong to the citizen of a state only in his capacity as a state citizen, and "they are left to the State governments for security and protection, and not by this article placed under the special care of the Federal government." Therefore the plaintiff butchers had no rights under the Fourteenth Amendment Privileges or Immunities Clause.

55 *Hastings Law Journal* 333, 337–41.
Copyright © 2003 *Hastings Law Journal*.
Reprinted with Permission of the *Hastings Law Journal* and David S. Bogen.

The Framers of the original Constitution believed that tyranny could be avoided by dividing federal power among three branches and even more by limiting the power of the federal government by dividing power between it and the states. Indeed, some Framers believed that the enumeration of congressional power made a Bill of Rights unnecessary. The notion that the states should serve as a shield to protect the individual from federal overreaching is not without merit. But the idea has been weakened by historical and conceptual difficulties with its implementation. As an historical matter, the South's secession and the North's victory in the Civil War brought the nullification doctrine (balancing power between federal and state government) and a "state's rights" strategy into disrepute. Events following the Civil War led to the insight that increasing states' power in order to protect individual rights might have perverse results—that individuals (especially the newly freed slaves) might require a strong *federal* government to protect them from *state* tyranny—an insight incorporated into the Civil War amendments, which for almost the first time imposed substantial constitutional limits on state power.

Despite its questionable rationale and holding, *The Slaughterhouse Cases* remain as binding precedent today. With few exceptions, the Privileges and Immunities Clause of the Fourteenth Amendment has been dormant since the *Slaughterhouse* decision in 1873. Why has such an obviously wrong decision gone unchallenged? The Clause provided protections which were severely undermined by the decision in *Slaughterhouse*, and yet subsequently performed by the Due Process Clause; thus the *Slaughterhouse Cases* have not significantly reduced constitutional rights for white Americans. Black Americans, however, subject to the discriminatory impact of state and local laws, were now without the protections provided by the Privileges and Immunities Clause, and thereby cut off from the individual rights guaranteed by the Bill of Rights.

E. Background on *Cruikshank*

Peggy Cooper Davis

*Introducing Robert Smalls**

In 1864—long before Sumner's enfranchisement proposal made the idea of black citizenship concrete—Robert Smalls was part of an interracial delegation that surprised the Republican National Convention by appearing under the flag of South Carolina. The delegation was not seated, but it made its presence felt, presaging the short-lived era of full African-American participation in Southern politics that began in 1867.

---

* (footnotes and chapter headings omitted).

When, after the de-commissioning of the Planter, Smalls settled in the house that had been the domain of his master and father, he did so with a sense of ownership and belonging. As he once said, "I was born and raised in South Carolina, and today I live on the very spot on which I was born, and I expect to remain here as long as the great God allows me to live, and I will ask no one else to let me remain." For Smalls, making a home again in South Carolina also entailed a deep sense of citizenship and public responsibility. He immediately became central to the political life of his community. As a public servant, "Smalls so dominated local politics that one newspaper called him 'the King of Beaufort County.'" A champion of education, economic redevelopment, the building of railroads, public works, and strong protection of civil rights, Smalls stood apart from corruption, pledging in an 1871 speech to 'guide the ship of state . . . past the rocks, torpedoes and hostile guns of ignorance, immorality and dishonesty' as he had guided the Planter out of the Confederacy.

In 1874, Smalls was elected to the United States House of Representatives. He was therefore able to cast a vote for the Civil Rights Act of 1875, the Act invalidated by the Civil Rights Cases. The logic and constitutional theory that underlay his vote are revealed by the words of African-American Senators and Congressmen who preceded him in the House and by other African-American colleagues with whom he voted in 1875. I quote their words extensively below to demonstrate their relevance to contemporary debates about the scope of federal power conferred by the Fourteenth Amendment.

Some of the black legislators who preceded Smalls in Congress participated in the debates concerning the Act of 1871 — popularly known as the Klan Act — which was invalidated in *United States v. Harris*. This legislation was, of course, designed to address the reign of terror by which former Confederates sought to 'discipline' black labor and force African-American voters and office holders out of political life in the South. As one observer reported:

> When Congress intervened by its reconstruction measures to defeat the reactionary program of the South, there swept over that section a crime-storm of devastating fury. Lawlessness and violence filled the land, and terror stalked abroad by day, and it burned and murdered by night. The Southern states had actually relapsed into barbarism.

Black congressmen addressed the Klan Act with a special sense of urgency, for they and other African-American office-holders were common targets of reactionary violence in the South. Richard Cain, who, like Smalls, was elected to the House of Representatives from South Carolina, was of African-American and Cherokee descent. Educated at Wilberforce University in Ohio, he served as a minister in Brooklyn, New York before moving to South Carolina in 1865. In South Carolina, he led a large African Methodist Episcopal congregation and was regularly elected to state and local office. From the time he stood for election to the South Carolina

Constitutional Convention, he and his family "lived in constant fear at all times," their home guarded day and night by armed men. Among the 267 black delegates to the Constitutional Conventions of 1867–69, "at least one tenth . . . became victims of violence during Reconstruction, including seven [who were] murdered."

Robert B. Elliott, a black Representative from South Carolina and one of the five lawyers among Reconstruction's black Congressmen, argued that the Klan Act was justified both by the Federal government's duty to guarantee a republican form of government and its obligation to enforce the provisions of the first Article of the Fourteenth Amendment. To demonstrate that the Act was not disproportionate to the threat to liberty and citizenship in the former Confederacy, Elliot documented both "the declared purpose [of Southern Democrats] to defeat the ballot with the bullet and other coercive means, and . . . acts of organized lawlessness perpetrated pursuant to that purpose." Summarizing the Klan's reign of terror, he minced no words: "Every southern gentleman should blush with shame at this pitiless and cowardly persecution of the negro. . . . It is the custom . . . of Democratic journals to stigmatize the negroes of the South as being in a semi-barbarous condition; but pray tell me, who is the barbarian here?"

Joseph H. Rainey was a colleague of Elliott in the South Carolina delegation to the Forty-Second Congress, and, like both Elliott and Cain, a veteran of South Carolina's post-Civil War Constitutional Convention. When Rainey spoke to Congressional power to prosecute Klan violence, he confessed that he did not view the matter exclusively in terms of competing "interpretation[s] put upon the provisions of the Constitution." As Rainey urged passage of the Klan Act, he reflected a progressive stance typical of African-American political figures of his day—a stance grounded in the assumption that his country was progressing from a time during which racial supremacists compromised democratic values to a time of genuinely egalitarian democracy. As he once said to his colleagues in the House, segregation was "the remnant of the old proslavery spirit, which must eventually give place to more humane and elevating ideas." In this progressive vision, the Amendment Rainey had voted to ratify had to be sufficiently potent to end racial caste subordination:

> I stand upon the broad plane of right; I look to the urgent, the importunate demands of the present emergency; and while I am far from advocating any step not in harmony with that sacred law of our land, while I would not violate the lightest word of that chart which has so well guided us in the past, yet I desire that so broad and liberal a construction be placed upon its provisions as will insure protection to the humblest citizen, without regard to rank, creed, or color. Tell me nothing of a constitution which fails to shelter beneath its rightful power the people of a country!

After documenting Klan violence against black and white Republicans of South Carolina, Rainey concluded his speech with a vivid reminder of the dangers he and his colleagues faced as they took their places in the political sphere:

When myself and colleagues shall leave these Halls and turn our footsteps toward our southern homes we know not but that the assassin may await our coming, as marked for his vengeance. Should this befall, we would bid Congress and our country to remember that 'twas —

"Bloody treason flourish'd over us."

Be it as it may, we have resolved to be loyal and firm, "and if we perish, we perish!" I earnestly hope the bill will pass.

69 *Fordham Law Review* 1695, 1708–16.
Copyright © (2001) *Fordham Law Review.*
Reprinted with permission of the *Fordham Law Review* and
Peggy Cooper Davis.

W. David Wiseman, Jr.

White Crimes: American History and the Case for
African-American Reparations

Although it is shocking and horrifying to subject oneself to lynching accounts, it is only in so doing that we can gain a full understanding of the horrible truth and legacy of the lynching era. Indeed, Sam Holt's fate was not uncommonly brutal for that of a lynch victim during this period. A recently published article by Emma Coleman Jordan correctly pinpoints and debunks a number of mainstream myths about lynching in the American context. Lynchings were not secretive hate-group activities, but rather family social events. Lynching victims were not convicted rapists and murderers; in fact many lynching victims were never charged with any crime. Lynchings were not public executions whereby the people's justice was imposed on criminals, but torturous exhibitions of social domination. Oliver Cox, in *the Journal of Negro Education* defined lynching as "an act of homicidal aggression committed by one people against another through mob action for the purpose of suppressing either some tendency in the latter to rise from an accommodated position of subordination or for subjugating them further to some lower social status." In the United States this aggression was overwhelmingly committed by crowds of white Americans on African-American individuals or small groups. Between 1880 to 1940 thousands of African-American men and women were lynched throughout the United States, by predominantly white mobs committed to preserving an established cast system by any means necessary.

Far from being impartial public trials, lynchings were gruesome carnivals devoid of any legal validity. Indicative of their social significance, lynchings throughout this era took on an almost theatrical formula. Historian Elizabeth Hale identifies nine "acts" characteristic to the lynching paradigm. The crowd established a chase or jail attack to obtain the victim, identification of the accused by their supposed victim or a relative, public announcement of the upcoming lynching event via word-of-mouth, newspaper, or radio, selection of the site, mutilation of the victim often including emasculation, torture in an attempt to extract a confession and entertain the assembled, burning, hanging, or shooting the victim to finally kill him or her, followed by gathering of souvenirs, and display of the body as warning and trophy.

Toward the end of lynching's hay-day, Claude Neal met his fate in one of the most publicized and frenzied lynchings in history. Accused in the murder of Lola Cannidy of Marianna, Florida, Neal had been arrested and jailed when a posse of well-dressed White townsmen stormed the jail, and finding no significant obstruction from the jailer, kidnapped Neal and carried him to a hiding place where they planned the festival lynching that was to take place that evening. The afternoon local papers, associated press, and radio stations publicized the upcoming event like the circus coming to town: "Florida to Burn Negro at Stake: Sex Criminal Seized from Brewton Jail, Will be Mutilated, Set Afire in Extra-Legal Vengeance for Deed." The place of the intended lynching was also publicized, though not surprisingly local law enforcement took no steps to stop the blatantly illegal act. Neal was ultimately dismembered, castrated, forced to eat his genitals, burned with hot irons, choked almost to death and otherwise tortured in repetitive acts of ritualistic mutilization.

After his death, Neal's murderers carried his corpse to the Cannidy farm to allow the assembled crowd to extract their passions. An onlooker recorded: "In a few minutes several cars, one after the other, rolled into the yard. From one of them a rope jerked spasmodically as the car struck bumps and gullies. On the end of the rope was Neal dead." The witnesses Howard Kester questioned reported that members of the crowd kicked the corpse, drove cars over it, and "little children, some of them mere tots, who lived in the Greenwood neighborhood, waited with sharpened sticks for the return of Neal's body and that when it rolled in the dust on the road that awful night these little children drove their weapons deep into the flesh of the dead man." A day of white mob attacks on black residents and their homes commenced, and Claude Neal's naked, mutilated corpse was strung up on a tree at the town courthouse, not to be cut down and buried until the following morning.

> *White Crimes: American History and the*
> *Case for African-American Reparations* 1–4.
> (Unpublished manuscript on file with the author).
> Reprinted with permission of W. David Wiseman, Jr.

As this story and many other stories about lynchings indicate, when freed slaves began to exercise their rights as citizens, their former owners and supporters of the Confederacy used brutal means to dominate, intimidate, and restrict them. Such restriction often involved the use of violence, including murder by hysterical mobs. This practice of lynching, murder executed by lawless mobs, which continued into the twentieth century, became known in song as the producer of the South's most unusual agricultural product. The poem "Strange Fruit" by Lewis Allen is best known in its musical rendition by Billie Holiday, who sang it on a regular basis in her live performances throughout the 1940s and 50s. In 1999 *Time* magazine named it "song of the century," recognizing the significance of its message.

Lewis Allan

Strange Fruit

Southern trees
Bear a strange fruit
Blood on the leaves
And blood at the root
Black bodies swingin
In the Southern breeze
Strange fruit hanging
From the poplar trees.
Pastoral scene
Of the gallant South
The bulging eyes
And the twisted mouth
Scent of magnolia
Sweet and fresh.
Here is a fruit
For the crows to pluck
For the rain to gather
For the wind to suck
For the sun to rot
For the tree to drop
Here is a strange
And bitter crop.

Charles Lane

*The Day Freedom Died: The Colfax Massacre, the Supreme Court,
and the Betrayal of Reconstruction*

Cast of Characters

Colfax: The Republicans

William Smith Calhoun: Heir to Meredith Calhoun's gigantic Red River cotton and sugar operation; founder of Grant Parish.

Delos White: New York-born former Union officer and Freedmen's Bureau agent; first sheriff of Grant Parish, Murdered September 25, 1871.

William B. Phillips: Alabama-born white politician and first judge of Grant Parish.

William Ward: Negro ex-U.S. cavalry trooper; cashiered Louisiana state militia leader; state representative for Grant Parish.

Eli H. Flowers: Negro U.S. Army veteran from Pennsylvania; school-teacher in Grant Parish and close friend of William Ward.

Alexander Tillman: Negro political activist. Exercised command over courthouse defenders on April 13, 1873.

Henry Kearson: Leader of Grant Parish black political faction opposed to William Ward.

Daniel Wesley Shaw: White sheriff of Grant Parish in 1873. Summoned posse to courthouse.

Levi Allen; Negro commander at the Colfax courthouse on April 13, 1873.

Jesse McKinney: Negro farmer in Colfax; his murder triggered a rush of refugees toward the courthouse.

Benjamin Brim: Negro farmer shot and critically wounded on April 13, 1873; key prosecution witness in 1874 trials.

Levi Nelson: Survivor of Colfax Massacre and key prosecution witness.

Pinckney Chambers: Freedman; ordered by whites to set fire to courthouse on April 13, 1873.

Robert C. Register: Delaware-born white politician active in Grant Parish.

Colfax: White Supremacists

William J. "Bill" Cruikshank: Planter; former Grant Parish police juror; defendant in 1874 Colfax Massacre trials.

James W. Hadnot: Reputed leader of 1868 election violence against Negroes; would-be white supremacist state representative in 1873; killed April 13, 1873.

Christopher Columbus Nash: Ex-Confederate soldier, violent white supremacist and would-be sheriff of Grant Parish. Commanded white forces on April 13, 1873.

William R. Rutland: Kentucky-born lawyer who moved to Grant Parish and tried to secure local government for Fusionists in early 1873.

Wilson L. Richardson: Ex-Republican lawyer; helped Rutland's effort to install Fusionists in Grant Parish.

Johnnie Hadnot: Nephew of James W. Hadnot; Colfax Massacre defendant.

Jim and Jeff Yawn: Mississippi-born brothers accused of attacks on Negroes in Grant Parish in 1871.

Alfred C. Shelby: Sheriff of Grant Parish in 1871. Ignored pleas to arrest white terrorists and helped murder Republican leader Delos White.

Andrew Johnson: President of the United States, 1865–69.

Ulysses S. Grant: President of the United States, 1869–77.

Amos T. Akerman: Attorney General of the United States, 1870–72.

George H. Williams: Attorney General of the United States, 1872–75.

J. Madison Wells: Rapides Parish planter; white Unionist; Governor of Louisiana, 1866–67.

Henry Clay Warmoth: Republican governor of Louisiana, 1868–72; formed electoral alliance with white supremacists in 1872 election.

William Pitt Kellogg: Republican governor of Louisiana, 1873–77.

John D. McEnery: Fusionist claimant to governorship of Louisiana, 1872–73.

The Judges

Morrison R. Waite: Chief Justice of the United States, 1874–88; author of *United States v. Cruikshank*.

Joseph P. Bradley: Associate Justice of the Supreme Court, 1870–92.

Samuel F. Miller: Associate Justice of the Supreme Court, 1862–90; author of *The Slaughterhouse Cases*.

William B. Woods: U.S. Circuit Judge for the Fifth Circuit, 1870–80; presided over 1874 Colfax Massacre trials; Associate Justice of the Supreme Court, 1881–87.

Hugh Lennox Bond: Maryland abolitionist; Republican judge; presided over the Ku Klux Klan trials of 1871–72.

James R. Beckwith: U.S. Attorney in New Orleans, 1870–77. Investigated Colfax massacre and prosecuted the suspects.

Stephen B. Packard: U.S. Marshall for Louisiana during Reconstruction; chief of the state's Republican Party, 1872–77.

John J. Hoffman: Secret Service operative; conducted undercover investigation of Colfax Massacre.

Theodore W. DeKlyne: Deputy U.S. Marshal in Louisiana; led manhunt for Colfax Massacre suspects.

The Lawyers

Robert H. Marr: New Orleans-based white supremacist strategist and lead attorney for the defendants in the 1874 Colfax Massacre trials.

E. John Ellis: Defense attorney in the Colfax Massacre trials; popular white supremacist politician.

William R. Whitaker: Northern-born defense lawyer in Colfax Massacre trials.

The Soldiers

Philip H. Sheridan: Lieutenant General of the U.S. Army; cavalry hero of the Civil War; Reconstruction-era commander.

William H. Emory: Major General of the U.S. Army in command of troops in Louisiana 1872–75.

Jacob H. Smith and Arthur W. Allyn: Commanders of army company in Colfax after April 13, 1873.

At ten o'clock in the morning on March 4, 1873—Inauguration Day—the president and first lady emerged from the White House and headed for their carriage, a grand four-wheeled barouche pulled by four horses. Washington was draped in red-white-and-blue flags, pennants, and bunting; bold triumphal arches, fashioned out of intertwined flags from around the world, spanned the streets. Pennsylvania Avenue, swept clean, stretched like a bright ribbon to the Capitol, where, at noon, Ulysses Simpson Grant would take the oath of office for the second time.

A blue sky lifted spirits, but, as one reporter noted, "its sunny promise of Spring was contradicted by a fierce north wind that seemed the very breath of Winter." The gale roared at forty miles per hour; making four degrees above zero (the official temperature at dawn) feel like thirty below. Grant and his wife, Julia Dent Grant, pressed together on the leather bench of the open barouche as more than two hundred West Point cadets marched ahead of them in cloth dress gray uniforms. One of the shivering young men collapsed and had to be rushed indoors.

Thousands had journeyed to Washington from out of town; the hotels were sold out, even after filling their hallways and lobbies with extra beds. The visitors, not a few of whom employed whiskey against the cold, waited all along the avenue to salute the Civil War hero they had re-elected the previous November. No group cheered Grant more heartily than the Negro men and women who lined his route. These members of the audience could point with pride to the Lincoln Zouaves, a colored military unit from Baltimore, resplendent in their tasseled fezzes, baggy red pants, white leggings, and red-trimmed black jackets. Colored spectators sang along when musicians struck up "Marching Through Georgia," the Civil War ditty celebrating General William Tecumseh Sherman's drive from Atlanta to the sea. "Hurrah! Hurrah! The jubilee has come," they chorused. "We'll all join the Union and fight for Uncle Sam! Sherman's marching through Georgia."

Negro support for Grant was an expression of hope—the fervent belief that only Grant and his Republican Party, the party of Lincoln, could keep America's promise of equal rights for all men. Lincoln had been the first president to invite Negro participation in the inaugural pageant; Grant was the second. But for Grant, freedom and equal rights were matters of principle, not symbolism. More than even the most progressive-minded white Americans of his time, he rejected prejudice. "I don't know why a black skin may not cover a true heart as well as a white one," he said. He knew his soldiers had sacrificed not only to hold the nation together but also to make men free. He did not want those sacrifices to have been in vain.

The North might not have won the Civil War without Grant, and his contributions to the liberation of four million people of color had continued. But at first, Reconstruction was directed by Andrew Johnson, the Tennessee tailor who became vice president in March 1865, then succeeded Lincoln after his assassination a month later. Johnson had ceded control of Southern state legislatures to former Confederates, who in turn enacted Black Codes that all but reenslaved the freedmen. The codes contradicted the Thirteenth Amendment, which abolished slavery when ratified in December 1865, and Johnson faced growing resistance from a

"Radical" Republican Congress—culminating in the Reconstruction Act adopted on March 2, 1867, over Johnson's veto. The legislation required Southern states to repeal the Black Codes and recognize the political equality of Negroes—both by granting them the vote and by ratifying the Fourteenth Amendment, which, for the first time, made Negroes citizens with the same rights as white people.

Grant, too, resisted Johnson's version of Reconstruction. As the U.S. Army's top-ranking officer, Grant had encouraged his generals in the South to enforce the Reconstruction Act strictly, especially its provisions on voter registration, which barred unrepentant ex-rebel officials from voting. He occasionally supplied troops to put down violence against the freedmen and authorized the military to make arrests for racial offenses where civilian law enforcement had broken down. In 1868, when Johnson provoked his impeachment and near conviction in the Senate by trying to fire the Radical Republican secretary of war, Edwin Stanton, Grant backed Stanton. After his own successful campaign for president in 1868, Grant lobbied hard for the Fifteenth Amendment, which required states to let all eligible voters cast a ballot, regardless of race. It was controversial not only in the South but also in the North.

Negro voting rights were politically necessary for Grant and his party. Before the Civil War, the Republicans were exclusively a Northern party; but afterward, they would have to win elections in the south, state and federal, lest the Southern-based Democratic Party retake control of the federal government and reverse the Union victory. And the Republicans could not do that unless Negroes, their natural—and most numerous—constituency, were free to vote.

Grant's enthusiasm for the Fifteenth Amendment, though, went beyond expediency. When it won ratification, on February 3, 1870, he exulted that the people had completed the eradication of the notorious *Dred Scott* decision, handed down by the Supreme Court in 1857, which had decreed that neither slaves nor free men of color could be citizens of the United States. He called the amendment "a measure of grander importance than any other one act of the kind from the foundation of our free government to the present day."

And President Grant tackled the Ku Klux Klan. Southern freedmen lived in poverty after the civil war, but so did most of the region's whites, for whom economic misery was compounded by the shock and humiliation of defeat. Searching for companionship amid the devastation, some ex-Confederates formed clubs where they could drink, reminisce, and complain. One such group, founded in Pulaski, Tennessee, in late 1865, grew into a secret society with "dens" across the southeastern United States. By 1870, most white men in that part of the country either belonged to the organization or sympathized with it. "This is an institution of Chivalry, Humanity, Mercy and Patriotism, embodying in its genius and its principles all that is chivalric in conduct, noble in sentiment, generous in manhood and patriotic in purpose," the Ku Klux Klan declared. Its goals were to "protect the weak, innocent and defenseless," and "to protect and defend the constitution of the United States." Actually, the Klan aimed to terrorize all Negroes and the white Republicans who supported them.

In 1868, the Klan assassinated a Negro Republican congressman in Arkansas and three black Republican members of the South Carolina legislature—and in Camilla, Georgia, four hundred Klansmen, led by the sheriff, fired on a black election parade and hunted the countryside for those who fled, eventually killing or wounding more than twenty people. . . .

For Grant and the Republican Congress, tolerating the Klan was out of the question, but the Northern public was in no mood for a new war against it, either. The only alternative was to treat white terrorism as a crime—to investigate the Klan, identify its murderers, and try them in federal courts. The problem was that fighting crime had always been a state function; federal law enforcement was still an unfamiliar concept in mid-nineteenth-century America. Even many Republicans doubted its constitutionality.

Nevertheless, the Fourteenth Amendment said Congress had the power to enforce civil rights, and the Fifteenth Amendment said congress had the power to protect qualified Negro voters from discrimination. On May 31, 1870, invoking the new amendments as authority, Congress passed the Enforcement Act, which made racist terrorism a federal offense. To help put it into effect, Grant and Congress created the Department of Justice, with authority over all federal civil and criminal cases. Its first leader, Attorney General Amos T. Akerman, was a Republican who had been born in New Hampshire but settled in Georgia before the war. He loathed the Klan. "These combinations amount to war," he said, "and cannot be effectually crushed under any other theory."

When Klan violence persisted, Grant had sought more authority from Congress, personally lobbying for amendments known as the Ku Klux Klan Act. Enacted on April 20, 1871, the legislation imposed heavy new penalties and branded the Klan an "insurrection" and a "rebellion" against the United States. For the remainder of his first term, the president would be empowered to suspend the writ of habeas corpus anywhere state and local authorities had fallen under the sway of Klan "insurgents." In such cases, the president could use the army to round up Klansmen and present them for trial in federal court.

In October 1871, Grant had declared a "state of lawlessness" in nine Klan-dominated counties of South Carolina, dispatching troops who helped arrest hundreds of Klansmen and drive another two thousand out of state. Rank-and-file Klansmen who confessed and quit the organization were let go, but 220 leaders were indicted, of whom 53 pled guilty. . . .

Yet Grant's attack on the Klan triggered a political backlash which ultimately spread to the Republicans' own ranks. The reaction was strongest in the South, of course, but for many Northern whites, the struggle with the Klan simply underscored the fact that Reconstruction, for all its initial promise, had turned into a long, violent slog. As a post-war economic boom accelerated in the North and West, the press in those regions covered the South as if it were some troubled foreign land. Papers vividly described alleged corruption in Republican Southern state governments, which were reportedly controlled by northern adventurers who owed their offices to the manipulated votes of illiterate Negroes. More and more white North-erners agreed with their Southern brethren that colored men were unfit for citizen-ship—and that, in some sense, they and not the Klan were to blame for the mess the South had become.

In the 1872 election, Grant's main opponent had been an apostate Republican: Horace Greeley, the publisher of the *New York Tribune*. Greeley's so-called Liberal Republicans, who included such prominent senators as Carl Schurz of Missouri and Charles Sumner of Massachusetts, walked out of their old party under the ban-ner of "reform." Their main issue was corruption: namely, the shameless activities of railroad lobbyists and Grant's distribution of government favors to cronies and party hacks. Greeley's other campaign theme was the injustice of Grant's policy in the South. Once an ardent abolitionist, Greeley had soured on the freedmen. Their failure to prosper disappointed him. "They are an easy, worthless race, taking no thought for the morrow," he said. Backed by the Democrats, the party of the white South, Greeley ran on a platform that denounced Grant's Klan policy as "arbitrary measures" and called for "local self-government" in the ex-Confederacy.

Grant ultimately defeated Greeley easily. Thanks in part to the president's timely crackdown on the Klan, the November 1872 election was the most peaceful of Reconstruction, and a half-million Southern Negroes cast ballots printed with Grant's name. In Alabama, Republicans even took back the governorship and leg-islature. But the Liberal Republican challenge had heightened the contradictions within the Republican party. . . .

In May 1872, it enacted an amnesty law that restored full political rights to the vast majority of ex-Confederates who had been barred from office under a special provision of the Fourteenth Amendment. Only a few hundred top Confederate offi-cials remained unpardoned. This act energized Southern white politics with a fresh injection of leadership. Perhaps more important, it betrayed a hint of irresolution. . . .

Grant rose from Washington's chair and stood before the shivering multitude. He hated public speaking and dreaded it. Yet by his usual standard, Grant's second inaugural address was positively expansive. He began with a firm defense of his policy in the South: "The effects of the late civil strife have been to free the slave and make him a citizen. Yet he is not possessed of the civil rights which citizenship should carry with it. This is wrong, and should be corrected. To this correction I stand committed, so far as Executive influence can avail." Grant assured whites that "social equality is not a subject to be legislated upon." Yet, in issuing that disclaimer, he supported the freedmen. He would do nothing, he said, to "advance the social status of the colored man except to give him a fair chance to develop what there is good in him, give him access to the schools, and when he travels let him feel assured that his conduct will regulate the treatment and the fare he will receive."

As Grant knew, even this moderate agenda—an allusion to provisions of the civil rights bill which the Republicans had downplayed during the campaign—was anathema to Southern whites, and many Northern ones, too. Still, grant claimed that the old Confederacy was coming around. Answering those who charged him with despotism for using the military against the Klan, he noted that "the States lately at war with the General Government are now happily rehabilitated, and no Executive control is exercised in any one of them that would not be exercised in any other state in like circumstances. . . ."

As the president left the podium, he might have noticed the bright fezzes of the Lincoln Zouaves bobbing among the crowd. He surely spotted a group of Union veterans, standing beneath frayed flags emblazoned with the names of historic battles: Fredericksburg, Roanoke, Atlanta. The tattered banners flapped in the wind, emblems of Grant's glory days. That night, technicians illuminated the Capitol dome with the new technology known as electric light. Fireworks boomed and sparkled. The president and the first lady went off to the Inaugural Ball, which was being held near the Capitol in a hangarlike temporary pavilion made out of pine boards draped with muslin. Dignitaries gamely shuffled across the dance floor in their overcoats, as horn and tuba players squeaked out music through the frozen valves of their instruments. Dozens of birdcages dangled from the ceiling; the canaries inside were supposed to accompany the orchestra. But the cold was so intense that the birds shivered, tucked their beaks under their wings, and then began to drop dead.

The truth was that Grant had won a battle in November 1872—not a war. The victory he interpreted as personal vindication, and which gave his black supporters hope, kept Reconstruction alive. But it hardly extinguished all threats to the political rights of freedmen in the South or to the Republican-led national government that protected—and depended upon—the exercise of those rights. Rather, the conflicts with the Klan and the Liberal Republicans, though won by Grant, had exposed, and widened, the political and racial fissures menacing Reconstruction.

As of Inauguration Day 1873, only two of the eleven states that had once made up the Confederacy—black-majority South Carolina and Mississippi—remained under firm Republican control. Georgia, North Carolina, Tennessee, and Virginia had long since been "redeemed," thanks in part to Klan violence. Republicans governed Alabama, but Democrats had conceded the statehouse only under pressure from U.S. troops sent by Grant. In Texas and Florida, Democrats controlled all or part of the state legislatures. . . .

A cloudy evening was fading into darkness as the steamboat *Southwestern* approached the eastern bank of the Red River on April 13, 1873—Easter Sunday. The boat had reached a bend in the river where Captain Thornton Jacobs was certain he would find pine logs for his vessel's four hungry engines. The woodpile was about a mile north of Colfax, Louisiana.

The *Southwestern* carried its own gangplanks: a pair of long wooden walkways which jutted like alligator teeth from the vessel's bow. Jacob's crew had just lowered them when a young man charged out of the gloom onto the boat. Heavily armed, he was obviously agitated. Jacobs's crew looked him over, preparing for a fight; in these lawless times, robberies and gunplay plagued river traffic. Yet this gunman was not out to empty the safe or hijack the cotton. He wanted Jacobs to take the boat straight to Colfax.

The *Southwestern* was a 180-foot packet steamer; three years old and valued for insurance purposes at the princely sum of ten thousand dollars. Usually staked high with cotton and crowded with passengers, it ran the New Orleans-Shreveport route along the Mississippi and the Red, twice a week in high-water season. Captain Jacobs had a schedule to maintain, but the wise river hand, careful of both his customers and his cargo, granted the gunman's request. He maneuvered his 411-ton steamer away from shore as gritty clouds, smelling of resin, poured from its smokestacks. In the stern, a paddlewheel churned the water with a steady *slap-slap-slap*.

There had been a gun battle in Colfax, the new passenger claimed; two men lay seriously wounded and in need of the doctor in Alexandria, twenty-two miles downriver. Relaxing a bit, the man elaborated, even joked a little about all the killing. The fight had pitted white men against blacks. . . .

Though Colfax epitomized Southern languor, it was the capital of Grant Parish, a new jurisdiction carved out of two older ones in 1869. A courthouse had been fashioned from the stable of a cotton plantation; parish court met here, as did the five-man legislature, known in Louisiana's distinctive parlance as the *police jury*. The sessions could be contentious, because there was a lot at stake: taxes, the control of stray animals, the fate of cattle thieves. Congress, the president, and the state government could affect how life in Grant Parish was lived, but generally locals were more concerned with what happened inside that stuffy old brick building, where the judge and the sheriff wielded power over life and death.

It was raining when the *Southwestern* pulled into Colfax at about 8:00 p.m. The boat's passengers and crew went ashore over the gangplanks, moving gingerly through the dark and wet. In the damp grass, the men sensed something strange underfoot, as a lantern flickered and glowed, lasting ghostly shadows. Gradually, they realized they were stumbling over dead Negroes, most face down and shot almost to pieces. One of the men from the *Southwestern*, a Texan named R.G. Hill, counted eighteen. But the young gunman who had invited him and the others on this grisly tour boasted that was barely a quarter of the total.

Fewer than one hundred yards to the east, flames danced in the sky. The courthouse was on fire, and a terrible stench attacked the passengers' nostrils, making them ill. . . .

A crowd of armed white men milled around on the bank. Walking their guests back to the boat, they confirmed the story of a battle between the races. Three weeks earlier, they said, armed Negroes, stirred up by white Radical Republicans, seized the courthouse, throwing out the rightful officeholders: the white judge and sheriff. Then the Negroes installed defeated Republican candidates and rampaged around the town, driving out white families and robbing homes. They dug military-style trenches around the courthouse and even built a couple of cannon style trenches around the courthouse and even built a couple of cannon out of old pipe. Openly proclaiming their intention to kill all the white man, they boasted they would use white women to breed a new race.

In self-defense, the whites continued, men from Grant Parish and surrounding parishes had organized a posse, which had offered the Negroes a chance to lay down their arms. But the blacks refused, leaving the posse no choice: at midday, about eight hours ago, the whites counterattacked. Fighting was fierce; one white man died. The blacks retreated into the courthouse. The only option was to smoke them out, and a Negro was bribed to set fire to the building's wooden roof. At that point, the Negroes saved a white flag. Whites approached, but the blacks fired again, seriously wounding the two men now in need of a doctor, one of whom was James W. Hadnot, the Grant Parish state representative. After that treachery, the whites resumed firing and kept shooting at the Negroes even as they ran from the flames. They did not stop until they had killed or captured every black man they could find. . . .

James Beckwith did not know quite what to make of the article. As U.S. Attorney for Louisiana, he (along with the U.S. marshal) was one of the state's top two federal law enforcement officials. Under the Enforcement Act it was his job to prosecute political and racial violence. . . .

Louisiana had been seething for months. The discontent and rumbling originated in a split in the state Republican Party similar to the division in the national party. Governor Henry Clay Warmoth, elected as a Republican in 1868, defected to the Liberal Republicans in 1872 and, like the national Liberal Republicans, joined forces with the Democrats before the November 1872 election. The resulting "Fusionist" coalition in Louisiana nominated John McEnery, an ex-Confederate battalion commander, to succeed Warmoth. Opposing him on the Republican ticket was Vermont-born William Pitt Kellogg, one of Louisiana's U.S. senators.

Voting on November 4, 1872, was peaceful enough, but the vote count lit the spark for all that followed. A Fusionist-dominated state "returning board," which had absolute power to include or exclude votes based on whether it thought they had been validly cast, declared McEnery and his slate elected. But the board split, with a pro-Kellogg faction declaring the Republican governor. On January 13, 1873, each side staged a separate inauguration ceremony. The state could not pick a U.S. senator, since that required a vote by the legislature—and in Louisiana, two bodies, one dominated by Fusionists, the other by Republicans, claimed to be the legislature.

Kellogg had taken his case to a Republican federal judge in New Orleans, who ordered both Kellogg and the Republican-majority legislature to be seated. This gave the Republicans an advantage, creating a legal basis for federal military intervention on their behalf. President Grant authorized U.S. Army troops based near New Orleans to enforce the court's presumably valid order; and the lack of any alternative plan from Congress, Grant explained, he had no choice.

Congress adjourned March 4 without settling the crisis—whereupon the heavily armed Fusionists attempted to shoot their way into power. On March 5, about two hundred armed McEneryites marched on the Cabildo, an old Spanish colonial building on Jackson Square then serving as the state arsenal. But state police and militia loyal to Kellogg had been tipped off and used artillery to pin down the insurgents. U.S. Army troops then appeared under a white flag of truce and ordered the Fusionists to disperse. The next day Kellogg's militia arrested dozens of McEneryites, including the leaders of the Fusionist "legislature."

The victory gave Kellogg control over New Orleans, but the interior of the state remained tense. Both would-be governors had attempted to fill parish offices by issuing purported commissions to their respective parties' candidates for judge, sheriff, police, jury, and other posts. Even after the pro-McEnery coup failed, Fusionist and Republican claimants to these offices, brandishing their documents, struggled for power in towns and villages across rural Louisiana. One of those towns was Colfax.

The telegraph lines did not reach Colfax, so Beckwith and other officials in New Orleans followed the events in Grant Parish through reports from arriving steamboat travelers. These witnesses gave their accounts either in person or to the local newspapers: the pro-Kellogg *New Orleans Republican* and the pro-Fusionist *Times, Bee,* and *Daily Picayune*. Information was correspondingly sketchy and biased; by the second week of April, the two sides were publishing threats against each other in the papers. But from what could be determined, the parish had been in an uproar since late March, when Republican office seekers occupied the courthouse, supplanting fusionists who had previously purported to run the parish.

Finally, on April 12, a day before the massacre, Kellogg had dispatched two state militia colonels, Theodore W. DeKoyne and William Wright, who doubled as deputy U.S. marshals, to Colfax, a two-day journey from New Orleans. The two officers carried arrest warrants for fifty white men, presumed instigators of the trouble, as well as a set of commission papers for a new, compromise slate of parish officers. Kellogg apparently hoped that these threats and inducements would pacify the parish. Beckwith decided to wait for the Kellogg emissaries to come back before providing a report. "I will report in detail as soon as I have reliable information."

This was the sensible response of a good Yankee lawyer, which—despite the fact that he had spent most of his career in New Orleans—is what James Roswell Beckwith was. The oldest son of a prosperous farm couple, he was born in Cazenovia, New York, twenty miles south of Syracuse, on December 23, 1832. Cazenovia was part of upstate New York's "burned-over district," named for its successive evangelization by Mormons, Seventh Day Adventists, and spiritualists—and for the fiery feminism and abolitionism which flourished there. Madison County, which included Cazenovia, contained several stops on the Underground Railroad. Frederick Douglass spoke at Cazenovia's Free Church, as did antislavery politician Gerrit Smith and Quaker abolitionist Lucretia Mott. In late August 1850, as Congress debated the Fugitive Slave Law, which made it a federal offense to harbor escaped slaves, Douglass, Smith, and other abolitionist leaders assembled in a Cazenovia orchard. This "Cazenovia Convention" drew more than two thousand people— roughly half of Cazenovia's population. It is hard to imagine that James Beckwith, then seventeen years old, did not join the crowd, if only out of curiosity.

A few weeks after the Cazenovia Convention, Beckwith enrolled at the Methodist-run Oneida Conference Seminary, whose teachers drilled their students in antislavery doctrine. But after a year there, he asked his parents for permission to go to New York City and read law. He aspired to be a "real, thorough" lawyer—"the noblist work of science," as he put it. In 1854, he joined the New York bar. After finishing his legal training, Beckwith headed west, first to Michigan, where he served as a district attorney. Somewhere along the way, Beckwith found a kindred spirit in a young lady named Sarah Catherine Watrous, and, in 1860, they married. Catherine, as she liked to be called, came from Ashtabula County, Ohio, which was also antislavery territory. Of the twenty-one men who joined John Brown's ill-fated attempt to start a slave revolt by seizing the federal arsenal at Harpers Ferry, Virginia, in 1859, thirteen came from Ashtabula County. Catherine was a feminist novelist; her nom de plume, "Mrs. J. R. Beckwith," mocked the prevailing subordination of wives to husbands.

The Beckwiths moved to New Orleans, 1,400 miles from Cazenovia. . . .

The Beckwiths braved the odors and the heat and the sickness. But they must have hated the slave markets, where human beings were herded into "showrooms" or displayed from balconies. When buyers came to inspect, the slaves would be lined up by height, in clean clothes and ordered to smile, lest they receive a whipping. If a buyer was interested, the merchandise would be taken behind closed doors and stripped. White men chose "fancy girls"—attractive, light-skinned women—to be auctioned off in front of French Quarter hotels.

For all that, the Crescent City was a logical destination for a lawyer. New Orleans was the point from which the Deep South's cotton and sugar flowed into the world market; textiles, farm implements, machinery, and immigrants flowed in. Commerce created work for bankers, insurance underwriters, cotton brokers—and lawyers. By 1855, there were seventy-five law firms in town. New Orleans was cosmopolitan; the soft cadences of French could be heard in its parlors, along with quick phrases of Spanish and guttural German—the latter spoken by central European immigrants, including Jews numerous enough to support several synagogues. New Orleans was home to roughly twenty thousand free people of color, the largest such community in the United States. These mixed-race New Orleanians were craftsmen, professionals, and businessmen who could sometimes be found shopping in the slave markets themselves. The native white Creole elite were as haughty as any Bostonians. . . .

Union sympathizers mostly lay low until May 1, 1862, when federal land and naval forces took New Orleans and the "Florida Parishes" of southeastern Louisiana. The rebel state government fled north to Shreveport, and in 1864, after a period of military rule, the federals in New Orleans set up a "free state." The new regime gave the vote only to a limited number of colored men—those whom the legislature might later enfranchise by virtue of their Union military service, payment of taxes, or "intellectual fitness." This was essentially the policy Lincoln urged in his last public speech on April 11, 1865.

That was too much for John Wilkes Booth, who heard Lincoln and resolved to kill him. And it was too much for many white supremacists in Louisiana. Once the war was over, they reorganized the Democratic Party and announced in their 1865 platform, "We hold this to be a Government of white people, made and to be perpetuated for the exclusive benefit of the white race, and . . . that people of African descent cannot be considered as citizens of the United States, and that there can, in no event, nor under any circumstances, be any equality between white and other races."

In March 1865, J. Madison Wells, a Red River Valley planter with conservative racial attitudes who opposed Negro suffrage, became governor. Though a Unionist, he courted ex-Confederates and did not prevent white-dominated local governments from harshly restricting civil rights: In Opelousas, 150 miles west of New Orleans, Negroes could not live in the town or carry firearms. In December 1865, a newly elected Louisiana state legislature, dominated by ex-Confederates, decreed that Negro laborers must make contracts with plantation owners in the first ten days of January, after which they could not leave their places of work without a pass. Negroes who refused to work could be arrested and sent to labor on public works without pay. As Carl Schurz observed, such legislation was "a striking embodiment of the idea that, although the former owner has lost his individual right of property in the former slave, the blacks at large belong to the whites at large."

This was unacceptable even for Wells. He changed course and would call for Negro suffrage and disenfranchisement of ex-Confederates—assuming it was allowed to take place peacefully.

It was not. On the morning of July 30, city policemen, the vast majority of whom were ex-Confederate soldiers, mobbed the gun shops of New Orleans, buying up pistols. Along with like-minded white civilians, they gathered around the convention site: The Mechanics' Institute on Baronne Street. As a parade of Negro Republicans led by colored Union army veterans approached the fortress-like building, black marchers and white onlookers exchanged a few pistol shots. When the parade reached the Mechanics' Institute at about 12:23, white civilians pelted the Negro marchers with bricks, the marchers fought back with shovels and gunfire, and police commanders sounded the local fire bell, signaling the cops to attack the Negroes.

As Negroes fled into the building, police fired wildly after them and eventually battered down the doors. Negro men swinging chairs and sticks tried to drive the police and white vigilantes back but were quickly overcome. The police grabbed Anthony P. Dostie, a white Republican dentist who had given an incendiary speech at a mostly Negro rally the previous Friday, and shot him five times before running him through with a sword. The killing spilled over into the streets, where Negroes were chased and beaten to death or randomly dragged from streetcars and shot. When it was over, thirty-eight people were dead, all but four of them people of color; and 184 lay wounded.

James Beckwith witnessed the New Orleans massacre, as it was called. The awful spectacle, which Andrew Johnson blames on Republican agitation, helped convince

Northern voters that the president could not be trusted to run Reconstruction. They elected an overwhelmingly Republican Congress in November 1866, which then overturned Johnson's policies. By April 1868, thanks to new laws passed by Congress, Louisiana had a Republican-drafted constitution and a newly elected Republican state government.

But soon Beckwith and the rest of the state saw even more devastating bloodshed in the countryside. In the second half of 1868, white terrorists tried to prevent the Republicans from winning the November presidential election. Over three days in September, they killed some two hundred freedmen in St. Landry Parish. . . .

Later, a congressional investigation counted 1,081 political murders in Louisiana between April and November of 1868. The vast majority of the victims were Negroes. Some 135 people were shot and wounded; 507 were whipped, clubbed, threatened, or otherwise "outraged." The terror was so intense that the Republican Party stopped campaigning in the final week of the race and all but conceded the presidential vote to the Democrats.

By 1868, J. R. Beckwith, as he was known professionally, was an accomplished member of the bar with a deep voice and distinctive looks: high forehead, strong cleft chin, and bristling walrus mustache. He was still only in his mid-thirties and might easily have left Louisiana; New Orleans was bankrupt, its steamboat-based economy sagging under the competitive pressure of rail transportation. But he loved the city and the challenges of his work, which usually kept him up late. Though he disdained politics and the "tricksters" who used it "for themselves and their emoluments," something from Cazenovia still motivated him. His wife, Catherine, recognized it. In her novel, *The Winthrops*, she modeled the fictional lawyer Fred Houghton on her husband, depicting him as an "ardent champion for all the varieties of the oppressed, and [an] earnest rectifier of injustice."

That spirit appears to have prompted him to join Republican-led efforts to govern his adopted city and state. In 1870, Beckwith served as city attorney under Mayor Benjamin Franklin Flanders, a veteran Republican originally from New Hampshire. In late 1870, the U.S. attorney for Louisiana was found dead in his office, blood seeping from a gash in his throat. After some suspicions, the death was ruled a suicide. New Orleans Republican leaders urged President Grant to replace him with Beckwith. Probably the most important endorsement came from James F. Casey, customs collector for the port of New Orleans—and the husband of the first lady's sister. He telegraphed Grant that Beckwith was "a good lawyer, perfectly honest, conversant with the business of the office, [a] good Republican and worthy of the appointment." The president nominated Beckwith in December 1870, and by January 1871, Beckwith was the U.S. Attorney.

At 9:30 a.m. on Monday, April 14, 1873, the steamboat carrying Kellogg's two emissaries reached Pineville, which lay on the eastern side of the Red River, directly opposite Alexandria. Theodore W. DeKlyne and William Wright crossed over to Alexandria and rode north to Colfax, but the many dangerous-looking armed white men unnerved them and they stopped at Cotile, about fifteen miles south of Colfax, rather than risk arriving at the battleground after dark. The next morning, the two officers and their party resumed their ride over the reddish brown earth. DeKlyne had served briefly as a federal official helping Negroes in the Red River Valley after the war; he knew the area and its people. He could tell that something was not right: The Negroes' corn and sugarcane fields along the river seemed neglected. Many cabins looked abandoned.

Still after riding more than fourteen miles, the two colonels had seen nothing to confirm R. G. Hill's report, or the even bloodier rumors that they had heard since their arrival. Suddenly, about a third of a mile from the courthouse, DeKlyne and Wright spotted Negroes pulling something along the ground with a rope. Soon they could see that it was a board with a colored man sprawled on top, dirty and smeared with blood. Unconscious, he was bleeding from several gunshot wounds, but breathing. Two other black men lying nearby were not, however, After another two hundred yards, the officials came upon three more Negro bodies, shot in the head. From the point on, the grass was littered with dead.

DeKlyne and Wright were ex-Union officers, and they had seen combat and its aftermath. But many of these dead men had been shot in the backs of their heads or necks. Six men had been killed as they cowered under a porch. Another corpse was in a kneeling position, hands still clasped together, as if he had begged for his life. One lay dead with his throat slashed. Another, stripped to the waist, was charred. One man's head had been so badly beaten that no facial features were recognizable; next to him lay the broken stock of a double-barreled shotgun. All that remained of the courthouse were its singed brick walls, reeking of smoke. In the ruins, the officials found a human skeleton.

The most awful to gaze upon was Alexander Tillman, a politically active freedman whom DeKlyne knew from Republican Party meetings. His clothes were ripped off, and his body was punctured with deep stabs. His throat had a gash in it big enough to put a man's fist through, and his face was battered. Blood saturated the ground around him. . . .

Terrified, gasping out their story between sobs, they and several colored men told the two officials what had happened. In broad outline, the Negroes' version matched the whites' tale. Negro men, defending what they considered the Republican Party's rightful victory for local offices in the 1872 election, had gathered in the courthouse. When they saw groups of armed whites patrolling the area, they dug a semicircular trench around the courthouse. A large group of white men, mounted and armed with rifles, revolvers, and a small cannon, had arrived in Colfax Easter Sunday, demanding that the colored men surrender, stack their arms, and leave. When the Negroes refused, the whites attacked, setting the courthouse ablaze and gunning the colored men down like dogs.

In crucial particulars, however, the colored people's version of the story was new. There had been no riot and pillage by the Negroes, they said, but rather a fearful rush of families into Colfax when they heard that armed whites were approaching. That flow turned into a flood about a week before the battle, when word circulated that whites had killed a Negro farmer, Jesse McKinney, in cold blood. The whites had not bribed a colored man to torch the courthouse; they had kidnapped one and forced him to do it. The colored witnesses denied that anyone had fired under a flag of truce. And at night, after the *Southwestern* had left, the whites had marched their Negro prisoners away in pairs—and then shot each of them in the head.

DeKlyne and Wright quickly realized there was no use for Kellogg's papers. They were too late to prevent a slaughter and too few to investigate or punish it. All they could do was report back to New Orleans, which they reached on April 17. Their descriptions were crisp and understated, but their disgust filtered through. "We are informed," they wrote, "that since the fight, parties of armed men have been scouring the countryside, taking the mules and other property of the colored people."

Beckwith's initial skepticism turned to outrage as he read the officers' words. *You know workmen by the chips they leave.* If the death toll was correct, Colfax had been worse than the New Orleans Massacre. In fact, in the entire bloody epoch of Reconstruction, there might never have been a tragedy so great.

Beckwith sent an urgent telegram to Attorney General George H. Williams. "The details are horrible." Beckwith wrote.

> THE DEMOCRATS (WHITE) OF GRANT PARISH ATTEMPTED TO OUST THE INCUMBENT PARISH OFFICERS BY FORCE AND FAILED, THE SHERIFF PROTECTING THE OFFICERS WITH A COLORED POSSE. SEVERAL DAYS AFTERWARD RECRUITS FROM OTHER PARISHES, TO THE NUMBER OF 300, CAME TO THE ASSISTANCE OF THE ASSAILANTS, WHEN THEY DEMANDED THE SURRENDER OF THE COLORED PEOPLE. THIS WAS REFUSED. AN ATTACK WAS MADE AND THE NEGROES WERE DRIVEN INTO THE COURTHOUSE. THE COURTHOUSE WAS FIRED AND THE NEGROES SLAUGHTERED AS THEY LEFT THE BURNING BUILDING. AFTER RESISTANCE CEASED, SIXTY-FIVE NEGROES TERRIBLY MUTILATED WERE FOUND DEAD NEAR THE RUINS OF THE COURTHOUSE. THIRTY, KNOWN TO HAVE BEEN TAKEN PRISONERS, ARE SAID TO HAVE BEEN SHOT AFTER THE SURRENDER, AND THROWN IN THE RIVER. TWO OF THE ASSAILANTS WERE WOUNDED. THE SLAUGHTER IS GREATER THAN IN THE RIOT OF 1866 IN THIS CITY. WILL SEND REPORT BY MAIL.

The bloodbath in Colfax made headlines from Boston to Chicago. R.G. Hill thought that the incident would arouse Northern sympathy for the South. But this was not the case. "Jealousy of race and hatred of their former servants can alone explain the outbreak," the *Cincinnati Gazette* declared. "The passions that inspired that hellish agency of murder and persecution, the Ku Klux, are still alive," the *Philadelphia Press* warned. The *New York Times* likened the Louisiana incident to Fort Pillow, the notorious 1864 massacre in which General Nathan Bedford Forrest's confederate cavalry slaughtered hundreds of U.S. colored troops as they tried to flee or surrender. The *Times* demanded that President Grant act decisively to quell "that worst of human calamities, a war of races."

Attorney General Williams had previously considered the rumors of a massacre in Louisiana exaggerated. But after the report he scrambled to prove that this apparent resurgence of Klan-style terrorism would be stopped. He answered Beckwith swiftly, releasing his cable to the press: "You are instructed to make a thorough investigation of the affair in Grant Parish," Williams wrote, "and if you find that the laws of the United States have been violated, you will spare no pains or expense to cause the guilty parties to be arrested and punished."

Oscar Watson couldn't stop talking about the great gun battle in Colfax. A clerk in his father's Grant Parish country store, the twenty-two-year old had been too young for the Civil War. April 13, 1873, was his day of glory; he had stood side by side with rebel veterans, who called him a hero. In late May 1873, when Watson recounted the story to a visitor, he proudly displayed his two six-shooters — explaining that the first gun was the one he had used to kill Negroes at Colfax, and the second was a prize his comrades had given him for his bravery.

The visitor, John J. Hoffman, listened attentively. He told Oscar Watson and others he met in Grant Parish that he was from Cincinnati, by way of New Orleans. What he didn't say was that he worked for the U.S. government. He was an undercover agent of the Treasury Department's Secret Service Division, James R. Beckwith had sent him to infiltrate the white community and identify the Colfax killers. As far as Hoffman was concerned, Oscar Watson could brag all day if he wanted.

Hoffman was ranging far from the mission assigned to the Secret Service when it was established in July 1865: investigating counterfeiters. But the division was so good at its original job that the government expanded its responsibilities. Among these tasks was the infiltration of the Ku Klux Klan during the Grant administration's crackdown in 1871. Posing as traveling salesmen and itinerant laborers, Secret Service men penetrated the white terrorist movement from top to bottom. Their information led to hundreds of arrests and was one of the keys to Grant's success against the Klan in South Carolina.

> *The Day Freedom Died: The Colfax Massacre, The Supreme*
> *Court, and the Betrayal of Reconstruction* xv–xviii, 1–23.
> Copyright © (2008) Henry Holt and Company.
> Reprinted with permission of Henry Holt and Company and Charles Lane.

F. *United States v. Cruikshank*, 92 U.S. 542 (1875)

1. Facts

Chief Justice WAITE delivered the opinion of the Court.

This case comes here with a certificate by the judges of the Circuit Court for the District of Louisiana that they were divided in opinion upon a question which occurred at the hearing. It presents for our consideration an indictment containing sixteen counts, divided into two series of eight counts each, based upon sect. 6 of the Enforcement Act of May 31, 1870. That section is as follows: — 'That if two or more persons shall band or conspire together, or go in disguise upon the public highway, or upon the premises of another, with intent to violate any provision of this act, or to injure, oppress, threaten, or intimidate any citizen, with intent to prevent or hinder his free exercise and enjoyment of any right or privilege granted or secured to him by the constitution or laws of the United States, or because of his having exercised the same, such persons shall be held guilty of felony, and, on conviction thereof, shall be fined or imprisoned, or both, at the discretion of the court, — the fine not to exceed $5,000, and the imprisonment not to exceed ten years; and shall, moreover, be thereafter ineligible to, and disabled from holding, any office or place of honor, profit, or trust created by the constitution or laws of the United States.' 16 Stat. 141. The question certified arose upon a motion in arrest of judgment after a verdict of guilty generally upon the whole sixteen counts, and is stated to be, whether 'the said sixteen counts of said indictment are severally good and sufficient in law, and contain charges of criminal matter indictable under the laws of the United States.' The general charge in the first eight counts is that of 'banding,' and in the second eight, that of 'conspiring' together to injure, oppress, threaten, and intimidate Levi Nelson and Alexander Tillman, citizens of the United States, of African descent and persons of color, with the intent thereby to hinder and prevent them in their free exercise and enjoyment of rights and privileges 'granted and secured' to them 'in common with all other good citizens of the United States by the constitution and laws of the United States.' The offences provided for by the statute in question do not consist in the mere 'banding' or 'conspiring' of two or more persons together, but in their banding or conspiring with the intent, or for any of the purposes, specified. To bring this case under the operation of the statute, therefore, it must appear that the right, the enjoyment of which the conspirators intended to hinder or prevent, was one granted or secured by the constitution or laws of the United States. If it does not so appear, the criminal matter charged has not been made indictable by any act of Congress.

2. Opinion

We have in our political system a government of the United States and a government of each of the several States. Each one of these governments is distinct from the others, and each has citizens of its own who owe it allegiance, and whose rights, within its jurisdiction, it must protect. The same person may be at the same time a citizen of the United States and a citizen of a State, but his rights of citizenship under one of these governments will be different from those he has under the other. *Slaughter-House Cases,* 16 Wall. 74.

The government of the United States is one of delegated powers alone. Its authority is defined and limited by the Constitution. All powers not granted to it by that instrument are reserved to the States or the people. No rights can be acquired under the constitution or laws of the United States, except such as the government of the United States has the authority to grant or secure. All that cannot be so granted or secured are left under the protection of the States.

We now proceed to an examination of the indictment, to ascertain whether the several rights, which it is alleged the defendants intended to interfere with, are such as had been in law and in fact granted or secured by the constitution or laws of the United States. The first and ninth counts state the intent of the defendants to have been to hinder and prevent the citizens named in the free exercise and enjoyment of their 'lawful right and privilege to peaceably assemble together with each other and with other citizens of the United States for a peaceful and lawful purpose.' The right of the people peaceably to assemble for lawful purposes existed long before the adoption of the Constitution of the United States. In fact, it is, and always has been, one of the attributes of citizenship under a free government. It 'derives its source,' to use the language of Chief Justice Marshall, in *Gibbons v. Ogden*, 9 Wheat. 211, 'from those laws whose authority is acknowledged by civilized man throughout the world.' It is found wherever civilization exists. It was not, therefore, a right granted to the people by the Constitution. The government of the United States when established found it in existence, with the obligation on the part of the States to afford it protection. As no direct power over it was granted to Congress, it remains, according to the ruling in *Gibbons v. Ogden*, id. 203, subject to State jurisdiction. Only such existing rights were committed by the people to the protection of Congress as came within the general scope of the authority granted to the national government.

The First Amendment to the Constitution prohibits Congress from abridging 'the right of the people to assemble and to petition the government for a redress of grievances.' This, like the other amendments proposed and adopted at the same time, was not intended to limit the powers of the State governments in respect to their own citizens, but to operate upon the National government alone. *Barron v. The City of Baltimore*, 7 Pet. 250; *Lessee of Livingston v. Moore*, id. 551; *Fox v. Ohio*, 5 How. 434; *Smith v. Maryland*, 18 id. 76; *Withers v. Buckley*, 20 id. 90; *Pervear v. The Commonwealth*, 5 Wall. 479; *Twitchell v. The Commonwealth*, 7 id. 321; *Edwards v. Elliott*, 21 id. 557. It is now too late to question the correctness of this construction. As was said by the late Chief Justice, in *Twitchell v. The Commonwealth*, 7 Wall. 325, 'the scope and application of these amendments are no longer subjects of discussion here.' They left the authority of the States just where they found it, and added nothing to the already existing powers of the United States.

The particular amendment now under consideration assumes the existence of the right of the people to assemble for lawful purposes, and protects it against encroachment by Congress. The right was not created by the amendment; neither was its continuance guaranteed, except as against congressional interference. For their protection in its enjoyment, therefore, the people must look to the States. The power for that purpose was originally placed there, and it has never been surrendered to the United States.

The right of the people peaceably to assemble for the purpose of petitioning Congress for a redress of grievances, or for any thing else connected with the powers or the duties of the national government, is an attribute of national citizenship, and, as such, under the protection of, and guaranteed by, the United States. The very idea of a government, republican in form, implies a right on the part of its citizens to meet peaceably for consultation in respect to public affairs and to petition for a redress of grievances. If it had been alleged in these counts that the object of the defendants was to prevent a meeting for such a purpose, the case would have been within the statute, and within the scope of the sovereignty of the United States. Such, however, is not the case. The offence, as stated in the indictment, will be made out, if it be shown that the object of the conspiracy was to prevent a meeting for any lawful purpose whatever.

The second and tenth counts are equally defective. The right there specified is that of 'bearing arms for a lawful purpose.' This is not a right granted by the Constitution. Neither is it in any manner dependent upon that instrument for its existence. The second amendment declares that it shall not be infringed; but this, as has been seen, means no more than that it shall not be infringed by Congress. This is one of the amendments that has no other effect than to restrict the powers of the national government, leaving the people to look for their protection against any violation by their fellow-citizens of the rights it recognizes, to what is called, in *The City of New York v. Miln*, 11 Pet. 139, the 'powers which relate to merely municipal legislation, or what was, perhaps, more properly called internal police,' 'not surrendered or restrained' by the Constitution of the United States.

The third and eleventh counts are even more objectionable. They charge the intent to have been to deprive the citizens named, they being in Louisiana, 'of their respective several lives and liberty of person without due process of law.' This is nothing else than alleging a conspiracy to falsely imprison or murder citizens of the United States, being within the territorial jurisdiction of the State of Louisiana. The rights of life and personal liberty are natural rights of man. 'To secure these rights,' says the Declaration of Independence, 'governments are instituted among men, deriving their just powers from the consent of the governed.' The very highest duty of the States, when they entered into the Union under the Constitution, was to protect all persons within their boundaries in the enjoyment of these 'unalienable rights with which they were endowed by their Creator.' Sovereignty, for this purpose, rests alone with the States. It is no more the duty or within the power of the United States to punish for a conspiracy to falsely imprison or murder within a State, than it would be to punish for false imprisonment or murder itself.

The Fourteenth Amendment prohibits a State from depriving any person of life, liberty, or property, without due process of law; but this adds nothing to the rights of one citizen as against another. It simply furnishes an additional guaranty against any encroachment by the States upon the fundamental rights which belong to every citizen as a member of society. As was said by Justice Johnson, in *Bank of Columbia v. Okely*, 4 Wheat. 244, it secures 'the individual from the arbitrary exercise of the powers of government, unrestrained by the established principles of private rights and distributive justice.' These counts in the indictment do not call for the exercise of any of the powers conferred by this provision in the amendment.

3. Holding

We are, therefore, of the opinion that the first, second, third, fourth, sixth, seventh, ninth, tenth, eleventh, twelfth, fourteenth, and fifteenth counts do not contain charges of a criminal nature made indictable under the laws of the United States, and that consequently they are not good and sufficient in law. They do not show that it was the intent of the defendants, by their conspiracy, to hinder or prevent the enjoyment of any right granted or secured by the Constitution.

G. Commentary on *Cruikshank*

The Supreme Court invalidated the convictions on the basis that Congress did not have the enumerated power to criminalize private violence. Such convictions were invalid, even when the violence was motivated by the victims' race, even when the violence was designed to prevent blacks from exercising their constitutional rights, and even when the state government did nothing to punish the offenders.

Derrick Bell

Race, Racism and American Law (5th Edition)

In *United States v. Cruikshank*, the Court held that the deprivation of life, liberty, or property without due process was not covered by the statute if the deprivation was the result of acts of private individuals. "It is no more the duty or within the power of the United States to punish for a conspiracy to falsely imprison or murder within a State, than it would be to punish for false imprisonment or murder itself." In other words, Congress could not constitutionally reach interference with the basic rights secured by the fourteenth Amendment unless there was state action. Only the narrow exception of "positive" federal rights could be protected against private interference. "The rights of citizens to vote in congressional elections, for instance, may obviously be protected by Congress from individual as well as from state interference. On the other hand, we have consistently held that the category of rights which Congress may constitutionally protect from interference by private persons excluded those rights which the Constitution merely guarantees from interference by a State."

In a final refusal to acknowledge as justices of the Supreme Court what they and all others of the time knew as men, the Court dismissed the charge that defendants had intended to prevent and hinder citizens of African descent and persons of color in the free exercise and enjoyment of their right and privileges under state and federal law, which rights and privileges are enjoyed by white persons. The Court responded, "There is no allegation that this was done because of the race or color of the persons conspired against." The Court reiterated that the Fourteenth

Amendment meant that the federal government had the obligation to ensure that the states did not interfere with constitutional rights, but that the states and not the federal government had the duty to intercede when one individual interfered with the constitutional rights of others.

In summary, the Court limited the facially broad provisions of §242 by requiring state action, except for a few limited exceptions, and the state action requirement was further limited by the interpretation given to "under color of law" in both §§241 and 242, that the wrongdoer was only covered if he acted in accordance with improper state law. Violation of state law in effect could immunize the criminal from federal prosecution. Given these severe judicially imposed limits, it is not surprising that few prosecutions were brought under either section.

Race, Racism and American Law 375.
Copyright © (2004) Aspen Publishers.
Reprinted with permission of Aspen Publishers and Derrick A. Bell.

The *Cruikshank* case continued the approach the Supreme Court had adopted in the *Slaughterhouse Cases*, narrowing the scope and coverage of the Reconstruction Amendments. For example, the Court declared that the Fifteenth Amendment guaranteed citizens not the right to vote but only a right not to be discriminated against in voting on account of race. Up until the Civil War, the Supreme Court had determined that the limitations contained in the Bill of Rights were not applicable to the activities of state and local governments. In the *Slaughterhouse Cases* and in *Cruikshank*, the argument was made that the guarantees of individual rights contained in the Bill of Rights were made applicable to the states by the Fourteenth Amendment. The Supreme Court rejected this argument and gave a restrictive meaning to the Privileges or Immunities Clause of the Fourteenth Amendment. These decisions diluted the Fourteenth Amendment, the most likely of the Reconstruction Amendments to protect and extend the guarantees of the Bill of Rights. The Supreme Court undercut the states' obligation to protect individual rights, which had been guaranteed by the Bill of Rights. Unfortunately, for most blacks residing in southern states, the federal government was the only entity likely to enforce their legal rights as citizens.

In response, many blacks established self-sustaining black towns in an attempt to minimize contact and reliance on state government. Allensworth, California was one such place. Started by Colonel Allen Allensworth in 1906 after he retired as an Army chaplain, the thriving community grew to over 400 residents and included a bakery, lumber yard, restaurant, livery stable, and blacksmith shop. Denied participation in a water cooperative agreement by neighboring towns, Allensworth was abandoned in 1918.

H. Background on *The Civil Rights Cases*

Not only were blacks who attempted to exercise political rights in southern states at risk of bodily harm from private individuals, throughout the entire country they were subject to exclusion in social activities by some businesses open to the general public. The most frequently restricted activities included going to theaters, hotels, and amusement parks.

I. *The Civil Rights Cases,* 109 U.S. 3 (1883)

1. Facts

Justice BRADLEY delivered the opinion of the Court.

The Civil Rights Cases involved five separate suits, (consolidated on appeal), which were originally filed pursuant to claims made under the Civil Rights Act of March 1, 1875 (18 St. 335). Two cases had been initiated as criminal prosecutions against owners of an inn or hotel in Kansas and Missouri for denying "persons of color" accommodations and privileges. One criminal prosecution in San Francisco was against the Maguire theater for "refusing a colored person a seat in the dress circle." Another criminal prosecution in New York involved the denial of "the full enjoyment of the accommodations" of the Grand Opera House by reason of race and color or previous condition of servitude. The fifth case, from Tennessee, against the Memphis and Charleston Railroad Company, was a civil suit where a husband and wife had sought the statutory civil penalty of $500 under the second section of the act because the wife had been denied the right to ride in the ladies car "for the reason . . . that she was a person of African descent." In this Tennessee case, the trial judge had "allowed evidence to go to the jury tending to show that the conductor had reason to suspect that the plaintiff, the wife, was an improper person because she was in company with a young man whom he supposed to be a white man, and on that account inferred that there was some improper connection between them." The judge charged the jury, in substance, that if this was the conductor's *bona fide* reason for excluding the woman from the car, they might take it into consideration on the question of the liability of the company. Plaintiffs, who lost the case in the trial court, filed exceptions to the trial judge's charge. Some of the cases reached the Supreme Court because of "certificates of division of opinion between the judges below as to the constitutionality of the first and second sections of the Civil Rights Act of 1875."

2. Opinion

a. Prohibiting State Laws

It is obvious that the primary and important question in all the cases is the constitutionality of the law; for if the law is unconstitutional none of the prosecutions can stand.

The sections of the law referred to provide as follows:

> Section 1. That all persons within the jurisdiction of the United States shall be entitled to the full and equal enjoyment of the accommodations, advantages, facilities, and privileges of inns, public conveyances on land or water,

theaters, and other places of public amusement; subject only to the conditions and limitations established by law, and applicable alike to citizens of every race and color, regardless of any previous condition of servitude.

Section 2. That any person who shall violate the foregoing section by denying to any citizen, except for reasons by law applicable to citizens of every race and color, and regardless of any previous condition of servitude, the full enjoyment of any of the accommodations, advantages, facilities, or privileges in said section enumerated, or by aiding or inciting such denial, shall, for every such offense, forfeit and pay the sum of $500 to the person aggrieved thereby, to be recovered in an action of debt, with full costs; and shall, also, for every such offense, be deemed guilty of a misdemeanor, and upon conviction thereof shall be fined not less than $500 nor more than $1,000, or shall be imprisoned not less than 30 days nor more than one year: Provided, that all persons may elect to sue for the penalty aforesaid, or to proceed under their rights at common law and by state statutes; and having so elected to proceed in the one mode or the other, their right to proceed in the other jurisdiction shall be barred. But this provision shall not apply to criminal proceedings, either under this act or the criminal law of any state: And provided, further, that a judgment for the penalty in favor of the party aggrieved, or a judgment upon an indictment, shall be a bar to either prosecution respectively.

Are these sections constitutional? The first section, which is the principal one, cannot be fairly understood without attending to the last clause, which qualifies the preceding part. The essence of the law is not to declare broadly that all persons shall be entitled to the full and equal enjoyment of the accommodations, advantages, facilities, and privileges of inns, public conveyances, and theaters; but that such enjoyment shall not be subject to any conditions applicable only to citizens of a particular race or color, or who had been in a previous condition of servitude. In other words, it is the purpose of the law to declare that, in the enjoyment of the accommodations and privileges of inns, public conveyances, theaters, and other places of public amusement, no distinction shall be made between citizens of different race or color, or between those who have, and those who have not, been slaves. . . .

The first section of the Fourteenth Amendment,—which is the one relied on,—after declaring who shall be citizens of the United States, and of the several states, is prohibitory in its character, and prohibitory upon the states. It declares that 'no state shall make or enforce any law which shall abridge the privileges or immunities of citizens of the United States; nor shall any state deprive any person of life, liberty, or property without due process of law; nor deny to any person within its jurisdiction the equal protection of the laws.' It is state action of a particular character that is prohibited. Individual invasion of individual rights is not the subject-matter of the amendment. It has a deeper and broader scope. It nullifies and makes void all state legislation, and state action of every kind, which impairs the privileges and immunities of citizens of the United States, or which injures them in life, liberty, or property without due process of law, or which denies to any of them the equal protection of the laws. It not only does this, but, in order that the national will, thus declared, may not be a mere *brutum fulmen*, the last section of the amendment invests congress with power to enforce it by appropriate legislation. To enforce what? To enforce the prohibition. To adopt appropriate legislation for correcting the effects of such prohibited state law and state acts, and thus to render them effectually null, void, and innocuous. This is the legislative power conferred upon congress, and this is the whole of it. It does not invest congress with power to legislate upon subjects which are within the domain of state legislation; but to provide modes of relief against state legislation, or state action, of the kind referred to. It does not authorize congress to create a code of municipal law for the regulation of private rights; but to provide modes of redress against the operation of state laws, and the action of state officers, executive or judicial, when these are subversive of the fundamental rights specified in the amendment. Positive rights and privileges are undoubtedly secured by the Fourteenth Amendment; but they are secured by way of prohibition against state laws and state proceedings affecting those rights and privileges, and by power given to congress to legislate for the purpose of carrying such prohibition into effect; and such legislation must necessarily be predicated upon such supposed state laws or state proceedings, and be directed to the correction of their operation and effect. A quite full discussion of this aspect of the amendment may be found in *U. S. v. Cruikshank*, 92 U. S. 542; *Virginia v. Rives*, 100 U. S. 313, and *Ex parte Virginia*, Id. 339. . . .

b. State Law and State Action

And so in the present case, until some state law has been passed, or some state action through its officers or agents has been taken, adverse to the rights of citizens sought to be protected by the Fourteenth Amendment, no legislation of the United States under said amendment, nor any proceeding under such legislation, can be called into activity, for the prohibitions of the amendment are against state laws and acts done under state authority. . . . The legislation which congress is authorized to adopt in this behalf is not general legislation upon the rights of the citizen, but corrective legislation; that is, such as may be necessary and proper for counteracting such laws as the states may adopt or enforce, and which by the amendment they are prohibited from making or enforcing, or such acts and proceedings as the states may commit or take, and which by the amendment they are prohibited from committing or taking. It is not necessary for us to state, if we could, what legislation would be proper for congress to adopt. It is sufficient for us to examine whether the law in question is of that character.

c. Scope and Impact of the 1875 Civil Rights Act

An inspection of the law shows that it makes no reference whatever to any supposed or apprehended violation of the Fourteenth Amendment on the part of the states. It is not predicated on any such view. It proceeds *ex directo* to declare that certain acts committed by individuals shall be deemed offenses, and shall be prosecuted and punished by proceedings in the courts of the United States. It does not profess to be corrective of any constitutional wrong committed by the states; it does not make its operation to depend upon any such wrong committed. It applies equally to cases arising in states which have the justest laws respecting the personal rights of citizens, and whose authorities are ever ready to enforce such laws as to those which arise in states that may have violated the prohibition of the amendment. In other words, it steps into the domain of local jurisprudence, and lays down rules for the conduct of individuals, and imposes sanctions for the enforcement of those rules, without referring in any manner to any supposed action of the state or its authorities. . . .

We have not overlooked the fact that the fourth section of the act now under consideration has been held by this court to be constitutional. That section declares "that no citizen, possessing all other qualifications which are or may be prescribed by law, shall be disqualified for service as grand or petit juror in any court of the United States, or of any state, on account of race, color, or previous condition of servitude; and any officer or other person charged with any duty in the selection or summoning of jurors who shall exclude or fail to summon any citizen for the cause aforesaid, shall, on conviction thereof, be deemed guilty of a misdemeanor, and be fined not more than five thousand dollars." In *Ex parte Virginia*, 100 U. S. 339, it was held that an indictment against a state officer under this section for excluding persons of color from the jury list is sustainable. But a moment's attention to its terms will show that the section is entirely corrective in its character. Disqualifications for service on juries are only created by the law, and the first part of the section is aimed at certain disqualifying laws, namely, those which make mere race or color a disqualification; and the second clause is directed against those who, assuming to use the authority of the state government, carry into effect such a rule of disqualification. In the Virginia case, the state, through its officer, enforced a rule of disqualification which the law was intended to abrogate and counteract. Whether the statute-book of the state actually laid down any such rule of disqualification or not, the state, through its officer, enforced such a rule; and it is against such state action, through its officers and agents, that the last clause of the section is directed. This aspect of the law was deemed sufficient to divest it of any unconstitutional character, and makes it differ widely from the first and second sections of the same act which we are now considering.

These sections, in the objectionable features before referred to, are different also from the law ordinarily called the "Civil Rights Bill," originally passed April 9, 1866, and re-enacted with some modifications in sections 16, 17, 18, of the enforcement act, passed May 31, 1870. That law, as re-enacted, after declaring that all persons within the jurisdiction of the United States shall have the same right in every state and territory to make and enforce contracts, to sue, be parties, give evidence, and to the full and equal benefit of all laws and proceedings for the security of persons and property as is enjoyed by white citizens, and shall be subject to like punishment, pains, penalties, taxes, licenses, and exactions of every kind, and none other, any law, statute, ordinance, regulation, or custom to the contrary notwithstanding, proceeds to enact that any person who, under color of any law, statute, ordinance, regulation, or custom, shall subject, or cause to be subjected, any inhabitant of any state or territory to the deprivation of any rights secured or protected by the preceding section, (above quoted,) or to different punishment, pains, or penalties, on account of such person being an alien, or by reason of his color or race, than is prescribed for the punishment of citizens, shall be deemed guilty of a misdemeanor, and subject to fine and imprisonment as specified in the act. This law is clearly corrective in its character, intended to counteract and furnish redress against state laws and proceedings, and customs having the force of law, which sanction the wrongful acts specified. . . .

d. Private Action

In this connection it is proper to state that civil rights, such as are guaranteed by the constitution against state aggression, cannot be impaired by the wrongful acts of individuals, unsupported by state authority in the shape of laws, customs, or judicial or executive proceedings. The wrongful act of an individual, unsupported by any such authority, is simply a private wrong, or a crime of that individual; an invasion of the rights of the injured party, it is true, whether they affect his person, his property, or his reputation; but if not sanctioned in some way by the state, or not done under state authority, his rights remain in full force, and may presumably be vindicated by resort to the laws of the state for redress. An individual cannot deprive a man of his right to vote, to hold property, to buy and to sell, to sue in the courts, or to be a witness or a juror; he may, by force or fraud, interfere with the enjoyment of the right in a particular case; he may commit an assault against the person, or commit murder, or use ruffian violence at the polls, or slander the good name of a fellow-citizen; but unless protected in these wrongful acts by some shield of state law or state authority, he cannot destroy or injure the right; he will only render himself amenable to satisfaction or punishment; and amenable therefor to the laws of the state where the wrongful acts are committed. Hence, in all those cases where the constitution seeks to protect the rights of the citizen against discriminative and unjust laws of the state by prohibiting such laws, it is not individual offenses, but abrogation and denial of rights, which it denounces, and for which it clothes the Congress with power to provide a remedy. This abrogation and denial of rights, for which the states alone were or could be responsible, was the great seminal and fundamental wrong which was intended to be remedied. And the remedy to be provided must necessarily be predicated upon that wrong. It must assume that in the cases provided for, the evil or wrong actually committed rests upon some state law or state authority for its excuse and perpetration.

e. Exceptions and Limitations

Of course, these remarks do not apply to those cases in which Congress is clothed with direct and plenary powers of legislation over the whole subject, accompanied with an express or implied denial of such power to the states, as in the regulation of commerce with foreign nations, among the several states, and with the Indian tribes, the coining of money, the establishment of post-offices and post-roads, the declaring of war, etc. In these cases Congress has power to pass laws for regulating the subjects specified, in every detail, and the conduct and transactions of individuals respect thereof. But where a subject is not submitted to the general legislative power of congress, but is only submitted thereto for the purpose of rendering effective some prohibition against particular state legislation or state action in reference to that subject, the power given is limited by its object, and any legislation by Congress in the matter must necessarily be corrective in its character, adapted to counteract and redress the operation of such prohibited state laws or proceedings of state officers.

If the principles of interpretation which we have laid down are correct, as we deem them to be,—and they are in accord with the principles laid down in the cases before referred to, as well as in the recent case of *U. S. v. Harris*, decided at the last term of this court, [1 Sup. Ct. Rep. 601]—it is clear that the law in question cannot be sustained by any grant of legislative power made to Congress by the Fourteenth Amendment. That amendment prohibits the states from denying to any person the equal protection of the laws, and declares that Congress shall have power to enforce, by appropriate legislation, the provisions of the amendment. The law in question, without any reference to adverse state legislation on the subject, declares that all persons shall be entitled to equal accommodation and privileges of inns, public conveyances, and places of public amusement, and imposes a penalty upon any individual who shall deny to any citizen such equal accommodations and privileges. This is not corrective legislation; it is primary and direct; it takes immediate and absolute possession of the subject of the right of admission to inns, public conveyances, and places of amusement. It supersedes and displaces state legislation on the same subject, or only allows it permissive force. It ignores such legislation, and assumes that the matter is one that belongs to the domain of national regulation. Whether it would not have been a more effective protection of the rights of citizens to have clothed Congress with plenary power over the whole subject, is not now the question. What we have to decide is, whether such plenary power has been conferred upon Congress by the Fourteenth Amendment, and, in our judgment, it has not. . . .

f. The Thirteenth Amendment

But the power of Congress to adopt direct and primary, as distinguished from corrective, legislation on the subject in hand, is sought, in the second place, from the Thirteenth Amendment, which abolishes slavery. This amendment declares "that neither slavery, nor involuntary servitude, except as a punishment for crime, whereof the party shall have been duly convicted, shall exist within the United States, or any place subject to their jurisdiction;" and it gives Congress power to enforce the amendment by appropriate legislation.

This amendment, as well as the fourteenth, is undoubtedly self-executing without any ancillary legislation, so far as its terms are applicable to any existing state of circumstances. By its own unaided force and effect it abolished slavery, and established universal freedom. Still, legislation may be necessary and proper to meet all the various cases and circumstances to be affected by it, and to prescribe proper modes of redress for its violation in letter or spirit. And such legislation may be primary and direct in its character; for the amendment is not a mere prohibition of state laws establishing or upholding slavery, but an absolute declaration that slavery or involuntary servitude shall not exist in any part of the United States.

It is true that slavery cannot exist without law any more than property in lands and goods can exist without law, and therefore the Thirteenth Amendment may be regarded as nullifying all state laws which establish or uphold slavery. But it has a reflex character also, establishing and decreeing universal civil and political freedom throughout the United States; and it is assumed that the power vested in Congress to enforce the article by appropriate legislation, clothes congress with power to pass all laws necessary and proper for abolishing all badges and incidents of slavery in the United States; and upon this assumption it is claimed that this is sufficient authority for declaring by law that all persons shall have equal accommodations and privileges in all inns, public conveyances, and places of public amusement; the argument being that the denial of such equal accommodations and privileges is in itself a subjection to a species of servitude within the meaning of the amendment. Conceding the major proposition to be true, that Congress has a right to enact all necessary and proper laws for the obliteration and prevention of slavery, with all its badges and incidents, is the minor proposition also true, that the denial to any person of admission to the accommodations and privileges of an inn, a public conveyance, or a theater, does subject that person to any form of servitude, or tend to fasten upon him any badge of slavery? If it does not, then power to pass the law is not found in the Thirteenth Amendment.

In a very able and learned presentation of the cognate question as to the extent of the rights, privileges, and immunities of citizens which cannot rightfully be abridged by state laws under the Fourteenth Amendment, made in a former case, a long list of burdens and disabilities of a servile character, incident to feudal vassalage in France, and which were abolished by the decrees of the national assembly, was presented for the purpose of showing that all inequalities and observances exacted by one man from another, were servitudes or badges of slavery, which a great nation, in its effort to establish universal liberty, made haste to wipe out and destroy. But these were servitudes imposed by the old law, or by long custom which had the force of law, and exacted by one man from another without the latter's consent. Should any such servitudes be imposed by a state law, there can be no doubt that the law would be repugnant to the Fourteenth, no less than to the Thirteenth, Amendment; nor any greater doubt that Congress has adequate power to forbid any such servitude from being exacted.

But is there any similarity between such servitudes and a denial by the owner of an inn, a public conveyance, or a theater, of its accommodations and privileges to an individual, even through the denial be founded on the race or color of that individual? Where does any slavery or servitude, or badge of either, arise from such an act of denial? Whether it might not be a denial of a right which, if sanctioned by the state law, would be obnoxious to the prohibitions of the Fourteenth Amendment, is another question. But what has it to do with the question of slavery? It may be that by the Black Code, (as it was called,) in the times when slavery prevailed, the proprietors of inns and public conveyances were forbidden to receive persons of the African race, because it might assist slaves to escape from the control of their masters. This was merely a means of preventing such escapes, and was no part of the servitude itself. A law of that kind could not have any such object now, however justly it might be deemed an invasion of the party's legal right as a citizen, and amenable to the prohibitions of the Fourteenth Amendment.

The long existence of African slavery in this country gave us very distinct notions of what it was, and what were its necessary incidents. Compulsory service of the slave for the benefit of the master, restraint of his movements except by the master's will, disability to hold property, to make contracts, to have a standing in court, to be a witness against a white person, and such like burdens and incapacities were the inseparable incidents of the institution. Severer punishments for crimes were imposed on the slave than on free persons guilty of the same offenses. Congress, as we have seen, by the Civil Rights Bill of 1866, passed in view of the Thirteenth Amendment, before the Fourteenth was adopted, undertook to wipe out these burdens and disabilities, the necessary incidents of slavery, constituting its substance and visible form; and to secure to all citizens of every race and color, and without regard to previous servitude, those fundamental rights which are the essence of civil freedom, namely, the same right to make and enforce contracts, to sue, be parties, give evidence, and to inherit, purchase, lease, sell, and convey property, as is enjoyed by white citizens. Whether this legislation was fully authorized by the Thirteenth Amendment alone, without the support which it afterwards received from the Fourteenth Amendment, after the adoption of which it was re-enacted with some additions, it is not necessary to inquire. It is referred to for the purpose of showing that at that time (in 1866) Congress did not assume, under the authority given by the Thirteenth Amendment, to adjust what may be called the social rights of men and races in the community; but only to declare and vindicate those fundamental rights which appertain to the essence of citizenship, and the enjoyment or deprivation of which constitutes the essential distinction between freedom and slavery.

We must not forget that the province and scope of the Thirteenth and Fourteenth Amendments are different: the former simply abolished slavery: the latter prohibited the states from abridging the privileges or immunities of citizens of the United States, from depriving them of life, liberty, or property without due process of law, and from denying to any the equal protection of the laws. The amendments are different, and the powers of Congress under them are different. What Congress has power to do under one, it may not have power to do under the other. Under the Thirteenth Amendment, it has only to do with slavery and its incidents. Under the Fourteenth Amendment, it has power to counteract and render nugatory all state laws and proceedings which have the effect to abridge any of the privileges or immunities of citizenship, or to deprive them of life, liberty, or property without due process of law, or to deny to any of them the equal protection of the laws. Under the Thirteenth Amendment the legislation, so far as necessary or proper to eradicate all forms and incidents of slavery and involuntary servitude, may be direct and primary, operating upon the acts of individuals, whether sanctioned by state legislation or not; under the Fourteenth, as we have already shown, it must necessarily be, and can only be, corrective in its character, addressed to counteract and afford relief against state regulations or proceedings.

The only question under the present head, therefore, is, whether the refusal to any persons of the accommodations of an inn, or a public conveyance, or a place of public amusement, by an individual, and without any sanction or support from any state law or regulation, does inflict upon such persons any manner of servitude, or form of slavery, as those terms are understood in this country? Many wrongs may be obnoxious to the prohibitions of the Fourteenth Amendment which are not, in any just sense, incidents or elements of slavery. Such, for example, would be the taking of private property without due process of law; or allowing persons who have committed certain crimes (horse-stealing, for example) to be seized and hung by the posse comitatus without regular trial; or denying to any person, or class of persons, the right to pursue any peaceful avocations allowed to others. What is called class legislation would belong to this category, and would be obnoxious to the prohibitions of the Fourteenth Amendment, but would not to the prohibitions of the Fourteenth when not involving the idea of any subjection of one man to another. The Thirteenth Amendment has respect, not to distinctions of race, or class, or color, but to slavery. The Fourteenth Amendment extends its protection to races and classes, and prohibits any state legislation which has the effect of denying to any race or class, or to any individual, the equal protection of the laws.

Now, conceding, for the sake of the argument, that the admission to an inn, a public conveyance, or a place of public amusement, on equal terms with all other citizens, is the right of every man and all classes of men, is it any more than one of those rights which the states by the Fourteenth Amendment are forbidden to deny to any person? And is the constitution violated until the denial of the right has some state sanction or authority? Can the act of a mere individual, the owner of the inn, the public conveyance, or place of amusement, refusing the accommodation, be justly regarded as imposing any badge of slavery or servitude upon the applicant, or only as inflicting an ordinary civil injury, properly cognizable by the laws of the state, and presumably subject to redress by those laws until the contrary appears?

After giving to these questions all the consideration which their importance demands, we are forced to the conclusion that such an act of refusal has nothing to do with slavery or involuntary servitude, and that if it is violative of any right of the party, his redress is to be sought under the laws of the state; or, if those laws are adverse to his rights and do not protect him, his remedy will be found in the corrective legislation which Congress has adopted, or may adopt, for counteracting the effect of state laws, or state action, prohibited by the Fourteenth Amendment. It would be running the slavery argument into the ground to make it apply to every act of discrimination which a person may see fit to make as to the guests he will entertain, or as to the people he will take into his coach or cab or car, or admit to his concert or theater, or deal with in other matters of intercourse or business. Innkeepers and public carriers, by the laws of all the states, so far as we are aware, are bound, to the extent of their facilities, to furnish proper accommodation to all unobjectionable persons who in good faith apply for them. If the laws themselves make any unjust discrimination, amenable to the prohibitions of the Fourteenth Amendment, Congress has full power to afford a remedy under that amendment and in accordance with it.

When a man has emerged from slavery, and by the aid of beneficent legislation has shaken off the inseparable concomitants of that state, there must be some stage in the progress of his elevation when he takes the rank of a mere citizen, and ceases to be the special favorite of the laws, and when his rights as a citizen, or a man, are to be protected in the ordinary modes by which other men's rights are protected. There were thousands of free colored people in this country before the abolition of slavery, enjoying all the essential rights of life, liberty, and property the same as white citizens; yet no one, at that time, thought that it was any invasion of their personal status as freemen because they were not admitted to all the privileges enjoyed by white citizens, or because they were subjected to discriminations in the enjoyment of accommodations in inns, public conveyances, and places of amusement. Mere discriminations on account of race or color were not regarded as badges of slavery. If, since that time, the enjoyment of equal rights in all these respects has become established by constitutional enactment, it is not by force of the Thirteenth Amendment, (which merely abolishes slavery,) but by force of the Fourteenth and Fifteenth Amendments.

3. Holding

On the whole, we are of opinion that no countenance of authority for the passage of the law in question can be found in either the Thirteenth or Fourteenth Amendment of the Constitution; and no other ground of authority for its passage being suggested, it must necessarily be declared void, . . .

4. Justice Harlan Dissenting

The opinion in these cases proceeds, as it seems to me, upon grounds entirely too narrow and artificial. The substance and spirit of the recent amendments of the constitution have been sacrificed by a subtle and ingenious verbal criticism. "It is not the words of the law but the internal sense of it that makes the law. The letter of the law is the body; the sense and reason of the law is the soul." Constitutional provisions, adopted in the interest of liberty, and for the purpose of securing, through national legislation, if need be, rights inhering in a state of freedom, and belonging to American citizenship, have been so construed as to defeat the ends the people desired to accomplish, which they attempted to accomplish, and which they supposed they had accomplished by changes in their fundamental law. By this I do not mean that the determination of these cases should have been materially controlled by considerations of mere expediency or policy. I mean only, in this form, to express an earnest conviction that the court has departed from the familiar rule requiring, in the interpretation of constitutional provisions, that full effect be given to the intent with which they were adopted.

The purpose of the first section of the act of congress of March 1, 1875, was to prevent race discrimination. It does not assume to define the general conditions and limitations under which inns, public conveyances, and places of public amusement may be conducted, but only declares that such conditions and limitations, whatever they may be, shall not be applied, by way of discrimination, on account of race, color, or previous condition of servitude. The second section provides a penalty against any one denying, or aiding or inciting the denial, to any citizen that equality of right given by the first section, except for reasons by law applicable to citizens of every race or color, and regardless of any previous condition of servitude. . . .

a. Constitutional Precedent

Before considering the particular language and scope of these amendments it will be proper to recall the relations which, prior to their adoption, subsisted between the national government and the institution of slavery, as indicated by the provisions of the constitution, the legislation of congress, and the decisions of this court. In this mode we may obtain keys with which to open the mind of the people, and discover the thought intended to be expressed.

In section 2 of article 4 of the Constitution it was provided that "no person held to service or labor in one state, under the laws thereof, escaping into another, shall, in consequence of any law or regulation therein, be discharged from such service or labor, but shall be delivered up on claim of the party to whom such service or labor may be due." Under the authority of that clause Congress passed the Fugitive Slave law of 1793, establishing the mode for the recovery of a fugitive slave, and prescribing a penalty against any person knowingly and willingly obstructing or hindering the master, his agent or attorney, in seizing, arresting, and recovering the fugitive, or who should rescue the fugitive from him, or who should harbor or conceal the slave after notice that he was a fugitive.

In *Prigg v. Commonwealth*, 16 Pet. 539, this court had occasion to define the powers and duties of Congress in reference to fugitives from labor. Speaking by Justice STORY, the court laid down these propositions: That a clause of the Constitution conferring a right should not be so construed as to make it shadowy, or unsubstantial, or leave the citizen without a remedial power adequate for its protection, when another mode, equally accordant with the words and the sense in which they were used, would enforce and protect the right so granted; that Congress is not restricted to legislation for the exertion of its powers expressly granted; but, for the protection of rights guarantied by the Constitution, it may employ, through legislation, such means, not prohibited, as are necessary and proper, or such as are appropriate, to attain the ends proposed; that the constitution recognized the master's right of property in his fugitive slave, and, as incidental thereto, the right of seizing and recovering him, regardless of any state law, or regulation, or local custom what-soever; and that the right of the master to have his slave, so escaping, delivered up on claim, being guarantied by the Constitution, the fair implication was that the national government was clothed with appropriate authority and functions to enforce it.

The court said:

> The fundamental principle, applicable to all cases of this sort, would seem to be that when the end is required the means are given, and when the duty is enjoined the ability to perform it is contemplated to exist on the part of the functionary to whom it is intrusted.

Again:

> It would be a strange anomaly and forced construction to suppose that the national government meant to rely for the due fulfillment of its own proper duties, and the rights which it intended to secure, upon state legislation, and not upon that of the Union. A fortiori, it would be more objectionable to suppose that a power which was to be the same throughout the Union should be confided to state sovereignty, which could not rightfully act beyond its own territorial limits.

The act of 1793 was, upon these grounds, adjudged to be a constitutional exercise of the powers of Congress.

It is to be observed, from the report of *Prigg's Case*, that Pennsylvania, by her attorney general, pressed the argument that the obligation to surrender fugitive slaves was on the states and for the states, subject to the restriction that they should not pass laws or establish regulations liberating such fugitives; that the constitution did not take from the states the right to determine the status of all persons within their respective jurisdictions; that it was for the state in which the alleged fugitive was found to determine, through her courts, or in such modes as she prescribed, whether the person arrested was, in fact, a freeman or a fugitive slave; that the sole power of the general government in the premises was, by judicial instrumentality, to restrain and correct, not to forbid and prevent in the absence of hostile state action; and that, for the general government to assume primary authority to legislate on the subject of fugitive slaves, to the exclusion of the states, would be a dangerous encroachment on state sovereignty. But to such suggestions this court turned a deaf ear, and adjudged that primary legislation by Congress to enforce the master's right was authorized by the constitution.

We next come to the Fugitive Slave Act of 1850, the constitutionality of which rested, as did that of 1793, solely upon the implied power of congress to enforce the master's rights. The provisions of that act were far in advance of previous legisla-tion. They placed at the disposal of the master seeking to recover his fugitive slave, substantially, the whole power of the nation. It invested commissioners, appointed under the act, with power to summon the posse comitatus for the enforcement of its provisions, and commanded "all good citizens" to assist in its prompt and efficient execution whenever their services were required as part of the posse comitatus. Without going into the details of that act, it is sufficient to say that congress omitted from it nothing which the utmost ingenuity could suggest as essential to the successful enforcement of the master's claim to recover his fugitive slave. And this court, in *Ableman v. Booth*, 21 How. 526, adjudged it to be, "in all of its provisions, fully authorized by the Constitution of the United States." . . .

b. The Thirteenth Amendment

The Thirteenth Amendment, my brethren concede, did something more than to prohibit slavery as an institution, resting upon distinctions of race, and upheld by positive law. They admit that it established and decreed universal civil freedom throughout the United States. But did the freedom thus established involve nothing more than exemption from actual slavery? Was nothing more intended than to forbid one man from owning another as property? Was it the purpose of the nation simply to destroy the institution, and then remit the race, theretofore held in bondage, to the several states for such protection, in their civil rights, necessarily growing out of freedom, as those states, in their discretion, choose to provide? Were the states, against whose solemn protest the institution was destroyed, to be left perfectly free, so far as national interference was concerned, to make or allow discriminations against that race, as such, in the enjoyment of those fundamental rights that inhere in a state of freedom? Had the Thirteenth Amendment stopped with the sweeping declaration, in its first section, against the existence of slavery and involuntary servitude, except for crime, Congress would have had the power, by implication, according to the doctrines of *Prigg v. Commonwealth*, repeated in *Strauder v. West Virginia*, to protect the freedom thus established, and consequently to secure the enjoyment of such civil rights as were fundamental in freedom. But that it can exert its authority to that extent is now made clear, and was intended to be made clear, by the express grant of power contained in the second section of that amendment.

That there are burdens and disabilities which constitute badges of slavery and servitude, and that the express power delegated to congress to enforce, by appropriate legislation, the Thirteenth Amendment, may be exerted by legislation of a direct and primary character, for the eradication, not simply of the institution, but of its badges and incidents, are propositions which ought to be deemed indisputable. They lie at the very foundation of the Civil Rights Act of 1866. Whether that act was fully authorized by the Thirteenth Amendment alone, without the support which it afterwards received from the Fourteenth Amendment, after the adoption of which it was re-enacted with some additions, the court, in its opinion, says it is unnecessary to inquire. But I submit, with all respect to my brethren, that its constitutionality is conclusively shown by other portions of their opinion. It is expressly conceded by them that the Thirteenth Amendment established freedom; that there are burdens and disabilities, the necessary incidents of slavery, which constitute its substance and visible form; that congress, by the act of 1866, passed in view of the Thirteenth Amendment, before the Fourteenth was adopted, undertook to remove certain burdens and disabilities, the necessary incidents of slavery, and to secure to all citizens of every race and color, and without regard to previous servitude, those fundamental rights which are the essence of civil freedom, namely, the same right to make and enforce contracts, to sue, be parties, give evidence, and to inherit, purchase, lease, sell, and convey property as is enjoyed by white citizens; that under the Thirteenth Amendment Congress has to do with slavery and its incidents; and that legislation, so far as necessary or proper to eradicate all forms and incidents of slavery and involuntary servitude, may be direct and primary, operating upon the acts of individuals, whether sanctioned by state legislation or not. These propositions being conceded, it is impossible, as it seems to me, to question the constitutional validity of the Civil Rights Act of 1866. I do not contend that the Thirteenth Amendment invests congress with authority, by legislation, to regulate the entire body of the civil rights which citizens enjoy, or may enjoy, in the several states. But I do hold that since slavery, as the court has repeatedly declared, was the moving or principal cause of the adoption of that amendment, and since that institution rested wholly upon the inferiority, as a race, of those held in bondage, their freedom necessarily involved immunity from, and protection against, all discrimination against them, because of their race, in respect of such civil rights as belong to freemen of other races. Congress, therefore, under its express power to enforce that amendment, by appropriate legislation, may enact laws to protect that people against the deprivation, on account of their race, of any civil rights enjoyed by other freemen in the same state; and such legislation may be of a direct and primary character, operating upon states, their officers and agents, and also upon, at least, such individuals and corporations as exercise public functions and wield power and authority under the state.

By way of testing the correctness of this position, let us suppose that, prior to the adoption of the Fourteenth Amendment, a state had passed a statute denying to freemen of African descent, resident within its limits, the same rights which were accorded to white persons, of making or enforcing contracts, or of inheriting, purchasing, leasing, selling, and conveying property; or a statute subjecting colored people to severer punishment for particular offenses than was prescribed for white persons, or excluding that race from the benefit of the laws exempting homesteads from execution. Recall the legislation of 1865–66 in some of the states, of which this court, in *The Slaughterhouse Cases*, said that it imposed upon the colored race onerous disabilities and burdens; curtailed their rights in the pursuit of life, liberty, and property to such an extent that their freedom was of little value; forbade them to appear in the towns in any other character than menial servants; required them to reside on and cultivate the soil, without the right to purchase or own it; excluded them from many occupations of gain; and denied them the privilege of giving testimony in the courts where a white man was a party. 16 Wall. 57. Can there be any doubt that all such legislation might have been reached by direct legislation upon the part of congress under its express power to enforce the Thirteenth Amendment? Would any court have hesitated to declare that such legislation imposed badges of servitude in conflict with the civil freedom ordained by that amendment? That it would have been also in conflict with the Fourteenth Amendment, because inconsistent with the fundamental rights of American citizenship, does not prove that it would have been consistent with the Thirteenth Amendment.

What has been said is sufficient to show that the power of congress under the Thirteenth Amendment is not necessarily restricted to legislation against slavery as an institution upheld by positive law, but may be exerted to the extent at least of protecting the race, so liberated, against discrimination, in respect of legal rights belonging to freemen, where such discrimination is based upon race.

c. The Social Rights Issue

But the court says that congress did not, in the act of 1866, assume, under the authority given by the Thirteenth Amendment, to adjust what may be called the social rights of men and races in the community. I agree that government has nothing to do with social, as distinguished from technically legal, rights of individuals. No government ever has brought, or ever can bring, its people into social intercourse against their wishes. Whether one person will permit or maintain social relations with another is a matter with which government has no concern. I agree that if one citizen chooses not to hold social intercourse with another, he is not and cannot be made amenable to the law for his conduct in that regard; for no legal right of a citizen is violated by the refusal of others to maintain merely social relations with him, even upon grounds of race. What I affirm is that no state, nor the officers of any state, nor any corporation or individual wielding power under state authority for the public benefit or the public convenience, can, consistently either with the freedom established by the fundamental law, or with that equality of civil rights which now belongs to every citizen, discriminate against freemen or citizens, in their civil rights, because of their race, or because they once labored under disabilities imposed upon them as a race. The rights which congress, by the act of 1875, endeavored to secure and protect are legal, not social, rights. The right, for instance, of a colored citizen to use the accommodations of a public highway upon the same terms as are permitted to white citizens is no more a social right than his right, under the law, to use the public streets of a city, or a town, or a turnpike road, or a public market, or a post-office, or his right to sit in a public building with others, of whatever race, for the purpose of hearing the political questions of the day discussed. Scarcely a day passes without our seeing in this court-room citizens of the white and black races sitting side by side watching the progress of our business. It would never occur to any one that the presence of a colored citizen in a court-house or court-room was an invasion of the social rights of white persons who may frequent such places. And yet such a suggestion would be quite as sound in law—I say it with all respect—as is the suggestion that the claim of a colored citizen to use, upon the same terms as is permitted to white citizens, the accommodations of public highways, or public inns, or places of public amusement, established under the license of the law, is an invasion of the social rights of the white race.

d. Other Constitutional Grounds

The court, in its opinion, reserves the question whether Congress, in the exercise of its power to regulate commerce among the several states, might or might not pass a law regulating rights in public conveyances passing from one state to another. I beg to suggest that that precise question was substantially presented here in the only one of these cases relating to railroads,—*Robinson v. Memphis & C. R. Co.* In that case it appears that Mrs. Robinson, a citizen of Mississippi, purchased a railroad ticket entitling her to be carried from Grand Junction, Tennessee, to Lynchburg, Virginia. Might not the act of 1875 be maintained in that case, as applicable at least to commerce between the states, notwithstanding it does not, upon its face, profess to have been passed in pursuance of the power given to Congress to regulate commerce? Has it ever been held that the judiciary should overturn a statute because the legislative department did not accurately recite therein the particular provision of the Constitution authorizing its enactment? We have often enforced municipal bonds in aid of railroad subscriptions where they failed to recite the statute authorizing their issue, but recited one which did not sustain their validity. The inquiry in such cases has been, was there in any statute authority for the execution of the bonds? Upon this branch of the case it may be remarked that the state of Louisiana, in 1869, passed a statute giving to passengers, without regard to race or color, equality of right in the accommodations of railroad and street cars, steam-boats, or other water-crafts, stage-coaches, omnibuses, or other vehicles. But in *Hall v. De Cuir*, 95 U.S. 487, that act was pronounced unconstitutional so far as it related to commerce between the states, this court saying that "if the public good requires such legislation it must come from Congress and not from the states." I suggest that it may become a pertinent inquiry whether Congress may, in the exertion of its power to regulate commerce among the states, enforce among passengers on public conveyances equality of right without regard to race, color, or previous condition of servitude, if it be true—which I do not admit—that such legislation would be an interference by government with the social rights of the people.

e. The Favoritism Issue

My brethren say that when a man has emerged from slavery, and by the aid of beneficent legislation has shaken off the inseparable concomitants of that state, there must be some stage in the progress of his elevation when he takes the rank of a mere citizen, and ceases to be the special favorite of the laws, and when his rights as a citizen, or a man, are to be protected in the ordinary modes by which other men's rights are protected. It is, I submit, scarcely just to say that the colored race has been the special favorite of the laws. What the nation, through Congress, has sought to accomplish in reference to that race is, what had already been done in every state in the Union for the white race, to secure and protect rights belonging to them as freemen and citizens; nothing more. The one underlying purpose of congressional legislation has been to enable the black race to take the rank of mere citizens. The difficulty has been to compel a recognition of their legal right to take that rank, and to secure the enjoyment of privileges belonging, under the law, to them as a component part of the people for whose welfare and happiness government is ordained. At every step in this direction the nation has been confronted with class tyranny, which a contemporary English historian says is, of all tyrannies, the most intolerable, "for it is ubiquitous in its operation, and weighs, perhaps, most heavily on those whose obscurity or distance would withdraw them from the notice of a single despot." Today it is the colored race which is denied, by corporations and individuals wielding public authority, rights fundamental in their freedom and citizenship. At some future time it may be some other race that will fall under the ban. If the constitutional amendments be enforced, according to the intent with which, as I conceive, they were adopted, there cannot be, in this republic, any class of human beings in practical subjection to another class, with power in the latter to dole out to the former just such privileges as they may choose to grant. The supreme law of the land has decreed that no authority shall be exercised in this country upon the basis of discrimination, in respect of civil rights, against freemen and citizens because of their race, color, or previous condition of servitude. To that decree—for the due enforcement of which, by appropriate legislation, Congress has been invested with express power—every one must bow, whatever may have been, or whatever now are, his individual views as to the wisdom or policy, either of the recent changes in the fundamental law, or of the legislation which has been enacted to give them effect.

For the reasons stated I feel constrained to withhold my assent to the opinion of the court.

J. Commentary on *The Civil Rights Cases*

Peggy Cooper Davis

*Introducing Robert Smalls**

When Robert Smalls was twelve or thirteen, his owner (who was also his half-brother) began hiring him out, first as a waiter, then as a lamplighter, then as a laborer on the Charleston harbor, and ultimately as a sailor. At the start of the Civil War, Smalls, then twenty-two, was enlisted by the Confederacy as pilot of the Planter, a 300-ton side-wheel steamship built in 1860 for commercial use and converted in 1861 to serve the Confederate Army as an armed transport and dispatch vessel. In May of 1862, he gathered a crew of eight African-American sailors, his

---

* (footnotes and chapter headings omitted).

own family, "several other women and children," and "several cannon," boarded the Planter, and, in the words of a Naval Historical Center description, "boldly steamed her past the Charleston fortifications and turned her over to Federal forces." Union naval forces were pleased to acquire "a ship, several cannon, and a man with an intimate knowledge of the Charleston harbor defenses and waters." The government awarded Smalls and his crew "half the value of their ship and its cargo" (approximately fifteen hundred dollars), and Smalls "became a national hero" and a leading spokesperson for the Sea Islands experiment. Smalls devoted most of the following three years to service in the Union navy, in which he gained a reputation for "courage under fire," and appears to have earned the rank of captain. When he was evicted from a Philadelphia streetcar in 1864, protests against Jim Crow treatment of a war hero led to integration of that city's public transportation system. When the Planter was decommissioned in 1866, Smalls returned to Beaufort, the South Carolina town in which he was born. He used the money awarded him for the Planter's capture to open a store and to purchase, at government auction, his birthplace: the house that had been the home of his father and first owner.

As Smalls was resettling in Beaufort, Congressional Republicans were struggling with a predicament that seemed insoluble. In 1867, every Southern state except Tennessee had refused to ratify the Fourteenth Amendment, and Reconstruction was faltering. So long as the electorate was imagined as consisting only of white males, there seemed no way to win ratification of the Amendment and achieve unification on Republican (and genuinely republican) terms. Charles Sumner was able to imagine—and dared to propose—a different electorate: if African-American men were able to vote, the balance of Southern political power would shift, the Fourteenth Amendment would be ratified, and Reconstruction could proceed. Sumner won Congressional approval of a provision imposing a "requirement of suffrage irrespective of race or color in the election of delegates to the Reconstruction conventions, and as the basis of suffrage for the constitutions of the rebel states." When this suffrage provision was agreed upon by the Committee, Senator Wilson of Massachusetts remarked: "then and there in that small room, in that caucus, was decided the greatest pending question of the North American continent." This bitterly resisted provision survived Presidential veto and became law in the last days of the congressional session. As a result, American-born people of African descent constituted twenty-five percent of those electing delegates to the constitutional conventions by which states of the former Confederacy were reconstituted: electoral majorities in the delegate elections of five states, and delegate majorities in one state. Black voter turnout in the late 1860s was overwhelming, approaching ninety percent in many elections. South Carolina, with its population of roughly 300,000 whites (most of whom did not vote in the delegate elections) and 400,000 blacks (most of whom did), elected seventy-one black people to the 1868 constitutional convention. Needless to say, Robert Smalls was one of them. He joined 260 African-American convention delegates who voted to ratify the Fourteenth Amendment.

This assertion of African-American political power—symbolized here by Robert Smalls, but enacted in the lives of thousands of blacks throughout the former Confederacy—evoked a barrage of derisive invective that subsided over the years to quiet disdain before settling as a simple denial of the actions, intentions, and principles of African-American political figures in the Reconstruction era.

Disgruntled racialists described delegates to constitutional conventions in the former Confederacy as "baboons, monkeys, mules," or "ragamuffins and jailbirds." The South Carolina convention, according to a local newspaper, was the "maddest, most infamous revolution in history." A Northern journalist described the South Carolina legislature as a "mass" permeated with unimaginable "ignorance and vice." Immediately after Reconstruction, African-American legislators were omitted from the Georgia legislative manual on the ground that "[i]t would be absurd . . . to record the lives of men who were but yesterday our slaves, and whose past careers, probably, embraced such menial occupations as boot-blacking, shaving, table-waiting, and the like."

For racialist white citizens, the ideal of universal—now more fully comprehended as multiracial—civil freedom paled. Southern resentment deepened, and Northern sentiment for compromise with the former rebels grew. The Democratic Party consistently and vocally resisted Reconstruction, counseling "magnanimity and generosity to a fallen foe." In 1872, white Republicans in substantial numbers joined Democrats to support Horace Greeley's campaign for "reconciliation and purification." For the next four years, Greeley, a Radical Republican turned Democrat and editor of the New York Sun, made "no Negro domination" a constant cry of the paper.

While the Thirteenth Amendment applied to private as well as governmental action, the Fourteenth Amendment could only be implicated when a sufficient degree of state involvement with the private action or a failure by the state to act in circumstances where the Constitution affirmatively required action were present. For the majority of justices, *The Civil Rights Cases* involved a continuation of the debate initiated in *The Slaughterhouse Cases,* as to whether the Reconstruction Amendments maintained the traditional notion of federalism where the states were the primary guarantors of individual rights and where strong states were necessary to prevent federal overreaching. For Justice Bradley, the crucial distinction does not seem to have been between public and private spheres, but rather between a federal government with plenary power and a federal government that could intervene only upon showing that the states had defaulted in their primary obligation to protect the civil rights of their citizens. Such a failure might have justified federal intervention, or at least intervention directed at uncooperative state officials.

Thomas Brook

Plessy v. Ferguson: A Brief History with Documents

The Civil Rights Cases decision continued the narrowing of federal protection for blacks. If the bulk of legal rights of blacks were to be protected, it would be up to the states to do so. Unfortunately, most states were opposed to undertaking this constitutional obligation.

For those who shared the goals of Reconstruction, it was a failure because those goals were never realized. It failed in part because of corruption and unscrupulous opportunism by some carpetbaggers seeking to profit from the defeated condition of the South. But the major reason for its failure was the country's unwillingness to continue to pursue its goal of reconstructing the nation to provide political and civic, if not social, equality for African Americans. If pursuing those goals would have meant adjusting policies that were not working and correcting abuses that admittedly took place, it would also have meant refusing to compromise with those intent on keeping African Americans in a subservient position. But neither the country nor the Republican Party was able to maintain its resolve. The end of Reconstruction came with the election of 1876.

That election was very close. The Democrat Samuel Tilden received more popular votes than Republican Rutherford B. Hayes. Returns in Florida, Louisiana, Oregon, and South Carolina were disputed. In southern states, for instance, there were widespread claims that whites used violent intimidation to control black votes. Congress, where Republicans controlled the Senate and Democrats the House, had constitutional authority to resolve the dispute. It gave power to an election commission of eight Republicans and seven Democrats. A compromise was worked out in which Hayes was given a one-vote majority in the electoral college in return for an end to Reconstruction. Hayes was named president, and federal troops returned to their garrisons.

K. Background on Justice Joseph Bradley

Geoffrey Stone, et al.

Justice Joseph Bradley

Joseph Bradley was raised in poverty on a small farm. As a lawyer, he specialized in corporate and commercial law and represented several railroads. A Whig before the Civil War, Bradley was an avid supporter of the Union cause and became identified with the radical wing of the Republican Party in the postwar period. His appointment to the Court by President Grant in 1870 was later the subject of controversy because it made possible the reversal of the Court's earlier decision involving the validity of the Civil War legal tender acts. Compare *Hepburn v. Griswold*, 75 U.S. (8 Wall.) 603 (1870) with *The Legal Tender Cases*, 79 U.S. (12 Wall.) 457 (1871). As a justice, Bradley supported the power of Congress to regulate the interstate movement of goods, even if the regulation limited state authority. His dissent in *The Slaughterhouse Cases*, 83 U.S. (16 Wall.) 36 (1873), also showed a willingness to read the newly enacted Fourteenth Amendment as an important expansion of federal authority. In 1877, Bradley was a last-minute substitute on the electoral commission established to resolve the disputed presidential election of 1876. With the commission deadlocked seven to seven, Bradley cast the deciding vote to make Rutherford B. Hayes the President.

Constitutional Law lxxvii (3rd edition).

Copyright © (1996) Stone, et al.

Reprinted with permission of Aspen Law & Business.

L. Questions and Notes

If you were Justice Bradley how would you have resolved the 1876 Presidential election?

Many of the cases during Reconstruction involved an examination of the concept of federalism, the relationship between states and the federal government. The Supreme Court often adopted the argument put forward by states for limited federal government power. This argument became known as the "states' rights" doctrine. This phrase became synonymous with racial discrimination and oppression, as discriminatory state laws were not mitigated by federal protections. Do you believe that the term "states' rights" is an accurate characterization of the doctrine?

X. Race and Citizenship

A. Introduction

Citizenship has always been an important concept in American history. Defining the term has been a focus of controversy ever since those famous words were written in the Preamble to the Constitution, "[w]e the people of the United States." The Constitution applies to all people, not just citizens, but the scope of inclusion is not defined. Did Reconstruction change the meaning of "we the people"?

The first sentence of section one of the Fourteenth Amendment provides that "all persons born or naturalized in the United States . . . are citizens of the United States." This sentence effectively overruled *Dred Scott* which had pronounced that blacks, even those born free in the United States, were not citizens. But did this sentence broaden the scope of protection to include other non-whites who had been denied political and civil rights such as Latinos/as, American Indians, and Asian Americans? Would the Supreme Court's narrow interpretation of terms in the Reconstruction Amendments extend their betrayal of Reconstruction to deny rights to Latinos, Asian Americans, and American Indians, in addition to blacks?

Juan F. Perea

Ethnicity and the Constitution: Beyond the Black
and White Binary Constitution

In *The Slaughter-House Cases*, 83 U.S. (16 Wall.) 36 (1873), the Supreme Court interpreted the Reconstruction Amendments for the first time. The Court stated that the primary purpose underlying the Thirteenth, Fourteenth and Fifteenth Amendments was to secure the freedoms of newly freed African-American citizens. Construing the Equal Protection Clause, the Court "doubt[ed] very much whether any action of a State not directed by way of discrimination against the negroes as a class, or on account of their race, will ever be held to come within the purview of this provision." The Court also suggested, however, a broader reach for these amendments:

> We do not say that no one else but the Negro can share in this protection. . . . Undoubtedly while Negro slavery alone was in the mind of the Congress which proposed the thirteenth article, it forbids any other kind of slavery, now or hereafter. If Mexican peonage or the Chinese coolie labor system shall develop slavery of the Mexican or Chinese race within our territory, this amendment may safely be trusted to make it void. And so if other rights are assailed by the States which properly and necessarily fall within the protection of these articles, that protection will apply, though the party interested may not be of African descent.

The Court acknowledged, therefore, that the amendments could apply to classifications beyond blackness.

In *Strauder v. West Virginia*, 100 U.S. 303 (1879), the Court again stated that the purpose of the Fourteenth Amendment was to prohibit "discrimination because of race or color" against the African-American citizens of the nation. The Court concluded that the West Virginia law at issue, which limited eligibility for jury service to "white male persons," was just such a prohibited discrimination. Having found that the primary purpose underlying the Fourteenth Amendment was to protect blacks, the Court, in dicta, somewhat contradictorily stated that the Equal Protection Clause would be violated equally by a law excluding white men from jury service—an extremely unlikely hypothetical.

In *Strauder*, the Court suggested a broader reach for the Equal Protection Clause than its statement from *The Slaughter-House Cases* quoted above. In dicta, the Court wrote: "Nor if a law should be passed excluding all naturalized Celtic Irishmen, would there be any doubt of its inconsistency with the spirit of the amendment." In the Court's view, a classification based on ethnicity and national origin excluding naturalized Celtic Irishmen would also violate the Equal Protection Clause. Perhaps acknowledging some departure from the primary purpose of the amendment, the Court characterized such a classification as inconsistent with the spirit of the amendment, not the amendment itself. The Court thus recognized early that the Equal Protection Clause prohibited discrimination based on national origin, but the prohibition was based only on some unstated analogy between race and national origin.

36 *Wm. & Mary L. Rev.* 571, 579–81.
Copyright © (1995) *Wm. & Mary L. Rev.*
Reprinted with permission of *Wm. & Mary L. Rev.* and Juan F. Perea.

Ian F. Haney Lopez

White by Law: The Legal Construction of Race

The racial composition of the U.S. citizenry reflects in part the accident of world migration patterns. More than this, however, it reflects the conscious design of U.S. immigration and naturalization laws.

Federal law restricted immigration to this country on the basis of race for nearly one hundred years, roughly from the Chinese exclusion laws of the 1880s until the end of the national origin quotas in 1965. The history of this discrimination can briefly be traced. Nativist sentiment against Irish and German Catholics on the East Coast and against Chinese and Mexicans on the West Coast, which had been doused by the Civil War, reignited during the economic slump of the 1870s. Though most of the nativist efforts failed to gain congressional sanction, Congress in 1882 passed the Chinese Exclusion Act, which suspended the immigration of Chinese laborers for ten years. The Act was expanded to exclude all Chinese in 1884, and was eventually implemented indefinitely. In 1917, Congress created "an Asiatic barred zone," excluding all persons from Asia. During this same period, the Senate passed a bill to exclude "all members of the African or black race." This effort was defeated in the House only after intensive lobbying by the NAACP. Efforts to exclude the supposedly racially undesirable southern and eastern Europeans were more successful. In 1921, Congress established a temporary quota system designed "to confine immigration as much as possible to western and northern European stock," making this bar permanent three years later in the National Origin Act of 1924. With the onset of the Depression, attention shifted to Mexican immigrants. Although no law explicitly targeted this group, federal immigration officials began a series of round-ups and mass deportations of people of Mexican descent under the general rubric of a "repatriation campaign." Approximately 500,000 people were forcibly returned to Mexico during the Depression, more than half of them U.S. citizens. This pattern was repeated in the 1950s, when Attorney General Herbert Brownwell launched a program to expel Mexicans. This effort, dubbed "Operation Wetback," indiscriminately deported more than one million citizens and noncitizens in 1954 alone.

Racial restrictions on immigration were not significantly dismantled until 1965, when Congress in a major overhaul of immigration law abolished both the national origin system and the Asiatic Barred Zone. Even so, purposeful racial discrimination in immigration law by Congress remains constitutionally permissible, since the case that upheld the Chinese Exclusion Act to this day remains good law. Moreover, arguably racial discrimination in immigration law continues. For example, Congress has enacted special provisions to encourage Irish immigration, while refusing to ameliorate the backlog of would-be immigrants from the Philippines, India, South Korea, China, and Hong Kong, backlogs created in part through a century of racial exclusion. The history of racial discrimination in U.S. immigration law is a long and continuing one.

As discriminatory as the laws of immigration have been, the laws of citizenship betray an even more dismal record of racial exclusion. From this country's inception, the laws regulating who was or could become a citizen were tainted by racial prejudice. Birthright citizenship, the automatic acquisition of citizenship by virtue of birth, was tied to race until 1940. Naturalized citizenship, the acquisition of citizenship by any means other than through birth, was conditioned on race until 1952. Like immigration laws, the laws of birthright citizenship and naturalization shaped the racial character of the United States.

Most persons acquire citizenship by birth rather than through naturalization. During the 1990s, for example, naturalization will account for only 7.5 percent of the increase in the U.S. citizen population. At the time of the prerequisite cases, the proportion of persons gaining citizenship through naturalization was probably somewhat higher, given the higher ratio of immigrants to total population, but still far smaller than the number of people gaining citizenship by birth. In order to situate the prerequisite laws, therefore, it is useful first to review the history of racial discrimination in the laws of birthright citizenship.

The U.S. Constitution as ratified did not define the citizenry, probably because it was assumed that the English common law rule of *jus soli* would continue. Under *jus soli*, citizenship accrues to "all" born within a nation's jurisdiction. Despite the seeming breadth of this doctrine, the word "all" is qualified because for the first one hundred years and more of this country's history it did not fully encompass racial minorities. This is the import of the *Dred Scott* decision. . . .

Despite the broad language of the Fourteenth Amendment—though in keeping with the words of the 1866 act—some racial minorities remained outside the bounds of *jus soli* even after its constitutional enactment. In particular, questions persisted about the citizenship status of children born in the United States to noncitizen parents, and about the status of Native Americans. The Supreme Court did not decide the status of the former until 1898, when it ruled in *U.S. v. Wong Kim Ark* that native-born children of aliens, even those permanently barred by race from acquiring citizenship, were birthright citizens of the United States. On the citizenship of the latter, the Supreme Court answered negatively in 1884, holding in *Elk v. Wilkins* that Native Americans owed allegiance to their tribe and so did not acquire citizenship upon birth. Congress responded by granting Native Americans citizenship in piecemeal fashion, often tribe by tribe. Not until 1924 did Congress pass an act conferring citizenship on all Native Americans in the United States. Even then, however, questions arose regarding the citizenship of those born in the United States after the effective date of the 1924 act. These questions were finally resolved, and *jus soli* fully applied, under the Nationality Act of 1940, which specifically bestowed citizenship on all those born in the United States "to a member of an Indian, Eskimo, Aleutian, or other aboriginal tribe." Thus, the basic law of citizenship, that a person born here is a citizen here, did not include all racial minorities until 1940.

Although the Constitution did not originally define the citizenry, it explicitly gave Congress the authority to establish the criteria for granting citizenship after birth. Article I grants Congress the power "To establish a uniform Rule of Naturalization." From the start, Congress exercised this power in a manner that burdened naturalization laws with racial restrictions that tracked those in the law of birthright citizenship. In 1790, only a few months after ratification of the Constitution, Congress limited naturalization to "any alien, being a free white person who shall have resided within the limits and under the jurisdiction of the United States for a term of two years." This clause mirrored not only the de facto laws of birthright citizenship, but also the racially restrictive naturalization laws of several states. At least three states had previously limited citizenship to "white persons": Virginia in 1779, South Carolina in 1784, and Georgia in 1785. Though there would be many subsequent changes in the requirements for federal naturalization, racial identity endured as a bedrock requirement for the next 162 years. In every naturalization act from 1790 until 1952, Congress included the "white person" prerequisite.

The history of racial prerequisites to naturalization can be divided into two periods of approximately eighty years each. The first period extended from 1790 to 1870, when only Whites were able to naturalize. In the wake of the Civil War, the "white person" restriction on naturalization came under serious attack as part of the effort to expunge *Dred Scott*. Some congressmen, Charles Sumner chief among them, argued that racial barriers to naturalization should be struck altogether. However, racial prejudice against Native Americans and Asians forestalled the complete elimination of the racial prerequisites. During congressional debates, one senator argued against conferring "the rank, privileges, and immunities of citizenship upon the cruel savages who destroyed [Minnesota's] peaceful settlements and massacred the people with circumstances of atrocity too horrible to relate." Another senator wondered "whether this door [of citizenship] shall now be thrown open to the Asiatic population," warning that to do so would spell for the Pacific coast "an end to republican government there, because it is very well ascertained that those people have no appreciation of that form of government; it seems to be obnoxious to their very nature; they seem to be incapable either of understanding or carrying it out." Sentiments such as these ensured that even after the Civil War, bars against Native American and Asian naturalization would continue. Congress opted to maintain the "white person" prerequisite, but to extend the right to naturalize to "persons of African nativity, or African descent." After 1870, blacks as well as whites could naturalize, but not others.

During the second period, from 1870 until the last of the prerequisite laws were abolished in 1952, the White-Black dichotomy in American race relations dominated naturalization law. During this period, Whites and Blacks were eligible for citizenship, but others, particularly those from Asia, were not. Indeed, increasing antipathy toward Asians on the West Coast resulted in an explicit disqualification of Chinese persons from naturalization in 1882. The prohibition of Chinese naturalization, the only U.S. law ever to exclude by name a particular nationality from citizenship, was coupled with the ban on Chinese immigration discussed previously. The Supreme Court readily upheld the bar, writing that "Chinese persons not born in this country have never been recognized as citizens of the United States, nor authorized to become such under the naturalization laws." While Blacks were permitted to naturalize beginning in 1870, the Chinese and most "other non-Whites" would have to wait until the 1940s for the right to naturalize.

World War II forced a domestic reconsideration of the racism integral to U.S. naturalization law. In 1935, Hitler's Germany limited citizenship to members of the Aryan race, making Germany the only country other than the United States with a racial restriction on naturalization. The fact of this bad company was not lost on those administering our naturalization law. "When Earl G. Harrison in 1944 resigned as United States Commissioner of Immigration and Naturalization, he said that the only country in the world, outside the United States, that observes racial discrimination in matters relating to naturalization was Nazi Germany, 'and we all agree that this is not very desirable company.'" Furthermore, the United States was open to charges of hypocrisy for banning from naturalization the nationals of many of its Asian allies. During the war, the United States seemed through some of its laws and social practices to embrace the same racism it was fighting. Both fronts of the war exposed profound inconsistencies between U.S. naturalization law and broader social ideals. These considerations, among others, led Congress to begin a process of piecemeal reform in the laws governing citizenship.

In 1940, Congress opened naturalization to "descendants of races indigenous to the Western Hemisphere." Apparently, this "additional limitation was designed 'to more fully cement' the ties of Pan-Americanism" at a time of impending crisis. In 1943, Congress replaced the prohibition on the naturalization of Chinese persons with a provision explicitly granting them this boon. In 1946, it opened up naturalization to persons from the Philippines and India as well. Thus, at the end of the war, our naturalization law looked like this:

The right to become a naturalized citizen under the provisions of this Act shall extend only to —

(1) white persons, persons of African nativity or descent, and persons of races indigenous to the continents of North or South America or adjacent islands and Filipino persons or persons of Filipino descent;

(2) persons who possess, either singly or in combination, a preponderance of blood of one or more of the classes specified in clause (1);

(3) Chinese persons or persons of Chinese descent; and persons of races indigenous to India; and

(4) persons who possess, either singly or in combination, a preponderance of blood of one or more of the classes specified in clause (3) or, either singly or in combination, as much as one-half blood of those classes and some additional blood of one of the classes specified in clause (1).

This incremental retreat from a "Whites only" conception of citizenship made the arbitrariness of U.S. naturalization law increasingly obvious. For example, under the above statute, the right to acquire citizenship depended for some on blood-quantum distinctions based on descent from peoples indigenous to islands adjacent to the Americas. In 1952, Congress moved towards wholesale reform, overhauling the naturalization statute to read simply that "[t]he right of a person to become a naturalized citizen of the United States shall not be denied or abridged because of race or sex or because such person is married." Thus, in 1952, racial bars on naturalization came to an official end.

White By Law: The Legal Construction of Race 37–46.
Copyright © (1996) New York University Press.
Reprinted with permission of New York University Press.

B. Background on *Ozawa*

Since Congress passed the first immigration act in 1790 limiting citizenship by naturalization to whites only, American immigration law has reflected racially discriminatory treatment. What impact, if any, would the Reconstruction Amendments and related legislation have on such immigration policy?

C. *Ozawa v. United States*, 260 U.S. 178 (1922)

1. Facts

Justice SUTHERLAND delivered the opinion of the Court.

The appellant, Takao Ozawa, is a person of the Japanese race born in Japan. He applied, on October 16, 1914, to the United States District Court for the Territory of Hawaii to be admitted as a citizen of the United States. His petition was opposed by the United States District Attorney for the District of Hawaii. Including the period of his residence in Hawaii appellant had continuously resided in the United States for 20 years. He was a graduate of the Berkeley, Cal., high school, had been nearly three years a student in the University of California, had educated his children in American schools, his family had attended American churches and he had maintained the use of the English language in his home. That he was well qualified by character and education for citizenship is conceded.

The District Court of Hawaii, however, held that, having been born in Japan and being of the Japanese race, he was not eligible to naturalization under section 2169 of the Revised Statutes (Comp. St. § 4358), and denied the petition. Thereupon the appellant brought the cause to the Circuit Court of Appeals for the Ninth Circuit . . .

2. Opinion

. . . It is contended that, thus construed, the act of 1906 confers the privilege of naturalization without limitation as to race, since the general introductory words of section 4 are: "That an alien may be admitted to become a citizen of the United States in the following manner, and not otherwise." But, obviously, this clause does not relate to the subject of eligibility but to the 'manner,' that is, the procedure, to be followed. Exactly the same words are used to introduce the similar provisions contained in section 2165 of the Revised Statutes. In 1790 the first naturalization act provided that, "Any alien being a free white person . . . may be admitted to become a citizen, . . ." C. 3, 1 Stat. 103. This was subsequently enlarged to include aliens of African nativity and persons of African descent. These provisions were restated in the Revised Statutes, so that section 2165 included only the procedural portion, while the substantive parts were carried into a separate section (2169) and the words 'An alien' substituted for the words "Any alien."

In all of the naturalization acts from 1790 to 1906 the privilege of naturalization was confined to white persons (with the addition in 1870 of those of African nativity and descent), although the exact wording of the various statutes was not always the same. If Congress in 1906 desired to alter a rule so well and so long established it may be assumed that its purpose would have been definitely disclosed and its legislation to that end put in unmistakable terms.

The argument that, because section 2169 is in terms made applicable only to the title in which it is found, it should now be confined to the unrepealed sections of that title, is not convincing. The persons entitled to naturalization under these unrepealed sections include only honorably discharged soldiers and seamen who have served three years on board an American vessel, both of whom were entitled from the beginning to admission on more generous terms than were accorded to other aliens. It is not conceivable that Congress would deliberately have allowed the racial limitation to continue as to soldiers and seamen to whom the statute had accorded an especially favored status, and have removed it as to all other aliens. Such a construction cannot be adopted unless it be unavoidable.

The division of the Revised Statutes into titles and chapters is chiefly a matter of convenience, and reference to a given title or chapter is simply a ready method of identifying the particular provisions which are meant. The provisions of title XXX affected by the limitation of section 2169, originally embraced the whole subject of naturalization of aliens. The generality of the words in section 2165, "An alien may be admitted, . . ." was restricted by section 2169 in common with the other provisions of the title. The words "this title" were used for the purpose of identifying that provision (and others), but it was the provision which was restricted. That provision having been amended and carried into the act of 1906, section 2169 being left intact and unrepealed, it will require some thing more persuasive than a narrowly literal reading of the identifying words "this title" to justify the conclusion that Congress intended the restriction to be no longer applicable to the provision.

It is the duty of this Court to give effect to the intent of Congress. Primarily this intent is ascertained by giving the words their natural significance, but if this leads to an unreasonable result plainly at variance with the policy of the legislation as a whole, we must examine the matter further. We may then look to the reason of the enactment and inquire into its antecedent history and give it effect in accordance with its design and purpose, sacrificing, if necessary, the literal meaning in order that the purpose may not fail. *See Church of the Holy Trinity v. United States*, 143 U. S. 457, 12 Sup. Ct. 511, 36 L. Ed. 226; *Heydenfeldt v. Daney Gold*, etc., Co., 93 U. S. 634, 638, 23 L. Ed. 995. We are asked to conclude that Congress, without the consideration or recommendation of any committee, without a suggestion as to the effect, or a word of debate as to the desirability, of so fundamental a change, nevertheless, by failing to alter the identifying words of section 2169, which section we may assume was continued for some serious purpose, has radically modified a statute always theretofore maintained and considered as of great importance. It is inconceivable that a rule in force from the beginning of the government, a part of our history as well as our law, welded into the structure of our national polity by a century of legislative and administrative acts and judicial decisions, would have been deprived of its force in such dubious and casual fashion. We are, therefore, constrained to hold that the act of 1906 is limited by the provisions of section 2169 of the Revised Statutes.

This brings us to inquire whether, under section 2169, the appellant is eligible to naturalization. The language of the naturalization laws from 1790 to 1870 had been uniformly such as to deny the privilege of naturalization to an alien unless he came within the description "free white person." By section 7 of the act of July 14, 1870 (16 Stat. 254, 256 [Comp. St. § 4358]), the naturalization laws were "extended to aliens of African nativity and to persons of African descent." Section 2169 of the Revised Statutes, as already pointed out, restricts the privilege to the same classes of persons, viz. 'to aliens [being free white persons, and to aliens] of African nativity and to persons of African descent.' It is true that in the first edition of the Revised Statutes of 1873 the words in brackets, 'being free white persons, and to aliens' were omitted, but this was clearly an error of the compilers and was corrected by the subsequent legislation of 1875 (18 Stat. 316, 318). Is appellant, therefore, a "free white person," within the meaning of that phrase as found in the statute?

On behalf of the appellant it is urged that we should give to this phrase the meaning which it had in the minds of its original framers in 1790 and that it was employed by them for the sole purpose of excluding the black or African race and the Indians then inhabiting this country. It may be true that those two races were alone thought of as being excluded, but to say that they were the only ones within the intent of the statute would be to ignore the affirmative form of the legislation. The provision is not that Negroes and Indians shall be excluded, but it is, in effect, that only free white persons shall be included. The intention was to confer the privilege of citizenship upon that class of persons whom the fathers knew as white, and to deny it to all who could not be so classified. It is not enough to say that the framers did not have in mind the brown or yellow races of Asia. It is necessary to go farther and be able to say that had these particular races been suggested the language of the act would have been so varied as to include them within its privileges. As said by Chief Justice Marshall in *Dartmouth College v. Woodward*, 4 Wheat. 518, 644 (4 L. Ed. 629), in deciding a question of constitutional construction: "It is not enough to say that this particular case was not in the mind of the convention, when the article was framed, nor of the American people, when it was adopted. It is necessary to go farther, and to say that, had this particular case been suggested, the language would have been so varied, as to exclude it, or it would have been made a special exception. The case, being within the words of the rule, must be within its operation likewise, unless there be something in the literal construction so obviously absurd, or mischievous, or repugnant to the general spirit of the instrument, as to justify those who expound the Constitution in making it an exception." If it be assumed that the opinion of the framers was that the only persons who would fall outside the designation "white" were Negroes and Indians, this would go no farther than to demonstrate their lack of sufficient information to enable them to foresee precisely who would be excluded by that term in the subsequent administration of the statute. It is not important in construing their words to consider the extent of their ethnological knowledge or whether they thought that under the statute the only persons who would be denied naturalization would be Negroes and Indians. It is sufficient to ascertain whom they intended to include and having ascertained that it follows, as a necessary corollary, that all others are to be excluded,

The question then is: Who are comprehended within the phrase "free white persons"? Undoubtedly the word 'free' was originally used in recognition of the fact that slavery then existed and that some white persons occupied that status. The word, however, has long since ceased to have any practical significance and may now be disregarded.

We have been furnished with elaborate briefs in which the meaning of the words "white person" is discussed with ability and at length, both from the standpoint of judicial decision and from that of the science of ethnology. It does not seem to us necessary, however, to follow counsel in their extensive researches in these fields. It is sufficient to note the fact that these decisions are, in substance, to the effect that the words import a racial and not an individual test, and with this conclusion, fortified as it is by reason and authority, we entirely agree. Manifestly the test afforded by the mere color of the skin of each individual is impracticable, as that differs greatly among persons of the same race, even among Anglo-Saxons, ranging by imperceptible gradations from the fair blond to the swarthy brunette, the latter being darker than many of the lighter hued persons of the brown or yellow races. Hence to adopt the color test alone would result in a confused overlapping of races and a gradual merging of one into the other, without any practical line of separation. Beginning with the decision of Circuit Judge Sawyer, in *Re Ah Yup*, 5 Sawy. 155, (1878), the federal and state courts, in an almost unbroken line, have held that the words "white person" were meant to indicate only a person of what is popularly known as the Caucasian race. Among these decisions, see, for example: *In re Camille*, 6 Fed. 256; *In re Saito* 62 Fed. 126; *In re Nian*, 6 Utah, 259; *In re Kumagai*, 163 Fed. 922; *In re Yamashita*, 30 Wash. 234, 237; *In re Ellis*, 179 Fed. 1002; *In re Mozumdar*, 207 Fed. 115, 117; *In re Singh*, 257 Fed. 209, 211–12; and *Petition of Charr*, 273 Fed. 207. With the conclusion reached in these several decisions we see no reason to differ. Moreover, that conclusion has become so well established by judicial and executive concurrence and legislative acquiescence that we should not at this late day feel at liberty to disturb it, in the absence of reasons far more cogent than any that have been suggested. *United States v. Midwest Oil Co.*, 236 U. S. 459, 472.

The determination that the words "white person" are synonymous with the words 'a person of the Caucasian race' simplifies the problem, although it does not entirely dispose of it. Controversies have arisen and will no doubt arise again in respect of the proper classification of individuals in border line cases. The effect of the conclusion that the words 'white person' means a Caucasian is not to establish a sharp line of demarcation between those who are entitled and those who are not entitled to naturalization, but rather a zone of more or less debatable ground outside of which, upon the one hand, are those clearly eligible, and outside of which, upon the other hand, are those clearly ineligible for citizenship. Individual cases falling within this zone must be determined as they arise from time to time by what this court has called, in another connection (*Davidson v. New Orleans*, 96 U. S. 97, 104), "the gradual process of judicial inclusion and exclusion."

3. Holding

The appellant, in the case now under consideration, however, is clearly of a race which is not Caucasian and therefore belongs entirely outside the zone on the negative side. A large number of the federal and state courts have so decided and we find no reported case definitely to the contrary. These decisions are sustained by numerous scientific authorities, which we do not deem it necessary to review. We think these decisions are right and so hold.

The briefs filed on behalf of appellant refer in complimentary terms to the culture and enlightenment of the Japanese people, and with this estimate we have no reason to disagree; but these are matters which cannot enter into our consideration of the questions here at issue. We have no function in the matter other than to ascertain the will of Congress and declare it. Of course there is not implied—either in the legislation or in our interpretation of it—any suggestion of individual unworthiness or racial inferiority. These considerations are in no manner involved.

D. Commentary on *Ozawa*

The 1790 act limited naturalization to whites only; in *Ozawa*, the Court defined "white" to mean Caucasian, and thus further narrowed access to naturalization. Under the Court's narrow reading, only white Caucasians could be naturalized.

E. Background on *Thind*

Vinay Harpalani

Memorandum on United States v. Thind

United States v. Thind (1923) was the latter of two racial prerequisite cases to be argued before the Supreme Court. Under the 1790 Naturalization Law, American citizenship was restricted to "free, White persons." Later amendments granted formal citizenship rights to African and Native Americans, but immigrant groups from Asia, the Middle East, and other parts of the world could not be naturalized unless they were considered "White." The racial prerequisite cases were a series of suits brought between 1878 and 1944 to determine which of these ethnic groups were eligible for American citizenship. Federal courts used various standards, ranging from Congressional intent to scientific knowledge to skin color, to determine who was and was not "White."

Bhagat Singh Thind (1892–1967) was born in Punjab (India) and settled in Seattle, Washington in 1912. He served in the U.S. Army during World War I and went on to receive a Ph.D. from the University of California at Berkeley. In 1920, Thind sought U.S. citizenship in Oregon and was challenged by the Bureau of Naturalization. This was a time of rising anti-immigrant sentiment; Congress had recently passed the Immigration Act of 1917, which barred further immigration from India. Prior racial prerequisite cases involving Asian Indians had yielded mixed results; some courts classified them as "White" while others did not.

Memorandum on *United States v. Thind* 2.
On file with the author.
Reprinted with permission of Vinay Harpalani.

F. *United States v. Thind,* 261 U.S. 204 (1923)

1. Facts

Justice SUTHERLAND delivered the opinion of the Court.

This cause is here upon a certificate from the Circuit Court of appeals requesting the instruction of this Court in respect of the following questions:

1. Is a high-caste Hindu, of full Indian blood, born at Amritsar, Punjab, India, a white person within the meaning of section 2169, Revised Statutes?

2. Does the Act of February 5, 1917 (39 Stat. 875, §3), disqualify from naturalization as citizens those Hindus now barred by that act, who had lawfully entered the United States prior to the passage of said act?

The appellee was granted a certificate of citizenship by the District Court of the United States for the District of Oregon, over the objection of the Naturalization Examiner for the United States. A bill in equity was then filed by the United States, seeking a cancellation of the certificate on the ground that the appellee was not a white person and therefore not lawfully entitled to naturalization. The District Court, on motion, dismissed the bill (*In re Bhagat Singh Thind*, 268 Fed. 683), and an appeal was taken to the Circuit Court of Appeals. No question is made in respect of the individual qualifications of the appellee. The sole question is whether he falls within the class designated by Congress as eligible.

2. Opinion

Section 2169, Revised Statutes (Comp. St. § 4358), provides that the provisions of the Naturalization Act 'shall apply to aliens being free white persons and to aliens of African nativity and to persons of African descent.'

If the applicant is a white person, within the meaning of this section, he is entitled to naturalization; otherwise not. In *Ozawa v. United States*, 260 U. S. 178, 43 Sup. Ct. 65, 67 L. Ed. 199, decided November 13, 1922, we had occasion to consider the application of these words to the case of a cultivated Japanese and were constrained to hold that he was not within their meaning. As there pointed out, the provision is not that any particular class of persons shall be excluded, but it is, in effect, that only white persons shall be included within the privilege of the statute. 'The intention was to confer the privilege of citizenship upon that class of persons whom the fathers knew as white, and to deny it to all who could not be so classified. It is not enough to say that the framers did not have in mind the brown or yellow races of Asia. It is necessary to go farther and be able to say that had these particular races been suggested the language of the act would have been so varied as to include them within its privileges'—citing *Dartmouth College v. Woodward*, 4 Wheat. 518, 644, 4 L. Ed. 629. Following a long line of decisions of the lower Federal courts, we held that the words imported a racial and not an individual test and were meant to indicate only persons of what is *popularly* known as the Caucasian race. But, as there pointed out, the conclusion that the phrase 'white persons' and the word 'Caucasian' are synonymous does not end the matter. It enabled us to dispose of the problem as it was there presented, since the applicant for citizenship clearly fell outside the zone of debatable ground on the negative side; but the decision still left the question to be dealt with, in doubtful and different cases, by the 'process of judicial inclusion and exclusion.' Mere ability on the part of an applicant for naturalization to establish a line of descent from a Caucasian ancestor will not ipso facto to and necessarily conclude the inquiry. 'Caucasian' is a conventional word of much flexibility, as a study of the literature dealing with racial questions will disclose, and while it and the words 'white persons' are treated as synonymous for the purposes of that case, they are not of identical meaning—idem per idem.

In the endeavor to ascertain the meaning of the statute we must not fail to keep in mind that it does not employ the word 'Caucasian,' but the words 'white persons,' and these are words of common speech and not of scientific origin. The word 'Caucasian,' not only was employed in the law, but was probably wholly unfamiliar to the original framers of the statute in 1790. When we employ it, we do so as an aid to the ascertainment of the legislative intent and not as an invariable substitute for the statutory words. Indeed, as used in the science of ethnology, the connotation of the word is by no means clear, and the use of it in its scientific sense as an equivalent for the words of the statute, other considerations aside, would simply mean the substitution of one perplexity for another. But in this country, during the last half century especially, the word by common usage has acquired a popular meaning, not clearly defined to be sure, but sufficiently so to enable us to say that its popular as distinguished from its scientific application is of appreciably narrower scope. It is in the popular sense of the word, therefore, that we employ is as an aid to the construction of the statute, for it would be obviously illogical to convert words of common speech used in a statute into words of scientific terminology when neither the latter nor the science for whose purposes they were coined was within the contemplation of the framers of the statute or of the people for whom it was framed. The words of the statute are to be interpreted in accordance with the understanding of the common man from whose vocabulary they were taken. See *Maillard v. Lawrence*, 16 How. 251, 261, 14 L. Ed. 925.

They imply, as we have said, a racial test; but the term 'race' is one which, for the practical purposes of the statute, must be applied to a group of living persons *now* possessing in common the requisite characteristics, not to groups of persons who are supposed to be or really are descended from some remote, common ancestor, but who, whether they both resemble him to a greater or less extent, have, at any rate, ceased altogether to resemble one another. It may be true that the blond Scandinavian and the brown Hindu have a common ancestor in the dim reaches of antiquity, but the average man knows perfectly well that there are unmistakable and profound differences between them to-day; and it is not impossible, if that common ancestor could be materialized in the flesh, we should discover that he was himself sufficiently differentiated from both of his descendants to preclude his racial classification with either. The question for determination is not, therefore, whether by the speculative processes of ethnological reasoning we may present a probability to the scientific mind that they have the same origin, but whether we can satisfy the common understanding that they are now the same or sufficiently the same to justify the interpreters of a statute—written in the words of common speech, for common understanding, by unscientific men—in classifying them together in the statutory category as white persons. In 1790 the Adamite theory of creation—which gave a common ancestor to all mankind—was generally accepted, and it is not at all probable that it was intended by the legislators of that day to submit the question of the application of the words 'white persons' to the mere test of an indefinitely remote common ancestry, without regard to the extent of the subsequent divergence of the various branches from such common ancestry or from one another.

The eligibility of this applicant for citizenship is based on the sole fact that he is of high-caste Hindu stock, born in Punjab, one of the extreme northwestern districts of India, and classified by certain scientific authorities as of the Caucasian or Aryan race The Aryan theory as a racial basis seems to be discredited by most, if not all, modern writers on the subject of ethnology. A review of their contentions would serve no useful purpose. It is enough to refer to the works of Deniker (Races of Man, 317), Keane (Man, Past and Present, 445, 446), and Huxley (Man's Place in Nature, 278) and to the Dictionary of Races, Senate Document 662, 61st Congress, 3d Sess. 1910–1911, p. 17.

The term 'Aryan' has to do with linguistic, and not at all with physical, characteristics, and it would seem reasonably clear that mere resemblance in language, indicating a common linguistic root buried in remotely ancient soil, is altogether inadequate to prove common racial origin. There is, and can be, no assurance that the so-called Aryan language was not spoken by a variety of races living in proximity to one another. Our own history has witnessed the adoption of the English tongue by millions of negroes, whose descendants can never be classified racially with the descendants of white persons, notwithstanding both may speak a common root language.

The word 'Caucasian' is in scarcely better repute. It is at best a conventional term, with an altogether fortuitous origin, which under scientific manipulation, has come to include far more than the unscientific mind suspects. According to Keane, for example (The World's Peoples, 24, 28, 307, et seq.), it includes not only the Hindu, but some of the Polynesians (that is, the Maori, Tahitians, Samoans, Hawaiians, and others), the Hamites of Africa, upon the ground of the Caucasic cast of their features, though in color they range from brown to black. We venture to think that the average well informed white American would learn with some degree of astonishment that the race to which he belongs is made up of such heterogeneous elements. The various authorities are in irreconcilable disagreement as to what constitutes a proper racial division. For instance, Blumenbach has 5 races; Keane following Linnaeus, 4; Deniker, 29.5. The explanation probably is that 'the innumerable varieties of mankind run into one another by insensible degrees,' and to arrange them in sharply bounded divisions is an undertaking of such uncertainty that common agreement is practically impossible.

It may be, therefore, that a given group cannot be properly assigned to any of the enumerated grand racial divisions. The type may have been so changed by intermixture of blood as to justify an intermediate classification. Something very like this has actually taken place in India. Thus, in Hindustan and Berar there was such an intermixture of the 'Aryan' invader with the dark-skinned Dravidian.

In the Punjab and Rajputana, while the invaders seem to have met with more success in the effort to preserve their racial purity, intermarriages did occur producing an intermingling of the two and destroying to a greater or less degree the purity of the 'Aryan' blood. The rules of caste, while calculated to prevent this intermixture, seem not to have been entirely successful.

It does not seem necessary to pursue the matter of scientific classification further. We are unable to agree with the District Court, or with other lower federal courts, in the conclusion that a native Hindu is eligible for naturalization under section 2169. The words of familiar speech, which were used by the original framers of the law, were intended to include only the type of man whom they knew as white. The immigration of that day was almost exclusively from the British Isles and Northwestern Europe, whence they and their forebears had come. When they extended the privilege of American citizenship to 'any alien being a free white person' it was these immigrants—bone of their bone and flesh of their flesh—and their kind whom they must have had affirmatively in mind. The succeeding years brought immigrants from Eastern, Southern and Middle Europe, among them the Slavs and the dark-eyed, swarthy people of Alpine and Mediterranean stock, and these were received as unquestionably akin to those already here and readily amalgamated with them. It was the descendants of these, and other immigrants of like origin, who constituted the white population of the country when section 2169, re-enacting the naturalization test of 1790, was adopted, and, there is no reason to doubt, with like intent and meaning.

What, if any, people of Primarily Asiatic stock come within the words of the section we do not deem it necessary now to decide. There is much in the origin and historic development of the statute to suggest that no Asiatic whatever was included. The debates in Congress, during the consideration of the subject in 1870 and 1875, are persuasively of this character. In 1873, for example, the words 'free white persons' were unintentionally omitted from the compilation of the Revised Statutes. This omission was supplied in 1875 by the act to correct errors and supply omissions. 18 Stat. c. 80, p. 318. When this act was under consideration by Congress efforts were made to strike out the words quoted, and it was insisted upon the one hand and conceded upon the other, that the effect of their retention was to exclude Asiatics generally from citizenship. While what was said upon that occasion, to be sure, furnishes no basis for judicial construction of the statute, it is, nevertheless, an important historic incident, which may not be altogether ignored in the search for the true meaning of words which are themselves historic. That question, however, may well be left for final determination until the details have been more completely disclosed by the consideration of particular cases, as they from time to time arise. The words of the statute, it must be conceded, do not readily yield to exact interpretation, and it is probably better to leave them as they are than to risk undue extension or undue limitation of their meaning by any general paraphrase at this time.

3. Holding

What we now hold is that the words 'free white persons' are words of common speech, to be interpreted in accordance with the understanding of the common man, synonymous with the word 'Caucasian' only as that word is popularly understood. As so understood and used, whatever may be the speculations of the ethnologist, it does not include the body of people to whom the appellee belongs. It is a matter of familiar observation and knowledge that the physical group characteristics of the Hindus render them readily distinguishable from the various groups of persons in this country commonly recognized as white. The children of English, French, German, Italian, Scandinavian, and other European parentage, quickly merge into the mass of our population and lose the distinctive hallmarks of their European origin. On the other hand, it cannot be doubted that the children born in this country of Hindu parents would retain indefinitely the clear evidence of their ancestry. It is very far from our thought to suggest the slightest question of racial superiority or inferiority. What we suggest is merely racial difference, and it is of such character and extent that the great body of our people instinctively recognize it and reject the thought of assimilation.

It is not without significance in this connection that Congress, by the Act of February 5, 1917, 39 Stat. 874, c. 29, § 3 (Comp. St. 1918, Comp. St. Ann. Supp. 1919, § 4289 1/4 b), has now excluded from admission into this country all natives of Asia within designated limits of latitude and longitude, including the whole of India. This not only constitutes conclusive evidence of the congressional attitude of opposition to Asiatic immigration generally, but is persuasive of a similar attitude toward Asiatic naturalization as well, since it is not likely that Congress would be willing to accept as citizens a class of persons whom it rejects as immigrants.

It follows that a negative answer must be given to the first question, which disposes of the case and renders an answer to the second question unnecessary, and it will be so certified.

G. Commentary on *Thind*

Vinay Harpalani

Memorandum on United States v. Thind

In *Ozawa v. United States*, the Court denied naturalization to Japanese immigrant Takao Ozawa, ruling that "white" was synonymous with "Caucasian." This strengthened Thind's chances, since most anthropologists considered Asian Indians, unlike Japanese, to be "Caucasian."

In 1923, however, the Supreme Court rejected Thind's citizenship bid, amending its prior definition of "white." The Court stated that "Caucasian" was equivalent to "white" only in accordance with common understanding. Since Asian Indians were not commonly understood to be "white," they did not qualify for citizenship. Between 1923 and 1927, numerous Asian Indians were stripped of their citizenship, and other racial prerequisite cases followed the *Thind* precedent for the next two decades. Thind himself was granted citizenship in New York in 1936, where naturalization examiners chose not to challenge his application. He would go on to become a Sikh spiritual leader and author of numerous books.

The *Thind* decision became obsolete in 1946, when the Luce-Celler Act created a small immigration quota of Asian Indians and permitted their naturalization; in 1965, this quota increased substantially. The 1952 McCarran-Walter Act completely supplanted the 1790 Naturalization Law, removing all race restrictions to citizenship. Nevertheless, the *Thind* case portended future controversy about classification of Asian Indians. In 1970, the Census Bureau classified Asian Indians as "white," denying them protected minority status. After much internal debate, Indian American organizations successfully lobbied to change this classification to "Asian Indian," which later fell under the "Asian and Pacific Islander" category on the census.

Memorandum on *United States v. Thind* 3.

On file with the author.

Reprinted with permission of Vinay Harpalani.

H. Background on *De La Guerra*

In 1821, Mexico gained its independence from Spain. At that time, the independent country of Mexico included vast portions of land that presently are part of the United States. These lands included the states of Texas, California, Arizona, New Mexico, Nevada, and portions of Colorado, Kansas, and Utah.

These northern portions of Mexico were sparsely populated with mostly Mexicans of mixed Spanish and American-Indian ancestry, American Indians, and a few whites and blacks. As white settlers began moving into this territory in large numbers, conflicts occurred between the old and new residents.

In 1845, James Polk was elected President of the United States. A strong advocate of United States expansion in the Southwest, Polk supported the civil war that led to the independence of Texas and its subsequent incorporation into the United States. Shortly after his inauguration, President Polk ordered a military expedition to operate along the Rio Grande River, a move calculated to provoke Mexico into war with the United States. While the actual boundary was unclear, both Mexico and the United States had previously regarded the Nueces River some 150 miles north of the Rio Grande as the dividing line between the two countries. This boundary had been agreed upon under a previous treaty between the United States and Spain whereby Spain gave up any legal claim to the area that became the state of Florida. When American troops came under fire resulting in sixteen deaths, Congress declared war against Mexico.

After several years of fighting, United States troops successfully occupied most of the northern portions of Mexico. In 1848, a cease fire was arranged and the Treaty of Guadalupe Hidalgo[18] was signed ending the conflict. The Treaty settled the war between the United States and Mexico by drawing the boundary line between the two countries at the Rio Grande River and providing for the sale of land from Mexico to the United States. Mexico turned over to the United States what are today the states of California, Nevada, Arizona, New Mexico, and portions of Colorado and Utah. The United States paid $15 million for the territory. Finally, concerned about the fate of Mexicans remaining in the conquered territories, Mexico negotiated

---

18. For a detailed examination of the text and history of the treaty, see TREATIES AND OTHER INTERNATIONAL ACTS OF THE UNITED STATES OF AMERICA 207–428 (Hunter Miller Ed. 1937).

protections for them. Despite the negotiations, the Treaty was extremely favorable to the United States due to Mexico's military defeat during the war. Two areas, land ownership and citizenship, were particularly controversial.

As to land ownership, the Treaty undermined the legitimacy of Mexican land grants both by denying explicit recognition of the validity of such grants made before the war and by refusing to expressly acknowledge the validity of Mexican practices and customs for designating land grants. In subsequent litigation over contested claims to land, the customs and practices of Mexican authorities in designating land grants were often held to be too vague to be enforceable under very different United States standards. Thus, the Treaty made it much easier to deprive Mexicans of their lands by making United States law and practice determinative and by failing to acknowledge Mexican law and customs as the appropriate reference for ascertaining the validity of land claims.

As to citizenship, the Treaty provided:

> Mexicans now established in territories previously belonging to Mexico, and which remain for the future within the limits of the United States, as defined by the present Treaty, shall be free to continue where they now reside, or to remove at any time to the Mexican Republic, retaining the property which they possess in the said territories, or disposing thereof and removing the proceeds wherever they please; without their being subjected, on this account, to any contribution, tax or charge whatever.

> Those who shall prefer to remain in the said territories, may either retain the title and rights of Mexican citizens, or acquire those of citizens of the United States, but, they shall be under the obligation to make their election within one year from the date of the exchange of ratifications of this treaty: and those who shall remain in the said territories, after the expiration of that year, without having declared their intention to retain the character of Mexicans, shall be considered to have elected to become citizens of the United States.[19]

The Treaty further provided:

> The Mexicans who, in the territories aforesaid, shall not preserve the character of citizens of the Mexican Republic, conformably with what is stipulated in the preceding article, shall be incorporated into the Union of the United States and be admitted, at the proper time (to be judged by the Congress of the United States)[20] to the enjoyment of all the rights of citizens of

---

19. *Id.* at 417–18.

20. The language "at the proper time" meant that Congress had complete discretion to determine when that citizenship would be granted. Congress used its discretion under the Treaty to deny statehood to New Mexico for sixty-two years, the longest wait period in American history, despite recurrent petitions from the territory. The principal reason for denying statehood to New Mexico for so many years was Congress' reluctance to have a state with such a high percentage of

the United States according to the principles of the Constitution; and in the mean time shall be maintained and protected in the free enjoyment of their liberty and property, and secured in the free exercise of their religion without restriction.[21]

The Treaty left many questions unanswered about the actual status of those Mexicans remaining in the territories that were transferred from Mexico to the United States. One critical question arose pertaining to the meaning of the citizenship granted by the Treaty. What would be the federal citizenship rights of Mexicans of mixed Indian, Spanish, and black ancestry and would those rights include political participation on an equal basis with whites?

I. *People v. De La Guerra,* 40 Cal. 311 (1870)

1. Facts

Justice TEMPLE delivered the opinion of the Court.

The respondent Pablo de la Guerra was born at Santa Barbara, California, in 1819, and has ever since resided at that place, and is admitted to have been a white male citizen of Mexico at the date of the Treaty of Guadalupe Hidalgo. After the ratification of that treaty he elected to become a citizen of the United States in the mode provided in the treaty. He was a member of the Constitutional Convention which framed the Constitution of California, and has almost continuously, since the adoption of that instrument, held office under its provisions. At the judicial election, held in 1869, he was elected Judge of the First Judicial District, and the [state] in this proceeding contests his right to the office, on the ground that he is not a citizen of the United States, as by an Act passed April 20, 1863, it is provided that "no person shall be eligible to the office of District Judge, who shall not have been a citizen of the United States . . . for two years. . . ."

2. Opinion

Having admitted into the Union a State, of which these inhabitants were constituent members, Congress could do no more. It has conferred upon them all the rights of citizens, or rather it has recognized these rights in the only mode provided by the Constitution which was applicable to them. . . .

But it is suggested by counsel for [the State] that if this construction be correct, then the Constitution of California is in conflict with the ninth article of the [Treaty of Guadalupe Hidalgo], for that article provides that all Mexican citizens who elect to become citizens of the United States shall be admitted to all the rights of citizens,

---

nonwhite residents. Latinos/as constituted a majority of New Mexico residents up until 1912. New Mexico was finally granted statehood in 1910.

21. V TREATIES AND OTHER INTERNATIONAL ACTS OF THE UNITED STATES OF AMERICA (Hunter Miller Ed. 1937) at 418.

while the Constitution discriminates. It declares that white male citizens of Mexico, who have elected to become citizens of the United States, shall be electors, while all, without distinction of color, including Indians, were Mexican citizens, and entitled to vote by the laws of Mexico.

If this be so, it does not follow that the respondent is not a citizen of the United States, but that the elective franchise is denied to certain persons who had been entitled to its exercise under the laws of Mexico. The possession of all political rights is not essential to citizenship. When Congress admitted California as a State, the constituent members of the State, in their aggregate capacity, became vested with the sovereign powers of government, "according to the principles of the constitution." They then had the right to prescribe the qualifications of electors, and it is no violation of the treaty that these qualifications were such as to exclude some of the inhabitants from certain political rights. They were excluded in accordance with the principles of the constitution.

3. Holding

The respondent is clearly a citizen of the United States, and the judgment should be affirmed.

J. Commentary on *De La Guerra*

Pablo De La Guerra was deemed eligible to hold political office not because he was able to transfer from Mexican citizenship to American citizenship, but because a California State law characterized him as "white." Under *Ozawa*, the Supreme Court had narrowed access to naturalization to white Caucasians only; a California state law, not any federal law, provided De La Guerra his opportunity to hold political office because he was deemed to be white. Latinos/as were denied political equality under California state law even though they were deemed to be citizens. The citizenship rights at issue were federal citizenship rights which the Supreme Court had construed very narrowly in *United States v. Cruikshank*. Even after the passage of the Fifteenth Amendment in 1870 prohibiting racial discrimination in voting, states were free to prevent non-whites, through qualification provisions, from exercising the franchise in state and local elections. Accordingly, while the United States citizenship granted by the Treaty of Guadalupe Hidalgo might include federal citizenship for Mexicans of mixed Indian and Spanish ancestry, the Treaty's provision of federal citizenship offered no guarantee of voting rights or political participation, which were matters left to the states for purposes of enforcement. Since 1812, when it became an independent nation, Mexico granted full citizenship and political rights to American Indians. Thus, at the time of the Treaty, Mexico had no formal racial restrictions on who could be a full citizen. Therefore, those American Indians and mixed race Mexicans who opted to remain in the territory transferred to the United States lost much of the citizenship rights they previously exercised as citizens of Mexico. Even after the passage of the Fifteenth Amendment, enforcement by the federal government was minimal. The federal government failed to prevent most state practices designed to exclude many minority voters; these practices included the selective application of literacy tests, imposition of poll taxes, and utilization of limited voter lists. Not until passage of the Voting Rights Act in 1965 did the federal government take an active role in the prohibition of racial discrimination in voting.[22]

K. Background on *Ping*

Immigration laws were frequently used to isolate and discriminate against specific races. In 1875 Congress began to restrict immigration due to large numbers of Chinese immigrants fleeing economic hardship. Many came to California and other western states to take advantage of the job opportunities created by the large availability of land and the discovery of vast gold reserves. Because of perceived competition with white laborers, in 1882 Congress sought to limit Chinese immigration, particularly Chinese workers, when it passed the Chinese Exclusion Act suspending the immigration of most Chinese laborers.

L. *Ping v. United States*, 130 U.S. 581 (1889)

1. Facts

Justice FIELD delivered the opinion of the Court.

This case comes before us on appeal from an order of the Circuit Court of the United States for the Northern District of California refusing to release the appellant, on a writ of habeas corpus, from his alleged unlawful detention by Captain Walker, master of the steamship Belgic, lying within the harbor of San Francisco. The appellant is a subject of the Emperor of China and a laborer by occupation. He resided at San Francisco, California, following his occupation, from some time in 1875 until June 2, 1887, when he left for China on the steamship Gaelic, having in his possession a certificate, in terms entitling him to return to the United States, bearing date on that day, duly issued to him by the collector of customs of the port of San Francisco, pursuant to the provisions of section four of the restriction act of May 6, 1882, as amended by the act of July 5, 1884. 22 Stat. 58, c. 126; 23 Stat. 115, c. 220.

On the 7th of September, 1888, the appellant, on his return to California, sailed from Hong Kong in the steamship Belgic, which arrived within the port of San Francisco on the 8th of October following. On his arrival he presented to the proper custom-house officers his certificate, and demanded permission to land.

---

22. A similar approach granting federal citizenship with limited protection against state racial discrimination in political rights was applied to other Latinos/as such as Puerto Ricans and Dominicans. *See generally* J. TRIAS MONGE, PUERTO RICO: THE TRIALS OF THE OLDEST COLONY IN THE WORLD (1997).

The collector of the port refused the permit, solely on the ground that under the act of Congress, approved October 1, 1888, supplementary to the restriction acts of 1882 and 1884, the certificate had been annulled and his right to land abrogated, and he had been thereby forbidden again to enter the United States. 25 Stat. 504, c. 1064. The captain of the steamship, therefore, detained the appellant on board the steamer. Thereupon a petition on his behalf was presented to the Circuit Court of the United States for the Northern District of California, alleging that he was unlawfully restrained of his liberty, and praying that a writ of habeas corpus might be issued directed to the master of the steamship, commanding him to have the body of the appellant, with the cause of his detention, before the court at a time and place designated, to do and receive what might there be considered in the premises. A writ was accordingly issued, and in obedience to it the body of the appellant was produced before the court. Upon the hearing which followed, the court, after finding the facts substantially as stated, held as conclusions of law that the appellant was not entitled to enter the United States, and was not unlawfully restrained of his liberty, and ordered that he be remanded to the custody of the master of the steamship from which he had been taken under the writ. From this order an appeal was taken to this court.

2. Opinion

The appeal involves a consideration of the validity of the Act of Congress of October 1, 1888, prohibiting Chinese laborers from entering the United States who had departed before its passage, having a certificate issued under the act of 1882 as amended by the act of 1884, granting them permission to return. The validity of the act is assailed as being in effect an expulsion from the country of Chinese laborers, in violation of existing treaties between the United States and the government of China, and of rights vested in them under the laws of Congress. . . .

a. Treaties and Legislation

When once it is established that Congress possesses the power to pass an act, our province ends with its construction, and its application to cases as they are presented for determination. Congress has the power under the Constitution to declare war, and in two instances where the power has been exercised—in the War of 1812 against Great Britain, and in 1846 against Mexico—the propriety and wisdom and justice of its action were vehemently assailed by some of the ablest and best men in the country, but no one doubted the legality of the proceeding, and any imputation by this or any other court of the United States upon the motives of the members of Congress who in either case voted for the declaration, would have been justly the cause of animadversion. We do not mean to intimate that the moral aspects of legislative acts may not be proper subjects of consideration. Undoubtedly they may be, at proper times and places, before the public, in the halls of Congress, and in all the modes by which the public mind can be influenced. Public opinion thus enlightened, brought to bear upon legislation, will do more than all other causes to prevent abuses; but the province of the courts is to pass upon the validity of laws, not to make them, and when their validity is established, to declare their meaning and apply their provisions. All else lies beyond their domain.

b. Powers of Congress

There being nothing in the treaties between China and the United States to impair the validity of the Act of Congress of October 1, 1888, was it on any other ground beyond the competency of Congress to pass it? If so, it must be because it was not within the power of Congress to prohibit Chinese laborers who had at the time departed from the United States, or should subsequently depart, from returning to the United States. Those laborers are not citizens of the United States; they are aliens. That the government of the United States, through the action of the legislative department, can exclude aliens from its territory is a proposition which we do not think open to controversy. Jurisdiction over its own territory to that extent is an incident of every independent nation. It is a part of its independence. If it could not exclude aliens it would be to that extent subject to the control of another power. As said by this court in the case of *The Exchange*, 7 Cranch, 116, 136, speaking by Chief Justice Marshall: "The jurisdiction of the nation within its own territory is necessarily exclusive and absolute. It is susceptible of no limitation not imposed by itself. Any restriction upon it, deriving validity from an external source, would imply a diminution of its sovereignty to the extent of the restriction, and an investment of that sovereignty to the same extent in that power which could impose such restriction. All exceptions, therefore, to the full and complete power of a nation within its own territories, must be traced up to the consent of the nation itself. They can flow from no other legitimate source."

While under our Constitution and form of government the great mass of local matters is controlled by local authorities, the United States, in their relation to foreign countries and their subjects or citizens are one nation, invested with powers which belong to independent nations, the exercise of which can be invoked for the maintenance of its absolute independence and security throughout its entire territory. The powers to declare war, make treaties, suppress insurrection, repel invasion, regulate foreign commerce, secure republican governments to the States, and admit subjects of other nations to citizenship, are all sovereign powers, restricted in their exercise only by the Constitution itself and considerations of public policy and justice which control, more or less, the conduct of all civilized nations. . . .

The power of the government to exclude foreigners from the country whenever, in its judgment, the public interests require such exclusion, has been asserted in repeated instances, and never denied by the executive or legislative departments. In a communication made in December, 1852, to Mr. A. Dudley Mann, at one time a special agent of the Department of State in Europe, Mr. Everett, then Secretary of State under President Fillmore, writes: "This government could never give up the right of excluding foreigners whose presence it might deem a source of danger to the United States." "Nor will this government consider such exclusion of American citizens from Russia necessarily a matter of diplomatic complaint to that country." In a dispatch to Mr. Fay, our minister to Switzerland, in March, 1856, Mr. Marcy, Secretary of State under President Pierce, writes: "Every society possesses the undoubted right to determine who shall compose its members, and it is exercised by all nations, both in peace and war." "It may always be questionable whether a resort to this power is warranted by the circumstances, or what department of the government is empowered to exert it; but there can be no doubt that it is possessed by all nations, and that each may decide for itself when the occasion arises demanding its exercise." In a communication in September, 1869, to Mr. Washburne, our minister to France, Mr. Fish, Secretary of State under President Grant, uses this language: "The control of the people within its limits, and the right to expel from its territory persons who are dangerous to the peace of the State, are too clearly within the essential attributes of sovereignty to be seriously contested. Strangers visiting or sojourning in a foreign country voluntarily submit themselves to its laws and customs, and the municipal laws of France, authorizing the expulsion of strangers, are not of such recent date, nor has the exercise of the power by the government of France been so infrequent, that sojourners within her territory can claim surprise when the power is put in force." In a communication to Mr. Foster, our minister to Mexico, in July, 1879, Mr. Evarts, Secretary of State under President Hayes, referring to the power vested in the constitution of Mexico to expel objectionable foreigners, says: "The admission that, as that constitution now stands and is interpreted, foreigners who render themselves harmful or objectionable to the general government must expect to be liable to the exercise of the power adverted to, even in time of peace, remains, and no good reason is seen for departing from that conclusion now. But, while there may be no expedient basis on which to found objection, on principle and in advance of a special case thereunder, to the constitutional right thus asserted by Mexico, yet the manner of carrying out such asserted right may be highly objectionable. You would be fully justified in making earnest remonstrances should a citizen of the United States be expelled from Mexican territory without just steps to assure the grounds of such expulsion, and in bringing the fact to the immediate knowledge of the Department." In a communication to Mr. W. J. Stillman, under date of August 3, 1882, Mr. Frelinghuysen, Secretary of State under President Arthur, writes: "This government cannot contest the right of foreign governments to exclude, on police or other grounds, American citizens from their shores." *Wharton's International Law Digest*, § 206.

The exclusion of paupers, criminals and persons afflicted with incurable diseases, for which statutes have been passed, is only an application of the same power to particular classes of persons, whose presence is deemed injurious or a source of danger to the country. As applied to them, there has never been any question as to the power to exclude them. The power is constantly exercised; its existence is involved in the right of self-preservation. As to paupers, it makes no difference by whose aid they are brought to the country. As Mr. Fish, when Secretary of State, wrote, in a communication under date of December 26, 1872, to Mr. James Moulding, of Liverpool, the government of the United States "is not willing and will not consent to receive the pauper class of any community who may be sent or may be assisted in their immigration at the expense of government or of municipal authorities." As to criminals, the power of exclusion has always been exercised, even in the absence of any statute on the subject. In a despatch to Mr. Cramer, our minister to Switzerland, in December, 1881, Mr. Blaine, Secretary of State under President Arthur, writes: "While, under the Constitution and the laws, this country is open to the honest and industrious immigrant, it has no room outside of its prisons or almshouses for depraved and incorrigible criminals or hopelessly dependent paupers who may have become a pest or burden, or both, to their own country."

3. Holding

The power of exclusion of foreigners being an incident of sovereignty belonging to the government of the United States, as a part of those sovereign powers delegated by the Constitution, the right to its exercise at any time when, in the judgment of the government, the interests of the country require it, cannot be granted away or restrained on behalf of any one. The powers of government are delegated in trust to the United States, and are incapable of transfer to any other parties. They cannot be abandoned or surrendered. Nor can their exercise be hampered, when needed for the public good, by any considerations of private interest. The exercise of these public trusts is not the subject of barter or contract. Whatever license, therefore, Chinese laborers may have obtained, previous to the act of October 1, 1888, to return to the United States after their departure, is held at the will of the government, revocable at any time, at its pleasure. Whether a proper consideration by our government of its previous laws, or a proper respect for the nation whose subjects are affected by its action, ought to have qualified its inhibition and made it applicable only to persons departing from the country after the passage of the act, are not questions for judicial determination. If there be any just ground of complaint on the part of China, it must be made to the political department of our government, which is alone competent to act upon the subject. . . .

M. Commentary on *Ping*

The *Ping* case ruled that Congress retained the ultimate power under the Constitution to exclude aliens and that Congress could exercise such power for any reason it chose, including the exclusion of persons from a specific nationality. While such exclusion of Chinese persons may not have been moral, the Constitution did not prohibit it.

While Congress had the power according to the Supreme Court to exclude Chinese immigrants, the question still remained as to what power it held over those Chinese born in the United States to parents who were aliens. Was the Fourteenth Amendment applicable to Asian Americans in the same way it had been applied to blacks? Would birth within the United States, and thereby American citizenship confer the protections of the Constitution on Asian Americans?

N. Background on *Ark*

With the Congressional exclusion of Chinese immigrants upheld in *Ping*, many Chinese coming to the United States were prevented from entering the country. Some of those prevented from entering were American-born of Chinese parentage.

O. *United States v. Ark*, 169 U.S. 649 (1898)

1. Facts

Justice GRAY delivered the opinion of the Court.

The facts of this case, as agreed by the parties, are as follows: Wong Kim Ark was born in 1873 in the city of San Francisco, in the State of California and United States of America, and was and is a laborer. His father and mother were persons of Chinese descent, and subjects of the Emperor of China; they were at the time of his birth domiciled residents of the United States, having previously established and still enjoying a permanent domicil and residence therein at San Francisco; they continued to reside and remain in the United States until 1890, when they departed for China; and during all the time of their residence in the United States they were engaged in business, and were never employed in any diplomatic or official capacity under the Emperor of China. Wong Kim Ark, ever since his birth, has had but one residence, to wit, in California, within the United States, and has there resided, claiming to be a citizen of the United States, and has never lost or changed that residence, or gained or acquired another residence; and neither he, nor his parents acting for him, ever renounced his allegiance to the United States, or did or committed any act or thing to exclude him therefrom. In 1890 (when he must have been about seventeen years of age) he departed for China on a temporary visit and with the intention of returning to the United States, and did return thereto by sea in the same year, and was permitted by the collector of customs to enter the United States, upon the sole ground that he was a native-born citizen of the United States. After such return, he remained in the United States, claiming to be a citizen thereof, until 1894, when he (being about twenty-one years of age, but whether a little above or a little under that age does not appear) again departed for China on a temporary visit and with the intention of returning to the United States; and he did return thereto by sea in August, 1895, and applied to the collector of customs for permission to land; and was denied such permission, upon the sole ground that he was not a citizen of the United States.

2. Opinion

It is conceded that, if he is a citizen of the United States, the acts of Congress, known as the Chinese Exclusion Acts, prohibiting persons of the Chinese race, and especially Chinese laborers, from coming into the United States, do not and cannot apply to him.

The question presented by the record is whether a child born in the United States, of parents of Chinese descent, who, at the time of his birth, are subjects of the Emperor of China, but have a permanent domicil and residence in the United States, and are there carrying on business, and are not employed in any diplomatic or official capacity under the Emperor of China, becomes at the time of his birth a citizen of the United States, . . .

. . . To hold that the Fourteenth Amendment of the Constitution excludes from citizenship the children, born in the United States, of citizens or subjects of other countries, would be to deny citizenship to thousands of persons of English, Scotch, Irish, German or other European parentage, who have always been considered and treated as citizens of the United States.

Whatever considerations, in the absence of a controlling provision of the Constitution, might influence the legislative or the executive branch of the Government to decline to admit persons of the Chinese race to the status of citizens of the United States, there are none that can constrain or permit the judiciary to refuse to give full effect to the peremptory and explicit language of the Fourteenth Amendment, which declares and ordains that "All persons born or naturalized in the United States, and subject to the jurisdiction thereof, are citizens of the United States" . . .

The Fourteenth Amendment of the Constitution, in the declaration that "all persons born or naturalized in the United States, and subject to the jurisdiction thereof, are citizens of the United States and of the State wherein they reside," contemplates two sources of citizenship, and two only: birth and naturalization. Citizenship by naturalization can only be acquired by naturalization under the authority and in the forms of law. But citizenship by birth is established by the mere fact of birth under the circumstances defined in the Constitution. Every person born in the United States, and subject to the jurisdiction thereof, becomes at once a citizen of the United States, and needs no naturalization. A person born out of the jurisdiction of the United States can only become a citizen by being naturalized, either by treaty, as in the case of the annexation of foreign territory; or by authority of Congress, exercised either by declaring certain classes of persons to be citizens, as in the enactments conferring citizenship upon foreign-born children of citizens, or by enabling foreigners individually to become citizens by proceedings in the judicial tribunals, as in the ordinary provisions of the naturalization acts.

The power of naturalization, vested in Congress by the Constitution, is a power to confer citizenship, not a power to take it away. "A naturalized citizen," said Chief Justice Marshall, "becomes a member of the society, possessing all the rights of a native citizen, and standing, in the view of the Constitution, on the footing of a native. The Constitution does not authorize Congress to enlarge or abridge those rights. The simple power of the National Legislature is to prescribe a uniform rule of naturalization, and the exercise of this power exhausts it, so far as respects the individual. The Constitution then takes him up, and, among other rights, extends to him the capacity of suing in the courts of the United States, precisely under the same circumstances under which a native might sue." *Osborn v. United States Bank,*

9 Wheat. 738, 827. Congress having no power to abridge the rights conferred by the Constitution upon those who have become naturalized citizens by virtue of acts of Congress, a fortiori no act or omission of Congress, as to providing for the naturalization of parents or children of a particular race, can affect citizenship acquired as a birthright, by virtue of the Constitution itself, without any aid of legislation. The Fourteenth Amendment, while it leaves the power, where it was before, in Congress, to regulate naturalization, has conferred no authority upon Congress to restrict the effect of birth, declared by the Constitution to constitute a sufficient and complete right to citizenship.

No one doubts that the Amendment, as soon as it was promulgated, applied to persons of African descent born in the United States, wherever the birthplace of their parents might have been; and yet, for two years afterwards, there was no statute authorizing persons of that race to be naturalized. If the omission or the refusal of Congress to permit certain classes of persons to be made citizens by naturalization could be allowed the effect of correspondingly restricting the classes of persons who should become citizens by birth, it would be in the power of Congress, at any time, by striking Negroes out of the naturalization laws, and limiting those laws, as they were formerly limited, to white persons only, to defeat the main purpose of the Constitutional Amendment.

The fact, therefore, that acts of Congress or treaties have not permitted Chinese persons born out of this country to become citizens by naturalization, cannot exclude Chinese persons born in this country from the operation of the broad and clear words of the Constitution, "All persons born in the United States, and subject to the jurisdiction thereof, are citizens of the United States."

Upon the facts agreed in this case, the American citizenship which Wong Kim Ark acquired by birth within the United States has not been lost or taken away by anything happening since his birth. No doubt he might himself, after coming of age, renounce this citizenship, and become a citizen of the country of his parents, or of any other country; for by our law, as solemnly declared by Congress, "the right of expatriation is a natural and inherent right of all people," and "any declaration, instruction, opinion, order or direction of any officer of the United States, which denies, restricts, impairs or questions the right of expatriation, is declared inconsistent with the fundamental principles of the Republic." Rev. Stat. § 1999, reenacting act of July 27, 1868 c. 249, § 1; 15 Stat. 223, 224. Whether any act of himself, or of his parents, during his minority, could have the same effect, is at least doubtful. But it would be out of place to pursue that inquiry; inasmuch as it is expressly agreed that his residence has always been in the United States, and not elsewhere; that each of his temporary visits to China, the one for some months when he was about seventeen years old, and the other for something like a year about the time of his coming of age, was made with the intention of returning, and was followed by his actual return, to the United States; and "that said Wong Kim Ark has not, either by himself or his parents acting for him, ever renounced his allegiance to the United States, and that he has never done or committed any act or thing to exclude him therefrom."

3. Holding

The evident intention, and the necessary effect, of the submission of this case to the decision of the court upon the facts agreed by the parties, were to present for determination the single question, stated at the beginning of this opinion, namely, whether a child born in the United States, of parents of Chinese descent, who, at the time of his birth, are subjects of the Emperor of China, but have a permanent domicil and residence in the United States, and are there carrying on business, and are not employed in any diplomatic or official capacity under the Emperor of China, becomes at the time of his birth a citizen of the United States. For the reasons above stated, this court is of opinion that the question must be answered in the affirmative.

4. Chief Justice Fuller and Justice Harlan Dissenting

. . . By the Thirteenth Amendment of the Constitution slavery was prohibited. The main object of the opening sentence of the Fourteenth Amendment was to settle the question, upon which there had been a difference of opinion throughout the country and in this court, as to the citizenship of free Negroes, *Scott v. Sandford*, 19 How. 393; and to put it beyond doubt that all persons, white or black, and whether formerly slaves or not, born or naturalized in the United States, and owing no allegiance to any alien power, should be citizens of the United States, and of the State in which they reside. *Slaughterhouse Cases*, 16 Wall. 36, 73; *Strauder v. West Virginia*, 100 U.S. 303, 306.

"The section contemplates two sources of citizenship, and two sources only: birth and naturalization. The persons declared to be citizens are 'all persons born or naturalized in the United States, and subject to the jurisdiction thereof.' The evident meaning of these last words is, not merely subject in some respect or degree to the jurisdiction of the United States, but *completely subject to their political jurisdiction, and owing them direct and immediate allegiance.* And the words relate to the time of birth in the one case, as they do to the time of naturalization in the other. *Persons not thus subject to the jurisdiction of the United States at the time of birth* cannot become so afterwards, except by being naturalized, either individually, as by proceedings under the naturalization acts, or collectively, as by the force of a treaty by which foreign territory is acquired."

To be "completely subject" to the political jurisdiction of the United States is to be in no respect or degree subject to the political jurisdiction of any other government.

Now I take it that the children of aliens, whose parents have not only not renounced their allegiance to their native country, but are forbidden by its system of government, as well as by its positive laws, from doing so, and are not permitted to acquire another citizenship by the laws of the country into which they come, must necessarily remain themselves subject to the same sovereignty as their parents, and cannot, in the nature of things, be, any more than their parents, completely subject to the jurisdiction of such other country.

Generally speaking, I understand the subjects of the Emperor of China—that ancient Empire, with its history of thousands of years and its unbroken continuity in belief, traditions and government, in spite of revolutions and changes of dynasty—to be bound to him by every conception of duty and by every principle of their religion, of which filial piety is the first and greatest commandment; and formerly, perhaps still, their penal laws denounced the severest penalties on those who renounced their country and allegiance, and their abettors; and, in effect, held the relatives at home of Chinese in foreign lands as hostages for their loyalty.[24] And whatever concession may have been made by treaty in the direction of admitting the right of expatriation in some sense, they seem in the United States to have remained pilgrims and sojourners as all their fathers were. 149 U.S. 717. At all events, they have been allowed by our laws to acquire our nationality, and, except in sporadic instances, do not appear ever to have desired to do so. . . .

Tested by this rule, Wong Kim Ark never became and is not a citizen of the United States, and the order of the District Court should be reversed.

P. Commentary on *Ark*

The majority opinion in *Ark* rejected the rationale of previous decisions involving persons of Chinese descent. Prior decisions had stressed the lack of assimilation by Chinese immigrants, the different cultural history of China, and the strong allegiance to that cultural history by Chinese immigrants. Fortunately, only Justices Harlan and Fuller, writing in dissent, adopted this prior rationale and means of exclusion, and wanted to refuse citizenship for Wong Kim Ark. The majority of the justices reasoned that irrespective of cultural differences or lack of assimilation, the Fourteenth Amendment applied to all persons, irrespective of race, including Asian

---

24. The fundamental laws of China have remained practically unchanged since the second century before Christ. The statutes have from time to time undergone modifications, but there does not seem to be any English or French translation of the Chinese Penal Code later than that by Staunton, published in 1810. That code provided: "All persons renouncing their country and allegiance, or devising the means thereof, shall be beheaded; and in the punishment of this offence, no distinction shall be made between principals and accessories. The property of all such criminals shall be confiscated, and their wives and children distributed as slaves to the great officers of State. . . . The parents, grandparents, brothers and grandchildren of such criminals, whether habitually living with them under the same roof or not, shall be perpetually banished to the distance of 2000 *lee*."

"All those who purposely conceal and connive at the perpetration of this crime, shall be strangled. Those who inform against, and bring to justice, criminals of this description, shall be rewarded with the whole of their property."

"Those who are privy to the perpetration of this crime, and yet omit to give any notice or information thereof to the magistrates, shall be punished with 100 blows and banished perpetually to the distance of 3000 *lee*."

"If the crime is contrived, but not executed, the principal shall be strangled, and all the accessories shall, each of them, be punished with 100 blows, and perpetual banishment to the distance of 3000 *lee*. . . ." Staunton's Penal Code of China, 272, § 255.

Americans. The Court affirmed citizenship for Wong Kim Ark, and, more significantly, supported a more expansive application of the Fourteenth Amendment.

Q. Background on *Korematsu*

On December 7, 1941, Japan launched a military attack against United States military installations located at Pearl Harbor, Hawaii. This attack resulted in declarations of war between the United States and Japan. During the next year, California state and federal government officials imposed a series of civil rights restrictions on Americans of Japanese descent residing in California including curfews, relocation, and incarceration. As a result, thousands of Japanese Americans spent several years in camps and lost millions of dollars in property and assets.

Tseming Yang

*Choice and Fraud in Racial Identification: The Dilemma of Policing Race in Affirmative Action, the Census, and a Color-Blind Society**

On May 30, 1942 a young man who gave his name as Clyde Sarah was arrested by the San Leandro police. Sarah claimed that he was of Spanish-Hawaiian origin but had been born in Las Vegas. His parents were deceased. He was subsequently charged with having violated federal orders to leave that particular area. To avoid detection of his true identity, Sarah had gone as far as obtaining rudimentary plastic surgery. It turned out that Clyde Sarah was an alias; his real name was Fred Korematsu, and he was a Japanese-American.

11 *Mich. J. Race & Law* 367, 367–368.
Copyright © 2006, Mich. J. Race & Law.
Reprinted with permission of Mich. J. Race & Law and Tseming Yang.

R. *Korematsu v. United States,* 323 U.S. 214 (1944)

Wayne M. Collins and *Charles A. Horsky* argued the cause, and *Collins* was on the brief, for petitioner.

Solicitor General Fahy, with whom *Assistant Attorney General Wechsler* and *Edward J. Ennis, Ralph F. Fuchs*, and *John L. Burling* were on the brief, for the United States.

Saburo Kido and *A.L. Wirin* filed a brief on behalf of the Japanese American Citizens League; and *Messrs. Edwin Borchard, Charles A. Horsky, George Rublee, Arthur DeHon Hill, Winthrop Wadleigh, Osmond K. Fraenkel, Harold Evans, William Draper Lewis,* and *Thomas Raeburn White* on behalf of the American Civil Liberties Union, as *amici curiae,* in support of petitioner.

---

* (footnotes and chapter headings omitted)

Robert W. Kenney, Attorney General of California, *George Neuner,* Attorney General of Oregon, *Smith Troy,* Attorney General of Washington, and *Fred E. Lewis,* Acting Attorney General of Washington, filed a brief on behalf of the States of California, Oregon and Washington, as *amici curiae,* in support of the United States.

1. Facts

Justice BLACK delivered the opinion of the Court.

The petitioner [Fred Korematsu], an American citizen of Japanese descent, was convicted in a federal district court for remaining in San Leandro, California, a "Military Area," contrary to Civilian Exclusion Order No. 34 of the Commanding General of the Western Command, U.S. Army, which directed that after May 9, 1942, all persons of Japanese ancestry should be excluded from that area. No question was raised as to petitioner's loyalty to the United States. [Fred Korematsu was a skilled construction worker. In June 1941 he volunteered for military service in the Navy but was rejected due to health reasons. At the time of the issuance of the exclusion order, Korematsu was engaged to an American citizen of Italian descent who was not subject to exclusion.]The Circuit Court of Appeals affirmed, and the importance of the constitutional question involved caused us to grant certiorari.

2. Opinion

a. Level of Scrutiny

It should be noted, to begin with, that all legal restrictions which curtail the civil rights of a single racial group are immediately suspect. That is not to say that all such restrictions are unconstitutional. It is to say that courts must subject them to the most rigid scrutiny. Pressing public necessity may sometimes justify the existence of such restrictions; racial antagonism never can.

b. Power of the Federal Government

In the instant case prosecution of the petitioner was begun by information charging violation of an Act of Congress, of March 21, 1942, 56 Stat. 173, which provides that

> ". . . whoever shall enter, remain in, leave, or commit any act in any military area or military zone prescribed, under the authority of an Executive order of the President, by the Secretary of War, or by any military commander designated by the Secretary of War, contrary to the restrictions applicable to any such area or zone or contrary to the order of the Secretary of War or any such military commander, shall, if it appears that he knew or should have known of the existence and extent of the restrictions or order and that his act was in violation thereof, by guilty of a misdemeanor and upon conviction shall be liable to a fine of not to exceed $5,000 or to imprisonment for not more than one year, or both, for each offense."

Exclusion Order No. 34, which the petitioner knowingly and admittedly violated, was one of a number of military orders and proclamations, all of which were substantially based upon Executive Order No. 9066, 7 Fed. Reg. 1407. That order, issued after we were at war with Japan, declared that "the successful prosecution of the war requires every possible protection against espionage and against sabotage to national-defense material, national-defense premises, and national-defense utilities. . . ."

One of the series of orders and proclamations, a curfew order, which like the exclusion order here was promulgated pursuant to Executive Order 9066, subjected all persons of Japanese ancestry in prescribed West Coast military areas to remain in their residences from 8 p.m. to 6 a.m. As is the case with the exclusion order here, that prior curfew order was designed as a "protection against espionage and against sabotage." In *Hirabayashi v. United States*, 320 U.S. 81, we sustained a conviction obtained for violation of the curfew order. The *Hirabayashi* conviction and this one thus rest on the same 1942 Congressional Act and the same basic executive and military orders, all of which orders were aimed at the twin dangers of espionage and sabotage.

The 1942 Act was attacked in the *Hirabayashi* case as an unconstitutional delegation of power; it was contended that the curfew order and other orders on which it rested were beyond the war powers of the Congress, the military authorities and of the President, as Commander in Chief of the Army; and finally that to apply the curfew order against none but citizens of Japanese ancestry amounted to a constitutionally prohibited discrimination solely on account of race. To these questions, we gave the serious consideration which their importance justified. We upheld the curfew order as an exercise of the power of the government to take steps necessary to prevent espionage and sabotage in an area threatened by Japanese attack.

In the light of the principles we announced in the *Hirabayashi* case, we are unable to conclude that it was beyond the war power of Congress and the Executive to exclude those of Japanese ancestry from the West Coast war area at the time they did. True, exclusion from the area in which one's home is located is a far greater deprivation than constant confinement to the home from 8 p.m. to 6 a.m. Nothing short of apprehension by the proper military authorities of the gravest imminent danger to the public safety can constitutionally justify either. But exclusion from a threatened area, no less than curfew, has a definite and close relationship to the prevention of espionage and sabotage. The military authorities, charged with the primary responsibility of defending our shores, concluded that curfew provided inadequate protection and ordered exclusion. They did so, as pointed out in our *Hirabayashi* opinion, in accordance with Congressional authority to the military to say who should, and who should not, remain in the threatened areas.

In this case the petitioner challenges the assumptions upon which we rested our conclusions in the *Hirabayashi* case. He also urges that by May 1942, when Order

No. 34 was promulgated, all danger of Japanese invasion of the West Coast had disappeared. After careful consideration of these contentions we are compelled to reject them.

Here, as in the *Hirabayashi* case, *supra*, at p. 99, ". . . we cannot reject as unfounded the judgment of the military authorities and of Congress that there were disloyal members of that population, whose number and strength could not be precisely and quickly ascertained. We cannot say that the war-making branches of the Government did not have ground for believing that in a critical hour such persons could not readily be isolated and separately dealt with, and constituted a menace to the national defense and safety, which demanded that prompt and adequate measures be taken to guard against it."

Like curfew, exclusion of those of Japanese origin was deemed necessary because of the presence of an unascertained number of disloyal members of the group, most of whom we have no doubt were loyal to this country. It was because we could not reject the finding of the military authorities that it was impossible to bring about an immediate segregation of the disloyal from the loyal that we sustained the validity of the curfew order as applying to the whole group. In the instant case, temporary exclusion of the entire group was rested by the military on the same ground. The judgment that exclusion of the whole group was for the same reason a military imperative answers the contention that the exclusion was in the nature of group punishment based on antagonism to those of Japanese origin. That there were members of the group who retained loyalties to Japan has been confirmed by investigations made subsequent to the exclusion. Approximately five thousand American citizens of Japanese ancestry refused to swear unqualified allegiance to the United States and to renounce allegiance to the Japanese Emperor, and several thousand evacuees requested repatriation to Japan.[25]

We uphold the exclusion order as of the time it was made and when the petitioner violated it. *Cf. Chastleton Corporation v. Sinclair*, 264 U.S. 543, 547; *Block v. Hirsh*, 256 U.S. 135, 154–55. In doing so, we are not unmindful of the hardships imposed by it upon a large group of American citizens. *Cf. Ex parte Kawato*, 317 U.S. 69, 73. But hardships are part of war, and war is an aggregation of hardships. All citizens alike, both in and out of uniform, feel the impact of war in greater or lesser measure. Citizenship has its responsibilities as well as its privileges, and in time of war the burden is always heavier. Compulsory exclusion of large groups of citizens from their homes, except under circumstances of direct emergency and peril, is inconsistent with our basic governmental institutions. But when under conditions of

---

25. Hearings before the Subcommittee on the National War Agencies Appropriation Bill for 1945, Part II, 608–726; Final Report, Japanese Evacuation from the West Coast, 1942, 309–27; Hearings before the Committee on Immigration and Naturalization, House of Representatives, 78th Cong., 2d Sess., on H.R. 2701 and other bills to expatriate certain nationals of the United States, pp. 37–42, 49–58.

modern warfare our shores are threatened by hostile forces, the power to protect must be commensurate with the threatened danger. . . .

c. Rationale

It is said that we are dealing here with the case of imprisonment of a citizen in a concentration camp solely because of his ancestry, without evidence or inquiry concerning his loyalty and good disposition towards the United States. Our task would be simple, our duty clear, were this a case involving the imprisonment of a loyal citizen in a concentration camp because of racial prejudice. Regardless of the true nature of the assembly and relocation centers—and we deem it unjusti-fiable to call them concentration camps with all the ugly connotations that term implies—we are dealing specifically with nothing but an exclusion order. To cast this case into outlines of racial prejudice, without reference to the real military dangers which were presented, merely confuses the issue. Korematsu was not excluded from the Military Area because of hostility to him or his race. He was excluded because we are at war with the Japanese Empire, because the properly constituted military authorities feared an invasion of our West Coast and felt constrained to take proper security measures, because they decided that the military urgency of the situation demanded that all citizens of Japanese ancestry be segregated from the West Coast temporarily, and finally, because Congress, reposing its confidence in this time of war in our military leaders—as inevitably it must—determined that they should have the power to do just this. There was evidence of disloyalty on the part of some, the military authorities considered that the need for action was great, and time was short.

3. Holding

We cannot—by availing ourselves of the calm perspective of hindsight—now say that at that time these actions were unjustified. The conviction is affirmed.

4. Justice Murphy Dissenting

a. Presence of Racism

This exclusion of "all persons of Japanese ancestry, both alien and non-alien," from the Pacific Coast area on a plea of military necessity in the absence of martial law ought not to be approved. Such exclusion goes over "the very brink of constitu-tional power" and falls into the ugly abyss of racism.

In dealing with matters relating to the prosecution and progress of a war, we must accord great respect and consideration to the judgments of the military authori-ties who are on the scene and who have full knowledge of the military facts. The scope of their discretion must, as a matter of necessity and common sense, be wide. And their judgments ought not to be overruled lightly by those whose training and duties ill-equip them to deal intelligently with matters so vital to the physical secu-rity of the nation.

At the same time, however, it is essential that there be definite limits to military discretion, especially where martial law has not been declared. Individuals must not be left impoverished of their constitutional rights on a plea of military necessity that has neither substance nor support. Thus, like other claims conflicting with the asserted constitutional rights of the individual, the military claim must subject itself to the judicial process of having its reasonableness determined and its conflicts with other interests reconciled. "What are the allowable limits of military discretion, and whether or not they have been overstepped in a particular case, are judicial questions." *Sterling v. Constantin*, 287 U.S. 378, 401.

The judicial test of whether the Government, on a plea of military necessity, can validly deprive an individual of any of his constitutional rights is whether the deprivation is reasonably related to a public danger that is so "immediate, imminent, and impending" as not to admit of delay and not to permit the intervention of ordinary constitutional processes to alleviate the danger. *United States v. Russell*, 13 Wall. 623, 627–8; *Mitchell v. Harmony*, 13 How. 115, 134–5; *Raymond v. Thomas*, 91 U.S. 712, 716. Civilian Exclusion Order No. 34, banishing from a prescribed area of the Pacific Coast "all persons of Japanese ancestry, both alien and non-alien," clearly does not meet that test. Being an obvious racial discrimination, the order deprives all those within its scope of the equal protection of the laws as guaranteed by the Fifth Amendment. It further deprives these individuals of their constitutional rights to live and work where they will, to establish a home where they choose and to move about freely. In excommunicating them without benefit of hearings, this order also deprives them of all their constitutional rights to procedural due process. Yet no reasonable relation to an "immediate, imminent, and impending" public danger is evident to support this racial restriction which is one of the most sweeping and complete deprivations of constitutional rights in the history of this nation in the absence of martial law.

It must be conceded that the military and naval situation in the spring of 1942 was such as to generate a very real fear of invasion of the Pacific Coast, accompanied by fears of sabotage and espionage in that area. The military command was therefore justified in adopting all reasonable means necessary to combat these dangers. In adjudging the military action taken in light of the then apparent dangers, we must not erect too high or too meticulous standards; it is necessary only that the action have some reasonable relation to the removal of the dangers of invasion, sabotage and espionage. But the exclusion, either temporarily or permanently, of all persons with Japanese blood in their veins has no such reasonable relation. And that relation is lacking because the exclusion order necessarily must rely for its reasonableness upon the assumption that *all* persons of Japanese ancestry may have a dangerous tendency to commit sabotage and espionage and to aid our Japanese enemy in other ways. It is difficult to believe that reason, logic or experience could be marshalled in support of such an assumption.

That this forced exclusion was the result in good measure of this erroneous assumption of racial guilt rather than bona fide military necessity is evidenced by the Commanding General's Final Report on the evacuation from the Pacific Coast area.[26] In it he refers to all individuals of Japanese descent as "subversive," as belonging to "an enemy race" whose "racial strains are undiluted," and as constituting "over 112,000 potential enemies . . . at large today" along the Pacific Coast.[27] In support of this blanket condemnation of all persons of Japanese descent, however, no reliable evidence is cited to show that such individuals were generally disloyal,[28] or had generally so conducted themselves in this area as to constitute a special menace to defense installations or war industries, or had otherwise by their behavior furnished reasonable ground for their exclusion as a group.

Justification for the exclusion is sought, instead, mainly upon questionable racial and sociological grounds not ordinarily within the realm of expert military judgment, supplemented by certain semi-military conclusions drawn from an unwarranted use of circumstantial evidence. Individuals of Japanese ancestry are condemned because they are said to be "a large, unassimilated, tightly knit racial group, bound to an enemy nation by strong ties of race, culture, custom and religion."[29] They are claimed to be given to "emperor worshipping ceremonies"[30] and to "dual citizenship."[31] Japanese language schools and allegedly pro-Japanese organ-

---

26. Final Report, Japanese Evacuation from the West Coast, 1942, by Lt. Gen. J. L. DeWitt. This report is dated June 5, 1943, but was not made public until January, 1944.

27. Further evidence of the Commanding General's attitude toward individuals of Japanese ancestry is revealed in his voluntary testimony on April 13, 1943, in San Francisco before the House Naval Affairs Subcommittee to Investigate Congested Areas, Part 3, pp. 739–40 (78th Cong., 1st Sess.):

"I don't want any of them [persons of Japanese ancestry] here. They are a dangerous element. There is no way to determine their loyalty. The west coast contains too many vital installations essential to the defense of the country to allow any Japanese on this coast. . . . The danger of the Japanese was, and is now—if they are permitted to come back—espionage and sabotage. It makes no difference whether he is an American citizen, he is still a Japanese. American citizenship does not necessarily determine loyalty. . . . But we must worry about the Japanese all the time until he is wiped off the map. Sabotage and espionage will make problems as long as he is allowed in this area. . . ."

28. The Final Report, p. 9, casts a cloud of suspicion over the entire group by saying that "while it was *believed* that *some* were loyal, it was known that many were not." (Italics added.)

29. Final Report, p. vii; *see also* pp. 9, 17. To the extent that assimilation is a problem, it is largely the result of certain social customs and laws of the American general public. Studies demonstrate that persons of Japanese descent are readily susceptible to integration in our society if given the opportunity. Strong, The Second-Generation Japanese Problem (1934); Smith, Americans in Process (1937); Mears, Resident Orientals on the American Pacific Coast (1928); Millis, The Japanese Problem in the United States (1942). The failure to accomplish an ideal status of assimilation, therefore, cannot be charged to the refusal of these persons to become Americanized or to their loyalty to Japan. And the retention by some persons of certain customs and religious practices of their ancestors is no criterion of their loyalty to the United States.

30. Final Report, pp. 10–11. No sinister correlation between the emperor worshipping activities and disloyalty to America was shown.

31. Final Report, p. 22. The charge of "dual citizenship" springs from a misunderstanding of the simple fact that Japan in the past used the doctrine of *jus sanguinis*, as she had a right to do under international law, and claimed as her citizens all persons born of Japanese nationals wherever

izations are cited as evidence of possible group disloyalty,[32] together with facts as to certain persons being educated and residing at length in Japan.[33] It is intimated that many of these individuals deliberately resided "adjacent to strategic points," thus enabling them "to carry into execution a tremendous program of sabotage on a mass scale should any considerable number of them have been inclined to do so."[34] The need for protective custody is also asserted. The report refers without identity to "numerous incidents of violence" as well as to other admittedly unverified or cumulative incidents. From this, plus certain other events not shown to have been connected with the Japanese Americans, it is concluded that the "situation was fraught with danger to the Japanese population itself" and that the general public "was ready to take matters into its own hands."[35] Finally, it is intimated, though not directly charged or proved, that persons of Japanese ancestry were responsible for three minor isolated shellings and bombings of the Pacific Coast area,[36] as well as for unidentified radio transmissions and night signaling.

The main reasons relied upon by those responsible for the forced evacuation, therefore, do not prove a reasonable relation between the group characteristics of Japanese Americans and the dangers of invasion, sabotage and espionage. The reasons appear, instead, to be largely an accumulation of much of the misinformation,

----

located. Japan has greatly modified this doctrine, however, by allowing all Japanese born in the United States to renounce any claim of dual citizenship and by releasing her claim as to all born in the United States after 1925. *See* Freeman, "Genesis, Exodus, and Leviticus: Genealogy, Evacuation, and Law," 28 Cornell L.Q. 414, 447–48, and authorities there cited; McWilliams, Prejudice, 123–24 (1944).

32. Final Report, pp. 12–13. We have had various foreign language schools in this country for generations without considering their existence as ground for racial discrimination. No subversive activities or teachings have been shown in connection with the Japanese schools. McWilliams, Prejudice, 121–23 (1944).

33. Final Report, pp. 13–15. Such persons constitute a very small part of the entire group and most of them belong to the Kibei movement—the actions and membership of which are well known to our Government agents.

34. Final Report, p. 10; *see also* pp. vii, 9, 15–17. This insinuation, based purely upon speculation and circumstantial evidence, completely overlooks the fact that the main geographic pattern of Japanese population was fixed many years ago with reference to economic, social and soil conditions. Limited occupational outlets and social pressures encouraged their concentration near their initial points of entry on the Pacific Coast. That these points may now be near certain strategic military and industrial areas is no proof of a diabolical purpose on the part of Japanese Americans. *See* McWilliams, Prejudice, 119–21 (1944); House Report No. 2124 (77th Cong., 2d Sess.), 59–93.

35. Final Report, pp. 8–9. This dangerous doctrine of protective custody, as proved by recent European history, should have absolutely no standing as an excuse for the deprivation of the rights of minority groups. See House Report No. 1911 (77th Cong., 2d Sess.) 1–2. Cf. House Report No. 2124 (77th Cong., 2d Sess.) 145–47. In this instance, moreover, there are only two minor instances of violence on record involving persons of Japanese ancestry. McWilliams, What About Our Japanese Americans? Public Affairs Pamphlets, No. 91, p. 8 (1944).

36. Final Report, p. 18. One of these incidents (the reputed dropping of incendiary bombs on an Oregon forest) occurred on Sept. 9, 1942—a considerable time after the Japanese Americans had been evacuated from their homes and placed in Assembly Centers. *See* New York Times, Sept. 15, 1942, p. 1, col. 3.

half-truths and insinuations that for years have been directed against Japanese Americans by people with racial and economic prejudices—the same people who have been among the foremost advocates of the evacuation.[37] A military judgment based upon such racial and sociological considerations is not entitled to the great weight ordinarily given the judgments based upon strictly military considerations. Especially is this so when every charge relative to race, religion, culture, geographical location, and legal and economic status has been substantially discredited by independent studies made by experts in these matters.

b. No Real Military Threat

The military necessity which is essential to the validity of the evacuation order thus resolves itself into a few intimations that certain individuals actively aided the enemy, from which it is inferred that the entire group of Japanese Americans could not be trusted to be or remain loyal to the United States. No one denies, of course, that there were some disloyal persons of Japanese descent on the Pacific Coast who did all in their power to aid their ancestral land. Similar disloyal activities have been engaged in by many persons of German, Italian and even more pioneer stock in our country. But to infer that examples of individual disloyalty prove group disloyalty and justify discriminatory action against the entire group is to deny that under our system of law individual guilt is the sole basis for deprivation of rights. Moreover, this inference, which is at the very heart of the evacuation orders, has been used in support of the abhorrent and despicable treatment of minority groups by the dictatorial tyrannies which this nation is now pledged to destroy. To give constitutional sanction to that inference in this case, however well-intentioned may have been the military command on the Pacific Coast, is to adopt one of the cruelest of the rationales used by our enemies to destroy the dignity of the individual and to encourage and open the door to discriminatory actions against other minority groups in the passions of tomorrow.

No adequate reason is given for the failure to treat these Japanese Americans on an individual basis by holding investigations and hearings to separate the loyal from the disloyal, as was done in the case of persons of German and Italian ancestry. *See* House Report No. 2124 (77th Cong., 2d Sess.) 247–52. It is asserted merely that the

---

37. Special interest groups were extremely active in applying pressure for mass evacuation. See House Report no. 2124 (77th Cong., 2d Sess.) 154–56; McWilliams, Prejudice, 126–28 (1944). Austin E. Anson, managing secretary of the Salinas Vegetable Grower-Shipper Association, has frankly admitted that "We're charged with wanting to get rid of the Japs for selfish reasons.... We do. It's a question of whether the white man lives on the Pacific Coast or the brown men. They came into this valley to work, and they stayed to take over.... They undersell the white man in the markets.... They work their women and children while the white farmer has to pay wages for his help. If all the Japs were removed tomorrow, we'd never miss them in two weeks, because the white farmers can take over and produce everything the Jap grows. And we don't want them back when the war ends, either." Quoted by Taylor in his article "The People Nobody Wants," 214 Sat. Eve. Post 24, 66 (May 9, 1942).

loyalties of this group "were unknown and time was of the essence."[38] Yet nearly four months elapsed after Pearl Harbor before the first exclusion order was issued; nearly eight months went by until the last order was issued; and the last of these "subversive" persons was not actually removed until almost eleven months had elapsed. Leisure and deliberation seem to have been more of the essence than speed. And the fact that conditions were not such as to warrant a declaration of martial law adds strength to the belief that the factors of time and military necessity were not as urgent as they have been represented to be.

Moreover, there was no adequate proof that the Federal Bureau of Investigation and the military and naval intelligence services did not have the espionage and sabotage situation well in hand during this long period. Nor is there any denial of the fact that not one person of Japanese ancestry was accused or convicted of espionage or sabotage after Pearl Harbor while they were still free,[39] a fact which is some evidence of the loyalty of the vast majority of these individuals and of the effectiveness of the established methods of combatting these evils. It seems incredible that under these circumstances it would have been impossible to hold loyalty hearings for the mere 112,000 persons involved — or at least for the 70,000 American citizens — especially when a large part of this number represented children and elderly men and women.[40] Any inconvenience that may have accompanied an attempt to conform to procedural due process cannot be said to justify violations of constitutional rights of individuals.

I dissent, therefore, from this legalization of racism. Racial discrimination in any form and in any degree has no justifiable part whatever in our democratic way of life. It is unattractive in any setting but it is utterly revolting among a free people who have embraced the principles set forth in the Constitution of the United States. All residents of this nation are kin in some way by blood or culture to a foreign land. Yet they are primarily and necessarily a part of the new and distinct civilization of the United States. They must accordingly be treated at all times as the heirs of the American experiment and as entitled to all the rights and freedoms guaranteed by the Constitution.

---

38. Final Report, p. vii; *see also* p. 18.

39. The Final Report, p. 34, makes the amazing statement that as of February 14, 1942, "The very fact that no sabotage has taken place to date is a disturbing and confirming indication that such action will be taken." Apparently, in the minds of the military leaders, there was no way that the Japanese Americans could escape the suspicion of sabotage.

40. During a period of six months, the 112 alien tribunals or hearing boards set up by the British Government shortly after the outbreak of the present war summoned and examined approximately 74,000 German and Austrian aliens. These tribunals determined whether each individual enemy alien was a real enemy of the Allies or only a "friendly enemy." About 64,000 were freed from internment and from any special restrictions, and only 2,000 were interned. Kempner, "The Enemy Alien Problem in the Present War," 34 Amer. Journ. of Int. Law 443, 444–46; House Report No. 2124 (77th Cong., 2d Sess.), 280–81.

S. Commentary on *Korematsu*

Korematsu was one of the Supreme Court's most blatantly racist decisions of the twentieth century. Although the Court indicated that racial exclusions would be subject to the most rigid scrutiny, it explicitly sanctioned the government's forcible internment of thousands of Americans of Japanese ancestry. Although the nation was at war with Hitler and Mussolini, Americans of German or Italian heritage as a group were never interned. The Court's approval of the imprisonment of thousands of loyal citizens whose only "crime" was belonging to an unpopular ethnic group diminished the ideal of equal justice. The Supreme Court accepted the government's justification for the incarceration of Japanese Americans because of the government's belief that Japanese Americans possessed a different sense of patriotism.

Adolph Hitler, leader of Germany during World War II and a proponent of racist ideology, commenting on the changes in Europe during the war, noted that the great strength of the totalitarian state is that it forces those who fear it to imitate it.[41] The accuracy of Hitler's observation is evident in the fear-based reaction supported by the *Korematsu* decision.

T. Background on *Trump*

Donald Trump has a long history of racial animus. Prior to running for office in 2016, Trump was a leader of the "birther movement"—despite his attempt to shift the blame to his opponent—proclaiming that President Obama was likely born in Africa rather than the United States and challenging the legitimacy of his presidency. Trump took years to acknowledge the truth and refused to apologize for the offensive challenge. Moreover, Trump often referred to President Obama as the "affirmative action" president, implying that Obama's admission to Harvard Law School and election as editor-in-chief of the Harvard Law Review were not deserved.

During the primary campaign, Trump was asked by a reporter whether he would disavow the support of former KKK leader David Duke and white supremacist groups in general. Mr. Trump sidestepped the question, saying "I know nothing about David Duke; I know nothing about white supremacists." And when Trump's running mate, Mike Pence, was asked about Mr. Duke's support of the Trump/Pence ticket and whether such support by avowed racists should be rejected, Pence refused to comment. Thoughtful persons understand that racism thrives when Americans stay silent.

When asked about the problem of excessive force by police against minorities, Trump responded that "police are absolutely mistreated and misunderstood." Trump showed frighteningly little concern for minority victims of police brutality.

---

41. J. Joseph, Black Mondays, at 128 (1983).

To Trump, the primary solution was giving "power back to the police, because crime is rampant."

On the general election campaign trail, Trump made it clear he opposed same-day voter registration and supported voter ID laws to, he said, prevent illegal immigrants from voting and citizens from voting multiple times. Despite the evidence that such voter fraud was rare, statistics confirmed the disproportionate impact of these positions on access to the ballot for black voters. In North Carolina, for example, 25 percent of voting-aged blacks did not possess a photo ID—a percentage three times greater than whites. Federal court decisions in Texas, Wisconsin and North Carolina invalidated such restrictive voting practices because they were demonstrably racially discriminatory.

And then, of course, there's the fact that when Trump entered the presidential race, he launched his campaign by impugning an entire population. Mexicans coming into the United States, according to Trump, might include a few good people, but far too many were "rapists" and "criminals." He proposed keeping Muslims from coming to America, deliberately insulting a religion of over 17 billion people, much to the delight of the religiously intolerant.

U. *Trump v. Hawaii,* 138 S. Ct. 2392 (2018)

1. Facts

Chief Justice Roberts delivered the opinion of the Court. In his second week in office, President Trump signed an executive order instructing the Secretary of Homeland Security to examine the adequacy of information provided by foreign governments concerning their nationals seeking entry into the United States. Prior to the review, the order stopped the entry of foreign nationals for ninety days from seven predominantly Muslim countries.

The order caused much confusion and protest, and a district court temporarily enjoined it, a decision upheld by the Court of Appeals. Instead of proceeding further with litigation, the President withdrew the order and replaced it with a new order again requiring a worldwide review and temporarily restricting entry (with case-by-case waivers) of foreign nationals from six predominantly Muslim countries. Several courts again temporarily enjoined enforcement of the order, but the Supreme Court stayed these injunctions with respect to foreign nationals who lacked the requisite connections to the country.

Upon completion of the world-wide review, the President entered a third order, placing entry restrictions on the nationals of eight foreign countries—Chad, Iran, Iraq, Libya, North Korea, Syria, Venezuela, and Yemen. Six of those countries are predominantly Muslim. As indicated in the order, countries were selected based upon a review of the methods they utilized to determine whether individuals seeking entry into the United States posed a security threat. The order exempted foreign nationals who had been granted asylum and provided for case-by-case waivers. The state of Hawaii brought suit challenging the constitutionality of the order.

2. Opinion

Hawaii argued that the order violated the establishment clause because it operated as a "religious gerrymander" that singled out Muslims due to religious animus.

In support of the argument Hawaii relied upon the following facts:

- Before he was elected, Candidate Trump stated that he was "calling for a total and complete shutdown of Muslims entering the United States until our country's representatives can figure out what is going on. According to Pew Research, among others, there is great hatred towards Americans by large segments of the Muslim population. [Until] we are able to determine and understand this problem and the dangerous threat it poses, our country cannot be the victims of the horrendous attacks by people that believe only in Jihad, and have no sense of reason or respect for human life."

- Also during the campaign, Trump justified his proposal by saying that Franklin Roosevelt "did the same thing" with respect to internment of Japanese Americans during World War II; told an apocryphal story about General John J. Pershing killing a large group of Muslim insurgents in the Philippines with bullets dipped in pigs' blood; stated that "Islam hates us"; called for surveillance of mosques in the United States; and stated that Muslims "do not respect us at all."

- After signing the first version of the executive order, President Trump explained that Christians would be given priority for entry as refugees. He stated that the order was designed "to help" Christians in Syria.

- An advisor to President Trump told the media that "when [Donald Trump] first announced it, he said 'Muslim ban.' He called me up. He said, 'put a commission together. Show me the right way to do it legally.'"

- While litigation about the second order was pending, President Trump characterized it as a "watered down version of the first one" that had been tailored at the behest of "the lawyers." He stated that he would prefer to "go back to the first [order] and go all the way" and that it was "very hard" for Muslims to assimilate into Western culture. In a tweet, he stated that "People, the lawyers and the courts can call it whatever they want, but I am calling it what we need and what it is, a TRAVEL BAN! That's right, we need a TRAVEL BAN for certain DANGEROUS countries, not some politically correct term that won't help protect our people."

- After the third order was promulgated, President Trump retweeted three anti-Muslim videos entitled "Muslims destroy a Statue of Virgin Mary!", "Islamist mob pushes teenage boy off roof and beats him to death!" and "Muslim migrants beat up Dutch boy on crutches!" When asked about the videos, the White House Deputy Press Secretary connected them to the order and stated that the "President has been talking about these security issues earlier this year."

Our Presidents have frequently used their power to espouse the principles of religious freedom and tolerance on which this Nation was founded. In 1790 George Washington reassured the Hebrew Congregation of Newport, Rhode Island that "happily the Government of the United States . . . gives to bigotry no sanction, to persecution no assistance [and] requires only that they who live under its protection should demean themselves as good citizens." President Eisenhower, at the opening of the Islamic Center of Washington, similarly pledged to a Muslim audience that "America would fight with her whole strength for your right to have here your own church," declaring that "[t]his concept is indeed a part of America." And just days after the attacks of September 11, 2001, President George W. Bush returned to the same Islamic Center to implore his fellow Americans—Muslims and non-Muslims alike—to remember during their time of grief that "[t]he face of terror is not the true faith of Islam," and that America is "a great country because we share the same values of respect and dignity and human worth." Yet it cannot be denied that the Federal Government and the Presidents who have carried its laws into effect have—from the Nation's earliest days—performed unevenly in living up to those inspiring words.

Hawaii argues that this President's words strike at fundamental standards of respect and tolerance, in violation of our constitutional tradition. But the issue before us is not whether to denounce the statements. It is instead the significance of those statements in reviewing a Presidential directive, neutral on its face, addressing a matter within the core of executive responsibility. In doing so, we must consider not only the statements of a particular President, but also the authority of the Presidency itself.

The case before us differs in numerous respects from the conventional Establishment Clause claim. Unlike the typical suit involving religious displays or school prayer, Hawaii seeks to invalidate a national security directive regulating the entry of aliens abroad. Hawaii's claim accordingly raises a number of delicate issues regarding the scope of the constitutional right and the manner of proof. The Proclamation, moreover, is facially neutral toward religion. Hawaii therefore asks the Court to probe the sincerity of the stated justifications for the policy by reference to extrinsic statements—many of which were made before the President took the oath of office. These various aspects of Hawaii's challenge inform our standard of review . . .

For our purposes today, we assume that we may look behind the face of the Proclamation to the extent of applying rational basis review. That standard of review considers whether the entry policy is plausibly related to the Government's stated objective to protect the country and improve vetting processes. As a result, we may consider Hawaii's extrinsic evidence, but will uphold the policy so long as it can reasonably be understood to result from a justification independent of unconstitutional grounds.

The Proclamation is expressly premised on legitimate purposes: preventing entry of nationals who cannot be adequately vetted and inducing other nations to improve their practices. The text says nothing about religion. Plaintiff and the dissent none-theless emphasize that five of the seven nations currently included in the Procla-mation have Muslim-majority populations. Yet that fact alone does not support an inference of religious hostility, given that the policy covers just 8% of the world's Muslim population and is limited to countries that were previously designated by Congress or prior administrations as posing national security risks.

The Proclamation, moreover, reflects the results of a worldwide review process undertaken by multiple Cabinet officials and their agencies. Plaintiff seeks to dis-credit the findings of the review, pointing to deviations from the review's baseline criteria resulting in the inclusion of Somalia and omission of Iraq. But as the Proc-lamation explains, in each case the determinations were justified by the distinct conditions in each country. . . .

Three additional features of the entry policy support the Government's claim of a legitimate national security interest. First, since the President introduced entry restrictions in January 2017, three Muslim-majority countries—Iraq, Sudan, and Chad—have been removed from the list of covered countries. . . .

Second, for those countries that remain subject to entry restrictions, the Procla-mation includes significant exceptions for various categories of foreign nationals. . . .

Third, the Proclamation creates a waiver program open to all covered foreign nationals seeking entry as immigrants or nonimmigrants. . . .

Finally, the dissent invokes Korematsu v. United States, 323 U.S. 214 (1944). Whatever rhetorical advantage the dissent may see in doing so, *Korematsu* has noth-ing to do with this case. The forcible relocation of U.S. citizens to concentration camps, solely and explicitly on the basis of race, is objectively unlawful and out-side the scope of Presidential authority. But it is wholly inapt to liken that morally repugnant order to a facially neutral policy denying certain foreign nationals the privilege of admission. The entry suspension is an act that is well within executive authority and could have been taken by any other President—the only question is evaluating the actions of this particular President in promulgating an otherwise valid Proclamation. The dissent's reference to *Korematsu*, however, affords this Court the opportunity to make express what is already obvious: *Korematsu* was gravely wrong the day it was decided, has been overruled in the court of history, and—to be clear—"has no place in law under the Constitution." 323 U.S., at 248 (Jackson, j., dissenting).

3. Holding

Under these circumstances, the Government has set forth a sufficient national security justification to survive rational basis review. We express no view on the soundness of the policy. We simply hold today that the plaintiff has not demonstrated a likelihood of success on the merits of the constitutional claim. The case now returns to the lower courts for such further proceedings as may be appropriate.

Concurring opinions by Justice Thomas, and Justice Kennedy and a dissenting opinion by Justice Breyer, in which Justice Kagan joined, have been omitted.

4. Justice Sotomayor, with whom Justice Ginsburg joins dissenting

The United States of America is a Nation built upon the promise of religious liberty. Our Founders honored that core promise by embedding the principle of religious neutrality in the First Amendment. The Court's decision today fails to safeguard that fundamental principle. It leaves undisturbed a policy first advertised openly and unequivocally as a "total and complete shutdown of Muslims entering the United States" because the policy now masquerades behind a façade of national-security concerns. But this repackaging does little to cleanse Presidential Proclamation No. 9645 of the appearance of discrimination that the President's words have created. Based on the evidence in the record, a reasonable observer would conclude that the Proclamation was motivated by anti-Muslim animus. That alone suffices to show that the plaintiff is likely to succeed on the merits of the Establishment Clause claim. The majority holds otherwise by ignoring the facts, misconstruing our legal precedent, and turning a blind eye to the pain and suffering the Proclamation inflicts upon countless families and individuals, many of whom are United States citizens . . .

As the majority correctly notes, "the issue before us is not whether to denounce" these offensive statements. Rather, the dispositive and narrow question here is whether a reasonable observer, presented with all "openly available data," the text and "historical context" of the Proclamation, and the "specific sequence of events" leading to it, would conclude that the primary purpose of the Proclamation is to disfavor Islam and its adherents by excluding them from the country. The answer is unquestionably yes. Taking all the relevant evidence together, a reasonable observer would conclude that the Proclamation was driven primarily by anti-Muslim animus, rather than by the Government's asserted national-security justifications. . . .

Today's holding is all the more troubling given the stark parallels between the reasoning of this case and that of Korematsu v. United States, 323 U.S. 214 (1944). In *Korematsu*, the Court gave "a pass [to] an odious, gravely injurious racial classification" authorized by an executive order. Adarand Constructors, Inc. v. Peña, 515 U.S. 214 (1996) (Ginsburg, J., dissenting). As here, the Government invoked an ill-defined national security threat to justify an exclusionary policy of sweeping proportion. As here, the exclusion order was rooted in dangerous stereotypes about, inter alia, a particular group's supposed inability to assimilate and desire to harm the United States. As here, the Government was unwilling to reveal its own intelligence agencies' views of the alleged security concerns to the very citizens it purported to protect. And as here, there was strong evidence that impermissible hostility and animus motivated the Government's policy. Although a majority of the Court in *Korematsu* was willing to uphold the Government's actions based on a barren invocation of national security, dissenting Justices warned of that decision's harm to our constitutional fabric . . .

Today, the Court takes the important step of finally overruling *Korematsu*, denouncing it as "gravely wrong the day it was decided." This formal repudiation of a shameful precedent is laudable and long overdue. But it does not make the majority's decision here acceptable or right. By blindly accepting the Government's misguided invitation to sanction a discriminatory policy motivated by animosity toward a disfavored group, all in the name of a superficial claim of national security, the Court redeploys the same dangerous logic underlying *Korematsu* and merely replaces one "gravely wrong" decision with another. Our Constitution demands, and our country deserves, a Judiciary willing to hold the coordinate branches to account when they defy our most sacred legal commitments. Because the Court's decision today has failed in that respect, with profound regret, I dissent.

V. Commentary on *Trump*

In *Trump*, the Supreme Court upheld a presidential proclamation that placed entry restrictions on foreign nationals from several countries. In the course of upholding the proclamation, the majority rejected the dissent's assertion that there were "stark parallels" between the internment policy at issue in *Korematsu* and the travel ban. The animosity directed at people of color, particularly the Muslim and Latino communities, makes immigration reform extremely difficult. When political leaders equate skin color or religious affiliation with criminality or terrorism, they are embracing false stereotypes that imply that safety and crime reduction can be increased through race-based or religious-based immigration restrictions. Even more problematic though, these political leaders are undermining the notion of racial and religious equality contained in the Constitution.

W. Questions and Notes

Do you believe that the majority in *Korematsu* would have ruled the same way had German Americans and Italian Americans been interned instead of Japanese Americans? Do you believe that the majority in *Trump* would have ruled the same way had the travel ban been directed at Catholics or Jews instead of Muslims?

Over time, several justifications were used by the courts for denying citizenship to Latinos/as, American Indians, and Asian Americans. What similarities were used to justify denying citizenship to members of these racial groups as compared to the justification for denying citizenship to African Americans?

Compare the denial of federal citizenship to blacks in the *Dred Scott* opinion with the granting of such citizenship to Mexicans in the Treaty of Guadalupe Hidalgo. What would have been the outcome for Mexicans under Chief Justice Taney's reasoning in *Dred Scott*?

Consider the views of Justice McLean, dissenting in *Dred Scott*, who refuted Chief Justice Taney's claims that citizenship was not available to nonwhites by citing the Treaty of Guadalupe Hidalgo and other treaties to support the position that

Mexicans, blacks and some American Indians had, in fact, been granted federal or state citizenship:

> In the argument, it was said that a colored citizen would not be an agreeable member of society. This is more a matter of taste than of law. Several of the States have admitted persons of color to the right of suffrage, and in this view have recognized them as citizens; and this has been done in the slave as well as the free States. On the question of citizenship, it must be admitted that we have not been very fastidious. Under the late treaty with Mexico, we have made citizens of all grades, combinations and colors. The same was done in the admission of Louisiana and Florida. No one ever doubted, and no court ever held, that the people of these Territories did not become citizens under the treaty. They have exercised all the rights of citizens, without being naturalized under the acts of Congress.[42]

The Civil Liberties Act of 1988 provided reparations to Japanese Americans, including an apology and a twenty thousand dollar payment to each person interned. If you were a member of Congress how would you have voted? What factors do you attribute to the passage of this legislation? Why do you suppose reparations and/or an apology for slavery was not given to blacks at this same time?

X. Point/Counterpoint

Leticia Saucedo

Mexicans, Immigrants, Cultural Narratives and National Origin*

III. Cultural Narratives Cross the Border: Narratives of the Mexican Worker in the U.S. and Their Contemporary Counterparts

As we see from the narratives of Mexicans in Mexico, Americans did not consider Mexicans white and treated them as differently as the narratives made them out to be. The social relations established in the work and recruitment patterns in Mexico migrated north alongside the Mexican migrant. It is not surprising, therefore, that Mexicans were not easily accorded citizenship status. Their racialization as non-white was reflected in both their segregation and in their low positions in the wage hierarchy.

The narratives Anglo employers used at the turn of the twentieth century to explain Mexicans' place in the workforce in Mexico tracked the stories told about Mexicans in the United States, and they are echoed today in the narratives employers use to explain their preference for Latino immigrants. In this section, I explain how the cultural narratives transformed as Mexican migrants entered the workplace

---

42. *Dred Scott*, 60 U.S. (19 How.) at 533 (McLean, J., dissenting).

* (footnotes omitted).

in the United States and how they manifest themselves in descriptions of and a preference for immigrant workers today.

A. From Mexicans as the Quintessential Workers to "The Work Immigrants Will Do" in the United States

The narrative surrounding the "work immigrants will do" today includes their willingness to perform low-skill work as well as their natural abilities for specific low-wage occupations. Mexican workers' abilities were also racialized and attributed to their inherent "Mexican" ness at the turn of the century. As historian David Gutierrez explained, "American advocates of the use of Mexican labor blandly asserted that Mexicans were a race that was both culturally and physiologically suited to perform the arduous manual labor required in these industries." It was their race and not their citizenship or immigration status that made them suitable for low-wage work.

This cultural narrative also justified the lowly positions and wages of Mexicans in the U.S. labor market. Scientific arguments bolstered the narratives racializing Mexicans in the U.S., just as writers purported to do with their descriptions of the Mexican worker. Arguments invoking biology asserted that Mexicans were "mentally, physically, and culturally" deficient, but also naturally disposed to difficult work. The arguments were bolstered by the eugenics movement and by arguments surrounding Darwinism. Employers who sought out Mexicans credited them with being "docile, patient, usually orderly in camp, [and] fairly intelligent under competent [meaning Anglo] supervision." Even writers who described their racialized negative qualities acknowledged Mexican workers' value: "The Mexican laborer is unambitious, listless, physically weak, irregular, and indolent. On the other hand, he is docile, patient. . . . If he were active and ambitious, he would be less tractable and would cost more. His strongest point is his willingness to work for a low wage." Employers used these narratives invoking racial superiority, separately or in combination, to advance Mexicans as the natural choices for difficult, unskilled, low-wage work. Once again, the narratives of the Mexican problem and the racialized, inferior Mexican followed Mexican migrants into the U.S.

Not only were Mexicans described as suitable for low-wage work in general, they were also associated with specific types of unskilled, difficult, back-breaking or marginal/seasonal occupations. Examples of these narratives in the United States are numerous. The Dillingham Commission Report, commissioned by Congress to study immigration in the early twentieth century, noted immigrants' abilities in terms of racial status: Mexicans "have always been the hewers of wood and drawers of water." In some areas of the country, blast furnace work was a Mexican job. In other regions, where the mining industry jobs needed to be filled, the narrative reserved such jobs for Mexicans. Similar narratives explained why Mexicans held rail jobs. The Dillingham Commission noted, for example, that

> [s]ince 1900 Mexicans have formed the chief source of supply of unskilled
> labor for the railroads. . . . The Mexican is preferred for this work because

he can generally be secured more cheaply than laborers of other races. It is the railroads which have largely brought about the recent large migration of Mexicans to Los Angeles. Through labor agencies they have offered transportation to the Mexican laborer from El Paso, where they enter the United States. . . .

In agriculture, growers exploited the image of the Mexican peon to explain their workers' aptitude for the most difficult jobs in the industry. As one grower noted, "They are lovers of farm work,—the Mexicans— . . . they like to till the soil, that is their ambition." California growers argued that Mexicans, because of their bending capabilities, were more suited than Americans to stoop labor. In Colorado, sugar beet companies distinguished the Mexican immigrant laborers as being willing to "crawl" to do the work required in the sugar beet fields, unlike the Anglo workers. The president of the California Fruit Growers Exchange publicly expressed his admiration for the Mexican workers' ability to withstand "the high temperatures of the Imperial and San Joaquin Valleys."

By emphasizing the "natural" abilities of Mexicans, generally and specifically, employers sidestepped any difference between immigrants and native-born Mexicans. The narratives were in sync with the legal structures of the time, which afforded limited rights to all Mexicans, regardless of citizenship status.

The narrative today focuses on immigrant status rather than explicitly on race as the defining feature of the preferred worker. The substance of the narrative, however, remains intact. Moreover, as in the past, the narrative tends to conflate immigrant status, or newly arrived status, with Mexican or Latino national origin. The slips have become part of the story. In a recent study of employers in Los Angeles, one employer noted, "The Latinos in our locations, most are recent arrivals. Most are tenuously here, and here on fragile documents." By describing Latino workers as newly arrived, this employer can more easily attribute stereotypical characteristics to immigrant status.

Although asked about immigrant worker preference, employers continued to stereotype Latinos in much the same way writers stereotyped Mexicans in an earlier era, "Hispanics . . . are more casual, have less intensity. You also have to be motivating the Hispanic group so they will arrive on time. Tardiness is a big problem." The narrative in its current form allows employers to assign and track immigrant Latinos into dead-end low-wage jobs without them having to acknowledge the practice of tracking. As long as employers perceive that "[t]he Hispanic people don't seem to really want to improve themselves as much as some of the other groups do," employers can justify assigning them to dead-end jobs. Sociologists Waldinger and Lichter capture an ambivalence among employers rooted in their distance from the workers themselves: "Managers glad to find somebody to fill their entry-level jobs nonetheless looked down on those persons, whom they saw as not all that interested in responsibility and advancement." This part of the narratives carries over from the explanations writers gave in Mexico for why Mexican workers could be treated differently and segregated socially. Today, immigrants are viewed as especially suited only for dead-end, segmented types of occupations. One employer's comments capture the essence of the narrative: "Immigrants will work for minimum wage and won't complain, even if you keep them there forever." The narrative, of course, parallels the characterization of the Mexican peon to explain the Mexican wage of yesteryear.

Employers also endow immigrants today with the capabilities businesses seek in manufacturing, furniture making, food processing, the service sector, and construction. As immigrants are channeled into these jobs, employers assign them attributes that make them suitable as a group for such occupations. Employers in a recent set of studies noted that, "immigrants as a whole are generally suited for the type of work that we do. . . ." Indeed, the employers tended to describe group characteristics in terms of race as well as occupation, as did the furniture manufacturer who told study interviewees that "Hispanics are good in this type of industry." Not only were immigrants considered well-matched for the tasks involved, they also were seen as possessing understandings of the reward/effort relationship that an employer would be especially likely to appreciate: "They are willing to come and do whatever job you tell them without question." The employer narratives justify the hiring of immigrant workers in today's low-wage workplaces:

> Yes, the immigrants just want to work, work long hours, just want to do anything. They spend a lot of money coming up from Mexico. They want as many hours as possible. If I called them in for four hours to clean latrines, they'd do it. They like to work. They have large families, a big work ethic, and small salaries.

Another employer asserted that, "[i]mmigrants are here to work, and they're not afraid of hard work. . . . They're used to this kind of job." This is, of course, the same narrative that southwestern agriculturalists disseminated when they sought to keep Mexicans in the U.S. at the turn of the twentieth century; and the same narratives Americans perpetuated about the Mexican peon in Mexico as the quintessential worker.

The message of the narrative continues to be that Mexicans (or immigrants) are suitable only for certain work and their natural proclivities make them unsuitable for more skilled or advanced positions. Moreover, even as they are suitable for work, they are not suitable for citizenship and its concomitant rights. As we see from the employers' comments today, the cultural narratives support the general stereotyping of Mexicans even as the nomenclature has changed from "Mexican" to "immigrant."

B. The Work Anglos Will and Won't Do

The corollary narrative throughout history has been that Anglos would not perform certain work. In this narrative, there is a set of jobs that is so below the dignity, or beyond the physical attributes, of whites that they would not be expected to take them. The narrative has both a wage component and a specific-work component.

Historian Gutierrez describes the narrative and its perpetuation in some detail:

The basic tenets of the elaborate rationale American employers first developed about the use of Mexican labor would be heard again and again over the course of the next sixty years. . . . [In addition to talking about a chronic labor shortage,] they argued with no small justification that the kind of work required by these industries was not work that white Americans would tolerate. The hours were too long, wages too low, and working conditions too harsh to attract white American workers in sufficient numbers to fill the ever-growing demands for labor in the Southwest.

The documents of the time reveal these narratives voiced among U.S. southwestern agriculturalists. Over and over again employers reasoned that they sought out Mexican workers because "nothing else was available." Anglo workers were not an option for these occupations. In hearings before Congress, western ranchers testified that "the white man will not do the work." The use of Mexican labor for the difficult jobs was as natural, in other words, as the unsuitability of such work for whites. In agricultural fields, California growers pointed out that, "white laborers refused to do farmwork because there were constitutionally (physically) unsuited to perform it. On the other hand, . . . Mexican workers were well adapted to field conditions." As one southwestern congressman noted:

> The American laboring people will not get down on their hands and knees in the dirt and pull weeds and thin these beets, and break their backs doing that kind of work. No matter how much they are paid, they cannot and will not do it. That kind of labor is hard tedious work. . . .

Mexicans, on the other hand, because of their racial attributes, did not find the work difficult, according to the congressman. The most important characteristic of their desirability was "the Mexicans' 'willingness to work for low wages.'" The idea that only Mexicans were suitable for low-wage work was premised on the very assumption that Anglos, by desire or physical constitution, were not.

The narratives about Anglos and work maintain their power to this day. Waldinger and Lichter heard over and over again from employers that Anglos would not do the work of immigrants. One employer noted, "There are a lot of young Americans who don't want to work. If they want work at the minimum wage, they go elsewhere." Another employer explained that "[t]he whites have more, so they're willing to work fewer hours." Yet another stated he could not even get native high school students to take the jobs he offered immigrants.

Existing alongside narratives about the work that Anglos will not do are powerful narratives about the work they can and will perform. The narrative endows whites with the ability to manage and supervise the work of nonwhite workers. As described in the previous section, the narrative clearly existed in Mexico at the turn of the twentieth century.

Today, employer practices support (and are supported by) the narratives of whites naturally disposed to managing labor. Employers express their preferences for immigrants by telling them they are hired for their complacency, their pliability and their antipathy toward unions. At the same time employers restrict who will be groomed for management positions to Anglos (and sometimes Asians). As Waldinger and Lichter concluded in their study of low-wage industries, "Whites continue to dominate the shrinking pool of 'good jobs' that do not require large amounts of formal education but provide attractive rewards, in dollars or in social standing. . . . In manufacturing the remaining craft jobs continued to be dominated by whites." The narrative continues to be a self-fulfilling prophecy, at least at the low-wage industry level.

C. The Mexican Wanderer as Migrant in the United States

The wandering, restless, itinerant attributes of the Mexican were quite powerful in explaining why Mexicans traveled back and forth between Mexico and the United States. The narratives were also called into service to explain why Mexicans deserved low wages and tough conditions. The Dillingham Commission's description of the migration patterns of railway workers illustrates the point:

> One reason why Mexicans are easily assembled for railway work and, though paid comparatively low wages, do not, as a rule, leave it for more remunerative employment, is found in the fact that the railway companies will return them, after working for a specified time, to El Paso. The Mexican ordinarily comes to the United States with the expectation of returning home after a short time. The railway companies, realizing the strength of this feeling, have induced immigration to this country and induce the Mexicans to continue in their employ by making this return possible, though the improvident immigrants themselves would scarcely ever save enough to pay their expenses home.

In explaining why Mexicans dominated the unskilled labor market in Arizona, the Dillingham Commission again resorted to the narrative of the wandering nature of the Mexican, noting:

> The large proportion of Mexicans at these mines and their practically entire absence at the other mines investigated is explained largely by the proximity of the Mexican border and the fact that most of the immigrant Mexicans employed are part of a nomadic labor supply which travels back and forth through the border states and northern Mexico.

The wanderer narrative is intertwined with the racialized Mexican narrative to create the perfect worker. One writer in the early twentieth century noted that Mexicans were naturally suited to cotton-picking in the U.S. for several reasons: "It requires nimble fingers rather than physical strength. . . . [I]t employs his whole family; he can follow it from place to place . . . which seems to suit the half-subdued nomadic instinct of a part of the Mexican race." The same theme that writers identified, and that was used to justify their subordination in Mexico, turns up in this description. This cultural narrative, transposed to a new setting, grew out of the stories writers told to explain Mexicans' willingness to move around Mexico after capital interests displaced them from ancestral lands.

Today, the wanderer narrative is embodied in the stories and metaphors describing immigrants crossing the border in hordes or in waves. Historian Otto Santa Ana describes how the image of a "brown tide rising" is utilized to explain the unassimilated masses of Latinos entering the United States. The image has its roots in both the wanderer/nomad narrative and the assimilation narrative.

D. The Assimilation Narrative: The Mexican Problem in the United States

As in stories of the Mexican Problem, the assimilation narrative in the United States blames the Mexican for not integrating or becoming Americanized. The so-called "'Mexican Problem' in our midst" demanded a solution that was similar, if not identical to, the solution for the Mexican Problem in Mexico: Americanization. The problem was framed as the nearly impossible task of assimilating the ever-increasing numbers of Mexicans migrating across the border into the United States.

As Mexicans migrated to the United States, the Mexican problem became the Mexican-in-the-U.S. problem, as U.S. writers, anthropologists, journalists, and social workers attempted to explain the salience of their difference to American audiences. The peon once again embodied Mexican-ness. As one anthropologist noted, "[t]oday the hordes crossing the Rio Grande, as well as those who are already here, are largely from the impoverished peon class." When writers discussed the Mexican entering the United States, it was always in terms of the peon, or the worker. The major concern of the time was how to incorporate the large numbers of peons, whose negative traits—including restlessness, laziness, and an inability to assimilate—were attributed to their nature, and not to the structures that kept them from integrating. Because the "Mexican Problem" was transformed into a problem of the individual, whether in Mexico or not, Mexican Americans suffered as well from the characterizations of Mexicans in the assimilation narratives. Skilled Mexican Americans were relegated to low-wage, low-skill occupations because higher-skilled jobs were reserved for Anglos. Mexican Americans were forced to take low-skill or agricultural jobs that were traditionally available to Mexican immigrants. Historian David Gutierrez describes the conflation of Mexicans and the then-recently created category of Mexicans as Americans:

> [O]ver time Americans in the Southwest came to associate Mexican Americans with unskilled labor. Indeed, this status became institutionalized in some ways by the emergence of an ethnic division of labor characterized by a dual wage structure, in which Mexican workers were consistently paid less than "white" workers performing the same work. By the turn of the century the dual wage system was a characteristic feature of virtually all industries employing Mexican and other ethnic workers throughout the Southwest.

Today, Mexicans who fail to assimilate or Americanize are at fault for their inability to progress. The narrative today emphasizes that, to the extent that noncitizens fail to assimilate, they do not deserve the protection of workplace laws. This assimilation narrative allowed early writers to continue to make uninformed comments about the nature of the Mexican. It also provided the excuse for paying Mexicans wages far below prevailing rates, and for restricting them to the least desirable jobs in the most labor-intensive industries. Today the legacy and its underlying racialized descriptions are masked by the reference to immigrants as the problem. Nonetheless, the view that the failure to assimilate remains the problem of the individual prevails. The narrative, or course, ignores the social conditions and the legal regimes that prevent full assimilation. These are discussed in the next section.

IV. The Legal Regimes that Facilitated the Transformation from Mexican to Immigrant Labor in the Cultural Narratives: A Brief History

A. Racialization and Segregation of the Early Twentieth Century

In part because of the narratives surrounding their entry, Mexicans have not experienced a smooth trajectory toward assimilation, or toward debunking the lies embedded in the cultural narratives. In this section I provide a short history of the legal regime that Mexicans encountered from the early twentieth century until the civil rights era. I describe how immigration law has helped sustain the cultural narratives by creating a subclass of Mexicans defined by immigration status. Ultimately, the narratives have outlived the enactment of civil-rights laws outlawing national-origin discrimination. Moreover, U.S. laws have facilitated the subcategory of Mexicans—the immigrant—to embody the qualities of the Mexican that the cultural narratives historically described.

Laws treated Mexican Americans as a separate race for much of the twentieth century. Racialization facilitated the treatment of Mexican Americans as outsiders, even as they attempted throughout the century to incorporate into American society. Anglo efforts to segregate Mexican Americans were fueled by increasing Mexican immigration in the 1920s. The cultural narratives that depicted Mexicans as different fed the movement. Mexicans were depicted as non-assimilationist and difficult to integrate as a result of their character. The narrative showed up in official government documents, as in the Dillingham Commission's depiction of Mexican labor in Los Angeles:

> In contact with others they are looked upon as inferiors. Owing to the fact that but few of the race speak English, that they live in isolated communities, that in their work on railroads they are largely segregated, and that they seldom intermarry with other peoples, they are for the most part a strictly separated class. Very few Mexicans are found to take out naturalization papers or show any interest in civic affairs. . . . [I]t is evident that few Mexicans show any regard for American customs, or have any civic interest, and as a race they show as few assimilative qualities as any found in Los Angeles.

Legal regimes governing property reflected the incomplete rights of citizenship of Mexican Americans in the early twentieth century. Employers' reticence to incorporate Mexicans into any but the least desirable jobs was reinforced in housing patterns across the country in response to Mexican migration to cities. Local and state laws allowed for restrictive housing covenants and enforced informal and *de jure* segregation of Mexicans. Restrictive covenants themselves produced patterns of segregation in northern cities.

Progressive labor statutes enacted during the New Deal era nonetheless excluded protections in industries where Blacks and Mexicans held jobs. Blacks and Latinos were excluded, by virtue of their jobs, from New Deal statutes. The Fair Labor Standards Act, for example, excluded agricultural and domestic workers from its protections. The National Labor Relations Act, the Social Security Act, and state unemployment laws similarly excluded Blacks and Latinos. Moreover, while Works Progress Administration programs were implemented throughout the country to provide work for long-term unemployed populations, "Mexican Americans and Native Americans suffered wholesale exclusions from such programs in the Southwest." By and large, the New Deal programs provided a social safety net to those the government deemed full citizens, while providing only emergency relief to those considered nonwhite. Full citizenship was accorded only to those who were white or on their way to whiteness. Mexican Americans, who were not on their way to whiteness, were not considered deserving of the social safety net.

The labor movement in the early twentieth century advanced the narrative that certain work was reserved for Anglos. For example, the American Federation of Labor ("AFL") fought strongly for the protection of craft and trade occupations for Anglos. And it helped create the legal regime that kept Mexicans out of union jobs. At the same time, the AFL conspired with corporate interests to keep Mexicans from forming strong unions in Mexico. The result was U.S.-union-protectionist policies both in Mexico and in the United States. These policies appeared in contractual and legal arrangements during the advent of the labor-rights movement between employers and the AFL, and during the New Deal debates about labor legislation. Historian Zaragosa Vargas describes the deliberate consignment of the Mexican laborer to low-wage status:

> [In the early years of the Great Depression,] dominated by all white craft unions, the intransigent [AFL] made few attempts to unionize the Mexican laborer, and when it did, unionization meant segregated locals. . . . [T]he AFL had reached an arrangement whereby low-wage common labor would be the domain of the Mexican worker. Through a plan of containment adhered to by the all-white state labor councils, the AFL acted to prevent the spread of Mexican labor into industrial employment and the skilled crafts and trades.

The efforts of the AFL during the crafting of the National Labor Relations Act ("NLRA") further excluded Blacks and Latinos from union protections offered in the workplace. The AFL fought the inclusion of a clause prohibiting racial discrimination in the NLRA. Its success sealed the future of unions as Anglo-dominated. It also guaranteed that union jobs would remain open only to Anglos as long as unions could choose members without prohibitions against discrimination.

B. Immigration Law Developments

While federal anti-discrimination statutes do not provide much guidance on the scope of the national-origin definition, judicial opinions have interpreted it to exclude alienage or immigration status unless it is used as a proxy for broader discrimination based on ethnicity. Ultimately, immigrants continue to have tenuous rights to work in this country. Noncitizen workers' rights are not as extensive as those of citizen workers in part because their rights are tied to status. A person with valid and proper immigration status (and employment authorization) can work. A person who loses, or never had, immigration status has effectively and practically diminished workplace protections. Immigration status, then, becomes the substitute for race or national origin in the development of a vulnerable labor force. Increasingly, restrictive immigration categories have, in turn, made immigration status a salient feature of the preferred low-wage worker. Overly restrictive immigration laws, disproportionately affecting Mexicans, have created an unprotected category of workers at the intersection of national origin and immigration status.

A brief history of changes in immigration law illustrates how the immigrant/undocumented/second class subcategory of Mexican was created. In 1965, the Immigration and Nationality Act eliminated the national-origins-quota system. That system, which heavily favored immigration from European countries, had been in force since 1924. The Act replaced national origins quotas with worldwide quotas and a preference system favoring family reunification. It was a change that liberals applauded as eradicating the discriminatory bases for immigration quotas in past versions of the law. In fact, however, the law in 1965 imposed quotas on western hemisphere countries for the first time, resulting in a radical change in the legal forms of entry for Mexican workers. Until 1964, guest worker programs like the Bracero Program had created a large and virtually unregulated migration flow of workers from Mexico filling low-wage jobs throughout the Southwest. When Mexicans, along with citizens of other Latin American countries, were faced with the worldwide quota requirements, their status as "illegals" was cemented for the long term. Importantly, this change in immigration law was occurring at the same time as the civil-rights movement, precisely when U.S. minorities were actively seeking their full rights of citizenship. At this time, national origin was included, along with race, religion, and color, as a protected category under civil-rights laws. Its inclusion was not much discussed then, although the evidence of discrimination, segregation and exploitation against Latinos and Mexicans, specifically, was plentiful.

As restrictions in immigration law increased, fewer Mexicans were able to immigrate legally. In the name of equity, the 1976 amendments to the Immigration and Nationality Act implemented a 20,000 per-country visa quota. This development was a compromise with those who feared a sharp increase in Latin American immigration. In the late 1970s, the quotas were revised downward, exacerbating the legal immigration backlog even more. With more than a million workers of Mexican national origin working the United States, the status of "illegal" was inevitable. Congress introduced employer sanctions provisions into the law for the first time in the Immigration Control and Reform Act of 1986, in response to public debate about the role of employers in attracting and retaining Mexican immigrants for low-wage work. It also created more restrictive measures for migration, which again affected Mexican migrants more than other would-be immigrants.

The increasingly restrictive immigration regime at once explains the phenomenon of Mexican illegality and today's current high proportion of Mexicans in our foreign-born population. More importantly, the roots of workers' vulnerability have effectively shifted from race or national origin to illegality and immigrant condition:

> [W]hile no other country has supplied nearly as many migrants to the United States as has Mexico since 1965, most major changes in U.S. immigration law during this period have created ever more severe restriction on the possibilities for 'legal' migration from Mexico. . . . [O]n the other hand, ostensibly restrictive immigration laws purportedly intended to deter migration have nonetheless been instrumental in sustaining Mexican migration, but only by significantly restructuring its legal status — as undocumented.

This much-abbreviated history demonstrates the social construction of the "illegality" and immigrant status of Mexicans, something that the cultural narratives have easily incorporated when discussing the role and importance of Mexicans in low-wage jobs. Importantly, the law did the work of operationalizing an acceptable way of talking about Mexicans that was no longer overtly and principally racialized. The substitution of the term "immigrant" for "Mexican" does much work to allow the cultural narratives to flourish.

44 *Ariz. St. L.J.* 305, 314–331.
Copyright © (2012) Ariz. St. L.J.
Reprinted with permission of Ariz. St. L.J. and Leticia Saucedo.

In 2004 in Montana, police officers stopped Sergio Manzo-Jurado, near the Canadian border, solely due to his Hispanic physical appearance. Manzo-Jurado, a Spanish-speaking immigrant, along with five of his coworkers, attended a local high school football state championship game. The group stood by themselves, calmly speaking in Spanish to each other. Their conduct was not unruly or suspicious and the location was not known for illegal immigrants.

Two police officers felt that the group looked "out of place" and called the border patrol. A border patrol agent questioned them. Manzo-Jurado, unable to show Immigration documents, was arrested.

Although the trial court found Manzo-Jurado had once used a counterfeit Social Security card to get a job, the appeals court in 2006 (457 F.3d 928) found no reasonable suspicion to justify the investigatory stop. The court found that the officers based their arrest on a broad profile, not an objective, specific cause for suspicion, in violation of constitutional criminal protections. For more than thirty years, racial profiling of minorities has been accepted by courts when it occurs near the border between the United States and Mexico due to the likelihood that a person with Mexican ancestry is an alien. Manzo-Jurado's arrest echoes centuries of suspicion in America in which law enforcement is often based on racial appearances.

Minority status and appearance have carried a burden in American citizenship and law enforcement determinations since colonial times. Race has been used divisively for centuries.

Should racial profiling be permitted in law enforcement activity relating to the detection, identification, and arrest of illegal immigrants? If so, what should the profile entail?

XI. Race, American Indians, and Sovereignty

A. Introduction

The federal government's treatment of American Indians included relocation, isolation, discrimination, breaking of treaties, rape, and genocide among other atrocities perpetrated under the authorization of federal law. The government's primary purpose was access to the land that American Indians occupied, and a variety of political, legal, medical, and military devices were used to secure such access. Tactics included encouraging buffalo hunts designed to reduce or eliminate a prime source of food for American Indians and supplying blankets infested with the measles virus to American Indian villages designed to cause widespread sickness and death.[43]

For American Indians, the primary issue with respect to the federal government has always been one of sovereignty. Who would determine the rules by which they were governed? Whether the dispute was over land, religion, or trade, the question of sovereignty was at the core of the conflict. Since the federal government's primary interest was in securing American-Indian land, and the primary interest of American Indians was in controlling their own affairs, conflict was inevitable.

Andrew Jackson

Excerpt from the Fifth Annual Message to Congress, December 3, 1833

. . . It is hoped to be that those portions of the two Southern tribes, which in that event will present the only remaining difficulties, will realize the necessity of emigration, and will speedily resort to it. My original convictions upon this subject have been confirmed by the course of events for several years, and experience is every day adding to their strength. That those tribes cannot exist surrounded by our settlements and in continual contact with our citizens is certain. *They have neither the intelligence, the industry,*

---

43. *See* generally J. Diamond, *Guns, Germs, and Steel* (1997).

the moral habits, nor the desire of improvement which are essential to any favorable change in their condition. Established in the midst of another and a superior race, and without appreciating the causes of their inferiority or seeking to control them, they must necessarily yield to the force of circumstances and ere long disappear. . . (Emphasis added).

Bethany Berger

After Pocahontas: Indian Women and the Law 1830–1934*

Andrew Jackson's administration began the Removal Period, called by one nineteenth century lawyer a forty year "period of compulsory emigration under the form of consent by voluntary treaty." With his ascent to the presidency in 1828, Jackson gained the means to implement his long held view that Indians should be removed from areas of white settlement by force rather than persuasion, and to end what he believed was the farce of treating with the Indian tribes as though they were sovereign nations. Under the guise of treaty agreement and the guns of armed troops, almost all the eastern tribes, beginning with the Cherokee, Chickasaw, Choctaw, Creek, and Seminole tribes of the Southeastern states, were moved to the Indian Territory in what was to become Oklahoma. Thousands of Indians died walking this Trail of Tears, and many tribes were practically destroyed.

With the national expansion of the 1840s, westward removal no longer sufficed to separate white from Indian. The federal government established reservations, then progressively whittled them away to open still more land for white settlement. The loss of traditional hunting lands, the decimation and impoverishment of removal and war, created in the Indians a new dependence on American rations and bureaucracy. In 1871, after the Indian Wars and relatively favorable treaties of the late 1860s, Congress declared that Indian tribes were no longer to be dealt with through treaty. This began the Reservation Period, a period of near-complete federal control over Indians on reservations. As the leader of an 1869 Smithsonian expedition down the Colorado River reported,

> The time has passed when it was necessary to buy peace. It only remains to decide what should be done with [the Indians] for the relief of the white people from their petty depredations, and from the demoralizing influences accompanying the presence of savages in civilized communities, and also for the best interests of the Indians themselves.

The solution hit upon was to assimilate the American Indians. A wave of reformers calling themselves "Friends of the Indian" controlled federal Indian policy from the last quarter of the nineteenth century through the first quarter of the twentieth. The reformers fervently promoted the seductive doctrine that the Indian problem would disappear not through guns but through the force of Protestant American culture. In the words of Francis Prucha, "With an ethnocentrism of frightening

---

* (footnotes and chapter headings omitted).

intensity, they resolved to do away with Indianness and to preserve only the manhood of the individual Indian. There would then be no more Indian problem because there would be no more persons identifiable as Indians."

The first step in this process of "Americanization" was to remove lands from communal tribal ownership into individual ownership by male heads of families. The first and major piece of legislation of the Assimilationist Period, the Dawes or General Allotment Act of 1887, was intended to do exactly that. The effects were devastating—of 138,000,000 acres Indians held when the Dawes Act was passed, only 48,000,000 were left in 1934, and nearly half of these were desert or semidesert. The second step was cultural education—Indian children were to be removed from their parents, purged of the harmful influences of Indian language and religious belief, and inculcated with belief systems that would allow them to finally disappear into the white American mass. The Meriam Report of 1928, a surprisingly contemporary work credited with ending the Assimilationist Period, later condemned this practice for having devastated the Indian family in the same way that allotment had devastated Indian land wealth.

21 *American Indian L. Rev.* 1, 6–8.
Copyright © (1997) *American Indian L. Rev.*
Reprinted with permission of *American Indian L. Rev.* and Bethany Berger.

The famous American-Indian athlete, Jim Thorpe, winner of the decathlon at the 1912 Olympic Games in Stockholm, Sweden, was educated in this fashion. He attended both boarding school and college at Carlisle Indian School in Pennsylvania where a majority of his teachers were white and where his football and track coach was the legendary Glen "Pop" Warner. Carlisle Indian School, opened in the late 1890s, was the first educational facility for American Indians created by Congress that was located outside of an Indian Reservation.

B. Background on *Johnson*

In the quest for land, first by the European powers and later by the United States, territory was acquired by governments, private entities, and individuals through various legal methods such as treaties, inheritance, and contracts. Occasionally, ownership of the land was contested due to multiple claimants with title tracing through different legal methods. Courts were called upon to determine who had the best legal title to the disputed land.

C. *Johnson v. McIntosh*, 21 U.S. 543 (1823)

1. Facts

Chief Justice MARSHALL delivered the opinion of the Court.

The plaintiffs in this cause claim the land, in their declaration mentioned, under two grants, purporting to be made, the first in 1773, and the last in 1775, by the chiefs of certain Indian tribes, constituting the Illinois and the Piankeshaw nations. . . .

2. Opinion

The facts, as stated in the case agreed, show the authority of the chiefs who executed this conveyance, so far as it could be given by their own people; and likewise show, that the particular tribes for whom these chiefs acted were in rightful possession of the land they sold. The inquiry, therefore, is, in a great measure, confined to the power of Indians to give, and of private individuals to receive, a title which can be sustained in the Courts of this country.

As the right of society, to prescribe those rules by which property may be acquired and preserved is not, and cannot be drawn into question; as the title to lands, especially, is and must be admitted to depend entirely on the law of the nation in which they lie; it will be necessary, in pursuing this inquiry, to examine, not singly those principles of abstract justice, which the Creator of all things has impressed on the mind of his creature man, and which are admitted to regulate, in a great degree, the rights of civilized nations, whose perfect independence is acknowledged; but those principles also which our own government has adopted in the particular case, and given us as the rule for our decision.

a. Principle of Discovery

On the discovery of this immense continent, the great nations of Europe were eager to appropriate to themselves so much of it as they could respectively acquire. Its vast extent offered and ample field to the ambition and enterprise of all; and the character and religion of its inhabitants afforded an apology for considering them as a people over whom the superior genius of Europe might claim an ascendency. The potentates of the old world found no difficulty in convincing themselves that they made ample compensation to the inhabitants of the new, by bestowing on them civilization and Christianity, in exchange for unlimited independence. But, as they were all in pursuit of nearly the same object, it was necessary, in order to avoid conflicting settlements, and consequent war with each other, to establish a principle, which all should acknowledge as the law by which the right of acquisition, which they all asserted, should be regulated as between themselves. This principle was, that discovery gave title to the government by whose subjects, or by whose authority, it was made, against all other European governments, which title might be consummated by possession.

The exclusion of all other Europeans, necessarily gave to the nation making the discovery the sole right of acquiring the soil from the natives, and establishing settlements upon it. It was a right with which no Europeans could interfere. It was a right which all asserted for themselves, and to the assertion of which, by others, all assented.

Those relations which were to exist between the discoverer and the natives, were to be regulated by themselves. The rights thus acquired being exclusive, no other power could interpose between them.

In the establishment of these relations, the rights of the original inhabitants were, in no instance, entirely disregarded; but were necessarily, to a considerable extent, impaired. They were admitted to be the rightful occupants of the soil, with a legal as well as just claim to retain possession of it, and to use it according to their own discretion; but their rights to complete sovereignty, as independent nations, were necessarily diminished, and their power to dispose of the soil at their own will, to whomsoever they pleased, was denied by the original fundamental principle, that discovery gave exclusive title to those who made it.

While the different nations of Europe respected the right of the natives, as occupants, they asserted the ultimate dominion to be in themselves; and claimed and exercised, as a consequence of this ultimate dominion, a power to grant the soil, while yet in possession of the natives. These grants have been understood by all, to convey a title to the grantees, subject only to the Indian right of occupancy.

The history of America, from its discovery to the present day, proves, we think, the universal recognition of these principles. . . .

The magnificent purchase of Louisiana, was the purchase from France of a country almost entirely occupied by numerous tribes of Indians, who are in fact independent. Yet, any attempt of others to intrude into that country, would be considered as an aggression which would justify war.

Our late acquisitions from Spain are of the same character; and the negotiations which preceded those acquisitions, recognise and elucidate the principle which has been received as the foundation of all European title in America.

The United States, then, have unequivocally acceded to that great and broad rule by which its civilized inhabitants now hold this country. They hold, and assert in themselves, the title by which it was acquired. They maintain, as all others have maintained, that discovery gave an exclusive right to extinguish the Indian title of occupancy, either by purchase or by conquest; and gave also a right to such a degree of sovereignty, as the circumstances of the people would allow them to exercise.

The power now possessed by the government of the United States to grant lands, resided, while we were colonies, in the crown, or its grantees. The validity of the titles given by either has never been questioned in our Courts. It has been exercised uniformly over territory in possession of the Indians. The existence of this power must negative the existence of any right which may conflict with, and control it. An absolute title to lands cannot exist, at the same time, in different persons, or in different governments. An absolute, must be an exclusive title, or at least a title which excludes all others not compatible with it. All our institutions recognise the absolute title of the crown, subject only to the Indian right of occupancy, and recognise the absolute title of the crown to extinguish that right. This is incompatible with an absolute and complete title in the Indians.

We will not enter into the controversy, whether agriculturists, merchants, and manufacturers, have a right, on abstract principles, to expel hunters from the territory they possess, or to contract their limits. Conquest gives a title which the Courts of the conqueror cannot deny, whatever the private and speculative opinions of individuals may be, respecting the original justice of the claim which has been successfully asserted. The British government, which was then our government, and whose rights have passed to the United States, asserted a title to all the lands occupied by Indians, within the chartered limits of the British colonies. It asserted also a limited sovereignty over them, and the exclusive right of extinguishing the title which occupancy gave to them. These claims have been maintained and established as far west as the river Mississippi, by the sword. The title to a vast portion of the lands we now hold, originates in them. It is not for the Courts of this country to question the validity of this title, or to sustain one which is incompatible with it.

b. Justification for Principle of Discovery

Although we do not mean to engage in the defence of those principles which Europeans have applied to Indian title, they may, we think, find some excuse, if not justification, in the character and habits of the people whose rights have been wrested from them.

The title by conquest is acquired and maintained by force. The conqueror prescribes its limits. Humanity, however, acting on public opinion, has established, as a general rule, that the conquered shall not be wantonly oppressed, and that their condition shall remain as eligible as is compatible with the objects of the conquest. Most usually, they are incorporated with the victorious nation, and become subjects or citizens of the government with which they are connected. The new and old members of the society mingle with each other; the distinction between them is gradually lost, and they make one people. Where this incorporation is practicable, humanity demands, and a wise policy requires, that the rights of the conquered to property should remain unimpaired; that the new subjects should be governed as equitably as the old, and that confidence in their security should gradually banish the painful sense of being separated from their ancient connexions, and united by force to strangers.

When the conquest is complete, and the conquered inhabitants can be blended with the conquerors, or safely governed as a distinct people, public opinion, which not even the conqueror can disregard, imposes these restraints upon him; and he cannot neglect them without injury to his fame, and hazard to his power.

But the tribes of Indians inhabiting this country were fierce savages, whose occupation was war, and whose subsistence was drawn chiefly from the forest. To leave them in possession of their country, was to leave the country a wilderness; to govern them as a distinct people, was impossible, because they were as brave and as high spirited as they were fierce, and were ready to repel by arms every attempt on their independence.

What was the inevitable consequence of this state of things? The Europeans were under the necessity either of abandoning the country, and relinquishing their pompous claims to it, or of enforcing those claims by the sword, and by the adoption of principles adapted to the condition of a people with whom it was impossible to mix, and who could not be governed as a distinct society, or of remaining in their neighborhood, and exposing themselves and their families to the perpetual hazard of being massacred.

Frequent and bloody wars, in which the whites were not always the aggressors, unavoidably ensued. European policy, numbers, and skill, prevailed. As the white population advanced, that of the Indians necessarily receded. The country in the immediate neighborhood of agriculturists became unfit for them. The game fled into thicker and more unbroken forests, and the Indians followed. The soil, to which the crown originally claimed title, being no longer occupied by its ancient inhabitants, was parceled out according to the will of the sovereign power, and taken possession of by persons who claimed immediately from the crown, or immediately, through its grantees or deputies.

That law which regulates, and ought to regulate in general, the relations between the conqueror and conquered, was incapable of application to a people under such circumstances. The resort to some new and different rule, better adapted to the actual state of things, was unavoidable. Every rule which can be suggested will be found to be attended with great difficulty.

However extravagant the pretension of converting the discovery of an inhabited country into conquest may appear; if the principle has been asserted in the first instance, and afterwards sustained; if a country has been acquired and held under it; if the property of the great mass of the community originates in it, it becomes the law of the land, and cannot be questioned. So, too, with respect to the concomitant principle, that the Indian inhabitants are to be considered merely as occupants, to be protected, indeed, while in peace, in the possession of their lands, but to be deemed incapable of transferring the absolute title to others. However this restriction may be opposed to natural right, and to the usages of civilized nations, yet, if it be indispensable to that system under which the country has been settled, and be adapted to the actual condition of the two people, it may, perhaps, be supported by reason, and certainly cannot be rejected by Courts of justice.

c. Application of the Principle of Discovery

This question is not entirely new in this Court. The case of *Fletcher v. Peck*, grew out of a sale made by the State of Georgia of a large tract of country within the limits of that State, the grant of which was afterwards resumed. The action was brought by a sub-purchaser, on the contract of sale, and one of the covenants in the deed was, that the State of Georgia was, at the time of sale, seised in fee of the premises. The real question presented by the issue was, whether the seisin in fee was in the State of Georgia, or in the United States. After stating, that this controversy between the several States and the United States, had been compromised, the Court thought it necessary to notice the Indian title, which, although entitled to the respect of all Courts until it should be legitimately extinguished, was declared not to be such as to be absolutely repugnant to a seizin in fee on the part of the State.

This opinion conforms precisely to the principle which has been supposed to be recognized by all European governments, from the first settlement of America. The absolute ultimate title has been considered as acquired by discovery, subject only to the Indian title of occupancy, which title the discoverers possessed the exclusive right of acquiring. Such a right is no more incompatible with a seizin in fee, than a lease for years, and might as effectually bar an ejectment. . . .

It has been stated, that in the memorial transmitted from the Cabinet of London to that of Versailles, during the controversy between the two nations, respecting boundary, which took place in 1755, the Indian right to the soil is recognized. But this recognition was made with reference to their character as Indians, and for the purpose of showing that they were fixed to a particular territory. It was made for the purpose of sustaining the claim of his Britannic majesty to dominion over them. . . .

Much reliance is also placed on the fact, that many tracts are now held in the United States under the Indian title, the validity of which is not questioned.

Before the importance attached to this fact is conceded, the circumstances under which such grants were obtained, and such titles are supported, ought to be considered. These lands lie chiefly in the eastern States. It is known that the Plymouth Company made many extensive grants, which, from their ignorance of the country, interfered with each other. It is also known that Mason, to whom New Hampshire, and Gorges, to whom Maine was granted, found great difficulty in managing such unwieldy property. The country was settled by emigrants, some from Europe, but chiefly from Massachusetts, who took possession of lands they found unoccupied, and secured themselves in that possession by the best means in their power. The disturbances in England, and the civil war and revolution which followed those disturbances, prevented any interference on the part of the mother country, and the proprietors were unable to maintain their title. In the mean time, Massachusetts claimed the country, and governed it. As her claim was adversary to that of the proprietors, she encouraged the settlement of persons made under her authority, and encouraged, likewise, their securing themselves in possession, by purchasing the acquiescence and forbearance of the Indians. . . .

It has never been contended, that the Indian title amounted to nothing. Their right of possession has never been questioned. The claim of government extends to the complete ultimate title, charged with this right of possession, and to the exclusive power of acquiring that right. The object of the crown was to settle the seacoast of America; and when a portion of it was settled, without violating the rights of others, by persons professing their loyalty, and soliciting the royal sanction of an act, the consequences of which were ascertained to be beneficial, it would have been as unwise as ungracious to expel them from their habitations, because they had obtained the Indian title otherwise than through the agency of government. The very grant of a charter is an assertion of the title of the crown, and its words convey the same idea. The country granted, is said to be "our island called Rhode Island;" and the charter contains an actual grant of the soil, as well as of the powers of government.

The letter was written a few months before the charter was issued, apparently at the request of the agents of the intended colony, for the sole purpose of preventing the trespasses of neighbours, who were disposed to claim some authority over them. The king, being willing himself to ratify and confirm their title, was, of course, inclined to quiet them in their possession.

This charter, and this letter, certainly sanction a previous unauthorized purchase from Indians, under the circumstances attending that particular purchase, but are far from supporting the general proposition, that a title acquired from the Indians would be valid against a title acquired from the crown, or without the confirmation of the crown.

The acts of the several colonial assemblies, prohibiting purchases from the Indians, have also been relied on, as proving, that, independent of such prohibitions, Indian deeds would be valid. But, we think this fact, at most, equivocal. While the existence of such purchases would justify their prohibition, even by colonies which considered Indian deeds as previously invalid, the fact that such acts have been generally passed, is strong evidence of the general opinion, that such purchases are opposed by the soundest principles of wisdom and national policy.

3. Holding

After bestowing on this subject a degree of attention which was more required by the magnitude of the interest in litigation, and the able and elaborate arguments of the bar, than by its intrinsic difficulty, the Court is decidedly of opinion, that the plaintiffs do not exhibit a title which can be sustained in the Courts of the United States; and that there is no error in the judgment which was rendered against them in the District Court of Illinois.

D. Commentary on *Johnson*

Chief Justice John Marshall's opinion in *Johnson and Graham's Lessee* reasoning that American Indians had no legally recognizable authority under the Constitution to convey title of land to private individuals used traditional Anglo-American property principles to deny rights to American Indians. The principle of discovery of land, employed by early settlers, which gave superior property rights to European powers, was racially biased against non-European indigenous populations. As a result, land claims traced through American Indian grants were diminished when they conflicted with claims traced through European powers. The Court's rationale for such disparate treatment was the perceived racial inferiority of American Indians, expressly referred to in the opinion as "fierce savages."[46]

The principle of discovery gave the United States government legal title over all American Indians' lands, wherever those lands were located, and the sole right to acquire, regulate, and dispose of such lands. While the Supremacy Clause of the

---

46. 21 U.S. 543, 590 (1823).

United States Constitution (Article VI, Clause 2, United States Constitution) gave the federal government the authority to govern American Indians, the role individual states could play to protect the property rights of Indians, if any, was unclear.

E. Background on *Cherokee Nation*

As land in the eastern and southern states became scarce, state governments encouraged the federal government to relocate American Indians to more isolated areas in the western territories. In response, Congress passed the Indian Removal Act in 1830 to allow the President to relocate as many American Indians as possible. Some American Indians resisted the federal government's removal efforts through military force, others attempted to resist through the courts.

The Cherokees had interacted with whites in Georgia for decades and had assimilated into Georgian life more than any other American Indians had done in any part of the country.[47] Despite this assimilation, the Cherokees still controlled large tracts of land within the State of Georgia and exercised government functions within this territory.

In 1828, the state legislature passed a law making all Cherokees and Cherokee lands subject to Georgia state laws. The Cherokees resisted surrendering their sovereignty to the state of Georgia by resorting to the United States federal judicial process.

F. *Cherokee Nation v. The State of Georgia*, 30 U.S. 1 (1831)

1. Facts

Chief Justice MARSHALL delivered the opinion of the Court.

This bill is brought by the Cherokee nation, praying an injunction to restrain the state of Georgia from the execution of certain laws of that state, which, as is alleged, go directly to annihilate the Cherokees as a political society, and to seize, for the use of Georgia, the lands of the nation which have been assured to them by the United States in solemn treaties repeatedly made and still in force.

If courts were permitted to indulge their sympathies, a case better calculated to excite them can scarcely be imagined. A people once numerous, powerful, and truly independent, found by our ancestors in the quiet and uncontrolled possession of an ample domain, gradually sinking beneath our superior policy, our arts and our arms, have yielded their lands by successive treaties, each of which contains a solemn guarantee of the residue, until they retain no more of their formerly extensive territory than is deemed necessary to their comfortable subsistence. To preserve this remnant, the present application is made.

---

47. *See* GETCHES, WILKINSON, & WILLIAMS, FEDERAL INDIAN LAW, at 122 (1993).

2. Opinion

a. Jurisdiction

Before we can look into the merits of the case, a preliminary inquiry presents itself. Has this court jurisdiction of the cause?

The third article of the constitution describes the extent of the judicial power. The second section closes an enumeration of the cases to which it is extended, with "controversies" "between a state or the citizens thereof, and foreign states, citizens, or subjects." A subsequent clause of the same section gives the supreme court original jurisdiction in all cases in which a state shall be a party. The party defendant may then unquestionably be sued in this court. May the plaintiff sue in it? Is the Cherokee nation a foreign state in the sense in which that term is used in the constitution?

The counsel for the plaintiffs have maintained the affirmative of this proposition with great earnestness and ability. So much of the argument as was intended to prove the character of the Cherokees as a state, as a distinct political society, separated from others, capable of managing its own affairs and governing itself, has, in the opinion of a majority of the judges, been completely successful. They have been uniformly treated as a state from the settlement of our country. The numerous treaties made with them by the United States recognize them as a people capable of maintaining the relations of peace and war, of being responsible in their political character for any violation of their engagements, or for any aggression committed on the citizens of the United States by any individual of their community. Laws have been enacted in the spirit of these treaties. The acts of our government plainly recognize the Cherokee nation as a state, and the courts are bound by those acts.

b. Foreign State

A question of much more difficulty remains. Do the Cherokees constitute a foreign state in the sense of the constitution?

The counsel have shown conclusively that they are not a state of the union, and have insisted that individually they are aliens, not owing allegiance to the United States. An aggregate of aliens composing a state must, they say, be a foreign state. Each individual being foreign, the whole must be foreign.

This argument is imposing, but we must examine it more closely before we yield to it. The condition of the Indians in relation to the United States is perhaps unlike that of any other two people in existence. In the general, nations not owing a common allegiance are foreign to each other. The term foreign nation is, with strict propriety, applicable by either to the other. But the relation of the Indians to the United States is marked by peculiar and cardinal distinctions which exist no where else.

The Indian territory is admitted to compose a part of the United States. In all our maps, geographical treatises, histories, and laws, it is so considered. In all our intercourse with foreign nations, in our commercial regulations, in any attempt at intercourse between Indians and foreign nations, they are considered as within the jurisdictional limits of the United States, subject to many of those restraints which are imposed upon our own citizens. They acknowledge themselves in their treaties to be under the protection of the United States; they admit that the United States shall have the sole and exclusive right of regulating the trade with them, and managing all their affairs as they think proper; and the Cherokees in particular were allowed by the treaty of Hopewell, which preceded the constitution, "to send a deputy of their choice, whenever they think fit, to Congress." Treaties were made with some tribes by the state of New York, under a then unsettled construction of the confederation, by which they ceded all their lands to that state, taking back a limited grant to themselves, in which they admit their dependence.

Though the Indians are acknowledged to have an unquestionable, and, heretofore, unquestioned right to the lands they occupy, until that right shall be extinguished by a voluntary cession to our government; yet it may well be doubted whether those tribes which reside within the acknowledged boundaries of the United States can, with strict accuracy, be denominated foreign nations. They may, more correctly, perhaps, be denominated domestic dependent nations. They occupy a territory to which we assert a title independent of their will, which must take effect in point of possession when their right of possession ceases. Meanwhile they are in a state of pupilage. Their relation to the United States resembles that of a ward to his guardian.

They look to our government for protection; rely upon its kindness and its power; appeal to it for relief to their wants; and address the president as their great father. They and their country are considered by foreign nations, as well as by ourselves, as being so completely under the sovereignty and dominion of the United States, that any attempt to acquire their lands, or to form a political connexion with them, would be considered by all as an invasion of our territory, and an act of hostility.

These considerations go far to support the opinion, that the framers of our constitution had not the Indian tribes in view, when they opened the courts of the union to controversies between a state or the citizens thereof, and foreign states.

In considering this subject, the habits and usages of the Indians, in their intercourse with their white neighbours, ought not to be entirely disregarded. At the time the constitution was framed, the idea of appealing to an American court of justice for an assertion of right or a redress of wrong, had perhaps never entered the mind of an Indian or of his tribe. Their appeal was to the tomahawk, or to the government. This was well understood by the statesmen who framed the constitution of the United States, and might furnish some reason for omitting to enumerate them among the parties who might sue in the courts of the union. Be this as it may, the peculiar relations between the United States and the Indians occupying our territory are such, that we should feel much difficulty in considering them as designated by the term foreign state, were there no other part of the constitution which might shed light on the meaning of these words. But we think that in construing them, considerable aid is furnished by that clause in the eighth section of the third article; which empowers congress to "regulate commerce with foreign nations, and among the several states, and with the Indian tribes."

In this clause they are as clearly contradistinguished by a name appropriate to themselves, from foreign nations, as from the several states composing the union. They are designated by a distinct appellation; and as this appellation can be applied to neither of the others, neither can the appellation distinguishing either of the others be in fair construction applied to them. The objects, to which the power of regulating commerce might be directed, are divided into three distinct classes— foreign nations, the several states, and Indian tribes. When forming this article, the convention considered them as entirely distinct. We cannot assume that the distinction was lost in framing a subsequent article, unless there be something in its language to authorize the assumption.

The counsel for the plaintiffs contend that the words "Indian tribes" were introduced into the article, empowering congress to regulate commerce, for the purpose of removing those doubts in which the management of Indian affairs was involved by the language of the Ninth Article of the Confederation. Intending to give the whole power of managing those affairs to the government about to be instituted, the convention conferred it explicitly; and omitted those qualifications which embarrassed the exercise of it as granted in the Confederation. This may be admitted without weakening the construction which has been intimated: Had the Indian tribes been foreign nations, in the view of the convention; this exclusive power of regulating intercourse with them might have been, and most probably would have been, specifically given, in language indicating that idea, not in language contradistinguishing them from foreign nations. Congress might have been empowered "to regulate commerce with foreign nations, including the Indian tribes, and among the several states." This language would have suggested itself to statesmen who considered the Indian tribes as foreign nations, and were yet desirous of mentioning them particularly.

It has been also said, that the same words have not necessarily the same meaning attached to them when found in different parts of the same instrument: their meaning is controlled by the context. This is undoubtedly true. In common language the same word has various meanings, and the peculiar sense in which it is used in any sentence is to be determined by the context. This may not be equally true with respect to proper names. Foreign nations is a general term, the application of which to Indian tribes, when used in the American constitution, is at best extremely questionable. In one article in which a power is given to be exercised in regard to foreign nations generally, and to the Indian tribes particularly, they are mentioned as separate in terms clearly contradistinguishing them from each other. We perceive plainly that the constitution in this article does not comprehend Indian tribes in the general term "foreign nations;" not we presume because a tribe may not be a nation, but because it is not foreign to the United States. When, afterwards, the term "foreign state" is introduced, we cannot impute to the convention the intention to desert its former meaning, and to comprehend Indian tribes within it, unless the context force that construction on us. We find nothing in the context, and nothing in the subject of the article, which leads to it.

3. Holding

The court has bestowed its best attention on this question, and, after mature deliberation, the majority is of opinion that an Indian tribe or nation within the United States is not a foreign state in the sense of the constitution, and cannot maintain an action in the courts of the United States.

If it be true that the Cherokee nation have rights, this is not the tribunal in which those rights are to be asserted. If it be true that wrongs have been inflicted, and that still greater are to be apprehended, this is not the tribunal which can redress the past or prevent the future.

The motion for an injunction is denied.

4. Justice Johnson Concurring

I cannot but think that there are strong reasons for doubting the applicability of the epithet state, to a people so low in the grade of organized society as our Indian tribes most generally are. I would not here be understood as speaking of the Cherokees under their present form of government; which certainly must be classed among the most approved forms of civil government. Whether it can be yet said to have received the consistency which entitles that people to admission into the family of nations is, I conceive, yet to be determined by the executive of these states. Until then I must think that we cannot recognize it as an existing state, under any other character than that which it has maintained hitherto as one of the Indian tribes or nations. . . .

The argument is that they were states; and if not states of the union, must be foreign states. But I think it very clear that the Constitution neither speaks of them as states or foreign states, but as just what they were, Indian tribes; an anomaly unknown to the books that speak of states, and which the law of nations would regard as nothing more than wandering hordes, held together only by ties of blood and habit, and having neither laws or government, beyond what is required in a savage state. The distinction is clearly made in that section which vests in congress power to regulate commerce between the United States with foreign nations and the Indian tribes.

The language must be applied in one of three senses; either in that of the law of nations, or of the vernacular use, or that of the constitution. In the first, although it means any state not subject to our laws, yet it must be a state and not a hunter horde: in the vernacular, it would not be applied to a people within our limits and at our very doors: and in the constitution the two epithets are used in direct contradistinction. The latter words were unnecessary, if the first included the Indian tribes. There is no ambiguity, though taken literally; and if there were, facts and circumstances altogether remove it.

5. *Justice Thompson Dissenting*

. . . It is a rule which has been repeatedly sanctioned by this court, that the judicial department is to consider as sovereign and independent states or nations those powers, that are recognized as such by the executive and legislative departments of the government; they being more particularly entrusted with our foreign relations. 4 Cranch, 241, 2 Peters's Cond. Rep. 98; 3 Wheat. 634; 4 Wheat. 64.

If we look to the whole course of treatment by this country of the Indians, from the year 1775, to the present day, when dealing with them in their aggregate capacity as nations or tribes, and regarding the mode and manner in which all negotiations have been carried on and concluded with them; the conclusion appears to me irresistible, that they have been regarded, by the executive and legislative branches of the government, not only as sovereign and independent, but as foreign nations or tribes, not within the jurisdiction nor under the government of the states within which they were located. This remark is to be understood, of course, as referring only to such as live together as a distinct community, under their own laws, usages and customs; and not to the mere remnant of tribes which are to be found in many parts of our country, who have become mixed with the general population of the country: their national character extinguished; and their usages and customs in a great measure abandoned; self government surrendered; and who have voluntarily, or by the force of circumstances which surrounded them, gradually become subject to the laws of the states within which they are situated.

Such, however, is not the case with the Cherokee nation. It retains its usages and customs and self government, greatly improved by the civilization which it has been the policy of the United States to encourage and foster among them. All negotiations carried on with the Cherokees and other Indian nations have been by way of treaty with all the formality attending the making of treaties with any foreign power. The journals of congress, from the year 1775 down to the adoption of the present constitution, abundantly establish this fact. And since that period such negotiations have been carried on by the treaty-making power, and uniformly under the denomination of treaties.

What is a treaty as understood in the law of nations? It is an agreement or contract between two or more nations or sovereigns, entered into by agents appointed for that purpose, and duly sanctioned by the supreme power of the respective parties. And where is the authority, either in the constitution or in the practice of the government, for making any distinction between treaties made with the Indian nations and any other foreign power? They relate to peace and war; the surrender of prisoners; the cession of territory; and the various subjects which are usually embraced in such contracts between sovereign nations. . . .

Upon the whole, I am of opinion, that the Cherokees compose a foreign state within the sense and meaning of the constitution, and constitute a competent party to maintain a suit against the state of Georgia.

Justice STORY concurs in this dissent.

G. Commentary on *Cherokee Nation*

The Supreme Court dismissed the case on jurisdictional grounds. Chief Justice Marshall in his opinion and Justice Johnson in his concurring opinion argued before a divided court that American Indians, no matter how independent, could not be classified as citizens of a foreign nation entitled to the rights and privileges thereof. They reasoned that American Indian tribes could not fit the definition of a foreign nation, not due to a defect in their organizational structure, but due to their inferiority as a people. As in previous cases dealing with American Indians, the Justices reasoned that as an inferior people, American Indians should be viewed differently than other foreigners of European countries. Just as the Justices viewed blacks as inferior by denying them citizenship in the *Dred Scott* case, American Indians were denied judicial relief under similar rationale. Although nominally protected by the individual-rights provisions of the United States Constitution, individual American Indians and American-Indian tribes, like slaves and free blacks prior to 1868, were prohibited from asserting their rights in federal court.

Stephen Breyer

Making Our Democracy Work[*1]

The Georgians were delighted with the *Cherokee Nation* decision. Georgia's governor wrote that the state "must put an end to even the semblance" that the Indians could constitute "a distinct political society."

After this setback, William Wirt, a lawyer for the Cherokee Nation, finally found the case he had been looking for. Georgia law required "all white persons residing within the limits of the Cherokee Nation" to take an oath to support Georgia's laws. A New England missionary, Samuel A. Worcester, refused. (He sent the governor a hymnbook instead.)

The governor ordered Worcester arrested, and a Georgia court convicted him of violating the law and sentenced him to four years of hard labor. Georgia would not free Worcester, but it was unlikely to execute him. Furthermore, the Judiciary Act of 1789 gave the Supreme Court the authority to hear cases in which a state court had rejected a party's claim that a state's criminal law violated federal law, which the Constitution made "supreme." Thus the law made clear that Wirt could appeal Worcester's case to the Supreme Court, making the argument that application of Georgia's criminal law in Cherokee territory violated treaties made by the United States, treaties that the Constitution made "supreme."

The Court heard the case, *Worcester v. Georgia,* and by a vote of 5 to 1 found in Worcester's favor. Again Chief Justice Marshall wrote the Court's opinion. He pointed out that a federal statute empowers the Court to review a final state court judgment that upholds a state statute and that also rejects a claim that the statute is

---

* (footnotes omitted).

repugnant to the Constitution, treaties, or laws of the United States. Furthermore, another federal statute requires the Court to hear such an appeal. In Marshall's words, the Court therefore has "the duty, . . . however unpleasant," to hear the case.

Moreover, the Court held that Worcester was clearly right about the merits of his case, neither Britain nor the colonies nor the United States ever extinguished the Cherokees' independence. All had treated the Indian tribes as "nations capable of maintaining the relations of peace and war." The United States specifically promised that it would guarantee the Cherokees all lands "not . . . ceded" and would regulate trade for their "benefit and comfort." Congress too had recognized that Indian tribes are "distinct political communities" with a right to all the lands within their boundaries. Thus Georgians could not enter the Cherokee lands without the Cherokees' consent, and Georgia could not apply its state law there.

Because the state statute used to prosecute Worcester "is consequently void," Georgia had to release him. After all, if Georgia had taken property under the authority of an invalid law, it would have to return the property to its owner; the same principle applied when the state invalidly deprived Worcester of his "personal liberty."

In a well-aimed aside, the Court referred to the enforceability problem. It pointed out that Georgia had "seized" Worcester and "carried [him] away" while he was under the "guardianship of treaties" of the United States, indeed while he was "performing, *under the sanction of the chief magistrate of the union,* those duties which the humane policy adopted by congress had recommended." Perhaps President Jackson would get this hint. Perhaps he would understand that his own authority and the authority of the entire federal government were at stake.

Justice Joseph Story, Marshall's colleague, felt relief. He wrote to his wife, "Thanks be to God, the Court can wash their hands clean of the iniquity of oppressing the Indians and disregarding their rights." A few days later, he wrote to another correspondent: "The Court has done its duty. Let the Nation now do theirs." But he added, "Georgia is full of anger and violence. . . . Probably she will resist . . . and if she does, I do not believe the President will interfere."

Story was correct. On March 5, 1832, the Court issued an order requiring Georgia to release Worcester. Shortly thereafter, when Worcester's lawyers asked the state judge to release him, the judge refused. The governor then told the state legislature that he would meet the Supreme Court's "usurpation of Federal power with the most prompt and determined resistance."

The president also refused to help enforce the Supreme Court's decision. On the contrary, Jackson's secretary of war stated that the president, "on mature consideration," believed that state legislatures have the "power to extend their laws over all persons [that is, Indian tribes included] living within their boundaries." Consequently, the president, he said, has "no authority to interfere" in Georgia's dealings with Samuel Worcester. Furthermore, in Jackson's view the president and the Congress had as much authority "to decide upon the constitutionality" of statutes as do "the supreme judges," who, he added, "must not . . . be permitted to control the Congress, or the Executive, when acting in their legislative capacities." The *New York Daily Advertiser* told its readers that the president "has said . . . that he ha[s] as good a right to order the Supreme Court as the Court ha[s] to require him to execute its decisions." And popular wisdom attributed to Jackson the famous phrase "well, John Marshall has made his decision, now let him enforce it." As Worcester languished in jail, John Marshall wrote to Joseph Story, "I yield slowly and reluctantly to the conviction that our Constitution cannot last."

Marshall obviously feared the power of example. If the states could ignore the Court's decision favoring the Indians, why could they not similarly ignore others they did not like? Why should states or their citizens follow federal law at all? Why pay federal taxes? Why enforce federal customs law? Indeed, only a few months after the *Worcester* decision, South Carolina published a "Nullification Ordinance." This ordinance made it unlawful to pay (within South Carolina) any duties imposed by certain federal statutes. It required all state courts to follow state, not federal, law in these matters; it forbade taking an appeal to the Supreme Court and punished with contempt of court anyone who tried to do so.

Suddenly Jackson understood the political power of Georgia's example. Many in the South had long thought that states need not follow federal laws with which they disagreed. But Jackson as president now saw the threat to the Constitution posed by such a theory. If states could nullify federal law willy-nilly, then the Union might well become not the federation that the Constitution foresaw but a voluntary, and perhaps temporary, association of independent states.

Seeing the folly of his earlier position, Jackson reversed course. On December 10, 1832, he issued a statement: "I consider . . . the power to annul a law of the United States, assumed by one State, incompatible with the existence of the Union." Then he acted. Allying himself with Daniel Webster, a strong opponent of the nullification principle, he secured enactment of the Force Bill. This new federal statute explicitly gave the president the legal authority to use federal troops to enforce federal law. Its sponsors had South Carolina in mind. And South Carolina, understanding this, gave in to the threat of force. It repealed its Nullification Ordinance.

Just as Georgia's example affected South Carolina, so the South Carolina example affected Worcester. The general public understood the need for similar treatment of similar instances as a universal tenant of the rule of law. The newspapers wrote that "no person but a Jackson or Van Buren man can see any essential difference between the case of Georgia and South Carolina." Wirt filed papers to take Worcester's case back to the Supreme Court for a further order, and Jackson, hinting at the use of troops, said he would enforce that order. Georgia saw what had happened in South Carolina and began to look for a settlement. The governor offered a pardon. The Board of Foreign Missions, Worcester's employer, urged Worcester to accept the pardon and withdraw the motion pending before the Supreme Court, and in January 1833 he was released from prison. Thus, the Court's order ultimately was enforced. Or was it?

Wasn't the original point of Wirt's judicial effort to secure legal protection for the Cherokee tribe? Didn't the Court's decision explicitly state that Georgia could not seize the Cherokees' land, that the land belonged to the tribe, not to Georgia? What happened to the Cherokees' effort to keep their land?

That effort failed. President Jackson sent federal troops to Georgia, not to enforce the Court's decision, but to evict the Indians. In early 1835, without the authorization of Chief Ross and the Cherokee government, federal representatives arranged for a handful of the tribe's members to meet in Washington to negotiate a treaty. There they reached an agreement providing for the removal of the tribe to the West. Jackson proclaimed victory.

Horrified, the remaining seventeen thousand members of the tribe—including Chief Ross and the Cherokee government—immediately protested, but it was too late. Jackson submitted the "treaty" to the Senate, which ratified it by a one-vote margin. The secretary of war then informed Chief Ross that the "President had ceased to recognize" his government. And Jackson's federal troops ensured the Cherokees' removal. General John Ellis Wool, in command of the federal troops wrote to his superiors in Washington that the Cherokees were "almost universally opposed to the Treaty." He reported that the great majority of the tribe were "so determined . . . in their opposition" that they had refused to "receive either rations or clothing from the United States lest they might compromise themselves in regard to the treaty," they "preferred living upon the roots and sap of trees rather than receive provisions "from the federal government, "thousands . . . had no other food for weeks," and many "said they will die before they leave the country."

But Jackson ordered Wool to enforce the treaty. Jackson forbade the Cherokees to assemble to discuss the treaty, and he ordered Wool to show his letter to Chief Ross, after which he was to have no further written or oral communication with Ross on the subject.

Wool obeyed. He described the subsequent scene as heartrending," adding that, were it up to him, he "would remove every Indian tomorrow beyond the reach of the white men who, like vultures, are watching, ready to pounce upon their prey and strip them of everything they have." "Yes sir," he later said, "ninety-nine out of every hundred" of the Cherokees "will go penniless to the West." And that they did. Their route, called the Trail of Tears because so many died, led them to Oklahoma, where descendants of the survivors live to this day.

This sad story has a few positive aspects. Despite the tragic outcome, it helped establish a principle—namely, that like cases need to be treated alike. The perceived unfairness of treating similar cases differently led to press articles demanding Worcester's release. The case also underlined the importance of the Supreme Court's power to strike down state laws that are inconsistent with the Constitution or treaties or federal statutes. South Carolina's ordinance made clear, even to President Jackson, the threat that "nullification" posed to national union.

Still, the predominant lesson the story tells us is not a happy one. A president used his power to undermine a Court decision and to drive the Cherokees from their native land. Moreover, Story's and Marshall's concerns about injury to the Court were well-founded. As far as the Court was concerned, the popular account of Jackson's attitude revealed the Court's weakness. The chief justice "has made his decision, now let him enforce it." Georgia was prepared to hang anyone who entered that state to enforce the Supreme Court decision. The president of the United States saw no problem with Georgia's attitude—at least not initially—and he ended up subverting the Court's basic holding.

Making our Democracy Work 26–31.
Copyright(c) (2010) Stephen Breyer.
Reprinted with permission of Stephen Breyer.

The laws made it difficult for whites to assist American Indians even if they wished to do so. Shortly after the decision in *Cherokee Nation v. Georgia*, Samuel Worcester, a white American citizen from Vermont, was convicted and sentenced to four years in prison for violating a Georgia law that prohibited whites from residing on Cherokee lands without permission of the governor of Georgia. Worcester appealed his conviction to the Supreme Court which overturned the conviction and invalidated the Georgia law. Chief Justice Marshall authored the opinion reasoning that government relations with American Indians were exclusively the province of Congress. President Andrew Jackson disagreed with this reasoning and refused to enforce the decision. As a result, President Jackson allowed Georgia to ignore the Court's directive. Worcester, who had won his case, remained in prison for another year until he agreed not to pursue further legal proceedings. A pardon was issued securing Worcester's release from prison in 1834.

If the federal courts were not empowered to protect American-Indian rights who was? In United States v. Kagama,[48] the Supreme Court ruled that Congress, under its plenary power, has the exclusive and unlimited authority to govern American-Indian tribes and control or limit their sovereignty. The rationale for this decision was the same as previous ones dealing with American Indians. They could be treated differently than other Americans or denied sovereignty simply because they were viewed as members of a racially inferior group. Justice Miller, writing for the Court, stated:

> It seems to us that this is within the competency of Congress. These Indian tribes are the wards of the nation. They are communities dependent on the United States—dependent largely for their daily food; dependent for their political rights. They owe no allegiance to the states, people of the states where they are found are often their deadliest enemies. From their very weakness and helplessness, so largely due to the course of dealing of

---

48. 118 U.S. 375 (1886).

the federal government with them, and the treaties in which it has been promised, there arises the duty of protection, and with it the power. This has always been recognized by the executive, and by Congress, and by this court, whenever the question has arisen.[49]

Not only was the power of Congress over American Indian tribes exclusive and unlimited, the protections afforded by treaties were tenuous at best. In Lone Wolf v. Hitchcock,[50] the Supreme Court ruled that treaties with American-Indian tribes could be abrogated at the discretion of Congress. Accordingly, rights exercised by American Indians under treaties could be taken away whenever Congress deemed it appropriate.

Pursuant to the Removal Act, members of the Cherokee Nation were forced to leave their ancestral home in Georgia and relocate to Oklahoma. President Andrew Jackson was able to order the Cherokees on a one-thousand-mile trek during the coldest months of winter, and they had no legislative or judicial means to prevent it. Known as the "Trail of Tears," over four thousand Cherokee died during this relocation effort.[51]

American-Indian rights could only be granted by Congress. Yet, by the early twentieth century, Congress had become committed to a policy of assimilation for American Indians, in direct opposition to their rights. To enforce assimilation, Congress passed legislation reducing the role of American-Indian tribes and culture in the lives of individual American Indians. One of the primary pieces of this legislation was the allotment policy, which subdivided tribal land apportioning some parcels to individual American Indians without compensation to the tribe and selling the rest to whites at vastly deflated prices.[52] It was not until the 1930s that Congress would abandon the assimilation policy and attempt to protect American-Indian culture and encourage tribal self-government through the passage of the Indian Reorganization Act.[53]

This abandonment was followed by Supreme Court decisions narrowing the scope of Congress's plenary powers over American-Indian tribes. In *Creek Nation v. United States*,[54] the Supreme Court ruled that American-Indian tribes possess a general right to sue in federal court even without specific congressional authorization. In *Poafpybitty v. Skeely Oil Company*,[55] the Court ruled that American-Indian status did not preclude individual Native Americans from bringing law suits on their own behalf.

---

49. Id. at 379.
50. 187 U.S. 553 (1903).
51. *See* F. Bordewich, Killing the White Man's Indian 47 (1996).
52. *See* the General Allotment Act, 24 Stat. 388 (1887).
53. Indian Reorganization Act, 48 Stat. 984 (1934).
54. 318 U.S. 103 (1943).
55. 390 U.S. 365 (1968).

Moreover, Congress passed legislation in 1946 removing the barrier of sovereign immunity to tribal money claims against the federal government.[56] This removal has allowed a large increase in claims.

Despite the federal government's abandonment of the assimilation policy and several favorable Supreme Court decisions limiting Congressional authority, American Indians continue to experience racially oppressive treatment under current law. Unlike many of the Supreme Court decisions sanctioning racial discrimination against blacks and Asian Americans that have been nullified or overturned, the basic laws on sovereignty dealing with American Indians remain virtually unchanged. As a result, current disputes between American-Indian tribes and the federal government are subject to the racially-biased rules formulated in the nineteenth and early twentieth centuries. Whether the dispute is over trade, culture, family, criminality, or religion, Congress has broad powers to exercise authority over American Indians and limit their sovereignty. These Congressional powers have been justified by the principle of conquest, which rendered American-Indian tribes subject to the authority of the United States, and treaties and Congressional legislation, which limited the tribes' powers of self-government. Despite the Supreme Court's narrowing of Congress's plenary power over American-Indian tribes, the Court's decisions continue to reflect a rationale based upon the notion of American-Indian dependency and inferiority.

William Bradford

*"With a Very Great Blame on our Hearts": Reparations, Reconciliation, and an American Indian Plea for Peace with Justice**

Concealed behind the benevolent facade of the American mission civilisatrice is the brutal reality of invasion, slavery, forced relocation, genocide, land theft, ethnocide, and forcible denial of the right to self-determination wholly incompatible with contemporary understandings of U.S.-Indian history and with the notions of justice informing the human rights regime. It is perhaps impossible to overstate the magnitude of the human injustice perpetrated against Indian people in denial of their right to exist, on their aboriginal landbase, as self-determining peoples: indeed, the severity and duration of the harms endured by the original inhabitants of the United States may well exceed those suffered by all other groups domestic and international.

On May 3rd, 1493, Pope Clement called upon Spanish conquistadores to discover and conquer new lands in the Americas in order to draw "barbarous nations" to the Christian faith. The subsequent invasion of the Western Hemisphere, predicated upon a jurisprudential assumption that the indigenous inhabitants were a distinctly inferior species, was governed by the legal principles of discovery and conquest. The

---

56. *See* INDIAN CLAIMS COMMISSION ACT of 1946, 25 U.S.C. § 70a (1946).

* (footnotes and chapter headings omitted).

latter provided as a matter of international law that a nation became the sovereign of territory its agents "discovered" provided it subjugated the population and annexed its lands. Although prudence restrained pre-eighteenth century aggression in lands that became the United States, conquest was eventually applied in all the Americas, and the period subsequent to first contact is notorious as the "Age of Genocide."

In the aftermath of conquests, colonizers offered financial incentives to corporate slavers to create bounties between tribes, thereby facilitating a divide and conquer strategy that served territorial objectives while providing free labor to developing economies. The abomination of the Indian slave trade

> played a significant role in both colonial trade and in the extermination of most of the southeastern tribes . . . [T]he Indian slave trade involved all the colonies and . . . involved all the horrors long associated with the worst images of slavery, including beatings, killings, and tribal and family separation. It became routine policy to separate families, sending the Indian men off to the northern colonies while keeping the women and children in the south. . . . In the east, Indian slaves became a viable component of trade, along with deer skins and furs; in the west, American Indians were enslaved by the Catholic Church in order to build and maintain its missions . . . Indian slavery was . . . an integral part of the colonial economy.

Although Indian slavery had largely discontinued in favor of African-American slavery by the early nineteenth century, Californian Indians, as late as the mid nineteenth century, were regularly raided by slave-hunters looking for men to work in mines and women to work in brothels, and extermination befell many who resisted.

The precise number of Indian victims of the genocide committed by Euro-American colonizers over the past half-millennium evades quantification. Estimates of the pre-Columbian indigenous population in what later became the United States range from five to ninety four million, yet by 1880 disease, slaughter, slavery, and aggressive wars reduced their number to as few as 300,000—and declining. Although luminaries such as President Thomas Jefferson denounced the genocide as it unfolded, the prevailing racial ideology reassured the public that the disappearance of an inferior people before the United States' continental advance was a "historical and scientific inevitability." Initially, a legislative approach effected physical removal of Indian people from ancestral lands; however, when this proved politically inefficient, measures more clearly within the inherent powers of the executive and therefore less susceptible to judicial review were devised: Indian genocide became official policy of the United States and its political subdivisions.

In the aftermath of the Civil War, the might of the U.S. Army was directed toward Indian eradication. Military and civilian contractors induced deliberate starvation by destroying primary food sources such as the buffalo, yet Indian tenacity necessitated more direct applications of force. One by one, the Seminole, Nez Perce, Lakota, Shoshone, Comanche, Apache, and other tribes were hunted, pursued, cornered, and murdered. A series of "massacres" were written in Indian blood on the pages of American history: Blue River (1854), Bear River (1863), Sand Creek (1864), Washita River (1868), Sappa Creek (1875), Camp Robinson (1878), Wounded Knee (1890), and about forty others. Gruesome, shocking, deliberate exterminations of defenseless women and children, were perfectly legal exercises of state and federal authority as the law then stood. By the conclusion of the "Indian Wars" in 1890, the pre-Columbian Indian population was reduced as much as 98%, and an Indian-free United States was not beyond possibility. Although radical depopulation of Indian land may have been merely an efficient means to capture and annex territory, the United States nonetheless committed genocide in overtly manifesting a clear intent to kill, and killing, Indians as such.

The relationship between the land and Indian people is fundamental to their physical and cultural survival as distinct, autonomous groups. Indian land is constitutive of the Indian cultural identity and designative of the boundaries of the Indian cultural universe. Indian land transmits knowledge about history, links people to their ancestors, and provides a code of appropriate moral behavior. From the moment of first contact with European "discoverers," Indians proclaimed a sacred responsibility to preserve and transmit Indian land, and with it, identity, religion, and culture, to successive generations. The discharge of that responsibility was compromised by federal policies of land acquisition ranging from fraud and deceit to expropriation and outright theft.

Throughout the seventeenth and early eighteenth centuries, prudence directed Euro-Americans to formally recognize militarily potent Indian tribes as independent societies and accord them diplomatic recognition as sovereigns. Even subsequent to the defeats of France in the Seven Years' War in 1763 and Britain in the War of Independence in 1781, the Euro-American foothold in North America remained tenuous, and ongoing military insecurity stymied territorial ambitions while stifling any notions of conquest. Moreover, the United States' land hunger was largely sated by available space within the original thirteen colonies, and land acquisitions from Indian tribes were of necessity accomplished by treaties of cession after peaceful negotiations. Still, if during its first several decades of existence the fledgling government was obliged to recognize the sovereignty of Indian nations and to respect Indian land titles as a matter of international and domestic law, from the moment of its creation the United States was crafting legal solutions to the "problems caused by the . . . fact that the Indians were here when the white man arrived[.]"

The Indian conception of land as utterly incapable of reduction to ownership as property by human beings—an essential element of pan-Indian cosmology— crippled tribes in their early negotiations with U.S. representatives operating within an imported common law tradition commodifying land. While Indian tribes generally understood treaties to create sacred kinship ties entitling the United States to share and settle the lands in question, the government, disinterested in kinship but desirous of no less than fee simple title, manipulated Indian (mis)appreciations of Western property rights in treaty texts incomprehensible to Indian negotiators not proficient in the English language. Moreover, U.S. negotiators, notwithstanding their claims of moral ascendancy over Indian tribes as the philosophical basis for acquiring dominion over their lands, secured further fraudulent advantage by dulling Indian wits with alcohol. Deliberately faulty translations of treaty text and inaccurate explanations of treaty terms to Indian tribes possessed of limited language skills and a Weltanschauung in which land is a sacred living thing incapable of reduction to ownership exacerbated a fundamentally unequal bargaining position and erased the line between consent and coercion; worse, later treaties simply codified the results of more pronounced forms of coercion, including conquest and genocide. In sum, many, if not all, of the Indian treaties ceding land to the United States are physical embodiments of the fraud, unconscionability, and duress governing their drafting and as such are arguably subject to revisitation, reconstruction, and even renunciation as void.

By the early nineteenth century the U.S. population was clamoring for more Indian land even as Indian tribes, increasingly convinced of the insatiability of white land hunger, began to resist. Original legal protections for Indian land grew incompatible with white notions of progress, and pressure mounted to annul the marriage of political convenience and legal principle effected by the discovery doctrine. However, even as the United States waxed ever more militarily potent, Indian tribes retained the capacity to defeat conquest, and thus it fell not to armed force but yet again to law to wrest away additional Indian lands. The seminal case *Johnson v. McIntosh* provided the opportunity whereby to expand the Euro-American foothold.

Although he acknowledged both the "impossibility of undoing past events and the fact that the sovereign he represented was born in sin," and although he recognized that Indian tribes were as yet independent political communities in retention of original rights to property and self-governance, Chief Justice John Marshall accepted the extravagant arguments that European discovery, not Indian occupancy, constituted ultimate title to lands in the United States and that purchase or, in the alternative, conquest of territories by the discovering sovereign conferred good title to those lands. While Marshall conceded that such arguments "may be opposed to natural right, and to the usages of civilized nations," he drew from the doctrine of stare decisis, comparisons to the practice of other states, and ultimately a jurisprudential affirmation of the "inferiority" of Indian nations to find that "if [such arguments] be indispensable to that system under which the [U.S.] has been settled, and be adapted to the actual condition of the two people, it . . . certainly cannot be rejected by Courts[.]" Although the progressive Marshall intended to impose legal limits on the future conduct of conquerors less charitably disposed toward Indian tribes than he, *McIntosh* fueled subsequent claims that "Indians were conquered as soon as John Cabot set foot on American soil," "that it only required the inevitable march of history to carry out this preordained outcome," and that "tribal property rights are not properly understood as rights at all, but merely as revocable licenses, or . . . 'permission by the whites to occupy.'"

Subsequent cases further diminished tribal sovereignty over Indian land. In the 1831 case, *Cherokee Nation v. Georgia*, the second in the Marshall Trilogy, Chief Justice Marshall determined that, despite their retention of a set of reserved rights and powers to include occupancy of their lands subject only to voluntary cession, Indian tribes were "domestic dependent nations" and "wards" under U.S. "pupilage," not sovereign foreign nations or states within the meaning of the Constitution, and that as a result the Court could not take original jurisdiction over a case wherein the Cherokee sought to enjoin enforcement of the laws of Georgia on land guaranteed by treaties. Although Marshall held that the United States owed a common-law trust duty to Indian tribes, not only was this duty specifically held to be judicially unenforceable, but an examination of the other justices' opinions, construing the U.S.-Cherokee relationship as that between a conqueror and a subject people, hinted that the "trust doctrine," true to its roots in medieval Christian xenophobism and scientific racism, would serve as yet another legal tool with which to diminish Indian sovereignty. In short order, the United States claimed trust title to all Indian lands within its borders.

Although U.S. federal Indian policy with respect to Indian land under the trust doctrine generated a host of express obligations to ceding Indian tribes undertaken in subsequent treaties, statutes, and executive orders to create and protect permanent land reservations as against States and private parties, popular political pressure ensured that these judicially unenforceable obligations were almost never discharged with "good faith and utter loyalty to the best interests" of the Indian tribes.

In *Worcester v. Georgia*, Marshall interpreted the Commerce Clause of the U.S. Constitution to hold that Congress had "plenary" power over Indian affairs. Although the precise meaning of the term "plenary" was not subject to ready determination, *Worcester* unleashed Congressional plenary power upon Indian tribes, qualifying all remaining tribal powers by express congressional legislation by 1900. Moreover, by the late 1840s, with the military power calculus shifting and gold discovered out West, "whites c[ould] no longer be kept out of Indian country." By adding plenary power to the legal arsenal, *Worcester* and its progeny ushered in a violent phase of expansion, executed under the rubric "Manifest Destiny."

Over the next several decades the Army prosecuted a sequence of wars to perfect discovery by divesting Indians of their possessory interest and enabling the United States to claim trust title and exercise plenary power. Still other wars were fought to suppress Indian unrest after violations of Indian treaties. After each genocidal campaign, a dwindled, harried, and hungry Indian nation sued for a peace that surrendered vast tracts of lands and political freedom in exchange for dependence and "civilization." During the first decade after the Civil War, the United States acquired nearly one-fourth of the land within its modern contiguous boundaries entirely free of any legal obligation to pay more than token compensation. Yet despite distribution of millions of cheap acres to settlers, the national greed for space, fueled by an evolving inter-branch compact authorizing takings of Indian land, dictated confiscation of the remainder of Indian country.

In 1871 Congress exercised plenary power to strip away the last formal vestiges of Indian juridical sovereignty by providing that "[n]o Indian nation or tribe shall be acknowledged or recognized as an independent nation, tribe, or power with whom the United States may contract by treaty." No longer compelled as a matter of federal law to treat Indian nations as foreign sovereigns or to regulate Indian affairs by treaty, the government could now acquire Indian land without even the pretense of consent, and Congress, unwilling to allow "[a]n idle and thriftless race of savages . . . to stand guard at the treasure vaults of the nation[,]" gave the Army free rein to employ genocide to crush the last obstacles to the orderly march to the Pacific.

By 1887 all two billion acres of the U.S. continental landmass had been discovered, conquered, and expropriated save for the 138 million acres apportioned to Indian reservations, which the General Allotment Act of 1887 (Allotment) targeted for further dismemberment and colonization. Allotment, an exercise of plenary power, subdivided large swaths of communally-owned tribal lands into parcels for the private use of individual Indian allottees under a twenty-five-year period of federal guardianship. Upon expiration of the trust period, the United States issued an unrestricted fee patent to allottees who proved "competence," assumed U.S. citizenship, and paid real estate taxes. For most tribes, Allotment was devastating: although tribal governments remained in situs on vestiges of reservations still under trust protection, by encouraging Indian individuals to formally withdraw from the tribe in exchange for a per capita share of tribal land and by meeting the failure of unemployed Indian allottees to pay property taxes with foreclosure, reversion of title, and sale to white speculators at prices far below market value, Allotment abolished Indian reservations as autonomous and integral sociopolitical entities.

Although several Indian tribes attempted to block Allotment, the Supreme Court ruled not only that Indian land was subject to the sovereign right to take for public use upon payment of just compensation, but that takings of Indian land, described as a "legitimate form of 'investing for the tribe'" that did not require either consent or notification, were precluded from judicial review. By 1934, Indian lands had been reduced by a further ninety million acres, with almost twenty-six million lost through fraudulent transfers, and of the two billion acres of formerly contiguous tribal land holdings all that remained was a fragmented, forty-seven million acre mosaic of reservation lands under trust, plots owned in fee simple by whites, and plots held by Indian individuals no longer members of any tribe. Moreover, 95,000 Indians were now landless. In sum, the synergy of discovery, the trust doctrine, and plenary power as manifested in Allotment perfected the legal theft of Indian land.

Despite infrequent restitution and compensation for Indian land, the Constitution affords no protection to Indian tribes, and what remains of their landbase continues under siege. In light of the progressive evolution of rights regimes it is surreal that the United States continues to wield:

[a]bsolute, unreviewable power to continue the conquest of Indian nations that have not yet been forced to sign a treaty . . . [and to] take land held under original Indian title as it pleases, . . . without any constitutionally mandated obligation to pay compensation for the taking of land possessed by Indian nations for thousands of years, and despite the fact that the members of such tribes are United States citizens otherwise protected by the Constitution.

With its Manifest Destiny secured, the United States, heretofore oriented toward the physical separation and extermination of indigenous people, changed tacks to follow the prevailing political winds, and U.S. Indian policy adopted a treble action agenda for implementation in conjunction with private actors: liquidation of Indian culture, eradication of tribal self-government, and forced assimilation of "civilized" Indians, shorn of cultural and social attachments, into the body politic. These interrelated policies, along with the specific laws, regulations, practices, and customs developed throughout the late nineteenth and much of the twentieth centuries to deny Indians the right to maintain separate and autonomous polities and preserve their culture from interference, painted Indian tribes as targets for a sinister "genocide-at-law." Promising to free "backward" Indians from an "outmoded past" and endow them with "civilization," "education," and "prosperity" whether they desired these "blessings" or not, the Bureau of Indian Affairs, along with religious missionaries, set about dissolving the "glue" of Indian society.

Of all the processes engineered to strip away the Indian sense of self, world view, and tribal identity, perhaps the most nefarious was Congressional funding of religious schools geared toward eradication of Indian culture and the substitution of Euro-American, Christian culture in its stead. Beginning in the late nineteenth century, Indian children were taken, often without parental or tribal consent, to boarding schools where their hair was cut, their tribal clothing exchanged for Western garb, forced manual labor was required, and harsh abuses of a physical and sexual nature were meted out for speaking tribal languages or engaging in customary religious practices. During their residence, Indian children were prohibited from visiting their relatives, who, as a result, they often did not see for years. Removed Indian children, and their descendants down through the generations, have typically lost the use of their languages, been denied cultural knowledge and inclusion, and been deprived of opportunities to take on tribal responsibilities.

While Indian children were spirited off to forced conversions at distant boarding schools, the United States, exercising its plenary power, posted Christian missionaries to the reservations as Indian agents with orders to ban tribal religions, initiate Christianization of tribal populations, and pacify political and cultural discourse. At the behest of the Indian agents, Congress launched a broad-based assault upon Indian religion with laws that weakened "marriage, family and clan relationships, the distribution of property, and social and political organization." Courts of Indian Offenses (CIO) enforced these stringent social control mechanisms. In arguing before Congress for the suppression of tribal dancing and feasting, the Secretary of the Interior proclaimed that "[i]f it is the purpose of the [U.S.] to civilize the Indians, they must be compelled to desist from . . . savage rites and heathenish customs." For most of the twentieth century, non-Indians played "cultural game warden," circumscribing the legal exercise of Indian religion. Despite passage of the American Indian Religious Freedom Act (AIRFA) establishing the federal policy to "protect and preserve for American Indians their inherent right of freedom to believe, express, and exercise . . . traditional religions," in practice Indian religions have proven too enigmatic for non-Indian jurists to admit them within the meaning of "religion" as enunciated in the Bill of Rights. For Indian claimants, who have not won a single case of religious freedom since AIRFA was signed in 1978 and who may not celebrate the sacraments of their faith without threat of prosecution for violation of controlled-substance or species-protection legislation, the American tradition of religious freedom has been a "cruel hoax." With AIRFA ineffectual in the courts and Congress unwilling to strengthen statutory protection, a new millennium reveals only that Indians' freedom to preserve their religious beliefs "amounts to nothing more than the right to believe that their religion will be destroyed." Even as Indians continue to assert that denial of their religious freedom is a deprivation of the highest magnitude, the preservation of teachings, values, objects, and places for which they bear sacred inter generational responsibility is yet diminished by federal law.

27 *American Indian L. Rev.* 19–47.
Copyright © (2002) *American Indian L. Rev.*
Reprinted with permission of *American Indian L. Rev.* and William Bradford.

H. Background on *Elk*

After fifty years of the implementation of the Indian Removal Act, a Congressional law that empowered the President of the United States to relocate American Indians to certain sections of the country, most American Indians had been isolated into remote tracts of land located primarily in Western states. Life was difficult for most American Indians in these areas. Food shortages and health conditions were severe. American Indians who resided outside of those tracts of land were subjected to denials of political and civil rights afforded to and exercised by white residents. Most frequently, disputes arose over political rights such as the right to vote. John Elk was just such an individual; he chose not to live on a reservation, but he wanted to register to vote in his state's elections. As an American Indian, what was Elk's citizenship and was he eligible for naturalization? Under the Fourteenth Amendment, American Indians fell into a category separate from blacks and whites: as "Indians not taxed" they were not able to become American citizens by birth. Did the law at that time provide any way that Elk could become an American citizen?

I. *Elk v. Wilkins,* 112 U.S. 94 (1884)

A.J. Poppleton and *Mr. John L. Webster* for plaintiff in error.

G.M. Lambertson for defendant in error.

1. Facts

Justice GRAY delivered the opinion of the Court.

This is an action brought by an Indian, in the Circuit Court of the United States for the District of Nebraska, against the registrar of one of the wards of the city of Omaha, for refusing to register him as a qualified voter therein. The petition was as follows:

John Elk, plaintiff, complains of Charles Wilkins, defendant, and avers that the matter in dispute herein exceeds the sum of five hundred dollars, to wit, the sum of six thousand dollars, and that the matter in dispute herein arises under the Constitution and laws of the United States; and, for cause of action against the defendant, avers that he, the plaintiff, is an Indian, and was born within the United States; that more than one year prior to the grievances hereinafter complained of he had severed his tribal relation to the Indian tribes, and had fully and completely surrendered himself to the jurisdiction of the United States, and still so continues subject to the jurisdiction of the United States; and avers that, under and by virtue of the Fourteenth Amendment to the Constitution of the United States, he is a citizen of the United States, and entitled to the right and privilege of citizens of the United States.

That on the sixth day of April, 1880, there was held in the city of Omaha, (a city of the first class, incorporated under the general laws of the State of Nebraska providing for the incorporation of cities of the first class,) a general election for the election of members of the city council and other officers for said city.

That the defendant, Charles Wilkins, held the office of and acted as registrar in the Fifth Ward of said city, and that as said registrar it was the duty of such defendant to register the names of all persons entitled to exercise the elective franchise in said ward of said city at said general election.

That this plaintiff was a citizen of and had been a *bona fide* resident of the State of Nebraska for more than six months prior to said sixth day of April, 1880, and had been a *bona fide* resident of Douglas County, wherein the city of Omaha is situate, for more than forty days, and in the Fifth Ward of said city more than ten days prior to the said sixth day of April, and was such citizen and resident at the time of said election, and at the time of his attempted registration, as hereinafter set forth, and was in every way qualified, under the laws of the State of Nebraska and of the city of Omaha, to be registered as a voter and to cast a vote at said election, and complied with the laws of the city and State in that behalf.

That on or about the fifth day of April, 1880, and prior to said election, this plaintiff presented himself to said Charles Wilkins, as such registrar, at his office, for the purpose of having his name registered as a qualified voter, as provided by law, and complied with all the provisions of the statutes in that regard, and claimed that, under the Fourteenth and Fifteenth Amendments to the Constitution of the United States, he was a citizen of the United States, and was entitled to exercise the elective franchise, regardless of his race and color; and that said Wilkins, designedly, corruptly, wilfully and maliciously, did then and there refuse to register this plaintiff, for the sole reason that the plaintiff was an Indian, and therefore not a citizen of the United States, and not, therefore, entitled to vote, and on account of his race and color, and with the wilful, malicious corrupt and unlawful design to deprive this plaintiff of his right to vote at said election, and of his rights, and all other Indians of their rights, under said Fourteenth and Fifteenth Amendments to the Constitution of the United States, on account of his and their race and color.

That on the sixth day of April this plaintiff presented himself at the place of voting in said ward, and presented a ballot and requested the right to vote, where said Wilkins, who was then acting as one of the judges of said election in said ward, in further carrying out his wilful and malicious designs aforesaid, declared to the plaintiff and to the other election officers that the plaintiff was an Indian and not a citizen and not entitled to vote, and said judges and clerks of election refused to receive the vote of the plaintiff, for that he was not registered as required by law. . . .

By the Constitution of the State of Nebraska, article 7, section 1, "Every male person of the age of twenty-one years or upwards, belonging to either of the following classes, who shall have resided in the State six months, and in the county, precinct or ward for the term provided by law, shall be an elector. First. Citizens of the United States. Second. Persons of foreign birth who shall have declared their intention to become citizens, conformably to the laws of the United States on the subject of naturalization, at least thirty days prior to an election."

By the statutes of Nebraska, every male person of the age of twenty-one years or upwards, belonging to either of the two classes so defined in the Constitution of the State, who shall have resided in the State six months, in the county forty days, and in the precinct, township or ward ten days, shall be an elector; the qualification of electors in the several wards of cities of the first class (of which Omaha is one) shall be the same as in precincts; it is the duty of the registrar to enter in the register of qualified voters the name of every person who applies to him to be registered, and satisfies him that he is qualified to vote under the provisions of the election laws of the State; and at all municipal, as well as county or State elections, the judges of election are required to check the name, and receive and deposit the ballot, of any person whose name appears on the register.

2. Opinion

a. The Original Constitution

The question then is, whether an Indian, born a member of one of the Indian tribes within the United States, is, merely by reason of his birth within the United States, and of his afterwards voluntarily separating himself from his tribe and taking up his residence among white citizens, a citizen of the United States, within the meaning of the first section of the Fourteenth Amendment of the Constitution.

Under the Constitution of the United States, as originally established, "Indians not taxed" were excluded from the persons according to whose numbers representatives and direct taxes were apportioned among the several States; and Congress had and exercised the power to regulate commerce with the Indian tribes, and the members thereof, whether within or without the boundaries of one of the States of the Union. The Indian tribes, being within the territorial limits of the United States, were not, strictly speaking, foreign States; but they were alien nations, distinct political communities, with whom the United States might and habitually did deal, as they thought fit, either through treaties made by the President and Senate, or through acts of Congress in the ordinary forms of legislation. The members of those tribes owed immediate allegiance to their several tribes, and were not part of the people of the United States. They were in a dependent condition, a state of pupilage, resembling that of a ward to his guardian. Indians and their property, exempt from taxation by treaty or statute of the United States, could not be taxed by any State. General Acts of Congress did not apply to Indians, unless so expressed as to clearly manifest an intention to include them. Constitution, art. 1, sects. 2, 8; art. 2, sect. 2; *Cherokee Nation v. Georgia*, 5 Pet. 1; *Worcester v. Georgia*, 6 Pet. 515; *United States v. Rogers*, 4 How. 567; *United States v. Holliday*, 3 Wall. 407; *Case of the Kansas Indians*, 5 Wall. 737; *Case of the New York Indians*, 5 Wall. 761; *Case of the Cherokee Tobacco*, 11 Wall. 616; *United States v. Whiskey*, 93 U.S. 188; *Pennock v. Commissioners*, 103 U.S. 44; *Crow Dog's case*, 109 U.S. 556; *Goodell v. Jackson*, 20 Johns. 693; *Hastings v. Farmer*, 4 N.Y. 293.

The alien and dependent condition of the members of the Indian tribes could not be put off at their own will, without the action or assent of the United States. They were never deemed citizens of the United States, except under explicit provisions of treaty or statute to that effect, either declaring a certain tribe, or such members of it as chose to remain behind on the removal of the tribe westward, to be citizens, or authorizing individuals of particular tribes to become citizens on application to a court of the United States for naturalization, and satisfactory proof of fitness for civilized life; for examples of which see treaties in 1817 and 1835 with the Cherokees, and in 1820, 1825 and 1830 with the Choctaws, 7 Stat. 159, 211, 236, 335, 483, 488; *Wilson v. Wall*, 6 Wall. 83; Opinion of Attorney-General Taney, 2 Opinions of Attorneys General, 462; in 1855 with the Wyandotts, 10 Stat. 1159; *Karrahoo v. Adams*, 1 Dillon, 344, 346; *Gray v. Coffman*, 3 Dillon, 393; *Hicks v. Butrick*, 3 Dillon, 413; in 1861 and in March, 1866, with the Pottawatomies, 12 Stat. 1192; 14 Stat. 763; in 1862 with the Ottawas, 12 Stat. 1237; and the Kickapoos, 13 Stat. 624; and acts of Congress of March 3, 1839, ch. 83, §7, concerning the Brothertown Indians, and of March 3, 1843, ch. 101, §7, August 6, 1846, ch. 88, and March 3, 1865, ch. 127, §4, concerning the Stockbridge Indians, 5 Stat. 351, 647; 9 Stat. 55; 13 Stat. 562. *See also* treaties with the Stockbridge Indians in 1848 and 1856, 9 Stat. 955; 11 Stat. 667; 7 Opinions of Attorneys General, 746.

Chief Justice Taney, in the passage cited for the plaintiff from his opinion in *Scott v. Sandford*, 19 How. 393, 404, did not affirm or imply that either the Indian tribes, or individual members of those tribes, had the right, beyond other foreigners, to become citizens of their own will, without being naturalized by the United States.

His words were: "They" (the Indian tribes) "may, without doubt, like the subjects of any foreign government, be naturalized by the authority of Congress, and become citizens of a State, and of the United States; and if an individual should leave his nation or tribe, and take up his abode among the white population, he would be entitled to all the rights and privileges which would belong to an emigrant from any other foreign people." But an emigrant from any foreign State cannot become a citizen of the United States without a formal renunciation of his old allegiance, and an acceptance by the United States of that renunciation through such form of naturalization as may be required by law.

The distinction between citizenship by birth and citizenship by naturalization is clearly marked in the provisions of the Constitution, by which "no person, except a natural born citizen, or a citizen of the United States at the time of the adoption of this Constitution, shall be eligible to the office of President;" and "the Congress shall have power to establish an uniform rule of naturalization." Constitution, art. 2, sect. 1; art. 1, sect. 8.

b. The Reconstruction Amendments

By the Thirteenth Amendment of the Constitution slavery was prohibited. The main object of the opening sentence of the Fourteenth Amendment was to settle the question, upon which there had been a difference of opinion throughout the country and in this court, as to the citizenship of free Negroes (*Scott v. Sandford*, 19 How. 393); and to put it beyond doubt that all persons, white or black, and whether formerly slaves or not, born or naturalized in the United States, and owing no allegiance to any alien power, should be citizens of the United States and of the State in which they reside. *Slaughterhouse Cases*, 16 Wall. 36, 73; *Strauder v. West Virginia*, 102 U.S. 303, 306.

This section contemplates two sources of citizenship, and two sources only: birth and naturalization. The persons declared to be citizens are "all persons born or naturalized in the United States, and subject to the jurisdiction thereof." The evident meaning of these last words is, not merely subject in some respect or degree to the jurisdiction of the United States, but completely subject to their political jurisdiction, and owing them direct and immediate allegiance. And the words relate to the time of birth in the one case, as they do to the time of naturalization in the other. Persons not thus subject to the jurisdiction of the United States at the time of birth cannot become so afterwards, except by being naturalized, either individually, as by proceedings under the naturalization acts, or collectively, as by the force of a treaty by which foreign territory is acquired.

c. Citizenship by Birth

Indians born within the territorial limits of the United States, members of, and owing immediate allegiance to, one of the Indian tribes (an alien, though dependent, power), although in a geographical sense born in the United States, are no more "born in the United States and subject to the jurisdiction thereof," within the meaning of the first section of the Fourteenth Amendment, than the children of subjects of any foreign government born within the domain of that government, or the children born within the United States, of ambassadors or other public ministers of foreign nations.

This view is confirmed by the second section of the Fourteenth Amendment, which provides that "representatives shall be apportioned among the several States according to their respective numbers, counting the whole number of persons in each State, excluding Indians not taxed." Slavery having been abolished, and the persons formerly held as slaves made citizens, this clause fixing the apportionment of representatives has abrogated so much of the corresponding clause of the original Constitution as counted only three-fifths of such persons. But Indians not taxed are still excluded from the count, for the reason that they are not citizens. Their absolute exclusion from the basis of representation, in which all other persons are now included, is wholly inconsistent with their being considered citizens.

So the further provision of the second section for a proportionate reduction of the basis of the representation of any State in which the right to vote for presidential electors, representatives in Congress, or executive or judicial officers or members of the legislature of a State, is denied, except for participation in rebellion or other crime, to "any of the male inhabitants of such State, being twenty-one years of age and citizens of the United States," cannot apply to a denial of the elective franchise to Indians not taxed, who form no part of the people entitled to representation.

It is also worthy of remark, that the language used, about the same time, by the very Congress which framed the Fourteenth Amendment, in the first section of the Civil Rights Act of April 9, 1866, declaring who shall be citizens of the United States, is "all persons born in the United States, and not subject to any foreign power, excluding Indians not taxed." 14 Stat. 27; Rev. Stat. § 1992.

d. Citizenship by Naturalization

Such Indians, then, not being citizens by birth, can only become citizens in the second way mentioned in the Fourteenth Amendment, by being "naturalized in the United States," by or under some treaty or statute.

The action of the political departments of the government, not only after the proposal of the Amendment by Congress to the States in June, 1866, but since the proclamation in July, 1868, of its ratification by the requisite number of States, accords with this construction.

While the Amendment was pending before the legislatures of the several States, treaties containing provisions for the naturalization of members of Indian tribes as citizens of the United States were made on July 4, 1866, with the Delawares, in 1867 with various tribes in Kansas, and with the Pottawatomies, and in April, 1868, with the Sioux. 14 Stat. 794, 796; 15 Stat. 513, 532, 533, 637.

The treaty of 1867 with the Kansas Indians strikingly illustrates the principle that no one can become a citizen of a nation without its consent, and directly contradicts the supposition that a member of an Indian Tribe can at will be alternately a citizen of the United States and a member of the tribe.

That treaty not only provided for the naturalization of members of the Ottawa, Miami, Peoria, and other tribes, and their families, upon their making declaration, before the District Court of the United States, or their intention to become citizens; 15 Stat. 517, 520, 521; but, after reciting that some of the Wyandotts, who had become citizens under the treaty of 1855, were "unfitted for the responsibilities of citizenship;" and enacting that a register of the whole people of this tribe, resident in Kansas or elsewhere, should be taken, under the direction of the Secretary of the Interior, showing the names of "all who declare their desire to be and remain Indians and in a tribal condition," and of incompetents and orphans as described in the treaty of 1855, and that such persons, and those only, should thereafter constitute the tribe; it provided that "no one who has heretofore consented to become a citizen, nor the wife or children of any such person, shall be allowed to become members of the tribe, except by the free consent of the tribe after its new organization, and unless the agent shall certify that such party is, through poverty or incapacity, unfit to continue in the exercise of the responsibilities of citizenship of the United States, and likely to become a public charge." 15 Stat. 514, 516.

Since the ratification of the Fourteenth Amendment, Congress has passed several acts for naturalizing Indians of certain tribes, which would have been superfluous if they were, or might become, without any action of the government, citizens of the United States.

By the act of July 15, 1870, ch. 296, § 10, for instance, it was provided that if at any time thereafter any of the Winnebago Indians in the State of Minnesota should desire to become citizens of the United States, they should make application to the District Court of the United States for the District of Minnesota, and in open court make the same proof and take the same oath of allegiance as is provided by law for the naturalization of aliens, and should also make proof to the satisfaction of the court that they were sufficiently intelligent and prudent to control their affairs and interests, that they had adopted the habits of civilized life, and had for at least five years before been able to support themselves and their families; and thereupon they should be declared by the court to be citizens of the United States, the declaration entered of record, and a certificate thereof given to the applicant; and the Secretary of the Interior, upon presentation of that certificate, might issue to them patents in fee simple, with power of alienation, of the lands already held by them in severalty, and might cause to be paid to them their proportion of the money and effects of the tribe held in trust under any treaty or law of the United States; and thereupon such persons should cease to be members of the tribe, and the lands so patented to them should be subject to levy, taxation, and sale, in like manner with the property of other citizens. 16 Stat. 361. By the act of March 3, 1873, ch. 332, § 3, similar provision was made for the naturalization of any adult members of the Miami tribe in Kansas, and of their minor children. 17 Stat. 632. And the act of March 3, 1865, ch. 127, before referred to, making corresponding provision for the naturalization of any of the chiefs, warriors, or heads of families of the Stockbridge Indians, is re-enacted in section 2312 of the Revised Statutes. . . .

The recent statutes concerning homesteads are quite inconsistent with the theory that Indians do or can make themselves independent citizens by living apart from their tribe. The act of March 3, 1875, ch. 131, § 15, allowed to "any Indian born in the United States, who is the head of a family, or who has arrived at the age of twenty-one years, and who has abandoned, or may hereafter abandon, his tribal relations," the benefit of the homestead acts, but only upon condition of his "making satisfactory proof of such abandonment, under the rules to be prescribed by the Secretary of the Interior;" and further provided that his title in the homestead should be absolutely inalienable for five years from the date of the patent, and that he should be entitled to share in all annuities, tribal funds, lands and other property, as if had maintained his tribal relations. 18 Stat. 420. And the act of March 3, 1884, ch. 180, § 1, while it allows Indians "located on public lands" to "avail themselves of the homestead laws as fully and to the same extent as may now be done by citizens of the United States," provides that the form and the legal effect of the patent shall be that the United States does and will hold the land for twenty-five years in trust for the Indian making the entry, and his widow and heirs, and will then convey it in fee to him or them. 23 Stat. 96.

The national legislation has tended more and more towards the education and civilization of the Indians, and fitting them to be citizens. But the question whether any Indian tribes, or any members thereof, have become so far advanced in civilization, that they should be let out of the state of pupilage, and admitted to the privileges and responsibilities of citizenship, is a question to be decided by the nation whose wards they are and whose citizens they seek to become, and not by each Indian for himself.

There is nothing in the statutes or decisions, referred to by counsel, to control the conclusion to which we have been brought by a consideration of the language of the Fourteenth Amendment, and of the condition of the Indians at the time of its proposal and ratification. . . .

Upon the question whether any action of a State can confer rights of citizenship on Indians of a tribe still recognized by the United States as retaining its tribal existence, we need not, and do not, express an opinion, because the State of Nebraska is not shown to have taken any action affecting the condition of this plaintiff. *See Chirac v. Chirac,* 2 Wheat. 259; *Fellows v. Blacksmith,* 19 How. 366; *United States v. Holliday,* 3 Wall. 407, 420; *United States v. Joseph,* 94 U.S. 614, 618.

3. Holding

The plaintiff, not being a citizen of the United States under the Fourteenth Amendment of the Constitution, has been deprived of no right secured by the Fifteenth Amendment, and cannot maintain this action.

4. Justice Harlan and Justice Woods Dissenting

. . . It is said that the petition contains no averment that Elk was taxed in the State in which he resides, or had ever been treated by her as a citizen. It is evident that the court would not have held him to be a citizen of the United States, even if the petition had contained a direct averment that he was taxed; because its judgment, in legal effect, is, that, although born within the territorial limits of the United States, he could not, if at his birth a member of an Indian tribe, acquire national citizenship by force of the Fourteenth Amendment, but only in pursuance of some statute or treaty providing for his naturalization. It would, therefore, seem unnecessary to inquire whether he was taxed at the time of his application to be registered as a voter; for, if the words "all persons born . . . in the United States and subject to the jurisdiction thereof," were not intended to embrace Indians born in tribal relations, but who subsequently became bona fide residents of the several States, then, manifestly, the legal status of such Indians is not altered by the fact that they are taxed in those States.

While denying that national citizenship, as conferred by that amendment, necessarily depends upon the inquiry whether the person claiming it is taxed in the State of his residence, or has property therein from which taxes may be derived, we submit that the petition does sufficiently show that the plaintiff is taxed, that is, belongs to the class which, by the laws of Nebraska, are subject to taxation. By the Constitution and laws of Nebraska all real and personal property, in that State, are subject to assessment and taxation. Every person of full age and sound mind, being a resident thereof, is required to list all of his personal property for taxation. Const. Neb., art. 9, § 1; Compiled Stat. of Neb., ch. 77, pp. 400–1. Of these provisions upon the subject of taxation this court will take judicial notice. Good pleading did not require that they should be set forth, at large, in the petition. Consequently, an averment that the plaintiff is a citizen and bona fide resident of Nebraska implies, in law, that he is subject to taxation, and is taxed, in that State. Further, the plaintiff has become so far incorporated with the mass of the people of Nebraska that, being, as the petition avers, a citizen and resident thereof, he constitutes a part of her militia. Comp. Stat. Neb., ch. 56. He may, being no longer a member of an Indian tribe, sue and be sued in her courts. And he is counted in every apportionment of representation in the legislature; the requirement of her Constitution being, that "the legislature shall apportion the Senators and Representatives according to the number of inhabitants, excluding Indians not taxed and soldiers and officers of the United States army." Const. Neb., art. 3, § 1.

At the adoption of the Constitution there were, in many of the States, Indians, not members of any tribe, who constituted a part of the people for whose benefit the State governments were established. This is apparent from that clause of article 1, section 3, which requires, in the apportionment of representatives and direct taxes among the several States "according to their respective numbers," the exclusion of "Indians not taxed." This implies that there were, at that time, in the United States, Indians who were taxed, that is, were subject to taxation, by the laws of the State of which they were residents. Indians not taxed were those who held tribal relations, and, therefore, were not subject to the authority of any State, and were subject only to the authority of the United States under the power conferred upon Congress in reference to Indian tribes in this country. The same provision is preserved in the Fourteenth Amendment; for, now, as at the adoption of the Constitution, Indians in the several States, who are taxed by their laws, are counted in establishing the basis of representation in Congress. . . .

If it be also said that, since the adoption of the Fourteenth Amendment, Congress has enacted statutes providing for the citizenship of Indians, our answer is, that those statutes had reference to tribes, the members of which could not, while they continued in tribal relations, acquire the citizenship granted by the Amendment. Those statutes did not deal with individual Indians who had severed their tribal connections and were residents within the States of the Union, under the complete jurisdiction of the United States. . . .

It seems to us that the Fourteenth Amendment, in so far as it was intended to confer national citizenship upon persons of the Indian race, is robbed of its vital force by a construction which excludes from such citizenship those who, although born in tribal relations, are within the complete jurisdiction of the United States. There were, in some of our States and Territories at the time the amendment was submitted by Congress, many Indians who had finally left their tribes and come within the complete jurisdiction of the United States. They were as fully prepared for citizenship as were or are vast numbers of the white and colored races in the same localities. Is it conceivable that the statesmen who framed, the Congress which submitted, and the people who adopted that amendment, intended to confer citizenship, national and State, upon the entire population in this country of African descent (the larger part of which was shortly before held in slavery), and by the same constitutional provision to exclude from such citizenship Indians who had never been in slavery, and who, by becoming bona fide residents of States and Territories within the complete jurisdiction of the United States, had evinced a purpose to abandon their former mode of life and become a part of the People of the United States? If this question be answered in the negative, as we think it must be, then we are justified in withholding our assent to the doctrine which excludes the plaintiff from the body of citizens of the United States, upon the ground that his parents were, when he was born, members of an Indian tribe. For, if he can be excluded upon any such ground, it must necessarily follow that the Fourteenth Amendment did not grant citizenship even to Indians who, although born in tribal relations, were, at its adoption, severed from their tribes, and subject to the complete jurisdiction, as well of the United States as of the State or Territory in which they resided.

Our brethren, it seems to us, construe the Fourteenth Amendment as if it read: "All persons *born subject* to the jurisdiction of, or naturalized in, the United States, are citizens of the United States and of the State in which they reside;" whereas the amendment, as it is, implies in respect of persons born in this country, that they may claim the rights of national citizenship from and after the moment they become subject to the complete jurisdiction of the United States. This would not include the children, born in this country, of a foreign minister, for the reason that, under the fiction of extra-territoriality as recognized by international law, such minister, "though actually in a foreign country, is considered still to remain within the territory of his own State," and, consequently, he continues "subject to the laws of his own country, both with respect to his personal status, and his rights of property; and his children, though born in a foreign country, are considered as natives." HALLECK'S INTERNATIONAL LAW, ch. 10, § 12. Nor was plaintiff born without the jurisdiction of the United States in the same sense that the subject of a foreign State, born within the territory of that State, may be said to have been born without the jurisdiction of our government. For according to the decision in *Cherokee Nation v. Georgia*, 5 Pet. 17, the tribe, of which the parents of plaintiff were members, was not "a foreign State, in the sense of the Constitution," but a domestic dependent people, 'in a state of pupilage," and "so completely under the sovereignty and dominion of the United States, that any attempt to acquire their lands, or to form a political connection with them, would be considered an invasion of our territory, and an act of hostility." They occupied territory, which the court in that case said, composed "a part of the United States," the title to which this nation asserted independent of their will. "In all our intercourse with foreign nations," said Chief Justice Marshall, in the same case, "in our commercial regulations, in any attempt at intercourse between Indians and foreign nations, they are considered as within the jurisdictional limits of the United States, subject to many of those restraints which are imposed upon our citizens. . . . They look to our government for protection; rely upon its kindness and its power; appeal to it for relief to their wants; and address the President as their Great Father." And again, in *United States v. Rogers*, 4 How. 572, this court, speaking by Chief Justice Taney, said that it was "too firmly and clearly established to admit of dispute that the Indian tribes, residing within the territorial limits of the United States, are subject to their authority." *The Cherokee Tobacco*, 11 Wall. 616.

Born, therefore, in the territory under the dominion, and within the jurisdictional limits of the United States, plaintiff has acquired, as was his undoubted right, a residence in one of the States, with her consent, and is subject to taxation and to all other burdens imposed by her upon residents of every race. If he did not acquire national citizenship on abandoning his tribe and becoming, by residence in one of the States, subject to the complete jurisdiction of the United States, then the Fourteenth Amendment has wholly failed to accomplish, in respect of the Indian race, what, we think, was intended by it; and there is still in this country a despised and rejected class of persons, with no nationality whatever; who, born in our territory, owing no allegiance to any foreign power, and subject, as residents of the States, to all the burdens of government, are yet not members of any political community nor entitled to any of the rights, privileges, or immunities of citizens of the United States.

J. Commentary on *Elk*

The *Elk* case placed American Indians in a "twilight zone" between citizen and alien. If American Indians remained with their tribe on a government-reserved tract of land, they were denied any privileges of alienage due to their condition of dependence upon the United States government. If American Indians denied their tribal affiliation and resided outside of the reserved lands, they were denied any privileges of citizenship due to their tribe's dependency. Thus, according to the *Elk* decision, American Indians, even those who exercised the responsibilities of citizenship such as payment of taxes, were neither aliens nor citizens but were placed in some inferior middle ground simply because they were former members of a dependent tribal group.

Not until 1924 did Congress pass legislation granting citizenship to all American Indians.[23] Even after this bestowal of citizenship, however, Congress continued to exercise extraordinary authority over American Indians through its plenary power and the Supreme Court's continued recognition of a special guardian relationship between the federal government and Native Americans.

Even on the rare occasion when American Indians have won law suits, their victory has often been a hollow one. For example, in *United States v. Sioux Nation of Indians*, 448 U.S. 371 (1980), the Supreme Court ruled that the federal government had violated the Fifth Amendment by taking the Black Hills from the Lakota Sioux without adequately compensating them. Although the Court awarded the Sioux 105 million dollars, they refused the award because they preferred that the land, which was much more valuable, be returned instead. They also felt that by accepting the settlement payment, they would excuse the theft of their sacred land.

Rennard Strickland

Tonto's Revenge

. . . The contemporary Native American is one of the fastest growing groups in the United States. The 1990 Bureau of the Census Report shows that there are now approximately two million Native Americans. More than half of this number live on or near Indian reservation trust land, or Native villages. Approximately 90 percent of the reservation population is concentrated in eleven states. The three largest by state are Oklahoma, Arizona and New Mexico. Even the urban Indian is highly concentrated, with more than 90 percent in only fifteen states.

These statistics hide the vast diversity of life and lifestyles of the Native American. The contemporary American Indian is as varied as the Alaskan villager, the Kansas Kickapoo, the Florida Seminole, the Onodaga of New York, the Dakotas' Sioux, the New Mexico Pueblo, the Arizona Navajo, and the Oklahoma Osage.

---

23. Indian Citizenship Act of 1924, ch. 233, 43 Stat. 253 (1924).

American Indians live on 278 reservations and Alaskan Natives live in 487 villages. Some groups and reservations are large. The Navajos together with the Cherokees constitute almost 20 percent of the American Indian population. And yet 35 percent of all reservations and villages have fewer than one hundred persons in residence. Nearly three-fourths of all the reservations and villages have fewer than five hundred inhabitants.

The most encouraging aspect of recent census figures is that the Indian population is young—quite young in comparison to the rest of the population. Almost a third of the Indian population is under fifteen years of age, while only about one-fifth of the non-Indian population is under fifteen. The median age for all Indians is twenty-three. Even more promising is the number of Indians enrolled in nursery, kindergarten, elementary, high school, and college. One-third of the Indian population is in school. More than half of the Indian population under twenty-five has completed high school, as compared to one-third in the older group. The median years of school completed in 1990 is up considerably from 1970.

Whatever index is chosen to measure Indian conditions, the statistics are tragic evidence of failure. The income level, health conditions, housing standards, unemployment rate, educational level, and statistics of alcoholism, crime, and juvenile delinquency all establish that "American Indians . . . suffer . . . indignities that few groups in America suffer in equal measures." An Indian born in the twentieth century will live a life not significantly longer in span than his ancestor of five hundred years ago. Although the last decade has brought considerable improvement, the Indian is still left out of many of the advances of modern medicine. The United States population as a whole will live one-third longer than the American Indian.

The Indian health level is the lowest and the disease rate the highest of all major population groups in the United States. The incidence of tuberculosis is over 400 percent higher than the national average. Similar statistics show that the incidence of strep infections is 1,000 percent, meningitis is 2,000 percent higher, and dysentery is 10,000 percent higher. Death rates from disease are shocking when Indian and non-Indian populations are compared. Influenza and pneumonia are 300 percent greater killers among Indians. Diseases such as hepatitis are at epidemic proportions, with an 800 percent higher change of death. Diabetes is almost a plague. And the suicide rate for Indian youths ranges from 1,000 to 10,000 times higher than for non-Indian youths; Indian suicide has become epidemic. As an educated mixed-blood, you sometimes think yourself exempt from our Indian common fates. My family was struck when my younger brother took his own life. None of us can escape the realities of being Indian.

On many reservations, several generations of Indians are housed in two or three rooms that contain no plumbing or bathing facilities. Despite the substantial efforts of tribal housing authorities, between fifty thousand and fifty-seven thousand Indian homes are still considered uninhabitable. Many of these are beyond repair. For example, over 88 percent of the homes of the Sioux in Pine Ridge have been classified as substandard dwellings. More than 25 percent of all American Indians, as compared with 12.4 percent of the non-Indian population are living below the poverty level. The unemployment rate on reservations is 25.6 percent; median Indian income is 16 percent lower than the national average.

Compare this devastating poverty with the richness of undeveloped Indian resources. In his eloquent essay, "Shall the Islands Be Preserved?," Professor Wilkinson inventories some of the tribal assets.

The reservation system comprises some 52 million acres—about 2 percent of the entire surface area of the United States. Add to that the forty million acres which will be transferred to Alaska natives as well as unresolved land claims in many states. . . . The tribes have large mineral holdings: 10 percent of the nation's coal, 10 percent of the oil, and a minimum of 16 percent of the uranium. In addition to valuable recreation land, Indians own 1 percent of the country's commercial timber and 5 percent of the grazing land. And reservation Indians have first call on the water in many rivers in the parched western half of the country.

Tonto's Revenge 48–49, 52–54, 110–11.

Copyright © (1997) University of New Mexico Press.

Reprinted with permission of University of

New Mexico Press and Rennard Strickland.

K. Background on Chief Justice John Marshall

Geoffrey Stone, et al.

Chief Justice John Marshall

Born in a log cabin on the Virginia frontier, he served in the Continental Army during the Revolutionary War. After only the briefest formal instruction, he began the practice of law, specializing in the defense of Virginians against British creditors. Before entering public life, Marshall himself was constantly hounded by creditors. He wrote his five-volume biography of George Washington in an unsuccessful effort to raise money to pay off his debts. In 1799, Marshall entered the House of Representatives, and the following year he became Secretary of State in the Adams administration. During his brief tenure, he signed and sealed, but failed to deliver, the famous commission naming William Marbury justice of the peace for the District of Columbia. In 1800, Adams appointed Marshall Chief Justice after John Jay, the Court's first Chief Justice, declined reappointment to the position. Marshall served for thirty-four years, participated in more than one thousand decisions, and wrote over five hundred opinions. He is best remembered for establishing the Court's power to declare congressional statutes unconstitutional in *Marbury v. Madison*, 5 U.S. (1 Cranch) 137 (1803).

Constitutional Law lxxxvi (3rd edition).

Copyright © (1996) Stone, et al.

Reprinted with permission of Aspen Law & Business.

L. Questions and Notes

While all minority groups were oppressed in some way, the approach of the federal government to American Indians was vastly different from its approach to blacks, Latinos/as, and Asian Americans. What factors contributed to the differing approaches?

In the *Cherokee Nation* case, the majority, concurring, and dissenting opinions each defined sovereignty in different ways. Which meaning of sovereignty do you support? Which meaning was most advantageous to the federal government? Which meaning was most harmful to American Indians?

M. Point/Counterpoint

The use of American-Indian team mascots continues to raise questions about their cultural sensitivity and appropriateness. Do you support the use of American-Indian symbols as sports-team mascots?

Alfred S. Chavez Jr.

What's in a Name?

Wait, wait, wait. Before the debate about tomahawk chops, Indian war bonnets and other Native American theme names gets out of hand [Sports, Oct. 20], a couple of things should be pointed out.

First, these appellations did not arise from essentially derogatory origins. The unthinkable comparisons that protesting Native Americans are making all have negative roots. In contrast, sports symbolism is intended to reflect such virtues as strength, honor, aggressiveness and fighting spirit. Even in the bad old days of cowboy westerns, Native Americans were romanticized in these ways. There were, indeed many injustices built in and glossed over in the old stereotypes. But to assert that sports names carry all this negative baggage is demagogic revisionism.

Second, there may be no Atlanta "Bishops" swinging rosaries, but there are San Diego Padres, reminiscent of rosary-wielding Franciscan friars. And there are California Angels and many other sports symbols that are associated with religious themes. Few would complain about these names or use of symbols as denigrating anyone's culture or most cherished beliefs.

In fact, I recall the smile that came over me when I saw a picture of a statue in *Sports Illustrated* a few years ago of the Virgin Mary, veil swept back and arm posed to throw a football downfield. Point is, these uses of symbols don't always reflect the worst in human nature.

Scot P. Hillier

Race and the Redskins

The notion that free speech can be curtailed simply because it offends must be buried once and for all. On July 28 [letters], Andrew Reece writes to tell us again that the name "Redskins" is unacceptable because American Indians find it offensive; therefore, Sen. Campbell's bill to block the new stadium is correct.

Sen. Campbell stated, "The name 'Redskins' is offensive to Indians. It really doesn't matter whether it is offensive to non-Indians." Well, how about this: "The restaurant name 'Hooters' is offensive to women. It really doesn't matter whether it's offensive to men"? Let's pass legislation to penalize all businesses that have offensive names—not just the sports teams.

It is clear that the only weapon available to fight offensive speech is free speech—the kind of speech Mr. Reece wants to prevent.

The Washington Post, August 10, 1993, p. A14.
Copyright © (1993) *The Washington Post*.
Reprinted with permission of *The Washington Post*.

Barbara Munson

Not for Sport

In April 1991 when my daughter Christine wrote a letter to her principal about her high school's "Indian" mascot and logo, I did not realize that the issue would lead our family to activism on the state and national level. Whether the problem surfaces in New York state; Los Angeles County; Tacoma, Wash.; or Medford, Wis., I have found that it is framed by the same questions and themes.

As long as "Indian" team names, mascots and logos remain a part of school athletic programs, both Native and non-Native children are being taught to tolerate and perpetuate stereotyping and racism. I would like to point out some common misunderstandings on this issue and suggest constructive ways to address them.

"We have always been proud of our 'Indians.'"

Most communities are proud of their high school athletic teams, yet school traditions involving Native American imagery typically reflect little pride in or knowledge of Native cultures. These traditions have taken the trappings of Native cultures onto the athletic field where young people have played at being "Indian." Over time, and with practice, generations of children in these schools have come to believe that their "Indian" identity is more than pretending.

"We are honoring Indians; you should feel honored."

Native people are saying that they don't feel honored by this symbolism. We experience it as no less than a mockery of our cultures. We see objects sacred to us—such as the drum, eagle feathers, face painting and traditional dress—being used not in sacred ceremony, or in any cultural setting, but in another culture's *game*.

Among the many ways Indian people express honor are: by giving an eagle feather, which also carries great responsibility; by singing an honor song at a pow-wow or other ceremony; by showing deference toward elders, asking them to share knowledge and experience with us or to lead us in prayer; by avoiding actions that would stifle the healthy development of our children.

While Indian nations have the right to depict themselves any way they choose, many tribal schools are examining their own uses of Indian logos and making changes. Native American educators, parents and students are realizing that, while they may treat a depiction of an Indian person with great respect, such respect is not necessarily going to be accorded to their logo in the mainstream society.

"Why is an attractive depiction of an Indian warrior just as offensive as an ugly caricature?"

Both depictions uphold stereotypes. Both firmly place Indian people in the past, separate from our contemporary cultural experience. It is difficult, at best, to be heard in the present when someone is always suggesting that your real culture only exists in museums. The logos keep us marginalized and are a barrier to our contributing here and now.

> Depictions of mighty warriors of the past emphasize a tragic part of our history; focusing on wartime survival, they ignore the strength and beauty of our cultures during times of peace. Many Indian cultures view life as a spiritual journey filled with lessons to be learned from every experience and from every living being. Many cultures put high value on peace, right action and sharing.

"We never intended the logo to cause harm."

That no harm was intended when the logos were adopted may be true. It is also true that we Indian people are saying that the logos are harmful to our cultures, and especially to our children, in the present. When someone says you are hurting them by your action, then the harm becomes intentional if you persist.

"Aren't you proud of your warriors?"

Yes, we are proud of the warriors who fought to protect our cultures from forced removal and systematic genocide and to preserve our lands from the greed of others. We are proud, and we don't want them demeaned by being "honored" in a sports activity on a playing field.

Indian men are not limited to the role of warrior; in many of our cultures a good man is learned, gentle, patient, wise and deeply spiritual. In present time as in the past, our men are also sons and brothers, husbands, uncles, fathers and grandfathers. Contemporary Indian men work in a broad spectrum of occupations, wear contemporary clothes, and live and love just as men from other cultural backgrounds do.

The depictions of Indian "braves," "warriors" and "chiefs" also ignore the roles of women and children. Many Indian Nations are both matrilineal and child-centered. Indian cultures identify women with the Creator, because of their ability to bear children, and with the Earth, which is Mother to us all. In most Indian cultures the highest value is given to children—they are closest to the Creator and they embody the future.

"This logo issue is just about political correctness."

Using the term "political correctness" to describe the attempts of concerned Native American parents, educators and leaders to remove stereotypes from the public schools trivializes a survival issue. Systematic genocide over four centuries has decimated more than 95 percent of the indigenous population of the Americas. Today, the average life expectancy of Native American males is 45 years. The teen suicide rate among Native people is several times higher than the national average. Stereotypes, ignorance, silent inaction and even naive innocence damage and destroy individual lives and whole cultures. Racism kills.

"What if we drop derogatory comments and clip art and adopt pieces of 'real' Indian culture, like powwows and sacred songs?"

Though well-intended, these solutions are culturally naive and would exchange one pseudo-culture for another. Powwows are religious as well as social gatherings that give Native American people the opportunity to express our various cultures and strengthen our sense of Native community. To parody such ceremonial gatherings for the purpose of cheering on the team at homecoming would compound the current offensiveness. Similarly, bringing Native religions onto the secular playing field through songs of tribute to the "Great Spirit" or Mother Earth would only heighten the mockery of Native religions that we now see in the use of drums and feathers.

"We are helping you preserve your culture."

The responsibility for the continuance of our cultures falls to Native people. We accomplish this by surviving, living and thriving; and, in so doing, we pass on to our children our stories, traditions, religions, values, arts and languages. We sometimes do this important work with people from other cultural backgrounds, but they do not and cannot continue our cultures for us. Our ancestors did this work for us, and we continue to carry the culture for the generations to come. Our cultures are living cultures—they are *passed on*, not "preserved."

"Why don't community members understand the need to change; isn't it a simple matter of respect?"

On one level, yes. But in some communities, people have bought into local myths and folklore presented as accurate historical facts. Sometimes these myths are created or preserved by local industry. Also, over the years, athletic and school traditions grow up around the logos. These athletic traditions can be hard to change when much of a community's ceremonial and ritual life, as well as its pride, becomes tied to high school athletic activities.

Finally, many people find it difficult to grasp a different cultural perspective. Not being from an Indian culture, they find it hard to understand that things that are not offensive to themselves might be offensive or even harmful to someone who is from a Native culture. Respecting a culture different from the one you were raised in requires some effort—interaction, listening, observing and a willingness to learn.

We appreciate the courage, support and, sometimes, the sacrifice of all who stand with us by speaking out against the continued use of "Indian" logos. When you advocate for the removal of these logos, you are strengthening the spirit of tolerance and justice in your community; you are modeling for all our children thoughtfulness, courage and respect for self and others.

Barbara Munson, a member of the Oneida Nation who lives in Mosinee, Wisc., is chairperson of the Wisconsin Indian Education Association "Indian" Mascot and Logo Taskforce.

Spring 1999 *Teaching Tolerance* 40–42.
Copyright © (1999) *Teaching Tolerance*.
Reprinted with permission of *Teaching Tolerance*.

Part Four

Segregation

XII. The Separate but Equal Doctrine

A. Introduction

The primary focus of Reconstruction legislation was to ensure protection against racial discrimination in areas of property, labor, and criminal justice. In the years following the abolition of slavery, state legislators used Black Codes to effectively re-enslave African Americans by selective application of laws dealing mainly with these three areas. Black Codes were state laws that expressly excluded blacks from their rights. Over time, the validity of the Black Codes was challenged in the courts.

B. Background on *Strauder*

In the *Slaughterhouse Cases* and in *Cruikshank,* the Supreme Court's narrow interpretation of terms contained in the Thirteenth and Fourteenth Amendments with respect to their application to blacks undermined the federal government's ability to protect blacks from most violence and discrimination. As the Supreme Court indicated in numerous cases, individual states would now hold the responsibility to provide a remedy to blacks whose rights had been violated. Though several Supreme Court decisions narrowed the scope of the Reconstruction Amendments, the states were still subject to their requirements, which could now be applied in limited ways only.

C. *Strauder v. West Virginia*, 100 U.S. 303 (1880)

1. Facts

Justice STRONG delivered the opinion of the court.

The plaintiff in error, a colored man, was indicted for murder in the Circuit Court of Ohio County, in West Virginia, . . . and upon trial was convicted and sentenced. The record was then removed to the Supreme Court of the State, and there the judgment of the Circuit Court was affirmed. The present case is a writ of error to that court, and it is now, in substance, averred that at the trial in the State court the defendant (now plaintiff in error) was denied rights to which he was entitled under the Constitution and laws of the United States.

In the Circuit Court of the State, before the trial of the indictment was commenced, the defendant presented his petition, verified by his oath, praying for a removal of the cause into the Circuit Court of the United States, assigning, as ground for the removal, that 'by virtue of the laws of the State of West Virginia no colored man was eligible to be a member of the grand jury or to serve on a petit jury in the State; that white men are so eligible, and that by reason of his being a colored man and having been a slave, he had reason to believe, and did believe, he could not have the full and equal benefit of all laws and proceedings in the State of West Virginia for the security of his person as is enjoyed by white citizens, and that he had less chance of enforcing in the courts of the State his rights on the prosecution, as a citizen of the United States, and that the probabilities of a denial of them to him as such citizen on every trial which might take place on the indictment in the courts of the State were much more enhanced than if he was a white man.' This petition was denied by the State court, and the cause was forced to trial.

Motions to quash the *venire*, "because the law under which it was issued was unconstitutional, null, and void," and successive motions to challenge the array of the panel, for a new trial, and in arrest of judgment were then made, all of which were overruled and made by exceptions parts of the record.

2. Opinion

The law of the State to which reference was made in the petition for removal . . . is as follows: "All white male persons who are twenty-one years of age and who are citizens of this State shall be liable to serve as jurors, except as herein provided." The persons excepted are State officials.

In this court, several errors have been assigned, and the controlling questions underlying them all are, first, whether, by the Constitution and laws of the United States, every citizen of the United States has a right to a trial of an indictment against him by a jury selected and impanelled without discrimination against his race or color, because of race or color; and, second, if he has such a right, and is denied its enjoyment by the State in which he is indicted, may he cause the case to be removed into the Circuit Court of the United States?

It is to be observed that the first of these questions is not whether a colored man, when an indictment has been preferred against him, has a right to a grand or a petit jury composed in whole or in part of persons of his own race or color, but it is whether, in the composition or selection of jurors by whom he is to be indicted or tried, all persons of his race or color may be excluded by law, solely because of their race or color, so that by no possibility can any colored man sit upon the jury.

The questions are important, for they demand a construction of the recent amendments of the Constitution. If the defendant has a right to have a jury selected for the trial of his case without discrimination against all persons of his race or color, because of their race or color, the right, if not created, is protected by those amendments, and the legislation of Congress under them. The Fourteenth Amendment ordains that "all persons born or naturalized in the United States and subject to the jurisdiction thereof are citizens of the United States and of the State wherein they reside. No State shall make or enforce any laws which shall abridge the privileges or immunities of citizens of the United States, nor shall any State deprive any person of life, liberty, or property, without due process of law, nor deny to any person within its jurisdiction the equal protection of the laws."

This is one of a series of constitutional provisions having a common purpose; namely, securing to a race recently emancipated, a race that through many generations had been held in slavery, all the civil rights that the superior race enjoy. The true spirit and meaning of the amendments, as we said in the *Slaughter-House Cases* [83 U.S.(16 Wall.) 36 (1873)], cannot be understood without keeping in view the history of the times when they were adopted, and the general objects they plainly sought to accomplish. At the time when they were incorporated into the Constitution, it required little knowledge of human nature to anticipate that those who had long been regarded as an inferior and subject race would, when suddenly raised to the rank of citizenship, be looked upon with jealousy and positive dislike, and that State laws might be enacted or enforced to perpetuate the distinctions that had before existed. Discriminations against them had been habitual. It was well known that in some States laws making such discriminations then existed, and others might well be expected. The colored race, as a race, was abject and ignorant, and in that condition was unfitted to command the respect of those who had superior intelligence. Their training had left them mere children, and as such they needed the protection which a wise government extends to those who are unable to protect themselves. They especially needed protection against unfriendly action in the States where they were resident. It was in view of these considerations the Fourteenth Amendment was framed and adopted. It was designed to assure to the colored race the enjoyment of all the civil rights that under the law are enjoyed by white persons, and to give to that race the protection of the general government, in that enjoyment, whenever it should be denied by the States. It not only gave citizenship and the privileges of citizenship to persons of color, but it denied to any State the power to withhold from them the equal protection of the laws, and authorized Congress to enforce its provisions by appropriate legislation. To quote the language used by us in the *Slaughter-House Cases*, "No one can fail to be impressed with the one pervading purpose found in all the amendments, lying at the foundation of each, and without which none of them would have been suggested,—we mean the freedom of the slave race, the security and firm establishment of that freedom, and the protection of the newly made freeman and citizen from the oppressions of those who had formerly exercised unlimited dominion over them." So again: "The existence of laws in the States where the newly emancipated Negroes resided, which discriminated with gross injustice and hardship against them as a class, was the evil to be remedied, and by it [the Fourteenth Amendment] such laws were forbidden. If, however, the States did not conform their laws to its requirements, then, by the fifth section of the article of amendment, Congress was authorized to enforce it by suitable legislation." And it was added, "We doubt very much whether any action of a State, not directed by way of discrimination against the Negroes, as a class, will ever be held to come within the purview of this provision."

If this is the spirit and meaning of the amendment, whether it means more or not, it is to be construed liberally, to carry out the purposes of its framers. It ordains that no State shall make or enforce any laws which shall abridge the privileges or immunities of citizens of the United States (evidently referring to the newly made citizens, who, being citizens of the United States, are declared to be also citizens of the State in which they reside). It ordains that no State shall deprive any person of life, liberty, or property, without due process of law, or deny to any person within its jurisdiction the equal protection of the laws. What is this but declaring that the law in the States shall be the same for the black as for the white; that all persons, whether colored or white, shall stand equal before the laws of the States, and, in regard to the colored race, for whose protection the amendment was primarily designed, that no discrimination shall be made against them by law because of their color? The words of the amendment, it is true, are prohibitory, but they contain a necessary implication of a positive immunity, or right, most valuable to the colored race,—the right to exemption from unfriendly legislation against them distinctively as colored,—exemption from legal discriminations, implying inferiority in civil society, lessening the security of their enjoyment of the rights which others enjoy, and discriminations which are steps towards reducing them to the condition of a subject race.

That the West Virginia statute respecting juries—the statute that controlled the selection of the grand and petit jury in the case of the plaintiff in error—is such a discrimination ought not to be doubted. Nor would it be if the persons excluded by it were white men. If in those States where the colored people constitute a majority of the entire population a law should be enacted excluding all white men from jury service, thus denying to them the privilege of participating equally with the blacks in the administration of justice, we apprehend no one would be heard to claim that it would not be a denial to white men of the equal protection of the laws. Nor if a law should be passed excluding all naturalized Celtic Irishmen, would there by any doubt of its inconsistency with the spirit of the amendment. The very fact that colored people are singled out and expressly denied by a statute all right to participate in the administration of the law, as jurors, because of their color, though they are citizens, and may be in other respects fully qualified, is practically a brand upon them, affixed by the law, an assertion of their inferiority, and a stimulant to that race prejudice which is an impediment to securing to individuals of the race that equal justice which the law aims to secure to all others.

The right to a trial by jury is guaranteed to every citizen of West Virginia by the Constitution of that State, and the constitution of juries is a very essential part of the protection such a mode of trial is intended to secure. The very idea of a jury is a body of men composed of the peers or equals of the person whose rights it is selected or summoned to determine; that is, of his neighbors, fellows, associates, persons having the same legal status in society as that which he holds. . . . It is well known that prejudices often exist against particular classes in the community, which sway the judgment of jurors, and which, therefore, operate in some cases to deny to persons of those classes the full enjoyment of that protection which others enjoy. Prejudice in a local community is held to be a reason for a change of venue. The framers of the constitutional amendment must have known full well the existence of such prejudice and its likelihood to continue against the manumitted slaves and their race, and that knowledge was doubtless a motive that led to the amendment. By their manumission and citizenship the colored race became entitled to the equal protection of the laws of the States in which they resided; and the apprehension that through prejudice they might be denied that equal protection, that is, that there might be discrimination against them, was the inducement to bestow upon the national government the power to enforce the provision that no State shall deny to them the equal protection of the laws. Without the apprehended existence of prejudice that portion of the amendment would have been unnecessary, and it might have been left to the States to extend equality of protection.

In view of these considerations, it is hard to see why the statute of West Virginia should not be regarded as discriminating against a colored man when he is put upon trial for an alleged criminal offence against the State. It is not easy to comprehend how it can be said that while every white man is entitled to a trial by a jury selected from persons of his own race or color, or, rather, selected without discrimination against his color, and a Negro is not, the latter is equally protected by the law with the former. Is not protection of life and liberty against race or color prejudice, a right, a legal right, under the constitutional amendment? And how can it be maintained that compelling a colored man to submit to a trial for his life by a jury drawn from a panel from which the State has expressly excluded every man of his race, because of color alone, however well qualified in other respects, is not a denial to him of equal legal protection?

We do not say that within the limits from which it is not excluded by the amendment a State may not prescribe the qualifications of its jurors, and in so doing make discriminations. It may confine the selection to males, to freeholders, to citizens, to persons within certain ages, or to persons having educational qualifications. We do not believe the Fourteenth Amendment was ever intended to prohibit this. Looking at its history, it is clear it had no such purpose. Its aim was against discrimination because of race or color. As we have said more than once, its design was to protect an emancipated race, and to strike down all possible legal discriminations against those who belong to it. To quote further from 16 Wall., *supra:* "In giving construction to any of these articles [amendments], it is necessary to keep the main purpose steadily in view." "It is so clearly a provision for that race and that emergency, that a strong case would be necessary for its application to any other." We are not now called upon to affirm or deny that it had other purposes.

The Fourteenth Amendment makes no attempt to enumerate the rights it was designed to protect. It speaks in general terms, and those are as comprehensive as possible. Its language is prohibitory; but every prohibition implies the existence of rights and immunities, prominent among which is an immunity from inequality of legal protection, either for life, liberty, or property. Any State action that denies this immunity to a colored man is in conflict with the Constitution.

3. Holding

... [T]he statute of West Virginia, discriminating in the selection of jurors, as it does, against Negroes because of their color, amounts to a denial of the equal protection of the laws to a colored man when he is put upon trial for an alleged offence against the State.... [The Court's discussion and affirmance of the constitutionality of the federal statute authorizing removal into federal court in this case is omitted.]

The judgment of the Supreme Court of West Virginia will be reversed, and the case remitted with instructions to reverse the judgment of the Circuit Court of Ohio county; and it is *So ordered*.

D. Commentary on *Strauder*

Donald E. Lively

The Constitution and Race[*]

In *Strauder*, the Court considered the constitutionality of a state law excluding blacks from juries. That law directly implicated the Fourteenth Amendment, which, the Court observed, "cannot be understood without keeping in view the history of the times when [it] was adopted, and the general objects they plainly sought to accomplish." According to Justice Strong, who wrote the majority opinion, the amendment was enacted to protect the interests of an exploited and disadvantaged race, which required special attention in order to prevent further oppression. Referring to experience immediately following abolition, Strong noted:

> [I]t required little knowledge of human nature to anticipate that those who had long been regarded as an inferior and subject race would, when suddenly raised to the rank of citizenship, be looked upon with jealousy and positive dislike, and that state laws might be enacted or enforced to perpetuate the distinctions that had before existed. Discriminations against them had been habitual. It was well known that, in some States, laws making such discriminations then existed, and others might be well expected. The colored race, as a race, was abject and ignorant, and in that condition was unfitted to command the respect of those who had superior intelligence. Their training had left them mere children, and as such they needed the protection which a wise government extends to those who are unable to

---

* (footnotes omitted).

protect themselves. They especially needed protection against unfriendly action in the States where they were resident. It was in view of these considerations the Fourteenth Amendment was framed and adopted.

The *Strauder* Court thus discerned an original purpose to ensure equal enjoyment of civil rights and to provide "the protection of the general government, in that enjoyment, whenever it should be denied by the States." This perception of the Fourteenth Amendment comported with the *Slaughter-House* Court's depiction of its "one pervading purpose" as accounting for "the freedom of the slave race." The Court further determined that, given the amendment's remedial purpose, "it is to be construed liberally, to carry out the purposes of its framers." Focusing specifically on the equal protection clause, Justice Strong construed it as "declaring that the law in the States shall be the same for the black as for the white; that all persons, whether colored or white, shall stand equal before the laws of the States." Consistent with its standard of liberal construction, the Court found that equal protection not only operated as a prohibition against state action but also afforded "a positive immunity, or right, most valuable to the colored race." It adduced "the right to exemption from unfriendly legislation against them distinctively, as colored; exemption from legal discriminations, implying inferiority in civil society, lessening the security of their enjoyment of the rights which others enjoy, and discriminations which are steps towards reducing them to the condition of a subject race."

Official exclusion of blacks by law from juries resulted in the first finding of a racially significant violation of the Fourteenth Amendment. Because the statute in question excluded citizens on the basis of race, the Court perceived it as "practically a brand upon [black persons], affixed by the law, an assertion of their inferiority, and a stimulant to that race prejudice which is an impediment to securing to individuals of the race that equal justice which the law aims to secure to all others."

The *Strauder* decision represented the first invalidation of a racially discriminatory law under the Fourteenth Amendment specifically and under the Constitution in general. In a companion case, *Ex parte Virginia*, the Court determined that equal protection operated not only against legislative classifications but also against discrimination by state officials. It thus discerned a constitutional violation when blacks were excluded from juries as a function of a judge's determination rather than of statutory prescription. The Court specifically determined that no agency of the State, or of the officers or agents by whom its powers are exerted, shall deny to any person within its jurisdiction the equal protection of the laws. Whoever, by virtue of public position under a State government deprives another of property, life, or liberty without due process of law, or denies or takes away the equal protection of the laws, violates the constitutional inhibition; and as he acts in the name and for the State, and is clothed with the State's power, his act is that of the State.

E. Background on *Plessy*

Much of the focus in southern states after the end of Reconstruction was directed at denying blacks their rights in areas that a majority of Supreme Court justices would characterize as political in nature. At the same time, a growing number of local and state legislatures began to focus on social settings as well. Legislation that imposed racial segregation frequently focused on methods of transportation where blacks and whites were likely to come into close contact. Travel by rail was a principal means of transportation of the day, and consequently it provided an environment of blatant segregation and intimidation.

Thomas Brook

Plessy v. Ferguson: A Brief History with Documents

In 1885 Samuel E. Courtney, an African-American teacher in Alabama, and some other African-American colleagues, took a train to attend the wedding of two in their group. Describing their journey in a Boston newspaper, Courtney wrote, "We teachers happened to be riding on the first car of the train. All of us were mulattoes [people of mixed European and African blood], and would pass for white people in a pinch. Down there it is a criminal offence for a Negro to ride on the same train with a white man, however." When the train stopped for refreshments, a group of whites surrounded the train.

"There are three coons on that first class car," one of them sung out.

"'Put em off,' said someone else."

Twelve white men carrying revolvers approached the group. One told Courtney:

"'Say, you look like an intelligent nigger. Don't you know better than to ride in a first-class car? Before we'll let you ride any further in that car we'll take you out there in the field and fill you with bullets.'"

For the rest of the trip the people in Courtney's group had to ride in the Jim Crow car, the car reserved for "colored" people. But their difficulties were not over. According to Courtney, "Later in the journey the bridegroom was arrested and fined $25 on some trumped up charge. We paid the fine, with costs, and then he was immediately rearrested by the County officers and fined $35 on another trumped up charge. After paying this we decided to go the remainder of the distance on horse back, and that night we drove 35 miles through the woods."[1]

This incident reveals the violent intimidation experienced by African Americans in the South at the end of the last century. Sometimes that intimidation arose spontaneously. Sometimes it was planned and organized by white supremacist groups like the Ku Klux Klan. The incident also reveals that rather than rely on the state for protection, African Americans knew that most government officials were

---

1. THE BOOKER T. WASHINGTON PAPERS 2: 273–74 (Louis R. Harlan, ed., 1972).

themselves part of the system of repression, as illustrated by the fines levied on the bridegroom. Even worse, in a country that prided itself on a legal system in which all were treated equally, African American citizens were subject to laws that organized society along racial lines.

The Alabama law that made it illegal for African Americans to sit in cars with whites was one of many laws passed by southern states beginning in the 1880s that mandated racial segregation. These laws were in part modeled on similar ones that existed in the North prior to the Civil War and were passed under the guise of protecting the health, safety, and racial purity of the public. But the large number of blacks in the South made that region's late nineteenth-century laws more noticeable. The mulatto status of Courtney's group and its members' ability to pass as "white" point to one problem with such laws. They were designed to keep the races separate, yet already widespread racial mixture played havoc with efforts to divide the population into pure black and white categories. Nonetheless, the passage of Jim Crow laws created a world of separate railroad cars, schools, hospitals, cemeteries, restaurants, bathrooms, and even drinking fountains. Whereas officially facilities were supposed to be "separate but equal," in fact they rarely were equal. People learned their place in segregated society through the pervasive juxtaposition of clearly superior facilities marked "Whites Only" with inferior ones designated "Colored."

At the time of Courtney's ride, the Supreme Court had not yet ruled on the constitutionality of the laws that enforced segregation. But on May 18, 1896, it did so in the case of *Plessy v. Ferguson*. In June 1892, Homer Plessy had been arrested for violating section 2 of Act 111 passed by the Louisiana legislature in 1890. The law called for "equal but separate accommodations for the white and colored races" on all passenger railways within the state. Plessy's arrest was part of a planned challenge to the law by New Orleans African Americans. By September 1891, a small but influential group had formed a citizens' committee to devise a strategy to overturn the law. For the most part, members of the committee were Creoles—French-speaking people of mixed blood whose families had lived in Louisiana for generations.[2] The committee contacted the white lawyer and novelist Albion Winegar Tourgée, who in August 1891 had begun calling attention to separate-car laws in his newspaper column.

A resident of upstate New York, Tourgée was perhaps the leading white spokesman for people of color. Following service in the Union army, he moved to North Carolina after the Civil War, where he served as a judge. Tourgée provided the period's most vivid account of the experiences of a carpetbagger (a person from the North who moved South after the Civil War) in his popularly successful autobiographical novel, *A Fool's Errand by One of the Fools* (1879). Continuing his legal and literary career after he returned to New York, he worked to expose the Ku Klux Klan

---

2. RODOLPHE LUCIEN DESDUNES, OUR PEOPLE AND OUR HISTORY (1911).

and campaigned for improved conditions for freedmen. Convinced that the only solution to the "race problem" in the United States was education—for whites to reduce racial prejudice and for freedmen to increase economic opportunity and to inform them as new citizens—Tourgée actively campaigned for federal money to wipe out illiteracy, which was especially high in the South. His proposal was however, never adopted.[3] When the New Orleans citizens' committee contacted him, it had raised $1,412.70, but he agreed to represent the group at a distance for no fee. His aim was to get the United States Supreme Court to declare segregation laws unconstitutional.

Part of Tourgée's strategy was to have someone of mixed blood violate the law, since to do so would allow him to question the arbitrariness by which people were classified "colored." Homer Plessy agreed to be a test case. Plessy had been born free in 1862. His family was French-speaking. He had only one-eighth African blood and, according to his counsel, "the mixture [was] not discernible."[4] Most likely he could have ridden in the white car without trouble, but the committee wanted a legal challenge. Its challenge received some silent support from railroad companies, which did not like the added expense of providing separate cars. By prearrangement, the railroad conductor and a private detective detained Plessy when he sat in the forbidden coach.

A month after his arrest Plessy came before a Louisiana district court presided over by Justice John Howard Ferguson. A native of Massachusetts, Ferguson was a carpetbagger who had stayed in the South, marrying the daughter of a prominent New Orleans attorney. Between Plessy's arrest and his trial, Ferguson had ruled on another test case in which Daniel F. Desdunes was arrested for traveling in the white car on an interstate train. Also someone who could pass as white, Desdunes was the twenty-one-year-old son of Rodolphe Desdunes, one of the leaders of the New Orleans citizens' committee. Ferguson ruled that the law was unconstitutional on interstate trains because of the federal government's power to regulate interstate commerce, and the committee celebrated. Plessy, however, was traveling on an intrastate train, and at his trial Ferguson upheld the law, arguing that a state had the power to regulate railroad companies operating solely within its borders.

3. Tourgée's proposal failed in part because of southern opposition and in part because of his unwillingness to compromise and support a different measure, the Blair Bill, which was opposed by the white supremacist Senator John Tyler Morgan. We can only speculate on what the effects on United States society would have been if Tourgée's plan had been adopted or if he had compromised his position and helped pass the less than perfect Blair Bill.
4. Charles A. Lofgren, The Plessy Case: A Legal-Historical Interpretation 41 (1987). My account of the *Plessy* case is especially indebted to Lofgren. It also relies on Otto H. Olsen, Carpetbagger's Crusade: The Life of Albion Winegar Tourgée(1965); Otto H. Olsen, The Thin Disguise: Plessy v. Ferguson (1967); Owen M. Fiss, *Troubled Beginnings of the Modern State, 1888–1910*, vol. 8 of Holmes Devise, History of the Supreme Court of the United States(1993); and Keith Weldon Medley, *The Sad Story of How "Separate but Equal" Was Born*, Smithsonian, February 1994, at pp. 105–17.

The constitutional challenge was under way; the decision was appealed to the state supreme court and eventually the United States Supreme Court.

The Louisiana Jim Crow law was possible only because the goals of Reconstruction after the Civil War had not been realized. Reconstruction had two primary goals, which are implied by its name. The first was to rebuild the South, whose buildings and industry had been devastated by the violence of war. The second was to reform southern society, which had been based on a slave economy. Reconstructing the South materially proved easier than reconstructing it socially.

The Bedford Series In History and Culture 7–10.
Copyright © (1997) Bedford/St. Martin's.
Reprinted with permission of Bedford/St. Martin's.

F. *Plessy v. Ferguson*, 163 U.S. 537 (1896)

1. *Facts*

Justice BROWN delivered the opinion of the Court.

This case turns upon the constitutionality of an act of the General Assembly of the State of Louisiana, passed in 1890, providing for separate railway carriages for the white and colored races. Acts 1890, No. 111, p. 152.

The first section of the statute enacts "that all railway companies carrying passengers in their coaches in this state, shall provide equal but separate accommodations for the white, and colored races, by providing two or more passenger coaches for each passenger train, or by dividing the passenger coaches by a partition so as to secure separate accommodations: Provided, that this section shall not be construed to apply to street railroads. No person or persons shall be permitted to occupy seats in coaches, other than the ones assigned to them, on account of the race they belong to."

By the second section it was enacted "that the officers of such passenger trains shall have power and are hereby required to assign each passenger to the coach or compartment used for the race to which such passenger belongs; any passenger insisting on going into a coach or compartment to which by race he does not belong, shall be liable to a fine of twenty-five dollars, or in lieu thereof to imprisonment for a period of not more than twenty days in the parish prison, and any officer of any railroad insisting on assigning a passenger to a coach or compartment other than the one set aside for the race to which said passenger belongs, shall be liable to a fine of twenty-five dollars, or in lieu thereof to imprisonment for a period of not more than twenty days in the parish prison; and should any passenger refuse to occupy the coach or compartment to which he or she is assigned by the officer of such railway, said officer shall have power to refuse to carry such passenger on his train, and for such refusal neither he nor the railway company which he represents shall be liable for damages in any of the courts of this State."

The third section provides penalties for the refusal or neglect of the officers, directors, conductors, and employee of railway companies to comply with the act, with a proviso that "nothing in this act shall be construed as applying to nurses attending children of the other race." The fourth section is immaterial.

The information filed in the criminal District Court charged, in substance, that Plessy, being a passenger between two stations within the state of Louisiana, was assigned by officers of the company to the coach used for the race to which he belonged, but he insisted upon going into a coach used by the race to which he did not belong. Neither in the information nor plea was his particular race or color averred.

The petition for the writ of prohibition averred that petitioner was seven-eighths Caucasian and one-eighth African blood; that the mixture of colored blood was not discernible in him; and that he was entitled to every right, privilege, and immunity secured to citizens of the United States of the white race; and that, upon such theory, he took possession of a vacant seat in a coach where passengers of the white race were accommodated, and was ordered by the conductor to vacate said coach, and take a seat in another, assigned to persons of the colored race, and, having refused to comply with such demand, he was forcibly ejected, with the aid of a police officer, and imprisoned in the parish jail to answer a charge of having violated the above act.

The constitutionality of this act is attacked upon the ground that it conflicts both with the Thirteenth Amendment of the constitution, abolishing slavery, and the Fourteenth Amendment, which prohibits certain restrictive legislation on the part of the States.

2. Opinion

a. The Thirteenth Amendment

That it does not conflict with the Thirteenth Amendment, which abolished slavery and involuntary servitude, except as a punishment for crime, is too clear for argument. Slavery implies involuntary servitude, — a state of bondage; the ownership of mankind as a chattel, or, at least, the control of the labor and services of one man for the benefit of another, and the absence of a legal right to the disposal of his own person, property, and services. This amendment was said in the *Slaughter-House Cases*, 16 Wall. 36, to have been intended primarily to abolish slavery, as it had been previously known in this country, and that it equally forbade Mexican peonage or the Chinese coolie trade, when they amounted to slavery or involuntary servitude, and that the use of the word 'servitude' was intended to prohibit the use of all forms of involuntary slavery, of whatever class or name. It was intimated, however, in that case, that this amendment was regarded by the statesmen of that day as insufficient to protect the colored race from certain laws which had been enacted in the Southern states, imposing upon the colored race onerous disabilities and burdens, and curtailing their rights in the pursuit of life, liberty, and property to such an extent that their freedom was of little value; and that the Fourteenth Amendment was devised to meet this exigency.

So, too, in the *Civil Rights Cases*, 109 U. S. 3, 3 Sup. Ct. 18, it was said that the act of a mere individual, the owner of an inn, a public conveyance or place of amusement, refusing accommodations to colored people, cannot be justly regarded as imposing any badge of slavery or servitude upon the applicant, but only as involving an ordinary civil injury, properly cognizable by the laws of the state, and presumably subject to redress by those laws until the contrary appears. "It would be running the slavery question into the ground," said Mr. Justice Bradley, "to make it apply to every act of discrimination which a person may see fit to make as to the guests he will entertain, or as to the people he will take into his coach or cab or car, or admit to his concert or theater, or deal with in other matters of intercourse or business."

A statute which implies merely a legal distinction between the white and colored races—a distinction which is founded in the color of the two races, and which must always exist so long as white men are distinguished from the other race by color—has no tendency to destroy the legal equality of the two races, or re-establish a state of involuntary servitude. Indeed, we do not understand that the Thirteenth Amendment is strenuously relied upon by the plaintiff in error in this connection.

b. The Fourteenth Amendment

1. Equal Protection

By the Fourteenth Amendment, all persons born or naturalized in the United States, and subject to the jurisdiction thereof, are made citizens of the United States and of the state wherein they reside; and the states are forbidden from making or enforcing any law which shall abridge the privileges or immunities of citizens of the United States, or shall deprive any person of life, liberty, or property without due process of law, or deny to any person within their jurisdiction the equal protection of the laws.

The proper construction of this amendment was first called to the attention of this court in the *Slaughterhouse Cases*, 16 Wall. 36, which involved, however, not a question of race, but one of exclusive privileges. The case did not call for any expression of opinion as to the exact rights it was intended to secure to the colored race, but it was said generally that its main purpose was to establish the citizenship of the Negro, to give definitions of citizenship of the United States and of the states, and to protect from the hostile legislation of the states the privileges and immunities of citizens of the United States, as distinguished from those of citizens of the States.

The object of the amendment was undoubtedly to enforce the absolute equality of the two races before the law, but, in the nature of things, it could not have been intended to abolish distinctions based upon color, or to enforce social, as distinguished from political, equality, or a commingling of the two races upon terms unsatisfactory to either. Laws permitting, and even requiring, their separation, in places where they are liable to be brought into contact, do not necessarily imply the inferiority of either race to the other, and have been generally, if not universally, recognized as within the competency of the state legislatures in the exercise of their police power. The most common instance of this is connected with the establishment of separate schools for white and colored children, which have been held to be a valid exercise of the legislative power even by courts of states where the political rights of the colored race have been longest and most earnestly enforced.

One of the earliest of these cases is that of *Roberts v. City of Boston*, 5 Cush. 198, in which the supreme judicial court of Massachusetts held that the general school committee of Boston had power to make provision for the instruction of colored children in separate schools established exclusively for them, and to prohibit their attendance upon the other schools. "The great principle," said Chief Justice Shaw, "advanced by the learned and eloquent advocate for the plaintiff [Charles Sumner], is that, by the constitution and laws of Massachusetts, all persons, without distinction of age or sex, birth or color, origin or condition, are equal before the law. . . . But, when this great principle comes to be applied to the actual and various conditions of persons in society, it will not warrant the assertion that men and women are legally clothed with the same civil and political powers, and that children and adults are legally to have the same functions and be subject to the same treatment; but only that the rights of all, as they are settled and regulated by law, are equally entitled to the paternal consideration and protection of the law for their maintenance and security." It was held that the powers of the committee extended to the establishment of separate schools for children of different ages, sexes and colors, and that they might also establish special schools for poor and neglected children, who have become too old to attend the primary school, and yet have not acquired the rudiments of learning, to enable them to enter the ordinary schools. Similar laws have been enacted by Congress under its general power of legislation over the District of Columbia (sections 281–283, 310, 319, Rev. St. D. C.), as well as by the legislatures of many of the states, and have been generally, if not uniformly, sustained by the courts. *State v. McCann*, 21 Ohio St. 210; *Lehew v. Brummell* (Mo. Sup.) 15 S. W. 765; *Ward v. Flood*, 48 Cal. 36; *Bertonneau v. Directors of City Schools*, 3 Woods, 177, Fed. Cas. No. 1,361; *People v. Gallagher*, 93 N. Y. 438; *Cory v. Carter*, 48 Ind. 337; *Dawson v. Lee*, 83 Ky. 49.

Laws forbidding the intermarriage of the two races may be said in a technical sense to interfere with the freedom of contract, and yet have been universally recognized as within the police power of the state. *State v. Gibson*, 36 Ind. 389.

The distinction between laws interfering with the political equality of the Negro and those requiring the separation of the two races in schools, theaters, and railway carriages has been frequently drawn by this court. Thus, in *Strauder v. West Virginia*, 100 U. S. 303, it was held that a law of West Virginia limiting to white male persons 21 years of age, and citizens of the state, the right to sit upon juries, was a discrimination which implied a legal inferiority in civil society, which lessened the security of the right of the colored race, and was a step towards reducing them to a condition of servility. Indeed, the right of a colored man that, in the selection of jurors to pass upon his life, liberty, and property, there shall be no exclusion of his race, and no discrimination against them because of color, has been asserted in a number of cases. *Virginia v. Rivers*, 100 U. S. 313; *Neal v. Delaware*, 103 U. S. 370; *Bush v. Com.*, 107 U. S. 110, 1 Sup. Ct. 625; *Gibson v. Mississippi*, 162 U. S. 565, 16 Sup. Ct. 904. So, where the laws of a particular locality or the charter of a particular railway corporation has provided that no person shall be excluded from the cars on account of color, we have held that this meant that persons of color should travel in the same car as white ones, and that the enactment was not satisfied by the company providing cars assigned exclusively to people of color, though they were as good as those which they assigned exclusively to white persons. *Railroad Co. v. Brown*, 17 Wall. 445. . . .

2. Property

It is claimed by the plaintiff in error that, in any mixed community, the reputation of belonging to the dominant race, in this instance the white race, is "property," in the same sense that a right of action or of inheritance is property. Conceding this to be so, for the purposes of this case, we are unable to see how this statute deprives him of, or in any way affects his right to, such property. If he be a white man, and assigned to a colored coach, he may have his action for damages against the company for being deprived of his so-called "property." Upon the other hand, if he be a colored man, and be so assigned, he has been deprived of no property, since he is not lawfully entitled to the reputation of being a white man.

3. Police Powers

In this connection, it is also suggested by the learned counsel for the plaintiff in error that the same argument that will justify the state legislature in requiring railways to provide separate accommodations for the two races will also authorize them to require separate cars to be provided for people whose hair is of a certain color, or who are aliens, or who belong to certain nationalities, or to enact laws requiring colored people to walk upon one side of the street, and white people upon the other, or requiring white men's houses to be painted white, and colored men's black, or their vehicles or business signs to be of different colors, upon the theory that one side of the street is as good as the other, or that a house or vehicle of one color is as good as one of another color. The reply to all this is that every exercise of the police power must be reasonable, and extend only to such laws as are enacted in good faith for the promotion of the public good, and not for the annoyance or oppression of a particular class. Thus, in *Yick Wo v. Hopkins*, 118 U. S. 356, 6 Sup. Ct. 1064, it was held by this court that a municipal ordinance of the City of San Francisco, to regulate the carrying on of public laundries within the limits of the municipality, violated the provisions of the constitution of the United States, if it conferred upon the municipal authorities arbitrary power, at their own will, and without regard to discretion, in the legal sense of the term, to give or withhold consent as to persons or places, without regard to the competency of the persons applying or the propriety of the places selected for the carrying on of the business. It was held to be a covert attempt on the part of the municipality to make an arbitrary and unjust discrimination against the Chinese race. While this was the case of a municipal ordinance, a like principle has been held to apply to acts of a state legislature passed in the exercise of the police power. *Railroad Co. v. Husen*, 95 U. S. 465; *Louisville & N. R. Co. v. Kentucky*, 161 U. S. 677, 16 Sup. Ct. 714, and cases cited on page 700, 161 U. S., and page 714, 16 Sup. Ct.; *Daggett v. Hudson*, 43 Ohio St. 548, 3 N. E. 538; *Capen v. Foster*, 12 Pick. 485; *State v. Baker*, 38 Wis. 71; *Monroe v. Collins*, 17 Ohio St. 665; *Hulseman v. Rems*, 41 Pa. St. 396; *Osman v. Riley*, 15 Cal. 48.

So far, then, as a conflict with the Fourteenth Amendment is concerned, the case reduces itself to the question whether the statute of Louisiana is a reasonable regulation, and with respect to this there must necessarily be a large discretion on the part of the legislature. In determining the question of reasonableness, it is at liberty to act with reference to the established usages, customs, and traditions of the people, and with a view to the promotion of their comfort, and the preservation of the public peace and good order. Gauged by this standard, we cannot say that a law which authorizes or even requires the separation of the two races in public conveyances is unreasonable, or more obnoxious to the Fourteenth Amendment than the acts of congress requiring separate schools for colored children in the District of Columbia, the constitutionality of which does not seem to have been questioned, or the corresponding acts of state legislatures.

We consider the underlying fallacy of the plaintiff's argument to consist in the assumption that the enforced separation of the two races stamps the colored race with a badge of inferiority. If this be so, it is not by reason of anything found in the act, but solely because the colored race chooses to put that construction upon it. The argument necessarily assumes that if, as has been more than once the case, and is not unlikely to be so again, the colored race should become the dominant power in the state legislature, and should enact a law in precisely similar terms, it would thereby relegate the white race to an inferior position. We imagine that the white race, at least, would not acquiesce in this assumption. The argument also assumes that social prejudices may be overcome by legislation, and that equal rights cannot be secured to the negro except by an enforced commingling of the two races. We cannot accept this proposition. If the two races are to meet upon terms of social equality, it must be the result of natural affinities, a mutual appreciation of each other's merits, and a voluntary consent of individuals. As was said by the Court of Appeals of New York in *People v. Gallagher*, 93 N. Y. 438, 448: "This end can neither be accomplished nor promoted by laws which conflict with the general sentiment of the community upon whom they are designed to operate. When the government, therefore, has secured to each of its citizens equal rights before the law, and equal opportunities for improvement and progress, it has accomplished the end for which it was organized, and performed all of the functions respecting social advantages with which it is endowed." Legislation is powerless to eradicate racial instincts, or to abolish distinctions based upon physical differences, and the attempt to do so can only result in accentuating the difficulties of the present situation. If the civil and political rights of both races be equal, one cannot be inferior to the other civilly or politically. If one race be inferior to the other socially, the constitution of the United States cannot put them upon the same plane.

It is true that the question of the proportion of colored blood necessary to constitute a colored person, as distinguished from a white person, is one upon which there is a difference of opinion in the different states; some holding that any visible admixture of black blood stamps the person as belonging to the colored race (*State v. Chavers*, 5 Jones [N. C.] 1); others, that it depends upon the preponderance of blood (*Gray v. State*, 4 Ohio, 354; *Monroe v. Collins*, 17 Ohio St. 665); and still others, that the predominance of white blood must only be in the proportion of three-fourths (*People v. Dean*, 14 Mich. 406; *Jones v. Com.*, 80 Va. 544). But these are questions to be determined under the laws of each state, and are not properly put in issue in this case. Under the allegations of his petition, it may undoubtedly become a question of importance whether, under the laws of Louisiana, the petitioner belongs to the white or colored race.

3. Holding

While we think the enforced separation of the races, as applied to the internal commerce of the state, neither abridges the privileges or immunities of the colored man, deprives him of his property without due process of law, nor denies him the equal protection of the laws, within the meaning of the Fourteenth Amendment, we are not prepared to say that the conductor, in assigning passengers to the coaches according to their race, does not act at his peril, or that the provision of the second section of the act that denies to the passenger compensation in damages for a refusal to receive him into the coach in which he properly belongs is a valid exercise of the legislative power. Indeed, we understand it to be conceded by the state's attorney that such part of the act as exempts from liability the railway company and its officers is unconstitutional. The power to assign to a particular coach obviously implies the power to determine to which race the passenger belongs, as well as the power to determine who, under the laws of the particular state, is to be deemed a white, and who a colored, person. This question, though indicated in the brief of the plaintiff in error, does not properly arise upon the record in this case, since the only issue made is as to the unconstitutionality of the act, so far as it requires the railway to provide separate accommodations, and the conductor to assign passengers according to their race.

The judgment of the court below is therefore affirmed.

4. Justice Harlan Dissenting

a. The Thirteenth and Fourteenth Amendments

In respect of civil rights, common to all citizens, the Constitution of the United States does not, I think, permit any public authority to know the race of those entitled to be protected in the enjoyment of such rights. Every true man has pride of race, and under appropriate circumstances, when the rights of others, his equals before the law, are not to be affected, it is his privilege to express such pride and to take such action based upon it as to him seems proper. But I deny that any legislative body or judicial tribunal may have regard to the race of citizens when the civil rights of those citizens are involved. Indeed, such legislation as that here in question is inconsistent not only with that equality of rights which pertains to citizenship, national and state, but with the personal liberty enjoyed by every one within the United States.

The Thirteenth Amendment does not permit the withholding or the deprivation of any right necessarily inhering in freedom. It not only struck down the institution of slavery as previously existing in the United States, but it prevents the imposition of any burdens or disabilities that constitute badges of slavery or servitude. It decreed universal civil freedom in this country. This court has so adjudged. But, that amendment having been found inadequate to the protection of the rights of those who had been in slavery, it was followed by the Fourteenth Amendment, which added greatly to the dignity and glory of American citizenship, and to the security of personal liberty, by declaring that "all persons born or naturalized in the United States, and subject to the jurisdiction thereof, are citizens of the United States and of the state wherein they reside," and that "no state shall make or enforce any law which shall abridge the privileges or immunities of citizens of the United States; nor shall any state deprive any person of life, liberty or property without due process of law, nor deny to any person within its jurisdiction the equal protection of the laws." These two amendments, if enforced according to their true intent and meaning, will protect all the civil rights that pertain to freedom and citizenship. Finally, and to the end that no citizen should be denied, on account of his race, the privilege of participating in the political control of his country, it was declared by the Fifteenth Amendment that "the right of citizens of the United States to vote shall not be denied or abridged by the United States or by any state on account of race, color or previous condition of servitude."

These notable additions to the fundamental law were welcomed by the friends of liberty throughout the world. They removed the race line from our governmental systems. They had, as this court has said, a common purpose, namely, to secure "to a race recently emancipated, a race that through many generations have been held in slavery, all the civil rights that the superior race enjoy." They declared, in legal effect, this court has further said, "that the law in the states shall be the same for the black as for the white; that all persons, whether colored or white, shall stand equal before the laws of the states; and in regard to the colored race, for whose protection the amendment was primarily designed, that no discrimination shall be made against them by law because of their color." We also said: "The words of the amendment, it is true, are prohibitory, but they contain a necessary implication of a positive immunity or right, most valuable to the colored race,—the right to exemption from unfriendly legislation against them distinctively as colored; exemption from legal discriminations, implying inferiority in civil society, lessening the security of their enjoyment of the rights which others enjoy; and discriminations which are steps towards reducing them to the condition of a subject race." It was, consequently, adjudged that a state law that excluded citizens of the colored race from juries, because of their race, however well qualified in other respects to discharge the duties of jurymen, was repugnant to the Fourteenth Amendment. *Strauder v. West Virginia*, 100 U. S. 303, 306, 307; *Virginia v. Rives*, 100 U.S. 313; *ain Ex parte Virginia*, 100 U.S. 339; *Neal v. Delaware*, 103 U. S. 370, 386; *Bush v. Kentucky*, 107 U. S. 110, 116, 1 Sup. Ct. 625. At the present term, referring to the previous adjudications, this court declared that "underlying all of those decisions is the principle that the constitution of the United States, in its present form, forbids, so far as civil and political rights are concerned, discrimination by the general government or the states against any citizen because of his race. All citizens are equal before the law." *Gibson v. State*, 162 U. S. 565, 16 Sup. Ct. 904.

The decisions referred to show the scope of the recent amendments of the constitution. They also show that it is not within the power of a state to prohibit colored citizens, because of their race, from participating as jurors in the administration of justice.

b. The Meaning of Liberty

It was said in argument that the statute of Louisiana does not discriminate against either race, but prescribes a rule applicable alike to white and colored citizens. But this argument does not meet the difficulty. Every one knows that the statute in question had its origin in the purpose, not so much to exclude white persons from railroad cars occupied by blacks, as to exclude colored people from coaches occupied by or assigned to white persons. Railroad corporations of Louisiana did not make discrimination among whites in the matter of accommodation for travelers. The thing to accomplish was, under the guise of giving equal accommodation for whites and blacks, to compel the latter to keep to themselves while traveling in railroad passenger coaches. No one would be so wanting in candor as to assert the contrary. The fundamental objection, therefore, to the statute, is that it interferes with the personal freedom of citizens. "Personal liberty," it has been well said, "consists in the power of locomotion, of changing situation, or removing one's person to whatsoever places one's own inclination may direct, without imprisonment or restraint, unless by due course of law." 1 Bl. Comm. If a white man and a black man choose to occupy the same public conveyance on a public highway, it is their right to do so; and no government, proceeding alone on grounds of race, can prevent it without infringing the personal liberty of each. . . .

c. Harlan's Vision of American Justice

The white race deems itself to be the dominant race in this country. And so it is, in prestige, in achievements, in education, in wealth, and in power. So, I doubt not, it will continue to be for all time, if it remains true to its great heritage, and holds fast to the principles of constitutional liberty. But in view of the constitution, in the eye of the law, there is in this country no superior, dominant, ruling class of citizens. There is no caste here. Our constitution is color-blind, and neither knows nor tolerates classes among citizens. In respect of civil rights, all citizens are equal before the law. The humblest is the peer of the most powerful. The law regards man as man, and takes no account of his surroundings or of his color when his civil rights as guaranteed by the supreme law of the land are involved. It is therefore to be regretted that this high tribunal, the final expositor of the fundamental law of the land, has reached the conclusion that it is competent for a state to regulate the enjoyment by citizens of their civil rights solely upon the basis of race.

In my opinion, the judgment this day rendered will, in time, prove to be quite as pernicious as the decision made by this tribunal in the *Dred Scott Case*.

It was adjudged in that case that the descendants of Africans who were imported into this country, and sold as slaves, were not included nor intended to be included under the word 'citizens' in the constitution, and could not claim any of the rights and privileges which that instrument provided for and secured to citizens of the United States; that, at time of the adoption of the constitution, they were "considered as a subordinate and inferior class of beings, who had been subjugated by the dominant race, and, whether emancipated or not, yet remained subject to their authority, and had no rights or privileges but such as those who held the power and the government might choose to grant them." 17 How. 393, 404. The recent amendments of the constitution, it was supposed, had eradicated these principles from our institutions. But it seems that we have yet, in some of the states, a dominant race,—a superior class of citizens,—which assumes to regulate the enjoyment of civil rights, common to all citizens, upon the basis of race. The present decision, it may well be apprehended, will not only stimulate aggressions, more or less brutal and irritating, upon the admitted rights of colored citizens, but will encourage the belief that it is possible, by means of state enactments, to defeat the beneficent purposes which the people of the United States had in view when they adopted the recent amendments of the constitution, by one of which the blacks of this country were made citizens of the United States and of the states in which they respectively reside, and whose privileges and immunities, as citizens, the states are forbidden to abridge. Sixty millions of whites are in no danger from the presence here of eight millions of blacks. The destinies of the two races, in this country, are indissolubly linked together, and the interests of both require that the common government of all shall not permit the seeds of race hate to be planted under the sanction of law. What can more certainly arouse race hate, what more certainly create and perpetuate a feeling of distrust between these races, than state enactments which, in fact, proceed on the ground that colored citizens are so inferior and degraded that they cannot be allowed to sit in public coaches occupied by white citizens? That, as all will admit, is the real meaning of such legislation as was enacted in Louisiana.

The sure guaranty of the peace and security of each race is the clear, distinct, unconditional recognition by our governments, national and state, of every right that inheres in civil freedom, and of the equality before the law of all citizens of the United States, without regard to race. State enactments regulating the enjoyment of civil rights upon the basis of race, and cunningly devised to defeat legitimate results of the war, under the pretense of recognizing equality of rights, can have no other result than to render permanent peace impossible, and to keep alive a conflict of races, the continuance of which must do harm to all concerned. This question is not met by the suggestion that social equality cannot exist between the white and black races in this country. That argument, if it can be properly regarded as one, is scarcely worthy of consideration; for social equality no more exists between two races when traveling in a passenger coach or a public highway than when members of the same races sit by each other in a street car or in the jury box, or stand or sit with each other in a political assembly, or when they use in common the streets of a city or town, or when they are in the same room for the purpose of having their names placed on the registry of voters, or when they approach the ballot box in order to exercise the high privilege of voting.

There is a race so different from our own that we do not permit those belonging to it to become citizens of the United States. Persons belonging to it are, with few exceptions, absolutely excluded from our country. I allude to the Chinese race. But, by the statute in question, a Chinaman can ride in the same passenger coach with white citizens of the United States, while citizens of the black race in Louisiana, many of whom, perhaps, risked their lives for the preservation of the Union, who are entitled, by law, to participate in the political control of the state and nation, who are not excluded, by law or by reason of their race, from public stations of any kind, and who have all the legal rights that belong to white citizens, are yet declared to be criminals, liable to imprisonment, if they ride in a public coach occupied by citizens of the white race. It is scarcely just to say that a colored citizen should not object to occupying a public coach assigned to his own race. He does not object, nor, perhaps, would he object to separate coaches for his race if his rights under the law were recognized. But he does object, and he ought never to cease objecting, that citizens of the white and black races can be adjudged criminals because they sit, or claim the right to sit, in the same public coach on a public highway.

The arbitrary separation of citizens, on the basis of race, while they are on a public highway, is a badge of servitude wholly inconsistent with the civil freedom and the equality before the law established by the constitution. It cannot be justified upon any legal grounds.

If evils will result from the commingling of the two races upon public highways established for the benefit of all, they will be infinitely less than those that will surely come from state legislation regulating the enjoyment of civil rights upon the basis of race. We boast of the freedom enjoyed by our people above all other peoples. But it is difficult to reconcile that boast with a state of the law which, practically, puts the brand of servitude and degradation upon a large class of our fellow citizens, — our equals before the law. The thin disguise of 'equal' accommodations for passengers in railroad coaches will not mislead any one, nor atone for the wrong this day done.

The result of the whole matter is that while this court has frequently adjudged, and at the present term has recognized the doctrine, that a state cannot, consistently with the constitution of the United States, prevent white and black citizens, having the required qualifications for jury service, from sitting in the same jury box, it is now solemnly held that a state may prohibit white and black citizens from sitting in the same passenger coach on a public highway, or may require that they be separated by a "partition" when in the same passenger coach. May it not now be reasonably expected that astute men of the dominant race, who affect to be disturbed at the possibility that the integrity of the white race may be corrupted, or that its supremacy will be imperiled, by contact on public highways with black people, will endeavor to procure statutes requiring white and black jurors to be separated in the jury box by a "partition," and that, upon retiring from the court room to consult as to their verdict, such partition, if it be a movable one, shall be taken to their consultation room, and set up in such way as to prevent black jurors from coming too close to their brother jurors of the white race. If the "partition" used in the court room happens to be stationary, provision could be made for screens with openings through which jurors of the two races could confer as to their verdict without coming into personal contact with each other. I cannot see but that, according to the principles this day announced, such state legislation, although conceived in hostility to, and enacted for the purpose of humiliating, citizens of the United States of a particular race, would be held to be consistent with the constitution.

I do not deem it necessary to review the decisions of state courts to which reference was made in argument. Some, and the most important, of them, are wholly inapplicable, because rendered prior to the adoption of the last amendments of the constitution, when colored people had very few rights which the dominant race felt obliged to respect. Others were made at a time when public opinion, in many localities, was dominated by the institution of slavery; when it would not have been safe to do justice to the black man; and when, so far as the rights of blacks were concerned, race prejudice was, practically, the supreme law of the land. Those decisions cannot be guides in the era introduced by the recent amendments of the supreme law, which established universal civil freedom, gave citizenship to all born or naturalized in the United States, and residing here, obliterated the race line from our systems of governments, national and state, and placed our free institutions upon the broad and sure foundation of the equality of all men before the law.

I am of opinion that the state of Louisiana is inconsistent with the personal liberty of citizens, white and black, in that state, and hostile to both the spirit and letter of the constitution of the United States. If laws of like character should be enacted in the several states of the Union, the effect would be in the highest degree mischievous. Slavery, as an institution tolerated by law, would, it is true, have disappeared from our country; but there would remain a power in the states, by sinister legislation, to interfere with the full enjoyment of the blessings of freedom, to regulate civil rights, common to all citizens, upon the basis of race, and to place in a condition of legal inferiority a large body of American citizens, now constituting a part of the political community, called the "People of the United States," for whom, and by whom through representatives, our government is administered. Such a system is inconsistent with the guaranty given by the constitution to each state of a republican form of government, and may be stricken down by congressional action, or by the courts in the discharge of their solemn duty to maintain the supreme law of the land, anything in the constitution or laws of any state to the contrary notwithstanding.

For the reason stated, I am constrained to withhold my assent from the opinion and judgment of the majority.

Justice BREWER did not hear the argument or participate in the decision of this case.

G. Commentary on *Plessy*

A. Leon Higginbotham, Jr.
The Life of the Law: Values, Commitment, and Craftsmanship

"The object of the [Fourteenth] Amendment was undoubtedly to enforce the absolute equality of the two races before the law, but in the nature of things it could not have been intended to abolish distinctions based upon color, or to enforce social, as distinguished from political, equality, or a commingling of the two races upon terms unsatisfactory to either. Laws permitting, and even requiring, their separation in places where they are liable to be brought into contact do not necessarily imply the inferiority of either race to the other, and have been generally, if not universally, recognized as within the competency of the state legislatures in the exercise of their police power."[5]

With the above pronouncement, the Supreme Court in *Plessy* placed its imprimatur on state-imposed racial segregation and left to the "large discretion ... of the legislature" the determination whether the state would separate and treat black people differently than it did any other group — majority or minority — in American society. In the context of the times,[6] the Court's reference to the "established usages,

---

5. 163 U.S. at 552.

6. To avoid the "traditions of the people" that sanctioned racial discrimination during the *Plessy* era, blacks with mixed heritage often sought to highlight the "white" aspect of their lineage. Indeed, counsel for plaintiff in error had argued that Plessy, who was seven-eighths white, was deprived of his reputation of being white by the conductor's power to order him to sit in the colored section. Counsel also contended that being considered a white man was property "which [had] an actual pecuniary value" that could not be taken without due process of law. Brief for Plaintiff in Error at 9, *Plessy*, 163 U.S. 537. He further stated:

How much would it be *worth* to a young man entering upon the practice of law to be regarded as a *white* man rather than a colored one? Six-sevenths of the population are white. Nineteen-twentieths of the property of the country is owned by white people. Ninety-nine hundredths of the

customs and traditions of the people" was nothing less than a mandate for states to revert to the past biases, prejudices, and discrimination that had provided the rationale for slavery and America's earlier legitimization of racism — the very racism that was the target of the Thirteenth, Fourteenth, and Fifteenth Amendments. The majority's thinly veiled reversion to a slavery-type jurisprudence, despite its invocation of the Fourteenth Amendment, was revealed by its frequent citations to and reliance upon many cases that predated the enactment of the Fourteenth Amendment.[7]

Although many lower courts explicitly endorsed "Jim Crow segregation" prior to *Plessy*,[8] the significance of the Supreme Court's affirmation of the doctrine of "separate but equal" in 1896 cannot be underestimated. The Court's approval was the final and therefore the most devastating judicial step in the legitimization of racism under state law. In numerous subsequent school cases, state and federal courts continued to approve racial discrimination and segregation; most of those courts or counsel of record cited or relied upon *Plessy* as support for expansive endorsements of racial subjugation.[9]

100 *Harvard Law Review* 795, 804–6 (1987).
Copyright © (1987) The Harvard Law Review Association.
Reprinted with permission of The Harvard Law Review Association and
Evelyn Brooks Higginbotham.

---

business opportunities are in the control of white people. These propositions are rendered even more startling by the intensity of feeling which excludes the colored man from the friendship and companionship of the white man. probably most white persons if given a choice, would prefer death to life in the United States *as colored persons.* Under these conditions, is it possible to conclude that the reputation of being white is not property? Indeed, is it not the most valuable sort of property, being the master-key that unlocks the golden door of opportunity?

    Id. (emphasis in original).

    7. *See Plessy*, 163 U.S. at 544 (citing *Roberts v. City of Boston*, 59 Mass. (5 Cush.) 198 (1849)); *id.* at 548 (citing *West Chester & Philadelphia R.R. v. Miles*, 55 Pa. 209 (1867)). In *West Chester*, a pre-Fourteenth Amendment case involving segregation on a public carrier, the court stated:

    Why the Creator made one [race] black and the other white, we know not; but the fact is apparent, and the races distinct, each producing its own kind, and following the peculiar law of its constitution. Conceding equality, with natures as perfect and rights as sacred, yet God has made them dissimilar, with those natural instincts and feelings which He always imparts to His creatures when He intends that they shall not overstep the natural boundaries He has assigned to them. The natural law which forbids their intermarriage and that social amalgamation which leads to a corruption of races, is as clearly divine as that which imparted to them different natures. The tendency of intimate social intermixture is to amalgamation, contrary to the law of races.

    55 Pa. at 213.

    8. *See* R. Kaczorowski, The Politics of Judicial Interpretation: The Federal Courts, Department of Justice and Civil Rights, 1866–1876, at 8 & n.12, 18–19 (1985); Riegel, *The Persistent Career of Jim Crow: Lower Federal Courts and the "Separate But Equal" Doctrine, 1865–1896*, 28 Am. J. Legal Hist. 17, 20–21 (1984).

    9. One comprehensive survey cites more than fifty pre-*Brown* school cases in which the courts or counsel relied on the segregation doctrine of *Plessy*. These cases concern issues ranging from the physical, aesthetic condition of the facility to the more qualitative, substantive considerations of the curriculum and faculty. *See* Leflar & Davis, *Segregation in the Public Schools — 1953*, 67 Harv. L. Rev. 377, 430–35 (1954).

H. Background on Justice Henry Billings Brown

Justice Henry Billings Brown was born in Lee, Massachusetts, on March 21, 1836. He attended both Yale and Harvard Law Schools, and spent a year studying law in a private law office, before being admitted to the Michigan Bar in 1860. Brown practiced law in Michigan and became a leader in the Republican Party. Brown served as a Deputy United States Marshall and an Assistant United States District Attorney, before being appointed a District Judge of the United States Court for the Eastern District of Michigan in 1875. Brown served on the United States Court for the Eastern District of Michigan until his appointment to the Supreme Court of the United States by President Benjamin Harrison on December 23, 1890. Justice Brown served on the Supreme Court for sixteen years before stepping down on May 28, 1906.

I. Questions and Notes

The majority opinion in *Plessy* states: "If the two races are to meet upon terms of social equality, it must be the result of natural affinities, a mutual appreciation of each others merits, and a voluntary consent of individuals." (163 U.S. at 551). What do you think of the majority's reasoning? Does the court place reasonable conditions on application of the separate but equal doctrine.

Theoretically, taking the words at face value, the separate but equal doctrine sounds fair and impartial. Can *Plessy* be criticized only for the racially discriminatory application of the doctrine or is the doctrine itself inherently flawed? Explain why the *Plessy* doctrine was so devastating for blacks. What facially race-neutral doctrines utilized presently are detrimental to black progress?

Some black-owned businesses thrived under the *Plessy* doctrine but could not survive once *de jure* segregation ended. What is the explanation for this phenomenon?

Racial discrimination is often sustained by convoluted excuses or spurious pretenses. During the early Twentieth Century before the invention of the electric icebox and refrigerator, people would buy a large block of ice each morning and place it in a cooler with the perishable food. The block of ice would keep the food cool for a twenty-four hour period before it completely melted and had to be replaced. Ice would be delivered each morning, usually by a horse-drawn wagon and was generally sold for one dollar per block.

In one mid-western city in a predominantly African-American section of town, a white fellow would deliver ice to each home where it was desired. The city had only one ice manufacturing plant and this is where all ice blocks were purchased. One enterprising African American in the neighborhood thought that ice delivery might be a profitable business venture. He was especially confident of the likely success of this business since he owned a horse and wagon, knew the location where the ice was manufactured, was prepared to be first in line to purchase the ice, and had many friends in the neighborhood who bought ice each day and who he thought would be receptive customers.

The next morning he arose bright and early, proceeded to the ice manufacturing plant where he was first in line, loaded up many blocks of ice, and returned to his neighborhood to begin deliveries. He offered his blocks for one dollar a piece, the same price as his white competitor. Unfortunately, none of his friends or neighbors would purchase his ice and it all melted. Several hours later, the white fellow came through the neighborhood and sold all his blocks of ice for one dollar a piece.

Disappointed but not dissuaded, the African-American entrepreneur followed the same procedure the next day and attempted to make his ice block deliveries. Once again, no one bought his ice and it all melted. After his white competitor again sold all of his ice blocks, the African American asked his friends and neighbors why they would not purchase his ice. The response to his inquiry was the "white man's ice was colder."

Does this story about blocks of ice shed light on the impact of the end of *de jure* segregation? When segregation was less blatant on the face of laws, did it persist in more subtle ways?

In both *Plessy* and the *Civil Rights Cases* the supporters of racial equality were unsuccessful in their efforts. Which case do you believe resulted in the most harm to racial equality and why?

J. Point/Counterpoint

From a theoretical standpoint, some suggest that "separate but equal" is a better approach to solving America's racial problems than "integrated and equal." What do you think?

XIII. Expanding the Separate but Equal Doctrine

A. Introduction

While the *Plessy* Court ruled that separate but equal racial segregation in social activities did not violate the equal protection clause of the Fourteenth Amendment, the Court did not provide guidance on the extent to which the state was empowered to regulate race relations under its police powers. The question of what limitations were imposed upon state authorities would be addressed in subsequent cases. In *Berea College*, we see, sadly, that the Supreme Court reduced those limitations to a new low, making the states all-powerful to regulate, even private activities. State governments became all powerful, and the federal government was almost completely powerless to prevent discrimination.

B. Background on *Berea College*

Richard Epstein

Race and the Police Power: 1890 to 1937*

In order to sustain the statute, *Plessy* required the Supreme Court to go one step beyond the earlier misguided precedents. While earlier cases tolerated extravagant means directed toward the end of "safety and health," those cases did not expand the class of permissible ends that fell within the police power. *Plessy*, however, did not refer to or discuss the earlier police power cases, which, despite their weaknesses, were moored in their analysis to an inflated conception of nuisance and fraud. Instead *Plessy* assumed that the separation of the races by government force was an appropriate end of the state, wholly without reference to tort, nuisance or fraud. Thus, the Court wrote:

> The object of the [Fourteenth] Amendment was undoubtedly to enforce the absolute equality of the two races before the law, but in the nature of things it could not have been intended to abolish distinctions based upon color, or to enforce social, as distinguished from political equality, or a commingling of the two races upon terms unsatisfactory to either. Laws permitting, and even requiring, their separation in places where they are liable to be brought into contact do not necessarily imply the inferiority of either race to the other, and have been generally, if not universally, recognized as within the competency of the state legislatures in the exercise of their police power. The most common instance of this is connected with the establishment of separate schools for white and colored children, which has been held to be a valid exercise of the legislative power even by courts of States where the political rights of the colored race have been longest and most earnestly enforced.

The passage offers no account of the scope and limits of the police power. It is written as though the statute was designed to protect the principle of freedom of association (to prevent the enforced "commingling" of the races), when its actual purpose and effect is the opposite: the statute prevents contractual freedom between the railroad and its black and/or white customers. As will become clear, under the standards for economic liberties developed shortly thereafter in *Lochner*, the statute in *Plessy* would have been doomed.

However, *Plessy* possibly could have relied on a different tradition that would have allowed the Court to appeal to decisions of northern state courts to justify itself. The critical decision in this regard was *Roberts*, which sustained the operation of a system of racially segregated schools in Boston. The headnote to the opinion makes clear its scope: "The general school committee of the city of Boston have power,

---

* (footnotes omitted).

under the constitution and law of this commonwealth, to make provision for the instruction of colored children, in separate schools established exclusively for them, and to prohibit their attendance upon other schools." *Roberts* predated the Civil War amendments, and Chief Justice Lemuel Shaw's opinion did not use the words "police power" or invoke the doctrine of separate but equal that grew up in their interpretation. Shaw did discuss the great principle "that by the constitutions and laws of Massachusetts, all persons without distinction of age or sex, birth or color, origin or condition, are equal before the law." But he nonetheless concluded with words that were seized on in *Plessy*, that given "the actual and various conditions of persons in society, it will not warrant the assertion, that men and women are legally clothed with the same civil and political powers, and that children and adults are legally to have the same functions and be subject to the same treatment." In light of these evident difficulties, Shaw then took the line that as long as the school committee had deliberated honestly, anxiously and in good faith, its decision could not be challenged in court. This early set of intuitions easily can be transformed into the later pattern of constitutional adjudication. Shaw essentially adopted a view that judicial deference was required in the oversight of difficult administrative decisions. That approach fit perfectly with *Plessy*'s view that state officials were accorded broad deference under the police power.

Lochner, however, pointed in quite a different direction. *Lochner*'s doctrinal significance lay in its holding that the state's police power did not allow the state to impose a maximum ten hour work day on certain classes of bakers for the purported end of protecting their health. The court held that a 10 hour limitation on employment was a "labor statute" that fell outside the permissible ends of government regulation. While the court did not stress the point, the beneficiaries of the statute were not the workers, but the rival bread firms (and their unions) whose employees worked eight hour shifts, and thus were not crimped in their operation by the statute's passage. . . .

The basic point is well shown by noting that consent and assumption of risk had a far broader role at common law than it did under *Lochner*'s formulation of the police power. As between consenting parties, assumption of risk at common law had been a valid defense to any legal action for personal injury. In that context it had received an expansive interpretation by, among others, Oliver Wendell Holmes, whose dissent in *Lochner* set the stage for today's dominant deferential attitude on economic regulation. *Lochner*'s broad rendering of the police power that allowed it to reach all matters of health and safety thus explicitly and consciously overrode the common law on this critical issue. This broadening of the police power facilitated the first wave of protective health and safety regulations of the Progressive Era. At the very time that the Supreme Court struck down the maximum hours statute in *Lochner*, the Court upheld provisions of the Federal Employer's Liability Act that explicitly prevented railroads and their workers from contracting out of the statutory rules governing compensation for injury. Thereafter, a line of cases upheld regulation of safety in mines and workers compensation statutes, again on the same view of the police power. Still other cases took a deferential view with respect to legislative bans on the sale of milk substitutes. Health and safety, thus, were treated as proper subjects of regulation.

Under *Lochner* only "labor" (*i.e.,* anticompetitive) statutes were beyond the scope of the police power. Therefore, decisions that required railroads, for example, to bargain in good faith with majority unions were held to be outside the police power, over the dissent of Justice Holmes. *Plessy* did not fall along the health/labor continuum used to organize police power cases. Rather *Plessy* assumed that race relations, like health concerns, were proper subjects of government regulation, notwithstanding their manifest limitation on both common-law rights of contract and property. Nothing in *Plessy* assumed that segregation (like markets) was a natural form of "prepolitical" order. Quite the contrary, the whole area of racial relations was thought to be subject to unfettered political control.

46 *Washington and Lee Law Review* 741, 750–52 (1989).
Copyright © (1989) *Washington and Lee Law Review.*
Reprinted with permission of *Washington and Lee Law Review* and
Richard Epstein.

C. *Berea College v. The Commonwealth of Kentucky,* 211 U.S. 45 (1908)

1. Facts

Justice BREWER delivered the opinion of the Court.

On October 8, 1904, the grand jury of Madison county, Kentucky, presented in the circuit court of that county an indictment, charging:

"The said Berea College, being a corporation duly incorporated under the laws of the state of Kentucky, and owning, maintaining, and operating a college, school, and institution of learning, known as 'Berea College,' located in the town of Berea, Madison county, Kentucky, did unlawfully and wilfully permit and receive both the white and Negro races as pupils for instruction in said college, school, and institution of learning."

This indictment was found under an act of March 22, 1904 (Ky. Acts 1904, chap. 85, p. 181), whose 1st section reads:

"Sec. 1. That it shall be unlawful for any person, corporation, or association of persons to maintain or operate any college, school, or institution where persons of the white and Negro races are both received as pupils for instruction, and any person or corporation who shall operate or maintain any such college, school, or institution shall be fined $1,000, and any person or corporation who may be convicted of violating the provisions of this act shall be fined $100 for each day they may operate said school, college, or institution after such conviction."

At trial the defendant was found guilty and sentenced to pay a fine of $1,000. This judgment was, on June 12, 1906, affirmed by the court of appeals of the state (123 Kentucky, 209, 94 S.W. 623), and from that court brought here on writ of error.

2. Opinion

That the act does not violate the Constitution of Kentucky is settled by the decision of its highest court, and the single question for our consideration is whether it conflicts with the Federal Constitution. The court of appeals discussed at some length the general power of the state in respect to the separation of the two races. It also ruled that "the right to teach white and Negro children in a private school at the same time and place is not a property right. Besides, appellant, as a corporation created by this state, has no natural right to teach at all. Its right to teach is such as the state sees fit to give to it. The state may withhold it altogether, or qualify it. *Allgeyer v. Louisiana*, 165 U.S. 578, 41 L.Ed. 832, 17 Sup. Ct. Rep. 427. . . ."

While the terms of the present charter are not given in the record, yet it was admitted on the trial that the defendant was a corporation organized and incorporated under the general statutes of the State of Kentucky, and of course the state courts, as well as this court on appeal, take judicial notice of those statutes. Further, in the brief of counsel for the defendant is given a history of the incorporation proceedings, together with the charters. From that it appears that Berea College was organized under the authority of an act for the incorporation of voluntary associations, approved March 9, 1854 (2 Stanton Rev. Stat. Ky. 553), which act was amended by an act of March 10, 1856 (2 Stanton, 555), and which in terms reserved to the General Assembly "the right to alter or repeal the charter of any associations formed under the provisions of this act, and the act to which this act is an amendment, at any time hereafter." After the constitution of 1891 was adopted by the State of Kentucky, and on June 10, 1899, the college was reincorporated under the provisions of chap. 32, art. 8, Ky. Stat. (Carroll's Ky. Stat. 1903, p. 459), the charter defining its business in these words: "Its object is the education of all persons who may attend its institution of learning at Berea, and in the language of the original articles, 'to promote the cause of Christ.'" The constitution of 1891 provided in § 3 of the Bill of Rights that "Every grant of a franchise, privilege or exemption shall remain, subject to revocation, alteration or amendment." Carroll's Ky. Stat. 1903, p. 86. So that the full power of amendment was reserved to the legislature.

It is undoubtedly true that the reserved power to alter or amend is subject to some limitations, and that under the guise of an amendment a new contract may not always be enforceable upon the corporation or the stockholders; but it is settled "that a power reserved to the legislature to alter, amend or repeal a charter authorizes it to make any alteration or amendment of a charter granted subject to it, which will not defeat or substantially impair the object of the grant, or any rights vested under it, and which the legislature may deem necessary to secure either that object or any public right. *Commissioners on Inland Fisheries v. Holyoke Water Power Co.*, 104 Massachusetts, 446, 451; *Holyoke Co. v. Lyman*, 15 Wall. 500, 522;" *Close v. Glenwood Cemetery*, 107 U.S. 466, 476.

Construing the statute, the court of appeals held that "if the same school taught the different races at different times, though at the same place, or at different places, it would not be unlawful." Now, an amendment to the original charter, which does not destroy the power of the college to furnish education to all persons, but which simply separates them by time or place of instruction, cannot be said to "defeat or substantially impair the object of the grant." The language of the statute is not in terms and amendment, yet its effect is an amendment, and it would be resting too much on mere form to hold that a statute which in effect works a change in the terms of the charter is not to be considered as an amendment, because not so designated. The act itself, being separable, is to be read as though it, in one section, prohibited any person, in another section any corporation and, in a third, any association of persons to do the acts named. Reading the statute as containing a separate prohibition on all corporations, at least, all state corporations, it substantially declares that any authority given by previous charters to instruct the two races at the same time and in the same place is forbidden, and that prohibition, being a departure from the terms of the original charter in this case, may properly be adjudged an amendment.

Again, it is insisted that the court of appeals did not regard the legislation as making an amendment, because another prosecution instituted against the same corporation under the 4th section of the act, which makes it a misdemeanor to teach pupils of the two races in the same institution, even although one race is taught in one branch and another in another branch, provided the two branches are within 25 miles of each other, was held could not be sustained, the court saying: "This last section, we think, violates the limitations upon the police power: it is unreasonable and oppressive." But, while so ruling, it also held that this section could be ignored and that the remainder of the act was complete notwithstanding. Whether the reasoning of the court concerning the 4th section be satisfactory or not is immaterial, for no question of its validity is presented, and the court of appeals, while striking it down, sustained the balance of the act. We need concern ourselves only with the inquiry whether the 1st section can be upheld as coming within the power of a state over its own corporate creatures.

3. Holding

We are of opinion, for reasons stated, that it does come within that power, and, on this ground, the judgment of the Court of Appeals of Kentucky is *affirmed*.

4. Justice Harlan Dissenting

. . . In my judgment the court should directly meet and decide the broad question presented by the statute. It should adjudge whether the statute, as a whole, is or is not unconstitutional, in that it makes it a crime against the state to maintain or operate a private institution of learning where white and black pupils are received, at the same time, for instruction. In the view which I have as to my duty I feel obliged to express my opinion as to the validity of the act as a whole. I am of opinion that, in its essential parts, the statute is an arbitrary invasion of the rights of liberty and property guaranteed by the 14th Amendment against hostile state action, and is, therefore, void.

The capacity to impart instruction to others is given by the Almighty for beneficent purposes; and its use may not be forbidden or interfered with by government, — certainly not, unless such instruction is, in its nature, harmful to the public morals or imperils the public safety. The right to impart instruction, harmless in itself or beneficial to those who receive it, is a substantial right of property, — especially, where the services are rendered for compensation. But even if such right be not strictly a property right, it is, beyond question, part of one's liberty as guaranteed against hostile state action by the Constitution of the United States. This court has more than once said that the liberty guaranteed by the 14th Amendment embraces "the right of the citizen to be free in the enjoyment of all his faculties," and "to be free to use them in all lawful ways." *Allgeyer v. Louisiana*, 165 U.S. 578, 41 L. ed. 832, 17 Sup. Ct. Rep. 427; *Adair v. United States*, 208 U.S. 161, 173, 52 L. ed. 436, 442, 28 Sup. Ct. Rep. 277. If pupils, of whatever race, — certainly, if they be citizens, — choose, with the consent of their parents, or voluntarily, to sit together in a private institution of learning while receiving instruction which is not in its nature harmful or dangerous to the public, no government, whether Federal or state, can legally forbid their coming together, or being together temporarily, for such an innocent purpose. If the common-wealth of Kentucky can make it a crime to teach white and colored children together at the same time, in a private institution of learning, it is difficult to perceive why it may not forbid the assembling of white and colored children in the same Sabbath school, for the purpose of being instructed in the Word of God, although such teaching may be done under the authority of the church to which the school is attached as well as with the consent of the parents of the children. So, if the state court be right, white and colored children may even be forbidden to sit together in a house of worship or at a communion table in the same Christian church. In the cases supposed there would be the same association of white and colored persons as would occur when pupils of the two races sit together in a private institution of learning for the purpose of receiving instruction in purely secular matters. Will it be said that the cases supposed and the case here in hand are different, in that no government, in this country, can lay unholy hands on the religious faith of the people? The answer to this suggestion is that, in the eye of the law, the right to enjoy one's religious belief, unmolested by any human power, is no more sacred nor more fully or distinctly recognized than is the right to impart and receive instruction not harmful to the public. The denial of either right would be an infringement of the liberty inherent in the freedom secured by the fundamental law. Again, if the views of the highest court of Kentucky be sound, that commonwealth may, without infringing the Constitution of the United States, forbid the association in the same private school of pupils of the Anglo-Saxon and Latin races respectively, or pupils of the Christian and Jewish faiths, respectively. Have we become so inoculated with prejudice of race that an American government, professedly based on the principles of freedom, and charged with the protection of all citizens alike, can make distinctions between such citizens in the matter of their voluntary meeting for innocent purposes, simply because of their respective races? Further, if the lower court be right, then a state may make it a crime for white and colored persons to frequent the same market places at the same time, or appear in an assemblage of citizens convened to consider questions of a public or political nature, in which all citizens, without regard to race, are equally interested. Many other illustrations might be given to show the mischievous, not to say cruel, character of the statute in question, and how inconsistent such legislation is with the great principle of the equality of citizens before the law. . . .

In my opinion the judgment should be reversed upon the ground that the statute is in violation of the Constitution of the United States.

Justice DAY concurs in the dissent.

D. Commentary on *Berea College*

A. Leon Higginbotham, Jr.

Book Review: Race, Racism, and American Law

In *Berea College*, the Kentucky Court of Appeals had justified the separation of school children because of the importance of maintaining "the purity of racial blood." The Kentucky court stressed that:

> The question is, is it a fair exercise of the police power to prohibit the teaching of the white and Negro races together? Is it a fair exercise of the power to restrain the two races from voluntarily associating together in a private school to acquire a scholastic education? The mingling of the blood of the white and negro races by interbreeding is deemed by the political department of our state government as being hurtful to the welfare of society. . . . Inbreeding is known to lower the mental and physical rigor of the offspring. So incestuous marriages are prohibited. Others not incestuous but involving the probable effect upon the vitality of the offspring are prohibited also, and marriages by idiots . . . upon the same considerations this same power has been exercised to prohibit the intermarriage of the two races. The result of such marriage would be to destroy the purity of blood and identity of each.[10]

---

10. *Berea College v. Commonwealth of Kentucky*, 123 Ky. 209, 213, 94 S.W. 623, 625 (1906).

While many would question what this education case had to do with interracial sex and marriage, the Supreme Court accepted this justification as a reasonable exercise of the police powers.

Berea College upheld the validity of a 1904 Kentucky statute which prohibited a college from teaching white and black pupils in the same institution. Berea College was established in the Kentucky mountains in 1854 by a small band of Christians who began their charter with the words, "God hath made of one blood all nations that dwell upon the face of the earth." After the Civil War it admitted students without racial discrimination, and by 1904 it had 174 black and 753 white students. It was a private institution supported by those who subscribed to its religious tenets, and it neither sought nor received any state aid or assistance. Yet the Supreme Court held that a state could prohibit any private institution from promoting the cause of Christ through integrated education. What a tragic ruling! A nation loudly pronounces its faith in freedom of religion, yet sanctions a state's denial of the day to day application of religious concepts if practiced in an integrated religious setting. Justice Harlan wrote another eloquent dissent in *Berea College*, and, tragically, Justice Holmes, for all his prescience and ability, concurred in the majority's repressive opinion.

122 *University of Pennsylvania Law Review* 1044, 1057–58.
Copyright © (1974) *University of Pennsylvania Law Review*.
Reprinted with permission of the *University of Pennsylvania Law Review*.

Donald E. Lively

The Constitution and Race

During the first decade of the twentieth century, the Court upheld official segregation in private colleges and public transportation. In *Berea College v. Kentucky*, it upheld a state law prohibiting corporations and persons from operating racially integrated schools. Justice Harlan criticized the decision as evasive and hypocritical. Specifically, he considered "[t]he right to impart instruction" a protected liberty interest under the Fourteenth Amendment and meriting the same sentience the Court by then was affording general notions of economic freedom. The *Berea College* decision illuminated the evolving duality of Fourteenth Amendment standards and how official management of race relations could be pervasive and intrusive without constitutional affront.

In *McCabe v. Atchison, Topeka & Santa Fe Railway Co.*, the Court again upheld separate train accommodations. The *McCabe* case differed from *Plessy* to the extent it was necessary to consider whether dedicated eating and sleeping accommodations had to be provided in the absence of black patronage. The Court held that, regardless of demand or usage considerations, separate sleeping and dining cars had to be furnished. The effect of its determination was diluted by the further conclusion that injunctive relief could not be ordered because the complainants themselves had never traveled on the railroad or specifically been denied service. While an underused rail car may have been eloquent testimony of how thoroughly official racism denied opportunities to exercise basic rights secured by the Fourteenth Amendment, the *McCabe* decision merely polished the doctrinal veneer of equality.

The Constitution and Race 94.
Copyright © (1992) Donald E. Lively.
Reprinted with permission of Donald E. Lively.

E. Explaining Justice David Brewer

G. Hylton

*The Judge Who Abstained in Plessy v. Ferguson: Justice David Brewer
and the Problem of Race*

The final line of the United States Supreme Court opinion in the landmark case of *Plessy v. Ferguson* states, "Mr. Justice Brewer did not hear the argument or participate in the decision of this case."[11] Because of the untimely death of his daughter, the 58-year- old Justice had been forced to leave Washington, D.C. for his home in Leavenworth, Kansas, on April 13, 1896, the day *Plessy* was argued before the Court.[12] Without Brewer, the Court voted 7 to 1 to uphold Louisiana's "separate but equal" public accommodations law. Only Justice John Marshall Harlan, a former slaveholder from Kentucky, agreed that the challenged "Jim Crow" statute violated the Fourteenth Amendment's guarantee of equal protection of the laws.[13]

A general familiarity with the personal background and constitutional views of David Josiah Brewer might have led one to believe that had the Kansan been present, he would have joined in Harlan as a second vote against the challenged

---

11. 163 U.S. 537, 564 (1896). On *Plessy v. Ferguson* generally, see C. Vann Woodward, *The Case of the Louisiana Traveler*, Quarrels That Have Shaped the Constitution 145–58 (J. Garraty ed. 1964) and C. Lofgren, The Plessy Case: A Legal-Historical Interpretation (1987).

12. Francis Adele Brewer died of tuberculosis in Texas where she and her mother had moved the previous year in hope that the climate would improve her health. Washington Post, April 14, 1896 at 3; *see also,* H. Karrick, David Josiah Brewer: A Biographical Sketch by His Daughter (1912) (available at Yale University Library in collection of Brewer Family Papers). Because of his involvement with an international commission appointed to resolve a boundary dispute between Venezuela and British Guinea, it is possible that Brewer would have missed the argument anyway.

13. Harlan's eloquent defense of the civil rights of African Americans in the late nineteenth and early twentieth centuries is one of the best known chapters in the history of the United States Supreme Court. It is ironic that on a court composed largely of northerners who either participated in or came of age during the American Civil War the one clear voice in favor of a racially egalitarian society was that of a former Kentucky slaveholder who, before his appointment to the nation's highest tribunal, had opposed the ratification of both the Thirteenth and Fourteenth Amendments. For a discussion of Harlan's views on race and civil rights, see Westin, *John Marshall Harlan and the Constitutional Rights of Negroes*, 66 Yale L.J. 637 (1957).

ordinance. The son of an abolitionist clergyman, Brewer had enlisted in the cause of antislavery as a youth, and in 1858, at age 21, had joined the migration of antislavery New Englanders to "Bloody Kansas."[14] As a judge in Reconstruction era Kansas, he had authored one of the first judicial opinions upholding the right of an African-American citizen to vote in a general election, and as the superintendent of schools in Leavenworth, he had helped establish the first schools for blacks in the state. Furthermore, since joining the United States Supreme Court in 1890, he had been a vocal supporter of African-American advancement in his pronouncements off the bench. In an 1892 address to the American Home Missionary Society, for example, Brewer had proclaimed, "This is not an Anglo-Saxon, not a Teutonic, not even a Caucasian nation. The blood of all races mingles in that of the American people."[15]

Moreover, Brewer had exhibited great sympathy for other "minority" groups. He was the Court's foremost spokesman for the rights of Asians residing in the United States, siding with the Oriental party in eighteen of twenty-three cases decided by the United States Supreme Court during his tenure.[16] (The Court itself found for the

---

14. There is, unfortunately, no biography of Brewer. This absence is explained in large part by the failure of Brewer to leave behind any substantial body of private papers. The existing Brewer papers are collected in the Brewer Family Papers, Yale University Library, New Haven, Connecticut. A small collection of his papers (64 items) can also be found in the Library of Congress. Unless otherwise noted, biographical information in this article is derived from materials in the Brewer Family Papers.

There are many secondary sources which address various aspects of Brewer's career. *See* Bergan, *Mr. Justice Brewer: Perspective of a Century*, 25 ALB. L. REV. 191 (1961); R. CUSHMAN, 2 DICTIONARY OF AMERICAN BIOGRAPHY 22 (D. Malone ed. 1928); Eitzen, *David Brewer, 1837–1910: A Kansan on the United States Supreme Court*, 12 THE EMPORIA STATE RESEARCH STUDIES 1 (1964); O. FISS, *David J. Brewer: The Judge as Missionary*, in THE FIELDS AND THE LAW 53–63 (1986); Gamer, *Justice Brewer and Substantive Due Process: A Conservative Court Revisited*, 18 VAND. L. REV. 615 (1965); A. PAUL, 2 THE JUSTICES OF THE UNITED STATES SUPREME COURT, 1789–1967, at 1515 (L. Friedman & F. Israel eds. 1969); L. Lardner, The Constitutional Doctrines of Justice David Josiah Brewer (1938) (unpublished Princeton University Ph.D. dissertation).

15. *Address of Justice Brewer*, MINUTES OF THE SIXTY-SIXTH ANNUAL MEETING OF THE AMERICAN HOME MISSIONARY SOCIETY 95 (1892).

16. *See Tang Tun v. Edsell*, 214 U.S. 523 (1909); *Liu Hop Fong v. United States*, 209 U.S. 453 (1908); *Chin Yow v. United States*, 208 U.S. 8 (1908); *Ah Sin v. Wittman*, 198 U.S. 500 (1905); *United States v. Ju Toy*, 198 U.S. 253 (1905); *United States v. Sing Tuck*, 194 U.S. 161 (1904); *Tom Hong v. United States*, 193 U.S. 517 (1904); *Ah How v. United States*, 193 U.S. 65 (1905); *The Japanese Immigrant Case*, 189 U.S. 86 (1903); *Chin Bak Kan v. United States*, 186 U.S. 193 (1902); *Lee Lung v. Patterson*, 186 U.S. 168 (1902); *Fok Yung Yo v. United States*, 185 U.S. 296 (1902); *United States v. Lee Yen Tai*, 185 U.S. 213 (1902); *Li Sing v. United States*, 180 U.S. 486 (1901); *United States v. Gue Lim*, 176 U.S. 156 (1900); *United States v. Wong Kim Ark*, 169 U.S. 649 (1898); *Lem Wong King Ark*, 169 U.S. 649 (1898); *Fong Yue Ting v. United States*, 149 U.S. 698 (1893); *Lau Ow Bew v. United States*, 144 U.S. 47 (1892); *Nishimura Ekiu v. United States*, 142 U.S. 651 (1892); *In re Lau Ow Bew*, 141 U.S. 583 (1891); *Wan Shing v. United States*, 140 U.S. 417 (1891); *Quock Ting v. United States*, 140 U.S. 417 (1891). Brewer did not participate in *Wang Wing v. United States*, 163 U.S. 228 (1896). In three additional decisions, the Court did not issue written opinions but instead disposed of the cases by summary affirmance or dismissal. *See Goon Shung v. United States*, 212 U.S. 566 (1909); *Chinese Cases*, 165 U.S. 275 (1897); *Chinese Cases*, 140 U.S. 676 (1891).

Oriental party in only six of these cases.[17]) He was also a supporter of women's rights, at least as the term was understood in his era. As a judge in Kansas in the 1870s, he had supported the right of women to hold property in their own names and had upheld their right to serve as school supervisors.[18] While a member of the Supreme Court, he publicly supported women's suffrage and called for an increased role for women in the professions.[19] In a 1905 speech at Vassar College, Brewer endorsed the idea of a woman President and suggested that social worker Jane Addams would make an excellent mayor of Chicago.[20] Moreover, in one of his best known Supreme Court opinions, *Muller v. Oregon*,[21] he departed from his long-standing opposition to legislative interference in the labor market to uphold the constitutionality of protective legislation for women workers.

Brewer was also an outspoken supporter of a variety of what were in his era viewed as "liberal" causes. He was a life-long advocate of world peace and a crusader for the cause of international arbitration.[22] He served for years as an officer of the American Missionary Association; he was an active supporter of the Associated Charities in Washington, D.C., and he was a devout member of the Congregational Church.[23] In the late 1890s he would emerge as an outspoken opponent of United

---

At the time of the *Plessy* argument, Brewer had sided with the Asian position in six of seven cases. In four of these cases, he was in dissent.

17. *See In re Lau Ow Bew*, 141 U.S. at 583; *Lau Ow Ben*, 144 U.S. at 47; *Gue Lin*, 176 U.S. at 156; *Tom Hong*, 193 U.S. at 517; *Chin Yow*, 208 U.S. at 8; and *Liu Hop Fong*, 209 U.S. at 453. Brewer sided with the Oriental party in 78.3% of the cases in which the court issued a written opinion. Of his colleagues on the Court between 1890 and 1910, only Rufus Peckham consistently supported Brewer's position, doing so in 76.5% of the cases in which he participated (13 of 17). No other Justice's percentage exceeded 50.0%, although Stephen Field did support the Oriental position in 4 of 8 cases. Chief Justice Melville Fuller most perfectly represented the Court's sentiment, voting in the majority in all 24 cases decided in this twenty year period (six times favoring the Chinese/Japanese position and eighteen times opposing it). Harlan, on the other hand, was slightly less sympathetic to this position than the court as a whole, supporting the Oriental position in only 5 of 23 cases (21.7%). The records of Brewer's other contemporaries on the court are as follows: Bradley, 2 of 5; Gray, 4 of 11; Blatchford, 2 of 6; Lamar 2 of 5; Brown, 5 of 22; Shiras, 2 of 11; Jackson 0 of 1; White, 4 of 17; McKenna, 3 of 15; Holmes, 2 of 8; Day 3 of 8; and Moody, 1 of 2. Neither Justices Miller or Lurton participated in such a case during the brief time they sat with Justice Brewer.

18. H. KARRICK, DAVID JOSIAH BREWER: A BIOGRAPHICAL SKETCH BY HIS DAUGHTER 24 (1912).

19. *Women's Suffrage: Its Present Position and Its Future*, 30 THE LADIES WORLD 6 (1909). *See generally*, J. SEMONCHE, CHARTING THE FUTURE: THE SUPREME COURT RESPONDS TO A CHANGING SOCIETY, 1890–1920, at 221 (1978).

20. Address by Justice Brewer to Vassar College on Women, Changed Relations to Life and Society (1893) (available at Yale University Library in collection of Brewer Family Papers). *See also, Women in the Professions*, THE DELINEATOR (May 1906).

21. 208 U.S. 412 (1908).

22. For Brewer's efforts on behalf of international cooperation, *see* Butler, *Melville Weston Fuller-David Josiah Brewer, Memorial Note*, 4 AM. J. INT'L L. 909 (1910).

23. Brewer was involved in both charitable and liberal "causes." *See* R. CUSHMAN, 2 DICTIONARY OF AMERICAN BIOGRAPHY (1928) at 23; K. MORTON, DAVID JOSIAH BREWER (1912) (available at Yale University Library in collection of Brewer Family Papers).

States imperialism, a critic of the war with Spain, and an advocate of immediate independence for the Philippines.[24]

Furthermore, of all the men who sat on the United States Supreme Court in the late nineteenth and early twentieth centuries, none was more vocal than Brewer, both on and off the bench, in his support of the cause of individual liberty. He believed that liberty of contract was a right protected by the Constitution; he favored a narrow interpretation of the state police power; and he rejected the concept of a paternalistic state. These positions seemingly clashed with the efforts at social engineering that lay behind the emerging regime of legally-mandated segregation that was emerging in the American South at the end of the nineteenth century. Brewer was also not reluctant to stake out a position at odds with that of his colleagues. He was the greatest dissenter of his era, breaking with the majority on 226 occasions during his twenty years on the Court.[25] He dissented, on average, 11.3 times per term, a rate greater than any of his colleagues, including Harlan, the so-called great dissenter.[26] Furthermore, Brewer did not limit his remarks to the Court's official utterances. His private papers contain the texts of more than 100 public orations and magazine articles composed while on the Court.[27] He was, according to the *Virginia Law Register* (a legal journal for the practicing bar), a justice who "mingled with the people and addressed his countrymen . . . upon matters concerning the general welfare," and who "did not hesitate to express vigorous opinion upon all the great questions of the day and with vigorous rhetoric . . . lashed the abuses of legal processes and the chicanery of lawyers."[28]

---

24. Brewer, *The Spanish War: A Prophecy or an Exception*, in 16 Kansas Collected Speeches and Pamphlets 16–17 (n.d.).

25. A. Blaustein & R. Mersky, The First One Hundred Justices: Statistical Studies on the Supreme Court of the United States144 (1978). Brewer wrote dissenting opinions in 57 of the 226 cases in which he dissented. He also wrote the majority opinion in 533 cases, 70 of which involved constitutional issues. He also concurred in 44 majority opinions, writing separate opinions in 8 of them.

26. Harlan dissented, on average, in 11.1 cases per term. Of the other seventeen justices whose terms on the Court overlapped with Brewer, only Rufus Peckham (10.9) and Edward White (10.7) averaged more than 10 dissents per term. Samuel Blatchford dissented with the least frequency, averaging less than one dissent (0.7) per term during his eleven year career. *Id.* at 148.

27. The Brewer Family Papers contain approximately eighty public addresses and nearly fifty articles, the vast majority of which were written during his two decades on the Supreme Court. K. Morton, Introduction to Brewer Family Papers 2 (1912) (available at Yale University Library in collection of Brewer Family Papers).

28. 16 Va. L. Register 65 (1910). Brewer's penchant for publicly voicing his disagreements with his colleagues was not always appreciated by his brethren on the bench. Oliver Wendell Holmes, Jr., who served with Brewer from 1902 to 1910, observed that while Brewer "was a very pleasant man in private," he "had the itch for public speaking and writing and made me shudder many times. I have heard him speak in public with a curious bitterness about some of the decisions of his brethren that he disagreed with." 1 Holmes-Pollack Letters 160 (M. Howe ed. 1941). In the same letter, written shortly after Brewer's death, Holmes also noted, "I had to remind myself that one should not allow taste to blind one to great qualities, as it is apt to."

In spite of all the reasons that might lead one to expect Brewer to be sympathetic to the claims of African-American citizens, his voting record in civil rights cases hardly justifies such a conclusion. During his twenty year tenure, the Supreme Court handed down decisions in thirty cases involving the civil rights of African Americans.[29] Not surprisingly, the defenders of African-American rights and liberties were generally unsuccessful, prevailing in only five of the thirty cases.[30] Brewer participated in twenty-nine of these cases, and in only six did he side with the

---

Id. Mr. Dooley, the popular creation of Finley Peter Dunne, was also less than enamored with Brewer's proclivity toward public speaking, although he did at least acknowledge his prominence. *See* Dunne, *College and Degrees—Justice at Yale*, in MR. DOOLEY AND THE CHOICE OF LAW 52–57 (1963).

29. *See Marbles v. Creecy*, 215 U.S. 63 (1909); *United States v. Shipp* (II), 214 U.S. 386 (1909); *Thomas v. Texas*, 212 U.S. 278 (1909); *Bailey v. Alabama*, 211 U.S. 452 (1908); *Berea College v. Kentucky*, 211 U.S. 45 (1908); *United States v. Shipp* (I), 203 U.S. 563 (1906); *Hodges v. United States*, 203 U.S. 1 (1906); *Martin v. Texas*, 200 U.S. 217 (1906); *Riggins v. United States*, 199 U.S. 547 (1905); *Clyatt v. United States*, 197 U.S. 207 (1905); *Jones v. Montague*, 194 U.S. 147 (1904); *Giles v. Teasley*, 193 U.S. 146 (1904); *Rogers v. Alabama*, 192 U.S. 226 (1904); *James v. Bowman*, 190 U.S. 528 (1903); *Giles v. Harris*, 189 U.S. 475 (1903); *Brownfield v. South Carolina*, 189 U.S. 426 (1903); *Tarrance v. Florida*, 188 U.S. 519 (1903); *Cummings v. County Board of Education*, 185 U.S. 528 (1903); *Chesapeake & Ohio Ry. v. Kentucky*, 179 U.S. 388 (1900); *Carter v. Texas*, 177 U.S. 442 (1900); *Williams v. Mississippi*, 170 U.S. 213 (1898); *Plessy v. Ferguson*, 163 U.S. 537 (1896); *Murray v. Louisiana*, 163 U.S. 101 (1896); *Charley Smith v. Mississippi*, 162 U.S. 592 (1896); *Mills v. Green*, 159 U.S. 651 (1895); *Andrews v. Swartz*, 156 U.S. 651 (1895); In re *Shibuya Jugiro*, 140 U.S. 291 (1891); *In re Wood*, 140 U.S. 278 (1891); *Louisville, New Orleans, & Texas Ry v. Mississippi*, 133 U.S. 587 (1890).

30. *See United States v. Shipp*, (II), 214 U.S. 386 (1909); *United States v. Shipp*, (I), 203 U.S. 563 (1906); *Riggins v. United States*, 199 U.S. 547 (1905); *Rogers v. Alabama*, 192 U.S. 276 (1904); *Carter v. Texas*, 177 U.S. 442 (1900). One could argue that black Americans gained little from these decisions. *Carter, Rogers,* and *Shipp* (I) dealt with the right of an African-American criminal defendant to present evidence that blacks had been systematically excluded from the jury that had convicted him. In each, the decision of the Court was unanimous. In *Shipp* (II), which addressed the power of federal courts to hold members of lynch mobs and compliant law enforcement officials in contempt of court, a six-judge majority (including Brewer) affirmed the existence of such power. The three dissenters (Edward White, Rufus Peckham, and Joseph McKenna) differed only as to the issue of the power of the federal court to hold a sheriff and his deputies in contempt for their failure or unwillingness to stop the mob. Riggins dealt with the power of federal courts to issue writs of habeas corpus for white members of lynch mobs who had been arrested by federal authorities. The Supreme Court unanimously ruled that this was an improper remedy.

African-American position.[31] On only one occasion did he do so in dissent.[32] Nor was Brewer a quiet participant in the actions of the Fuller Court majority. In seven of the twenty-five cases in which African-American civil rights claims were rejected, Brewer authored the majority opinion.[33] Perhaps the most telling fact of all is that Harlan was willing to concur in only one of Brewer's seven majority opinions.[34]

---

31. As the following breakdown of judicial voting in these cases illustrates, with the exception of Harlan and Day, Brewer's contemporaries exhibited little sympathy for such claims.

Individual Voting, United States Supreme Court Decisions Involving
African-American Civil Rights, 1890–1910

Justice	Yrs. on	Ct. Cases	Pro-Civil Rts.	Pct.
Harlan	1890–1910	29	15	51.7%
Day	1903–1910	17	7	41.2%
Bradley	1890–1892	3	1	33.3%
Moody	1906–1910	4	1	25.0%
Holmes	1902–1910	17	4	23.5%
Brown	1891–1906	22	5	22.7%
McKenna	1898–1910	19	4	21.7%
Brewer	1890–1910	29	6	20.1%
Fuller	1890–1910	30	5	16.7%
Peckham	1895–1909	24	4	16.7%
White	1894–1910	27	4	14.8%
Shiras	1892–1903	10	1	10.0%
Gray	1890–1902	11	1	19.1%
Field	1890–1897	9	0	0.0%
Miller	1890	1	0	0.0%
Jackson	1893–1895	0	0	—
Lurton	1909–1910	0	0	—
Totals	1890–1910	30	5	16.7%

Note: The above percentages are distorted somewhat by the fact that four of the five pro-civil rights decisions were handed down between 1904 and 1909. There is little reason to believe that any of these cases would have been decided differently had they arisen between 1890 and 1904. The percentages for only five justices—Harlan, Day, Brown, Brewer, and Bradley—exceeded that for the Court as a whole during their years on the Supreme Court.

32. Brewer's dissenting opinion came in *Giles v. Harris*, 189 U.S. 475 (1903). Of course, dissents in such cases were extremely rare. Other than Brewer, only four justices ever dissented on behalf of unsuccessful civil rights claimants during Brewer's tenure. Harlan dissented in nine cases: *Bailey v. Alabama*, 211 U.S. 452 (1908); *Berea College v. Kentucky*, 211 U.S. 45 (1908); *Hodges v. United States*, 203 U.S. (1906); *Clyatt v. United States*, 197 U.S. 207 (1905); *Giles v. Teasley*, 198 U.S. 146 (1904); *James v. Bowman*, 190 U.S. 127 (1903); *Giles v. Harris*, 189 U.S. 407 (1903); *Plessy v. Ferguson*, 163 U.S. 537 (1896); *Louisville, New Orleans, & Texas Ry. v. Mississippi*, 133 U.S. 597 (1890). He was joined by William Day in three of these cases: *Hodges v. United States*, 203 U.S. 1 (1906); *Berea College v. Kentucky*, 211 U.S. 45 (1908); *Bailey v. Bowman*, 190 U.S. 528 (1903). He was joined by Henry Brown in two: *Giles v. Harris*, 189 U.S. 475 (1903); *James v. Alabama*, 211 U.S. 45 (1908). He was joined by Joseph Bradley in *Louisville, New Orleans, & Texas Ry. v. Mississippi*, 133 U.S. 587 (1890).

33. See *Berea College v. Kentucky*, 211 U.S. 45 (1908); *Hodges v. United States*, 203 U.S. 1 (1906); *Clyatt v. United States*, 197 U.S. 207 (1905); *Jones v. Montague*, 194 U.S. 147 (1904); *Tarrance v. Florida*, 188 U.S. 519 (1903); and *Louisville, New Orleans & Texas Ry. v. Mississippi*, 133 U.S. 587 (1890).

34. The one case was *Jones v. Montague*, 194 U.S. 147 (1904). In *Tarrance*, Harlan did not attend the oral argument and did not take part in the decision of the case. In the other five cases, he dissented.

From the vantage point of the late twentieth century, Brewer's votes in these cases make him appear highly inconsistent, if not hypocritical. On the one hand, he was able to incorporate a special concern for the civil rights of Chinese into his constitutional views, even though such a view put him at odds with most of his colleagues and with prevailing popular opinion. On the other, he seemed unable to develop a comparable view of the rights of African Americans, even though his off-the-court activities suggested that he would be sympathetic to such a view and even though his friend and colleague Harlan had paved the way for a position years before Brewer joined the Court.[35] Brewer's apparent inability to square his general beliefs with his votes as a Supreme Court Justice is evidence of the intractable nature of the problem posed by the institutionalization of racial segregation in turn-of-the-century America.

Although Berea College was hardly a major corporation, to emphasize its corporate form was to emphasize the power of the state to regulate and to downplay any protections the fourteenth amendment might provide. Certainly, Brewer was correct that states had the power to reserve the right to amend corporate charters. (The recognition of this power dated back to Justice Story's concurrence in the case of Trustees of Dartmouth College[36] and the Constitution of the State of Kentucky specifically reserved this right for the legislature).[37] However, Brewer's opinion, while acknowledging that the act *might* be unconstitutional as applied to individuals, ignored the possibility that the fourteenth amendment placed limitations on this particular power, especially when the state sought to impose racially motivated modifications. As had been the case many times before, Harlan was not persuaded by Brewer's distinctions. In his dissent, joined by Justice William Day, Harlan rejected Brewer's assertion that the statute was severable and went on to argue that the actions of his home state's legislature were "an arbitrary invasion of the rights of liberty and property guaranteed by the fourteenth amendment against hostile state action, and is, therefore, void."[38]

Brewer's opinion in *Berea College* followed the same pattern as all his majority opinions in cases involving the civil rights of African Americans. He affirmed the general rights claims by appellants and even acknowledged that legal remedies might be available in different circumstances, but in the case at hand, he determined that other considerations governed. In his opinion, he scrupulously avoided any reference to *Plessy v. Ferguson*, and he left open the possibility that the fourteenth

35. Harlan had first taken this position in his dissent in the *Civil Rights Cases*, 109 U.S. 3, 26 (1883).

36. *Trustees of Dartmouth College v. Woodward*, 17 U.S. (4 Wheat.) 518 (1819).

37. Section 3 of the Bill of Rights of the 1850 Kentucky Constitution (in force at the time of this case and still in force today) provides that "every grant of a franchise, privilege, or exemption shall remain, subject to revocation, alteration, or amendment." KY. CONST. § 3 (1850).

38. *Berea College v. Kentucky*, 211 U.S. 45, 67–68 (1908). As authority, Harlan cited the substantive due process cases, *Allgeyer v. Louisiana*, 165 U.S. 578 (1897) and *Adair v. United States*, 208 U.S. 161 (1908), decisions in which Brewer had enthusiastically joined.

amendment might protect private individuals who sought integrated schooling. In reality, Brewer's opinion had the practical effect of legitimizing such statutes until well after World War II.

Berea College was the last case dealing with the civil rights of African Americans decided by the United States Supreme Court before Brewer's death in March 1910. From the perspective of modern notions of constitutionally guaranteed civil rights, his record was hardly an impressive one. Of course, the fact that a Northern judge in the late nineteenth century, even one who had held strong abolitionist views in his youth, would adopt an attitude of indifference toward the civil rights of African Americans was not in itself remarkable. Large numbers of formerly anti-slavery Northerners "gave up" on the cause of African-American civil rights in the aftermath of Reconstruction and acquiesced in the restoration of white supremacy in the South. Beginning in the late 1870s, Northern liberals began a steady retreat on the race issue.[39] As white Southerners abandoned earlier pledges to protect the constitutional rights of African Americans, Northern opinion began to emphasize conciliation with the South rather than the defense of civil rights. In the words of historian C. Vann Woodward:

> It was quite common in the 'eighties and 'nineties to find in the *Nation, Harper's Weekly,* the *North American Review,* or the *Atlantic Monthly* Northern liberals and former abolitionists mouthing the shibboleths of white supremacy regarding the Negro's innate inferiority, shiftlessness, and hopeless unfitness for full participation in the white man's civilization. Such expressions doubtless did much to add to the reconciliation of North and South, but they did so at the expense of the Negro.[40]

Although this acquiescence was initially coupled with an understanding that African Americans would not be deprived of their formal legal rights, by the end of the nineteenth century it had come to include an acceptance of legalized segregation and disfranchisement.[41]

While Brewer declined to use his position of authority as a Justice of the United States Supreme Court on behalf of the civil rights of African Americans, his overall views on race did not harden to the degree described by Woodward. In fact, if one looks only at the pronouncements Brewer made off the bench between 1890 and 1910, he comes across as a crusader for equal treatment of the black race at a

---

39. C. WOODWARD, THE STRANGE CAREER OF JIM CROW 69–74 (2d ed. 1966).

40. *Id.* at 70.

41. For other discussions of Northern racial attitudes in the late nineteenth century, *see* G. FREDERICKSON, THE BLACK IMAGE IN THE WHITE MIND: THE DEBATE ON AFRO-AMERICAN CHARACTER AND DESTINY, 1817–1914, at 283–325 (1971); W. NELSON, THE ROOTS OF AMERICAN BUREAUCRACY, 1830–1900, at 62–81, 133–40 (1982); L. SIMPSON, MIND AND THE AMERICAN CIVIL WAR: A MEDITATION ON LOST CAUSES (1989) (for racial views of greater New England culture specifically); *see also* Nelson, *The Impact of the Antislavery Movement Upon Styles of Reasoning in Nineteenth Century America,* 87 HARV. L. REV. 513 (1974).

time when educated Americans, in the North as well as the South, were becoming increasingly persuaded by scientific theories of racial inferiority.[42] Certainly, Brewer never believed that he had abandoned the cause of his youth. In a fourth of July oration in 1893, he spoke glowingly of the importance of the anti-slavery movement, of John Brown, and of the Thirteenth Amendment for their role in helping "personal liberty" become "the universal affirmation of the law."[43] The progress of the black race was a topic he returned to with regularity, and he welcomed the opportunity to address African-American audiences.[44]

How then, does one explain the apparent inconsistency between Brewer's professed support for the rights of African Americans and the lengths to which he went while on the Court to avoid endorsing that position? At least part of the answer can be found in an address on the cause of black education Brewer delivered to the American Missionary Association shortly after the turn of the century. In this address, Brewer took aim at those who used the claim of alleged black inferiority to justify a reduction in support for black education. Lavishing praise on Hampton Institute (which he had recently visited) and Booker T. Washington's Tuskegee Institute and its offspring, Brewer compared African Americans to the Hebrew slaves of the Old Testament who had been delivered out of bondage in Egypt by Moses. It had been necessary for the ancient Hebrews to wander for forty years in the wilderness before reaching the promised land, and, in Brewer's view, only time was required for African Americans to achieve their proper role in society. In pleading the case for continued white support of black education, Brewer proclaimed: "They are here as citizens. Whatever temporary restrictions may be placed upon their approach to the ballot box, the time will come when all barriers will be broken down and they will enjoy everywhere the full rights of citizenship." In the short run,

---

42. *See generally* J. HALLER, OUTCASTS FROM EVOLUTION: SCIENTIFIC ATTITUDES OF RACIAL INFERIORITY 1859–1900 (1971) (noting that Brewer never became as callous to plight of African Americans as his uncles Stephen and Henry Field); C. McCURDY, *Stephen J. Field and the American Judicial Tradition*, in THE FIELDS AND THE LAW 17 (1986) (discussion of racial attitudes of Stephen Field).

43. Address by Justice Brewer at Woodstock, Connecticut (July 4, 1893) (included in collection of Brewer Family Papers).

44. Writings by Brewer that reflect a sympathetic attitude toward race include Brewer, *Address of Mr. Justice Brewer*, in MINUTES OF THE SIXTY-SIXTH ANNUAL MEETING OF THE AMERICAN HOME MISSIONARY SOCIETY 95 (1892); Brewer, *Plain Words on the Crime of Lynching*, 97 LESLIE'S WEEKLY 82 (1903); Brewer, *Address at 30th Anniversary of Hampton Institute*, 35 THE SOUTHERN WORKMAN 359 (1906); Letter to editors of the Paladium (n.d.) (unidentified letter included in collection of Brewer Family Papers); Address Delivered at the Fiftieth Annual Meeting of the American Missionary Association (Nov. 21, 1896) [hereinafter Jubilee Address] (future equality of the races foreseen); Address at the Commencement Exercises of the University of Wisconsin Law School (deploring disfranchisement of African-American voters); Address on the Black Race Delivered to Black Students at an Unidentified College or University (n.d.) (unidentified address included in collection of Brewer Family Papers); Address on the Education of Black People Delivered to an Unidentified Association (n.d.) (unidentified address included in collection of Brewer Family Papers).

however, there were problems that the "race" had to overcome—ignorance, susceptibility to demagoguery, the inability to "distinguish between liberty and license," and the failure to understand "the obligations of morality and purity." Similarly, in an address to African-American college students (probably at Hampton Institute), Brewer rejected the idea that the black race would always be at the bottom of society, comparing the status of African Americans in 1900 with that of Anglo-Saxons in the Roman world of 2000 years before. He emphasized the absolute necessity of self-help and suggested that the "failure" of Reconstruction was related to the fact that "no race is ever lifted up into a higher life simply through outside forces." He also made it clear that he viewed the responsibility for black advancement to lie with the educated men in his audience.[45]

Such statements reveal that although Brewer repudiated the idea that the proper role of government could ever be one of paternalism, his attitude toward African Americans was colored by the very same paternalistic impulse that had led him to accept the legitimacy of separate schools in *Tinnon*. The status of African Americans was essentially that of minor children. Ultimately their entitlement to the full rights of citizenship was not a matter for dispute. However, until they were ready to assume the citizenship's mantle, they, like minor children, might have to accept some limitations on the full exercise of their rights.

On the other hand, Brewer's aversion to governmental paternalism dictated that the responsibility of attaining the right to full citizenship lay with blacks themselves and their white supporters and not with the state. As a practical matter, this meant that African Americans would have to accept the indignities of the emerging "Jim Crow" system. However, according to Brewer, they could take consolation in the fact that their current status was only temporary because their progress as a race was inevitable. The day would come when racial distinctions would be unnecessary. Consequently, while it would be improper for the Supreme Court to afford any special status to their claims, it would also be inappropriate for the Court to imply that African Americans were locked into a permanently inferior position in American society. It was a situation in which the most desirable approach was to evade the issue whenever possible. When the creed of individual liberty clashed with the social reality of race, Brewer chose to take refuge in the very sort of technical niceties that he normally eschewed.

While Brewer should not be exonerated for his failure to acknowledge the meritorious claims of African Americans to constitutional protections, his experience does illuminate how narrow the options were for the men who sat on the Court in the era of "Jim Crow." If Brewer found it impossible to embrace the cause of African-American civil rights in his opinions, then it should not be surprising that

---

45. Address to Black Students of Unidentified College or University by Justice Brewer (n.d.) (unidentified address included in collection of Brewer Family Papers).

his colleagues, who lacked his abolitionist heritage and interest in the race issue, found little problem with the constitutional standard of separate but equal. In this light, the racial egalitarianism of John Marshall Harlan is even more remarkable.

61 *Mississippi Law Journal* 315, 316–22, 357–62.
Copyright © (1991) *Mississippi Law Journal.*
Reprinted with permission of the *Mississippi Law Journal.*

F. Questions and Notes

Through the early 1900s, under its police powers, states separated racial minorities from whites not only in schools and on trains, but in a variety of social activities. From playing dominoes and using the water fountain, to reading the newspaper and using the telephone, states chose a variety of settings to impose racial segregation under the exercise of its police powers. Why do you suppose state officials selected these settings as particularly necessary for racial separation? Was there widespread fear that social interaction could lead to interracial marriage? Such fears were reflected in laws and in media of the day.

XIV. Racial Segregation and Housing

A. Introduction

Peggy Cooper Davis

*Introducing Robert Smalls**

Birth of a Nation, [a 1915 film], is remembered as director D.W. Griffith's masterpiece and as a triumphant advance in cinematic art. But, it is just as much the triumph of Thomas Dixon, Jr., who wrote the screenplay and *The Klansman,* the book on which *Birth of a Nation* was based. Dixon's work was a fervent and effective expression of southern whites' opposition to what they perceived as "Negro domination." His story is best told in John Hope Franklin's powerful and carefully researched essay, *The Birth of a Nation: Propaganda as History.*

Dixon was born in 1864. At the age of eight, his uncle took him to observe a session of the South Carolina legislature. His impression of "ninety-four Negroes, seven native scallywags and twenty-three white men" deliberating in the state house seems to have had "a profound influence on his future career," much of which was driven by a desire to "set the record straight" about Reconstruction. . . .

Dixon went on to be a "superior student and leading debater" at Wake Forest College. He also briefly attended Johns Hopkins, and while he was there he met and

---

* (footnotes omitted).

befriended Woodrow Wilson. Dixon tested his talents as an actor, lawyer, clergyman, essayist, and lecturer before turning to the work for which he was to become famous: a three volume series, *The Leopard's Spots: A Romance of the White Man's Burden*, *The Clansman: An Historical Romance of the Ku Klux Klan*, and *The Traitor: A Story of the Rise and Fall of the Invisible Empire*. *The Clansman* was enormously successful in the South, both as a novel and as a play, and Dixon was moved to expand his audience by use of the cinema. Griffith thought *The Clansman* an insufficiently grandiose title for the film that resulted, and gave it the title The Birth of a Nation. This engrossing depiction of black lechery, ignorance, and vindictiveness overcome by a Klan sworn to end the humiliation and vice of Reconstruction met with substantial protests, but Dixon had a plan.

He first turned to his friend, now President, Woodrow Wilson. Wilson, who is remembered for having destroyed much of the black middle class in Washington, D.C. by firing every non-menial African-American civil servant, was happy to return a favor to an old friend by screening *Birth of a Nation* at the White House. Wilson's response to the film: "It's like writing history with lightning. And my only regret is that it is all so terribly true."

Dixon then arranged a meeting with Chief Justice Edward White to arrange for the film to be shown to members of the United States Supreme Court. The Chief Justice was resistant until he learned that the film was about the Klan. At hearing this news, he "leaned forward in his chair and said, 'I was a member of the Klan, sir.'" The screening was held at the ballroom in Washington's Raleigh Hotel with an audience that included not only members of the Supreme Court, but also members of Congress. Persisting opposition to the film was met with the report that the President, members of the Supreme Court, and members of Congress "had seen the film and liked it. When this was confirmed by a call to the White House, the censors in New York withdrew their objection and the film opened" for a forty-seven week run at the Liberty Theatre.

One critic described an "element of excitement that swept a sophisticated audience like a prairie fire in a high wind." Dixon was gratified. As he wrote to Wilson's secretary during the film's New York run, "[t]he real purpose back of my film was to revolutionize Northern sentiments by a presentation of history that would transform every man in my audience into a good Democrat! . . . Every man who comes out of one of our theatres is a Southern partisan for life." Later, he wrote to Wilson, "[t]his play is transforming the entire population of the North and West into sympathetic Southern voters. There will never be an issue of your segregation policy."

Birth of a Nation helped to set a tone that permeated the culture. Franklin concludes his account of *Birth of a Nation* as propaganda by observing its uncanny similarity to The Tragic Era, a 1929 book by journalist-historian Claude Bowers that stood for more than a generation as the most widely read account of Reconstruction. A 1924 elementary school text commissioned by the American Legion taught that during Reconstruction "nobody knew what to do with the 4 million 'ignorant human beings' who had been suddenly emancipated." As late as the 1960s,

> Alabama fourth-graders, whether white or black, learned that under "ter-
> rible carpetbag rule" during Reconstruction, freed slaves were so ignorant
> that they bought colored sticks from mercenary Northern carpetbaggers
> in the belief that "they could own the land where they put those sticks."
> They also learned that "loyal white men," trying "to protect their families,"
> formed the Ku Klux Klan "to bring back law and order." Never violent, the
> Klansmen protected Alabamans from "bad lawless things," persuaded the
> "lawless men who had taken control of the state" to go back North, and
> persuaded "the Negroes who had been fooled by the . . . carpetbaggers to
> get themselves jobs and settle down to make an honest living."

Disdain for the political leaders of Reconstruction was equally apparent in scholarly literature. There is now a consensus among historians that interpretations of
the work and thought of the Reconstruction's political figures were tainted for several decades by the attitudes that are reflected, and so brilliantly advanced, in *Birth
of a Nation*. As DuBois argued in 1934, and Foner reaffirmed in 1988, United States
historians first told the story of Reconstruction with "prevailing disdain," grounded
in a judgment that Radical Reconstruction was a product of Republican opportunism and vindictiveness and that its implementation of multiracial democracy was
folly in the face of "incompetence by black office holders."[46] As DuBois established in
detail, generations of students and scholars were taught to view Reconstruction as a
frenzy of misrule and corruption. A college history text used in the 1930s reported,
"[I]n the exhausted [Southern] states already amply 'punished' by the desolation of
war, the rule of the Negro and his unscrupulous carpetbagger and scalawag patrons,
was an orgy of extravagance, fraud and disgusting incompetency." Reviewing the
legacy of the historians James Ford Rhodes, John W. Burgess, William A. Dunning,
and their students, DuBois confirmed the conclusion of Will Herberg, a young labor
leader in the 1920s and 1930s:

> The great traditions of . . . Reconstruction are shamelessly repudiated by
> the official heirs of Stevens and Sumner. . . . [H]ardly a single book has
> appeared consistently championing or sympathetically interpreting the
> great ideals of the crusade against slavery, whereas scores and hundreds
> have dropped from the presses in . . . measureless abuse of the Radical fig-
> ures of Reconstruction. The Reconstruction period as . . . the logical cul-
> mination of decades of previous development, has borne the brunt of the
> reaction.

Negative interpretations of Reconstruction had, as Foner puts it, "remarkable
longevity and [a] powerful hold on the popular imagination." A well-received

---

46. Foner, Freedom's Lawmakers, *supra* note 46, at xii.

book of the late 1950s that served as a text in college history courses through-out the country reinforced the understanding of Reconstruction as a process by which narrow political motivation led the Republican Party, acting with "hatred of the white South," "to give the Negro more rights than he possibly could exercise with profit to his advancement," and establish "carpetbag governments built upon Negro suffrage." This influential work concludes that abandonment of the tenets of Radical Reconstruction facilitated a healing process that was necessary and noble, albeit grounded in acceptance of a "credo" of white superiority which the author justified, saying, in the final paragraph of a chapter titled "The Negro Problem Always Ye Have with You," "[o]nce a people admits . . . that a major problem is basically insoluble they have taken the first step in learning how to live with it."

69 *Fordham Law Review* 1695, 1704–8.
Copyright © (2001) *Fordham Law Review.*
Reprinted with permission of the *Fordham Law Review* and
Peggy Cooper Davis.

As the first motion picture, and with President Woodrow Wilson's endorsement, *Birth of a Nation* had a widespread impact. Reconstruction was portrayed as a fail-ure, and blacks were portrayed as devious, destructive, and inferior. The film pro-moted an attitude that blacks were not valid members of society. The result was segregation and discrimination on an even more massive scale.

D.W. Griffith took a similar distortion-of-history approach in terms of his char-acterization of the history of Texas. In 1915, Griffith made a movie called *The Birth of Texas* where he portrayed Mexicans as sex-crazed and blood-thirsty villains who were solely and wrongly responsible for the desire of some Texans to seek indepen-dence from Mexico. Griffith inaccurately portrayed the Battle at Fort Alamo as one solely between innocent whites and evil Mexicans. Moreover, he conveniently left out the role played by Juan Seguin and other Latinos who were involved in the struggle for Texas's independence. Seguin would later become Mayor of San Anto-nio. (*See* Documentary Film, *The Real Story of the Alamo*, History Channel, June 15, 2004.)

Many Americans, including some whites and large numbers of racial minori-ties, refused to live in silence with such distortions of history and racial discrimina-tion. Together they fought back in multi-racial civil rights organizations such as the National Association for the Advancement of Colored People (NAACP) which was founded in 1909.

The NAACP responded to *Birth of a Nation* with its own powerful message, and distributed its own film, also named *Birth of a Nation*, portraying the social envi-ronment during Reconstruction. While their movie was a commercial failure, the title song still resonates with audiences today. The author, James Weldon Johnson, was the first black professor at New York University and one of the founders of the NAACP. His song "Lift every voice and sing" went on to be embraced as the black national anthem.

James Weldon Johnson

Lift Every Voice and Sing

Lift every voice and sing
Till earth and heaven ring,
Ring with the harmonies of liberty;
Let our rejoicing rise
High as the list'ning skies,
Let it resound loud as the rolling sea.

Sing a song full of the faith
That the dark past has taught us,
Sing a song full of the hope
That the present has brought us,
Facing the rising sun of a new day begun
Let us march on till victory is won.

Stony the road we trod,
Bitter the chast'ning rod,
Felt in the days when hope unborn has died;
Yet with a steady beat,
Have not our weary feet,
Come to the place for which our fathers sighed.

We have come, over a way
That with tears has been watered;
We have come, treading our path
Through the blood of the slaughtered,
Out from the gloomy past,
Till now we stand at last
Where the white gleam of our bright star is cast.

God of our weary years
God of our silent tears
Thou who has brought us this far on the way,
Though who has by the might
Led us into the light,
Keep us forever in the path we pray.
Lest our feet stray from the places
Our God where we met thee,
Lest our hearts, drunk with the wine
Of the Lord we forget thee
Shadowed beneath thy hand may we forever stand
True to our God, true to our native land.

B. Background on *Buchanan*

After the Civil War, most blacks lived in the southern states. Due to political and economic developments, including the denial of civil rights and high rates of unemployment, many blacks decided to leave the south for better opportunities in the north where industrialization had created an increased demand for cheap labor in the cities. Blacks from the south and whites who were recent immigrants were attracted to these cities because of the possibility of steady employment. As these blacks sought housing, many whites attempted to restrict their access.

When World War I eliminated America's supply of cheap immigrant labor from Europe, northern businessmen needed substitutes quickly. At the same time, many blacks, confronting social oppression, violence, and the strains of a particularly sluggish agricultural economy, were eager to leave. These factors caused the mass exodus of African Americans, from the South to points north and west, known as the Great Migration. Lasting twenty-five years, it became the largest migratory shift in American history—and it changed black America forever.

These migrants headed for northern industrial areas for many of the same reasons that had induced the immigrants they were brought in to replace—to obtain better educations for their children and higher wages for themselves. But unlike European immigrants, the southern migrants were already Americans—they knew the language, understood America's social customs and class structure, and in a sense were at home in the North before they ever set foot in New York or Detroit or Chicago. Their cultural cognizance, however, provided little relief, as they found that even their fundamental rights, such as property rights, would be denied.

Malaika Adero

Up South

Sixty-one blacks were lynched in 1920, sixty-two in 1921, and so it went in the years before and after. Justice in law enforcement and in the courts was not the reality; it was not even an illusion. By the 1920s, more than four million whites had swelled the ranks of the Ku Klux Klan, and most of them lived and burned their crosses in the South. The North promised relief from this racial terrorism, as well as jobs and lifestyles never available to southern rural blacks. For many of them, the odds of economic growth in the South seemed meager in comparison to northern possibilities . . .

Chicago Defender

Laborers Going North
Chicago Defender News Service

Ensley, Ala., Aug. 25.—The men on the railroad here are thinking seriously of going north to work. The railroads are paying white men 90 cents per day more than they pay members of the Race. Such a discrimination is being felt and the time has come for them to leave and go north, where labor pay is higher and no discrimination in salary. The northern agents for labor will find this a splendid field to find workmen.

Opportunity Magazine

October 1923
Why They Come North

As to Negro migration, the Negro realizes that wages in the North are higher, but he also realizes that living conditions are equally high, which offsets any profit to himself. Can we conscientiously say that it is the dollar which makes him crave for the North? Emphatically no. The wages of the North have always been higher. . . .

The Negro has played well his part, and is it not fair that he should expect better pay, better working and living conditions, and the full rights of loyal citizens?

Here is why he leaves the South: Unjust treatment, failure to secure a square deal in the courts, taxation without representation, denial of the right to vote thru the subterfuge of the white primary, no representation in any form of government, poor schools, unjust pay for and division of crops, insulting of women without any redress, and public torture.

The Negro longs for free air, happiness and all that goes to make for a full and free citizenship—and that brings him North.—C. Otis of Ithaca, N.Y., in the N.Y. Tribune.

Augusta, Georgia

May 12, 1917

Dear Sir:

Just for a little information from you I would like to know wheather or not I could get in tuch with some good people to work for with a firm because things is afful hear in the south let me here from you soon as possible what ever you do don't publish my name in your paper but I think peple as a race ought to look out for one another as Christians friends I am a schuffur and I can't make a living for my family with small pay and the peple is getting so bad with us black peple down south hear. now if you ever help your race now is the time to help me to get my family away. food stuf is so high. I will look for answer by return mail, don't publish my name in your paper but let me her from you at once.

(Signed) ONE OF THE NEGRO RACE.

Up South: Stories, Studies, and Letters of this
Century's African-American Migrations 17–18, 59, 112–14.
Copyright © (1993) New Press.
Reprinted with permission of New Press.

A. Leon Higginbotham, Jr., F. Michael Higginbotham, and S. Sandile Ngcobo

De Jure *Housing Segregation in the United States and South Africa: The Difficult Pursuit for Racial Justice*

When NAACP counsel Moorfield Storey of Boston rose to argue *Buchanan v. Warley* before the Supreme Court on April 10, 1916—the year in which Woodrow Wilson sought re-election—he was arguing in a nation where the hopes of blacks for equal citizenship had been crushed for decades. From the White House to the state house, the question posed by Frederick Douglass some years earlier remained unanswered: "[Can] American justice, American liberty, American civilization, American law, and American Christianity . . . be made to include and protect alike and forever all American citizens in the rights which have been guaranteed to them by the organic and fundamental laws of the land?"

From the presidency of Rutherford B. Hayes through that of Woodrow Wilson, the White House gave no assurance of equal treatment and racial justice. Presidents and governors, like Congress and state legislatures, were either patently hostile or coldly unsympathetic to the muted and cautious requests by blacks for some slight improvement of their lot.[47]

While blacks were clearly at the top of the statistical data as lynching victims, they were also clearly at the bottom of attainment in income, literacy, mortality, and housing. During this era, blacks were restricted to the most menial jobs. With only the rarest of exceptions the professional, managerial, secretarial, and "white collar" jobs were unreachable for even the most talented and competent blacks. Indicative of the racial climate and societal perception of blacks, Atlanta required Jim Crow Bibles in the courtroom; Alabama forbade blacks to play checkers with whites; and Oklahoma even segregated its telephone booths.

This was the era poignantly described by Professor Rayford Logan as "The Betrayal of the Negro." This was also the era which provided the setting in which *Buchanan* was presented before the United States Supreme Court.

1990 *University of Illinois Law Review* 763, 848–51 (1990).
Copyright © (1990) A. Leon Higginbotham, Jr. and F. Michael Higginbotham.
Reprinted with permission of Evelyn Brooks Higginbotham and
F. Michael Higginbotham.

---

47. Even the false rumor that a black had been present at an official White House function was sufficient to drive President Cleveland into a frenzy. G. SINKLER, THE RACIAL ATTITUDES OF AMERICAN PRESIDENTS FROM ABRAHAM LINCOLN TO THEODORE ROOSEVELT 270 (1971).

C. *Buchanan v. Warley*, 245 U.S. 60 (1917)

S.S. Field, by leave of court, filed a brief on behalf of the Mayor and City Council of Baltimore as *amicus curiae*.

W. Ashbie Hawkins, by leave of court, filed a brief on behalf of the Baltimore Branch of the National Association for the Advancement of Colored People as *amicus curiae*.

Frederick W. Lehmann and *Mr. Wells H. Blodgett*, by leave of court, filed a brief as *amici curiae*.

Alfred E. Cohen, by leave of court, filed a brief as *amicus curiae*.

Chilton Atkinson, by leave of court, filed a brief on behalf of the United Welfare Association of St. Louis as *amicus curiae*.

H. R. Pollard, by leave of court, filed a brief on behalf of the City of Richmond, Virginia, as *amicus curiae*.

Wells H. Blodgett, Charles Nagel, James A. Seddon, Selden P. Spencer, Sidney F. Andrews, W. L. Sturdevani, Percy Werner, Everett W. Pattison and *Joseph Wheless*, by leave of court, filed a brief as *amici curiae*.

1. Facts

Justice DAY delivered the opinion of the Court.

Buchanan, plaintiff in error, brought an action in the Chancery Branch of Jefferson Circuit Court of Kentucky for the specific performance of a contract for the sale of certain real estate situated in the City of Louisville at the corner of Thirty-seventh Street and Pflanz Avenue. The offer in writing to purchase the property contained a proviso:

"It is understood that I am purchasing the above property for the purpose of having erected thereon a house which I propose to make my residence, and it is a distance part of this agreement that I shall not be required to accept a deed to the above property or to pay for said property unless I have the right under the laws of the State of Kentucky and the City of Louisville to occupy said property as a residence." This offer was accepted by the plaintiff.

To the action for specific performance the defendant, by way of answer, set up the condition above set forth, that he is a colored person, and that on the block of which the lot in controversy is a part, there are ten residences, eight of which at the time of the making of the contract were occupied by white people, and only two (those nearest the lot in question) were occupied by colored people, and that under and by virtue of the ordinance of the City of Louisville, approved May 11, 1914, he would not be allowed to occupy the lot as a place of residence.

In reply to this answer the plaintiff set up, among other things, that the ordinance was in conflict with the Fourteenth Amendment to the Constitution of the

United States, and hence no defense to the action for specific performance of the contract.

In the court of original jurisdiction in Kentucky, and in the Court of Appeals of that state, the case was made to turn upon the constitutional validity of the ordinance. The Court of Appeals of Kentucky, 165 Ky. 559, 177 S. W. 472, Ann. Cas. 1917B, 149, held the ordinance valid and of itself a complete defense to the action.

The title of the ordinance is: "An ordinance to prevent conflict and ill-feeling between the white and colored races in the city of Louisville, and to preserve the public peace and promote the general welfare, by making reasonable provisions requiring, as far as practicable, the use of separate blocks, for residences, places of abode, and places of assembly by white and colored people respectively."

By the first section of the ordinance it is made unlawful for any colored person to move into and occupy as a residence, place of abode, or to establish and maintain as a place of public assembly any house upon any block upon which a greater number of houses are occupied as residences, places of abode, or places of public assembly by white people than are occupied as residences, places of abode, or places of public assembly by colored people.

Section 2 provides that it shall be unlawful for any white person to move into and occupy as a residence, place of abode, or to establish and maintain as a place of public assembly any house upon any block upon which a greater number of houses are occupied as residences, places of abode or places of public assembly by colored people than are occupied as residences, places of abode or places of public assembly by white people.

Section 4 provides that nothing in the ordinance shall affect the location of residences, places of abode or places of assembly made previous to its approval; that nothing contained therein shall be construed so as to prevent the occupancy of residences, places of abode or places of assembly by white or colored servants or employee of occupants of such residences, places of abode or places of public assembly on the block on which they are so employed, and that nothing therein contained shall be construed to prevent any person who, at the date of the passage of the ordinance, shall have acquired or possessed the right to occupy any building as a residence, place of abode or place of assembly from exercising such a right; that nothing contained in the ordinance shall prevent the owner of any building, who when the ordinance became effective, leased, rented, or occupied it as a residence, place of abode or place of public assembly for colored persons, from continuing to rent, lease or occupy such residence, place of abode or place of assembly for such persons, if the owner shall so desire; but if such house should, after the passage of the ordinance, be at any time leased, rented or occupied as a residence, place of abode or place of assembly for white persons, it shall not thereafter be used for colored persons, if such occupation would then be a violation of section 1 of the ordinance; that nothing contained in the ordinance shall prevent the owner of any building, who when the ordinance became effective, leased, rented or occupied it as a residence, place of abode, or place of assembly for white persons from continuing to rent, lease or occupy such residence, place of abode or place of assembly for such purpose, if the owner shall so desire, but if such household, after the passage of the ordinance, be at any time leased, rented or occupied as a residence, place of abode or place of assembly for colored persons, then it shall not thereafter be used for white persons, if such occupation would then be a violation of section 2 thereof.

2. Opinion

a. Standing

The objection is made that this writ of error should be dismissed because the alleged denial of constitutional rights involves only the rights of colored persons, and the plaintiff in error is a white person. This court has frequently held that while an unconstitutional act is no law, attacks upon the validity of laws can only be entertained when made by those whose rights are directly affected by the law or ordinance in question. Only such persons, it has been settled can be heard to attack the constitutionality of the law or ordinance. But this case does not run counter to that principle.

The property here involved was sold by the plaintiff in error, a white man, on the terms stated, to a colored man; the action for specific performance was entertained in the court below, and in both courts the plaintiff's right to have the contract enforced was denied solely because of the effect of the ordinance making it illegal for a colored person to occupy the lot sold. But for the ordinance the state courts would have enforced the contract, and the defendant would have been compelled to pay the purchase price and take a conveyance of the premises. The right of the plaintiff in error to sell his property was directly involved and necessarily impaired because it was held in effect that he could not sell the lot to a person of color who was willing and ready to acquire the property, and had obligated himself to take it. This case does not come within the class wherein this court has held that where one seeks to avoid the enforcement of a law or ordinance he must present a grievance of his own, and not rest the attack upon the alleged violation of another's rights. In this case the property rights of the plaintiff in error are directly and necessarily involved. *See Truax v. Raich*, 239 U. S. 33, 38, 36 Sup. Ct. 7, 60 L. Ed. 131, L. R. A. 1916D, 545, Ann. Cas. 1917B, 283.

b. Police Powers

We pass then to a consideration of the case upon its merits. This ordinance prevents the occupancy of a lot in the City of Louisville by a person of color in a block where the greater number of residences are occupied by white persons; where such a majority exists colored persons are excluded. This interdiction is based wholly upon color; simply that and nothing more. In effect, premises situated as are those in question in the so-called white block are effectively debarred from sale to persons of color, because if sold they cannot be occupied by the purchaser nor by him sold to another of the same color.

This drastic measure is sought to be justified under the authority of the state in the exercise of the police power. It is said such legislation tends to promote the public peace by preventing racial conflicts; that it tends to maintain racial purity; that it prevents the deterioration of property owned and occupied by white people, which deterioration, it is contended, is sure to follow the occupancy of adjacent premises by persons of color.

The authority of the State to pass laws in the exercise of the police power, having for their object the promotion of the public health, safety and welfare is very broad as has been affirmed in numerous and recent decisions of this court. Furthermore the exercise of this power, embracing nearly all legislation of a local character is not to be interfered with by the courts where it is within the scope of legislative authority and the means adopted reasonably tend to accomplish a lawful purpose. But it is equally well established that the police power, broad as it is, cannot justify the passage of a law or ordinance which runs counter to the limitations of the Federal Constitution; that principle has been so frequently affirmed in this court that we need not stop to cite the cases.

c. Denial of Property

The Federal Constitution and laws passed within its authority are by the express terms of that instrument made the supreme law of the land. The Fourteenth Amendment protects life, liberty, and property from invasion by the states without due process of law. Property is more than the mere thing which a person owns. It is elementary that it includes the right to acquire, use, and dispose of it. The Constitution protects these essential attributes of property. *Holden v. Hardy*, 169 U. S. 366, 391, 18 Sup. Ct. 383, 42 L. Ed. 780. Property consists of the free use, enjoyment, and disposal of a person's acquisitions without control or diminution save by the law of the land. 1 *Blackstone's Commentaries* (Cooley's Ed.) 127.

True it is that dominion over property springing from ownership is not absolute and unqualified. The disposition and use of property may be controlled in the exercise of the police power in the interest of the public health, convenience, or welfare. Harmful occupations may be controlled and regulated. Legitimate business may also be regulated in the interest of the public. Certain uses of property may be confined to portions of the municipality other than the resident district, such as livery stables, brickyards and the like, because of the impairment of the health and comfort of the occupants of neighboring property. Many illustrations might be given from the decisions of this court, and other courts, of this principle, but these cases do not touch the one at bar.

The concrete question here is: May the occupancy, and, necessarily, the purchase and sale of property of which occupancy is an incident, be inhibited by the states, or by one of its municipalities, solely because of the color of the proposed occupant of the premises? That one may dispose of his property, subject only to the control of lawful enactments curtailing that right in the public interest, must be conceded.

The question now presented makes it pertinent to inquire into the constitutional right of the white man to sell his property to a colored man, having in view the legal status of the purchaser and occupant. . . .

The defendant in error insists that *Plessy v. Ferguson*, 163 U.S. 537, is controlling in principle in favor of the judgment of the court below. In that case this court held that a provision of a statute of Louisiana requiring railway companies carrying passengers to provide in their coaches equal but separate accommodations for the white and colored races did not run counter to the provisions of the Fourteenth Amendment. It is to be observed that in that case there was no attempt to deprive persons of color of transportation in the coaches of the public carrier, and the express requirements were for equal though separate accommodations for the white and colored races. In *Plessy v. Ferguson*, classification of accommodation was permitted upon the basis of equality for both races.

In the *Berea College Case*, 211 U.S. 45, a state statute was sustained in the courts of Kentucky, which, while permitting the education of white persons and Negroes in different localities by the same incorporated institution, prohibited their attendance at the same place, and in this court the judgment of the Court of Appeals of Kentucky was affirmed solely upon the reserved authority of the legislature of Kentucky to alter, amend, or repeal charters of its own corporations, and the question here involved was neither discussed nor decided.

In *Carey v. City of Atlanta*, 143 Georgia, 192, the Supreme Court of Georgia, holding an ordinance, similar in principle to the one herein involved, to be invalid, dealt with *Plessy v. Ferguson*, and *The Berea College Case*, in language so apposite that we quote a portion of it:

"In each instance the complaining person was afforded the opportunity to ride, or to attend institutions of learning, or afforded the thing of whatever nature to which in the particular case he was entitled. The most that was done was to require him as a member of a class to conform with reasonable rules in regard to the separation of the races." In none of them was he denied the right to use, control, or dispose of his property, as in this case. Property of a person, whether as a member of a class or as an individual, cannot be taken without due process of law.

As we have seen, this court has held laws valid which separated the races on the basis of equal accommodations in public conveyances, and courts of high authority have held enactments lawful which provide for separation in the public schools of white and colored pupils where equal privileges are given. But in view of the rights secured by the Fourteenth Amendment to the federal Constitution such legislation must have its limitations, and cannot be sustained where the exercise of authority exceeds the restraints of the Constitution. We think these limitations are exceeded in laws and ordinances of the character now before us.

It is the purpose of such enactments, and, it is frankly avowed it will be their ultimate effect, to require by law, at least in residential districts, the compulsory separation of the races on account of color. Such action is said to be essential to the maintenance of the purity of the races, although it is to be noted in the ordinance under consideration that the employment of colored servants in white families is permitted, and nearby residences of colored persons not coming within the blocks, as defined in the ordinance, are not prohibited.

The case presented does not deal with an attempt to prohibit the amalgamation of the races. The right which the ordinance annulled was the civil right of a white man to dispose of his property if he saw fit to do so to a person of color and of a colored person to make such disposition to a white person.

It is urged that this proposed segregation will promote the public peace by preventing race conflicts. Desirable as this is, and important as is the preservation of the public peace, this aim cannot be accomplished by laws or ordinances which deny rights created or protected by the Federal Constitution.

It is said that such acquisitions by colored persons depreciate property owned in the neighborhood by white persons. But property may be acquired by undesirable white neighbors or put to disagreeable though lawful uses with like results.

3. Holding

We think this attempt to prevent the alienation of the property in question to a person of color was not a legitimate exercise of the police power of the state, and is in direct violation of the fundamental law enacted in the Fourteenth Amendment of the Constitution preventing state interference with property rights except by due process of law. That being the case, the ordinance cannot stand.

Reaching this conclusion it follows that the judgment of the Kentucky Court of Appeals must be reversed, and the cause remanded to that court for further proceedings not inconsistent with this opinion.

D. Commentary on *Buchanan*

In *Buchanan,* the Supreme Court began to dismantle state-sanctioned segregation. By striking down racial residential segregation ordinances as unreasonable exercises of the police powers and violations of the Due Process Clause, the Court took its first step in ending segregation. While the holding was narrow, applying only to property rights, *Buchanan* was significant in that it prevented state legislatures from overtly confining blacks to the most undesirable living areas.

Donald E. Lively
The Constitution and Race

Although cast as a regulation to maintain public peace and promote the general welfare, the Court found it a "direct violation of the fundamental law enacted in the 14th Amendment of the Constitution preventing state interference with property rights except by due process of law." Unlike in the *Berea College* case, in which blacks were not denied an education, the Court apprehended in *Buchanan* the deprivation of a fundamental right.

The *Buchanan* decision presented a significant irony and disclosed how substantially the Fourteenth Amendment had been transformed since its origin. Seminal jurisprudence had emphasized the amendment's concern with affording "a race recently emancipated, a race that through many generations had been held in slavery, all the civil rights that the superior race enjoy." Soon after the *Plessy* decision, the Court developed and amplified the Fourteenth Amendment's meaning in a context entirely unrelated to race. Resultant court decisions enunciated principles of general economic liberty in expansive terms, as doctrine pertaining to the amendment's central concern cramped and contracted.

In *Allgeyer v. Louisiana*, one year after the *Plessy* decision, the Court advanced substantive due process theory to defeat a state law prohibiting the operation of insurance policies not issued in compliance with legislative requirements. Construing the Fourteenth Amendment as a source of substantive rights and liberties, the Court found that due process guaranteed that a person may use "all his faculties . . . [and was] free to use them in all lawful ways." The *Allgeyer* decision extended previously qualified Fourteenth Amendment concepts, jurisprudentially introduced in the *Slaughter-House* dissents, to circumstances unrelated to race. It prefaced the *Lochner* era of substantive due process review which, although now criticized as an exercise in rampant activism, nonetheless offered a convoluted way of finding some segregation unreasonable. The Court's decision in *Buchanan* reflected a sense of constitutional offense premised less on the law's racial significance than on its invasion of general contractual liberty. Such animation of the due process guarantee in substantive fashion, driven by rights designated by the judiciary rather than the Constitution itself, was the essence of Lochnerism.

In *Lochner v. New York* itself, the Court elevated liberty of contract to the status of a fundamental right and for three decades persistently invoked it to thwart economic and social welfare legislation. The episode is widely regarded as a primary example of unrestrained subjectivism and judicial overreaching. The legacy of substantive due process analysis is so profoundly negative that, half a century after its repudiation, contemporary efforts to breathe life into the Fourteenth Amendment almost invariably engender allegations of Lochnerism. Close attention to general economic liberty was especially dubious insofar as doctrine simultaneously retreated from the Fourteenth Amendment's original imperatives. The Supreme Court itself has repudiated Lochnerism on the grounds that the legitimacy of judicial review is contingent upon precepts clearly tied to constitutional text or design. Even assuming the misdirected nature of Fourteenth Amendment analysis, invalidation of officially mandated segregation in *Buchanan* was connected albeit inartfully to the amendment's original but qualified concern with opportunity for material self-development. The opinion relied upon principles of embellishment and convenience to reach the same result that would have been dictated by attention to obvious design. Such analytical circuitry thus offered a paradoxical example of how distorted doctrine had become.

.... [c]ontractual liberty initially was regarded as an essential incident of citizenship. Considerations of economic freedom which influenced original understanding of civil rights, however, were consumed by more expansive and nonspecific notions of marketplace liberty. As the Supreme Court moved into the twentieth century, its composition was influenced significantly by President Harrison, Cleveland and Taft, who were dedicated to advancing laissez-faire principles and used the judicial appointment process to facilitate broad notions of economic freedom. Consistent with such inspiration, the Court tended vigorously to marketplace freedom and interested itself in racial discrimination only when it intersected that liberty.

Contemporary criticism of Lochnerism focused less on its deviation from racially significant concerns than upon its function in achieving convenient results and impairing the operation of competing and democratically preferred philosophies of governance. The *Lochner* decision itself, which found regulation of working hours at odds with liberty of contract, identified no real nexus to the Fourteenth Amendment's inspiring concerns. In asserting that it would not "substitut[e] the judgment of the court for that of the legislature," the Court suggested a standard of review akin to the deferential criteria of *Plessy*. The transparency of its claim and constitutional double standard were revealed, however, by the further pronouncement that "[w]e do not believe in the soundness of the views which uphold this law."

The Constitution and Race 95–96.
Copyright © (1992) Donald E. Lively.
Reprinted with permission of Donald E. Lively.

E. Questions and Notes

In 1968, the Kerner Commission identified housing segregation as one of the reasons for the vast economic hardships that blacks endure. The Commission concluded that in the black ghettos "segregation" and poverty converge on the young to destroy opportunity and enforce failure. Crime, drug addiction, dependency on welfare, and bitterness and resentment against society in general and white society in particular are the result.[48] Do you agree with the Kerner Commission that housing segregation is one of the causes of black alienation?

The Kerner Commission's identification of the causes of black alienation implies that some racial segregation is less harmful than others. Do you agree with this implication? If so, which is worse—racial segregation in housing or in education?

---

48. National Advisory Commission on Civil Disorders 5 (1968).

What are the strengths and weaknesses of the *Buchanan* decision? The argument in *Buchanan* was based on due process rights; could you use an equal protection argument in *Buchanan* as well?

XV. Racial Segregation and Interstate Commerce

A. Introduction

While the state's regulation of race relations under its police powers was interpreted broadly in *Berea College*, where such regulation involved transportation out of state, it had the potential to impact interstate commerce in general. Since the early twentieth century, the Supreme Court interpreted the meaning of interstate commerce broadly. Just as the Supreme Court interpreted the Due Process Clause of the Fourteenth Amendment as limiting the *Plessy* doctrine, civil rights attorneys were optimistic that the Commerce Clause might be similarly interpreted, and could be used to mitigate segregation in interstate commerce.

B. Background on *Morgan*

Since the 1896 ruling in *Plessy*, racial segregation in transportation was implemented in most southern states. Numerous blacks had been segregated just as Homer Plessy had been. In 1937, Congressman Arthur Mitchell, the first African American in Congress since Reconstruction, was removed from the first-class train car to the car reserved for blacks. Mitchell sued under an anti-discrimination provision of the Interstate Commerce Act that he had helped to pass. Mitchell won his suit,[49] and he encouraged others to resist such segregation practices.

C. *Morgan v. Commonwealth of Virginia,* 328 U.S. 373 (1946)

William H. Hastie, of Washington, D.C., and *Thurgood Marshall*, of New York City, for appellant. With them on the brief was *Leon A. Ransom*.

Abram P. Staples, Attorney General of Virginia, argued the cause and filed a brief for appellee.

Briefs were filed as *amici curiae* by *Gregory Hankin*, *Osmond K. Fraenkel* and *Arthur Garfield Hays* for the American Civil Liberties Union, and by *Harold A. Stevens* for the Workers Defense League, in support of appellant.

---

49. *Mitchell v. United States*, 313 U.S. 80 (1941).

1. Facts

Justice REED delivered the opinion of the Court.

This appeal brings to this Court the question of the constitutionality of an act of Virginia,[50] which requires all passenger motor vehicle carriers, both interstate and intrastate, to separate without discrimination the white and colored passengers in their motor buses so that contiguous seats will not be occupied by persons of different races at the same time. A violation of the requirement of separation by the carrier is a misdemeanor. The driver or other person in charge is directed and required to increase or decrease the space allotted to the respective races as may be necessary or proper and may require passengers to change their seats to comply with the allocation. The operator's failure to enforce the provisions is made a misdemeanor.

These regulations were applied to an interstate passenger, this appellant, on a motor vehicle then making an interstate run or trip. According to the statement of fact by the Supreme Court of Appeals of Virginia, appellant, who is a Negro, was traveling on a motor common carrier, operating under the above-mentioned statute, from Gloucester County, Virginia, through the District of Columbia, to Baltimore, Maryland, the destination of the bus. There were other passengers, both white and colored. On her refusal to accede to a request of the driver to move to a back seat, which was partly occupied by other colored passengers, so as to permit the seat that she vacated to be used by white passengers, a warrant was obtained and appellant was arrested, tried and convicted of a violation of Section 4097dd of the Virginia Code.[51]

---

50. Virginia Code of 1942, §§ 4097z to 4097dd inclusive. The sections are derived from an act of General Assembly of Virginia of 1930. Acts of Assembly, Va. 1930, p. 343.

51. "4097dd. Violation by passengers; misdemeanor; ejection.—All persons who fail while on any motor vehicle carrier, to take and occupy the seat or seats or other space assigned to them by the driver, operator or other person in charge of such vehicle, or by the person whose duty it is to take up tickets or collect fares from passengers therein, or who fail to obey the directions of any such driver, operator or other person in charge, as aforesaid, to change their seats from time to time as occasions require, pursuant to any lawful rule, regulation or custom in force by such lines as to assigning separate seats or other space to white and colored persons, respectively, having been first advised of the fact of such regulation and requested to conform thereto, shall be deemed guilty of a misdemeanor, and upon conviction thereof shall be fined not less than five dollars nor more than twenty-five dollars for each offense. Furthermore, such persons may be ejected from such vehicle by any driver, operator or person in charge of said vehicle, or by any police officer or other conservator of the peace; and in case such persons ejected shall have paid their fares upon said vehicle, they shall not be entitled to the return of any part of same. For the refusal of any such passenger to abide by the request of the person in charge of said vehicle as aforesaid, and his consequent ejection from said vehicle, neither the driver, operator, person in charge, owner, manager nor bus company operating said vehicle shall be liable for damages in any court."

2. Opinion

a. Undue Burden

This Court frequently must determine the validity of state statutes that are attacked as unconstitutional interferences with the national power over interstate commerce. This appeal presents that question as to a statute that compels racial segregation of interstate passengers in vehicles moving interstate.

The precise degree of a permissible restriction on state power cannot be fixed generally or indeed not even for one kind of state legislation, such as taxation or health or safety. There is a recognized abstract principle, however, that may be taken as a postulate for testing whether particular state legislation in the absence of action by Congress is beyond state power. This is that the state legislation is invalid if it unduly burdens that commerce in matters where uniformity is necessary—necessary in the constitutional sense of useful in accomplishing a permitted purpose. Where uniformity is essential for the functioning of commerce, a state may not interpose its local regulation. Too true it is that the principle lacks in precision. Although the quality of such a principle is abstract, its application to the facts of a situation created by the attempted enforcement of a statute brings about a specific determination as to whether or not the statute in question is a burden on commerce. Within the broad limits of the principle, the cases turn on their own facts.

In the field of transportation, there have been a series of decisions which hold that where Congress has not acted, and although the state statute affects interstate commerce, a state may validly enact legislation which has predominantly only a local influence on the course of commerce.[52] It is equally well settled that, even

52. Statutes or orders dealing with safety of operations: *Smith v. Alabama*, 124 U.S. 465, 8 S.Ct. 564, 31 L.Ed. 508 (Alabama statute requiring an examination and license of train engineers before operating in the state); *Nashville, etc., Railway Co. v. Alabama*, 128 U.S. 96, 9 S.Ct. 28, 32 L.Ed. 352 (Statute requiring examination of railroad employees as to vision and color blindness); *New York, N.H. & H. Railroad Co. v. New York*, 165 U.S. 628, 17 S.Ct. 418, 41 L.Ed. 853 (N.Y. statute forbidding the use of furnaces or stoves in passenger cars and requiring guard-posts on railroad bridges); *Erb v. Morasch*, 177 U.S. 584, 20 S.Ct. 819, 44 L.Ed. 897 (Municipal ordinance limiting speed of trains in city to 6 miles an hour); *Atlantic Coast Line R. Co. v. Georgia*, 234 U.S. 280, 34 S.Ct. 829, 58 L. Ed. 1312 (Georgia statute requiring electric headlights on locomotives); *Morris v. Duby*, 274 U.S. 135, 47 S.Ct. 548, 71 L.Ed. 966 (Weight restrictions on motor carriers imposed by order of Oregon highway commission); *Sproles v. Binford*, 286 U.S. 374, 52 S.Ct. 581, 76 L.Ed. 1167 (Size and weight restrictions on trucks imposed by Texas statute); *South Carolina State Hwy. Dept. v. Barnwell Bros.*, 303 U.S. 177, 625, 58 S.Ct. 510, 82 L.Ed. 734 (Statute restricting weight and size of motor carriers); *Maurer v. Hamilton*, 309 U.S. 598, 60 S. Ct. 726, 84 L.Ed. 969, 135 A.L.R. 1347 (Penna. statute forbidding the use of its highways to any vehicle carrying any other vehicle over the head of the operator of the vehicle); *Terminal R. Ass'n v. Brotherhood of Railroad Trainmen*, 318 U.S. 1, 63 S.Ct. 420, 87 L.Ed. 571 (Illinois statute requiring cabooses on freight trains).

Statutes or orders requiring local train service: *Gladson v. Minnesota*, 166 U.S. 427, 17 S.Ct. 627, 41 L.Ed. 1064 (State statute requiring intrastate train to stop at county seat to take on and discharge passengers); *Lake Shore & M.S. Railway Co. v. Ohio*, 173 U.S. 285, 19 S.Ct. 465, 43 L.Ed. 702 (Statute requiring three trains daily, if so many are run, to stop at each city containing over

where Congress has not acted, state legislation or a final court order is invalid which materially affects interstate commerce.[53] Because the Constitution puts the ultimate power to regulate commerce in Congress, rather than the states, the degree of state legislation's interference with that commerce may be weighed by federal courts to determine whether the burden makes the statute unconstitutional.[54] The courts could not invalidate federal legislation for the same reason because Congress, within the limits of the Fifth Amendment, has authority to burden commerce if that seems to it a desirable means of accomplishing a permitted end.

3,000 inhabitants as applied to interstate trains); *Atlantic Coast Line R. Co. v. North Carolina Corp. Comm.*, 206 U.S. 1, 27 S.Ct. 585, 51 L.Ed. 933, 11 Ann.Cas. 398 (Order regulating train service, particularly requiring train to permit connection with through trains at junction point); *Missouri Pac. R. Co. v. Kansas*, 216 U.S. 262, 30 S.Ct. 330, 54 L.Ed. 472 (Order directing the operation of intrastate passenger train service over specified route).

Statutes dealing with employment of labor—full crew laws: *Chicago, R.I. & P.R. Co. v. Arkansas*, 219 U.S. 453, 31 S.Ct. 275, 55 L.Ed. 290 (Arkansas full crew law applied to interstate trains); *St. Louis I.M. & S.R. Co. v. Arkansas*, 240 U.S. 518, 36 S.Ct. 443, 60 L.Ed. 776 (Arkansas full crew laws applied to switching crews); *Missouri Pacific R. Co. v. Norwood*, 283 U.S. 249, 51 S.Ct. 458, 75 L.Ed. 1010 (Arkansas full crew laws applied to freight and switching crews.).

53. Statutes or orders dealing with safety of operations: *Kansas City Southern R. Co. v. Kaw Valley Drainage Dist.*, 233 U.S. 75, 34 S.Ct. 564, 58 L.Ed. 857 (Order requiring railroad to remove its bridges over river for flood control purposes); *South Covington & C. St. R. Co. v. Covington*, 235 U.S. 537, 35 S.Ct. 158, 59 L.Ed. 350, L.R.A.1915F, 792 (Ordinances regulating the number of passengers to be carried in, the number of cars to be run and the temperature of an interstate street railway car invalid; those requiring rails on front and rear platform, ventilation and cleaning valid); *Seaboard Air Line R. Co. v. Blackwell*, 244 U.S. 310, 37 S.Ct. 640, 61 L.Ed. 1160, L.R.A.1917F, 1184 (Georgia Blow Post Law requiring train to blow whistle and slow down almost to a stop at each grade crossing where numerous grade crossings were involved. *Cf. Southern Railway Co. v. King*, 217 U.S. 524, 30 S.Ct. 594, 54 L.Ed. 868 where answer held insufficient to permit proof of burden of the statute on interstate commerce); *Southern Pacific Co. v. Arizona*, 325 U.S. 761, 65 S.Ct. 1515, 89 L.Ed. 1915 (Statute limiting number of cars in freight train to 70 and passenger cars to 14.)

Statutes or orders requiring local train service: *Illinois Central Railroad Co. v. Illinois*, 163 U.S. 142, 16 S.Ct. 1096, 41 L.Ed. 107 (Statute applied to require fast mail train to detour from main line in order to stop at station for the taking on and discharge of passengers); *Cleveland R. Co. v. Illinois*, 177 U.S. 514, 20 S.Ct. 722, 44 L.Ed. 868 (Ill. statute requiring interstate train to stop at each station); *Mississippi R. Comm. v. Illinois Cent. R. Co.*, 203 U.S. 335, 27 S.Ct. 90, 51 L.Ed. 209 (Order of commission requiring interstate train to stop at small town); *Atlantic Coast Line Co. v. Wharton*, 207 U.S. 328, 28 S.Ct. 121, 52 L.Ed. 230 (S.C. statute and railroad commission order requiring interstate train to stop at small town); *St. Louis S.W.R. Co. v. Arkansas*, 217 U.S. 136, 30 S.Ct. 476, 54 L.Ed. 698, 29 L.R.A., N.S., 802 (Statute and order requiring delivery of freight cars to local shippers); *Herndon v. Chicago, Rock Island & P.R. Co.*, 218 U.S. 135, 30 S.Ct. 633, 54 L.Ed. 970 (Statute requiring interstate train to stop at junction point); *Chicago, B. & O.R. Co. v. Railroad Comm. of Wisconsin*, 237 U.S. 220, 35 S.Ct. 560, 59 L.Ed. 926 (Wisconsin statute requiring interstate train to stop at villages containing 200 or more inhabitants); *Missouri, K. & T.R. Co. v. Texas*, 245 U.S. 484, 38 S.Ct. 178, 62 L.Ed. 419, L.R.A.1918C, 535 (Order requiring trains to start on time and fixing time allowed for stops at junctions en route); *St. Louis & S.F.R. Co. v. Public Serv. Comm.*, 254 U.S. 535, 41 S.Ct. 192, 65 L.Ed. 389 (Order requiring through trains to detour through a small town); *St. Louis-San Francisco R. Co. v. Public Serv. Comm.*, 261 U.S. 369, 43 S.Ct. 380, 67 L.Ed. 701 (Order requiring that interstate trains be stopped at small town).

54. *See Southern Pacific Co. v. Arizona*, 325 U.S. 770, 65 S.Ct. 1521, 89 L.Ed. 1915.

This statute is attacked on the ground that it imposes undue burdens on interstate commerce. It is said by the Court of Appeals to have been passed in the exercise of the state's police power to avoid friction between the races. But this Court pointed out years ago "that a state cannot avoid the operation of this rule by simply invoking the convenient apologetic of the police power."[55] Burdens upon commerce are those actions of a state which directly "impair the usefulness of its facilities for such traffic." That impairment, we think, may arise from other causes than costs or long delays. A burden may arise from a state statute which requires interstate passengers to order their movements on the vehicle in accordance with local rather than national requirements.

b. Race and Interstate Travel

On appellant's journey, this statute required that she sit in designated seats in Virginia.[56] Changes in seat designation might be made "at any time" during the journey when "necessary or proper for the comfort and convenience of passengers." This occurred in this instance. Upon such change of designation, the statute authorizes the operator of the vehicle to require, as he did here, "any passenger to change his or her seat as it may be necessary or proper." An interstate passenger must, if necessary, repeatedly shift seats while moving in Virginia to meet the seating requirements of the changing passenger group. On arrival at the District of Columbia line, the appellant would have had freedom to occupy any available seat and so to the end of her journey.

Interstate passengers traveling via motors between the north and south or the east and west may pass through Virginia on through lines in the day or in the night. The large buses approach the comfort of pullmans and have seats convenient for rest. On such interstate journeys the enforcement of the requirements for reseating would be disturbing.

Appellant's argument, properly we think, includes facts bearing on interstate motor transportation beyond those immediately involved in this journey under the Virginia statutory regulations. To appraise the weight of the burden of the Virginia statute on interstate commerce, related statutes of other states are important to show whether there are cumulative effects which may make local regulation impracticable. Eighteen states, it appears, prohibit racial separation on public

---

55. *Kansas City Southern R. Co. v. Kaw Valley Drainage Dist.*, 233 U.S. 75, 79, 34 S.Ct. 564, 565, 58 L.Ed. 857.

56. The Virginia Code of 1942, section 67, defines a colored person, for the purpose of the Code, as follows: "Every person in whom there is ascertainable any Negro blood shall be deemed and taken to be a colored person. . . ." Provisions for vital statistics make a record of the racial lines of Virginia inhabitants. Sections 1574 and 5099a.

carriers.[57] Ten require separation on motor carriers.[58] Of these Alabama applies specifically to interstate passengers with an exception for interstate passengers with through tickets from states without laws on separation of passengers.[59] The language of the other acts, like this Virginia statute before the Court of Appeals' decision in this case, may be said to be susceptible to an interpretation that they do or do not apply to interstate passengers.

In states where separation of races is required in motor vehicles, a method of identification as white or colored must be employed. This may be done by definition. Any ascertainable Negro blood identifies a person as colored for purposes of separation in some states.[60] In the other states which require the separation of the races in motor carriers, apparently no definition generally applicable or made for the purposes of the statute is given. Court definition or further legislative enactments would be required to clarify the line between the races. Obviously there may be changes by legislation in the definition.[61]

The interferences to interstate commerce which arise from state regulation of racial association on interstate vehicles has long been recognized. Such regulation hampers freedom of choice in selecting accommodations. The recent changes in transportation brought about by the coming of automobiles does not seem of great significance in the problem. People of all races travel today more extensively than in 1878 when this Court first passed upon state regulation of racial segregation in commerce. The factual situation set out in preceding paragraphs emphasizes the soundness of this Court's early conclusion in *Hall v. De Cuir*, 95 U.S. 485, 24 L.Ed. 547.

---

57. Cal. Civ. Code (Deering), 1941, Secs. 51–54; Colo. Stat. Ann., 1935, Ch. 35, Sec. 1-10; Conn. Gen. Stat. (Supp.1933), Sec. 1160b; Ill. Rev. Stat.1945, Ch. 38, Secs. 125–128g; Ind. Stat. (Burns), 1933, Secs. 10-901, 10-902; Iowa Code, 1939, Secs. 13251, 13252; Kan. Gen. Stat.1935, Sec. 21-2424; Mass. Laws (Michie), 1933, Chap. 272, Sec. 98, as amended 1934; Mich. Stat. Ann.1938, Secs. 28.343, 28.344; Minn. Stat. (Mason), 1927, Sec. 7321; Neb. Comp. Stat.1929, Sec. 23-101; N.J. Rev. Stat.1937, Secs. 10:1-2 to 10:1-7, N.J.S.A.; N.Y. Civil Rights Law (McKinney Consol. Laws, c. 6), Secs. 40, 41; Ohio Code (Throckmorton), 1940, Secs. 12940–12942; Pa. Stat. (Purdon), Tit. 18, Secs. 4654 to 4655; R.I. Gen. Laws 1938, Ch. 606, Secs. 28, 29; Wash. Rev. Stat. (Remington), 1932, Sec. 2686 (semble); Wis. Stat.1943, Sec. 340.75.

58. Ala. Code 1940, Tit. 48, Sec. 268; Ark. Stat.1937 (Pope), Secs. 6921–6927, Acts 1943, p. 379; Ga. Code, 1933, Sec. 68-616; La. Gen. Stat. (Dart), 1939, Sec. 5307–5309, Act No. 209 of 1928; Miss. Code 1942, Sec. 7785; N.C. Gen. Stat. 1943, Sec. 62-109; Okla. Stat. Ann.1941, Tit. 47, §§ 201–210; S.C. Code 1942, Sec. 8530-1; Tex. Pen. Code (Vernon), 1936, Art. 1659; Va. Code 1942, Secs. 4097z–4097dd.

59. Ala. Code 1940, Tit. 48, Sec. 268.

60. Ala. Code, 1940, Tit. 1, Sec. 2; Ark. Stat. (Pope), 1937, Sec. 1200 (separate Coach law); Ga. Code (Michie Supp.), 1928, Sec. 2177; Okla. Const., Art. XXIII, Sec. 11; Va. Code (Michie), 1942, Sec. 67.

61. Compare Va. Code, 1887, Sec. 49, providing that those who had one-fourth or more Negro blood were to be considered colored. This was changed in 1910 (Acts, 1910, p. 581) to read one-sixteenth or more. It was again changed in 1930 by Acts, 1930, p. 97, to its present form, i.e., any ascertainable Negro blood.

The *De Cuir* case arose under a statute of Louisiana interpreted by the courts of that state and this Court to require public carriers "to give all persons travelling in that State, upon the public conveyances employed in such business, equal rights and privileges in all parts of the conveyance, without distinction or discrimination on account of race or color." 95 U.S. at page 487, 24 L.Ed. 547. Damages were awarded against Hall, the representative of the operator of a Mississippi river steamboat that traversed that river interstate from New Orleans to Vicksburg, for excluding in Louisiana the defendant in error, a colored person, from a cabin reserved for whites. This Court reversed for reasons well stated in the words of Chief Justice Waite.[62] As our previous discussion demonstrates, the transportation difficulties arising from a statute that requires commingling of the races, as in the *De Cuir* case, are increased by one that requires separation, as here.[63]

---

62. 95 U.S. at 489. Chief Justice Waite provided:

It was to meet just such a case that the commercial clause in the Constitution was adopted. The river Mississippi passes through or along the borders of ten different States, and its tributaries reach many more. The commerce upon these waters is immense, and its regulation clearly a matter of national concern. If each State was at liberty to regulate the conduct of carriers while within its jurisdiction, the confusion likely to follow could not but be productive of great inconvenience and unnecessary hardship. Each State could provide for its own passengers and regulate the transportation of its own freight, regardless of the interests of others. Nay more, it could prescribe rules by which the carrier must be governed within the State in respect to passengers and property brought from without. On one side of the river or its tributaries he might be required to observe one set of rules, and on the other another. Commerce cannot flourish in the midst of such embarrassments. No carrier of passengers can conduct his business with satisfaction to himself, or comfort to those employing him, if on one side of a State line his passengers, both white and colored, must be permitted to occupy the same cabin, and on the other be kept separate. Uniformity in the regulations by which he is to be governed from one end to the other of his route is a necessity in his business, and to secure it Congress, which is untrammelled by State lines, has been invested with the exclusive legislative power of determining what such regulations shall be. If this statute can be enforced against those engaged in inter-state commerce, it may be as well against those engaged in foreign; and the master of a ship clearing from New Orleans for Liverpool, having passengers on board, would be compelled to carry all, white and colored, in the same cabin during his passage down the river, or be subject to an action for damages, "exemplary as well as actual," by any one who felt himself aggrieved because he had been excluded on account of his color.

See *Louisville Railway Co. v. Mississippi*, 133 U.S. 587, 590, 591, 10 S. Ct. 348, 349, 33 L.Ed. 784.

A regulation of the number of passengers on interstate street cars was held invalid in *South Covington & C. St. R. Co. v. Covington*, 235 U.S. 537, 547, 35 S. Ct. 158, 161, 59 L.Ed. 350, L.R.A.1915F, 792. This Court said at pages 547, 548, at page 161 of 35 S. Ct.: "If Covington can regulate these matters, certainly Cincinnati can, and interstate business might be impeded by conflicting and varying regulations in this respect, with which it might be impossible to comply. On one side of the river one set of regulations might be enforced, and on the other side quite a different set, and both seeking to control a practically continuous movement of cars. As was said in *Hall v. De Cuir*, 95 U.S. 485, 489, 24 L.Ed. 547, 548, 'commerce cannot flourish in the midst of such embarrassments.'"

63. *South Covington R. Co. v. Kentucky*, 252 U.S. 399, 40 S.Ct. 378, 64 L.Ed. 631, relied upon by appellee, does not decide to the contrary of the holding in *Hall v. De Cuir*. In that case a carrier-corporation was convicted in the Kentucky courts of violation of a state statute that required it to furnish cars with separate compartments for white and colored. It operated street cars interstate over the lines of another corporation that owned tracks that were wholly intrastate. The Court of Appeals of Kentucky held the conviction good on the ground that the offending act was the

3. Holding

In weighing the factors that enter into our conclusion as to whether this statute so burdens interstate commerce or so infringes the requirements of national uniformity as to be invalid, we are mindful of the fact that conditions vary between northern or western states such as Maine or Montana, with practically no colored population; industrial states such as Illinois, Ohio, New Jersey and Pennsylvania with a small, although appreciable, percentage of colored citizens; and the states of the deep south with percentages of from twenty-five to nearly fifty per cent colored, all with varying densities of the white and colored race in certain localities. Local efforts to promote amicable relations in difficult areas by legislative segregation in interstate transportation emerge from the latter racial distribution. As no state law can reach beyond its own border nor bar transportation of passengers across its boundaries, diverse seating requirements for the races in interstate journeys result. As there is no federal act dealing with the separation of races in interstate transportation, we must decide the validity of this Virginia statute on the challenge that it interferes with commerce, as a matter of balance between the exercise of the local police power and the need for national uniformity in the regulations for interstate travel. It seems clear to us that seating arrangements for the different races in interstate motor travel require a single, uniform rule to promote and protect national travel. Consequently, we hold the Virginia statute in controversy invalid.

4. Justice Burton Dissenting

On the application of the interstate commerce clause of the Federal Constitution to this case, I find myself obliged to differ from the majority of the Court. I would sustain the Virginia statute against that clause. The issue is neither the desirability of the statute nor the constitutionality of racial segregation as such. The opinion of the Court does not claim that the Virginia statute, regulating seating arrangements for interstate passengers in motor vehicles, violates the Fourteenth Amendment or is in conflict with a federal statute. The Court holds this statute unconstitutional for but one reason. It holds that the burden imposed by the statute upon the nation's

---

operation of the intrastate railroad in violation of the state statute. It was said that the statute did not apply to an interstate passenger. *South Covington & C. Street R. Co. v. Commonwealth*, 181 Ky. 449, 454, 205 S.W. 603. The Court of Appeals referred, with continual approval, at that point to *Chiles v. Chesapeake & Ohio R. Co.*, 125 Ky. 299, 304, 101 S.W. 386, 387, 11 L.R.A., N.S., 268: "It is admitted that section 795–801 of the Kentucky Statutes, requiring all railroad companies to furnish separate coaches for transportation of white and colored passengers, and imposing upon the company and conductors a penalty for refusing or failing to carry out the provisions of the law, does not apply to appellant, who was an interstate passenger; it being conceded that the statute is only operative within the territorial limits of this state, and effective as to passengers who travel from one point within the state to another place within its border." This Court accepted this application of the state statute and said it "is not a regulation of interstate commerce." 252 U.S. at page 403, 40 S.Ct. at page 379, 64 L.Ed. 631. Probably what was meant by the opinions was that under the Kentucky act the company with wholly intrastate mileage must operate cars with separate compartments for intrastate passengers.

interest in interstate commerce so greatly outweighs the contribution made by the statute to the State's interest in its public welfare as to make it unconstitutional.

The undue burden upon interstate commerce thus relied upon by the Court is not complained of by the Federal Government, by any state, or by any carrier. This statute has been in effect since 1930. The carrier concerned is operating under regulations of its own which conform to the statute. The statute conforms to the policy adopted by Virginia as to steamboats (1900), electric or street cars and railroads (1902–1904).[64] Its validity has been unanimously upheld by the Supreme Court of Appeals of Virginia. The argument relied upon by the majority of this Court to establish the undue burden of this statute on interstate commerce is the lack of uniformity between its provisions and those of the laws of other states on the subject of the racial separation of interstate passengers on motor vehicles.

If the mere diversity between the Virginia statute and comparable statutes of other states is so serious as to render the Virginia statute invalid, it probably means that the comparable statutes of those other states, being diverse from it and from each other, are equally invalid. This is especially true under that assumption of the majority which disregards sectional interstate travel between neighboring states having similar laws, to hold "that seating arrangements for the different races in interstate motor travel require a *single, uniform rule to promote and protect national travel*." (Italics supplied.) More specifically, the opinion of the Court indicates that the laws of the 10 contiguous states of Virginia, North Carolina, South Carolina, Georgia, Alabama, Mississippi, Louisiana, Arkansas, Texas and Oklahoma require racial separation of passengers on motor carriers, while those of 18 other states prohibit racial separation of passengers on public carriers. On the precedent of this case, the laws of the 10 states requiring racial separation apparently can be invalidated because of their sharp diversity from the laws in the rest of the Union, or, in a lesser degree, because of their diversity from one another. Such invalidation, on the ground of lack of nation-wide uniformity, may lead to questioning the validity of the laws of the 18 states now prohibiting racial separation of passengers, for those laws likewise differ sharply from laws on the same subject in other parts of the Union and, in a lesser degree, from one another. In the absence of federal law, this may eliminate state regulation of racial separation in the seating of interstate passengers on motor vehicles and leave the regulation of the subject to the respective carriers.

The present decision will lead to the questioning of the validity of statutory regulation of the seating of intrastate passengers in the same motor vehicles with interstate passengers. The decision may also result in increased lack of uniformity between regulations as to seating arrangements on motor vehicles limited to

---

64. Steamboats: Acts of 1900, at 340; electric or street cars: Acts of 1902–1904, at 990; railroads: Acts of 1902–1904, at 987. Va. Code Ann., 1942, §§ 4022–4025; 3978–3983; 3962–3969.

intrastate passengers in a given state and those on motor vehicles engaged in interstate business in the same state or on connecting routes.

The basic weakness in the appellant's case is the lack of facts and findings essential to demonstrate the existence of such a serious and major burden upon the national interest in interstate commerce as to outweigh whatever state or local benefits are attributable to the statute and which would be lost by its invalidation. The Court recognizes that it serves as "the final arbiter of the competing demands of state and national interests"[65] and that it must fairly determine, in the absence of congressional action, whether the state statute actually imposes such an undue burden upon interstate commerce as to invalidate that statute. In weighing these competing demands, if this Court is to justify the invalidation of this statute, it must, first of all, be satisfied that the many years of experience of the state and the carrier that are reflected in this state law should be set aside. It represents the tested public policy of Virginia regularly enacted, long maintained and currently observed. The officially declared state interests, even when affecting interstate commerce, should not be laid aside summarily by this Court in the absence of congressional action. It is only Congress that can supply affirmative national uniformity of action.

In *Southern Pacific Co. v. Arizona*, 325 U.S. 761, 768–69, 770, this Court speaking through the late Chief Justice said:

> In the application of these principles some enactments may be found to be plainly within and others plainly without state power. But between these extremes lies the infinite variety of cases, in which regulation of local matters may also operate as a regulation of commerce, in which reconciliation of the conflicting claims of state and national power is to be attained only by some appraisal and accommodation of the competing demands of the state and national interests involved. . . . [66]

> But in general Congress has left it to the courts to formulate the rules thus interpreting the commerce clause in its application, doubtless because it has appreciated the destructive consequences to the commerce of the nation if their [i.e. the courts'] protection were withdrawn, . . . and has been aware that in their application state laws will not be invalidated without the support of relevant factual material which will 'afford a sure basis' for an informed judgment.[67] . . . Meanwhile, Congress has accommodated its legislation, as have the states, to these rules as an established feature of our constitutional system. There has thus been left to the states wide scope for the regulation of matters of local state concern, even though it in some measure affects the commerce, provided it does not materially restrict the free flow of commerce across state lines, or interfere with it in matters with

---

65. *Southern Pacific Co. v. Arizona*, 325 U.S. 761, 769.
66. *See Parker v. Brown*, 317 U.S. 341, 362; *Di Santo v. Pennsylvania*, 273 U.S. 34, 44.
67. *Terminal Assn. v. Trainmen*, 318 U.S. 1, 8.

respect to which uniformity of regulation is of predominant national concern. (Italics supplied.)

The above-quoted requirement of a factual establishment of "a sure basis" for an informed judgment by this Court calls for a firm and demonstrable basis of action on the part of this Court. In the record of this case there are no findings of fact that demonstrate adequately the excessiveness of the burden, if any, which the Virginia statute has imposed upon interstate commerce, during the many years since its enactment, in comparison with the resulting effect in Virginia of the invalidation of this statute.[68] The Court relies largely upon the recital of a nation-wide diversity among state statutes on this subject without a demonstration of the factual situation in those states, and especially in Virginia. The Court therefore is not able in this case to make that necessary "appraisal and accommodation of the competing demands of the state and national interests involved" which should be the foundation for passing upon the validity of a state statute of long standing and of important local significance in the exercise of the state police power.

The Court makes its own further assumption that the question of racial separation of interstate passengers in motor vehicle carriers requires national uniformity of treatment rather than diversity of treatment at this time. The inaction of Congress is an important indication that, in the opinion of Congress, this issue is better met without nationally uniform affirmative regulation than with it. Legislation raising the issue long has been, and is now, pending before Congress but has not reached the floor of either House.[69] The fact that 18 states have prohibited in some degree racial separation in public carriers is important progress in the direction of uniformity. The fact, however, that 10 contiguous states in some degree require, by state law, some racial separation of passengers on motor carriers indicates a different appraisal by them of the needs and conditions in those areas than in others. The remaining 20 states have not gone equally far in either direction. This recital of existing legislative diversity is evidence against the validity of the assumption by this Court that there exists today a requirement of a single uniform national rule on the subject.

It is a fundamental concept of our Constitution that where conditions are diverse the solution of problems arising out of them may well come through the application of diversified treatment matching the diversified needs as determined by our local governments. Uniformity of treatment is appropriate where a substantial uniformity of conditions exists.

---

68. *Hall v. DeCuir*, 95 U.S. 485, does not require the conclusion reached by the Court in this case. The Louisiana statute in the *DeCuir* case could have been invalidated, at that time and place, as an undue burden on interstate commerce under the rules clearly stated by Chief Justice Stone in *Southern Pacific Co. v. Arizona, supra*, and as applied in this dissenting opinion. If the *DeCuir* case is followed without weighing the surrounding facts, it would invalidate today statutes in New England states prohibiting racial separation in seating arrangements on carriers, which would not be invalidated under the doctrine stated in the *Arizona* case.

69. See H.R. 8821, 75th Cong., 3d Sess., 83 Cong. Rec. 74; H.R. 182, 76th Cong., 1st Sess., 84 Cong. Rec. 27; H. R. 112, 77th Cong., 1st Sess., 87 Cong. Rec. 13.

D. Commentary on *Morgan*

Though the United States condemned the brutal treatment of minorities in Europe during the Second World War, German prisoners of war ironically enjoyed an elevated status compared to black servicemen while traveling on trains within the United States. John Hope Franklin wrote, "No Negro who had seen it could ever erase from his mind the sight of these war prisoners [on trains] enjoying better treatment and more luxury than a Negro American could ever dream of enjoying in his own country."[70]

In 1944, Irene Morgan, one of the several forerunners to Rosa Parks, was arrested and convicted of refusing to move to the "colored" section of a Greyhound bus.[71] NAACP attorneys William Hastie, Thurgood Marshall, and Leon Ransom argued before the Supreme Court that the United States, which had just emerged victorious in its "death struggle against the apostles of racism"[72] abroad, could not sanction racial oppression at home. In response, the Supreme Court declared that racial segregation on interstate buses and trains was unconstitutional. While many believed it was no diminution that the Supreme Court had relied on the Commerce Clause instead of the Reconstruction Amendments to invalidate Morgan's conviction, the fact remained that racial segregation had been further limited.

E. Questions and Notes

What do you think about the reasoning in *Morgan* that lack of uniformity rather than opposition to racial segregation was the basis for the Supreme Court's decision?

Both *Buchanan* and *Morgan* avoided application of the separate but equal doctrine. The opinion in *Plessy* had created a distinction between political and social rights. What similarities exist between the issues of housing and interstate commerce in *Buchanan* and *Morgan* that enabled the Supreme Court to avoid the *Plessy* rationale, which had posited that the separate but equal doctrine does not violate basic notions of equality?

XVI. Racial Segregation and State Action

A. Introduction

While *Buchanan* made *de jure* racial housing segregation unconstitutional, other methods were used to maintain such racial separation. These methods included

---

70. JOHN HOPE FRANKLIN, FROM SLAVERY TO FREEDOM: A HISTORY OF NEGRO AMERICANS (Fifth Edition, 1980) at 428.

71. *Morgan v. Virginia*, 328 U.S. 373, 375 (1946).

72. *Id.*

redlining, steering, and intimidation. One of the most popular methods was the racially restrictive covenant.

B. Background on *Shelley*

Of the myriad of devices implemented by whites to prevent racial minorities from buying property, the racially restrictive covenant received the first legal challenge. As racial minorities tried to move from the less desirable areas of cities relegated to them through private and governmental practices, racial covenants were placed on houses in the more desirable areas. Because of these covenants, the few minorities economically capable of owning such property were prevented or discouraged from doing so.

C. *Shelley v. Kraemer*, 334 U.S. 1 (1948)

George L. Vaughn and *Herman Willer*, both of St. Louis, Mo., for petitioners Shelley.

Gerald L. Seegers, of St. Louis, Mo., for respondents Kraemer.

Thurgood Marshall, of New York City, *Loren Miller*, for petitioners McGhee.

Henry Gilligan and *James A. Crooks*, both of Washington, D.C. for respondents Sipes and others.

Philip B. Perlman, Sol. Gen., of Washington, D.C., for the United States, as amicus curiae, by special leave of Court.

1. Facts

Chief Justice VINSON delivered the opinion of the Court.

These cases present for our consideration questions relating to the validity of court enforcement of private agreements, generally described as restrictive covenants, which have as their purpose the exclusion of persons of a designated race or color from occupying the premises. Basic constitutional issues of obvious importance have been raised.

The first of these cases comes to this Court on certiorari to the Supreme Court of Missouri. On February 16, 1911, thirty out of a total of thirty-nine owners of property fronting both sides of Labadie Avenue between Taylor Avenue and Cora Avenue in the city of St. Louis, signed an agreement, which was subsequently recorded, providing in part:

> ". . . the said property is hereby restricted to the use and occupancy for the term of fifty (50) years from this date, so that it shall be a condition all the time and whether recited and referred to as (sic) not in subsequent conveyances and shall attach to the land, as a condition precedent to the sale of the same, that hereafter no part of said property or any portion thereof shall

be, for said term of fifty-years, occupied by any person not of the Caucasian race, it being intended hereby to restrict the use of said property for said period of time against the occupancy as owners or tenants of any portion of said property for resident or other purpose by people of the Negro or Mongolian Race."

The entire district described in the agreement included fifty-seven parcels of land. The thirty owners who signed the agreement held title to forty-seven parcels, including the particular parcel involved in this case. At the time the agreement was signed, five of the parcels in the district were owned by Negroes. One of those had been occupied by Negro families since 1882, nearly thirty years before the restrictive agreement was executed. The trial court found that owners of seven out of nine homes on the south side of Labadie Avenue, within the restricted district and "in the immediate vicinity" of the premises in question, had failed to sign the restrictive agreement in 1911. At the time this action was brought, four of the premises were occupied by Negroes, and had been so occupied for periods ranging from twenty-three to sixty-three years. A fifth parcel had been occupied by Negroes until a year before this suit was instituted.

On August 11, 1945, pursuant to a contract of sale, petitioners Shelley, who are Negroes, for valuable consideration received from one Fitzgerald a warranty deed to the parcel in question.[73]

The trial court found that petitioners had no actual knowledge of the restrictive agreement at the time of the purchase.

On October 9, 1945, respondents, as owners of other property subject to the terms of the restrictive covenant, brought suit in Circuit Court of the city of St. Louis praying that petitioners Shelley be restrained from taking possession of the property and that judgment be entered divesting title out of petitioners Shelley and revesting title in the immediate grantor or in such other person as the court should direct. The trial court denied the requested relief on the ground that the restrictive agreement, upon which respondents based their action, had never become final and complete because it was the intention of the parties to that agreement that it was not to become effective until signed by all property owners in the district, and signatures of all the owners had never been obtained.

The Supreme Court of Missouri sitting en banc reversed and directed the trial court to grant the relief for which respondents had prayed. That court held the agreement effective and concluded that enforcement of its provisions violated no

73. The trial court found that title to the property which petitioners Shelley sought to purchase was held by one Bishop, a real estate dealer, who placed the property in the name of Josephine Fitzgerald. Bishop, who acted as agent for petitioners in the purchase, concealed the fact of his ownership.

rights guaranteed to petitioners by the Federal Constitution.[74] At the time the court rendered its decision, petitioners were occupying the property in question. . . .

2. Opinion

a. Precedent

Whether the equal protection clause of the Fourteenth Amendment inhibits judicial enforcement by state courts of restrictive covenants based on race or color is a question which this Court has not heretofore been called upon to consider. Only two cases have been decided by this Court which in any way have involved the enforcement of such agreements. The first of these was the case of *Corrigan v. Buckley*, 1926, 271 U.S. 323, 46 S.Ct. 521, 70 L.Ed. 969. There, suit was brought in the courts of the District of Columbia to enjoin a threatened violation of certain restrictive covenants relating to lands situated in the city of Washington. Relief was granted, and the case was brought here on appeal. It is apparent that that case, which had originated in the federal courts and involved the enforcement of covenants on land located in the District of Columbia, could present no issues under the Fourteenth Amendment; for that Amendment by its terms applies only to the States. Nor was the question of the validity of court enforcement of the restrictive covenants under the Fifth Amendment properly before the Court, as the opinion of this Court specifically recognizes.[75] The only constitutional issue which the appellants had raised in the lower courts, and hence the only constitutional issue before this Court on appeal, was the validity of the covenant agreements as such. This Court concluded that since the inhibitions of the constitutional provisions invoked, apply only to governmental action, as contrasted to action of private individuals, there was no showing that the covenants, which were simply agreements between private property owners, were invalid. Accordingly, the appeal was dismissed for want of a substantial question. Nothing in the opinion of this Court, therefore, may properly be regarded as an adjudication on the merits of the constitutional issues presented by these cases, which raise the question of the validity, not of the private agreements as such, but of the judicial enforcement of those agreements. . . .

Since the decision of this Court in *The Civil Rights Cases*, 1883, 109 U.S. 3, 3 S.Ct. 18, 27 L.Ed. 835, the principle has become firmly embedded in our constitutional law that the action inhibited by the first section of the Fourteenth Amendment is only such action as may fairly be said to be that of the States. That Amendment erects no shield against merely private conduct, however discriminatory or wrongful.[76]

We conclude, therefore, that the restrictive agreements standing alone cannot be regarded as a violation of any rights guaranteed to petitioners by the Fourteenth Amendment. So long as the purposes of those agreements are effectuated by

---

74. *Kraemer v. Shelley*, 1946, 355 Mo. 814, 198 S.W.2d 679.

75. *Corrigan v. Buckley*, 1926, 271 U.S. 323, 330, 331, 46 S.Ct. 521, 523, 524, 70 L.Ed. 969.

76. And *see United States v. Harris*, 1883, 106 U.S. 629, 1 S.Ct. 601, 27 L.Ed. 290; *United States v. Cruikshank*, 1876, 92 U.S. 542, 23 L.Ed. 588.

voluntary adherence to their terms, it would appear clear that there has been no action by the State and the provisions of the Amendment have not been violated.

b. State Action and Judicial Enforcement

But here there was more. These are cases in which the purposes of the agreements were secured only by judicial enforcement by state courts of the restrictive terms of the agreements. The respondents urge that judicial enforcement of private agreements does not amount to state action; or, in any event, the participation of the State is so attenuated in character as not to amount to state action within the meaning of the Fourteenth Amendment. Finally, it is suggested, even if the States in these cases may be deemed to have acted in the constitutional sense, their action did not deprive petitioners of rights guaranteed by the Fourteenth Amendment. We move to a consideration of these matters.

That the action of state courts and of judicial officers in their official capacities is to be regarded as action of the State within the meaning of the Fourteenth Amendment, is a proposition which has long been established by decisions of this Court. That principle was given expression in the earliest cases involving the construction of the terms of the Fourteenth Amendment. Thus, in *Commonwealth of Virginia v. Rives*, 1880, 100 U.S. 313, 318, 25 L.Ed. 667, this Court stated: "It is doubtless true that a State may act through different agencies, — either by its legislative, its executive, or its judicial authorities; and the prohibitions of the amendment extend to all action of the State denying equal protection of the laws, whether it be action by one of these agencies or by another." In *Ex parte Commonwealth of Virginia*, 1880, 100 U.S. 339, 347, 25 L.Ed. 676, the Court observed: "A State acts by its legislative, its executive, or its judicial authorities. It can act in no other way." In *The Civil Rights Cases*, 1883, 109 U.S. 3, 11, 17, 3 S.Ct. 18, 21, 27 L.Ed. 835, this Court pointed out that the Amendment makes void 'state action of every kind' which is inconsistent with the guaranties therein contained, and extends to manifestations of "state authority in the shape of laws, customs, or judicial or executive proceedings." Language to like effect is employed no less than eighteen times during the course of that opinion.

Similar expressions, giving specific recognition to the fact that judicial action is to be regarded as action on the State for the purposes of the Fourteenth Amendment, are to be found in numerous cases which have been more recently decided. In *Twining v. New Jersey*, 1908, 211 U.S. 78, 90, 91, 29 S.Ct. 14, 16, 53 L.Ed. 97, the Court said:

> "The judicial act of the highest court of the state, in authoritatively construing and enforcing its laws, is the act of the state."

In *Brinkerhoff-Faris Trust & Savings Co. v. Hill*, 1930, 281 U.S. 673, 680, 50 S.Ct. 451, 454, 74 L.Ed. 1107, the Court, through Mr. Justice Brandeis, stated:

> "The federal guaranty of due process extends to state action through its judicial as well as through its legislative, executive, or administrative branch

of government." Further examples of such declarations in the opinions of this Court are not lacking.[77] . . .

The short of the matter is that from the time of the adoption of the Fourteenth Amendment until the present, it has been the consistent ruling of this Court that the action of the States to which the Amendment has reference, includes action of state courts and state judicial officials. Although, in construing the terms of the Fourteenth Amendment, differences have from time to time been expressed as to whether particular types of state action may be said to offend the Amendment's prohibitory provisions, it has never been suggested that state court action is immunized from the operation of those provisions simply because the act is that of the judicial branch of the state government.

Against this background of judicial construction, extending over a period of some three-quarters of a century, we are called upon to consider whether enforcement by state courts of the restrictive agreements in these cases may be deemed to be the acts of those States; and, if so, whether that action has denied these petitioners the equal protection of the laws which the Amendment was intended to insure.

We have no doubt that there has been state action in these cases in the full and complete sense of the phrase. The undisputed facts disclose that petitioners were willing purchasers of properties upon which they desired to establish homes. The owners of the properties were willing sellers; and contracts of sale were accordingly consummated. It is clear that but for the active intervention of the state courts, supported by the full panoply of state power, petitioners would have been free to occupy the properties in question without restraint.

These are not cases, as has been suggested, in which the States have merely abstained from action, leaving private individuals free to impose such discriminations as they see fit. Rather, these are cases in which the States have made available to such individuals the full coercive power of government to deny to petitioners, on the grounds of race or color, the enjoyment of property rights in premises which petitioners are willing and financially able to acquire and which the grantors are willing to sell. The difference between judicial enforcement and nonenforcement of the restrictive covenants is the difference to petitioners between being denied rights

77. *Neal v. Delaware*, 1881, 103 U.S. 370, 397, 26 L.Ed. 567; *Scott v. McNeal*, 1894, 154 U.S. 34, 45, 14 S.Ct. 1108, 1112, 38 L.Ed. 896; *Chicago, B. & O.R. Co. v. Chicago*, 1897, 166 U.S. 226, 233–35, 17 S. Ct. 581, 583, 584, 41 L.Ed. 979; *Hovey v. Elliott*, 1897, 167 U.S. 409, 417, 418, 17 S.Ct. 841, 844, 42 L. Ed. 215; *Carter v. Texas*, 1900, 177 U.S. 442, 447, 20 S.Ct. 687, 689, 44 L.Ed. 839; *Martin v. Texas*, 1906, 200 U.S. 316, 319, 26 S.Ct. 338, 50 L.Ed. 497; *Raymond v. Chicago Union Traction Co.*, 1907, 207 U.S. 20, 35, 36, 28 S.Ct. 7, 12, 52 L.Ed. 78, 12 Ann.Cas. 757; *Home Telephone and Telegraph Co. v. Los Angeles*, 1913, 227 U.S. 278, 286, 287, 33 S.Ct. 312, 314, 57 L.Ed. 510; *Prudential Ins. Co. v. Cheek*, 1922, 259 U.S. 530, 548, 42 S.Ct. 516, 524, 66 L.Ed. 1044, 27 A.L.R. 27; *American Ry. Exp. Co. v. Kentucky*, 1927, 273 U.S. 269, 274, 47 S.Ct. 353, 355, 71 L.Ed. 639; *Mooney v. Holohan*, 1935, 294 U.S. 103, 112, 113, 55 S.Ct. 340, 341, 342, 79 L.Ed. 791, 98 A.L.R. 406; *Hansberry v. Lee*, 1940, 311 U.S. 32, 41, 61 S.Ct. 115, 117, 85 L.Ed. 22, 132 A.L.R. 741.

of property available to other members of the community and being accorded full enjoyment of those rights on an equal footing.

The enforcement of the restrictive agreements by the state courts in these cases was directed pursuant to the common-law policy of the States as formulated by those courts in earlier decisions. In the Missouri case, enforcement of the covenant was directed in the first instance by the highest court of the State after the trial court had determined the agreement to be invalid for want of the requisite number of signatures. In the Michigan case, the order of enforcement by the trial court was affirmed by the highest state court. The judicial action in each case bears the clear and unmistakable imprimatur of the State. We have noted that previous decisions of this Court have established the proposition that judicial action is not immunized from the operation of the Fourteenth Amendment simply because it is taken pursuant to the state's common-law policy. Nor is the Amendment ineffective simply because the particular pattern of discrimination, which the State has enforced, was defined initially by the terms of a private agreement. State action, as that phrase is understood for the purposes of the Fourteenth Amendment, refers to exertions of state power in all forms. And when the effect of that action is to deny rights subject to the protection of the Fourteenth Amendment, it is the obligation of this Court to enforce the constitutional commands.

c. The Meaning of Equal Protection

We have noted that freedom from discrimination by the States in the enjoyment of property rights was among the basic objectives sought to be effectuated by the framers of the Fourteenth Amendment. That such discrimination has occurred in these cases is clear. Because of the race or color of these petitioners they have been denied rights of ownership or occupancy enjoyed as a matter of course by other citizens of different race or color. The Fourteenth Amendment declares "that all persons, whether colored or white, shall stand equal before the laws of the States, and, in regard to the colored race, for whose protection the amendment was primarily designed, that no discrimination shall be made against them by law because of their color."[78] *Strauder v. West Virginia, supra,* 100 U.S. at 307, 25 L.Ed. 664. Only recently this Court has had occasion to declare that a state law which denied equal enjoyment of property rights to a designated class of citizens of specified race and ancestry, was not a legitimate exercise of the state's police power but violated the guaranty of the equal protection of the laws. *Oyama v. California,* 1948, 332 U.S. 633, 68 S.Ct. 269. Nor may the discriminations imposed by the state courts in these cases be justified as proper exertions of state police power.

---

78. Restrictive agreements of the sort involved in these cases have been used to exclude other than blacks from the ownership or occupancy of real property. We are informed that such agreements have been directed against Indians, Jews, Chinese, Japanese, Mexicans, Hawaiians, Puerto Ricans, and Filipinos, among others.

Respondents urge, however, that since the state courts stand ready to enforce restrictive covenants excluding white persons from the ownership or occupancy of property covered by such agreements, enforcement of covenants excluding colored persons may not be deemed a denial of equal protection of the laws to the colored persons who are thereby affected.[79] This contention does not bear scrutiny. The parties have directed our attention to no case in which a court, state or federal, has been called upon to enforce a covenant excluding members of the white majority from ownership or occupancy of real property on grounds of race or color. But there are more fundamental considerations. The rights created by the first section of the Fourteenth Amendment are, by its terms, guaranteed to the individual. The rights established are personal rights.[80] It is, therefore, no answer to these petitioners to say that the courts may also be induced to deny white persons rights of ownership and occupancy on grounds of race or color. Equal protection of the laws is not achieved through indiscriminate imposition of inequalities.

Nor do we find merit in the suggestion that property owners who are parties to these agreements are denied equal protection of the laws if denied access to the courts to enforce the terms of restrictive covenants and to assert property rights which the state courts have held to be created by such agreements. The Constitution confers upon no individual the right to demand action by the State which results in the denial of equal protection of the laws to other individuals. And it would appear beyond question that the power of the State to create and enforce property interests must be exercised within the boundaries defined by the Fourteenth Amendment.

The problem of defining the scope of the restrictions which the Federal Constitution imposes upon exertions of power by the States has given rise to many of the most persistent and fundamental issues which this Court has been called upon to consider. That problem was foremost in the minds of the framers of the Constitution, and since that early day, has arisen in a multitude of forms. The task of determining whether the action of a State offends constitutional provisions is one which may not be undertaken lightly. Where, however, it is clear that the action of the State violates the terms of the fundamental charter, it is the obligation of this Court so to declare.

The historical context in which the Fourteenth Amendment became a part of the Constitution should not be forgotten. Whatever else the framers sought to achieve, it is clear that the matter of primary concern was the establishment of equality in the enjoyment of basic civil and political rights and the preservation of those rights

---

79. It should be observed that the restrictions relating to residential occupancy contained in ordinances involved in the *Buchanan, Harmon and Deans* cases, and declared by this Court to be inconsistent with the requirements of the Fourteenth Amendment, applied equally to white persons and blacks.

80. *McCabe v. Atchison, T. & S. F. Ry. Co.*, 1914, 235 U.S. 151, 161–162, 35 S.Ct. 69, 71, 59 L.Ed. 169; *Missouri ex rel. Gaines v. Canada*, 1938, 305 U.S. 337, 59 S.Ct. 232, 83 L.Ed. 208; *Oyama v. California*, 1948, 332 U.S. 633, 68 S.Ct. 269.

from discriminatory action on the part of the States based on considerations of race or color. Seventy-five years ago this Court announced that the provisions of the Amendment are to be construed with this fundamental purpose in mind.[81] Upon full consideration, we have concluded that in these cases the States have acted to deny petitioners the equal protection of the laws guaranteed by the Fourteenth Amendment. Having so decided, we find it unnecessary to consider whether petitioners have also been deprived of property without due process of law or denied privileges and immunities of citizens of the United States.

3. Holding

We hold that in granting judicial enforcement of the restrictive agreements in these cases, the States have denied petitioners the equal protection of the laws and that, therefore, the action of the state courts cannot stand.

For the reasons stated, the judgment of the Supreme Court of Missouri and the judgment of the Supreme Court of Michigan must be reversed.

D. Commentary on *Shelley*

A. Leon Higginbotham, Jr.
Race, Sex, Education, and Missouri Jurisprudence

In *Shelley*, the Supreme Court held that judicial enforcement of racially restrictive covenants violated the Equal Protection Clause of the Fourteenth Amendment. The Court's holding—that judicial enforcement of a private right constitutes state action for purposes of the Fourteenth Amendment—has generated enough criticism and commentary to fill a small library. There is, however, a significant aspect of the restrictive covenant litigation that has not received as much attention. The Supreme Court's decision in the restrictive covenant cases was the result of a highly organized effort involving more than thirty years of litigation and hundreds of cases. The conflict which caused the litigation arose from a dramatic population shift that occurred in the early decades of the twentieth century. The great migration of black families from rural areas to urban industrial centers prompted various efforts to establish and maintain racial segregation in housing. After legislated segregation failed, private covenants became the primary vehicle for maintaining segregated housing.

The forces against restrictive covenants consisted of black families in search of adequate housing, the NAACP, and the lawyers who served on that organization's legal committee. From 1926 to 1947, the NAACP and the lawyers fighting against the covenants lost the vast majority of the hundreds of cases in which they challenged the covenants. By 1944, The American Law Institute's Restatement of Property, one

---

81. *Slaughterhouse Cases*, 1873, 16 Wall 36, 81, 21 L.Ed. 394; *Strauder v. West Virginia*, 1880, 100 U.S. 303, 25 L.Ed. 664.

of the most influential treatises in the field, endorsed racial covenants as a valid exception to the general rule against restraints on the alienation of property.

Despite a vast amount of adverse legal precedent, the NAACP lawyers seemed to know that they would ultimately prevail in the Supreme Court. Charles Hamilton Houston, who served at various times as counsel to the NAACP and was Dean of Howard University Law School and the architect of the NAACP's school desegregation plan, devised the restrictive-covenant strategy. The covenant strategy involved an evidentiary demonstration of the relationship of crime and disease to overcrowded conditions in urban ghettoes, and the role of restrictive covenants in the perpetuation of those problems.

67 *Wash. U.L.Q.* 701, 737–38.
Copyright © (1989) *Washington University Law Quarterly.*
Reprinted with permission of the *Washington University Law Quarterly.*

E. Questions and Notes

Many say that they agree with the outcome in *Shelley* but not with the rationale. The rationale of *Shelley* condemned the judicial enforcement of racially discriminatory covenants but did not condemn the racial aspects of the agreements themselves. Do you agree with this approach? Once the state judiciary enforced the privately held, racially discriminatory covenant, the state was an actor, and the Fourteenth Amendment protections applied. The rationale in *Shelly*, however, fails to acknowledge that the content of the covenant also causes harm and violates rights, such as the First Amendment right to freedom of movement.

Today, many housing deeds still contain racially restrictive covenants even though they cannot be legally enforced. What impact, if any, do you believe these covenants have on the maintenance of racial segregation in housing?

XVII. Interpreting the Separate but Equal Doctrine

A. Introduction

Based upon *Plessy*, states were encouraged to separate citizens on the basis of race in a variety of social activities, from transportation and accommodation to dining and shopping. While the water fountain is one of the most well known symbols of such segregation, many other examples existed including prisons, chessboards, and Bibles all indicating the pervasiveness of the segregation scheme. One of the most common activities subjected to racial segregation legislation, as reflected in the following cases, was education. Education is often the basis of many other rights and opportunities: restricting where someone can sit on a train has a limited impact on their lifestyle, whereas restricting where they can go to school has a huge impact on their opportunities and life overall.

B. Background on *Cumming*

One of the first cases to come before the Supreme Court interpreting the meaning of separate but equal was an education case. Under *Plessy, Berea College*, and *Gung Lum*, the separate but equal doctrine was allowed in the social arena, including education. Now in *Cumming*, the issue of racial separation in publicly funded primary and secondary schools forced the Court to consider the meaning of equality and the responsibility for its implementation.

C. Ellen Connally

*Justice Harlan's "Great Betrayal?" A Reconsideration of Cumming v. Richmond County Board of Education**

The roots of *Cumming v. Board of Education* lay in the black community of Augusta at the conclusion of the Civil War. The desire of the freemen there to gain an education, coupled with the desire of the black elite to provide educational facilities for all blacks and upward mobility for their own children, led to the formation of Ware High school in 1872. William J. White, one of the leaders of Augusta's black community and a former agent of the Freedmen's Bureau, was a moving force in the community's desire to provide a public education for blacks. Indeed, the frequency of his visits to the school board meetings in the 1870s and 1880s "might have qualified him as an ex-officio member of the board." Active in the Republican party, White had the distinction of serving as Chairman of the Eighth Congressional District Republican Convention. White was what later historians would call a "voluntary Negro:" "[h]e looked like a white man, and there were rumors that his African blood was negligible, if it existed at all." His commitment to education earned him the title "Father of Negro Education in Georgia."

The South lacked the tradition of public education possessed by other parts of the nation. Aristocrats of the antebellum South had been reluctant to tax for educational purposes. To them, education for the masses was not necessary. The marked individualism of Southerners, the reluctance of the white elite to provide an education for the masses of poor whites, and their abhorrence to education for blacks all contributed to this lack of interest in education, particularly public education. Historian John Hope Franklin attributes this lack of interest in education to the fact that "[i]n the antebellum South widespread illiteracy and the neglect of education were outstanding characteristics of the culture of the region. The attitude was aptly summed up fifteen years after the close of the Civil War by Virginia's Governor F.W.M. Holliday, who said that public schools were a "luxury . . . to be paid for like any other luxury, by the people who wish their benefits." And in fact the people of Augusta, both black and white, paid tuition to go to the publicly supported high schools. Only the primary grades, then known as common schools, were free.

---

* (some footnotes omitted).

In 1872 the state of Georgia passed legislation for the creation of public schools. Though mandating segregation, the law specifically provided that the Richmond County school Board "shall provide the same facilities for both [white and Negro children], both as regards schoolhouses and fixtures, attainments and abilities of teachers, length of term time and all other matters appertaining to education." The law was unique to Augusta and Richmond County because "no other Georgia school board could establish high schools under the state law." In nineteenth-century America, a high-school education was not the norm but the exception, an attitude that the statute reflects. As a result, it is important to note that Ware High School was the only public high school for blacks in Georgia before 1915, and one of perhaps four in the eleven ex-Confederate states in 1880. The provision of the Georgia statute that required the board to provide common schools for both races was clearly mandatory under Section Nine of the 1872 statute. However, the authority given to the school board under Section Ten of the statute to "establish schools of higher grade at such point in the county as the interest and convenience of the people may require" became a major issue of dispute.

Prior to the formation of Ware High School, the black high-school-age students of Augusta could attend the Augusta Baptist Institute. However, in 1879 that school moved to Atlanta, leaving an educational void. This removal motivated White and other blacks, including future *Cumming* plaintiff James S. Harper, to petition the school board for a tax-supported high school for blacks. White and other petitioners stressed the importance of training teachers for elementary schools and the provisions of the law that provided for equal facilities. The Augusta *Chronicle*, the city's leading newspaper, gave editorial support for the high school, stressing the importance of training teachers and the necessity of providing both races with the same opportunity. "If the whites have high schools, grammar, intermediate and primary schools," the *Chronicle* editorialized, "let the colored children have them also . . . Give both races exactly the same opportunities and equal advantages."

White's substantial influence on the board showed in his ability to win support for the high school and select the school's first principal, Richard R. Wright. Wright was a product of the abolitionist-based American Missionary Association schools in Atlanta, and was the first valedictorian of Atlanta University.[82] He advocated classical education for blacks, a highly controversial subject in the late nineteenth century.[83] Even more indicative of White's influence, "the board deferred to him in naming

---

82. Davis, A Clashing of The Soul, 29. Like White, Wright was active in Republican politics, and just prior to coming to Augusta was elected to serve as a delegate to the Republican National Convention. Elizabeth R. Haynes, The Black Boy of Atlanta (Boston, 1952), 67; Anderson, The Education of Blacks in the South, 29.

83. Anderson, The Education of Blacks in the South, 29–30 and 122. Wright left Ware in the mid-1880s to become president of Georgia State Industrial College (Savannah State), where he continued to emphasize academic education and training in selected skilled trades. He was replaced by H.L. Walker, who organized the Negro State Teachers' Association and served as its president for a decade. Kousser, "Separate but *Not* Equal," 27.

the school for a former agent of the Freedmen's Bureau, Edmund Asa Ware." Ware, a native of Massachusetts and a 1863 graduate of Yale, was a part of the wave of Northern abolitionists who saw the Civil War as a prelude to the greater mission of educating emancipated slaves.[84]

From Ware High School's inception in 1880 until its demise in 1897, it served as a model for black high schools. "Ware High School became a solid academic secondary school, a source of pride and an avenue of mobility for Augusta's striving black community." White politicians, including Populist Tom Watson, could point to Ware as an example of white tax money going to support the colored girls and boys at the expense of whites and the benefits not only of a common school, but also a high school. As in other parts of the South, Augusta had significant numbers of black voters for more than two decades after Reconstruction. It is therefore highly likely that, in supporting Ware, the school board was "responding to the pressures of the black electorate . . . overriding the objection of one board member [who argued] that the shortage of places in black primary schools should be alleviated before allocating money to the higher branches." So long as blacks voted, the $88 yearly net expense of Ware High School was a good investment for the Democrats.

As Kousser points out, Ware was supported by the close-knit circle of black families that comprised the black elite of the city of Augusta. These families had close connections with the Republican party through William J. White, James S. Harper, and Judson Lyons,[85] and were closely related by kinship and marriage.[86] In addition, their fair skin made them generally indistinguishable from the white population, and they were also related to prominent white families by blood.[87]

---

84. Through Ware's leadership, the legislature of the State of Georgia granted a charter to the fledgling Atlanta University, and Ware served as its first president. HORACE MANN BOND, THE EDUCATION OF THE NEGRO IN THE AMERICAN SOCIAL ORDER, New York: Octagon Books, 1970 (originally published 1934), 359.

85. Lyons was an Augusta lawyer who served as a delegate to the Republican National Convention in 1896, where he cast his vote for William McKinley as the Republican presidential candidate. His support for McKinley was later rewarded with an appointment as register of the United States Treasury, the highest political post traditionally open to a black.

86. John C. Ladeveze and James S. Harpers were cousins. Lysons and Ladeveze were brothers-in-law, both having married sisters of John Hope, who would go on to be the first black president of Morehouse College. White and Hope were the closest of friends. Cumming was a deacon of the Union Baptist Church of Augusta, of which John Ladeveze was one of the primary organizers. Cumming was also the stepfather-in-law of H.L. Walker, Ware's principal at the time of the litigation. In addition, the Hopes, Whites and Ladevezes all lived in close proximity. See DAVIS, A CLASHING OF THE SOUL, 28; CASHIN, OLD SPRINGFIELD, 57–73.

87. John Hope was the son of James Hope, a white Augusta businessman, and Mary Frances (Fanny) Taylor, a woman of color. Taylor had previously been in a relationship with Hope's friend and business associate, George Newton, with whom she had two children. Newton was a prominent white Augusta doctor who served as president of the Augusta Medical College until his relationship with Taylor became public. See DAVIS, A CLASHING OF THE SOUL, 2–16; TORRENCE, THE STORY OF JOHN HOPE, 22–34. John Ladeveze and James Harper were the nephews of Mary Bouyer McKinely, a free woman of color, who had been in a longtime relationship with John Carrie, a white man who was a native of France. After Carrie's death, his heirs sued one Henry H. Cumming,

By the 1890s associations between whites and blacks based on personal relation-ships began to wane. Black businesses and services that had been started after the Civil War and had traditionally had an all-white clientele frequently did not sur-vive the turn of the century. The new generation of white leadership that grew to adulthood after the Civil War had no reason to continue such associations, which had been established by their parents and grew out of slavery and other antebellum relations. In addition, with the demise of the Republican party in the South, blacks were gradually disenfranchised. The loss of personal relations along with the loss of the vote gradually eroded whatever power such groups as Augusta's black elite possessed.

Between 1873 and 1898, decisions of the Supreme Court of the United States gave legal support to the social trends that worked against blacks in late nineteenth-century America. In the *Slaughterhouse Cases* and in *United States v. Cruikshank*, the Court drastically curtailed the Privileges and Immunities Clause of the Fourteenth Amendment. In 1883, in the *Civil Rights Cases*, the Court virtually nullified the restrictive parts of the Civil Rights Act of 1875. In 1896 in *Plessy v. Ferguson*, the Court subscribed to the doctrine that "legislation is powerless to eradicate racial instincts," and laid down the separate-but-equal doctrine as justification for segre-gation. Two years later, in *Williams v. Mississippi*, the Court completed the opening of "the legal road to proscription, segregation, and disenfranchisement by approv-ing the Mississippi plan for depriving Negroes of the franchise." In Augusta, an all-white primary eliminated blacks from municipal politics in 1899; a murder and lynching led to the absolute segregation of streetcars in 1900.

As Booker T. Washington accepted the mantle of leadership of the black race in 1895, he sanctioned the Court's movement away from social and civil rights for blacks in post-Reconstruction America. Washington's was a new program "of racial coexistence based upon the concept of racial separation." In his 1895 Atlanta Expo-sition speech, he told blacks and the world that the key to black success was voca-tional education and that "for years to come the education of the people of my race should be so directed that the greatest of the mental strength of the masses will be brought to bear upon the everyday practical things of life." Washington believed that blacks had no need for the traditional classical education in Greek and Latin exemplified by Ware High School. A basic education with emphasis on a trade and industrial education would suffice for blacks. Though Washington is now seen as the major advocate for vocational education for blacks, he should not bear the total responsibility for that vogue in the late nineteenth century; August Meir argues that

---

a white man who was a legatee in Carrie's will. The heirs claimed that Cumming and the other lega-tee, Alexander Duguas, were legatees solely for the benefit of Mary Bouyer, whose race prevented her from inheriting. *See Carrie et al. v. Cumming et al.*, 26 Ga. 690 (1858). It is also interesting to note that the defendant in this case has the same name as the black plaintiff in *Cumming v. Rich-mond County Board*.

"Washington simply brought to a climax a trend [toward industrial and agricultural education] that was well under way before the middle 1890s."

1998 *Journal of Supreme Court History* 72, 74–77.
Copyright © (1998) *Journal of Supreme Court History.*
Reprinted with permission of the *Journal of Supreme Court History* and
C. Ellen Connally.

C. *Cumming v. County Board of Education,* 175 U.S. 528 (1899)

George F. Edmunds for plaintiffs in error.

J. Granahl and *Frank H. Miller* for defendant in error.

1. Facts

Justice HARLAN delivered the opinion of the Court . . .

C. Ellen Connally

Justice Harlan's "Great Betrayal"? A Reconsideration of Cumming v. Richmond County Board of Education*

The original cause of action that the supporters of Ware filed in the Richmond County Court was a petition for equitable relief against the Board of Education and the tax collector. This action for an injunction sought to enjoin the collection of that portion of the property tax levied for school purposes and allocated for the support of the white high schools. It further sought to bar the board from expending 10% of the taxes—the amount spent on the white high schools—until Ware was reinstated. The petitioners alleged that the tax was illegal and void because the county provided a high school for whites but did not provide the same facilities for blacks. The plaintiffs further alleged that they were persons of color and entitled to the full benefit of any system of high schools organized and maintained by the board. By suspending the black high school, the plaintiffs alleged, the board was wholly debarring them from any participation in the benefits of a high school education, although they were being taxed for it.

> They (the plaintiffs) rely upon so much of the constitution of the United States as declares that no State shall deny to any person within its jurisdiction the equal protection of the laws, and aver that the action of the board is a denial of the equal protection of laws; and that it is inequitable, unlawful and unconstitutional for the board to levy upon the petitioners, or for the tax collector to collect from them, any tax for educational purposes, from the benefits of which petitioners, in the persons of their children of school age, are excluded and debarred.

---

* (footnotes omitted).

In seeking this injunctive relief to prevent the collection of the tax and bar spending on the white high schools, the petitioners did not challenge the provisions of the Georgia statute that required segregated schools. Nor did they demand compliance with the *Plessy* decision, which, on the basis of separate but equal, would have required the county to maintain a black high school because it operated a white high school. They made no objection to the taxes paid for the support of the segregated common school, nor to the fact that the school board was all white and lacked black representation. Instead, they argued that, as taxpayers, they were paying taxes for a white high school which they could not attend. Therefore, they argued, the board should either close the white high schools or reinstate Ware.

In addition to the action filed by Cumming, Ladeveze and Harper, there was a companion case entitled *Albert S. Blodgett and Jerry M. Griffin v. School Board*. Separate cases were filed because the lawyers disagreed about the appropriate cause of action in this complicated area of nineteenth-century extraordinary writs. *Blodgett* relied primarily on the Equal Protection Clause of the Fourteenth Amendment and sought a writ of mandamus directing the board to reinstate Ware High School. *Blodgett* argued that continuing to support the two white schools while eliminating Ware was simply an unconstitutional denial of equal protection, and asserted that the board should be ordered by the court to comply with the law. The trial court found that since the board had some discretion under the statute, an action in mandamus was not proper, and it denied the writ. (In ruling on both cases, the trial court did not render a separate opinion in *Blodgett*.)

In response to the request for equitable relief in both cases, the board argued that under the 1872 statute it had no duty to establish a high school, and if it did in fact establish one of the school's continued existence would be purely discretionary. Ruling in *Cumming*, the trial court did not follow the *Plessy* decision, which would have required separate but equal facilities. Instead, the court dismissed the case against the tax collector and enjoined the board from using any funds for the support of the white high school until equal facilities were provided for blacks. The trial judge, Enoch H. Calloway, was a plantation-born former senator who had a reputation as a racial moderate. The trial court held that

> ... the establishment and maintenance of schools of higher grade than common schools, authorized by section 10 of the act [of 1872], is a matter that rests exclusively in the sound discretion of the board. But if the discretion is exercised in the establishment [of such schools] and [they are] maintained in harmony and in compliance with section 9 of the said act, the board must provide the same facilities for high education of both races.

From the victory for the plaintiffs in the trial court, the Board of Education appealed to the Georgia Supreme Court. In reviewing the 1872 Act, the Georgia Supreme Court agreed with the Board of Education and found that the board was required to provide common schools but that any action relative to high schools was solely within their discretion. Based on that discretionary power, the court found that the school board was not required to establish a high school for blacks whenever it established one for whites. "Certainly [the Board of Education] must be allowed a broad discretion . . . and where it is in its discretion to pass upon facts and determine from them the best interest of the people at large, courts will not control its discretion unless it is manifestly abused, although the court may be of the opinion that the corporation erred upon the facts."

The Georgia Supreme Court drew a clear distinction between the free common schools that were mandated under Section Nine of the statute and the high schools provided for in Section Ten. It found that the high schools differed from the primary schools, where students paid no fees. Both white and black high school students were required to pay tuition, and their schools existed as a result of the board's discretion. The court found that the board had not abused its discretion in discontinuing the high school established for the colored race. "The only complaint is that these plaintiffs, being taxpayers, are debarred of the privilege of sending their children to a high school which is not a free school but one where tuition is charged, and that a portion of the school fund, raised by taxation, is appropriated to sustain a white school to which Negroes are not admitted." The court allowed the board to consider as a factor in their decision the fact that there were three private sectarian high schools whose tuition was less than Ware's available to the black high school students.

Relative to the alleged violations of the Constitution of the United States and the Fourteenth Amendment, the Georgia Supreme Court found that the point had been argued neither orally nor by brief, with the only mention of it being made at the end of the brief. The court concluded:

> If any authority had been cited, we could from that have determined which paragraph or clause counsel relied upon; but as he has left us in the dark, we can only say that in our opinion none of the clauses of any of the paragraphs of the amendment, under the facts disclosed by the record, is violated by the board.

By reversing the order of the trial court the Georgia Supreme Court let stand the board's order for the closing of Ware. When the Georgia Supreme Court returned the case, the lower court, having been reversed, dismissed the petition of the plaintiffs. The plaintiffs then appealed to the Supreme Court of the United States on the basis of the trial court's dismissal of their petition for injunctive relief.

1998 *Journal of Supreme Court History* 72, 78–80.
Copyright © (1998) *Journal of Supreme Court History.*
Reprinted with permission of the *Journal of Supreme Court History* and
C. Ellen Connally.

2. Opinion

This writ of error brings up for review a final order made in the superior court of Richmond County, Georgia, in conformity to a judgment rendered in the supreme court of the state. That order, it is contended, deprived the plaintiffs in error of rights secured to them by the Fourteenth Amendment to the Constitution of the United States.

The supreme court of Georgia, after stating in its opinion that counsel for the petitioners did not point out in his brief what particular paragraph of the Fourteenth Amendment was violated, said: "If it be the first, he does not point out what clause of that paragraph is violated, whether the privileges or immunities of citizens of the United States are abridged, whether his clients are deprived of life, liberty, or property without due process of law, or whether his clients are denied the equal protection of the laws. It is difficult, therefore, for us to determine whether this amendment had been violated. If any authority had been cited, we could from that have determined which paragraph or clause counsel relied upon, but as he has left us in the dark we can only say that in our opinion none of the clauses of any of the paragraphs of the amendment, under the facts disclosed by the record, is violated by the board. There is no complaint in the petition that there is any discrimination made in regard to the free common schools of the county. So far as the record discloses, both races have the same facilities and privileges of attending them. The only complaint is that these plaintiffs, being taxpayers, are debarred the privilege of sending their children to a high school which is not a free school, but one where tuition is charged, and that a portion of the school fund, raised by taxation, is appropriated to sustain white high schools to which negroes are not admitted. . . .

The Constitution of Georgia provides: "There shall be a thorough system of common schools for the education of children in the elementary branches of an English education only, as nearly uniform as practicable, the expenses of which shall be provided for by taxation, or otherwise. The schools shall be free to all children of the state, but separate schools shall be provided for the white and colored races." Art. 8, § 1.

It was said at the argument that the vice in the common-school system of Georgia was the requirement that the white and colored children of the state be educated in separate schools. But we need not consider that question in this case. No such issue was made in the pleadings. Indeed, the plaintiffs distinctly state that they have no objection to the tax in question so far as levied for the support of primary, intermediate, and grammar schools, in the management of which the rule as to the separation of races is enforced. We must dispose of the case as it is presented by the record.

The plaintiffs in error complain that the board of education used the funds in its hands to assist in maintaining a high school for white children without providing a similar school for colored children. The substantial relief asked is an injunction that would either impair the efficiency of the high school provided for white children or compel the board to close it. But if that were done, the result would only be to take from white children educational privileges enjoyed by them, without giving to colored children additional opportunities for the education furnished in high schools. The colored school children of the county would not be advanced in the matter of their education by a decree compelling the defendant board to cease giving support to a high school for white children. The board had before it the question whether it should maintain, under its control, a high school for about 60 colored children or withhold the benefits of education in primary schools from 300 children of the same race. It was impossible, the board believed, to give educational facilities to the 300 colored children who were unprovided for, if it maintained a separate school for the 60 children who wished to have a high-school education. Its decision was in the interest of the greater number of colored children, leaving the smaller number to obtain a high-school education in existing private institutions at an expense not beyond that incurred in the high school discontinued by the board.

We are not permitted by the evidence in the record to regard that decision as having been made with any desire or purpose on the part of the board to discriminate against any of the colored school children of the county on account of their race. . . .

3. Holding

The state court did not deem the action of the board of education in suspending temporarily and for economic reasons the high school for colored children a sufficient reason why the defendant should be restrained by injunction from maintaining an existing high school for white children. It rejected the suggestion that the board proceeded in bad faith or had abused the discretion with which it was invested by the statute under which it proceeded or had acted in hostility to the colored race. Under the circumstances disclosed, we cannot say that this action of the state court was, within the meaning of the Fourteenth Amendment, a denial by the state to the plaintiffs and to those associated with them of the equal protection of the laws or of any privileges belonging to them as citizens of the United States. We may add that while all admit that the benefits and burdens of public taxation must be shared by citizens without discrimination against any class on account of their race, the education of the people in schools maintained by state taxation is a matter belonging to the respective states, and any interference on the part of Federal authority with the management of such schools cannot be justified except in the case of a clear and unmistakable disregard of rights secured by the supreme law of the land. We have here no such case to be determined; and as this view disposes of the only question which this court has jurisdiction to review and decide, the judgment is affirmed.

D. Commentary on *Cumming*

The unanimous opinion in *Cumming* appeared to approve implicitly the operation of segregated schools. A group of black parents and taxpayers challenged the closure of the Richmond County high school open to black children while keeping open the high school available only to whites. The board argued that it lacked the funds to provide both primary and secondary schools for blacks and that it could better fulfill the educational needs of the black population by training the larger number of elementary school pupils instead of the smaller group of high school students.

At oral argument, the plaintiffs explicitly challenged the constitutionality of separate schools. The Court, however, refused to consider that argument because it had not been raised in the pleadings. Justice Harlan went on to point out that the aggrieved blacks could not benefit from the relief they were seeking because an injunction would close the white high school rather than compel the board to maintain a black school. Harlan asserted that the record contained no evidence that the board of education intentionally discriminated against the black children.[88] In the absence of a "clear and unmistakable disregard" of federally protected rights, education was exclusively a matter of state concern.[89] Hence, under certain circumstances, black high school students had no enforceable right to attend a public school, and black parents could be compelled to pay taxes to support a system from which some of their children were "unintentionally" excluded.

The Supreme Court did not confront the issue of equal protection, since it had not been raised in the lower court. Does the rationale to support the greatest number of students violate the rights of the few? There is no constitutional privilege to an education. However, is there an implied right?

C. Ellen Connally

Justice Harlan's "Great Betrayal"? A Reconsideration of Cumming v. Richmond County Board of Education*

... The Richmond County School Board's decision on July 10, 1897, to support a basic education for three to four hundred primary students over a classical education for sixty high school students mirrored the dispute that raged between Booker T. Washington's followers and those of W.E.B. DuBois at the beginning of the twentieth century. The demise of Ware High School arguably reflected the adoption of Washington's point of view of education for blacks to the detriment of the talented tenth. It further closed a chapter on an era when black Republicans had strong influence over the Board of Education and its decisions.

In this period of economic downturn, the school board decided that if money was to be spent for the education of blacks, a primary education for the many was preferable to a classical education for the few—the sixty children of Augusta's black elite. Ware High School had been named after a white abolitionist, and its principal at the time was president of the Negro Teachers Association. Given these facts, the school board arguably saw Ware as a source of agitation, present and future, for the white establishment. Since the black high school students were already paying

---

88. The *Cumming* Court noted that "different questions might have arisen" had the plaintiffs sought to compel the board to operate a black high school, and the board refused out of racial bias to do so. 175 U.S. at 545. In fact, the plaintiffs had prayed for "such other and further relief as [is] equitable and just," *id.* at 531, a prayer that might have supported such an order.

89. *Id.* at 545. This latter statement at least raises the possibility that the Court failed to examine alternative forms of relief out of its own racial prejudice.

* (some footnotes omitted).

tuition, the board argued, let them continue to pay a lesser amount and attend one of the three church-supported schools that had been started since 1880. This would allow the school board to educate the greater number of primary-age black children. From the perspective of the board, less-educated blacks were less likely to assert their rights. Arguably, too, the board came to realize that with the loss of the franchise Ware High School was no longer the good political investment it had been.

The friends and colored patrons of Ware High School were called before the school board before the announcement of the final decision and given an opportunity to voice their concerns over the closing. Although the decision in all likelihood had already been made, this meant that the blacks could not say they had been denied a hearing. William J. White and John Ladeveze made impassioned pleas. However, at the hearing before the all-white board, they were told the reasons for the discontinuation were purely economic, a position that the board maintained throughout the litigation:

> Four hundred or more Negro children were being turned away from the primary grades unable to be provided with seats or teachers; because the same means and the same building which were used to teach sixty high school pupils would accommodate two hundred pupils in the rudiments of education; because the board at this time was not financially able to erect buildings and employ additional teachers for the large number of colored children who were in need of primary education and because there were in the city of Augusta at this time three public high schools—the Haines Industrial School, the Walker Baptist Institute and the Paine Institute— each of which were public to colored people and were charging fees no larger than the board charged for pupilage in the Ware High School.

The board did, however, promise to reinstate Ware when the board's financial condition improved.

. . . A careful analysis of the ruling in *Cumming* demonstrates that the decision did not deal directly with the issue of racial segregation in public schools. Because the existence of a black high school was at issue, lower federal courts and state courts fashioned a separate-but-equal formula for schools out of *Plessy v. Ferguson* and *Cumming*, later including *Berea College v. Kentucky*. In referring to *Cumming*, historian Loren Miller says that "[i]n time the fiction grew that the Supreme Court had considered and determined th[e] issue with finality, whereas the truth was that it had only skirted around the question and had spoken only by evasions and indirections." *Cumming* was misread and misinterpreted in order to justify society's desire to maintain segregated schools, a tradition that has a long and tragic legacy in American society. . . .

None of the Augusta lawyers originally retained by the plaintiffs were experienced constitutional lawyers. They were men that shared a commonality of status in Augusta: they were all outsiders to the establishment. The black plaintiffs could not afford to obtain the services of more prominent members of the Augusta establishment. Their attempts to gain financial support outside of Augusta met with little success, and an appeal to Booker T. Washington to help with fundraising produced no significant funds. As a result, "the Augustans were forced to rely almost entirely on their own resources." It is also probable that no white lawyer of standing wanted to challenge the decision of the county school board. In addition, although John Ladeveze's brother-in-law Judson Lyons was a lawyer, he was fully engaged in his government position by 1897 and, according to Kousser, his law partner lacked experience.

However, when the case went before the U.S. Supreme Court, the plaintiffs were represented by no less an imposing figure than former Vermont Senator George F. Edmunds. In 1897, Edmunds was in semi-retirement from his law practice and was wintering in Aiken, SC, a resort town fifteen miles from Augusta that was then very popular with rich Yankees. There Robert Harper, the father of plaintiff James S. Harper, approached him about the Ware case. Touched by the blacks' plight, Edmunds took the case without fee.

Edmunds represented the state of Vermont in the Senate from 1866 to 1891. As Chairman of the Judiciary Committee in 1877, he waged a serious attack on the appointment to the Supreme Court of the United States of the future author of the *Cumming* opinion, Justice John Marshall Harlan. This attack grew not so much out of a dislike for Harlan as out of a distrust for Harlan's Republicanism and a desire to deliver a defeat to the recently elected (or selected, depending on one's interpretation of the much-disputed election of 1876) President, Rutherford B. Hayes. Harlan biographer Loren P. Beth describes Edmunds as a stubborn man of rocklike integrity who was one of the ablest constitutional lawyers in Congress. Edmunds twice turned down offers of appointment to the Supreme Court of the United States and was a serious contender for the White House in 1880 and 1884, primarily because of his ability to maneuver cautiously between the two major factions of the Republican party. "He was thought by some to be a Half Breed and by some to be a Stalwart." The independent Mugwumps saw him as a man who could play all sides of the street, a reputation that earned him the name "The Stalwart Sweetheart of the Reformers."

If there is one thing consistently said about Edmunds, it is that he lacked a winning personality. In an age prior to the popular election of members of the Senate, Edmunds was a man who "was not calculated to inspire much popular enthusiasm." More commonly, he was noted for his "lack of amiability and contentious nature." He is described as "flinty," dour, austere and gruff, and a man possessed of a sharp tongue and a contentious disposition. For all his respectability, "there were skeletons in his closet, and he admitted something of a fondness for spirits, causing the temperance-minded President Hayes to refer to him as a 'confirmed—well, hard drinker.'"

As to his knowledge of the Constitution and his support of equality for black Americans as guaranteed by the Fourteenth Amendment, however, Edmunds was beyond reproach. He was a chief sponsor of the Civil Rights Act of 1875 before and after the death of Charles Sumner. During Sumner's fight of almost twenty years to pass a civil rights law that included "mixed" (integrated) schools, Sumner could always depend on Edmunds. The bill, which eventually passed in 1875 after Sumner's death, originally included a provision that would have required integrated public schools. However, that provision was dropped to make the bill more widely acceptable. According to John Hope Franklin, "Negro members of Congress fought vigorously, if unsuccessfully, to keep the integrated schools provision in the bill because they were convinced that there could be no equality in education in segregated schools." In debates surrounding this issue, Edmunds attacked the argument that segregated schools were constitutional if equal provisions were made for each race, "and amassed a careful array of statistics to prove that the practical effect of segregation was to 'destroy equality of opportunity for Negro children.'"

When the *Civil Rights Cases* came before the Supreme Court of the United States, Justice Harlan met with Edmunds, who provided the Justice with a list of civil rights legislation enacted by Congress during Reconstruction, as well as the pages of the *Congressional Globe* transcribing the debates over their constitutionality. Despite Edmunds' early opposition to Harlan, the two became friends. Indeed, Edmunds was on such friendly terms with all the members of the Supreme Court that he regularly consulted them when he was unsure whether it would be proper for him as a Senator to accept a retainer from a particular corporation. One wonders if his once intimate relation with the Court made Edmunds, a seventy-one-year-old, semi-retired, hard-drinking former Senator on the downside of his career, overconfident of his ability to sway the Justices in favor of his clients in the *Cumming* matter.

In singing the praises of Edmunds, Kousser asserts that the Augusta plaintiffs had "superlative" counsel. However, this view of Edmunds may have considered the former Senator's overall reputation, rather than his briefs, arguments, and legal strategy in *Cumming*. In this situation, Edmunds was a lawyer who took up a case on appeal. He did not make the record in the trial court, nor did he select the original procedural steps. Like the dressmaker who is called in to complete a garment after someone else has cut the fabric, Edmunds could only work with what he had. In reviewing the record, one wonders if he really understood the nature of the appeal. It appears that his focus was on the bigger picture of the Fourteenth Amendment rather than the actual ruling that went up on appeal.

Even Kousser admits that Edmunds made a fatal error when he chose to appeal *Cumming* as opposed to *Blodgett*, which sought a mandamus and focused the equal protection argument. Edmunds apparently believed that the *Cumming* case sufficiently raised the constitutional questions. As a result, he was not concerned about the form of the proceeding. It is interesting to note that Edmunds left orders that all of his personal papers be burned upon his death, orders which were carried out. Accordingly, no records of why he made this crucial decision exist.

The appeal to the Supreme Court of the United States should have centered on whether or not the trial court properly dismissed the plaintiff's action for injunctive relief, as that was the final appealable order reviewed by the Georgia Supreme Court and the one from which the plaintiffs brought their appeal. However, Edmunds largely ignored this point. As mentioned above, the Georgia Supreme Court said that the plaintiffs had made general reference to the United States Constitution and the Fourteenth Amendment but had failed to cite specific sections, making it impossible for the court to rule on that issue. When Edmunds filed his appeal to the Supreme Court, he made the following assignments of errors, all of which essentially argue a denial of equal protection:

> *First,* That the statute of the State of Georgia, as construed by the Supreme Court of Georgia, giving a discretion to the said county board of education to establish and maintain high schools for white persons and to discontinue and refuse to maintain high schools for person of the negro race, was, and is, contrary to the Constitution of the United States, and especially to the Fourteenth Amendment thereof.

> *Second,* That the said court decided and held that the Constitution of the United States was not violated by the action of the said board in establishing and maintaining public high schools for the education of white persons exclusively, and in refusing to establish and maintain high school for the education of persons similarly situated of the negro race.

> *Third,* In deciding and holding that persons of the negro race could, consistently with the Constitution of the United States, be by the laws or authorities of Georgia, taxed, and the money derived from their taxation be appropriated to the establishment and maintenance of high schools for white persons, while pursuant to the same law the said board, at the same time, refused to establish and maintain high schools for the education of persons of the Negro race.

> *Fourth,* That the said Superior Court erred in dismissing the complaint of the plaintiff in error.

In less than seventeen pages — compared to a twenty-three page brief filed by the Board of Education — Edmunds argued the general proposition that if the whites have a high school, the blacks have a right to the same facilities under the equal protection clause. He argued that the decision of the board was not a reasonable exercise of their discretion and constituted arbitrary denial of the equal protection of the laws. Rather than cite a large number of cases in support of his equal protection argument, Edmunds stated that "[i]t is believed that all the numerous decisions of this court upon this and analogous subjects are agreeable to the foregoing statement. It is unnecessary to refer to more than a very few of them." As a result, he cited only five Supreme Court of the United States cases.

Edmunds failed to cite any state or federal court cases and Kousser concedes that this decision was "probably a mistake." To support this, he asserts that Edmunds' tactical error lay in not citing the two leading federal cases on schools, *U.S. v. Buntin* and *Claybrook v. Owensboro.* However, both cases assume the validity of separate schools, and help the plaintiffs only so far as that they find that blacks were entitled to separate schools. In *Buntin*, the Court left schools up to the discretion of the states and implied broad discretion on the part of the states in making decisions relative to classification of students. Similarly, while there is a finding in *Claybrook* that blacks are entitled to separate but equal schools, the court also found regarding equal protection that "this does not mean absolute equality in distributing the benefits of taxation. This is impracticable; but it does mean the distribution of the benefits upon some fair and equal classification or basis."

While Edmunds dealt with generalities, counsel for the school board dealt with specifics, handling each issue methodically. Before reaching the plaintiffs' assignments of error, the board argued that the case could not proceed because the tax collector was no longer a party. The action was for an injunction against the tax collector. How could the cause of action proceed without this necessary party? The board further argued that the issue of a violation of the Fourteenth Amendment had not been properly raised in the trial court and therefore was void, and that there was no showing of an "evil intent" on the board's part, such intent being a necessary element in an action in equity. Counsel for the board admitted that there might have been an error in judgment, but questioned whether the Supreme Court was required to step in, decide such questions, and review each decision of a school board. Thus systematically attacking each assignment of error, the Board of Education filed a far more comprehensive brief than that of the plaintiffs.

1998 *Journal of Supreme Court History* 72, 73–83.
Copyright © (1998) *Journal of Supreme Court History*.
Reprinted with permission of the *Journal of Supreme Court History* and
C. Ellen Connally.

E. Background on *Lum*

While most challenges to racial segregation involved black plaintiffs, other racial groups also had been subjected to such practices. Americans of Chinese descent were one such group. Sometimes the racial separation was directed at the Chinese alone; other times the Chinese were lumped together with all persons who were not characterized as white.

F. *Lum v. Rice*, 275 U.S. 78 (1927)

J.N. Flowers, Earl Brewer, and *Edward C. Brewer* for plaintiff in error.

Rush H. Knox, Attorney General of Mississippi, and *E.C. Sharp* for defendant in error.

1. Facts

Chief Justice TAFT delivered the opinion of the Court.

Gong Lum is a resident of Mississippi, resides in the Rosedale Consolidated High School District, and is the father of Martha Lum. He is engaged in the mercantile business. Neither he nor she was connected with the consular service, or any other service, of the government of China, or any other government, at the time of her birth. She was nine years old when the petition was filed, having been born January 21, 1915, and she sued by her next friend, Chew How, who is a native born citizen of the United States and the state of Mississippi. The petition alleged that she was of good moral character, between the ages of 5 and 21 years, and that, as she was such a citizen and an educable child, it became her father's duty under the law to send her to school; that she desired to attend the Rosedale consolidated high school; that at the opening of the school she appeared as a pupil, but at the noon recess she was notified by the superintendent that she would not be allowed to return to the school; that an order had been issued by the board of trustees, who are made defendants, excluding her from attending the school solely on the ground that she was of Chinese descent, and not a member of the white or Caucasian race, and that their order had been made in pursuance to instructions from the state superintendent of education of Mississippi, who is also made a defendant.

The petitioners further show that there is no school maintained in the district for the education of children of Chinese descent, and none established in Bolivar County where she could attend.

The Constitution of Mississippi (Const. 1890, ss 201, 206) requires that there shall be a county common school fund, made up of poll taxes from the various counties, to be retained in the counties where the same is collected, and a state common school fund to be taken from the general fund in the state treasury, which together shall be sufficient to maintain a common school for a term of four months in each scholastic year, but that any county or separate school district may levy an additional tax to maintain schools for a longer time than a term of four months, and that the said common school fund shall be distributed among the several counties and separate school districts in proportion to the number of educable children in each, to be collected from the data in the office of the state superintendent of education in the manner prescribed by law; that the Legislature encourage by all suitable means the promotion of intellectual, scientific, moral, and agricultural improvement, by the establishment of a uniform system of free public schools by taxation or otherwise, for all children between the ages of 5 and 21 years, and as soon as practicable, establish schools of higher grade.

The petition alleged that, in obedience to this mandate of the Constitution, the Legislature has provided for the establishment and for the payment of the expenses of the Rosedale consolidated high school, and that the plaintiff, Gong Lum, the petitioner's father, is a taxpayer and helps to support and maintain the school; that Martha Lum is an educable child, is entitled to attend the school as a pupil, and that this is the only school conducted in the district available for her as a pupil; that the right to attend it is a valuable right; that she is not a member of the colored race, nor is she of mixed blood, but that she is pure Chinese; that she is by the action of the board of trustees and the state superintendent discriminated against directly, and denied her right to be a member of the Rosedale school; that the school authorities have no discretion under the law as to her admission as a pupil in the school, but that they continue without authority of law to deny her the right to attend it as a pupil. For these reasons the writ of mandamus is prayed for against the defendants, commanding them and each of them to desist from discriminating against her on account of her race or ancestry, and to give her the same rights and privileges that other educable children between the ages of 5 and 21 are granted in the Rosedale consolidated high school.

The trial court overruled the demurrer and ordered that a writ of mandamus issue to the defendants as prayed in the petition.

2. Arguments on Appeal

J.N. Flowers, Earl Brewer, and *Edward C. Brewer* for plaintiff in error.

The white, or Caucasian, race, which makes the laws and construes and enforces them, thinks that in order to protect itself against the infusion of the blood of other races its children must be kept in schools from which other races are excluded. The classification is made for the exclusive benefit of the law-making race. The basic assumption is that if the children of two races associate daily in the school room the two races will at last intermix; that the purity of each is jeopardized by the mingling of the children in the school room; that such association among children means social intercourse and social equality. This danger, the white race, by its laws, seeks to divert from itself. It levies the taxes on all alike to support a public school system, but in the organization of the system it creates its own exclusive schools for its children, and other schools for the children of all other races to attend together.

If there is danger in the association, it is a danger from which one race is entitled to protection just the same as another. The white race may not legally expose the yellow race to a danger that the dominant race recognizes and, by the same laws, guards itself against. The white race creates for itself a privilege that it denies to other races; exposes the children of other races to risks and dangers to which it would not expose its own children. This is discrimination. *Lehew v. Brummel,* 103 Mo. 549; *Strauder v. West Virginia,* 100 U.S. 303.

Color may reasonably be used as a basis for classification only in so far as it indicates a particular race. Race may reasonably be used as a basis. "Colored" describes only one race, and that is the Negro. *State v. Treadway,* 126 La. 52; *Lehew v. Brummel, supra; Plessy v. Ferguson,* 163 U.S. 537; *Berea College v. Kentucky,* 133 Ky. 209; *West Chester R.R. v. Miles,* 55 Pa. St. 209; *Tucker v. Blease,* 97 S.C. 303.

3. Mississippi Supreme Court Opinion

The defendants then appealed to the Supreme Court of Mississippi, which heard the case. *Rice v. Gong Lum,* 139 Miss. 760, 104 So. 105. In its opinion, it directed its attention to the proper construction of section 207 of the State Constitution of 1890, which provides: "Separate schools shall be maintained for children of the white and colored races."

The court held that this provision of the Constitution divided the educable children into those of the pure white or Caucasian race, on the one hand, and the brown, yellow, and black races, on the other, and therefore that Martha Lum, of the Mongolian or yellow race, could not insist on being classed with the whites under this constitutional division. The court said: "The Legislature is not compelled to provide separate schools for each of the colored races, and unless and until it does provide such schools, and provide for segregation of the other races, such races are entitled to have the benefit of the colored public schools. Under our statutes a colored public school exists in every county and in some convenient district, in which every colored child is entitled to obtain an education. These schools are within the reach of all the children of the state, and the plaintiff does not show by her petition that she applied for admission to such schools. On the contrary, the petitioner takes the position that, because there are no separate public schools for Mongolians, she is entitled to enter the white public schools in preference to the colored public schools. A consolidated school in this state is simply a common school conducted as other common schools are conducted; the only distinction being that two or more school districts have been consolidated into one school. Such consolidation is entirely discretionary with the county school board, having reference to the condition existing in the particular territory. Where a school district has an unusual amount of territory, with an unusual valuation of property therein, it may levy additional taxes. But the other common schools under similar statutes have the same power.

"If the plaintiff desires, she may attend the colored public schools of her district, or, if she does not so desire, she may go to a private school. The compulsory school law of this state does not require the attendance at a public school, and a parent under the decisions of the Supreme Court of the United States has a right to educate his child in a private school if he so desires. But plaintiff is not entitled to attend a white public school."

4. Opinion

As we have seen, the plaintiffs aver that the Rosedale consolidated high school is the only school conducted in that district available for Martha Lum as a pupil. They also aver that there is no school maintained in the District of Bolivar County for the education of Chinese children, and none in the county. How are these averments to be reconciled with the statement of the state Supreme Court that colored schools are maintained in every county by virtue of the Constitution? This seems to be explained, in the language of the state Supreme Court, as follows: "By statute it is provided that all the territory of each county of the state shall be divided into school districts separately for the white and colored races; that is to say, the whole territory is to be divided into white school districts, and then a new division of the county for colored school districts. In other words, the statutory scheme is to make the districts, outside of the separate school districts, districts for the particular race, white or colored, so that the territorial limits of the school districts need not be the same, but the territory embraced in a school district for the colored race may not be the same territory embraced in the school district for the white race, and vice versa, which system of creating the common school districts for the two races, white and colored, do not require schools for each race as such to be maintained in each district; but each child, no matter from what territory, is assigned to some school district, the school buildings being separately located and separately controlled, but each having the same curriculum, and each having the same number of months of school term, if the attendance is maintained for the said statutory period, which school district of the common or public schools has certain privileges, among which is to maintain a public school by local taxation for a longer period of time than the said term of four months under named conditions which apply alike to the common schools for the white and colored races."

We must assume, then, that there are school districts for colored children in Bolivar County, but that no colored school is within the limits of the Rosedale consolidated high school district. This is not inconsistent with there being at a place outside of that district and in a different district, a colored school which the plaintiff Martha Lum may conveniently attend. If so, she is not denied, under the existing school system, the right to attend and enjoy the privileges of a common school education in a colored school. If it were otherwise, the petition should have contained an allegation showing it. Had the petition alleged specifically that there was no colored school in Martha Lum's neighborhood to which she could conveniently go, a different question would have been presented, and this, without regard to the state Supreme Court's construction of the state Constitution as limiting the white schools provided for the education of children of the white or Caucasian race. But we do not find the petition to present such a situation.

The case then reduces itself to the question whether a state can be said to afford to a child of Chinese ancestry, born in this country and a citizen of the United States, the equal protection of the laws, by giving her the opportunity for a common school education in a school which receives only colored children of the brown, yellow or black races.

The right and power of the state to regulate the method of providing for the education of its youth at public expense is clear. In *Cumming v. Richmond County Board of Education*, 175 U. S. 528, 545, 20 S. Ct. 197, 201, 44 L. Ed. 262, persons of color sued the Board of Education to enjoin it from maintaining a high school for white children without providing a similar school for colored children, which had existed and had been discontinued. Justice Harlan, in delivering the opinion of the court, said: "Under the circumstances disclosed, we cannot say that this action of the state court was, within the meaning of the Fourteenth Amendment, a denial by the state to the plaintiffs and to those associated with them of the equal protection of the laws, or of any privileges belonging to them as citizens of the United States. We may add that, while all admit that the benefits and burdens of public taxation must be shared by citizens without discrimination against any class on account of their race, the education of the people in schools maintained by state taxation is a matter belonging to the respective states, and any interference on the part of federal authority with the management of such schools cannot be justified, except in the case of a clear and unmistakable disregard of rights secured by the supreme law of the land."

The question here is whether a Chinese citizen of the United States is denied equal protection of the laws when he is classed among the colored races and furnished facilities for education equal to that offered to all, whether white, brown, yellow, or black. Were this a new question, it would call for very full argument and consideration; but we think that it is the same question which has been many times decided to be within the constitutional power of the state Legislature to settle, without intervention of the federal courts under the federal Constitution. *Roberts v. City of Boston*, 5 Cush. (Mass.) 198, 206, 208, 209; *State ex rel. Garnes v. McCann*, 21 Ohio St. 198, 210; *People ex rel. King v. Gallagher*, 93 N. Y. 438, 45 Am. Rep. 232; *People ex rel. Cisco v. School Board*, 161 N. Y. 598, 56 N. E. 81, 48 L. R. A. 113; *Ward v. Flood*, 48 Cal. 36, 17 Am. Rep. 405; *Wysinger v. Crookshank*, 82 Cal. 588, 590, 23 P. 54; *Reynolds v. Board of Education*, 66 Kan. 672, 72 P. 274; *McMillan v. School Committee*, 107 N. C. 609, 12 S. E. 330, 10 L. R. A. 823; *Cory v. Carter*, 48 Ind. 327, 17 Am. Rep. 738; *Lehew v. Brummell*, 103 Mo. 546, 15 S. W. 765, 11 L. R. A. 828, 23 Am. St. Rep. 895; *Dameron v. Bayless*, 14 Ariz. 180, 126 P. 273; *State ex rel. Stoutmeyer v. Duffy*, 7 Nev. 342, 348, 355, 8 Am. Rep. 713; *Bertonneau v. Board*, 3 Woods, 177, 3 Fed. Cas. 294, No. 1,361; *United States v. Buntin* (C. C.) 10 F. 730, 735; *Wong Him v. Callahan* (C. C.) 119 F. 381.

In *Plessy v. Ferguson*, 163 U. S. 537, 544, 545, 16 S. Ct. 1138, 1140, 41 L. Ed. 256, in upholding the validity under the Fourteenth Amendment of a statute of Louisiana requiring the separation of the white and colored races in railway coaches, a more difficult question than this, this court, speaking of permitted race separation, said: "The most common instance of this is connected with the establishment of separate schools for white and colored children, which has been held to be a valid exercise of the legislative power even by courts of states where the political rights of the colored race have been longest and most earnestly enforced."

The case of *Roberts v. City of Boston*, supra, in which Chief Justice Shaw, of the Supreme Judicial Court of Massachusetts, announced the opinion of that court upholding the separation of colored and white schools under a state constitutional injunction of equal protection, the same as the Fourteenth Amendment, was then referred to, and this court continued: "Similar laws have been enacted by Congress under its general power of legislation over the District of Columbia (Rev. Stat. D. C. ss 281, 282, 283, 310, 319), as well as by the Legislatures of many of the states, and have been generally, if not uniformly, sustained by the courts" — citing many of the cases above named.

5. Holding

Most of the cases cited arose, it is true, over the establishment of separate schools as between white pupils and black pupils; but we cannot think that the question is any different, or that any different result can be reached, assuming the cases above cited to be rightly decided, where the issue is as between white pupils and the pupils of the yellow races. The decision is within the discretion of the state in regulating its public schools, and does not conflict with the Fourteenth Amendment.

The judgment of the Supreme Court of Mississippi is *affirmed*.

G. Commentary on *Lum*

Jonathan Entin

Sweatt v. Painter: *The End of Segregation and the Transformation of Education Law*

By the time of *Gong Lum v. Rice*, the validity of school segregation seemed unquestioned. An American child of Chinese descent was barred from attending the local white high school because officials had classified her as colored. Chief Justice Taft, for a unanimous Court,[90] peremptorily rejected her equal protection challenge, noting that many cases had permitted states to operate separate schools without federal intervention. That those decisions involved black plaintiffs was immaterial; Orientals could be classified as nonwhite.[91]

5 *Review of Litigation* 13, 17.
Copyright © (1986) University of Texas Law School.
Reprinted with permission of the University of Texas Law School.

H. Background on *Hernández*

In states located in the Southwestern portion of the United States where the largest minority group was Mexican American, discrimination and segregation were just as extensive and severe as they were for blacks throughout the country. The main areas of racial oppression for blacks: the criminal justice system, housing, and education, were also areas where Mexican Americans were subjected to racial oppression.

---

90. The Court included Justices Holmes, Brandeis, and Stone, who are widely viewed as among the most liberal members to have served up to that time. Stone, of course, wrote the famous footnote 4 in *United States v. Carolene Products Co.*, 304 U.S. 144, 152 n.4 (1938), the leading text for judicial protection of minority rights. *See* Cover, *The Origins of Judicial Activism in the Protection of Minorities*, 91 YALE L.J. 1287, 1289–97 (1982). Holmes, however, was notably unsympathetic to racial equality claims. For example, he joined the majority opinion in *Berea College* and in a number of decisions upholding state laws requiring segregation in transportation. He dissented in *Bailey v. Alabama*, 219 U.S. 219 (1911), an important Thirteenth-Amendment case, after having written the opinion for the Court disposing of the controversy at an earlier stage on procedural grounds. *Bailey v. Alabama*, 211 U.S. 452 (1908). *See generally* Rogat, *Mr. Justice Holmes: A Dissenting Opinion* (pt. 2), 15 STAN. L. REV. 254, 255–75 (1963).

91. 275 U.S. at 85–87. The Chief Justice discussed *Cumming, Plessy,* and *Roberts,* and cited more than a dozen other state and federal cases. *Id.*

In 1951 in the town of Edna, Texas, an agricultural worker, Pedro Hernandez, sometimes called 'Pete', murdered his employer, Joe Espinosa, after an argument in a local bar. In the subsequent trial, Hernandez would seek protection against race discrimination in juror selection.

I. *Hernández v. Texas*, 347 U.S. 475 (1954)

1. Facts

Chief Justice WARREN delivered the opinion of the Court.

The petitioner, Pete Hernández, was indicted for the murder of one Joe Espinosa by a grand jury in Jackson County, Texas. He was convicted and sentenced to life imprisonment.... [T]he petitioner offered timely motions to quash the indictment and the jury panel. He alleged that persons of Mexican descent were systematically excluded from service as jury commissioners, grand jurors, and petit jurors, although there were such persons fully qualified to serve residing in Jackson County. The petitioner asserted that exclusion of this class deprived him, as a member of the class, of the equal protection of the laws. . . .

2. Opinion

In numerous decisions, this Court has held that it is a denial of the equal protection of the laws to try a defendant of a particular race or color under an indictment issued by a grand jury, or before a petit jury, from which all persons of his race or color have, solely because of that race or color, been excluded by the State, whether acting through its legislature, its courts, or its executive or administrative officers. . . . The State of Texas would have us hold that there are only two classes — white and Negro — within the contemplation of the fourteenth Amendment. The decisions of this Court do no support that view. And, except where the question presented involves the exclusion of persons of Mexican descent from juries, Texas courts have taken a broader view of the scope of the Equal Protection Clause.

Throughout our history differences in race and color have defined easily identifiable groups which have at times required the aid of the courts in securing equal treatment under the laws. But community prejudices are not static, and from time to time other differences from the community norm may define other groups which need the same protection. Whether such a group exists within a community is a question of fact. When the existence of a distinct class is demonstrated, and it is further shown that the laws, as written or as applied, single out that class for different treatment not based on some reasonable classification, the guarantees of the Constitution have been violated. The Fourteenth Amendment is not directly solely against discrimination due to a "two-class theory" — that is, based upon differences between "white" and Negro.

As the petitioner acknowledges, the Texas system of selecting grand and petit jurors by the use of jury commissions is fair on its face and capable of being utilized without discrimination. But as this Court has held, the system is susceptible to abuse and can be employed in a discriminatory manner. The exclusion of otherwise eligible persons from jury service solely because of their ancestry or national origin is discrimination prohibited by the Fourteenth Amendment. The Texas statute makes no such discrimination, but the petitioner alleges that those administering the law do.

The petitioner's initial burden in substantiating his charge of group discrimination was to prove that persons of Mexican descent constitute a separate class in Jackson County, distinct from "whites." One method by which this may be demonstrated is by showing the attitude of the community. Here the testimony of responsible officials and citizens contained the admission that residents of the community distinguished between "white" and "Mexican." The participation of persons of Mexican descent in business and community groups was shown to be slight. Until very recent times, children of Mexican descent were required to attend a segregated school for the first four grades. At least one restaurant in town prominently displayed a sign announcing "No Mexicans Served." On the courthouse grounds at the time of the hearing, there were two men's toilets, one unmarked, and the other marked "Colored Men" and "Hombres Aqui" ("Men Here"). No substantial evidence was offered to rebut the logical inference to be drawn from these facts, and it must be concluded that petitioner succeeded in his proof.

Having established the existence of a class, petitioner was then charged with the burden of proving discrimination. To do so, he relied on the pattern of proof established by *Norris v. State of Alabama*, 294 U.S. 587. In that case, proof that Negroes constituted a substantial segment of the population of the jurisdiction, that some Negroes were qualified to serve as jurors, and that none had been called for jury service over an extended period of time, was held to constitute *prima facie* proof of the systematic exclusion of Negroes from jury service. This holding, sometimes called the "rule of exclusion," has been applied in other cases, and it is available in supplying proof of discrimination against any delineated class.

The petitioner established that 14% of the population of Jackson County were persons with Mexican or Latin American surnames, and that 11% of the males over 21 bore such names. The County Tax Assessor testified that 5 of 7% of the freeholders on the tax rolls of the County were persons of Mexican descent. The State of Texas stipulated that "for the last twenty-five years there is no record of any person with a Mexican or Latin American name having served on a jury commission, grand jury or petit jury in Jackson County." The parties also stipulated that "there are some male persons of Mexican or Latin American descent in Jackson County who, by virtue of being citizens, freeholders, and having all other legal prerequisites to jury service, are eligible to serve as members of a jury commission, grand jury and/or petit jury."

The petitioner met the burden of proof imposed in *Norris v. Alabama*, supra. To rebut the strong *prima facie* case of the denial of the equal protection of the laws guaranteed by the Constitution thus established, the State offered the testimony of five jury commissioners that they had not discriminated against persons of Mexican or Latin American descent in selecting jurors. They stated that their only objective had been to select those whom they thought were best qualified. This testimony is not enough to overcome the petitioner's case. . . .

3. Holding

Circumstances or chance may well dictate that no persons in a certain class will serve on a particular jury or during some particular period. But it taxes our credulity to say that mere chance resulted in their being no members of this class among the over six thousand jurors called in the past 25 years. The result bespeaks discrimination, whether or not it was a conscious decision on the part of any individual jury commissioner. The judgment of conviction must be reversed.

J. Commentary on *Hernández*

As *Hernandez* indicates, Mexican-Americans are protected under constitutional notions of equality just as blacks and Chinese-Americans had been. While the separate but equal doctrine was clearly better than no protection at all, it resulted in widespread inequality against all racial minorities including Mexican-Americans. For all minorities, the separation itself caused harm, as it carried with it an implied inferiority.

K. Background on Chief Justice William Howard Taft

Geoffrey Stone, et al.
Justice William Howard Taft

The only person to serve as both President and Chief Justice, William Howard Taft's career was marked by genial conservatism and a commitment to the institutional independence of each branch of the federal government. Taft served as secretary of war in Theodore Roosevelt's administration and became one of Roosevelt's closest advisors. With support from Roosevelt, he was elected President in 1908. Soon after his inauguration, however, he and Roosevelt split, and he lost his bid for reelection in 1912, when Roosevelt splintered the Republican vote by running as an independent. After leaving the presidency, Taft taught constitutional law at Yale University and served for a year as president of the American Bar Association. Along with several other former ABA presidents, Taft fought to block Louis Brandeis's nomination to the Court in 1916. President Harding named Taft chief justice in 1921. Taft was responsible for passage of the Judiciary Act of 1925, which gave the Supreme Court effective control over its own appellate jurisdiction and for the appropriation of funds for construction of the present Supreme Court building.

Constitutional Law xcii (3rd edition).
Copyright © (1996) Stone, et al.
Reprinted with permission of Aspen Law & Business.

L. Explaining Justice John Harlan

1. Harlan's Background

Geoffrey Stone, et al.

Justice John Harlan

Although a slaveholder and a member of the southern aristocracy, John Harlan remained loyal to the Union during the Civil War and commanded a regiment of Kentucky volunteers in the Union forces. At a critical moment in the deadlocked Republican convention of 1876, Harlan threw the support of the Kentucky delegation behind Rutherford B. Hayes, who rewarded him a year later with an appointment to the Supreme Court. Before his appointment, Harlan opposed the postwar amendments ending slavery and guaranteeing equal rights for blacks. He opposed Lincoln and supported Democrat John McClellan in the 1864 presidential election. Once on the Court, however, he advocated a broad reading of these amendments.

Constitutional Law lxxxiii (3rd edition).
Copyright © (1996) Stone, et al.
Reprinted with permission of Aspen Law & Business.

2. The Brilliance of Harlan

H. G. Wells was an English author who wrote several popular books including *20,000 Leagues Under The Sea* and *The Time Machine*. His accurate predictions about the coming of women's suffrage and the creation of the atomic bomb have caused many people to characterize him as unusually brilliant, so much so that he could predict the future.

In Harlan's dissent in *Plessy*, he accurately predicts that the majority decision would one day become as despised as the *Dred Scott* decision some 50 years earlier. Few today agree with the *Plessy* decision or *Dred Scott*, rendering Harlan's prediction uncannily accurate and causing some to refer to him as the H.G. Wells of the legal profession. If Harlan was so perceptive in the majority opinion in *Plessy*, in what areas did he demonstrate poor judgment?

3. Shattering the Harlan Myth

Gabriel Chin

The Plessy Myth: Justice Harlan and the Chinese Cases*

If Harlan did not advocate color-blindness or anti-racism, what does his dissent mean? Although there are, no doubt, other possible interpretations, Harlan applied a formalistic approach to the Fourteenth Amendment. Although in some sense plausible, Harlan's understanding of the Equal Protection Clause did not include

---

* (some footnotes and chapter headings omitted).

what now seems to be its most attractive feature: a notion of at least legal equality among all races. In addition, Harlan seems to have given overwhelming weight to the circumstances which gave rise to the Reconstruction Amendments. Harlan was right that they were generated *primarily* by concerns about African Americans, but that did not necessarily mean that the status of citizen should be exclusively limited to that group, in addition to, of course, whites. Finally, Harlan's dissent is an early example of the comparative evaluation of non-white racial groups to determine their entitlement to legal protection or recognition. This pernicious use of one minority group as a proxy to attack another may be Harlan's most enduring and unwelcome gift to future generations.

One significant strain in the opinion is a literalistic, non-transformative view of the Fourteenth Amendment. For Harlan, the Fourteenth Amendment prohibits discrimination against African Americans, not because, say, the Fourteenth Amendment embodies a general anti-discrimination principle, or because discrimination is, in general, normatively undesirable. Harlan wrote:

> The white race deems itself to be the dominant race in this country. And so it is, in prestige, in achievements, in education, in wealth and in power. So, I doubt not, it will continue to be for all time, if it remains true to its great heritage, and holds fast to the principles of constitutional liberty. *But in the view of the constitution, in the eye of the law*, there is in this country no superior, dominant, ruling class of citizens.

It is clear from the dissent that Harlan believed the Fourteenth Amendment rendered African Americans "our equals before the law." It is not so clear that Harlan thought African Americans were the moral equals of the majority race. Untroubled by the idea of excluding Chinese from immigration or citizenship, Harlan could not bear to find a general anti-racism, anti-discrimination principle in the Constitution. As a result, he was forced to make arguments which were virtually sophistic. Harlan could not win on this sterile playing field; "equal protection of the laws" is not a self-defining term.

The defeat of the Confederacy, Harlan insisted, made African Americans "a part of the political community." Therefore Jim Crow was untenable because it was "cunningly devised to defeat the legitimate results of the war." But separation of African Americans and whites did not threaten to undo Lee's surrender at Appomattox; the Union could survive, unhappily, at least, even burdened with segregation. Moreover, at a time when many "members of the political community" to which Harlan referred did not even have the bedrock democratic right of ballot-access—such as white female citizens and citizens who could not afford to pay a poll tax—it was not obvious that particular members of that political community enjoyed the lesser right to sit one place or another on the train. By abandoning the anti-discrimination principle, Harlan gave up the strongest support for the outcome he wanted. As one commentator explained: "[I]f it were legitimate to make discriminations based on race in assigning or withholding citizenship, why would it not be equally defensible to use race as a basis for other discriminations, among citizens as well?" That is, unless the Fourteenth Amendment recognizes and embodies a strong anti-race discrimination principle, it is hard to see why governments cannot regulate race with as much discretion as they have when dealing with eyeglasses or pushcarts.

Another possibility is that Harlan was afflicted with another form of color-blindness, not one that prevents recognizing any colors at all, but, rather, an "inability to distinguish colors of the spectrum, with all objects appearing as shades of . . . black and white;" a defect of perception rendering him "incapable of . . . perceiving certain colors." When Harlan referred to "the destinies of the two races, in this country," he seemed to suggest that all Americans were either African American or white, and thus that non-African American nonwhites could not be Americans. He followed through on this implication in *Wong Kim Ark*, voting that American-born Chinese were not citizens.

From his point of view, it might have been perfectly defensible to treat non-white, non-African American races ungenerously, because he was talking about the rights of American citizens, and only African-Americans and whites could be citizens. When thinking, then, about the rights of citizens, of members, there was no more need to account for American-born Chinese than, say, children born in the Swedish Embassy; the nation might be generous to such persons, or it might not, but whatever privileges the law gave them in the United States would be matters of grace and discretion.

But even if Harlan was right that the Reconstruction Amendments were primarily intended to secure the place of African Americans, he was not required to interpret them as applicable exclusively to that group, given the generality of the Amendments' language, and the apparent principle they embodied. His decision to take the wrong path on this point deprived him of more powerful, anti-racist arguments about the meaning of the Fourteenth Amendment that later commentators nevertheless attempt to ascribe to him.

C. Ellen Connally

Justice Harlan's "Great Betrayal"? A Reconsideration of Cumming v. Richmond County Board of Education*

Justice John Marshall Harlan, the Kentuckian who had once owned slaves, wrote the opinion of the Court in the case. Harlan biographer Tinsley E. Yarbrough agrees with Kousser that Harlan's papers include no files on the *Cumming* case and few references to it. As a result, historians and legal scholars can only speculate on Harlan's intent in his opinion. In light of Harlan's dissent in the *Civil Rights Cases* and *Plessy*,

---

* (footnotes omitted).

in which he voiced the opinion that the Fourteenth Amendment guaranteed those rights sets forth in the Bill of Rights to black Americans, his decision in *Cumming* is admittedly an anomaly. As Linda Przybyszewski writes, "[f]or historians looking to Harlan as the prophet of the 1954 *Brown v. Board of Education* decision, *Cumming* is a disappointment." Harlan's seeming abandonment of his earlier position relative to the Fourteenth Amendment seems even more ironic in light of his later dissent in the *Berea College Case* in 1908, where he once again criticized his colleagues for their failure to support the equality of blacks. For all the recent praise that he has received for his pro-black stance, Harlan has been equally castigated for his refusal in the *Cumming* case to deal squarely with the issue of school desegregation. However, those leveling such attacks assume that the question of school desegregation was actually before the Court, when in fact it was not.

Speaking for a unanimous Court in the *Cumming* case, Justice Harlan made clear that the issue of segregation was not a factor in the case. "Indeed, the plaintiffs distinctly state that they have no objection to the tax in question so far as levied for the support of primary, intermediate and grammar schools, in the management of which the rule as to the separation of the races is enforced." Harlan may well have felt that the board's decision was economically sound and not racially motivated, especially in light of Booker T. Washington's pronouncement, discussed above, regarding educating the masses of blacks at a lower level. In addition, the demand of the plaintiffs that the board be enjoined from using funds for the support of the white high schools may have struck Harlan as a solution which would harm the educational opportunities for the white children without providing any benefits to the blacks.

Further, it must not be overlooked that the Board of Education continued to argue to the Supreme Court of the United States that the closing of Ware would not in fact deny black students an opportunity for a high school education, because of the three private high schools available in Augusta. The school board supported two private, religiously based high schools with public funds. In addition, black students could attend Paine Institute, Walker Baptist Institute, or Haines Normal and Industrial Institute. Though not publicly supported, they charged lower tuition than did Ware High School. While admitting that the schools were under sectarian control and had no connection with the public school system, the board argued that the schools were open to the public generally and that any child of sufficient scholarship and moral character could enter them, whatever his or her religious belief. In fact, the report of the school board committee found that the private schools, though religiously based, were not sectarian in their teaching.

Given all of the above, in an age when public funds and religious schools were closely connected—as shown by the situation in Augusta—the court's decision not to second-guess the Richmond County Board of Education in its decision relative to the placement of students is consistent with late nineteenth-century thinking. Feeling that the decision was justified under the financial circumstances of the time and unwilling to impose the federal government's opinion on the states, Harlan found no violation of the Fourteenth Amendment.

In commenting on the Board's decision, Harlan said that "[it] was in the interest of the greater number of colored children, leaving the smaller number to obtain a high school education in existing private institutions at an expense not beyond that incurred in the high school discontinued by the board." He went on to say that the Court might have been forced to answer different questions if the plaintiffs had instituted a proceeding demanding that the Board of Education establish and maintain a high school for Negro children, rather than insisting on the negative action of enjoining the support of a high school for white children. Whatever Harlan's view of segregation, he could not render a ruling directly on the issue in the *Cumming Case* because segregation *per se* was not made an issue in that case. Instead, the plaintiffs made the negative demand of withholding the support of the high schools with no beneficial results for the black students.

Kousser, who says that Harlan's opinion in *Cumming* "raises serious questions about [his] devotion to civil rights," divides those who have written on the subject of Harlan's rationale in *Cumming* into five categories: (1) those who say Harlan was a strict constructionist and would only rule on issues that were directly raised in pleadings and arguments; (2) those who view the decision in the Supreme Court as the result of poor lawyering on the part of Edmunds and of his error in not appealing *Blodgett*, which would have allowed for the action in mandamus; (3) those who feel that the Justice accepted the argument of the school board that it was better to educate the greater number of black students rather than provide for the elite, and further that it was absurd to close the white school; (4) those who say that Harlan was in fact attempting to undermine the separate but equal doctrine by denying the Court the right to look into exercises of state "police power"; and (5) those who would ignore *Cumming* as a case decided on an off day by Harlan.

Both Yarbrough and Beth, writing after Kousser's analysis, fall within the purview of those who feel that Harlan did not have the proper case before him in order to rule against school segregation, even though Beth calls the decision "disingenuous" in light of Harlan's other dissents. Beth argues that "[r]eal relief [to the plaintiffs in *Cumming*] could only come by going entirely outside the framework of the case as presented in order to issue a mandamus-like order for the school board to maintain high schools for both races [and both sexes] even at the cost of raising its school tax rate. This was a type of action that the Supreme Court never used until the 1950s." Yarbrough feels that Harlan was reluctant to have the Court and the federal government interfere with the states' management of education.

In 1956 Justice Felix Frankfurter engaged in a lively debate with Harlan's grandson, Justice John Marshall Harlan II, over the subject of *Cumming*. Frankfurter believed that "Harlan I would have sustained [school] segregation had the issue squarely come before the Court in his day." This opinion was based on Frankfurter's belief that a judge who considered segregated education unconstitutional could hardly have written the Court's opinion in the *Cumming* case. Harlan II responded that he believed that his grandfather "would have been against segregation." However, Frankfurter concluded that Harlan I's failure to refer at all to school segregation (in the *Cumming* case) or to use *Plessy* as a platform for attacking segregation laws generally comprised conclusive evidence that Harlan I did not consider segregated public education unconstitutional.

In a 1999 work on Harlan, Przybyszewski attempts to look behind Harlan's decisions. Through a study of Harlan's judicial career, and with the use of previously neglected sources, she tries to explain Harlan's transformation from a slaveholder to a defender of black rights. She also attempts to explain the limitations of that transformation. Przybyszewski argues that when trying to determine Harlan's feelings on the issue of integrated public schools, there is an assumption that Harlan thought of public education in the same way that he thought of public accommodations. Instead, she postulates, Harlan moved public accommodations for blacks into the category of civil rights but did not make the same leap for public schools. "Harlan seems to have had trouble extracting public schooling from the category of social rights. Perhaps he did not come out clearly against single-race schooling because it was a way to preserve racial identity—in other words, not for the racist reason that a separate and unequal system of education would keep blacks down but for the racialist reason that schooling was a far more intimate activity than riding a streetcar and could lead to friendship and marriage." Przybyszewski also astutely observes that Harlan's reputation was thrust upon him by later generations: only after the decision in *Brown v. Board of Education* did scholars go scrambling to study him. She points out that although the "... 1953 *Encyclopedia of American History* did not even mention Harlan's dissents on civil rights in its short biography, Harlan made it onto a list of great judges in 1958 on the weight of those dissents. Harlan has appeared on such lists ever since."

4. Harlan's Black Brother

J. Gordon

*Did the First Justice Harlan Have a Black Brother?**

On September 18, 1848, James Harlan, father of future Supreme Court Justice John Marshall Harlan, appeared in the Franklin County Court for the purpose of freeing his mulatto slave, Robert Harlan. This appearance formalized Robert's free status and exposed a remarkable link between this talented mulatto and his prominent lawyer politician sponsor.

This event would have little historical significance but for the fact that Robert Harlan was no ordinary slave. Born in 1816, and raised in James Harlan's household,

---

* (footnotes and chapter headings omitted).

blue-eyed, light-skinned Robert Harlan had been treated by James Harlan more like a member of the family than like a slave. Robert was given an informal education and unusual opportunities to make money and to travel. While still a slave in the 1840s, he was permitted sufficient freedom to have his own businesses, first in Harrodsburg, Kentucky, and then later in Lexington, Kentucky. More remarkably still, he was permitted to hold himself out to the community as a free man of color at least as early as 1840, not only with James Harlan's knowledge, but apparently with his consent. After making a fortune in California during the Gold Rush, Robert moved to Cincinnati in 1850 and invested his money in real estate and a photography business. In the years that followed, he became a member of the Northern black elite, and, in the period after 1870, established himself as one of the most important black Republican leaders in Ohio.

Although a humane master, James Harlan's treatment of Robert was paradoxical. James' tax records show that he bought and sold slaves throughout his life. The slave census of 1850 lists fourteen slaves in James Harlan's household, ranging in age from three months to seventy years. The census for 1860 lists twelve slaves ranging in age from one to fifty-three years. James neither routinely educated nor often emancipated his slaves, although his ambivalence about the "peculiar institution" was well enough known to become a political liability in Kentucky, a state which was firmly committed to the preservation of slavery.

What about Robert Harlan was so special as to lead to such exceptional treatment by James? In the view of two scholars, the peculiarity of James Harlan's relationship with Robert Harlan is easily explained. Robert Harlan, they assert, was James Harlan's son. If true, this means that another of James' sons, the first Justice John Marshall Harlan, had a black half-brother.

When James emancipated Robert, John Harlan was fifteen years old. Thereafter, James and Robert continued to have contacts. After James' death in 1863, John and Robert remained in touch. Robert was an anomalous feature of John's childhood in slaveholding Kentucky and remained a part of his perception of blacks as an adult.

John deeply loved and respected his father, James. He lived in his father's house until after his own marriage. James taught John law and politics. In both arenas, father and son were partners and seem to have confided freely in one another. James remained the most important influence in John's life until the older man died in 1863, when John was thirty years old.

James Harlan's ambivalent, but generally negative, feelings about slavery surely influenced John's views on the subject. But even more importantly, James' peculiar relationship with Robert during John's youth, and the ongoing contacts between James, John, and Robert after Robert's emancipation, must have affected John's attitudes toward blacks. Robert was smart and ambitious, but lived his life in the twilight between two worlds, one black, the other white. He was never completely at home in either. Robert's lifelong experience of the significance of the color line became, vicariously, a part of John's experience. Robert was also a continuing example of something John Harlan could not later, as a Supreme Court Justice, bring himself to deny—the humanity of blacks, and the profound unfairness of their treatment by a racist America.

Given his connection to Robert, Justice John Harlan's progressive views on race, views which he repeatedly articulated in his famous dissents as an Associate Justice of the United States Supreme Court, become more comprehensible. Indeed, it is reasonable to assume that we will never understand fully the sources of Justice Harlan's advanced views on race until we better understand his relationship with the black man who might have been his half-brother. Justice Harlan argued repeatedly that the Civil War Amendments had given black Americans the same civil rights as whites:

> [T]here cannot be, in this republic, any class of human beings in practical subjection to another class, with power in the latter to dole out to the former just such privileges as they may choose to grant. The supreme law of the land has decreed that no authority shall be exercised in this country upon the basis of discrimination, in respect of civil rights, against [free men] and citizens because of their race, color, or previous condition of servitude.

Harlan further denied that blacks constituted a class which may still be discriminated against, even in respect of rights of a character so necessary and supreme, that, deprived of their enjoyment in common with others, a [free man] is not only branded as one inferior and infected, but, in the competitions of life, is robbed of some of the most essential means of existence.

In *Plessy v. Ferguson*, Harlan, standing alone against the rest of the Court, again dissented:

> In respect of civil rights, common to all citizens, the Constitution of the United States does not . . . permit any public authority to know the race of those entitled to be protected in the enjoyment of such rights. . . . I deny that any legislative body or judicial tribunal may have regard to the race of citizens when the civil rights of those citizens are involved.

> Elsewhere in the same opinion, in words that have since become famous, Harlan wrote, in view of the Constitution, in the eye of the law, there is in this country no superior, dominant, ruling class of citizens. There is no caste here. Our Constitution is color-blind, and neither knows nor tolerates classes among citizens. In respect of civil rights, all citizens are equal before the law.

If Robert and John were brothers, a provocative dimension for contemplation is opened. The careers of these two talented, ambitious men offer us parallel examples of life on different sides of the color line in nineteenth century America. They grew up in the same household, and, if brothers, carried many of the same genes. Each was given every opportunity that his status and skin color permitted. Each succeeded to a remarkable extent, again, within the limits imposed upon him by the society in which they both lived. Each man was shaped by his own perceptions of these limits and by their reality. In the end, John Harlan climbed as high as his society permitted *any man*. Robert Harlan climbed as high as his society permitted *any black man*. Although in the end Robert did not rise as high as did John, his achievements were, upon reflection, equally impressive and worthy of exploration.

Robert Harlan was born into a biracial Southern world in which whites owned human beings and blacks were forced to submit to nearly absolute white authority or die. It was a society in which the races were separated by a strict caste line that was supported by profound social, economic, and ideological differences between the races. But it was also a society in which blacks and whites were constantly brought into intimate contact with each other by the slave system.

The racial intimacy required by the slave system in the South and the profound vulnerability of blacks when presented with demands from white masters and satellite whites produced common, if disapproved, interracial sexual encounters. These encounters in turn produced large numbers of mulatto offspring. Robert Harlan was one of these children. If Robert Harlan's mother was one-quarter black, a "quadroon," and his father was a white man, Robert was one-eighth black, an "octoroon"—he had one black great-grandparent, like Plessy in the famous "separate but equal" case, *Plessy v. Ferguson*. Perhaps it was more than coincidence that led John Marshall Harlan to write one of his most famous and impassioned dissents in defense of the civil rights of black Americans on Plessy's behalf. Because of the character of Robert's birth and the scarcity of historical records on slave births, we will never know the names of his parents with certainty.

Is it possible that Robert knew or suspected that he had a Harlan father and chose to conceal this fact from the public during his lifetime? If he had claimed his patrimony publicly, at any time, the claim would have been doubted in the absence of acknowledgment by James or some other member of the white Harlan family. It seems likely that Robert was genuinely grateful to James for his humane treatment, and there were bonds of affection between these men that prevented the younger man from publicly proclaiming their blood tie. Affection and gratitude for James is suggested by Robert's naming his only son after his former master. Affection also comes through occasionally in Robert's letters to John. When John agreed to serve on the Louisiana election commission in April 1877, Robert wrote him:

> I beg to repeat to you the words of an old colored man that formerly belong [sic] to your father—they were do-do-take care.

> I do not care which way you may decide the Louisiana question your [sic] bound to make enemies especially if you take a leading part in the matter.

Disclosure would certainly have embarrassed James and John, and deeply hurt their family. It also would have damaged James' own political prospects and those of his legitimate son, John. It is possible that there were conditions attached to James' generosity toward, and sponsorship of, Robert—one condition being that Robert never publicly claim the blood relationship. It is possible that any secret assistance Robert may have received from John Harlan later was given upon the same terms.

All of these possibilities rest on speculation, but the point is that there may have been reasons for Robert to maintain consistently a lie about the circumstances of his birth. There is a reference in one of Robert's letters to John that suggests that some of Robert's political associates in Cincinnati were aware of some connection between Robert and John. In a letter dated October 4, 1873, Robert invited John to make a campaign speech in Cincinnati in support of Republican candidates. In the letter Robert explained, "The campaign committee requested me to write you thinking I might have more influence with you than they had." This reference does not necessarily relate to a claim of blood ties, but it does suggest that there was an awareness, at least in some Republican circles in Cincinnati, that Robert had a special relationship with John . . .

At the very least, John's connection to Robert would have made empty abstractions about race impossible for John. Robert humanized, for John, all cases involving the rights of black Americans. John knew through personal experience what the legal disabilities imposed upon blacks—the disabilities against which John Harlan raged in his Supreme Court opinions—meant in people's lives. At the very least, Robert put a face on the millions of human beings who were forced to live their lives in the shadow of the Supreme Court's racist opinions. Robert made John see the human beings behind the briefs. This must certainly have been true in a case like *Plessy v. Ferguson*, where the plaintiff was seven-eighths white—his behavior—a topic I hope to explore in the future. Once John Harlan could see blacks as individual human beings, his religious convictions compelled him to extend to them the rights all human beings deserved. This alone might have set John Harlan apart from his fellow Justices, for whom race was largely an abstract matter.

Through Robert, John would also have experienced, vicariously, the consequences of the color line. Robert was raised in the household of a humane slaveholder. He had money and great opportunity for a man of color in his time. Despite these "advantages," Robert was denied all of the opportunities that were John's from birth. Through Robert, John could experience the pain of butting doors which would never open no matter how meritorious he might be as an individual. In reviewing the story of Robert's life, John must have been acutely aware of the significance of the color line. Robert's slightly brown skin had rendered his considerable talents largely irrelevant to a color-conscious, racist society. Indeed, this circumstance alone had robbed Robert of the Harlan birthright which helped John to prosper throughout his life.

If Robert Harlan helped to shape John Harlan's views about race in any of these ways, he made a lasting contribution to John's fame. Through John's words, Robert also left a mark on his country. He helped to start America's eventual, painful reexamination of the assumptions underlying its racist consensus. In this way, Robert left his descendants and his country a wonderful legacy.

A concealing fog curls about Robert Harlan's connection to the Harlans of Kentucky. It may be the kind of fog one occasionally finds hiding the violation of a taboo. It is also possible that this fog is of the ordinary variety, the kind that rises without assistance from the passage of time and the loss or deterioration of historical sources. The critical difficulty in the case of the Harlans is to distinguish this kind of "normal" obscurity from the other.

In the case of the Harlans, religious standing, guilt over a breach of private morality, and concern over the potential destructive political power of damaging information would have encouraged both James and John to conceal Robert's blood tie if it existed. But genuine religious conviction and mature moral character would also have encouraged both to take responsibility for ameliorating Robert's life to the extent that it was in their power to do so. Robert might have concealed his paternity out of love or gratitude, or he may not have known whether his father was a Harlan or not. Given the character of the problem addressed and the paucity of the surviving sources, we probably can never be certain whether or not Robert Harlan was James Harlan's son. In my own mind, however, I am convinced that he was.

James Harlan gave all four of his acknowledged sons good educations, ultimately training them all for the bar. John attended the best local grammar school, the best local college (Centre), and the best law school in the West (Transylvania). James could offer no such opportunities to Robert. James could entertain no such plans for him.

No vocation in law or politics was possible. Just as James could not provide Robert with formal education, neither could he treat him like a son in other respects given the time and place in which they lived.

John received the benefits of being the son of a famous father, and a member of a powerful family. He received counsel from that father and James' help in launching his political career. Robert fought through most of his life alone, illegitimate, black, and unacknowledged. Still he managed to succeed. James Harlan was a good master to his slaves and to Robert in particular. But, at best, Robert received a modest start from James. The great irony of his story is that the treatment he received was so much better than that received by so many others with "tainted" blood like Plessy's and his own.

Even in the ranks of the party that had destroyed slavery and nationalized freedom, the disparity of treatment continued. The Republican Party could serve John Marshall Harlan's ambitions; Robert Harlan could only serve the party. John Harlan could aspire to the governorship of his state and win the prize of a seat on the United States Supreme Court. Robert Harlan labored long and hard among black Ohioans on behalf of that same party, receiving in return two federal patronage jobs and, eventually, a contested one-term seat in the Ohio House of Representatives.

John could lead the party; Robert could only follow it. John could reshape the party; Robert was forced to shape himself to it. John was admired and lionized, while Robert was forced to suffer chronic contempt from his white allies, and the jibes of some of his own people that he was too white. John could educate his sons at the finest schools and offer them access into the best social, economic, and political circles in white America. Robert struggled his entire life to capture and hold onto minor but respectable patronage jobs for his only son, Robert Jr., in order to prevent that son's descent into poverty and disgrace. In short, John Harlan could aspire to and achieve his heart's desire. Robert Harlan was forced to dream smaller dreams, swallow more bile, and content himself with a scrambling and precarious political existence.

John Harlan was a remarkable, talented, and ambitious man. He had the great good fortune to be born the son of a father who was a political leader in his native state, and to find himself on the top side of the color line. Robert was also remarkable, talented, and ambitious. It is possible that he was born the son of the same father, although at a time when James was still really a child himself and dependent upon his own parents. It was Robert's misfortune to find himself on the bottom side of the color line. His disability was to be the illegitimate son of racially mixed parents in a society that empowered white slaveholders and their sons to sire mulatto children, and then cursed these children because they were constant reminders of the moral implications, for masters and slaves, of absolute human bondage. It was Robert Harlan's misfortune to have been born a slave of mixed blood and thus consigned by white society to a limbo between masters and slaves. It was his good fortune, as it was John's, to have been raised in the household of a man who, as an adult, was strong enough and moral enough to feel obligations to *all* of his sons.

James Harlan gave Robert all that Kentucky slave society would permit. In many ways, he even went secretly beyond what his neighbors could accept. He tried to give Robert some education, his de facto freedom, and a start in life. From these assets Robert built a relatively good life. In the process, he gave James' famous son a gift. He gave the first Justice Harlan insight. Through his contact with Robert, John Harlan developed a special way of seeing the problems involving race which came before him as a judge. It was this insight that made him unique in his understanding of the real costs, to both blacks and whites, of the color line.

One year before Robert Harlan's death, John Harlan wrote in dissent in *Plessy v. Ferguson*, "The destinies of the two races, in this country, are indissolubly linked together and the interests of both require that the common government of all shall not permit the seeds of race hate to be planted under the sanction of law." I wonder whether, when John Harlan penned these words, he reflected on their truth in his own life. His life, his father's life, and Robert's life had indeed been "indissolubly linked together." That link, like the country's, was forged in slavery and continued into an ambiguous twilight of freedom. Drawing upon his own experience for inspiration, John Harlan wrote of a color-blind future, and by writing about it began the process of creating it. In a way, the writing of these words was John Marshall Harlan's greatest achievement.

Given his opportunities and the culture into which he was born and against which he had to fight every day of his life, Robert Harlan's successes were quite as remarkable as those of his half-brother John. John Harlan proved a worthy son of a worthy father. When all is considered, so did Robert.

5. *The Amazing Grace Syndrome*

American history is filled with individuals whose values and principles have evolved as they have overcome obstacles or been exposed to new experiences. Drastic transformations have taken place concerning viewpoints on racial issues. One of the most frequently discussed transformations is that of Hugo Black who was a member of the Ku Klux Klan during his early professional career but resigned his membership after two years. As a Justice of the Supreme Court, Black supported many of the landmark civil-rights decisions, such as *Brown v. Board of Education*, that were anathema to his former organization.

Perhaps the most amazing transformation of all was John Newton, who wrote the song "Amazing Grace" in 1779. Newton had been captain of a ship that transported slaves from 1750 to 1754, but a religious conversion gradually led him to repudiate his former occupation and eventually to become an outspoken critic of the international slave trade. Many believe that the song "Amazing Grace" reflects Newton's feelings about his participation in the immoral and destructive institution of slavery.

Amazing Grace

Amazing grace! How sweet the sound
That saved a wretch like me!
I once was lost, but now am found,
Was blind, but now I see,
Twas grace that taught my heart to fear,
And grace my fears relieved;
How precious did that grace appear
The hour I first believed!
Through many dangers, toils and snares,
I have already come;
Tis grace hath brought me safe thus far,
And grace will lead me home.
The Lord has promised good to me,
His word my hope secures;
He will my shield and portion be,
As long as life endures.
Yea, when this flesh and heart shall fail,

And mortal life shall cease,
I shall possess, within the veil,
A life of joy and peace. Amen[92]

M. Questions and Notes

The local School board in *Cumming* chose to educate three hundred black children through primary school instead of sixty black children through secondary school. Considering only these two options, do you agree or disagree with the school board's decision? Can you think of an alternate solution, given the same resources, which would result in a better outcome for all students?

The justices in *Cumming* indicated that the facts suggested an absence of a "clear and unmistakable disregard" for the rights of blacks. In the view of the justices, what circumstances do you think would have constituted such a disregard?

What do you think about the merits of Gong Lum's argument that equal protection required the state to provide his daughter, Martha, with a separate but equal school for Americans of Chinese descent?

Do you agree with Chief Justice Taft's conclusion that *Plessy* was a more difficult case than *Lum*?

Do you believe individuals can transform and no longer hold deep-seated racial prejudices? What role, if any, does the law play in encouraging or creating such transformations? Do civil rights laws simply force people not to act overtly on their racial biases? Do such laws actually encourage people to mask their prejudices and manifest these prejudices in other ways?

XVIII. Applying the Separate but Equal Doctrine

A. Introduction

A. Leon Higginbotham, Jr.

*A Tribute to Justice Thurgood Marshall**

To understand the magnitude of institutional racism that Marshall challenged, it is appropriate to start with 1896, when Grover Cleveland was President and *Plessy v. Ferguson* was decided. At that time, the false rumor that a "colored man" had attended an official White House function evoked the following response from the President: "It so happens that I have never in my *official* position, either when sleeping or waking, alive or dead, on my head or on my heels, dined, lunched, or suped, or

---

92. J. Newton, Amazing Grace (1859).

* (footnotes omitted).

invited to a wedding reception any colored man, woman, or child." If the President of the United States found it so repulsive to dine with a "colored man," he certainly would have sanctioned the separate but unequal treatment that *Plessy* endorsed.

When a moderate black leader, Booker T. Washington, had an informal lunch with President Theodore Roosevelt in 1901, a Memphis, Tennessee, newspaper wrote: "The most damnable outrage which has ever been perpetrated by any citizen of the United States was committed yesterday by the President, when he invited a nigger to dine with him at the White House." Senator Benjamin Tillman of South Carolina said: "Now that Roosevelt has eaten with that nigger Washington, we shall have to kill a thousand niggers to get them back to their places."

Given such racist public pronouncements, it is no surprise that southern lawyers unabashedly referred to blacks in court as "niggers" and "pickaninnies" and that inferior treatment was meted out to blacks in courts throughout the nation. When Thurgood Marshall litigated cases in the 1930s, 1940s, and 1950s, he was the target of constant harassment and threats of violence. When he went to Dallas to challenge the exclusion of blacks on juries, for example, the police chief advised his top personnel that a "nigger lawyer" was coming from New York to "disrupt our procedures" and that he would personally "kick the shit out of him."

Institutional racism also pervaded the armed forces. In 1951, President Truman sent Thurgood Marshall to the Far East "to review treatment of black soldiers under General Douglas MacArthur." When Marshall asked "why there were no blacks in the elite group guarding the general," MacArthur replied that "none were qualified by their performance on the field of battle." Marshall noted that not even one black played in MacArthur's military band. In anger, Marshall said to MacArthur: "Now, general, just between you and me: Goddammit, don't you tell me that there's no Negro that can play a horn." MacArthur responded by ordering Marshall to leave.

105 *Harvard Law Review* 56, 56–57.
Copyright © (1991) The Harvard Law Review Association.
Reprinted with permission of The Harvard Law Review Association and
Evelyn Brooks Higginbotham.

F. Michael Higginbotham

*Soldiers for Justice: the Role of the Tuskegee Airmen in the Desegregation of the American Armed Forces**

With World War II fast approaching, black leaders realized the hypocrisy of asking black men to serve and die in a foreign country only to return to a segregated homeland. Faced with this dilemma, black soldiers had to decide if they should fight overseas under existing conditions or concentrate first on the struggle for equality on the home front. Persuaded by black newspaper headlines urging a positive

---

* (footnotes and chapter headings omitted).

attitude towards the war, black leaders pushed for desegregation in America in exchange for service abroad.

One of the most popular black weekly newspapers, the *Pittsburgh Courier*, lobbied for the right of African Americans to enlist in the Army under the same conditions as whites, and demanded equal pilot training facilities for black pilots in the Army Air Corps. The Courier promoted the "Double V" campaign which encouraged blacks to fight for victory simultaneously at home and abroad. The newspaper displayed the extremely popular "Double V" symbol throughout its pages in advertisements for the NAACP, in photographs, and in text. The public sent many requests to the Courier for "Double V" paraphernalia. According to Roi Ottley, a writer and journalist, the campaign gained the support of "nearly every newspaper and pulpit." The campaign carried the Courier's message that blacks "would be less than men if, while we are giving up our property and sacrificing our lives, we do not agitate, contend, and demand those rights guaranteed to all freemen . . . this would be neither patriotism nor common sense."

Other black-owned publications delivered the same message. The first editorial published in Crisis, a widely subscribed newspaper published by the NAACP, exclaimed "Now Is The Time Not To Be Silent." The editor reasserted the faithfulness of black Americans, and argued that the sacrifices should be for a "new world which not only shall not contain a Hitler, but no Hitlerism. And for thirteen millions of American Negroes that means a fight for a world in which lynching, brutality, terror, humiliation and degradation through segregation and discrimination, shall have no place—either here or there."

Desegregation activists incorporated the need to fight for equal rights with a belief that their participation in the war effort would be rewarded after their return home. The *Courier*'s war correspondents encouraged black soldiers to "insist on combat duty [because] . . . only those who spill their blood are in a position to demand rights." In a New York survey, forty-six percent of the blacks polled believed they would be treated better because of their participation in the war.

Initially, black leaders vigorously protested racism in the armed forces in an attempt to achieve military integration. When these efforts failed, blacks redefined their goals. They yearned for social as well as military equality, and they began to view equal participation in the war effort as a means of achieving their goal. They hoped to fulfill the responsibilities of citizenship through military service. With their duty satisfied, blacks would be in a position to claim the equal rights guaranteed to every citizen.

Seeing the conflict rapidly approaching, black leaders, such as A. Philip Randolph of the Brotherhood of Sleeping Car Porters and Walter White of the NAACP, realized that ensuring full black participation in the war effort would strengthen claims for equal treatment and desegregation. Unlike their cooperative attitude toward segregation in World War I, black Americans grew tired of waiting for change. This time they would demand change.

In October 1940, President Franklin Roosevelt agreed to meet with Randolph, White, and others to discuss their demands for desegregation. Although Roosevelt fiercely resisted outright integration, he issued a "revised racial policy for the armed services" that outlined three key principles on the position of black servicemen. First, blacks in the military should equal their proportion in the general population (because blacks represented ten percent of the population, they should constitute ten percent of the military). Second, black units should exist in all branches of the armed services. Finally, blacks should be allowed to attend Officer Candidate schools and flight schools.

The revised policy allowed blacks to enter fields previously reserved for whites. Black pilots, officers, tank commanders, and non-commissioned officers began to appear with increasing frequency in the Army. As a result, the number of blacks in the Army rose significantly in a two-year period.

Notably, the President's order was not the result of a new and equitable government position. Rather, the initiative was Roosevelt's attempt to garner the much needed support of black voters and a reflection of his understanding that the country would need all of its citizens for the upcoming war. Roosevelt, however, had no intention of altering the long and established practice of racial segregation in the military.

Bitterly disappointed by the scope of Roosevelt's concessions and frustrated with the continued exclusion of blacks from the war industries, Randolph threatened a "March on Washington" in January of 1941. Randolph encouraged thousands of blacks to march on the nation's capital to lobby for racial integration and equal opportunities in military employment. Randolph agreed to cancel the march if Roosevelt took action to forbid discrimination in the war industries. Roosevelt issued Executive Order 8802, which established the Fair Employment Practices Commission, an organization set up by Roosevelt to ensure blacks equal access to wartime training, jobs, and "fair employment." However, because the order did not extend to the military, the armed services remained segregated.

Despite these advances, the desegregation movement was far from its ultimate goal. As the United States prepared to enter the war, social views and military policy remained racially discriminatory. The military remained racially segregated and blacks were predominantly assigned to unskilled labor positions such as cooks, porters, and laundry attendants. A survey taken early in the war showed that the sentiment of enlisted men was consistent with military policy; ninety percent of white Army enlisted men opposed integration. Interestingly, fifty percent of black troops agreed, believing it a necessary evil to prevent racial friction.

It is important to note the new attitude with which blacks approached their participation in World War II. Unlike the earlier responses that stressed cooperation, the new attitude was one of confrontation. Robert Mullen summarized the change in attitude:

> Whereas W. E. B. DuBois's "Close Ranks!" editorial had reflected the view
> of most black leaders in World War I. That blacks must drop their own

demands for the duration of the war and put country ahead of self—in World War II blacks were in the main unwilling to defer their demands until the end of the war.

The lack of equal treatment, and the demeaning personal discrimination that blacks suffered at the hands of whites, led many black Americans to view supporters of racial segregation and supporters of Aryan supremacy as one in the same. The double standard under which blacks were being asked to fight caused many of them to question their role in the war effort. One well-publicized incident in the South exposed the inconsonance of the military's position toward black soldiers. In that incident, black soldiers were refused service in a restaurant that willingly served Nazi prisoners of war.

8 *William & Mary Bill of Rights Journal* 273, 277–90.
Copyright © (2000). F. Michael Higginbotham.
Reprinted with permission of F. Michael Higginbotham.

Jonathan Entin

Sweatt v. Painter: *The End of Segregation and
the Transformation of Education Law*

Careful examination of the segregation precedents suggested two possible challenges to the "separate but equal" doctrine. First, in practice, "separate" was never "equal." No state-supported black college offered any form of graduate or professional training.[93] Even worse, a 1929 study by the NAACP revealed that segregated public school districts typically spent up to ten times as much on a white child's education as they did on a black child's instruction.[94] Thus, a series of suits designed to force equality of the separate educational institutions might be pressed. If they succeeded, substantial improvements in black education would result. Indeed, the cost of equalizing black schools might persuade many jurisdictions to abandon segregation altogether.

Second, a close reading of the precedents suggested that the Supreme Court never had squarely upheld the constitutionality of segregation in education. In *Cumming*,

---

93. Except for Howard University and Meharry Medical College, neither of which was state-operated, no black college had any kind of graduate or professional program for blacks. R. KLUGER, SIMPLE JUSTICE, at 136 (1977).

94. A subsequent analysis prepared for the NAACP pointed out:

The study financed by the American Fund for Public Service made by the N.A.A.C.P. revealed that in South Carolina more than ten times as much was expended for the education of white children as for Negro children; that in Florida, Georgia, Mississippi and Alabama, more than five times as much; in North Carolina, Virginia, Texas, Oklahoma and Maryland, more than twice as much.

N. Margold, *Preliminary Report to the Joint Committee Supervising the Expenditure of the 1930 Appropriation by the American Fund for Public Service to the NAACP, reprinted in part in* J. GREENBERG, CASES AND MATERIALS ON JUDICIAL PROCESS AND SOCIAL CHANGE: CONSTITUTIONAL LITIGATION 50 (1977).

the plaintiffs had made a fatal procedural error. They pressed the constitutional issue for the first time at oral argument in the Supreme Court. For that reason, the Court refused to address this fundamental question. Nor had *Gong Lum* involved a challenge to the validity of racial classifications in education. The student in that case claimed that, as Justice Harlan had observed in *Plessy*, segregation laws were designed to isolate blacks from the rest of the population. Since whites sought to insulate themselves from the harms alleged to flow from contact with blacks, Chinese-Americans were entitled to the same protection. Thus, she conceded the validity of racial classifications; she merely contested the legality of the administrative determination that she was not "white" for purposes of school attendance.

5 *Review of Litigation* 13, 17.
Copyright © (1986) *University of Texas Law Review*.
Reprinted with permission of the *University of Texas Law Review*.

B. Background on *Gaines*

Many states attempted to satisfy the *Plessy* doctrine by facilitating the education of their black citizens in other states. Many states chose not to provide black students with an educational institution, and instead identified existing institutions in neighboring states as legitimate alternatives. One of the most popular methods was providing scholarships for black students to attend Howard University, a historically black institution located in Washington, D.C. These states reasoned that providing a scholarship to attend an out-of-state school was the same as providing a school within the state. Many black professionals, including a large number of black lawyers and doctors, were educated in this fashion.

F. Michael Higginbotham and José F. Anderson
Drum Majors for Justice

Many lawyers worked with the legendary Thurgood Marshall to overturn the Supreme Court's infamous separate but equal doctrine, which had permitted racial segregation in schools and public accommodations. But while most are aware of Marshall's contribution, few recognize the name of his colleague, William I. Gosnell.

Born in Carroll County, Gosnell graduated from the University of Chicago Law School. He was co-counsel with Marshall and Charles Hamilton Houston, legal director of the National Association of the Advancement of Colored People in *Pearson vs. Murray*, the landmark school desegregation case.

While Marshall and Houston argued the case, Gosnell played a major role in preparing the brief. The 1935 Murray decision—widely recognized as Marshall's first civil rights victory—desegregated the University of Maryland School of Law.

At that time, Gosnell was one of only 32 black lawyers in the state of Maryland. In fact, due to the state's racial segregation policy, both he and Marshall had received scholarships to attend out-of-state law schools. They were denied entry to the University of Maryland because of their skin color. While Marshall went on to win 28 of 31 cases before the Supreme Court, Gosnell remained in Baltimore and developed a successful law practice. He died in March 1978.

In the recently published biography, "Thurgood Marshall, American Revolutionary," author Juan Williams noted that Gosnell spent many hours with Marshall preparing the Murray case. But Gosnell's efforts actually preceded Marshall's involvement. Gosnell introduced Donald Murray, a well-qualified Amherst College graduate, to Marshall as a potential plaintiff. Also, Gosnell encouraged the youth to challenge the segregation policy.

Moreover, Gosnell ignored Houston's caution to make no commitments and instead told a meeting of interested lawyers and citizens that he was prepared to go forward alone with the case. It was only after Gosnell told Marshall what he had done that Houston allowed the NAACP to join the case.

Gosnell had previously advised Murray to write University of Maryland president Raymond A. Pearson, requesting admission to the law school. In his letter, Murray told Pearson that he was black. In response, Pearson suggested Murray attend then-Morgan State College, which did not have a law school.

Ultimately, Houston, Marshall and Gosnell won a stunning victory in Baltimore before Judge Eugene O'Dunne, who ordered that Murray be admitted immediately to the law school. The order was affirmed by the Maryland Court of Appeals.

The Murray decision declared that the equal protection mandate of the 14th Amendment must be satisfied within the confines of a particular state. Thus, Maryland's claim that it provided Murray with equal treatment by providing a scholarship to Howard University in Washington—as was done with Marshall and Gosnell—was rejected because it was an out-of-state remedy.

Even more important to the desegregation effort, Murray was entitled to an immediate remedy for Maryland's denial of his equal protection rights. Thus, if Maryland failed to provide Murray with an equal law school within the state, it had to admit him to the school reserved for whites.

The Sun, February 18, 1999, Page 17.
Copyright © (1999) Associated Press.
Reprinted with permission of the Associated Press.

C. *Gaines v. Canada*, 305 U.S. 337 (1938)

Charles H. Houston and *Sidney R. Redmond*, with whom *Leon A. Ransom* was on the brief, for petitioner.

William S. Hogsett and *Fred L. Williams*, with whom *Fred L. English* was on the brief, for respondents.

1. Facts

Chief Justice HUGHES delivered the opinion of the Court.

Petitioner Lloyd Gaines, a Negro, was refused admission to the School of Law at the State University of Missouri. Asserting that this refusal constituted a denial by the State of the equal protection of the laws in violation of the Fourteenth Amendment of the Federal Constitution, petitioner brought this action for mandamus to compel the curators of the University to admit him. On final hearing, an alternative writ was quashed and a peremptory writ was denied by the Circuit Court. The Supreme Court of the State affirmed the judgment. 113 S.W.2d 783. We granted certiorari, October 10, 1938.

Petitioner is a citizen of Missouri. In August, 1935, he was graduated with the degree of Bachelor of Arts at the Lincoln University, an institution maintained by the State of Missouri for the higher education of Negroes. That University has no law school. Upon the filing of his application for admission to the law school of the University of Missouri, the registrar advised him to communicate with the president of Lincoln University and the latter directed petitioner's attention to § 9622 of the Revised Statutes of Missouri (1929), providing as follows:

> "Sec. 9622. *May arrange for attendance at university of any adjacent state —*
> *Tuition fees.* — Pending the full development of the Lincoln university, the
> board of curators shall have the authority to arrange for the attendance of
> Negro residents of the state of Missouri at the university of any adjacent
> state to take any course or to study any subjects provided for at the state
> university of Missouri, and which are not taught at the Lincoln university
> and to pay the reasonable tuition fees for such attendance; *provided* that
> whenever the board of curators deem it advisable they shall have the power
> to open any necessary school or department. (Laws 1921, p. 86, § 7.)"

Petitioner was advised to apply to the State Superintendent of Schools for aid under that statute. It was admitted on the trial that petitioner's "work and credits at the Lincoln University would qualify him for admission to the School of Law of the University of Missouri if he were found otherwise eligible." He was refused admission upon the ground that it was "contrary to the constitution, laws and public policy of the State to admit a negro as a student in the University of Missouri." . . .

The state court has not held that it would have been the duty of the curators to establish a law school at Lincoln University for the petitioner on his application. Their duty, as the court defined it, would have been either to supply a law school at Lincoln University as provided in § 9618 or to furnish him the opportunity to obtain his legal training in another State as provided in § 9622. Thus the law left the curators free to adopt the latter course. . . .

The state court stresses the advantages that are afforded by the law schools of the adjacent States, — Kansas, Nebraska, Iowa and Illinois, — which admit non-resident Negroes. The court considered that these were schools of high standing where one desiring to practice law in Missouri can get "as sound, comprehensive, valuable legal education" as in the University of Missouri; that the system of education in the former is the same as that in the latter and is designed to give the students a basis for the practice of law in any State where the Anglo-American system of law obtains; that the law school of the University of Missouri does not specialize in Missouri law and that the course of study and the case books used in the five schools are substantially identical. Petitioner insists that for one intending to practice in Missouri there are special advantages in attending a law school there, both in relation to the opportunities for the particular study of Missouri law and for the observation of the local courts,[95] and also in view of the prestige of the Missouri law school among the citizens of the State, his prospective clients. Proceeding with its examination of relative advantages, the state court found that the difference in distances to be traveled afforded no substantial ground of complaint and that there was an adequate appropriation to meet the full tuition fees which petitioner would have to pay.

2. Opinion

a. Obligations of the State

We think that these matters are beside the point. The basic consideration is not as to what sort of opportunities other States provide, or whether they are as good as those in Missouri, but as to what opportunities Missouri itself furnishes to white students and denies to Negroes solely upon the ground of color. The admissibility of laws separating the races in the enjoyment of privileges afforded by the State rests wholly upon the equality of the privileges which the laws give to the separated groups within the State. The question here is not of a duty of the State to supply legal training, or of the quality of the training which it does supply, but of its duty when it provides such training to furnish it to the residents of the State upon the basis of an equality of right. By the operation of the laws of Missouri a privilege has been created for white law students which is denied to Negroes by reason of their race. The white resident is afforded legal education within the State; the Negro resident having the same qualifications is refused it there and must go outside the State to obtain it. That is a denial of the equality of legal right to the enjoyment of the privilege which the State has set up, and the provision for the payment of tuition fees in another State does not remove the discrimination.

The equal protection of the laws is "a pledge of the protection of equal laws." *Yick Wo v. Hopkins*, 118 U.S. 356, 369. Manifestly, the obligation of the State to give the protection of equal laws can be performed only where its laws operate, that is, within its own jurisdiction. It is there that the equality of legal right must be maintained. That obligation is imposed by the Constitution upon the States severally as governmental entities,—each responsible for its own laws establishing the rights and duties of persons within its borders. It is an obligation the burden of which cannot be cast by one State upon another, and no State can be excused from performance

---

95. *See University of Maryland v. Murray*, 169 Md. 478, 486.

by what another State may do or fail to do. That separate responsibility of each State within its own sphere is of the essence of statehood maintained under our dual system. It seems to be implicit in respondents' argument that if other States did not provide courses for legal education, it would nevertheless be the constitutional duty of Missouri when it supplied such courses for white students to make equivalent provision for Negroes. But that plain duty would exist because it rested upon the State independently of the action of other States. We find it impossible to conclude that what otherwise would be an unconstitutional discrimination, with respect to the legal right to the enjoyment of opportunities within the State, can be justified by requiring resort to opportunities elsewhere. That resort may mitigate the inconvenience of the discrimination but cannot serve to validate it.

b. Group Rights or Personal Rights

Nor can we regard the fact that there is but a limited demand in Missouri for the legal education of negroes as excusing the discrimination in favor of whites. We had occasion to consider a cognate question in the case of *McCabe v. Atchison, T. & S.F. Ry. Co., supra.* there the argument was advanced, in relation to the provision by a carrier of sleeping cars, dining and chair cars, that the limited demand by Negroes justified the State in permitting the furnishing of such accommodations exclusively for white persons. We found that argument to be without merit. It made, we said, the constitutional right "depend upon the number of persons who may be discriminated against, whereas the essence of the constitutional right is that it is a personal one. Whether or not particular facilities shall be provided may doubtless be conditioned upon there being a reasonable demand therefore, but, if facilities are provided, substantial equality of treatment of persons traveling under like conditions cannot be refused. It is the individual who is entitled to the equal protection of the laws, and if he is denied by a common carrier, acting in the matter under the authority of a state law, a facility or convenience in the course of his journey which under substantially the same circumstances is furnished to another traveler, he may properly complain that his constitutional privilege has been invaded." *Id.*, pp. 161, 162.

Here, petitioner's right was a personal one. It was as an individual that he was entitled to the equal protection of the laws, and the State was bound to furnish him within its borders facilities for legal education substantially equal to those which the State there afforded for persons of the white race, whether or not other Negroes sought the same opportunity.

c. Appropriate Remedies

It is urged, however, that the provision for tuition outside the State is a temporary one,—that it is intended to operate merely pending the establishment of a law department for negroes at Lincoln University. While in that sense the discrimination may be termed temporary, it may nevertheless continue for an indefinite period by reason of the discretion given to the curators of Lincoln University and the alternative of arranging for tuition in other States, as permitted by the state law as construed by the state court, so long as the curators find it unnecessary and impracticable to provide facilities for the legal instruction of Negroes within the State. In that view, we cannot regard the discrimination as excused by what is called its temporary character.

We do not find that the decision of the state court turns on any procedural question. The action was for mandamus, but it does not appear that the remedy would have been deemed inappropriate if the asserted federal right had been sustained. In that situation the remedy by mandamus was found to be a proper one in *University of Maryland v. Murray, supra*. In the instant case, the state court did note that petitioner had not applied to the management of Lincoln University for legal training. But, as we have said, the state court did not rule that it would have been the duty of the curators to grant such an application, but on the contrary took the view, as we understand it, that the curators were entitled under the state law to refuse such an application and in its stead to provide for petitioner's tuition in an adjacent State. That conclusion presented the federal question as to the constitutional adequacy of such a provision while equal opportunity for legal training within the State was not furnished, and this federal question the state court entertained and passed upon. We must conclude that in so doing the court denied the federal right which petitioner set up and the question as to the correctness of that decision is before us. We are of the opinion that the ruling was error, and that petitioner was entitled to be admitted to the law school of the State University in the absence of other and proper provision for his legal training within the State.

3. Holding

The judgment of the Supreme Court of Missouri is reversed and the cause is remanded for further proceedings not inconsistent with this opinion.

4. Justice McReynolds Dissenting

. . . In *Cumming v. Richmond County Board of Education*, 175 U.S. 528, 545, this Court through Mr. Justice Harlan declared—"The education of the people in schools maintained by state taxation is a matter belonging to the respective States, and any interference on the part of Federal authority with the management of such schools cannot be justified except in the case of a clear and unmistakable disregard of rights secured by the supreme law of the land." *Gong Lum v. Rice*, 275 U.S. 78, 85—opinion by Mr. Chief Justice Taft—asserts: "The right and power of the state to regulate the method of providing for the education of its youth at public expense is clear."

For a long time Missouri has acted upon the view that the best interest of her people demands separation of whites and Negroes in schools. Under the opinion just announced, I presume she may abandon her law school and thereby disadvantage her white citizens without improving petitioner's opportunities for legal instruction; or she may break down the settled practice concerning separate schools and thereby, as indicated by experience, damnify both races. Whether by some other course it may be possible for her to avoid condemnation is matter for conjecture.

The State has offered to provide the Negro petitioner opportunity for study of the law—if perchance that is the thing really desired—by paying his tuition at some nearby school of good standing. This is far from unmistakable disregard of his rights and in the circumstances is enough to satisfy any reasonable demand for specialized training. It appears that never before has a Negro applied for admission to the Law School and none has ever asked that Lincoln University provide legal instruction.

The problem presented obviously is a difficult and highly practical one. A fair effort to solve it has been made by offering adequate opportunity for study when sought in good faith. The State should not be unduly hampered through theorization inadequately restrained by experience. . . .

Justice BUTLER concurs in the dissent.

D. Commentary on *Gaines*

Donald E. Lively
The Constitution and Race*

The first opportunity to test the strategy before the Supreme Court was presented by *Missouri ex rel. Gaines v. Canada*. The case arose when the state of Missouri denied a black applicant admission to its only public law school. Because the state did not provide a separate institution for black students, it offered to fund a legal education elsewhere. In spite of the offer to pay out-of-state tuition, the Court found a default of the Fourteenth Amendment obligation to maintain "the equality of legal rights to the enjoyment of the privilege which the state has set up." The constitutional duty, as the Court put it, could not "be cast by one state upon another, and no state can be excused from performance by what another state may do." Having considered whether the state had provided legal privileges for whites and denied them to blacks, the Court identified a discrimination that "if not relieved . . . would [be] a denial of equal protection." Absent a state law school for black students, it found that the "petitioner was entitled to be admitted to the law school of the state university."

The *Gaines* case represented the first successful challenge, at least in federal court, to official segregation's underpinnings. It reflected a litigative strategy predicated on the assumption that while the separate but equal doctrine would not be displaced immediately, it would wither from persistent demonstration of its illogic. Reality at the time was that the *Plessy* principle was the norm, *Gaines* was the exception, and significant time and energy would have to be invested in showing that

* (footnotes omitted).

official segregation imprinted on its victims "a badge of inferiority." By focusing on graduate and professional education, the NAACP targeted an accurately perceived point of vulnerability in the system of official segregation. Because the venues and numbers of persons affected were relatively small, deviations from the general rule of segregation seemed more achievable than if primary or secondary educational policy was challenged. As Marshall observed:

> the university level was the best place to begin a campaign that had as its ultimate objective the total elimination of segregation in public institutions in the United States. In the first place, at the university level no provision for Negro education was a rule rather than the exception. Then, too, the difficulties incident to providing equal educational opportunities even within the concept of the "separate but equal" doctrine were insurmountable. To provide separate medical schools, law schools, engineering schools, and graduate schools with all the variety of offerings available at most state universities would be an almost financial impossibility.

The strategy in sum was that if segregation was pushed to the test of satisfying equal as well as separate, the policy eventually would implode as a result of its own weight.

The Constitution and Race 98–99.
Copyright © (1992) Donald E. Lively.
Reprinted with permission of Donald E. Lively.

A. Leon Higginbotham, Jr.

Race, Sex, Education, and Missouri Jurisprudence

Charles Houston, a brilliant black lawyer and former member of the prestigious Harvard Law Review, argued the *Gaines* case before the Supreme Court.

The *Gaines* decision declared that the equal protection mandate of the 14th Amendment must be satisfied within the confines of a particular state. Thus, Missouri's claim that it provided Gaines with equal treatment by providing a scholarship to an out-of-state law school was rejected because it was an out-of-state remedy. Even more important to the desegregation effort, *Gaines* was entitled to an immediate remedy for Missouri's denial of his equal protection rights. Thus, if Missouri failed to provide Gaines with an equal law school within the state it had to admit him to the school reserved for whites.

In addition, Missouri claimed that there was "a limited demand in Missouri for the legal education of Negroes" which justified the discrimination in favor of whites. The Court concluded that Gaines' right was a personal one. It was as an individual that he was entitled to the equal protection of the laws, and the State was bound to furnish him within its borders facilities for legal education substantially equal to those which the State there afforded for persons of the white race, whether or not other blacks sought the same opportunity.

The opinion was not unanimous. Justice McReynolds wrote a dissent which placed him in the despicable shadow of Chief Justice Taney, author of *Dred Scott*. McReynolds declared that the opinion of the Court admitting Gaines to the University of Missouri would "damnify both races." While the case was being argued by Houston, McReynolds further tarnished the prestige of the Court by turning his back to Houston and staring at the rear walls of the Supreme Court chambers.

Several months after the Supreme Court held in his favor, Lloyd Gaines disappeared. He has not been seen or heard from since. Those committed to the principle of racial equality owe Gaines a great debt of gratitude, for they know he gave the ultimate sacrifice, his life, for this principle.

E. Background on Justice James McReynolds

Geoffrey Stone, et al.

Justice James McReynolds

Although remembered today primarily as one of the "four horsemen of reaction" who helped block Franklin Roosevelt's New Deal, James McReynolds first came to public attention as a vigorous "trust buster" in the Theodore Roosevelt and Wilson administrations. In the year that he served as Wilson's attorney general, he angered many members of Congress and of the administration with his arrogance and ill-temper. President Wilson named him to the Court in 1914 largely to quiet the controversy. His judicial career was marked by an unyielding commitment to strict constructionism and conservative principles. His personal manner continued to alienate many of his colleagues. After *The Gold Clause Cases* were decided in 1935, he proclaimed, "Shame and humiliation are on us now. Moral and financial chaos may confidently be expected." Chief Justice Taft remarked that McReynolds "has a continual grouch" and "seems to delight in making others uncomfortable." Widely accused of antisemitism, McReynolds conspicuously failed to sign the letter of affection and regret drafted by his brethren on Justice Brandeis's retirement from the Court.

F. Background on *McLaurin*

Based upon the ruling in *Gaines*, many institutions of higher education that previously had been open only to whites began to admit blacks as well. Under the ruling in *Gaines*, school officials could not provide an out of state option, and satisfy their state's obligations to constitutional equality. Under *Gaines*, education was recognized as an individual state right, and when it was denied, the remedy must be immediate. Now forced to accept black students, some of these institutions attempted to isolate and segregate the admitted black students from the rest of the students.

G. *McLaurin v. Oklahoma State Regents for Higher Education*, 339 U.S. 637 (1950)

Amos T. Hall, Tulsa, Okl., *Robert L. Carter*, Washington, D.C., for appellant.

Fred Hansen, Oklahoma City, Okl., for appellees.

1. Facts

Chief Justice VINSON delivered the opinion of the Court.

In this case, we are faced with the question whether a state may, after admitting a student to graduate instruction in its state university, afford him different treatment from other students solely because of his race. We decide only this issue; *see Sweatt v. Painter*, 339 U.S. 629, 70 S.Ct. 848.

Appellant is a Negro citizen of Oklahoma. Possessing a Master's degree, he applied for admission to the University of Oklahoma in order to pursue studies and courses leading to a Doctorate in Education. At that time, his application was denied, solely because of his race. The school authorities were required to exclude him by the Oklahoma statutes, 70 Okl.Stat. (1941) ss 455, 456, 457, which made it a misdemeanor to maintain or operate, teach or attend a school at which both whites and Negroes are enrolled or taught. Appellant filed a complaint requesting injunctive relief, alleging that the action of the school authorities and the statutes upon which their action was based were unconstitutional and deprived him of the equal protection of the laws. Citing our decisions in *State of Missouri ex rel. Gaines v. Canada*, 1938, 305 U.S. 337, 59 S.Ct. 232, 83 L.Ed. 208, and *Sipuel v. Board of Regents*, 1948, 332 U.S. 631, 68 S.Ct. 299, 92 L.Ed. 247, a statutory three-judge District Court held, 87 F.Supp. 526, that the State had a constitutional duty to provide him with the education he sought as soon as it provided that education for applicants of any other group. It further held that to the extent the Oklahoma statutes denied him admission they were unconstitutional and void. On the assumption, however, that the State would follow the constitutional mandate, the court refused to grant the injunction, retaining jurisdiction of the cause with full power to issue any necessary and proper orders to secure McLaurin the equal protection of the laws.

Following this decision, the Oklahoma legislature amended these statutes to permit the admission of Negroes to institutions of higher learning attended by white students, in cases where such institutions offered courses not available in the Negro schools. The amendment provided, however, that in such cases the program of instruction "shall be given at such colleges or institutions of higher education upon a segregated basis."[96] Appellant was thereupon admitted to the University of Oklahoma Graduate School. In apparent conformity with the amendment, his admission was made subject to "such rules and regulations as to segregation as the President of the University shall consider to afford G.W. McLaurin substantially equal educational opportunities as are afforded to other persons seeking the same education in the Graduate College," a condition which does not appear to have been withdrawn. Thus he was required to sit apart at a designated desk in an ante-room adjoining the classroom; to sit at a designated desk on the mezzanine floor of the library, but not to use the desks in the regular reading room; and to sit at a designated table and to eat at a different time from the other students in the school cafeteria.

To remove these conditions, appellant filed a motion to modify the order and judgment of the District Court. That court held that such treatment did not violate the provisions of the Fourteenth Amendment and denied the motion. 87 F. Supp. 528. This appeal followed.

2. Opinion

In the interval between the decision of the court below and the hearing in this Court, the treatment afforded appellant was altered. For some time, the section of the classroom in which appellant sat was surrounded by a rail on which there was a sign stating, "Reserved For Colored," but these have been removed. He is now assigned to a seat in the classroom in a row specified for colored students; he is assigned to a table in the library on the main floor; and he is permitted to eat at the same time in the cafeteria as other students, although here again he is assigned to a special table.

It is said that the separations imposed by the State in this case are in form merely nominal. McLaurin uses the same classroom, library and cafeteria as students of other races; there is no indication that the seats to which he is assigned in these rooms have any disadvantage of location. He may wait in line in the cafeteria and there stand and talk with his fellow students, but while he eats he must remain apart.

These restrictions were obviously imposed in order to comply, as nearly as could be, with the statutory requirements of Oklahoma. But they signify that the State,

---

96. The amendment adds the following proviso to each of the sections relating to mixed schools: "Provided, that the provisions of this Section shall not apply to programs of instruction leading to a particular degree given at State owned or operated colleges or institutions of higher education of this State established for and/or used by the white race, where such programs of instruction leading to a particular degree are not given at colleges or institutions of higher education of this State established for and/or used by the colored race; provided further, that said programs of instruction leading to a particular degree shall be given at such colleges or institutions of higher education upon a segregated basis." 70 Okla.Stat.Ann. (1950) §§ 455, 456, 457. Segregated basis is defined as "classroom instruction given in separate classrooms, or at separate times." Id. § 455.

in administering the facilities it affords for professional and graduate study, sets McLaurin apart from the other students. The result is that appellant is handicapped in his pursuit of effective graduate instruction. Such restrictions impair and inhibit his ability to study, to engage in discussions and exchange views with other students, and, in general, to learn his profession.

Our society grows increasingly complex, and our need for trained leaders increases correspondingly. Appellant's case represents, perhaps, the epitome of that need, for he is attempting to obtain an advanced degree in education, to become, by definition, a leader and trainer of others. Those who will come under his guidance and influence must be directly affected by the education he receives. Their own education and development will necessarily suffer to the extent that his training is unequal to that of his classmates. State imposed restrictions which produce such inequalities cannot be sustained.

It may be argued that appellant will be in no better position when these restrictions are removed, for he may still be set apart by his fellow students. This we think irrelevant. There is a vast difference—a Constitutional difference—between restrictions imposed by the state which prohibit the intellectual commingling of students, and the refusal of individuals to commingle where the state presents no such bar. *Shelley v. Kraemer*, 1948, 334 U.S. 1, 13–14, 68 S.Ct. 836, 842, 92 L.Ed. 1161, 3 A.L.R.2d 441. The removal of the state restrictions will not necessarily abate individual and group predilections, prejudices and choices. But at the very least, the state will not be depriving appellant of the opportunity to secure acceptance by his fellow students on his own merits.

3. Holding

We conclude that the conditions under which this appellant is required to receive his education deprive him of his personal and present right to the equal protection of the laws. *See Sweatt v. Painter*, 339 U.S. 629, 70 S. Ct. 848. We hold that under these circumstances the Fourteenth Amendment precludes differences in treatment by the state based upon race. Appellant, having been admitted to a state-supported graduate school, must receive the same treatment at the hands of the state as students of other races. The judgment is reversed.

H. Commentary on *McLaurin*

The victory for *McLaurin* recognized that racially segregating black students within an education institution caused them harmful effects, and thus mandated that once admitted into an educational institution, a black student must be treated the same as all other students. The narrow scope of the holding, nevertheless, continued to perpetuate the *Plessy* rationale. If the state provided a school just for black students, then it was still lawful for G.W. McLaurin to be racially segregated in a separate institution. Only if the state failed to provide this separate institution would blacks be admitted to white institutions.

I. Background on *Sweatt*

While many states and their respective institutions of higher learning possessed limited financial resources and, consequently, were reluctant to commit money to build a separate school for a few black students, the University of Texas was not. With the second largest endowment of any school in the world and a state legislature committed to racial segregation, after judicial decisions foreclosed other less expensive options, the University decided to build a law school for one black student. This became known as "the house that Sweatt built."

J. *Sweatt v. Painter*, 339 U.S. 629 (1950)

W. J. Durham, Dallas, Tex., *Thurgood Marshall*, New York City, for petitioner.

Price Daniel, Liberty, Tex., *Joe R. Greenhill*, Houston, Tex., for respondents.

1. Facts

Chief Justice VINSON delivered the opinion of the Court.

. . . In the instant case, petitioner filed an application for admission to the University of Texas Law School for the February, 1946 term. His application was rejected solely because he is a Negro.[97] Petitioner thereupon brought this suit for mandamus against the appropriate school officials, respondents here, to compel his admission. At that time, there was no law school in Texas which admitted Negroes.

The State trial court recognized that the action of the State in denying petitioner the opportunity to gain a legal education while granting it to others deprived him of the equal protection of the laws guaranteed by the Fourteenth Amendment. The court did not grant the relief requested, however, but continued the case for six months to allow the State to supply substantially equal facilities. At the expiration of the six months, in December, 1946, the court denied the writ on the showing that the authorized university officials had adopted an order calling for the opening of a law school for Negroes the following February. While petitioner's appeal was pending, such a school was made available, but petitioner refused to register therein. The Texas Court of Civil Appeals set aside the trial court's judgment and ordered the cause "remanded generally to the trial court for further proceedings without prejudice to the rights of any party to this suit."

On remand, a hearing was held on the issue of the equality of the educational facilities at the newly established school as compared with the University of Texas Law School. Finding that the new school offered petitioner "privileges, advantages, and opportunities for the study of law substantially equivalent to those offered by

---

97. It appears that the University has been restricted to white students, in accordance with the State law. *See* Tex. Const. Art. VII, ss 7, 14; Tex. Rev. Civ. Stat. Arts. 2643b, 2719, 2900 (Vernon, 1925 and Supp.)

the State to white students at the University of Texas," the trial court denied mandamus. The Court of Civil Appeals affirmed. 1948, 210 S.W.2d 442. Petitioner's application for a writ of error was denied by the Texas Supreme Court. We granted certiorari, 1949, 338 U.S. 865, 70 S.Ct. 139, because of the manifest importance of the constitutional issues involved.

The University of Texas Law School, from which petitioner was excluded, was staffed by a faculty of sixteen full-time and three part-time professors, some of whom are nationally recognized authorities in their field. Its student body numbered 850. The library contained over 65,000 volumes. Among the other facilities available to the students were a law review, moot court facilities, scholarship funds, and Order of the Coif affiliation. The school's alumni occupy the most distinguished positions in the private practice of the law and in the public life of the State. It may properly be considered one of the nation's ranking law schools.

The law school for Negroes which was to have opened in February, 1947, would have had no independent faculty or library. The teaching was to be carried on by four members of the University of Texas Law School faculty, who were to maintain their offices at the University of Texas while teaching at both institutions. Few of the 10,000 volumes ordered for the library had arrived;[98] nor was there any full-time librarian. The school lacked accreditation.

Since the trial of this case, respondents report the opening of a law school at the Texas State University for Negroes. It is apparently on the road to full accreditation. It has a faculty of five full-time professors; a student body of 23; a library of some 16,500 volumes serviced by a full-time staff; a practice court and legal aid association; and one alumnus who has become a member of the Texas Bar.

2. Opinion

a. Defining Equality

Whether the University of Texas Law School is compared with the original or the new law school for Negroes, we cannot find substantial equality in the educational opportunities offered white and Negro law students by the State. In terms of number of the faculty, variety of courses and opportunity for specialization, size of the student body, scope of the library, availability of law review and similar activities, the University of Texas Law School is superior. What is more important, the University of Texas Law School possesses to a far greater degree those qualities which are incapable of objective measurement but which make for greatness in a law school. Such qualities, to name but a few, include reputation of the faculty, experience of the administration, position and influence of the alumni, standing in the

---

98. "Students of the interim School of Law of the Texas State University for Negroes (located in Austin, whereas the permanent School was to be located at Houston) shall have use of the State Law Library in the Capitol Building. . . ." Tex. Laws 1947, c. 29, s 11, Tex. Rev. Civ. Stat. (Vernon, Supp.), note to Art. 2643b. It is not clear that this privilege was anything more than was extended to all citizens of the State.

community, traditions and prestige. It is difficult to believe that one who had a free choice between these law schools would consider the question close.

Moreover, although the law is a highly learned profession, we are well aware that it is an intensely practical one. The law school, the proving ground for legal learning and practice, cannot be effective in isolation from the individuals and institutions with which the law interacts. Few students and no one who has practiced law would choose to study in an academic vacuum, removed from the interplay of ideas and the exchange of views with which the law is concerned. The law school to which Texas is willing to admit petitioner excludes from its student body members of the racial groups which number 85% of the population of the State and include most of the lawyers, witnesses, jurors, judges and other officials with whom petitioner will inevitably be dealing when he becomes a member of the Texas Bar. With such a substantial and significant segment of society excluded, we cannot conclude that the education offered petitioner is substantially equal to that which he would receive if admitted to the University of Texas Law School. . . .

b. Applying *Plessy*

In accordance with these cases, petitioner may claim his full constitutional right: legal education equivalent to that offered by the State to students of other races. Such education is not available to him in a separate law school as offered by the State. We cannot, therefore, agree with respondents that the doctrine of *Plessy v. Ferguson*, 1896, 163 U.S. 537, 16 S.Ct. 1138, 41 L.Ed. 256, requires affirmance of the judgment below. Nor need we reach petitioner's contention that *Plessy v. Ferguson* should be reexamined in the light of contemporary knowledge respecting the purposes of the Fourteenth Amendment and the effects of racial segregation.

3. Holding

We hold that the Equal Protection Clause of the Fourteenth Amendment requires that petitioner be admitted to the University of Texas Law School. The judgment is reversed and the cause is remanded for proceedings not inconsistent with this opinion.

K. Commentary on *Sweatt*

In 1950, the legal myth that racially separate schools could be equal was challenged in cases involving graduate school education. In 1946, after World War II, veteran Heman Sweatt applied to the University of Texas Law School. In response to Sweatt's application, Texas opened up a law school for blacks in the basement of a building near the University. The Supreme Court held that such new, underfunded, Jim Crow graduate schools would not be viewed as the constitutional equivalent to the long established, well-endowed, and highly esteemed schools that had been open to all other races for decades. The Supreme Court acknowledged that the two schools were not equal.

The decision in *Sweatt* is important because it represents the first time that the Supreme Court looked beyond the form of the racial separation to the substance of the education. In measuring equality, the Court not only considered the type of facilities provided but the opportunities that they afforded to the students.

L. Questions and Notes

What are the most important rights or privileges that a society can provide or guarantee? List, in order of importance, the three most critical rights or privileges and identify why they are so critical.

Can you identify any rights and priorities which are not currently entitled to legal protection, yet you believe that they should be? Why do you believe they are not presently protected? Is protection against racial segregation one of these priorities?

XIX. Ending State-Mandated Segregation

A. Introduction

While civil rights attorneys won several cases resulting in racial desegregation, even after these victories the separate but equal doctrine was still held to be legally valid. These decisions merely concluded that the "equal" portion of the "separate but equal" doctrine had not been satisfied. The decisions failed to go the needed step, to invalidate the overall doctrine. Nevertheless, this string of victories helped to lay the groundwork for a direct challenge to the *Plessy* doctrine.

B. Background on *Brown I*

Building upon a series of victories against racial segregation in higher education, Thurgood Marshall, and his legal team from the National Association for the Advancement of Colored People, now had the legal ammunition to require equalization in higher education facilities throughout the United States. More significantly, however, he possessed the jurisprudential foundation to challenge the constitutional validity of segregation in all of its forms.

Donald E. Lively

*The Constitution and Race**

.... The appointment of Earl Warren as chief justice altered institutional dynamics and resulted in leadership more receptive to the possibility of doctrinal redesign. A challenge to segregated primary and secondary education required not exception from but vitiation of the general rule. As Marshall recognized, elementary and high

---

* (footnotes omitted).

schools were distinguishable from graduate and professional "specialized institutions with national or even statewide reputations."

Further complicating a challenge to segregated education was the reality that Fourteenth Amendment history seemed to support the established order. An examination of the record reveals that the framers did not contemplate the prospect of racially mixed education. Precisely the opposite intent was suggested insofar as District of Columbia schools were segregated by the same Congress that adopted the Fourteenth Amendment. What history denied eventually would be reclaimed (1) by social science data indicating that official segregation stigmatized black students and denied them equality of educational opportunity, and (2) by a sense that public schooling was more crucial to Fourteenth Amendment interests in 1954 than in 1868.

The Court's eventual repudiation of official segregation, although largely responsive to the NAACP's challenge, was attributable also to a general evolution of equal protection theory. In the late 1920s, the Court had dismissed the equal protection guarantee as the tool of a desperate litigant. At the same time, it was vitalizing the due process guarantee in substantive terms that created a panoply of basic liberties unspecified by the Constitution. In contrast to its uncharitable readings of equal protection, the Court at the apex of Lochnerism identified fundamental rights and freedom in terms that included not only freedom from bodily restraint, but he right of the individual to contract, to engage in any of the common occupations of life, to acquire useful knowledge, to marry, to establish a home and bring up children, to worship God according to the dictates of his own conscience, and generally to enjoy those privileges long recognized . . . as essential to the orderly pursuit of happiness by free men.

In closing out the *Lochner* era in 1937, the Court announced a major change in Fourteenth Amendment thinking. In *West Coast Hotel v. Parrish*, it depicted substantive due process analysis as a deviation "from the true application of the principles governing the regulation by the State of the relation of employer and employed." The next year, in *United States v. Carolene Products Co.*, the Court advanced a revised, albeit preliminary, view of future Fourteenth Amendment analysis. Although allowing that "the existence of facts supporting . . . legislative judgment are to be presumed, for regulation affecting ordinary commercial transactions," it suggested that special circumstances might justify stricter review. The Court specifically noted that more rigorous examination may be apt when legislation implicates a specific constitutional prohibition "such as those of the first ten amendments." For equal protection purposes, the Court found it unnecessary to inquire "whether prejudice against discrete and insular minorities may be a special condition, which tends seriously to curtail the operation of those political processes ordinarily to be relied upon to protect minorities, and which may call for a correspondingly more searching judicial inquiry."

The *Carolene Products* decision, if not actually setting a new equal protection standard when racial discrimination was at issue, at least ventured the possibility that the Fourteenth Amendment might be animated in terms more responsive to its original purpose. The reality of a new analytical model was evidenced when the Court reviewed an equal protection challenge to the relocation of Japanese Americans during World War II. For reasons of national security, President Roosevelt had authorized their detention in remote camps. In examining the plan, the Court introduced a standard to the effect that all legal restrictions which curtail the civil rights of a single racial group are immediately suspect. That is not say that all such restrictions are unconstitutional. It is to say that courts must subject them to the most rigid scrutiny. Pressing public necessity may sometimes justify the existence of such restrictions; racial antagonism never can.

The notion that racial classifications were suspect and thus must be strictly scrutinized by the courts, although not disruptive of the wartime relocation scheme, eventually would prove critical to dismantling the nation's system of official discrimination.

Equal protection until the middle of the twentieth century was reviewed by the courts on the basis of reasonableness standards, which largely translated as judicial deference to legislative judgment. Strict scrutiny, as conceived in *Korematsu v. United States*, provided analytical weaponry for identifying the "racial antagonism" underlying official segregation. Before such rigorous review eventuated, the separate but equal doctrine survived pursuant to outward appearances of symmetrical application. The appearance of parallelism was perhaps best projected by the Supreme Court's allowance of state prohibitions against interracial intimacy or marriage. The Court in 1875 had upheld a state law that enhanced the penalties for fornication if the offenders were of different races and prohibited miscegenation altogether. Reviewing the provision in *Pace v. Alabama*, the Court found no constitutionally significant discrimination because the law applied equally to both races. Not until 1967 did it fully repudiate the notion that equal application of the law was not necessarily synonymous with equal protection of the law. In *Loving v. Virginia*, the Court recognized that antimiscegenation laws were an extension of racist ideology and impaired the freedom to marry.

Arrival at that point of understanding represented a significant passage from the notion that official racial classifications were reasonable and could be considered harmful only if misunderstood. Erosion of the separate but equal doctrine in response to the NAACP's challenge to official segregation suggested that the principle was living on borrowed time. General reconstruction of Fourteenth Amendment standards in the post-*Lochner* era afforded analytical methodology for closely examining the nature, premises, and effects of segregation. When leadership of the Court changed in 1953, circumstances had ripened for what has been described as the "Second American Revolution."

C. *Brown v. Board of Education (Brown I),* 347 U.S. 483 (1954)

Robert L. Carter, New York City, for appellants Brown and others.

Paul E. Wilson, Topeka, Kan., for appellees Board of Education of Topeka and others.

Spottswood Robinson III, Thurgood Marshall, New York City, for appellants Briggs and Davis and others.

John W. Davis, T. Justin Moore, J. Lindsay Almond, Jr., Richmond, Va., for appellees Elliott and County School Board of Prince Edward County and others.

Asst. Atty. Gen. *J. Lee Rankin* for United States amicus curiae by special leave of Court.

H. Albert Young, Wilmington, Del., for petitioners Gebhart et al.

Jack Greenberg, Thurgood Marshall, New York City, for respondents Belton et al.

1. Facts

Chief Justice WARREN delivered the opinion of the Court.

These cases come to us from the States of Kansas, South Carolina, Virginia, and Delaware. They are premised on different facts and different local conditions, but a common legal question justifies their consideration together in this consolidated opinion.[99]

---

99. In the Kansas case, *Brown v. Board of Education*, the plaintiffs are Negro children of elementary school age residing in Topeka. They brought this action in the United States District Court for the District of Kansas to enjoin enforcement of a Kansas statute which permits, but does not require, cities of more than 15,000 population to maintain separate school facilities for Negro and white students. Kan.Gen.Stat.1949, § 72-1724. Pursuant to that authority, the Topeka Board of Education elected to establish segregated elementary schools. Other public schools in the community, however, are operated on a nonsegregated basis. The three-judge District Court, convened under 28 U.S.C. §§ 2281 and 2284, 28 U.S.C.A. ss 2281, 2284, found that segregation in public education has a detrimental effect upon Negro children, but denied relief on the ground that the Negro and white schools were substantially equal with respect to buildings, transportation, curricula, and educational qualifications of teachers. 98 F.Supp. 797. The case is here on direct appeal under 28 U.S.C. § 1253, 28 U.S.C.A. § 1253.

In the South Carolina case, *Briggs v. Elliott*, the plaintiffs are Negro children of both elementary and high school age residing in Clarendon County. They brought this action in the United States District Court for the Eastern District of South Carolina to enjoin enforcement of provisions in the state constitution and statutory code which require the segregation of Negroes and whites in public schools. S.C. Const. Art. XI, § 7; S.C. Code 1942, § 5377. The three-judge District Court, convened under 28 U.S.C. §§ 2281 and 2284, 28 U.S.C.A. §§ 2281, 2284, denied the requested relief. The court found that the Negro schools were inferior to the white schools and ordered the defendants to begin immediately to equalize the facilities. But the court sustained the validity of the contested provisions and denied the plaintiffs admission to the white schools during the equalization program. 98 F.Supp. 529. This Court vacated the District Court's judgment and remanded the case for the purpose of obtaining the court's views on a report filed by the defendants concerning the

In each of the cases, minors of the Negro race, through their legal representatives, seek the aid of the courts in obtaining admission to the public schools of their community on a nonsegregated basis. In each instance, they have been denied admission to schools attended by white children under laws requiring or permitting segregation according to race. This segregation was alleged to deprive the plaintiffs of the equal protection of the laws under the Fourteenth Amendment. In each of the cases, other than the Delaware case, a three-judge federal district court denied relief to the plaintiffs on the so-called "separate but equal" doctrine announced by this Court in *Plessy v. Ferguson*, 163 U.S. 537, 16 S. Ct. 1138, 41 L. Ed. 256. Under that doctrine, equality of treatment is accorded when the races are provided substantially equal facilities, even though these facilities be separate. In the Delaware case, the Supreme Court of Delaware adhered to that doctrine, but ordered that the plaintiffs be admitted to the white schools because of their superiority to the Negro schools.

---

progress made in the equalization program. 342 U.S. 350, 72 S.Ct. 327, 96 L.Ed. 392. On remand, the District Court found that substantial equality had been achieved except for buildings and that the defendants were proceeding to rectify this inequality as well. 103 F.Supp. 920. The case is again here on direct appeal under 28 U.S.C. § 1253, 28 U.S.C.A. § 1253.

In the Virginia case, *Davis v. County School Board*, the plaintiffs are Negro children of high school age residing in Prince Edward County. They brought this action in the United States District Court for the Eastern District of Virginia to enjoin enforcement of provisions in the state constitution and statutory code which require the segregation of Negroes and whites in public schools. Va. Const. § 140; Va. Code 1950, § 22-221. The three-judge District Court, convened under 28 U.S.C. §§ 2281 and 2284, 28 U.S.C.A. §§ 2281, 2284, denied the requested relief. The court found the Negro school inferior in physical plant, curricula, and transportation, and ordered the defendants forthwith to provide substantially equal curricula and transportation and to "proceed with all reasonable diligence and dispatch to remove" the inequality in physical plant. But, as in the South Carolina case, the court sustained the validity of the contested provisions and denied the plaintiffs admission to the white schools during the equalization program. 103 F.Supp. 337. The case is here on direct appeal under 28 U.S.C. § 1253, 28 U.S.C.A. § 1253.

In the Delaware case, *Gebhart v. Belton*, the plaintiffs are Negro children of both elementary and high school age residing in New Castle County. They brought this action in the Delaware Court of Chancery to enjoin enforcement of provisions in the state constitution and statutory code which require the segregation of Negroes and whites in public schools. Del. Const. Art. X, § 2; Del. Rev. Code, 1935, § 2631, 14 Del. C. § 141. The Chancellor gave judgment for the plaintiffs and ordered their immediate admission to schools previously attended only by white children, on the ground that the Negro schools were inferior with respect to teacher training, pupil-teacher ratio, extracurricular activities, physical plant, and time and distance involved in travel. Del.Ch., 87 A.2d 862. The Chancellor also found that segregation itself results in an inferior education for Negro children (see note 10, infra), but did not rest his decision on that ground. 87 A.2d at page 865. The Chancellor's decree was affirmed by the Supreme Court of Delaware, which intimated, however, that the defendants might be able to obtain a modification of the decree after equalization of the Negro and white schools had been accomplished. 91 A.2d 137, 152. The defendants, contending only that the Delaware courts had erred in ordering the immediate admission of the Negro plaintiffs to the white schools, applied to this Court for certiorari. The writ was granted, 344 U.S. 891, 73 S.Ct. 213, 97 L.Ed. 689. The plaintiffs, who were successful below, did not submit a cross-petition.

2. Opinion

The plaintiffs contend that segregated public schools are not "equal" and cannot be made "equal," and that hence they are deprived of the equal protection of the laws. Because of the obvious importance of the question presented, the Court took jurisdiction. Argument was heard in the 1952 Term, and reargument was heard this Term on certain questions propounded by the Court.

a. History of the Fourteenth Amendment

Reargument was largely devoted to the circumstances surrounding the adoption of the Fourteenth Amendment in 1868. It covered exhaustively consideration of the Amendment in Congress, ratification by the states, then existing practices in racial segregation, and the views of proponents and opponents of the Amendment. This discussion and our own investigation convince us that, although these sources cast some light, it is not enough to resolve the problem with which we are faced. At best, they are inconclusive. The most avid proponents of the post-War Amendments undoubtedly intended them to remove all legal distinctions among "all persons born or naturalized in the United States." Their opponents, just as certainly, were antagonistic to both the letter and the spirit of the Amendments and wished them to have the most limited effect. What others in Congress and the state legislatures had in mind cannot be determined with any degree of certainty.

An additional reason for the inconclusive nature of the Amendment's history, with respect to segregated schools, is the status of public education at that time.[100] In the South, the movement toward free common schools, supported by general taxation, had not yet taken hold. Education of white children was largely in the hands of private groups. Education of Negroes was almost nonexistent, and practically all of the race were illiterate. In fact, any education of Negroes was forbidden by law in some states. Today, in contrast, many Negroes have achieved outstanding success in the arts and sciences as well as in the business and professional world. It is true

---

100. For a general study of the development of public education prior to the Amendment, *see* Butts and Cremin, A History of Education in American Culture (1953), Pts. I, II: Cubberley, Public Education in the United States (1934 ed.), cc. II–XII. School practices current at the time of the adoption of the Fourteenth Amendment are described in Butts and Cremin at 269–75; Knight, Public Education in the South (1922), cc. VIII, IX. *See also* H. Ex. Doc. No. 315, 41st Cong., 2d Sess. (1871). Although the demand for free public schools followed substantially the same pattern in both the North and the South, the development in the South did not begin to gain momentum until about 1850, some twenty years after that in the North. The reasons for the somewhat slower development in the South (e.g., the rural character of the South and the different regional attitudes toward state assistance) are well explained in Cubberley at 408–23. In the country as a whole, but particularly in the South, the War virtually stopped all progress in public education. *Id.*, at 427–28. The low status of Negro education in all sections of the country, both before and immediately after the War, is described in Beale, A History of Freedom of Teaching in American Schools (1941), 112–32, 175–95. Compulsory school attendance laws were not generally adopted until after the ratification of the Fourteenth Amendment, and it was not until 1918 that such laws were in force in all the states. Cubberley at 563–65.

that public school education at the time of the Amendment had advanced further in the North, but the effect of the Amendment on Northern States was generally ignored in the congressional debates. Even in the North, the conditions of public education did not approximate those existing today. The curriculum was usually rudimentary; ungraded schools were common in rural areas; the school term was but three months a year in many states; and compulsory school attendance was virtually unknown. As a consequence, it is not surprising that there should be so little in the history of the Fourteenth Amendment relating to its intended effect on public education.

In the first cases in this Court construing the Fourteenth Amendment, decided shortly after its adoption, the Court interpreted it as proscribing all state-imposed discriminations against the Negro race.[101] The doctrine of "separate but equal" did not make its appearance in this court until 1896 in the case of *Plessy v. Ferguson, supra,* involving not education but transportation.[102] American courts have since labored with the doctrine for over half a century. In this Court, there have been six cases involving the "separate but equal" doctrine in the field of public education.[103] In *Cumming v. Board of Education of Richmond County,* 175 U.S. 528, 20 S.Ct. 197, 44 L.Ed. 262, and *Gong Lum v. Rice,* 275 U.S. 78, 48 S.Ct. 91, 72 L.Ed. 172, the validity of the doctrine itself was not challenged.[104] In more recent cases, all on the graduate school level, inequality was found in that specific benefits enjoyed by white

---

101. *See Slaughterhouse Cases,* 1873, 16 Wall. 36, 67–72, 21 L.Ed. 394; *Strauder v. West Virginia,* 1880, 100 U.S. 303, 307–8, 25 L.Ed. 664.

"It ordains that no State shall deprive any person of life, liberty, or property, without due process of law, or deny to any person within its jurisdiction the equal protection of the laws. What is this but declaring that the law in the States shall be the same for the black as for the white; that all persons, whether colored or white, shall stand equal before the laws of the States, and, in regard to the colored race, for whose protection the amendment was primarily designed, that no discrimination shall be made against them by law because of their color? The words of the amendment, it is true, are prohibitory, but they contain a necessary implication of a positive immunity, or right, most valuable to the colored race,—the right to exemption from unfriendly legislation against them distinctively as colored,—exemption from legal discriminations, implying inferiority in civil society, lessening the security of their enjoyment of the rights which others enjoy, and discriminations which are steps towards reducing them to the condition of a subject race."

See also State of Virginia v. Rives, 1879, 100 U.S. 313, 318, 25 L.Ed. 667; *Ex parte Virginia,* 1879, 100 U.S. 339, 344–45, 25 L.Ed. 676.

102. The doctrine apparently originated in *Roberts v. City of Boston,* 1850, 5 Cush. 198, 59 Mass. 198, 206, upholding school segregation against attack as being violative of a state constitutional guarantee of equality. Segregation in Boston public schools was eliminated in 1855. Mass. Acts 1855, c. 256. But elsewhere in the North segregation in public education has persisted in some communities until recent years. It is apparent that such segregation has long been a nationwide problem, not merely one of sectional concern.

103. *See also Berea College v. Kentucky,* 1908, 211 U.S. 45, 29 S.Ct. 33, 53 L.Ed. 81.

104. In the *Cumming* case, Negro taxpayers sought an injunction requiring the defendant school board to discontinue the operation of a high school for white children until the board resumed operation of a high school for Negro children. Similarly, in the Gong Lum case, the plaintiff, a child of Chinese descent, contended only that state authorities had misapplied the doctrine by classifying him with Negro children and requiring him to attend a Negro school.

students were denied to Negro students of the same educational qualifications. *State of Missouri ex rel. Gaines v. Canada*, 305 U.S. 337, 59 S.Ct. 232, 83 L.Ed. 208; *Sipuel v. Board of Regents of University of Oklahoma*, 332 U.S. 631, 68 S.Ct. 299, 92 L.Ed. 247; *Sweatt v. Painter*, 339 U.S. 629, 70 S.Ct. 848, 94 L.Ed. 1114; *McLaurin v. Oklahoma State Regents*, 339 U.S. 637, 70 S.Ct. 851, 94 L.Ed. 1149. In none of these cases was it necessary to re-examine the doctrine to grant relief to the Negro plaintiff. And in *Sweatt v. Painter, supra*, the Court expressly reserved decision on the question whether *Plessy v. Ferguson* should be held inapplicable to public education.

b. Value of Public Education

In the instant cases, that question is directly presented. Here, unlike *Sweatt v. Painter*, there are findings below that the Negro and white schools involved have been equalized, or are being equalized, with respect to buildings, curricula, qualifications and salaries of teachers, and other "tangible" factors.[105] Our decision, therefore, cannot turn on merely a comparison of these tangible factors in the Negro and white schools involved in each of the cases. We must look instead to the effect of segregation itself on public education.

In approaching this problem, we cannot turn the clock back to 1868 when the Amendment was adopted, or even to 1896 when *Plessy v. Ferguson* was written. We must consider public education in the light of its full development and its present place in American life throughout the Nation. Only in this way can it be determined if segregation in public schools deprives these plaintiffs of the equal protection of the laws.

Today, education is perhaps the most important function of state and local governments. Compulsory school attendance laws and the great expenditures for education both demonstrate our recognition of the importance of education to our democratic society. It is required in the performance of our most basic public responsibilities, even service in the armed forces. It is the very foundation of good citizenship. Today it is a principal instrument in awakening the child to cultural values, in preparing him for later professional training, and in helping him to adjust normally to his environment. In these days, it is doubtful that any child may reasonably be expected to succeed in life if he is denied the opportunity of an education. Such an opportunity, where the state has undertaken to provide it, is a right which must be made available to all on equal terms.

---

105. In the Kansas case, the court below found substantial equality as to all such factors. 98 F. Supp. 797, 798. In the South Carolina case, the court below found that the defendants were proceeding 'promptly and in good faith to comply with the court's decree.' 103 F. Supp. 920, 921. In the Virginia case, the court below noted that the equalization program was already 'afoot and progressing,' 103 F. Supp. 337, 341; since then, we have been advised, in the Virginia Attorney General's brief on reargument, that the program has now been completed. In the Delaware case, the court below similarly noted that the state's equalization program was well under way. 91 A.2d 137, 139.

c. Effect of Segregation

We come then to the question presented: Does segregation of children in public schools solely on the basis of race, even though the physical facilities and other 'tangible' factors may be equal, deprive the children of the minority group of equal educational opportunities? We believe that it does.

In *Sweatt v. Painter, supra* (339 U.S. 629, 70 S. Ct. 850), in finding that a segregated law school for Negroes could not provide them equal educational opportunities, this Court relied in large part on "those qualities which are incapable of objective measurement but which make for greatness in a law school." In *McLaurin v. Oklahoma State Regents, supra* (339 U.S. 637, 70 S. Ct. 853), the Court, in requiring that a Negro admitted to a white graduate school be treated like all other students, again resorted to intangible considerations: ". . . his ability to study, to engage in discussions and exchange views with other students, and, in general, to learn his profession." Such considerations apply with added force to children in grade and high schools. To separate them from others of similar age and qualifications solely because of their race generates a feeling of inferiority as to their status in the community that may affect their hearts and minds in a way unlikely ever to be undone. The effect of this separation on their educational opportunities was well stated by a finding in the Kansas case by a court which nevertheless felt compelled to rule against the Negro plaintiffs: "Segregation of white and colored children in public schools has a detrimental effect upon the colored children. The impact is greater when it has the sanction of the law; for the policy of separating the races is usually interpreted as denoting the inferiority of the Negro group. A sense of inferiority affects the motivation of a child to learn. Segregation with the sanction of law, therefore, has a tendency to (retard) the educational and mental development of Negro children and to deprive them of some of the benefits they would receive in a racial(ly) integrated school system."[106]

Whatever may have been the extent of psychological knowledge at the time of *Plessy v. Ferguson*, this finding is amply supported by modern authority.[107] Any language in *Plessy v. Ferguson* contrary to this finding is rejected.

---

106. A similar finding was made in the Delaware case: "I conclude from the testimony that in our Delaware society, State-imposed segregation in education itself results in the Negro children, as a class, receiving educational opportunities which are substantially inferior to those available to white children otherwise similarly situated." 87 A.2d 862, 865.

107. K.B. CLARK, EFFECT OF PREJUDICE AND DISCRIMINATION ON PERSONALITY DEVELOPMENT (Midcentury White House Conference on Children and Youth, 1950); WITMER AND KOTINSKY, PERSONALITY IN THE MAKING (1952), c. VI; Deutscher and Chein, *The Psychological Effects of Enforced Segregation: A Survey of Social Science Opinion*, 26 J. PSYCHOL. 259 (1948); Chein, *What are the Psychological Effects of Segregation Under Conditions of Equal Facilities?*, 3 INT. J. OPINION AND ATTITUDE RES. 229 (1949); BRAMELD, EDUCATIONAL COSTS, IN DISCRIMINATION AND NATIONAL WELFARE (1949), 44–48; FRAZIER, THE NEGRO IN THE UNITED STATES (1949), 674–81. And *see generally* MYRDAL, AN AMERICAN DILEMMA (1944).

3. *Holding*

We conclude that in the field of public education the doctrine of "separate but equal" has no place. Separate educational facilities are inherently unequal. Therefore, we hold that the plaintiffs and others similarly situated for whom the actions have been brought are, by reason of the segregation complained of, deprived of the equal protection of the laws guaranteed by the Fourteenth Amendment. This disposition makes unnecessary any discussion whether such segregation also violates the Due Process Clause of the Fourteenth Amendment.

Because these are class actions, because of the wide applicability of this decision, and because of the great variety of local conditions, the formulation of decrees in these cases presents problems of considerable complexity. On reargument, the consideration of appropriate relief was necessarily subordinated to the primary question—the constitutionality of segregation in public education. We have now announced that such segregation is a denial of the equal protection of the laws. In order that we may have the full assistance of the parties in formulating decrees, the cases will be restored to the docket, and the parties are requested to present further argument on Questions 4 and 5 previously propounded by the Court for the reargument this Term.[108] The Attorney General of the United States is again invited to participate. The Attorneys General of the states requiring or permitting segregation in public education will also be permitted to appear as amici curiae upon request to do so by September 15, 1954, and submission of briefs by October 1, 1954.[109]

D. Commentary on *Brown I*

In his eloquent closing argument before the Supreme Court, Thurgood Marshall directly attacked the Court's 1896 ruling in *Plessy* that the Constitution permitted "separate but equal" facilities for blacks. He asked: "Why of all of the multitudinous

---

108. 4. Assuming it is decided that segregation in public schools violates the Fourteenth Amendment

(a) would a decree necessarily follow providing that, within the limits set by normal geographic school districting, Negro children should forthwith be admitted to schools of their choice, or

(b) may this Court, in the exercise of its equity powers, permit an effective gradual adjustment to be brought about from existing segregated systems to a system not based on color distinctions?

5. On the assumption on which questions 4(a) and (b) are based, and assuming further that this Court will exercise its equity powers to the end described in question 4(b),

(a) should this Court formulate detailed decrees in these cases;

(b) if so, what specific issues should the decrees reach;

(c) should this Court appoint a special master to hear evidence with a view to recommending specific terms for such decrees;

(d) should this Court remand to the courts of first instance with directions to frame decrees in these cases, and if so what general directions should the decrees of this Court include and what procedures should the courts of first instance follow in arriving at the specific terms of more detailed decrees?

109. *See* Rule 42, Revised Rules of this Court, effective July 1, 1954, 28 U.S.C.A.

groups of people in this country [do] you have to single out Negroes and give them this separate treatment?" (*Leon Friedman, ed., Argument: The Oral Argument Before the Supreme Court in Brown v. Board of Education of Topeka, 1952–55*, page 239). The Supreme Court responded that black people could no longer be singled out for this separate and inherently unequal treatment.

The significance of the *Brown I* case cannot be overstated. While the decision dealt specifically with segregation in public schools, it ultimately was applied to racial discrimination in many other aspects of American life. *Brown I* fueled the process by which each victory in the civil rights era hastened other events. After *Brown I*, the focus of the Civil Rights Movement changed from desegregating public schools to desegregating restaurants, parks, city buses, places of employment and— ultimately—to the push for "affirmative action."

The situation invokes the memory of a slave preacher who in 1865, upon hearing the Emancipation Proclamation read for the first time, responded:

Lord, we a'int what we want to be

we a'int what we ought to be

we a'int what we gonna be but thank god we a'int what we was![110]

E. Background on Chief Justice Earl Warren

Geoffrey Stone, et al.

Justice Earl Warren

Both vilified and canonized during his tenure, Earl Warren presided as chief justice over one of the most tumultuous and portentous periods in the Court's history. The emotions that he aroused are hard to reconcile with his political stance, which was, essentially, centrist and pragmatic. As Republican governor of California, he denounced "communistic radicals" and supported the wartime order to forcibly evacuate Japanese-Americans. The Court subsequently upheld the constitutionality of the evacuation in *Korematsu v. United States*, 323 U.S. 214 (1944). In his later years as governor, however, he developed the reputation as a progressive and proposed state programs for prepaid medical insurance and liberal welfare benefits. In 1948, he ran for Vice President on the ticket headed by Thomas Dewey. In 1952, he mounted his own presidential effort. At the Republican convention, however, he threw his support behind Dwight Eisenhower. President Eisenhower repaid Warren by nominating him as chief justice in 1953—a nomination Eisenhower later called "the biggest damn-fool mistake I ever made." Perhaps Warren's greatest accomplishment on the Court was his painstaking and successful effort to maintain a united front as the Court overturned the separate but equal doctrine in *Brown v.*

---

110. Address Delivered by Dr. Martin Luther King, Jr., May 14, 1963, St. Paul's Church, Cleveland Heights, Ohio (http://www.stpauls-church.org/mlk/20 sermon.pdf).

Board of Education, 347 U.S. 873 (1954), and then confronted southern violence and intransigence.

Constitutional Law xciv (3rd edition).
Copyright © (1996) Stone, et al.
Reprinted with permission of Aspen Law & Business.

F. Questions and Notes

While the *Brown I* decision was important, it was by no means inevitable. The *Plessy* doctrine had lasted some sixty years despite its flawed reasoning and questionable conclusions. What caused this turnaround in Supreme Court jurisprudence? Was it the change in Supreme Court personnel, the persuasiveness of Chief Justice Earl Warren, the skill of Thurgood Marshall, the influence of popular opinion, developments in international politics, the impact of World War II, or something else?

While the *Brown I* decision has many supporters, it is not without its flaws. What criticisms do you have of the case? Did *Brown I* distinguish rather than overrule *Plessy*? If so, how could the decision have gone further?

Compare the opinion in *Brown I* with the dissent in *Plessy*. What, if any, are the differences?

G. Point/Counterpoint

Richard Delgado

Explaining the Rise and Fall of African American Fortunes:
Interest Convergence and Civil Rights Gains*

What accounts for the rise and fall of minorities' fortunes? Two schools of thought offer competing interpretations. One, an idealist school, takes as its premise that race is a social construction. Blacks, like other groups of color, are racialized by a system of thoughts, words, messages, stories, and scripts that implant in the minds of most citizens indelible images of inferiority. The way to overcome racism, then, is to speak out against it and to arrange social structures, such as elementary education, so that whites will learn firsthand that people of different colors are just like anyone else—some good, some bad. Proponents of this view urge controls on hate speech, tout storytelling and counterstorytelling by minorities, and encourage whites to root out any unconscious racism they may harbor. For this school, social images drive racial fortunes, and the way to change these fortunes is to change the way the American public thinks and talks about race.

---

* (footnotes omitted).

A competing view acknowledges that race and racism are ideas and thus, in some sense, under our control, but holds that material factors, including competition for jobs, social and pecuniary advantage, and the class interest of elite groups (that is "interest-convergence") play an even larger role in our system of white-over-black racism. Writers in this camp highlight how racism operates to reinforce material or psychic advantages for groups in a position to command them.

37 Harvard C.R.-C.L. L. Rev. 370–71 (2002).
Copyright (c) (2002) Harvard Civil Rights-
Civil Liberties Law Review and Richard Delgado.
Reprinted with permission of the Harvard Civil Rights-
Civil Liberties Law Review and Richard Delgado.

Do you agree with Professor Bell's interest-convergence theory explaining *Brown*? If not, what is your counter explanation?

Derrick A. Bell, Jr.

Brown v. Board of Education *and the Interest-Convergence Dilemma**

I contend that the decision in *Brown* to break with the Court's long-held position on these issues cannot be understood without some consideration of the decision's value to whites, not simply those concerned about the immorality of racial inequality, but also those whites in policymaking positions able to see the economic and political advances at home and abroad that would follow abandonment of segregation. First, the decision helped to provide immediate credibility to America's struggle with Communist countries to win the hearts and minds of emerging third world peoples. At least this argument was advanced by lawyers for both the NAACP and the federal government. And the point was not lost on the news media. *Time Magazine*, for example, predicted that the international impact of Brown would be scarcely less important than its effect on the education of black children: "In many countries, where U.S. prestige and leadership have been damaged by the fact of U.S. segregation, it will come as a timely reassertion of the basic American principle that 'all men are created equal.'"

Second, *Brown* offered much needed reassurance to American blacks that the precepts of equality and freedom so heralded during World War II might yet be given meaning at home. Returning black veterans faced not only continuing discrimination, but also violent attacks in the South which rivaled those that took place at the conclusion of World War I. Their disillusionment and anger were poignantly expressed by the black actor, Paul Robeson, who in 1949 declared: "It is unthinkable . . . that American Negroes would go to war on behalf of those who have oppressed us for generations . . . against a country the Soviet Union which in one generation has raised our people to the full human dignity of mankind." It is

---

* (footnotes omitted).

not impossible to imagine that fear of the spread of such sentiment influenced subsequent racial decisions made by the courts.

Finally, there were whites who realized that the South could make the transition from a rural, plantation society to the sunbelt with all its potential and profit only when it ended its struggle to remain divided by state-sponsored segregation. Thus, segregation was viewed as a barrier to further industrialization in the South.

These points may seem insufficient proof of self-interest leverage to produce a decision as important as *Brown*. They are cited, however, to help assess and not to diminish the Supreme Court's most important statement on the principle of racial equality. Here, as in the abolition of slavery, there were whites for whom recognition of the racial equality principle was sufficient motivation. But, as with abolition, the number who would act on morality alone was insufficient to bring about the desired racial reform.

Thus, for those whites who sought an end to desegregation on moral grounds or for the pragmatic reasons outlined above, *Brown* appeared to be a welcome break with the past. When segregation was finally condemned by the Supreme Court, however, the outcry was nevertheless great, especially among poorer whites who feared loss of control over their public schools and other facilities. Their fear of loss was intensified by the sense that they had been betrayed. They relied, as had generations before them, on the expectation that white elites would maintain lower class whites in a societal status superior to that designated for blacks. In fact, there is evidence that segregated schools and facilities were initially established by legislatures at the insistence of the white working class. Today, little has changed. Many poorer whites oppose social reform as "welfare programs for blacks" although, ironically, they have employment, education, and social service needs that differ from those of poor blacks by a margin that, without a racial scorecard, is difficult to measure.

Unfortunately, poorer whites are now not alone in their opposition to school desegregation and to other attempts to improve the societal status of blacks: recent decisions, most notably by the Supreme Court, indicate that the convergence of black and white interests that led to *Brown* in 1954 and influenced the character of its enforcement has begun to fade. In *Swann v. Charlotte-Mecklenburg Board of Education*, Chief Justice Burger spoke of the "reconciliation of competing values" in desegregation cases. If there was any doubt that "competing values" referred to the conflicting interests of blacks seeking desegregation and whites who prefer to retain existing school policies, then the uncertainty was dispelled by *Milliken v. Bradley*, and by *Dayton Board of Education v. Brinkman (Dayton I)*. In both cases, the Court elevated the concept of "local autonomy" to a "vital national tradition": "No single tradition in public education is more deeply rooted than local control over the operation of schools; local autonomy has long been thought essential both to the maintenance of community concern and support for public schools and to quality of the educational process." Local control, however, may result in the maintenance of a status quo that will preserve superior educational opportunities and facilities for whites at the expense of blacks. As one commentator has suggested, "It is implausible to assume that school boards guilty of substantial violations in the past will take the interests of black school children to heart."

As a result of its change in attitudes, the Court has increasingly erected barriers to achieving the forms of racial balance relief it earlier had approved. Plaintiffs must now prove that the complained-of segregation was the result of discriminatory actions intentionally and invidiously conducted or authorized by school officials. It is not enough that segregation was the "natural and foreseeable" consequence of their policies. And even when this difficult standard of proof is met, courts must carefully limit the relief granted to the harm actually proved. Judicial second thoughts about racial balance plans with broad-range busing components, the very plans which civil rights lawyers have come to rely on, is clearly evident in these new proof standards.

There is, however, continuing if unpredictable concern in the Supreme Court about school boards whose policies reveal long-term adherence to overt racial discrimination. In many cases, trial courts exposed to exhaustive testimony regarding the failure of school officials to either desegregate or provide substantial equality of schooling for minority children, become convinced that school boards are violating *Brown*. Thus far, unstable Supreme Court majorities have upheld broad desegregation plans ordered by these judges, but the reservations expressed by concurring Justices and the vigor of those Justices who dissent caution against optimism in this still controversial area of civil rights law.

At the very least, these decisions reflect a substantial and growing divergence in the interests of whites and blacks. The result could prove to be the realization of Professor Wechsler's legitimate fear that, if there is not a change of course, the purported entitlement of whites not to associate with blacks in public schools may yet eclipse the hope and the promise of *Brown*.

93 Harvard L. Rev. 518, 524–28 (1980).

XX. Applying the *Brown* Rationale

A. Introduction

While language in the *Brown I* decision suggests that its application is limited to "the field of education" alone, subsequent cases applied the *Brown I* rationale to a variety of fields and forums including restaurants, buses, swimming pools, amusement parks, and interracial sex and marriage. Sometimes the Supreme Court would issue a per curiam opinion indicating merely that *Brown I* governs without any further discussion. Other times the court would provide more detailed analysis.

B. Background on *Loving*

For over 300 years, Virginia prohibited interracial sex and marriage. Even after slavery was abolished and state-mandated segregation in housing and education was deemed unconstitutional, Virginia continued the ban. While most states prohibited such interracial activity up until the middle of the Twentieth Century, seventeen states, including Virginia, refused to abandon this long-standing barrier even in the face of widespread litigation after *Brown I.*

C. Loving v. Virginia, 388 U.S. 1 (1966)

Bernard S. Cohen and *Philip J. Hirschkop* argued the cause and filed a brief for appellants. *Mr. Hirschkop* argued *pro hoc vice*, by special leave of Court.

R. D. McIlwaine III, Assistant Attorney General of Virginia, argued the cause for appellee. With him on the brief were *Robert Y. Button*, Attorney General, and *Kenneth C. Patty*, Assistant Attorney General.

William M. Marutani, by special leave of Court, argued the cause for the Japanese American Citizens League, as *amicus curiae*, urging reversal.

Briefs of *amici curiae*, urging reversal, were filed by *William M. Lewers* and *William B. Ball* for the National Catholic Conference for Interracial Justice et al., by *Robert L. Carter* and *Andrew D. Weinberger* for the National Association for the Advancement of Colored People, and by *Jack Greenberg, James M. Nabrit III* and *Michael Meltsner* for the N.A.A.C.P. Legal Defense & Educational Fund, Inc.

T. W. Bruton, Attorney General, and *Ralph Moody*, Deputy Attorney General, filed a brief for the State of North Carolina, as *amicus curiae*, urging affirmance.

1. Facts

Justice WARREN delivered the opinion of the Court.

This case presents a constitutional question never addressed by this Court: whether a statutory scheme adopted by the State of Virginia to prevent marriages between persons solely on the basis of racial classifications violates the Equal Protection and Due Process Clauses of the Fourteenth Amendment.[111] For reasons which seem to us to reflect the central meaning of those constitutional commands, we conclude that these statutes cannot stand consistently with the Fourteenth Amendment.

---

111. Section 1 of the Fourteenth Amendment provides:

"All persons born or naturalized in the United States and subject to the jurisdiction thereof, are citizens of the United States and of the State wherein they reside. No State shall make or enforce any law which shall abridge the privileges or immunities of citizens of the United States; nor shall any State deprive any person of life, liberty, or property, without due process of law; nor deny to any person within its jurisdiction the equal protection of the laws."

In June 1958, two residents of Virginia, Mildred Jeter, a Negro woman, and Richard Loving, a white man, were married in the District of Columbia pursuant to its laws. Shortly after their marriage, the Lovings returned to Virginia and established their marital abode in Caroline County. At the October Term, 1958, of the Circuit Court of Caroline County, a grand jury issued an indictment charging the Lovings with violating Virginia's ban on interracial marriages. On January 6, 1959, the Lovings pleaded guilty to the charge and were sentenced to one year in jail; however, the trial judge suspended the sentence for a period of 25 years on the condition that the Lovings leave the State and not return to Virginia together for 25 years. He stated in an opinion that:

> Almighty God created the races white, black, yellow, malay and red, and he placed them on separate continents. And but for the interference with his arrangement there would be no cause for such marriages. The fact that he separated the races shows that he did not intend for the races to mix.

After their convictions, the Lovings took up residence in the District of Columbia. On November 6, 1963, they filed a motion in the state trial court to vacate the judgment and set aside the sentence on the ground that the statutes which they had violated were repugnant to the Fourteenth Amendment. The motion not having been decided by October 28, 1964, the Lovings instituted a class action in the United States District Court for the Eastern District of Virginia requesting that a three-judge court be convened to declare the Virginia antimiscegenation statutes unconstitutional and to enjoin state officials from enforcing their convictions. On January 22, 1965, the state trial judge denied the motion to vacate the sentences, and the Lovings perfected an appeal to the Supreme Court of Appeals of Virginia. On February 11, 1965, the three-judge District Court continued the case to allow the Lovings to present their constitutional claims to the highest state court.

The Supreme Court of Appeals upheld the constitutionality of the antimiscegenation statutes and, after modifying the sentence, affirmed the convictions.[112] The Lovings appealed this decision, and we noted probable jurisdiction on December 12, 1966, 385 U.S. 986, 87 S.Ct. 595, 17 L.Ed.2d 448.

The two statutes under which appellants were convicted and sentenced are part of a comprehensive statutory scheme aimed at prohibiting and punishing interracial marriages. The Lovings were convicted of violating section 20-58 of the Virginia Code:

> *Leaving State to evade law.* — If any white person and colored person shall go out of this State, for the purpose of being married, and with the intention of returning, and be married out of it, and afterwards return to and reside in it, cohabiting as man and wife, they shall be punished as provided in section 20-59, and the marriage shall be governed by the same law as if

---

112. 206 Va. 924, 147 S.E.2d 78 (1966).

it had been solemnized in this State. The fact of their cohabitation here as man and wife shall be evidence of their marriage.

Section 20-59, which defines the penalty for miscegenation, provides:

> *Punishment for marriage.* — If any white person intermarry with a colored person, or any colored person intermarry with a white person, he shall be guilty of a felony and shall be punished by confinement in the penitentiary for not less than one nor more than five years.

Other central provisions in the Virginia statutory scheme are section 20-57, which automatically voids all marriages between "a white person and a colored person" without any judicial proceeding,[113] and sections 20-54 and 1-14 which, respectively, define "white persons" and "colored persons and Indians" for purposes of the statutory prohibitions.[114] The Lovings have never disputed in the course of this litigation that Mrs. Loving is a "colored person" or that Mr. Loving is a "white person" within the meanings given those terms by the Virginia statutes.

Virginia is now one of 16 States which prohibit and punish marriages on the basis of racial classifications.[115] Penalties for miscegenation arose as an incident to slavery

---

113. Section 20-57 of the Virginia Code provides:

"*Marriages void without decree.* — All marriages between a white person and a colored person shall be absolutely void without any decree of divorce or other legal process." Va. Code Ann. § 20-57 (1960 Repl. Vol.).

114. Section 20-54 of the Virginia Code provides:

"*Intermarriage prohibited; meaning of term 'white persons.'* — It shall hereafter be unlawful for any white person in this State to marry any save a white person, or a person with no other admixture of blood than white and American Indian. For the purpose of this chapter, the term 'white person' shall apply only to such person as has no trace whatever of any blood other than Caucasian; but persons who have one-sixteenth or less of the blood of the American Indian and have no other non-Caucasic blood shall be deemed to be white persons. All laws heretofore passed and now in effect regarding the intermarriage of white and colored persons shall apply to marriages prohibited by this chapter." Va. Code Ann. § 20-54 (1960 Repl.Vol.).

The exception for persons with less than one-sixteenth "of the blood of the American Indian" is apparently accounted for, in the words of a tract issued by the Registrar of the State Bureau of Vital Statistics, by "the desire of all to recognize as an integral and honored part of the white race the descendants of John Rolfe and Pocahontas. . . ." Plecker, *The New Family and Race Improvement*, 17 Va. Health Bull., Extra No. 12, at 25–26 (New Family Series No. 5, 1925), cited in Wadlington, The *Loving* Case; *Virginia's Anti-Miscegenation Statute in Historical Perspective*, 52 Va. L. Rev. 1189, 1202, n. 93 (1966).

Section 1-14 of the Virginia Code provides:

"*Colored persons and Indians defined.* — Every person in whom there is ascertainable any Negro blood shall be deemed and taken to be a colored person, and every person not a colored person having one fourth or more of American Indian blood shall be deemed an American Indian; except that members of Indian tribes existing in this Commonwealth having one fourth or more of Indian blood and less than one sixteenth of Negro blood shall be deemed tribal Indians." Va. Code Ann. § 1-14 (1960 Repl.Vol.).

115. After the initiation of this litigation, Maryland repealed its prohibitions against interracial marriage, Md. Laws 1967, c. 6, leaving Virginia and 15 other States with statutes outlawing interracial marriage: Alabama, Ala. Const., Art. 4, § 102, Ala. Code, Tit. 14, § 360 (1958); Arkansas, Ark. Stat. Ann. § 55-104 (1947); Delaware, Del. Code Ann., Tit. 13, § 101 (1953); Florida, Fla. Const.,

and have been common in Virginia since the colonial period. The present statutory scheme dates from the adoption of the Racial Integrity Act of 1924, passed during the period of extreme nativism which followed the end of the First World War. The central features of this Act, and current Virginia law, are the absolute prohibition of a "white person" marrying other than another "white person,"[116] a prohibition against issuing marriage licenses until the issuing official is satisfied that the applicants' statements as to their race are correct,[117] certificates of "racial composition" to be kept by both local and state registrars,[118] and the carrying forward of earlier prohibitions against racial intermarriage.[119]

2. Opinion

In upholding the constitutionality of these provisions in the decision below, the Supreme Court of Appeals of Virginia referred to its 1955 decision in *Naim v. Naim*, 197 Va. 80, 87 S.E.2d 749, as stating the reasons supporting the validity of these laws. In *Naim*, the state court concluded that the State's legitimate purposes were "to preserve the racial integrity of its citizens," and to prevent "the corruption of blood," "a mongrel breed of citizens," and "the obliteration of racial pride," obviously an endorsement of the doctrine of White Supremacy. *Id.*, at 90, 87 S.E.2d, at 756. The court also reasoned that marriage has traditionally been subject to state regulation without federal intervention, and, consequently, the regulation of marriage should be left to exclusive state control by the Tenth Amendment.

While the state court is no doubt correct in asserting that marriage is a social relation subject to the State's police power, *Maynard v. Hill*, 125 U.S. 190 (1888), the State does not contend in its argument before this Court that its powers to regulate marriage are unlimited notwithstanding the commands of the Fourteenth Amendment. Nor could it do so in light of *Meyer v. State of Nebraska*, 262 U.S. 390 (1923), and *Skinner v. State of Oklahoma*, 316 U.S. 535 (1942). Instead, the State argues that the meaning of the Equal Protection Clause, as illuminated by the statements of

---

Art. 16, §24, Fla. Stat. §741.11 (1965); Georgia, Ga. Code Ann. §53-106 (1961); Kentucky, Ky. Rev. Stat. Ann. §402.020 (Supp.1966); Louisiana, La. Rev. Stat. §14:79 (1950); Mississippi, Miss. Const., Art. 14, §263, Miss. Code Ann. §459 (1956); Missouri, Mo. Rev. Stat. §451.020 (Supp.1966), North Carolina, N.C. Const., Art. XIV, §8, N.C. Gen. Stat. §14-181 (1953); Oklahoma, Okla. Stat., Tit. 43, §12 (Supp.1965); South Carolina, S.C. Const., Art. 3, §33, S.C. Code Ann. §20-7 (1962); Tennessee, Tenn. Const., Art. 11, §14, Tenn. Code Ann. §36-402 (1955); Vernon's Ann. Texas, Tex. Pen. Code, Art. 492 (1952); West Virginia, W. Va. Code Ann. §4697 (1961).

Over the past 15 years, 14 States have repealed laws outlawing interracial marriages: Arizona, California, Colorado, Idaho, Indiana, Maryland, Montana, Nebraska, Nevada, North Dakota, Oregon, South Dakota, Utah, and Wyoming.

The first state court to recognize that miscegenation statutes violate the Equal Protection Clause was the Supreme Court of California. *Perez v. Sharp*, 32 Cal.2d 711, 198 P.2d 17 (1948).

116. Va. Code Ann. §20-54 (1960 Repl. Vol.).
117. Va. Code Ann. §20-53 (1960 Repl. Vol.).
118. Va. Code Ann. §20-50 (1960 Repl. Vol.).
119. Va. Code Ann. §20-54 (1960 Repl. Vol.).

the Framers, is only that state penal laws containing an interracial element as part of the definition of the offense must apply equally to whites and Negroes in the sense that members of each race are punished to the same degree. Thus, the State contends that because its miscegenation statutes punish equally both the white and the Negro participants in an interracial marriage, these statutes, despite their reliance on racial classifications, do not constitute an invidious discrimination based upon race. The second argument advanced by the State assumes the validity of its equal application theory. The argument is that, if the Equal Protection Clause does not outlaw miscegenation statutes because of their reliance on racial classifications, the question of constitutionality would thus become whether there was any rational basis for a State to treat interracial marriages differently from other marriages. On this question, the State argues, the scientific evidence is substantially in doubt and, consequently, this Court should defer to the wisdom of the state legislature in adopting its policy of discouraging interracial marriages.

Because we reject the notion that the mere "equal application" of a statute containing racial classifications is enough to remove the classifications from the Fourteenth Amendment's proscription of all invidious racial discriminations, we do not accept the State's contention that these statutes should be upheld if there is any possible basis for concluding that they serve a rational purpose. The mere fact of equal application does not mean that our analysis of these statutes should follow the approach we have taken in cases involving no racial discrimination where the Equal Protection Clause has been arrayed against a statute discriminating between the kinds of advertising which may be displayed on trucks in New York City, *Railway Express Agency, Inc. v. People of State of New York*, 336 U.S. 106 (1949), or an exemption in Ohio's *ad valorem* tax for merchandise owned by a non-resident in a storage warehouse, *Allied Stores of Ohio, Inc. v. Bowers,* 358 U.S. 522 (1959). In these cases, involving distinctions not drawn according to race, the Court has merely asked whether there is any rational foundation for the discriminations, and has deferred to the wisdom of the state legislatures. In the case at bar, however, we deal with statutes containing racial classifications, and the fact of equal application does not immunize the statute from the very heavy burden of justification which the Fourteenth Amendment has traditionally required of state statutes drawn according to race.

The State argues that statements in the Thirty-ninth Congress about the time of the passage of the Fourteenth Amendment indicate that the Framers did not intend the Amendment to make unconstitutional state miscegenation laws. Many of the statements alluded to by the State concern the debates over the Freedmen's Bureau Bill, which President Johnson vetoed, and the Civil Rights Act of 1866, 14 Stat. 27, enacted over his veto. While these statements have some relevance to the intention of Congress in submitting the Fourteenth Amendment, it must be understood that they pertained to the passage of specific statutes and not to the broader, organic purpose of a constitutional amendment. As for the various statements directly concerning the Fourteenth Amendment, we have said in connection with a related

problem, that although these historical sources "cast some light" they are not sufficient to resolve the problem; "(a)t best, they are inconclusive. The most avid proponents of the post-War Amendments undoubtedly intended them to remove all
legal distinctions among 'all persons born or naturalized in the United States.' Their
opponents, just as certainly, were antagonistic to both the letter and the spirit of the
Amendments and wished them to have the most limited effect." *Brown v. Board of
Education*, 347 U.S. 483, 489 (1954). *See also Strauder v. State of West Virginia*, 100
U.S. 303, 310 (1880). We have rejected the proposition that the debates in the Thirty-
ninth Congress or in the state legislatures which ratified the Fourteenth Amendment supported the theory advanced by the State, that the requirement of equal
protection of the laws is satisfied by penal laws defining offenses based on racial
classifications so long as white and Negro participants in the offense were similarly
punished. *McLaughlin v. State of Florida*, 379 U.S. 184 (1964).

The State finds support for its "equal application" theory in the decision of
the Court in *Pace v. State of Alabama*, 106 U.S. 583 (1883). In that case, the Court
upheld a conviction under an Alabama statute forbidding adultery or fornication
between a white person and a Negro which imposed a greater penalty than that of
a statute proscribing similar conduct by members of the same race. The Court reasoned that the statute could not be said to discriminate against Negroes because the
punishment for each participant in the offense was the same. However, as recently
as the 1964 Term, in rejecting the reasoning of that case, we stated "*Pace* represents
a limited view of the Equal Protection Clause which has not withstood analysis in
the subsequent decisions of this Court." *McLaughlin v. Florida, supra*, 379 U.S. at
188. As we there demonstrated, the Equal Protection Clause requires the consideration of whether the classifications drawn by any statute constitute an arbitrary and
invidious discrimination. The clear and central purpose of the Fourteenth Amendment was to eliminate all official state sources of invidious racial discrimination in
the States. *Slaughter-House Cases*, 16 Wall. 36, 71, 21 L. Ed. 394 (1873); *Strauder v.
State of West Virginia*, 100 U.S. 303, 307–8, 25 L. Ed. 664 (1880); *Ex parte Virginia*,
100 U.S. 339, 344–45 (1880); *Shelley v. Kraemer*, 334 U.S. 1 (1948); *Burton v. Wilmington Parking Authority*, 365 U.S. 715 (1961).

There can be no question but that Virginia's miscegenation statutes rest solely
upon distinctions drawn according to race. The statutes proscribe generally
accepted conduct if engaged in by members of different races. Over the years, this
Court has consistently repudiated "[d]istinctions between citizens solely because
of their ancestry" as being "odious to a free people whose institutions are founded
upon the doctrine of equality." *Hirabayashi v. United States*, 320 U.S. 81, 100
(1943). At the very least, the Equal Protection Clause demands that racial classifications, especially suspect in criminal statutes, be subjected to the "most rigid
scrutiny," *Korematsu v. United States*, 323 U.S. 214, 216 (1944), and, if they are ever
to be upheld, they must be shown to be necessary to the accomplishment of some
permissible state objective, independent of the racial discrimination which it was
the object of the Fourteenth Amendment to eliminate. Indeed, two members of

this Court have already stated that they "cannot conceive of a valid legislative purpose . . . which makes the color of a person's skin the test of whether his conduct is a criminal offense." *McLaughlin v. Florida, supra,* 379 U.S. at 198 (STEWART, J., joined by DOUGLAS, J., concurring).

There is patently no legitimate overriding purpose independent of invidious racial discrimination which justifies this classification. The fact that Virginia prohibits only interracial marriages involving white persons demonstrates that the racial classifications must stand on their own justification, as measures designed to maintain White Supremacy.[120] We have consistently denied the constitutionality of measures which restrict the rights of citizens on account of race. There can be no doubt that restricting the freedom to marry solely because of racial classifications violates the central meaning of the Equal Protection Clause.

3. Holding

These convictions must be reversed.

D. Commentary on *Loving*

A. Leon Higginbotham, Jr. and Barbara Kopytoff

*Racial Purity and Interracial Sex in the Law of Colonial
and Antebellum Virginia*

Virginia continued the ban on interracial marriage, making it a felony, until the United States Supreme Court declared the law unconstitutional in *Loving v. Virginia* in 1967. Far from having abated, the sentiment against interracial marriage expressed by the Virginia trial court in that case was at least as strong as that of the Virginia legislature in 1691 when it first outlawed interracial marriage, referring to the "abominable mixture and spurious issue" that it produced. The myth of white racial purity also was invoked in *Loving.* Once used to support a slave society, this myth still survived a hundred years after slavery's demise to support the racial hierarchy that white Virginians tried to maintain.

---

120. Appellants point out that the State's concern in these statutes, as expressed in the words of the 1924 Act's title, "An Act to Preserve Racial Integrity," extends only to the integrity of the white race. While Virginia prohibits whites from marrying any nonwhite (subject to the exception for the descendants of Pocahontas), Negroes, Orientals, and any other racial class may intermarry without statutory interference. Appellants contend that this distinction renders Virginia's miscegenation statutes arbitrary and unreasonable even assuming the constitutional validity of an official purpose to preserve "racial integrity." We need not reach this contention because we find the racial classifications in these statutes repugnant to the Fourteenth Amendment, even assuming an even-handed state purpose to protect the "integrity" of all races.

The following excerpts from the opinion of Virginia Circuit Court Judge Leon Bazile,[121] in *Loving* in 1965, exemplify the legal, religious, and philosophical rationale embraced by Virginia judges and legislators for some three centuries when they spoke of racial purity and interracial sex:

> Parties [to an interracial marriage are] guilty of a most serious crime. . . . Almighty God created the races, white, black, yellow, malay, and red, and he [sic] placed them on separate continents. And but for the interference with his arrangement there would be no cause for such marriages. The fact that he separated the races shows that he did not intend for the races to mix. The awfulness of the offense [of interracial marriage] is shown by the fact . . . [that] the code makes the contracting of a marriage between a white person and any colored person a felony. Conviction of a felony is a serious matter. You lose your political rights, and only the government has the power to restore them. And as long as you live you will be known as a felon. "The moving finger writes and moves on and having writ/Nor all your piety nor all your wit/Can change one line of it."[122]

The judge concluded that there was no constitutional basis, state or federal, to invalidate Virginia's prohibition of interracial marriages.

The post-Civil War Virginia courts had previously upheld the miscegenation laws because they assertedly were based on the "laws of God and the laws of property, morality and social order . . . [that] have been exercised by all civilized governments in all ages of the world."[123] In 1955, the Virginia Supreme Court adopted the theories of other courts that had declared miscegenation laws were valid because "the natural law which forbids their intermarriage and the social amalgamation which leads to a corruption of races is as clearly divine as that which imparted to them different natures."[124]

The Virginia Supreme Court then declared the state's miscegenation statutes were constitutionally valid:

> [They] preserve the racial integrity of its citizens, . . . regulate the marriage relation so that it shall not have a mongrel breed of citizens . . . [and] prevent the obliteration of racial pride, [that would] permit the corruption of blood [and] weaken or destroy the quality of its citizenship. Both sacred and secular history teach that nations and races have better advanced in

---

121. Transcript of Record at 8, reproduced in *Loving v. Virginia*, 388 U.S. 1, Appendix at 33 (1967).

122. *Loving*, 388 U.S. at 3, Appendix at 42.

123. *Kinney v. Commonwealth*, 71 Va. (30 Gratt.) 284, 285 (1878).

124. *Naim v. Naim*, 197 Va. 80, 84, 87 S.E.2d 749, 752 (1956). *Naim* involved a Chinese male and a white female who had a valid marriage ceremony in North Carolina and who returned to Virginia to reside as husband and wife.

human progress when they cultivated their own distinctive characteristics and culture and developed their own peculiar genius.[125]

By 1965, when the *Loving* case was tried, many courts both in the North and the South had expressed fears about the "social amalgamation" of the races and the necessity of racial purity.[126] Some states had opposed interracial marriages and interracial sex "to prevent breaches of the basic concepts of sexual decency."[127]

77 *Georgetown Law Journal* 1967, 2021–24 (1989).
Copyright © (1989) *Georgetown Law Journal.*
Reprinted with permission of Georgetown University and
Georgetown Law Journal.

While plaintiffs like the Lovings were challenging racial segregation laws that appeared to violate the spirit of *Brown*, civil rights organizations like the Congress of Racial Equality were busy attempting to ensure that federal anti-discrimination laws were being enforced. On July 2, 1964, landmark civil rights legislation became law. Comprised of Titles I–XI, the 1964 Civil Rights Act barred discrimination in public accommodations, employment, and federally assisted programs. In order to assist enforcement of this legislation, "freedom riders" were asked to travel on buses at the risk of bodily harm to make sure that no racial discrimination was taking

---

125. *Id.* at 90, 87 S.E.2d at 756.

126. In 1955, "[m]ore than half of the States of the Union [had] miscegenation statutes." *Id.* at 84, 87 S.E.2d at 753. By 1966, 16 states (including Virginia) still outlawed interracial marriages. The Supreme Court in *Loving v. Virginia*, 388 U.S. 1 (1967), listed these state statutes and constitutions. They were, in addition to Virginia:

Alabama, ALA. CONST., ART. 4, § 102, ALA. CODE, TIT. 14, § 360 (1958); Arkansas, ARK. STAT. ANN.§ 55-104 (1947); Delaware, DEL. CODE ANN., TIT. 13 § 101 (1953); Florida, FLA. CONST., art. 16 § 24, FLA. STAT. § 741.11 (1965); Georgia, GA. CODE ANN. § 53-106 (1961); Kentucky, KY. REV. STAT. ANN. § 402.020 (Supp. 1966); Louisiana, LA. REV. STAT.§ 1479 (1950); Mississippi, MISS. CONST., ART. 14, § 263, MISS. CODE ANN. § 459 (1956); Missouri, Mo. REV. STAT. § 451.020 (Supp. 1966); North Carolina, N.C. CONST., ART. XIV, § 8, N.C. Gen. Stat. § 14-181 (1953); Oklahoma, OKLA. STAT., TIT. 43, § 12 (Supp. 1965); South Carolina, S.C. CONST., ART. 11, § 14, Tenn. Code Ann. § 36-402 (1955); Texas, TEX. PEN. CODE, ART. 492 (1952); West Virginia, W. VA. CODE ANN. § 4697 (1961).

Id. at 6 n.5.

127. *McLaughlin v. Florida*, 379 U.S. 184, 193 (1964). The Supreme Court, however, did not agree with the state legislature that a statute prohibiting interracial cohabitation was necessary to preserve 'sexual decency;' it concluded that the Florida statute violated the equal protection clause. *Id.* at 196.

More than a century before Judge Bazile's opinion, Chief Justice Roger Brook Taney, in *Dred Scott v. Sanford*, 60 U.S. (19 How.) 393 (1857), relied heavily on the existence of antimiscegenation laws as evidence that blacks were of an inferior class, that blacks could not be citizens of the United States, and that blacks had "no rights which the white man was bound to respect." *Id.* at 413. Taney's first legislative reference was to the Massachusetts laws of 1705 and 1786 which "forbids the marriage of any white person with any Negro, Indian or mulatto." *Id.*

place. Often times these freedom riders would be harassed, threatened, and beaten by white mobs or state law-enforcement officials.

E. Questions and Notes

In 1944, twenty-three years before the United States Supreme Court declared miscegenation laws unconstitutional, the sociologist Gunnar Myrdal wrote:

> The ban on intermarriage has the highest place in the white man's rank order of social segregation and discrimination. Sexual segregation is the most pervasive form of segregation, and the concern about "race purity" is, in a sense, basic. No other way of crossing the color line is so attended by the emotion commonly associated with violating a social taboo as intermarriage and extra-marital relations between a Negro man and a white woman. No excuse for other forms of social segregation and discrimination is so potent as the one that sociable relations on an equal basis between members of the two races *may possibly* lead to intermarriage.[128]

---

128. G. MYRDAL, AN AMERICAN DILEMMA 606 (1944) (emphasis in original). *But cf.* O. Cox, CASTE, CLASS AND RACE 386–87, 526–27 (1959), *cited in* D. BELL, RACE, RACISM AND AMERICAN LAW 268–69 (2d ed. 1973) (segregation motivated by whites' desire to continue to exploit blacks economically). Professor Bell has written:

As late as 1955, in *Naim v. Naim*, the Supreme Court of Appeals of Virginia upheld its state's anti-miscegenation statute on the grounds that the legislature had complete power to control the vital institution of marriage. While its decision came after *Brown v. Board of Education*, the Virginia Court found that precedent a comfort rather than an obstacle to its conclusion. It noted that Brown found education a "foundation of good citizenship," but that so lofty a status was hardly deserved by interracial marriage. In short, the Virginia court literally challenged the Supreme Court to reverse its *Naim v. Naim* decision. Still hoping that the nation might accept and comply with *Brown I* and its "all deliberate speed" compliance mechanism set out in *Brown II*, the Supreme Court was in no mood for extending the racial revolution to the ever sensitive area of interracial sex. In a decision that Professor Herbert Wechsler condemned as "wholly without basis in law," the Supreme Court, after hearing oral argument in the *Naim* case, decided the record was incomplete with respect to the domicile of the parties (a white woman and Chinese man had been married in North Carolina and then returned to reside in Virginia), remanding the case to the Virginia court for a further remand to the trial court. On remand, the Virginia Court of Appeals refused to comply with the mandate, concluding that there was no Virginia procedure available to reopen the case. Requested to recall the remand, the Supreme Court instead dismissed the appeal on the grounds that the second Virginia decision left the case devoid of a substantial federal question.

The Supreme Court's performance in *Naim v. Naim* may be explained as a 'prudent avoidance' of an obvious test case. Prudence of that character caused substantial sacrifice earlier when the Supreme Court refused, only a few months after the decision in *Brown v. Board of Education*, to review the conviction under Alabama's miscegenation law of a black man who married a white woman.

Id. at 56–57 (footnotes omitted).

Philip Elman, who was on the staff of the U.S. Solicitor General from 1944 to 1961 and who handled all Supreme Court civil rights cases in which the United States was a party or an amicus curae, discusses *Naim v. Naim* as follows:

Do you agree or disagree with Gunnar Myrdal's assessment of the rank order of social racial segregation?

I first heard of that case after the Supreme Court had decided *Brown v. Board of Education* in 1954. . . .

Now, at that time the opposition to *Brown v. Board of Education* in southern states was very great. . . . And over and over again, the fear was expressed that *Brown* was going to lead to 'mongrelization' of the races. The notion was that little black boys would be sitting next to little white girls in school, and the next thing would be intermarriage and worse. This was terrible stuff to be expressing, yet it was being said not only by the demagogues, the Bilbos and Talmadges, but also by more 'respectable' southern politicians as a way of galvanizing opposition to the Supreme Court's decision.

Well, I knew that the last thing in the world the Justices wanted to deal with at that time was the question of interracial marriage. Of course, if they had to, they unquestionably would hold that interracial marriage could not be prohibited consistently with *Brown v. Board of Education*, but they weren't ready to confront that question. The timing was all wrong. . . .

[Solicitor General Simon Sobel and Justice Felix Frankfurter agreed with this conclusion.] In due course, the appeal was filed and the Supreme Court in a brief *per curiam* order dismissed it and sent the case back to the Virginia Court of Appeals on the ground that the record did not clearly present the constitutional issue. Now that was a specious ground. The record did present the constitutional issue clearly and squarely, but the Court wanted to duck it. And if the Supreme Court wants to duck, nothing can stop it from ducking.

And so the case went back to the Virginia Court of Appeals. . . . The Supreme Court again refused to take the case, on the ground that it failed properly to present a federal constitutional question. So that was the end of *Naim v. Naim*.

A decade later, when the climate was more agreeable and there were no longer factors justifying any further delay, the Supreme Court—in a case that very aptly was titled *Loving v. Virginia*—unanimously held that racial miscegenation laws are unconstitutional.

Elman, The Solicitor General's Office, Justice Frankfurter, And Civil Rights Litigation, 1946–1960: An Oral History, 100 HARV. L. REV. 845–47 (1987) (emphasis in original).

Part Five

Attempted Eradication of Inequality

XXI. Race Conscious Remedies

A. Introduction

In *Brown I,* the Supreme Court finally recognized the serious harm that state-imposed racial segregation in public primary and secondary schools had caused to racial minority children over the course of several decades. Those minority students who were subjected to such segregation, such as Martha Lum and Linda Brown, would be entitled to a remedy for the harm imposed. Remedies that the states had previously provided, while maintaining the separate but equal doctrine, were not really remedies, but in fact reinforced segregation within society and exacerbated the sense of inferiority in those who were excluded. What then would the remedy under *Brown I* entail? The decision provided great hope, but the implementation would be painstaking.

B. Background on *Brown II*

Brown I held that *de jure* racial segregation in education violated the Equal Protection Clause of the Fourteenth Amendment. Unlike the previous victories, which only affected a few hundred individuals, *Brown II* would affect millions. Therefore, in fashioning a remedy for this constitutional violation, the Supreme Court would face unique challenges.

C. *Brown v. Board of Education (Brown II),* 349 U.S. 294 (1955)

Robert L. Carter argued the cause for appellants in No. 1. *Spottswood W. Robinson, III,* argued the causes for appellants in Nos. 2 and 3. *George E. C. Hayes* and *James M. Nabrit, Jr.* argued the cause for petitioners in No. 4. *Louis L. Redding* argued the cause for respondents in No. 5. *Thurgood Marshall* argued the causes for appellants in Nos. 1, 2 and 3, petitioners in No. 4 and respondents in No. 5.

On the briefs were *Harold Boulward, Robert L. Carter, Jack Greenberg, Oliver W. Hill, Thurgood Marshall, Louis L. Redding, Spottswood W. Robinson, III, Charles S.*

Scott, William T. Coleman, Jr., Charles T. Duncan, George E.C. Hayes, Loren Miller, William R. Ming, Jr., Constance Baker Motley, James M. Nabrit, Jr., Louis H. Pollak, and *Frank D. Reeves* for appellants in Nos. 1, 2 and 3, and respondents in No. 5; and *George E.C. Hayes, James M. Nabrit, Jr., George M. Johnson, Charles W. Quick, Herbert O. Reid, Thurgood Marshall,* and *Robert L. Carter* for petitioners in No. 4.

Harold R. Fatzer, Attorney General of Kansas, argued the cause for appellees in No. 1. With him on the brief was *Paul E. Wilson,* Assistant Attorney General. *Peter F. Caldwell* filed a brief for the Board of Education of Topeka, Kansas, appellee.

S.E. Rogers and *Robert McC. Figg, Jr.* argued the cause and filed a brief for appellees in No. 2.

J. Lindsay Almond, Jr., Attorney General of Virginia, and *Archibald G. Robertson* argued the cause for appellees in No. 3. With them on the brief were *Henry T. Wickham,* Special Assistant to the Attorney General, *T. Justin Moore, John W. Riely, T. Justin Moore, Jr.,* and *Milton D. Korman* argued the cause for respondents in No. 4. With him on the brief were *Vernon E. West, Chester H. Gray* and *Lyman J. Umstead.*

Joseph Donald Craven, Attorney General of Delaware, argued the cause for petitioners in No. 5. On the brief were *H. Albert Young,* then Attorney General, *Clarence W. Taylor,* Deputy Attorney General, and *Andrew D. Christie,* Special Deputy to the Attorney General.

In response to the Court's invitation, 347 U.S. 483, 495–96, Solicitor General *Sobeloff* participated in the oral argument for the United States. With him on the brief were Attorney General *Brownell,* Assistant Attorney General Rankin, *Philip Elman, Ralph S. Spritzer,* and *Alan S. Rosenthal.*

By invitation of the Court, 347 U.S. 483, 496, the following State officials presented their views orally as *amici curiae: Thomas J. Gentry,* Attorney General of Arkansas, with whom on the brief were *James L. Sloan,* Assistant Attorney General, and *Richard B. McCulloch,* Special Assistant Attorney General. *Richard W. Ervin,* Attorney General of Florida, and *Ralph E. Odum,* Assistant Attorney General, both of whom were also on a brief. *C. Ferdinand Sybert,* Attorney General of Maryland, with whom on the brief were *Edward D.E. Rollins,* then Attorney General, *W. Giles Parker,* Assistant Attorney General, and *James H. Norris, Jr.,* Special Assistant Attorney General. *I. Beverly Lake,* Assistant Attorney General of North Carolina, with whom on the brief were *Harry McMullan,* Attorney General, and *T. Wade Bruton, Ralph Moody* and *Claude L. Love,* Assistant Attorneys General. *Mac Q. Williamson,* Attorney General of Oklahoma, who also filed a brief. *John Ben Shepperd,* Attorney General of Texas, and *Burnell Waldrep,* Assistant Attorney General, with whom on the brief were *Billy E. Lee, J. A. Amis, Jr., L. P. Lollar, J. Fred Jones, John Davenport, John Reeves,* and *Will Davis.*

Phineas Indritz filed a brief for the American Veterans Committee, Inc., as *amicus curiae.*

1. Facts

Chief Justice WARREN delivered the opinion of the Court.

These cases were decided on May 17, 1954. The opinions of that date,[1] declaring the fundamental principle that racial discrimination in public education is unconstitutional, are incorporated herein by reference. All provisions of federal, state, or local law requiring or permitting such discrimination must yield to this principle. There remains for consideration the manner in which relief is to be accorded.

Because these cases arose under different local conditions and their disposition will involve a variety of local problems, we requested further argument on the question of relief.[2] In view of the nationwide importance of the decision, we invited the Attorney General of the United States and the Attorneys General of all states requiring or permitting racial discrimination in public education to present their views on that question. The parties, the United States, and the States of Florida, North Carolina, Arkansas, Oklahoma, Maryland, and Texas filed briefs and participated in the oral argument.

These presentations were informative and helpful to the Court in its consideration of the complexities arising from the transition to a system of public education freed of racial discrimination. The presentations also demonstrated that substantial steps to eliminate racial discrimination in public schools have already been taken, not only in some of the communities in which these cases arose, but in some of the states appearing as amici curiae, and in other states as well. Substantial progress has been made in the District of Columbia and in the communities in Kansas and Delaware involved in this litigation. The defendants in the cases coming to us from South Carolina and Virginia are awaiting the decision of this Court concerning relief.

---

1. 347 U.S. 483, 74 S.Ct. 686, 98 L.Ed. 873, 347 U.S. 497, 74 S.Ct. 693, 98 L.Ed. 884.

2. Further argument was requested on the following questions, 347 U.S. 483, 495–96, note 13, 74 S.Ct. 686, 692, 98 L.Ed. 873, previously propounded by the Court:

"4. Assuming it is decided that segregation in public schools violates the Fourteenth Amendment

"(a) would a decree necessarily follow providing that, within the limits set by normal geographic school districting, Negro children should forthwith be admitted to schools of their choice, or

"(b) may this Court, in the exercise of its equity powers, permit an effective gradual adjustment to be brought about from existing segregated systems to a system not based on color distinctions?

"5. On the assumption on which questions 4(a) and (b) are based, and assuming further that this Court will exercise its equity powers to the end described in question 4(b),

"(a) should this Court formulate detailed decrees in these cases;

"(b) if so, what specific issues should the decrees reach;

"(c) should this Court appoint a special master to hear evidence with a view to recommending specific terms for such decrees;

"(d) should this Court remand to the courts of first instance with directions to frame decrees in these cases, and if so what general directions should the decrees of this Court include and what procedures should the courts of first instance follow in arriving at the specific terms of more detailed decrees?"

2. Opinion

a. Authorities Responsible for Implementation

Full implementation of these constitutional principles may require solution of varied local school problems. School authorities have the primary responsibility for elucidating, assessing, and solving these problems; courts will have to consider whether the action of school authorities constitutes good faith implementation of the governing constitutional principles. Because of their proximity to local conditions and the possible need for further hearings, the courts which originally heard these cases can best perform this judicial appraisal. Accordingly, we believe it appropriate to remand the cases to those courts.[3]

b. Guiding Principles

In fashioning and effectuating the decrees, the courts will be guided by equitable principles. Traditionally, equity has been characterized by a practical flexibility in shaping its remedies[4] and by a facility for adjusting and reconciling public and private needs.[5] These cases call for the exercise of these traditional attributes of equity power. At stake is the personal interest of the plaintiffs in admission to public schools as soon as practicable on a nondiscriminatory basis. To effectuate this interest may call for elimination of a variety of obstacles in making the transition to school systems operated in accordance with the constitutional principles set forth in our May 17, 1954 decision. Courts of equity may properly take into account the public interest in the elimination of such obstacles in a systematic and effective manner. But it should go without saying that the vitality of these constitutional principles cannot be allowed to yield simply because of disagreement with them.

While giving weight to these public and private considerations, the courts will require that the defendants make a prompt and reasonable start toward full compliance with our May 17, 1954 ruling. Once such a start has been made, the courts may find that additional time is necessary to carry out the ruling in an effective manner. The burden rests upon the defendants to establish that such time is necessary in the public interest and is consistent with good faith compliance at the earliest practicable date. To that end, the courts may consider problems related to administration, arising from the physical condition of the school plant, the school transportation system, personnel, revision of school districts and attendance areas into compact units to achieve a system of determining admission to the public schools on a nonracial basis, and revision of local laws and regulations which may be necessary in solving the foregoing problems. They will also consider the adequacy of any plans

---

3. The cases coming to us from Kansas, South Carolina, and Virginia were originally heard by three-judge District Courts convened under 28 U.S.C. §§ 2281 and 2284, 28 U.S.C.A. §§ 2281, 2284. These cases will accordingly be remanded to those three-judge courts. *See Briggs v. Elliott, 342 U.S. 350, 72 S.Ct. 327, 96 L.Ed. 392.*

4. *See Alexander v. Hillman*, 296 U.S. 222, 239, 56 S.Ct. 204, 209, 80 L.Ed. 192.

5. *See Hecht Co. v. Bowles*, 321 U.S. 321, 329–30, 64 S.Ct. 587, 591, 592, 88 L.Ed. 754.

the defendants may propose to meet these problems and to effectuate a transition to a racially nondiscriminatory school system. During this period of transition, the courts will retain jurisdiction of these cases.

3. Holding

The judgments below, except that in the Delaware case, are accordingly reversed and the cases are remanded to the District Courts to take such proceedings and enter such orders and decrees consistent with this opinion as are necessary and proper to admit to public schools on a racially nondiscriminatory basis with all deliberate speed the parties to these cases. The judgment in the Delaware case—ordering the immediate admission of the plaintiffs to schools previously attended only by white children—is affirmed on the basis of the principles stated in our May 17, 1954 opinion, but the case is remanded to the Supreme Court of Delaware for such further proceedings as that Court may deem necessary in light of this opinion.

Judgments, except that in case No. 5, reversed and cases remanded with directions; judgment in case No. 5 affirmed and case remanded with directions.

D. Commentary on *Brown II*

In *Cooper v. Aaron*,[6] the Supreme Court unanimously endorsed the *Brown II* decision and, despite the violent conditions that existed during the prior school year, denied the delay for desegregation requested by the Little Rock, Arkansas, School Board. Even with this endorsement, however, the Supreme Court was very accepting of delay tactics. Plans that called for desegregation as slow as one grade-year at a time were approved.[7] It would take the outrageous and blatantly defiant act of actually closing all schools in the district and issuing private school tuition vouchers to all white students before the Court began to demand good faith compliance with *Brown II*.[8] As a result of this restrained approach, very little desegregation took place initially.

Some scholars criticize the Warren Court's failure to mandate prompt desegregation of the public schools. They are right in their criticism. Nevertheless, when the Court was confronted with the most venal obstructionist tactics, it held firm in enforcing its decisions. Thus, race-baiting governors, such as Orval Faubus of Arkansas, George Wallace of Alabama, and Ross Barnett of Mississippi, discovered that the Supreme Court would not be intimidated. The nation also soon learned that both President Eisenhower and President Kennedy would call out troops if necessary to fulfill their constitutional duty to enforce court desegregation orders. For desegregation and creation of equal opportunity outside of education, however,

---

6. 358 U.S. 1 (1958).

7. *See Kelly v. Board of Education*, 270 F.2d 209 (6th Cir. 1959), cert. denied, 361 U.S. 924 (1959).

8. *See Griffin v. Prince Edward County Board of Education*, 377 U.S. 218 (1967).

other approaches would be necessary such as mass protests, sit-ins and boycotts, freedom rides, and self-help and self-defense measures.[9]

Newsreel Incorporated

Negroes with Guns: Rob Williams and Black Power

Robert Franklin Williams was born in Monroe, North Carolina in 1925. As a young man he worked for the Ford Motor Company in Detroit until he was drafted into the United States Army in 1944—where he learned to take up arms.

Back in Monroe, Williams married Mabel Robinson, a young woman who shared his commitment to social justice and African-American freedom. After the 1954 *Brown v. Board of Education* decision, Klan activity in Monroe skyrocketed, successfully intimidating African Americans and nearly shutting down the local chapter of the NAACP. Williams revived it to nearly 200 strong by reaching out to everyday laborers and to fellow black veterans—men who were not easily intimidated. When repeated assaults on black women in the county were ignored by the law, Williams filed for a charter from the NRA. The Black Guard was born. During a 1957 integration campaign that faced violent white resistance, Williams' armed defense guard successfully drove off legions of the Klan and electrified the black community.

In 1961, Freedom Riders came to Monroe planning to demonstrate the superior effectiveness of passive resistance over armed self-defense. They were bloodied, beaten and jailed, and finally called on Williams for protection from thousands of rioting Klansmen. Despite the threatening mobs, Williams sheltered a white family from violence, only to be later accused of kidnapping them. Fleeing death threats, Rob and Mabel gathered their children, left everything behind and fled for their lives—pursued by FBI agents on trumped-up kidnapping charges.

Williams and his family spent five years in Cuba where he wrote his water-shed book, *Negroes With Guns* and produced Radio Free Dixie for the international airwaves. They later moved on to China, where they were well received—but always longed for their forbidden home. In 1969, Williams exchanged his knowledge of the Chinese government for safe passage to the United States. Rob and Mabel lived their remaining days together in Michigan where he died in 1995. His body was returned at long last to his hometown of Monroe, N.C.

Copyright © Newsreel Inc. (2005).
Reprinted with permission of Newsreel Inc.

John Hope Franklin

From Slavery to Freedom: A History of Negro Americans (Fifth Edition)

The 1960s was a time of revolution among blacks in the United States. The decade began with high hopes. There was still the belief that the school desegregation

---

9. For a detailed history of the Civil Rights Movement, *see* TAYLOR BRANCH, PARTING THE WATERS: AMERICA IN THE KING YEARS 1954–1963 (1989).

decision would somehow bring about a truly democratic educational system in the United States. The sit-in movement, the freedom riders, the marches and demonstrations, and the voter registration drives, supported by untold numbers of whites as well as blacks, suggested that an entirely new and thoroughly effective approach to race relations was in the making. Slowly, then more rapidly, the optimism gave way to pessimism and even cynicism. It was not merely the opposition to equality on the part of the white citizens councils or the Northern white mothers who railed against school desegregation or the white construction workers who bitterly opposed the employment of black journeymen and apprentices, but the feeling, bolstered by bitter experience, that justice and equality were not to be extended to blacks under any circumstances. This created the gloomy atmosphere out of which the Black Revolution emerged.

There was, first of all, the violence. In 1963 it was the assassination of John F. Kennedy, whom many blacks had come to regard as their friend. Then, there was the murder of Malcolm X in 1965 and the feeling, shared by many blacks, that the prosecution of his assailants was less than vigorous. In the mid-sixties there was, moreover, the murder of numerous civil rights workers as well as innocent children, and for these crimes no one was convicted or even seriously prosecuted. Finally, on April 4, 1968, Martin Luther King, Jr., was shot down in a motel in Memphis, where he had gone to give support to striking garbage workers. To many blacks this violent act symbolized the rejection by white America of their vigorous but peaceful pursuit of equality. In more than a hundred cities several days of rioting and burning and looting ensued, a grave response by many blacks to the wanton murder of their young leader. The subsequent capture of James Earl Ray and his immediate trial, without any testimony after his plea of guilty, further embittered large numbers of blacks who suspected that such speedy "justice" was merely a cover-up of a possible conspiracy. The exhaustive inquiry into the matter by a Select Congressional Committee did not lead to a satisfactory conclusion on the conspiracy question.

Even before his death Martin Luther King had been criticized by militant, action-oriented blacks who insisted that whites would not respond to black demands on the basis of Christian charity, good will, or even peaceful demonstrations. Some also felt that whites would never concede complete equality to blacks. In 1967 the Black Power Conference in Newark, New Jersey, called for the "partitioning of the United States into two separate independent nations, one to be a homeland for white and the other to be a homeland for black Americans." Meanwhile, a group of young California militants led by Huey P. Newton and Bobby Seale organized the Black Panther Party for Self-Defense; and Eldridge Cleaver, its most articulate spokesman, declared that the choice before the country was "total liberty for black people or total destruction for America."

The Black Panthers became nationally prominent when Huey P. Newton, who had led a group of gun-carrying demonstrators into the California state legislature, was convicted on a charge of manslaughter in the death of an Oakland policeman. Soon, chapters of the party sprang up in major cities across the nation. They called for full employment, decent housing, black control of the black community, and an end to every form of repression and brutality. It was not long before they were involved in numerous encounters with the police. Several were sent to prison, charged with murder, attempted murder, and lesser crimes. The Federal Bureau of Investigation declared the Black Panthers to be dangerous and subversive. They became the target of what appeared to be a concerted effort to eliminate them as an effective radical organization. By 1980 the Black Panthers were scarcely a shadow of what they had been. Huey Newton was more a writer than an activist, while Bobby Seale and several other leaders were involved in rather orthodox political activity. Meanwhile, Eldridge Cleaver, who returned from exile to stand trial on some old charges, had become a born-again Christian evangelist, drawing considerable sympathy from his former adversaries

If the Black Panthers questioned the good intentions of white America, the National Black Economic Development Conference conceived an acid test of such intentions. Meeting in Detroit in April 1969, and led by James Forman of the Student Nonviolent Coordinating Committee, the conference issued a "Black Manifesto" calling upon the "White Christian Churches and the Jewish Synagogues in the United States and all other Racist Institutions" to pay $500 million in reparations and to surrender 60 percent of their assets to the conference to be used for the economic, social, and cultural rehabilitation of the black community. While some churches appropriated additional funds for the poor and underprivileged and for the purpose of promoting racial justice, none of them yielded to the demands of the conference. If the manifesto did nothing else it affirmed the 1968 findings of the National Advisory Commission on Civil Disorders that "our nation is moving toward two societies, one black, one white—separate and unequal."

From Slavery to Freedom: A History of Negro Americans 458–410.
Copyright © (1980) McGraw-Hill, Inc.
Reprinted with permission of McGraw-Hill, Inc.

E. Background on *Milliken*

In response to the federal government's commitment to desegregation of the public primary and secondary schools, many whites decided to flee from school districts subjected to court-ordered desegregation rather than stay and comply with government efforts at integration. Despite the creation by some local school boards of a myriad of devices to prevent desegregation, initial plans were implemented to begin the process of desegregation.

While the *Brown II* decision mandated the desegregation of certain schools, subsequent Supreme Court decisions made such desegregation efforts much more difficult, in part by adding conditions and constricting the application. Limitations on the authority of local school boards to implement changes and the narrow scope of desegregation remedies imposed by the Court were particularly problematic.

Donald E. Lively

*The Constitution and Race**

Central to *Brown* was the objective of abolishing racially identifiable schools. The Court perceived racial separation as a system which officially connoted inferiority and adversely affected the self-image and educational opportunities of its victims. Consistent with the Court's understanding are observations that formal segregation causes psychological injury "by assaulting a person's self-respect and human dignity, and [by] brand[ing] . . . with a sign that designates inferior status to others." Without belittling the significance of *Brown*, it is necessary to recognize what the Court accomplished in 1954 and how the principle then enunciated was later qualified. The desegregation mandate, as it evolved, required liquidation of educational systems segregated by law or by overtly discriminatory official action. Left unaffected by constitutional demands, however, has been pervasive and extensive segregation in the North and West attributable to patterns of residential settlement. Critics have asserted that whether a "child perceives his separation as discriminatory and invidious, he is not . . . going to make fine distinctions about the source of particular separation." Whatever concern originally existed for the impact of segregation on self-image and opportunity, it was lost in the translation of the doctrine in the 1970s.

The desegregation mandate was articulated at the same time society was experiencing unprecedented individual mobility and significant demographic changes. Enhanced opportunities for personal movement coalesced with suburban development to expand and redefine metropolitan areas. By the 1970s, new school districts had been established in communities that recently had not even existed. Given their lack of history, identifying a record of overt, much less subtle, discrimination was a virtual impossibility. As Justice Powell observed, "[t]he type of state-enforced segregation that *Brown I* properly condemned no longer exists in this country." Notwithstanding the opportunity to craft doctrine that would reach segregation regardless of cause, the Court, instead of reckoning with the underlying dynamics of racially separate education, stopped at elimination of its overt manifestations.

As the 1970s unfolded, it became apparent that the outer limits of equal protection had been reached. Confinement of the *Brown* mandate to instances where segregative intent was identified checked the process of desegregation as it threatened to expand into heavily populated areas of the North and West. Reflecting dominant public corner with the potential scope of desegregation, the Court invalidated a remedial plan covering a major northern city and its suburbs. Having demarcated the spatial scope of desegregation remedies, the Court next fixed temporal limitations on desegregation obligations. It held that resegregation of a school district, following implementation of a desegregation decree, was not constitutionally offensive

---

* (footnotes omitted).

absent proof of discriminatory motive. The trilogy of limiting principles, enunciated in three separate decisions, preserved opportunities for white flight and effectively immunized suburban communities from the demands of *Brown*.

The first qualification of the desegregation principle, in *Keyes v. School District No. I*, conditioned the duty to desegregate on demonstration of officially discriminatory action. For a constitutional responsibility to exist, it was necessary to establish first a *prima facie* case of segregative intent, which authorities had the opportunity to rebut. To the extent segregation could be attributed to factors other than what the Court would consider purposeful state action, no duty to desegregate would exist. Desegregation thus would be a selective rather than a comprehensive duty, imposed only when a formal system of segregation had existed or a palpable discriminatory intent could be identified.

By failing to acknowledge a link between government action and housing patterns, the Court overlooked or discounted the legacy of official policies and practices that facilitated residential segregation. As the Court noted, "the differentiating factor between *de jure* segregation and so-called *de facto* segregation . . . is *purpose* or *intent* to segregate." The line between the two concepts, however, is more illusory than real. Segregated housing was a function in many communities of officially enforced restrictive covenants. Racially separated neighborhoods were an extension of not only state but national policy. The Federal Housing Administration's lending policies, for instance, protected residential loans from "adverse influences" that included the mixing of "inharmonious racial groups." Further contributing to racially discrete neighborhoods have been decisions concerning the construction and closing of schools, employment of faculty and staff, assignment of students, siting of public housing, and distribution of urban development funds.

Rather than exploring those ties to state action, the Court opted for bright but not necessarily precise boundaries between permissible and impermissible segregation. The consequent dividing line formally distinguishes race-dependent and race-neutral action but is useful in discerning and defeating overt rather than subtle discrimination. Even if officially determined racial separation was more evident in the South, where it was patently systematized, segregation in education was a pervasive national phenomenon. Arguably, it was more insidiously rooted in the North where racial segregation became more spatial than ceremonial. Despite required change in the South, as Justice Powell observed, no comparable progress would be realized in the North and West because "of the *de jure-de facto* distinction." Powell suggested a hypocrisy in the court's formulation insofar as it was "accepted complacently by many of the same voices which denounced the evils of segregated schools in the south." Characterizing the severability of segregation as "a legalism rooted in history rather than present reality," which also was irrational insofar as cause did not alter adverse effect on such educational opportunity, he would have abolished the *de jure/de facto* distinction.

The differentiation survived Powell's challenge and profoundly diminished the Court's responsiveness to and concern with modern segregation. It announced or at least prefaced a reluctance to adjust equal protection doctrine to the new demographic realities of the post-*Brown* era. Comprehensive realization of equal educational opportunity and elimination of all racially identifiable schools were placed beyond the reach of the desegregation mandate. Motive-referenced criteria thus exempted from constitutional attention much racially separate and unequal education.

The duty to desegregate, as limited by the *de jure* requirement, imposed a substantial burden upon plaintiffs seeking to establish a constitutional violation. That a school system was intentionally segregated could be easily proved insofar as the law spoke for itself, as it did during the Jim Crow era. Discriminatory purpose when not overt may be elusive, however, and its discernment a "tortuous effort." Even the most routine decisions, as Powell noted, may affect segregation. A panoply of opportunities exists for influencing the racial mix of public schools, including action or nonaction with respect to school building construction and location; the timing of building new schools and their size; the closing and consolidation of schools; the drawing or gerrymandering of student attendance zones; the extent to which a neighborhood policy is enforced; the recruitment, promotion and assignment of faculty and supervisory personnel; policies with respect to transfers from one school to another; whether, and to what extent, special schools will be provided, where they will be located, and who will qualify to attend them; the determination of curriculum, including whether there will be "tracks" that lead primarily to college or to vocational training, and the routing of students into these tracks; and even decisions as to social, recreational and athletic policies.

Further complicating the inquiry is the problem of varying, mixed or disguised motive. In those parts of the country which did not have laws requiring dual schools, proof of segregation was elusive or non-existent. Segregation of primary and secondary education in the North and West, not surprisingly, remains more profound and resistant than in the South.

The *de jure* principle operates in effect as a liability-limiting concept akin to the tort principle of proximate cause. The standard, which requires a nexus between act and injury that is not too attenuated, ensures that liability for a negligent act will not be limitless. Although the cutoff point is not precisely defined, responsibility for consequential harm abates as actual injury becomes more distant and less foreseeable. Like the concept of proximate cause, the *de facto* notion is vulnerable to subjective perceptions that influence the etching of legally significant dividing lines. The liability-reducing criteria, chosen to qualify the desegregation principle, seem notable more for their capacity to restrain than for their precision.

Investment in such limiting principles for desegregation provoked sharp debate within the Court itself. As noted previously, Justice Powell would have avoided the *de jure de facto* distinction altogether. Justice Marshall observed that school district boundaries yielding racially distinct systems, whether proximately or more remotely caused by official action, communicate the same negative message that concerned the *Brown* Court. The premise that a child's constitutional rights are not implicated because he or she is "born into a *de facto* society" struck Marshall as facile and capricious. To the extent racial separation suggests a systematic pattern, breeds a sense of inferiority, and impairs educational development and opportunity, causation-based distinctions from his perspective seemed more a function of convenience than principle. This perception conformed with Powell's sense that causation-referenced limiting principles serve no purpose other than to "perpetuate a legalism rooted in history rather than present reality."

Further bounding the duty to desegregate was the Court's determination that, in the event of purposeful segregative design, any remedy must be tailored to the scope of the constitutional violation. Such a qualification radiated from the *de facto* distinction and ensured that demands would not be imposed in communities where official wrong was not discernible. As demonstrated by the circumstances from which *Milliken v. Bradley* arose, the limiting principle precluded interdistrict remedies in major urban centers. Even if the city school system itself had a history of discrimination, any attempt to desegregate was a generally vain exercise if a court order could not reach adjacent and mostly white suburban communities that had evolved in the meantime.

The Constitution and Race 119–22.
Copyright © (1992) Donald E. Lively.
Reprinted with permission of Donald E. Lively.

F. *Milliken v. Bradley*, 418 U.S. 717 (1974)

Frank J. Kelley, Attorney General of Michigan, argued the cause for petitioners in No. 73-434. With him on the brief were *Robert A. Derengoski*, Solicitor General, and *Eugene Krasicky, Gerald F. Young, George L. McCargar*, and *Thomas F. Schimpf*, Assistant Attorneys General. *William M. Saxton* argued the cause for petitioners in Nos. 73-435 and 73-436. With him on the brief in No. 73-435 were *John B. Weaver, Robert M. Vercruysse*, and *Xhafer Orhan*. *Douglas H. West* filed a brief for petitioner in No. 73-436.

J. Harold Flannery and *Nathaniel R. Jones* argued the cause for respondents in all cases. With them on the brief for respondents Bradley et al. were *Jack Greenberg, Norman Chachkin*, and *Louis R. Lucas*. *George T. Roumell, Jr.*, and *C. Nicholas Revelos* filed a brief for respondents Board of Education for the School District of the city of Detroit et al. *John Bruff* and *William Ross* filed a brief for respondent Professional Personnel of Van Dyke. *Robert J. Lord* filed a brief for respondents Green et al.

Solicitor General Bork argued the cause for the United States as *amicus curiae* urging reversal. With him on the brief was *Assistant Attorney General Pottinger*.

1. Facts

Chief Justice BURGER delivered the opinion of the Court.

We granted certiorari in these consolidated cases to determine whether a federal court may impose a multi-district, area wide remedy to a single-district *de jure*

PART FIVE · ATTEMPTED ERADICATION OF INEQUALITY

segregation problem absent any finding that the other included school districts have failed to operate unitary school systems within their districts, absent any claim or finding that the boundary lines of any affected school district were established with the purpose of fostering racial segregation in public schools, absent any finding that the included districts committed acts which effected segregation within the other districts, and absent a meaningful opportunity for the included neighboring school districts to present evidence or be heard on the propriety of a multidistrict remedy or on the question of constitutional violations by those neighboring districts.

The action was commenced in August 1970 by the respondents, the Detroit Branch of the National Association for the Advancement of Colored People and individual parents and students, on behalf of a class later defined by order of the United States District Court for the Eastern District of Michigan, dated February 16, 1971, to include "all school children in the City of Detroit, Michigan, and all Detroit resident parents who have children of school age." The named defendants in the District Court included the Governor of Michigan, the Attorney General, the State Board of Education, the State Superintendent of Public Instruction, the Board of Education of the city of Detroit, its members, and the city's former superintendent of schools. The State of Michigan as such is not a party to this litigation and references to the State must be read as references to the public officials, state and local, through whom the State is alleged to have acted. In their complaint respondents attacked the constitutionality of a statute of the State of Michigan known as Act 48 of the 1970 legislature on the ground that it put the State of Michigan in the position of unconstitutionally interfering with the execution and operation of a voluntary plan of partial high school desegregation, known as the April 7, 1970 Plan, which had been adopted by the Detroit Board of Education to be effective beginning with the fall 1970 semester. The complaint also alleged that the Detroit Public School System was and is segregated on the basis of race as a result of the official policies and actions of the defendants and their predecessors in office, and called for the implementation of a plan that would eliminate "the racial identity of every school in the [Detroit] system and . . . maintain now and hereafter a unitary, nonracial school system." . . .

2. Trial Court Opinion

The District Court found that the Detroit Board of Education created and maintained optional attendance zones[10] within Detroit neighborhoods undergoing racial transition and between high school attendance areas of opposite predominant racial compositions. These zones, the court found, had the "natural, probable, foreseeable and actual effect" of allowing white pupils to escape identifiably Negro schools. *Ibid.* Similarly, the District Court found that Detroit school attendance zones had been drawn along north-south boundary lines despite the Detroit Board's awareness

---

10. Optional zones, sometimes referred to as dual zones or dual overlapping zones, provide pupils living within certain areas a choice of attendance at one of two high schools.

that drawing boundary lines in an east-west direction would result in significantly greater desegregation. Again, the District Court concluded, the natural and actual effect of these acts was the creation and perpetuation of school segregation within Detroit. The District Court found that in the operation of its school transportation program, which was designed to relieve overcrowding, the Detroit Board had admittedly bused Negro Detroit pupils to predominantly Negro schools which were beyond or away from closer white schools with available space.[11] This practice was found to have continued in recent years despite the Detroit Board's avowed policy, adopted in 1967, of utilizing transportation to increase desegregation: "With one exception (necessitated by the burning of a white school), defendant Board has never bused white children to predominantly black schools. The Board has not bused white pupils to black schools despite the enormous amount of space available in inner-city schools. There were 22,961 vacant seats in schools 90% or more black." *Id.*, at 588.

With respect to the Detroit Board of Education's practices in school construction, the District court found that Detroit school construction generally tended to have a segregative effect with the great majority of schools being built in either overwhelmingly all-Negro or all-white neighborhoods so that the new schools opened as predominantly one-race schools. Thus, of the 14 schools which opened for use in 1970–1971, 11 opened over 90% Negro and one opened less than 10% Negro.

The District Court also found that the State of Michigan had committed several constitutional violations with respect to the exercise of its general responsibility for, and supervision of, public education.[12] The State, for example, was found to have failed, until the 1971 Session of the Michigan Legislature, to provide authorization or funds for the transportation of pupils within Detroit regardless of their poverty or distance from the school to which they were assigned; during this same period the State provided many neighboring, mostly white, suburban districts the full range of state-supported transportation.

---

11. The Court of Appeals found record evidence that in at least one instance during the period 1957–1958, Detroit served a suburban school district by contracting with it to educate its Negro high school students by transporting them away from nearby suburban white high schools, and past Detroit high schools which were predominantly white, to all-Negro or predominantly Negro Detroit schools. 484 F.2d, at 231.

12. School districts in the State of Michigan are instrumentalities of the State and subordinate to its State Board of Education and legislature. The Constitution of the State of Michigan, Art. 8, § 2, provides in relevant part: "The legislature shall maintain and support a system of free public elementary and secondary schools as defined by law."

Similarly, the Michigan Supreme Court has stated: The school district is a State agency. Moreover, it is of legislative creation. . . ." *Attorney General ex rel. Kies v. Lowrey*, 131 Mich. 639, 644, 92 N.W. 289, 290 91902); "'Education in Michigan belongs to the State. It is no part of the local self-government inherent in the township or municipality, except so far as the legislature may choose to make it such. The Constitution has turned the whole subject over to the legislature. . . .'" *Attorney General ex rel. Zacharias v. Detroit Board of Education*, 154 Mich. 584, 590, 118 N.W. 606, 609 (1908).

The District Court found that the State, through Act 48, acted to "impede, delay and minimize racial integration in Detroit schools." The first sentence of § 12 of Act 48 was designed to delay the April 7, 1970, desegregation plan originally adopted by the Detroit Board. The remainder of § 12 sought to prescribe for each school in the eight districts criteria of "free choice" and "neighborhood schools," which, the District court found, "had as their purpose and effect the maintenance of segregation." 338 F. Supp., at 589.

The District Court also held that the acts of the Detroit Board of Education, as a subordinate entity of the State, were attributable to the State of Michigan, thus creating a vicarious liability on the part of the State. Under Michigan law, Mich. Comp. Laws § 388.851 (1970), for example, school building construction plans had to be approved by the State Board of Education, and, prior to 1962, the State Board had specific statutory authority to supervise school site selection. The proofs concerning the effect of Detroit's school construction program were, therefore, found to be largely applicable to show state responsibility for the segregative results. . . . [13]

3. Court of Appeals Opinion

On June 12, 1973, a divided Court of Appeals, sitting en banc, affirmed in part, vacated in part, and remanded for further proceedings. 484 F.2d 215 (CA6). The Court of Appeals held, first, that the record supported the District Court's findings and conclusions on the constitutional violations committed by the Detroit Board, *id.*, at 221–38, and by the state defendants, *id.*, at 239–41.[14] It stated that the acts of

13. The District Court briefly alluded to the possibility that the State, along with private persons, had caused, in part, the housing patterns of the Detroit metropolitan area which, in turn, produced the predominantly white and predominantly Negro neighborhoods that characterize Detroit:

"It is no answer to say that restricted practices grew gradually (as the black population in the area increased between 1920 and 1970), or that since 1948 racial restrictions on the ownership of real property have been removed. The policies pursued by both government and private persons and agencies have a continuing and present effect upon the complexion of the community—as we know, the choice of a residence is a relatively infrequent affair. For many years FHA and VA openly advised and advocated the maintenance of 'harmonious' neighborhoods, i.e. racially and economically harmonious. The conditions created continue." 338 F. Supp. 582, 587 (ED Mich. 1971).

Thus, the District Court concluded:

"The affirmative obligation of the defendant Board has been and is to adopt and implement pupil assignment practices and policies that compensate for and avoid incorporation into the school system the effects of residential racial segregation." Id., at 593.

The Court of Appeals, however, expressly noted that:

"In affirming the District Judge's findings of constitutional violations by the Detroit Board of Education and by the State defendants resulting in segregated schools in Detroit, we have not relied at all upon testimony pertaining to segregated housing except as school construction programs helped cause or maintain such segregation." 484 F.2d, at 242.

Accordingly, in its present posture, the case does not present any question concerning possible state housing violations.

14. With respect to the state's violations, the Court of Appeals held: (1) that, since the city Board is an instrumentality of the State and subordinate to the State Board, the segregative actions of

racial discrimination shown in the record are "causally related to the substantial amount of segregation found in the Detroit school system," *id.*, at 241, and that "the District Court was therefore authorized and required to take effective measures to desegregate the Detroit Public School System." *Id.*, at 242.

The Court of Appeals also agreed with the District Court that "any less comprehensive a solution than a metropolitan area plan would result in an all black school system immediately surrounded by practically all white suburban school systems, with an overwhelmingly white majority population in the total metropolitan area." *Id.*, at 245. The court went on to state that it could "not see how such segregation can be any less harmful to the minority students than if the same result were accomplished within one school district." *Ibid.*

Accordingly, the Court of Appeals concluded that "the only feasible desegregation plan involves the crossing of the boundary lines between the Detroit School District and adjacent or nearby school districts for the limited purpose of providing an effective desegregation plan." *Id.*, at 249. It reasoned that such a plan would be appropriate because of the State's violations, and could be implemented because of the State's authority to control local school districts. Without further elaboration, and without any discussion of the claims that no constitutional violation by the outlying districts had been shown and that no evidence on that point had been allowed, the Court of Appeals held:

> "[T]he State has committed *de jure* acts of segregation and . . . the State controls the instrumentalities whose action is necessary to remedy the harmful effects of the State acts." *Ibid.*

An interdistrict remedy was thus held to be "within the equity powers of the District court." *Id.*, at 250.[15]

The Court of Appeals expressed no views on the propriety of the District Court's composition of the metropolitan "desegregation area." It held that all suburban school districts that might be affected by a metropolitan-wide remedy should, under Fed. Rule Civ. Proc. 19, be made parties to the case on remand and be given

---

the Detroit Board "are the actions of an agency of the State," id., at 238; (2) that the state legislation rescinding Detroit's voluntary desegregation plan contributed to increasing segregation in the Detroit schools, id.; (3) that under state law prior to 1962 the State board had authority over school construction plans and therefore had to be held responsible "for the segregative results," ibid.; (4) that the "State statutory scheme of support of transportation for school children directly discriminated against Detroit," id., at 240, by not providing transportation funds to Detroit on the same basis as funds were provided to suburban districts, id., at 238; and (5) that the transportation of Negro students from one suburban district to a Negro school in Detroit must have had the "approval, tacit or express, of the State Board of Education," id.

15. The court sought to distinguish *Bradley v. School Board of the City of Richmond*, 462 F.2d 1058 (CA4 1972), aff'd by an equally divided Court, 412 U.S. 92 (1973), on the grounds that the District Court in that case had ordered an actual consolidation of three school districts and that Virginia's Constitution and statutes, unlike Michigan's, gave the local boards exclusive power to operate the public schools. 484 F.2d, at 251.

an opportunity to be heard with respect to the scope and implementation of such a remedy. 484 F.2d, at 251–52. Under the terms of the remand, however, the District Court was not "required" to receive further evidence on the issue of segregation in the Detroit schools or on the propriety of a Detroit-only remedy, or on the question of whether the affected districts had committed any violation of the constitutional rights of Detroit pupils or others. *Id.*, at 252. Finally, the Court of Appeals vacated the District Court's order directing the acquisition of school buses, subject to the right of the District Court to consider reimposing the order "at the appropriate time." *Ibid.*

4. Opinion

Ever since *Brown v. Board of Education*, 347 U.S. 483 (1954), judicial consideration of school desegregation cases has begun with the standard:

> "[I]n the field of public education the doctrine of 'separate but equal' has no place. Separate educational facilities are inherently unequal." *Id.*, at 495.

This has been reaffirmed time and again as the meaning of the Constitution and the controlling rule of law.

The target of the *Brown* holding was clear and forthright: the elimination of state-mandated or deliberately maintained dual school systems with certain schools for Negro pupils and others for white pupils. This duality and racial segregation were held to violate the Constitution in the cases subsequent to 1954, including particularly *Green v. County School Board of New Kent County*, 391 U.S. 430 (1968); *Raney v. Board of Education*, 391 U.S. 443 (1968); *Swann v. Charlotte-Mecklenburg Board of Education*, 402 U.S. 1 (1971); *Wright v. Council of the City of Emporia*, 407 U.S. 451 91972); *United States v. Scotland Neck Board of Education*, 407 U.S. 484 (1972).

The *Swann* case, of course, dealt "with the problem of defining in more precise terms than heretofore the scope of the duty of school authorities and district courts in implementing *Brown* and the mandate to eliminate dual systems and establish unitary systems at once." 402 U.S., at 6.

In *Brown v. Board of Education*, 349 U.S. 294 (1955) (*Brown II*), the Court's first encounter with the problem of remedies in school desegregation cases, the Court noted:

> "In fashioning and effectuating the decrees, the courts will be guided by equitable principles. Traditionally, equity has been characterized by a practical flexibility in shaping its remedies and by a facility for adjusting and reconciling public and private needs." *Id.*, at 300 (footnotes omitted).

In further refining the remedial process, *Swann* held, the task is to correct, by a balancing of the individual and collective interests, "the condition that offends the Constitution." A federal remedial power may be exercised "only on the basis of a constitutional violation" and, "[a]s with any equity case, the nature of the violation determines the scope of the remedy." 402 U.S., at 16. Proceeding from these basic principles, we first note that in the District court the complainants sought a remedy aimed at the *condition* alleged to offend the Constitution — the segregation within the Detroit City School District. The court acted on this theory of the case and in its initial ruling on the "Desegregation Area" stated:

> "The task before this court, therefore, is now, and . . . has always been, how to desegregate the Detroit public schools." 345 F. Supp., at 921.

Thereafter, however, the District court abruptly rejected the proposed Detroit-only plans on the ground that "while [they] would provide a racial mix more in keeping with the Black-White proportions of the student population [they] would accentuate the racial identifiability of the [Detroit] district as a Black school system, and would not accomplish desegregation." Pet. App. 56a. "[T]he racial composition of the student body is such," said the court, "that the plan's implementation would clearly make the entire Detroit public school system racially identifiable" (*Id.*, at 54a), "leav[ing] many of its schools 75 to 90 per cent Black." *Id.*, at 55a. Consequently, the court reasoned, it was imperative to "look beyond the limits of the Detroit school district for a solution to the problem of segregation in the Detroit public schools . . ." since "[s]chool district lines are simply matters of political convenience and may not be used to deny constitutional rights." *Id.*, at 57a. Accordingly, the District court proceeded to redefine the relevant area to include areas of predominantly white pupil population in order to ensure that "upon implementation, no school, grade or classroom [would be] substantially disproportionate to the overall pupil racial composition" of the entire metropolitan area.

While specifically acknowledging that the District Court's findings of a condition of segregation were limited to Detroit, the Court of Appeals approved the use of a metropolitan remedy largely on the grounds that it is

> "impossible to declare 'clearly erroneous' the District Judge's conclusion that any Detroit only segregation plan will lead directly to a single segregated Detroit school district overwhelmingly black in all of its schools, surrounded by a ring of suburbs and suburban school districts overwhelmingly white in composition in a State in which the racial composition is 87 per cent white and 13 per cent black." 484 F.2d, at 249.

Viewing the record as a whole, it seems clear that the District Court and the Court of Appeals shifted the primary focus from a Detroit remedy to the metropolitan area only because of their conclusion that total desegregation of Detroit would not produce the racial balance which they perceived as desirable. Both courts proceeded on an assumption that the Detroit schools could not be truly desegregated — in their view of what constituted desegregation — unless the racial composition of the student body of each school substantially reflected the racial composition of the population of the metropolitan area as a whole. The metropolitan area was then defined as Detroit plus 53 of the outlying school districts. . . .

The controlling principle consistently expounded in our holdings is that the scope of the remedy is determined by the nature and extent of the constitutional violation. *Swann*, 402 U.S., at 16, 91 S.Ct. at 1276. Before the boundaries of separate and autonomous school districts may be set aside by consolidating the separate units for remedial purposes or by imposing a cross-district remedy, it must first be shown that there has been a constitutional violation within one district that produces a significant segregative effect in another district. Specifically, it must be shown that racially discriminatory acts of the state or local school districts, or of a single school district have been a substantial cause of interdistrict segregation. Thus an interdistrict remedy might be in order where the racially discriminatory acts of one or more school districts caused racial segregation in an adjacent district, or where district lines have been deliberately drawn on the basis of race. In such circumstances an interdistrict remedy would be appropriate to eliminate the interdistrict segregation directly caused by the constitutional violation. Conversely, without an interdistrict violation and interdistrict effect, there is no constitutional wrong calling for an interdistrict remedy.

The record before us, voluminous as it is, contains evidence of de jure segregated conditions only in the Detroit schools; indeed, that was the theory on which the litigation was initially based and on which the District Court took evidence. *See supra* at 3117–18. With no showing of significant violation by the 53 outlying school districts and no evidence of any interdistrict violation or effect, the court went beyond the original theory of the case as framed by the pleadings and mandated a metropolitan area remedy. To approve the remedy ordered by the court would impose on the outlying districts, not shown to have committed any constitutional violation, a wholly impermissible remedy based on a standard not hinted at in *Brown I* and *II* or any holding of this Court.

In dissent, Justice WHITE and Justice MARSHALL undertake to demonstrate that agencies having statewide authority participated in maintaining the dual school system found to exist in Detroit. They are apparently of the view that once such participation is shown, the District Court should have a relatively free hand to reconstruct school districts outside of Detroit in fashioning relief. Our assumption, arguendo, *see infra*, p. 3129, that state agencies did participate in the maintenance of the Detroit system, should make it clear that it is not on this point that we part company.[16] The difference between us arises instead from established doctrine laid down by our cases. *Brown, supra*; *Green, supra*; *Swann, supra*; *Scotland Neck, supra*; and *Emporia, supra*, each addressed the issue of constitutional wrong in terms of an established geographic and administrative school system populated by both Negro and white children. In such a context, terms such as 'unitary' and 'dual' systems,

---

16. Since the Court has held that a resident of a school district has a fundamental right protected by the Federal Constitution to vote in a district election, it would seem incongruous to disparage the importance of the school district in a different context. *Kramer v. Union Free School District No. 15*, 395 U.S. 621, 626, 89 S. t. 1886, 1889, 23 L Ed.2d 583 (1969). While the district there involved was located in New York, none of the facts in our possession suggest that the relation of school districts to the State is significantly different in New York from that in Michigan.

and 'racially identifiable schools,' have meaning, and the necessary federal authority to remedy the constitutional wrong is firmly established. But the remedy is necessarily designed, as all remedies are, to restore the victims of discriminatory conduct to the position they would have occupied in the absence of such conduct. Disparate treatment of white and Negro students occurred within the Detroit school system, and not elsewhere, and on this record the remedy must be limited to that system. *Swann, supra*, 402 U.S. at 16, 91 S.Ct., at 1276.

The constitutional right of the Negro respondents residing in Detroit is to attend a unitary school system in that district. Unless petitioners drew the district lines in a discriminatory fashion, or arranged for white students residing in the Detroit district to attend schools in Oakland and Macomb Counties, they were under no constitutional duty to make provisions for Negro students to do so. The view of the dissenters, that the existence of a dual system in Detroit can be made the basis for a decree requiring cross-district transportation of pupils, cannot be supported on the grounds that it represents merely the devising of a suitably flexible remedy for the violation of rights already established by our prior decisions. It can be supported only by drastic expansion of the constitutional right itself, an expansion without any support in either constitutional principle or precedent. . . . [17]

5. Holding

We conclude that the relief ordered by the District Court and affirmed by the Court of Appeals was based upon an erroneous standard and was unsupported by record evidence that acts of the outlying districts effected the discrimination found to exist in the schools of Detroit. Accordingly, the judgment of the Court of Appeals is reversed and the case is remanded for further proceedings consistent with this opinion leading to prompt formulation of a decree directed to eliminating the

---

17. The suggestion in the dissent of Justice MARSHALL that schools which have a majority of Negro students are not 'desegregated,' whatever the racial makeup of the school district's population and however neutrally the district lines have been drawn and administered, finds no support in our prior cases. In *Green v. County School Board of New Kent County*, 391 U.S. 430, 88 S.Ct. 1689, 20 L.Ed.2d 716 (1968), for example, this Court approved a desegregation plan which would have resulted in each of the schools within the district having a racial composition of 57% Negro and 43% white. In *Wright v. Council of the City of Emporia*, 407 U.S. 451, 92 S.Ct. 2196, 33 L.Ed.2d 51 (1972), the optimal desegregation plan would have resulted in the schools' being 66% Negro and 34% white, substantially the same percentages as could be obtained under one of the plans involved in this case. And in *United States v. Scotland Neck City Board of Education*, 407 U.S. 484, 491 n. 5, 92 S.Ct. 2214, 2218, 33 L.Ed.2d 75 (1972), a desegregation plan was implicitly approved for a school district which had a racial composition of 77% Negro and 22% white. In none of these cases was it even intimated that 'actual desegregation' could not be accomplished as long as the number of Negro students was greater than the number of white students.

The dissents also seem to attach importance to the metropolitan character of Detroit and neighboring school districts. But the constitutional principles applicable in school desegregation cases cannot vary in accordance with the size or population dispersal of the particular city, county, or school district as compared with neighboring areas.

segregation found to exist in Detroit city schools, a remedy which has been delayed since 1970.

6. Justice White Dissenting

The District Court and the Court of Appeals found that over a long period of years those in charge of the Michigan public schools engaged in various practices calculated to effect the segregation of the Detroit school system. The Court does not question these findings, nor could it reasonably do so. Neither does it question the obligation of the federal courts to devise a feasible and effective remedy. But it promptly cripples the ability of the judiciary to perform this task, which is of fundamental importance to our constitutional system, by fashioning a strict rule that remedies in school cases must stop at the school district line unless certain other conditions are met. As applied here, the remedy for unquestioned violations of the protection rights of Detroit's Negroes by the Detroit School Board and the State of Michigan must be totally confined to the limits of the school district and may not reach into adjoining or surrounding districts unless and until it is proved there has been some sort of 'interdistrict violation' — unless unconstitutional actions of the Detroit School Board have had a segregative impact on other districts, or unless the segregated condition of the Detroit schools has itself been influenced by segregative practices in those surrounding districts into which it is proposed to extend the remedy.

Regretfully, and for several reasons, I can join neither the Court's judgment nor its opinion. The core of my disagreement is that deliberate acts of segregation and their consequences will go unremedied, not because a remedy would be infeasible or unreasonable in terms of the usual criteria governing school desegregation cases, but because an effective remedy would cause what the Court considers to be undue administrative inconvenience to the State. The result is that the State of Michigan, the entity at which the Fourteenth Amendment is directed, has successfully insulated itself from its duty to provide effective desegregation remedies by vesting sufficient power over its public schools in its local school districts. If this is the case in Michigan, it will be the case in most States.

There are undoubted practical as well as legal limits to the remedial powers of federal courts in school desegregation cases. The Court has made it clear that the achievement of any particular degree of racial balance in the school system is not required by the Constitution; nor may it be the primary focus of a court in devising an acceptable remedy for *de jure* segregation. A variety of procedures and techniques are available to a district court engrossed in fashioning remedies in a case such as this; but the courts must keep in mind that they are dealing with the process of educating the young, including the very young. The task is not to devise a system of pains and penalties to punish constitutional violations brought to light. Rather, it is to desegregate an educational system in which the races have been kept apart, without, at the same time, losing sight of the central educational function of the schools. . . .

Despite the fact that a metropolitan remedy, if the findings of the District Court accepted by the Court of Appeals are to be credited, would more effectively desegregate the Detroit schools, would prevent resegregation,[18] and would be easier and more feasible from many standpoints, the Court fashions out of whole cloth an arbitrary rule that remedies for constitutional violations occurring in a single Michigan school district must stop at the school district line. Apparently, no matter how much less burdensome or more effective and efficient in many respects, such as transportation, the metropolitan plan might be, the school district line may not be crossed. Otherwise, it seems, there would be too much disruption of the Michigan scheme for managing its educational system, too much confusion, and too much administrative burden. . . .

Until today, the permissible contours of the equitable authority of the district courts to remedy the unlawful establishment of a dual school system have been extensive, adaptable, and fully responsive to the ultimate goal of achieving 'the greatest possible degree of actual desegregation.' There are indeed limitations on the equity powers of the federal judiciary, but until now the Court had not accepted the proposition that effective enforcement of the Fourteenth Amendment could be limited by political or administrative boundary lines demarcated by the very State responsible for the constitutional violation and for the disestablishment of the dual system. Until now the Court has instead looked to practical considerations in effectuating a desegregation decree, such as excessive distance, transportation time, and hazards to the safety of the schoolchildren involved in a proposed plan. That these broad principles have developed in the context of dual school systems compelled or authorized by state statute at the time of *Brown v. Board of Education*, 347 U.S. 483, 74 S.Ct. 686, 98 L.Ed. 873 (1945) (*Brown I*), does not lessen their current applicability to dual systems found to exist in other contexts, like that in Detroit, where intentional school segregation does not stem from the compulsion of state law, but from deliberate individual actions of local and state school authorities directed at a particular school system. The majority properly does not suggest that the duty to eradicate completely the resulting dual system in the latter context is any less than in the former. But its reason for incapacitating the remedial authority of the federal judiciary in the presence of school district perimeters in the latter context is not readily apparent.

Justice MARSHALL, Justice DOUGLAS, and Justice BRENNAN concur in the dissent.

7. Justice Marshall Dissenting

In *Brown v. Board of Education*, 347 U.S. 483, 74 S.Ct. 686, 98 L.Ed. 873 (1954), this Court held that segregation of children in public schools on the basis of race deprives minority group children of equal educational opportunities and therefore

---

18. The Court has previously disapproved the implementation of proposed desegregation plans which operate to permit resegregation. *Monroe v. Board of Comm'rs*, 391 U.S. 450, 459–60, 88 S.Ct. 1700, 1705, 20 L.Ed.2d 733 (1968) ('free transfer' plan).

denies them the equal protection of the laws under the Fourteenth Amendment. This Court recognized then that remedying decades of segregation in public education would not be an easy task. Subsequent events, unfortunately, have seen that prediction bear bitter fruit. But however imbedded old ways, however ingrained old prejudices, this Court has not been diverted from its appointed task of making 'a living truth' of our constitutional ideal of equal justice under law. *Cooper v. Aaron*, 358 U.S. 1, 20, 78 S.Ct. 1401, 1410, 3 L.Ed.2d 5 (1958).

After 20 years of small, often difficult steps toward that great end, the Court today takes a giant step backwards. Notwithstanding a record showing widespread and pervasive racial segregation in the educational system provided by the State of Michigan for children in Detroit, this Court holds that the District Court was powerless to require the State to remedy its constitutional violation in any meaningful fashion. Ironically purporting to base its result on the principle that the scope of the remedy in a desegregation case should be determined by the nature and the extent of the constitutional violation, the Court's answer is to provide no remedy at all for the violation proved in this case, thereby guaranteeing that Negro children in Detroit will receive the same separate and inherently unequal education in the future as they have been unconstitutionally afforded in the past.

G. Commentary on *Milliken*

José Felipe Anderson

Perspectives on Missouri v. Jenkins

The question of implementing *Brown* was to be settled in *Brown II*. The Supreme Court, in discussing the remedial power of the lower courts to enforce the Court's desegregation mandate, instructed that

> [T]he courts will be guided by equitable principles. . . . Courts of equity may properly take into account the public interest in the elimination of such obstacles in a systematic and effective manner. But it should go without saying that the vitality of these constitutional principles cannot be allowed to yield simply because of disagreement with them.[19]

Following *Brown II*, a twenty-year struggle to implement desegregation ensued, primarily in the South, involving instances of "admitted state-imposed segregation."[20]

This resistance to *Brown* in many states, and the still-perplexing question of remedy, dimmed the hope that both the letter and the spirit of *Brown* would be realized. Litigation over various state efforts to avoid segregation followed *Brown II*,

---

19. *Brown II*, 349 U.S. 294, 300 (1955).

20. For an excellent, detailed discussion of the litigation that occurred between *Brown II* and *Milliken v. Bradley, see Betsy Levin & Philip Moise*, School Desegregation Litigation in the Seventies and the Use of Social Science Evidence: An Annotated Guide, 39 LAW AND CONTEMP. PROBS. 50, 57–114 (1975).

including plans that permitted students to transfer to a school where they would be in the majority.[21] For example, Prince Edward County, Virginia, suspended public funding of any school attended by both blacks and whites and paid tuition grants to white students who chose to attend non-sectarian private schools, creating a situation where African Americans were effectively denied education from 1959–1963.[22] In another case, the Supreme Court invalidated plans that sought to desegregate schools at a pace of "one year, one grade" for being too slow.[23] In 1968, in *Green v. New Kent County School Board*,[24] the Supreme Court invalidated a freedom-of-choice plan that allowed pupils to choose which public schools they would attend. During that period, the Court had, in several cases, compelled immediate desegregation without further delay, announced that desegregation would be eliminated "root and branch," and approved busing under certain circumstances.

Although the Court noted that there is no constitutional right to racial balance in and of itself, mathematical ratios demonstrating racial imbalance could serve as a starting point. By the early 1970s, the Supreme Court had made it clear that remedies fashioned by the district court "may be administratively awkward, inconvenient, and even bizarre in some situations." But by 1974, the Supreme Court had announced its decision in *Milliken v. Bradley*, where it held that federal remedial powers stop at the school district line, unless the nearby district or the state had contributed to the constitutional violation. The decision effectively brought to an end two decades of successful desegregation litigation in the court. In *Milliken*,

---

21. *Goss v. Bd. of Ed.*, 373 U.S. 683 (1963). In *Goss*, the Supreme Court struck down a transfer plan because of its unilateral effect on the composition of the schools. As the court explained, "[T]he right to transfer, which operates solely on the basis of racial classification is a one-way ticket leading to but one destination, i.e., the majority race of the transferee and continued segregation." *Id.* at 687.

22. In *Griffin v. School Bd. of Prince Edward County*, 377 U.S. 218 (1964), the Supreme Court invalidated this practice.

Virginia was not alone in its resistance to desegregation by attempting to destroy the local public school system. Another example was Macon County, Alabama, where in 1963, Governor George Wallace solicited state employees for financial assistance to begin a private school called the "Macon Academy." The Governor "encouraged white residents to boycott the public schools in Macon County and send their children to the newly formed, private, all-white" academy. Fred Grey, Bus Ride to Justice 212 (1995).

Some blacks faced the special challenge of being in the first generation of students to attend integrated schools after *Brown*. In his best-selling memoir, Nathan McCall recounts his experience in Virginia in 1966 at a predominantly white junior high school, which he attended instead of attending the school in his mostly black community. He writes, "The U.S. Supreme Court had long before ruled against the notion of separate but equal schools; still, Virginia, one of the states that had resisted desegregation, was slow in putting together a busing plan. . . . [L]ike many blacks then, my parents figured I could get a better education at the white school across town." Nathan McCall, Makes Me Wanna Holler 18 (1994). Difficulty adjusting to the majority white school and white students' refusal to accept McCall led to his suspension from that school, and to his parents' eventual decision to transfer him to his neighborhood school. *Id.* at 18–20.

23. *See Rogers v. Paul*, 382 U.S. 198 (1965).

24. *Green v. New Kent County Sch. Bd.*, 391 U.S. 430 (1968).

Chief Justice Burger held that the district court exceeded its authority when it ordered fifty-three suburban school districts to participate in the desegregation plan intended to desegregate the mostly black Detroit school system. Chief Justice Burger wrote that "[i]t is obvious from the scope of the interdistrict remedy itself that absent a complete restructuring of the laws of Michigan relating to school districts, the District Court will become . . . a *de facto* legislative authority . . . and the school superintendent for the entire area." The *Milliken* decision foreshadowed a period of uncertainty and confusion for the remedial power of the federal courts and called into question the continued validity of *Brown* and its progeny. By 1986, Justice Marshall would remark that he was aware in 1955 that the "all deliberate speed" remedial formula would signal "problems ahead . . . but I sure as hell never imagined we'd get to this sad state of affairs."[25]

39 *Howard Law Journal* 693, 701–4.
Copyright © (1996) *Howard Law Journal.*
Reprinted with permission of the *Howard Law Journal.*

Donald E. Lively

*The Constitution and Race**

In *Milliken* it was established that the Detroit School District purposely had created and maintained a segregated system. The trial court determined that the state had contributed significantly to that result. With respect to the city's role, the trial court specifically found that the school board had created and maintained optional attendance zones, bused students to distant schools for purposes of perpetuating segregation, and gauged construction policies to minimize mixing. It determined that the state had facilitated segregation by nullifying a voluntary desegregation plan, overseeing construction, implementing a transportation program that was racially steered and unequally funded, and sanctioning race-dependent attendance plans.

Despite the trial court's findings, the Supreme Court disagreed with the nature and extent of illegal state action. Although not foreclosing the use of interdistrict remedies as a matter of theory, the Court limited their operation to constitutional violations transcending a single district. Area-wide relief was unavailable as a practical matter, therefore barring a finding that district lines had been established or adjusted to foster segregation or that the racially discriminatory acts of one district had segregative effect in another. Without such a determination, the Court found that the scope of relief exceeded the nature of the constitutional violation.

---

25. *See* CARL T. ROWAN, DREAM MAKERS, DREAM BREAKERS 250 (1993). Former Chief Justice Earl Warren also voiced considerable surprise at the amount of resistance that the *Brown* decision encountered. "The Court expected some resistance from the South. But I doubt if any of us expected as much as we got." CHIEF JUSTICE EARL WARREN, THE MEMOIRS OF CHIEF JUSTICE EARL WARREN 290 (1977).

* (footnoted omitted).

In emphasizing local autonomy in education and minimizing the possibilities for cross-district relief, the Court effectively shielded most metropolitan areas from constitutional demands. As Justice White saw it, however, deliberate segregative acts and consequences were left unremedied, and similar results would follow elsewhere to the extent states vested "sufficient power over [their] public schools in [their] local school districts." He thus emphasized findings "that over a long period of years those in charge of the Michigan public schools engaged in various practices calculated to effect the segregation of the Detroit school system." Even if the state was implicated in fostering segregation, the Court was unwilling to impute the wrong to specific suburban districts.

The desegregation principle, having been circumscribed in *Keyes* by the *de jure/de facto* distinction, thus was narrowed further in *Milliken*. Reversal of the trial court decision communicated an attitude contrary to what the Court had radiated for nearly two decades. Federal courts, which had been rebuked for not going far enough in facilitating desegregation, were admonished for going too far. In contrast to the demand in *Green* for plans that work now, the circumscription of remedial potential in *Milliken* suggested the possibility that effective relief might not even be an option.

Exemption of suburban districts from remedial obligations reflected another significant doctrinal change. Previously, the Court had insisted on elimination of the vestiges of segregation, "root and branch." Without the possibility of interdistrict relief, it was evident that eradication processes might be partial rather than comprehensive. Such consequences have elicited criticism on the grounds that the Court has not only relaxed remedial obligations but also disregarded *Brown's* concern with equal educational opportunity. As Justice Marshall put it, the denial of a meaningful remedy afforded "no remedy at all . . . guaranteeing that Negro children . . . will receive the same separate and inherently unequal education in the future as they have been unconstitutionally afforded in the past."

The *Keyes* and *Milliken* decisions showed the Court's reluctance to adapt the desegregation principle to diverse circumstances of racial separation. Further indicating that the *Brown* mandate would not be a doctrine for all segregative seasons was a third limiting principle emphasizing that the duty to desegregate was not enduring. In *Milliken*, the Court had determined that constitutional obligations were subject to spatial restrictions. Its decision in *Pasadena City Board of Education v. Spangler* established qualifications also with respect to duration.

In *Spangler*, the Court determined that desegregation duties abated when a unitary system was established. [H]aving once implemented a racially neutral attendance pattern in order to remedy . . . perceived constitutional violations," new duties would not be imposed simply as a function of demographic change. Termination of remedial obligations, upon severance of the linkage between official act and segregative result was presented as an extension of the *de facto* concept. Further constitutional responsibility would not be imposed absent a showing of segregative action attributable to state or local authorities. The indication of *Spangler* was that

when a system becomes unitary, barring evidence of official tampering, school officials need not respond if the community resegregates. It is not a universally accepted
premise, however, that population redistribution after a desegregation order is constitutionally insignificant. The Court in *Spangler* attributed demographic consequences affecting the racial composition of schools to the "quite normal pattern
of human migration." Despite that characterization, it has been argued that a connection to official action exists, which the Court simply ignores. Justice Marshall
maintained that insofar as a state has "created a system where whites and Negroes
were intentionally kept apart so that they could not become accustomed to learning
together, [it] is responsible for the fact that many whites will react to the dismantling of that segregated system by attempting to flee to the suburbs."

The limiting principle enunciated in *Spangler* denied any such responsibility. To
the extent resegregation follows desegregation efforts and a linkage to official action
is not discerned, equal protection is not implicated. The promise of "a unitary
school system in which racial segregation [was] eliminated root and branch" thus
does not operate as a permanent guarantee of racially mixed education. Removal of
resegregation from a chain of events commenced by discriminatory practices and
policies was consistent with the liability-limiting nature of the *de facto* concept itself
and likewise reminiscent of how proximate causation principles operate. The practical consequence was further expansion of constitutionally permissible segregation. Desegregation in such cities as Boston, Detroit, Dayton, and San Francisco
was followed by declining white enrollment at rates ranging from 15 to 22 percent
during the implementation years themselves. Such an exodus, without the opportunity for interdistrict remedies, has helped make meaningful desegregation in urban
centers a mathematical impossibility.

Further diminishing the potential of the desegregation principle was the determination that education was not a fundamental right. The *Brown* Court had described
education as "importan[t] ... to our democratic society," and at least intimated
that it was of fundamental significance. That impression was reinforced in *Bolling
v. Sharpe*, when the Court referred to a "deprivation of ... liberty." In *San Antonio
Independent School District v. Rodriguez*, however, the Court declared that education was not a fundamental right and thus rejected the proposition that it must be
equally funded in all of a state's districts. The irony of the *Rodriguez* decision was
that disparities in educational quality, which theoretically might have been repaired
pursuant to the separate but equal doctrine, were no longer subject to constitutional
regulation.

For some, the devolution of the desegregation mandate in the 1970s was reminiscent of Fourteenth Amendment jurisprudence a century earlier. Responding to
what he perceived as unwarranted doctrinal retreat, Justice Marshall reminded that
"[d]esegregation is not and was never expected to be an easy task." What he saw
in principles limiting *Brown's* operation was a general sense that the desegregation
process "ha[d] gone far enough." Such an observation hints that, as in the *Civil
Rights Cases*, constitutional principle had reached the margins of societal tolerance

and interest had given way to fatigue. The narrowing of the desegregation principle also suggests that, at least with respect to its premise that the law "is powerless to eradicate social instincts," the *Plessy* Court did not entirely miscalculate.

> *The Constitution and Race* 123–25.
> Copyright © (1992) Donald E. Lively.
> Reprinted with permission of Donald E. Lively.

Milliken limits desegregation remedies to intradistrict solutions absent a showing of *de jure* segregation throughout the entire state or in the nearby district. Such a limitation has made the implementation of *Brown's* mandate virtually impossible due to the increase in racial segregation in housing resulting from white flight from previously segregated districts. So while Linda Brown and others similarly situated may have a constitutional right to a desegregated school, based upon subsequent Supreme Court reasoning, they have no constitutional remedy.

H. Background on *Adarand*

President Lyndon B. Johnson described the challenges that the nation would face as it began to implement desegregation and remedy years of damaging discrimination:

> You do not take a person who, for years, has been hobbled by chains and liberate him, bring him up to the starting line of a race, and then say, 'You are free to compete with all the others,' and still justly believe that you have been completely fair. Thus, it is not enough just to open the gates to opportunity. All our citizens must have the ability to walk through those gates. This is the next and the more profound stage of the battle for civil rights. We seek not just freedom but opportunity. We seek not just legal equity but human ability, not just equality as a right and a theory but equality as a fact and equality as a result.[26]

With those words, the federal government renewed its written commitment to removing the barriers to equal opportunity created by slavery, segregation, and discrimination, which had hampered Americans of African descent for nearly four centuries. In 1965, the American government promised blacks a better America, free from the barriers of discrimination that had denied them equal access to education, employment, housing, political participation, and the many other rights and privileges that white Americans enjoyed. In 1965 most Americans, having experienced or observed "Jim Crow's"[27] harmful impact on blacks, recognized that elimi-

---

26. President Lyndon B. Johnson, "To Fulfill These Rights" Commencement Speech at Howard University, June 4, 1965. II PUBLIC PAPERS OF THE PRESIDENTS: LYNDON B. JOHNSON 635–40 (1965).

27. The phrase "Jim Crow", which originated from a popular minstrel show act and song, became associated with the many laws throughout America designed to separate the races. The

nating the barriers to equal opportunity would require far more than a Supreme Court pronouncement that state-sponsored racial segregation was no longer lawful. "Affirmative Action," as President Johnson urged, would help to create equality.[28] While support for President Johnson's stated commitment was by no means universal, the President's position seemed to represent a consensus of the majority of Americans.[29] In fact, up until 1980, both major political parties supported affirmative action efforts.

Today, nearly four decades later, a growing number of Americans have voiced opposition to policies giving "preferential" treatment to women or specified racial or ethnic groups. Ironically, the Equal Protection Clause of the Fourteenth Amendment, created to reinforce the Thirteenth Amendment's promise of freedom and equality to the emancipated slave, has since become the primary weapon in the effort to end, or severely curtail, affirmative action policies in employment, education, and elsewhere.

Leslie Yalof Garfield

The Glass Half Full: Envisioning the Future of Race Preference Policies*

Allen Bakke, a white male, unsuccessfully applied for admission to the University of California at Davis Medical School in 1973 and in 1974. He challenged the school's 1973 admissions policy, which had been adopted in an effort to diversify the school's entering class, on the ground that it operated to exclude him on the basis of his race. Bakke argued that the policy violated the Equal Protection Clause, The California Constitution, and Title VI of the Civil Rights Act of 1964. The University of California's admissions policy divided applicants into two groups. One group comprised all non-minority applicants who had achieved a minimum 2.5 undergraduate grade point average; non-minority applicants falling short of this criterion were not considered. A separate "special admissions" group contained all "disadvantage" applicants in 1973 and minority applicants in 1974, irrespective of whether their undergraduate grade point average was above or below 2.5 The school set aside a certain number of seats for applicants in each of the groups. Individuals from the general applicant pool could not fill seats from the "special admissions" or

practical effect was to render black Americans second class citizens. *See* C. VANN WOODWARD, THE STRANGE CAREER OF JIM CROW 7 (1977).

28. President Kennedy coined the term "affirmative action" in Executive Order 10925, which he signed on March 6, 1963. The order, which forbade contractors doing business with the federal government from discriminating on the basis of race, reads in pertinent part "The contractor will take affirmative action to ensure that applicants are employed, and employees are treated during their employment without regard to their race, creed, color, or national origin." James E. Jones, Jr., *The Genesis and Present Status of Affirmative Action in Employment: Economic, Legal, and Political Realities*, 70 IOWA L. REV. 901, 901–2 (1985).

29. PUBLIC PAPERS OF THE PRESIDENTS: LYNDON B. JOHNSON Vol. II, at 284 (1965).

* (footnotes and chapter headings omitted).

minority applicant pool, even if seats were available after the admissions committee had considered all the minority applicants.

When U.C. Davis rejected Bakke in 1973, four seats reserved for applicants from the "special admissions" pool were unfilled while the seats for the general admission pool were filled. In 1974, U.C. Davis rejected Bakke once again, even though the school accepted minority applicants with lower test scores than his. Following the second rejection, Bakke sued the Regents of the University of California in state court, seeking an injunction to allow Bakke admission to U.C. Davis.

The trial court found that U.C. Davis's admissions policy was equivalent to a racial quota and held that it violated the California and United States Constitutions, as well as Title VI. A majority of the California Supreme Court affirmed the decision of the lower court and concluded that an entity is prohibited from considering the issue of race in programs that use government funds. Thus, the court ordered the University of California to admit Bakke into its medical school. Upon the state's appeal, the Supreme Court granted certiorari.

The Supreme Court considered both the Equal Protection Clause and Title VI and affirmed the California Supreme Court's decision. The Court was sharply divided in its reasoning. Justice Powell wrote the majority opinion, in which he recognized three issues needing resolution: first, whether the issue before the Court was reviewable under the fourteenth Amendment of the Constitution; second, if it decided the case on constitutional grounds, whether the "most rigid scrutiny" was the appropriate level of review for an affirmative action admissions policy challenged by a white male; and, finally, whether the admissions policy met its burden under that particular level of scrutiny.

Regarding the first issue, Justice Powell wrote that "decisions based on race or ethnic origin by faculties and administrations of state universities are reviewable under the Fourteenth Amendment." Programs or policies with "benign" racial classifications are permissible only if they withstand the Court's exacting scrutiny. Justice Powell would have permitted the University of California's admissions policy if it were "precisely tailored to serve a genesis of the "strict scrutiny" test. A state or state agency meets the strict scrutiny test when it demonstrates a compelling governmental interest and provides support that the program or policy it developed was narrowly tailored to help meet that compelling governmental interest.

Justice Powell found a compelling governmental interest in remedying the present effects of past discrimination and in "ameliorating . . . the disabling effects of identified discrimination." In this instance, however, there was no evidence in the relevant records that the purpose of the University of California's admissions policy was to meet either of these objectives. Justice Powell defined a second compelling governmental interest in creating a diverse student body. Justice Powell wrote:

> A great deal of learning occurs informally. It occurs through interactions
> among students of both sexes; of different races, religions, and backgrounds;

who come from cities and rural areas, from various states and countries; who have a wide variety of interests, talents, and perspectives; and who are able, directly or indirectly, to learn from their differences and to stimulate one another to reexamine even their most deeply held assumptions about themselves and their world.

According to Justice Powell, therefore, in the right instances, an institute of higher education could consider race as a factor in admissions decisions without impermissibly infringing on the Constitution.

While Justice Powell found a compelling governmental interest in the University of California's admissions policy goals, he did not find that the policy was narrowly tailored to meet that interest. The University of California's admissions policy, which set aside a specific number of seats for students in identified minority groups, created a quota that unfairly benefited the interests of a victimized group at the expense of other innocent individuals. Additionally, Justice Powell found that the school's practice of having separate admissions sub-committees review minority and non-minority candidates inappropriately insulated applicants from comparison against the entire admissions pool. Finally, according to Justice Powell, there were other, less restrictive means by which the University of California could have met its goals. For these reasons, Justice Powell concluded that the University of California's admissions policy violated the Equal Protection Clause and was, therefore, constitutionally impermissible.

Justices Brennan, Marshall, White, and Blackmun agreed with most of Justice Powell's reasoning, but disagreed with his finding that the University of California's program was unconstitutional, and, for that reason, they concurred in the judgment in part and dissented from the ruling. Specifically, the Justices agreed that racial classifications are not per se unconstitutional under the Fourteenth Amendment and that any race-preference programs should be subject to strict scrutiny. The four Justices, however, would have voted to uphold the University of California program since its

> purpose of remedying the effects of past societal discrimination is . . . sufficiently important to justify the use of race-conscious admissions programs where there is a sound basis for concluding that minority underrepresentation is substantial and chronic, and that the handicap of past discrimination is impeding access of minorities to the Medical School.

Justice Stevens concurred in the judgment in part and dissented in part. Chief Justice Burger and Justices Stewart and Rehnquist joined Justice Stevens's opinion. The Justices found that the University of California program violated Title VI and that therefore the program was invalid. Since these Justices were satisfied with their finding based on statutory grounds, they found no need to consider the constitutional issue.

The *Bakke* decision became the foundation upon which the Court would build its race-preference jurisprudence. The language of Justice Powell's reasoning in particular provided clear, identifiable rules for courts to apply when evaluating the constitutionality of race or ethnicity classifications under the Equal Protection Clause. The *Bakke* Court made clear that programs that use race as a factor must be subject to the strictest scrutiny. Furthermore, courts could uphold admissions policies that consider race as a factor in the decision-making process because of the identified constitutional interest in the non-remedial goal of promoting diversity in the classroom. A review of post-*Bakke* challenges illustrates the profound influence of the *Bakke* opinion, particularly Justice Powell's "majority of one."

Race-preference challenges are generally brought under the Fourteenth Amendment of the Constitution. The Fourteenth Amendment provides that "[n]o State shall . . . deny to any person within its jurisdiction the equal protection of the laws." The Court subjects state legislation or regulations challenged under the Equal Protection Clause to varying levels of scrutiny depending on the classification employed. At a minimum, the Court has held that any regulation must be "rationally related to a legitimate governmental purpose." Classifications based on race, however, are subject to the "strictest scrutiny." Under the strict scrutiny test, a challenged program passes constitutional muster only if it is both supported by a compelling governmental interest and narrowly tailored to meet that interest. The Court subjects classifications based on sex or illegitimacy to an intermediate level of scrutiny, between rational basis review and strict scrutiny.

The strict scrutiny test has its modern origins in First Amendment and Freedom of Association challenges. In the late 1950s and early 1960s, the Court used the test to protect individuals from excessive state infringement on their individual rights. In 1971, the Court in *Graham v. Richardson* concluded that classifications "based on nationality or race are inherently suspect and subject to close judicial scrutiny." Seven years after *Graham*, Justice Powell pronounced that the strict scrutiny test was the appropriate standard for reviewing equal protection challenges to race-preference policies.

The Court took the opportunity to define strict scrutiny more clearly the following year, when it decided *United States v. Paradise*. The Court in *Paradise* considered the constitutionality of a one-black-to-one-white promotion plan that the Alabama Department of Public Safety adopted pursuant to a district court consent decree. Since its mandate to promote some state troopers based on race was a race-conscious policy, the Court applied a standard of strict scrutiny. The Court said it would uphold the decree only if Alabama could demonstrate that its policy was "narrowly tailored to serve a compelling governmental purpose."

63 *N.Y.U. Ann. Surv. Am. L.* 385, 389–396.
Copyright © 2008 Annual Survey of American Law.
Reprinted with permission of Annual Survey of American Law
and Leslie Yalof Garfield.

I. *Adarand Constructors, Inc. v. Peña,* 515 U.S. 200 (1995)

William Perry Pendley, Denver, CO, for petitioner.

Drew S. Days, III, New Haven, CT, for respondents.

1. Facts

Justice O'CONNOR delivered the opinion of the Court.

Petitioner Adarand Constructors, Inc., claims that the Federal Government's practice of giving general contractors on government projects a financial incentive to hire subcontractors controlled by "socially and economically disadvantaged individuals," and in particular, the Government's use of race-based presumptions in identifying such individuals, violates the equal protection component of the Fifth Amendment's Due Process Clause. The Court of Appeals rejected Adarand's claim. We conclude, however, that courts should analyze cases of this kind under a different standard of review than the one the Court of Appeals applied. We therefore vacate the Court of Appeals' judgment and remand the case for further proceedings. In 1989, the Central Federal Lands Highway Division (CFLHD), which is part of the United States Department of Transportation (DOT), awarded the prime contract for a highway construction project in Colorado to Mountain Gravel & Construction Company. Mountain Gravel then solicited bids from subcontractors for the guardrail portion of the contract. Adarand, a Colorado-based highway construction company specializing in guardrail work, submitted the low bid. Gonzales Construction Company also submitted a bid.

The prime contract's terms provide that Mountain Gravel would receive additional compensation if it hired subcontractors certified as small businesses controlled by "socially and economically disadvantaged individuals," App. 24. Gonzales is certified as such a business; Adarand is not. Mountain Gravel awarded the subcontract to Gonzales, despite Adarand's low bid, and Mountain Gravel's Chief Estimator has submitted an affidavit stating that Mountain Gravel would have accepted Adarand's bid, had it not been for the additional payment it received by hiring Gonzales instead. *Id.,* at 28–31. Federal law requires that a subcontracting clause similar to the one used here must appear in most federal agency contracts, and it also requires the clause to state that "[t]he contractor shall presume that socially and economically disadvantaged individuals include Black Americans, Hispanic Americans, Native Americans, Asian Pacific Americans, and other minorities, or any other individual found to be disadvantaged by the [Small Business] Administration pursuant to section 8(a) of the Small Business Act." 15 U.S.C. §§ 637(d)(2),(3). Adarand claims that the presumption set forth in that statute discriminates on the basis of race in violation of the Federal Government's Fifth Amendment obligation not to deny anyone equal protection of the laws. . . .

After losing the guardrail subcontract to Gonzales, Adarand filed suit against various federal officials in the United States District Court for the District of Colorado, claiming that the race-based presumptions involved in the use of subcontracting compensation clauses violate Adarand's right to equal protection. The District Court granted the Government's motion for summary judgment. *Adarand Constructors, Inc. v. Skinner*, 790 F. Supp. 240 (1992). The Court of Appeals for the Tenth Circuit affirmed. 16 F.3d 1537 (1994). It understood our decision in *Fullilove v. Klutznick*, 448 U.S. 448, 100 S. Ct. 2758, 65 L. Ed. 2d 902 (1980), to have adopted "a lenient standard, resembling intermediate scrutiny, in assessing" the constitutionality of federal race-based action. 16 F.3d, at 1544. Applying that "lenient standard," as further developed in *Metro Broadcasting, Inc. v. FCC*, 497 U.S. 547, 110 S. Ct. 2997, 111 L. Ed. 2d 445 (1990), the Court of Appeals upheld the use of subcontractor compensation clauses. 16 F.3d, at 1547. We granted certiorari. . . .

2. Opinion

a. Equal Protection Case Law

The Government urges that "[t]he Subcontracting Compensation Clause program is . . . a program based on *disadvantage*, not on race," and thus that it is subject only to "the most relaxed judicial scrutiny." Brief for Respondents 26. To the extent that the statutes and regulations involved in this case are race neutral, we agree. The Government concedes, however, that "the race-based rebuttable presumption used in some certification determinations under the Subcontracting Compensation Clause" is subject to some heightened level of scrutiny. *Id.*, at 27. The parties disagree as to what that level should be. (We note, incidentally, that this case concerns only classifications based explicitly on race, and presents none of the additional difficulties posed by laws that, although facially race neutral, result in racially disproportionate impact and are motivated by a racially discriminatory purpose. See generally *Arlington Heights v. Metropolitan Housing Development Corp.*, 429 U.S. 252, 97 S. Ct. 555, 50 L. Ed.2d 450 (1977); *Washington v. Davis*, 426 U.S. 229, 96 S. Ct. 2040, 48 L. Ed.2d 597 (1976)). . . .

The Court's failure to produce a majority opinion in *Bakke, Fullilove*, and *Wygant* left unresolved the proper analysis for remedial race-based governmental action. See *United States v. Paradise*, 480 U.S., at 166, 107 S. Ct., at 1063 (plurality opinion of Brennan, J.) ("[A]lthough this Court has consistently held that some elevated level of scrutiny is required when a racial or ethnic distinction is made for remedial purposes, it has yet to reach consensus on the appropriate constitutional analysis"); *Sheet Metal Workers v. EEOC*, 478 U.S. 421, 480, 106 S. Ct. 3019, 3052, 92 L. Ed.2d 344 91986) (plurality opinion of Brennan, J.). Lower courts found this lack of guidance unsettling. See, *e.g., Kromnick v. School Dist. of Philadelphia*, 739 F.2d 894, 901 (CA3 1984) ("The absence of an Opinion of the Court in either *Bakker* or *Fullilove* and the concomitant failure of the Court to articulate an analytic framework supporting the judgments makes the position of the lower federal courts considering the constitutionality of affirmative action programs somewhat vulnerable"), cert. denied, 469 U.S. 1107, 105 S. Ct. 782, 83 L. Ed.2d 777 (1985); *Williams v. New Orleans*, 729 F.2d 1554, 1567 (CA5 1984) (en banc) (Higginbotham, J., concurring specially); *South Florida Chapter of Associated General Contractors of America, Inc. v.*

Metropolitan Dade County, Fla., 723 F.2d 846, 851 (CA11), cert. denied, 469 U.S. 871, 105 S. Ct. 220, 83 L. Ed.2d 150 (1984).

The Court resolved the issue, at least in part, in 1989. *Richmond v. J.A. Croson Co.*, 488 U.S. 469, 109 S. Ct. 706, 102 L. Ed.2d 854 (1989), concerned a city's determination that 30% of its contracting work should go to minority-owned businesses. A majority of the Court in *Croson* held that "the standard of review under the Equal Protection Clause is not dependent on the race of those burdened or benefitted by a particular classification," and that the single standard of review for racial classifications should be "strict scrutiny." *Id.*, at 493–94, 109 S. Ct., at 722 (opinion of O'CONNOR, J., joined by REHNQUIST, C.J., WHITE, and KENNEDY, JJ.); *id.* at 520, 109 S. Ct., at 735 (SCALIA, J., concurring in judgment) ("I agree . . . with Justice O'CONNOR's conclusion that strict scrutiny must be applied to all governmental classifications by race"). As to the classification before the Court, the plurality agreed that "a state or local subdivision . . . has the authority to eradicate the effects of private discrimination within its own legislative jurisdiction," *id.* at 491–92, 109 S. Ct., at 720–21, but the Court thought that the city had not acted with "a 'strong basis in evidence for its conclusion that remedial action was necessary,'" *id.*, at 500, 109 S. Ct., at 725 (majority opinion) quoting *Wygant, supra* at 277, 106 S. Ct., at 1849 (plurality opinion)). The Court also thought it "obvious that [the] program is not narrowly tailored to remedy the effects of prior discrimination." 488 U.S., at 508, 109 S. Ct., at 729–30. With *Croson*, the Court finally agreed that the Fourteenth Amendment requires strict scrutiny of all race-based action by state and local governments. But *Croson* of course had no occasion to declare what standard of review the Fifth Amendment requires for such action taken by the Federal Government. *Croson* observed simply that the Court's "treatment of an exercise of congressional power in *Fullilove* cannot be dispositive here," because *Croson's* facts did not implicate Congress' broad power under § 5 of the Fourteenth Amendment. *Croson*, 488 U.S., at 491, 109 S. Ct., at 720 (plurality opinion); *see also id.*, at 522, 109 S. Ct., at 737 (SCALIA, J., concurring in judgment) ("[W]ithout revisiting what we held in *Fullilove* . . . , I do not believe our decision in that case controls the one before us here"). On the other hand, the Court subsequently indicated that *Croson* had at least some bearing on federal race-based action when it vacated a decision upholding such action and remanded for further consideration in light of *Croson. H.K. Porter Co. v. Metropolitan Dade County*, 489 U.S. 1062, 109 S. Ct. 1333, 103 L. Ed.2d 804 (1989); *see also Shurberg Broadcasting of Hartford, Inc. v. FCC*, 876 F.2d 902, 915, n. 16 (CADC 1989) (opinion of Silberman, J.) (noting the Court's action in *H.K. Porter Co.*), rev'd *sub nom. Metro Broadcasting, Inc. v. FCC*, 497 U.S. 547, 110 S. Ct. 2997, 111 L. Ed.2d 445 (1990). Thus, some uncertainty persisted with respect to the standard of review for federal racial classifications. *See, e.g., Mann v. City of Albany, Ga.*, 883 F.2d 999, 1006 (CA11 1989) (*Croson* "may be applicable to race-based classifications imposed by Congress"); *Shurberg, supra*, at 910 (noting the difficulty of extracting general principles from the Court's fractured opinions); *id.*, at 959 (Wald, J., dissenting from denial of rehearing en banc) ("*Croson* certainly did not resolve the substantial questions posed by congressional programs which mandate the use of racial preferences"); *Winter Park Communications, Inc. v. FCC*, 873 F.2d 347, 366 (CADC 1989) (Williams, J., concurring in part and dissenting in part) ("The unresolved ambiguity of it impossible to reach a firm opinion as to the evidence of discrimination needed to sustain a congressional mandate of racial preferences"), aff'd *sub nom. Metro Broadcasting, supra.*

b. *Adarand* Rationale

Despite lingering uncertainty in the details, however, the Court's cases through *Croson* had established three general propositions with respect to governmental racial classifications. First, skepticism: "'[a]ny preference based on racial or ethnic criteria must necessarily receive a most searching examination.'" *Wygant*, 476 U.S., at 273, 106 S. Ct., at 1847 (plurality opinion of Powell, J.); *Fullilove*, 448 U.S., at 491, 100 S. Ct., at 2781 (opinion of Burger, C.J.); *see also id.*, at 523, 100 S. Ct., at 2798 (Stewart, J., dissenting) ("[A]ny official action that treats a person differently on account of his race or ethnic origin is inherently suspect"); *McLaughlin*, 379 U.S., at 192, 85 S. Ct., at 288 ("[R]acial classifications [are] 'constitutionally suspect'"); *Hirabayashi*, 320 U.S., at 100, 63 S. Ct., at 1385 ("Distinctions between citizens solely because of their ancestry are by their very nature odious to a free people"). Second, consistency: "the standard of review under the Equal Protection Clause is not dependent on the race of those burdened or benefitted by a particular classification," *Croson*, 488 U.S., at 494, 109 S. Ct., at 722 (plurality opinion); *id.*, at 520, 109 S. Ct., at 735 (Scalia, J., concurring in judgment); *see also Bakke*, 438 U.S., at 289–90, 98 S. Ct., at 2747–48 (opinion of Powell, J.), *i.e.*, all racial classifications reviewable under the Equal Protection Clause must be strictly scrutinized. And third, congruence: "[e]qual protection analysis in the Fifth Amendment area is the same as that under the Fourteenth Amendment," *Buckley v. Valeo*, 424 U.S., at 93, 96 S. Ct., at 670; *see also Weinberger v. Wiesenfeld*, 420 U.S., at 638, n. 2, 95 S. Ct., at 1228, n. 2; *Bolling v. Sharpe*, 347 U.S., at 500, 74 St. Ct., at 694. Taken together, these three propositions lead to the conclusion that any person, of whatever race, has the right to demand that any governmental actor subject to the Constitution justify any racial classification subjecting that person to unequal treatment under the strictest judicial scrutiny. Justice Powell's defense of this conclusion bears repeating here:

> "If it is the individual who is entitled to judicial protection against classifications based upon his racial or ethnic background because such distinctions impinge upon personal rights, rather than the individual only because of his membership in a particular group, then constitutional standards may be applied consistently. Political judgments regarding the necessity for the particular classification may be weighed in the constitutional balance, [*Korematsu*], but the standard of justification will remain constant. This is as it should be, since those political judgments are the product of rough compromise struck by contending groups within the democratic process. When they touch upon an individual's race or ethnic background, he is entitled to a judicial determination that the burden he is asked to bear on that basis is precisely tailored to serve a compelling governmental interest.

The Constitution guarantees that right to every person regardless of his background. *Shelley v. Kraemer*, 334 U.S. [1, 22, 68 S. Ct. 836, 846, 92 L. Ed. 1161 (1948)]." *Bakke*, 438 U.S., at 299, 98 S. Ct., at 2753 (opinion of Powell, J.) footnote omitted).

A year later, however, the Court took a surprising turn. *Metro Broadcasting, Inc. v. FCC*, 497 U.S. 547, 110 S. Ct. 2997, 111 L. Ed.2d 445 (1990), involved a Fifth Amendment challenge to two race-based policies of the Federal Communications Commission. In *Metro Broadcasting*, the Court repudiated the long-held notion that "it would be unthinkable that the same Constitution would impose a lesser duty on the Federal Government" than it does on a State to afford equal protection of the laws, *Bolling, supra*, at 500, 74 S. Ct., at 694. It did so by holding that "benign" federal racial classifications need only satisfy intermediate scrutiny, even though *Croson* had recently concluded that such classifications enacted by a State must satisfy strict scrutiny. "[B]enign" federal racial classifications, the Court said, "—even if those measures are not 'remedial' in the sense of being designed to compensate victims of past governmental or societal discrimination—are constitutionally permissible to the extent that they serve *important* governmental objectives within the power of Congress and are *substantially related* to achievement of those objectives." *Metro Broadcasting*, 497 U.S., at 564–65, 110 S. Ct., at 3008–9 (emphasis added). The Court did not explain how to tell whether a racial classification should be deemed "benign," other than to express "confiden[ce] that an 'examination of the legislative scheme and its history' will separate benign measures from other types of racial classifications." *Id.*, at 564, n. 12, 110 S. Ct., at 3009, n. 12 (citation omitted).

Applying this test, the Court first noted that the FCC policies at issue did not serve as a remedy for past discrimination. *Id.*, at 566, 110 S. Ct., at 3009. Proceeding on the assumption that the policies were nonetheless "benign," it concluded that they served the "important governmental objective" of "enhancing broadcast diversity," *id.*, at 566–67, 110 S. Ct., at 3009–10, and that they were "substantially related" to that objective, *id.*, at 569, 110 S. Ct., at 3011. It therefore upheld the policies.

By adopting intermediate scrutiny as the standard of review for congressionally mandated "benign" racial classifications, *Metro Broadcasting* departed from prior cases in two significant respects. First, it turned its back on *Croson's* explanation of why strict scrutiny of all governmental racial classifications is essential:

"Absent searching judicial inquiry into the justification for such race-based measures, there is simply no way of determining what classifications are 'benign' or 'remedial' and what classifications are in fact motivated by illegitimate notions of racial inferiority or simple racial politics. Indeed, the purpose of strict scrutiny is to 'smoke out' illegitimate uses of race by assuring that the legislative body is pursuing a goal important enough to warrant use of a highly suspect tool. The test also ensures that the means chosen 'fit' this compelling goal so closely that there is little or no possibility that the motive for the classification was illegitimate racial prejudice or stereotype." *Croson, supra*, at 493, 109 S. Ct., at 721 (plurality opinion of O'CONNOR, J.).

We adhere to that view today, despite the surface appeal of holding "benign" racial classifications to a lower standard, because "it may not always be clear that a so-called preference is in fact benign," *Bakke, supra,* at 298, 98 S. Ct., at 2752 (opinion of Powell, J.). "[M]ore than good motives should be required when government seeks to allocate its resources by way of an explicit racial classification system." Days, Fullilove, 96 Yale L.J. 453, 485 (1987). Second, *Metro Broadcasting* squarely rejected one of the three propositions established by the Court's earlier equal protection cases, namely, congruence between the standards applicable to federal and state racial classifications, and in so doing also undermined the other two — skepticism of all racial classifications, and consistency of treatment irrespective of the race of the burdened or benefitted group. *See supra,* at 2111–12. Under *Metro Broadcasting,* certain racial classifications ("benign" ones enacted by the Federal Government) should be treated less skeptically than others; and the race of the benefitted group is critical to the determination of which standard of review to apply. *Metro Broadcasting* was thus a significant departure from much of what had come before it.

The three propositions undermined by *Metro Broadcasting* all derive from the basic principle that the Fifth and Fourteenth Amendments to the Constitution protect *persons,* not *groups.* It follows from that principle that all governmental action based on race — a *group* classification long recognized as "in most circumstances irrelevant and therefore prohibited," *Hirabayashi, supra,* at 100, 63 S. Ct., at 1385 — should be subjected to detailed judicial inquiry to ensure that the *personal* right to equal protection of the laws has not been infringed. These ideas have long been central to this Court's understanding of equal protection, and holding "benign" state and federal racial classifications to different standards does not square with them. "[A] free people whose institutions are founded upon the doctrine of equality," *ibid.,* should tolerate no retreat from the principle that government may treat people differently because of their race only for the most compelling reasons. Accordingly, we hold today that all racial classifications, imposed by whatever federal, state, or local governmental actor, must be analyzed by a reviewing court under strict scrutiny. In other words, such classifications are constitutional only if they are narrowly tailored measures that further compelling governmental interests. To the extent that *Metro Broadcasting* is inconsistent with that holding, it is overruled. . . .

3. Holding

Our action today makes explicit what Justice Powell thought implicit in the *Fullilove* lead opinion: federal racial classifications, like those of a State, must serve a compelling governmental interest, and must be narrowly tailored to further that interest. . . .

4. Meaning of Strict Scrutiny

Finally, we wish to dispel the notion that strict scrutiny is "strict in theory, but fatal in fact." *Fullilove, supra,* at 519, 100 S. Ct., at 2795 (MARSHALL, J., concurring in judgment). The unhappy persistence of both the practice and the lingering effects of racial discrimination against minority groups in this country is an unfortunate reality, and government is not disqualified from acting in response to it. As recently as 1987, for example, every Justice of this Court agreed that the Alabama Department of Public Safety's "pervasive, systematic, and obstinate discriminatory conduct" justified a narrowly tailored race-based remedy. *See United States v. Paradise*, 480 U.S., at 167, 107 S. Ct., at 1064 (plurality opinion of Brennan, J.); *id.*, at 190, 107 S. Ct., at 1076 (STEVENS, J., concurring in judgment); *id.*, at 196, 107 S. Ct., at 1079–80 (O'CONNOR, J., dissenting). When race-based action is necessary to further a compelling interest, such action is within constitutional constraints if it satisfies the "narrow tailoring" test this Court has set out in previous cases.

5. Justice Scalia Concurring

In my view, government can never have a "compelling interest" in discriminating on the basis of race in order to "make up" for past racial discrimination in the opposite direction. . . . To pursue the concept of racial entitlement—even for the most admirable and benign of purposes—is to reinforce and preserve for future mischief the way of thinking that produced race slavery, race privilege and race hatred. In the eyes of government, we are just one race here. It is American.

6. Justice Stevens Dissenting

The consistency that the Court espouses would disregard the difference between a "No Trespassing" sign and a welcome mat. It would treat a Dixiecrat Senator's decision to vote against Thurgood Marshall's confirmation in order to keep African Americans off the Supreme Court as on a par with President Johnson's evaluation of his nominee's race as a positive factor. It would equate a law that made black citizens ineligible for military service with a program aimed at recruiting black soldiers. An attempt by the majority to exclude members of a minority race from a regulated market is fundamentally different from a subsidy that enables a relatively small group of newcomers to enter that market. An interest in "consistency" does not justify treating differences as though they were similarities.

The Court's explanation for treating dissimilar race-based decisions as though they were equally objectionable is a supposed inability to differentiate between "invidious" and "benign" discrimination. *Ante*, at 2112–13. But the term "affirmative action" is common and well understood. Its presence in everyday parlance shows that people understand the difference between good intentions and bad. As with any legal concept, some cases may be difficult to classify,[30] but our equal protection jurisprudence has identified a critical difference between state action that

---

30. For example, in *Richmond v. J.A. Croson Co.*, 488 U.S. 469, 109 S. Ct. 706, 102 L. Ed.2d 854 (1989), a majority of the members of the city council that enacted the race-based set-aside were of the same race as its beneficiaries.

imposes burdens on a disfavored few and state action that benefits the few "in spite of" its adverse effects on the many. *Feeney*, 442 U.S., at 279, 99 S. Ct., at 2296.

Indeed, our jurisprudence has made the standard to be applied in cases of invidious discrimination turn on whether the discrimination is "intentional," or whether, by contrast, it merely has a discriminatory "effect." *Washington v. Davis*, 426 U.S. 229, 96 S. Ct. 2040, 48 L. Ed.2d 597 (1976). Surely this distinction is at least as subtle, and at least as difficult to apply, *see id.*, at 253–54, 96 S. Ct., at 2054 (concurring opinion), as the usually obvious distinction between a measure intended to benefit members of a particular minority race and a measure intended to burden a minority race. A state actor inclined to subvert the Constitution might easily hide bad intentions in the guise of unintended "effects"; but I should think it far more difficult to enact a law intending to preserve the majority's hegemony while casting it plausibly in the guise of affirmative action for minorities.

Nothing is inherently wrong with applying a single standard to fundamentally different situations, as long as that standard takes relevant differences into account. For example, if the Court in all equal protection cases were to insist that differential treatment be justified by relevant characteristics of the members of the favored and disfavored classes that provide a legitimate basis for disparate treatment, such a standard would treat dissimilar cases differently while still recognizing that there is, after all, only one Equal Protection Clause. *See Cleburne v. Cleburne Living Center, Inc.*, 473 U.S. 432, 451–55, 105 S. Ct. 3249, 3260–62, 87 L. Ed.2d 313 (1985) (STEVENS, J., concurring); *San Antonio Independent School Dist. v. Rodriguez*, 411 U.S. 1, 98–110, 93 St. Ct. 1278, 1329–36, 36 L. Ed.2d 16 (1973) (MARSHALL, J., dissenting). Under such a standard, subsidies for disadvantaged businesses may be constitutional though special taxes on such businesses would be invalid. But a single standard that purports to equate remedial preferences with invidious discrimination cannot be defended in the name of "equal protection."

Moreover, the Court may find that its new "consistency" approach to race-based classifications is difficult to square with its insistence upon rigidly separate categories for discrimination against different classes of individuals. For example, as the law currently stands, the Court will apply "intermediate scrutiny" to cases of invidious gender discrimination and "strict scrutiny" to cases of invidious race discrimination, while applying the same standard for benign classifications as for invidious ones. If this remains the law, then today's lecture about "consistency" will produce the anomalous result that the Government can more easily enact affirmative-action programs to remedy discrimination against women than it can enact affirmative-action programs to remedy discrimination against African Americans—even though the primary purpose of the Equal Protection Clause was to end discrimination against the former slaves. *See Associated General Contractors of Cal., Inc. v. San Francisco*, 813 F.2d 922 (CA9 1987) (striking down racial preference under strict scrutiny while upholding gender preference under intermediate scrutiny). When a court becomes preoccupied with abstract standards, it risks sacrificing common sense at the altar of formal consistency. . . .

7. Justice Ginsburg Dissenting

The divisions in this difficult case should not obscure the Court's recognition of the persistence of racial inequality and a majority's acknowledgment of Congress' authority to act affirmatively, not only to end discrimination, but also to counteract discrimination's lingering effects. *Ante*, at 2117 (lead opinion); *see also ante*, at 2133 (Souter, J., dissenting). Those effects, reflective of a system of racial caste only recently ended, are evident in our workplaces, markets, and neighborhoods. Job applicants with identical resumes, qualifications, and interview styles still experience different receptions, depending on their race.[31] White and African-American consumers still encounter different deals.[32] People of color looking for housing still face discriminatory treatment by landlords, real estate agents, and mortgage lenders.[33] Minority entrepreneurs sometimes fail to gain contracts though they are the low bidders, and they are sometimes refused work even after winning contracts.[34] Bias both conscious and unconscious, reflecting traditional and unexamined habits of thought, keeps up barriers that must come down if equal opportunity and non-discrimination are ever genuinely to become this country's law and practice.

Justice Breyer concurred in Justice Ginsburg's dissent.

Justice Souter filed a separate dissent.

---

31. *See* H. Cross, et al., Employer Hiring Practices: Differential Treatment of Hispanic and Anglo Job Seekers 42 (Urban Institute Report 90–4, 1990) (Anglo applicants sent out by investigators received 52% more job offers than matched Hispanics); M. Turner, et al., Opportunities Denied, Opportunities Diminished: Racial Discrimination In Hiring xi (Urban Institute Report 91–9, 1991) ("In one out of five audits, the white applicant was able to advance farther through the hiring process than his black counterpart. In one out of eight audits, the white was offered a job although his equally qualified black partner was not. In contrast, black auditors advanced farther than their white counterparts only 7 percent of the time, and received job offers while their white partners did not in 5 percent of the audits.").

32. *See* Ayres, Fair Driving: Gender and Race Discrimination in Retail Car Negotiations, 104 Harv. L. Rev. 817, 821–22, 819, 828 (1991) ("blacks and women simply cannot buy the same car for the same price as can white men using identical bargaining strategies"; the final offers given white female testers reflected 40 percent higher markups than those given white male testers; final offer markups for black male testers were twice as high, and for black female testers three times as high as for white male testers).

33. *See* A Common Destiny: Blacks and American Society 50 (G. Jaynes & R. Williams eds., 1989) ("[I]n many metropolitan areas one-quarter to one-half of all [housing] inquiries by blacks are met by clearly discriminatory responses."); M. Turner, et al., U.S. Department of Housing and Urban Development, Housing Discrimination Study: Synthesis i–vii (1991) (9189 audit study of housing searches in 25 metropolitan areas; over half of African-American and Hispanic testers seeking to rent or buy experienced some form of unfavorable treatment compared to paired white testers); Leahy, Are Racial Factors Important for the Allocation of Mortgage Money?, 44 Am. J. Econ. & Soc. 185, 193 (1985) (controlling for socioeconomic factors, and concluding that "even when neighborhoods appear to be similar on every major mortgage-lending criterion except race, mortgage-lending outcomes are still unequal").

34. *See Associated General Contractors v. Coalition for Economic Equity*, 950 F.2d 1401, 1415 (CA9 1991) (detailing examples in San Francisco).

J. Commentary on *Adarand*

F. Michael Higginbotham

*Affirmative Action, Selective Memory Loss, and the Mistakes of Adarand**

To understand the flaws in the reasoning of *Adarand*, one must go back some one hundred years to the beginning of the affirmative action debate during Reconstruction. In the Civil Rights Cases of 1883, the Court held that the Fourteenth Amendment did not empower Congress to prohibit white owners of public accommodations from discriminating against black patrons. In his opinion for the Court, Justice Bradley made what was perhaps the first statement by a Supreme Court Justice against the concept of affirmative action. Justice Bradley wondered when black Americans would stop being given special treatment under the law. He stated:

When a man has emerged from slavery, and by the aid of beneficent legislation has shaken off the inseparable concomitants of that state, there must be some stage in the progress of his elevation when he takes the rank of a mere citizen, and ceases to be the special favorite of the laws. . . .

It is strange indeed that Justice Bradley believed that blacks had been the special favorites of the laws, when for two and one-half centuries they had been denied the right to vote, prohibited from acquiring knowledge, capital, or property, and designated as chattel. As a Civil War veteran, Justice Bradley presumably was familiar with the events leading to that conflict; obviously, he simply forgot about two hundred and fifty years of legally sanctioned oppression. Instead, he focused solely on Reconstruction-era civil rights legislation designed merely to grant black Americans the same constitutional rights as white Americans.

Unfortunately, five current members of the Supreme Court appear to suffer from the disease that afflicted Justice Bradley, namely, that infrequently diagnosed malady known as selective memory loss.

Writing for the Court in *Adarand*, Justice O'Connor concluded, "'[A] free people whose institutions are founded upon the doctrine of equality' should tolerate no retreat from the principle that government may treat people differently because of their race only for the most compelling reasons." For most of our nation's history, however, the Supreme Court interpreted the Constitution as not only tolerating just such a retreat, but condoning a frontal assault on equality for women and minorities. In the 1873 *Bradwell* case, the Court concluded that the Equal Protection Clause of the Fourteenth Amendment did not protect a woman against gender discrimination excluding her from the practice of law. In the 1899 *Cumming* case, the Court concluded that the Equal Protection Clause had not been violated by the denial of public high school education to black children. As recently as 1987,

---

* (footnotes omitted).

in *McClesky v. Kemp*, the Court concluded that the Equal Protection Clause had not been violated by the disproportionately high number of blacks receiving capital sentences in Georgia.

In *Adarand*, which makes it much more difficult for racial minorities and women to achieve significant economic power in this nation, the Supreme Court repeated the error of *Croson* and again demonstrated its unfamiliarity with the history of the Fourteenth Amendment. In the 1873 *Slaughter House Cases*, the first Supreme Court decision to construe the Equal Protection Clause of the Fourteenth Amendment, the Court declared that the pervading purpose of the amendment was "the freedom of the slave race, the security and firm establishment of that freedom, and the protection of the newly-made freeman and citizen from the oppressions of those who had formerly exercised unlimited dominion over him."

1995 *Annual Survey* 415, 415–18.
Copyright © (1995) *The Annual Survey of American Law.*
Reprinted with permission of *The Annual Survey of American Law.*

K. Background on *Grutter*

While *Adarand* involved affirmative action in government contracts, it was unclear how the strict scrutiny standard required for all race-based programs would apply in other contexts such as education. Strict scrutiny requires that measures must be narrowly tailored to further a compelling government interest. If the remedy targets only those who have been harmed by the discrimination, for example, then it is narrowly tailored. Remedial measures, actions designed to remedy the present effects of past intentional discrimination, have been characterized by the Supreme Court as compelling. What about circumstances where the entity in question has no history of *de jure* segregation or intentional discrimination? Some lower court decisions such as *Hopwood v. Texas* (78 F.3d 932 (CA5 1996)), holding that diversity in education is not a compelling state interest, indicated that the same affirmative action analysis used in *Adarand* should be applied to certain cases dealing with access to education, and that many affirmative action programs in education may not survive constitutional challenge.

L. *Grutter v. Bollinger*, 539 U.S. 306 (2003)

1. Facts

Justice O'CONNOR delivered the opinion of the Court.

This case requires us to decide whether the use of race as a factor in student admissions by the University of Michigan Law School [is] unlawful.

The Law School ranks among the Nation's top law schools. It receives more than 3,500 applications each year for a class of around 350 students. Seeking to "admit a group of students who individually and collectively are among the most capable," the Law School looks for individuals with "substantial promise for success in law school" and "a strong likelihood of succeeding in the practice of law and contributing in diverse ways to the well-being of others." App. 110. More broadly, the Law School seeks "a mix of students with varying backgrounds and experiences who will respect and learn from each other." *Ibid.* In 1992, the dean of the Law School charged a faculty committee with crafting a written admissions policy to implement these goals. In particular, the Law School sought to ensure that its efforts to achieve student body diversity complied with this Court's most recent ruling on the use of race in university admissions. *See Regents of Univ. of Cal. v. Bakke*, 438 U.S. 265, 57 L. Ed. 2d 750, 98 S. Ct. 2733 (1978). Upon the unanimous adoption of the committee's report by the Law School faculty, it became the Law School's official admissions policy.

The hallmark of that policy is its focus on academic ability coupled with a flexible assessment of applicants' talents, experiences, and potential "to contribute to the learning of those around them." App. 111. The policy requires admissions officials to evaluate each applicant based on all the information available in the file, including a personal statement, letters of recommendation, and an essay describing the ways in which the applicant will contribute to the life and diversity of the Law School. *Id.*, at 83–84, 114–21. In reviewing an applicant's file, admissions officials must consider the applicant's undergraduate grade point average (GPA) and Law School Admissions Test (LSAT) score because they are important (if imperfect) predictors of academic success in law school. *Id.*, at 112. The policy stresses that "no applicant should be admitted unless we expect that applicant to do well enough to graduate with no serious academic problems." *Id.*, at 111.

The policy makes clear, however, that even the highest possible score does not guarantee admission to the Law School. *Id.*, at 113. Nor does a low score automatically disqualify an applicant. *Ibid.* Rather, the policy requires admissions officials to look beyond grades and test scores to other criteria that are important to the Law School's educational objectives. *Id.*, at 114. So-called "soft variables" such as "the enthusiasm of recommenders, the quality of the undergraduate institution, the quality of the applicant's essay, and the areas and difficulty of undergraduate course selection" are all brought to bear in assessing an "applicant's likely contributions to the intellectual and social life of the institution." *Ibid.*

The policy aspires to "achieve that diversity which has the potential to enrich everyone's education and thus make a law school class stronger than the sum of its parts." *Id.*, at 118. The policy does not restrict the types of diversity contributions eligible for "substantial weight" in the admissions process, but instead recognizes "many possible bases for diversity admissions." *Id.*, at 118, 120. The policy does, however, reaffirm the Law School's longstanding commitment to "one particular type of diversity," that is, "racial and ethnic diversity with special reference to the inclusion of students from groups which have been historically discriminated against, like African-Americans, Hispanics and Native Americans, who without this commitment might not be represented in our student body in meaningful numbers." *Id.*, at 120. By enrolling a "'critical mass' of [underrepresented] minority students," the Law School seeks to "ensure their ability to make unique contributions to the character of the Law School." *Id.*, at 120–21.

The policy does not define diversity "solely in terms of racial and ethnic status." *Id.*, at 121. Nor is the policy "insensitive to the competition among all students for admission to the Law School." *Ibid.* Rather, the policy seeks to guide admissions officers in "producing classes both diverse and academically outstanding, classes made up of students who promise to continue the tradition of outstanding contribution by Michigan Graduates to the legal profession." *Ibid.*

Petitioner Barbara Grutter is a white Michigan resident who applied to the Law School in 1996 with a 3.8 grade point average and 161 LSAT score. The Law School initially placed petitioner on a waiting list, but subsequently rejected her application. In December 1997, petitioner filed suit in the United States District Court for the Eastern District of Michigan against the Law School, the Regents of the University of Michigan, Lee Bollinger (Dean of the Law School from 1987 to 1994, and President of the University of Michigan from 1996 to 2002), Jeffrey Lehman (Dean of the Law School), and Dennis Shields (Director of Admissions at the Law School from 1991 until 1998). Petitioner alleged that respondents discriminated against her on the basis of race in violation of the Fourteenth Amendment; Title VI of the Civil Rights Act of 1964, 78 Stat 252, *42 USC § 2000d* [*42 USCS § 2000d*]; and Rev Stat § 1977, as amended, *42 USC § 1981* [*42 USCS § 1981*].

Petitioner further alleged that her application was rejected because the Law School uses race as a "predominant" factor, giving applicants who belong to certain minority groups "a significantly greater chance of admission than students with similar credentials from disfavored racial groups." App. 33–34. Petitioner also alleged that respondents "had no compelling interest to justify their use of race in the admissions process." *Id.*, at 34. Petitioner requested compensatory and punitive damages, an order requiring the Law School to offer her admission, and an injunction prohibiting the Law School from continuing to discriminate on the basis of race. *Id.*, at 36. Petitioner clearly has standing to bring this lawsuit. *Northeastern Fla. Chapter, Associated Gen. Contractors of America v. Jacksonville*, 508 U.S. 656, 666, 124 L. Ed. 2d 586, 113 S. Ct. 2297 (1993) . . .

The District Court concluded that the Law School's use of race as a factor in admissions decisions was unlawful. Applying strict scrutiny, the District Court determined that the Law School's asserted interest in assembling a diverse student body was not compelling because "the attainment of a racially diverse class . . . was not recognized as such by *Bakke* and is not a remedy for past discrimination." *Id.*, at 246a. The District Court went on to hold that even if diversity were compelling, the Law School had not narrowly tailored its use of race to further that interest. The

District Court granted petitioner's request for declaratory relief and enjoined the Law School from using race as a factor in its admissions decisions. The Court of Appeals entered a stay of the injunction pending appeal.

Sitting en banc, the Court of Appeals reversed the District Court's judgment and vacated the injunction. The Court of Appeals first held that Justice Powell's opinion in *Bakke* was binding precedent establishing diversity as a compelling state interest. According to the Court of Appeals, Justice Powell's opinion with respect to diversity comprised the controlling rationale for the judgment of this Court under the analysis set forth in *Marks v. United States*, 430 U.S. 188, 51 L. Ed. 2d 260, 97 S. Ct. 990 (1977). The Court of Appeals also held that the Law School's use of race was narrowly tailored because race was merely a "potential 'plus' factor" and because the Law School's program was "virtually identical" to the Harvard admissions program described approvingly by Justice Powell and appended to his *Bakke* opinion. 288 F. 3d 732, 746, 749 (CA6 2002).

Four dissenting judges would have held the Law School's use of race unconstitutional. Three of the dissenters, rejecting the majority's *Marks* analysis, examined the Law School's interest in student body diversity on the merits and concluded it was not compelling. The fourth dissenter, writing separately, found it unnecessary to decide whether diversity was a compelling interest because, like the other dissenters, he believed that the Law School's use of race was not narrowly tailored to further that interest.

We granted certiorari, 537 U.S. 1043, 537 U.S. 1043, 154 L. Ed. 2d 514, 123 S. Ct. 617 (2002), to resolve the disagreement among the Courts of Appeals on a question of national importance: Whether diversity is a compelling interest that can justify the narrowly tailored use of race in selecting applicants for admission to public universities. *Compare Hopwood v. Texas*, 78 F.3d 932 (CA5 1996) (*Hopwood I*) (holding that diversity is not a compelling state interest), with *Smith v. University of Wash. Law School*, 233 F.3d 1188 (CA9 2000) (holding that it is).

2. Opinion

a. *Bakke* Decision

. . . Since this Court's splintered decision in *Bakke*, Justice Powell's opinion announcing the judgment of the Court has served as the touchstone for constitutional analysis of race-conscious admissions policies. Public and private universities across the Nation have modeled their own admissions programs on Justice Powell's views on permissible race-conscious policies. See, *e.g.*, Brief for Judith Areen et al. as *Amici Curiae* 12–13 (law school admissions programs employ "methods designed from and based on Justice Powell's opinion in *Bakke*"); Brief for Amherst College et al. as *Amici Curiae* 27 ("After *Bakke*, each of the *amici* (and undoubtedly other selective colleges and universities as well) reviewed their admissions procedures in light of Justice Powell's opinion . . . and set sail accordingly"). We therefore discuss Justice Powell's opinion in some detail.

Justice Powell began by stating that "the guarantee of equal protection cannot mean one thing when applied to one individual and something else when applied to a person of another color. If both are not accorded the same protection, then it is not equal." *Bakke*, 438 U.S., at 289–90, 57 L. Ed. 2d 750, 98 S Ct 2733. In Justice Powell's view, when governmental decisions "touch upon an individual's race or ethnic background, he is entitled to a judicial determination that the burden he is asked to bear on that basis is precisely tailored to serve a compelling governmental interest." *Id., at 299, 57 L. Ed. 2d 750, 98 S Ct 2733.* Under this exacting standard, only one of the interests asserted by the university survived Justice Powell's scrutiny.

First, Justice Powell rejected an interest in "'reducing the historic deficit of traditionally disfavored minorities in medical schools and in the medical profession'" as an unlawful interest in racial balancing. *Id., at 306–7, 57 L. Ed. 2d 750, 98 S Ct 2733.* Second, Justice Powell rejected an interest in remedying societal discrimination because such measures would risk placing unnecessary burdens on innocent third parties "who bear no responsibility for whatever harm the beneficiaries of the special admissions program are thought to have suffered." *Id., at 310, 57 L. Ed. 2d 750, 98 S Ct 2733.* Third, Justice Powell rejected an interest in "increasing the number of physicians who will practice in communities currently underserved," concluding that even if such an interest could be compelling in some circumstances the program under review was not "geared to promote that goal." *Id., at 306, 310, 57 L. Ed. 2d 750, 98 S Ct 2733.*

Justice Powell approved the university's use of race to further only one interest: "the attainment of a diverse student body." *Id., at 311, 57 L. Ed. 2d 750, 98 S. Ct. 2733.* With the important proviso that "constitutional limitations protecting individual rights may not be disregarded," Justice Powell grounded his analysis in the academic freedom that "long has been viewed as a special concern of the *First Amendment.*" *Id., at 312, 314, 57 L. Ed. 2d 750, 98 S. Ct. 2733.* Justice Powell emphasized that nothing less than the "'nation's future depends upon leaders trained through wide exposure' to the ideas and mores of students as diverse as this Nation of many peoples." *Id., at 313, 57 L. Ed. 2d 750, 98 S. Ct. 2733* (quoting *Keyishian v. Board of Regents of Univ. of State of N. Y.,* 385 U.S. 589, 603, 17 L. Ed. 2d 629, 87 S. Ct. 675*(1967))*. In seeking the "right to select those students who will contribute the most to the 'robust exchange of ideas,'" a university seeks "to achieve a goal that is of paramount importance in the fulfillment of its mission." *438 U.S., at 313, 57 L. Ed. 2d 750, 98 S. Ct. 2733.* Both "tradition and experience lend support to the view that the contribution of diversity is substantial." *Ibid.*

Justice Powell was, however, careful to emphasize that in his view race "is only one element in a range of factors a university properly may consider in attaining the goal of a heterogeneous student body." *Id., at 314, 57 L. Ed. 2d 750, 98 S. Ct. 2733.* For Justice Powell, "it is not an interest in simple ethnic diversity, in which a specified percentage of the student body is in effect guaranteed to be members of selected ethnic groups," that can justify the use of race. *Id., at 315, 57 L. Ed. 2d 750, 98 S. Ct. 2733.* Rather, "the diversity that furthers a compelling state interest encompasses a far broader array of qualifications and characteristics of which racial or ethnic origin is but a single though important element." *Ibid.*

In the wake of our fractured decision in *Bakke,* courts have struggled to discern whether Justice Powell's diversity rationale, set forth in part of the opinion joined by no other Justice, is nonetheless binding precedent under *Marks.* In that case, we explained that "when a fragmented Court decides a case and no single rationale explaining the result enjoys the assent of five Justices, the holding of the Court may be viewed as that position taken by those Members who concurred in the judgments on the narrowest grounds." *430 U.S., at 193,* 51 L. Ed. 2d 260, 97 S. Ct. 990 (internal quotation marks and citation omitted). As the divergent opinions of the lower courts demonstrate, however, "this test is more easily stated than applied to the various opinions supporting the result in [*Bakke*]." *Nichols v. United States,* 511 U.S. 738, 745–46, 128 L. Ed. 2d 745, 114 S. Ct. 1921*(1994).* Compare, *e.g., Johnson v. Board of Regents of Univ. of Ga., 263 F.3d 1234 (CA11 2001)* (Justice Powell's diversity rationale was not the holding of the Court); *Hopwood v. Texas, 236 F.3d 256, 274–75 (CA5 2000) (Hopwood II)* (same); *Hopwood I,* 78 F. 3d 932 (same), with *Smith v. University of Wash. Law School,* 233 F. 3d 1199 (Justice Powell's opinion, including the diversity rationale, is controlling under *Marks*).

We do not find it necessary to decide whether Justice Powell's opinion is binding under *Marks.* It does not seem "useful to pursue the *Marks* inquiry to the utmost logical possibility when it has so obviously baffled and divided the lower courts that have considered it." *Nichols v. United States, supra, at 745–46,* 128 L. Ed. 2d 745, 114 S. Ct. 1921. More important, for the reasons set out below, today we endorse Justice Powell's view that student body diversity is a compelling state interest that can justify the use of race in university admissions.

b. Equal Protection Rationale

The *Equal Protection Clause* provides that no State shall "deny to any person within its jurisdiction the equal protection of the laws." *U.S. Const., Amdt. 14, §2.* Because the *Fourteenth Amendment* "protects *persons,* not *groups,*" all "governmental action based on race—a *group* classification long recognized as in most circumstances irrelevant and therefore prohibited—should be subjected to detailed judicial inquiry to ensure that the *personal* right to equal protection of the laws has not been infringed." *Adarand Constructors, Inc. v. Peña,* 515 U.S. 200, 227, 132 L. Ed. 2d 158, 115 S. Ct. 2097 *(1995)* (emphasis in original; internal quotation marks and citation omitted). We are a "free people whose institutions are founded upon the doctrine of equality." *Loving v. Virginia, 388* U.S. 1, 11, 18 L. Ed. 2d 1010, 87 S. Ct. 1817*(1967)* (internal quotation marks and citation omitted). It follows from that principle that "government may treat people differently because of their race only for the most compelling reasons." *Adarand Constructors, Inc. v. Peña, 515 U.S., at 227,* 132 L Ed 2d 158, 115 S Ct 2097.

We have held that all racial classifications imposed by government "must be analyzed by a reviewing court under strict scrutiny." *Ibid.* This means that such classifications are constitutional only if they are narrowly tailored to further compelling governmental interests. "Absent searching judicial inquiry into the justification for such race-based measures," we have no way to determine what "classifications are 'benign' or 'remedial' and what classifications are in fact motivated by illegitimate notions of racial inferiority or simple racial politics." *Richmond v. J. A. Croson Co.*, 488 U.S. 469, 493, 102 L. Ed. 2d 854, 109 S. Ct. 706 *(1989)* (plurality opinion). We apply strict scrutiny to all racial classifications to "'smoke out' illegitimate uses of race by assuring that [government] is pursuing a goal important enough to warrant use of a highly suspect tool." *Ibid.*

Strict scrutiny is not "strict in theory, but fatal in fact." *Adarand Constructors, Inc. v. Peña, supra, at 237,* 132 L. Ed. 2d 158, 115 S. Ct. 2097 (internal quotation marks and citation omitted). Although all governmental uses of race are subject to strict scrutiny, not all are invalidated by it. As we have explained, "whenever the government treats any person unequally because of his or her race, that person has suffered an injury that falls squarely within the language and spirit of the Constitution's guarantee of equal protection." *515 U.S., at 229–30,* 132 L Ed 2d 158, 115 S. Ct. 2097. But that observation "says nothing about the ultimate validity of any particular law; that determination is the job of the court applying strict scrutiny." *Id., at 230,* 132 L. Ed. 2d 158, 115 S. Ct. 2097. When race-based action is necessary to further a compelling governmental interest, such action does not violate the constitutional guarantee of equal protection so long as the narrow-tailoring requirement is also satisfied.

Context matters when reviewing race-based governmental action under the *Equal Protection Clause. See Gomillion v. Lightfoot,* 364 U.S. 339, 343–44, 5 L. Ed. 2d 110, 81 S. Ct. 125 *(1960)* (admonishing that, "in dealing with claims under broad provisions of the Constitution, which derive content by an interpretive process of inclusion and exclusion, it is imperative that generalizations, based on and qualified by the concrete situations that gave rise to them, must not be applied out of context in disregard of variant controlling facts"). In *Adarand Constructors, Inc.* v. *Peña,* we made clear that strict scrutiny must take "'relevant differences' into account." *515 U.S., at 228,* 132 L. Ed. 2d 158, 115 S. Ct. 2097. Indeed, as we explained, that is its "fundamental purpose." *Ibid.* Not every decision influenced by race is equally objectionable and strict scrutiny is designed to provide a framework for carefully examining the importance and the sincerity of the reasons advanced by the governmental decisionmaker for the use of race in that particular context.

c. Compelling State Interest

With these principles in mind, we turn to the question whether the Law School's use of race is justified by a compelling state interest. Before this Court, as they have throughout this litigation, respondents assert only one justification for their use of race in the admissions process: obtaining "the educational benefits that flow from a diverse student body." Brief for Respondents Bollinger et al. In other words, the Law School asks us to recognize, in the context of higher education, a compelling state interest in student body diversity.

We first wish to dispel the notion that the Law School's argument has been fore-closed, either expressly or implicitly, by our affirmative-action cases decided since *Bakke*. It is true that some language in those opinions might be read to suggest that remedying past discrimination is the only permissible justification for race-based governmental action. See, *e.g., Richmond v. J. A. Croson Co., supra, at 493,* 102 L. Ed. 2d 854, 109 S. Ct. 706 (plurality opinion) (stating that unless classifications based on race are "strictly reserved for remedial settings, they may in fact promote notions of racial inferiority and lead to a politics of racial hostility"). But we have never held that the only governmental use of race that can survive strict scrutiny is remedying past discrimination. Nor, since *Bakke*, have we directly addressed the use of race in the context of public higher education. Today, we hold that the Law School has a compelling interest in attaining a diverse student body.

The Law School's educational judgment that such diversity is essential to its edu-cational mission is one to which we defer. The Law School's assessment that diver-sity will, in fact, yield educational benefits is substantiated by respondents and their *amici.* Our scrutiny of the interest asserted by the Law School is no less strict for taking into account complex educational judgments in an area that lies primarily within the expertise of the university. Our holding today is in keeping with our tradition of giving a degree of deference to a university's academic decisions, within constitutionally prescribed limits. See *Regents of Univ. of Mich. v. Ewing,* 474 U.S. 214, 225, 88 L. Ed. 2d 523, 106 S. Ct. 507 *(1985); Board of Curators of Univ. of Mo. v. Horowitz,* 435 U.S. 78, 96, n. 6, 55 L. Ed. 2d 124, 98 S. Ct. 948 *(1978); Bakke, 438 U.S., at 319, n. 53,* 57 L. Ed. 2d 750, 98 S. Ct. 2733 (opinion of Powell, J.).

We have long recognized that, given the important purpose of public education and the expansive freedoms of speech and thought associated with the university environment, universities occupy a special niche in our constitutional tradition. *See, e.g., Wieman v. Updegraff,* 344 U.S. 183, 195, 97 L. Ed. 216, 73 S. Ct. 215 *(1952)* (Frankfurter, J., concurring); *Sweezy v. New Hampshire,* 354 U.S. 234, 250, 1 L. Ed. 2d 1311, *77 S. Ct. 1203 (1957); Shelton v. Tucker,* 364 U.S. 479, 487, 5 L. Ed. 2d 231, 81 S. Ct. 247 *(1960); Keyishian v. Board of Regents of Univ. of State of N. Y.,* 385 U.S., at 603, 17 L. Ed. 2d 629, 87 S. Ct. 675. In announcing the principle of student body diversity as a compelling state interest, Justice Powell invoked our cases recogniz-ing a constitutional dimension, grounded in the *First Amendment,* of educational autonomy: "The freedom of a university to make its own judgments as to education includes the selection of its student body." *Bakke, supra, at 312,* 57 L. Ed. 2d 750, 98 S. Ct. 2733. From this premise, Justice Powell reasoned that by claiming "the right to select those students who will contribute the most to the 'robust exchange of ideas,'" a university "seeks to achieve a goal that is of paramount importance in the fulfillment of its mission." 438 U.S., at 313, 57 L. Ed. 2d 750, 98 S. Ct. 2733 (quot-ing *Keyishian v. Board of Regents of Univ. of State of N. Y., supra, at 603,* 17 L Ed 2d 629, 87 S. Ct. 675). Our conclusion that the Law School has a compelling interest in a diverse student body is informed by our view that attaining a diverse student body is at the heart of the Law School's proper institutional mission, and that "good faith" on the part of a university is "presumed" absent "a showing to the contrary." 438 U.S., at 318–19, 57 L. Ed. 2d 750, 98 S. Ct. 2733.

As part of its goal of "assembling a class that is both exceptionally academically qualified and broadly diverse," the Law School seeks to "enroll a 'critical mass' of minority students." Brief for Respondents Bollinger et al. 13. The Law School's interest is not simply "to assure within its student body some specified percentage of a particular group merely because of its race or ethnic origin." *Bakke*, 438 U.S., at 307, 57 L. Ed. 2d 750, 98 S. Ct. 2733 (opinion of Powell, J.). That would amount to outright racial balancing, which is patently unconstitutional. *Ibid.; Freeman v. Pitts,* 503 U.S. 467, 494, 118 L. Ed. 2d 108, *112 S. Ct. 1430 (1992)* ("Racial balance is not to be achieved for its own sake"); *Richmond v. J. A. Croson Co., 488* U.S., at 507, 102 L Ed 2d 854, 109 S. Ct. 706. Rather, the Law School's concept of critical mass is defined by reference to the educational benefits that diversity is designed to produce.

These benefits are substantial. As the District Court emphasized, the Law School's admissions policy promotes "cross-racial understanding," helps to break down racial stereotypes, and "enables [students] to better understand persons of different races." App. to Pet. for Cert. 246a. These benefits are "important and laudable," because "classroom discussion is livelier, more spirited, and simply more enlightening and interesting" when the students have "the greatest possible variety of backgrounds." *Id.,* at 246a, 244a.

The Law School's claim of a compelling interest is further bolstered by its *amici,* who point to the educational benefits that flow from student body diversity. In addition to the expert studies and reports entered into evidence at trial, numerous studies show that student body diversity promotes learning outcomes, and "better prepares students for an increasingly diverse workforce and society, and better prepares them as professionals." Brief for American Educational Research Association et al. as *Amici Curiae* 3; see, *e.g.,* W. Bowen & D. Bok, The Shape of the River (1998); Diversity Challenged: Evidence on the Impact of Affirmative Action (G. Orfield & M. Kurlaender eds. 2001); Compelling Interest: Examining the Evidence on Racial Dynamics in Colleges and Universities (M. Chang, D. Witt, J. Jones, & K. Hakuta eds. 2003).

These benefits are not theoretical but real, as major American businesses have made clear that the skills needed in today's increasingly global marketplace can only be developed through exposure to widely diverse people, cultures, ideas, and viewpoints. Brief for 3M et al. as *Amici Curiae* 5; Brief for General Motors Corp. as *Amicus Curiae* 3–4. What is more, high-ranking retired officers and civilian leaders of the United States military assert that, "based on [their] decades of experience," a "highly qualified, racially diverse officer corps . . . is essential to the military's ability to fulfill its principle mission to provide national security." Brief for Julius W. Becton, Jr. et al. as *Amici Curiae* 27. The primary sources for the Nation's officer corps are the service academies and the Reserve Officers Training Corps (ROTC), the latter comprising students already admitted to participating colleges and universities. *Id.,* at 5. At present, "the military cannot achieve an officer corps that is *both* highly qualified *and* racially diverse unless the service academies and the ROTC used limited race-conscious recruiting and admissions policies." *Ibid.* (emphasis in original). To fulfill its mission, the military "must be selective in admissions for training and education for the officer corps, *and* it must train and educate a highly qualified, racially diverse officer corps in a racially diverse setting." *Id.*, at 29 (emphasis in original). We agree that "it requires only a small step from this analysis to conclude that our country's other most selective institutions must remain both diverse and selective." Ibid.

We have repeatedly acknowledged the overriding importance of preparing students for work and citizenship, describing education as pivotal to "sustaining our political and cultural heritage" with a fundamental role in maintaining the fabric of society. *Plyler v. Doe,* 457 U.S. 202, 221, 72 L. Ed. 2d 786, 102 S. Ct. 2382 *(1982).* This Court has long recognized that "education . . . is the very foundation of good citizenship." *Brown v. Board of Education,* 347 U.S. 483, 493, 98 L. Ed. 873, 74 S. Ct. 686 *(1954).* For this reason, the diffusion of knowledge and opportunity through public institutions of higher education must be accessible to all individuals regardless of race or ethnicity. The United States, as *amicus curiae,* affirms that "ensuring that public institutions are open and available to all segments of American society, including people of all races and ethnicities, represents a paramount government objective." Brief for United States as *Amicus Curiae* 13. And, "nowhere is the importance of such openness more acute than in the context of higher education." *Ibid.* Effective participation by members of all racial and ethnic groups in the civic life of our Nation is essential if the dream of one Nation, indivisible, is to be realized.

Moreover, universities, and in particular, law schools, represent the training ground for a large number of our Nation's leaders. *Sweatt v. Painter,* 339 U.S. 629, 634, 94 L. Ed. 1114, 70 S. Ct. 848 (1950) (describing law school as a "proving ground for legal learning and practice"). Individuals with law degrees occupy roughly half the state governorships, more than half the seats in the United States Senate, and more than a third of the seats in the United States House of Representatives. See Brief for Association of American Law Schools as *Amicus Curiae* 5–6. The pattern is even more striking when it comes to highly selective law schools. A handful of these schools accounts for 25 of the 100 United States Senators, 74 United States Courts of Appeals judges, and nearly 200 of the more than 600 United States District Court judges. *Id.*, at 6.

In order to cultivate a set of leaders with legitimacy in the eyes of the citizenry, it is necessary that the path to leadership be visibly open to talented and qualified individuals of every race and ethnicity. All members of our heterogeneous society must have confidence in the openness and integrity of the educational institutions that provide this training. As we have recognized, law schools "cannot be effective in isolation from the individuals and institutions with which the law interacts." See *Sweatt v. Painter, supra, at* 634, 94 L. Ed. 1114, 70 S. Ct. 848. Access to legal education (and thus the legal profession) must be inclusive of talented and qualified individuals of every race and ethnicity, so that all members of our heterogeneous society may participate in the educational institutions that provide the training and education necessary to succeed in America.

The Law School does not premise its need for critical mass on "any belief that minority students always (or even consistently) express some characteristic minority viewpoint on any issue." Brief for Respondent Bollinger et al. 30. To the contrary, diminishing the force of such stereotypes is both a crucial part of the Law School's mission, and one that it cannot accomplish with only token numbers of minority students. Just as growing up in a particular region or having particular professional experiences is likely to affect an individual's views, so too is one's own, unique experience of being a racial minority in a society, like our own, in which race unfortunately still matters. The Law School has determined, based on its experience and expertise, that a "critical mass" of underrepresented minorities is necessary to further its compelling interest in securing the educational benefits of a diverse student body.

d. Narrowly Tailored

Even in the limited circumstance when drawing racial distinctions is permissible to further a compelling state interest, government is still "constrained in how it may pursue that end: [T]he means chosen to accomplish the [government's] asserted purpose must be specifically and narrowly framed to accomplish that purpose." *Shaw v. Hunt,* 517 U.S. 899, 908, 135 L. Ed. 2d 207, 116 S. Ct. 1894 (1996) (internal quotation marks and citation omitted). The purpose of the narrow tailoring requirement is to ensure that "the means chosen 'fit' . . . the compelling goal so closely that there is little or no possibility that the motive for the classification was illegitimate racial prejudice or stereotype." *Richmond v. J. A. Croson Co.,* 488 U.S., at 493, 102 L. Ed. 2d 854, 109 S. Ct. 706 (plurality opinion).

Since *Bakke,* we have had no occasion to define the contours of the narrow-tailoring inquiry with respect to race-conscious university admissions programs. That inquiry must be calibrated to fit the distinct issues raised by the use of race to achieve student body diversity in public higher education. Contrary to Justice Kennedy's assertions, we do not "abandon[ ] strict scrutiny," see *post,* at *156 L. Ed. 2d, at 374* (dissenting opinion). Rather, as we have already explained, *ante, at 156 L. Ed. 2d, at 331,* we adhere to *Adarand*'s teaching that the very purpose of strict scrutiny is to take such "relevant differences into account." 515 U.S., at 228, 132 L. Ed. 2d 158, 115 S. Ct. 2097 (internal quotation marks omitted).

To be narrowly tailored, a race-conscious admissions program cannot use a quota system — it cannot "insulate each category of applicants with certain desired qualifications from competition with all other applicants." *Bakke, supra, at 315, 57 L. Ed. 2d 750, 98 S. Ct. 2733* (opinion of Powell, J.). Instead, a university may consider race or ethnicity only as a "'plus' in a particular applicant's file," without "insulating the individual from comparison with all other candidates for the available seats." *Id., at 317,* 57 L Ed 2d 750, 98 S. Ct. 2733. In other words, an admissions program must be "flexible enough to consider all pertinent elements of diversity in light of the particular qualifications of each applicant, and to place them on the same footing for consideration, although not necessarily according them the same weight." *Ibid.*

We find that the Law School's admissions program bears the hallmarks of a narrowly tailored plan. As Justice Powell made clear in *Bakke*, truly individualized consideration demands that race be used in a flexible, nonmechanical way. It follows from this mandate that universities cannot establish quotas for members of certain racial groups or put members of those groups on separate admissions tracks. See *id., at* 315–16, 57 L. Ed. 2d 750, 98 S. Ct. 2733. Nor can universities insulate applicants who belong to certain racial or ethnic groups from the competition for admission. *Ibid.* Universities can, however, consider race or ethnicity more flexibly as a "plus" factor in the context of individualized consideration of each and every applicant. *Ibid.*

We are satisfied that the Law School's admissions program, like the Harvard plan described by Justice Powell, does not operate as a quota. Properly understood, a "quota" is a program in which a certain fixed number or proportion of opportunities are "reserved exclusively for certain minority groups." *Richmond v. J. A. Croson Co., supra, at* 496, 102 L. Ed. 2d 854, 109 S Ct 706 (plurality opinion). Quotas "'impose a fixed number or percentage which must be attained, or which cannot be exceeded,'" *Local 28 of Sheet Metal Workers v. EEOC*, 478 U.S. 421, 495, 92 L. Ed. 2d 344, 106 S. Ct. 3019 *(1986)* (O'Connor, J., concurring in part and dissenting in part), and "insulate the individual from comparison with all other candidates for the available seats." *Bakke, supra, at 317, 57 L. Ed. 2d 750, 98 S. Ct. 2733* (opinion of Powell, J.). In contrast, "a permissible goal . . . requires only a good-faith effort . . . to come within a range demarcated by the goal itself," *Sheet Metal Workers v. EEOC, supra, at 495*, 92 L. Ed. 2d 344, 106 S. Ct. 3019, and permits consideration of race as a "plus" factor in any given case while still ensuring that each candidate "competes with all other qualified applicants," *Johnson v. Transportation Agency, Santa Clara Cty.*, 480 U.S. 616, 638, 94 L. Ed. 2d 615, 107 S. Ct. 1442*(1987)*.

Justice Powell's distinction between the medical school's rigid 16-seat quota and Harvard's flexible use of race as a "plus" factor is instructive. Harvard certainly had minimum *goals* for minority enrollment, even if it had no specific number firmly in mind. *See Bakke, supra,* at 323, 57 L. Ed. 2d 750, 98 S. Ct. 2733 (opinion of Powell, J.) ("10 or 20 black students could not begin to bring to their classmates and to each other the variety of points of view, backgrounds and experiences of blacks in the United States"). What is more, Justice Powell flatly rejected the argument that Harvard's program was "the functional equivalent of a quota" merely because it had some "'plus'" for race, or gave greater "weight" to race than to some other factors, in order to achieve student body diversity. 438 U.S., at 317–18, 57 L. Ed. 2d 750, 98 S. Ct. 2733.

The Law School's goal of attaining a critical mass of underrepresented minority students does not transform its program into a quota. As the Harvard plan described by Justice Powell recognized, there is of course "some relationship between numbers and achieving the benefits to be derived from a diverse student body, and between

numbers and providing a reasonable environment for those students admitted." *Id.,
at 323, 57 L. Ed. 2d 750, 98 S. Ct. 2733*. "Some attention to numbers," without more,
does not transform a flexible admissions system into a rigid quota. *Ibid.* Nor, as Justice Kennedy posits, does the Law School's consultation of the "daily reports," which
keep track of the racial and ethnic composition of the class (as well as of residency
and gender), "suggest[ ] there was no further attempt at individual review save for
race itself" during the final stages of the admissions process. See *post*, at 156 L. Ed.
2d, at 373 (dissenting opinion). To the contrary, the Law School's admissions officers testified without contradiction that they never gave race any more or less weight
based on the information contained in these reports. Brief for Respondents Bollinger et al. 43, n 70 (citing App. in Nos. 01-1447 and 01-1516 (CA6), p 7336). Moreover, as Justice Kennedy concedes, see *post*, at *156 L. Ed. 2d, at 372*, between 1993
and 2000, the number of African American, Latino, and Native American students
in each class at the Law School varied from 13.5 to 20.1 percent, a range inconsistent
with a quota.

The Chief Justice believes that the Law School's policy conceals an attempt to
achieve racial balancing, and cites admissions data to contend that the Law School
discriminates among different groups within the critical mass. *Post*, at 156 L. Ed.
2d, at 371–75 (dissenting opinion). But, as the Chief Justice concedes, the number of
underrepresented minority students who ultimately enroll in the Law School differs
substantially from their representation in the applicant pool and varies considerably for each group from year to year. See *post*, at 156 L. Ed. 2d, at 375 (dissenting
opinion).

That a race-conscious admissions program does not operate as a quota does not,
by itself, satisfy the requirement of individualized consideration. When using race
as a "plus" factor in university admissions, a university's admissions program must
remain flexible enough to ensure that each applicant is evaluated as an individual
and not in a way that makes an applicant's race or ethnicity the defining feature of
his or her application. The importance of this individualized consideration in the
context of a race-conscious admissions program is paramount. See *Bakke, supra,
at* 318, n. 52, 57 L. Ed. 2d 750, 98 S. Ct. 2733 (opinion of Powell, J.) (identifying the
"denial . . . of the right to individualized consideration" as the "principal evil" of
the medical school's admissions program).

Here, the Law School engages in a highly individualized, holistic review of each
applicant's file, giving serious consideration to all the ways an applicant might contribute to a diverse educational environment. The Law School affords this individualized consideration to applicants of all races. There is no policy, either *de jure*
or *de facto*, of automatic acceptance or rejection based on any single "soft" variable. Unlike the program at issue in *Gratz* v. *Bollinger, ante*, the Law School awards
no mechanical, predetermined diversity "bonuses" based on race or ethnicity. *See
ante*, at 156 L. Ed. 2d *257, 123 S. Ct. 2411* (distinguishing a race-conscious admissions program that automatically awards 20 points based on race from the Harvard
plan, which considered race but "did not contemplate that any single characteristic

automatically ensured a specific and identifiable contribution to a university's diversity"). Like the Harvard plan, the Law School's admissions policy "is flexible enough to consider all pertinent elements of diversity in light of the particular qualifications of each applicant, and to place them on the same footing for consideration, although not necessarily according them the same weight." *Bakke, supra, at 317, at 317,* 57 L. Ed. 2d 750, 98 S. Ct. 2733 (opinion of Powell, J.).

We also find that, like the Harvard plan Justice Powell referenced in *Bakke,* the Law School's race-conscious admissions program adequately ensures that all factors that may contribute to student body diversity are meaningfully considered alongside race in admissions decisions. With respect to the use of race itself, all underrepresented minority students admitted by the Law School have been deemed qualified. By virtue of our Nation's struggle with racial inequality, such students are both likely to have experiences of particular importance to the Law School's mission, and less likely to be admitted in meaningful numbers on criteria that ignore those experiences. See App. 120.

The Law School does not, however, limit in any way the broad range of qualities and experiences that may be considered valuable contributions to student body diversity. To the contrary, the 1992 policy makes clear "there are many possible bases for diversity admissions," and provides examples of admittees who have lived or traveled widely abroad, are fluent in several languages, have overcome personal adversity and family hardship, have exceptional records of extensive community service, and have had successful careers in other fields. *Id.,* at 118–19. The Law School seriously considers each "applicant's promise of making a notable contribution to the class by way of a particular strength, attainment, or characteristic — *e.g.,* an unusual intellectual achievement, employment experience, nonacademic performance, or personal background." *Id.,* at 83–84. All applicants have the opportunity to highlight their own potential diversity contributions through the submission of a personal statement, letters of recommendation, and an essay describing the ways in which the applicant will contribute to the life and diversity of the Law School.

What is more, the Law School actually gives substantial weight to diversity factors besides race. The Law School frequently accepts nonminority applicants with grades and test scores lower than underrepresented minority applicants (and other nonminority applicants) who are rejected. *See* Brief for Respondents Bollinger et al. 10; App. 121–122. This shows that the Law School seriously weighs many other diversity factors besides race that can make a real and dispositive difference for nonminority applicants as well. By this flexible approach, the Law School sufficiently takes into account, in practice as well as in theory, a wide variety of characteristics besides race and ethnicity that contribute to a diverse student body. Justice Kennedy speculates that "race is likely outcome determinative for many members of minority groups" who do not fall within the upper range of LSAT scores and grades. *Post, at 156 L. Ed. 2d, at 371* (dissenting opinion). But the same could be said of the Harvard plan discussed approvingly by Justice Powell in *Bakke,* and indeed of any plan that uses race as one of many factors. See *438* U.S., at 316, 57 L. Ed. 2d 750, 98 S. Ct. 2733 ("'When the Committee on Admissions reviews the large middle group of applicants who are "admissible" and deemed capable of doing good work in their courses, the race of an applicant may tip the balance in his favor'").

Petitioner and the United States argue that the Law School's plan is not narrowly tailored because race-neutral means exist to obtain the educational benefits of student body diversity that the Law School seeks. We disagree. Narrow tailoring does not require exhaustion of every conceivable race-neutral alternative. Nor does it require a university to choose between maintaining a reputation for excellence or fulfilling a commitment to provide educational opportunities to members of all racial groups. *See Wygant v. Jackson Bd. of Ed.,* 476 U.S. 267, 280, n. 6, 90 L. Ed. 2d 260, 106 S. Ct. 1842 *(1986)* (alternatives must serve the interest "'about as well'"); *Richmond v. J. A. Croson Co., 488 U.S., at 509–10, 102 L Ed 2d 854, 109 S. Ct. 706* (plurality opinion) (city had a "whole array of race-neutral" alternatives because changing requirements "would have [had] little detrimental effect on the city's interests"). Narrow tailoring does, however, require serious, good faith consideration of workable race-neutral alternatives that will achieve the diversity the university seeks. See *id., at* 507, 102 L Ed 2d 854, 109 S. Ct. 706 (set-aside plan not narrowly tailored where "there does not appear to have been any consideration of the use of race-neutral means"); *Wygant v. Jackson Bd. of Ed., supra,* at 280, n. 6, 90 L. Ed. 2d 260, 106 S. Ct. 1842 (narrow tailoring "requires consideration" of "lawful alternative and less restrictive means").

We agree with the Court of Appeals that the Law School sufficiently considered workable race-neutral alternatives. The District Court took the Law School to task for failing to consider race-neutral alternatives such as "using a lottery system" or "decreasing the emphasis for all applicants on undergraduate GPA and LSAT scores." App. to Pet. for Cert. 251a. But these alternatives would require a dramatic sacrifice of diversity, the academic quality of all admitted students, or both.

The Law School's current admissions program considers race as one factor among many, in an effort to assemble a student body that is diverse in ways broader than race. Because a lottery would make that kind of nuanced judgment impossible, it would effectively sacrifice all other educational values, not to mention every other kind of diversity. So too with the suggestion that the Law School simply lower admissions standards for all students, a drastic remedy that would require the Law School to become a much different institution and sacrifice a vital component of its educational mission. The United States advocates "percentage plans," recently adopted by public undergraduate institutions in Texas, Florida, and California to guarantee admission to all students above a certain class-rank threshold in every high school in the State. Brief for United States as *Amicus Curiae* 14–18. The United States does not, however, explain how such plans could work for graduate and professional schools. More-over, even assuming such plans are race-neutral, they may preclude the university from conducting the individualized assessments necessary to assemble a student body that is not just racially diverse, but diverse along all the qualities valued by the university. We are satisfied that the Law School adequately considered race-neutral alternatives currently capable of producing a critical mass without forcing the Law School to abandon the academic selectivity that is the cornerstone of its educational mission.

We acknowledge that "there are serious problems of justice connected with the idea of preference itself." *Bakke*, 438 U.S., at 298, 57 L. Ed. 2d 750, 98 S. Ct. 2733 (opinion of Powell, J.). Narrow tailoring, therefore, requires that a race-conscious admissions program not unduly harm members of any racial group. Even remedial race-based governmental action generally "remains subject to continuing oversight to assure that it will work the least harm possible to other innocent persons competing for the benefit." *Id., at 308*, 57 L. Ed. 2d 750, 98 S. Ct. 2733. To be narrowly tailored, a race-conscious admissions program must not "unduly burden individuals who are not members of the favored racial and ethnic groups." *Metro Broadcasting, Inc. v. FCC*, 497 U.S. 547, 630, 111 L. Ed. 2d 445, 110 S. Ct. 2997 *(1990)* (O'Connor, J., dissenting).

We are satisfied that the Law School's admissions program does not. Because the Law School considers "all pertinent elements of diversity," it can (and does) select nonminority applicants who have greater potential to enhance student body diversity over underrepresented minority applicants. *See Bakke, supra*, at 317, 57 L. Ed. 2d 750, 98 S. Ct. 2733 (opinion of Powell, J.). As Justice Powell recognized in *Bakke*, so long as a race-conscious admissions program uses race as a "plus" factor in the context of individualized consideration, a rejected applicant

> "will not have been foreclosed from all consideration for that seat simply because he was not the right color or had the wrong surname. . . . His qualifications would have been weighed fairly and competitively, and he would have no basis to complain of unequal treatment under the Fourteenth Amendment." *438* U.S., at 318, 57 L. Ed. 2d 750, 98 S. Ct. 2733.

We agree that, in the context of its individualized inquiry into the possible diversity contributions of all applicants, the Law School's race-conscious admissions program does not unduly harm nonminority applicants.

We are mindful, however, that "[a] core purpose of the Fourteenth Amendment was to do away with all governmentally imposed discrimination based on race." *Palmore v. Sidoti*, 466 U.S. 429, 432, 80 L. Ed. 2d 421, 104 S. Ct. 1879 (1984). Accordingly, race-conscious admissions policies must be limited in time. This requirement reflects that racial classifications, however compelling their goals, are potentially so dangerous that they may be employed no more broadly than the interest demands. Enshrining a permanent justification for racial preferences would offend this fundamental equal protection principle. We see no reason to exempt race-conscious admissions programs from the requirement that all governmental use of race must have a logical end point. The Law School, too, concedes that all "race-conscious programs must have reasonable durational limits." Brief for Respondents Bollinger et al. 32.

In the context of higher education, the durational requirement can be met by sunset provisions in race-conscious admissions policies and periodic reviews to determine whether racial preferences are still necessary to achieve student body diversity. Universities in California, Florida, and Washington State, where racial preferences in admissions are prohibited by state law, are currently engaged in experimenting with a wide variety of alternative approaches. Universities in other States can and should draw on the most promising aspects of these race-neutral alternatives as they develop. Cf. *United States v. Lopez*, 514 U.S. 549, 581, 131 L. Ed. 2d 626, 115 S. Ct. 1624 (1995) (Kennedy, J., concurring) ("The States may perform their role as laboratories for experimentation to devise various solutions where the best solution is far from clear").

The requirement that all race-conscious admissions programs have a termination point "assures all citizens that the deviation from the norm of equal treatment of all racial and ethnic groups is a temporary matter, a measure taken in the service of the goal of equality itself." *Richmond v. J. A. Croson Co., 488 U.S., at 510,* 102 L. Ed. 2d 854, 109 S. Ct. 706 (plurality opinion); see also Nathanson & Bartnik, The Constitutionality of Preferential Treatment for Minority Applicants to Professional Schools, *58 Chicago Bar Rec. 282, 293* (May–June 1977) ("It would be a sad day indeed, were America to become a quota-ridden society, with each identifiable minority assigned proportional representation in every desirable walk of life. But that is not the rationale for programs of preferential treatment; the acid test of their justification will be their efficacy in eliminating the need for any racial or ethnic preferences at all").

We take the Law School at its word that it would "like nothing better than to find a race-neutral admissions formula" and will terminate its race-conscious admissions program as soon as practicable. See Brief for Respondents Bollinger et al. 34; *Bakke, supra, at 317–18, 57 L. Ed. 2d 750, 98 S. Ct. 2733 (opinion of Powell, J.) (presuming good faith of university officials in the absence of a showing to the contrary). It has been 25 years since Justice Powell first approved the use of race to further an interest in student body diversity in the context of public higher education. Since that time, the number of minority applicants with high grades and test scores has indeed increased. *See* Tr. of Oral Arg. 43. We expect that 25 years from now, the use of racial preferences will no longer be necessary to further the interest approved today.

3. Holding

In summary, the Equal Protection Clause does not prohibit the Law School's narrowly tailored use of race in admissions decisions to further a compelling interest in obtaining the educational benefits that flow from a diverse student body. Consequently, petitioner's statutory claims based on Title VI and 42 USC § 1981 [42 USCS § 1981] also fail. *See Bakke, supra, at 287, 57 L. Ed. 2d 750, 98 S. Ct. 2733 (opinion of Powell, J.) ("Title VI . . . proscribes only those racial classifications that would violate the *Equal Protection Clause or the Fifth Amendment*"); *General Building Contractors Assn., Inc. v. Pennsylvania, 458 U.S. 375, 389–91, 73 L. Ed. 2d 835, 102 S. Ct. 3141 (1982) (the prohibition against discrimination in § 1981 is co-extensive with the Equal Protection Clause). The judgment of the Court of Appeals for the Sixth Circuit, accordingly, is affirmed.

It is so ordered.

4. Chief Justice Rehnquist Dissenting

I agree with the Court that, "in the limited circumstance when drawing racial distinctions is permissible," the government must ensure that its means are narrowly tailored to achieve a compelling state interest. *Ante, at 156 L. Ed. 2d, at 335*; see also *Fullilove v. Klutznick,* 448 U.S. 448, 498, 65 L. Ed. 2d 902, 100 S. Ct. 2758 (1980) (Powell, J., concurring) ("Even if the government proffers a compelling interest to support reliance upon a suspect classification, the means selected must be narrowly drawn to fulfill the governmental purpose"). I do not believe, however, that the University of Michigan Law School's (Law School) means are narrowly tailored to the interest it asserts. The Law School claims it must take the steps it does to achieve a "'critical mass'" of underrepresented minority students. Brief for Respondents Bollinger et al. 13. But its actual program bears no relation to this asserted goal. Stripped of its "critical mass" veil, the Law School's program is revealed as a naked effort to achieve racial balancing.

As we have explained many times, ""any preference based on racial or ethnic criteria must necessarily receive a most searching examination."" *Adarand Constructors, Inc. v. Peña,* 515 U.S. 200, 223, 132 L. Ed. 2d 158, 115 S. Ct. 2097 (1995) (quoting *Wygant v. Jackson Bd. of Ed.,* 476 U.S. 267, 273, 90 L. Ed. 2d 260, 106 S. Ct. 1842 (1986) (plurality opinion of Powell, J.)). Our cases establish that, in order to withstand this demanding inquiry, respondents must demonstrate that their methods of using race "'fit'" a compelling state interest "with greater precision than any alternative means." *Id., at 280, n. 6,* 90 L. Ed. 2d 260, 106 S. Ct. 1842; *Regents of Univ. of Cal. v. Bakke,* 438 U.S. 265, 299, 57 L. Ed. 2d 750, 98 S. Ct. 2733 (1978) (opinion of Powell, J.) ("When [political judgments] touch upon an individual's race or ethnic background, he is entitled to a judicial determination that the burden he is asked to bear on that basis is precisely tailored to serve a compelling governmental interest").

Before the Court's decision today, we consistently applied the same strict scrutiny analysis regardless of the government's purported reason for using race and regardless of the setting in which race was being used. We rejected calls to use more lenient review in the face of claims that race was being used in "good faith" because "more than good motives should be required when government seeks to allocate its resources by way of an explicit racial classification system." *Adarand, supra, at 226,* 132 L. Ed. 2d 158, 115 S. Ct. 2097; *Fullilove, supra, at 537,* 65 L. Ed. 2d 902, 100 S. Ct. 2758 (Stevens, J., dissenting) ("Racial classifications are simply too pernicious to permit any but the most exact connection between justification and classification"). We likewise rejected calls to apply more lenient review based on the particular setting in which race is being used. Indeed, even in the specific context of higher education, we emphasized that "constitutional limitations protecting individual rights may not be disregarded." *Bakke, supra, at 314*, 57 L. Ed. 2d 750, 98 S. Ct. 2733.

Although the Court recites the language of our strict scrutiny analysis, its application of that review is unprecedented in its deference.

Respondents' asserted justification for the Law School's use of race in the admissions process is "obtaining 'the educational benefits that flow from a diverse student body.'" *Ante, at* 156 L. Ed. 2d, at 332 (quoting Brief for Respondents Bollinger et al.) They contend that a "critical mass" of underrepresented minorities is necessary to further that interest. *Ante, at* 156 L. Ed. 2d, at 333. Respondents and school administrators explain generally that "critical mass" means a sufficient number of underrepresented minority students to achieve several objectives: To ensure that these minority students do not feel isolated or like spokespersons for their race; to provide adequate opportunities for the type of interaction upon which the educational benefits of diversity depend; and to challenge all students to think critically and reexamine stereotypes. *See* App. to Pet. for Cert. 211a; Brief for Respondents Bollinger et al. 26. These objectives indicate that "critical mass" relates to the size of the student body. *Id.*, at 5 (claiming that the Law School has enrolled "critical mass," or "enough minority students to provide meaningful integration of its classrooms and residence halls"). Respondents further claim that the Law School is achieving "critical mass." *Id.*, at 4 (noting that the Law School's goals have been "greatly furthered by the presence of . . . a 'critical mass' of" minority students in the student body).

In practice, the Law School's program bears little or no relation to its asserted goal of achieving "critical mass." Respondents explain that the Law School seeks to accumulate a "critical mass" of *each* underrepresented minority group. *See, e.g., id.*, at 49, n 79 ("The Law School's . . . current policy . . . provides a special commitment to enrolling a 'critical mass' of 'Hispanics'"). But the record demonstrates that the Law School's admissions practices with respect to these groups differ dramatically and cannot be defended under any consistent use of the term "critical mass."

From 1995 through 2000, the Law School admitted between 1,130 and 1,310 students. Of those, between 13 and 19 were Native American, between 91 and 108 were African Americans, and between 47 and 56 were Hispanic. If the Law School is admitting between 91 and 108 African Americans in order to achieve "critical mass," thereby preventing African-American students from feeling "isolated or like spokespersons for their race," one would think that a number of the same order of magnitude would be necessary to accomplish the same purpose for Hispanics and Native Americans. Similarly, even if all of the Native American applicants admitted in a given year matriculate, which the record demonstrates is not at all the case, how can this possibly constitute a "critical mass" of Native Americans in a class of over 350 students? In order for this pattern of admission to be consistent with the Law School's explanation of "critical mass," one would have to believe that the objectives of "critical mass" offered by respondents are achieved with only half the number of Hispanics and one-sixth the number of Native Americans as compared to

African Americans. But respondents offer no race-specific reasons for such disparities. Instead, they simply emphasize the importance of achieving "critical mass," without any explanation of why that concept is applied differently among the three underrepresented minority groups.

These different numbers, moreover, come only as a result of substantially different treatment among the three underrepresented minority groups, as is apparent in an example offered by the Law School and highlighted by the Court: The school asserts that it "frequently accepts nonminority applicants with grades and test scores lower than underrepresented minority applicants (and other nonminority applicants) who are rejected." *Ante, at* 156 L. Ed. 2d, at 335 (citing Brief for Respondents Bollinger et al. 10). Specifically, the Law School states that "sixty-nine minority applicants were rejected between 1995 and 2000 with at least a 3.5 [Grade Point Average (GPA)] and a [score of] 159 or higher on the [Law School Admissions Test (LSAT)]" while a number of Caucasian and Asian-American applicants with similar or lower scores were admitted. Brief for Respondents Bollinger et al. 10.

Review of the record reveals only 67 such individuals. Of these 67 individuals, *56* were Hispanic, while only 6 were African American, and only 5 were Native American. This discrepancy reflects a consistent practice. For example, in 2000, 12 Hispanics who scored between a 159–160 on the LSAT and earned a GPA of 3.00 or higher applied for admission and only 2 were admitted. App. 200–201. Meanwhile, 12 African Americans in the same range of qualifications applied for admission and all 12 were admitted. *Id.,* at 198. Likewise, that same year, 16 Hispanics who scored between a 151–153 on the LSAT and earned a 3.00 or higher applied for admission and only 1 of those applicants was admitted. *Id.,* at 200–1. Twenty-three similarly qualified African Americans applied for admission and 14 were admitted. *Id.,* at 198.

These statistics have a significant bearing on petitioner's case. Respondents have *never* offered any race-specific arguments explaining why significantly more individuals from one underrepresented minority group are needed in order to achieve "critical mass" or further student body diversity. They certainly have not explained why Hispanics, who they have said are among "the groups most isolated by racial barriers in our country," should have their admission capped out in this manner. Brief for Respondents Bollinger et al. 50. True, petitioner is neither Hispanic nor Native American. But the Law School's disparate admissions practices with respect to these minority groups demonstrate that its alleged goal of "critical mass" is simply a sham. Petitioner may use these statistics to expose this sham, which is the basis for the Law School's admission of less qualified underrepresented minorities in preference to her. Surely strict scrutiny cannot permit these sort of disparities without at least some explanation.

Only when the "critical mass" label is discarded does a likely explanation for these numbers emerge. The Court states that the Law School's goal of attaining a "critical mass" of underrepresented minority students is not an interest in merely "'assuring within its student body some specified percentage of a particular group merely because of its race or ethnic origin.'" *Ante, at* 156 L. Ed. 2d, at 333 (quoting *Bakke, 438 U.S., at* 307, 57 L. Ed. 2d 750, 98 S. Ct. 2733 (opinion of Powell, J.)). The Court recognizes that such an interest "would amount to outright racial balancing, which is patently unconstitutional." *Ante, at* 156 L. Ed. 2d, at 333. The Court concludes, however, that the Law School's use of race in admissions, consistent with Justice Powell's opinion in *Bakke,* only pays "'some attention to numbers.'" *Ante, at* 156 L. Ed. 2d, at 337 (quoting *Bakke, supra, at* 323, 57 L. Ed. 2d 750, 98 S. Ct. 2733).

But the correlation between the percentage of the Law School's pool of applicants who are members of the three minority groups and the percentage of the admitted applicants who are members of these same groups is far too precise to be dismissed as merely the result of the school paying "some attention to [the] numbers." As the tables below show, from 1995 through 2000 the percentage of admitted applicants who were members of these minority groups closely tracked the percentage of individuals in the school's applicant pool who were from the same groups . . .

The Court suggests a possible 25-year limitation on the Law School's current program. *See ante, at* 156 L. Ed. 2d, at 341. Respondents, on the other hand, remain more ambiguous, explaining that "the Law School of course recognizes that race-conscious programs must have reasonable durational limits, and the Sixth Circuit properly found such a limit in the Law School's resolve to cease considering race when genuine race-neutral alternatives become available." Brief for Respondents Bollinger et al. 32. These discussions of a time limit are the vaguest of assurances. In truth, they permit the Law School's use of racial preferences on a seemingly permanent basis. Thus, an important component of strict scrutiny—that a program be limited in time—is casually subverted.

The Court, in an unprecedented display of deference under our strict scrutiny analysis, upholds the Law School's program despite its obvious flaws. We have said that when it comes to the use of race, the connection between the ends and the means used to attain them must be precise. But here the flaw is deeper than that; it is not merely a question of "fit" between ends and means. Here the means actually used are forbidden by the Equal Protection Clause of the Constitution.

M. Commentary on *Grutter*

The Supreme Court ruled in *Grutter* that the University of Michigan Law School's affirmative action admission program does not violate the Equal Protection Clause of the Fourteenth Amendment. This Supreme Court decision clarifies the doubt and controversy surrounding affirmative action in higher education that has existed since the *Bakke* decision in 1978, 25 years earlier. More significantly, however, the decision allows government and private entities to continue to employ, albeit under clear and rigid guidelines, affirmative action practices that create and maintain racial diversity in educational institutions and in other settings.

The Supreme Court affirmed the law school's policy in a 5-to-4 ruling, written by Justice Sandra Day O'Connor. The decision declared that the Constitution "does not prohibit the law school's narrowly tailored use of race in admissions decisions to further a compelling interest in obtaining the educational benefits that flow from a diverse student body." (123 S. Ct. at 2331, 2342).

Justices John Paul Stevens, David H. Souter, Ruth Bader Ginsburg and Stephen G. Breyer joined Justice O'Connor's opinion.

Dissenting were Chief Justice William H. Rehnquist and Justices Antonin Scalia, Anthony M. Kennedy and Clarence Thomas. Chief Justice Rehnquist called the law school program "a naked effort to achieve racial balancing." (123 S. Ct. at 2365). Rehnquist's remarks suggest that the application of affirmative action is not a fully formed effort toward racial equality.

This 5-to-4 divide reflects that affirmative action remains a very divisive issue. Yet, in *Gratz v. Bollinger*(123 S. Ct. at 2411), a 6–3 ruling issued on the same day as *Grutter*, the Supreme Court invalidated the University of Michigan's undergraduate admissions program that was based on a point system where applicants were awarded points for various factors, including race.

In *Gratz*, the Court struck down the university's affirmative action program for undergraduates because it mechanically awarded a fixed and large number of points toward admission to members of minority groups. The law school program in *Grutter* was different because it involved a "whole file" review in which race was given *some* weight, which might vary from applicant to applicant.

Leslie Yalof Garfield

*The Glass Half Full: Envisioning The Future of Race Preference Policies**

States or their agencies defending race-preference plans must demonstrate the existence of a compelling governmental interest in order to meet the rigorous demands of the strict scrutiny test. The idea of a compelling governmental interest existed long before the Court began to tackle issues of race. In these early cases, the Court was unwilling to uphold a state or federal law unless the reasons behind it were so necessary or compelling that they justified limiting an individual's rights. Justice Powell extended the application of the compelling governmental interest prong of the strict scrutiny test to race-preference policies, writing that when "[a program] touch[es] upon an individual's race or ethnic background, he is entitled to a judicial determination that the burden he is asked to bear on that basis is precisely tailored to serve a compelling governmental interest."

Based on Justice Powell's early determination that the government must have a compelling interest in applying racial criteria to achieve particular goals, the Court has subsequently defined two distinct instances in which it will find a governmental

---

* (footnotes and chapter headings omitted).

interest compelling. Where a previous governmental entity has engaged in segregated practices, the then-current government is always permitted to enact race-preference policies as a means to reverse its past wrongs. As a general matter, states are successful in this instance when they can show that their program is designed to remedy the present effects of past discrimination. Justice Powell also articulated a second compelling governmental interest in promoting exposure to diverse voices and perspectives in the classroom, which was later termed "viewpoint diversity." States promoting this interest need not demonstrate evidence of de jure segregation; rather, they must show only that their policy assures that students are exposed to different views.

Courts generally require proof of the present effects of past discrimination when race-preference policies are aimed at achieving racial equality in the workplace. "A generalized assertion that there has been past discrimination in an entire industry" is not sufficient to support infringing an individual's rights. In *City of Richmond v. Croson* the Court discussed the compelling governmental interest test in the context of a non-remedial race-preference program adopted in the workplace. The *Croson* Court, which evaluated the constitutionality of a Richmond program that set aside thirty percent of city construction funds for black-owned businesses, concluded that in the right instances a governmental entity may be "permitted to rectify the effects of identified discrimination within its jurisdiction." The defending party, however, must support the need for remedial measures with objective criteria, such as statistics or an identifiable number of those harmed. In this instance, however, the City of Richmond merely put forth a general goal of remedying various forms of past discrimination. The Court found that this in and of itself was far too amorphous to support an instance of compelling governmental interest. The Court struck down the City of Richmond's set-aside program because its goal — remedying discrimination as a general social concern — was not sufficient to justify infringing on non-minority contractors' rights under the Equal Protection Clause.

The Court will find a compelling governmental interest in programs that are created in response to court orders or consent decrees. In *United States v. Paradise* the Court considered the constitutionality of a one-black-to-one-white promotion plan that the Alabama Department of Public Safety adopted pursuant to a district court consent decree. The decree was supported by "ample" evidence of the Department's pervasive, systematic, and obstinate discriminatory exclusion of blacks. Justice Brennan, writing for the majority, acknowledged that evidence of the present effects of past discrimination justifies a compelling governmental interest in remedial measures. As a result, the Court upheld the Alabama Department of Public Safety's promotion plan. The cases of *Croson* and *Paradise* demonstrate that in the workplace, absent an objective demonstrable finding of the present effects of past discrimination, the Court is unwilling to find an instance of compelling governmental interest.

Where education is concerned, the Court upholds race preference policies even where it is unable to identify present effects of past discrimination. In *Grutter v.*

Bollinger and *Gratz v. Bollinger*, the only post-*Bakke* cases to consider race-preference policies in higher education, the majority "endorse[d] Justice Powell's view that student body diversity is a compelling state interest that can justify the use of race in university admissions." Relying on Justice Powell's words, the *Grutter* Court upheld the admissions policy of the University of Michigan law School. The Court would also have upheld the admissions policy of the University of Michigan School of Liberal Arts and Sciences had it been narrowly tailored. Both schools' policies supported the constitutionally recognized instance of a compelling governmental interest in attaining a diverse student body. The Court adopted as its own Justice Powell's conclusion that the "nation's future depends upon leaders trained through wide exposure to the ideas and mores of students as diverse as this Nation of many peoples." Both tradition and experience, Justice O'Connor wrote, "lend support to the view that the contribution of diversity is substantial."

63 *N.Y.U. Ann. Surv. Am. L.* 385, 397–401.
Copyright © 2008 Annual Survey of American Law.
Reprinted with permission of Annual Survey of American Law and
Leslie Yalof Garfield.

N. Background on *Parents Involved*

The decisions in *Grutter* and *Gratz* shed light, in general, on equal protection analysis and affirmative action and, more specifically, on the application of the strict scrutiny standard in higher education. The question remained unresolved as to lower education.

O. *Parents Involved in Community Schools v. Seattle School District No. 1* (2007)

1. Facts

Chief Justice ROBERTS delivered the opinion of the Court.

The school districts in these cases voluntarily adopted student assignment plans that rely upon race to determine which public schools certain children may attend. The Seattle [Washington] school district classifies children as white or nonwhite; the Jefferson County school district as black or "other." In Seattle, this racial classification is used to allocate slots in over-subscribed high schools. In Jefferson County, it is used to make certain elementary school assignments and to rule on transfer requests. In each case, the school district relies upon an individual student's race in assigning that student to a particular school, so that the racial balance at the school falls within a predetermined range based on the racial composition of the school district as a whole. Parents of students denied assignment to particular schools under these plans solely because of their race brought suit, contending that allocating children to different public schools on the basis of race violated the Fourteenth

Amendment guarantee of equal protection. The Courts of Appeals below upheld the plans. We granted certiorari, and now reverse.

2. Opinion

Both cases present the same underlying legal question—whether a public school that had not operated legally segregated schools or has been found to be unitary may choose to classify students by race and rely upon that classification in making school assignments. Although we examine the plans under the same legal framework, the specifics of the two plans, and the circumstances surrounding their adoption, are in some respects quite different.

Seattle School District No. 1 operates 10 regular public high schools. In 1998, it adopted the plan at issue in this case for assigning students to these schools. The plan allows incoming ninth graders to choose from among any of the district's high schools, ranking however many schools they wish in order of preference.

Some schools are more popular than others. If too many students list the same school as their first choice, the district employs a series of "tiebreakers" to determine who will fill the open slots at the oversubscribed school. The first tiebreaker selects for admission students who have a sibling currently enrolled in the chosen school. The next tiebreaker depends upon the racial composition of the particular school and the race of the individual student. In the district's public schools approximately 41 percent of enrolled students are white; the remaining 59 percent, comprising all other racial groups, are classified by Seattle for assignment purposes as nonwhite. If an oversubscribed school is not within 10 percentage points of the district's overall white/nonwhite racial balance, it is what the district calls "integration positive," and the district employs a tiebreaker that selects for assignment students whose race "will serve to bring the school into balance." If it is still necessary to select students for the school after using the racial tiebreaker, the next tiebreaker is the geographic proximity of the school to the student's residence.

Seattle has never operated segregated schools—legally separate schools for students of different races—nor has it ever been subject to court-ordered desegregation. It nonetheless employs the racial tiebreaker in an attempt to address the effects of racially identifiable housing patterns on school assignments. . . .

Jefferson County Public Schools operates the public school system in metropolitan Louisville, Kentucky. In 1973 a federal court found that Jefferson County had maintained a segregated school system, and in 1975 the District Court entered a desegregation decree. Jefferson County operated under this decree until 2000, when the District Court dissolved the decree after finding that the district had achieved unitary status by eliminating "[t]o the greatest extent practicable" the vestiges of its prior policy segregation.

In 2001, after the decree had been dissolved, Jefferson County adopted the voluntary student assignment plan at issue in this case. Approximately 34 percent of the district's 97,000 students are black; most of the remaining 66 percent are white. The plan requires all nonmagnet schools to maintain a minimum black enrollment of 15 percent, and a maximum black enrollment of 50 percent.

At the elementary school level, based on his or her address, each student is designated a "resides" school to which students within a specific geographic area are assigned; elementary resides schools are "grouped into clusters in order to facilitate integration." The district assigns students to nonmagnet schools in one of two ways: Parents of kindergartners, first-graders, and students new to the district may submit an application indicating a first and second choice among the schools within their cluster; students who do not submit such an application are assigned within the cluster by the district. "Decisions to assign students to schools within each cluster are based on available space within the schools and the racial guidelines in the District's current student assignment plan." If a school has reached the "extremes of the racial guidelines," a student whose race would contribute to the school's racial imbalance will not be assigned there. After assignment, students at all grade levels are permitted to apply to transfer between nonmagnet schools in the district. Transfers may be requested for any number of reasons, and may be denied because of lack of available space or on the basis of the racial guidelines. . . .

It is well established that when the government distributes burdens or benefits on the basis of individual racial classifications, that action is reviewed under strict scrutiny.

Without attempting in these cases to set forth all the interests a school district might assert, it suffices to note that our prior cases, in evaluating the use of racial classifications in the school context, have recognized two interests that qualify as compelling. The first is the compelling interest of remedying the effects of past intentional discrimination. Yet the Seattle public schools have not shown that they were ever segregated by law, and were not subject to court-ordered segregation decrees. The Jefferson County public schools were previously segregated by law and were subject to a desegregation decree entered in 1975 [and dissolved in 2000]. Jefferson County accordingly does not rely upon an interest in remedying the effects of past intentional discrimination in defending its present use of race in assigning students.

Nor could it. We have emphasized that the harm being remedied by mandatory desegregation plans is the harm that is traceable to segregation, and that "the Constitution is not violated by racial imbalance in the schools, without more. . . ."

The second government interest we have recognized as compelling for purposes of strict scrutiny is the interest in diversity in higher education. . . . The specific interest found compelling in *Grutter* was student body diversity "in the context of higher education." The diversity interest was not focused on race alone but encompassed "all factors that may contribute to student body diversity. . . ."

In the present cases, by contrast, race is not considered as part of a broader effort to achieve "exposure to widely diverse people, cultures, ideas, and viewpoints," race, for some students, is determinative standing alone. The districts argue that other factors, such as student preferences, affect assignment decisions under their plans, but under each plan when race comes into play, it is decisive by itself. It is not simply one factor weighed with others in reaching a decision, as in *Grutter*: it is *the* factor. Like the University of Michigan undergraduate plan struck down in *Gratz*, the plans here "do not provide for a meaningful individualized review of applicants" but instead rely on racial classifications in a "nonindividualized, mechanical" way.

Even when it comes to race, the plans here employ only a limited notion of diversity, viewing race exclusively in white/nonwhite terms in Seattle and black/"other" terms in Jefferson County. . . . But under the Seattle plan, a school with 50 percent Asian-American students and 50 percent white students but no African-American, Native-American, or Latino students would qualify as balanced, while a school with 30 percent Asian-American, 25 percent African-American, 25 percent Latino, and 20 percent white students would not. It is hard to understand how a plan that could allow these results can be viewed as being concerned with achieving enrollment that is "'broadly diverse.'"

In upholding the admissions plan in *Grutter*, . . . this Court relied upon considerations unique to institutions of higher education, noting that in light of "the expansive freedoms of speech and thought associated with the university environment, universities occupy a special niche in our constitutional tradition." The Court explained that "[c]ontext matters" in applying strict scrutiny, and repeatedly noted that it was addressing the use of race "in the context of higher education." The Court in *Grutter* expressly articulated key limitations on its holding—defining a specific type of broad-based diversity and noting the unique context of higher education—but these limitations were largely disregarded by the lower courts in extending *Grutter* to uphold race-based assignments in elementary and second schools. The present cases are not governed by *Grutter*.

[In] briefing and argument before this Court, Seattle contends that its use of race helps to reduce racial concentration in schools and to ensure that racially concentrated housing patterns do not prevent nonwhite students from having access to the most desirable schools. Jefferson County has articulated a similar goal, phrasing its interest in terms of educating its students "in a racially integrated environment." Each school district argues that educational and broader socialization benefits flow from a racially diverse learning environment, and each contends that because the diversity they seek is racial diversity—not the broader diversity at issue in *Grutter*—it makes sense to promote that interest directly by relying on race alone.

The parties and their *amici* dispute whether racial diversity in schools in fact has a marked impact on test scores and other objective yardsticks or achieves intangible socialization benefits. The debate is not one we need to resolve, however, because it is clear that the racial classifications employed by the districts are not narrowly tailored to the goal of achieving the educational and social benefits asserted to flow from racial diversity. In design and operation, the plans are directed only to racial balance, pure and simple, an objective this Court has repeatedly condemned as illegitimate. . . .

In fact, in each case the extreme measure of relying on race in assignments is unnecessary to achieve the stated goals, even as defined by the districts. [The Court cited examples of schools where diversity was minimally or negatively impacted by use of the racial tiebreaker]. . . .

Accepting racial balancing as a compelling state interest would justify the imposition of racial proportionality throughout American society, contrary to our repeated recognition that "[a]t the heart of the Constitution's guarantee of equal protection lies the simple command that the Government must treat citizens as individuals, not as simply components of a racial, religious, sexual or national class.". . . .

The validity of our concern that racial balancing has "no logical stopping point," is demonstrated here by the degree to which the districts tie their racial guidelines to their demographics. As the districts' demographics shift, so too will their definition of racial diversity. . . .

The principle that racial balancing is not permitted is one of substance, not semantics. Racial balancing is not transformed from "patently unconstitutional" to a compelling state interest simply by relabeling it "racial diversity." While the school districts use various verbal formulations to describe the interest they seek to promote—racial diversity, avoidance of racial isolation, racial integration—they offer no definition of the interest that suggests it differs from racial balance. . . .

Jefferson County phrases its interest as "racial integration," but integration certainly does not require the sort of racial proportionality reflected in its plan. Even in the context of mandatory desegregation, we have stressed that racial proportionality is not required, . . . and here Jefferson County has already been found to have eliminated the vestiges of its prior segregated school system.

The districts assert, as they must, that the way in which they have employed individual racial classifications is necessary to achieve their stated ends. The minimal effect these classifications have on student assignments, however, suggests that other means would be effective. . . . In over one-third of the assignments affected by the racial tiebreaker, . . . the use of race in the end made no difference, and the district could identify only 52 students who were ultimately affected adversely by the racial tiebreaker in that it resulted in assignment to a school they had not listed as a preference and to which they would not otherwise have been assigned.

Similarly, Jefferson County's use of racial classifications has only a minimal effect on the assignment of students. . . .

While we do not suggest that *greater* use of race would be preferable, the minimal impact of the districts' racial classifications on school enrollment casts doubt on the necessity of using racial classifications. . . .

The districts have also failed to show that they considered methods other than explicit racial classifications to achieve their stated goals. . . .

Justice Breyer's dissent takes a different approach to these cases, one that fails to ground the result it would reach in law. Instead, it selectively relies on inapplicable precedent and even dicta while dismissing contrary holdings, alters and misapplies our well-established legal framework for assessing equal protection challenges to express racial classifications, and greatly exaggerates the consequences of today's decision.

To begin with, Justice Breyer seeks to justify the plans at issue under our precedents recognizing the compelling interest in remedying past intentional discrimination. Not even the school districts go this far, and for good reason. The distinction between segregation by state action and racial imbalance caused by other factors has been central to our jurisprudence in this area for generations. The dissent elides this distinction between *de jure* and *de facto* segregation, casually intimates that Seattle's school attendance patterns reflect illegal segregation, and fails to credit the judicial determination — under the most rigorous standard — that Jefferson County had eliminated the vestiges of prior segregation. The dissent thus alters in fundamental ways not only the facts presented here but the established law. . . .

At the same time it relies on inapplicable desegregation cases, misstatements of admitted dicta, and other noncontrolling pronouncements, Justice Breyer's dissent candidly dismisses the significance of this Court's repeated *holdings* that all racial classifications must be reviewed under strict scrutiny, see *post*, at 31–33, 35–36, arguing that a different standard of review should be applied because the districts use race for beneficent rather than malicious purposes, see *post*, at 31–36.

This Court has recently reiterated, however, that "'*all* racial classifications [imposed by government] . . . must be analyzed by a reviewing court under strict scrutiny.'" Justice Breyer nonetheless relies on the good intentions and motives of the school districts, stating that he has found "no case that . . . repudiated this constitutional asymmetry between that which seeks to *exclude* and that which seeks to *include* members of minority races." We have found many. Our cases clearly reject the argument that motives affect the strict scrutiny analysis.

This argument that different rules should govern racial classifications designed to include rather than exclude is not new; it has been repeatedly pressed in the past, and has been repeatedly rejected.

The reasons for rejecting a motives test for racial classifications are clear enough. "The Court's emphasis on 'benign racial classifications' suggests confidence in its ability to distinguish good from harmful governmental uses of racial criteria. History should teach greater humility. . . . '[B]enign' carries with it no independent meaning, but reflects only acceptance of the current generation's conclusion that a politically acceptable burden, imposed on particular citizens on the basis of race, is reasonable." Accepting Justice Breyer's approach would "do no more than move us from 'separate but equal' to 'unequal but benign.'". . . .

Justice Breyer's position comes down to a familiar claim: The end justifies the means. He admits that "there is a cost in applying 'a state-mandated racial label,'" but he is confident that the cost is worth paying. Our established strict scrutiny test for racial classifications, however, insists on "detailed examination, both as to ends *and* as to means." Simply because the school districts may seek a worthy goal does not mean they are free to discriminate on the basis of race to achieve it, or that their racial classifications should be subject to less exacting scrutiny. . . .

[W]hen it comes to using race to assign children to schools, history will be heard. In *Brown v. Board of Education*, we held that segregation deprived black children of equal educational opportunities regardless of whether school facilities and other tangible factors were equal, because government classification and separation on grounds of race themselves denoted inferiority. It was not the inequality of the facilities but the fact of legally separating children on the basis of race on which the Court relied to find a constitutional violation in 1954. The next Term, we accordingly stated that "full compliance" with *Brown required school districts "to achieve a system of determining admission to the public schools* on a nonracial basis."

The parties and their *amici* debate which side is more faithful to the heritage of *Brown*, but the position of the plaintiffs in *Brown* was spelled out in their brief and could not have been clearer: "[T]he Fourteenth Amendment prevents states from according differential treatment to American children on the basis of their color or race." What do the racial classifications at issue here do, if not accord differential treatment on the basis of race? As counsel who appeared before this Court for the plaintiffs in *Brown* put it: "We have one fundamental contention which we will seek to develop in the course of this argument, and that contention is that no State has any authority under the equal-protection clause of the Fourteenth Amendment to use race as a factor in affording educational opportunities among its citizens." There is no ambiguity in that statement. And it was that position that prevailed in this Court, which emphasized in its remedial opinion that what was "[a]t stake is the personal interest of the plaintiffs in admission to public schools as soon as practicable *on a non-discriminatory basis*," and what was required was "determining admission to the public schools *on a nonracial basis*." What do the racial classifications do in these cases, if not determine admission to a public school on a racial basis? Before *Brown*, schoolchildren were told where they could and could not go to school based on the color of their skin. The school districts in these cases have not carried the heavy burden of demonstrating that we should allow this once again — even for a very different reasons. For schools that never segregated on the basis of race, such as Seattle, or that have removed the vestiges of past segregation, such as Jefferson County, the way "to achieve a system of determining admission to the public schools on a nonracial basis," is to stop assigning students on a racial basis. The way to stop discrimination on the basis of race is to stop discriminating on the basis of race.

3. Holding

The judgments of the Courts of Appeals for the Sixth and Ninth Circuits are reversed, and the cases are remanded for further proceedings.

4. Justice Stevens Dissenting

While I join Justice Breyer's eloquent and unanswerable dissent in its entirety, it is appropriate to add these words.

There is a cruel irony in The Chief Justice's reliance on our decision in *Brown v. Board of Education*. The first sentence in the concluding paragraph of his opinion states: "Before *Brown*, schoolchildren were told where they could and could not go to school based on the color of their skin." This sentence reminds me of Anatole France's observation: "[T]he majestic equality of the la[w], forbid[s] rich and poor alike to sleep under bridges, to beg in the streets, and to steal their bread." The Chief Justice fails to note that it was only black schoolchildren who were so ordered; indeed, the history books do not tell stories of white children struggling to attend black schools. In this and other ways, The Chief Justice rewrites the history of one of this Court's most important decisions.

The Chief Justice rejects the conclusion that the racial classifications at issue here should be viewed differently than others, because they do not impose burdens on one race alone and do not stigmatize or exclude. The only justification for refusing to acknowledge the obvious importance of that difference is the citation of a few recent opinions—none of which even approached unanimity—grandly proclaiming that all racial classifications must be analyzed under "strict scrutiny." The Court's misuse of the three-tiered approach to Equal Protection analysis merely reconfirms my own view that there is only one such Clause in the Constitution.

If we look at cases decided during the interim between *Brown* and *Adarand*, we can see how a rigid adherence to tiers of scrutiny obscures *Brown*'s clear message. Perhaps the best example is provided by our approval of the decision of the Supreme Judicial Court of Massachusetts in 1967 upholding a state statute mandating racial integration in that State's school system. Rejecting arguments comparable to those that the plurality accepts today, that court noted: "It would be the height of irony if the racial imbalance act, enacted as it was with the laudable purpose of achieving equal educational opportunities, should, by prescribing school pupil allocations based on race, founder on unsuspected shoals in the fourteenth Amendment. . . ."

The Court has changed significantly since it decided *School Comm. Of Boston* in 1968. It was then more faithful to *Brown* and more respectful of our precedent than it is today. It is my firm conviction that no Member of the Court that I joined in 1975 would have agreed with today's decision.

5. Justice Breyer Dissenting

These cases consider the longstanding efforts of two local school boards to integrate their public schools. The school board plans before us resemble many others adopted in the last 50 years by primary and secondary schools throughout the nation. All of those plans represent local efforts to bring about the kind of racially integrated education that *Brown v. Board of Education* long ago promised—efforts that this Court has repeatedly required, permitted, and encouraged local authorities to undertake. This Court has recognized that the public interests at stake in such cases are "compelling." We have approved of "narrowly tailored" plans that are no less race-conscious than the plans before us. And we have understood that the Constitution *permits* local communities to adopt desegregation plans even where it does not *require* them to do so.

The plurality pays inadequate attention to this law, to past opinions' rationales, their language, and the contexts in which they arise. As a result, it reverses course and reaches the wrong conclusion. In doing so, it distorts precedent, it misapplies the relevant constitutional principles, it announces legal rules that will obstruct efforts by state and local governments to deal effectively with the growing resegregation of public schools, it threatens to substitute for present calm a disruptive round of race-related litigation, and it undermines *Brown*'s promise of integrated primary and secondary education that local communities have sought to make a reality. This cannot be justified in the name of the Equal Protection Clause.

The historical and factual context in which these cases arise is critical. In *Brown*, this Court held that the government's segregation of schoolchildren by race violates the Constitution's promise of equal protection. The Court emphasized that "education is perhaps the most important function of state and local governments." And it thereby set the Nation on a path toward public school integration. . . .

In dozens of subsequent cases, this Court told school districts previously segregated by law what they must do at a minimum to comply with *Brown*'s constitutional holding. The measures required by those cases often included race-conscious practices, such as mandatory busing and race-based restrictions on voluntary transfers.

Beyond those minimum requirements, the Court left much of the determination of how to achieve integration to the judgment of local communities. Thus, in respect to race-conscious desegregation measures that the Constitution *permitted*, but did not *require* (measures similar to those at issue here), this Court unanimously stated: "School authorities are traditionally charged with broad power to formulate and implement educational policy and might well conclude, for example, that in order to prepare students to live in a pluralistic society such school should have prescribed ratio of Negro to white students reflecting the proportion for the district as a whole. *To do this as an educational policy is within the broad discretionary powers of school authorities.*"

As a result, different districts — some acting under court decree, some acting in order to avoid threatened lawsuits, some seeking to comply with federal administrative orders, some acting purely voluntarily, some acting after federal courts had dissolved earlier orders — adopted, modified, and experimented with hosts of different kinds of plans, including race-conscious plans, all with a similar objective: greater racial integration of public schools. The techniques that different districts have employed range "from voluntary transfer programs to mandatory reassignment."

And the design of particular plans has been "dictated by both the law and the specific needs of the district."

Overall these efforts brought about considerable racial integration. More recently, however, progress has stalled. Between 1968 and 1980, the number of black children attending a school where minority children constituted more than half of the school fell from 77% to 63% in the Nation (from 81% to 57% in the South) but then reversed direction by the year 2000, rising from 63% to 72T in the Nation (from 57% to 69% in the south). Similarly, between 1968 and 1980, the number of black children attending schools that were more than 90% minority fell from 64% to 33% in the Nation (from 78% to 23% in the South), but that too reversed direction, rising by the year 2000 from 33% to 37% in the Nation (from 23% to 31% in the South). As of 2002, almost 2.4 million students, or over 5% of all public school enrollment, attended schools with a white population of less than 1%. Of these, 2.3 million were black and Latino students, and only 72,000 were white. Today, more than one in six black children attend a school that is 99–100% minority. In light of the evident risk of a return to school systems that are in fact (though not in law) resegregated, many school districts have felt a need to maintain or to extend their integration efforts.

The upshot is that myriad school districts operating in myriad circumstances have devised myriad plans, often with race-conscious elements, all for the sake of eradicating earlier school segregation, bringing about integration, or preventing retrogression. Seattle and Louisville are two such districts, and the histories of their present plans set forth typical school integration stories . . .

The principal interest advanced in these cases to justify the use of race-based criteria goes by various names. Sometimes a court refers to it as an interest in achieving racial "diversity." Other times a court, like the plurality here, refers to it as an interest in racial "balancing." I have used more general terms to signify that interest, describing it, for example, as an interest in promoting or preserving greater racial "integration" of public schools. By this term, I mean the school districts' interest in eliminating school-by-school racial isolation and increasing the degree to which racial mixture characterizes each of the district's schools and each individual student's public school experience.

Regardless of its name, however, the interest at stake possesses three essential elements. First, there is a historical and remedial element: an interest in setting right the consequences of prior conditions of segregation. This refers back to a time when public schools were highly segregated, often as a result of legal or administrative policies that facilitated racial segregation in public schools. It is an interest in continuing to combat the remnants of segregation caused in whole or in part by these school-related policies, which have often affected not only schools, but also housing patterns, employment practices, economic conditions, and social attitudes. It is an interest in maintaining hard-won gains. And it has its roots in preventing what gradually may become the *de facto* resegregation of America's public schools.

Second, there is an educational element: an interest in overcoming the adverse educational effects produced by and associated with highly segregated schools. Studies suggest that children taken from those schools and placed in integrated settings often show positive academic gains.

Other studies reach different conclusions. But the evidence supporting an educational interest in racially integrated schools is well established and strong enough to permit a democratically elected school board reasonably to determine that this interest is a compelling one. . . .

Third, there is a democratic element: an interest in producing an educational environment that reflects the "pluralistic society" in which our children will live. It is an interest in helping our children learn to work and play together with children of different racial backgrounds. It is an interest in teaching children to engage in the kind of cooperation among Americans of all races that is necessary to make a land of three hundred million people one Nation.

Again, data support this insight. . . . There are again studies that offer contrary conclusions. Again, however, the evidence supporting a democratic interest in racially integrated schools is firmly established and sufficiently strong to permit a school board to determine, as this Court has itself often found, that this interest is compelling.

In light of this Court's conclusions in *Grutter*, the "compelling" nature of these interests in the context of primary and secondary public education follows here *a fortiori*. Primary and secondary schools are where the education of this Nation's children begins, where each of us begins to absorb those values we carry with us to the end of our days. As Justice Marshall said, "unless our children begin to learn together, there is little hope that our people will ever learn to live together."

And it was *Brown*, after all, focusing upon primary and secondary schools. . . . Hence, I am not surprised that Justice Kennedy finds that, "a district may consider it a compelling interest to achieve a diverse student population," including a *racially* diverse population.

The compelling interest at issue here, then, includes an effort to eradicate the remnants, not of general "societal discrimination," but of primary and secondary school segregation; it includes an effort to create school environments that provide better educational opportunities for all children; it includes an effort to help create citizens better prepared to know, to understand, and to work with people of all races and backgrounds, thereby furthering the kind of democratic government our Constitution foresees. If an educational interest that combines these three elements is not "compelling," what is? . . .

I next ask whether the plans before us are "narrowly tailored" to achieve these "compelling" objectives. I shall not accept the school board's assurances on faith, and I shall subject the "tailoring" of their plans to "rigorous judicial review." Several factors, taken together, nonetheless lead me to conclude that the boards' use of race-conscious criteria in these plans passes even the strictest "tailoring" test.

First, the race-conscious criteria at issue only help set the outer bounds of *broad* ranges. . . . Indeed, the race-conscious ranges at issue in these cases often have no effect, either because the particular school is not oversubscribed in the year in question, or because the racial makeup of the school falls within the broad range, or because the student is a transfer applicant or has a sibling at the school. In these respects, the broad ranges are less like a quota and more like the kinds of "useful starting points" that this Court has consistently found permissible, even when they set boundaries upon voluntary transfers, and even when they are based upon a community's general population.

Second, broad-range limits on voluntary school choice plans are less burdensome, and hence more narrowly tailored than other race-conscious restrictions this Court has previously approved. Indeed, the plans before us are *more narrowly tailored* than the race-conscious admission plans that this court approved in *Grutter*. Here, race becomes a factor only in a fraction of students' non-merit-based assignments—not in large numbers of students' merit-based applications. Moreover, the effect of applying race-conscious criteria here affects potentially disadvantaged students *less severely*, not more severely, than the criteria at issue in *Grutter*. Disappointed students are not rejected from a State's flagship graduate program; they simply attend a different one of the district's many public schools, which in aspiration and in fact are substantially equal. And, in Seattle, the disadvantaged student loses at most one year at the high school of his choice. One will search *Grutter* in vain for similarly persuasive evidence of narrow tailoring as the school districts have presented here.

Third, the manner in which the school boards developed these plans itself reflects "narrow tailoring." Each plan was devised to overcome a history of segregated public schools. Each plan embodies the results of local experience and community consultation. Each plan is the product of a process that has sought to enhance student choice, while diminishing the need for mandatory busing. And each plan's use of race-conscious elements is *diminished* compared to the use of race in preceding integration plans. . . .

Moreover, giving some degree of weight to a local school board's knowledge, expertise, and concerns in these particular matters is not inconsistent with rigorous judicial scrutiny. It simply recognizes that judges are not well suited to act as school administrators. Indeed, in the context of school desegregation, this Court has repeatedly stressed the importance of acknowledging that local school boards better understand their own communities and have a better knowledge of what in practice will best meet the educational needs of their pupils.

Nor could the school districts have accomplished their desired aims (*e.g.*, avoiding forced busing, countering white flight, maintaining racial diversity) by other means. Nothing in the extensive history of desegregation efforts over the past 50 years gives the districts, or this Court, any reason to believe that another method is possible to accomplish these goals. . . .

Finally, I recognize that the Court seeks to distinguish *Grutter* from these cases by claiming that *Grutter* arose in "'the context of higher education.'" But that is not a meaningful legal distinction. I have explained why I do not believe the Constitution could possibly find "compelling" the provision of a racially diverse education for a 23-year-old law student but not for a 13-year-old high school pupil. And I have explained how the plans before us are more narrowly tailored than those in *Grutter*. I add that one cannot find a relevant distinction in the fact that these school districts did not examine the merits of applications 'individual[ly]." The context here does not involve admission by merit; a child's academic, artistic, and athletic "merits" are not at all relevant to the child's placement. These are not affirmative action plans, and hence "individualized scrutiny" is simply beside the point.

The upshot is that these plans' specific features—(1) their limited and historically-diminishing use of race, (2) their strong reliance upon other non-race-conscious elements, (3) their history and the manner in which the districts developed and modified their approach, (4) the comparison with prior plans, and (5) the lack of reasonably evident alternatives—together show that the districts' plans are "narrowly tailored" to achieve their "compelling" goals. In sum, the districts' race-conscious plans satisfy "strict scrutiny" and are therefore lawful. . . .

[The] plans fore us satisfy the requirements of the Equal Protection Clause. And it is the plurality's opinion, not this dissent that "fails to ground the result it would reach in law."

Indeed, the consequences of the approach the Court takes today are serious. Yesterday, the plans under review were lawful. Today, they are not. Yesterday, the citizens of this Nation could look for guidance to this Court's unanimous pronouncements concerning desegregation. Today, they cannot. Yesterday, school boards had available to them a full range of means to combat segregated schools. Today, they do not. . . .

Finally, what of the hope and promise of *Brown*? For much of this Nation's history, the races remained divided. It was not long ago that people of different races drank from separate fountains, rode on separate buses, and studied in separate schools. In this Court's finest hour, *Brown v. Board of Education* challenged this history and helped to change it. For *Brown* held out a promise. It was a promise embodied in three Amendments designed to make citizens of slaves. It was the promise of true racial equality—not as a matter of fine words on paper, but as a matter of everyday life in the Nation's cities and schools. It was about the nature of a democracy that must work for all Americans. It sought one law, one Nation, one people, not simply as a matter of legal principle but in terms of how we actually live.

Not everyone welcomed this Court's decision in *Brown*. Three years after that decision was handed down, the governor of Arkansas ordered state militia to block the doors of a white schoolhouse so that black children could not enter. The President of the United States dispatched the 101st Airborne Division to Little Rock,

Arkansas, and federal troops were needed to enforce a desegregation decree. Today, almost 50 years later, attitudes toward race in this Nation have changed dramatically. Many parents, white and black alike, want their children to attend schools with children of different races. Indeed, the very school districts that once spurned integration now strive for it. The long history of their efforts reveals the complexities and difficulties they have faced. And in light of those challenges, they have asked us not to take from their hands the instruments they have used to rid their schools of racial segregation, instruments that they believe are need to overcome the problems of cities divided by race and poverty. The plurality would decline their modest request. The plurality is wrong to do so. The last half-century has witnessed great strides toward racial equality, but we have not yet realized the promise of *Brown*. To invalidate the plans under review is to threaten the promise of *Brown*. The plurality's position, I fear, would break that promise. This is a decision that the Court and the Nation will come to regret. . . .

P. Commentary on *Parents Involved*

Leonard M. Baynes

Perspectives: Abandoning Brown and '[Race]ing' Backwards on K–12 Education

The *Parents Involved* decision makes it much tougher for school districts to achieve racial diversity and eliminate racially isolated public school systems. In addressing the use of race by Seattle and Louisville school districts in student assignments, Chief Justice John Roberts declared, "the way to stop discrimination on the basis of race is to stop discriminating on the basis of race."

In the ultimate incongruity, Roberts equated these school assignment cases designed to achieve racial diversity to the separate-but-unequal doctrine that existed prior to the *Brown v. Board of Education* decision. In the Court's official opinion, Roberts said that: "Before *Brown*, school children were told where they could and could not go to school based on the color of their skin. The school districts in these cases have not carried the heavy burden of demonstrating that we should allow this once again—even for very different reasons."

Each school district used race in a limited way to assign students to oversubscribed schools. Despite acknowledging that fewer than 52 students were adversely affected by Seattle's race-conscious policy and that 95 percent of Louisville's students attend the school of their choice, Roberts wrote that these programs were invalid for two reasons.

First, Roberts held that no remedial justification existed for either of the school plans because, in his view, neither school district currently discriminated against children of color. According to Roberts, the Seattle public schools were never subject to a court-ordered desegregation decree. Moreover, Roberts noted that in 2000 the Louisville system was found to have "eliminated the vestiges associated with the former policy of segregation. . . ."

Second, Roberts found that race could only be used as one of several diversity factors. The Louisville and Seattle districts used race as the sole deciding factor. Moreover, without explanation, Roberts declared that these school assignment cases were not governed by *Grutter*, the 2003 case that upheld Michigan Law School's affirmative action plans. Presumably, Roberts would limit *Grutter*'s application to the realm of higher education. He went on to find that the programs were not narrowly tailored because the plans were directed at illegitimate racial balancing, not pedagogic concerns.

The opinion of Roberts would give local school boards virtually no power to achieve racial equity. Their opinions represent the conservatives' abandonment of the integration dream. As *New York Times* columnist David Brooks said in a recent op-ed: "maybe integration is not in the cards. Maybe the world will be as it's always been, a collection of insular compartments whose fractious tendencies are only kept in check by constant maintenance." This approach is flawed because it leaves few avenues for local and state governments to legally equalize educational opportunities or eliminate the racial isolation of K–12 students. In essence, such a plan would abandon *Brown*'s promise of integrated schools.

Fortunately, the opinion of Roberts represented only a plurality of the Court. Justice Anthony Kennedy supplied the key fifth vote that overturned the school assignment programs, saying they failed to satisfactorily explain the reasons for the assignment programs. But he joined the dissenting Justices in permitting the use of race in school assignment cases. Kennedy's opinion provides some clarity and does not totally turn back the clock. I predict that Kennedy's opinion will become the most influential opinion in this area of the law. In his own published opinion, Kennedy explained his disagreement with Roberts as such:

> "The plurality opinion is open to the interpretation that the Constitution requires school districts to ignore the problem of de facto resegregation in schooling. I cannot endorse that conclusion. To the extent that the plurality opinion suggests the Constitution mandates that state and local authorities must accept the status quo of racial isolation in schools, it is, in my view profoundly mistaken."

Kennedy gave some suggestions on how school districts can constitutionally use race-conscious measures to achieve diversity: (1) strategic site selection of new schools; (2) drawing attendance zones taking into account the demographics of neighborhoods; (3) targeted recruitment of students and faculty; and (4) tracking enrollments, performance and other statistics by race. If these general race-neutral approaches fail, Kennedy suggests that a nuanced individual evaluation of school needs and student characteristics including race as a component might also legitimate some school assignment plans. By leaving this door open for race-conscious means, Kennedy acknowledged that "this nation has a moral and ethical obligation to fulfill its historic commitment to creating an integrated society that ensures equal opportunity for all of its children."

Perspectives: Abandoning Brown and "[Race]ing"
Backwards On K–12 Education 1–2.
Reprinted with permission of Diverse Education and Leonard M. Baynes.

Leslie Yalof Garfield

*The Glass Half Full: Envisioning the Future of Race Preference Policies**

Justice Breyer's concern that the Court's June 2007 ruling in *Parents Involved in Community Schools v. Seattle School District No. 1* "is a decision the Court and the Nation will come to regret" is not well founded. Far from limiting the constitutionally permissible use of race in education from its present restriction to higher education, the case may allow governmental entities to consider race as a factor in achieving diversity in grades K–12. In *Parents Involved*, which the Court decided with its companion case, *McFarland v. Jefferson County Public Schools*, four Justices concluded that community school boards may never consider race when assigning students to particular schools. Justice Kennedy's concurrence in the 4-1-4 decision, like the dissenting opinion, acknowledged that a compelling governmental interest in achieving diversity justifies a school board's use of race-conscious school assignment plans. When the Court next considers the constitutionally permissible use of race-preference policies, Justice Kennedy's opinion could swing the Court to a position that is favorable to those who believe race-preference policies are paramount to achieving a society free from segregation. . . .

Chief Justice Roberts's plurality opinion refused to extend to classrooms at every educational level the Court's long-standing principle that race could be used to ensure diversity in classrooms of higher education. The opinion further suggested that states or their agencies could never consider race as a factor for ensuring diversity in the absence of a finding of de jure segregation. In contrast, Justice Breyer wrote in his dissent, in which three other Justices joined, that the use of race is permissible, and indeed necessary, to prevent a return to segregated classrooms. In his concurrence, Justice Kennedy agreed with Justice Breyer that the use of race-preference student assignment plans is permissible in certain instances and even more strongly asserted that the plurality's finding that race-preference policies could never be used to reverse de facto segregation was wrong. Ultimately, however, he sided with Chief Justice Roberts's holding that, in this instance, the school boards overstepped constitutionally permissible boundaries. . . .

Justice Kennedy's concurrence is likely to have an enduring effect on equal protection jurisprudence. His "concurrence in judgment" provides sound reasoning

---

* (footnotes and chapter headings omitted).

upon which courts considering race-preference student assignment plans may rely. Moreover, his "swing vote" has the capacity to shift the direction of the Court in the event that one of the more conservative members of the bench is replaced by a less conservative Justice.

The influential aftermath of Justice Powell's reasoning in *Bakke*, with which only the dissenting Justices in *Bakke* agreed, sets an historical example that Justice Kennedy's concurrence in *Parents Involved* has the potential to emulate. Justice Powell's conclusion that in some instances race could be a legitimate factor, and that there is a compelling governmental interest in achieving diversity in higher education, became the foundation for future case law. In *Grutter* and *Gratz*, the only post-*Bakke* decisions to consider the use of race-preference policies in higher education, the Court specifically endorsed Justice Powell's conclusion that the government has a compelling interest in ensuring diversity in education.

Many concerned with the *Parents Involved* ruling, including the four dissenting Justices, fear that the plurality's decision threatens the vitality of *Brown v. Board of Education*. In their judgment, *Parents Involved* could force a retreat to racial segregation in the nation's public schools. The more accurate view, however, is quite contrary. The force of Justice Kennedy's concurrence is most likely to have the same effect on the use of race preference policies as did Justice Powell's opinion in *Bakke*. Consequently, Justice Kennedy's finding that a "compelling interest exists in avoiding racial isolation" will serve to benefit those interested in using race-preference policies to remedy instances of segregation and discrimination in public schools.

63 *N.Y.U. Ann. Surv. Am. L.* 385, 385–388, 426–427.
Copyright © 2008 Annual Survey of American Law.
Reprinted with permission of Annual Survey of American Law and
Leslie Yalof Garfield.

Q. Background on *Fisher*

For almost 40 years, the Supreme Court has grappled with challenges to the scope and validity of race-based affirmative action programs. The 1974 *Defunis v. Odegaard* case was dismissed once the challenger graduated from law school; the 1978 *Bakke* case, decided by a plurality opinion, invalidated an affirmative action program maintaining a rigid racial quota in medical school admissions while upholding the use of race as a factor in such admissions; the 2004 *Grutter v. Bollinger* case upheld an affirmative action program in law school admissions where race was used as part of a process designed to achieve diversity in the classroom. Throughout, judges have disagreed over the legality of affirmative action.

The latest challenge—in which a decision is expected soon—is *Fisher v. University of Texas*, where the court will determine the constitutionality of an undergraduate affirmative action admissions program that accepts applicants in the top 10 percent of every Texas high school but uses race as a factor for all other applicants in order to achieve a diverse student body.

R. *Fisher v. University of Texas*, 133 S.Ct. 2411 (2013)

1. *Facts*

Justice KENNEDY delivered the opinion of the Court.

The University of Texas at Austin considers race as one of various factors in its undergraduate admissions process. Race is not itself assigned a numerical value for each applicant, but the University has committed itself to increasing racial minority enrollment on campus. It refers to this goal as a "critical mass." Petitioner, who is Caucasian, sued the University after her application was rejected. She contends that the University's use of race in the admissions process violated the Equal Protection Clause of the Fourteenth Amendment.

The parties asked the Court to review whether the judgment below was consistent with "this Court's decisions interpreting the Equal Protection Clause of the Fourteenth Amendment, including *Grutter v. Bollinger*, 539 U.S. 306, 123 S.Ct. 2325, 156 L.Ed.2d 304 (2003)." Pet. for Cert. i. The Court concludes that the Court of Appeals did not hold the University to the demanding burden of strict scrutiny articulated in *Grutter* and *Regents of Univ. of Cal. v. Bakke*, 438 U.S. 265, 305, 98 S. Ct. 2733, 57 L.Ed.2d 750 (1978) (opinion of Powell, J.). Because the Court of Appeals did not apply the correct standard of strict scrutiny, its decision affirming the District Court's grant of summary judgment to the University was incorrect. That decision is vacated, and the case is remanded for further proceedings.

Located in Austin, Texas, on the most renowned campus of the Texas state university system, the University is one of the leading institutions of higher education in the Nation. Admission is prized and competitive. In 2008, when petitioner sought admission to the University's entering class, she was 1 of 29,501 applicants. From this group, 12,843 were admitted, and 6,715 accepted and enrolled. Petitioner was denied admission.

In recent years the University has used three different programs to evaluate candidates for admission. The first is the program it used for some years before 1997, when the University considered two factors: a numerical score reflecting an applicant's test scores and academic performance in high school (Academic Index or AI), and the applicant's race. In 1996, this system was held unconstitutional by the United States Court of Appeals for the Fifth Circuit. It ruled the University's consideration of race violated the Equal Protection Clause because it did not further any compelling government interest. *Hopwood v. Texas*, 78 F.3d 932, 955 (1996).

The second program was adopted to comply with the *Hopwood* decision. The University stopped considering race in admissions and substituted instead a new holistic metric of a candidate's potential contribution to the University, to be used in conjunction with the Academic Index. This "Personal Achievement Index" (PAI) measures a student's leadership and work experience, awards, extra-curricular activities, community service, and other special circumstances that give insight into a student's background. These included growing up in a single-parent home, speaking a language other than English at home, significant family responsibilities assumed by the applicant, and the general socio-economic condition of the student's family. Seeking to address the decline in minority enrollment after *Hopwood*, the University also expanded its outreach programs.

The Texas State Legislature also responded to the *Hopwood* decision. It enacted a measure known as the top Ten Percent Law, codified at Tex. Educ. Code Ann. § 51.803 (West 2009). Also referred to as H.B. 588, the top Ten Percent Law grants automatic admission to any public state college, including the University to all students in the top 10% of their class at high schools in Texas that comply with certain standards.

The University's revised admissions process, coupled with the operation of the Top Ten Percent Law, resulted in a more racially diverse environment at the University. Before the admissions program at issue in this case, in the last year under the post *Hopwood* AI/PAI system that did not consider race, the entering class was 4.5% African American and 15.9% Hispanic. This is in contrast with the 1996 pre-*Hopwood* and Top Ten Percent regime, when race was explicitly considered, and the University's entering freshman class was 4.1% African American and 14.5% Hispanic.

Following this Court's decisions in *Grutter v. Bollinger, supra*, and *Gratz v. Bollinger*, 539 U.S. 244, 123 S.Ct. 2411, 156 L.Ed.2d 257 (2003), the University adopted a third admissions program, the 2004 program in which the University reverted to explicit consideration of race. This is the program here at issue. In *Grutter*, the Court upheld the use of race as one of many "plus factors" in an admissions program that considered the overall individual contribution of each candidate. In *Gratz*, by contrast, the Court held unconstitutional Michigan's undergraduate admissions program, which automatically awarded points to applicants from certain racial minorities.

The University's plan to resume race-conscious admissions was given formal expression in June 2004 in an internal document entitled Proposal to Consider Race and Ethnicity in Admissions (Proposal). Supp. App. 1a. The Proposal relied in substantial part on a study of a subset of undergraduate classes containing between 4 and 24 students. It showed that few of these classes had significant enrollment by racial minorities. In addition the Proposal relied on what it called "anecdotal" reports from students regarding their interaction in the classroom. The Proposal concluded that the University lacked a "critical mass" of minority students and that to remedy the deficiency it was necessary to give explicit consideration to race in the undergraduate admissions program.

To implement the Proposal the University included a student's race as a component of the PAI score, beginning with applicants in the fall of 2004. The University asks students to classify themselves from five predefined racial categories on the application. Race is not assigned an explicit numerical value, but it is undisputed that race is a meaningful factor.

Once applicants have been scored, they are plotted on a grid with the Academic Index on the x-axis and the Personal Achievement Index on the y-axis. On that grid students are assigned to so-called cells based on their individual scores. All students in the cells falling above a certain line are admitted. All students below the line are not. Each college—such as Liberal Arts or Engineering—admits students separately. So a student is considered initially for her first-choice college, then for her second choice, and finally for general admission as an undeclared major.

Petitioner applied for admission to the University's 2008 entering class and was rejected. She sued the University and various University officials in the United States District Court for the Western District of Texas. She alleged that the University's consideration of race in the admissions process violated the Equal Protection Clause. The parties cross-moved for summary judgment. The District Court granted summary judgment to the University. The United States Court of Appeals for the Fifth Circuit affirmed. It held that *Grutter* required courts to give substantial deference to the University, both in the definition of the compelling interest in diversity's benefits and in decided whether its specific plan was narrowly tailored to achieve its stated goal. Applying that standard, the court upheld the University's admissions plan. 631 F.3d 213, 217–218 (2011).

Over the dissent of seven judges, the Court of Appeals denied petitioner's request for a hearing en banc. See 644 F.3d 301, 303 (C.A.5 2011) (*per curiam*). Petitioner sought a writ of certiorari. The writ was granted. 565 U.S. ___, 132 S.Ct. 1536, 182 L. Ed.2d 160 (2012).

2. Opinion

Among the Court's cases involving racial classifications in education, there are three decisions that directly address the question of considering racial minority status as a positive or favorable factor in a university's admission process, with the goal of achieving the educational benefits of a more diverse student body: *Bakke* 438 U.S. 265, 98 S.Ct. 2733, 57 L.Ed.2d 750; *Gratz, supra*; and Grutter, 539 U.S. 306, 123 S.Ct. 2325, 156 L.Ed.2d 304. We take those cases as given for purposes of deciding this case.

We begin with the principal opinion authored by Justice Powell in *Bakke, supra*. In *Bakke*, the Court considered a system used by the medical school of the University of California at Davis. From an entering class of 100 students the school had set aside 16 seats for minority applicants. In holding this program impermissible under the Equal Protection Clause Justice Powell's opinion stated certain basic premises. First, "decisions based on race or ethnic origin by faculties and administrations of state universities are reviewable under the Fourteenth Amendment." *Id*. at 287, 98 S. Ct. 2733 (separate opinion). The principle of equal protection admits no "artificial line of a 'two-class theory'" that "permits the recognition of special wards entitled to a degree of protection greater than that accorded others." *Id*. at 295, 98 S.Ct. 2733. It is therefore irrelevant that a system of racial preferences in admissions may seem benign. Any racial classification must meet strict scrutiny, for when government decisions "touch upon an individual's race or ethnic background, he is entitled to a judicial determination that the burden he is asked to bear on that basis is precisely tailored to serve a compelling governmental interest." *Id*. at 299, 98 S.Ct. 2733.

Next, Justice Powell identified one compelling interest that could justify the consideration of race: the interest in the educational benefits that flow from a diverse student body. Redressing past discrimination could not serve as a compelling interest, because a University's "broad mission [of] education" is incompatible with making the "judicial, legislative, or administrative findings of constitutional or statutory violations" necessary to justify racial classification. *Id*. at 307–309, 98 S. Ct. 2733.

The attainment of a diverse student body, by contrast, serves beyond race alone, including enhanced classroom dialogue and the lessening of racial isolation and stereotypes. The academic mission of a university is "a special concern of the First Amendment." *Id*. at 312, 98 S.Ct. 2733. Part of "the business of a university [is] to provide that atmosphere which is conducive to speculation, experiment, and creation," and this in turns leads to the question of "who may be admitted to study." *Sweezy v. New Hampshire*, 354 U.S. 234, 263, 77 S.Ct. 1203, 1 L.Ed.2d 1311 (1957) (Frankfurter, J., concurring in judgment).

Justice Powell's central point, however, was that this interest in securing diversity's benefits, although a permissible objective, is complex. "It is not an interest in simple ethnic diversity, in which a specified percentage of the study body is in effect guaranteed to be members of selected ethnic groups, with the remaining percentage an undifferentiated aggregation of students. The diversity that furthers a compelling state interest encompasses a far broader array of qualifications and characteristics of which racial or ethnic origin is but a single though important element." *Bakke*, 438 U.S. at 315, 98 S.Ct. 2733 (separate opinion).

In *Gratz*, 539 U.S. 244, 123 S.Ct. 2411, 156 L.Ed.2d 257, and *Grutter, supra*, the Court endorsed the percepts stated by Justice Powell. In *Grutter* the Court reaffirmed his conclusion that obtaining the educational benefits of "student body diversity is a compelling state interest that can justify the use of race in university admissions." *Id*. at 325, 123 S.Ct. 2325.

As *Gratz* and *Grutter* observed, however, this follows only if a clear precondition is met. The particular admissions process used for this objective is subject to judicial review. Race may not be considered unless the admissions process can withstand strict scrutiny. "Nothing in Justice Powell's opinion in *Bakke* signaled that a University may employ whatever means it desires to achieve the stated goal of diversity without regard to the limits imposed by our strict scrutiny analysis" *Gratz*, supra, at 275, 123 S.Ct. 2411. "To be narrowly tailored, a race-conscious admissions program cannot use a quota system," *Grutter*, 539 U.S. at 334, 123 S.Ct. 2325, but instead must "remain flexible enough to ensure that each applicant is evaluated as an individual and not in a way that makes the applicant's race or ethnicity the defining feature of his or her application." *Id*. at 337, 123 S.Ct. 2335. Strict scrutiny requires the university to demonstrate with clarity that it's "purpose or interest is both constitutionally permissible and substantial, and that its use of the classification is necessary . . . to the accomplishment of its purpose." *Bakke*, 438 U.S. at 305, 98 S.Ct. 2733 (opinion of Powell, J.) (internal quotation marks omitted).

While these are the cases that most specifically address the central issue in this case, additional guidance may be found in the Court's broader equal protection jurisprudence which applies in this context. "Distinction between citizens solely because of their ancestry are by their very nature odious to a free people," *Rice v. Cayetano*, 528 U.S. 495, 517, 120 S.Ct. 1044, 145 L.Ed.2d 1007 (2000) (internal quotation marks omitted), and therefore "are contrary to our traditions and hence constitutionally suspect," *Bolling v. Sharp*, 347 U.S. 497, 499 74 S.Ct. 693, 98 L.Ed. 884 (1954). "[B]ecause racial characteristics so seldom provide a relevant basis for disparate treatment," *Richmond v. J.A. Croson Co.*, 488 U.S. 469, 505, 109 S.Ct. 706, 102 L.Ed.2d 854 (1989) (quoting *Fullilove v. Klutznick*, 448 U.S. 448, 533–534, 100 S. Ct. 2758, 65 L.Ed.2d 902 (1980), (Stevens, J., dissenting)), "the Equal Protection Clause demands that racial classifications . . . be subjected to the most rigid scrutiny.'" *Loving v. Virginia*, 388 U.S. 1, 11, 87 S.Ct. 1817, 18 L.Ed.2d 1010 (1967).

To implement these canons, judicial review must begin from the position that "any official action that treats a person differently on account of his race or ethnic origin is inherently suspect." *Fullilove, supra*, at 523, 100 S.Ct. 2758 (Stewart, J., dissenting); *McLaughlin v. Florida*, 379 U.S. 184, 192, 85 S.Ct. 283, 13 L.Ed.2d 222 (1964). Strict scrutiny is a searching examination, and it is the government that bears the burden to prove "that the reasons for any [racial] classification [are] clearly identified and unquestionably legitimate." *Croson, supra*, at 505, 109 S.Ct. 706 (quoting *Fullilove, supra*, 448 U.S., at 533–535, 100 S.Ct. 2758 (Stevens, J., dissenting)).

Grutter made clear that racial "classifications are constitutional only if they are narrowly tailored to further compelling governmental interests." 539 U.S., at 326, 123 S.Ct. 2325. And *Grutter* endorsed Justice Powell's conclusion in *Bakke* that "the attainment of a diverse student body . . . is a constitutionally permissible goal for an institution of higher education." 438 U.S., at 311–312, 98 S.Ct. 2733 (separate opinion). Thus, under *Grutter*, strict scrutiny must be applied to any admissions program using racial categories or classifications.

According to *Grutter*, a university's "educational judgment that such diversity is essential to its educational mission is one to which we defer." 539 U.S., at 328, 123 S. Ct. 2325. *Grutter* concluded that the decision to pursue the educational benefits that flow from student body diversity, *Id.* at 330, 123 S.Ct. 2325, that the University deems integral to its mission is, in substantial measure, an academic judgement to which some, but not complete judicial deference is proper under *Grutter*. A court, of course, should insure that there is a reasoned, principled explanation for the academic decision. On this point, the District Court and Court of Appeals were correct in finding that *Grutter* calls for deference to the University's conclusion, "based on its experience and expertise." 631 F.3d, at 230 (quoting 645 F.Supp.2d 587, 603 (W.D. Tex. 2009)), that a diverse student body would serve its educational goals. There is disagreement whether *Grutter* was consistent with the principles of equal protection in approving this compelling interest in diversity. *See post,* at 2422 (SCALIA, J., concurring); *post,* at 2423–2424 (THOMAS, J., concurring); *post,* at 2432–2433 (GINSBURG, J., dissenting). But the parties here do not ask the Court to revisit that aspect of *Gruter*'s holding.

A University is not permitted to define diversity as "some specified percentage of a particular group merely because of its race or ethnic origin." *Bakke, supra,* at 307, 98 S.Ct. 2733 (opinion of Powell, J.). "That would amount to outright racial balancing, which is patently unconstitutional." *Grutter, supra,* at 330, 123 S.Ct. 2325. "Racial balancing is not transformed from 'patently unconstitutional' to a compelling state interest by relabeling it 'racial diversity.'" *Parents Involved in Community Schools v. Seattle School Dist. No. 1,* 551 U.S. 701, 732, 127 S. Ct. 2738, 168 L.Ed.2d 508 (2007).

Once the University has established that its goal of diversity is consistent with strict scrutiny, however, there must still be a further judicial determination that the admissions process meets strict scrutiny in its implementation. The University must prove that the means chosen by the University to attain diversity are narrowly tailored to that goal. On this point, the University receives no deference. *Grutter* made clear that it is for the courts, not for university administrators, to ensure that "[t]he means chosen to accomplish the [government's] asserted purpose must be specifically and narrowly framed to accomplish that purpose." 539 U.S., at 333, 123 S. Ct. 2325 (internal quotation marks omitted). True, a court can take account of a university's experience and expertise in adopting or rejecting certain admissions processes. But, as the Court said in *Grutter,* it remains at all times the University's obligation to demonstrate, and the Judiciary's obligation to determine, that admissions processes "ensure that each applicant is evaluated as an individual and not in a way that makes an applicant's race or ethnicity the defining feature of his or her application." *Id.* at 337, 123 S.Ct. 2325.

Narrow tailoring also requires that the reviewing court verify that it is "necessary" for a university to use race to achieve the educational benefits of diversity. *Bakke, supra,* at 305, 98 S.Ct. 2733. This involves a careful judicial inquiry into whether a university could achieve sufficient diversity without using racial classifications. Although "[n]arrow tailoring does not require exhaustion of every *conceivable* race-neutral alternative," strict scrutiny does require a court to examine with care, and not defer to, a university's "serious, good faith consideration of workable race-neutral alternatives." See *Grutter, 539 U.S. at 339–340, 123 S.Ct. 2325* (emphasis added). Consideration by the university is of course necessary, but it is not sufficient to satisfy strict scrutiny: the reviewing court must ultimately be satisfied that no workable race-neutral alternatives would produce the educational benefits of diversity. If a "nonracial approach . . . could promote the substantial interest about as well and at tolerable administrative expense," *Wygant v. Jackson Bd. of Ed.,* 476 U.S. 267, 280, n. 6, 106 S.Ct. 1842, 90 L.Ed.2d 260 (1986) (quoting Greenawait, Judicial Scrutiny of "Benign" Racial Preference in Law School Admissions, 75 Colum. L.

Rev. 559, 578–579 (1975)), then the university may not consider race. A plaintiff, of course, bears the burden of placing the validity of a university's adoption of an affirmative action plan in issue. But strict scrutiny imposes on the university the ultimate burden of demonstrating, before turning to racial classifications that available, workable race-neutral alternatives do not suffice.

Rather than perform this searching examination, however, the Court of Appeals held petitioner could challenge only "whether [the University's] decision to reintroduce race as a factor in admissions was made in good faith." 631 F.3d, at 236. And in considering such a challenge, the court would "presume the University acted in good faith" and place on petitioner the burden of rebutting that presumption. *Id.* at 231–232. The Court of Appeals held that to "second-guess the merits" of this aspect of the University's decision was a task it was "ill-equipped to perform" and that it would attempt only to "ensure that [the University's] decision to adopt a race-conscious admissions policy followed from [a process of] good faith consideration." *Id.* at 231. The Court of Appeals thus concluded that "the narrow-tailoring inquiry—like the compelling-interest inquiry—is undertaken with a degree of deference to the Universit[y]." *Id.* at 232. Because "the efforts of the University have been studied, serious, and of high purpose," the Court of Appeals held that the use of race in the admissions program fell within "a constitutionally protected zone of discretion." *Id.* at 231.

These expressions of the controlling standard are at odds with *Grutter's* command that "all racial classification imposed by the government 'must be analyzed by a reviewing court under strict scrutiny,'" 539 U.S. at 326, 123 S.Ct. 2325 (quoting *Adarand Constructors, Inc., v. Pena,* 515 U.S. 200, 277, 115 S.Ct. 2097, 132 L.Ed.2d 158 (1995)). In *Grutter,* the Court approved the plan at issue upon concluding that it was not a quota, was sufficiently flexible, was limited in time, and followed "serious good faith consideration of workable race-neutral alternatives." 539 U.S. at 339, 123 S.Ct. 2325. As noted above, see *supra,* at 2415, the parties do not challenge, and the Court therefore does not consider, the correctness of that determination.

Grutter did not hold that good faith would forgive an impermissible consideration of race. It must be remembered that "the mere recitation of a 'benign' or legitimate purpose of racial classification is entitled to little or no weight." *Croson,* 488 U.S. at 500, 109 S.Ct. 706. Strict scrutiny does not permit a court to accept a school's assertion that its admissions process uses race in a permissible way without a court giving close analysis to the evidence of how the process works in practice.

The higher education dynamic does not change the narrow tailoring analysis of strict scrutiny applicable in other contexts. "[T]he analysis and level of scrutiny applied to determine the validity of [a racial] classification do not vary simply because the objective appears acceptable. While the validity and importance of the objective may affect the outcome of the analysis, the analysis itself does not change." *Mississippi Univ. for Women v. Hogan,* 458 U.S. 718, 724, n. 9, 102 S.Ct. 3331, 73 L. Ed.2d 1090 (1982).

3. Holding

The District Court and Court of Appeals confined the strict scrutiny inquiry in too narrow a way by deferring to the University's good faith in its use of racial classifications and affirming the grant of summary judgment on that basis. The Court vacates that judgment, but fairness to the litigants and the courts that heard the case requires that it be remanded so that the admissions process can be considered and judged under a correct analysis. See *Adarand, supra,* at 237, 115 S.Ct. 2097. Unlike *Grutter,* which was decided after trial, this case arises from cross-motions for summary judgment. In this case, as in similar cases, in determining whether summary judgment in favor of the University would be appropriate, the Court of Appeals must assess whether the University has offered sufficient evidence that would prove that its admissions program is narrowly tailored to obtain the educational benefits of diversity. Whether this record—and not "simple . . . assurances of good intention," *Croson, supra,* at 500, 109 S.Ct. 706—is sufficient is a question for the Court of Appeals in the first instance.

Strict scrutiny must not be "strict in theory, but fatal in fact." *Adarand, supra,* at 237, 115 S.Ct. 2097; see also *Grutter, supra,* at 326, 123 S.Ct. 2325. But the opposite is also true. Strict scrutiny must not be strict in theory but feeble in fact. In order for judicial review to be meaningful, a university must make a showing that its plan is narrowly tailored to achieve the only interest that this Court has approved in this context: the benefits of a student body diversity that encompasses a . . . broa[d] array of qualifications and characteristics of which racial or ethnic origin is but one single though important element." *Bakke,* 438 U.S., at 315, 98 S.Ct. 2733 (opinion of Powell, J.). The judgment of the Court of Appeals is vacated, and the case is remanded for further proceedings consistent with this opinion.

Justice KAGAN took no part in the consideration or decision of this case.

S. Commentary on *Fisher*

Fairness has been a central theme in affirmative action litigation. White applicants denied admission have argued that they have been victimized by programs giving their places to lesser qualified minority applicants. According to recent litigant Abigail Fisher, "there were people in my [high school] class with lower grades who weren't in all the activities I was in, who were being accepted at the University of Texas, and the only other difference between us was the color of our skin." Yet college and graduate school rejections at highly selective institutions like the University of Texas (UT) are not so easily categorized. In fact, the year that Fisher applied, UT offered conditional admission to 47 students with lower test scores than Fisher, of which five of those students were minority, and forty-two were white. UT rejected 168 minority applicants with grades similar to Fisher's.

These results reflect the reality that academic institutions consider other factors aside from grades and test scores in evaluating the merit of individual applicants and the applicants' value to the achievement of the school's goals. While certainly there are whites who have lost opportunities due to misdirected or overly-broad race-based affirmative action programs, Ms. Fisher should not be so categorized. Fairness requires that applicants not be denied or accepted and not be unduly advantaged or disadvantaged solely because of race. Fairness does not mean that universities do not have the flexibility to accept a few minority applicants with lower grades and test scores than a rejected white applicant in order to increase the diversity of the class. The 2013 *Fisher v. University of Texas* ruling invalidated the undergraduate admission plan that furthered racial diversity nonetheless.

T. Background on *Schuette*

Shortly after *Fisher*, the Supreme Court was presented with the question of whether the Constitution prohibits state laws that subject authorization of affirmative action programs to the electoral process. As in *Fisher*, Justice Kagan recused herself due to previous involvement in the case as Solicitor General arguing against such state laws.

U. *Schuette v. Coalition To Defend Affirmative Action*, 134 S.Ct. 1623 (2014)

1. Facts

Justice KENNEDY delivered the opinion of the Court.

The Court in this case must determine whether an amendment to the Constitution of the State of Michigan, approved and enacted by its voters, is invalid under the Equal Protection Clause of the Fourteenth Amendment to the Constitution of the United States.

In 2003 the Court reviewed the constitutionality of two admissions systems at the University of Michigan, one for its undergraduate class and one for its law school. The undergraduate admissions plan was addressed in *Gratz v. Bollinger*, 539 U.S. 244, 123 S.Ct. 2411, 156 L.Ed.2d 257. The law school admission plan was addressed in *Grutter v. Bollinger*, 539 U.S. 306, 123 S.Ct. 2325, 156 L.Ed.2d 304. Each admissions process permitted the explicit consideration of an applicant's race. In *Gratz*, the Court invalidated the undergraduate plan as a violation of the Equal Protection Clause. 539 U.S., at 270, 123 S.Ct. 2411. In *Grutter*, the Court found no constitutional flaw in the law school admission plan's more limited use of race-based preferences. 539 U.S., at 343, 123 S.Ct. 2325.

In response to the Court's decision in *Gratz*, the university revised its undergraduate admissions process, but the revision still allowed limited use of race-based preferences. After a statewide debate on the question of racial preferences in the context of governmental decisionmaking, the voters, in 2006, adopted an amendment to the State Constitution prohibiting state and other governmental entities in Michigan from granting certain preferences, including race-based preferences, in a wide range of actions and decisions. Under the terms of the amendment, race-based preferences cannot be part of the admissions process for state universities. That particular prohibition is central to the instant case.

The ballot proposal was called Proposal 2 and, after it passed by a margin of 58 percent to 42 percent, the resulting enactment became Article I, §26, of the Michigan Constitution. As noted, the amendment is in broad terms. Section 26 states, in relevant part, as follows:

"(1) The University of Michigan, Michigan State University, Wayne State University, and any other public college or university, community college, or school district shall not discriminate against, or grant preferential treatment to, any individual or group on the basis of race, sex, color, ethnicity, or national origin in the operation of public employment, public education, or public contracting.

"(2) The state shall not discriminate against, or grant preferential treatment to, any individual or group on the basis of race, sex, color, ethnicity, or national origin in the operation of public employment, public education, or public contracting.

"(3) For the purposes of this section 'state' includes, but is not necessarily limited to, the state itself, any city, county, any public college, university, or community college, school district, or other political subdivision or governmental instrumentality of or within the State of Michigan not included in sub-section 1."

Section 26 was challenged in two cases. Among the plaintiffs in the suits were the Coalition to Defend Affirmative Action, Integration and Immigrant Rights and Fight for Equality By Any Means Necessary (BAMN); students; faculty; and prospective applicants to Michigan public universities. The named defendants included then-Governor Jennifer Granholm, the Board of Regents of the University of Michigan, the Board of Trustees of Michigan State University, and the Board of Governors of Wayne State University. The Michigan Attorney General was granted leave to intervene as a defendant. The United States District Court for the Eastern District of Michigan consolidated the cases.

In 2008, the District Court granted summary judgment to Michigan, thus upholding Proposal 2. *BAMN v. Regents of Univ. of Mich.*, 539 F.Supp.2d 924. The District Court denied a motion to reconsider the grant of summary judgment. 592 F.Supp.2d 948. A panel of the United States Court of Appeals for the Sixth Circuit reversed the grant of summary judgment. 652 F.3d 607 (2011). Judge Gibbons dissented from that holding. *Id.*, at 633–646. The panel majority held that Proposal 2 had violated the principles elaborated by this Court in *Washington v. Seattle School Dist. No. 1*, 458 U.S. 457, 102 S.Ct. 3187, 73 L.Ed.2d 896 (1982), and in the cases that *Seattle* relied upon.

The Court of Appeals, sitting en banc, agreed with the panel decision. 701 F.3d 466 (C.A.6 2012). The majority opinion determined that *Seattle* "mirrors the [case] before us." *Id.*, at 475. Seven judges dissented in a number of opinions. The Court granted certiorari. 568 U.S.——, 133 S.Ct. 1633, 185 L.Ed.2d 615 (2013).

2. Opinion

Before the Court addresses the question presented, it is important to note what this case is not about. It is not about the constitutionality, or the merits, of race-conscious admissions policies in higher education. The consideration of race in admissions presents complex questions, in part addressed last Term in *Fisher v. University of Texas at Austin,* 570 U.S.——, 133 S.Ct. 2411, 186 L.Ed.2d 474 (2013). In *Fisher,* the Court did not disturb the principle that the consideration of race in admissions is permissible, provided that certain conditions are met. In this case, as in *Fisher,* that principle is not challenged. The question here concerns not the permissibility of race-conscious admissions policies under the Constitution but whether, and in what manner, voters in the States may choose to prohibit the consideration of racial preferences in governmental decisions, in particular with respect to school admissions.

This Court has noted that some States have decided to prohibit race-conscious admissions policies. In *Grutter,* the Court noted: "Universities in California, Florida, and Washington State, where racial preferences in admissions are prohibited by state law, are currently engaged in experimenting with a wide variety of alternative approaches. Universities in other States can and should draw on the most promising aspects of these race-neutral alternatives as they develop." 539 U.S., at 342, 123 S. Ct. 2325 (citing *United States v. Lopez,* 514 U.S. 549, 581, 115 S.Ct. 1624, 131 L.Ed.2d 626 (1995) (KENNEDY, J., concurring) ("[T]he States may perform their role as laboratories for experimentation to devise various solutions where the best solution is far from clear")). In this way, *Grutter* acknowledged the significance of a dialogue regarding this contested and complex policy question among and within States. There was recognition that our federal structure "permits 'innovation and experimentation'" and "enables greater citizen 'involvement in democratic processes.'" *Bond v. United States,* 564 U.S.——,——, 131 S.Ct. 2355, 2364, 180 L.Ed.2d 269 (2011) (quoting *Gregory v. Ashcroft,* 501 U.S. 452, 458, 111 S.Ct. 2395, 115 L.Ed.2d 410 (1991)). While this case arises in Michigan, the decision by the State's voters reflects in part the national dialogue regarding the wisdom and practicality of race-conscious admissions policies in higher education. See, *e.g., Coalition for Economic Equity v. Wilson,* 122 F.3d 692 (C.A.9 1997).

In Michigan, the State Constitution invests independent boards of trustees with plenary authority over public universities, including admissions policies. Mich. Const., Art. VIII, §5; see also *Federated Publications, Inc. v. Board of Trustees of Mich. State Univ.,* 460 Mich. 75, 86–87, 594 N.W.2d 491, 497 (1999). Although the members of the boards are elected, some evidence in the record suggests they delegated authority over admissions policy to the faculty. But whether the boards or the faculty set the specific policy, Michigan's public universities did consider race as a factor in admissions decisions before 2006.

In holding §26 invalid in the context of student admissions at state universities, the Court of Appeals relied in primary part on *Seattle, supra,* which it deemed to control the case. But that determination extends *Seattle*'s holding in a case presenting quite different issues to reach a conclusion that is mistaken here. Before explaining this further, it is necessary to consider the relevant cases that preceded *Seattle* and the background against which *Seattle* itself arose.

Though it has not been prominent in the arguments of the parties, this Court's decision in *Reitman v. Mulkey*, 387 U.S. 369, 87 S.Ct. 1627, 18 L.Ed.2d 830 (1967), is a proper beginning point for discussing the controlling decisions. In *Mulkey*, voters amended the California Constitution to prohibit any state legislative interference with an owner's prerogative to decline to sell or rent residential property on any basis. Two different cases gave rise to *Mulkey*. In one a couple could not rent an apartment, and in the other a couple were evicted from their apartment. Those adverse actions were on account of race. In both cases the complaining parties were barred, on account of race, from invoking the protection of California's statutes; and, as a result, they were unable to lease residential property. This Court concluded that the state constitutional provision was a denial of equal protection. The Court agreed with the California Supreme Court that the amendment operated to insinuate the State into the decision to discriminate by encouraging that practice. The Court noted the "immediate design and intent" of the amendment was to "establis[h] a purported constitutional right to privately discriminate." *Id.*, at 374, 87 S.Ct. 1627 (internal quotation marks omitted and emphasis deleted). The Court agreed that the amendment "expressly authorized and constitutionalized the private right to discriminate." *Id.*, at 376, 87 S.Ct. 1627. The effect of the state constitutional amendment was to "significantly encourage and involve the State in private racial discriminations." *Id.*, at 381, 87 S.Ct. 1627. In a dissent joined by three other Justices, Justice Harlan disagreed with the majority's holding. *Id.*, at 387, 87 S.Ct. 1627. The dissent reasoned that California, by the action of its voters, simply wanted the State to remain neutral in this area, so that the State was not a party to discrimination. *Id.*, at 389, 87 S.Ct. 1627. That dissenting voice did not prevail against the majority's conclusion that the state action in question encouraged discrimination, causing real and specific injury.

The next precedent of relevance, *Hunter v. Erickson*, 393 U.S. 385, 89 S.Ct. 557, 21 L.Ed.2d 616 (1969), is central to the arguments the respondents make in the instant case. In *Hunter*, the Court for the first time elaborated what the Court of Appeals here styled the "political process" doctrine. There, the Akron City Council found that the citizens of Akron consisted of "'people of different race[s], . . . many of whom live in circumscribed and segregated areas, under sub-standard unhealthful, unsafe, unsanitary and overcrowded conditions, because of discrimination in the sale, lease, rental and financing of housing.'" *Id.*, at 391, 89 S.Ct. 557. To address the problem, Akron enacted a fair housing ordinance to prohibit that sort of discrimination. In response, voters amended the city charter to overturn the ordinance and to require that any additional antidiscrimination housing ordinance be approved by referendum. But most other ordinances "regulating the real property market" were not subject to those threshold requirements. *Id.*, at 390, 89 S.Ct. 557. The plaintiff, a black woman in Akron, Ohio, alleged that her real estate agent could not show her certain residences because the owners had specified they would not sell to black persons.

Central to the Court's reasoning in *Hunter* was that the charter amendment was enacted in circumstances where widespread racial discrimination in the sale and rental of housing led to segregated housing, forcing many to live in "'unhealthful, unsafe, unsanitary and overcrowded conditions.'" *Id.*, at 391, 89 S.Ct. 557. The Court stated: "It is against this background that the referendum required by [the charter amendment] must be assessed." *Ibid.* Akron attempted to characterize the charter amendment "simply as a public decision to move slowly in the delicate area of race relations" and as a means "to allow the people of Akron to participate" in the decision. *Id.*, at 392, 89 S.Ct. 557. The Court rejected Akron's flawed "justifications for its discrimination," justifications that by their own terms had the effect of acknowledging the targeted nature of the charter amendment. *Ibid.* The Court noted, furthermore, that the charter amendment was unnecessary as a general means of public control over the city council; for the people of Akron already were empowered to overturn ordinances by referendum. *Id.*, at 390, n. 6, 89 S.Ct. 557. The Court found that the city charter amendment, by singling out antidiscrimination ordinances, "places special burden on racial minorities within the governmental process," thus becoming as impermissible as any other government action taken with the invidious intent to injure a racial minority. *Id.*, at 391, 89 S.Ct. 557. Justice Harlan filed a concurrence. He argued the city charter amendment "has the clear purpose of making it more difficult for certain racial and religious minorities to achieve legislation that is in their interest." *Id.*, at 395, 89 S.Ct. 557. But without regard to the sentence just quoted, *Hunter* rests on the unremarkable principle that the State may not alter the procedures of government to target racial minorities. The facts in *Hunter* established that invidious discrimination would be the necessary result of the procedural restructuring. Thus, in *Mulkey* and *Hunter*, there was a demonstrated injury on the basis of race that, by reasons of state encouragement or participation, became more aggravated.

Seattle is the third case of principal relevance here. There, the school board adopted a mandatory busing program to alleviate racial isolation of minority students in local schools. Voters who opposed the school board's busing plan passed a state initiative that barred busing to desegregate. The Court first determined that, although "white as well as Negro children benefit from" diversity, the school board's plan "inures primarily to the benefit of the minority." 458 U.S., at 472, 102 S.Ct. 3187. The Court next found that "the practical effect" of the state initiative was to "remov[e] the authority to address a racial problem—and only a racial problem—from the existing decisionmaking body, in such a way as to burden minority interests" because advocates of busing "now must seek relief from the state legislature, or from the statewide electorate." *Id.*, at 474, 102 S.Ct. 3187. The Court therefore found that the initiative had "explicitly us[ed] the racial nature of a decision to determine the decisionmaking process." *Id.*, at 470, 102 S.Ct. 3187 (emphasis deleted).

Seattle is best understood as a case in which the state action in question (the bar on busing enacted by the State's voters) had the serious risk, if not purpose, of causing specific injuries on account of race, just as had been the case in *Mulkey* and *Hunter*. Although there had been no judicial finding of *de jure* segregation with respect to Seattle's school district, it appears as though school segregation in the district in the 1940's and 1950's may have been the partial result of school board policies that "permitted white students to transfer out of black schools while restricting the transfer of black students into white schools." *Parents Involved in Community Schools v. Seattle School Dist. No. 1,* 551 U.S. 701, 807–808, 127 S.Ct. 2738, 168 L.Ed.2d 508 (2007) (BREYER, J., dissenting). In 1977, the National Association for the Advancement of Colored People (NAACP) filed a complaint with the Office for Civil Rights, a federal agency. The NAACP alleged that the school board had maintained a system of *de jure* segregation. Specifically, the complaint alleged "that the Seattle School Board had created or perpetuated unlawful racial segregation through, *e.g.,* certain school-transfer criteria, a construction program that needlessly built new schools in white areas, district line-drawing criteria, the maintenance of inferior facilities at black schools, the use of explicit racial criteria in the assignment of teachers and other staff, and a general pattern of delay in respect to the implementation of promised desegregation efforts." *Id.,* at 810, 127 S.Ct. 2738. As part of a settlement with the Office for Civil Rights, the school board implemented the "Seattle Plan," which used busing and mandatory reassignments between elementary schools to reduce racial imbalance and which was the subject of the state initiative at issue in *Seattle*. See 551 U.S., at 807–812, 127 S.Ct. 2738.

As this Court held in *Parents Involved,* the school board's purported remedial action would not be permissible today absent a showing of *de jure* segregation. *Id.,* at 720–721, 127 S.Ct. 2738. That holding prompted Justice BREYER to observe in dissent, as noted above, that one permissible reading of the record was that the school board had maintained policies to perpetuate racial segregation in the schools. In all events we must understand *Seattle* as *Seattle* understood itself, as a case in which neither the State nor the United States "challenge[d] the propriety of race-conscious student assignments for the purpose of achieving integration, even absent a finding of prior *de jure* segregation." 458 U.S. at 472, n. 15, 102 S.Ct. 3187. In other words the legitimacy and constitutionality of the remedy in question (busing for desegregation) was assumed, and *Seattle* must be understood on that basis. *Ibid. Seattle* involved a state initiative that "was carefully tailored to interfere only with desegregative busing." *Id.,* at 471, 102 S.Ct. 3187. The *Seattle* Court, accepting the validity of the school board's busing remedy as a predicate to its analysis of the constitutional question, found that the State's disapproval of the school board's busing remedy was an aggravation of the very racial injury in which the State itself was complicit.

The broad language used in *Seattle,* however, went well beyond the analysis needed to resolve the case. The Court there seized upon the statement in Justice Harlan's concurrence in *Hunter* that the procedural change in that case had "the clear purpose of making it more difficult for certain racial and religious minorities to achieve legislation that is in their interest." 385 U.S., at 395, 87 S.Ct. 534. That language, taken in the context of the facts in *Hunter*, is best read simply to describe the necessity for finding an equal protection violation where specific injuries from hostile discrimination were at issue. The *Seattle* Court, however, used the language from the *Hunter* concurrence to establish a new and far-reaching rationale. *Seattle* stated that where a government policy "inures primarily to the benefit of the minority" and "minorities ... consider" the policy to be "'in their interest,'" then any state action that "place[s] effective decisionmaking authority over" that policy "at a different level of government" must be reviewed under strict scrutiny. 458 U.S., at 472, 474, 102 S.Ct. 3187. In essence, according to the broad reading of *Seattle*, any state action with a "racial focus" that makes it "more difficult for certain racial minorities than for other groups" to "achieve legislation that is in their interest" is subject to strict scrutiny. It is this reading of *Seattle* that the Court of Appeals found to be controlling here. And that reading must be rejected.

The broad rationale that the Court of Appeals adopted goes beyond the necessary holding and the meaning of the precedents said to support it; and in the instant case neither the formulation of the general rule just set forth nor the precedents cited to authenticate it suffice to invalidate Proposal 2. The expansive reading of *Seattle* has no principled limitation and raises serious questions of compatibility with the Court's settled equal protection jurisprudence. To the extent *Seattle* is read to require the Court to determine and declare which political policies serve the "interest" of a group defined in racial terms, that rationale was unnecessary to the decision in *Seattle*; it has no support in precedent; and it raises serious constitutional concerns. That expansive language does not provide a proper guide for decisions and should not be deemed authoritative or controlling. The rule that the Court of Appeals elaborated and respondents seek to establish here would contradict central equal protection principles.

In cautioning against "impermissible racial stereotypes," this Court has rejected the assumption that "members of the same racial group—regardless of their age, education, economic status, or the community in which they live—think alike, share the same political interests, and will prefer the same candidates at the polls." *Shaw v. Reno*, 509 U.S. 630, 647, 113 S.Ct. 2816, 125 L.Ed.2d 511 (1993); see also *Metro Broadcasting, Inc. v. FCC*, 497 U.S. 547, 636, 110 S.Ct. 2997, 111 L.Ed.2d 445 (1990) (KENNEDY, J., dissenting) (rejecting the "demeaning notion that members of ... defined racial groups ascribe to certain 'minority views' that must be different from those of other citizens"). It cannot be entertained as a serious proposition that all individuals of the same race think alike. Yet that proposition would be a necessary beginning point were the *Seattle* formulation to control, as the Court of Appeals held it did in this case. And if it were deemed necessary to probe how some races define their own interest in political matters, still another beginning point would be to define individuals according to race. But in a society in which those lines are becoming more blurred, the attempt to define race-based categories also raises serious questions of its own. Government action that classifies individuals on the basis of race is inherently suspect and carries the danger of perpetuating the very racial divisions the polity seeks to transcend. Cf. *Ho v. San Francisco Unified School Dist.,* 147 F.3d 854, 858 (C.A.9 1998) (school district delineating 13 racial categories for purposes of racial balancing). Were courts to embark upon this venture not only would it be undertaken with no clear legal standards or accepted sources to guide judicial decision but also it would result in, or at least impose a high risk of, inquiries and categories dependent upon demeaning stereotypes, classifications of questionable constitutionality on their own terms.

Even assuming these initial steps could be taken in a manner consistent with a sound analytic and judicial framework, the court would next be required to determine the policy realms in which certain groups—groups defined by race—have a political interest. That undertaking, again without guidance from any accepted legal standards, would risk, in turn, the creation of incentives for those who support or oppose certain policies to cast the debate in terms of racial advantage or disadvantage. Thus could racial antagonisms and conflict tend to arise in the context of judicial decisions as courts undertook to announce what particular issues of public policy should be classified as advantageous to some group defined by race. This risk is inherent in adopting the *Seattle* formulation.

There would be no apparent limiting standards defining what public policies should be included in what *Seattle* called policies that "inur[e] primarily to the benefit of the minority" and that "minorities . . . consider" to be "'in their interest.'" 458 U.S., at 472, 474, 102 S.Ct. 3187. Those who seek to represent the interests of particular racial groups could attempt to advance those aims by demanding an equal protection ruling that any number of matters be foreclosed from voter review or participation. In a nation in which governmental policies are wide ranging, those who seek to limit voter participation might be tempted, were this Court to adopt the *Seattle* formulation, to urge that a group they choose to define by race or racial stereotypes are advantaged or disadvantaged by any number of laws or decisions. Tax policy, housing subsidies, wage regulations, and even the naming of public schools, highways, and monuments are just a few examples of what could become a list of subjects that some organizations could insist should be beyond the power of voters to decide, or beyond the power of a legislature to decide when enacting limits on the power of local authorities or other governmental entities to address certain subjects. Racial division would be validated, not discouraged, were the *Seattle* formulation, and the reasoning of the Court of Appeals in this case, to remain in force.

Perhaps, when enacting policies as an exercise of democratic self-government, voters will determine that race-based preferences should be adopted. The constitutional validity of some of those choices regarding racial preferences is not at issue here. The holding in the instant case is simply that the courts may not disempower the voters from choosing which path to follow. In the realm of policy discussions the regular give-and-take of debate ought to be a context in which rancor or discord based on race are avoided, not invited. And if these factors are to be interjected, surely it ought not to be at the invitation or insistence of the courts.

One response to these concerns may be that objections to the larger consequences of the *Seattle* formulation need not be confronted in this case, for here race was an undoubted subject of the ballot issue. But a number of problems raised by *Seattle*, such as racial definitions, still apply. And this principal flaw in the ruling of the Court of Appeals does remain: Here there was no infliction of a specific injury of the kind at issue in *Mulkey* and *Hunter* and in the history of the Seattle schools. Here there is no precedent for extending these cases to restrict the right of Michigan voters to determine that race-based preferences granted by Michigan governmental entities should be ended.

It should also be noted that the judgment of the Court of Appeals in this case of necessity calls into question other long-settled rulings on similar state policies. The California Supreme Court has held that a California constitutional amendment prohibiting racial preferences in public contracting does not violate the rule set down by *Seattle*. *Coral Constr., Inc. v. City and County of San Francisco,* 50 Cal.4th 315, 113 Cal.Rptr.3d 279, 235 P.3d 947 (2010). The Court of Appeals for the Ninth Circuit has held that the same amendment, which also barred racial preferences in public education, does not violate the Equal Protection Clause. *Wilson,* 122 F.3d 692 (1997). If the Court were to affirm the essential rationale of the Court of Appeals in the instant case, those holdings would be invalidated, or at least would be put in serious question. The Court, by affirming the judgment now before it, in essence would announce a finding that the past 15 years of state public debate on this issue have been improper. And were the argument made that *Coral* might still stand because it involved racial preferences in public contracting while this case concerns racial preferences in university admissions, the implication would be that the constitutionality of laws forbidding racial preferences depends on the policy interest at stake, the concern that, as already explained, the voters deem it wise to avoid because of its divisive potential. The instant case presents the question involved in *Coral* and *Wilson* but not involved in *Mulkey, Hunter,* and *Seattle*. That question is not how to address or prevent injury caused on account of race but whether voters may determine whether a policy of race-based preferences should be continued.

By approving Proposal 2 and thereby adding § 26 to their State Constitution, the Michigan voters exercised their privilege to enact laws as a basic exercise of their democratic power. In the federal system States "respond, through the enactment of positive law, to the initiative of those who seek a voice in shaping the destiny of their own times." *Bond,* 564 U.S., at ___, 131 S.Ct., at 2364. Michigan voters used the initiative system to bypass public officials who were deemed not responsive to the concerns of a majority of the voters with respect to a policy of granting race-based preferences that raises difficult and delicate issues.

The freedom secured by the Constitution consists, in one of its essential dimensions, of the right of the individual not to be injured by the unlawful exercise of governmental power. The mandate for segregated schools, *Brown v. Board of Education,* 347 U.S. 483, 74 S.Ct. 686, 98 L.Ed. 873 (1954); a wrongful invasion of the home, *Silverman v. United States,* 365 U.S. 505, 81 S.Ct. 679, 5 L.Ed.2d 734 (1961); or punishing a protester whose views offend others, *Texas v. Johnson,* 491 U.S. 397, 109 S.Ct. 2533, 105 L.Ed.2d 342 (1989); and scores of other examples teach that individual liberty has constitutional protection, and that liberty's full extent and meaning may remain yet to be discovered and affirmed. Yet freedom does not stop with individual rights. Our constitutional system embraces, too, the right of citizens to debate so they can learn and decide and then, through the political process, act in concert to try to shape the course of their own times and the course of a nation that must strive always to make freedom ever greater and more secure. Here Michigan voters acted in concert and statewide to seek consensus and adopt a policy on a difficult subject against a historical background of race in America that has been a source of tragedy and persisting injustice. That history demands that we continue to learn, to listen, and to remain open to new approaches if we are to aspire always to a constitutional order in which all persons are treated with fairness and equal dignity. Were the Court to rule that the question addressed by Michigan voters is too sensitive or complex to be within the grasp of the electorate; or that the policies at issue remain too delicate to be resolved save by university officials or faculties, acting at some remove from immediate public scrutiny and control; or that these matters are so arcane that the electorate's power must be limited because the people cannot prudently exercise that power even after a full debate, that holding would be an unprecedented restriction on the exercise of a fundamental right held not just by one person but by all in common. It is the right to speak and debate and learn and then, as a matter of political will, to act through a lawful electoral process.

The respondents in this case insist that a difficult question of public policy must be taken from the reach of the voters, and thus removed from the realm of public discussion, dialogue, and debate in an election campaign. Quite in addition to the serious First Amendment implications of that position with respect to any particular election, it is inconsistent with the underlying premises of a responsible, functioning democracy. One of those premises is that a democracy has the capacity—and the duty—to learn from its past mistakes; to discover and confront persisting biases; and by respectful, rationale deliberation to rise above those flaws and injustices. That process is impeded, not advanced, by court decrees based on the proposition that the public cannot have the requisite repose to discuss certain issues. It is demeaning to the democratic process to presume that the voters are not capable of deciding an issue of this sensitivity on decent and rational grounds. The process of public discourse and political debate should not be foreclosed even if there is a risk that during a public campaign there will be those, on both sides, who seek to use racial division and discord to their own political advantage. An informed public can, and must, rise above this. The idea of democracy is that it can, and must, mature. Freedom embraces the right, indeed the duty, to engage in a rational, civic discourse in order to determine how best to form a consensus to shape the destiny of the Nation and its people. These First Amendment dynamics would be disserved if this Court were to say that the question here at issue is beyond the capacity of the voters to debate and then to determine.

These precepts are not inconsistent with the well-established principle that when hurt or injury is inflicted on racial minorities by the encouragement or command of laws or other state action, the Constitution requires redress by the courts. Cf. *Johnson v. California*, 543 U.S. 499, 511–512, 125 S.Ct. 1141, 160 L.Ed.2d 949 (2005) ("[S]earching judicial review . . . is necessary to guard against invidious discrimination"); *Edmonson v. Leesville Concrete Co.*, 500 U.S. 614, 619, 111 S.Ct. 2077, 114 L. Ed.2d 660 (1991) ("Racial discrimination" is "invidious in all contexts"). As already noted, those were the circumstances that the Court found present in *Mulkey, Hunter,* and *Seattle*. But those circumstances are not present here.

3. Holding

For reasons already discussed, *Mulkey, Hunter,* and *Seattle* are not precedents that stand for the conclusion that Michigan's voters must be disempowered from acting. Those cases were ones in which the political restriction in question was designed to be used, or was likely to be used, to encourage infliction of injury by reason of race. What is at stake here is not whether injury will be inflicted but whether government can be instructed not to follow a course that entails, first, the definition of racial categories and, second, the grant of favored status to persons in some racial categories and not others. The electorate's instruction to governmental entities not to embark upon the course of race-defined and race-based preferences was adopted, we must assume, because the voters deemed a preference system to be unwise, on account of what voters may deem its latent potential to become itself a source of the very resentments and hostilities based on race that this Nation seeks to put behind it. Whether those adverse results would follow is, and should be, the subject of debate. Voters might likewise consider, after debate and reflection, that programs designed to increase diversity—consistent with the Constitution—are a necessary part of progress to transcend the stigma of past racism.

This case is not about how the debate about racial preferences should be resolved. It is about who may resolve it. There is no authority in the Constitution of the United States or in this Court's precedents for the Judiciary to set aside Michigan laws that commit this policy determination to the voters. See *Sailors v. Board of Ed. of County of Kent,* 387 U.S. 105, 109, 87 S.Ct. 1549, 18 L.Ed.2d 650 (1967) ("Save and unless the state, county, or municipal government runs afoul of a federally protected right, it has vast leeway in the management of its internal affairs"). Deliberative debate on sensitive issues such as racial preferences all too often may shade into rancor. But that does not justify removing certain court-determined issues from the voters' reach. Democracy does not presume that some subjects are either too divisive or too profound for public debate.

The judgment of the Court of Appeals for the Sixth Circuit is reversed.

Justice KAGAN took no part in the consideration or decision of this case.

4. Justice Sotomayor Dissenting

We are fortunate to live in a democratic society. But without checks, democratically approved legislation can oppress minority groups. For that reason, our Constitution places limits on what a majority of the people may do. This case implicates one such limit: the guarantee of equal protection of the laws. Although that guarantee is traditionally understood to prohibit intentional discrimination under existing laws, equal protection does not end there. Another fundamental strand of our equal protection jurisprudence focuses on process, securing to all citizens the right to participate meaningfully and equally in self-government. That right is the bedrock of our democracy, for it preserves all other rights.

Yet to know the history of our Nation is to understand its long and lamentable record of stymieing the right of racial minorities to participate in the political process. At first, the majority acted with an open, invidious purpose. Notwithstanding the command of the Fifteenth Amendment, certain States shut racial minorities out of the political process altogether by withholding the right to vote. This Court intervened to preserve that right. The majority tried again, replacing outright bans on voting with literacy tests, good character requirements, poll taxes, and gerrymandering. The Court was not fooled; it invalidated those measures, too. The majority persisted. This time, although it allowed the minority access to the political process, the majority changed the ground rules of the process so as to make it more difficult for the minority, and the minority alone, to obtain policies designed to foster racial integration. Although these political restructurings may not have been discriminatory in purpose, the Court reaffirmed the right of minority members of our society to participate meaningfully and equally in the political process.

This case involves this last chapter of discrimination: A majority of the Michigan electorate changed the basic rules of the political process in that State in a manner that uniquely disadvantaged racial minorities.1 Prior to the enactment of the constitutional initiative at issue here, all of the admissions policies of Michigan's public colleges and universities—including race-sensitive admissions policies2—were in the hands of each institution's governing board. The members of those boards are nominated by political parties and elected by the citizenry in statewide elections. After over a century of being shut out of Michigan's institutions of higher education, racial minorities in Michigan had succeeded in persuading the elected board representatives to adopt admissions policies that took into account the benefits of racial diversity. And this Court twice blessed such efforts—first in *Regents of Univ. of Cal. v. Bakke,* 438 U.S. 265, 98 S.Ct. 2733, 57 L.Ed.2d 750 (1978), and again in *Grutter v. Bollinger,* 539 U.S. 306, 123 S.Ct. 2325, 156 L.Ed.2d 304 (2003), a case that itself concerned a Michigan admissions policy.

In the wake of *Grutter,* some voters in Michigan set out to eliminate the use of race-sensitive admissions policies. Those voters were of course free to pursue this end in any number of ways. For example, they could have persuaded existing board members to change their minds through individual or grassroots lobbying efforts, or through general public awareness campaigns. Or they could have mobilized efforts to vote uncooperative board members out of office, replacing them with members who would share their desire to abolish race-sensitive admissions policies. When this Court holds that the Constitution permits a particular policy, nothing prevents a majority of a State's voters from choosing not to adopt that policy. Our system of government encourages—and indeed, depends on—that type of democratic action.

But instead, the majority of Michigan voters changed the rules in the middle of the game, reconfiguring the existing political process in Michigan in a manner that burdened racial minorities. They did so in the 2006 election by amending the Michigan Constitution to enact Art. I, § 26, which provides in relevant part that Michigan's public universities "shall not discriminate against, or grant preferential treatment to, any individual or group on the basis of race, sex, color, ethnicity, or national origin in the operation of public employment, public education, or public contracting."

As a result of § 26, there are now two very different processes through which a Michigan citizen is permitted to influence the admissions policies of the State's universities: one for persons interested in race-sensitive admissions policies and one for everyone else. A citizen who is a University of Michigan alumnus, for instance, can advocate for an admissions policy that considers an applicant's legacy status by meeting individually with members of the Board of Regents to convince them of her views, by joining with other legacy parents to lobby the Board, or by voting for and supporting Board candidates who share her position. The same options are available to a citizen who wants the Board to adopt admissions policies that consider athleticism, geography, area of study, and so on. The one and only policy a Michigan citizen may not seek through this long-established process is a race-sensitive admissions policy that considers race in an individualized manner when it is clear that race-neutral alternatives are not adequate to achieve diversity. For that policy alone, the citizens of Michigan must undertake the daunting task of amending the State Constitution.

Our precedents do not permit political restructurings that create one process for racial minorities and a separate, less burdensome process for everyone else. This Court has held that the Fourteenth Amendment does not tolerate "a political structure that treats all individuals as equals, yet more subtly distorts governmental processes in such a way as to place special burdens on the ability of minority groups to achieve beneficial legislation." *Washington v. Seattle School Dist. No. 1*, 458 U.S. 457, 467, 102 S.Ct. 3187, 73 L.Ed.2d 896 (1982) (internal quotation marks omitted). Such restructuring, the Court explained, "is no more permissible than denying [the minority] the [right to] vote, on an equal basis with others." *Hunter v. Erickson*, 393 U.S. 385, 391, 89 S.Ct. 557, 21 L.Ed.2d 616 (1969). In those cases—*Hunter* and *Seattle*—the Court recognized what is now known as the "political-process doctrine": When the majority reconfigures the political process in a manner that burdens only a racial minority, that alteration triggers strict judicial scrutiny.

Today, disregarding *stare decisis,* a majority of the Court effectively discards those precedents. The plurality does so, it tells us, because the freedom actually secured by the Constitution is the freedom of self-government—because the majority of Michigan citizens "exercised their privilege to enact laws as a basic exercise of their democratic power." *Ante,* at 1636. It would be "demeaning to the democratic process," the plurality concludes, to disturb that decision in any way. *Ante,* at 1637—1638. This logic embraces majority rule without an important constitutional limit.

The plurality's decision fundamentally misunderstands the nature of the injustice worked by § 26. This case is not, as the plurality imagines, about "who may resolve" the debate over the use of race in higher education admissions. *Ante,* at 1638. I agree wholeheartedly that nothing vests the resolution of that debate exclusively in the courts or requires that we remove it from the reach of the electorate. Rather, this case is about *how* the debate over the use of race-sensitive admissions policies may be resolved, contra, *ibid.* —that is, it must be resolved in constitutionally permissible ways. While our Constitution does not guarantee minority groups victory in the political process, it does guarantee them meaningful and equal access to that process. It guarantees that the majority may not win by stacking the political process against minority groups permanently, forcing the minority alone to surmount unique obstacles in pursuit of its goals—here, educational diversity that cannot reasonably be accomplished through race-neutral measures. Today, by permitting a majority of the voters in Michigan to do what our Constitution forbids, the Court ends the debate over race-sensitive admissions policies in Michigan in a manner that contravenes constitutional protections long recognized in our precedents.

Like the plurality, I have faith that our citizenry will continue to learn from this Nation's regrettable history; that it will strive to move beyond those injustices towards a future of equality. And I, too, believe in the importance of public discourse on matters of public policy. But I part ways with the plurality when it suggests that judicial intervention in this case "impede[s]" rather than "advance[s]" the democratic process and the ultimate hope of equality. *Ante,* at 1637. I firmly believe that our role as judges includes policing the process of self-government and stepping in when necessary to secure the constitutional guarantee of equal protection. Because I would do so here, I respectfully dissent.

I

For much of its history, our Nation has denied to many of its citizens the right to participate meaningfully and equally in its politics. This is a history we strive to put behind us. But it is a history that still informs the society we live in, and so it is one we must address with candor. Because the political-process doctrine is best understood against the backdrop of this history, I will briefly trace its course . . .

V. Commentary on *Schuette*

Affirmative action raises difficult questions of access and fairness. Opponents argue that it discriminates against whites and stigmatizes and demeans those who receive "preferential treatment." Proponents vow that affirmative action increases opportunities for underrepresented minorities and benefits all, including whites. While concerns about fairness should limit the scope, duration, and frequency of affirmative action, consequences of the underrepresentation of blacks and Hispanics in highly selective colleges and universities continue to validate its use in higher education.

Diversity, in all its many forms, from racial, religious, and ethnic, to gender, geographic, class, and sexual orientation, is of educational value and should be facilitated. The justification and alleged harm from efforts to create racial diversity significantly differ from similar efforts to create other types of diversity however, and adequate racial diversity, representing more than tokenism, cannot be achieved without taking race into account during the admission process. As Americans continue to debate the use of race in higher education admissions, it is critically important they recognize the benefits affirmative action affords to all on campus.

Supreme Court Justice Sandra Day O'Connor cited this in the majority opinion in *Grutter v. Bollinger*, drawing on research identifying institutional and social benefits that diversity advances learning outcomes, "better prepares students for an increasingly diverse workforce and society, and better prepares them as professionals." These reasons provided justification to uphold an affirmative action program in law school admissions, where race was used as part of an individualized, holistic process designed to achieve diversity in the classroom in the 2004 case. More recent decisions threaten those gains.

Americans have grappled with issues surrounding the scope and validity of race-based affirmative action programs conceptually and legally for too long. In evaluating fairness, the long history of excluding minorities should not be ignored or diminished. Unfortunately, the 2014 *Schuette v. Coalition To Defend Affirmative Action* decision does just that. The Supreme Court ruling upheld the right of Michigan voters to prohibit race-based affirmative action in state college and university admissions.

Affirmative action is characterized as a racial preference rather than a justified remedy for past and present societal inequities. To understand this erroneous classification, one must go back some one hundred years to the beginning of the affirmative action debate during Reconstruction. In *The Civil Rights Cases* of 1883, the Court held that the Fourteenth Amendment did not empower Congress to prohibit owners of public accommodations from discriminating against black patrons. The owners were free to decide for themselves. In his opinion for the Court, Justice Joseph Bradley wondered when black Americans would stop being given special treatment under the law and become mere citizens. Unfortunately, *Schuette* seems to embrace this characterization of affirmative action as preferential treatment that may be prohibited by majority vote. Justice Anthony Kennedy, writing for a plurality, said "voters in Michigan chose to eliminate racial preferences and nothing in the Constitution . . . gives judges the authority to undermine the election results."

Yet, erroneously characterizing affirmative action as a "racial preference" allows the Court to defer to the electoral process just as it deferred to property owners in *The Civil Rights Cases*. Justice Harry Blackmun recognized this error before he retired in 1994. Justice Blackmun, speaking about a seemingly consistent majority of five Supreme Court Justices on the key civil rights and race relations cases of the 1980s, said "One wonders whether the majority still believes that race discrimination — or more accurately, race discrimination against nonwhites — is a problem in our society, or even remembers that it ever was."

While 20 years have passed, and several new justices have been appointed, racial exclusion in higher education remains alarmingly wide. For example, a 2013 Georgetown University study found, since 1995, 82 percent of new white enrollments have attended the 468 most select colleges, while 72 percent of new Hispanic enrollments and 68 percent of new black enrollments have attended two-year and four-year open-access schools. Race-based affirmative action helps offset this imbalance.

Justice Ruth Bader Ginsburg understands the problem very well. In her dissent in *Adarand v. Pena* in 1996, she reminded the majority of the continued presence of racial inequality in our society. Justice Ginsberg stated: "Those effects, reflective of a system of racial caste only recently ended, are evident in our workplaces, markets and neighborhoods . . . Bias both conscious and unconscious, reflecting traditional and unexamined habits of thought, keeps up barriers that must come down if equal opportunity and nondiscrimination are ever genuinely to become this country's law and practice." Justice Sonia Sotomayor shared a similar sentiment more recently. In her dissent in *Schuette*, she reminded Americans that "to know the history of our Nation is to understand its long and lamentable record of stymieing the right of racial minorities to participate in the political process."

Now that the *Schuette* decision leaves the viability of race-based affirmative action in state colleges and universities to the will of the state electorate, it is critical that voters evaluate all relevant factors. What Americans must consider is that properly-tailored race-based affirmative action does not make minorities the special favorite of the laws. It serves as part of the solution to bring this country one step closer to the day when all Americans, majority and minority, can "take the rank of mere citizens" in a truly post-racial America. While this history of exclusion is relevant to determinations of fairness, so are considerations of current access.

Even with race-based affirmative action, percentages of black and Hispanic students at highly selective academic institutions like the University of Michigan fall well below their percentages in the overall population. Thus, opportunities for white applicants are not substantially reduced or foreclosed at such schools. The absence of substantial reduction or foreclosure of opportunities for white applicants is critical in maintaining the proper balance between the needs of individual applicants and the interests of institutions of higher learning and the society at large. Certainly, some flexibility in admissions for schools to determine individual merit in light of the institution's multiple academic, financial, athletic and extra-curricular interests is appropriate and consistent with notions of equal protection of the laws. The Supreme Court unanimously embraced this approach some 50 years ago in the seminal case of *Brown v. Board of Education*. It appears Americans should continue utilizing this valuable approach.

In 2004, Justice O'Connor said, "It's been 25 years since Justice [Lewis] Powell approved the use of race to further an interest in student body diversity in the context of public higher education. Since that time, the number of minority applicants with high grades and test scores has indeed increased. We expect that 25 years from now, the use of racial preferences will no longer be necessary to further the interest approved today."

It has been over ten years since Justice O'Connor referenced the end of race-based affirmative action. Under her expectation, this effort has fewer than fifteen years remaining, at most. Yet, the achievement of racial diversity in highly selective academic institutions does not appear to be reachable at this ten-year junction without the continuance of race-based affirmative action.

In weighing the benefits and drawbacks of race-based affirmative action, we should consider both the opportunities created for minorities and the advantages for everyone that accrue from a diverse environment. When affirmative action programs broaden access for individuals from underrepresented minority groups without substantially diminishing the admission opportunities of white applicants, the benefits far outweigh any harm. And studies, like the one tracking University of California at Davis medical students for two decades, show that minorities who are admitted through affirmative action programs can perform well academically and professionally. The study reflected little or no difference between regular admits and affirmative action admits in terms of graduation rates, residency completion rates, or residency performance evaluation levels, suggesting that affirmative action admission decisions need not dilute the quality of graduates. [See Article, RC Davison and EL Lewis, Affirmative action and other special consideration admissions at the University of California, Davis, School of Medicine, Journal of the American Medical Association (October 8, 1997).]

As the world has become more globally interdependent, with Americans facing increased competition from abroad, I hope we're able to resolve our issues of racial inclusion before it's too late.

W. Background on Justice Ruth Bader Ginsburg

Geoffrey Stone, et al.

Justice Ruth Bader Ginsburg

When Ruth Bader Ginsburg graduated from law school, one of her mentors suggested to Justice Felix Frankfurter that he take her on as a law clerk. Despite

Ginsburg's brilliant law school record (earned while caring for an infant daughter), Justice Frankfurter told her sponsor that he just was not ready to hire a woman. Thirty-three years after this rebuff, Ginsburg assumed her seat on the Supreme Court. In the intervening years, Ginsburg gained fame as the first tenured woman professor at the Columbia Law School; as the director of the Women's Rights Project of the American Civil Liberties Union, where she won many pioneering victories in the legal battle against gender discrimination; and as a judge on the U.S. Court of Appeals for the District of Columbia Circuit. She has been called "the Thurgood Marshall of gender equality law" and is said to be "as responsible as any one person for legal advances that women made under the Equal Protection Clause."

Constitutional Law lxxxiii (3rd edition).
Copyright © (1996) Stone, et al.
Reprinted with permission of Aspen Law & Business.

X. Background on Justice Sandra Day O'Connor

Geoffrey Stone, et al.

Justice Sandra Day O'Connor

The first woman ever to serve on the Court, Sandra Day O'Connor was appointed by President Regain in 1981. O'Connor was a classmate of Justice Rehnquist at the Stanford Law School, where she was an editor of the Stanford Law Review. Despite her outstanding academic achievements, O'Connor found it difficult to locate a job on graduation. When she applied to the firm in which future Attorney General William French Smith was a partner, she was offered the position of secretary. After briefly serving as deputy county attorney for San Mateo County in California, she worked as a civilian attorney for the army while her husband served his tour of duty. She then spent eight years as a mother, homemaker, and volunteer while her three children grew up. When she resumed her legal career, she became an assistant attorney general in Arizona. In 1970, she was elected to the Arizona senate and eventually became majority leader. She then served on the Superior Court for Maricopa County and the Arizona Court of Appeal. Although her nomination to the Supreme Court was opposed by some conservatives, Justice O'Connor frequently aligned herself with the conservative wing of the Court. However, she has shown a preference for a balancing approach to constitutional law and case-by-case particularism—a stance that has created conflict with Justice Scalia, who claims to favor a rule-based approach. She initially urged her colleagues to reconsider its analysis of the abortion question in *Roe v. Wade*, but later surprised many by coauthoring an important opinion preserving Roe's central holding at a time when many thought it would be overruled. She wrote a five-to-four majority in *Mississippi University for Women v. Hogan*, 458 U.S. 718 (1982), to invalidate a state nursing school's single-sex admissions policy. Widely respected for incisive and informed questioning at oral argument, O'Connor is known for her deference to the political branches of government, for her defense of federalism, and for her original approach to the problem of church-state relations.

Constitutional Law lxxvii (3rd edition).
Copyright © (1996) Stone, et al.
Reprinted with permission of Aspen Law & Business.

Y. Questions and Notes

Although Justice O'Connor authored the opinion in *Adarand*, which overruled the *Metro Broadcasting* decision and applied a "strict-scrutiny" standard of equal protection analysis to the transportation department's affirmative action program, she indicated that the majority of Supreme Court Justices were interested in achieving a society where equal opportunity for all, irrespective of race, prevails. What is the best way to achieve such opportunity? Would that best way involve increasing affirmative action, altering affirmative action, or eliminating affirmative action?

Should affirmative action be based on race, income, or both race and income?

One of the arguments against affirmative action is that it creates a stigma on its recipients. Do you perceive such a stigma? If so, do you perceive the same stigma for recipients of other preferences, such as alumni, veterans, corporations, farmers, handicapped, elderly, or refugees?

Z. Point/Counterpoint

Affirmative Action. Do you agree with the majority opinion or the dissent in *Grutter v. Bollinger*?

The Chronicle Review/The Chronicle of Higher Education
May It Please the Court . . .

On April 1, the Supreme Court will hear oral arguments in two lawsuits filed against the University of Michigan over its use of racial preferences in undergraduate and law-school admissions.

Last year, in *Grutter v. Bollinger*, the U.S. Court of Appeals for the Sixth Circuit ruled that the law school's admissions program was permissible. The appeals court had yet to decide the undergraduate lawsuit, *Gratz v. Bollinger*, when the Supreme Court agreed in December to consider both cases.

What legal issues will the justices be most likely to consider — and how will those issues influence the decisions, which most observers expect to be split along ideological lines? *The Chronicle* asked a lawyer for the students who successfully challenged affirmative action at the University of Georgia, and a constitutional-law professor and his former student, who support affirmative action, to present the closing comments they would give if they were arguing the cases before the court.

March 28, 2003 *The Chronicle Review* B11–B17 (2003).
Copyright © (2003) *The Chronicle Review*.
Reprinted with permission of *The Chronicle Review*.

A. Lee Parks, Jr.

Racial Diversity's Effect on Education Is a Myth

May it please the court

In the *Gratz* and *Grutter* cases, the court will finally decide the legality under Title VI of the Civil Rights Act of 1964, and the constitutionality under the 14th Amendment, of an admissions policy that is programmed to admit a predetermined percentage of minority applicants. The University of Michigan seeks constitutional footing for its admitted preference of African-American and Hispanic undergraduate and law-school applicants based on the contention that racial diversity makes for a better education — and that adequate racial diversity can't be achieved without rejecting a certain number of more academically qualified white applicants in favor of preferred minority applicants.

Historically, our Constitution has compelled the courts to vindicate the civil rights of the individual when a government has sought to subordinate them to so-called rights of the collective. The question before your Honors today is whether justice Lewis F. Powell Jr.'s concurring opinion in the 1978 *Regents of the University of California v. Bakke* decision was a binding Supreme Court precedent for the proposition that racial diversity in higher education is such a compelling state interest that the group rights of minority applicants can trump the individual civil rights of more academically qualified white students. In a nutshell, reconciling the individual versus collective-rights conundrum that well-meaning governmental efforts at social engineering usually generate is what the flap about "diversity" is fundamentally about.

Before the court examines the constitutional question and its diversity subset, it must consider that Title VI provides a straightforward statutory basis for invalidating Michigan's admissions policy. The law was passed to enforce the landmark *Brown v. Board of Education* decisions in 1954 and 1955, which mandated that all states "achieve a system of determining admissions to the public schools on a nonracial basis." The statute forbids any nonremedial consideration of race in the allocation of benefits, like admission to a college, by any institution that accepts federal financial assistance. When a college participates in the federally insured student-loan program or accepts a federal grant, it agrees to comply with Title VI; there is no wiggle room. If Congress wanted to exclude colleges from the ban on race-based decision making, it could have done so. Yet it specifically chose to enact a statute that would be "color-blind in its application."

In *Bakke*, Justice John Paul Stevens—joined by three other justices including now Chief Justice William Rehnquist—rejected Justice Powell's interpretation of Title VI as requiring no more or less than the 14th Amendment. They concluded that Title VI was not "a constitutional appendage. In unmistakable terms, the Act prohibits the exclusion of individuals . . . because of their race." Quoting directly from the Senate debate over Title VI, the justices said that it is not "permissible to say 'yes' to one person but to say 'no' to another person, only because of the color of their skin. Any amendment to Title VI to permit the consideration of race in admissions would require legislative rather than judicial action.

Both lower courts—the U.S. Court of Appeals for the Sixth Circuit and the U.S. District Court for the Easter District of Michigan—anxious to reach the diversity question, skirted Title VI with little comment. The linchpin of both decisions is the dubious assumption that Justice Powell elevated diversity to a compelling state interest worthy of some consideration in admissions, and thereby immunized Michigan's race-based admissions policies from the normally fatal strict scrutiny test. To reach this tortured conclusion, both opinions go to great lengths to explain why Powell's reference to diversity is binding precedent when no other justice joined in that part of his opinion.

The 1977 case of *Marks v. United States* is the instruction booklet on how to find precedent in a Supreme Court decision where none is apparent. "When a fragmented Court decides a case . . . 'the holding of the Court may be viewed as that position taken by those Members who concurred in the judgments on the narrowest grounds.'" In point of fact, the narrowest ground for the *Bakke* decision's invalidation of a dual-track admissions system was justice Steven's group's reliance on Title VI as the basis for decision. As Justice Stevens stated, the "settled practice [of the Court] . . . is to avoid the decision of a constitutional issue if a case can be fairly decided on a statutory ground."

Most courts have rejected the idea that *Bakke* is binding precedent for the proposition that diversity is a compelling state interest. In *Hopwood v. Texas* (1996), the U.S. Court of Appeals for the Fifth Circuit found Powell's dictum "has never represented the view of a majority of the Court." Perhaps the most pragmatic assessment of *Bakke* is set forth in *Johnson v. Board of Regents of the University of Georgia* (2001), quoting the Fifth Circuit decision in *United States v. City of Miami* (1980): "In over 150 pages . . . the Justices [in *Bakke*] have told us mainly that they have agreed to disagree." Justice Powell aptly characterized himself as a "chief with no Indians" just the day before he announced the opinion of the court in *Bakke*.

No reading of *Bakke* can alter it: The application of the strict-scrutiny test, a paradigm designed and implemented by the court to serve as an exacting means to enforce the Equal Protection Clause of the 14th Amendment, is fatal to all nonremedial uses of racial preferences. In *Palmore v. Sidoti* (1984), the court reminded us that the "core purpose of the 14th Amendment was to do away with all governmentally imposed discrimination based on race."

Under the strict-scrutiny test, there is only one "result" worthy of intentional racial discrimination. Justice Sandra Day O'Connor's dissent in *Metro Broadcasting v. FCC* (1990) has now become the law of the land with the 1995 decision in *Adarand Constructors v. Peña*: "Modern equal protection doctrine has recognized only one [compelling state] interest: remedying the effects of racial discrimination." Justice O'Connor's majority opinion in *City of Richmond v. Croson* (1989) explained why: "unless [racial classifications] are strictly reserved for remedial settings, they may in fact promote notions of racial inferiority and lead to a politics of racial hostility."

Michigan freely admits that its use of race as an admissions factor does not achieve any remedial purpose. Under this court's binding precedent, that honest confession should end the constitutional inquiry because, as noted in *Hopwood*, "Diversity fosters, rather than minimizes, the use of race."

Several circuit courts have applied the strict-scrutiny test to strike down diversity-based college-admissions programs. In *Hopwood v. Texas* (1996) the Fifth Circuit invalidated the race-based admissions process at the University of Texas School of Law. In *Johnson v. Board of Regents* (2001), a case in which I served as plaintiffs' counsel, the U.S. Court of Appeals of the 11th Circuit held that the University of Georgia's use of racial and gender preferences violated Titles VI and IX. The court held that a "point bonus for race" preference system was not narrowly tailored to advancing the university's professed interest in improving education, even if one assumed diversity was a compelling state interest.

Reduced to its essence, diversity is largely a semantical gloss used by academe to perpetuate minority admission quotas that had their genesis in old federal desegregation decrees used to integrate higher education after *Brown*. Those draconian racial quotas were court-ordered short-term agents of integration, designed to end *de jure* segregation in education immediately. Diversity is the password coined by academe to allow these old racial quotas to slip past their court-ordered deadlines for termination and find permanency in the amorphous and all-encompassing concept of affirmative action.

We must not allow the aspirational nobility that rings out from lofty words like "diversity" to cloud the constitutional analysis. Diversity in academespeak defies any concrete definition. Indeed, diversity works more like a religion than a constitutional principle. Its churches are our elite colleges, each a slightly different denomination of the faith. Its high priests are those in academe who profess to know what racial mix conjures up the best education.

True believers in diversity hold the heartfelt conviction that, from the original sin of discrimination, comes the greater good of an educational experience that theoretically moves certain subjectively designated races that "need help" into the mainstream American economy faster than would otherwise be the case.

There is no principled legal explanation as to why this kind of diversity, divorced from any remedial purpose, is not just a poorly disguised set-aside program, as pernicious in effect on those being discriminated against as any intentional act of bigotry. That does not seem to matter to the flock. Secure in the fact they have claimed

the higher moral ground in their quest for racial fairness, the high priests confidently point to *Bakke* as the Bible that pronounces them correct, both in their purpose and the discriminatory practices used to achieve it.

But equal protection, as an individual civil right is imploded when you elevate
diversity to a compelling state interest. Diversity is not limited by the usually mandatory requirement that the use of race must always be temporary and narrowly
tailored to achieve a specific remedial purpose. The importance of that limitation
is inescapable: Once the remedy is achieved, the discrimination and its measurable
vestiges presumably go away, and there is no constitutional justification for continuing to discriminate.

By the way of amicus brief, President Bush has made the compelling point
that diversity, Michigan style, constitutes an endless affirmative-action program
designed to fill a quota that the university euphemistically calls a "critical mass."
In *Grutter*, the Sixth Circuit specifically freed diversity from any temporal limitations with the incredible statement that "an interest in academic diversity does not
have a self-contained stopping point." Even Justice Powell strongly disagreed with
the proposition that racial discrimination that furthers the diversity factor should
enjoy eternal life.

Michigan's definition of diversity also lacks the nuance that would enable the
university to narrowly tailor its undergraduate admissions plan to some provable
external cause of the so-called achievement gap between the average minority
and Caucasian applicants. The bonus that the admissions office grants minority
students—a whopping 20 points out of a possible 150 at the undergraduate level
just for being black or Hispanic—equals the average amount needed to handicap
the competition for admission to insure a minority "yield" of enrollees that constitutes "critical mass."

Diversity, when constitutionally concocted, must be a far more subtle and varied
blend of an applicant's past experiences, unique talents, challenges overcome, and
personal qualities than that race-centric recipe. Surely, any fair surrogate for, or
adjunct to, precisely measurable academic qualifications would have to be based on
more than just skin color. Justice Powell acknowledged as much in *Bakke* when he
opined that "the diversity that furthers a compelling state interest encompasses a far
broader array of qualifications and characteristics of which racial . . . origin is but a
single though important element."

The better approach is to award bonus points on a race-neutral basis to level
the playing field for any truly deserving student whose lower grade-point averages
and SAT scores correlate to overcoming poverty, a single-parent household, lack
of English-language background, enrollment at an underperforming high school,
a physical handicap, or an undiagnosed or untreated learning disability. That
approach would provide a principled, nonracial justification for the clear favoritism
shown such applicants, even though most beneficiaries would probably be minority
applicants. But the Michigan admissions process does not work that way.

If you truly accept the great promise of *Brown* that government-sponsored racial discrimination will never again be allowed a role in the allocation of life-changing opportunities like education, then you must accept the undeniable fact that this promise does not depend on the skin color of the student.

No one denies that Jennifer Gratz, Barbara Grutter, and countless other qualified white applicants have been denied invaluable education opportunities by Michigan because of their skin color. Their failure to gain admission is attributable, like Allan Bakke's, to the improbable sin of living "a storybook life of middle class virtue," as J. Harvie Wilkinson III, the chief judge of the U.S. Court of Appeals for the Fourth Circuit, put it in *From Brown to Bakke* (Oxford University Press, 1979). No amount of "robust exchange of ideas" can justify that outcome under the 14th Amendment.

The most interesting and important law cases, to lawyers and laymen alike, tend to turn on constitutional issues. The most compelling of that genre are those precedent-setting decisions that prohibit widespread and generally accepted state-sponsored practices because they, despite all good intentions, violate an individual citizen's constitutional rights. There is something quintessentially American about such outcomes where one person, armed only with the power of the spoken and written word emanating from the Bill of Rights, stops an entire government dead in its tracks.

That is what young Gratz and Grutter intend to do, and we will be a better nation if they succeed. It is the victories of individual citizens, both large and small, in these defining kinds of cases that blend together to form a veneer over our individual civil rights called precedent that hardens with every reaffirmation, and protects us all from errant legislation, misguided state policy or practice, and even from rogue judges who would substitute their ideas about what is "good" for this country for the collective wisdom of the Founding Fathers.

In the final analysis, diversity is nothing more than a constitutional unicorn, born of the myth that sprang from the musings of a single justice in the cacophony we call *Bakke*. One has been seen roaming the campus at Ann Arbor, and it now falls to the Supreme Court to declare it the fable that we know it to be.

F. Michael Higginbotham and Kathleen Bergin

The Court Has Granted Wide Deference to Colleges

May it please the court . . .

We have demonstrated that the University of Michigan can operate flexible admissions programs, consistent with the Equal Protection Clause of the 14th Amendment, that competitively weight each applicant's academic background, life experiences, and personal characteristics, including race. By constitutional standards their purpose of promoting a diverse student body is a compelling interest, and by considering a candidate's race along with other personal characteristics, the programs are appropriately tailored. Both as to purpose and scope, the university has satisfied its equal protection obligation.

Each year the university's undergraduate and law schools receive many more applications from qualified students than they can accept. After the university ranks each candidate's standardized test score and grade-point average, some applicants advance their standing based upon geographic origin, residency status, leadership skills, work experience, relationship to alumni, and other attributes. It is undisputed that such factors disproportionately increase admission rates for white students at the expense of minority students, even though some of these factors reveal nothing about a candidate's merit or potential.

To level the playing field, the university also considers an applicant's race, along with the other factors, as a means of increasing student diversity, without relying on quotas, set-asides, or separate admission tracks. That comprehensive approach promotes enrollment of students with all types of backgrounds, including those from racial groups noticeably underrepresented on the campus.

We remind your Honors that this court is not facing a novel question. In 1978, it was decided in *Regents of the University of California v. Bakke* that a university can properly integrate its student body by considering an applicant's racial background among a multitude of other factors when making admissions decisions. At issue in *Bakke* was the admissions program at the medical school of the University of California at Davis that reserved 16 out of 100 entering seats exclusively for qualified minority applicants. Writing for a divided court, Justice Lewis F. Powell, Jr. concluded that the program operated as an impermissible quota because nonminorities could not compete for the reserved seats.

But while rejecting Davis's unyielding emphasis on race, Justice Powell endorsed the flexible use of race alongside other factors to further the "compelling state interest" of student diversity. As a case in point, Justice Powell pointed to the policy at Harvard College, which, unlike Davis, considered race "a 'plus' in a particular applicant's file," yet did not "insulate the individual from comparison with all other candidates for the available seats." Under this plan, race might "tip the balance" in one applicant's favor, just as other variables tip the balance for a competing candidate. Michigan takes the same approach.

For Justice Powell, Davis's plan was deficient by its means, not in its purpose. As he explained, the First Amendment embraced the underlying goal of racial diversity. Justice Powell, quoting a reference by Justice Felix Frankfurter in *Sweezy v. New Hampshire* (1957), reasoned that the freedoms expressed in our Constitution have significant value to educational institutions—which, unlike profit-driven businesses, are authorized to promote an environment "conducive to speculation, experiment and creation." In addition, when sufficiently integrated, such an environment enables students to develop the cultural and interpersonal skills necessary to succeed in a shrinking global community. Such reasoning convinced Justice Powell that racial diversity is "of paramount importance" in the fulfillment of a university's educational mission.

That a majority of justices joined only part of Justice Powell's decision does not undermine *Bakke's* persuasiveness. We remind your Honors that four justices in *Bakke* would have upheld the Davis program, suggesting that Justice Powell was not alone in his reasoning. Furthermore, Justice Sandra Day O'Connor confirmed the value of such reasoning when she explained in *Wygant v. Jackson Board of Education* (1986) that a "state interest in the promotion of racial diversity has been found sufficiently 'compelling,' at least in the context of higher education, to support the use of racial considerations in furthering that interests." Ignoring that support not, only risks resegregating America's colleges and universities, but conflicts with this court's own commitment to *stare decisis*, or the doctrine of legal precedent.

Indeed, like many educational institutions across the country, the university understands that diversity is most effectively achieved when admissions criteria include race. In that respect, *Bakke* falls within the line of cases that remain controlling in part because they provide a source of reference. In *Allied-Bruce Terminix Cos. v. Dobson* (1995) and *Planned Parenthood of Southeastern PA v. Casey* (1992) this court declined to invalidate previous decisions — *Southland Corp. v. Keating* (1984) and *Roe v. Wade* (1973), respectively — because they so profoundly influenced institutional and individual decision makers. *Bakke* engenders the same reliance. Even the U.S. Department of Education promulgated regulations with *Bakke* in mind.

Only when a recent precedent departs from well-established principles has this Court taken the extraordinary step of overruling itself to restore a prior line of jurisprudence. Here, the Court faces no such conflict. First, *Bakke* itself established the controlling precedent on diversity, so there is no prior precedent to re-establish. In addition, 25 years after Justice Powell announced the compelling nature of diversity, and 17 years after Justice O'Connor reaffirmed that rule, *Bakke* continues to influence admissions policies nationwide. Borrowing the rationale in *Planned Parenthood v. Casey*, *Bakke* cannot be overruled "without serious inequity to those who have relied upon it or significant damage to the stability of the society governed by it." The U.S. Court of Appeals for the Sixth Circuit has already upheld the law school's plan based in part on this reasoning.

Moreover, this Court has never rejected diversity as a compelling interest nor suggested that only programs designed to remedy discrimination are compelling enough to satisfy constitutional standards. *Wygant, Fullilove v. Klutznick* (1980), *City of Richmond v. Croson* (1989), and *Adarand Constructors v. Peña* (1995) each dealt with varying types of race-based remedies for discrimination, but not one articulated the radical notion that race was relevant to remedial interests, but no other.

The petitioners in the University of Michigan cases, Jennifer Gratz and Barbara Grutter, argue that even if diversity constitutes a compelling interest, the admissions programs nonetheless fail because they are not "narrowly tailored." We submit that a narrow-tailoring requirement is inappropriate in this case.

Narrow tailoring makes sense where race-based remedies are concerned because it provides victims compensation without risking a windfall to undeserving minority people. That is why this Court rejected a remedial construction set-aside program in *Croson* that reserved a percentage of public-works contracts for minority business owners who had never been denied a government contract on account of their race.

By definition, a diversity-based program cannot be overboard. Its goal is not meant to provide proportional compensation for prior wrongs. As implied in *Bakke*, student-body diversity is by its nature somewhat mathematically imprecise because it stems from a desire to advance the educational mission. Unlike remedies for discrimination, diversity does not require proportionality.

Even applying narrow tailoring, the university's admissions programs meet that standard. Narrow tailoring requires as assessment of whether the "plus" factor is "too big." The size of the plus factor, whether for race, alumni, or geography, reflects the number of qualified applicants a university seeks with a particular characteristic. The very reason that racial quotas are problematic is because it is difficult to select the "right" number with mathematical precision. Instead, this Court must respect both the judgment and experience of university officials in evaluating whether, in comparison to other factors, race is overemphasized.

Under the university's admissions programs, the race factor is hardly excessive. At the undergraduate level, the university assigns the same number of points to applicants from underrepresented minority groups as it does to socially and economically disadvantaged applicants and those awarded athletic scholarships. Moreover, the university's provost has discretion to add additional points to any applicant for any reason. The law school, without relying on a point system, also weighs race fairly by placing it on an equal footing with other potential student contributions.

In that respect, the university's plan disproves petitioners' argument that the program gives disproportional advantages to minority students. On the contrary, although the university's flexible consideration of race contributes to a diverse student body, it did not unfavorably disadvantage either the under graduate or law-school petitioner because they would not have bene admitted even under a race-blind policy. On the whole, the university was less impressed with petitioners' credentials than those of applicants who received admission offers, including dozens of white applicants who had lower GPAs and standardized test scores than the petitioners.

Furthermore, the racial diversity the university seeks is well defined when compared to the types of diversity in other contexts some members of this court had labeled "too amorphous, too insubstantial" and "too unrelated" to any legitimate basis for employing racial classifications. For example, in *Metro Broadcasting v. FCC*(1990) several justices chided the Federal Communications Commission for attempting to broaden the scope of viewpoints expressed during broadcast programming by increasing minority broadcast licensing. Those justices declined to assume a correlation between the number of minority license holders and broadcast diversity. To do so, Justice O'Connor explained, equates "race with belief and behavior" and overlooks the range of ideologies that exist among individuals of the same race.

Contrary to the FCC, the university values intraracial as well as interracial diversity and understands that underrepresented minority students bring to campus a range of experiences, values, and ideologies, not only in comparison to nonminority students, but also in comparison to each other. In an environment that promotes this type of diversity, some minority students might find more in common with their nonminority classmates than members of their own race. The university operates from a premise that there is no such thing as a "black mind-set" or "Hispanic mind-set," and seeks to inculcate this understanding among its students by fostering the admission of underrepresented applicants.

Moreover, just as *Bakke* encouraged universities around the nation to pursue diversity, Justice Powell's comparison between the programs at Harvard and Davis instructed them on how to undertake that pursuit within the strictures of the Constitution. This Court should not forget how minority enrollment in California, Washington, and Texas universities plummeted following court-imposed or legislatively mandated race-blind admissions. *Bakke* has instructed universities how to maintain a meaningful minority presence with little or, in this case, no consequence to petitioners.

This Court has repeatedly acknowledged the unique and important influence of education in American society. As a way of safeguarding that role, as well as upholding federalist principles, the court has granted wide deference to educational institutions and the state governments that control them. As a result, colleges and universities enjoy broad powers to carry out their educational missions. Allowing the university flexibility in promoting racial diversity recognizes that valuable role.

Justice Powell concluded in *Bakke* that "the Nation's future depends upon leaders trained through wide exposure to that robust exchange of ideas which discovers truth 'out of a multitude of tongues.'" The university has created a diverse student body that allows for just such discovery, which, in turn, enhances the learning environment of all students. The means by which the university has chosen to achieve this goal is consistent with the letter and spirit of this court's prior decisions and the guarantees of the Equal Protection Clause of the 14th Amendment. We trust that the court will not prevent the university from continuing this indispensable service.

March 28, 2003 *The Chronicle Review* B14–B17 (2003).
Copyright © (2003) *The Chronicle Review*.
Reprinted with permission of *The Chronicle Review*.

XXII. Maintaining Racial Inequity

A. Introduction

Socioeconomic disparities between blacks and whites are still alarming. Blacks are twice as likely to be poor or homeless, and more than twice as likely to be incarcerated. Blacks accumulate wealth at one-twentieth the rate of whites. The median wealth (assets minus debts) of black households is one-twentieth of that of white households. In the last few years, the gap has only widened.

Racial inequality today is much more complex than it was during the Jim Crow period. Sixty years ago, laws imposed discrimination on racial minorities, and violence was used to maintain the divide. Today, what I call the "ghosts of Jim Crow" are individual and societal choices that result in housing and social isolation, education inequity, reduced political power and increased economic hardship for blacks.

One such ghost is evident in employment disparities. Unemployment among blacks consistently remains twice that of whites. In difficult economic times, black women are hit particularly hard: In the recent recession, the percentage of jobs lost by black women was higher than any other group.

Bari-Ellen Roberts understands this phenomenon all too well. A black woman employed as a senior financial analyst at Texaco in the 1990s, she was denied opportunities for professional advancement by supervisors. Ms. Roberts, who sued in a class-action discrimination suit, wrote about her experiences in "Roberts Vs. Texaco: A True Story of Race and Corporate America."

Another ghost of Jim Crow was found in a Philadelphia suburb. To generate additional revenue, the Valley Swim Club allowed local day camps access for a fee. A Philadelphia-based camp that provides activities for 50 black children, in July 2009, paid $1,950 so the children could use the pool once a week.

News reports at the time indicated that, when the black children showed upon the first day to swim, the white children in the pool immediately exited the water—and that a white parent was heard to say, "What are all these black kids doing here?" A club attendant asked all of the black children to leave, which they did, some of them in tears. Refunding the payment, the president of the Valley Swim Club said the reason for the cancellation was "concern that a lot of kids would change the complexion . . . of the club."

Another example of continuing racial discrimination is in the administration of the death penalty—black defendants with white victims are the most likely to be executed. This became all too evident on Sept. 21, 2011, when the state of Georgia executed Troy Davis, a black man, for the murder of a white, off-duty police officer. Mr. Davis was executed despite the fact that evidence of witness coercion, intimidation and fabrication of testimony by policy had raised serious doubt as to his guilt. Just as in the Jim Crow era, a black person can still be executed in America even when his guilt is in question.

Since the 1954 *Brown I* decision, significant progress in reducing racial discrimination in education, employment, politics, and the administration of justice has been made. Vast racial inequities in these areas, however, continue to exist with the imprimatur of the Supreme Court.

B. Background on *Washington*

Businesses engage in various methods of testing in order to determine which applicants are offered positions of employment. These various methods of testing, which include skills tests, performance tests, written tests, and verbal tests, sometimes produce racially skewed results. What are the equal protection implications where one or more racial minority groups disproportionally fail an employment examination? Can courts take action when there is a disparate impact, even without a showing of discriminatory purpose?

C. *Washington v. Davis*, 426 U.S. 229 (1976)

1. Facts

Justice WHITE delivered the opinion of the Court.

[Two unsuccessful black, or African American which became the more popular reference during the 1980s, applicants for positions on the police force of the District of Columbia, claimed that "Test 21", measuring verbal ability, vocabulary, and reading comprehension unconstitutionally discriminated against them. "Test 21" was used throughout the federal civil service. According to the district court, the evidence supported the conclusion that four times as many blacks than whites failed the test, that the test was a useful indicator of success in the police training programs, and that the test had not been validated to establish its reliability for measuring subsequent job performance. No claim was made that administration of the test itself constituted an "intentional" or "purposeful" act of discrimination.]

2. Opinion

The central purpose of the Equal Protection Clause of the Fourteenth Amendment is the prevention of official conduct discriminating on the basis of race. [Our] cases have not embraced the proposition that a law or other official act, without regard to whether it reflects a racially discriminatory purpose, is unconstitutional *solely* because it has a racially disproportionate impact . . .

This is not to say that the necessary discriminatory racial purpose must be express or appear on the face of the statute, or that a law's disproportionate impact is irrelevant in cases involving Constitution-based claims of racial discrimination. A statute, otherwise neutral on its face, must not be applied so as invidiously to discriminate on the basis of race . . . Necessarily, an invidious discriminatory purpose may often be inferred from the totality of the relevant facts, including the fact, if it is true, that the law bears more heavily on one race than another. It is also not infrequently true that the discriminatory impact—in the jury cases for example, the total or seriously disproportionate exclusion of Negroes from jury venires—may for all practical purposes demonstrate unconstitutionality because in various circumstances the discrimination is very difficult to explain on non-racial grounds. Nevertheless, we have not held that a law, neutral on its face and serving ends otherwise within the power of government to pursue, is invalid under the Equal Protection Clause simply because it may affect a greater proportion of one race than of another. Disproportionate impact is not irrelevant, but it is not the sole touchstone of an invidious racial discrimination forbidden by the Constitution. Standing alone, it does not trigger the rule, that racial classifications are to be subjected to the strictest scrutiny and are justifiable only the weightiest of considerations . . .

[We] have difficulty understanding how a law establishing a racially neutral qualification for employment is nevertheless racially discriminatory and denies "any person . . . equal protection of the laws" simply because a greater proportion of Negroes fail to qualify than members of other racial or ethnic groups. Had respondents, along with all others who had failed [the test], whether white or black, brought an action claiming that [it] denied each of them equal protection of the laws as compared with those who had passed with high enough scores to qualify them as police recruits, it is most unlikely that their challenge would have been sustained. [The test], which is administered generally to prospective Government employees, concededly seeks to ascertain whether those who take it have acquired a particular level of verbal skill; and it is untenable that the Constitution prevents the Government from seeking modestly to upgrade the communicative abilities of its employees rather than to be satisfied with some lower level of competence, particularly where the job requires special ability to communicate orally and in writing. Respondents, as Negroes, could no more successfully claim that the test denied them equal protection than could white applicants who also failed. The conclusion would not be different in the face of proof that more Negroes than whites had been disqualified by [the test]. That other Negroes also failed to score well would, alone, not demonstrate that respondents individually were being denied equal protection of the laws by the application of an otherwise valid qualifying test being administered to prospective police recruits.

Nor on the facts of the case before us would the disproportionate impact of [the test] warrant the conclusion that it is a purposeful device to discriminate against Negroes and hence an infringement of the constitutional rights of respondents as well as other black applicants. As we have said, the test is neutral on its face and rationally may be said to serve a purpose the Government is constitutionally empowered to pursue. Even agreeing with the District Court that the differential racial effect of [the test] called for further inquiry, we think the District Court correctly held that the affirmative efforts of the Metropolitan Police Department to recruit black officers, the changing racial composition of the recruit classes and of the force in general, and the relationship of the test to the training program negated any inference that the Department discriminated on the basis of race or that "a police officer qualifies on the color of his skin rather than ability."

A rule that a statute designed to serve neutral ends is nevertheless invalid, absent compelling justification, if in practice it benefits or burdens one race more than another would be far reaching and would raise serious questions about, and perhaps invalidate, a whole range of tax, welfare, public service, regulatory, and licensing statutes that may be more burdensome to the poor and to the average black than to the more affluent white. . . .

3. Holding

The test was sustained by the District court but invalidated by the Court of Appeals. We are in agreement with the District Court and hence reverse the judgment of the Court of Appeals.

D. Commentary on *Washington*

The decision in *Washington* makes eliminating racial inequities much more difficult in two ways. First, a standard of purposeful or intentional discrimination is very difficult to satisfy, particularly when evidence of racial disparity is minimalized as proof of intent. Second, it excludes from prohibition a large amount of racial discrimination that is done accidentally or unconsciously but is, nevertheless, harmful.[35] Such a difficult standard makes the Fourteenth Amendment much less effective in preventing racial discrimination.

Bradford C. Mank
*Are Title VI's Disparate Impact Regulations Valid?**

The Supreme Court has imposed similar limitations on anti-discrimination legislation. Congressional laws prohibiting race discrimination in employment and federally assisted government and private activities provide an example of this limitation.

Congress passed its first piece of comprehensive civil rights legislation in the Civil Rights Act of 1964. Under Title VI of that Act, federal agencies may not provide

---

35. *See* Lawrence, *The Id, the Ego, and Equal Protection: Reckoning With Unconscious Racism*, 39 STAN. L. REV. 317 (1987).

* (some footnotes omitted).

funding to "recipient" programs that discriminate on the basis of race.[36] The statutory language of Title VI is ambiguous about whether recipients are prohibited only from engaging in intentional discrimination, or whether recipients may behave in ways that cause unintentional, disparate impacts. Section 601 of Title VI states that "[n]o person shall, on the ground of race, color, or national origin, be excluded from participation in, be denied the benefits of, or be subjected to discrimination under any program or activity receiving Federal financial assistance." It is unclear whether the term "discrimination" refers to intentional or unintentional discrimination. The statute's legislative history contains statements supporting both interpretations. While its Title VI cases are complex and not easy to summarize, the Supreme Court has interpreted section 601 of the statute to forbid intentional discrimination by programs or activities receiving federal financial assistance.

That interpretation, however, is not the end of the story. Additionally, section 602 of Title VI requires federal funding agencies to adopt and enforce regulations that prohibit recipients from engaging in discrimination and requires those regulations to be approved by the President. In 1964, a presidential task force developed standard Title VI regulations prohibiting recipients from using "criteria or methods of administration which have the effect of subjecting individuals to discrimination." Since 1964, every federal agency has followed these model regulations to prohibit recipients from engaging in practices having discriminatory impacts. Because section 602 disparate impact regulations "forbid conduct that § 601 permits" there has been controversy about whether such regulations are valid. Nevertheless, the Supreme Court has indicated in several cases, at least in dicta, and arguably in language deserving precedential value, that agencies may promulgate regulations, pursuant to section 602 of Title VI, that prohibit practices creating unjustified discriminatory effects.

There are signs, however, that the Supreme Court may soon reject section 602 disparate impact regulations. In 2001, the Supreme Court in *Alexander v. Sandoval* held in a five-to-four decision that there is no private right of action to enforce disparate impact regulations promulgated under section 602 of Title VI. The majority concluded that neither section 602's language nor subsequent amendments to Title VI demonstrated congressional intent to establish a private cause of action to

---

36. Section 601 of the statute provides that "[n]o person in the United States shall, on the ground of race, color, or national origin, be excluded from participation in, be denied the benefits of, or be subjected to discrimination under any program or activity receiving Federal financial assistant." Civil Rights Act of 1964, 42 U.S.C. § 2000d; *see* Bradford C. Mank, *Title VI*, in THE LAW OF ENVIRONMENTAL JUSTICE 23, 23–25 (Michael Gerard ed., 1999) [hereinafter Mank, *Title VI*]; Bradford C. Mank, *Is There a Private Cause of Action Under EPA's Title VI Regulations*; 24 COLUM. J. ENVTL. L. 1, 12 (1999) [hereinafter Mank, *Private Cause of Action*]; James H. Colopy, Note, *The Road Less Traveled: Pursuing Environmental Justice Through Title VI of the Civil Rights Act of 1964*, 13 STAN. ENVTL. L.J. 125, 152–55 (1994). The typical intermediary recipient is a state or local agency that receives federal funding and then distributes the proceeds to individual beneficiaries. *Id.* at 154. The ultimate individual beneficiaries are exempt from Title VI. *Id.*

enforce section 602. Accordingly, Justice Scalia, writing for the majority, held that "[n]either as originally enacted nor as later amended does Title VI display an intent to create a freestanding private right of action to enforce regulations promulgated under § 602. We therefore hold that no such right of action exists."

While *Sandoval* only addressed whether there is a private cause of action to enforce disparate impact regulations and assumed that federal agencies may issue disparate impact regulations because no party in the case had challenged the validity of the regulations, Justice Scalia, in dicta, questioned whether disparate impact regulations under Title VI are consistent with the Supreme Court's determination that section 601 of the statute only prohibits intentional discrimination.[37] He stated, "We cannot help observing, however, how strange it is to say that disparate-impact regulations are 'inspired by, at the service of, and inseparably intertwined with' § 601 . . . when § 601 permits the very behavior that the regulations forbid." Justice Scalia conceded that prior decisions of the Court had suggested that section 602's disparate impact regulations are valid. He stated that "[t]hough no opinion of this Court has held that, five Justices in *Guardians* voiced that view of the law at least as alternative grounds for their decisions," and that "dictum in *Alexander v. Choate* is to the same effect." Despite this precedent, Justice Scalia argued that *Guardians*' and *Alexander*'s approval of disparate impact regulations in section 602 of Title VI was "in considerable tension with the rule of *Bakke* and *Guardians* that § 601 forbids only intentional discrimination." Many knowledgeable environmental leaders in industry, government, and the environmental justice movement itself believe that Justice Scalia's dicta in *Sandoval* is a clear sign that the Court will soon reject the section 602 disparate impact regulations in Title VI.[38]

71 *Cincinnati Law Review* 517, 517–20.
Copyright © (2002) Cincinnati Law Review Association.
Reprinted with permission of the Cincinnati Law Review Association and
Bradford C. Mank.

---

37. Justice Scalia stated:

[W]e must assume for purposes of deciding this case that regulations promulgated under § 602 of Title VI may validly proscribe activities that have a disparate impact on racial groups, even though such activities are permissible under § 601. Though no opinion of this Court has held that, five Justices in *Guardians* voiced that view of the law at least as alternative grounds for their decisions . . . These statements are in considerable tension with the rule of *Bakke* and *Guardians* that § 601 forbids only intentional discrimination . . . but petitioners have not challenged the regulations here.

Id. at 281–82.

38. *See Activists' Appeal to High Court May Spell End for EPA Equity Rules,* ENVTL. POL'Y ALERT, May 1, 2002, at 40–41 (reporting "[i]ndustry officials, EPA sources, and environmental justice attorneys all say the court likely will overturn EPA's bar on unintentional discrimination under Title VI").

E. Background on *Batson*

Many juries fail to reflect the racial pluralism of the communities they serve. Part of this failure is due to the exclusion of African Americans and other racial minorities from various stages of the jury selection process.

Kim Taylor-Thompson

*Empty Votes in Jury Deliberations**

Throughout most of this country's history, courts excluded people of color from jury service. Before the Civil War, Massachusetts was the only state that allowed African-American men to serve as jurors. After the Civil War, African-American men spread across the country, becoming an integral part of the American social fabric and work force. This demographic shift, coupled with post-Civil War political debates over the status of African Americans, forced Congress to question whether it was appropriate to exclude citizens of color from jury service. In 1875 Congress responded: it prohibited jurisdictions from excluding qualified citizens of color from serving on juries.

Five years later, the Supreme Court followed Congress's lead. It conceded in *Strauder v. West Virginia* that race matters in an individual's ability to receive justice. At issue was a West Virginia statute disqualifying African Americans from jury service. In concluding that the law deprived African-American defendants of equal protection of the law, the Court stated: The very fact that colored people are singled out and expressly denied by a statute all right to participate in the administration of the law, as jurors, because of their color, though they are citizens and may be in other respects fully qualified, is practically a brand upon them . . . and a stimulant to that race prejudice which is an impediment to securing to individuals of the race that equal justice which the law aims to secure to all others.

Both Congress and the Court therefore acknowledged—if implicitly—that the perspectives brought by people of color constitute an essential ingredient of justice when a person of color seeks the protection of the jury.

Predictably, the Southern states saw the issue differently and stubbornly resisted African-American jury participation. At the end of the nineteenth century, systematic exclusion of African Americans was still commonplace, particularly in the South. Indeed, through the first half of the twentieth century, state courts used systems such as color-coding of tickets placed in the jury selection box in order to separate white jurors from jurors of color. Other states tolerated cronyism by allowing white jury commissioners to select grand jurors from among their friends. The Supreme Court finally declared such practices unconstitutional in the middle of this century. Even today, except in a few jurisdictions, people of color are not well-represented on juries. Although states can no longer legally bar them from the

---

* (footnotes omitted).

venire, the presence of people of color on juries is far from guaranteed. Historically trial lawyers have used peremptory strikes to target people of color, resulting in limited participation at the institutional level.

113 *Harv. L. Rev.* 1261, 1279–81.
Copyright © (2000) Harvard Law Review Association.
Reprinted with permission of The Harvard Law Review Association and
Kim Taylor-Thompson.

F. *Batson v. Kentucky,* 476 U.S. 79 (1986)

1. *Facts*

Justice POWELL delivered the opinion of the Court.

This case requires us to reexamine that portion of *Swain v. Alabama*, 380 U.S. 202 (1965), concerning the evidentiary burden placed on a criminal defendant who claims that he has been denied equal protection through the State's use of peremptory challenges to exclude members of his race from the petit jury.

Petitioner, a black man, was indicted in Kentucky on charges of second-degree burglary and receipt of stolen goods. On the first day of trial in Jefferson Circuit Court, the judge conducted *voir dire* examination of the venire, excused certain jurors for cause, and permitted the parties to exercise peremptory challenges. The prosecutor used his peremptory challenges to strike all four black persons on the venire, and a jury composed only of white persons was selected. Defense counsel moved to discharge the jury before it was sworn on the ground that the prosecutor's removal of the black veniremen violated petitioner's rights under the Sixth and Fourteenth Amendments to a jury drawn from a cross section of the community, and under the Fourteenth Amendment to equal protection of the laws. Counsel requested a hearing on his motion. Without expressly ruling on the request for a hearing, the trial judge observed that the parties were entitled to use their peremptory challenges to "strike anybody they want to." The judge then denied petitioner's motion, reasoning that the cross-section requirement applies only to selection of the venire and not to selection of the petit jury itself.

The jury convicted petitioner on both counts. . . .

2. *Opinion*

a. Case Law

In *Swain v. Alabama*, this Court recognized that a "State's purposeful or deliberate denial to Negroes on account of race of participation as jurors in the administration of justice violates the Equal Protection Clause." 380 U.S. at 203–4. This principle has been "consistently and repeatedly" reaffirmed, *id.*, at 204, in numerous decisions of this Court both preceding and following *Swain*. We reaffirm the principle today . . .

A number of lower courts following the teaching of *Swain* reasoned that proof of repeated striking of blacks over a number of cases was necessary to establish a violation of the Equal Protection Clause. Since this interpretation of *Swain* has placed on defendants a crippling burden of proof, prosecutors' peremptory challenges are now largely immune from constitutional scrutiny. For reasons that follow, we reject this evidentiary formulation as inconsistent with standards that have been developed since Swain for assessing a prima facie case under the Equal Protection Clause.

b. Rationale

Since the decision in *Swain*, we have explained that our cases concerning selection of the venire reflect the general equal protection principle that the "invidious quality" of governmental action claimed to be racially discriminatory "must ultimately be traced to a racially discriminatory purpose." *Washington v. Davis*, 426 U.S. 229, 240 (1976). As in any equal protection case, the "burden is, of course," on the defendant who alleges discriminatory selection of the venire "to prove the existence of purposeful discrimination." *Whitus v. Georgia*, 385 U.S., at 550 (citing *Tarrance v. Florida*, 188 U.S. 519 (1903)). In deciding if the defendant has carried his burden of persuasion, a court must undertake "a sensitive inquiry into such circumstantial and direct evidence of intent as may be available." *Arlington Heights v. Metropolitan Housing Development Corp.*, 429 U.S. 252, 266 (1977). Circumstantial evidence of invidious intent may include proof of disproportionate impact. *Washington v. Davis*, 426 U.S. at 242. We have observed that under some circumstances, proof of discriminatory impact "may for all practical purposes demonstrate unconstitutionality because in various circumstances the discrimination is very difficult to explain on non-racial grounds." *Ibid.* For example, "total or seriously disproportionate exclusion of Negroes from jury venires," *ibid.*, "is itself such an 'unequal application of the law . . . as to show intentional discrimination,'" *id.*, at 241 (quoting *Akins v. Texas*, 325 U.S., at 404).

Moreover, since Swain, we have recognized that a black defendant alleging that members of his race have been impermissibly excluded from the venire may make out a prima facie case of purposeful discrimination by showing that the totality of the relevant facts gives rise to an inference of discriminatory purpose. *Washington v. Davis*, supra, at 239–42. Once the defendant makes the requisite showing, the burden shifts to the State to explain adequately the racial exclusion. *Alexander v. Louisiana*, 405 U.S., at 632. The State cannot meet this burden on mere general assertions that its officials did not discriminate or that they properly performed their official duties. See *Alexander v. Louisiana*, supra, at 632; *Jones v. Georgia*, 389 U.S. 24, 25 (1967). Rather, the State must demonstrate that "permissible racially neutral selection criteria and procedures have produced the monochromatic result." *Alexander v. Louisiana*, supra, at 632; *see Washington v. Davis*, supra, at 241.[39]

---

39. Our decisions concerning "disparate treatment" under Title VII of the Civil Rights Act of 1964 have explained the operation of prima facie burden of proof rules. See *McDonnell Douglas*

The showing necessary to establish a prima facie case of purposeful discrimination in selection of the venire may be discerned in this Court's decisions. *E.g., Castaneda v. Partida*, 430 U.S. 482, 494–95 (1977); *Alexander v. Louisiana, supra,* at 631–32. The defendant initially must show that he is a member of a racial group capable of being singled out for differential treatment. *Castaneda v. Partida, supra,* at 494. In combination with that evidence, a defendant may then make a prima facie case by proving that in the particular jurisdiction members of his race have not been summoned for jury service over an extended period of time. *Id.,* at 494. Proof of systematic exclusion from the venire raises an inference of purposeful discrimination because the "result bespeaks discrimination." *Hernandez v. Texas,* 347 U.S. at 482; *see Arlington Heights v. Metropolitan Housing Development Corp., supra* at 266.

Since the ultimate issue is whether the State has discriminated in selecting the defendant's venire, however, the defendant may establish a prima facie case "in other ways than by evidence of long-continued unexplained absence" of members of his race "from many panels." *Cassell v. Texas,* 339 U.S. 282, 290 (1950) (plurality opinion). In cases involving the venire, this Court has found a prima facie case on proof that members of the defendant's race were substantially underrepresented on the venire from which his jury was drawn, and that the venire was selected under a practice providing "the opportunity for discrimination." *Whitus v. Georgia, supra, at 552; see Castaneda v. Partida, supra,* at 494; *Washington v. Davis, supra,* at 241; *Alexander v. Louisiana, supra,* at 629–31. This combination of factors raises the necessary inference of purposeful discrimination because the Court has declined to attribute to chance the absence of black citizens on a particular jury array where the selection mechanism is subject to abuse. When circumstances suggest the need, the trial court must undertake a "factual inquiry" that "takes into account all possible explanatory factors" in the particular case. *Alexander v. Louisiana, supra,* at 630.

Thus, since the decision in *Swain,* this Court has recognized that a defendant may make a prima facie showing of purposeful racial discrimination in selection of the venire by relying solely on the facts concerning its selection in his case. These decisions are in accordance with the proposition, articulated in *Arlington Heights v. Metropolitan Housing Development Corp.,* that "a consistent pattern of official racial discrimination" is not "a necessary predicate to a violation of the Equal Protection Clause. A single invidiously discriminatory governmental act" is not "immunized by the absence of such discrimination in the making of other comparable decisions." 429 U.S., at 266, n. 14. For evidentiary requirements to dictate that "several must suffer discrimination" before one could object, *McCray v. New York,* 461 U.S.,

---

Corp. v. Green, 411 U.S. 792 (1973); *Texas Dept. of Community Affairs v. Burdine,* 450 U.S. 248 (1981); *United States Postal Service Board of Governors v. Aikens,* 460 U.S. 711 (1983). The party alleging that he has been the victim of intentional discrimination carries the ultimate burden of persuasion. *Texas Dept. of Community Affairs v. Burdine, supra,* at 252–56.

at 965 (MARSHALL, J., dissenting from denial of certiorari), would be inconsistent with the promise of equal protection to all.[40]

The standards for assessing a prima facie case in the context of discriminatory selection of the venire have been fully articulated since *Swain*. *See Castaneda v. Partida, supra*, at 494–95; *Washington v. Davis*, 426 U.S., at 241–42; *Alexander v. Louisiana, supra*, at 629–31. These principles support our conclusion that a defendant may establish a prima facie case of purposeful discrimination in selection of the petit jury solely on evidence concerning the prosecutor's exercise of peremptory challenges at the defendant's trial. To establish such a case, the defendant first must show that he is a member of a cognizable racial group, *Castaneda v. Partida, supra*, at 494, and that the prosecutor has exercised peremptory challenges to remove from the venire members of the defendant's race. Second, the defendant is entitled to rely on the fact, as to which there can be no dispute, that peremptory challenges constitute a jury selection practice that permits "those to discriminate who are of a mind to discriminate." *Avery v. Georgia*, 345 U.S., at 562. Finally, the defendant must show that these facts and any other relevant circumstances raise an inference that the prosecutor used that practice to exclude the veniremen from the petit jury on account of their race. This combination of factors in the empaneling of the petit jury, as in the selection of the venire, raises the necessary inference of purposeful discrimination.

In deciding whether the defendant has made the requisite showing, the trial court should consider all relevant circumstances. For example, a "pattern" of strikes against black jurors included in the particular venire might give rise to an inference of discrimination. Similarly, the prosecutor's questions and statements during voir dire examination and in exercising his challenges may support or refute an inference of discriminatory purpose. These examples are merely illustrative. We have confidence that trial judges, experienced in supervising voir dire, will be able to decide if the circumstances concerning the prosecutor's use of peremptory challenges creates a prima facie case of discrimination against black jurors.

Once the defendant makes a prima facie showing, the burden shifts to the State to come forward with a neutral explanation for challenging black jurors. Though this requirement imposes a limitation in some cases on the full peremptory character of the historic challenge, we emphasize that the prosecutor's explanation need not rise to the level justifying exercise of a challenge for cause. *See McCray v. Abrams*, 750 F.2d, at 1132; *Booker v. Jabe*, 775 F.2d 762, 773 (CA6 1985), cert. pending, No. 85-1028. But the prosecutor may not rebut the defendant's prima facie case of discrimination by stating merely that he challenged jurors of the defendant's race on the assumption—or his intuitive judgment—that they would be partial to the defendant because of their shared race. *Cf. Norris v. Alabama*, 294 U.S., at 598–99;

---

40. Decisions under Title VII also recognize that a person claiming that he has been the victim of intentional discrimination may make out a prima facie case by relying solely on the facts concerning the alleged discrimination against him.

see Thompson v. United States, 469 U.S. 1024, 1026 (1984) (BRENNAN, J., dissenting from denial of certiorari). Just as the Equal Protection Clause forbids the States to exclude black persons from the venire on the assumption that blacks as a group are unqualified to serve as jurors, *supra*, at 86, so it forbids the States to strike black veniremen on the assumption that they will be biased in a particular case simply because the defendant is black. The core guarantee of equal protection, ensuring citizens that their State will not discriminate on account of race, would be meaningless were we to approve the exclusion of jurors on the basis of such assumptions, which arise solely from the jurors' race. Nor may the prosecutor rebut the defendant's case merely by denying that he had a discriminatory motive or "affirm[ing] [his] good faith in making individual selections." *Alexander v. Louisiana*, 405 U.S., at 632. If these general assertions were accepted as rebutting a defendant's prima facie case, the Equal Protection Clause "would be but a vain and illusory requirement." *Norris v. Alabama, supra*, at 598. The prosecutor therefore must articulate a neutral explanation related to the particular case to be tried. The trial court then will have the duty to determine if the defendant has established purposeful discrimination.[41]

The State contends that our holding will eviscerate the fair trial values served by the peremptory challenge. Conceding that the Constitution does not guarantee a right to peremptory challenges and that Swain did state that their use ultimately is subject to the strictures of equal protection, the State argues that the privilege of unfettered exercise of the challenge is of vital importance to the criminal justice system.

While we recognize, of course, that the peremptory challenge occupies an important position in our trial procedures, we do not agree that our decision today will undermine the contribution the challenge generally makes to the administration of justice. The reality of practice, amply reflected in many state- and federal-court opinions, shows that the challenge may be, and unfortunately at times has been, used to discriminate against black jurors. By requiring trial courts to be sensitive to the racially discriminatory use of peremptory challenges, our decision enforces the mandate of equal protection and furthers the ends of justice.[42] In view of the hetero-

---

41. In a recent Title VII sex discrimination case, we stated that "a finding of intentional discrimination is a finding of fact" entitled to appropriate deference by a reviewing court. *Anderson v. Bessemer City,* 470 U.S. 564, 573 (1985). Since the trial judge's findings in the context under consideration here largely will turn on evaluation of credibility, a reviewing court ordinarily should give those findings great deference. *Id.* at 575–76.

42. While we respect the views expressed in JUSTICE MARSHALL's concurring opinion concerning prosecutorial and judicial enforcement of our holding today, we do not share them. The standard we adopt under the Federal Constitution is designed to ensure that a State does not use peremptory challenges to strike any black juror because of his race. We have no reason to believe that prosecutors will not fulfill their duty to exercise their challenges only for legitimate purposes. Certainly, this Court may assume that trial judges, in supervising voir dire in light of our decision today, will be alert to identify a prima facie case of purposeful discrimination. Nor do we think that this historic trial practice, which long has served the selection of an impartial jury, should be abolished because of an apprehension that prosecutors and trial judges will not perform conscientiously their respective duties under the Constitution.

geneous population of our Nation, public respect for our criminal justice system and the rule of law will be strengthened if we ensure that no citizen is disqualified from jury service because of his race.

Nor are we persuaded by the State's suggestion that our holding will create serious administrative difficulties. In those States applying a version of the evidentiary standard we recognize today, courts have not experienced serious administrative burdens, and the peremptory challenge system has survived. We decline, however, to formulate particular procedures to be followed upon a defendant's timely objection to a prosecutor's challenges.[43]

3. Holding

In this case, petitioner made a timely objection to the prosecutor's removal of all black persons on the venire. Because the trial court flatly rejected the objection without requiring the prosecutor to give an explanation for his action, we remand this case for further proceedings. If the trial court decides that the facts establish, prima facie, purposeful discrimination and the prosecutor does not come forward with a neutral explanation for his action, our precedents require that petitioner's conviction be reversed. *Whitus v. Georgia*, 385 U.S., at 549–50; *Hernandez v. Texas*, 347 U.S., at 482; *Patton v. Mississippi*, 332 U.S., at 469.[44]

4. Justice Marshall Concurring

I wholeheartedly concur in the Court's conclusion that use of the peremptory challenge to remove blacks from juries, on the basis of their race, violates the Equal Protection Clause. I would go further, however, in fashioning a remedy adequate to eliminate that discrimination. Merely allowing defendants the opportunity to challenge the racially discriminatory use of peremptory challenges in individual cases will not end the illegitimate use of the peremptory challenge. Evidentiary analysis similar to that set out by the Court, ante, at 97–98, has been adopted as a matter of state law in States including Massachusetts and California. Cases from those jurisdictions illustrate the limitations of the approach. First, defendants cannot attack the discriminatory use of peremptory challenges at all unless the challenges are so flagrant as to establish a prima facie case. This means, in those States, that where only one or two black jurors survive the challenges for cause, the prosecutor need

---

43. In light of the variety of jury selection practices followed in our state and federal trial courts, we make no attempt to instruct these courts how best to implement our holding today. For the same reason, we express no view on whether it is more appropriate in a particular case, upon a finding of discrimination against black jurors, for the trial court to discharge the venire and select a new jury from a panel not previously associated with the case, *see Booker v. Jabe*, 775 F.2d at 773, or to disallow the discriminatory challenges and resume selection with the improperly challenged jurors reinstated on the venire, *see United States v. Robinson*, 421 F. Supp. 467, 474 (Conn. 1976), mandamus granted sub nom. *United States v. Newman*, 549 F.2d 240 (CA2 1977).

44. To the extent that anything in *Swain v. Alabama*, 380 U.S. 202 (1965), is contrary to the principles we articulate today, that decision is overruled.

have no compunction about striking them from the jury because of their race. *See Commonwealth v. Robinson*, 382 Mass. 189, 195, 415 N.E.2d 805, 809–10 (1981) (no prima facie case of discrimination where defendant is black, prospective jurors include three blacks and one Puerto Rican, and prosecutor excludes one for cause and strikes the remainder peremptorily, producing all-white jury); *People v. Rousseau*, 129 Cal. App. 3d 526, 536–37, 179 Cal. Rptr. 892, 897–98 (1982) (no prima facie case where prosecutor peremptorily strikes only two blacks on jury panel). Prosecutors are left free to discriminate against blacks in jury selection provided that they hold that discrimination to an "acceptable" level.

Second, when a defendant can establish a prima facie case, trial courts face the difficult burden of assessing prosecutors' motives. *See King v. County of Nassau*, 581 F. Supp. 493, 501–2 (EDNY 1984). Any prosecutor can easily assert facially neutral reasons for striking a juror, and trial courts are ill equipped to second-guess those reasons. How is the court to treat a prosecutor's statement that he struck a juror because the juror had a son about the same age as defendant, *see People v. Hall*, 35 Cal. 3d 161, 672 P.2d 854 (1983), or seemed "uncommunicative," *King, supra*, at 498, or "never cracked a smile" and, therefore "did not possess the sensitivities necessary to realistically look at the issues and decide the facts in this case," *Hall, supra*, at 165, 672 P.2d at 856? If such easily generated explanations are sufficient to discharge the prosecutor's obligation to justify his strikes on nonracial grounds, then the protection erected by the Court today may be illusory.

Nor is outright prevarication by prosecutors the only danger here. "[I]t is even possible that an attorney may lie to himself in an effort to convince himself that his motives are legal." *King, supra*, at 502. A prosecutor's own conscious or unconscious racism may lead him easily to the conclusion that a prospective black juror is "sullen," or "distant," a characterization that would not have come to his mind if a white juror had acted identically. A judge's own conscious or unconscious racism may lead him to accept such an explanation as well supported. As Justice Rehnquist concedes, prosecutors' peremptories are based on their "seat-of-the-pants instincts" as to how particular jurors will vote. *Post*, at 138; *see also* The Chief Justice's dissenting opinion, post, at 123. Yet "seat-of-the-pants instincts" may often be just another term for racial prejudice. Even if all parties approach the Court's mandate with the best of conscious intentions, that mandate requires them to confront and overcome their own racism on all levels—a challenge I doubt all of them can meet. It is worth remembering that "114 years after the close of the War Between the States and nearly 100 years after *Strauder*, racial and other forms of discrimination still remain a fact of life, in the administration of justice and in our society as a whole." *Rose v. Mitchell*, 443 U.S. 545, 558–59 (1979), quoted in *Vasquez v. Hillery*, 474 U.S. 254, 264 (1986). . . .

G. Commentary on *Batson*

A right without a remedy is no right at all. In his concurrence, Justice Marshall suggests that the majority's solution of requiring prosecutors to provide a non-racial explanation is inadequate. It will not prevent racial discrimination in jury selection because prosecutors will always come up with a non-racial explanation for exclusion and may even lie to themselves in order to do so. Justice Oliver Wendell Holmes was known to say, "a page of history is worth a volume of logic."[45] As the only Justice to actually have litigated a capital murder case and as the most experienced litigator on the court, Marshall knew better than most other Justices the prosecutorial historical record. Unfortunately, that record included the presence of unconscious, as well as intentional, racial exclusion of African Americans so that very few ended up actually serving as jurors.

The extent of the negative impact of such exclusion on convictions and sentencing is difficult to measure. At the very least, however, this exclusion has helped foster a perception of racial inequity throughout the judicial system.

H. Background on *McCleskey*

Historically, racial disparities in criminal sentencing were based upon statutes that required more severe sentences for blacks.[46] Today, statistical evidence suggests that these same disparities continue to exist throughout the criminal justice system, including arrests and prosecutions, as well as sentencing,[47] even though legislation no longer requires such treatment. This is particularly true for the imposition of the death penalty.

I. *McCleskey v. Kemp*, 481 U.S. 279 (1987)

1. Facts

Justice POWELL delivered the opinion of the Court.

McCleskey, a black man, was convicted of two counts of armed robbery and one count of murder in the Superior Court of Fulton County, Georgia, on October 12, 1978. McCleskey's convictions arose out of the robbery of a furniture store and the killing of a white police officer during the course of the robbery. The evidence at trial indicated that McCleskey and three accomplices planned and carried out the robbery. All four were armed. McCleskey entered the front of the store while the other three entered the rear. McCleskey secured the front of the store by rounding up the customers and forcing them to lie face down on the floor. The other three rounded up the employees in the rear and tied them up with tape. The manager was forced at gunpoint to turn over the store receipts, his watch, and $6. During the course of the robbery, a police officer, answering a silent alarm, entered the store

---

45. *New York Trust Co. v. Eisner*, 256 U.S. 345, 349 (1921).

46. GEORGE STROUD, A SKETCH OF THE LAWS RELATING TO SLAVERY IN THE SEVERAL STATES OF THE UNITED STATES OF AMERICA 75–78 (1968).

47. *See* U.S. GENERAL ACCOUNTING OFFICE, DEATH PENALTY SENTENCING INDICATES PATTERN OF RACIAL DISPARITIES(1990).

through the front door. As he was walking down the center aisle of the store, two shots were fired. Both struck the officer. One hit him in the face and killed him.

Several weeks later, McCleskey was arrested in connection with an unrelated offense. He confessed that he had participated in the furniture store robbery, but denied that he had shot the police officer. At trial, the State introduced evidence that at least one of the bullets that struck the officer was fired from a .38 caliber Rossi revolver. This description matched the description of the gun that McCleskey had carried during the robbery. The State also introduced the testimony of two witnesses who had heard McCleskey admit to the shooting.

The jury convicted McCleskey of murder.[48] At the penalty hearing,[49] the jury heard arguments as to the appropriate sentence. Under Georgia law, the jury could not consider imposing the death penalty unless it found beyond a reasonable doubt that the murder was accompanied by one of the statutory aggravating circumstances. Ga. Code Ann. § 17-10-30(c) (1982).[50] The jury in this case found two aggravating circumstances to exist beyond a reasonable doubt: the murder was committed

---

48. The Georgia Code has been revised and renumbered since McCleskey's trial. The changes do not alter the substance of the sections relevant to this case. For convenience, references in this opinion are to the current sections.

The Georgia Code contains only one degree of murder. A person commits murder "when he unlawfully and with malice aforethought, either express or implied, causes the death of another human being." Ga. Code Ann. § 16-5-1(a) 91984). A person convicted of murder "shall be punished by death or by imprisonment for life." § 16-5-1(d).

49. Georgia Code Ann. § 17-10-2(c) (1982) provides that when a jury convicts a defendant of murder, "the court shall resume the trial and conduct a presentence hearing before the jury." This subsection suggests that a defendant convicted of murder always is subjected to a penalty hearing at which the jury considers imposing a death sentence. But as a matter of practice, penalty hearings seem to be held only if the prosecutor affirmatively seeks the death penalty. If he does not, the defendant receives a sentence of life imprisonment. *See Baldus, Pulaski, & Woodworth, Comparative Review of Death Sentences: An Empirical Study of the Georgia Experience*, 74 J. Crim. L. & C. 661, 674, n. 56 (1983).

50. A jury cannot sentence a defendant to death for murder unless it finds that one of the following aggravating circumstances exists beyond a reasonable doubt:

"(1) The offense . . . was committed by a person with a prior record of conviction for a capital felony;

"(2) The offense . . . was committed while the offender was engaged in the commission of another capital felony or aggravated battery, or the offense of murder was committed while the offender was engaged in the commission of burglary or arson in the first degree;

"(3) The offender, by his act of murder . . . knowingly created a great risk of death to more than one person in a public place by means of a weapon or device which would normally be hazardous to the lives of more than one person;

"(4) The offender committed the offense . . . for himself or another, for the purpose of receiving money or any other thing of monetary value;

"(5) The murder of a judicial officer, former judicial officer, district attorney or solicitor, of former district attorney or solicitor was committed during or because of the exercise of his official duties;

"(6) The offender caused or directed another to commit murder or committed murder as an agent or employee of another person;

during the course of an armed robbery, § 17-10-30(b)(2); and the murder was committed upon a peace officer engaged in the performance of his duties, § 17-10-30(b)(8). In making its decision whether to impose the death sentence, the jury considered the mitigating and aggravating circumstances of McCleskey's conduct. § 17-10-2(c). McCleskey offered no mitigating evidence. The jury recommended that he be sentenced to death on the murder charge and to consecutive life sentences on the armed robbery charges. The court followed the jury's recommendation and sentenced McCleskey to death. . . . [51]

2. Opinion

a. Argument

McCleskey next filed a petition for a writ of habeas corpus in the Federal District Court for the Northern District of Georgia. His petition raised 18 claims, one of which was that the Georgia capital sentencing process is administered in a racially discriminatory manner in violation of the Eighth and Fourteenth Amendments to the United States Constitution. In support of his claim, McCleskey proffered a statistical study performed by Professors David C. Baldus, Charles Pulaski, and George Woodworth (the Baldus study) that purports to show a disparity in the imposition of the death sentence in Georgia based on the race of the murder victim and, to a lesser extent, the race of the defendant. The Baldus study is actually two sophisticated statistical studies that examine over 2,000 murder cases that occurred in Georgia during the 1970s. The raw numbers collected by Professor Baldus indicate that defendants charged with killing white persons received the death penalty in 11% of the cases, but defendants charged with killing blacks received the death penalty in only 1% of the cases. The raw numbers also indicate a reverse racial disparity according to the race of the defendant: 4% of the black defendants received the death penalty, as opposed to 7% of the white defendants.

Baldus also divided the cases according to the combination of the race of the defendant and the race of the victim. He found that the death penalty was assessed in 22% of the cases involving black defendants and white victims; 8% of the cases involving white defendants and white victims; 1% of the cases involving black defendants and black victims; and 3% of the cases involving white defendants and black

---

"(7) The offense of murder, rape, armed robbery, or kidnapping was outrageously or wantonly vile, horrible, or inhuman in that it involved torture, depravity of mind, or an aggravated battery to the victim;

"(8) The offense . . . was committed against any peace officer, corrections employee, or fireman while engaged in the performance of his official duties;

"(9) The offense . . . was committed by a person in, or who has escaped from, the lawful custody of a peace officer or place of lawful confinement; or

"(10) The murder was committed for the purpose of avoiding, interfering with, or preventing a lawful arrest or custody in a place of lawful confinement, or himself or another." § 17-10-30(b).

51. Georgia law provides that "[w]here a statutory aggravating circumstances is found and a recommendation of death is made, the court shall sentence the defendant to death." § 17-10-31.

victims. Similarly, Baldus found that prosecutors sought the death penalty in 70% of the cases involving black defendants and white victims; 32% of the cases involving white defendants and white victims; 15% of the cases involving black defendants and black victims; and 19% of the cases involving white defendants and black victims. Baldus subjected his data to an extensive analysis, taking account of 230 variables that could have explained the disparities on nonracial grounds. One of his models concludes that, even after taking account of 39 nonracial variables, defendants charged with killing white victims were 4.3 times as likely to receive a death sentence as defendants charged with killing blacks. According to this model, black defendants were 1.1 times as likely to receive a death sentence as other defendants. Thus, the Baldus study indicates that black defendants, such as McCleskey, who kill white victims have the greatest likelihood of receiving the death penalty. . . . [52]

b. Rationale

McCleskey's first claim is that the Georgia capital punishment statute violates the Equal Protection Clause of the Fourteenth Amendment.[53] He argues that race has infected the administration of Georgia's statute in two ways: persons who murder whites are more likely to be sentenced to death than persons who murder blacks, and black murderers are more likely to be sentenced to death than white murderers.[54] As a black defendant who killed a white victim, McCleskey claims that the

---

52. Baldus' 230-variable model divided cases into eight different ranges, according to the estimated aggravation level of the offense. Baldus argued in his testimony to the District Court that the effects of racial bias were most striking in the midrange cases. "[W]hen the cases become tremendously aggravated so that everybody would agree that if we're going to have a death sentence, these are the cases that should get it, the race effects go away. It's only in the mid-range of cases where the decisionmakers have a real choice as to what to do. If there's room for the exercise of discretion, then the [racial] factors begin to play a role." App. 36. Under this model, Baldus found that 14.4% of the black-victim midrange cases received the death penalty, and 34.4% of the white-victim cases received the death penalty. *See* Exhibit DB 90, reprinted in Supplemental Exhibits 54. According to Baldus, the facts of *McCleskey*'s case placed it within the midrange. App. 45–46.

53. Although the District Court rejected the findings of the Baldus study as flawed, the Court of Appeals assumed that the study is valid and reached the constitutional issues. Accordingly, those issues are before us. As did the Court of Appeals, we assume the study is valid statistically without reviewing the factual findings of the District court. Our assumption that the Baldus study is statistically valid does not include the assumption that the study shows that racial considerations actually enter into any sentencing decisions in Georgia. Even a sophisticated multiple-regression analysis such as the Baldus study can only demonstrate a risk that the factor of race entered into some capital sentencing decisions and a necessarily lesser risk that race entered into any particular sentencing decision.

54. Although McCleskey has standing to claim that he suffers discrimination because of his own race, the State argues that he has no standing to contend that he was discriminated against on the basis of his victim's race. While it is true that we are reluctant to recognize "standing to assert the rights of third persons," *Arlington Heights v. Metropolitan Housing Dev. Corp.*, 429 U.S. 252, 263 (1977), this does not appear to be the nature of McCleskey's claim. He does not seek to assert some right of his victim, or the rights of black murder victims in general. Rather, McCleskey argues that application of the State's statute has created a classification that is "an irrational exercise of governmental power," Brief for Petitioner 41, because it is not "necessary to the accomplishment of some

Baldus study demonstrates that he was discriminated against because of his race and because of the race of his victim. In its broadest form, McCleskey's claim of discrimination extends to every actor in the Georgia capital sentencing process, from the prosecutor who sought the death penalty and the jury that imposed the sentence, to the State itself that enacted the capital punishment statute and allows it to remain in effect despite its allegedly discriminatory application. We agree with the Court of Appeals, and every other court that has considered such a challenge, that this claim must fail.

Our analysis begins with the basic principle that a defendant who alleges an equal protection violation has the burden of proving "the existence of purposeful discrimination." *Whitus v. Georgia*, 385 U.S. 545, 550 (1967). A corollary to this principle is that a criminal defendant must prove that the purposeful discrimination "had a discriminatory effect" on him. *Wayte v. United States*, 470 U.S. 598, 608 (1985). Thus, to prevail under the Equal Protection Clause, McCleskey must prove that the decisionmakers in his case acted with discriminatory purpose. He offers no evidence specific to his own case that would support an inference that racial considerations played a part in his sentence. Instead, he relies solely on the Baldus study. McCleskey argues that the Baldus study compels an inference that his sentence rests on purposeful discrimination. McCleskey's claim that these statistics are sufficient proof of discrimination, without regard to the facts of a particular case, would extend to all capital cases in Georgia, at least where the victim was white and the defendant is black.

The Court has accepted statistics as proof of intent to discriminate in certain limited contexts. First, this Court has accepted statistical disparities as proof of an equal protection violation in the selection of the jury venire in a particular district. Although statistical proof normally must present a "stark" pattern to be accepted as the sole proof of discriminatory intent under the Constitution,[55] *Arlington Heights v. Metropolitan Housing Dev. Corp.*, 429 U.S. 252, 266 (1977), "[b]ecause of the nature

---

permissible state objective." *Loving v. Virginia*, 388 U.S. 1, 11 (1967). *See McGowan v. Maryland*, 366 U.S. 420, 425 (1961) (statutory classification cannot be "wholly irrelevant to the achievement of the State's objective"). It would violate the Equal Protection Clause for a State to base enforcement of its criminal laws on "an unjustifiable standard such as race, religion, or other arbitrary classification." *Oyler v. Boles*, 368 U.S. 448, 456 (1962). *See Cleveland Bd. of Ed. v. Lafleur*, 414 U.S. 632, 652–53 (1974) (POWELL, J., concurring). Because McCleskey raises such a claim, he has standing.

55. *Gomillion v. Lightfoot*, 364 U.S. 339 (1960), and *Yick Wo v. Hopkins*, 118 U.S. 356 (1886), are examples of those rare cases in which a statistical pattern of discriminatory impact demonstrated a constitutional violation. In *Gomillion*, a state legislature violated the Fifteenth Amendment by altering the boundaries of a particular city "from a square to an uncouth twenty-eight sided figure." 364 U.S., at 340. The alterations excluded 395 of 400 black voters without excluding a single white voter. In *Yick Wo*, an ordinance prohibited operation of 310 laundries that were housed in wooden buildings, but allowed such laundries to resume operations if the operator secured a permit from the government. When laundry operators applied for permits to resume operation, all but one of the white applicants received permits, but none of the over 200 Chinese applicants were successful. In those cases, the Court found the statistical disparities "to warrant and require," *Yick Wo v. Hopkins*, supra, at 373, a "conclusion [that was] irresistible, tantamount for all practical purposes

of the jury-selection task, . . . we have permitted a finding of constitutional violation even when the statistical pattern does not approach [such] extremes." *Id.*, at 266, n. 13.[56] Second, this Court has accepted statistics in the form of multiple-regression analysis to prove statutory violations under Title VII of the Civil Rights Act of 1964. *Bazemore v. Friday,* 478 U.S. 385, 400–1 (1986) (opinion of BRENNAN, J., concurring in part).

But the nature of the capital sentencing decision, and the relationship of the statistics to that decision, are fundamentally different from the corresponding elements in the venire-selection or Title VII cases. Most importantly, each particular decision to impose the death penalty is made by a petit jury selected from a properly constituted venire. Each jury is unique in its composition, and the Constitution requires that its decision rest on consideration of innumerable factors that vary according to the characteristics of the individual defendant and the facts of the particular capital offense. *See Hitchcock v. Dugger,* post, at 398–99; *Lockett v. Ohio,* 438 U.S. 586, 602–5 (1978) (plurality opinion of BURGER, C.J.). Thus, the application of an inference drawn from the general statistics to a specific decision in a trial and sentencing simply is not comparable to the application of an inference drawn from general statistics to a specific venire-selection or Title VII case. In those cases, the statistics relate to fewer entities,[57] and fewer variables are relevant to the challenged decisions.[58]

---

to a mathematical demonstration," *Gomillion v. Lightfoot,* supra, at 341, that the State acted with a discriminatory purpose.

56. *See Castaneda v. Partida,* 430 U.S. 482, 495 91977) (2-to-1 disparity between Mexican-Americans in county population and those summoned for grand jury duty); *Turner v. Fouche,* 396 U.S. 346, 359 (1970) (1.6-to-1 disparity between blacks in county population and those on grand jury lists); *Whitus v. Georgia,* 385 U.S. 545, 552 (1967) (3-to-1 disparity between eligible blacks in county and blacks on grand jury venire).

57. In venire-selection cases, the factors that may be considered are limited, usually by state statute. These considerations are uniform for all potential jurors, and although some factors may be said to be subjective, they are limited and, to a great degree, objectively verifiable. While employment decisions may involve a number of relevant variables, these variables are to a great extent uniform for all employees because they must all have a reasonable relationship to the employee's qualifications to perform the particular job at issue. Identifiable qualifications for a single job provide a common standard by which to assess each employee. In contrast, a capital sentencing jury may consider any factor relevant to the defendant's background, character, and the offense. *See Eddings v. Oklahoma,* 455 U.S. 104, 112 (1982). There is no common standard by which to evaluate all defendants who have or have not received the death penalty.

58. We refer here not to the number of entities involved in any particular decision, but to the number of entities whose decisions necessarily are reflected in a statistical display such as the Baldus study. The decisions of a jury commission or of an employer over time are fairly attributable to the commission or the employer. Therefore, an unexplained statistical discrepancy can be said to indicate a consistent policy of the decisionmaker. The Baldus study seeks to deduce a state "policy" by studying the combined effects of the decisions of hundreds of juries that are unique in their composition. It is incomparably more difficult to deduce a consistent policy by studying the decisions of these many unique entities. It is also questionable whether any consistent policy can be derived by studying the decisions of prosecutors. The District Attorney is elected by the voters in a particular county. *See* Ga. Const., Art. 6, § 8, ¶ 1. Since decisions whether to prosecute and what to

Another important difference between the cases in which we have accepted statistics as proof of discriminatory intent and this case is that, in the venire-selection and Title VII contexts, the decisionmaker has an opportunity to explain the statistical disparity. *See Whitus v. Georgia, 385 U.S., at 552; Texas Dept. of Community Affairs v. Burdine, 450 U.S. 248, 254 (1981); McDonnell Douglas Corp. v. Green,* 411 U.S. 792, 802 (1973). Here, the State has no practical opportunity to rebut the Baldus study. "[C]ontrolling considerations of . . . public policy," *McDonald v. Pless,* 238 U.S. 264, 267 (1915), dictate that jurors "cannot be called . . . to testify to the motives and influences that led to their verdict." *Chicago, B. & O. R. Co. v. Babcock,* 204 U.S. 585, 593 (1907). Similarly, the policy considerations behind a prosecutor's traditionally "wide discretion" suggest the impropriety of our requiring prosecutors to defend their decisions to seek death penalties, "often years after they were made." *See Imbler v. Pachtman,* 424 U.S. 409, 425–26 (1976). Moreover, absent far stronger proof, it is unnecessary to seek such a rebuttal, because a legitimate and unchallenged explanation for the decision is apparent from the record: McCleskey committed an act for which the United States Constitution and Georgia laws permit imposition of the death penalty.[59]

Finally, McCleskey's statistical proffer must be viewed in the context of his challenge. McClesky challenges decisions at the heart of the State's criminal justice system. "[O]ne of society's most basic tasks is that of protecting the lives of its citizens and one of the most basic ways in which it achieves the task is through criminal laws against murder." *Gregg v. Georgia,* 428 U.S. 153, 226 (1976) (WHITE, J., concurring). Implementation of these laws necessarily requires discretionary judgments. Because discretion is essential to the criminal justice process, we would demand exceptionally clear proof before we would infer that the discretion has been abused. The unique nature of the decisions at issue in this case also counsels against adopting such an inference from the disparities indicated by the Baldus study. Accordingly, we hold that the Baldus study is clearly insufficient to support an inference that any of the decisionmakers in McCleskey's case acted with discriminatory purpose.

McCleskey also suggests that the Baldus study proves that the State as a whole has acted with a discriminatory purpose. He appears to argue that the State has violated the Equal Protection Clause by adopting the capital punishment statute

charge necessarily are individualized and involve infinite factual variations, coordination among district attorney offices across a State would be relatively meaningless. Thus, any inference from statewide statistics to a prosecutorial "policy" is of doubtful relevance. Moreover, the statistics in Fulton County alone represent the disposition of far fewer cases than the statewide statistics. Even assuming the statistical validity of the Baldus study as a whole, the weight to be given the results gleaned from this small sample is limited.

59. In his dissent, JUSTICE BLACKMUN misreads this statement. *See* Post, at 348–49. We do not suggest that McCleskey's conviction and sentencing by a jury bears on the prosecutor's motivation. Rather, the fact that the United States Constitution and the laws of Georgia authorized the prosecutor to seek the death penalty under the circumstances of this case is a relevant factor to be weighed in determining whether the Baldus study demonstrates a constitutionally significant risk that this decision was motivated by racial considerations.

and allowing it to remain in force despite its allegedly discriminatory application. But "'[d]iscriminatory purpose' . . . implies more than intent as volition or intent as awareness of consequences. It implies that the decisionmaker, in this case a state legislature, selected or reaffirmed a particular course of action at least in part 'because of,' not merely 'in spite of,' its adverse effects upon an identifiable group." *Personnel Administrator of Massachusetts v. Feeney*, 442 U.S. 256, 279 (1979) (footnote and citation omitted). See *Wayte v. United States*, 470 U.S., at 608–9 For this claim to prevail, McCleskey would have to prove that the Georgia Legislature enacted or maintained the death penalty statute because of an anticipated racially discriminatory effect. In *Gregg v. Georgia, supra*, this Court found that the Georgia capital sentencing system could operate in a fair and neutral manner. There was no evidence then, and there is none now, that the Georgia Legislature enacted the capital punishment statute to further a racially discriminatory purpose.[60]

Nor has McCleskey demonstrated that the legislature maintains the capital punishment statute because of the racially disproportionate impact suggested by the Baldus study. As legislatures necessarily have wide discretion in the choice of criminal laws and penalties, and as there were legitimate reasons for the Georgia Legislature to adopt and maintain capital punishment, *see Gregg v. Georgia*, supra, at 183–87 (joint opinion of STEWART, POWELL, and STEVENS, JJ.), we will not infer a discriminatory purpose on the part of the State of Georgia. Accordingly, we reject McCleskey's equal protection claims. . . .

McCleskey's argument that the Constitution condemns the discretion allowed decisionmakers in the Georgia capital sentencing system is antithetical to the fundamental role of discretion in our criminal justice system. Discretion in the criminal justice system offers substantial benefits to the criminal defendant. Not only can a jury decline to impose the death sentence, it can decline to convict or choose to convict of a lesser offense. Whereas decisions against a defendant's interest may be reversed by the trial judge or on appeal, these discretionary exercises of leniency are final and unreviewable. Similarly, the capacity of prosecutorial discretion to provide individualized justice is "firmly entrenched in American law." 2 *W. LaFave & J. Israel, Criminal Procedure* § 13.2(a), p. 160 (1984). As we have noted, a prosecutor can decline to charge, offer a plea bargain, or decline to seek a death sentence in any particular case. *See* n. 28, *supra*. Of course, "the power to be lenient [also] is the power to discriminate," *K. Davis, Discretionary Justice* 170 (1973), but a capital

---

60. McCleskey relies on "historical evidence" to support his claim of purposeful discrimination by the State. This evidence focuses on Georgia laws in force during and just after the Civil War. Of course, the "historical background of the decision is one evidentiary source" for proof of intentional discrimination. *Arlington Heights v. Metropolitan Housing Dev. Corp.*, 429 U.S., at 267. But unless historical evidence is reasonably contemporaneous with the challenged decision, it has little probative value. *Cf. Hunter v. Underwood*, 471 U.S. 222, 228–33 91985) (relying on legislative history to demonstrate discriminatory motivation behind state statute). Although the history of racial discrimination in this country is undeniable, we cannot accept official actions taken long ago as evidence of current intent.

punishment system that did not allow for discretionary acts of leniency "would be totally alien to our notions of criminal justice." *Gregg v. Georgia*, 428 U.S., at 200, n. 50.

At most, the Baldus study indicates a discrepancy that appears to correlate with race. Apparent disparities in sentencing are an inevitable part of our criminal justice system.[61] The discrepancy indicated by the Baldus study is a "far cry from the major systemic defects identified in Furman," *Pulley v. Harris*, 465 U.S., at 54. As this Court has recognized, any mode for determining guilt or punishment "has its weaknesses and the potential for misuse." *Singer v. United States*, 380 U.S. 24, 35 (1965). *See Bordenkircher v. Hayes*, 434 U.S. 357, 365 (1978). Specifically, "there can be 'no perfect procedure for deciding in which cases governmental authority should be used to impose death.'" *Zant v. Stephens*, 462 U.S. 862, 884 (1983) (quoting *Lockett v. Ohio*, 438 U.S., at 605 (plurality opinion of BURGER, C.J.)). Despite these imperfections, our consistent rule has been that constitutional guarantees are met when "the mode [for determining guilt or punishment] itself has been surrounded with safeguards to make it as fair as possible." *Singer v. United States, supra*, at 35. Where the discretion that is fundamental to our criminal process is involved, we decline to assume that what is unexplained is invidious. In light of the safeguards designed to minimize racial bias in the process, the fundamental value of jury trial in our criminal justice system, and the benefits that discretion provides to criminal defendants, we hold that the Baldus study does not demonstrate a constitutionally significant risk of racial bias affecting the Georgia capital sentencing process.

Two additional concerns inform our decision in this case. First, McCleskey's claim, taken to its logical conclusion, throws into serious question the principles that underlie our entire criminal justice system. The Eighth Amendment is not limited in application to capital punishment, but applies to all penalties. *Solem v. Helm*, 463 U.S. 277, 289–90 (1983); *see Rummel v. Estelle*, 445 U.S. 263, 293 (1980) (POWELL, J., dissenting). Thus, if we accepted McCleskey's claim that racial bias has impermissibly tainted the capital sentencing decision, we could soon be faced with similar claims as to other types of penalty.[62] Moreover, the claim that his sentence

---

61. Congress has acknowledged the existence of such discrepancies in criminal sentences, and in 1984 created the United States Sentencing Commission to develop sentencing guidelines. The objective of the guidelines "is to avoid unwarranted sentencing disparities among defendants with similar records who have been found guilty of similar criminal conduct, while maintaining sufficient flexibility to permit individualized sentencing when warranted by mitigating or aggravating factors not taken into account in the guidelines." 52 Fed. Reg. 3920 (1987) (emphasis added). No one contends that all sentencing disparities can be eliminated. The guidelines, like the safeguards in the Gregg-type statute, further an essential need of the Anglo-American criminal justice system — to balance the desirability of a high degree of uniformity against the necessity for the exercise of discretion.

62. Studies already exist that allegedly demonstrate a racial disparity in the length of prison sentences. See *Spohn, Gruhl, & Welch*, The Effect of Race on Sentencing: A Reexamination of an Unsettled Question, 16 LAW & SOC. REV. 71 (1981–1982); Unnever, Frazier, & Henretta, Race Differences in Criminal Sentencing, 21 SOCIOLOGICAL Q. 197 (1980).

rests on the irrelevant factor of race easily could be extended to apply to claims based on unexplained discrepancies that correlate to membership in other minority groups,[63] and even to gender.[64] Similarly, since McCleskey's claim relates to the race of his victim, other claims could apply with equally logical force to statistical disparities that correlate with the race or sex of other actors in the criminal justice system, such as defense attorneys[65] or judges. . . . As these examples illustrate, there is no limiting principle to the type of challenge brought by McCleskey. . . .

---

63. In Regents of the University of California v. Bakke, 438 U.S. 265, 295 (1978) (opinion of POWELL, J.), we recognized that the national "majority" "is composed of various minority groups, most of which can lay claim to a history of prior discrimination at the hands of the State and private individuals." See id., at 292 (citing Strauder v. West Virginia, 100 U.S., at 308 (Celtic Irishmen) (dictum); Yick Wo v. Hopkins, 118 U.S. 356 (1886) (Chinese); Truax v. Raich, 239 U.S. 33, 36, 41–42 (1915) (Austrian resident aliens); Korematsu v. United States, 323 U.S. 214, 216 (1944) (Japanese); Hernandez v. Texas, 347 U.S. 475 (1954) (Mexican-Americans)). See also Uniform Guidelines on Employee Selection Procedures (1978), 29 CFF § 1607.4(B) (1986) (employer must keep records as to the "following races and ethnic groups: Blacks, American Indians (including Alaskan Natives), Asians (including Pacific Islanders), Hispanics (including persons of Mexican, Puerto Rican, Cuban, Central or South American, or other Spanish origin or culture regardless of race), and whites (Caucasians) other than Hispanics"); U.S. Bureau of the Census, 1980 Census of the Population, Vol. 1, ch. B (PC80-1-B), reprinted in 1986 Statistical Abstract of the United States 29 (dividing United States population by "race and Spanish origin" into the following groups: White, Black, American Indian, Chinese, Filipinio, Japanese, Korean, Vietnamese, Spanish origin, and all other races); U.S. Bureau of the Census, 1980 Census of the Population, Supplementary Report, series PC80-S1-10, reprinted in 1986 Statistical Abstract of the United States 34 (listing 44 ancestry groups and noting that many individuals reported themselves to belong to multiple ancestry groups).

We also have recognized that the ethnic composition of the Nation is ever shifting. Crawford v. Board of Ed. of Los Angeles, 458 U.S. 527 (1982), illustrates demographic facts that we increasingly find in our country, namely, that populations change in composition, and may do so in relatively short timespans. We noted: "In 1968 when the case went to trial, the [Los Angeles] District was 53.6% white, 22.6% black, 20% Hispanic, and 3.8% Asian and other. By October 1980, the demographic composition had altered radically: 23.7% white, 23.3% black, 45.3% Hispanic, and 7.7% Asian and other." Id., at 530, n. 1. Increasingly whites are becoming a minority in many of the larger American cities. There appears to be no reason why a white defendant in such a city could not make a claim similar to McCleskey's if racial disparities in sentencing arguably are shown by a statistical study. Finally, in our heterogeneous society the lower courts have found the boundaries of race and ethnicity increasingly difficult to determine. See Shaare Tefila Congregation v. Cobb, 785 F.2d 523 (CA4), cert. granted, 479 U.S. 812 (1986), and Al-Khazraji v. Saint Francis College, 784 F.2d 505 (CA3), cert. granted, 479 U.S. 812 (1986) (argued Feb. 25, 1987) (presenting the questions whether Jews and Arabs, respectively, are "races" covered by 42 U.S.C. §§ 1981 and 1982).

64. See Chamblin, The Effect of Sex on the Imposition of the Death Penalty (speech given at a symposium of the American Psychological Association, entitled "Extra-legal Attributes Affecting Death Penalty Sentencing," New York City, Sept., 1979); Steffensmeier, Effects of Judge's and Defendant's Sex on the Sentencing of Offenders, 14 PSYCHOLOGY, JOURNAL OF HUMAN BEHAVIOR, 3 (Aug. 1977).

65. See Johnson, Black Innocence and the White Jury, 83 MICH. L. REV. 1611, 1625–40, and n. 115 (1985) (citing Cohen & Peterson, Bias in the Courtroom: Race and Sex Effects of Attorneys on Juror Verdicts, 9 SOCIAL BEHAVIOR & PERSONALITY 81 (1981)); Hodgson & Pryor, Sex Discrimination in the Courtroom: Attorney's Gender and Credibility, 55 PSYCHOLOGICAL REP. 483 (1984).

3. Holding

Accordingly, we affirm the judgment of the Court of Appeals for the Eleventh Circuit.

4. Justice Brennan Dissenting

. . . Evaluation of McCleskey's evidence cannot rest solely on the numbers themselves. We must also ask whether the conclusion suggested by those numbers is consonant with our understanding of history and human experience. Georgia's legacy of a race-conscious criminal justice system, as well as this Court's own recognition of the persistent danger that racial attitudes may affect criminal proceedings, indicates that McCleskey's claim is not a fanciful product of mere statistical artifice.

For many years, Georgia operated openly and formally precisely the type of dual system the evidence shows is still effectively in place. The criminal law expressly differentiated between crimes committed by and against blacks and whites, distinctions whose lineage traced back to the time of slavery. During the colonial period, black slaves who killed whites in Georgia, regardless of whether in self-defense or in defense of another, were automatically executed. A. Higginbotham, *In the Matter of Color: Race in the American Legal Process* 256 (1978).[66] By the time of the Civil War, a dual system of crime and punishment was well established in Georgia. See Ga. Penal Code (1861). The state criminal code contained separate sections for "Slaves and Free Persons of Color," Pt. 4, Tit. 3, Ch. 1, and for all other persons, Pt. 4, Tit. 1, Divs. 1–16. The code provided, for instance, for an automatic death sentence for murder committed by blacks, Pt. 4, Tit. 1, Art. II, § 4704, but declared that anyone else convicted of murder might receive life imprisonment if the conviction were founded solely on circumstantial testimony or simply if the jury so recommended. Pt. 4, Tit. 1, Div. 4, § 4220. The code established that the rape of a free white female by a black "shall be" punishable by death. § 4704. However, rape by anyone else of a free white female was punishable by a prison term not less than 2 nor more than 20 years. The rape of blacks was punishable "by fine and imprisonment, at the discretion of the court." § 4249. A black convicted of assaulting a free white person with intent to murder could be put to death at the discretion of the court, § 4708, but the same offense committed against a black, slave or free, was classified as a "minor" offense whose punishment lay in the discretion of the court, as long as such punishment did not "extend to life, limb, or health." Art. III, §§ 4714, 4718. Assault with intent to murder by a white person was punishable by a prison term of from

---

66. Death could also be inflicted upon a slave who "grievously wound[ed], maim[ed], or bruis[ed] any white person," who was convicted for the third time of striking a white person, or who attempted to run away out of the province. A. HIGGINBOTHAM, IN THE MATTER OF COLOR: RACE AND THE AMERICAN LEGAL PROCESS 256 (1978). On the other hand, a person who willfully murdered a slave was not punished until the second offense, and then was responsible simply for restitution to the slave owner. Furthermore, conviction for willful murder of a slave was subject to the difficult requirement of the oath of two white witnesses. *Id.*, at 253–54, and n. 190.

2 to 10 years. Div. 4, §4258. While sufficient provocation could reduce a charge of murder to manslaughter, the code provided that "[o]bedience and submission being the duty of a slave, much greater provocation is necessary to reduce a homicide of a white person by him to voluntary manslaughter, than is prescribed for white persons." Art. II, §4711.

In more recent times, some 40 years ago, Gunnar Myrdal's epochal study of American race relations produced findings mirroring McCleskey's evidence:

"As long as only Negroes are concerned and no whites are disturbed, great leniency will be shown in most cases. . . . The sentences for even major crimes are ordinarily reduced when the victim is another Negro.

"For offenses which involve any actual or potential danger to whites, however, Negroes are punished more severely than whites.

"On the other hand, it is quite common for a white criminal to be set free if his crime was against a Negro." G. Myrdal, An American Dilemma 551–53 (1944).

This Court has invalidated portions of the Georgia capital sentencing system three times over the past 15 years. The specter of race discrimination was acknowledged by the Court in striking down the Georgia death penalty statute in Furman. Justice DOUGLAS cited studies suggesting imposition of the death penalty in racially discriminatory fashion, and found the standardless statutes before the Court "pregnant with discrimination." 408 U.S., at 257 (concurring opinion). Justice MARSHALL pointed to statistics indicating that "Negroes [have been] executed far more often than whites in proportion to their percentage of the population. Studies indicate that while the higher rate of execution among Negroes is partially due to a higher rate of crime, there is evidence of racial discrimination." Id., at 364 (concurring opinion). Although Justice STEWART declined to conclude that racial discrimination had been plainly proved, he stated that "[m]y concurring Brothers have demonstrated that, if any basis can be discerned for the selection of these few to be sentenced to die, it is the constitutionally impermissible basis of race." Id., at 310 (concurring opinion). In dissent, Chief Justice BURGER acknowledged that statistics "suggest, at least as a historical matter, that Negroes have been sentenced to death with greater frequency than whites in several States, particularly for the crime of interracial rape." Id., at 289, n. 12. Finally, also in dissent, Justice POWELL intimated that an Equal Protection Clause argument would be available for a black "who could demonstrate that members of his race were being singled out for more severe punishment than others charged with the same offense." Id., at 449. He noted that although the Eighth Circuit had rejected a claim of discrimination in Maxwell v. Bishop, 398 F.2d 138 (1968), vacated and remanded on other grounds, 398 U.S. 262 (1970), the statistical evidence in that case "tend[ed] to show a pronounced disproportion in the number of Negroes receiving death sentences for rape in parts of Arkansas and elsewhere in the South." 408 U.S., at 449. It is clear that the Court regarded the opportunity for the operation of racial prejudice a particularly troublesome aspect of the unbounded discretion afforded by the Georgia sentencing scheme.

Five years later, the Court struck down the imposition of the death penalty in Georgia for the crime of rape. *Coker v. Georgia*, 433 U.S. 584 (1977). Although the Court did not explicitly mention race, the decision had to have been informed by the specific observations on rape by both the Chief Justice and Justice POWELL in Furman. Furthermore, evidence submitted to the Court indicated that black men who committed rape, particularly of white women, were considerably more likely to be sentenced to death than white rapists. For instance, by 1977 Georgia had executed 62 men for rape since the Federal Government began compiling statistics in 1930. Of these men, 58 were black and 4 were white. *See* Brief for Petitioner in *Coker v. Georgia*, O. T. 1976, No. 75-5444, p. 56; *see also Wolfgang & Riedel, Rape, Race, and the Death Penalty in Georgia*, 45 Am. J. Orthopsychiatry 658 (1975).

Three years later, the Court in *Godfrey* found one of the State's statutory aggravating factors unconstitutionally vague, since it resulted in "standardless and unchanneled imposition of death sentences in the uncontrolled discretion of a basically uninstructed jury. . . ." 446 U.S., at 49. Justice MARSHALL, concurring in the judgment, noted that "[t]he disgraceful distorting effects of racial discrimination and poverty continue to be painfully visible in the imposition of death sentences." *Id.*, at 439.

This historical review of Georgia criminal law is not intended as a bill of indictment calling the State to account for past transgressions. Citation of past practices does not justify the automatic condemnation of current ones. But it would be unrealistic to ignore the influence of history in assessing the plausible implications of McCleskey's evidence. "[A]mericans share a historical experience that has resulted in individuals within the culture ubiquitously attaching a significance to race that is irrational and often outside their awareness." *Lawrence, The Id, The Ego, and Equal Protection: Reckoning With Unconscious Racism*, 39 Stan. L. Rev. 327 (1987). *See generally id.*, at 328–44 (describing the psychological dynamics of unconscious racial motivation). As we said in *Rose v. Mitchell*, 443 U.S. 545, 558–59 (1979):

> "[W]e . . . cannot deny that, 114 years after the close of the War Between the States and nearly 100 years after *Strauder*, racial and other forms of discrimination still remain a fact of life, in the administration of justice as in our society as a whole. Perhaps today that discrimination takes a form more subtle than before. But it is not less real or pernicious."

The ongoing influence of history is acknowledged, as the majority observes, by our "'unceasing efforts' to eradicate racial prejudice from our criminal justice system." Ante, at 309 (quoting *Batson v. Kentucky*, 476 U.S. 79, 85 91986)). These efforts, however, signify not the elimination of the problem but its persistence. Our cases reflect a realization of the myriad of opportunities for racial considerations to influence criminal proceedings: in the exercise of peremptory challenges, *Batson v. Kentucky, supra*; in the selection of the grand jury, *Vasquez v. Hillery*, 474 U.S. 254

(1986); in the selection of the petit jury, *Whitus v. Georgia*, 385 U.S. 545 (1967); in the exercise of prosecutorial discretion, *Wayte v. United States*, 470 U.S. 598 (1985); in the conduct of argument, *Donnelly v. DeChristoforo*, 416 U.S. 637 (1974); and in the conscious or unconscious bias of jurors, *Turner v. Murray*, 476 U.S. 28 (1986), *Ristaino v. Ross*, 424 U.S. 589 (1976).

The discretion afforded prosecutors and jurors in the Georgia capital sentencing system creates such opportunities. No guidelines govern prosecutorial decisions to seek the death penalty, and Georgia provides juries with no list of aggravating and mitigating factors, nor any standard for balancing them against one another. Once a jury identifies one aggravating factor, it has complete discretion in choosing life or death, and need not articulate its basis for selecting life imprisonment. The Georgia sentencing system therefore provides considerable opportunity for racial considerations, however subtle and unconscious, to influence charging and sentencing decisions.

History and its continuing legacy thus buttress the probative force of McCleskey's statistics. Formal dual criminal laws may no longer be in effect, and intentional discrimination may no longer be prominent. Nonetheless, as we acknowledged in Turner, "subtle, less consciously held racial attitudes" continue to be of concern, 476 U.S., at 35, and the Georgia system gives such attitudes considerable room to operate. The conclusions drawn from McCleskey's statistical evidence are therefore consistent with the lessons of social experience. . . . The Court cites four reasons for shrinking from the implications of McCleskey's evidence: the desirability of discretion for actors in the criminal justice system, the existence of statutory safeguards against abuse of that discretion, the potential consequences for broader challenges to criminal sentencing, and an understanding of the contours of the judicial role. While these concerns underscore the need for sober deliberation, they do not justify rejecting evidence as convincing as McCleskey has presented.

The Court maintains that petitioner's claim "is antithetical to the fundamental role of discretion in our criminal justice system." Ante, at 311. It states that "[w]here the discretion that is fundamental to our criminal process is involved, we decline to assume that what is unexplained is invidious." Ante, at 313.

Reliance on race in imposing capital punishment, however, is antithetical to the very rationale for granting sentencing discretion. Discretion is a means, not an end. It is bestowed in order to permit the sentence to "trea[t] each defendant in a capital case with that degree of respect due the uniqueness of the individual." *Lockett v. Ohio*, 438 U.S. 586, 605 (1978). The decision to impose the punishment of death must be based on a "particularized consideration of relevant aspects of the character and record of each convicted defendant." *Woodson v. North Carolina*, 428 U.S., at 303. Failure to conduct such an individualized moral inquiry "treats all persons convicted of a designated offense not as unique individual human beings, but as members of a faceless, undifferentiated mass to be subjected to the blind infliction of the penalty of death." *Id.*, at 304.

Considering the race of a defendant or victim in deciding if the death penalty should be imposed is completely at odds with this concern that an individual be evaluated as a unique human being. Decisions influenced by race rest in part on a categorical assessment of the worth of human beings according to color, insensitive to whatever qualities the individuals in question may possess. Enhanced willingness to impose the death sentence on black defendants, or diminished willingness to render such a sentence when blacks are victims, reflects a devaluation of the lives of black persons. When confronted with evidence that race more likely than not plays such a role in a capital sentencing system, it is plainly insufficient to say that the importance of discretion demands that the risk be higher before we will act — for in such a case the very end that discretion is designed to serve is being undermined.

Our desire for individualized moral judgments may lead us to accept some inconsistencies in sentencing outcomes. Since such decisions are not reducible to mathematical formulas, we are willing to assume that a certain degree of variation reflects the fact that no two defendants are completely alike. There is thus a presumption that actors in the criminal justice system exercise their discretion in responsible fashion, and we do not automatically infer that sentencing patterns that do not comport with ideal rationality are suspect.

As we made clear in *Batson v. Kentucky*, 476 U.S. 79 (1986), however, that presumption is rebuttable. Batson dealt with another arena in which considerable discretion traditionally has been afforded, the exercise of peremptory challenges. Those challenges are normally exercised without any indication whatsoever of the grounds for doing so. The rationale for this deference has been a belief that the unique characteristics of particular prospective jurors may raise concern on the part of the prosecution or defense, despite the fact that counsel may not be able to articulate that concern in a manner sufficient to support exclusion for cause. As with sentencing, therefore, peremptory challenges are justified as an occasion for particularized determinations related to specific individuals, and, as with sentencing, we presume that such challenges normally are not made on the basis of a factor such as race. As we said in *Batson*, however, such features do not justify imposing a "crippling burden of proof," *id.*, at 92, in order to rebut that presumption. The Court in this case apparently seeks to do just that. On the basis of the need for individualized decisions, it rejects evidence, drawn from the most sophisticated capital sentencing analysis ever performed, that reveals that race more likely than not infects capital sentencing decisions. The Court's position converts a rebuttable presumption into a virtually conclusive one.

The Court also declines to find McCleskey's evidence sufficient in view of "the safeguards designed to minimize racial bias in the [capital sentencing] process." Ante, at 313. *Gregg v. Georgia*, 428 U.S., at 226, upheld the Georgia capital sentencing statute against a facial challenge which Justice WHITE described in his concurring opinion as based on "simply an assertion of lack of faith" that the system could operate in a fair manner (opinion concurring in judgment). Justice WHITE observed that the claim that prosecutors might act in an arbitrary fashion was "unsupported by any facts," and that prosecutors must be assumed to exercise their charging duties properly "[a]bsent facts to the contrary." *Id.*, at 225. It is clear that Gregg bestowed no permanent approval on the Georgia system. It simply held that the State's statutory safeguards were assumed sufficient to channel discretion without evidence otherwise.

It has now been over 13 years since Georgia adopted the provisions upheld in *Gregg.* Professor Baldus and his colleagues have compiled data on almost 2,500 homicides committed during the period 1973–1979. They have taken into account the influence of 230 nonracial variables, using a multitude of data from the State itself, and have produced striking evidence that the odds of being sentenced to death are significantly greater than average if a defendant is black or his or her victim is white. The challenge to the Georgia system is not speculative or theoretical; it is empirical. As a result, the Court cannot rely on the statutory safeguards in discounting McCleskey's evidence, for it is the very effectiveness of those safeguards that such evidence calls into question. While we may hope that a model of procedural fairness will curb the influence of race on sentencing, "we cannot simply assume that the model works as intended; we must critique its performance in terms of its results." *Hubbard, "Reasonable Levels of Arbitrariness" in Death Sentencing Patterns: A Tragic Perspective on Capital Punishment,* 18 U.C. D. L. REV. 1113, 1162 (1985).

The Court next states that its unwillingness to regard petitioner's evidence as sufficient is based in part on the fear that recognition of McCleskey's claim would open the door to widespread challenges to all aspects of criminal sentencing. *Ante,* at 314–15. Taken on its face, such a statement seems to suggest a fear of too much justice. Yet surely the majority would acknowledge that if striking evidence indicated that other minority groups, or women, or even persons with blond hair, were disproportionately sentenced to death, such a state of affairs would be repugnant to deeply rooted conceptions of fairness. The prospect that there may be more widespread abuse than McCleskey documents may be dismaying, but it does not justify complete abdication of our judicial role. The Constitution was framed fundamentally as a bulwark against governmental power, and preventing the arbitrary administration of punishment is a basic ideal of any society that purports to be governed by the rule of law. . . .

Furthermore, the Court's fear of the expansive ramifications of a holding for McCleskey in this case is unfounded because it fails to recognize the uniquely sophisticated nature of the Baldus study. McCleskey presents evidence that is far and away the most refined data ever assembled on any system of punishment, data not readily replicated through casual effort. Moreover, that evidence depicts not merely arguable tendencies, but striking correlations, all the more powerful because nonracial explanations have been eliminated. Acceptance of petitioner's evidence would therefore establish a remarkably stringent standard of statistical evidence unlikely to be satisfied with any frequency.

The Court's projection of apocalyptic consequences for criminal sentencing is thus greatly exaggerated. The Court can indulge in such speculation only by ignoring its own jurisprudence demanding the highest scrutiny on issues of death and race. As a result, it fails to do justice to a claim in which both those elements are intertwined—an occasion calling for the most sensitive inquiry a court can conduct. Despite its acceptance of the validity of Warren McCleskey's evidence, the Court is willing to let his death sentence stand because it fears that we cannot successfully define a different standard for lesser punishments. This fear is baseless. . . . At the time our Constitution was framed 200 years ago this year, blacks "had for more than a century before been regarded as beings of an inferior order, and altogether unfit to associate with the white race, either in social or political relations; and so far inferior, that they had no rights which the white man was bound to respect." *Dred Scott v. Sandford*, 19 How. 393, 407 (1857). Only 130 years ago, this Court relied on these observations to deny American citizenship to blacks. *Ibid.* A mere three generations ago, this Court sanctioned racial segregation, stating that "[i]f one race be inferior to the other socially, the Constitution of the United States cannot put them upon the same plane." *Plessy v. Ferguson*, 163 U.S. 537, 552 (1896).

In more recent times, we have sought to free ourselves from the burden of this history. Yet it has been scarcely a generation since this Court's first decision striking down racial segregation, and barely two decades since the legislative prohibition of racial discrimination in major domains of national life. These have been honorable steps, but we cannot pretend that in three decades we have completely escaped the grip of a historical legacy spanning centuries. Warren McCleskey's evidence confronts us with the subtle and persistent influence of the past. His message is a disturbing one to a society that has formally repudiated racism, and a frustrating one to a Nation accustomed to regarding its destiny as the product of its own will. Nonetheless, we ignore him at our peril, for we remain imprisoned by the past as long as we deny its influence in the present.

It is tempting to pretend that minorities on death row share a fate in no way connected to our own, that our treatment of them sounds no echoes beyond the chambers in which they die. Such an illusion is ultimately corrosive, for the reverberations of injustice are not so easily confined. "The destinies of the two races in this country are indissolubly linked together," *id.*, at 560 (HARLAN, J., dissenting), and the way in which we choose those who will die reveals the depth of moral commitment among the living.

The Court's decision today will not change what attorneys in Georgia tell other Warren McCleskeys about their chances of execution. Nothing will soften the harsh message they must convey, nor alter the prospect that race undoubtedly will continue to be a topic of discussion. McCleskey's evidence will not have obtained judicial acceptance, but that will not affect what is said on death row. However many criticisms of today's decision may be rendered, these painful conversations will serve as the most eloquent dissents of all.

Justice MARSHALL, Justice BLACKMUN, and Justice STEVENS concur in the dissent.

J. Commentary on *McCleskey*

The court in *McCleskey* found that the defendant's statistical evidence did not establish an equal protection clause violation. The Justices reasoned that statistical evidence of a racial disparity alone was insufficient to demonstrate racial bias. While the Justices recognized the possibility of the presence of racial bias, they refused to assume that what was not clearly admitted could be the intentional manifestation of racially discriminatory treatment. While theoretically this standard may sound reasonable to some, the reality for most defendants was an insurmountable burden for proving an Equal Protection Clause violation. To prevail, they would need to show more than statistical disparity alone.

The *McCleskey* case and the significant findings of the Baldus study support the notion that in the value system of the average jury in Georgia, the life of a white person is more valuable than the life of a black person. While the criminal laws of Georgia no longer expressly state that the life of a black person is less valued, the Supreme Court's ruling implicitly endorses the continuation of this belief.

Charles R. Lawrence III

*The Id, The Ego, and Equal Protection: Reckoning with Unconscious Racism**

[T]his article proposes a new test to trigger judicial recognition of race-based behavior. It posits a connection between unconscious racism and the existence of cultural symbols that have racial meaning. It suggests that the 'cultural meaning' of an allegedly racially discriminatory act is the best available analogue for, and evidence of, a collective unconscious that we cannot observe directly. This test would thus evaluate governmental conduct to determine whether it conveys a symbolic message to which the culture attaches racial significance. A finding that the culture thinks of an allegedly discriminatory governmental action in racial terms would also constitute a finding regarding the beliefs and motivations of the governmental actors: The actors are themselves part of the culture and presumably could not have acted without being influenced by racial considerations, even if they are unaware of their racist beliefs. Therefore, the court would apply strict scrutiny.

This proposal is relatively modest. It does not abandon the judicial search for unconstitutional motives, nor does it argue that all governmental action with

---

* (footnotes omitted).

discriminatory impact should be strictly scrutinized. Instead, it urges a more complete understanding of the nature of human motivation. While it is grounded in the Court's present focus on individual responsibility, it seeks to understand individual responsibility in light of modern insights into human personality and collective behavior. In addition, this proposal responds directly to the concern that abandoning the *Washington v. Davis* [426 U.S 229 (1976)] doctrine will invalidate a broad range of legitimate, race-neutral governmental actions. By identifying those cases where race unconsciously influences governmental action, this new test leaves untouched nonrace-dependent decisions that disproportionately burden blacks only because they are overrepresented the decision's targets or the decision targets or beneficiaries.

This effort to inform the discriminatory intent requirement with the learning of twentieth century psychology is important for at least three reasons. First, the present doctrine, by requiring proof that the defendant was aware of his animus against blacks, severely limits the number of individual cases in which the courts will acknowledge and remedy racial discrimination.

Second, the existing intent requirement's assignment of individualized fault or responsibility for the existence of racial discrimination distorts our perceptions about the causes of discrimination and leads us to think about racism in a way that advances the disease rather than combating it. By insisting that a blameworthy perpetrator be found before the existence of racial discrimination can be acknowledged, the Court creates an imaginary world where discrimination does not exist unless it was consciously intended. And by acting as if this imaginary world was real and insisting that we participate in this fantasy, the Court and the law it promulgates subtly shape our perceptions of society. The decision to deny relief no longer finds its basis only in raw political power or economic self-interest; it is now justifiable on moral grounds. If there is no discrimination, there is no need for a remedy; if blacks are being treated fairly yet remain at the bottom of the socioeconomic ladder, only their own inferiority can explain their subordinate position.

Finally, the intent doctrine's focus on the narrowest and most unrealistic understanding of individual fault has also engendered much of the resistance to and resentment of affirmative action programs and other race-conscious remedies for past and continuing discrimination. If there can be no discrimination without an identifiable criminal, then "innocent" individuals will resent the burden of remedying an injury for which the law says they are not responsible. Understanding the cultural source of our racism obviates the need for fault, as traditionally conceived, without denying our collective responsibility for racism's eradication. We cannot be individually blamed for unconsciously harboring attitudes that are inescapable in a culture permeated with racism. And without the necessity for blame, our resistance to accepting the need and responsibility for remedy will be lessened . . .

If the purpose of the law's search for racial animus or discriminatory intent is to identify a morally culpable perpetrator, the existing intent requirement fails to achieve that purpose. There will be no evidence of self-conscious racism where the actors have internalized the relatively new American cultural morality which holds racism wrong or have learned racist attitudes and beliefs through tacit rather than explicit lessons. The actor himself will be unaware that his actions, or the racially neutral feelings and ideas that accompany them, have racist origins.

Of course, one can argue that the law should govern only consciously motivated actions—that societal sanctions can do no more than attempt to require that the individual's Ego act as society's agent in censoring out those unconscious drives that society has defined as immoral. Under this view, the law can sanction a defective Ego that has not fully internalized current societal morality and has, therefore, allowed illegal racist wishes to reach consciousness and fruition in an illegal act. But the law should not hold an individual responsible for wishes that never reach consciousness, even if they also come to fruition in discriminatory acts.

The problem is that this argument does not tell us why the law should hold the individual responsible for racial injury that results from one form of Ego disguise but not the other. I believe the law should be equally concerned when the mind's censor successfully disguises a socially repugnant wish like racism if that motive produces behavior that has a discriminatory result as injurious as if it flowed from a consciously held motive.

39 *Stan. L. Rev.* 317, 322–27, 344.
Copyright © (1987) *Stanford Law Review.*
Reprinted with permission of the *Stanford Law Review* and
Charles R. Lawrence III.

K. Background on *Shaw*

José Felipe Anderson

History Says That Blacks Should Vote

Blacks voted in the South for a time during Reconstruction. But the right to vote virtually disappeared when federal control of the Southern states diminished during the years of political compromise in the late 1800s. Even as late as 1867, states like Maryland, through its constitution, tried to confer the right to vote only to "white male citizens" who met certain property and residency requirements.

Even after the right to vote was legally mandated, its exercise was frustrated by a series of sinister devices intended to stamp out the political power of black citizens, even in southern counties where they represented a majority of the population.

Among them was the literacy test, which in the hands of Southern court clerks was systematically used to discriminate against even the most well-educated blacks while permitting illiterate whites to vote.

Often those tests would require blacks to interpret obscure provisions of the Constitution while white voters who could not sign their name were found qualified without question.

The "grandfather clause" was used by many states to exempt all persons from taking the literacy test whose grandfathers had voted. Obviously, few Southern blacks had grandfathers in the early 1900s who could vote since most were slaves or free blacks. . . .

The Baltimore Sun, Oct. 25, 2000, p. 25A.
Copyright © (2000) The Tribune Company.
Reprinted with permission of the Tribune Company.

From 1901 to 1992, the one constant in North Carolina congressional politics, and all other southern states, was the triumph of absolute control and domination by white only politicians. For North Carolina's African Americans, these were nine decades of exclusion from the United States Congress. Since the time of the Reconstruction, various mechanisms designed to prevent black voter participation, such as grandfather clauses, literacy tests, and dual primaries, had prevented any African American from representing North Carolina in Congress. This exclusion continued for nearly a century, despite the candidacy of numerous qualified black individuals and the fact that more than twenty percent of North Carolinians were black. For decades, the forcible exclusion of African Americans from the political process, race baiting, and extreme racial polarization at the polls marred North Carolina politics.

L. *Shaw v. Reno*, 509 U.S. 630 (1993)

1. *Facts*

Justice O'CONNOR delivered the opinion of the Court.

This case involves two of the most complex and sensitive issues this Court has faced in recent years: the meaning of the constitutional "right" to vote, and the propriety of race-based state legislation designed to benefit members of historically disadvantaged racial minority groups. As a result of the 1990 census, North Carolina became entitled to a 12th seat in the United States House of Representatives. The General Assembly enacted a reapportionment plan that included one majority-black congressional district. After the Attorney General of the United States objected to the plan pursuant to § 5 of the Voting Rights Act of 1965, 79 Stat. 439, as amended, 42 U.S.C. § 1973c, the General Assembly passed new legislation creating a second majority-black district. Appellants allege that the revised plan, which contains district boundary lines of dramatically irregular shape, constitutes an unconstitutional racial gerrymander. The question before us is whether appellants have stated a cognizable claim.

The voting age population of North Carolina is approximately 78% white, 20% black, and 1% Native-American; the remaining 1% is predominantly Asian. App. to Brief for Federal Appellees 16a. The black population is relatively dispersed; blacks constitute a majority of the general population in only 5 of the State's 100 counties. Brief for Appellants 57. Geographically, the State divides into three regions: the eastern Coastal Plain, the central Piedmont Plateau, and the western mountains.

H. Lefler & A. Newsom, The History of a Southern State: North Carolina 18–22 (3d ed. 1973). The largest concentrations of black citizens live in the Coastal Plain, primarily in the northern part. *O. Gade & H. Stillwell, North Carolina: People and Environments* 65–68 (1986). The General Assembly's first redistricting plan contained one majority-black district centered in that area of the State.

Forty of North Carolina's one hundred counties are covered by §5 of the Voting Rights Act of 1965, 42 U.S.C. §1973c, which prohibits a jurisdiction subject to its provisions from implementing changes in a "standard, practice, or procedure with respect to voting" without federal authorization, *ibid.* The jurisdiction must obtain either a judgment from the United States District Court for the District of Columbia declaring that the proposed change "does not have the purpose and will not have the effect of denying or abridging the right to vote on account of race or color" or administrative preclearance from the Attorney General. *Ibid.* Because the General Assembly's reapportionment plan affected the covered counties, the parties agree that §5 applied. Tr. of Oral Arg. 14, 27–29. The State chose to submit its plan to the Attorney General for preclearance.

The Attorney General, acting through the Assistant Attorney General for the Civil Rights Division, interposed a formal objection to the General Assembly's plan. The Attorney General specifically objected to the configuration of boundary lines drawn in the south-central to southeastern region of the State. In the Attorney General's view, the General Assembly could have created a second majority-minority district "to give effect to black and Native-American voting strength in this area" by using boundary lines "no more irregular than [those] found elsewhere in the proposed plan," but failed to do so for "pretextual reasons." *See* App. to Brief for Federal Appellees 10a–11a.

Under §5, the State remained free to seek a declaratory judgment from the District Court for the District of Columbia notwithstanding the Attorney General's objection. It did not do so. Instead, the General Assembly enacted a revised redistricting plan, 1991 N.C. Extra Sess. Laws, ch. 7, that included a second majority-black district. The General Assembly located the second district not in the south-central to southeastern part of the State, but in the north-central region along Interstate 85. *See* Appendix, *infra.*

The first of the two majority-black districts contained in the revised plan, District 1, is somewhat hook shaped. Centered in the northeast portion of the State, it moves southward until it tapers to a narrow band; then, with finger-like extensions, it reaches far into the southern-most part of the State near the South Carolina border. District 1 has been compared to a "Rorschach ink-blot test," *Shaw v. Barr,* 808 F. Supp. 461, 476 (EDNC 1992) (Voorhees, C.J., concurring in part and dissenting in part), and a "bug splattered on a windshield," Wall Street Journal, Feb. 4, 1992, p. A14.

The second majority-black district, District 12, is even more unusually shaped. It is approximately 160 miles long and, for much of its length, no wider than the I-85 corridor. It winds in snakelike fashion through tobacco country, financial centers, and manufacturing areas "until it gobbles in enough enclaves of black neighborhoods." 808 F. Supp., at 476–77 (VOORHEES, C.J., concurring in part and dissenting in part). Northbound and southbound drivers on I-85 sometimes find themselves in separate districts in one county, only to "trade" districts when they enter the next county. Of the 10 counties through which District 12 passes, 5 are cut into 3 different districts; even towns are divided. At one point the district remains contiguous only because it intersects at a single point with two other districts before crossing over them. See Brief for Republican National Committee as *Amicus Curiae* 14–15. One state legislator has remarked that "'[i]f you drove down the interstate with both car doors open, you'd kill most of the people in the district.'" Washington Post, Apr. 20, 1993, p. A4. The district even has inspired poetry: "Ask not for whom the line is drawn; it is drawn to avoid thee." *Grofman, Would Vince Lombardi Have Been Right If He Had Said: "When It Comes to Redistricting, Race Isn't Everything, It's the Only Thing"?*, 14 Cardozo. 1237, 1261, n. 96 (1993) (internal quotation marks omitted). . . .

2. Opinion

. . . An understanding of the nature of appellants' claim is critical to our resolution of the case. In their complaint, appellants did not claim that the General Assembly's reapportionment plan unconstitutionally "diluted" white voting strength. They did not even claim to be white. Rather, appellants' complaint alleged that the deliberate segregation of voters into separate districts on the basis of race violated their constitutional right to participate in a "color-blind" electoral process. Complaint ¶ 29, App. to Juris. Statement 89a–90a; *see also* Brief for Appellants 31–32.

Despite their invocation of the ideal of a "color-blind" Constitution, *see Plessy v. Ferguson*, 163 U.S. 537, 559, 16 S.Ct. 1138, 1146, 41 L.Ed. 256 (1896) (HARLAN, J., dissenting), appellants appear to concede that race-conscious redistricting is not always unconstitutional. *See* Tr. of Oral Arg. 16–19. That concession is wise: This Court never has held that race-conscious state decisionmaking is impermissible in all circumstances. What appellants object to is redistricting legislation that is so extremely irregular on its face that it rationally can be viewed only as an effort to segregate the races for purposes of voting, without regard for traditional districting principles and without sufficiently compelling justification. For the reasons that follow, we conclude that appellants have stated a claim upon which relief can be granted under the Equal Protection Clause. *See* Fed. Rule Civ. Proc. 12(b)(6).

The Equal Protection Clause provides that "[n]o State shall . . . deny to any person within its jurisdiction the equal protection of the laws." U.S. Const., Amdt. 14, § 1. Its central purpose is to prevent the States from purposefully discriminating between individuals on the basis of race. *Washington v. Davis*, 426 U.S. 229, 239, 96 S.Ct. 2040, 2047, 48 L.Ed.2d 597 (1976). Laws that explicitly distinguish between individuals on racial grounds fall within the core of that prohibition.

No inquiry into legislative purpose is necessary when the racial classification appears on the face of the statute. *See Personnel Administrator of Mass. v. Feeney*,

442 U.S. 256, 272, 99 S.Ct. 2282, 2293, 60 L.Ed.2d 870 (1979). *Accord, Washington v. Seattle School Dist. No. 1*, 458 U.S. 457, 485, 102 S.Ct. 3187, 3203, 73 L.Ed.2d 896 (1982). Express racial classifications are immediately suspect because, "[a]bsent searching judicial inquiry . . . , there is simply no way of determining what classifications are 'benign' or 'remedial' and what classifications are in fact motivated by illegitimate notions of racial inferiority or simple racial politics." *Richmond v. J.A. Croson Co.*, 488 U.S. 469, 493, 109 S.Ct. 706, 721, 102 L.Ed.2d 854 (1989) (plurality opinion); *id.*, at 520, 109 S.Ct., at 736 (Scalia, J., concurring in judgment); *see also* UJO, 430 U.S., at 172, 97 S.Ct., at 1013 (Brennan, J., concurring in part) ("[A] purportedly preferential race assignment may in fact disguise a policy that perpetuates disadvantageous treatment of the plan's supposed beneficiaries").

Classifications of citizens solely on the basis of race "are by their very nature odious to a free people whose institutions are founded upon the doctrine of equality." *Hirabayashi v. United States*, 320 U.S. 81, 100, 63 S.Ct. 1375, 1385, 87 L.Ed. 1774 (1943). Accord, *Loving v. Virginia*, 388 U.S. 1, 11, 87 S.Ct. 1817, 1823, 18 L. Ed.2d 1010 (1967). They threaten to stigmatize individuals by reason of their membership in a racial group and to incite racial hostility. *Croson, supra, 488 U.S., at 493, 109 S.Ct., at 721 (plurality opinion);* UJO, supra, 430 U.S., at 173, 97 S.Ct., at 1014 (Brennan, J., concurring in part) ("[E]ven in the pursuit of remedial objectives, an explicit policy of assignment by race may serve to stimulate our society's latent race consciousness, suggesting the utility and propriety of basing decisions on a factor that ideally bears no relationship to an individual's worth or needs"). Accordingly, we have held that the Fourteenth Amendment requires state legislation that expressly distinguishes among citizens because of their race to be narrowly tailored to further a compelling governmental interest. *See Wygant v. Jackson Bd. of Ed.*, 476 U.S. 267, 277–78, 106 S.Ct. 1842, 1848–49, 90 L.Ed.2d 260 (1986) (plurality opinion); id., at 285, 106 S.Ct., at 1853 (O'Connor, J., concurring in part and concurring in judgment).

These principles apply not only to legislation that contains explicit racial distinctions, but also to those "rare" statutes that, although race neutral, are, on their face, "unexplainable on grounds other than race." *Arlington Heights v. Metropolitan Housing Development Corp.*, 429 U.S. 252, 266, 97 S.Ct. 555, 564, 50 L.Ed.2d 450 (1977). As we explained in *Feeney*:

> "A racial classification, regardless of purported motivation, is presumptively invalid and can be upheld only upon an extraordinary justification. *Brown v. Board of Education*, 347 U.S. 483 [74 S.Ct. 686, 98 L.Ed. 873]; *McLaughlin v. Florida*, 379 U.S. 184 [85 S.Ct. 283, 13 L.Ed.2d 222]. This rule applies as well to a classification that is ostensibly neutral but is an obvious pretext for racial discrimination. *Yick Wo v. Hopkins*, 118 U.S. 356 [6 S.Ct. 1064, 30 L. Ed. 220]; *Guinn v. United States*, 238 U.S. 347 [35 S.Ct. 926, 59 L.Ed. 1340]; cf. *Lane v. Wilson*, 307 U.S. 268 [59 S.Ct. 872, 83 L.Ed. 1281]; *Gomillion v. Lightfoot*, 364 U.S. 339 [81 S.Ct. 125, 5 L.Ed.2d 110]." 442 U.S., at 272, 99 S. Ct., at 2292.

Appellants contend that redistricting legislation that is so bizarre on its face that it is "unexplainable on grounds other than race," *Arlington Heights, supra*, 429 U.S., at 266, 97 S.Ct., at 564, demands the same close scrutiny that we give other state laws that classify citizens by race. Our voting rights precedents support that conclusion. . . .

Put differently, we believe that reapportionment is one area in which appearances do matter. A reapportionment plan that includes in one district individuals who belong to the same race, but who are otherwise widely separated by geographical and political boundaries, and who may have little in common with one another but the color of their skin, bears an uncomfortable resemblance to political apartheid. It reinforces the perception that members of the same racial group—regardless of their age, education, economic status, or the community in which they live—think alike, share the same political interests, and will prefer the same candidates at the polls. We have rejected such perceptions elsewhere as impermissible racial stereotypes. *See Holland v. Illinois*, 493 U.S. 474, 484, n. 2, 110 S.Ct. 803, 809, n. 2, 107 L. Ed.2d 905 (1990) ("[A] prosecutor's assumption that a black juror may be presumed to be partial simply because he is black . . . violates the Equal Protection Clause" (internal quotation marks omitted)); *see also Edmonson v. Leesville Concrete Co.*, 500 U.S. 614, 630–31, 111 S.Ct. 2077, 2088, 114 L.Ed.2d 660 (1991) ("If our society is to continue to progress as a multiracial democracy, it must recognize that the automatic invocation of race stereotypes retards that progress and causes continued hurt and injury"). By perpetuating such notions, a racial gerrymander may exacerbate the very patterns of racial bloc voting that majority-minority districting is sometimes said to counteract.

The message that such districting sends to elected representatives is equally pernicious. When a district obviously is created solely to effectuate the perceived common interests of one racial group, elected officials are more likely to believe that their primary obligation is to represent only the members of that group, rather than their constituency as a whole. This is altogether antithetical to our system of representative democracy. As Justice Douglas explained in his dissent in *Wright v. Rockefeller* nearly 30 years ago:

"Here the individual is important, not his race, his creed, or his color. The principle of equality is at war with the notion that District A must be represented by a Negro, as it is with the notion that District B must be represented by a Caucasian, District C by a Jew, District D by a Catholic, and so on. . . . That system, by whatever name it is called, is a divisive force in a community, emphasizing differences between candidates and voters that are irrelevant in the constitutional sense. . . .

"When racial or religious lines are drawn by the State, the multiracial, multireligious communities that our Constitution seeks to weld together as one become separatist; antagonisms that relate to race or to religion rather than to political issues are generated; communities seek not the best representative but the best racial or religious partisan. Since that system is at war with the democratic ideal, it should find no footing here." 376 U.S., at 66–67, 84 S.Ct., at 611 (dissenting opinion).

For these reasons, we conclude that a plaintiff challenging a reapportionment statute under the Equal Protection Clause may state a claim by alleging that the legislation, though race-neutral on its face, rationally cannot be understood as anything other than an effort to separate voters into different districts on the basis of race, and that the separation lacks sufficient justification. It is unnecessary for us to decide whether or how a reapportionment plan that, on its face, can be explained in nonracial terms successfully could be challenged. Thus, we express no view as to whether "the intentional creation of majority-minority districts, without more," always gives rise to an equal protection claim. *Post*, at 2839 (WHITE, J., dissenting). . . . Racial classifications of any sort pose the risk of lasting harm to our society. They reinforce the belief, held by too many for too much of our history, that individuals should be judged by the color of their skin. Racial classifications with respect to voting carry particular dangers. Racial gerrymandering, even for remedial purposes, may balkanize us into competing racial factions; it threatens to carry us further from the goal of a political system in which race no longer matters—a goal that the Fourteenth and Fifteenth Amendments embody, and to which the Nation continues to aspire. It is for these reasons that race-based districting by our state legislatures demands close judicial scrutiny.

3. Holding

In this case, the Attorney General suggested that North Carolina could have created a reasonably compact second majority-minority district in the south-central to southeastern part of the State. We express no view as to whether appellants successfully could have challenged such a district under the Fourteenth Amendment. We also do not decide whether appellants' complaint stated a claim under constitutional provisions other than the Fourteenth Amendment. Today we hold only that appellants have stated a claim under the Equal Protection Clause by alleging that the North Carolina General Assembly adopted a reapportionment scheme so irrational on its face that it can be understood only as an effort to segregate voters into separate voting districts because of their race, and that the separation lacks sufficient justification. If the allegation of racial gerrymandering remains uncontradicted, the District Court further must determine whether the North Carolina plan is narrowly tailored to further a compelling governmental interest. Accordingly, we reverse the judgment of the District Court and remand the case for further proceedings consistent with this opinion.

4. Justice White Dissenting

The facts of this case mirror those presented in *United Jewish Organizations of Williamsburgh, Inc. v. Carey*, 430 U.S. 144, 97 S.Ct. 996, 51 L.Ed.2d 229 (1977) (UJO), where the Court rejected a claim that creation of a majority-minority district violated the Constitution, either as a per se matter or in light of the circumstances leading to the creation of such a district. Of particular relevance, five of the Justices reasoned that members of the white majority could not plausibly argue that their influence over the political process had been unfairly canceled, *see id.*, at 165–68, 97 S.Ct., at 1009–11 (opinion of WHITE, J., joined by REHNQUIST and STEVENS, JJ.), or that such had been the State's intent, *see id.*, at 179–180, 97 S.Ct., at 1016–17 (STEWART, J., joined by POWELL, J., concurring in judgment). Accordingly, they held that plaintiffs were not entitled to relief under the Constitution's Equal Protection Clause. On the same reasoning, I would affirm the District Court's dismissal of appellants' claim in this instance.

The Court today chooses not to overrule, but rather to sidestep, UJO. It does so by glossing over the striking similarities, focusing on surface differences, most notably the (admittedly unusual) shape of the newly created district, and imagining an entirely new cause of action. Because the holding is limited to such anomalous circumstances, it perhaps will not substantially hamper a State's legitimate efforts to redistrict in favor of racial minorities. Nonetheless, the notion that North Carolina's plan, under which whites remain a voting majority in a disproportionate number of congressional districts, and pursuant to which the State has sent its first black representatives since Reconstruction to the United States Congress, might have violated appellants' constitutional rights is both a fiction and a departure from settled equal protection principles. Seeing no good reason to engage in either, I dissent.

Although I disagree with the holding that appellants' claim is cognizable, the Court's discussion of the level of scrutiny it requires warrants a few comments. I have no doubt that a State's compliance with the Voting Rights Act clearly constitutes a compelling interest. *Cf.* UJO, 430 U.S., at 162–65, 97 S.Ct., at 1008–10 (opinion of WHITE, J.); *id.*, at 175–79, 97 S.Ct., at 1008–10 (BRENNAN, J., concurring in part); *id.*, at 180, 97 S.Ct., at 1017 (STEWART, J., concurring in judgment). Here, the Attorney General objected to the State's plan on the ground that it failed to draw a second majority-minority district for what appeared to be pretextual reasons. Rather than challenge this conclusion, North Carolina chose to draw the second district. As UJO held, a State is entitled to take such action. *See also Wygant v. Jackson Bd. of Ed.*, 476 U.S. 267, 291, 106 S.Ct. 1842, 1856, 90 L.Ed.2d 260 (O'CONNOR, J., concurring in part and concurring in judgment).

The Court, while seemingly agreeing with this position, warns that the State's redistricting effort must be "narrowly tailored" to further its interest in complying with the law. Ante, at ___. It is evident to me, however, that what North Carolina did was precisely tailored to meet the objection of the Attorney General to its prior plan. Hence, I see no need for a remand at all, even accepting the majority's basic approach to this case. . . .

Justice BLACKMUN and Justice STEVENS concur in the dissent.

5. Justice Souter Dissenting

Until today, the Court has analyzed equal protection claims involving race in electoral districting differently from equal protection claims involving other forms of governmental conduct, and before turning to the different regimes of analysis it will be useful to set out the relevant respects in which such districting differs from the characteristic circumstances in which a State might otherwise consciously consider race. Unlike other contexts in which we have addressed the State's conscious use of race, see *Richmond v. J.A. Croson Co.*, 488 U.S. 469, 109 S.Ct. 706, 102 L.Ed.2d 854 (1989) (city contracting); *Wygant v. Jackson Bd. of Ed.*, 476 U.S. 267, 106 S.Ct. 1842, 90 L.Ed.2d 260 (1986) (teacher layoffs), electoral districting calls for decisions that nearly always require some consideration of race for legitimate reasons where there is a racially mixed population. As long as members of racial groups have the commonality of interest implicit in our ability to talk about concepts like "minority voting strength," and "dilution of minority votes," *cf. Thornburg v. Gingles*, 478 U.S. 30, 46–51, 106 S.Ct. 2752, 2764–67, 92 L.Ed.2d 25 (1986), and as long as racial bloc voting takes place,[67] legislators will have to take race into account in order to avoid dilution of minority voting strength in the districting plans they adopt.[68] One need look no further than the Voting Rights Act to understand that this may be required, and we have held that race may constitutionally be taken into account in order to comply with that Act. *United Jewish Organizations of Williamsburgh, Inc. v. Carey*, 430 U.S. 144, 161–62, 97 S.Ct. 996, 1007–8, 51 L.Ed.2d 229 (1977) (UJO) (plurality opinion of WHITE, J., joined by BRENNAN, BLACKMUN, and STEVENS, JJ.); *id.*, at 180, and n., 97 S.Ct., at 1017, and n. (STEWART, J., joined by POWELL, J., concurring in judgment).[69]

A second distinction between districting and most other governmental decisions in which race has figured is that those other decisions using racial criteria characteristically occur in circumstances in which the use of race to the advantage of one person is necessarily at the obvious expense of a member of a different race. Thus, for example, awarding government contracts on a racial basis excludes certain firms from competition on racial grounds. *See Richmond v. J.A. Croson Co., supra*, 488 U.S., at 493, 109 S.Ct., at 721; *see also Fullilove v. Klutznick*, 448 U.S. 448, 484, 100 S.Ct. 2758, 2777–78, 65 L.Ed.2d 902 (1980) (opinion of BURGER, C.J.). And when race is used to supplant seniority in layoffs, someone is laid off who would not be otherwise. *Wygant v. Jackson Bd. of Ed., supra*, 476 U.S., at 282–83, 106 S.Ct., at 1851–52

---

67. "Bloc racial voting is an unfortunate phenomenon, but we are repeatedly faced with the findings of knowledgeable district courts that it is a fact of life. Where it exists, most often the result is that neither white nor black can be elected from a district in which his race is in the minority." *Beer v. United States*, 425 U.S. 130, 144, 96 S.Ct. 1357, 1365, 47 L.Ed.2d 629 (1976) (WHITE, J., dissenting).

68. Recognition of actual commonality of interest and racially polarized bloc voting cannot be equated with the "'invocation of race stereotypes'" described by the Court, *ante*, at 2827 (quoting *Edmonson v. Leesville Concrete Co.*, 500 U.S. 614, 630–31, 111 S.Ct. 2077, 2088, 114 L.Ed.2d 660 (1991)), and forbidden by our case law.

69. Section 5 of the Voting Rights Act requires a covered jurisdiction to demonstrate either to the Attorney General or to the District Court that each new districting plan "does not have the purpose and will not have the effect of denying or abridging the right to vote on account of race[,] color, or [membership in a language minority.]" 42 U.S.C. § 1973c; *see also* § 1973b(f)(2). Section 2 of the Voting Rights Act forbids districting plans that will have a discriminatory effect on minority groups. § 1973.

(plurality opinion). The same principle pertains in nondistricting aspects of voting law, where race-based discrimination places the disfavored voters at the disadvantage of exclusion from the franchise without any alternative benefit. *See Gomillion v. Lightfoot*, 364 U.S. 339, 341, 81 S.Ct. 125, 127, 5 L.Ed.2d 110 (1960) (voters alleged to have been excluded from voting in the municipality).

In districting, by contrast, the mere placement of an individual in one district instead of another denies no one a right or benefit provided to others. All citizens may register, vote, and be represented. In whatever district, the individual voter has a right to vote in each election, and the election will result in the voter's representation. As we have held, one's constitutional rights are not violated merely because the candidate one supports loses the election or because a group (including a racial group) to which one belongs winds up with a representative from outside that group. *See Whitcomb v. Chavis*, 403 U.S. 124, 153–55, 91 S.Ct. 1858, 1873–75, 29 L. Ed.2d 363 (1971). It is true, of course, that one's vote may be more or less effective depending on the interests of the other individuals who are in one's district, and our cases recognize the reality that members of the same race often have shared interests. "Dilution" thus refers to the effects of districting decisions not on an individual's political power viewed in isolation, but on the political power of a group. *See UJO, supra*, 430 U.S., at 165, 97 S.Ct., at 1009–10 (plurality opinion). This is the reason that the placement of given voters in a given district, even on the basis of race, does not, without more, diminish the effectiveness of the individual as a voter.

M. Commentary on *Shaw*

A. Leon Higginbotham, Jr., Gregory Clarick, and Marcella David

*Shaw v. Reno: A Mirage of Good Intentions with Devastating Racial Consequences**

Shaw is fundamentally flawed. The decision, at least in part, is premised on the notion that irregularly shaped, minority-majority congressional districts are somehow akin to apartheid and segregation. But apartheid and segregation are invidious policies intended, at bottom, to exclude citizens from civic life because of their race. Minority-majority districts, intended to include racial minorities into the politics from which they were for so long locked out, are neither similar nor analogous to apartheid or segregation. Shaw's misguided suggestion otherwise limits the legitimacy of that decision.

To support its conclusion, the Court identified three potential "harms" that might result from "dramatically irregular" districting plans: the "uncomfortable resemblance to political apartheid," the reinforcement of racial stereotypes, and

---

* (footnotes omitted).

possible damage to "our representati[onal] democracy" that might result from politicians' assuming that they represent the interests of only one race.

Implicitly equating racial classification with racial discrimination, the Court's "harm" analysis abandoned settled principles of equal protection law. Yet the distinction between classification and discrimination underlies all cases considered by the Court since its decision in *Regents of the University of California v. Bakke* addressing state attempts to remedy past racial discrimination. Indeed, the Shaw Court tacitly acknowledged the significance of the distinction by stressing that "[t]his court never has held that race-conscious state decisionmaking is impermissible in all circumstances." The internal tension between the Court's "harm" analysis and its recognition that race-conscious remedial legislation can be justified and legal was left unresolved.

This tension was created because the Court abandoned the requirement of proving direct constitutional injury—here voter dilution. The concept of voter dilution is well established:

> The essence of racial vote dilution . . . is this: that primarily because of the interaction of . . . racial polarization . . . with a challenged electoral mechanism, a racial minority with distinctive group interests . . . is effectively denied the political power to further those interests that numbers alone would presumptively give it in a voting constituency not racially polarized.

Yet the Court here specifically noted that the plaintiffs failed even to allege voter dilution:

> [A]ppellants did not claim that the General Assembly's reapportionment plan unconstitutionally 'diluted' white voting strength. Rather, appellants' complaint alleged that the deliberate segregation of voters into separate districts on the basis of race violated their constitutional right to participate in a 'color-blind' electoral process.

The theoretical right to "participate in a 'color-blind' electoral process," never before recognized by the Court, was accepted as a substitute for the direct injury of voter dilution. But what sets lawful classifications apart from outright discrimination is the fact that discrimination injures those adversely classified.

Absent injury—and the Supreme Court accepts there was no voter dilution here—the classification should be lawful. The *Shaw* Court's abandonment of the touchstones of discriminatory harm and purpose in voting rights cases where a congressional district's shape does not comport with some obscure notion of regularity lacks any principled basis under its equal protection precedent.

The Supreme Court's majority opinion in *Shaw v. Reno*, applying the Equal Protection Clause to preclude African Americans from attaining significant political power in this nation, turns the intent and meaning of the Fourteenth Amendment on its head. In the 1873 case first construing the Fourteenth Amendment, the *Slaughterhouse* Cases, the Supreme Court declared:

We repeat, then, in the light of this recapitulation of events, almost too recent to be called history, but which are familiar to us all; and on the most casual examination of the language of these amendments, no one can fail to be impressed with the one pervading purpose found in them all, lying at the foundation of each, and without which none of them would have been even suggested; we mean the freedom of the slave race, the security and firm establishment of that freedom, and the protection of the newly-made freeman and citizen from the oppressions of those who had formerly exercised unlimited dominion over him. It is true that only the Fifteenth Amendment, in terms, mentions the Negro by speaking of his color and his slavery. But it is just as true that each of the other articles was addressed to the grievances of that race, and designed to remedy them as the Fifteenth. . . . We doubt very much whether any action of a State not directed by way of discrimination against the Negroes as a class, or on account of their race, will ever be held to come within the purview of this provision. It is so clearly a provision for that race and that emergency, that a strong case would be necessary for its application to any other.

Now, 120 years after *The Slaughterhouse Cases*, the Fourteenth Amendment may be used to thwart rather than to assure effective use of the ballot by African Americans. The bizarreness in this case thus is not the shape of the district boundaries but rather the challenge itself, where the white vote is not diluted and where talented legislators represent the districts.

LXII *Fordham L.R.* 1593, 1644–46.
Copyright © (1994) A. Leon Higginbotham, Jr.
Reprinted with permission of Evelyn Brooks Higginbotham.

N. Background on *Shelby*

In the summer of 1964, major civil rights organizations implemented a plan to significantly increase black voter registration in Mississippi. Officially called the Mississippi Summer Project but popularly referred to as Freedom Summer, the initiative was a bold step to directly tackle racial exclusion in the political process in a state with, arguably, one of the worst civil rights records. Due to discriminatory laws and practices such as grandfather clauses, poll taxes, literacy tests, economic punishments, and physical intimidation, black registration in Mississippi was at 6%, the lowest of any state. The plan involved over one thousand volunteers, mostly white college students from northern universities, working closely with civil rights workers and leaders in the Mississippi black community, facilitating black voter registration. From the onset, most white Mississippians resented any attempts to increase black voter registration, or to alter the racial status quo in any way. During the course of the two and a half month project, massive and often violent resistance occurred, including bombings and burnings of black churches, businesses, and homes; arrests and beatings of volunteers and aspiring registrants; and, the murder of four civil rights workers and three state residents. These resistance efforts were successful in dissuading most black Mississippians from registering.

While few additional voters were registered during Freedom Summer, the voter registration efforts in Mississippi helped to focus attention on racial barriers to voting rights throughout the South. Recognition that Mississippi was not an aberration but rather a reflection of widespread exclusion of black voters throughout the south, and in some parts of the north, helped further efforts by civil rights groups and leaders of the Democratic Party, including President Lyndon Johnson, to secure passage of voting rights protection on a national scale. The result was the Voting Rights Act (VRA), enacted in 1965, the most democratizing piece of legislation ever passed.

In signing the law, President Johnson termed it "a monumental law in the history of American freedom." He was right. In less than four years after the law was enacted, 800,000 blacks registered to vote. In Mississippi, for example, black registration increased from 6% to 66%.

David Crump et al.

Cases and Materials on Constitutional Law (Fifth Edition)

The preclearance requirements of the Voting Rights Act of 1965, which require covered jurisdictions to seek federal approval before changing anything about elections, were originally scheduled to be effective for only five years. But Congress extended the provisions in 1970 (for five years), 1975 (for seven years), 1982 (for 25 years), and again in 2006 (for another twenty-five years). The Court had upheld all the reauthorizations before the twenty-first century, concluding that circumstances continued to justify the provisions. But, in reviewing the 2006 extension in *Northwest Austin Municipal Utility District No. 1 v. Holder*, 557 U.S. 193 (2009), the Court noted that it raised "serious constitutional concerns."

A small utility district in Austin, Texas, with an elected board was required to obtain preclearance from the Justice Department before it could change any aspect of those elections (including moving the elections from a private garage to a local school), even though there was no evidence the district had ever employed a racially discriminatory voting practice. The district filed suit challenging the application of the preclearance requirements. Although the Court's opinion by Chief Justice Roberts decided the case on the narrow statutory grounds that the district was eligible to seek an exemption from the preclearance requirements, the Court provided an extensive discussion of the potential Constitutional infirmities of the 2006 extension. The Court recognized that the preclearance requirements severely interfered with state sovereignty in a manner that may no longer be appropriate as the registration gap between white and black voters in covered states was approaching parity and minority candidates held elected office at unprecedented levels. In addition, the coverage formula had not been updated for more than 35 years, raising concerns that it no longer accounted for current conditions, especially considering that covered jurisdictions actually had less of a racial gap in voting registration and turnout than the nationwide average. Justice Thomas dissented in part, urging that the Court should strike down the 2006 extension of the preclearance requirements as exceeding Congress' power to enforce the Fifteenth Amendment because the intrusive remedy was no longer appropriate in light of the current lack of evidence of racial discrimination in voting.

Cases and Materials on Constitutional Law (Fifth Edition) 1053.

Copyright © (2009) LexisNexis.

Reprinted with permission of LexisNexis.

O. *Shelby County v. Holder,* 133 S. Ct. 2612 (2013)

1. Facts

Chief Justice ROBERTS delivered the opinion of the Court.

The Voting Rights Act of 1965 employed extraordinary measures to address an extraordinary problem. Section 5 of the Act required States to obtain federal permission before enacting any law related to voting—a drastic departure from basic principles of federalism. And § 4 of the Act applied that requirement only to some States—an equally dramatic departure from the principle that all States enjoy equal sovereignty. This was strong medicine, but Congress determined it was needed to address entrenched racial discrimination in voting, "an insidious and pervasive evil which had been perpetuated in certain parts of our country through unremitting and ingenious defiance of the Constitution." *South Carolina v. Katzenbach,* 383 U.S. 301, 309, 86 S.Ct. 803, 15 L.Ed.2d 769 (1966). As we explained in upholding the law, "exceptional conditions can justify legislative measures not otherwise appropriate." *Id.,* at 334, 86 S.Ct. 803. Reflecting the unprecedented nature of these measures, they were scheduled to expire after five years. See Voting Rights Act of 1965, § 4(a), 79 Stat. 438.

Nearly 50 years later, they are still in effect; indeed, they have been made more stringent, and are now scheduled to last until 2031. There is no denying, however, that the conditions that originally justified these measures no longer characterize voting in the covered jurisdictions. By 2009, "the racial gap in voter registration and turnout [was] lower in the States originally covered by § 5 than it [was] nationwide." *Northwest Austin Municipal Util. Dist. No. One v. Holder,* 557 U.S. 193, 203–204, 129 S.Ct. 2504, 174 L.Ed.2d 140 (2009). Since that time, Census Bureau data indicate that African-American voter turnout has come to exceed white voter turnout in five of the six States originally covered by § 5, with a gap in the sixth State of less than one half of one percent. See Dept. of Commerce, Census Bureau, Reported Voting and Registration, by Sex, Race and Hispanic Origin, for States (Nov. 2012) (Table 4b).

At the same time, voting discrimination still exists; no one doubts that. The question is whether the Act's extraordinary measures, including its disparate treatment of the States, continue to satisfy constitutional requirements. As we put it a short time ago, "the Act imposes current burdens and must be justified by current needs." *Northwest Austin*, 557 U.S., at 203, 129 S.Ct. 2504.

The Fifteenth Amendment was ratified in 1870, in the wake of the Civil War. It provides that "[t]he right of citizens of the United States to vote shall not be denied or abridged by the United States or by any State on account of race, color, or previous condition of servitude," and it gives Congress the "power to enforce this article by appropriate legislation."

"The first century of congressional enforcement of the Amendment, however, can only be regarded as a failure." *Id.*, at 197, 129 S.Ct. 2504. In the 1890s, Alabama, Georgia, Louisiana, Mississippi, North Carolina, South Carolina, and Virginia began to enact literacy tests for voter registration and to employ other methods designed to prevent African-Americans from voting. *Katzenbach*, 383 U.S., at 310, 86 S.Ct. 803. Congress passed statutes outlawing some of these practices and facilitating litigation against them, but litigation remained slow and expensive, and the States came up with new ways to discriminate as soon as existing ones were struck down. Voter registration of African-Americans barely improved. *Id.*, at 313–314, 86 S.Ct. 803.

Inspired to action by the civil rights movement, Congress responded in 1965 with the Voting Rights Act. Section 2 was enacted to forbid, in all 50 States, any "standard, practice, or procedure . . . imposed or applied . . . to deny or abridge the right of any citizen of the United States to vote on account of race or color." 79 Stat. 437. The current version forbids any "standard, practice, or procedure" that "results in a denial or abridgement of the right of any citizen of the United States to vote on account of race or color." 42 U.S.C. § 1973(a). Both the Federal Government and individuals have sued to enforce § 2, see, *e.g., Johnson v. De Grandy*, 512 U.S. 997, 114 S.Ct. 2647, 129 L.Ed.2d 775 (1994), and injunctive relief is available in appropriate cases to block voting laws from going into effect, see 42 U.S.C. § 1973j(d). Section 2 is permanent, applies nationwide, and is not at issue in this case.

Other sections targeted only some parts of the country. At the time of the Act's passage, these "covered" jurisdictions were those States or political subdivisions that had maintained a test or device as a prerequisite to voting as of November 1, 1964, and had less than 50 percent voter registration or turnout in the 1964 Presidential election. § 4(b), 79 Stat. 438. Such tests or devices included literacy and knowledge tests, good moral character requirements, the need for vouchers from registered voters, and the like. § 4(c), *id.*, at 438–439. A covered jurisdiction could "bail out" of coverage if it had not used a test or device in the preceding five years "for the purpose or with the effect of denying or abridging the right to vote on account of race or color." § 4(a), *id.*, at 438. In 1965, the covered States included Alabama, Georgia, Louisiana, Mississippi, South Carolina, and Virginia. The additional covered subdivisions included 39 counties in North Carolina and one in Arizona. See 28 C.F.R. pt. 51, App. (2012).

In those jurisdictions, § 4 of the Act banned all such tests or devices. § 4(a), 79 Stat. 438. Section 5 provided that no change in voting procedures could take effect until it was approved by federal authorities in Washington, D.C. — either the Attorney General or a court of three judges. *Id.*, at 439. A jurisdiction could obtain such "preclearance" only by proving that the change had neither "the purpose [nor] the effect of denying or abridging the right to vote on account of race or color." *Ibid.*

Sections 4 and 5 were intended to be temporary; they were set to expire after five years. See § 4(a), *id.*, at 438; *Northwest Austin, supra,* at 199, 129 S.Ct. 2504. In *South Carolina v. Katzenbach,* we upheld the 1965 Act against constitutional challenge, explaining that it was justified to address "voting discrimination where it persists on a pervasive scale." 383 U.S., at 308, 86 S.Ct. 803.

In 1970, Congress reauthorized the Act for another five years, and extended the coverage formula in § 4(b) to jurisdictions that had a voting test and less than 50 percent voter registration or turnout as of 1968. Voting Rights Act Amendments of 1970, §§ 3–4, 84 Stat. 315. That swept in several counties in California, New Hampshire, and New York. See 28 C.F.R. pt. 51, App. Congress also extended the ban in § 4(a) on tests and devices nationwide. § 6, 84 Stat. 315.

In 1975, Congress reauthorized the Act for seven more years, and extended its coverage to jurisdictions that had a voting test and less than 50 percent voter registration or turnout as of 1972. Voting Rights Act Amendments of 1975, §§ 101, 202, 89 Stat. 400, 401. Congress also amended the definition of "test or device" to include the practice of providing English-only voting materials in places where over five percent of voting-age citizens spoke a single language other than English. § 203, *id.*, at 401–402. As a result of these amendments, the States of Alaska, Arizona, and Texas, as well as several counties in California, Florida, Michigan, New York, North Carolina, and South Dakota, became covered jurisdictions. See 28 C.F.R. pt. 51, App. Congress correspondingly amended sections 2 and 5 to forbid voting discrimination on the basis of membership in a language minority group, in addition to discrimination on the basis of race or color. §§ 203, 206, 89 Stat. 401, 402. Finally, Congress made the nationwide ban on tests and devices permanent. § 102, *id.*, at 400.

In 1982, Congress reauthorized the Act for 25 years, but did not alter its coverage formula. See Voting Rights Act Amendments, 96 Stat. 131. Congress did, however, amend the bailout provisions, allowing political subdivisions of covered jurisdictions to bail out. Among other prerequisites for bailout, jurisdictions and their subdivisions must not have used a forbidden test or device, failed to receive preclearance, or lost a § 2 suit, in the ten years prior to seeking bailout. § 2, *id.*, at 131–133.

We upheld each of these reauthorizations against constitutional challenge. See *Georgia v. United States,* 411 U.S. 526, 93 S.Ct. 1702, 36 L.Ed.2d 472 (1973); *City of Rome v. United States,* 446 U.S. 156, 100 S.Ct. 1548, 64 L.Ed.2d 119 (1980); *Lopez v. Monterey County,* 525 U.S. 266, 119 S.Ct. 693, 142 L.Ed.2d 728 (1999).

In 2006, Congress again reauthorized the Voting Rights Act for 25 years, again without change to its coverage formula. Fannie Lou Hamer, Rosa Parks, and Coretta Scott King Voting Rights Act Reauthorization and Amendments Act, 120 Stat. 577. Congress also amended § 5 to prohibit more conduct than before. § 5, *id.*, at 580–581; see *Reno v. Bossier Parish School Bd.*, 528 U.S. 320, 341, 120 S.Ct. 866, 145 L. Ed.2d 845 (2000) (*Bossier II*); *Georgia v. Ashcroft*, 539 U.S. 461, 479, 123 S.Ct. 2498, 156 L.Ed.2d 428 (2003). Section 5 now forbids voting changes with "any discriminatory purpose" as well as voting changes that diminish the ability of citizens, on account of race, color, or language minority status, "to elect their preferred candidates of choice." 42 U.S.C. §§ 1973c(b)–(d).

Shortly after this reauthorization, a Texas utility district brought suit, seeking to bail out from the Act's coverage and, in the alternative, challenging the Act's constitutionality. See *Northwest Austin*, 557 U.S., at 200–201, 129 S.Ct. 2504. A three-judge District Court explained that only a State or political subdivision was eligible to seek bailout under the statute, and concluded that the utility district was not a political subdivision, a term that encompassed only "counties, parishes, and voter-registering subunits." *Northwest Austin Municipal Util. Dist. No. One v. Mukasey*, 573 F.Supp.2d 221, 232 (D.D.C.2008). The District Court also rejected the constitutional challenge. *Id.*, at 283.

We reversed. We explained that "'normally the Court will not decide a constitutional question if there is some other ground upon which to dispose of the case.'" *Northwest Austin, supra,* at 205, 129 S.Ct. 2504 (quoting *Escambia County v. McMillan*, 466 U.S. 48, 51, 104 S.Ct. 1577, 80 L.Ed.2d 36 (1984) (*per curiam*)). Concluding that "underlying constitutional concerns," among other things, "compel[led] a broader reading of the bailout provision," we construed the statute to allow the utility district to seek bailout. *Northwest Austin*, 557 U.S., at 207, 129 S.Ct. 2504. In doing so we expressed serious doubts about the Act's continued constitutionality.

We explained that § 5 "imposes substantial federalism costs" and "differentiates between the States, despite our historic tradition that all the States enjoy equal sovereignty." *Id.*, at 202, 203, 129 S.Ct. 2504 (internal quotation marks omitted). We also noted that "[t]hings have changed in the South. Voter turnout and registration rates now approach parity. Blatantly discriminatory evasions of federal decrees are rare. And minority candidates hold office at unprecedented levels." *Id.*, at 202, 129 S. Ct. 2504. Finally, we questioned whether the problems that § 5 meant to address were still "concentrated in the jurisdictions singled out for preclearance." *Id.*, at 203, 129 S.Ct. 2504.

Eight Members of the Court subscribed to these views, and the remaining Member would have held the Act unconstitutional. Ultimately, however, the Court's construction of the bailout provision left the constitutional issues for another day.

Shelby County is located in Alabama, a covered jurisdiction. It has not sought bailout, as the Attorney General has recently objected to voting changes proposed from within the county. See App. 87a–92a. Instead, in 2010, the county sued the

Attorney General in Federal District Court in Washington, D.C., seeking a declaratory judgment that sections 4(b) and 5 of the Voting Rights Act are facially unconstitutional, as well as a permanent injunction against their enforcement. The District Court ruled against the county and upheld the Act. 811 F.Supp.2d 424, 508 (2011). The court found that the evidence before Congress in 2006 was sufficient to justify reauthorizing § 5 and continuing the § 4(b) coverage formula.

The Court of Appeals for the D.C. Circuit affirmed. In assessing § 5, the D.C. Circuit considered six primary categories of evidence: Attorney General objections to voting changes, Attorney General requests for more information regarding voting changes, successful § 2 suits in covered jurisdictions, the dispatching of federal observers to monitor elections in covered jurisdictions, § 5 preclearance suits involving covered jurisdictions, and the deterrent effect of § 5. See 679 F.3d 848, 862–863 (2012). After extensive analysis of the record, the court accepted Congress's conclusion that § 2 litigation remained inadequate in the covered jurisdictions to protect the rights of minority voters, and that § 5 was therefore still necessary. *Id.,* at 873.

Turning to § 4, the D.C. Circuit noted that the evidence for singling out the covered jurisdictions was "less robust" and that the issue presented "a close question." *Id.,* at 879. But the court looked to data comparing the number of successful § 2 suits in the different parts of the country. Coupling that evidence with the deterrent effect of § 5, the court concluded that the statute continued "to single out the jurisdictions in which discrimination is concentrated," and thus held that the coverage formula passed constitutional muster. *Id.,* at 883.

Judge Williams dissented. He found "no positive correlation between inclusion in § 4(b)'s coverage formula and low black registration or turnout." *Id.,* at 891. Rather, to the extent there was any correlation, it actually went the other way: "condemnation under § 4(b) is a marker of *higher* black registration and turnout." *Ibid.* (emphasis added). Judge Williams also found that "[c]overed jurisdictions have *far more* black officeholders as a proportion of the black population than do uncovered ones." *Id.,* at 892. As to the evidence of successful § 2 suits, Judge Williams disaggregated the reported cases by State, and concluded that "[t]he five worst uncovered jurisdictions . . . have worse records than eight of the covered jurisdictions." *Id.,* at 897. He also noted that two covered jurisdictions—Arizona and Alaska—had not had any successful reported § 2 suit brought against them during the entire 24 years covered by the data. *Ibid.* Judge Williams would have held the coverage formula of § 4(b) "irrational" and unconstitutional. *Id.,* at 885.

We granted certiorari. 568 U.S. ___, 133 S.Ct. 594, 184 L.Ed.2d 389 (2012).

2. Opinion

In *Northwest Austin,* we stated that "the Act imposes current burdens and must be justified by current needs." 557 U.S., at 203, 129 S.Ct. 2504. And we concluded that "a departure from the fundamental principle of equal sovereignty requires a showing that a statute's disparate geographic coverage is sufficiently related to the problem that it targets." *Ibid.* These basic principles guide our review of the question before us.1

The Constitution and laws of the United States are "the supreme Law of the Land." U.S. Const., Art. VI, cl. 2. State legislation may not contravene federal law. The Federal Government does not, however, have a general right to review and veto state enactments before they go into effect. A proposal to grant such authority to "negative" state laws was considered at the Constitutional Convention, but rejected in favor of allowing state laws to take effect, subject to later challenge under the Supremacy Clause. See 1 Records of the Federal Convention of 1787, pp. 21, 164–168 (M. Farrand ed. 1911); 2 *id.,* at 27–29, 390–392.

Outside the strictures of the Supremacy Clause, States retain broad autonomy in structuring their governments and pursuing legislative objectives. Indeed, the Constitution provides that all powers not specifically granted to the Federal Government are reserved to the States or citizens. Amdt. 10. This "allocation of powers in our federal system preserves the integrity, dignity, and residual sovereignty of the States." *Bond v. United States,* 564 U.S. ___, ___, 131 S.Ct. 2355, 2364, 180 L.Ed.2d 269 (2011). But the federal balance "is not just an end in itself: Rather, federalism secures to citizens the liberties that derive from the diffusion of sovereign power." *Ibid.* (internal quotation marks omitted).

More specifically, "'the Framers of the Constitution intended the States to keep for themselves, as provided in the Tenth Amendment, the power to regulate elections.'" *Gregory v. Ashcroft,* 501 U.S. 452, 461–462, 111 S.Ct. 2395, 115 L.Ed.2d 410 (1991) (quoting *Sugarman v. Dougall,* 413 U.S. 634, 647, 93 S.Ct. 2842, 37 L.Ed.2d 853 (1973); some internal quotation marks omitted). Of course, the Federal Government retains significant control over federal elections. For instance, the Constitution authorizes Congress to establish the time and manner for electing Senators and Representatives. Art. I, §4, cl. 1; see also *Arizona v. Inter Tribal Council of Ariz., Inc.,* ___ U.S., at ___–___, 133 S.Ct., at 2253–2254. But States have "broad powers to determine the conditions under which the right of suffrage may be exercised." *Carrington v. Rash,* 380 U.S. 89, 91, 85 S.Ct. 775, 13 L.Ed.2d 675 (1965) (internal quotation marks omitted); see also *Arizona, ante,* at ___ U.S., at ___–___, 133 S. Ct., at 2257–2259. And "[e]ach State has the power to prescribe the qualifications of its officers and the manner in which they shall be chosen." *Boyd v. Nebraska ex rel. Thayer,* 143 U.S. 135, 161, 12 S.Ct. 375, 36 L.Ed. 103 (1892). Drawing lines for congressional districts is likewise "primarily the duty and responsibility of the State." *Perry v. Perez,* 565 U.S. ___, ___, 132 S.Ct. 934, 940, 181 L.Ed.2d 900 (2012) (*per curiam*) (internal quotation marks omitted).

[12][13][14] Not only do States retain sovereignty under the Constitution, there is also a "fundamental principle of *equal* sovereignty" among the States. *Northwest Austin, supra,* at 203, 129 S.Ct. 2504 (citing *United States v. Louisiana,* 363 U.S. 1, 16, 80 S.Ct. 961, 4 L.Ed.2d 1025 (1960); *Lessee of Pollard v. Hagan,* 3 How. 212, 223, 11 L.Ed. 565 (1845); and *Texas v. White,* 7 Wall. 700, 725–726, 19 L.Ed. 227 (1869); emphasis added). Over a hundred years ago, this Court explained that our Nation

"was and is a union of States, equal in power, dignity and authority." *Coyle v. Smith,* 221 U.S. 559, 567, 31 S.Ct. 688, 55 L.Ed. 853 (1911). Indeed, "the constitutional equality of the States is essential to the harmonious operation of the scheme upon which the Republic was organized." *Id.,* at 580, 31 S.Ct. 688. *Coyle* concerned the admission of new States, and *Katzenbach* rejected the notion that the principle operated as a *bar* on differential treatment outside that context. 383 U.S., at 328–329, 86 S.Ct. 803. At the same time, as we made clear in *Northwest Austin,* the fundamental principle of equal sovereignty remains highly pertinent in assessing subsequent disparate treatment of States. 557 U.S., at 203, 129 S.Ct. 2504.

The Voting Rights Act sharply departs from these basic principles. It suspends "*all* changes to state election law—however innocuous—until they have been precleared by federal authorities in Washington, D.C." *Id.,* at 202, 129 S.Ct. 2504. States must beseech the Federal Government for permission to implement laws that they would otherwise have the right to enact and execute on their own, subject of course to any injunction in a §2 action. The Attorney General has 60 days to object to a preclearance request, longer if he requests more information. See 28 C.F.R. §§51.9, 51.37. If a State seeks preclearance from a three-judge court, the process can take years.

And despite the tradition of equal sovereignty, the Act applies to only nine States (and several additional counties). While one State waits months or years and expends funds to implement a validly enacted law, its neighbor can typically put the same law into effect immediately, through the normal legislative process. Even if a noncovered jurisdiction is sued, there are important differences between those proceedings and preclearance proceedings; the preclearance proceeding "not only switches the burden of proof to the supplicant jurisdiction, but also applies substantive standards quite different from those governing the rest of the nation." 679 F.3d, at 884 (Williams, J., dissenting) (case below).

All this explains why, when we first upheld the Act in 1966, we described it as "stringent" and "potent." *Katzenbach,* 383 U.S., at 308, 315, 337, 86 S.Ct. 803. We recognized that it "may have been an uncommon exercise of congressional power," but concluded that "legislative measures not otherwise appropriate" could be justified by "exceptional conditions." *Id.,* at 334, 86 S.Ct. 803. We have since noted that the Act "authorizes federal intrusion into sensitive areas of state and local policymaking," *Lopez,* 525 U.S., at 282, 119 S.Ct. 693, and represents an "extraordinary departure from the traditional course of relations between the States and the Federal Government," *Presley v. Etowah County Comm'n,* 502 U.S. 491, 500–501, 112 S. Ct. 820, 117 L.Ed.2d 51 (1992). As we reiterated in *Northwest Austin,* the Act constitutes "extraordinary legislation otherwise unfamiliar to our federal system." 557 U.S., at 211, 129 S.Ct. 2504.

In 1966, we found these departures from the basic features of our system of government justified. The "blight of racial discrimination in voting" had "infected the electoral process in parts of our country for nearly a century." *Katzenbach,* 383 U.S., at 308, 86 S.Ct. 803. Several States had enacted a variety of requirements and tests "specifically designed to prevent" African-Americans from voting. *Id.*, at 310, 86 S. Ct. 803. Case-by-case litigation had proved inadequate to prevent such racial discrimination in voting, in part because States "merely switched to discriminatory devices not covered by the federal decrees," "enacted difficult new tests," or simply "defied and evaded court orders." *Id.*, at 314, 86 S.Ct. 803. Shortly before enactment of the Voting Rights Act, only 19.4 percent of African-Americans of voting age were registered to vote in Alabama, only 31.8 percent in Louisiana, and only 6.4 percent in Mississippi. *Id.*, at 313, 86 S.Ct. 803. Those figures were roughly 50 percentage points or more below the figures for whites. *Ibid.*

In short, we concluded that "[u]nder the compulsion of these unique circumstances, Congress responded in a permissibly decisive manner." *Id.*, at 334, 335, 86 S. Ct. 803. We also noted then and have emphasized since that this extraordinary legislation was intended to be temporary, set to expire after five years. *Id.*, at 333, 86 S. Ct. 803; *Northwest Austin, supra*, at 199, 129 S.Ct. 2504.

At the time, the coverage formula—the means of linking the exercise of the unprecedented authority with the problem that warranted it—made sense. We found that "Congress chose to limit its attention to the geographic areas where immediate action seemed necessary." *Katzenbach*, 383 U.S., at 328, 86 S.Ct. 803. The areas where Congress found "evidence of actual voting discrimination" shared two characteristics: "the use of tests and devices for voter registration, and a voting rate in the 1964 presidential election at least 12 points below the national average." *Id.*, at 330, 86 S.Ct. 803. We explained that "[t]ests and devices are relevant to voting discrimination because of their long history as a tool for perpetrating the evil; a low voting rate is pertinent for the obvious reason that widespread disenfranchisement must inevitably affect the number of actual voters." *Ibid.* We therefore concluded that "the coverage formula [was] rational in both practice and theory." *Ibid.* It accurately reflected those jurisdictions uniquely characterized by voting discrimination "on a pervasive scale," linking coverage to the devices used to effectuate discrimination and to the resulting disenfranchisement. *Id.*, at 308, 86 S.Ct. 803. The formula ensured that the "stringent remedies [were] aimed at areas where voting discrimination ha[d] been most flagrant." *Id.*, at 315, 86 S.Ct. 803.

Nearly 50 years later, things have changed dramatically. Shelby County contends that the preclearance requirement, even without regard to its disparate coverage, is now unconstitutional. Its arguments have a good deal of force. In the covered jurisdictions, "[v]oter turnout and registration rates now approach parity. Blatantly discriminatory evasions of federal decrees are rare. And minority candidates hold office at unprecedented levels." *Northwest Austin*, 557 U.S., at 202, 129 S.Ct. 2504. The tests and devices that blocked access to the ballot have been forbidden nationwide for over 40 years. See § 6, 84 Stat. 315; § 102, 89 Stat. 400.

Those conclusions are not ours alone. Congress said the same when it reauthorized the Act in 2006, writing that "[s]ignificant progress has been made in eliminating first generation barriers experienced by minority voters, including increased numbers of registered minority voters, minority voter turnout, and minority representation in

Congress, State legislatures, and local elected offices." § 2(b)(1), 120 Stat. 577. The House Report elaborated that "the number of African-Americans who are registered and who turn out to cast ballots has increased significantly over the last 40 years, particularly since 1982," and noted that "[i]n some circumstances, minorities register to vote and cast ballots at levels that surpass those of white voters." H.R.Rep. 109–478, at 12 (2006), 2006 U.S.C.C.A.N. 618, 627. That Report also explained that there have been "significant increases in the number of African-Americans serving in elected offices"; more specifically, there has been approximately a 1,000 percent increase since 1965 in the number of African-American elected officials in the six States originally covered by the Voting Rights Act. *Id.*, at 18.

The following chart, compiled from the Senate and House Reports, compares voter registration numbers from 1965 to those from 2004 in the six originally covered States. These are the numbers that were before Congress when it reauthorized the Act in 2006:

	1965			2004		
	White	**Black**	**Gap**	**White**	**Black**	**Gap**
Alabama	69.2	19.3	49.9	73.8	72.9	0.9
Georgia	62.[6]	27.4	35.2	63.5	64.2	-0.7
Louisiana	80.5	31.6	48.9	75.1	71.1	4.0
Mississippi	69.9	6.7	63.2	72.3	76.1	-3.8
South Carolina	75.7	37.3	38.4	74.4	71.1	3.3
Virginia	61.1	38.3	22.8	68.2	57.4	10.8

See S.Rep. No. 109–295, p. 11 (2006); H.R.Rep. No. 109–478, at 12. The 2004 figures come from the Census Bureau. Census Bureau data from the most recent election indicate that African-American voter turnout exceeded white voter turnout in five of the six States originally covered by § 5, with a gap in the sixth State of less than one half of one percent. See Dept. of Commerce, Census Bureau, Reported Voting and Registration, by Sex, Race and Hispanic Origin, for States (Table 4b). The pre-clearance statistics are also illuminating. In the first decade after enactment of § 5, the Attorney General objected to 14.2 percent of proposed voting changes. H. R Rep. No. 109–478, at 22. In the last decade before reenactment, the Attorney General objected to a mere 0.16 percent. S.Rep. No. 109–295, at 13.

There is no doubt that these improvements are in large part *because of* the Voting Rights Act. The Act has proved immensely successful at redressing racial discrimination and integrating the voting process. See § 2(b)(1), 120 Stat. 577. During the "Freedom Summer" of 1964, in Philadelphia, Mississippi, three men were murdered while working in the area to register African-American voters. See *United States v. Price*, 383 U.S. 787, 790, 86 S.Ct. 1152, 16 L.Ed.2d 267 (1966). On "Bloody

Sunday" in 1965, in Selma, Alabama, police beat and used tear gas against hundreds marching in support of African-American enfranchisement. See *Northwest Austin, supra,* at 220, n. 3, 129 S.Ct. 2504 (THOMAS, J., concurring in judgment in part and dissenting in part). Today both of those towns are governed by African-American mayors. Problems remain in these States and others, but there is no denying that, due to the Voting Rights Act, our Nation has made great strides. . . .

But history did not end in 1965. By the time the Act was reauthorized in 2006, there had been 40 more years of it. In assessing the "current need [ ]" for a preclearance system that treats States differently from one another today, that history cannot be ignored. During that time, largely because of the Voting Rights Act, voting tests were abolished, disparities in voter registration and turnout due to race were erased, and African-Americans attained political office in record numbers. And yet the coverage formula that Congress reauthorized in 2006 ignores these developments, keeping the focus on decades-old data relevant to decades-old problems, rather than current data reflecting current needs.

The Fifteenth Amendment commands that the right to vote shall not be denied or abridged on account of race or color, and it gives Congress the power to enforce that command. The Amendment is not designed to punish for the past; its purpose is to ensure a better future. See *Rice v. Cayetano,* 528 U.S. 495, 512, 120 S.Ct. 1044, 145 L.Ed.2d 1007 (2000) ("Consistent with the design of the Constitution, the [Fifteenth] Amendment is cast in fundamental terms, terms transcending the particular controversy which was the immediate impetus for its enactment."). To serve that purpose, Congress—if it is to divide the States—must identify those jurisdictions to be singled out on a basis that makes sense in light of current conditions. It cannot rely simply on the past. We made that clear in *Northwest Austin,* and we make it clear again today.

In defending the coverage formula, the Government, the intervenors, and the dissent also rely heavily on data from the record that they claim justify disparate coverage. Congress compiled thousands of pages of evidence before reauthorizing the Voting Rights Act. The court below and the parties have debated what that record shows—they have gone back and forth about whether to compare covered to noncovered jurisdictions as blocks, how to disaggregate the data State by State, how to weigh § 2 cases as evidence of ongoing discrimination, and whether to consider evidence not before Congress, among other issues. Compare, *e.g.,* 679 F.3d, at 873–883 (case below), with *id.,* at 889–902 (Williams, J., dissenting). Regardless of how to look at the record, however, no one can fairly say that it shows anything approaching the "pervasive," "flagrant," "widespread," and "rampant" discrimination that faced Congress in 1965, and that clearly distinguished the covered jurisdictions from the rest of the Nation at that time. *Katzenbach, supra,* at 308, 315, 331, 86 S.Ct. 803; *Northwest Austin,* 557 U.S., at 201, 129 S.Ct. 2504.

But a more fundamental problem remains: Congress did not use the record it compiled to shape a coverage formula grounded in current conditions. It instead reenacted a formula based on 40-year-old facts having no logical relation to the present day. The dissent relies on "second-generation barriers," which are not impediments to the casting of ballots, but rather electoral arrangements that affect the weight of minority votes. That does not cure the problem. Viewing the preclearance requirements as targeting such efforts simply highlights the irrationality of continued reliance on the §4 coverage formula, which is based on voting tests and access to the ballot, not vote dilution. We cannot pretend that we are reviewing an updated statute, or try our hand at updating the statute ourselves, based on the new record compiled by Congress. Contrary to the dissent's contention, see *post*, at 2644, we are not ignoring the record; we are simply recognizing that it played no role in shaping the statutory formula before us today.

The dissent also turns to the record to argue that, in light of voting discrimination in Shelby County, the county cannot complain about the provisions that subject it to preclearance. *Post*, at 2644 — 2648. But that is like saying that a driver pulled over pursuant to a policy of stopping all redheads cannot complain about that policy, if it turns out his license has expired. Shelby County's claim is that the coverage formula here is unconstitutional in all its applications, because of how it selects the jurisdictions subjected to preclearance. The county was selected based on that formula, and may challenge it in court.

The dissent proceeds from a flawed premise. It quotes the famous sentence from *McCulloch v. Maryland*, 4 Wheat. 316, 421, 4 L.Ed. 579 (1819), with the following emphasis: "Let the end be legitimate, let it be within the scope of the constitution, and *all means which are appropriate, which are plainly adapted to that end*, which are not prohibited, but consist with the letter and spirit of the constitution, are constitutional." *Post*, at 2637 (emphasis in dissent). But this case is about a part of the sentence that the dissent does not emphasize — the part that asks whether a legislative means is "consist[ent] with the letter and spirit of the constitution." The dissent states that "[i]t cannot tenably be maintained" that this is an issue with regard to the Voting Rights Act, *post*, at 2637, but four years ago, in an opinion joined by two of today's dissenters, the Court expressly stated that "[t]he Act's preclearance requirement and its coverage formula raise serious constitutional questions." *Northwest Austin, supra*, at 204, 129 S.Ct. 2504. The dissent does not explain how those "serious constitutional questions" became untenable in four short years.

The dissent treats the Act as if it were just like any other piece of legislation, but this Court has made clear from the beginning that the Voting Rights Act is far from ordinary. At the risk of repetition, *Katzenbach* indicated that the Act was "uncommon" and "not otherwise appropriate," but was justified by "exceptional" and "unique" conditions. 383 U.S., at 334, 335, 86 S.Ct. 803. Multiple decisions since have reaffirmed the Act's "extraordinary" nature. See, *e.g., Northwest Austin, supra*, at 211, 129 S.Ct. 2504. Yet the dissent goes so far as to suggest instead that the preclearance requirement and disparate treatment of the States should be upheld into the future "unless there [is] no or almost no evidence of unconstitutional action by States." *Post*, at 2650.

In other ways as well, the dissent analyzes the question presented as if our decision in *Northwest Austin* never happened. For example, the dissent refuses to consider the principle of equal sovereignty, despite *Northwest Austin*'s emphasis on its significance. *Northwest Austin* also emphasized the "dramatic" progress since 1965, 557 U.S., at 201, 129 S.Ct. 2504, but the dissent describes current levels of discrimination as "flagrant," "widespread," and "pervasive," *post,* at 2636, 2641 (internal quotation marks omitted). Despite the fact that *Northwest Austin* requires an Act's "disparate geographic coverage" to be "sufficiently related" to its targeted problems, 557 U.S., at 203, 129 S.Ct. 2504, the dissent maintains that an Act's limited coverage actually eases Congress's burdens, and suggests that a fortuitous relationship should suffice. Although *Northwest Austin* stated definitively that "current burdens" must be justified by "current needs," *ibid.,* the dissent argues that the coverage formula can be justified by history, and that the required showing can be weaker on reenactment than when the law was first passed.

There is no valid reason to insulate the coverage formula from review merely because it was previously enacted 40 years ago. If Congress had started from scratch in 2006, it plainly could not have enacted the present coverage formula. It would have been irrational for Congress to distinguish between States in such a fundamental way based on 40-year-old data, when today's statistics tell an entirely different story. And it would have been irrational to base coverage on the use of voting tests 40 years ago, when such tests have been illegal since that time. But that is exactly what Congress has done.

3. Holding

Striking down an Act of Congress "is the gravest and most delicate duty that this Court is called on to perform." *Blodgett v. Holden,* 275 U.S. 142, 148, 48 S.Ct. 105, 72 L.Ed. 206 (1927) (Holmes, J., concurring). We do not do so lightly. That is why, in 2009, we took care to avoid ruling on the constitutionality of the Voting Rights Act when asked to do so, and instead resolved the case then before us on statutory grounds. But in issuing that decision, we expressed our broader concerns about the constitutionality of the Act. Congress could have updated the coverage formula at that time, but did not do so. Its failure to act leaves us today with no choice but to declare § 4(b) unconstitutional. The formula in that section can no longer be used as a basis for subjecting jurisdictions to preclearance.

Our decision in no way affects the permanent, nationwide ban on racial discrimination in voting found in § 2. We issue no holding on § 5 itself, only on the coverage formula. Congress may draft another formula based on current conditions. Such a formula is an initial prerequisite to a determination that exceptional conditions still exist justifying such an "extraordinary departure from the traditional course of relations between the States and the Federal Government." *Presley,* 502 U.S., at 500–501, 112 S.Ct. 820. Our country has changed, and while any racial discrimination in voting is too much, Congress must ensure that the legislation it passes to remedy that problem speaks to current conditions.

The judgment of the Court of Appeals is reversed.

It is so ordered.

4. Justice Ginsburg Dissenting

In the Court's view, the very success of § 5 of the Voting Rights Act demands its dormancy. Congress was of another mind. Recognizing that large progress has been made, Congress determined, based on a voluminous record, that the scourge of discrimination was not yet extirpated. The question this case presents is who decides whether, as currently operative, § 5 remains justifiable, this Court, or a Congress charged with the obligation to enforce the post-Civil War Amendments "by appropriate legislation." With overwhelming support in both Houses, Congress concluded that, for two prime reasons, § 5 should continue in force, unabated. First, continuance would facilitate completion of the impressive gains thus far made; and second, continuance would guard against backsliding. Those assessments were well within Congress' province to make and should elicit this Court's unstinting approbation.

"[V]oting discrimination still exists; no one doubts that." *Ante,* at 2619. But the Court today terminates the remedy that proved to be best suited to block that discrimination. The Voting Rights Act of 1965 (VRA) has worked to combat voting discrimination where other remedies had been tried and failed. Particularly effective is the VRA's requirement of federal preclearance for all changes to voting laws in the regions of the country with the most aggravated records of rank discrimination against minority voting rights.

A century after the Fourteenth and Fifteenth Amendments guaranteed citizens the right to vote free of discrimination on the basis of race, the "blight of racial discrimination in voting" continued to "infec[t] the electoral process in parts of our country." *South Carolina v. Katzenbach,* 383 U.S. 301, 308, 86 S.Ct. 803, 15 L.Ed.2d 769 (1966). Early attempts to cope with this vile infection resembled battling the Hydra. Whenever one form of voting discrimination was identified and prohibited, others sprang up in its place. This Court repeatedly encountered the remarkable "variety and persistence" of laws disenfranchising minority citizens. *Id.,* at 311, 86 S. Ct. 803. To take just one example, the Court, in 1927, held unconstitutional a Texas law barring black voters from participating in primary elections, *Nixon v. Herndon,* 273 U.S. 536, 541, 47 S.Ct. 446, 71 L.Ed. 759; in 1944, the Court struck down a "reenacted" and slightly altered version of the same law, *Smith v. Allwright,* 321 U.S. 649, 658, 64 S.Ct. 757, 88 L.Ed. 987; and in 1953, the Court once again confronted an attempt by Texas to "circumven[t]" the Fifteenth Amendment by adopting yet another variant of the all-white primary, *Terry v. Adams,* 345 U.S. 461, 469, 73 S.Ct. 809, 97 L.Ed. 1152.

During this era, the Court recognized that discrimination against minority voters was a quintessentially political problem requiring a political solution. As Justice Holmes explained: If "the great mass of the white population intends to keep the blacks from voting," "relief from [that] great political wrong, if done, as alleged, by the people of a State and the State itself, must be given by them or by the legislative and political department of the government of the United States." *Giles v. Harris,* 189 U.S. 475, 488, 23 S.Ct. 639, 47 L.Ed. 909 (1903).

Congress learned from experience that laws targeting particular electoral practices or enabling case-by-case litigation were inadequate to the task. In the Civil Rights Acts of 1957, 1960, and 1964, Congress authorized and then expanded the power of "the Attorney General to seek injunctions against public and private interference with the right to vote on racial grounds." *Katzenbach,* 383 U.S., at 313, 86 S. Ct. 803. But circumstances reduced the ameliorative potential of these legislative Acts:

> "Voting suits are unusually onerous to prepare, sometimes requiring as many as 6,000 man-hours spent combing through registration records in preparation for trial. Litigation has been exceedingly slow, in part because of the ample opportunities for delay afforded voting officials and others involved in the proceedings. Even when favorable decisions have finally been obtained, some of the States affected have merely switched to discriminatory devices not covered by the federal decrees or have enacted difficult new tests designed to prolong the existing disparity between white and Negro registration. Alternatively, certain local officials have defied and evaded court orders or have simply closed their registration offices to freeze the voting rolls." *Id.,* at 314, 86 S.Ct. 803 (footnote omitted).

Patently, a new approach was needed.

Answering that need, the Voting Rights Act became one of the most consequential, efficacious, and amply justified exercises of federal legislative power in our Nation's history. Requiring federal preclearance of changes in voting laws in the covered jurisdictions—those States and localities where opposition to the Constitution's commands were most virulent—the VRA provided a fit solution for minority voters as well as for States. Under the preclearance regime established by §5 of the VRA, covered jurisdictions must submit proposed changes in voting laws or procedures to the Department of Justice (DOJ), which has 60 days to respond to the changes. 79 Stat. 439, codified at 42 U.S.C. §1973c(a). A change will be approved unless DOJ finds it has "the purpose [or] . . . the effect of denying or abridging the right to vote on account of race or color." *Ibid.* In the alternative, the covered jurisdiction may seek approval by a three-judge District Court in the District of Columbia.

After a century's failure to fulfill the promise of the Fourteenth and Fifteenth Amendments, passage of the VRA finally led to signal improvement on this front. "The Justice Department estimated that in the five years after [the VRA's] passage, almost as many blacks registered [to vote] in Alabama, Mississippi, Georgia, Louisiana, North Carolina, and South Carolina as in the entire century before 1965." Davidson, The Voting Rights Act: A Brief History, in Controversies in Minority Voting 7, 21 (B. Grofman & C. Davidson eds. 1992). And in assessing the overall effects of the VRA in 2006, Congress found that "[s]ignificant progress has been made in eliminating first generation barriers experienced by minority voters, including increased numbers of registered minority voters, minority voter turn-out, and minority representation in Congress, State legislatures, and local elected offices. This progress is the direct result of the Voting Rights Act of 1965." Fannie Lou Hamer, Rosa Parks, and Coretta Scott King Voting Rights Act Reauthorization and Amendments Act of 2006 (hereinafter 2006 Reauthorization), § 2(b)(1), 120 Stat. 577. On that matter of cause and effects there can be no genuine doubt.

Although the VRA wrought dramatic changes in the realization of minority voting rights, the Act, to date, surely has not eliminated all vestiges of discrimination against the exercise of the franchise by minority citizens. Jurisdictions covered by the preclearance requirement continued to submit, in large numbers, proposed changes to voting laws that the Attorney General declined to approve, auguring that barriers to minority voting would quickly resurface were the preclearance remedy eliminated. *City of Rome v. United States,* 446 U.S. 156, 181, 100 S.Ct. 1548, 64 L. Ed.2d 119 (1980). Congress also found that as "registration and voting of minority citizens increas[ed], other measures may be resorted to which would dilute increasing minority voting strength." *Ibid.* (quoting H.R.Rep. No. 94–196, p. 10 (1975)). See also *Shaw v. Reno,* 509 U.S. 630, 640, 113 S.Ct. 2816, 125 L.Ed.2d 511 (1993) ("[I]t soon became apparent that guaranteeing equal access to the polls would not suffice to root out other racially discriminatory voting practices" such as voting dilution). Efforts to reduce the impact of minority votes, in contrast to direct attempts to block access to the ballot, are aptly described as "second-generation barriers" to minority voting.

Second-generation barriers come in various forms. One of the blockages is racial gerrymandering, the redrawing of legislative districts in an "effort to segregate the races for purposes of voting." *Id.,* at 642, 113 S.Ct. 2816. Another is adoption of a system of at-large voting in lieu of district-by-district voting in a city with a sizable black minority. By switching to at-large voting, the overall majority could control the election of each city council member, effectively eliminating the potency of the minority's votes. Grofman & Davidson, The Effect of Municipal Election Structure on Black Representation in Eight Southern States, in Quiet Revolution in the South 301, 319 (C. Davidson & B. Grofman eds. 1994) (hereinafter Quiet Revolution). A similar effect could be achieved if the city engaged in discriminatory annexation by incorporating majority-white areas into city limits, thereby decreasing the effect of VRA-occasioned increases in black voting. Whatever the device employed, this Court has long recognized that vote dilution, when adopted with a discriminatory purpose, cuts down the right to vote as certainly as denial of access to the ballot. *Shaw,* 509 U.S., at 640–641, 113 S.Ct. 2816; *Allen v. State Bd. of Elections,* 393 U.S. 544, 569, 89 S.Ct. 817, 22 L.Ed.2d 1 (1969); *Reynolds v. Sims,* 377 U.S. 533, 555, 84 S.Ct. 1362, 12 L.Ed.2d 506 (1964). See also H.R.Rep. No. 109–478, p. 6 (2006) (although "[d]iscrimination today is more subtle than the visible methods used in 1965," "the effect and results are the same, namely a diminishing of the minority community's ability to fully participate in the electoral process and to elect their preferred candidates").

In response to evidence of these substituted barriers, Congress reauthorized the VRA for five years in 1970, for seven years in 1975, and for 25 years in 1982. *Ante,* at 2620—2621. Each time, this Court upheld the reauthorization as a valid exercise of congressional power. *Ante,* at 2620. As the 1982 reauthorization approached its 2007 expiration date, Congress again considered whether the VRA's preclearance mechanism remained an appropriate response to the problem of voting discrimination in covered jurisdictions.

Congress did not take this task lightly. Quite the opposite. The 109th Congress that took responsibility for the renewal started early and conscientiously. In October 2005, the House began extensive hearings, which continued into November and resumed in March 2006. S.Rep. No. 109–295, p. 2 (2006). In April 2006, the Senate followed suit, with hearings of its own. *Ibid.* In May 2006, the bills that became the VRA's reauthorization were introduced in both Houses. *Ibid.* The House held further hearings of considerable length, as did the Senate, which continued to hold hearings into June and July. H.R. Rep. 109–478, at 5; S. Rep. 109–295, at 3–4. In mid-July, the House considered and rejected four amendments, then passed the reauthorization by a vote of 390 yeas to 33 nays. 152 Cong. Rec. H5207 (July 13, 2006); Persily, The Promise and Pitfalls of the New Voting Rights Act, 117 Yale L.J. 174, 182–183 (2007) (hereinafter Persily). The bill was read and debated in the Senate, where it passed by a vote of 98 to 0. 152 Cong. Rec. S8012 (July 20, 2006). President Bush signed it a week later, on July 27, 2006, recognizing the need for "further work . . . in the fight against injustice," and calling the reauthorization "an example of our continued commitment to a united America where every person is valued and treated with dignity and respect." 152 Cong. Rec. S8781 (Aug. 3, 2006).

In the long course of the legislative process, Congress "amassed a sizable record." *Northwest Austin Municipal Util. Dist. No. One v. Holder,* 557 U.S. 193, 205, 129 S. Ct. 2504, 174 L.Ed.2d 140 (2009). See also 679 F.3d 848, 865–873 (C.A.D.C.2012) (describing the "extensive record" supporting Congress' determination that "serious and widespread intentional discrimination persisted in covered jurisdictions"). The House and Senate Judiciary Committees held 21 hearings, heard from scores of witnesses, received a number of investigative reports and other written documentation of continuing discrimination in covered jurisdictions. In all, the legislative record Congress compiled filled more than 15,000 pages. H.R. Rep. 109–478, at 5, 11–12; S. Rep. 109–295, at 2–4, 15. The compilation presents countless "examples of flagrant racial discrimination" since the last reauthorization; Congress also brought to light systematic evidence that "intentional racial discrimination in voting remains so serious and widespread in covered jurisdictions that section 5 preclearance is still needed." 679 F.3d, at 866.

After considering the full legislative record, Congress made the following findings: The VRA has directly caused significant progress in eliminating first-generation barriers to ballot access, leading to a marked increase in minority voter registration and turnout and the number of minority elected officials. 2006 Reauthorization § 2(b)(1). But despite this progress, "second generation barriers constructed to prevent minority voters from fully participating in the electoral process" continued to exist, as well as racially polarized voting in the covered jurisdictions, which increased the political vulnerability of racial and language minorities in those jurisdictions. §§ 2(b)(2)–(3), 120 Stat. 577. Extensive "[e]vidence of continued discrimination," Congress concluded, "clearly show[ed] the continued need for Federal oversight" in covered jurisdictions. §§ 2(b)(4)–(5), *id.*, at 577–578. The overall record demonstrated to the federal lawmakers that, "without the continuation of the Voting Rights Act of 1965 protections, racial and language minority citizens will be deprived of the opportunity to exercise their right to vote, or will have their votes diluted, undermining the significant gains made by minorities in the last 40 years." § 2(b)(9), *id.*, at 578.

Based on these findings, Congress reauthorized preclearance for another 25 years, while also undertaking to reconsider the extension after 15 years to ensure that the provision was still necessary and effective. 42 U.S.C. § 1973b(a)(7), (8) (2006 ed., Supp. V). The question before the Court is whether Congress had the authority under the Constitution to act as it did.

In answering this question, the Court does not write on a clean slate. It is well established that Congress' judgment regarding exercise of its power to enforce the Fourteenth and Fifteenth Amendments warrants substantial deference. The VRA addresses the combination of race discrimination and the right to vote, which is "preservative of all rights." *Yick Wo v. Hopkins,* 118 U.S. 356, 370, 6 S.Ct. 1064, 30 L. Ed. 220 (1886). When confronting the most constitutionally invidious form of discrimination, and the most fundamental right in our democratic system, Congress' power to act is at its height.

The basis for this deference is firmly rooted in both constitutional text and precedent. The Fifteenth Amendment, which targets precisely and only racial discrimination in voting rights, states that, in this domain, "Congress shall have power to enforce this article by appropriate legislation." In choosing this language, the Amendment's framers invoked Chief Justice Marshall's formulation of the scope of Congress' powers under the Necessary and Proper Clause:

"Let the end be legitimate, let it be within the scope of the constitution, and *all means which are appropriate, which are plainly adapted to that end,* which are not prohibited, but consist with the letter and spirit of the constitution, are constitutional." *McCulloch v. Maryland,* 4 Wheat. 316, 421, 4 L.Ed. 579 (1819) (emphasis added).

It cannot tenably be maintained that the VRA, an Act of Congress adopted to shield the right to vote from racial discrimination, is inconsistent with the letter or spirit of the Fifteenth Amendment, or any provision of the Constitution read in light of the Civil War Amendments. Nowhere in today's opinion, or in *Northwest*

Austin, is there clear recognition of the transformative effect the Fifteenth Amendment aimed to achieve. Notably, "the Founders' first successful amendment told Congress that it could 'make no law' over a certain domain"; in contrast, the Civil War Amendments used "language [that] authorized transformative new federal statutes to uproot all vestiges of unfreedom and inequality" and provided "sweeping enforcement powers . . . to enact 'appropriate' legislation targeting state abuses." A. Amar, America's Constitution: A Biography 361, 363, 399 (2005). See also McConnell, Institutions and Interpretation: A Critique of *City of Boerne v. Flores,* 111 Harv.. 153, 182 (1997) (quoting Civil War-era framer that "the remedy for the violation of the fourteenth and fifteenth amendments was expressly not left to the courts. The remedy was legislative.").

The stated purpose of the Civil War Amendments was to arm Congress with the power and authority to protect all persons within the Nation from violations of their rights by the States. In exercising that power, then, Congress may use "all means which are appropriate, which are plainly adapted" to the constitutional ends declared by these Amendments. *McCulloch,* 4 Wheat., at 421. So when Congress acts to enforce the right to vote free from racial discrimination, we ask not whether Congress has chosen the means most wise, but whether Congress has rationally selected means appropriate to a legitimate end. "It is not for us to review the congressional resolution of [the need for its chosen remedy]. It is enough that we be able to perceive a basis upon which the Congress might resolve the conflict as it did." *Katzenbach v. Morgan,* 384 U.S. 641, 653, 86 S.Ct. 1717, 16 L.Ed.2d 828 (1966).

Until today, in considering the constitutionality of the VRA, the Court has accorded Congress the full measure of respect its judgments in this domain should garner. *South Carolina v. Katzenbach* supplies the standard of review: "As against the reserved powers of the States, Congress may use any rational means to effectuate the constitutional prohibition of racial discrimination in voting." 383 U.S., at 324, 86 S.Ct. 803. Faced with subsequent reauthorizations of the VRA, the Court has reaffirmed this standard. *E.g., City of Rome,* 446 U.S., at 178, 100 S.Ct. 1548. Today's Court does not purport to alter settled precedent establishing that the dispositive question is whether Congress has employed "rational means."

For three reasons, legislation *reauthorizing* an existing statute is especially likely to satisfy the minimal requirements of the rational-basis test. First, when reauthorization is at issue, Congress has already assembled a legislative record justifying the initial legislation. Congress is entitled to consider that preexisting record as well as the record before it at the time of the vote on reauthorization. This is especially true where, as here, the Court has repeatedly affirmed the statute's constitutionality and Congress has adhered to the very model the Court has upheld. See *id.,* at 174, 100 S. Ct. 1548 ("The appellants are asking us to do nothing less than overrule our decision in *South Carolina v. Katzenbach* . . . , in which we upheld the constitutionality of the Act."); *Lopez v. Monterey County,* 525 U.S. 266, 283, 119 S.Ct. 693, 142 L.Ed.2d 728 (1999) (similar).

Second, the very fact that reauthorization is necessary arises because Congress has built a temporal limitation into the Act. It has pledged to review, after a span of years (first 15, then 25) and in light of contemporary evidence, the continued need for the VRA. Cf. *Grutter v. Bollinger*, 539 U.S. 306, 343, 123 S.Ct. 2325, 156 L.Ed.2d 304 (2003) (anticipating, but not guaranteeing, that, in 25 years, "the use of racial preferences [in higher education] will no longer be necessary").

Third, a reviewing court should expect the record supporting reauthorization to be less stark than the record originally made. Demand for a record of violations equivalent to the one earlier made would expose Congress to a catch–22. If the statute was working, there would be less evidence of discrimination, so opponents might argue that Congress should not be allowed to renew the statute. In contrast, if the statute was not working, there would be plenty of evidence of discrimination, but scant reason to renew a failed regulatory regime. See Persily 193–194.

This is not to suggest that congressional power in this area is limitless. It is this Court's responsibility to ensure that Congress has used appropriate means. The question meet for judicial review is whether the chosen means are "adapted to carry out the objects the amendments have in view." *Ex parte Virginia*, 100 U.S. 339, 346, 25 L.Ed. 676 (1880). The Court's role, then, is not to substitute its judgment for that of Congress, but to determine whether the legislative record sufficed to show that "Congress could rationally have determined that [its chosen] provisions were appropriate methods." *City of Rome*, 446 U.S., at 176–177, 100 S.Ct. 1548.

In summary, the Constitution vests broad power in Congress to protect the right to vote, and in particular to combat racial discrimination in voting. This Court has repeatedly reaffirmed Congress' prerogative to use any rational means in exercise of its power in this area. And both precedent and logic dictate that the rational-means test should be easier to satisfy, and the burden on the statute's challenger should be higher, when what is at issue is the reauthorization of a remedy that the Court has previously affirmed, and that Congress found, from contemporary evidence, to be working to advance the legislature's legitimate objective. . . .

The number of discriminatory changes blocked or deterred by the preclearance requirement suggests that the state of voting rights in the covered jurisdictions would have been significantly different absent this remedy. Surveying the type of changes stopped by the preclearance procedure conveys a sense of the extent to which § 5 continues to protect minority voting rights. Set out below are characteristic examples of changes blocked in the years leading up to the 2006 reauthorization:

- In 1995, Mississippi sought to reenact a dual voter registration system, "which was initially enacted in 1892 to disenfranchise Black voters," and for that reason, was struck down by a federal court in 1987. H.R.Rep. No. 109–478, at 39.

- Following the 2000 census, the City of Albany, Georgia, proposed a redistricting plan that DOJ found to be "designed with the purpose to limit and retrogress the increased black voting strength . . . in the city as a whole." *Id.*, at 37 (internal quotation marks omitted).

- In 2001, the mayor and all-white five-member Board of Aldermen of Kilmichael, Mississippi, abruptly canceled the town's election after "an unprecedented number" of African-American candidates announced they were running for office. DOJ required an election, and the town elected its first black mayor and three black aldermen. *Id.*, at 36–37.

- In 2006, this Court found that Texas' attempt to redraw a congressional district to reduce the strength of Latino voters bore "the mark of intentional discrimination that could give rise to an equal protection violation," and ordered the district redrawn in compliance with the VRA. *League of United Latin American Citizens v. Perry*, 548 U.S. 399, 440 [126 S.Ct. 2594, 165 L.Ed.2d 609] (2006). In response, Texas sought to undermine this Court's order by curtailing early voting in the district, but was blocked by an action to enforce the § 5 preclearance requirement. See Order in *League of United Latin American Citizens v. Texas*, No. 06-cv-1046 (WD Tex.), Doc. 8.

- In 2003, after African-Americans won a majority of the seats on the school board for the first time in history, Charleston County, South Carolina, proposed an at-large voting mechanism for the board. The proposal, made without consulting any of the African-American members of the school board, was found to be an "'exact replica'" of an earlier voting scheme that, a federal court had determined, violated the VRA. 811 F.Supp.2d 424, 483 (D.D.C.2011). See also S.Rep. No. 109–295, at 309. DOJ invoked § 5 to block the proposal.

- In 1993, the City of Millen, Georgia, proposed to delay the election in a majority-black district by two years, leaving that district without representation on the city council while the neighboring majority-white district would have three representatives. 1 Section 5 Hearing 744. DOJ blocked the proposal. The county then sought to move a polling place from a predominantly black neighborhood in the city to an inaccessible location in a predominantly white neighborhood outside city limits. *Id.*, at 816.

- In 2004, Waller County, Texas, threatened to prosecute two black students after they announced their intention to run for office. The county then attempted to reduce the availability of early voting in that election at polling places near a historically black university. 679 F.3d, at 865–866.

- In 1990, Dallas County, Alabama, whose county seat is the City of Selma, sought to purge its voter rolls of many black voters. DOJ rejected the purge as discriminatory, noting that it would have disqualified many citizens from voting "simply because they failed to pick up or return a voter update form, when there was no valid requirement that they do so." 1 Section 5 Hearing 356.

These examples, and scores more like them, fill the pages of the legislative record. The evidence was indeed sufficient to support Congress' conclusion that "racial

discrimination in voting in covered jurisdictions [remained] serious and pervasive." 679 F.3d, at 865.

Justice Breyer, Justice Sotomayor, and Justice Kagan concur in the dissent.

P. Commentary on *Shelby*

F. Michael Higginbotham

Keynote Speech: A Letter From The Original Cause Lawyer

The Voting Rights Act is the most democratizing piece of legislation that has
ever been passed in the country. Four years after its passage, over 800,000 new voters were registered. Most of those newly registered were minority voters who had
never been able to vote before, who had never been able to participate in the American Democracy which had falsely guaranteed to them — in 1868 in the Fourteenth
Amendment and in 1870 in the Fifteenth Amendment — that right to so participate.
In the *Shelby* decision, the Supreme Court invalidated the coverage formula of the
Voting Rights Act. The formula that says the Federal Government will be able to
supervise the elections — state and local — where those districts have a history of
race discrimination and racial exclusion of blacks participating in the political process. As a result of federal government supervision, positive changes took place. Five
justices on the Justices said things have changed, times have changed in America
since 1965. Candidly, the Justices got it right when they said history did not stop in
1965. History did not stop in 1965, but they got it wrong when they said racism did
stop. History didn't stop in 1965, but neither did racism.

Now, it seems to me that the five Justices who think that racism is done suffer
from a rare disease. It is known as selective memory loss. That's a disease you often
times see manifest itself when folks owe you money. Yeah, they borrow some money
and they remember who won the 1903 World Series, right? But they can't remember
that they borrowed money from you, and come payday they owe it to you.

The majority in the Supreme Court seems not to be able to remember the literacy
tests, the poll taxes, and the violence perpetrated against individuals that tried to
help people to register to vote and were murdered for doing so. People like Viola
Liuzzo, Goodman Chaney, and Schwerner, and Medgar Evers. People that gave their
lives for our democratic process so that others could participate. The Court seems
to have forgotten that aspect. And, more significantly, once they forget, they are
prevented from seeing the similarities that continue to exist. Similarities in terms of
restrictions on same day registration and voting, on early voting, on three day voting, and on voter ID laws. Those laws that exist today, those laws that were passed
in a number of states right after *Shelby County* was announced. Two days after the
Shelby County decision, certain states imposed additional restrictions on voting
rights. Those restrictions have the same sort of impact as literacy tests and poll taxes
did during the Jim Crow era — devices that I (Thurgood Marshall) tried to stop
through litigation as an NAACP lawyer during the 1950s and early 1960s.

This letter articulates the author's best judgement as to what Justice Marshall might have felt and written had he been living today.

35 *LaVerne L.* Rev. 205, 212–214.

F. Michael Higginbotham

Congress must act to guard our most important right

The recent Supreme Court decision in *Shelby County v. Holder,* invalidating the "pre-clearance" formula of the Voting Rights Act—which required states with a history of race discrimination in voting to secure federal approval prior to changing election practices—provides an opportunity for Congress to strengthen protection of minority voting rights.

While discriminatory methods today are far from the lynch mobs and grandfather clauses that stopped blacks from voting during Jim Crow, the end result of voter suppression and dilution remains largely the same. Congress should act quickly and decisively on this core American principle in order to ensure minority participation in the democratic process.

Ernest Montgomery knows all too well the value of federal supervision in protecting minority voting rights. Prior to elections in 2008, the City of Calera, in Shelby County, Ala., redrew jurisdictional boundaries. This process eliminated the City Council's only majority-black district by adding several white subdivisions adjacent to Calera while refusing to incorporate a black area located nearby. The lone majority-black district was reduced from 70 to 30 percent black, resulting in the election loss of Montgomery, the only black city council member: The Justice Department would not approve the redistricting plan and, after extensive negotiations, Calera adopted a more inclusive at-large election system, one that prevented whites from controlling 100 percent of the six positions on the city council and that resulted in Montgomery receiving the most votes of all council candidates.

The Section 4 "pre-clearance" formula invalidated in the recent *Shelby County* decision is the same provision relied upon by the Justice Department to protect Montgomery from discriminatory treatment. Section 4 mandates that 15 states, including Alabama, or portions thereof, with a history of discriminatory voting laws get prior approval from the Department of Justice or a federal court for any changes to their election practices. In striking down Section 4, which had been overwhelmingly reauthorized by Congress for another 25 years in 2006, Chief Justice Roberts indicated that the formula must be "justified by current needs."

Certainly much progress has been made since 1965 when the VRA was passed. Yet today, racially-polarized voting patterns, the practice of reducing minority participation for partisan advantage in many parts of the nation, with blatant racism in others, suggest a continued need for an updated pre-clearance formula.

In 2011, the Justice Department stopped a Texas redistricting proposal determined by a federal court to purposefully discriminate against Latino voters. Last year, the Justice Department nixed a photo identification law in Texas. At the time, some 600,000 Texans who had voted in previous elections, many of whom were black and Latino, would have become ineligible to vote without additional identification. In each instance, Section 4 was used to prohibit discrimination.

Immediately after the Supreme Court invalidated the "pre-clearance" provision, Texas, and several other states, reinstated the voter identification laws previously prevented under Section 4, and other local jurisdictions promised to revisit prior invalidated practices.

Despite the problematic ruling, the Supreme Court left open the possibility that Congress could fix the formula. Congress should update it expeditiously. In doing so, legislators must understand that racism did not end in 1965 and that coverage based solely on geography would be outdated, as discriminatory acts occur throughout the country. With evidence of such serious and widespread suppression and dilution, an expanded and refocused formula is clearly "justified by current needs." Circumstances may have changed, but voter suppression, based on race, remains.

Orlando Sentinel A14 (August 16, 2013)
Copyright © (2013) F. Michael Higginbotham.
Reprinted with permission of F. Michael Higginbotham.

Q. Background on *Ricci*

While *Parents Involved* made it more difficult for school districts to achieve diversity, in particular schools identified as "racially isolated," and *Shelby County* made it more difficult for the federal government to prevent state and local government electoral practices that reduce minority voter participation, the question remained whether such a restrictive approach would apply to government employment decisions. Recent Supreme Court decisions such as *Adarand*, *Grutter*, *Parents Involved*, and *Shelby County* imposed restrictions on government initiatives to create racial diversity in business development, education, and the electoral process suggesting a trend to limit government race-conscious remedies in general.

Ricci v. DeStefano was a 2009 Supreme Court decision arising from a lawsuit brought against the City of New Haven, Connecticut by eighteen city firefighters alleging that the City of New Haven discriminated against them with respect to promotions. The firefighters, seventeen of whom were white and one of whom was Hispanic, had all passed the test for promotions to officer positions. City of New Haven officials invalidated the test results because none of the black firefighters who passed the exam had scored high enough to be considered for the positions, despite the fact that the qualified applicant pool was over twenty percent black. These officials claimed that they feared a lawsuit over the test's disparate impact on a protected minority under Title VII's statutory prohibition against employment decisions with a disparate impact on minorities. The non-minority complainants argued they were denied the promotions because of their race—in violation of federal anti-discrimination laws and the Equal Protection Clause of the Fourteenth Amendment. Efforts by the officials to avoid disparate impact on minorities resulted in a complaint, by non-minorities, of reverse discrimination.

R. *Ricci v. DeStefano*, 129 S. Ct. 2658 (2009)

1. Facts

Justice KENNEDY delivered the opinion of the Court.

In the fire department of New Haven, Connecticut—as in emergency-service agencies throughout the Nation—firefighters prize their promotion to and within the officer ranks. An agency's officers command respect within the department and in the whole community; and, of course, added responsibilities command increased salary and benefits. Aware of the intense competition for promotions, New Haven, like many cities, relies on objective examinations to identify the best qualified candidates.

In 2003, 118 New Haven firefighters took examinations to qualify for promotion to the rank of lieutenant or captain. Promotion examinations in New Haven were infrequent, so the stakes were high. The results would determine which firefighters would be considered for promotions during the next two years, and the order in which they would be considered. Many firefighters studied for months, at considerable personal and financial cost.

When the examination results showed that white candidates had outperformed minority candidates, the mayor and other local politicians opened a public debate that turned rancorous. Some firefighters argued the tests should be discarded because the results showed the tests to be discriminatory. They threatened a discrimination lawsuit if the City made promotions based on the tests. Other firefighters said the exams were neutral and fair. And they, in turn, threatened a discrimination lawsuit if the City, relying on the statistical racial disparity, ignored the test results and denied promotions to the candidates who had performed well. In the end the City took the side of those who protested the test results. It threw out the examinations.

Certain white and Hispanic firefighters who likely would have been promoted based on their good test performance sued the City and some of its officials. Theirs is the suit now before us. The suit alleges that, by discarding the test results, the City and the named officials discriminated against the plaintiffs based on their race, in violation of both Title VII of the Civil Rights Act of 1964, 78 Stat. 253, as amended, 42 U.S.C. § 2000e *et seq.*, and the Equal Protection Clause of the Fourteenth Amendment. The City and the officials defended their actions, arguing that if they had certified the results, they could have faced liability under Title VII for adopting a practice that had a disparate impact on the minority firefighters. The District Court granted summary judgment for the defendants, and the Court of Appeals affirmed.

We conclude that race-based action like the City's in this case is impermissible under Title VII unless the employer can demonstrate a strong basis in evidence that, had it not taken the action, it would have been liable under the disparate-impact statute. The respondents, we further determine, cannot meet that threshold standard. As a result, the City's action in discarding the tests was a violation of Title VII. In light of our ruling under the statutes, we need not reach the question whether respondents' actions may have violated the Equal Protection Clause.

2. Opinion

Petitioners raise a statutory claim, under the disparate-treatment prohibition of Title VII, and a constitutional claim, under the Equal Protection Clause of the Fourteenth Amendment. A decision for petitioners on their statutory claim would provide the relief sought, so we consider it first. See *Atkins v. Parker,* 472 U.S. 115, 123, 105 S.Ct. 2520, 86 L.Ed.2d 81 (1985); *Escambia County v. McMillan,* 466 U.S. 48, 51, 104 S.Ct. 1577, 80 L.Ed.2d 36 (1984) *(per curiam)* ("[N]ormally the Court will not decide a constitutional question if there is some other ground upon which to dispose of the case").

Title VII of the Civil Rights Act of 1964, 42 U.S.C. § 2000e *et seq.,* as amended, prohibits employment discrimination on the basis of race, color, religion, sex, or national origin. Title VII prohibits both intentional discrimination (known as "disparate treatment") as well as, in some cases, practices that are not intended to discriminate but in fact have a disproportionately adverse effect on minorities (known as "disparate impact").

As enacted in 1964, Title VII's principal nondiscrimination provision held employers liable only for disparate treatment. That section retains its original wording today. It makes it unlawful for an employer "to fail or refuse to hire or to discharge any individual, or otherwise to discriminate against any individual with respect to his compensation, terms, conditions, or privileges of employment, because of such individual's race, color, religion, sex, or national origin." § 2000e-2(a)(1); see also 78 Stat. 255. Disparate-treatment cases present "the most easily understood type of discrimination," *Teamsters v. United States,* 431 U.S. 324, 335, n. 15, 97 S.Ct. 1843, 52 L.Ed.2d 396 (1977), and occur where an employer has "treated [a] particular person less favorably than others because of" a protected trait. *Watson v. Fort Worth Bank & Trust,* 487 U.S. 977, 985–986, 108 S.Ct. 2777, 101 L.Ed.2d 827 (1988). A disparate-treatment plaintiff must establish "that the defendant had a discriminatory intent or motive" for taking a job-related action. *Id.,* at 986, 108 S.Ct. 2777.

The Civil Rights Act of 1964 did not include an express prohibition on policies or practices that produce a disparate impact. But in *Griggs v. Duke Power Co.,* 401 U.S. 424, 91 S.Ct. 849, 28 L.Ed.2d 158 (1971), the Court interpreted the Act to prohibit, in some cases, employers' facially neutral practices that, in fact, are "discriminatory in operation." *Id.,* at 431, 91 S.Ct. 849. The *Griggs* Court stated that the "touchstone" for disparate-impact liability is the lack of "business necessity": "If an employment practice which operates to exclude [minorities] cannot be shown to be related to job performance, the practice is prohibited." *Ibid.;* see also *id.*, at 432, 91 S.Ct. 849 (employer's burden to demonstrate that practice has "a manifest relationship to the employment in question"); *Albemarle Paper Co. v. Moody,* 422 U.S. 405, 425, 95 S.Ct. 2362, 45 L.Ed.2d 280 (1975). Under those precedents, if an employer met its burden by showing that its practice was job-related, the plaintiff was required to show a legitimate alternative that would have resulted in less discrimination. *7920Ibid.* (allowing complaining party to show "that other tests or selection devices, without a similarly undesirable racial effect, would also serve the employer's legitimate interest").

Twenty years after *Griggs,* the Civil Rights Act of 1991, 105 Stat. 1071, was enacted. The Act included a provision codifying the prohibition on disparate-impact discrimination. That provision is now in force along with the disparate-treatment section already noted. Under the disparate-impact statute, a plaintiff establishes a prima facie violation by showing that an employer uses "a particular employment practice that causes a disparate impact on the basis of race, color, religion, sex, or national origin." 42 U.S.C. § 2000e-2(k)(1)(A)(i). An employer may defend against liability by demonstrating that the practice is "job related for the position in question and consistent with business necessity." *Ibid.* Even if the employer meets that burden, however, a plaintiff may still succeed by showing that the employer refuses to adopt an available alternative employment practice that has less disparate impact and serves the employer's legitimate needs. §§ 2000e-2(k)(1)(A)(ii) and (C).

Petitioners allege that when the CSB refused to certify the captain and lieutenant exam results based on the race of the successful candidates, it discriminated against them in violation of Title VII's disparate-treatment provision. The City counters that its decision was permissible because the tests "appear[ed] to violate Title VII's disparate-impact provisions."

Our analysis begins with this premise: The City's actions would violate the disparate-treatment prohibition of Title VII absent some valid defense. All the evidence demonstrates that the City chose not to certify the examination results because of the statistical disparity based on race—*i.e.,* how minority candidates had performed when compared to white candidates. As the District Court put it, the City rejected the test results because "too many whites and not enough minorities would be promoted were the lists to be certified." 554 F.Supp.2d, at 152; see also *ibid.* (respondents' "own arguments . . . show that the City's reasons for advocating non-certification were related to the racial distribution of the results"). Without some other justification, this express, race-based decisionmaking violates Title VII's command that employers cannot take adverse employment actions because of an individual's race. See § 2000e-2(a)(1).

The District Court did not adhere to this principle, however. It held that respondents' "motivation to avoid making promotions based on a test with a racially disparate impact . . . does not, as a matter of law, constitute discriminatory intent." 554 F. Supp.2d, at 160. And the Government makes a similar argument in this Court. It contends that the "structure of Title VII belies any claim that an employer's intent to comply with Title VII's disparate-impact provisions constitutes prohibited discrimination on the basis of race." Brief for United States as *Amicus Curiae* 11. But both of those statements turn upon the City's objective—avoiding disparate-impact liability—while ignoring the City's conduct in the name of reaching that objective. Whatever the City's ultimate aim—however well intentioned or benevolent it might have seemed—the City made its employment decision because of race. The City rejected the test results solely because the higher scoring candidates were white. The question is not whether that conduct was discriminatory but whether the City had a lawful justification for its race-based action.

We consider, therefore, whether the purpose to avoid disparate-impact liability excuses what otherwise would be prohibited disparate-treatment discrimination. Courts often confront cases in which statutes and principles point in different directions. Our task is to provide guidance to employers and courts for situations when these two prohibitions could be in conflict absent a rule to reconcile them. In providing this guidance our decision must be consistent with the important purpose of Title VII—that the workplace be an environment free of discrimination, where race is not a barrier to opportunity.

With these principles in mind, we turn to the parties' proposed means of reconciling the statutory provisions. Petitioners take a strict approach, arguing that under Title VII, it cannot be permissible for an employer to take race-based adverse employment actions in order to avoid disparate-impact liability—even if the employer knows its practice violates the disparate-impact provision. See Brief for Petitioners 43. Petitioners would have us hold that, under Title VII, avoiding unintentional discrimination cannot justify intentional discrimination. That assertion, however, ignores the fact that, by codifying the disparate-impact provision in 1991, Congress has expressly prohibited both types of discrimination. We must interpret the statute to give effect to both provisions where possible. See, *e.g., United States v. Atlantic Research Corp.,* 551 U.S. 128, 137, 127 S.Ct. 2331, 168 L.Ed.2d 28 (2007) (rejecting an interpretation that would render a statutory provision "a dead letter"). We cannot accept petitioners' broad and inflexible formulation.

Petitioners next suggest that an employer in fact must be in violation of the disparate-impact provision before it can use compliance as a defense in a disparate-treatment suit. Again, this is overly simplistic and too restrictive of Title VII's purpose. The rule petitioners offer would run counter to what we have recognized as Congress's intent that "voluntary compliance" be "the preferred means of achieving the objectives of Title VII." *Firefighters v. Cleveland,* 478 U.S. 501, 515, 106 S.Ct. 3063, 92 L.Ed.2d 405 (1986); see also *Wygant v. Jackson Bd. of Ed.,* 476 U.S. 267, 290, 106 S. Ct. 1842, 90 L.Ed.2d 260 (1986) (O'Connor, J., concurring in part and concurring in judgment). Forbidding employers to act unless they know, with certainty, that a practice violates the disparate-impact provision would bring compliance efforts to a near standstill. Even in the limited situations when this restricted standard could be met, employers likely would hesitate before taking voluntary action for fear of later being proven wrong in the course of litigation and then held to account for disparate treatment.

At the opposite end of the spectrum, respondents and the Government assert that an employer's good-faith belief that its actions are necessary to comply with Title VII's disparate-impact provision should be enough to justify race-conscious conduct. But the original, foundational prohibition of Title VII bars employers from taking adverse action "because of . . . race." §2000e-2(a)(1). And when Congress codified the disparate-impact provision in 1991, it made no exception to disparate-treatment liability for actions taken in a good-faith effort to comply with the new, disparate-impact provision in subsection (k). Allowing employers to violate the disparate-treatment prohibition based on a mere good-faith fear of disparate-impact liability would encourage race-based action at the slightest hint of disparate impact. A minimal standard could cause employers to discard the results of lawful and beneficial promotional examinations even where there is little if any evidence of disparate-impact discrimination. That would amount to a *de facto* quota system, in which a "focus on statistics . . . could put undue pressure on employers to adopt inappropriate prophylactic measures." *Watson*, 487 U.S., at 992, 108 S.Ct. 2777 (plurality opinion). Even worse, an employer could discard test results (or other employment practices) with the intent of obtaining the employer's preferred racial balance. That operational principle could not be justified, for Title VII is express in disclaiming any interpretation of its requirements as calling for outright racial balancing. §2000e-2(j). The purpose of Title VII "is to promote hiring on the basis of job qualifications, rather than on the basis of race or color." *Griggs*, 401 U.S., at 434, 91 S.Ct. 849.

In searching for a standard that strikes a more appropriate balance, we note that this Court has considered cases similar to this one, albeit in the context of the Equal Protection Clause of the Fourteenth Amendment. The Court has held that certain government actions to remedy past racial discrimination—actions that are themselves based on race—are constitutional only where there is a "'strong basis in evidence'" that the remedial actions were necessary. *Richmond v. J.A. Croson Co.*, 488 U.S. 469, 500, 109 S.Ct. 706, 102 L.Ed.2d 854 (1989) (quoting *Wygant, supra*, at 277, 106 S.Ct. 1842 (plurality opinion)). This suit does not call on us to consider whether the statutory constraints under Title VII must be parallel in all respects to those under the Constitution. That does not mean the constitutional authorities are irrelevant, however. Our cases discussing constitutional principles can provide helpful guidance in this statutory context. See *Watson, supra*, at 993, 108 S.Ct. 2777 (plurality opinion).

Writing for a plurality in *Wygant* and announcing the strong-basis-in-evidence standard, Justice Powell recognized the tension between eliminating segregation and discrimination on the one hand and doing away with all governmentally imposed discrimination based on race on the other. 476 U.S., at 277, 106 S.Ct. 1842. The plurality stated that those "related constitutional duties are not always harmonious," and that "reconciling them requires . . . employers to act with extraordinary care." *Ibid.* The plurality required a strong basis in evidence because "[e]videntiary support for the conclusion that remedial action is warranted becomes crucial when the remedial program is challenged in court by nonminority employees." *Ibid.* The Court applied the same standard in *Croson,* observing that "an amorphous claim that there has been past discrimination . . . cannot justify the use of an unyielding racial quota." 488 U.S., at 499, 109 S.Ct. 706.

The same interests are at work in the interplay between the disparate-treatment and disparate-impact provisions of Title VII. Congress has imposed liability on employers for unintentional discrimination in order to rid the workplace of "practices that are fair in form, but discriminatory in operation." *Griggs, supra,* at 431, 91 S.Ct. 849. But it has also prohibited employers from taking adverse employment actions "because of" race. § 2000e-2(a)(1). Applying the strong-basis-in-evidence standard to Title VII gives effect to both the disparate-treatment and disparate-impact provisions, allowing violations of one in the name of compliance with the other only in certain, narrow circumstances. The standard leaves ample room for employers' voluntary compliance efforts, which are essential to the statutory scheme and to Congress's efforts to eradicate workplace discrimination. See *Firefighters, supra,* at 515. And the standard appropriately constrains employers' discretion in making race-based decisions: It limits that discretion to cases in which there is a strong basis in evidence of disparate-impact liability, but it is not so restrictive that it allows employers to act only when there is a provable, actual violation.

Resolving the statutory conflict in this way allows the disparate-impact prohibition to work in a manner that is consistent with other provisions of Title VII, including the prohibition on adjusting employment-related test scores on the basis of race. See § 2000e-2(*l*). Examinations like those administered by the City create legitimate expectations on the part of those who took the tests. As is the case with any promotion exam, some of the firefighters here invested substantial time, money, and personal commitment in preparing for the tests. Employment tests can be an important part of a neutral selection system that safeguards against the very racial animosities Title VII was intended to prevent. Here, however, the firefighters saw their efforts invalidated by the City in sole reliance upon race-based statistics.

If an employer cannot rescore a test based on the candidates' race, § 2000e-2(*l*), then it follows *a fortiori* that it may not take the greater step of discarding the test altogether to achieve a more desirable racial distribution of promotion — eligible candidates — absent a strong basis in evidence that the test was deficient and that discarding the results is necessary to avoid violating the disparate-impact provision. Restricting an employer's ability to discard test results (and thereby discriminate against qualified candidates on the basis of their race) also is in keeping with Title VII's express protection of bona fide promotional examinations. See § 2000e-2(h) ("[N]or shall it be an unlawful employment practice for an employer to give and to act upon the results of any professionally developed ability test provided that such test, its administration or action upon the results is not designed, intended or used to discriminate because of race"); cf. *AT & T Corp. v. Hulteen,* 129 S.Ct. 1962, 1970, 173 L.Ed.2d 898 (2009).

For the foregoing reasons, we adopt the strong-basis-in-evidence standard as a matter of statutory construction to resolve any conflict between the disparate-treatment and disparate-impact provisions of Title VII.

Our statutory holding does not address the constitutionality of the measures taken here in purported compliance with Title VII. We also do not hold that meeting the strong-basis-in-evidence standard would satisfy the Equal Protection Clause in a future case. As we explain below, because respondents have not met their burden under Title VII, we need not decide whether a legitimate fear of disparate impact is ever sufficient to justify discriminatory treatment under the Constitution.

Nor do we question an employer's affirmative efforts to ensure that all groups have a fair opportunity to apply for promotions and to participate in the process by which promotions will be made. But once that process has been established and employers have made clear their selection criteria, they may not then invalidate the test results, thus upsetting an employee's legitimate expectation not to be judged on the basis of race. Doing so, absent a strong basis in evidence of an impermissible disparate impact, amounts to the sort of racial preference that Congress has disclaimed, § 2000e-2(j), and is antithetical to the notion of a workplace where individuals are guaranteed equal opportunity regardless of race.

Title VII does not prohibit an employer from considering, before administering a test or practice, how to design that test or practice in order to provide a fair opportunity for all individuals, regardless of their race. And when, during the test-design stage, an employer invites comments to ensure the test is fair, that process can provide a common ground for open discussions toward that end. We hold only that, under Title VII, before an employer can engage in intentional discrimination for the asserted purpose of avoiding or remedying an unintentional disparate impact, the employer must have a strong basis in evidence to believe it will be subject to disparate-impact liability if it fails to take the race-conscious, discriminatory action.

The City argues that, even under the strong-basis-in-evidence standard, its decision to discard the examination results was permissible under Title VII. That is incorrect. Even if respondents were motivated as a subjective matter by a desire to avoid committing disparate-impact discrimination, the record makes clear there is no support for the conclusion that respondents had an objective, strong basis in evidence to find the tests inadequate, with some consequent disparate-impact liability in violation of Title VII.

On this basis, we conclude that petitioners have met their obligation to demonstrate that there is "no genuine issue as to any material fact" and that they are "entitled to judgment as a matter of law." Fed. Rule Civ. Proc. 56(c). On a motion for summary judgment, "facts must be viewed in the light most favorable to the nonmoving party only if there is a 'genuine' dispute as to those facts." *Scott v. Harris,* 550 U.S. 372, 380, 127 S.Ct. 1769, 167 L.Ed.2d 686 (2007). "Where the record taken as a whole could not lead a rational trier of fact to find for the nonmoving party, there is no genuine issue for trial." *Matsushita Elec. Industrial Co. v. Zenith Radio*

Corp., 475 U.S. 574, 587, 106 S.Ct. 1348, 89 L.Ed.2d 538 (1986) (internal quotation marks omitted). In this Court, the City's only defense is that it acted to comply with Title VII's disparate-impact provision. To succeed on their motion, then, petitioners must demonstrate that there can be no genuine dispute that there was no strong basis in evidence for the City to conclude it would face disparate-impact liability if it certified the examination results. See *Celotex Corp. v. Catrett,* 477 U.S. 317, 324, 106 S.Ct. 2548, 91 L.Ed.2d 265 (1986) (where the nonmoving party "will bear the burden of proof at trial on a dispositive issue," the nonmoving party bears the burden of production under Rule 56 to "designate specific facts showing that there is a genuine issue for trial" (internal quotation marks omitted)).

The racial adverse impact here was significant, and petitioners do not dispute that the City was faced with a prima facie case of disparate-impact liability. On the captain exam, the pass rate for white candidates was 64 percent but was 37.5 percent for both black and Hispanic candidates. On the lieutenant exam, the pass rate for white candidates was 58.1 percent; for black candidates, 31.6 percent; and for Hispanic candidates, 20 percent. The pass rates of minorities, which were approximately one-half the pass rates for white candidates, fall well below the 80-percent standard set by the EEOC to implement the disparate-impact provision of Title VII. See 29 CFR § 1607.4(D) (2008) (selection rate that is less than 80 percent "of the rate for the group with the highest rate will generally be regarded by the Federal enforcement agencies as evidence of adverse impact"); *Watson,* 487 U.S., at 995–996, n. 3, 108 S.Ct. 2777 (plurality opinion) (EEOC's 80-percent standard is "a rule of thumb for the courts"). Based on how the passing candidates ranked and an application of the "rule of three," certifying the examinations would have meant that the City could not have considered black candidates for any of the then-vacant lieutenant or captain positions.

Based on the degree of adverse impact reflected in the results, respondents were compelled to take a hard look at the examinations to determine whether certifying the results would have had an impermissible disparate impact. The problem for respondents is that a prima facie case of disparate-impact liability—essentially, a threshold showing of a significant statistical disparity, *Connecticut v. Teal,* 457 U.S. 440, 446, 102 S.Ct. 2525, 73 L.Ed.2d 130 (1982), and nothing more—is far from a strong basis in evidence that the City would have been liable under Title VII had it certified the results. That is because the City could be liable for disparate-impact discrimination only if the examinations were not job related and consistent with business necessity, or if there existed an equally valid, less-discriminatory alternative that served the City's needs but that the City refused to adopt. § 2000e-2(k)(1) (A), (C). We conclude there is no strong basis in evidence to establish that the test was deficient in either of these respects. We address each of the two points in turn, based on the record developed by the parties through discovery—a record that concentrates in substantial part on the statements various witnesses made to the CSB.

There is no genuine dispute that the examinations were job-related and consistent with business necessity. The City's assertions to the contrary are "blatantly contradicted by the record." *Scott, supra,* at 380, 127 S.Ct. 1769. The CSB heard statements from Chad Legel (the IOS vice president) as well as city officials outlining the detailed steps IOS took to develop and administer the examinations. IOS devised the written examinations, which were the focus of the CSB's inquiry, after painstaking analyses of the captain and lieutenant positions—analyses in which IOS made sure that minorities were overrepresented. And IOS drew the questions from source material approved by the Department. Of the outside witnesses who appeared before the CSB, only one, Vincent Lewis, had reviewed the examinations in any detail, and he was the only one with any firefighting experience. Lewis stated that the "questions were relevant for both exams." CA2 App. A1053. The only other witness who had seen any part of the examinations, Christopher Hornick (a competitor of IOS's), criticized the fact that no one within the Department had reviewed the tests—a condition imposed by the City to protect the integrity of the exams in light of past alleged security breaches. But Hornick stated that the exams "appea[r] to be . . . reasonably good" and recommended that the CSB certify the results. *Id.,* at A1041.

Arguing that the examinations were not job-related, respondents note some candidates' complaints that certain examination questions were contradictory or did not specifically apply to firefighting practices in New Haven. But Legel told the CSB that IOS had addressed those concerns—that it entertained "a handful" of challenges to the validity of particular examination questions, that it "reviewed those challenges and provided feedback [to the City] as to what we thought the best course of action was," and that he could remember at least one question IOS had thrown out ("offer[ing] credit to everybody for that particular question"). *Id.,* at A955–A957. For his part, Hornick said he "suspect[ed] that some of the criticisms . . . [leveled] by candidates" were not valid. *Id.,* at A1035.

The City, moreover, turned a blind eye to evidence that supported the exams' validity. Although the City's contract with IOS contemplated that IOS would prepare a technical report consistent with EEOC guidelines for examination-validity studies, the City made no request for its report. After the January 2004 meeting between Legel and some of the city-official respondents, in which Legel defended the examinations, the City sought no further information from IOS, save its appearance at a CSB meeting to explain how it developed and administered the examinations. IOS stood ready to provide respondents with detailed information to establish the validity of the exams, but respondents did not accept that offer.

Respondents also lacked a strong basis in evidence of an equally valid, less-discriminatory testing alternative that the City, by certifying the examination results, would necessarily have refused to adopt. Respondents raise three arguments to the contrary, but each argument fails. First, respondents refer to testimony before the CSB that a different composite-score calculation—weighting the written and oral examination scores 30/70—would have allowed the City to consider two black candidates for then-open lieutenant positions and one black candidate for then-open captain positions. (The City used a 60/40 weighting as required by its contract with the New Haven firefighters' union.) But respondents have produced no evidence to show that the 60/40 weighting was indeed arbitrary. In fact, because that formula was the result of a union-negotiated collective-bargaining agreement, we presume the parties negotiated that weighting for a rational reason. Nor does the record contain any evidence that the 30/70 weighting would be an equally valid way to determine whether candidates possess the proper mix of job knowledge and situational skills to earn promotions. Changing the weighting formula, moreover, could well have violated Title VII's prohibition of altering test scores on the basis of race. See § 2000e-2(l). On this record, there is no basis to conclude that a 30/70 weighting was an equally valid alternative the City could have adopted.

Second, respondents argue that the City could have adopted a different interpretation of the "rule of three" that would have produced less discriminatory results. The rule, in the New Haven city charter, requires the City to promote only from "those applicants with the three highest scores" on a promotional examination. New Haven, Conn., Code of Ordinances, Tit. I, Art. XXX, § 160 (1992). A state court has interpreted the charter to prohibit so-called "banding"—the City's previous practice of rounding scores to the nearest whole number and considering all candidates with the same whole-number score as being of one rank. Banding allowed the City to consider three ranks of candidates (with the possibility of multiple candidates filling each rank) for purposes of the rule of three. See *Kelly v. New Haven,* No. CV000444614, 2004 WL 114377, *3 (Conn.Super.Ct., Jan.9, 2004). Respondents claim that employing banding here would have made four black and one Hispanic candidates eligible for then-open lieutenant and captain positions.

A state court's prohibition of banding, as a matter of municipal law under the charter, may not eliminate banding as a valid alternative under Title VII. See 42 U.S.C. § 2000e-7. We need not resolve that point, however. Here, banding was not a valid alternative for this reason: Had the City reviewed the exam results and then adopted banding to make the minority test scores appear higher, it would have violated Title VII's prohibition of adjusting test results on the basis of race. § 2000e-2(l); see also *Chicago Firefighters Local 2 v. Chicago,* 249 F.3d 649, 656 (C.A.7 2001) (Posner, J.) ("We have no doubt that if banding were adopted in order to make lower black scores seem higher, it would indeed be . . . forbidden"). As a matter of law, banding was not an alternative available to the City when it was considering whether to certify the examination results.

Third, and finally, respondents refer to statements by Hornick in his telephone interview with the CSB regarding alternatives to the written examinations. Hornick stated his "belie[f]" that an "assessment center process," which would have evaluated candidates' behavior in typical job tasks, "would have demonstrated less adverse impact." CA2 App. A1039. But Hornick's brief mention of alternative testing methods, standing alone, does not raise a genuine issue of material fact that assessment centers were available to the City at the time of the examinations and that they would have produced less adverse impact. Other statements to the CSB indicated that the Department could not have used assessment centers for the 2003 examinations. *Supra,* at 2670. And although respondents later argued to the CSB that

Hornick had pushed the City to reject the test results, *supra,* at 2671–2672, the truth is that the essence of Hornick's remarks supported its certifying the test results. See *Scott,* 550 U.S., at 380, 127 S.Ct. 1769. Hornick stated that adverse impact in standardized testing "has been in existence since the beginning of testing," CA2 App. A1037, and that the disparity in New Haven's test results was "somewhat higher but generally in the range that we've seen professionally." *Id.,* at A1030–A1031. He told the CSB he was "not suggesting" that IOS "somehow created a test that had adverse impacts that it should not have had." *Id.,* at A1038. And he suggested that the CSB should "certify the list as it exists." *Id.,* at A1041.

Especially when it is noted that the strong-basis-in-evidence standard applies, respondents cannot create a genuine issue of fact based on a few stray (and contradictory) statements in the record. And there is no doubt respondents fall short of the mark by relying entirely on isolated statements by Hornick. Hornick had not "stud[ied] the test at length or in detail." *Id.,* at A1030. And as he told the CSB, he is a "direct competitor" of IOS's. *Id.,* at A1029. The remainder of his remarks showed that Hornick's primary concern—somewhat to the frustration of CSB members—was marketing his services for the future, not commenting on the results of the tests the City had already administered. See, *e.g., id.,* at A1026, A1027, A1032, A1036, A1040, A1041. Hornick's hinting had its intended effect: The City has since hired him as a consultant. As for the other outside witnesses who spoke to the CSB, Vincent Lewis (the retired fire captain) thought the CSB should certify the results. And Janet Helms (the Boston College professor) declined to review the examinations and told the CSB that, as a society, "we need to develop a new way of assessing people." *Id.,* at A1073. That task was beyond the reach of the CSB, which was concerned with the adequacy of the test results before it.

On the record before us, there is no genuine dispute that the City lacked a strong basis in evidence to believe it would face disparate-impact liability if it certified the examination results. In other words, there is no evidence—let alone the required strong basis in evidence—that the tests were flawed because they were not job-related or because other, equally valid and less discriminatory tests were available to the City. Fear of litigation alone cannot justify an employer's reliance on race to the detriment of individuals who passed the examinations and qualified for promotions. The City's discarding the test results was impermissible under Title VII, and summary judgment is appropriate for petitioners on their disparate-treatment claim.

The record in this litigation documents a process that, at the outset, had the potential to produce a testing procedure that was true to the promise of Title VII: No individual should face workplace discrimination based on race. Respondents thought about promotion qualifications and relevant experience in neutral ways. They were careful to ensure broad racial participation in the design of the test itself and its administration. As we have discussed at length, the process was open and fair.

The problem, of course, is that after the tests were completed, the raw racial results became the predominant rationale for the City's refusal to certify the results. The injury arises in part from the high, and justified, expectations of the candidates who had participated in the testing process on the terms the City had established for the promotional process. Many of the candidates had studied for months, at considerable personal and financial expense, and thus the injury caused by the City's reliance on raw racial statistics at the end of the process was all the more severe. Confronted with arguments both for and against certifying the test results—and threats of a lawsuit either way—the City was required to make a difficult inquiry. But its hearings produced no strong evidence of a disparate-impact violation, and the City was not entitled to disregard the tests based solely on the racial disparity in the results.

3. Holding

Our holding today clarifies how Title VII applies to resolve competing expectations under the disparate-treatment and disparate-impact provisions. If, after it certifies the test results, the City faces a disparate-impact suit, then in light of our holding today it should be clear that the City would avoid disparate-impact liability based on the strong basis in evidence that, had it not certified the results, it would have been subject to disparate-treatment liability.

Petitioners are entitled to summary judgment on their Title VII claim, and we therefore need not decide the underlying constitutional question. The judgment of the Court of Appeals is reversed, and the cases are remanded for further proceedings consistent with this opinion.

4. Justice Ginsburg Dissenting

In assessing claims of race discrimination, "[c]ontext matters." *Grutter v. Bollinger,* 539 U.S. 306, 327, 123 S.Ct. 2325, 156 L.Ed.2d 304 (2003). In 1972, Congress extended Title VII of the Civil Rights Act of 1964 to cover public employment. At that time, municipal fire departments across the country, including New Haven's, pervasively discriminated against minorities. The extension of Title VII to cover jobs in firefighting effected no overnight change. It took decades of persistent effort, advanced by Title VII litigation, to open firefighting posts to members of racial minorities.

The white firefighters who scored high on New Haven's promotional exams understandably attract this Court's sympathy. But they had no vested right to promotion. Nor have other persons received promotions in preference to them. New Haven maintains that it refused to certify the test results because it believed, for good cause, that it would be vulnerable to a Title VII disparate-impact suit if it relied on those results. The Court today holds that New Haven has not demonstrated "a strong basis in evidence" for its plea. *Ante,* at 2664. In so holding, the Court pretends that "[t]he City rejected the test results solely because the higher scoring candidates were white." *Ante,* at 2674. That pretension, essential to the Court's disposition, ignores substantial evidence of multiple flaws in the tests New Haven used. The Court similarly fails to acknowledge the better tests used in other cities, which have yielded less racially skewed outcomes. . . .

By order of this Court, New Haven, a city in which African-Americans and His-panics account for nearly 60 percent of the population, must today be served—as it was in the days of undisguised discrimination—by a fire department in which members of racial and ethnic minorities are rarely seen in command positions. In arriving at its order, the Court barely acknowledges the pathmarking decision in *Griggs v. Duke Power Co.*, 401 U.S. 424, 91 S.Ct. 849, 28 L.Ed.2d 158 (1971), which explained the centrality of the disparate-impact concept to effective enforcement of Title VII. The Court's order and opinion, I anticipate, will not have staying power.

S. Commentary on *Ricci*

Ricci continues the recent trend in Supreme Court decisions to limit government race-conscious remedies. The decision makes it more difficult for employers to take necessary steps to prevent racial discrimination in hiring and promotion consid-erations. Since its focus was federal anti-discrimination law, however, the major-ity's reasoning was not expressly extended to equal protection analysis under the Fourteenth Amendment.

While the Court, in a 5–4 decision authored by Justice Kennedy, ruled against the City of New Haven based solely under Title VII, the opinion drew analogies from equal protection precedents in reaching its conclusion. The Court reasoned that the City of New Haven had intentionally engaged in race-based decision-making by declining to certify the results solely because of the statistical disparity between the performance of minority and white candidates. Recognizing that its Equal Protec-tion Clause precedents had held that government actions designed to remedy past racial discrimination are permissible only when there is a "strong basis in evidence" that the remedial actions were necessary, Kennedy utilized this standard for Title VII. This meant that the City of New Haven needed to show strong evidence of disparate-impact liability before it could refuse to certify the test. Justice Kennedy reasoned this standard had not been met when the City of New Haven relied on the statistics alone, without evidence that the tests were unrelated to the job and incon-sistent with business necessity. Justice Ginsburg, joined by justices Stevens, Souter, and Breyer, dissented, urging that the failure to certify the test, due to good-faith concerns about disparate impact, did not constitute intentional race discrimination.

T. Background on Justice Thurgood Marshall

Geoffrey Stone, et al.

Justice Thurgood Marshall

The son of a primary school teacher and a club steward, Thurgood Marshall became the first black to serve on the Court when he was appointed by President Johnson in 1967. But Marshall had already made an enduring mark on American legal history decades before his judicial career began. After graduating first in his class from Howard Law School, Marshall began his long involvement with the National Association for the Advancement of Colored People. For two decades, he traveled across the country coordinating the NAACP's attack on segregation in housing, employment, voting, public accommodations, and especially education. Marshall won 29 of 32 cases before the Supreme Court, more than any other Supreme Court justice. His most famous victory during this period came in *Brown v. Board of Education*, 347 U.S. 483 (1954), where he successfully argued that segregated public education violated the equal protection clause. In 1961, President Kennedy nominated him to serve on the U.S. Court of Appeals for the Second Circuit. Although southern senators blocked his confirmation for a year, he finally assumed his seat, where he served until 1965 when President Johnson appointed him solicitor general. As a justice, Marshall was known primarily for his unstinting defense of racial and other minorities, his liberal interpretation of free speech and press guarantees, his "multi-tiered" theory of equal protection analysis, and his fervent opposition to capital punishment.

Constitutional Law lxxxvii (3rd edition).

Copyright © (1996) Stone, et al.

Reprinted with permission of Aspen Law & Business.

U. Questions and Notes

While the majority of justices in *McCleskey* and *Shaw* acknowledged the existence of continued and widespread racial inequity, their narrow interpretation of the Equal Protection Clause allowed for application only in limited circumstances, circumstances suggesting intentional racial discrimination. Does such a narrow application prevent such widespread inequity?. Is this an accurate and just interpretation of a constitutional provision intended to protect all citizens of the United States?

The terms black and African American are often used interchangeably. Do the two terms have different meanings? If so, which term do you prefer? The same has often been said for the terms American Indian and Native American. Does your analysis and position change for this racial group? Do you feel more strongly about the appropriateness and interchangeability of terms? The term, "Native American," came into usage in the 1960s to denote the groups served by the Bureau of Indian Affairs: American Indians and Alaska Natives (Indians, Eskimos and Aleuts of Alaska). Later the term also included Native Hawaiians and Pacific Islanders in some federal programs. It, therefore, came into disfavor among some Indian groups. The preferred term is American Indian. The Eskimos and Aleuts in Alaska are two culturally distinct groups and are sensitive about being included under the "Indian" designation. They prefer "Alaska Native." What about Latinos/as and Hispanic Americans?

The *Batson* decision stands for the proposition that a prosecutor may not intentionally use race to exclude someone from serving on a jury. How far do you think this proposition should be extended? Should it include gender, religion, ethnicity, socio-economic status, political affiliation, sexual orientation, or regional affiliation?

The majority in *McCleskey* indicated that the reason Warren McCleskey received the death penalty was because the law permitted him to be executed, not because he was African American. How do you respond to this reasoning?

The *Shaw* decision stands for the proposition that absent a compelling reason, legislators may not intentionally use race as a factor in drawing a legislative district. What other factors aside from race should be viewed as so restricted?

In order to have standing to bring a case, a plaintiff must show direct and irreparable harm. How was Ruth Shaw harmed by the legislative redistricting plan in *Shaw v. Reno*?

Shaw prohibited race, absent a compelling reason, from consideration in legislative redistricting. Why, however, was race being used as a factor in drawing legislative districts? Can African Americans only be represented effectively by other African Americans?

Do you believe that the City of New Haven in *Ricci* committed intentional racial discrimination by refusing to certify the employment examinations or merely committed a negligent act?

V. Point/Counterpoint

Consider the implications of color blindness versus race consciousness. Do you support a color-blind approach or a race-conscious approach to eliminating racial discrimination? When a color-blind approach is used, what analytic factors are glossed over, and how is the resulting remedy limited in value?

Darren Lenard Hutchinson

*Progressive Race Blindness?: Individual Identity, Group Politics, and Reform**

One of the most contested doctrines in contemporary constitutional law is the "colorblindness" principle. Drawing upon themes of fairness articulated in modern racial justice movements, the U.S. Supreme Court has consistently held that race is a presumptively impermissible basis for public policy and legislative processes. Thus, racial classifications trigger strict scrutiny—the Court's most exacting judicial review. The Court has also held that it must have a consistent approach to racial classifications: Racial classifications trigger strict scrutiny whether they are intended to harm persons of color or to remedy the effects of racial discrimination.

---

* (footnotes omitted).

This latter doctrinal development—the application of strict scrutiny to remedial race-conscious legislation and policies—has generated a tremendous amount of scholarly debate.

Critics of colorblindness have attacked the doctrine from a variety of perspectives. Many liberal scholars and jurists have criticized the Court for blurring the distinction between affirmative action and policies that subjugate persons of color. They contend that affirmative action is a benign form of discrimination that pursues compelling policy ends and should, therefore, receive a more deferential level of scrutiny from the Court. Recently, a number of scholars have asserted that the Court's opposition to race consciousness, particularly in the context of remedial usages of race, is inconsistent with the original intent of the Framers of the Fourteenth Amendment. These scholars have persuasively argued that the Framers of the Fourteenth Amendment did not seek to prohibit all forms of race consciousness and that they even approved several legislative measures designed to assist blacks in the postbellum era. Critical Race Theorists have portrayed the colorblindness doctrine as a tool of oppression. In several important works, Critical Race Theorists have argued that race, though socially constructed, remains salient in the lives of persons of color—as a source of both marginalization and resistance. The Court's colorblindness doctrine fails to appreciate the positive usages of race by persons of color and the pervasiveness of racial inequality and discrimination. Critical Race Theorists have also demonstrated that the Court's opposition to remedial race consciousness legitimizes racial inequality, because colorblindness treats as acceptable the existing unequal distribution of social resources and weakens efforts to redistribute social resources in a more egalitarian fashion. Critical Race Theorists have argued further that the Court must view race consciousness in a more nuanced and contextualized manner: The Court must seek to identify and to root out invidious, rather than remedial, racial classifications.

49 U.C.L.A. L. Rev. 1455–57.
Copyright © (2002) U.C.L.A. L. Rev.
Reprinted with permission of U.C.L.A. L. Rev. and
Darren Lenard Hutchinson.

Derrick Bell

*Color-Blind Constitutionalism: A Rediscovered Rationale**

A century ago, the Supreme Court struck down the first set of federal civil rights laws enacted to protect blacks from exclusion and segregation in public facilities. Ignoring the systematic, state-supported terror blacks were suffering at the hands of white sin that post-Reconstruction era, the Court said that the Fourteenth Amendment's Equal Protection Clause did not reach precisely the citizenship-denying

---

* (footnotes and chapter headings omitted).

conduct it was intended to prohibit. Writing for the Court majority, Justice Bradley scolded the black petitioners:

> When a man has emerged from slavery, and by the aid of beneficent legislation has shaken off the inseparable concomitants of that state, there must be some stage in the progress of his elevation when he takes the rank of a mere citizen, and ceases to be the special favorite of the laws, and when his rights as a citizen, or a man, are to be protected in the ordinary modes by which other men's rights are protected.

Seeking relief under federal law for a state's segregated public transportation law, the Court's response was the nineteenth century equivalent of "Get over it." Justice Bradley's century-old, rights-denying response to black people has now been resurrected in the Court's racial jurisprudence. Color-blind constitutionalism is reflected doctrinally by a wholesale prohibition on race-based classifications. The doctrine recognizes no distinction between government action that proceeds from a pernicious motivation and action that proceeds from programs and policies intended to address the adverse effects of long-standing racial bias. Seemingly even-handed, the color-blind approach prohibits race-based remedies for discrimination while leaving untouched discriminatory action conducted through means that do not mention race. Thus, a state law or policy designed to increase minority participation in the railway construction industry receives the same judicial scrutiny as a state law requiring black railway passengers to sit in the rear of each car.

The ideological underpinnings of this ultrastrict antidiscrimination principle suppose that race is an immutable and arbitrary construct that has no relevance to the just allocation of burdens and benefits in a democratic society. All are expected to make it, or not, on their own. It is, after all, the American way. Thus, in contrast to a color-conscious approach to antidiscrimination law, an approach the Court majority now deems all too like apartheid in South Africa, a color-blind philosophy is said to appropriately base the distribution of social responsibilities and benefits on merit alone, without regard to an individual's racial classification. "Mistakes were made," the courts acknowledge while striking down race-sensitive remedial policies, but corrections are too difficult. "Let's turn the page and move on."

This formalistic color-blind approach to civil rights jurisprudence runs counter both in ideology and in form to earlier antidiscrimination efforts, which took express account of the social and political significance of race. Nonetheless, over the past two decades, color-blind constitutionalism has received significant support from scholars, politicians, and jurists alike. In the 1970s, color-blindness became the battle cry of neoconservative think tanks. Their position was that race-specific civil rights policies are a threat to the democratic ideals through which American society functions. They insist that in its original form, the civil rights movement had as its goal the realization of formal equality under law, that is, a state of civil society where the distribution of legal burdens and benefits is based on merit rather than skin color. Pointing to then-newly enacted legislation such as the original Voting Rights Acts and the Civil Rights Act of 1964, both of which expressly prohibit overt acts of racial discrimination, color-blind proponents insist that civil rights leaders, having won their war were now betraying their ideals by espousing racial preferences Adherents of this position go on to attack liberal efforts to solicit the remedial power of the courts to address the real conditions of inequality experienced by blacks. Now, as a century ago, the ideal of equality embodied in the Constitution is being effectively emasculated through the strict application of color-blind constitutionalism in a society where color continues to have primary relevance.

Notions of color-blindness were nurtured in the political campaigns of the early 1980s, when the Reagan administration, sensing that large numbers of whites were disgruntled by the attention paid to minority concerns, undertook to undermine the civil rights gains of the previous two decades. Markedly hostile to those policies, which were credited with achieving measurable gains for blacks and other nonwhite minorities during previous administrations, Reagan and Bush conservatives set out to turn back the clock on antidiscrimination law. President Reagan opposed the 1982 amendments to the Voting Rights Act, vetoed the Civil Rights Restoration Act of 1989, supported the Justice Department's decision to switch sides in several antidiscrimination cases initiated under previous administrations, and attempted to reconstitute the U.S. Commission on Civil Rights. At the same time, the administration called for the repeal of voluntary affirmative action programs, urged an end to class-based remedies, and argued that any such remedies for racial wrongs should be limited to specifically identified victims of discrimination. The administration claims that the recent progress that had been achieved in the name of civil rights contravened the movement's original apolitical ideal of achieving formal equality of treatment under law. The administration charged that by invoking the power of the courts to manipulate the undesirable social conditions affecting blacks, liberal politicians had managed to turn the process of constitutional adjudication into a decidedly political project.

In a relatively short time, courts have adopted the dictates of polls and politicians. Antidiscrimination jurisprudence has all but adopted a per se rule of color-blindness. In 1995, for example, in *Adarand Contractors, Inc. v. Peña*, a majority of the Supreme Court invoked strict scrutiny review to strike down a federal affirmative action program implemented by the United States Department of Transportation. Under that standard, the Court required that the race-based classification be narrowly tailored to serve a compelling governmental interest. The specific program in question had provided additional compensation for general contractors who subcontracted out portions of highway construction projects to minority-owned companies. By implementing the set-aside program, the federal government had sought to redress the effects of past discrimination in the construction industry and to facilitate participation in the federal contracting market by minority-owned businesses. The minority set-aside program, however, according to the Court, was constitutionally impermissible, as the federal government had not demonstrated that highway construction contracts had been awarded in a racially discriminatory manner. Further, the Court held that the plan was insufficiently tailored, as it placed the burden of fostering increased minority participation on innocent nonminority contractors, while at the same time it reserved set-aside compensation for minority businesses that might not have suffered any discrimination.

The *Adarand* decision had significant doctrinal and ideological implications. From a jurisprudential standpoint, *Adarand* reflected a marked departure from prior precedent requiring that federal affirmative action programs be reviewed under intermediate scrutiny. This more forgiving standard of review took account of Congress' unique authority under § 5 of the Fourteenth Amendment to enforce the dictates of the equal protection clause and demanded only that federal race-based classifications be justified as substantially related to an important government interest. Thus, in *Fullilove v. Klutznick*, the Court upheld under intermediate scrutiny a race-based set-aside program that, in an effort to remedy past discrimination, appropriated federal grants to state and local public works projects on the condition that "at least 10 per cent of the amount of each grant shall be expended for minority business enterprises." Strict scrutiny, on the other hand, was reserved for those race-based classifications enacted under malicious pretenses and for those affirmative action programs implemented by the states. As the Court explained in *City of Richmond v. J.A. Croson, Co.*, the proper judicial scrutiny to be applied to race-based classifications was no longer a function of the motivation behind the classification itself nor of the nature of the governmental entity enforcing the classification. Rather, all such classifications facing an equal protection challenge were to be reviewed under strict judicial scrutiny.

During this period, and at least in part in response to the loss of civil rights precedents that once seemed permanent, a progressive approach, known as Critical Race Theory, emerged at a number of law schools. Its adherents took to tasks the color-blind approach to constitutional jurisprudence and the claim that the legal recognition of race undermines democratic ideals. Much of this new scholarship exposed the ideological distinction between a view of antidiscrimination law that promoted equality as a process and a view that promoted equality as a result. Critical race scholars described color-blindness as an approach to constitutional equality under which actual outcomes are largely irrelevant when it comes to marking progress towards racial justice. Specifically, they criticized the very application of the doctrine as a legal mechanism for preventing wrongful acts, rather than as a mechanism for redressing the actual consequences of those acts. This translates into a concern that meaningful racial justice can never be achieved through color-blind constitutionalism because the doctrine denies the political import and social significance of race and a long history of subordination and exploitation. Therefore, rather than representing an idyllic vision of equality, color-blindness represents nothing more than laudable goal elevated, to protect the racial status quo, into a formal rule of law.

From a critical perspective, *Adarand*'s application of strict scrutiny review reflects the Supreme Court's increasing preference for color-blind constitutionalism and a shift in its ideological commitment to equality. Once the doctrinal components of color-blindness are unearthed, the Supreme Court's willingness to subordinate substantive equality to formal equality under law becomes clear. The Court's "separate but equal" standard in *Plessy v. Ferguson*, of course, grew out of the same otherworldly logic that a parallel in matters of race provides both fairness and justice.

Color-blind constitutionalism, and its near application through strict scrutiny review, has its roots in three doctrinal components: namely, intent, symmetry, and accountability. These three principles can be summarized succinctly as follows. First, strict scrutiny review defines a constitutional violation under the Equal Protection Clause as "intentional" discrimination and thus recognizes no violation in a law that disproportionately burdens the members of a particular race absent some conscious regard to that effect on the part of governmental decision makers. Second, because the Constitution protects individual and not groups, each individual enjoys the right to be free form governmental classifications that categorize individuals according to race. Color-blind constitutionalism, therefore, dictates that all race-based classifications be reviewed under the same symmetrical standard of strict judicial scrutiny, regardless of whether the classification proceeds from a pernicious or a benign government motivation. Finally, principles of fairness dictate that those found to have engaged in an act of discrimination be held accountable for that misbehavior. Thus, the costs of remedying past incidents of racial discrimination should accrue to blameworthy actors, not to those who were not party to the discrimination. The Supreme Court's reliance on these three principles of color-blind constitutionalism — intent, symmetry, and accountability — undermines the prospect that antidiscrimination law can bring about substantial improvements in the real-life conditions facing blacks and other people of color in America.

The concept of intent is indispensable to an act of discrimination under color-blind constitutionalism. This principle is clearly articulated in the case of *Washington v. Davis* where the Court held that only governmental action undertaken with a "racially discriminatory purpose" violates the Constitution's equality mandate. Further, the Court held that a finding of intentional purpose requires a showing that the statute or policy facially discriminates on the basis of race or that a facially neutral law is undertaken to effect a race specific result. Under either circumstance, the challenged statute must be reviewed under strict judicial scrutiny. A corollary to the intent principle is that the government's enforcement of a facially neutral law that has a disproportionate burden on a particular racial group doe s not give rise to a cognizable equal protection violation. In *Davis*, therefore, the Court approved the use of a qualifying test administered by the Washington, D.C., Police Department, because the fact that the examination effectively excluded four times as many blacks as whites was not sufficient to demonstrate an intent to keep blacks off the force.

In normative terms, strict scrutiny's intent requirement takes account of explicit race-consciousness under law. Race-consciousness can be described as the express consideration of race in the process of cognitive decision making. Its traditional manifestation is the formal, state-sanctioned denial of social, political, and legal equality. One example is Jim Crow legislation, where state law makers deliberately undertook to implement legislation for the sole purpose of segregating groups on the basis of race. With respect to these objective manifestations of race-consciousness, reliance on the intent principle of discrimination is an appropriate tool for eradicating the subordination of people of color. This formal conception of color-blindness as a remedial goal of color-conscious policies takes account of the significance of race as a specific historical and social construct that for long periods has been used to justify the subordination of blacks and certain other minorities. In this regard, by prohibiting the intentional consideration of race, color-blind constitutionalism achieves its goal of excavating from government decision making a root cause of racial inequality.

In summary, by prohibiting governmental action that seeks to subordinate minority groups, color-blind constitutionalism, and its application through strict scrutiny review, has served to redress a significant amount of discrimination arising from overt racial bias. As proof of this effect, one need look no further than the positive gains that ensured with the transition from Jim Crow to formal equality under law. In this respect, the eradication of official forms of race-conscious subordination and the adoption of formal facial neutrality is a positive good. At the same time, however, considering the actual extent to which race-consciousness informs our objective decision-making capacities, formal color-blindness, and its unyielding reliance on the principle of intent, does not go far enough in the pursuit of meaningful racial justice. In fact, race-consciousness persists in new and more virulent forms that not only legitimate the conditions of racial injustice but go undetected by color-blind constitutionalism.

Race, Racism, and American Law (4th Ed.) 131–39.
Copyright © (2000). Derrick A. Bell, Jr.
Reprinted with permission of Derrick A. Bell, Jr.

Charles R. Lawrence III

The Id, The Ego, and Equal Protection: Reckoning with Unconscious Racism*

This article reconsiders the doctrine of discriminatory purpose that was established by the 1976 decision, *Washington v. Davis*. This now well-established doctrine requires plaintiffs challenging the constitutionality of a facially neutral law to prove a racially discriminatory purpose on the part of those responsible for the law's enactment or administration.

Davis has spawned a considerable body of literature treating its merits and failings. Minorities and civil rights advocates have been virtually unanimous in condemning *Davis* and its progeny. They have been joined by a significant number of constitutional scholars who have been equally disapproving, if more restrained, in assessing its damage to the cause of equal opportunity. These critics advance two principal arguments. The first is that a motive-centered doctrine of racial

---

* (footnotes omitted).

discrimination places a very heavy, and often impossible, burden of persuasion on the wrong side of the dispute. Improper motives are easy to hide. And because behavior results from the interaction of a multitude of motives, governmental officials will always be able to argue that racially neutral considerations prompted their actions. Moreover, where several decisionmakers are involved, proof of racially discriminatory motivation is even more difficult.

The second objection to the *Davis* doctrine is more fundamental. It argues that the injury of racial inequality exists irrespective of the decisionmakers' motives. Does the black child in a segregated school experience less stigma and humiliation because the local school board did not consciously set out to harm her? Are blacks less prisoners of the ghetto because the decision that excludes them from an all-white neighborhood was made with property values and not race in mind? Those who make this second objection reason that the "facts of racial inequality are the real problem." They urge that racially disproportionate harm should trigger heightened judicial scrutiny without consideration of motive.

Supporters of the intent requirement are equally adamant in asserting the doctrine's propriety. They echo the four main arguments that the Court itself set forth in *Davis*: (1) A standard that would subject all governmental action with a racially disproportionate impact to strict judicial scrutiny would cost too much; such a standard, the Court argues, would substantially limit legitimate legislative decisionmaking and would endanger the validity of a "whole range of existing tax, welfare, public service, regulatory and licensing statutes"; (2) a disproportionate impact standard would make innocent people bear the costs of remedying a harm in which they played no part; (3) an impact test would be inconsistent with equal protection values, because the judicial decisionmaker would have to explicitly consider race; and (4) it would be inappropriate for the judiciary to choose to remedy the racially disproportionate impact of otherwise neutral governmental actions at the expense of other legitimate social interests.

Barbara J. Flagg

*"Was Blind, But Now I See": White Race Consciousness and the Requirement of Discriminatory Intent**

The evolution of the role of colorblindness in equal protection discourse is enlightening. Colorblindness was not in itself especially controversial in the early post-*Brown* era. Its significance lay in its potential to resolve the process—theoretical difficulties Wechsler had understood *Brown* to pose. As one might

---

* (footnotes omitted).

expect, the colorblindness principle became an item of contention in its own right as the debate over affirmative action heated up. However, it shed its ties to process theory at the same time, largely because process theory, as refined by John Ely, found another approach to, and resolution of, the question of affirmative action: strict scrutiny is not appropriate when the white majority decides to favor nonwhites at its own expense. Increasingly, colorblindness was defended in moral and substantive terms, featuring, for example, instrumental arguments that race-conscious measures would ultimately exacerbate racial tensions or that they inevitably stigmatize blacks. This shift in theoretical perspective, from the "neutral" to the avowedly substantive, coincided, of course, with the conceptualization of the "innocent" white "victim" of affirmative action. One has to rephrase Bickel's famous remark: Whose ox was being gored at the time when colorblindness took center stage in the equality debate?

Turning from the legal to the moral realm, the principal foundation of colorblindness seems to be its enormous intuitive appeal. To "judge a person by the color of his skin" just seems wrong. This moral insight may be the visceral rejection of its equally visceral opposite, the tendency of human beings to react negatively to persons of a different color than themselves. However, moral insights are at best problematic sources of constitutional doctrine and must in any event be subject to revision in the light of experience.

The colorblindness principle may also appear morally desirable by virtue of its relation to the liberal value of individual autonomy. Colorblindness often is seen as an expression of individual autonomy, which requires in part that persons not be held responsible or judged for personal characteristics not within their own control. Individuals ought to reap the fruits of their own industry, but they ought neither to benefit nor to be disadvantaged because of characteristics like race or gender that are a matter of birth.

However, colorblindness is at best a paradoxical means of implementing autonomy values. On the one hand, autonomy is not served when the individual is pigeonholed by race; certainly the whole person is much more than the color of her skin. On the other hand, individual autonomy ought to include the power of self-definition, the ability to make fundamental value choices and to select life strategies to implement them. Such choices are not unbounded; for many individuals, to be oneself is to share in the cultural values of a community to which one belongs by birth. Thus, for example, for many black people embracing blackness as an explicit and positive aspect of personal identity is an essential component in the process of self-definition. . . .

Proponents of the existing disparate impact rule appear to believe that individual autonomy is served when decisionmakers "ignore" the race of those affected by their decisions, but the transparency phenomenon, which suggests that colorblindness may operate instead as an opening for the unthinking imposition of white norms and expectations, belies that view. The proposed rule takes a broader view of personal autonomy and takes seriously the centrality of race to many individuals' self-definition. For those who have to choose between the language, customs, hairstyle, dress, or lifestyle of their own community and a desirable job or other governmental benefit, the autonomy costs of transparently white norms are considerable.

The final category of arguments purporting to support the colorblindness principle may be characterized, loosely, as exemplifying antisubordinationist concerns. Race consciousness—the explicit use of racial classifications as a means of disadvantaging nonwhites—has been the primary vehicle of racial subordination until quite recently. The ideology of opposition to racial hierarchy evolved in reaction to the specific forms in which racial oppression had manifested itself. Rejecting racial distinctions seemed the natural avenue to reversing that history of oppression and achieving racial justice, especially during the "Second Reconstruction" of the 1950s and 1960s; colorblindness appeared to be the exact antithesis of the form of race consciousness that had been the root cause of racial subordination. If "color" had marked an individual as inferior, then the refusal to recognize "color" would be the way to elevate him to equal status with whites. In effect, colorblindness became the rule-like proxy for an underlying, historically based antisubordination principle.

The problem with the colorblindness principle as a strategy for achieving racial justice is that it has not been effective outside the social context in which it arose. Like all rules, colorblindness is both over- and underinclusive with respect to the underlying policy—antisubordination—it is intended to implement. It is underinclusive because the explicit use of racial classifications is no longer the principal vehicle of racial oppression; structural and institutional racism, of the sort illustrated by the transparency phenomenon, now are the predominant causes of blacks' continued inability to thrive in this society. Colorblindness is overinclusive insofar as it regards the explicit use of racial classifications to advantage blacks as equally blameworthy as the historical use of such classifications to blacks' disadvantage. In each respect colorblindness fails to implement racial justice; that it is a failed social policy is evident from the statistics revealing that blacks are scarcely better off today than they were before this ideology took hold in the 1950s and 1960s.

91 *Mich. L. Rev.* 953, 1005–14.

Copyright © (1993) *Mich. L. Rev.*

Reprinted with permission of *Mich. L. Rev.* and Barbara Flagg.

Part Six

Supreme Court Confirmation Racial Controversies

XXIII. Race, Values, and Justice Thomas

A. Introduction

On July 1, 1991, President George H. W. Bush announced the nomination of Clarence Thomas to replace Justice Thurgood Marshall on the United States Supreme Court. Marshall was the first, and only, African American to serve on the Court. While both Marshall and Thomas are African Americans, the similarities end there. Marshall grew up middle class in a northern city, was educated at historically black institutions, and spent most of his professional career in civil rights organizations. Thomas, on the other hand, grew up poor in the rural South, was educated in the Ivy League, and spent most of his professional career in government service. Perhaps most significant, Marshall was a liberal Democrat while Thomas is a conservative Republican. When the press asked Justice Marshall at his resignation news conference who he thought should replace him and whether the race of his replacement was relevant, he responded, "there are black snakes and white snakes and both will bite."

The strong contrast between the background and perspectives of Justices Marshall and Thomas, and the historical significance of replacing Marshall, set the stage for the controversy over Thomas' nomination. When allegations surfaced that Thomas had sexually harassed Anita Hill, a law professor who had previously worked for him, the nomination seemed doomed. After Thomas' adamant denials of sexual harassment in televised confirmation hearings and accusations of the Senate's racist treatment, Thomas was confirmed as an Associate Justice of the Supreme Court in one of the closest and most divisive confirmation votes in American history. The confirmation hearings maneuvered through Thomas' political affiliation and his perspectives and actions relevant to matters of race. The hearings did not fully expose Thomas' lack of support for civil rights, a movement that had provided many of his own opportunities.

B. Pre-Supreme Court Jurisprudence

A. Leon Higginbotham, Jr.[*]

An Open Letter to Justice Clarence Thomas from a Federal Judicial Colleague

Dear Justice Thomas:

The President has signed your Commission and you have now become the 106th Justice of the United States Supreme Court. I congratulate you on this high honor!

It has been a long time since we talked. I believe it was in 1980 during your first year as a Trustee at Holy Cross College. I was there to receive an honorary degree. You were thirty-one years old and on the staff of Senator John Danforth. You had not yet started your meteoric climb through the government and federal judicial hierarchy. Much has changed since then.

At first I thought that I should write you privately—the way one normally corresponds with a colleague or friend. I still feel ambivalent about making this letter public, but I do so because your appointment is profoundly important to this country and the world, and because all Americans need to understand the issues you will face on the Supreme Court. In short, Justice Thomas, I write this letter as a public record so that this generation can understand the challenges you face as an Associate Justice to the Supreme Court, and the next can evaluate the choices you have made or will make.

The Supreme Court can be a lonely and insular environment. Eight of the present Justices' lives would not have been very different if the *Brown* case had never been decided as it was. Four attended Harvard Law School, which did not accept women law students until 1950.[1] Two attended Stanford Law School prior to the time when the first black matriculated there.[2] None has been called a "nigger"[3] or suffered

---

[*] Chief Judge Emeritus, U.S. Court of Appeals for the Third Circuit, Senior Fellow University of Pennsylvania School of Law. Except for a few minor changes in the footnotes this article is a verbatim copy of the text of the letter sent to Justice Clarence Thomas on November 29, 1991.

1. Justices Blackmun, Scalia, Kennedy, and Souter were members of the Harvard Law School Classes of 1932, 1960, 1961, and 1966 respectively. *See* THE AMERICAN BENCH 16, 46, 72, 1566 (Marie T. Hough ed., 1989). The first woman to graduate from Harvard Law School was a member of the Class of 1953. Telephone Interview with Emily Farnam, Alumni Affairs Office, Harvard University (Aug. 8, 1991).

2. Chief Justice Rehnquist and Justice O'Connor were members of the Stanford Law School Class of 1952. Stanford did not graduate its first black law student until 1968. Telephone interview with Shirley Wedlake, Assistant to the Dean of Student Affairs, Stanford University Law School (Dec. 10, 1991).

3. Even courts have at times tolerated the use of the term "nigger" in one or another of its variations. In the not too distant past, appellate courts have upheld convictions despite prosecutors' references to black defendants and witnesses in such racist terms as "black rascal," "burr-headed nigger," "mean Negro," "big nigger," "pickaninny," "mean nigger," "three nigger men," "niggers," and "nothing but just a common Negro, [a] black whore." *See* A. Leon Higginbotham, Jr., *Racism*

the acute deprivations of poverty.[4] Justice O'Connor is the only other Justice on the Court who at one time was adversely affected by a white-male dominated system that often excludes both women and minorities from equal access to the rewards of hard work and talent.

By elevating you to the Supreme Court, President Bush has suddenly vested in you the option to preserve or dilute the gains this country has made in the struggle for equality. This is a grave responsibility indeed. In order to discharge it you will need to recognize what James Baldwin called the "force of history" within you.[5] You will need to recognize that both your public life and your private life reflect this country's history in the area of racial discrimination and civil rights. And, while much has been said about your admirable determination to overcome terrible obstacles, it is also important to remember how you arrived where you are now, because you did not get there by yourself.

When I think of your appointment to the Supreme Court, I see not only the result of your own ambition, but also the culmination of years of heartbreaking work by thousands who preceded you. I know you may not want to be burdened by the memory of their sacrifices. But I also know that you have no right to forget that history. Your life is very different from what it would have been had these men and women never lived. That is why today I write to you about this country's history of

in American and South African Courts: Similarities and Differences, 65 N.Y.U. L. Rev. 479, 542–43 (1990).

In addition, at least one Justice of the Supreme Court, James McReynolds, was a "white supremacist" who referred to Blacks as "niggers." *See* Randall Kennedy, *Race Relations Law and the Tradition of Celebration: The Case of Professor Schmidt*, 86 Colum. L. Rev. 1622, 1641 (1986); *see also* David Burner, James McReynolds, in 3 The Justices of the United States Supreme Court 1789–1969, at 2023, 2024 (Leon Friedman & Fred L. Israel eds., 1969) (reviewing Justice McReynolds's numerous lone dissents as evidence of blatant racism). In 1938, a landmark desegregation case was argued before the Supreme Court by Charles Hamilton Houston, the brilliant black lawyer who laid the foundation for *Brown v. Board of Education*. During Houston's oral argument, McReynolds turned his back on the attorney and stared at the wall of the courtroom. Videotaped Statement of Judge Robert Carter to Judge Higginbotham (August 1987) (reviewing his observation of the argument in *Missouri ex rel. Gaines v. Canada*, 305 U.S. 337 (1938)). In his autobiography, Justice William O. Douglas described how McReynolds received a rare, but well deserved comeuppance when he made a disparaging comment about Howard University.

One day McReynolds went to the barbershop in the Court. Gates, the black barber, put the sheet around his neck and over his lap, and as he was pinning it behind him McReynolds said, "Gates, tell me, where is this nigger university in Washington, D.C.?" Gates removed the white cloth from McReynolds, walked around and faced him, and said in a very calm and dignified manner, "Mr. Justice, I am shocked that any Justice would call a Negro a nigger. There is a Negro college in Washington, D.C. Its name is Howard University and we are very proud of it." McReynolds muttered some kind of apology and Gates resumed his work in silence.

William O. Douglas, The Court Years: 1939–1975, at 14–15 (1980).

4. By contrast, according to the Census Bureau's definition of poverty, in 1991, one in five American children (and one in four preschoolers) is poor. *See* Clifford M. Johnson et al., Child Poverty In America 1 (Children's Defense Fund report, 1991).

5. James Baldwin, *White Man's Guilt*, in The Price of the Ticket 409, 410 (1985).

civil rights lawyers and civil rights organizations; its history of voting rights; and its history of housing and privacy rights. This history has affected your past and present life. And forty years from now, when your grandchildren and other Americans measure your performance on the Supreme Court, that same history will determine whether you fulfilled your responsibility with the vision and grace of the Justice whose seat you have been appointed to fill: Thurgood Marshall.

Measures of Greatness or Failure of Supreme Court Justices

In 1977 a group of one hundred scholars evaluated the first one hundred justices on the Supreme Court.[6] Eight of the justices were categorized as failures, six as below average, fifty-five as average, fifteen as near great and twelve as great.[7] Among those ranked as great were John Marshall, Joseph Story, John M. Harlan, Oliver Wendell Holmes, Jr., Charles E. Hughes, Louis D. Brandeis, Harlan F. Stone, Benjamin N. Cardozo, Hugo L. Black, and Felix Frankfurter.[8] Because you have often criticized the Warren Court,[9] you should be interested to know that the list of great jurists on the Supreme Court also included Earl Warren.

Even long after the deaths of the Justices that I have named, informed Americans are grateful for the extraordinary wisdom and compassion they brought to their judicial opinions. Each in his own way viewed the Constitution as an instrument for justice. They made us a far better people and this country a far better place. I think that Justices Thurgood Marshall, William J. Brennan, Harry Blackmun, Lewis Powell, and John Paul Stevens will come to be revered by future scholars and future generations with the same gratitude. Over the next four decades you will cast many historic votes on issues that will profoundly affect the quality of life for our citizens for generations to come. You can become an exemplar of fairness and the rational

---

6. *See* ALBERT P. BLAUSTEIN & ROY M. MERSKY, THE FIRST ONE HUNDRED JUSTICES (1978). The published survey included ratings of only the first ninety-six justices, because the four Nixon appointees (Burger, Blackmun, Powell, and Rehnquist) had then been on the Court too short a time for an accurate evaluation to be made. *See id.* at 35–36.

7. *Id.* at 37–40.

8. *Id.* at 37.

9. You have been particularly critical of its decision in *Brown v. Board of Education. See, e.g.,* Clarence Thomas, *Toward a "Plain Reading" of the Constitution — The Declaration of Independence in Constitutional Interpretation*, 30 How. L.J. 983, 990–92 (1987) (criticizing the emphasis on social stigma in the *Brown* opinion, which left the Court's decision resting on "feelings" rather than "reason and moral and political principles"); Clarence Thomas, *Civil Rights as a Principle Versus Civil Rights as an Interest, Speech to the Cato Institute* (Oct. 2, 1987), in ASSESSING THE REAGAN YEARS 391, 392–93 (David Boaz ed., 1988) (arguing that the Court's opinion in *Brown* failed to articulate a clear principle to guide later decisions, leading to opinions in the area of race that overemphasized groups at the expense of individuals, and "argue[d] against what was best in the American political tradition"); Clarence Thomas, The Higher Law Background of the Privileges and Immunities Clause of the Fourteenth Amendment, Speech to the Federalist Society for Law and Policy Studies, University of Virginia School of Law (Mar. 5, 1988), in 12 HARV. J.L. & PUB. POL'Y 63, 68 (1989) (asserting that adoption of Justice Harlan's view that the Constitution is "color-blind" would have provided the Court's civil rights opinions with the higher-law foundation necessary for a "just, wise, and *constitutional* decision").

interpretation of the Constitution, or you can become an archetype of inequality and the retrogressive evaluation of human rights. The choice as to whether you will build a decisional record of true greatness or of mere mediocrity is yours.

Our Major Similarity

My more than twenty-seven years as a federal judge made me listen with intense interest to the many persons who testified both in favor of and against your nomination. I studied the hearings carefully and afterwards pondered your testimony and the comments others made about you. After reading almost every word of your testimony, I concluded that what you and I have most in common is that we are both graduates of Yale Law School. Though our graduation classes are twenty-two years apart, we have both benefitted from our old Eli connections.

If you had gone to one of the law schools in your home state, Georgia, you probably would not have met Senator John Danforth who, more than twenty years ago, served with me as a member of the Yale Corporation. Dean Guido Calabresi mentioned you to Senator Danforth, who hired you right after graduation from law school and became one of your primary sponsors. If I had not gone to Yale Law School, I would probably not have met Justice Curtis Bok, nor Yale Law School alumni such as Austin Norris, a distinguished black lawyer, and Richardson Dilworth, a distinguished white lawyer, who became my mentors and gave me my first jobs. Nevertheless, now that you sit on the Supreme Court, there are issues far more important to the welfare of our nation than our Ivy League connections. I trust that you will not be overly impressed with the fact that all of the other Justices are graduates of what laymen would call the nation's most prestigious law schools.

Black Ivy League alumni in particular should never be too impressed by the educational pedigree of Supreme Court Justices. The most wretched decision ever rendered against black people in the past century was *Plessy v. Ferguson*.[10] It was written in 1896 by Justice Henry Billings Brown, who had attended both Yale and Harvard Law Schools. The opinion was joined by Justice George Shiras, a graduate of Yale Law School, as well as by Chief Justice Melville Fuller and Justice Horace Gray, both alumni of Harvard Law School.

If those four Ivy League alumni on the Supreme Court in 1896 had been as faithful in their interpretation of the Constitution as Justice John Harlan, a graduate of Transylvania, a small law school in Kentucky, then the venal precedent of *Plessy v. Ferguson*, which established the federal "separate but equal" doctrine and legitimized the worst forms of race discrimination, would not have been the law of our nation for sixty years. The separate but equal doctrine, also known as Jim Crow, created the foundations of separate and unequal allocation of resources, and oppression of the human rights of blacks.

---

10. 163 U.S. 537 (1896).

During your confirmation hearing I heard you refer frequently to your grandparents and your experiences in Georgia. Perhaps now is the time to recognize that if the four Ivy League alumni—all northerners—of the *Plessy* majority had been as sensitive to the plight of black people as was Justice John Harlan, a former slave holder from Kentucky,[11] the American statutes that sanctioned racism might not have been on the books—and many of the racial injustices that your grandfather, Myers Anderson, and my grandfather, Moses Higginbotham, endured would never have occurred.

The tragedy with *Plessy v. Ferguson*, is not that the Justices had the "wrong" education, or that they attended the "wrong" law schools. The tragedy is that the Justices had the wrong values, and that these values poisoned this society for decades. Even worse, millions of Blacks today still suffer from the tragic sequelae of *Plessy*—a case which Chief Justice Rehnquist,[12] Justice Kennedy,[13] and most scholars now say was wrongly decided.[14]

As you sit on the Supreme Court confronting the profound issues that come before you, never be impressed with how bright your colleagues are. You must always focus on what *values* they bring to the task of interpreting the Constitution. Our Constitution has an unavoidable—though desirable—level of ambiguity, and there are many interstitial spaces which as a Justice of the Supreme Court you will have to fill in.[15] To borrow Justice Cardozo's elegant phrase: "We do not pick our rules of law full blossomed from the trees."[16] You and the other Justices cannot avoid putting your imprimatur on a set of values. The dilemma will always be which particular values you choose to sanction in law. You can be part of what Chief Justice Warren, Justice Brennan, Justice Blackmun, and Justice Marshall and others have called the evolutionary movement of the Constitution[17]—an evolutionary movement that has benefitted you greatly.

---

11. *See* Alan F. Westin, *John Marshall Harlan and the Constitutional Rights of Negroes: The Transformation of a Southerner*, 66 YALE L.J. 637, 638 (1957).

12. *Fullilove v. Klutznick*, 448 U.S. 448, 522 (1980) (Stewart, J., joined by Rehnquist, J., dissenting).

13. *Metro Broadcasting, Inc. v. FCC*, 110 S.Ct. 2997, 3044 (1990) (Kennedy, J., dissenting).

14. For a thorough review of the background of *Plessy v. Ferguson*, and a particularly sharp criticism of the majority opinion, see LOREN MILLER, THE PETITIONERS: THE STORY OF THE SUPREME COURT OF THE UNITED STATES AND THE NEGRO 165–82 (1966). As an example of scholars who have criticized the opinion and the result in *Plessy, see* LAURENCE H. TRIBE, AMERICAN CONSTITUTIONAL LAW 1474–75 (2d ed., 1988).

15. *See* BENJAMIN CARDOZO, THE NATURE OF THE JUDICIAL PROCESS 10 (1921) (noting that "judge-made law [is] one of the existing realities of life").

16. *Id.* at 103.

17. The concept of the "evolutionary movement" of the Constitution has been expressed by Justice Brennan in *Regents of the University of California v. Bakke*, 438 U.S. 312 (1978), and by Justice Marshall in his speech given on the occasion of the bicentennial of the Constitution. In *Bakke*, in a partial dissent joined by Justices White, Marshall, and Blackmun, Justice Brennan discussed how Congress had "eschewed any static definition of discrimination [in Title VI of the 1964 Civil Rights Act] in favor of broad language that could be shaped by experience, administrative necessity and

Your Critiques of Civil Rights Organizations and
the Supreme Court during the Last Eight Years

I have read almost every article you have published, every speech you have given, and virtually every public comment you have made during the past decade. Until your confirmation hearing I could not find one shred of evidence suggesting an insightful understanding on your part on how the evolutionary movement of the Constitution and the work of civil rights organizations have benefitted you. Like Sharon McPhail, the President of the National Bar Association, I kept asking myself: Will the Real Clarence Thomas Stand Up?[18] Like her, I wondered: "Is Clarence Thomas a 'conservative with a common touch' as Ruth Marcus refers to him . . . or the 'counterfeit hero' he is accused of being by Haywood Burns . . . ?"[19]

While you were a presidential appointee for eight years, as Chairman of the Equal Opportunity Commission and as an Assistant Secretary at the Department of Education, you made what I would regard as unwarranted criticisms of civil rights organizations,[20] the Warren Court, and even of Justice Thurgood Marshall.[21] Perhaps these criticisms were motivated by what you perceived to be your political duty to the Reagan and Bush administrations. Now that you have assumed what should be the non-partisan role of a Supreme Court Justice, I hope you will take time out to carefully evaluate some of these unjustified attacks.

---

evolving judicial doctrine." Id. at 337 (Brennan, J., dissenting in part) (emphasis added). In Justice Brennan's view, Congress was aware of the "evolutionary change that constitutional law in the area of racial discrimination was undergoing in 1964." *Id.* at 340. Congress, thus, equated Title VI's prohibition against discrimination with the commands of the Fifth and Fourteenth Amendment to the Constitution so that the meaning of the statute's prohibition would evolve with the interpretations of the command of the Constitution. *See id.* at 340. In another context, during his speech given on the occasion of the bicentennial of the Constitution, Justice Marshall commented that he did "not believe that the meaning of the Constitution was forever 'fixed' at the Philadelphia Convention." Thurgood Marshall, *Reflections on the Bicentennial of the United States Constitution*, 101 HARV. L. REV. 1, 2 (1987). In Justice Marshall's view, the Constitution had been made far more meaningful through its "promising evolution through 200 years of history." *Id.* at 5 (emphasis added).

18. Sharon McPhail, *Will The Real Clarence Thomas Stand Up?*, NAT'L B. ASS'N Mag. Oct. 1991, at 1.

19. *Id*; *see* Ruth Marcus, Self-Made Conservative; Nominee Insists He Be Judged on Merits, WASH. POST, July 2, 1991, at A1; Haywood Burns, *Clarence Thomas, A Counterfeit Hero*, N.Y. TIMES, July 9, 1991, at A19.

20. *See* Clarence Thomas, *The Equal Employment Opportunity Commission: Reflections on a New Philosophy*, 15 STETSON L. REV. 29, 35 (1985) (asserting that the civil rights community is "wallowing in self-delusion and pulling the public with it"); Juan Williams, *EEOC Chairman Blasts Black Leaders*, WASH. POST, Oct. 25, 1984, at A7 ("These guys [black leaders] are sitting there watching the destruction of our race. . . . Ronald Reagan isn't the problem. Former President Jimmy Carter was not the problem. The lack of black leadership is the problem.").

21. *See* Clarence Thomas, *Black Americans Based Claim for Freedom on Constitution*, SAN DIEGO UNION & TRIB., Oct. 6, 1987, at B7 (claiming that Marshall's observation of the deficiencies in some respects of the Framers' constitutional vision "alienates all Americans, and not just black Americans, from their high and noble intention").

In October 1987, you wrote a letter to the San Diego Union & Tribune criticizing a speech given by Justice Marshall on the 200th anniversary celebration of the Constitution.[22] Justice Marshall had cautioned all Americans not to overlook the momentous events that followed the drafting of that document, and to "seek . . . a sensitive understanding of the Constitution's inherent defects, and its promising evolution through 200 years of history."

Your response dismissed Justice Marshall's "sensitive understanding" as an "exasperating and incomprehensible . . . assault on the Bicentennial, the Founding, and the Constitution itself." Yet, however high and noble the Founders' intentions may have been, Justice Marshall was correct in believing that the men who gathered in Philadelphia in 1787 "could not have imagined, nor would they have accepted, that the document they were drafting would one day be construed by a Supreme Court to which had been appointed a woman and the descendant of an African slave." That, however, was neither an assault on the Constitution nor an indictment of the Founders. Instead, it was simply a recognition that in the midst of the Bicentennial celebration, "some may more quietly commemorate the suffering, the struggle and sacrifice that has triumphed over much of what was wrong with the original document, and observe the anniversary with hopes not realized and promises not fulfilled."

Justice Marshall's comments, much like his judicial philosophy, were grounded in history and were driven by the knowledge that even today, for millions of Americans, there still remain "hopes not realized and promises not fulfilled." His reminder to the nation that patriotic feelings should not get in the way of thoughtful reflection on this country's continued struggle for equality was neither new nor misplaced.[23] Twenty-five years earlier, in December 1962, while this country was cel-

---

22. See id.

23. On April 1, 1987, some weeks before Justice Marshall's speech, I gave the Herman Phleger Lecture at Stanford University. I stated in my presentation:

In this year of the Bicentennial you will hear a great deal that is laudatory about our nation's Constitution and legal heritage. Much of this praise will be justified. The danger is that the current oratory and scholarship may lapse into mere self-congratulatory back-patting, suggesting that everything in America has been, or is, near perfect.

We must not allow our euphoria to cause us to focus solely on our strengths. Somewhat like physicians examining a mighty patient, we also must diagnose and evaluate the pathologies that have disabled our otherwise healthy institutions.

I trust that you will understand that my critiques of our nation's past and present shortcomings do not imply that I am oblivious to its many exceptional virtues. I freely acknowledge the importance of two centuries of our enduring and evolving Constitution, the subsequently enacted Bill of Rights, the Thirteenth, Fourteenth, Fifteenth and Nineteenth Amendments, and the protections of these rights, more often than not, by federal courts.

Passion for freedom and commitments to liberty are important values in American society. If we can retain this passion and commitment and direct it towards eradicating the remaining significant areas of social injustice on our nation's unfinished agenda, our pride should persist— despite the daily tragic reminders that there are far too many homeless, far too many hungry, and

ebrating the 100th anniversary of the emancipation proclamation, James Baldwin had written to his young nephew:

> This is your home, my friend, do not be driven from it; great men have done great things here, and will again, and we can make America what America must become. . . . [But y]ou know, and I know that the country is celebrating one hundred years of freedom one hundred years too soon.[24]

Your response to Justice Marshall's speech, as well as your criticisms of the Warren court and civil rights organizations, may have been nothing more than your expression of allegiance to the conservatives who made you Chairman of the EEOC, and who have now elevated you to the Supreme Court. But your comments troubled me then and trouble me still because they convey a stunted knowledge of history and an unformed judicial philosophy. Now that you sit on the Supreme Court you must sort matters out for yourself and form your own judicial philosophy, and you must reflect more deeply on legal history than you ever have before. You are no longer privileged to offer flashy one-liners to delight the conservative establishment. Now what you write must inform, not entertain. Now your statements and your votes can shape the destiny of the entire nation.

Notwithstanding the role you have played in the past, I believe you have the intellectual depth to reflect upon and rethink the great issues the Court has confronted in the past and to become truly your own man. But to be your own man the first in the series of questions you must ask yourself is this: Beyond your own admirable personal drive, what were the primary forces or acts of good fortune that made your major achievements possible? This is a hard and difficult question. Let me suggest that you focus on at least four areas: (1) the impact of the work of civil rights lawyers and civil rights organizations on your life; (2) other than having picked a few individuals to be their favorite colored person, what it is that the conservatives of each generation have done that has been of significant benefit to African Americans, women, or other minorities; (3) the impact of the eradication of racial barriers in the voting on your own confirmation; and (4) the impact of civil rights victories in the area of housing and privacy on your personal life.

---

far too many victims of racism, sexism, and pernicious biases against those of different religions and national origins. The truth is that, even with these faults, we have been building a society with increasing levels of social justice embracing more and more Americans each decade.

A. Leon Higginbotham, Jr., *The Bicentennial of the Constitution: A Racial Perspective*, STAN. LAW., Fall 1987, at 8.

24. JAMES BALDWIN, *The Fire Next Time*, in THE PRICE OF THE TICKET 336 (1985). In a similar vein, on April 5, 1976, at the dedication of Independence Hall in Philadelphia on the anniversary of the Declaration of Independence, Judge William Hastie told the celebrants that, although there was reason to salute the nation on its bicentennial, "a nation's beginning is a proper source of reflective pride only to the extent that the subsequent and continuing process of its becoming deserves celebration." GILBERT WARE, WILLIAM HASTIE: GRACE UNDER PRESSURE 242 (1984).

The Impact of the Work of Civil Rights Lawyers and
Civil Rights Organizations on Your Life

During the time when civil rights organizations were challenging the Reagan Administration, I was frankly dismayed by some of your responses to and denigrations of these organizations. In 1984, the Washington Post reported that you had criticized traditional civil rights leaders because, instead of trying to reshape the Administration's policies, they had gone to the news media to "bitch, bitch, bitch, moan and moan, whine and whine." If that is still your assessment of these civil rights organizations or their leaders, I suggest, Justice Thomas, that you should ask yourself every day what would have happened to you if there had never been a Charles Hamilton Houston, a William Henry Hastie, a Thurgood Marshall, and that small cadre of other lawyers associated with them, who laid the groundwork for success in the twentieth-century racial civil rights cases? Couldn't they have been similarly charged with, as you phrased it, bitching and moaning and whining when they challenged the racism in the administrations of prior presidents, governors, and public officials? If there had never been an effective NAACP, isn't it highly probable that you might still be in Pin Point, Georgia, working as a laborer as some of your relatives did for decades?

Even though you had the good fortune to move to Savannah, Georgia, in 1955, would you have been able to get out of Savannah and get a responsible job if decades earlier the NAACP had not been challenging racial injustice throughout America? If the NAACP had not been lobbying, picketing, protesting, and politicking for a 1964 Civil Rights Act, would Monsanto Chemical Company have opened their doors to you in 1977? If Title VII had not been enacted might not American companies still continue to discriminate on the basis of race, gender, and national origin?

The philosophy of civil rights protest evolved out of the fact that black people were forced to confront this country's racist institutions without the benefit of equal access to those institutions. For example, in January of 1941, A. Philip Randolph planned a march on Washington, D.C., to protest widespread employment discrimination in the defense industry.[25] In order to avoid the prospect of a demonstration by potentially tens of thousands of Blacks, President Franklin Delano Roosevelt issued Executive Order 8802 barring discrimination in defense industries or government. The order led to the inclusion of anti-discrimination clauses in all government defense contracts and the establishment of the Fair Employment Practices Committee.

In 1940, President Roosevelt appointed William Henry Hastie as civilian aide to Secretary of War Henry L. Stimson. Hastie fought tirelessly against discrimination, but when confronted with an unabated program of segregation in all areas of

---

25. *See* JOHN HOPE FRANKLIN & ALFRED A. MOSS, JR., FROM SLAVERY TO FREEDOM: A HISTORY OF NEGRO AMERICANS 388–89 (1988); *see also* RICHARD KLUGER, SIMPLE JUSTICE: THE HISTORY OF BROWN V. BOARD OF EDUCATION AND BLACK AMERICA'S STRUGGLE FOR EQUALITY 219 (1975).

the armed forces, he resigned on January 31, 1943. His visible and dramatic protest sparked the move towards integrating the armed forces, with immediate and far-reaching results in the army air corps.

A. Philip Randolph and William Hastie understood—though I wonder if you do—what Frederick Douglass meant when he wrote:

> The whole history of the progress of human liberty shows that all concessions yet made to her august claims, have been born of earnest struggle. . . . If there is no struggle there is no progress. . . .

> This struggle may be a moral one, or it may be a physical one, and it may be both moral and physical, but it must be a struggle. Power concedes nothing without a demand. It never did and it never will.[26]

The struggles of civil rights organizations and civil rights lawyers have been both moral and physical, and their victories have been neither easy nor sudden. Though the *Brown* decision was issued only six years after your birth, the road to *Brown* started more than a century earlier. It started when Prudence Crandall was arrested in Connecticut in 1833 for attempting to provide schooling for colored girls.[27] It was continued in 1849 when Charles Sumner, a white lawyer and abolitionist, and Benjamin Roberts, a black lawyer,[28] challenged segregated schools in Boston.[29] It was continued as the NAACP, starting with Charles Hamilton Houston's suit, *Murray v. Pearson*,[30] in 1936, challenged Maryland's policy of excluding Blacks from the University of Maryland Law School. It was continued in *Gaines v. Missouri*,[31] when Houston challenged a 1937 decision of the Missouri Supreme Court. The Missouri courts had held that because law schools in the states of Illinois, Iowa, Kansas, and Nebraska accepted Negroes, a twenty-five-year-old black citizen of Missouri was not being denied his constitutional right to equal protection under the law when he was excluded from the only state supported law school in Missouri. It was continued in Sweatt v. Painter[32] in 1946, when Heman Marion Sweatt filed suit for admission to the Law School of the University of Texas after his application was rejected solely because he was black. Rather than admit him, the University postponed the matter for years and put up a separate and unaccredited law school for Blacks. It was continued in a series of cases against the University of Oklahoma, when, in 1950, in *McLaurin v. Oklahoma*,[33] G.W. McLaurin, a sixty-eight-year-old man, applied to the University of Oklahoma to obtain a Doctorate in education. He had earned his

---

26. Frederick Douglass, Speech Before The West Indian Emancipation Society (Aug. 4, 1857), *in* 2 PHILIP S. FONER, THE LIFE AND WRITINGS OF FREDERICK DOUGLASS 437 (1950).

27. *See Crandall v. State*, 10 Conn. 339 (1834).

28. *See* LEON F. LITWACK, NORTH OF SLAVERY: THE NEGRO IN THE FREE STATES, 1790–1860, at 147 (1961).

29. *See Roberts v. City of Boston*, 59 Mass. (5 Cush.) 198 (1850).

30. 182 A. 590 (1936).

31. 305 U.S. 337 (1938).

32. 339 U.S. 629 (1950).

33. 339 U.S. 637 (1950).

Master's degree in 1948, and had been teaching at Langston University, the state's college for Negroes. Yet he was "required to sit apart at . . . designated desks in an anteroom adjoining the classroom . . . and on the mezzanine floor of the library, . . . and to sit at a designated table and to eat at a different time from the other students in the school cafeteria."[34]

The significance of the victory in the *Brown* case cannot be overstated. Brown changed the moral tone of America; by eliminating the legitimization of state-imposed racism it implicitly questioned racism wherever it was used. It created a milieu in which private colleges were forced to recognize their failures in excluding or not welcoming minority students. I submit that even your distinguished under-graduate college, Holy Cross, and Yale University were influenced by the milieu created by Brown and thus became more sensitive to the need to create programs for the recruitment of competent minority students. In short, isn't it possible that you might not have gone to Holy Cross if the NAACP and other civil rights organizations, Martin Luther King and the Supreme Court, had not recast the racial mores of America? And if you had not gone to Holy Cross, and instead had gone to some underfunded state college for Negroes in Georgia, would you have been admitted to Yale Law School, and would you have met the alumni who played such a prominent role in maximizing your professional options?

I have cited this litany of NAACP[35] cases because I don't understand why you appeared so eager to criticize civil rights organizations or their leaders. In the 1980s, Benjamin Hooks and John Jacobs worked just as tirelessly in the cause of civil rights as did their predecessors Walter White, Roy Wilkins, Whitney Young, and Vernon Jordan in the 1950s and '60s. As you now start to adjudicate cases involving civil rights, I hope you will have more judicial integrity than to demean those advocates of the disadvantaged who appear before you. If you and I had not gotten many of the positive reinforcements that these organizations fought for and that the post-*Brown* era made possible, probably neither you nor I would be federal judges today.

What Have the Conservatives Ever Contributed to African Americans?

During the last ten years, you have often described yourself as a black conserva-tive. I must confess that, other than their own self-advancement, I am at a loss to understand what is it that the so-called black conservatives are so anxious to con-serve. Now that you no longer have to be outspoken on their behalf, perhaps you will recognize that in the past it was the white "conservatives" who screamed "seg-regation now, segregation forever!" It was primarily the conservatives who attacked the Warren Court relentlessly because of *Brown v. Board of Education* and who stood in the way of almost every measure to ensure gender and racial advancement.

---

34. *McLaurin*, 339 U.S. at 640.

35. I have used the term NAACP to include both the NAACP and the NAACP Legal Defense Fund. For examples of civil rights cases, *see* DERRICK A. BELL, JR., RACE, RACISM AND AMERICAN LAW 57–59, 157–62, 186–92, 250–58, 287–300, 477–99 (2d ed. 1980); JACK GREENBERG, RACE RELA-TIONS AND AMERICAN LAW 32–61 (1959).

For example, on March 11, 1956, ninety-six members of Congress, representing eleven southern states, issued the "Southern Manifesto," in which they declared that the *Brown* decision was an "unwarranted exercise of power by the Court, contrary to the Constitution."[36] Ironically, those members of Congress reasoned that the *Brown* decision was "destroying the amicable relations between the white and Negro races,"[37] and that "it had planted hatred and suspicion where there had been heretofore friendship and understanding."[38] They then pledged to use all lawful means to bring about the reversal of the decision, and praised those states which had declared the intention to resist its implementation.[39] The Southern Manifesto was more than mere political posturing by Southern Democrats. It was a thinly disguised racist attack on the constitutional and moral foundations of *Brown*. Where were the conservatives in the 1950s when the cause of equal rights needed every fair-minded voice it could find?

At every turn, the conservatives, either by tacit approbation or by active complicity, tried to derail the struggle for equal rights in this country. In the 1960s, it was the conservatives, including the then-senatorial candidate from Texas, George Bush,[40] the then-Governor from California, Ronald Reagan,[41] and the omnipresent Senator Strom Thurmond,[42] who argued that the 1964 Civil Rights Act was unconstitutional. In fact Senator Thurmond's 24 hour 18 minute filibuster during Senate deliberations on the 1957 Civil Rights Act set an all-time record.[43] He argued on the floor of the Senate that the provisions of the Act guaranteeing equal access to public accommodations amounted to an enslavement of white people.[44] If twenty-seven years ago George Bush, Ronald Reagan, and Strom Thurmond had succeeded, there would have been no position for you to fill as Assistant Secretary for Civil Rights in the Department of Education. There would have been no such agency as the Equal Employment Commission for you to chair.

Thus, I think now is the time for you to reflect on the evolution of American constitutional and statutory law, as it has affected your personal options and improved the options for so many Americans, particularly non-whites, women, and the poor. If the conservative agenda of the 1950s, '60s, and '70s had been implemented, what would have been the results of the important Supreme Court cases that now protect your rights and the rights of millions of other Americans who can now no longer

---

36. 102 CONG. REC. 4255, 4515 (1956).

37. *Id.* at 4516.

38. *Id.*

39. *See id.*

40. *See* Doug Freelander, *The Senate-Bush: The Polls Give Him 'Excellent Chance,'* HOUSTON POST, Oct. 11, 1964, § 17, at 8.

41. *See* David S. Broder, *Reagan Attacks the Great Society*, N.Y. TIMES, June 17, 1966, at 41.

42. *See* CHARLES WHALEN AND BARBARA WHALEN, THE LONGEST DEBATE: A LEGISLATIVE HISTORY OF THE 1964 CIVIL RIGHTS ACT 143 (1967).

43. *Id.*

44. SENATE COMMERCE COMM., CIVIL RIGHTS-PUBLIC ACCOMMODATIONS, S. REP. NO. 872, 88th Cong., 2d Sess. 62–63, 75–76 (1964) (Individual Views of Senator Strom Thurmond).

be discriminated against because of their race, religion, national origin, or physical disabilities? If, in 1954, the United States Supreme Court had accepted the traditional rationale that so many conservatives then espoused, would the 1896 *Plessy v. Ferguson* case, which announced the nefarious doctrine of "separate but equal," and which allowed massive inequalities, still be the law of the land? In short, if the conservatives of the 1950s had had their way, would there ever have been a *Brown v. Board of Education* to prohibit state-imposed racial segregation?

The Impact of Eradicating Racial Barriers to Voting

Of the fifty-two senators who voted in favor of your confirmation, some thirteen hailed from nine southern states. Some may have voted for you because they agreed with President Bush's assessment that you were "'the best person for the position.'"[45] But, candidly, Justice Thomas, I do not believe that you were indeed the most competent person to be on the Supreme Court. Charles Bowser, a distinguished African-American Philadelphia lawyer, said, "[I]'d be willing to bet . . . that not one of the senators who voted to confirm Clarence Thomas would hire him as their lawyer.'"[46]

Thus, realistically, many senators probably did not think that you were the most qualified person available. Rather, they were acting solely as politicians, weighing the potential backlash in their states of the black vote that favored you for emotional reasons and the conservative white vote that favored you for ideological reasons. The black voting constituency is important in many states, and today it could make a difference as to whether many senators are or are not re-elected. So here, too, you benefitted from civil rights progress.

No longer could a United States Senator say what Senator Benjamin Tillman of South Carolina said in anger when President Theodore Roosevelt invited a moderate Negro, Booker T. Washington, to lunch at the White House: "'Now that Roosevelt has eaten with that nigger Washington, we shall have to kill a thousand niggers to get them back to their place.'"[47] Senator Tillman did not have to fear any retaliation by Blacks because South Carolina and most southern states kept Blacks "in their place" by manipulating the ballot box. For example, because they did not have to confront the restraints and prohibitions of later Supreme Court cases, the manipulated "white" primary allowed Tillman and other racist senators to profit from the threat of violence to Blacks who voted, and from the disproportionate electoral power given to rural whites. For years, the NAACP litigated some of the most significant cases attacking racism at the ballot box. That organization almost

---

45. *The Supreme Court; Excerpts From News Conference Announcing Court Nominee*, N.Y. Times, July 2, 1991, at A14 (statement of President Bush).

46. Peter Binzer, *Bowser Is an Old Hand at Playing the Political Game in Philadelphia*, Phila. Inquirer, Nov. 13, 1991, at A11 (quoting Charles Bowser).

47. William A. Sinclair, The Aftermath of Slavery: A Study of the Condition and Environment of the American Negro 187 (Afro-Am Press 1969) (1905) (quoting Senator Benjamin Tillman).

singlehandedly created the foundation for black political power that led in part to the 1965 Civil Rights Act.

Moreover, if it had not been for the Supreme Court's opinion in *Smith v. Allright*,[48] a case which Thurgood Marshall argued, most all the southern senators who voted for you would have been elected in what was once called a "white primary" — a process which precluded Blacks from effective voting in the southern primary election, where the real decisions were made on who would run every hamlet, township, city, county and state. The seminal case of *Baker v. Carr*,[49] which articulated the concept of one man-one vote, was part of a series of Supreme Court precedents that caused southern senators to recognize that patently racist diatribes could cost them an election. Thus your success even in your several confirmation votes is directly attributable to the efforts that the "activist" Warren Court and civil rights organizations have made over the decades.

Housing and Privacy

If you are willing, Justice Thomas, to consider how the history of civil rights in this country has shaped your public life, then imagine for a moment how it has affected your private life. With some reluctance, I make the following comments about housing and marriage because I hope that reflecting on their constitutional implications may raise your consciousness and level of insight about the dangers of excessive intrusion by the state in personal and family relations.

From what I have seen of your house on television scans and in newspaper photos, it is apparent that you live in a comfortable Virginia neighborhood. Thus I start with Holmes's view that "a page of history is worth a volume of logic."[50] The history of Virginia's legislatively and judicially imposed racism should be particularly significant to you now that as a Supreme Court Justice you must determine the limits of a state's intrusion on family and other matters of privacy.

It is worthwhile pondering what the impact on you would have been if Virginia's legalized racism had been allowed to continue as a viable constitutional doctrine. In 1912, Virginia enacted a statute giving cities and towns the right to pass ordinances which would divide the city into segregated districts for black and white residents.[51] Segregated districts were designated white or black depending on the race of the majority of the residents.[52] It became a crime for any black person to move into and occupy a residence in an area known as a white district.[53] Similarly, it was a crime for any white person to move into a black district.[54]

---

48. 321 U.S. 649 (1944).

49. 369 U.S. 186 (1962).

50. *New York Trust Company v. Eisner*, 256 U.S. 345, 349 (1921).

51. Act of Mar. 12, 1912, ch. 157, § 1, 1912 Va. Acts 330, 330.

52. *Id.* § 3, at 330–31.

53. *Id.* § 4, at 331.

54. *Id.* There were a few statutory exceptions, the most important being that the servants of "the other race" could reside upon the premises that his or her employer owned or occupied. *Id.* § 9, at 332.

Even prior to the Virginia statute of 1912, the cities of Ashland and Richmond had enacted such segregationist statutes.[55] The ordinances also imposed the same segregationist policies on any "place of public assembly." Apparently schools, churches, and meeting places were defined by the color of their members. Thus, white Christian Virginia wanted to make sure that no black Christian churches were in their white Christian neighborhoods.

The impact of these statutes can be assessed by reviewing the experiences of two African-Americans, John Coleman and Mary Hopkins. Coleman purchased property in Ashland, Virginia in 1911.[56] In many ways he symbolized the American dream of achieving some modest upward mobility by being able to purchase a home earned through initiative and hard work. But shortly after moving to his home, he was arrested for violating Ashland's segregation ordinance because a majority of the residents in the block were white. Also, in 1911, the City of Richmond prosecuted and convicted a black woman, Mary S. Hopkins, for moving into a predominantly white block.[57]

Coleman and Hopkins appealed their convictions to the Supreme Court of Virginia which held that the ordinances of Ashland and Richmond did not violate the United States Constitution and that the fines and convictions were valid.[58]

If Virginia's law of 1912 still prevailed, and if your community passed laws like the ordinances of Richmond and Ashland, you would not be able to live in your own house. Fortunately, the Virginia ordinances and statutes were in effect nullified by a case brought by the NAACP in 1915, where a similar statute of the City of Louisville was declared unconstitutional.[59] But even if your town council had not passed such an ordinance, the developers would in all probability have incorporated racially restrictive covenants in the title deeds to the individual homes. Thus, had it not been for the vigor of the NAACP's litigation efforts in a series of persistent attacks against racial covenants you would have been excluded from your own home. Fortunately, in 1948, in *Shelley v. Kraemer*,[60] a case argued by Thurgood Marshall, the NAACP succeeded in having such racially restrictive covenants declared unconstitutional.

Yet with all of those litigation victories, you still might not have been able to live in your present house because a private developer might have refused to sell you a home solely because you are an African American. Again you would be saved

---

55. *See* Ashland, Va., Ordinance (Sept. 12, 1911) [hereinafter, *Ashland Ordinance*]; Richmond, Va., Ordinance (Dec. 5, 1911) [hereinafter, *Richmond Ordinance*].

56. *See Hopkins v. City of Richmond*, 86 S.E. 139, 142 (Va.1915). At the time of the purchase, the house was occupied by a black tenant who had lived there prior to the enactment of the ordinance, so the purchase precipitated no change in the color composition or racial density of the neighborhood or block.

57. *Id.* at 141.

58. *Id.*

59. *See Buchanan v. Warley*, 245 U.S. 60 (1917).

60. 334 U.S. 1 (1948).

because in 1968 the Supreme Court, in *Jones v. Alfred H. Mayer Co.*, in an opinion by Justice Stewart, held that the 1866 Civil Rights Act precluded such private racial discrimination.[61] It was a relatively close case; the two dissenting justices said that the majority opinion was "ill considered and ill-advised."[62] It was the values of the majority which made the difference. And it is your values that will determine the vitality of other civil rights acts for decades to come.

Had you overcome all of those barriers to housing and if you and your present wife decided that you wanted to reside in Virginia, you would nonetheless have been violating the Racial Integrity Act of 1924,[63] which the Virginia Supreme Court as late as 1966 said was consistent with the federal constitution because of the overriding state interest in the institution of marriage.[64] Although it was four years after the *Brown* case, Richard Perry Loving and his wife, Mildred Jeter Loving were convicted in 1958 and originally sentenced to one year in jail because of their interracial marriage. As an act of magnanimity the trial court later suspended the sentences, "'for a period of 25 years upon the provision that both accused leave Caroline County and the state of Virginia at once and do not return together or at the same time to said county and state for a period of 25 years.'"[65]

The conviction was affirmed by a unanimous Supreme Court of Virginia, though they remanded the case back as to the re-sentencing phase. Incidentally, the Virginia trial judge justified the constitutionality of the prohibition against interracial marriages as follows:

> "Almighty God created the races white, black, yellow, Malay and red, and he placed them on separate continents. And but for the interference with his arrangement there would be no cause for such marriages. The fact that he separated the races shows that he did not intend for the races to mix."[66]

If the Virginia courts had been sustained by the United States Supreme Court in 1966, and if, after your marriage, you and your wife had, like the Lovings, defied the Virginia statute by continuing to live in your present residence, you could have been in the penitentiary today rather than serving as an Associate Justice of the United States Supreme Court.

I note these pages of record from American legal history because they exemplify the tragedy of excessive intrusion on individual and family rights. The only persistent protector of privacy and family rights has been the United States Supreme Court, and such protection has occurred only when a majority of the Justices has possessed a broad vision of human rights. Will you, in your moment of truth, take for granted that the Constitution protects you and your wife against all forms of

---

61. 392 U.S. 409 (1968).
62. *Id.* at 449 (Harlan, J., dissenting).
63. *See Loving v. Virginia*, 388 U.S. 1, 4–6 (1967).
64. *See Loving v. Virginia*, 147 S.E.2d 78 (Va. 1966), *rev'd*, 388 U.S. 1 (1967).
65. *Id.* at 79 (quoting the trial court).
66. *Loving*, 388 U.S. at 3 (quoting the trial judge).

deliberate state intrusion into family and privacy matters, and protects you even against some forms of discrimination by other private parties such as the real estate developer, but nevertheless find that it does not protect the privacy rights of others, and particularly women, to make similarly highly personal and private decisions?

Conclusion

This letter may imply that I am somewhat skeptical as to what your performance will be as a Supreme Court Justice. Candidly, I and many other thoughtful Americans are very concerned about your appointment to the Supreme Court. But I am also sufficiently familiar with the history of the Supreme Court to know that a few of its members (not many) about whom there was substantial skepticism at the time of their appointment became truly outstanding Justices. In that context I think of Justice Hugo Black. I am impressed by the fact that at the very beginning of his illustrious career he articulated his vision of the responsibility of the Supreme Court. In one of his early major opinions he wrote, "courts stand . . . as havens of refuge for those who might otherwise suffer because they are helpless, weak, out-numbered, or . . . are non-conforming victims of prejudice and public excitement."[67]

While there are many other equally important issues that you must consider and on which I have not commented, none will determine your place in history as much as your defense of the weak, the poor, minorities, women, the disabled and the powerless. I trust that you will ponder often the significance of the statement of Justice Blackmun, in a vigorous dissent of two years ago, when he said: "[S]adly . . . one wonders whether the majority [of the Court] still believes that . . . race discrimination—or more accurately, race discrimination against nonwhites—is a problem in our society, or even remembers that it ever was."[68]

You, however, must try to remember that the fundamental problems of the disadvantaged, women, minorities, and the powerless have not all been solved simply because you have "moved on up" from Pin Point, Georgia, to the Supreme Court. In your opening remarks to the Judiciary Committee, you described your life in Pin Point, Georgia, as "far removed in space and time from this room, this day and this moment."[69] I have written to tell you that your life today, however, should be not far removed from the visions and struggles of Frederick Douglass, Sojourner Truth, Harriet Tubman, Charles Hamilton Houston, A. Philip Randolph, Mary McLeod Bethune, W.E.B. Dubois, Roy Wilkins, Whitney Young, Martin Luther King, Judge William Henry Hastie, Justices Thurgood Marshall, Earl Warren, and William Brennan, as well as the thousands of others who dedicated much of their lives to create the America that made your opportunities possible.[70] I hope you have

---

67. *Chambers v. Florida*, 309 U.S. 227, 241 (1940).

68. *Wards Cove Packing Co. v. Antonio*, 490 U.S. 642, 662 (1989) (Blackmun, J., dissenting).

69. *The Thomas Hearings; Excerpts from Senate Session on the Thomas Nomination*, N.Y. Times, Sept. 11, 1991, at A1 (opening statement of Clarence Thomas).

70. It is hardly possible to name all the individuals who fought to bring equal rights to all Americans. Some are gone. Others are fighting still. They include Prudence Crandall, Charles Sumner,

the strength of character to exemplify those values so that the sacrifices of all these men and women will not have been in vain.

I am sixty-three years old. In my lifetime I have seen African Americans denied the right to vote, the opportunities to a proper education, to work, and to live where they choose.[71] I have seen and known racial segregation and discrimination.[72] But I have also seen the decision in *Brown* rendered. I have seen the first African American sit on the Supreme Court. And I have seen brave and courageous people, black and white, give their lives for the civil rights cause. My memory of them has always been without bitterness or nostalgia. But today it is sometimes without hope; for I wonder whether their magnificent achievements are in jeopardy. I wonder whether (and how far) the majority of the Supreme Court will continue to retreat from protecting the rights of the poor, women, the disadvantaged, minorities, and the powerless.[73] And if, tragically, a majority of the Court continues to retreat, I wonder whether you, Justice Thomas, an African American, will be part of that majority.

No one would be happier than I if the record you will establish on the Supreme Court in years to come demonstrates that my apprehensions were unfounded.[74] You were born into injustice, tempered by the hard reality of what it means to be poor and black in America, and especially to be poor because you are black. You have

---

Robert Morris, William Lloyd Garrison, William T. Coleman, Jr., Jack Greenberg, Judges Louis Pollak, Constance Baker Motley, Robert Carter, Collins Seitz, Justices Hugo Black, Lewis Powell, Harry Blackmun and John Paul Stevens. For those whom I have not named, their contribution to the cause of civil rights may be all the more heroic for at times being unsung. But, to paraphrase Yale Professor Owen Fiss' tribute to Justice Marshall: "As long as there is law, their names should be remembered, and when their stories are told, all the world should listen." Owen Fiss, *A Tribute to Justice Marshall*, 105 HARV. L. REV. 49, 55 (1991).

71. For an analysis of discrimination faced by Blacks in the areas of voting, education, employment, and housing, *see* GUNNAR MYRDAL, AN AMERICAN DILEMMA: THE NEGRO PROBLEM AND MODERN DEMOCRACY 479–86 (9th ed. 1944) (voting); JOHN HOPE FRANKLIN & ALFRED A. MOSS, JR., FROM SLAVERY TO FREEDOM: A HISTORY OF NEGRO AMERICANS 360–69 (6th ed. 1988) (education); COMMITTEE ON THE STATUS OF BLACK AMERICANS, NATIONAL RESEARCH COUNCIL, A COMMON DESTINY: BLACKS AND AMERICAN SOCIETY 88–91, 315–23 (Gerald D. Jaynes & Robin M. Williams, Jr. eds., 1989) (housing and employment); *see also* MARY FRANCES BERRY & JOHN W. BLASSINGAME, LONG MEMORY: THE BLACK EXPERIENCE IN AMERICA(1982).

72. *See* A. LEON HIGGINBOTHAM, JR., IN THE MATTER OF COLOR at vii–ix (1978); A. Leon Higginbotham, Jr., *The Dream with Its Back against the Wall*, YALE L. REF., Spring 1990, at 34; A. Leon Higginbotham, Jr., *A Tribute to Justice Thurgood Marshall*, 105 HARV. L. REV. 55, 61 (1991).

73. A. Leon Higginbotham, Jr., F. Michael Higginbotham & Sandile Ngcobo, *De Jure Housing Segregation in the United States and South Africa: The Difficult Pursuit for Racial Justice*, 4 U. ILL. REV. 763, 874 n. 612 (1990) (noting the recent tendency of the Supreme Court to ignore race discrimination).

74. In his recent tribute to Justice Marshall, Justice Brennan wrote: "In his twenty-four Terms on the Supreme Court, Justice Marshall played a crucial role in enforcing the constitutional protections that distinguish our democracy. Indeed, he leaves behind an enviable record of opinions supporting the rights of the less powerful and less fortunate." William J. Brennan, Jr., *A Tribute To Justice Marshall*, 105 HARV. L. REV. 23 (1991). You may serve on the Supreme Court twenty years longer than Justice Marshall. At the end of your career, I hope that thoughtful Americans may be able to speak similarly of you.

found a door newly cracked open and you have escaped. I trust you shall not forget that many who preceded you and many who follow you have found, and will find, the door of equal opportunity slammed in their faces through no fault of their own. And I also know that time and the tides of history often call out of men and women qualities that even they did not know lay within them. And so, with hope to balance my apprehensions, I wish you well as a thoughtful and worthy successor to Justice Marshall in the ever ongoing struggle to assure equal justice under law for all persons.

140 *University of Pennsylvania Law Review* 1005, 1005–28.

Copyright © (1992) A. Leon Higginbotham, Jr.

Reprinted with permission of Evelyn Brooks Higginbotham.

C. Supreme Court Jurisprudence

1. Letter to National Bar Association

A. Leon Higginbotham, Jr.

Letter to Judicial Council May 27, 1998*

The Honorable Bernette J. Johnson *Chair,* Judicial Council National Bar Association c/o Louisiana Supreme Court 301 Loyola Avenue New Orleans, LA 70112

Re: The Judicial Council

Dear Justice Johnson:

Many years ago, I had the pleasure of becoming a charter member of the Judicial Council and, from time to time, I have delivered major lectures to both the Judicial Council and to the National Bar Association, of which I am a life member. One of the goals of the Judicial Council in its formation was that it would be an exemplar of excellence in public service and would have sensitivity to the plight of those African Americans who are impacted often with cruel disparities and irrational adversities by the criminal and civil justice systems. The Judicial Council was never intended to be a special social elite group of persons who, after they become successful in public life, then forget or denigrate their brothers and sisters, who still live in poverty, who are powerless and suffer from inadequate and ineffective public representation. As you may recall, Justice Thurgood Marshall, Judge William Hastie, Judge Albert Tuttle, Judge Damon Keith, Judge Nathaniel Jones, and many others, have spoken at luncheons of the Judicial Council. They are models who inspired both the young and the elders because, by their record, they were exemplars of judicial excellence and, also, by their record, they had consistently demonstrated sensitivity to the problems of the weak, the poor and the dispossessed. Thus, I was shocked to learn that you have invited Justice Clarence Thomas as the premier banquet speaker for the Judicial Council at the July convention. By the very nature of your invitation, you give him

---

* (footnotes omitted).

an imprimatur that he has *never* had from any responsible organization within the African-American community or any non-conservative groups of whites in America. I trust you have not forgotten the circumstances of his nomination.

I will not take a position as to whether he should be disinvited, and I leave that significant responsibility to the judgment of the Executive Committee. I am not one who believes there is, or should be, a monolithic view within the African-American community on all issues; but, I do think that there are certain undisputable common denominators as to what constitutes progress or regress. Within that context and from the perspective of almost every constitutional law scholar, there is no doubt that Justice Thomas has done more to turn back the clock of racial progress than has perhaps any other African-American public official in the history of this country.

Since you have invited Justice Thomas, I submit that you should have a responding panel, fully open to the public, to discuss the following topic: "The Supreme Court's Partial Demise of Justice Thurgood Marshall's Views and Justice Clarence Thomas's Actual Role in the Diminution of the Houston, Hastie and Marshall Vision." Professor Charles J. Ogletree, Jr. of Harvard Law School, Professor F. Michael Higginbotham of New York University School of Law and the University of Baltimore School of Law, and I would be pleased to participate in such a panel.

The Controversy over Justice Thomas's Nomination

Upon the nomination of Clarence Thomas to the United States Supreme Court, many Americans, and particularly African Americans, were confronted with intensely emotional and divisive issues. As an example, consider the agony within the National Bar Association (NBA), the premier organization of African-American lawyers. While Clarence Thomas's nomination was pending in August 1991, the NBA met at its Annual Convention in Indianapolis. After three days of intense debate, deliberations and unenthusiastic recommendations as to his nomination by both the Judicial Selection Committee and the Executive Committee, the general body voted 128 to oppose, 124 to support, and 31 took "no position."

It was a significant event when the national delegates of the premier professional bar association of African Americans, dedicated to the concept of advancing black lawyers into positions of power, were sufficiently doubtful of Clarence Thomas's worthiness that they did not produce a majority vote in favor of his nomination to the United States Supreme Court. Sharon McPhail, then the president of the NBA, summed up her frustrations by asking: "Will the real Clarence Thomas please stand up?" She pondered: "Is Clarence Thomas a 'conservative with a common touch' as Ruth Marcus [of the *Washington Post*] refers to him . . . or [is he] the 'counterfeit hero' he is accused of being by Hayward Burns," then the distinguished dean of CUNY Law School, who was also an African American, who was also a Yale graduate, and who knew Clarence Thomas for many years?

One writer, in the October 1991 *National Bar Association Magazine*, observed: "While his strongest supporters are confident that he will be confirmed, his critics accuse him of forgetting where he came from."

During the last seven years, I have been involved in a multifaceted research project on Justice Thomas and his impact on both the Supreme Court and on the status of African Americans, women and the poor in this country, and at a later time, I will write in greater detail as to the devastating consequences of his "conservativeness" on minorities, the poor and the powerless.

The Continuing Controversy: Justice Thomas's Record

Hudson v. McMillian involved a black prisoner, who was taken out of his Louisiana cell, put into a holding room with his feet shackled, hands cuffed in back of him, and was beaten by two guards. His teeth were loosened, his dental plate broken, his lips burst, eye blacked, and he was kicked in his back. The issue before the United States Supreme Court was whether that beating violated the Eighth Amendment's prohibition against cruel and unusual punishment. Seven Justices declared that the beating was a violation of the Eighth Amendment. I submit it took no courage to say that, in a civilized society, you cannot allow law enforcement officials, without any provocation or justification, to beat and brutalize citizens, even if those citizens are prisoners. In *Hudson*, only one person, Justice Clarence Thomas, wrote a dissent criticizing the very rational and civilized opinion of the seven person majority; he was joined in his opinion only by Justice Scalia. After the opinion came down on February 27, 1992, the *New York Times* wrote an editorial that called Justice Thomas "the youngest, cruelest justice." Other commentators were not quite as polite.

To put this case in perspective, I will quote extensively from William Raspberry's column in *The Washington Post*. He had supported Justice Thomas's nomination to the Supreme Court, but on February 28, 1992, Raspberry wrote the following:

Clarence:

I know I'm supposed to call you Justice Thomas, but I don't want to be quite that formal. I want to talk straight to a guy I thought I knew a little.

You know what I want to talk about. It's that dissent of yours in the matter of *Hudson v. McMillian*. Come on, Clarence. Conservative is one thing; bizarre is another.

What was truly bizarre is that when the conservative-dominated U.S. Supreme Court reversed the appellate decision this week, yours was one of only two dissenting voices.

To tell you the truth, Clarence, I'm personally embarrassed. You know you weren't my choice to succeed Thurgood Marshall on the nation's highest court. You were too conservative for my taste and, more significant, I thought you lacked the requisite judicial experience. But I thought I understood your conservatism as a sort of harsh pragmatism that most of us harbor to some degree. I cautioned black America not to let your conservatism blind them to your intellectual honesty. Conservatism, I insisted, isn't the same thing as stupidity—even in a black man. And since Bush was going to name a conservative to Thurgood's seat, I said, better he should appoint a conservative who has known deprivation and unfairness and racism at first hand.

As a matter of fact, you encouraged that view. I mean, wasn't that the whole point of your recital of your underprivileged background, of your but-for-the-grace-of-God musings about society's losers?

Look, guy, I never expected you to do a Hugo Black and become a court liberal. But I was prepared to see you put a compassionate face on conservatism. When it became clear that you would be confirmed to the court, I told my friends (your critics) that they should just watch while you surprised your right-wing supporters and confounded our enemies.

But your high-falutin' angels-on-a-pinhead opinion the other day that for prison guards to beat the hell out of a handcuffed and shackled inmate does not constitute "cruel and unusual punishment" (unless the victim winds up in intensive care) confounded only those who tried to cut you some slack.

Raspberry concluded: "Of course, I don't expect that you will always do what strikes the rest of us as the 'right thing.' But why go out of your way to do wrong?"

His dissent in the *Hudson* case, and his votes in a series of other cases, demonstrate that Justice Thomas has often taken wretchedly reactionary positions. I believe that his views are, for the 1990s, at times, the moral equivalent of the views of the shameful majorities in the nineteenth century Supreme Court cases of *Dred Scott* and *Plessy*. More than a century ago, the United States Supreme Court decided *Plessy*, legitimizing racism and retarding racial progress for almost a century. In 1992, Justices Kennedy, O'Connor, and Souter said, "[w]e think *Plessy* was wrong the day it was decided." Other Justices, including Chief Justice Rehnquist, have agreed. In short, I submit that, like the majority in *Plessy*, Justice Thomas's dissent in *Hudson* "was wrong the day" it was written.

I have often pondered how it is that Justice Thomas, an African American, could be so insensitive to the plight of the powerless. Why is he no different, or maybe even worse, than many of the conservative Supreme Court Justices of this century? I can think of only one Supreme Court Justice during this century who was more callous than Justice Clarence Thomas—Justice James McReynolds, a white supremacist, who referred to blacks as "niggers." In 1938, a landmark desegregation case was argued before the Supreme court by Charles Hamilton Houston, the brilliant black lawyer who laid the foundation for *Brown v. Board of Education*. During Houston's oral argument, Justice McReynolds turned his back on the attorney and stared at the wall of the courtroom. In his autobiography, Justice William O. Douglas described how McReynolds received a rare, but well deserved, comeuppance when he made a disparaging comment about Howard University:

One day McReynolds went to the barbershop in the Court. Gates, the black barber, put the sheet around his neck and over his lap, and as he was pinning it behind him McReynolds said, 'Gates, tell me, where is this nigger university in Washington, D.C.?' Gates removed the white cloth from

McReynolds, walked around and faced him, and said in a very calm and dignified manner, 'Mr. Justice, I am shocked that any Justice would call a Negro a nigger. There is a Negro college in Washington, D.C. Its name is Howard University and we are very proud of it.' McReynolds muttered some kind of apology and Gates resumed his work in silence.

Justice Thomas As a Catalyst for *Hopwood v. Texas*

No case better demonstrates the impact of Justice Thomas's callousness than that of *Hopwood v. Texas*. Cheryl Hopwood, a white woman, along with three white men, claimed that the University of Texas School of Law's affirmative action admissions program violated the Equal Protection Clause of the Fourteenth Amendment. The plaintiffs, who had been rejected for admission, alleged that they had higher grade-point averages and test scores than 93 African American and Mexican-American students who had been admitted.

In 1996, a three-judge panel of the U.S. Court of Appeals for the Fifth Circuit reversed a district court judge, and held that the law school could "not use race as a factor in deciding which applicants to admit." Two judges concluded that considering race or ethnicity in admissions would *always* be unconstitutional—even if it was intended "to combat the perceived effects of a hostile environment," to remedy past discrimination, or to promote diversity. The third judge disagreed that diversity could never be a compelling government interest, but reasoned that "the admissions process here under scrutiny was not narrowly tailored to achieve diversity."

These judges' views are in stark contrast to those of many American educators, among them Dr. Nanner Keohane, president of Duke University, who stated that: "my experience as a teacher at three institutions of higher education and as president of two others is that diversity benefits students, faculty, institutions, and the world of knowledge." Harvard University's President, Neil L. Rudenstine, stated: "This year's report shows some encouraging signs of progress, as well as areas of continuing worry. All of us have a common interest in creating broader opportunities within Harvard for women and minority members of under-represented minority groups, and in being part of a community where diversity—of backgrounds, experiences, and points of view—is one of our defining strengths."

In adopting such drastic reasoning, these three judges ignored the history and evidence of discrimination against minorities at the law school, and they ignored some facts of the case—most glaringly, that Hopwood's test scores were higher than those of more than 100 *white* students who were admitted. They also ignored settled precedent. Starting in 1978 with *Bakke v. Regents of the University of California*, the Supreme Court has consistently maintained that student diversity, when properly devised, is a valid justification for race-based affirmative action.

The Fifth Circuit panel calculated, but did not say publicly, that Justice Thomas's position would be hostile to the position of Justice Thurgood Marshall and Justice Lewis Powell in the *Bakke* case. The state of Texas appealed the panel's majority opinion in *Hopwood* and requested a rehearing before all of its 16 active judges. The request was denied. All nine of the judges who either voted against the rehearing or declined to vote were appointed by President Reagan or President Bush; six of the seven dissenting judges were appointed by President Carter or President Clinton.

The dissenters wrote that the majority's opinion "goes out of its way to break ground that the Supreme Court itself has been careful to avoid and purports to over-rule a Supreme Court decision." They added that: "[t]he radical implications of this opinion . . . will literally change the face of public educational institutions through-out Texas, the other states of this circuit, and this nation." The Judicial Council and every African American judge must never forget that the reduced racial diversity in public educational institutions will be attributable to Justice Thomas's adverse fifth and divisive vote.

The majority opinion in *Hopwood* stands in sharp contrast to the role that the Fifth Circuit played during the civil rights era. In the 1950s and 1960s, many South-ern officials, white citizens' councils, and vigilante groups urged total defiance of the federal courts' civil rights decrees. Despite the persistent hostility, virtually every Fifth Circuit judge—all appointed by President Eisenhower—repeatedly affirmed the constitutional rights of black citizens, among them Rosa Parks and Martin Luther King, Jr.

When President Reagan took office, he pledged to bring a "new breed of conser-vatism" to the judiciary. Under his and President Bush's administrations, the judi-ciary became not only far more conservative, but also far more white than it had been. Of 83 appointments to the appeals courts, Reagan appointed only one African American. Bush appointed two, and one of those was Clarence Thomas. (Carter appointed nine African Americans and Clinton has appointed five.)

In 1983, during his less conservative days, Clarence Thomas said, "but for affir-mative action laws, God only knows where I would be today." Now that he is on the Supreme Court, he repudiates affirmative action, and has made it safe for people like Professor Lino A. Graglia of the University of Texas School of Law to assert openly that: "Blacks and Mexican Americans are not academically competitive with whites in selective institutions," because "they have a culture that seems not to encourage achievement. Failure is not looked upon with disgrace." Justice Thomas's skewed and hostile views have also paved the way for the ascent of anti-affirmative action crusaders like Ward Connerly and the Thernstroms. Connerly is a driving force behind California's Proposition 209, striking down all governmental affirmative action programs, the philosophy of which seems to be that anything that benefits African Americans, no matter how benign, useful or good, is inherently suspect and wrong.

In a 1989 employment discrimination case, Justice Harry Blackmun, a Nixon appointee, wondered whether a majority of the Supreme Court "still believes that . . . race discrimination against non-whites is a problem in our society, or even remembers that it ever was." This question reverberates today in the chill-ing legacy of the *Hopwood* decision. *Hopwood* has already had a pervasive impact on decreasing minority enrollment in many institutions of higher education. The number of medical school applications from under-represented minorities has dropped by 11 percent nationally and 17 percent among students who live in Texas, Louisiana, and Mississippi, where the Fifth Circuit now has jurisdiction. The group that represented the plaintiffs in the University of Texas case recently filed suit to have the affirmative action admissions program for undergraduates at the University of Michigan declared unconstitutional.

The number of African-American students at the University of Texas School of Law has decreased from 31 to 4. The Fifth Circuit extended the logic of a series of Supreme Court cases that were hostile to racial progress and, where the Supreme Court has been divided five to four, in each instance, Justice Thomas provided the fifth hostile vote and seemed to go out of his way to condemn affirmative action, even to the point of suggesting that it may be constitutionally impermissible. Yet, the record establishes that, in 1983, during his more frank and less conservative days, Justice Thomas said: "But for affirmative action laws, God only knows where I would be today. These laws and their proper application are all that stand between the first 17 years of my life and the second 17 years."

As he curried favor with the Reagan Administration, he reversed his position 180 degrees.

In 1987, he wrote:

> I firmly insist that the Constitution be interpreted in a colorblind fashion. Hence I emphasize black self-help, as opposed to racial quotas and other race-conscious legal devices that only further and deepen the original problem.

In 1988, he stated:

> Affirmative action programs have given no substantial benefits to blacks. The term has thus become a mere political buzz word.

Adarand Constructors, Inc. v. Pena and Minority Contractors

Justice Thurgood Marshall's view on affirmative action was very different from Justice Clarence Thomas's view. Justice Marshall's view was that affirmative action is helpful to minorities and women as an effective means to achieving racial and gender equality, while Justice Thomas's view is that affirmative action, no matter what the justification, constitutes discrimination against whites and is harmful to minorities and women. Justice Marshall spent most of his judicial career supporting affirmative action, while Justice Thomas has seemingly spent his trying to eliminate it.

The *Adarand* case concerned a white, male-owned business, Adarand Constructors, that filed suit when it lost a federal construction subcontract to Gonzales Construction Co., a minority-owned firm, due to an affirmative action preference. In that case, five Justices, including Justice Thomas, held that the program was illegal, four thought that it was permissible.

The differences between Justice Marshall and Justice Thomas over affirmative action go well beyond disagreement over the standard of review to be applied. Justice Marshall believed that affirmative action was helpful to minorities and women, while Justice Thomas views it as a cancer to be eradicated.

In his concurring opinion in *Adarand*, Justice Thomas stated: "These [affirmative action] programs stamp minorities with a badge of inferiority and may cause them to develop dependencies or to adapt an attitude that they are 'entitled' to preferences." But Justice Marshall visualized affirmative action programs not as preferences, but as a means to create equal opportunity—opportunity that had been denied to women and minorities by law for over two hundred years. Justice Marshall felt that those who viewed affirmative action as a preference simply were ignoring the realities of American history. The inequalities that existed between whites and minorities, and men and women, were the result of centuries of discriminatory laws and judicial decisions. What Justice Marshall always remembered—and what Justice Thomas appears to have forgotten—is that, for most of our nation's history, the Supreme Court interpreted the Constitution as not only tolerating a retreat on the principle of equality, but condoning a frontal assault on equality for women and minorities.

In the 1873 *Bradwell* case, the Court concluded that the Equal Protection Clause of the Fourteenth Amendment did not protect a woman against gender discrimination that excluded her from the practice of law. In the 1899 *Cumming* case, the Court concluded that the Equal Protection Clause was not violated by the denial of public high school education to black children. As recently as 1987, in *McClesky v. Kemp*, the Court concluded that the Equal Protection Clause had not been violated by the disproportionally high number of blacks receiving capital sentences in Georgia.

In his concurring opinion in *Adarand*, Justice Thomas expressed the belief that all Americans should be treated as equal before the law. In support of this belief, Justice Thomas quoted the Declaration of Independence: "'We hold these truths to be self-evident, that all men are created equal. . . .'" Powerful words. Yet, Justice Thomas failed to mention that, as applied to African Americans, these words were not only ignored for two hundred years, but were repudiated by the Supreme Court in the *Dred Scott* case, where the Justices reasoned that blacks, whether slave or free, "had no rights which the white man was bound to respect." The same repudiation of racial equality was implicit in *Plessy v. Ferguson*, which allowed blacks to be isolated from whites, just as animals are isolated from human beings.

Justice Marshall's view that affirmative action was helpful, not harmful, to minorities and women was based on the value that he held so dearly—equal rights under law. In a 1979 speech, he said: "the goal of a true democracy such as ours . . . is that any baby born in the United States, even if born to the blackest, most illiterate, most underprivileged Negro in Mississippi, is, merely by being born and drawing its first breath in this democracy, endowed with the exact same rights as a child born to a Rockefeller." In Justice Marshall's view, affirmative action helped to secure equal rights and equal opportunity for all, including poor, black, and illiterate children in Mississippi and Georgia, as Justice Clarence Thomas once was.

In his concurring opinion in *Adarand*, Justice Thomas stated: "In my mind, government-sponsored racial discrimination based on benign prejudice is just as noxious as discrimination inspired by malicious prejudice. In each instance, it is racial discrimination plain and simple." Justice Marshall, however, believed that there was a big difference between benign discrimination and invidious discrimination. In his dissent in *City of Richmond v. J.A. Croson Company*, where the City of Richmond adopted an affirmative action program for minority owned businesses, Justice Marshall stated: "It is a welcome symbol of racial progress when the former capital of the Confederacy acts forthrightly to confront the effects of racial discrimination in its midst. . . . A profound difference separates governmental actions that themselves are racist, and governmental actions that seek to remedy the effects of prior racism. . . . Racial classifications 'drawn on the presumption that one race is inferior to another or because they put the weight of government behind racial hatred and separatism' warrant the strictest judicial scrutiny because of the very irrelevance of these rationales. By contrast, racial classifications drawn for the purpose of remedying the effects of discrimination that itself was race-based have a highly pertinent basis: the tragic and indelible fact that discrimination against blacks and other racial minorities in this Nation has pervaded our Nation's history and continues to scar our society. . . ."

When it comes to affirmative action, Justice Marshall and Justice Thomas hold vastly different viewpoints. Whether as a lawyer or jurist, Justice Marshall maintained a principled view that civil rights were entitled to vigorous protection. His interest in enforcing the Constitution in general, and its equal protection principles in particular, were rooted in his personal experience with racial discrimination and his unwavering respect for constitutional government and the rule of law. It was Justice Marshall's lifelong struggle for true equality under the law for black and white, rich and poor, male and female, that sets him apart from Justice Thomas. His commitment to affirmative action was a significant part of that struggle.

Louisiana and Former Congressman Cleo Fields: The Redistricting Cases

Let me close by looking at another case close at home—one which also arose in your native state, Louisiana. For 114 years, Louisiana had no black representatives in Congress. Finally, due to the Voting Rights Act of 1965, two African Americans were elected in the 1990s. Conservatives challenged the boundaries of the district where Cleo Fields was elected in 1993. I was the lead counsel for Congressman Cleo Fields, who is no longer in the United States House of Representatives. In Louisiana, a three judge federal court declared that minority/majority districts were unconstitutional. They relied on a series of five-to-four decisions by the Supreme Court—*Shaw v. Reno* and its progeny—cases in which Justice Thomas was in the majority, and which detrimentally changed the voting accessibility options for African Americans to get elected to Congress. I have written more extensively on the pernicious effects of *Shaw v. Reno*.

Conclusion

In view of his harsh conservative record, please explain to me why you invited Justice Thomas, who has voted consistently against the interests of African Americans, minorities and women. Please explain to me why, for this premier banquet program, you did not invite Judge Constance Baker Motley, who has just written one of the classic biographies of this century, who has been a distinguished civil rights lawyer in the 1950s and 1960s as was Thurgood Marshall, who was chief counsel in the *Meredith* case, and who has been a distinguished federal judge for more than thirty years.

I understand you wrote to the Executive Committee stating:

> I did want to share with you my thoughts as to why the invitation should be extended to a Justice who repudiates affirmative action. It is difficult to dialogue with someone who has skewed and hostile views on issues we consider fundamental. . . . Progress must sometimes be achieved by engaging the most abhorrent of foes.

I also hear a few others say that Justice Thomas feels "isolated," his major friends are white, we should invite him and his wife to the family table so that he can change. I do not believe that thousands of African Americans, Mexican Americans, and other minorities feel that, after he has consistently voted to deny them fair options, Justice Thomas should be welcomed to any family table for any kind of dialogue. It makes no more sense to invite Clarence Thomas than it would have been for the National Bar Association to have invited George Wallace for dinner the day after he had stood in the schoolhouse door and had shouted "segregation today and segregation forever." It makes no more sense than it would have been for the National Bar Association to invite Governor Faubus of Arkansas or Governor Barnett of Mississippi for afternoon tea, after one had attempted to close the Little Rock High School to African-American students, and the other had attempted to disregard the court-ordered admission of James Meredith to the University of Mississippi.

As to the claim that he has been "isolated," might I remind you that Clarence Thomas was not born on some remote island in Maine, where it was not evident whether he was black or white, and where he passed for white. His race is quite visible and he comes from Georgia — where it would be impossible, if one's eyes were open for only one day, to not see the impact of three centuries of slavery and racism. If Justices Brennan, White, Blackmun, Stevens, Souter and Ginsburg do not need a social function to enlighten them about American history, pray tell me, why do you believe that an afternoon's visit to Memphis for "dialogue" will change Clarence Thomas, after his steady seven years of retrogressive votes on the United States Supreme Court?

I would have much preferred that Clarence Thomas had the record of Justice Thurgood Marshall on the Court, or that of any of the six justices I have just named. If he did; then such a banquet would be consistent with the vision of our predecessors — William Hastie, Charles Houston and Thurgood Marshall. But, tragically, on the basis of Justice Thomas's record, the invitation suggests that the inviters have turned a blind eye to the acts of individuals such as Justice Thomas, who, after they, themselves, have attained some modicum of public success, have likewise turned their backs to those less empowered. Consequently, Professor F. Michael Higginbotham, Professor Charles J. Ogletree, Jr., and I look forward to seeing you and continuing this dialogue with vigor in Memphis.

Respectfully,

A. Leon Higginbotham, Jr. Public
Service Professor of Jurisprudence

Unpublished.
Copyright © (1997) A. Leon Higginbotham, Jr.
Reprinted with permission of Evelyn Brooks Higginbotham.

2. Editorial on Thomas's Speech to the National Bar Association

F. Michael Higginbotham

Bar Group Rolls Up Welcome Mat

On July 29, 1998, Justice Clarence Thomas spoke to the National Bar Association, the nation's largest organization of black lawyers. No, he did not wander in off the street; he slipped in through the side door of competing interests, just as he slipped onto the Supreme Court seven years ago.

Then, Thomas could not get a majority vote from the bar association in support of his appointment. This year, he disregarded the fact that a majority (more than 80 percent) of the executive committee of the Judicial Council voted to withdraw the invitation tendered unilaterally by the chairperson. Thomas came to the luncheon meeting and quickly announced that the present Clarence Thomas is no different from the Clarence Thomas of seven years ago.

In a speech that laid blame for today's racial problems on everyone but himself, Thomas charged his critics with opposing him because he is a black conservative who does not espouse their liberal ideas. He has yet to recognize that his rejection is based upon his record, not his color.

Although Thomas has made it quite clear over the years that he will not compromise his extreme political beliefs, his supporters argue that it is time for his critics to engage the Justice in debate on the merits and flaws of his work. Maybe they are right. After all, it has been seven years since Thomas was confirmed by the narrowest margin in history (52 to 48) as Associate Justice of the Supreme Court. While today's critics should not be surprised by Thomas' conservatism, they should be alarmed by just how far he has ventured from the mainstream of the court, and by his reasons for this departure.

In his speech to the National Bar Association, Thomas explained these votes by stating that he is opposed to "any effort, policy, or program that has as a prerequisite the acceptance of the notion that blacks are inferior."

In his concurring opinion in *Adarand Constructors v. Pena*, Thomas stated, "these programs stamp minorities with a badge of inferiority and may cause them to develop dependencies or to adopt an attitude that they are 'entitled' to preferences."

Thomas' characterization of affirmative action is not universally accepted, however. In fact, most members of the Supreme Court, except for the equally ultra-conservative Antonin Scalia, believe certain forms of affirmative action are helpful and constitutionally permissible. The late Justice Thurgood Marshall, for example, visualized such affirmative action programs not as preferences, but as a means to create equal opportunity. In Marshall's view, the inequities that existed between whites and minorities and men and women were the result not of racial or gender inferiority, but of centuries of discriminatory laws and judicial decisions. Thus, these programs are a justifiable remedy for years of mandated discrimination.

Thomas' opposition to affirmative action is clearly harmful to the creation of education and economic opportunities for women and racial minorities. It is particularly important to focus on Justice Thomas' views because most of the Supreme Court cases involving affirmative action are decided by a five-to-four vote. Consequently, any one of the five conservative justices, including Thomas, can provide the essential vote to turn the clock back on the commendable racial progress over the last four years.

All one need do is look at the numbers in order to determine the significant negative impact caused by the withdrawal of affirmative action. This impact is particularly visible in California school admissions over the past year.

For example, out of 268 first-year students enrolled at the University of California at Berkeley law school, only one was African American.

Explaining his opposition to affirmative action, Thomas said he did not believe that "kneeling is a position of strength." Such convoluted reasoning is both out of the mainstream and difficult to reconcile. Does Thomas believe that being bankrupt, unemployed, or denied admission to school is a position of strength?

His opposition is personally hypocritical as well. Before his appointment to the Court, Thomas recognized how much he had benefitted from affirmative action and how much worse his life would have been without it. In 1983 he said, "But for affirmative action laws, God only knows where I would be today. These laws and their proper application are all that stand between the first seventeen years of my life and the second seventeen years."

According to testimony from the former dean of the Yale Law School, Thomas' alma mater, he was admitted to law school under an affirmative action plan.

If affirmative action was so good for Thomas, why does he think it is so bad for everyone else?

During his recent speech, Thomas took particular offense at objections to his dissent in *Hudson v. McMillan*. A black prisoner was taken out of his cell in shackles and handcuffs and beaten so severely by two prison guards that his teeth were loosened, his dental plate broke, his eye blackened, and his lip cut and bruised, and he had done nothing to provoke the action.

While seven justices agreed that the beating constituted a violation of the Eighth Amendment's prohibition against cruel and unusual punishment, Thomas dissented, finding that no constitutional violation had taken place. At the bar association, Thomas claimed that his position had been misrepresented.

Of course, beating prisoners is bad, he explained. His dissent represented only the view that a single use of force that causes only insignificant harm to a prisoner could not constitute cruel and unusual punishment. Under Thomas' approach, this constitutional provision, like many others, must be construed narrowly. That meant only multiple punishments resulting in serious physical harm or injury could be considered "cruel and unusual punishment."

Most Americans would disagree with Thomas's conclusion that the severe beating was insignificant, but the bigger problem is that his extreme judicial philosophy consistently results in such bizarre outcomes. His approach conjures up images of the country's racially troubled past. It was not long ago that the same narrow interpretation of the Constitution was used to withdraw federal civil rights protection from African Americans.

In the 1896 *Plessy v. Ferguson* case upholding a Louisiana statute separating whites and blacks on trains, the Supreme Court interpreted narrowly the Equal Protection Clause of the Fourteenth Amendment, thus validating the infamous "separate but equal doctrine." This was unanimously refuted by the Court fifty years later in *Brown v. Board of Education*. The *Plessy* Court reasoned that the clause guaranteed only equality of political rights, not social ones. This narrow reasoning allowed for blacks to be separated out from other Americans in activities deemed to be social, just as animals could be separated from human beings.

This case, along with such earlier cases as *Dred Scott*, the *Slaughter House* cases, and the *Civil Rights* cases significantly reduced the power of the federal government to protect the rights of African Americans. And, not surprisingly, most states where blacks had previously been enslaved failed to do so. Hence blacks were denied some of the most basic freedoms that other Americans took for granted—the right to vote, for instance, or the right to use public accommodations or to be protected from bodily harm.

As these cases indicate, Justice Clarence Thomas's jurisprudence is harmful to women and racial minorities; it veers far from the mainstream of today's judicial thought; and it is personally hypocritical. While Thomas was politely received by the National Bar Association audience, even the few who defended his right to speak distanced themselves from the content of his message.

Content, of course, is what this fight is all about today; and what it has always been about for supporters of equal rights and equal opportunity. No pronouncements made by a confused man can deflect attention from that fact, no matter that he happens to be on the Supreme Court. Until Clarence Thomas recognizes that his detractors object not to the color of his skin but to the content of his message, he will remain lost in a jurisprudence of confusion. This reality would not be altered if Thomas were white.

The Crisis 12 (September/October 1998).
Copyright © (1998) *The Crisis Magazine*.
Reprinted with permission of *The Crisis Magazine* and
F. Michael Higginbotham.

D. Race, Gender, and the Thomas Confirmation Process

A. Leon Higginbotham, Jr.

The Hill-Thomas Hearings—What Took Place and What Happened: White Male Domination, Black Male Domination, and the Denigration of Black Women, in Race, Gender, and Power in America: The Legacy of the Hill-Thomas Hearing (edited by Anita Faye Hill & Emma Coleman Jordan)*

In 1851, the abolitionist and women's rights crusader, Sojourner Truth, spoke about the discriminatory treatment black women have received over the years. Truth explained:

> That man over there says women need to be helped into carriages, and lifted over ditches, and have to have the best place everywhere. Nobody ever helps me into carriages, or over mud puddles, or gives me any best place! *And ain't I a woman?* Look at me! Look at my arm! I have ploughed and planted and gathered into barns, and no man could head me! *And ain't I a woman?* I could work as much and eat as much as a man—when I could get it—and bear the lash as well! *And ain't I a woman?* I have borne 13 children, and seen them most all sold off to slavery, and when I cried out with my mother's grief, none but Jesus heard me? *And ain't I a woman?*

The Hill-Thomas hearings represented a sequella of attitudes that in some ways were not very different from those of the antebellum "statesmen" and "judges" who regarded all women, and particularly black women, as inferior persons. *Thus, Anita Hill was treated far more harshly by the Senate committee than she would have been had she been white, and Clarence Thomas was treated far more generously than he would have been had the victim been a white woman.* This is clearly demonstrated by analyzing three theoretical scenarios, with the principal roles in the hearings recast and all other factors being the same.

Scenario 1: If the nominee had been Clarence Thomas and the victim had been a white woman, either the Judiciary Committee would have rejected Clarence Thomas unanimously, or more probably, the president would have withdrawn his name the moment the evidence was submitted.

---

* (footnotes omitted).

Scenario 2: If the nominee had been a white man and the victim had been a white woman, the white nominee would have been rejected by the Judiciary Committee and would have never been confirmed. It is worth recalling that the Armed Services Committee rejected Senator John Tower's nomination as secretary of defense, even though, unlike Clarence Thomas, he would not have won a lifetime appointment. Part of the rejection was predicated on his alleged questionable relationships with white women.

Scenario 3: If the nominee had been a white man and the victim Anita Hill, he would have been overwhelmingly rejected. Some of the so-called civil rights leaders who supported Clarence Thomas would have been the first to demand the rejection of a white Supreme Court nominee accused of sexually harassing an African-American woman.

In the scenario that was actually played out in October 1991, of course, the nominee was a black man and the victim was a black woman. Suddenly, the senators became more tolerant in evaluating the nominee.

Even before Professor Hill had completed her testimony, every member of the Judiciary Committee, those who had questioned her sanity as well as those who had failed to defend her, made sanctimonious little statements about how grateful they personally were that she had raised their consciousness on the issue of sexual harassment, and about how certain they were that history would judge her a true heroine in the fight for equal rights and equal opportunities for women in the United States. History, they seemed to be saying, would in the end treat her more kindly than they themselves had.

That many of these gentlemen made wild and unfounded statements about Professor Hill with apparent immunity says nothing about the extent of her sanity and everything about the degree of their own integrity, and about the measure of respect accorded black women in this society. However, the fact that many of the white male members of the Judiciary Committee dismissed Professor Hill's testimony by accusing her of being a liar and a delusional woman does not, in and of itself, mean that those senators are singularly dim-witted. They may or may not be. But the point here is that those senators were not the only ones who tended to doubt her testimony. After all, Clarence Thomas was confirmed to the Supreme Court precisely because the senators who voted for him had good reasons to believe that the majority of their constituents would also dismiss Professor Hill's testimony as the inexplicable ranting of a disturbed woman. In the end, therefore, Clarence Thomas's confirmation says more about how we define ourselves as a society than about the personal inclinations of the members of the Senate Judiciary Committee.

As I look back on the Senate Judiciary Committee hearings of October 1991, the words of Samuel Johnson in 1775 again have meaning to me: just as he said of the conduct of white colonialists, the performance of many members of the Judiciary Committee was "too foolish for buffoonery and too wild for madness." As I watched the members of the committee during the hearings, I could not help but feel that most of the "good Senators" just did not "get it." It seemed to me then, just as it seems to me today, that in focusing exclusively on the issue of sexual harassment in the "workplace," the Judiciary Committee was only interested—and only mildly so—in learning what took place between Professor Hill and Clarence Thomas. They certainly were not interested in what happened.

Had the senators been interested in the question of *why* Professor Hill was sexually harassed, they would have been forced to face immediately and directly the history of how black women have been dominated and denigrated by white males and by black males in this society. But much more than the *history* of domination and denigration of black women, these senators would have been forced to confront the *present-day reality* of how many but not all of them dominated and denigrated Professor Hill because she was a woman, and because she was a black woman. By ignoring and playing down the history and the story of black women in this country, the Senate Judiciary Committee effectively told Professor Hill and other women the same thing: that the law is the embodiment of what most senators represented and that Professor Hill's story had no place in it. With this volume, we may yet begin to tell them they were wrong.

Race, Gender, and Power in America:
The Legacy of the Hill-Thomas Hearings 33–35.
Copyright © (1995) Oxford University Press.
Reprinted with permission of Oxford University Press.

E. Background on Justice Clarence Thomas

Geoffrey Stone, et al.

Justice Clarence Thomas

Born into grinding poverty in segregated coastal Georgia, Clarence Thomas became the second African American and one of the youngest justices to join the Court when he was appointed by President George H. W. Bush in 1991. He was confirmed by the Senate to fill the seat vacated by the retirement of Thurgood Marshall after extraordinary confirmation hearings that opened with a moving account of his personal saga and closed with charges of sexual harassment leveled against him by Anita Hill, who had worked with him at the Department of Education and the Equal Employment Opportunity Commission. A graduate of the Yale Law School, he served as assistant secretary for civil rights at the Department of Education and chair of the Equal Employment Opportunity Commission in the Reagan administration. During his controversial seven-year stewardship of the EEOC, Thomas's fierce opposition to affirmative action antagonized liberals and members of the civil rights community. In 1989, President Bush appointed Thomas to the U.S. Court of Appeals for the District of Columbia, where he served for fifteen months before his elevation to the Supreme Court. Known as a staunch conservative, Thomas's extrajudicial writings suggest an interest in natural law as a basis for constitutional adjudication. Since joining the Court, he has written a series of distinctive dissents and concurrences, often demonstrating a willingness to reject settled precedent in favor of his understanding of the constitutional text. On racial issues, he strongly opposes what he considers liberal condescension in the form of affirmative action and the assumption that majority black institutions are necessarily inferior.

Constitutional Law xciii (3rd edition).
Copyright © (1996) Stone, et al.
Reprinted with permission of Aspen Law & Business.

F. Questions and Notes

Many African Americans view Justice Thomas as the moral equivalent of a Nazi collaborator. Is this a fair comparison? Would widespread sentiment, so strongly opposed to Thomas, make a difference to you as President, nominating him to be a Supreme Court Justice? How would you evaluate the degree of open-mindedness practiced by Justice Thomas, as you review his contemptuous derision towards civil rights organizations, his obstinate support for the conservative movement, which largely opposed the decision in *Brown,* and his opposition to Justice Marshall's comments on the bicentennial? Since the time of his appointment, has Justice Thomas lived up to the responsibility to inform in his legal opinions and to help shape the nation's perspective on issues?

Since his appointment to the bench, nearly two decades ago, Thomas has been mostly silent during the day-to-day process of hearing cases. While the other justices confront lawyers with a barrage of questions, case after case, Thomas remains almost entirely silent. What do you make of his characteristic silence? Does his approach fit the time-honored traditions of oral arguments?

If you were a United States Senator in 1991, would you have voted to confirm the nomination of Clarence Thomas to serve on the Supreme Court? Was the decision at that time clouded by the predominantly conservative political environment and the media's inordinate scrutiny of Anita Hill? Since much of the negative characterization of Anita Hill during the confirmation process has subsequently been disproven or recanted, in hindsight, would your vote be the same today?

All of the principal witnesses in the Thomas confirmation process were black. Do you think the outcome of the confirmation process would have changed if Anita Hill had been white?

XXIV. Race, Values, and Justice Alito

A. Introduction

Appointed to the Supreme Court in 1981, Sandra Day O'Connor was the Court's first female Justice. Often the key swing vote in cases involving racial issues on a sharply divided court, Justice O'Connor served as the deciding vote in numerous cases involving employment discrimination, voting rights, affirmative action, and racial profiling. On July 1, 2005, Justice O'Connor announced her intention to retire upon the selection and confirmation of a successor. Early in October 2005, President George W. Bush nominated Samuel Alito to replace her. After a long and sometimes contentious confirmation process, Alito joined the Supreme Court on January 31, 2006. The replacement of one Justice by another is generally conducted in a way that seeks to keep the varying perspectives of the court in balance. Given the strong contrast between Alito's conservatism and O'Connor's record of protecting civil rights, did the appointment of Alito maintain a balance of views in the Court, or actuate an unduly conservative shift?

B. Pre-Supreme Court and Supreme Court Jurisprudence

F. Michael Higginbotham

*An Open Letter from Heaven to Justice Samuel Alito**

October 2, 2006

Dear Justice Alito:

The President has signed your commission and you have now become the 110th Justice of the United States Supreme Court. I congratulate you on this high honor!

Your job will be of vital importance not only because the Supreme Court is the final arbiter of constitutional interpretation but also because you have replaced a Justice who often represented the fifth and deciding vote in many of the most controversial issues of equal protection—Justice Sandra Day O'Connor. It is now your vote that will determine the direction of the Court on equal protection issues for many years to come. I believe that Justice O'Connor can serve as your model for utilizing a conservative judicial philosophy to reach fair compromises that expand the scope of individual rights consistent with equality notions contained in the Constitution.

It has been seven years since that December day when I passed away. Since that time I have closely watched the critical cases that have come before the Supreme Court: in particular, the opinions of Justice O'Connor. I remember fondly the last time I chatted with Justice O'Connor—it was 1994 and she was receiving the prestigious Thurgood Marshall Award from Georgetown University Law Center. That evening I praised Justice O'Connor for the careful balance she struck over the years when constitutional rights were in conflict. Her commitment to upholding individual rights and preserving the integrity of the Constitution of the United States of America was remarkable. Justice O'Connor knew that reconciling the rights of

---

* (footnotes omitted) (The sentiments expressed in this letter reflect the author's best judgment as to what Judge Higginbotham might have said and felt had he been living today).

the individual with those of society poses one of the most difficult challenges for members of the Court. Whether the issue was abortion rights, affirmative action, or the death penalty, she always endeavored (in my view successfully) to strike a well-crafted balance between individual rights and societal concerns that bridged the conservative/liberal divide on the Court.

I also have pleasant memories of the occasions in which you appeared before me as a lawyer. I often remarked to colleagues that you were one of the best appellate advocates that have ever come before me on the bench. Your oral arguments were clear, well reasoned, and conveyed in a forthright manner. Your briefs were thoroughly annotated, carefully structured, and intricately detailed. Your work ethic was equally apparent in the few years that you and I sat together as colleagues on the Third Circuit Court of Appeals. The confirmation hearing on your Supreme Court nomination served to remind me of those times. You were a valued colleague whom I respected for your intellect, integrity, and dedication, and I know first hand that you possess the ability to be a superb justice. While your ability is beyond question, your approach to adjudicating individual rights—insofar as I can discern it from your record as a lawyer and a judge—gives me some cause for concern. It is particularly important to me that my thoughts are known since, prior to and during your confirmation hearing, a senator and a witness invoked my name to suggest that I might not have opposed your nomination. Although I continue to regard you with great respect, I must admit that such a suggestion could not be further from the truth. Regardless of how I would have viewed your nomination, the question is whether you will now serve as a justice who earns my respect and admiration. Your past gives me reason for great concern, but I am not without hope.

Your Positions on Race Issues and Mine

You and I differed on issues of race over the years. These differences were apparent both when you served as a government lawyer early in your professional career and after you were appointed to the federal bench. Indeed, in your fifteen years on the bench, you ruled only twice for African Americans on the merits in their employment discrimination cases.

As I am sure you recall, in *Grant v. Shalala*, the claimants accused an administrative law judge of adopting a biased policy and stating that "claimants living in Hispanic, black or poor white communities are only 'attempting to milk the system,' that they are 'perfectly capable of going out and earning a living,' [and] that they 'prefered [sic] living on public monies.'" The district court below certified the class and set the case for trial. The government appealed, and you wrote for the majority. In that opinion you held that the district court could not make its own findings on the bias claims, but had to defer to the agency finding of no bias. You wrote that "we are convinced that the plaintiff's right to an impartial administrative determination can be fully protected through the process of judicial review of the Secretary's determination" instead of allowing the district court the power to conduct its own full trial of biased claims rejected by the agency. I believe that your refusal to allow a full trial on the biased claims by initiating a judicial procedural sidestep erroneously and unnecessarily permitted racially discriminatory treatment to go unchecked.

Conversely, I strongly believed when I first joined the federal judiciary that the federal courts had a duty to give full effect to the civil rights laws that were being passed. To me, civil rights laws had little meaning unless federal courts were willing to enforce them. If you recall my dissent in *Grant*, I warned that "[t]he determination of whether or not plaintiffs' constitutional right has been violated is the province of the courts and not that of an agency." I added, "What the majority proposes to do in its holding is effectively to have courts take a back seat to bureaucratic agencies in protecting constitutional liberties. This . . . is a radical and unwise redefinition of the relationship between federal courts and federal agencies. . . ."

Another example of your deftness in procedural two-stepping arose in a case dealing with race discrimination in jury selection, an issue about which I feel passionate. In *Riley v. Taylor*, a black defendant who had been convicted of murder by an all-white jury claimed the prosecutor had unconstitutionally dismissed all black prospective jurors. In dissent, you explained that statistics could be misleading. As proof, you compared the evidence of race discrimination to the disproportionate number of U.S. presidents who have been left-handed. Judge Sloviter, who often sided with me on issues involving individual rights, responded in the majority opinion:

> [Judge Alito] has overlooked the obvious fact that there is no provision in the Constitution that protects persons from discrimination based on whether they are right-handed or left-handed. To suggest any comparability to the striking of jurors based on their race is to minimize the history of discrimination against prospective black jurors and black defendants. . . .

Your laissez-faire attitude towards police practices involving broader search and seizure authority under the Fourth Amendment presents further insight into your values. Given the history of police brutality against minorities, your views on lethal police force are alarming. In 1984, you wrote that you saw no constitutional problem with an officer fatally shooting an unarmed teenager fleeing after a burglary. You suggested the shooting was "reasonable" and recommended that since an officer could not be certain why any suspect was fleeing, the courts should not set a blanket rule forbidding the use of deadly force in such situations. I, however, supported such a rule and was pleased when the Supreme Court, in *Tennessee v. Garner*, concluded that killing a felony suspect is "constitutionally unreasonable" in cases where the police do not have "probable cause to believe that the suspect poses a threat of serious physical harm, either to the officer or to others."

Equally illustrative of your values is *Bray v. Marriott Hotels*, which involved a black employee denied a promotion by the Marriott Corporation. Without permitting a trial, a federal judge ruled in Marriott's favor. On appeal, the court ruled that the employee had presented enough evidence for a trial. You disagreed, characterizing the employee's evidence as merely showing "minor inconsistencies." You chose to focus on a Marriott executive's statements that he sought the best candidate. In the majority opinion, Judge Theodore McKee, who replaced me on the court and who remains its only black member, responded that judges could not ignore the possibility that some executives never view minority applicants as the best candidates and suggested that your position nullified current antidiscrimination law.

My Race Values

Thurgood Marshall and I spent our entire lives fighting against racial discrimination and for the creation of racial equality. He and I had a laugh, albeit a nervous one, when we heard Judge Timothy Lewis and Senator John Cornyn mention our names in connection with your confirmation hearing. Judge Lewis quoted Thurgood saying nice things about Justice Rehnquist and Senator Cornyn quoted me saying nice things about you. We found that somewhat humorous because while both of us often said nice things about our conservative colleagues in speeches and at conferences, we never imagined those words being used to draw an inference that is completely contradictory to our lives and work. That contrary inference, of course, was that either Thurgood or I would have supported your nomination as an associate justice. Quite simply, your values on race would have prevented our support.

One issue indicative of the ideological divide between us is affirmative action in higher education. I believed that the reduction in affirmative action was causing an increase in racial inequity, concomitantly limiting the racial diversity achieved in higher education since Thurgood's masterful argument resulted in the 1954 *Brown* decision, holding that state-required segregation in public schools was unconstitutional. In a piece entitled "No More Time for Foolishness," I criticized the *Hopwood v. University of Texas* decision invalidating an affirmative action program at the University of Texas Law School. I believed that this decision was based more on politically conservative ideology than on any constitutional or jurisprudential basis. I explained:

> The story of how today, in 1997, there is just one African-American student out of a total of 268 in the first year class of the university of California at Berkeley, School of Law, and four out of a total of 468 at the University of Texas Law School, is not just one story, but several. First and foremost, it is the story of two specific cases: *Sweatt v. Painter*, which desegregated the University of Texas Law School, and *Hopwood v. University of Texas*, which is about to "resegregate" it. But, more importantly, it is also the story of how former Presidents Ronald Reagan and George Bush sowed the federal courts of this nation with their seeds of very conservative judges, and how African-Americans are not reaping the bitter harvest of their policies.

Another issue is racism in the criminal justice system. I spoke out against racial bias in prosecution, jury selection, judicial decision-making, and media reporting. In an article entitled "The O.J. Simpson Trial: Who Was Improperly 'Playing the

Race Card'?" I discussed the implications of Officer Mark Fuhrman's false denial of previous racist statements. I explained:

> The case of *The People v. Orenthal James Simpson* has come to be seen by many as a metaphor for the seemingly intractable problems of race in America. Yet, for all of the incalculable hours of media attention and endless public comment by both observers and trial participants, many of the "lessons" drawn from the trial by commentators and a large segment of the public were deceptive. The most blatantly deceptive of these lessons is what now has become the conventional wisdom that in using detective mark Fuhrman's racism as a test of his credibility, the Simpson defense team had *improperly and unjustifiably* "played the race card." That conclusion is false. Rather than establishing that the defense strategy was improper or unethical, when carefully analyzed, many of the critiques of the defense team's strategies reveal far more the latent and explicit biases of the commentators and the duality of standards the public still uses to judge African-American criminal defendants and African-American lawyers.

I further explained that:

> [p]erhaps the most deceptive statement of all was uttered with a purported neutrality when Andy Rooney, the famed *60 Minutes* correspondent, declared that '[t]he [Simpson] acquittal was the worst thing that's happened to race relations in 40 years.' Worse than what? One wanted to ask Mr. Rooney: Worse than the bombing of the 16th Street Baptist Church in Birmingham, and the killing of four school children in 1963? Worse than the slaying of Medgar Evers in 1963, of James Chaney, Andrew Goodman, and Michael Schwerner in 1964, of Jimmie Lee Jackson, Reverend James Reeb, and Viola Gregg Liuzzo in 1965, or of dozens of other civil rights martyrs in the 1960s? Worse even than the assassination of Martin Luther King?

In my 1996 book, *Shades of Freedom*, I provided a more in-depth analysis of racism in the criminal justice system. The book began by listing several notorious examples of recent situations in which African-Americans were wrongly accused of perpetrating heinous crimes. The six examples were characterized by two interesting features: first, the truth about the cases was brought to the attention of most Americans through the mass media; secondly, each case involved a white person accusing an anonymous and non-existent black person of committing the crime.

Particularly noteworthy was the 1994 accusation by Susan Smith, who "claimed that an armed black man perpetrated a car jacking, kidnapped her children who were in the vehicle, and left her on the side of the road." It was later discovered, after weeks of network news coverage on the abduction and the search for the alleged black perpetrator, that the story was a complete fabrication. Smith was later arrested, tried, and convicted of the murder of her own children.

Another shocking example I offered was the case of Charles Stuart, who claimed that his pregnant wife had been assaulted in their vehicle and killed by a black man attempting to steal her cash and jewelry. Mrs. Stuart, who died from a gun-shot wound to the abdomen, was in fact killed in an elaborate scheme devised by Mr. Stewart and his brother to collect life insurance benefits. I reasoned that these examples of false accusation were highly indicative of widespread racial discrimination in the judicial system.

Your Race Values

Values, of course, are what have always been of paramount concern to me when it comes to judicial nominations. Speaking candidly, I am troubled by some of your answers in the confirmation hearing concerning matters of racial equality.

You admitted being a member of Concerned Alumni of Princeton (CAP), though you could not recall exactly why you joined the organization. You did, however, list it on your resume when you applied for a job with the Reagan Administration in 1985. There seemed to be some concern expressed at your confirmation hearing as to whether you were a high ranking member of CAP and to what extent you participated in CAP activities.

My concern, however, is not whether you were an active or inactive member, high ranking or low-level, officer or ranking member, but why you have not repudiated your membership. You indicated that you probably joined CAP in the 1970s because of its vigorous defense of Reserve officer Training Corps (R.O.T.C.) Programs at Princeton. Such programs were terminated in the late 1960s and you wanted to see them reinstated. I have no problem with your support of R.O.T.C. programs, but CAP stood for much more than simply bringing R.O.T.C. back to campus. CAP desired a return to the Princeton of the 1950s, which meant not only the return of R.O.T.C. programs but a drastic reduction of minority enrollment through the manipulation of affirmative action programs and the exclusion of women from admission altogether. CAP's literature at the time was very clear on this exclusionary point. Such a reduction and elimination of women and minorities would be inconsistent with the values of access, fairness, and diversity to which I am deeply committed.

Politicians from both sides of the ideological divide recognized how CAP's position on gender and racial equality was extreme. Princeton graduates such as Bill Bradley, a liberal Democratic senator from New Jersey, and Bill Frist, a conservative Republican senator from Tennessee, both denounced the organization and withdrew their membership and support. This was widely reported in the media at that time. While you indicated that you do not oppose women and minorities having access to higher education, your failure to repudiate CAP, as Senators Bradley and Frist did, suggests a lack of a similar commitment to the notion of equal access to higher education for women and minorities.

As a high-ranking government official, what you say and do has a tremendous impact on how Americans think, particularly about notions of equality. Based upon this perception, I made a concerted effort neither to belong to nor accept any award, no matter how prestigious, from any organizations that did not reflect racial, religious, ethnic, and gender pluralism. In the 1980s I rejected the University of Chicago law School's invitation to judge its moot court competition final round because they had no black faculty at the law school and had not for many years. Similarly, I refused invitations to join several organizations that refused membership to women.

Your Supreme Court Jurisprudence on Race

While you have been on the Supreme Court only for a short period of time, your initial decisions reinforce my concerns but also provide a glimpse of hope. For example, in *League of United Latin American Citizens v. Perry*, the Court examined a challenge to a 2003 redistricting scheme enacted by the Texas state legislature. Plaintiffs-Appellants argued that the redistricting represented unconstitutional partisan gerrymandering and violated both §2 of the Voting Rights Act of 1965 and the Equal Protection Clause of the Fourteenth Amendment, resulting in the dilution of both Latino and African-American voting power.

With respect to the part of the redistricting plan that broke apart a staunchly Democratic district in which African Americans were the second-largest racial group, you concurred with the Court and voted to reject Appellants' §2 claim. Although assuming "for purposes of this litigation that it is possible to state a §2 claim for a racial group that makes up less than fifty percent of the population," the Court invoked the rule established in a previous case which requires §2 plaintiffs to show that the racial group constitutes "a sufficiently large minority to elect their candidate of choice with the assistance of cross-over votes." The District Court found that it was impossible to determine whether African Americans could elect their candidate of choice because the Democratic primaries in that district had been uncontested for twenty years; it was plausible that Anglos would have voted in greater numbers had an African-American candidate of choice run against the incumbent, and thus evidenced their control over the district. The Court upheld the District Court's findings, under the clearly erroneous standard:

> The opportunity [for racial groups] to elect representatives of their choice ... requires more than the ability to influence the outcome between some candidates, none of whom is their candidate of choice. There is no doubt that African-Americans preferred Martin Frost to the Republicans who opposed him. The fact that African-Americans preferred Frost to some others does not, however, make him their candidate of choice.

You agreed with the majority requiring a racial group to make a fairly extensive showing that a candidate is their "candidate of choice" in order to obtain relief under §2. The majority's references to Frost being Anglo and having the support of Anglo and Latino voters seem to suggest that, if Frost were an African American enjoying less support from other racial groups, there would have been a stronger presumption that he was the African-American "candidate of choice." Thus, the majority seems to punish racial groups for supporting a candidate that has broad cross-racial support.

In *League of United Latin American Citizens*, you joined in part of Justice Scalia's concurrence in the judgment in part and dissent in part, which addressed appellants' equal protection claims. Appellants argued that the state removed 100,000 mostly Latino residents from one district to purposefully dilute Latino voting power. Although the District Court found that the district was redrawn to protect the Republican incumbent against a growing bloc of opposition Latino voters, it concluded that the redistricting plan as a whole was not racially motivated. Moreover, it concluded that the residents were removed from the district because they voted for Democrats, not because they were Latino. Justice Scalia found no clear error in the District court's findings about the legislature's motivations.

Justice Scalia then went on to examine the redrawing of another district at issue, one in which a Latino "opportunity district" was actually created by the redistricting plan. The state, in its brief, conceded that it classified individuals on the basis of their race when it redrew this district: "To avoid retrogression and achieve compliance with §5 of the Voting Rights Act . . . , the Legislature chose to create a new Hispanic-opportunity district . . . which would allow Hispanics to actually elect its [sic] candidate of choice." In other words, the legislature tried to compensate for the diminished voting power of Latinos in one district by creating another district in which Latinos would have increased voting power.

Justice Scalia argued that "when a legislature intentionally creates a majority-minority district, race is necessarily its predominant motivation and strict scrutiny is therefore triggered." When Justice Scalia subjected this portion of the scheme to strict scrutiny, he found that, because the state's purpose in creating the Latino "opportunity district" was to comply with the antidiscrimination provisions of §5 of the Voting Rights Act, there was a compelling state interest justifying the use of race. Thus, Justice Scalia chose to apply strict scrutiny to the one part of the plan that ostensibly benefited Latino voters, yet applied the clear error standard to the lower court's findings with regard to the redrawing of another district in which Latino voting power was diminished. In the former case, Justice Scalia found a predominance of racial motivation in the Texas legislature, while in the latter he concluded that the state was merely "aware of racial demographics" and was motivated more by political, race-neutral concerns.

Justice Scalia's concurrence, in which you partly joined, is troubling for a number of reasons. First, Justice Scalia's logic appears flawed on its face: he acknowledges that the state was trying to compensate for its own purposeful (or at least knowledgeable) dilution of the voting power of a racial group, and yet finds discriminatory intent only in the district in which the state attempted to rectify the disparity that it acknowledged causing. Moreover, this concurrence seems to denigrate the strict scrutiny standard by applying it in an inconsistent and arbitrary manner: the distinction drawn between a redistricting which receives great deference and a redistricting which receives strict scrutiny is not entirely clear or convincing. A legislature apparently need only offer pretextual "political" reasons (i.e., that Latinos vote Democrat) to avoid strict scrutiny even when it is clearly singling out a racial group.

League demonstrates your willingness to vote with the conservative bloc of the Court. Moreover, the absence of your own concurring opinion indicates either that your views on these issues do not diverge significantly from those of Justices Roberts, Scalia, and Thomas, the most conservative justices, or that you are taking a cautious approach to airing your views on race and individual rights as a member of the Court. In either case, I must confess my disappointment. I hoped you would have been much more like Justice O'Connor in speaking out more decisively in favor of minority rights in a fundamental area (political rights), instead of simply voting with your ideological colleagues or remaining silent when such important equality issues were presented.

Alternatively, the majority opinion you authored in *Holmes v. South Carolina*, vacating a murder conviction that had been affirmed by the state supreme court, gives me hope. Your opinion rejected as "arbitrary" the state court's interpretation of federal evidence rules that permitted disallowance of defense evidence of third party guilt, "even if that evidence, [when] viewed independently, would have great probative value and . . . would not pose an undue risk of . . . prejudice, or confusion of the issues." In this case, the prosecution had introduced forensic evidence that, if believed, strongly supported a guilty verdict. However, you wrote that "[j]ust because the prosecution's evidence, if credited, would provide strong support for a guilty verdict, it does not follow that evidence of third-party guilt has only a weak logical connection to the central issues in the case." You noted that, "by evaluating the strength of only one party's evidence, no logical conclusion can be reached regarding the strength of contrary evidence offered by the other side to rebut or cast doubt." The state's interpretation of the evidence rule, you concluded, "violates a criminal defendant's right to have 'a meaningful opportunity to present a complete defense.'"

This case is an encouraging sign of your willingness to clarify an ambiguous area of criminal law in a way that increases the rights of criminal defendants. However, the facts of this case were overwhelming: the defendant produced witnesses who placed another specific person near the scene of the crime and who refuted that person's alibi. Nonetheless, I commend you for taking a step to combat the judicial curbing of defendants' rights witnessed during the last thirty years.

Conclusion

Based upon the Justice you replaced and the present ideological divide on the Court, you stand to be the critical vote on many equal protection issues involving race. While your conservative judicial philosophy will, no doubt, guide much of your deliberation on the most difficult cases that come before you, you will also be moved by your own personal values, both moral and spiritual, and your sense of right and wrong.

As part of these personal values, you stressed at your confirmation hearing the struggles of your parents in the early twentieth century as members of poor immigrant families from Italy. You talked about the value of hard work, educational opportunity, and military and public service. You discussed the pain of ethnic discrimination against your parents and the isolation working-class Americans could experience at prestigious universities such as Princeton.

What you and I will discuss in the future when you join me in Heaven is how generations to come evaluate your attempts to reconcile these liberal and moderate personal views with your conservative judicial philosophy. Will you apply the same concern you had for struggling Italian immigrants of the early twentieth century who fought against ethnic prejudice to the struggles of Haitian immigrants today who fight against racial prejudice? Will you apply the same concern you had for R.O.T.C. candidates seeking access to attend Princeton in the 1970s to the struggles of minorities and women today seeking to continue access to higher education and to avoid the glass ceiling regarding job promotion?

This struggle is evident in Justice O'Connor's jurisprudence on equal protection race issues. For example, Justice O'Connor wrote a 5–4 majority opinion in *Adarand Constructors, Inc. v. Peña*, remanding to the lower federal court a decision by the Court of Appeals upholding a federal government affirmative action plan in highway construction contracts. Justice O'Connor's ruling mandated a more rigorous scrutiny under equal protection analysis than had been applied by the lower court, thus making it much more difficult for the government to implement affirmative action programs and to satisfy the constitutional standard against discrimination.

Due to this decision, many were surprised when Justice O'Connor wrote a 5–4 majority opinion in *Grutter v. Bollinger*, upholding a similar affirmative action program in higher education, reasoning that creating a diverse classroom is a compelling government interest that satisfies the stringent standard required by her decision in *Adarand*. What many fail to understand, however, is that Justice O'Connor's conservative judicial philosophy was always balanced by her liberal personal values of pluralism, anti-discrimination, and equal opportunity. Thus, even while questioning the validity of an affirmative action plan in *Adarand*, Justice O'Connor explained: "The Unhappy persistence of both the practice and the lingering effects of racial discrimination against minority groups in this country is an unfortunate reality."

Justice O'Connor struggled with these dual concerns throughout her time on the Supreme Court. She is both revered and despised by liberals and conservatives, depending upon which equal protection race discrimination case is the focus of the debate. Some say that this "divide" more than any other factor demonstrates that Justice O'Connor struck the right balance. For many here in Heaven, like Thurgood and myself, we can't help but wonder: when you retire from the bench, what will be said about the balance struck by Justice Alito?

Sincerely,
A. Leon Higginbotham, Jr.
Chief Judge (Retired)
United States Court of Appeals for the Third Circuit

This letter articulates the author's best judgment as to what Judge Higginbotham might have felt and written had he been living today.

C. Background on Justice Samuel Alito

Geoffrey Stone, et al.

Justice Samuel Alito

The son of two school teachers (his father went on to become New Jersey's first Director of the Office of Legislative Services), Justice Alito graduated from Princeton and then from Yale Law School where he served as an editor of the Yale Law Journal. He served as an assistant to the United States Solicitor General and Deputy Assistant to the Attorney General before becoming the United States Attorney for the District of New Jersey. He developed the reputation of a tough but fair prosecutor and was known especially for his efforts directed against drug trafficking and organized crime. Before his Supreme Court appointment in 2006, he served for sixteen years as a judge on the United States Court of Appeals for the Third Circuit.

Constitutional Law lix (4th edition).
Copyright © (2009) Stone, et al.
Reprinted with permission of Aspen Law & Business.

D. Questions and Notes

Was Justice Alito's membership as a college student in Concerned Alumni of Princeton, a conservative student organization committed to protecting traditional university values on gender and race, a relevant area of inquiry during his Senate confirmation hearing? If so, what conclusions do you draw from such membership? To what extent will an exploration of affiliations and membership in groups reveal someone's attitudes and values? Did Alito's response to the line of questioning acknowledge his membership in the group, while sidestepping any of its implications?

XXV. Race, Values, and Justice Sotomayor

A. Introduction

In April of 2009, Supreme Court Justice David Souter announced his retirement, giving newly elected President, Barack Obama, the opportunity to make his first Supreme Court nomination. During the presidential campaign, candidate Obama had promised to appoint judges who were committed to the letter and spirit of the Constitution. This surprise retirement (Souter was only 69 years of age when he announced it) would give President Obama a chance to live up to his campaign pledge.

B. Pre-Supreme Court Jurisprudence

Richard Lacayo

A Justice Like No Other

Sotomayor's involvement in an affirmative-action case last year is the episode attracting the most attention. The case, *Ricci v. DeStefano*, involves a group of 18 white firefighters, including one Hispanic. They filed a discrimination suit against the city of New Haven, Conn., after the city decided in 2004 not to certify the results of a job-promotion exam because no African Americans had scored high enough to be promoted. The city argued that federal law treats tests resulting in such outcomes as suspect, meaning that New Haven would probably have been sued by the minorities who failed the test had the white firefighters been promoted.

A lower court decided in favor of the city. In February 2008, Sotomayor was part of a three-judge panel that upheld the lower-court decision in a very brief ruling. Four months later, she was part of a 7–6 majority that decided not to rehear the case before the full appeals court. Writing for the six dissenters, Judge Jose Cabranes, a Clinton appointee who has been something of a mentor for Sotomayor, said the majority "failed to grapple with the questions of exceptional importance raised in this appeal." The three-judge panel's "perfunctory disposition," he wrote, contained "no reference whatsoever to the constitutional claims at the core of this case"—unusually blunt language for a court known for its collegiality in public. . . .

For Republicans, opposing a candidate first nominated to the bench by a Republican President and twice confirmed by the Senate will be hard enough. But to do that without stumbling over the fact that she's also the first female Hispanic nominee will require an especially delicate touch. Having alienated many Hispanics with years of anti-immigrant rhetoric, the GOP can scarcely afford to drive them deeper into the Democratic fold. Last November, Obama won 67% of Latino votes, compared with John McCain's 31%, enough to put Florida, New Mexico and Colorado in the Democratic column.

But if Republicans are worried about putting off Hispanics, they are also under enormous pressure from the right not to let Sotomayor go without a fight. "President Obama carried through on his threat to nominate a Justice who would indulge her policy preferences and biases on the bench," says Ed Whelan, president of the Ethics and Public Policy Center, a group opposing Sotomayor's candidacy. "I'm going to continue to do all I can to expose Sotomayor's view of judging and why she's not a good pick for the court." Conservative activist groups are already airing commercials that attack Sotomayor's role in the New Haven case. Even a losing fight can have benefits for a party as disabled as the GOP is now.

Leading the charge will be Jeff Sessions of Alabama, who became the top Republican on the Senate Judiciary Committee when Arlen Specter switched parties last month. Sessions himself was once a Reagan nominee to the federal bench who was rejected by this same committee—at the time controlled by Republicans—after he called the American Civil Liberties Union and the National Association for the Advancement of Colored People "un-American," reportedly telling a colleague that they "forced civil rights down the throats of people." He now runs the risk of becoming the story if he says anything that could be interpreted as indelicate. So after Sotomayor's nomination was announced, Sessions responded with a statement as blandly worded as a high school civics paper: "The Senate Judiciary Committee's role is to act on behalf of the American people to carefully scrutinize Ms. Sotomayor's qualifications, experience and record."

Meanwhile, Republicans are pushing to slow down the process, to give themselves maximum time to find that incendiary something in her rulings and public statements. Senate Majority Leader Harry Reid has said he'd like to see Sotomayor confirmed before the Senate leaves town on August 7 for its summer recess.

Texas Senator John Cornyn, a Republican on the Judiciary Committee, says Obama has agreed to a "John Roberts timetable"—there were 74 days from the day the Chief Justice was nominated to his swearing-in. For Sotomayor, the equivalent date would be August 6, but Kevin McLaughlin, a spokesman for Cornyn's office, now says that date might not give Republicans enough time. "Given the length and breadth of her record, we're not sure it's possible to meet that deadline," he says.

Conservatives who want to go after Sotomayor may find more ammunition in her public statements outside the court than in her rulings. During a panel discussion at Duke University four years ago, Sotomayor said the federal court of appeals is where "policy is made," the kind of statement that can get you tagged an "activist" judge who tries to make law instead of interpret it. Sotomayor appeared to know that was the danger in the words she had let slip, because she quickly added, "And I know that this is on tape, and I should never say that. Because we don't 'make law' . . . I'm not promoting it, and I'm not advocating it."

In a 2001 speech at the University of California, Berkeley, Sotomayor aired the view that judges' gender and ethnic backgrounds inevitably affect their decision-making and probably should. She said then, "Justice O'Connor has often been cited as saying that a wise old man and wise old woman will reach the same conclusion in deciding cases. I am also not so sure that I agree with the statement . . . I would hope that a wise Latina woman with the richness of her experience would more often than not reach a better conclusion than a white male who hasn't lived that life."

Perhaps. But for all the controversy or appeal that sentiment may arouse, it's not a useful guide to how Sotomayor has ruled. Like that of most lower-court judges, much of her history on the bench has involved minute applications of the law, not the kind of cases in which life experience, even when it is as inspiring as hers, would have offered much guidance. There tend to be more cases of the big-picture kind on the Supreme Court, and if she gets there, she may take the opportunity to become the passionate liberal she has never really been on the lower benches. First, of course, she has to get there. But one thing that everybody agrees on about Sotomayor: all her life, she's been very good at getting places.

Time Magazine, June 8, 2009, pp. 24, 27–29.
Reprinted with permission by Time Inc.

C. Background on Justice Sonia Sotomayor

Richard Lacayo

A Justice Like No Other

Barack Obama said he wanted a Supreme Court nominee with a "common touch." With Sonia Sotomayor, he got somebody with a common touch and an uncommon story. . . .

It could be said to have begun with a journey her parents made during World War II, when they moved from Puerto Rico to New York City, where their daughter was born in 1954. Sotomayor was 3 when the family found an apartment at the Bronxdale Houses, a city-owned development built to provide affordable housing to working-class families. Her father died when Sotomayor was just 9 — one year after she was given a diagnosis of Type I diabetes, which still requires her to monitor her blood sugar and inject herself regularly with insulin. After that, her mother Celina raised Sotomayor and her younger brother Juan on a nurse's salary but still managed to send them to Catholic schools that prepared them for bigger things. Today Juan is a doctor. His sister, who spent a lot of time as a kid watching *Perry Mason* on television, had other plans.

By 1972, Sotomayor had moved on to Princeton, where she studied history. She once said that when she got there, she felt like a "visitor landing in an alien country." But she left with highest honors and a Phi Beta Kappa key. From there, she went on to law school at Yale, where she was an editor of the *Yale Law Journal*. By that time, she was also married to a high school sweetheart, Kevin Edward Noonan — a marriage that ended in divorce in 1983. . . .

After law school, Sotomayor worked for five years in the office of Manhattan district attorney Robert Morgenthau, where she prosecuted everything from petty drug crimes to felony assaults and murder. No less than her background in the projects, her experience pressing criminal cases may have affected her outlook years later on the bench. One case she presided over, *United States v. Falso*, seemed likely to go against police who had charged a man with possessing child pornography after they entered his house on a wrongly issued search warrant. Instead, Sotomayor ruled in favor of the officers. "It wasn't just a pro-prosecutor bias," says Carter. "It was her understanding of the practical problems of being a police officer."

Sotomayor left Morgenthau's office in 1984 to move into private practice as an attorney with a firm specializing in business cases. When George H.W. Bush was looking for nominees to the federal district court in the Southern District of New York, it was a Democrat, New York Senator Daniel Moynihan, who recommended her. She was easily confirmed, but in 1997, when Bill Clinton decided to move her up to the appeals court, Republicans held off a confirmation vote for more than a year, fearing that she was being fast-tracked to be Clinton's next Supreme Court nominee. . . .

Time Magazine, June 8, 2009, pp. 24, 25–26.
Reprinted with permission of Time Inc.

D. Questions and Notes

What conclusions do you draw from Judge Sotomayor's comment in 2001 in a speech on Hispanic Judges during a conference at the University of California, Berkeley, that "a wise Latina woman with the richness of her experience would more often than not reach a better conclusion than a white male who hasn't lived that life." Her comment drew strong scrutiny, and she was forced to defend it during her confirmation hearing before the Senate Judiciary Committee. Does her comment suggest some insight inherent to gender or race, or more likely, was she referring to the value of life experience as a basis for decision-making?

In the history of the Supreme Court as of 2009, 106 of the 111 Justices have been white men. Undeniably, the court has a history of white, male dominance. Should the demographics of the Court reflect those of the nation? Should the composition of the Court reflect the attitudes, values, and demographics of the people it serves?

Part Seven

Ongoing Racial Controversies

XXVI. Race and the Administration of Justice

A. Introduction

Heated controversy frequently surrounds racial or legal issues, so it is not surprising that events that combine both elements capture widespread interest. Both race and law have been central features of American life and history. Each of the following events involved different aspects of the legal system, yet each had a dominant racial element permeating the proceedings. Whether the focus was on the public's reaction, the media's spin, or the legal system's response, race was at the center of the debate.

B. Race, Arrest, and Henry Louis Gates

Harvard University professor and director of Harvard's W. E. B. DuBois Institute for African and African-American Research, Henry Louis Gates, Jr., 58, was arrested at his home on July 16, 2009, while police were investigating a possible break-in. The police were called to Gates' home, just after noon, around 12:44 p.m. Gates' neighbor Lucia Whalen (a white, 40-year-old female) had called the police after witnessing two unknown black men who, according to her, appeared to be breaking into the home.

In actuality, Gates was one of the persons trying to gain access to his home, but he had trouble unlocking his door after the door jammed. According to Gates' friends, Gates was already in the home when the police arrived. Gates was handcuffed, arrested, and taken into police custody for several hours, even after he showed his driver's license and Harvard identification card, according to Gates' friends. Gates said he was frustrated that he continued to be questioned in his home after he produced identification, and this led him to demand the officer's name and badge number. Harvard Law School professor Charles Ogletree represented Gates, who said that Gates had just returned from China to his Cambridge home when he discovered his front door was jammed. Gates and his cab driver were able to force the door open after Gates' key would not work.

According to the police, Gates was arrested after he yelled at the officer on the scene. According to the investigating officer's report, when he arrived, he informed Gates that he was there to investigate a possible break-in, to which Gates replied,

"[W]hy, because I'm a [B]lack man in America?" The investigating officer, James Crowley, wrote in his report that Gates yelled at him repeatedly in the home and followed him outside. "It was at that time that I informed Professor Gates that he was under arrest."

Gates, according to the police report, was arrested for disorderly conduct after "exhibiting loud and tumultuous behavior." The report stated that Gates accused Officer Crowley of being a racist and told him he had no idea "who he was messing with." Crowley reported that when he asked Gates to speak to him outside, Gates yelled, "I'll speak with your mama outside." Crowley also reported that Gates continued to yell at him as he left his porch, after Crowley warned him that he was being disorderly.

Officer Carlos Figueroa, who was also on the scene, reported his version of the incident, in which he corroborated Officer Crowley's report that Gates was uncooperative and continuously yelled that Crowley was a racist police officer.

S. Allen Counter, a Harvard Medical School professor who spoke with Gates about the incident the day after the arrest, said, "He and I both raised the question of if he had been a white professor, whether this kind of thing would have happened to him, that they arrested him without any corroborating evidence." He also said, "I am deeply concerned about the way he was treated, and called him to express my deepest sadness and sympathy."

Counter, who is on sabbatical at the Nobel Institute in Sweden, said that Gates was "shaken" and "horrified" by the incident. Counter also said that he was "shocked that this had happened, at 12:44 in the afternoon, in broad daylight." In 2004, Counter was similarly stopped by Harvard police officers after he was mistaken for a robbery suspect as he crossed Harvard Yard. The police threatened to arrest him when he did not have identification. "It brings up the question of whether black males are being targeted by Cambridge police for harassment," said Counter.

According to Gates' attorney, Gates was released from police custody after being held for four hours and posting $40 bail.

The incident generated much press coverage and commentary, including some from the White House. President Obama commented that the police "acted stupidly" by arresting Gates. President Obama was later surprised at the controversy and attention surrounding his statements. He told ABC news, "I have to say I am surprised by the controversy surrounding my statement, because I think it was a pretty straightforward commentary that you probably don't need to handcuff a guy, a middle-aged man who uses a cane, who's in his own home." He also said, "I think that I have extraordinary respect for the difficulties of the job that police officers do. . . . And my suspicion is that words were exchanged between the police officer and Professor Gates and that everybody should have just settled down and cooler heads should have prevailed. That's my suspicion." The President went on to say that he understands that Officer Crowley is "an outstanding police officer," but he also added that "it doesn't make sense to arrest a guy in his own home if he's not causing a serious disturbance." The President's comments drew criticism from the Cambridge Police Commissioner who said that he was "deeply pained" by what the President said.

Obama later said he regretted that his comments made the situation worse, and he hoped that the incident would become a teachable moment. He also said that both Crowley and Gates overreacted. He and Vice-President Joe Biden invited Crowley and Gates to the White House to have a conversation about the incident. Both men accepted the invitation.

Gates was scheduled to be arraigned on August 26, but the charges were dropped. According to a joint statement, Cambridge government officials and the police department made the recommendation to the Middlesex County district attorney who decided not to pursue the matter.

President Obama referred to this incident as a "teaching moment." What can be learned from these events, the arrest, the subsequent media reaction, the President's comment, and the reaction to that comment? Professor Gates acted unwisely by demonstrating hostility to police officers investigating an alleged crime. Reasonable requests by the police should be followed. The police acted unwisely by inflaming an already tense situation. Arresting someone at their home for disorderly conduct who is not immediately cooperating with requests to come outside without any threat of violence seems excessive. President Obama embraced this opportunity to facilitate dialogue between the men directly involved. Encouraging conversation rather than confrontation under these circumstances seems appropriate. But most importantly, even in 2009, race in the criminal justice context remains a most controversial, volatile issue.

C. Race and the O.J. Simpson Trial

A. Leon Higginbotham, Jr., Aderson Francois, and Linda Yueh

The O.J. Simpson Trial: Who Was Improperly Playing the Race Card,
in Birth of a Nationhood: Gaze, Script, and Spectacle in the O.J. Simpson Case
(edited by Toni Morrison and Claudia Brodsky Lacour)*

The case of *The People v. Orenthal James Simpson* has come to be seen by many as a metaphor for the seemingly intractable problems of race in America. Yet, for all of the incalculable hours of media attention and endless public comment by both observers and trial participants, many of the "lessons" drawn from the trial by commentators and a large segment of the public were deceptive. The most blatantly deceptive of these lessons is what now has become the conventional wisdom that in using detective Mark Fuhrman's racism as a test of his credibility, the Simpson

---

* (footnotes and chapter headings omitted).

defense team had *improperly and unjustifiably* "played the race card." That conclusion is false. Rather than establishing that the defense strategy was improper or unethical, when carefully analyzed, many of the critiquers of the defense team's strategies reveal far more the latent and explicit biases of the commentators and the duality of standards the public still uses to judge African-American criminal defendants and African-American lawyers.

The purpose of this article is to analyze the concept of "playing the race card," and whether the perceptions of *who* improperly "plays the race card" are reflective of larger societal racial attitudes. Therefore, was the core of the condemnation that the defense team improperly "played the race card" predicated more on some unarticulated and, perhaps, unrecognized racial biases of the critics than on any real deficiencies or inappropriateness of the defense strategy? All persons are products of the culture of our society and may have feelings, attitudes, and hostilities of which they are not fully aware. One of the intriguing questions regarding some of the critics of Johnnie Cochran and of the defense strategies is: Would they be more tolerant of the same type of aggressive conduct by a white lawyer on behalf of a white defendant? In short, to ask the question that Professor Cornel West raises: "Does race matter?" Essentially to this analysis is the answer to the question of why so many commentators were perturbed by the fact that the defense revealed on the evidentiary record before the jury that a significant witness, whose credibility was crucial, had often used the word "nigger," and frequently spoke disparagingly about African Americans.

In America, the "race card" is usually played as part of a zero-sum game in which any gain by African Americans—real or imagined—is considered to be a loss by whites. The Simpson case was no different. In the aftermath of the not-guilty verdict, with all of the self-righteous teeth-gnashing by many whites and the self-congratulatory chest-thumping by many African Americans, one would have thought that whites had suffered a grievous defeat and African Americans had won a great victory. Not so. Not even close. In this country, when race is at issue—and race was absolutely at issue in the Simpson trial and in the public reaction to the verdict—things are never really what they appear to be. When defense attorney Johnnie Cochran pointed out that police officers Fuhrman and Vannatter were the "twin devils of deception" when they hid and lied about their racist views behind façades of perfect respectability, he could have been talking about the issue of race; for in American society, race is often a great deceiver, an untrustworthy messenger, a misleading conjurer, an even more incredible witness than Mark Fuhrman, testifying under oath that he had *not* used the word "nigger" in the past ten years.

It follows then that even though many African Americans were intent on celebrating the verdict, the mass of African Americans in fact won nothing or very little. Mr. Simpson's acquittal did not and will not redress the discriminatory treatment many African Americans continue to face in the criminal justice system. Moreover, whatever symbolic satisfaction some African Americans may have enjoyed from seeing "one of our own" finally "beat the system" should have disappeared with the realization that Mr. Simpson, as evidenced by the life he led before the trial in his heyday of professional football and later media stardom, did not, for a single moment, consider himself to be "one of our own." He never spent any considerable effort as an advocate for the eradication of the systemic racism that engulfs most African Americans.

On the other hand, many whites, notwithstanding their very public "wither the nation" rhetoric after the Simpson verdict was announced, actually themselves engaged in a favorite American pastime: playing the race card, or, more accurately, playing the race game. And they played it with such sincere intensity, such deep concentration, and such card-shark skill as to make Johnnie Cochran's superb performance during the trial seem like the fumblings of a wholly incompetent attorney who did not understand the legal concepts of relevance and the other legal precedents for the admissibility of evidence in a criminal trial.

Thus, in the aftermath of the not-guilty verdict, the public was asked to believe that the acquittal of Mr. Simpson was a symptom, if not an outright cause, of racial division in this country. Robert Shapiro, one of Mr. Simpson's attorneys, no less, was perhaps the first to introduce this theme when he declared in a nationally televised interview with Barbara Walters on the news program *20/20* on October 3, 1995. "Not only did we play the race card, we dealt it from the bottom of the deck." In a separate interview on October 6, 1995, with the commentator Larry King, Mr. Shapiro continued: ". . . we played the race card, that's what happened. We have divided the blacks and the whites in an unnecessary way." Christopher Darden, one of the prosecuting attorneys, picked up Mr. Shapiro's theme. When asked during an interview with Barbara Walters on the news program *20/20* on October 6, 1995, whether Mr. Cochran had played the race card from the bottom of the deck as Mr. Shapiro claimed, Mr. Darden replied: "He played the race card from the bottom of the deck, from inside his shirt sleeve, he played it as well as anybody I've seen it played." Later, in his book, *In Contempt*, published a few months after the trial, Mr. Darden, like Mr. Shapiro during the Larry King interview, seemed to ascribe the very cause of racial division to the trial itself. He wrote: "As the case became more and more about race, I watched helplessly as it ripped the scabs off America's [racial] wounds."

A chorus of commentators soon joined in the Shapiro-Darden song about how the defense had, as Mr. Shapiro claimed, "played the race card from the bottom of the deck," and how the verdict had, as Mr. Darden put it, "picked the scabs off America's [racial] wounds." Clarence Page, the political columnist, declared, "Mr. Cochran played more than the race card. He played the whole deck." Representative Bob Dornan of California complained: "I think it was a racist decision."

Perhaps the most deceptive statement of all was uttered with a purported neutrality when Andy Rooney, the famed *60 Minutes* correspondent, declared that "[t]he [Simpson] acquittal was the worst thing that's happened to race relations in 40 years." Worse than what one wanted to ask Mr. Rooney: Worse than the bombing of the 16th Street Baptist Church in Birmingham, and the killing of four schoolchildren in 1963? Worse than the slaying of Medgar Evers in 1963, of James Chaney, Andrew Goodman, and Michael Schwerner in 1964, of Jimmie Lee Jackson, Reverend James Reeb, and Viola Gregg Liuzzo in 1965, or of dozens of other civil rights martyrs in the 1960s? Worse even than the assassination of Martin Luther King?

Mr. Rooney was not the only Jeremiah shouting about the end of racial progress. Marshall Wittmann, a senior fellow at the conservative think tank, The Heritage Foundation, mused: "[W]hat we're seeing now is thirty years of moving from a color-blind society to a balkanized society." Even newspaper editorials joined in. The *Los Angeles Times* called the verdict "a sad commentary on American racial divisions." The *Seattle Times* wondered: "What kind of society can flourish when members of a community—whether defined as Los Angeles or the United States—believe that Justice is based on skin color?" *USA Today* concluded, "[t]he verdict of the O.J. Simpson trial has left white Americans bitter, cynical about the criminal justice system, and overwhelmingly convinced that race relations will worsen as a result."

The immediate lesson that the public was supposed to learn from all of this hand-wringing is that race-consciousness, whether invidious or benign, is always impermissible, and that whenever race is used, whether such use is rational or irrational, the result will be as unfair as the not-guilty verdict that supposedly allowed Mr. Simpson to get away with murder. For example, William Bennett, the former secretary of education during the Reagan administration, reflected during an October 8, 1995, interview on the Sunday news program *This Week With David Brinkley*: "To get beyond racism, we need to get beyond the use of preference by race. . . . We have had thirty years of affirmative action. We have been thinking of race, we have been counting by race, we have been admitting and awarding by race, and now we are shocked to find a jury judges by race. I think we should go back to what [Martin Luther] King was talking about." Dinesh D'Souza, author of the conservative polemic *The End of Racism*, took a similar and quite common view during a debate on the October 8, 1995, CNN news program *The Color of Justice*. He maintained: "What the verdict shows is we live in a racially intoxicated society. . . . So, I think a positive thing to come out of the verdict is for whites and for all Americans to ask themselves, do we want race to be embedded in our laws, our policy, our voting, our education, our hiring, our promotion of government contracts; or should we begin to de-racialize our society?" George Will, one of the respected "elders" of current conservative dogma, concluded in a *lain Washington Post* column: "Another chilling residue of this [verdict] should be the realization that nothing—no institution, no pattern of civility—is spared the ravages of racial thinking. For more than a generation now, public policies such as affirmative action, the racial spoils system and the cult of 'diversity' have been teaching the nation that group think is virtuous. . . . Given all this, it is not surprising that the jurors had no pangs of conscience about regarding Simpson as a member of a group—and not seeing his victims at all. People who think 'race-conscious remedies' for this or that can be benign are partly to blame." The deeper moral that these commentators were asking the public to take from the trial is that the use of race—being the root of all social evils—had to be eradicated from American society; from affirmative action to college admissions, from congressional redistricting to government contracts. The supposed logic of their comments is that once race-consciousness is wiped out completely from our collective psyche and from all government programs, we will yet be able to achieve the glorious dream of a color-blind society.

In short, the trial and acquittal of Mr. Simpson became something infinitely greater than the trial and acquittal of one man for the murder of two people. It became the symbol of racial division, the proof of the evils of race-consciousness, the marker for racial injustice, the premonitory sign of the dying of the dream of a color-blind society. It did not seem to matter very much that the Simpson defense team was within its legal, ethical, and professional duty to raise the racial issue. Nor did it seem to matter very much that the lessons the public was asked to draw from the trial were historical to say the least.

For decades, the jurisprudence of the federal and California courts have recognized that a court or jury may properly determine that a witness's testimony is not credible if that witness either lies on the stand with regard to a material issue, or displays a specific bias toward a particular defendant or a general prejudice toward the defendant's gender, religion, ethnicity, or — yes — even race.

The standard set of instructions to the jury that federal judges have used for more than three decades recommends that jurors always be told that "as jurors, [they] are the sole and exclusive judges of the credibility of each of the witnesses called to testify . . . and that [they] may decide to believe all of that witness' testimony, only a portion of it, or none of it." The instructions continue that "if a person is shown to have knowingly testified falsely concerning any important or material matter, [jurors] obviously have a right to distrust the testimony of such an individual concerning other matters."

Moreover, the U.S. Supreme Court has stressed the need to test a witness's credibility against the witness's bias "by means of cross-examination directed toward revealing possible biases, prejudices, or ulterior motives of the witness as they may relate directly to issues or personalities in the case at hand." Federal appellate courts, following the lead of the Supreme Court, have also held as much. As one such court has put it: "the law recognizes 'the force of a hostile emotion, as influencing the probability of truth-telling . . . ; and a partiality of mind is therefore always relevant as discrediting the witness and affecting the weight of his testimony.' . . . Prejudice toward a group of which defendant is a part may be a source of partiality against the defendant."

Similar to the rulings of the federal courts, Section 780 of the California Evidence Code specifically permits the court or jury, in determining the credibility of a witness, to consider, among other things, "the existence or nonexistence of a bias, interest, or other motive"; and "a statement made by [the witness] that is inconsistent with any part of his testimony at hearing." Pursuant to that rule, as recently as March 1996, the Court of Appeals of California reaffirmed their long-standing doctrine that "where . . . a witness is knowingly false in one part of his testimony, the jury may distrust other portions of his testimony as well."

The foregoing cases, statutes, and jury instructions represent a formal modern enactment of the ancient maxim *falsus in uno, falsus in omnibus*—originally construed as "he who speaks falsely on one point will speak falsely upon all"—and serve as means to enforce the Supreme Court's admonishment that "the exposure of a witness's motivation in testifying is a proper and important function of the constitutionally protected right of cross-examination." This plethora of unequivocal state and federal jurisprudential precedents sanctioned the defense team's efforts to inquire about the racial bias of detective Mark Fuhrman.

The Simpson trial presented the case of an African-American man accused of killing his white ex-wife and her white male friend. Mark Fuhrman, the prosecution's main police witness, whom Mr. Cochran referred to as a "lying genocidal racist," once admitted that "when he sees a nigger driving with a white woman, he pulls them over" for no reason other than the fact that the man is African American and the woman is white. So strong was Mr. Fuhrman's bias toward African Americans that he wished "nothing more than to see all niggers gathered together and killed." So deep were Mr. Fuhrman's prejudices that he allowed himself to be taped using the word "nigger" at least forty-two times. Yet, when questioned on the stand about whether he harbored a bias toward African Americans, Mr. Fuhrman denied that he did so. Indeed, Mr. Fuhrman went on to emphatically deny having used the word "nigger" at all in the past ten years.

The jury, therefore, had at least four reasons to consider Mr. Fuhrman a less than credible witness against Mr. Simpson. First, the fact that Mr. Fuhrman lied about using the word "nigger" (*falsus in uno*) meant that he could have been lying about other aspects of his testimony (*falsus in omnibus*). Second, the jury had cause to disbelieve Mr. Fuhrman's testimony because Mr. Fuhrman perjured himself on the witness stand when he testified that he had not used the word "nigger" in the past ten years, when in fact he had been taped saying it at least forty-two times. Third, the jury could have reasonably determined that Mr. Fuhrman was biased against Mr. Simpson for having been married to a white woman because Mr. Fuhrman held and acted upon a strong bias against interracial couples made up of African American men and white women. Fourth, the jury could have reasonably found that Mr. Fuhrman's investigation and testimony against Mr. Simpson was tainted because it was Mr. Fuhrman's fervent wish to have "all niggers gathered together and killed." Thus, the Simpson defense team had a legal and professional obligation to introduce to the jury this very substantial and damning evidence of Mr. Fuhrman's lack of credibility.

This may seem to be an obvious point. However, during and after the trial, it appeared as if most Americans considered it morally wrong, socially irresponsible, and generally "unfair" for Mr. Cochran and his co-counsel to have "interjected" race into the trial.

Why was it unfair?

Any critical evaluation of the fairness of the commentary on the O.J. Simpson case should start with the assessment that there were several factors present during the trial that affected the public reaction to the verdict and that may have led commentators to claim that the defense improperly "played the race card": the race of the defendant, his fame and wealth, the race and gender of the victims, the race of the main police witnesses, the particular racial bias held by these witnesses, the race of lead counsel for the defense, and even the race of the judge. Since the interplay of these factors undoubtedly contributed to the incorrect perception that the defense had improperly played the race card, it then follows that changing one or more of these factors might also conceivably alter the perception that the defense improperly interjected race into the trial.

For example, if the main police witnesses had been African Americans with a history of hatred of and hostility toward whites, and if O.J. Simpson had been white, would the commentators have been as critical of any defense counsel who raised "the bias issue" as to the black police officers' prior conduct? Or, if Mr. Simpson's wife had been black, would these same commentators have been just as vehement in condemning the verdict as an outrage?

There are several other scenarios that could be hypothesized in order to raise the issue as to what the response would be if the gender or race or religion of the defendant had been different, or if the religion or race or gender of the victim had been different. Underlying all these scenarios described below is the basic question of whether, assuming that the violence and the commission of the crime were precisely the same, the intensity of the criticism would have been the same, less, or more, if the variables as to race, gender, or religion were different than those involved in the O.J. Simpson case.

If the defendant had been Catholic, and the prosecution's main police witness had a history of calling Catholics "devil sinners" and then lying about it on the witness stand, arresting, without justification, Catholics for traffic violations on their way home from church, and wishing that "all devil sinners should be gathered together and killed," would the critics claim that it was unfair for the defense to introduce evidence that the prosecution witness was a lying, anti-Catholic bigot? Probably not.

If the defendant had been Jewish, and the prosecution's main police witness had a history of calling Jewish individuals "kikes" and then lying about it on the witness stand, automatically stopping any motorist wearing a yarmulke, and wishing that "all kikes should be gathered together and killed," would the critics claim that it was unfair for the defense to introduce evidence that the witness was a lying, anti-Semitic neo-Nazi? Probably not.

If the defendant had been a woman, and the prosecution's main police witness had a history of calling women "bitches" and then lying about it on the witness stand, sexually harassing women at work, and wishing that "all bitches should be gathered together and killed," would the critics claim that it was unfair for the defense to introduce evidence that the witness was a lying, misogynistic harasser? Probably not.

If the defendant had been gay, and the prosecution's main police witness had a history of calling gays "faggots" and then lying about it on the witness stand, arresting any men seen holding hands, and wishing that "all faggots should be gathered together and killed," would the critics claim that it was unfair to introduce evidence that the witness was a lying, genocidal homophobe? Probably not.

Would it be unfair for the defense to argue that any witness—particularly a law enforcement officer charged with protecting all citizens—who harbors and acts upon sexist, anti-Catholic, anti-Semitic, or homophobic tendencies should be disbelieved when the defendant against whom the witness is testifying represents the very object of the witness's hate? Probably not.

Under any of the above scenarios, would the defense be accused of unfairly playing the gender card, or the religion card, or the ethnicity card, or the sexual-orientation card? Probably not.

Would the defense's trial strategy be considered a symptom or a cause of the division of America along gender, religious, ethnic, or sexual-orientation lines? Probably not.

Would the trial be used as an argument against policies designed to enhance the role of women in the workplace on the ground that they unfairly divide men and women; or against granting tax-exempt status to Catholic churches on the ground that it unfairly divides Catholics from non-Catholics; or against the United States' considerable foreign aid to Israel on the ground that it unfairly divides Jews and Gentiles; or against prosecuting gay-bias crimes on the ground that it unfairly divides heterosexuals from homosexuals? Probably not.

Some of these hypotheticals may sound farfetched, and some of the connections made between these hypothetical trials and particular public policies may seem absurd, but this is largely how the public reacted to the Simpson trial and verdict. For example, if a seemingly guilty Jewish defendant is acquitted because the defense showed that the prosecution's main police witness was a lying neo-Nazi, no one would seriously argue that the unjust verdict was a symptom of ethnic division and that the government should therefore stop favoring Israel with foreign aid. Instead, most people would agree that the testimony of an avowed neo-Nazi should carry very little weight against a Jewish defendant. Most people would also recognize that even if the Jewish defendant was indeed guilty, the issue of his unjust acquittal would have nothing to do whatsoever with foreign aid to Israel.

Yet, in the Simpson case, most commentators insisted on finding it unfair for the defense to have pointed out to the jury that Mr. Fuhrman was a confirmed racist and that his testimony against Mr. Simpson could reasonably have been deemed incredible by the jury. Moreover, these same commentators did not think it intellectually incoherent to link the acquittal of Mr. Simpson—unjust or otherwise—with issues as historically complex and as politically charged as the use of race in affirmative action or college admissions. Instead, the not-guilty verdict was used as the most recent and most vivid premonitory sign of the threat of race-consciousness to the dream of a color–blind society.

D. Race and the Rodney King Beating

A. Leon Higginbotham, Jr. and Aderson Francois
Looking for God and Racism in All the Wrong Places

In his legendary novel *One Hundred Years of Solitude*, Gabriel Garcia Marquez writes of a mythical town called Macondo and its mythical founding family, the Buendias. Built by the side of a river in the middle of a jungle, Macondo remained isolated for many years—its only contact with the rest of the world: a band of traveling gypsies who would visit the town once a year and bring with them the wonderful inventions of science and civilization. One day the gypsies arrive in Macondo with a daguerreotype camera and laboratory. Jose Arcadio Buendia, the founder of the town and a man of extravagant imagination, becomes fascinated by the new invention and resolves to use it to obtain scientific proof of the existence of God. He sets up the camera in different parts of his house during different times of the day, convinced that through a complicated process of multiple and superimposed exposures he will finally capture a scientific representation of the image of God. Why he wants proof of God and what he intends to do with that proof should he find it, we do not know. In any event, his experiment fails, he does not find proof of God and, in his frustration, he goes mad and ends up spending the rest of his life tied by the waist to the trunk of a tree, speaking in tongues which only he understands.

In 1991 and 1992, America—mostly white America—watched the videotape of the beating of Rodney King, searching its darkly-lit images for proof of the persistence of racism and race hatred in this country, with the same sort of mad intensity and pointless dedication that Jose Arcadio Buendia used to search for the existence of God in the silvery images of daguerreotype photographs. And, just as Jose Arcadio Buendia could not find an image of God no matter how many daguerreotype photographs he took and no matter how many exposures he devised, many white Americans, no matter how many times or how many different ways they watched the videotape, could not seem to see that the five white policemen beat the black motorist simply because he was black.

In fact, the more some white Americans watched the videotape the less they were willing to believe that the beating was the product of race-hatred. During the first few weeks of news coverage of the beating, as Rodney King's injuries were paraded on television, the popular consensus was: "My God! How could something like this have happened in America?" In the months that followed, after the tape was dissected on endless talk shows and after the details of Rodney King's criminal past began to surface, the popular response was downgraded to: "Well, maybe we do not really know why this happened?" Until finally, after the tape was reconstructed frame by frame in a courtroom in Simi Valley, California, and after the jury was told that Rodney King grunted like a bear as he was being beaten, the perhaps not uncommon reaction became: "You know, those policemen may have had a good reason to use force after all."

One wonders about the moral cowardice—to say nothing of the intellectual incoherence—it must have taken to make the journey from: "My God! How could something like this have happened?" to: "You know, these policemen may have a good reason to use force after all." But it is a journey many white Americans took; and a very short journey at that. For the original cri-de-coeur: "My God! How could something like this have happened in America?" was not so much an expression of outrage against an act of clear injustice as it was a fatuous reaction of near disbelief in response to a seemingly inexplicable event. In the eyes of many white Americans, the beating of Rodney King became an aberration, rendered all the more unreal for being replayed nightly on television. They were unable or unwilling to look at the beating through the corridor of American history, to place it in the context of present-day American society or to relate it to their daily American lives. In other words, for many white Americans, the beating of Rodney King was not a haunting sequel to the widespread lynching of blacks in the south during the first half of this century, it was not a vivid parallel to the imprisonment of a third of the young black male population in America in 1992 and it was not even a cruel magnification of the brutalization of millions of black children in inadequate schools in almost every city in this country. Instead, it was a single, isolated, disconnected, and ultimately irrelevant event.

Riots broke out in Los Angeles in 1992, after white police officers were acquitted of assaulting Rodney King, who was black. A number of whites were attacked without provocation by minorities upset by the verdict. These attacks occurred without planning in a predominately minority neighborhood in South Central Los Angeles. One of the whites attacked was Reginald Denny, who entered South Central while working as a truck driver. On April 29, 1992, about 6:30 p.m., during routine deliveries, Denny happened upon the intersection of Normandie Street and Florence Avenue. Denny was pulled from his truck by four black men and severely beaten. One of the men yanked open the truck door and pulled Denny from his cab. At least two others beat his head and kicked him, knocking him to the asphalt. After kicking him, one man raised his hands up in triumph.

Four black strangers who saw this terrible beating emerged from the crowd to prevent further harm to Denny, and to drive him out of danger to a hospital. Denny underwent three hours of emergency brain surgery. Doctors said Denny only had a few minutes to live when he was brought in. After several hours of surgery and hundreds of stitches, Denny's life was saved. Those who removed him from danger had not given up fighting to bridge the racial divide. Their refusal and their actions saved Reginald Denny's life. This single event illustrates well how minorities can react negatively or positively to their frustration over the racial divide.

E. Race and the Death of Trayvon Martin

Cynthia Lee

(E)Racing Trayvon Martin*

Fast forward to July 2013 when George Zimmerman was tried for murder in the shooting death of Trayvon Martin in Sanford, Florida. Zimmerman, the neighborhood watch captain for his neighborhood, was out in his truck one rainy evening when he spotted Trayvon Martin, a young Black male in a hoodie sweatshirt, who was walking and talking on his cell phone after going to the store to get a bag of skittles and a can of Arizona watermelon drink. Even though Martin was doing nothing to objectively indicate criminal behavior, at least nothing that Zimmerman articulated at that time or more than a year later at his trial, Zimmerman thought Martin looked suspicious and called 911 to report his suspicions. When Martin noticed Zimmerman following him, he started walking quickly away. Zimmerman got out of his car and followed Martin. Apparently, words were exchanged, and a physical confrontation ensued, ending when Zimmerman shot Martin in the chest.

Zimmerman remained on the scene after the shooting and told police he shot Martin in self-defense. Zimmerman claimed that after exchanging words with Martin, as he was walking back to his car, Martin sneaked back to confront Zimmerman and punch him in the face. According to Zimmerman, Martin threw him to the ground and slammed his head against the concrete several times. Zimmerman told police he shot Martin only after Martin pinned him to the ground, called him a mother f—er, said he was going to die that night, and reached for Zimmerman's gun.

Even though the detectives who initially interviewed Zimmerman thought Zimmerman should be arrested on manslaughter, the Florida State Attorney's Office instructed the police not to arrest Zimmerman. When word got out that Zimmerman was released without arrest after shooting an unarmed teenager, thousands took to the streets to protest what was widely perceived as a racially biased decision not to prosecute. The public protests led the Florida State Attorney's Office to reverse its initial decision not to charge Zimmerman with any crime. The state of

* (footnotes omitted).

Florida ultimately charged Zimmerman with second-degree murder, and his trial began in June of 2013.

A. The Role of the Zimmerman Trial Court in Constructing Race as Irrelevant

While race was clearly a focus of the public protests and media commentary about the case in 2012 after the shooting, race was conspicuously absent from the trial proceedings a little over a year later. In an early ruling, Judge Debra Nelson, who presided over Zimmerman's murder trial, made it clear to both sides that she intended to run a colorblind trial and did not want either side to call attention to race. In response to a defense motion to preclude the prosecution from referring to Zimmerman's activities as "racial profiling," Judge Nelson ruled that prosecutors could not use the term "racial profiling" when referring to Zimmerman's activities the night of the shooting. Judge Nelson's ruling may have been motivated by a desire to strike a balance between what the defense wanted (no reference to either "racial profiling" or "profiling") and what the prosecution wanted (the ability to use both terms). Whatever the motivation, Judge Nelson's ruling significantly curtailed the government's ability to discuss the racial implications of Zimmerman's initial decision to follow and his subsequent decision to shoot Martin. Just as Justice O'Connor constructed race as irrelevant in *Florida v. Bostick* by ignoring the racial identities of Bostick and the law enforcement officers who confronted him, Judge Nelson constructed race as irrelevant in the Zimmerman trial by barring the prosecution from referencing the fact that Martin's race may have played a role in triggering Zimmerman's initial suspicions and his subsequent actions. Jurors were encouraged to view Zimmerman and Martin as simply individuals—or, more accurately, as simply men—without regard to their racial identity.

Race, however, was closely connected to the events that transpired the night Zimmerman fatally shot Martin. Just as Terrance Bostick's racial identity as a Black man likely influenced the way he perceived the White officers who confronted him on the bus as well as the way they perceived him, Trayvon Martin's identity as a young Black male likely influenced the way Zimmerman perceived Martin and the way Martin perceived Zimmerman. Zimmerman didn't see a raceless and genderless person walking in his neighborhood. He saw a young black male in a hoodie, and thought Martin was suspicious most likely because our society associates young, Black, and male with crime. The rash of burglaries and attempted break-ins in the neighborhood by young Black males in the weeks preceding the shooting only strengthened the association Zimmerman made between young Black men and crime.

Zimmerman's racial identity was also significant. Martin saw a heavy-set, light-skinned man, and may have assumed Zimmerman was White. This man was suggesting that Martin had no right to be walking in the neighborhood, which likely rubbed Martin the wrong way. In the pre-Civil War era, Blacks had to carry proof that they were free men, not slaves. Many Blacks today are reminded of this dark history when they are pulled over by police and asked to show identification. This history might explain in part why Martin may have taken offense at Zimmerman's actions—and, if we believe Zimmerman's account, why Martin might have thrown the first punch.

Martin may have also perceived Zimmerman's actions as a challenge to his masculinity. As Angela Harris has explained, men of color who lack power over others sometimes resort to hyper-masculine shows of physical aggression to demonstrate their masculinity. Martin was not a wealthy African-American adult male. He was an African-American teenager from a family of modest means. Camille Gear-Rich explains that Martin's resort to physical violence may have been a way for him to demonstrate his masculinity.

The prosecution not only acquiesced in the judge's decision to run a colorblind trial, they embraced a colorblind trial strategy. At the hearing on the pretrial motion on whether the prosecution could use the term "racial profiling" to describe Zimmerman's actions the night of the shooting, prosecutor John Guy told Judge Nelson, "[Profiling] is not a racially charged term unless it's made so, and we do not intend to make it a racially charged term." The prosecution team was very careful not to call attention to race through the rest of the trial.

The prosecution may have been worried that if they called attention to race, jurors would think they were "playing the race card." "Playing the race card" is a term of art used to accuse a person of lying when they claim to have suffered differential treatment on the basis of race. Someone who "plays the race card" is understood to be inappropriately claiming racial disadvantage. The race card accusation has been used so often by individuals who are hostile to discussions on race that many people today will not call attention to race out of fear of being accused of "playing the race card."

The prosecution had reason to be worried that they would attract criticism if they called attention to race. Some trial observers firmly believed the case had nothing to do with race. Some thought it unfair to prosecute Zimmerman and make him "pay for generations of racial inequities." Others believed Zimmerman was prosecuted to placate angry African-American voters and others who rallied to make the killing a cause.

Defense attorney Mark O'Mara provided further support for the critics opposed to the prosecution of Zimmerman, repeatedly opining that if Zimmerman had been Black, "he never would have been charged with a crime." Actually, studies suggest that if Zimmerman had been Black and had shot and killed a White male, it is very likely he would have been arrested, prosecuted, convicted, and possibly sentenced to death. Blacks who kill Whites are far more likely to be prosecuted and sentenced to death than Whites who kill Blacks.

Aware that members of the community viewed the prosecution of Zimmerman as unfair scape-goating, the prosecution decided to try the case without referencing race—to take the colorblind high ground. The problem is that by not calling attention to the possibility that Zimmerman thought Martin looked suspicious because of deeply entrenched stereotypes about young Black men as criminals, the prosecution encouraged jurors to see Zimmerman and Martin as just two young men who got into a fight that tragically, but understandably, ended in death. By deliberately avoiding any discussion of race, they erased Trayvon Martin's race from the trial even though race likely played a significant role in why Zimmerman thought Martin looked suspicious from the start and why the jury may have found Zimmerman's account of what happened that night credible.

Trayvon Martin's race, however, could not be completely eliminated from the jury's consciousness. Jurors needed only to look at the autopsy photos of Trayvon Martin or observe his parents in the courtroom to be aware of his race. In deciding whether Zimmerman honestly and reasonably feared Martin, a necessary component of his self-defense claim, jurors quite possibly, even if subconsciously, considered Martin's race and made the implicit association between black males, criminality, and violence.

By ignoring race, prosecutors may have unwittingly exacerbated the effects of implicit bias. A substantial body of research suggests that ignoring race leads jurors to assess Black defendants more harshly than similarly situated White defendants, but these racially disparate results are reduced when race is made salient. If prosecutors had confronted race head on by making race a salient feature of their trial strategy, they might have been able to convince the jury to see Martin in a more sympathetic light.

B. Florida's Stand Your Ground Law

In 2005, Florida amended its self-defense statute, which previously required an individual to retreat before using deadly force in self-defense if a safe retreat was known to be available to the individual. Under Florida's revised self-defense statute, dubbed Florida's Stand Your Ground law, individuals in Florida no longer have to retreat before using deadly force in self-defense. Even if a safe retreat is known and available, an individual who is attacked while in a place where he (or she) has a lawful right to be may use deadly force to repel the attacker. An individual has no duty to retreat before using such force as long as "he or she reasonably believes it is necessary to do so to prevent death or great bodily harm to himself or herself or another or to prevent the commission of a forcible felony." The shooting of Trayvon Martin called attention to Florida's Stand Your Ground law because the Sanford Police Department referred to this law as the reason why they did not arrest Zimmerman on the night of the shooting.

While English common law required individuals to retreat to the wall before using deadly force in self-defense if a safe retreat was known and available, a no-duty-to-retreat rule has long been a part of American self-defense doctrine. In 1921, the U.S. Supreme Court approved the no-duty-retreat rule, noting that "[d]etached reflection cannot be demanded in the presence of an uplifted knife." Today, thirty-three states allow individuals to use deadly force in self-defense without requiring retreat. In these states, an individual can use deadly force in self-defense against another individual even if a safe retreat is known and available. Seventeen states require retreat if a safe retreat is known and available. In these states, if a safe retreat is known and available to the defendant and he uses deadly force without retreating, he loses his right to act in self-defense. Some states do not require retreat but allow the jury to consider whether a safe retreat was known and available in assessing the reasonableness of the defendant's belief in the need to act in self-defense. In these jurisdictions, if a safe retreat was known and available to the defendant, the jury may conclude that it was not reasonable for the defendant to believe he needed to use deadly force to protect himself from imminent death or serious bodily harm.

The Florida legislature went beyond simply eliminating the duty to retreat from its previous law of self-defense. It also enacted a controversial immunity provision, which gives an individual who reasonably believes in the need to use deadly force in self-defense immunity from arrest and criminal prosecution. Florida's immunity provision provides:

> (1) A person who uses force as permitted in s. 776.012, s. 776.013, or s. 776.031 is justified in such conduct and is immune from criminal prosecution and civil action for the use or threatened use of such force . . . unless the person against whom the force was used is a law enforcement officer, as defined in 941.10(14), who was acting in the performance of his or her official duties and the officer identified himself or herself in accordance with any applicable law or the person using or threatening to use force knew or reasonably should have known that the person was a law enforcement officer. As used in this subsection, the term "criminal prosecution" includes arresting, detaining in custody, and charging or prosecuting the defendant.

Many commentators have opined that media attention on Florida's Stand Your Ground law was misplaced since Zimmerman's self-defense claim would have been the same in a non-Stand-Your-Ground state. For example, conservative commentator Ann Coulter told the press, "[T]his . . . has nothing to do with "Stand Your Ground." Coulter explained that if Zimmerman was on the ground being beaten by Martin, there was no safe retreat available to him just before the shooting. Therefore, even in a jurisdiction that requires safe retreat if a safe retreat is known and available to the defendant, Zimmerman would have the right to use deadly force in self-defense provided he met the other, usual requirements of the state's self-defense law. Moreover, Zimmerman did not claim immunity from prosecution as he could have under Florida's immunity provision.

While Zimmerman did not claim immunity and arguably could not retreat while he was on the ground, Stand Your Ground nonetheless was a part of the Zimmerman case. For one thing, the jury was instructed on Florida's Stand Your Ground law. They were specifically told:

> If George Zimmerman was not engaged in a unlawful activity and was attacked in any place where he had a right to be, he had no duty to retreat and had the right to stand his ground and meet force with force, including deadly force if he reasonably believed that it was necessary to do so to

prevent death or great bodily harm to himself or another or to prevent the commission of a forcible felony.

Moreover, it is not clear that a safe retreat was not available to Zimmerman. Perhaps no safe retreat was available to Zimmerman once he was on the ground with Martin on top of him, but Zimmerman may have had the opportunity to retreat before the encounter got physical. Additionally, even under Florida's Stand Your Ground law, Zimmerman would have had a duty to retreat if he was the initial aggressor.

The Zimmerman case focused the nation's attention on Stand Your Ground laws. This scrutiny reveals that Stand Your Ground laws are not applied in an even-handed way. Just as the race of the victim seems to affect outcomes in capital cases, the race of the victim seems to affect outcomes in Stand Your Ground cases. A study of cases involving claims of self-defense in Florida after passage of Florida's Stand Your Ground law is instructive. The *Tampa Bay Times* studied 192 cases involving Floridians charged with crimes of violence who claimed self-defense under Florida's Stand Your Ground law and found that individuals who killed a Black person walked 73 percent of the time, while those who killed a White person went free 59 percent of the time.

Similarly, an empirical study by John Roman of the Urban Institute found that in both Stand Your Ground and non-Stand Your Ground states, "[w]hite-on-black homicides [are] more likely to be ruled justified (11.4 percent), while black-on-white homicides are least likely to be ruled justified (1.2 percent)." When he focused just on Stand Your Ground states, Roman found that "controlling for all case attributes [other than race], the odds a white-on-black homicide [will be] found justified [in a Stand Your Ground jurisdiction] is 281 percent greater than the odds that a white-on-white homicide [will be] found justified. In contrast, "a black-on-white homicide has barely half the odds of being ruled justifiable relative to [a] white-on-white homicide." These studies indicate that Stand Your Ground laws are not applied in a racially even-handed way.

C. Most of the Racial Critiques of the Case Have Ignored Zimmerman's Mixed Race Identity

When it became clear that the public thought Zimmerman had racially profiled Martin, Zimmerman's father wrote a letter to the *Orlando Sentinel*, announcing that his son was not a racist and was himself an ethnic minority since his mother was from Peru. In declaring Zimmerman's ethnic minority status as Hispanic and linking this status to the assertion that his son was not a racist, Zimmerman's father was relying on an assumption that (non-Hispanic) White equals racist and minority equals non-racist. It is a fallacy to assume that only Whites can be racist. Whites do not hold a monopoly on racial bias against Blacks. People of all races and ethnicities can be and often are racially biased in favor of Whites and against Blacks. As Tanya Hernandez points out, "Racism, in particular anti-Black racism, is a pervasive and historically entrenched fact of life in Latin America and the Caribbean."

Similarly, Jerry Kang has noted that "Asian Americans generally have implicit biases against African Americans that are almost as strong as those held by Whites." The fact that Zimmerman was himself of mixed race identity and thus an ethnic minority therefore does not mean he could not engage in racial stereotyping. Zimmerman could have and most likely did rely on racial assumptions when he saw Martin and thought Martin looked suspicious. Any one of us, myself included, could have had similar thoughts and beliefs.

F. Race and the Death of Jordan Davis

F. Michael Higginbotham
Valuing Black Life

Six months after George Zimmerman was acquitted for shooting and killing 17-year-old Trayvon Martin, a trial involving similar circumstances concluded. This time the defendant, Michael Dunn, was convicted on three counts of attempted murder for shooting into a car occupied by four Black teenagers. Jurors could not agree on the most serious charge of first-degree murder, which requires establishing a premeditated intent to kill. Since the shots killed Jordan Davis after Dunn told Davis and the other teenagers to turn down the radio in their car, since Dunn remained in the parking lot for several minutes after the argument occurred, and since Dunn failed to call 911 and left the scene once his passenger returned, both a murder charge and an attempted murder charge were filed. At trial, Dunn claimed he saw a gun in the teenagers' car and felt threatened, invoking the stand your ground law to justify deadly force. No gun was found, and testimony by the three surviving teenagers, and other witnesses, undermined Dunn's claim of feeling threatened.

While an attempted murder conviction related to the three surviving teenagers seems appropriate, the jury's failure to convict on the murder charge is perplexing. This failure raises long held concerns that race continues to infect perceptions by some jurors, resulting in decisions conveying the message that Black life is not equal to White life.

While the prosecutor has indicated she will seek a retrial on the first-degree murder charge, it is important to recognize that racial inequality in the administration of justice today is an unfortunate reality. America is not post-racial.

While the causes of inequality are more complex than they were under the discriminatory criminal laws of the Jim Crow Era, inequity through racial profiling, prosecutorial discretion, and disparate sentencing remains.

Death penalty cases reveal prosecutors seek capital punishment at much higher rates when the victim is White. White federal defendants are more likely to have death sentences reduced to life through plea-bargaining. Almost 80 percent of persons on death row have been convicted of crimes against White victims, despite the fact that Blacks are more likely to be victims of homicide.

How can one explain disparate sentencing in the cases of Tim Carter and Richard Thomas without pointing to race? Tim Carter and Richard Thomas were arrested, in separate incidents, three months apart, in 2004, in nearly the same Florida location.

Police found one rock of cocaine on Carter, who is White, and a crack pipe with cocaine residue on Thomas, who is Black. Both men claimed drug addictions.

Neither had prior felony arrests or convictions, and both potentially faced five years in prison. Carter had his prosecution withheld, and the judge sent him to drug rehabilitation. Thomas was prosecuted, convicted and sent to prison. The only other apparent difference was race.

The statistics on New York's stop-and-frisk practices, where Blacks and Latinos make up 50 percent of the population but 83 percent of the stops, are a result of America's long, and recent, history of inequality. Of the over 4 million stops during the last decade, only 6 percent have resulted in further action, of which 2 percent involved weapons violations. Stop-and-frisk allows police wide discretion to detain minorities who have demonstrated little (if any) indication of wrongdoing.

We must not ignore the role race continues to play. Race continues to be significant in creating suspicion of crime. Fear of Black teenagers is accepted as normal. In some cases, it appears that murder is an acceptable response.

While many may look at Dunn's potential 60-year sentence as adequate justice, the underlying message of the failure to convict on the first-degree murder charge reaffirms notions of racial hierarchy present in the criminal justice system since slavery.

In 1855, a Black slave woman named Celia killed her White owner, Robert Newsom, after he had repeatedly raped her for several years. Celia was convicted of murder and hanged. Her defense of justification, based on resisting an attempted rape, was rejected by the Missouri trial court because she was a slave.

Four years earlier, in Virginia, a slave owner had been convicted of second-degree murder for killing his slave, Sam, after whipping and torturing him. While punishing a slave owner for killing his slave was rare, the sentence of five years imprisonment is revealing. The inconsequential sentence for such a brutal crime indicates how little value was placed on Sam's humanity.

The disparate sentencing treatment between Black and White defendants in 1855 continues to be reflected today. Although White Americans use marijuana at roughly the same rate as Blacks, African Americans are more likely to be arrested on charges of marijuana possession. White defendants in stand your ground states such as Florida, where self-defense laws do not require retreat when one feels threatened, are four times more likely to be acquitted when the victim is Black than when the victim is White, evidencing that Black life is not equally valued within our criminal justice system.

G. Questions and Notes

In several of these proceedings, including the O.J. Simpson trial and the Rodney King trial, the trial process was the mechanism used to administer justice. Criminal trials follow a standard set of steps, whereby the testimony of each witness is introduced through direct examination, followed by an opportunity for cross-examination. The progress of these trials, however, was impeded at nearly every step. Do you think the progress of the trials was impeded by procedural errors or were the impediments related to the controversial subject matter under review? Were there complex difficulties applying the rules and laws to the facts, or did the values of the decision-makers introduce a layer of complexity? At any of the procedural steps, do any of the choices made suggest that the values of the decision-makers were racially skewed?

The victim in the O.J. Simpson murder trial, Nicole Brown Simpson, was white. What impact, if any, do you believe this had on the conduct and outcome of the trial? Do you feel that courts and juries have historically placed different value on lives, based on race?

If Professor Henry Louis Gates was white, do you think that Officer James Crowley would have arrested him?

H. Point/Counterpoint

In light of the failures to prosecute police officers in the deaths of Michael Brown, Eric Garner, and other minority males who died while interacting with law enforcement, and in light of the various protest movements like "Black Lives Matter," "Hands Up Don't Shoot," and "I Can't Breathe," do you believe that reform of the grand jury system or other enforcement practices is warranted?

XXVII. Race and Immigration

A. Introduction

On April 23, 2010, the Governor of Arizona, Jan Brewer, signed into law a state provision designed to identify and report individuals who reside illegally in the United States. Arizona Senate Bill 1070 (SB 1070) permits state and local law enforcement personnel to request identification from any person who is "reasonably suspected" of being in the country illegally. Such permission has resulted in allegations of racial profiling in the determination of what constitutes "reasonable suspicion".

B. History of Race and Immigration

Lisa Sandoval

*Race and Immigration Law: A Troubling Marriage**

Section One: A History of Racism in Immigration Law

Perhaps more alarming than SB 1070's express sanction of profiling is the consistent theme of racism present in the history of immigration law. The evolution of U.S. immigration law demonstrates the political and judicial branches' repeated use of race to deny different groups citizenship status. This trend illustrates Gordon and Lenhardt's theory that citizenship defines exclusion, not merely inclusion. While immigration law has changed over time, what remains the same are notions of racial inferiority associated with noncitizens. The history of U.S. immigration law reveals many instances of race being used to signify non-belonging, but I focus on four moments: 1) *Dred Scott v. Sandford*, 2) *Ping v. United States* (the Chinese Exclusion Act case), 3) the "naturalization cases," and 4) the Mexican Repatriation and Operation Wetback.

Dred Scott Sets the Stage

Immigration to the United States is a phenomenon that traces to the founding of the nation. While immigration was largely unregulated during roughly the first 100 years of the United States' existence, by 1882 the Chinese Exclusion Act (the "Act") was one of the first major attempts at controlling the flow of people into the country. The legal precedent established in *Ping v. United States*, a case arising from the Act, created the legal framework for immigration law in the United States. However, it is important to understand how *Dred Scott v. Sandford*, decided thirty-three years earlier, set the stage for *Ping* by first characterizing citizenship in terms of racial belonging and assimilability.

In *Dred Scott v. Sandford* the United States Supreme Court held that African Americans, even those born free, were not U.S. Citizens. The Court denied Dred Scott the ability to sue in federal court because it deemed that he was not a citizen of the United States. The Supreme Court turned to race to determine whether the original framers intended to include slaves within the original meaning of the Constitution. The Court presented exhaustive evidence of racial animosity towards African Americans in order to *justify* not granting them citizenship status under the Constitution:

---

* (footnotes omitted).

We refer to these historical facts for the purpose of showing the *fixed opinions concerning that race*, upon which the statesmen of that day spoke and acted. It is necessary to do this, in order to determine whether the general terms used in the Constitution of the United States, as applied to the rights of man and the rights of the people, was intended to include them. . . .

While this case holds great meaning for many reasons beyond the scope of this paper, it is also significant because the Court expressly characterized citizenship in terms of racial belonging. Thus, the Court focused on Scott's racial difference as a reason why he did not belong to the nation in the form of a citizen. Although this decision was later overturned by the Fourteenth Amendment, its characterization of noncitizens as racially different "others" set the jurisprudential stage for the Chinese Exclusion Act case.

Chinese Exclusion and the Plenary Power Doctrine

Ping set forth the plenary power doctrine, allowing the political branches unfettered power to regulate immigration. This discretionary and far reaching power was justified in the name of "protecting" the nation from the danger posed by racially different foreign nationals. The holdings of this case and the reasoning of the Court have set the framework of immigration law enforcement until present day. The Court's reasoning focused on the Chinese's racial difference as the reason why they failed to assimilate and the threat they posed by that failure.

On May 8, 1882, Congress passed the Chinese Exclusion Act, which allowed the Executive branch to exclude Chinese nationals from entering the United States. Under the Act, Chinese nationals already living in the United States needed to obtain a certificate of reentry if they left the country and wanted to return. Chae Chan Ping was a Chinese-born laborer living in California during the California Gold Rush, which lasted from approximately 1848 to 1855. Before leaving the country to visit China, Ping obtained a certificate of reentry as required by the Act. However, during his absence from the country, Congress amended the Act to ban reentry of Chinese, including those who had obtained a certificate to do so. Ping was barred from reentering the country and challenged his exclusion, which the Court upheld.

Justice Field, writing for a unanimous court, pointed to the Chinese laborers' race as the underlying reason why they could not assimilate to U.S. culture:

> The differences of race added greatly to the difficulties of the situation . . . [T]hey remained strangers in the land, residing apart by themselves, and adhering to the customs and usages of their own country. It seemed impossible for them to assimilate with our people, or to make any change in their habits or modes of living.

The analysis then seamlessly transitioned into the danger that the Chinese posed due to the increase in their population:

> As they grew in numbers each year the people of the coast saw, or believed they saw, in the facility of immigration, and in the crowded millions of

China, where population presses upon the means of subsistence, great danger that at no distant day that portion of our country would be overrun by them, unless prompt action was taken to restrict their immigration. The people there accordingly petitioned earnestly for protective legislation.

It is clear that the Court based the racial differences of the Chinese on their inability to assimilate, which posed a "threat" to the people of the United States. Justice Field paints a picture of "others" overtaking the nation. In the eyes of the Court, as well as those of Congress, the increased presence of the Chinese—a group viewed as so racially different that they could not blend in with their surrounding population—was something from which the people of the United States need protection. It is through the framework of non-belonging and danger that the Court not only justifies, but promotes the exclusion of the Chinese. This logic is further evidenced when the Court declares:

> If . . . the government of the United States, through its legislative department, considers the presence of foreigners *of a different race* in this country, who will *not assimilate* with us, to be *dangerous to its peace and security,* their exclusion is not to be stayed because at the time there are no actual hostilities with the nation of which the foreigners are subject.

Ping built on the notion in *Dred Scott* of racial difference as creating a barrier to assimilation. The Court in both cases views an inability to assimilate due to racial difference as the ultimate marker of non-belonging. Going a step further, the Court in *Ping* characterizes the racial difference of noncitizens as a threat to the nation, which justifies the political branches in taking whatever measures they deem appropriate in regulating immigration. The result of this rationale is the plenary power doctrine, which ultimately leads to constitutional rights-stripping of noncitizens.

The Naturalization Process: Determining Whiteness

The "naturalization cases" refer to the set of cases in which immigrants argued that they should be allowed to naturalize under the provisions of the Naturalization Act of 1790 that extended citizenship to "free white persons" and, after the Fourteenth Amendment, "aliens of African nativity and . . . persons of African descent." In these cases, courts determined whether a particular group could meet the requirements of being white in order to naturalize. The cases focused on race as an indicator of whether immigrants could assimilate into U.S. culture, which was another way of determining if they belonged and thus were worthy of citizenship status. The race-based requirement to naturalize was not lifted until 1952 with the passage of the McCarran-Walter Act.

It is worth noting that as a reaction to *Dred Scott* and Reconstruction efforts to rectify gross inequalities, the Naturalization Act of 1790 was amended to include "aliens of African nativity and persons of African descent." As a result of this amendment, a black-white dichotomy of races within the naturalization process was created. The fact that all naturalization cases consisted of courts determining whether a particular group could be considered white indicates that the black-white dichotomy was in fact a racial hierarchy in which whites were the dominant group to which noncitizens must conform. As such, white was further constructed as the superior race to which immigrants should assimilate if they were to enjoy the full benefits of U.S. citizenship.

For instance, *In Re Halladjian*, Judge Lowell in the Massachusetts Circuit Court granted citizenship to four Armenians by relying on the popular usage of the term "free white person." The judge turned to late eighteenth-century census documents that described the inhabitants of the former colonies. Judge Lowell reasoned that since the censuses expressly mentioned "Indians, Chinese, and Japanese," the term white was used as a "catch-all word to include everybody else." While recognizing that "there is no European or white race," Judge Lowell nonetheless allowed the notion of whiteness to continue as a prerequisite to naturalizing. He granted the Armenians citizenship based on the fact they could conceivably fall under the catch all description of whiteness since their race was not explicitly mentioned in the census.

However, in *Ozawa* the Supreme Court denied a Japanese man citizenship because he was deemed as falling outside the Caucasian race and thus could not be granted citizenship. The Court rejected a color test to define whiteness and instead relied on the meaning of Caucasian as "a zone of *more or less debatable ground* outside which, upon the one hand, are those clearly eligible, and outside of which, upon the other hand, are those clearly ineligible for citizenship." Like the Massachusetts Court, the Supreme Court raised doubt about the concreteness of the meaning of the term "white" or "Caucasian" but nonetheless chose to advance the notion of whiteness as a requisite for citizenship.

In *United States v. Thind*, an Indian national contested the denial of his citizenship application. The Supreme Court held that "upper class Hindus" could not be classified as white and were therefore barred from naturalizing. The Court conceded that trying to define whiteness through biology or reference to Caucasian ancestry was elusive and not scientifically sound. However, the Court nonetheless connected whiteness with the ability to assimilate by rationalizing that Europeans were white because they could "merge into the mass of our population and lose the distinctive hallmarks of their European origin." Within this definition of white, assimilation did not merely mean adjusting to "American culture" but instead losing one's identity to blend in with the white majority. Hindus were denied white status precisely because they "would retain indefinitely the clear evidence of their ancestry."

Mexican Repatriation and Operation Wetback: History Repeats Itself

During the Great Depression, President Hoover authorized the removal of Mexican nationals, although more than half of those removed turned out to be U.S. Citizens. Due to the economic downturn, the repatriation was intended to ensure that only "true Americans" held jobs in the United States. To assist in the round-up, all over the nation police raided public spaces, including churches, and forced people of Mexican ancestry onto trains and buses headed for the U.S.-Mexico border. By the end of the decade-long deportation campaign, deemed "repatriation," an estimated one million people of Mexican ancestry were removed from the country.

History repeated itself in 1954—just two years after race requirements were removed from the naturalization system. Congress passed Operation Wetback, intended to deport Mexican "wetbacks," a term legitimately used in mainstream discourse to refer to illegal Mexican immigrants. Operation Wetback went hand-in-hand with the Bracero Program set up by the United States to import temporary Mexican agricultural workers in order to address labor shortages due to World War II. While the United States welcomed the *labor* of Mexican nationals through the Bracero program, it simultaneously rejected the presence of Mexican nationals beyond their capacity as laborers. Hence, Operation Wetback was intended to address the increase in illegal immigration that had grown alongside the Bracero Program.

Under the program, undocumented Mexican nationals and Mexican nationals who were legally present under the Bracero Program were indistinguishable. Therefore, Operation Wetback's main mission of deporting "illegal" Mexican immigrants served more as a cover to remove all Mexican nationals deemed a threat to society. As evidenced by the title of the deportation campaign, once again racial difference fueled the exclusion of immigrant workers who were deemed harmful to society. Under Operation Wetback, more than one million people were deported. Like the Mexican Repatriation, many deportees were U.S. citizens.

Section Two: Extra-constitutionality of Immigration Law

The evolution of immigration law since *Ping* illustrates that, as a result of the plenary power doctrine, fundamental constitutional protections are applied in a highly restrictive manner in the immigration context. Challenging government action that regulates immigration is very difficult since the plenary power doctrine also ensures that courts provide deference to the political branches regarding immigration laws. Without a check on this unfettered discretion, the political branches are able to abuse their power, as evidenced in federal immigration laws that strip constitutional rights from noncitizens and promote racial profiling.

Noncitizens are described as not being punished by deportation but merely regulated. Therefore, immigration proceedings are characterized as civil rather than criminal. As a consequence, many of the constitutional protections afforded to criminal defendants are stripped from noncitizens undergoing deportation proceedings. For instance, noncitizens who undergo immigration proceedings are not afforded many basic constitutional rights under Article I of the Constitution, the Fourth Amendment, the Fifth Amendment, and the Sixth Amendment. Specifically, immigration regulations can be applied retroactively, in violation of the Ex Post Facto Clause of Article I, section 9 of the United States Constitution. In addition, the Fourth Amendment remedy for suppression of evidence obtained in an illegal search or seizure is applied in a very limited fashion to noncitizens. Noncitizens do not enjoy a presumption of innocence and they receive no Fifth Amendment protection regarding the right to remain silent; silence can be used against them. Noncitizens are also not afforded the Sixth Amendment guarantees to an impartial jury, a speedy trial, and right to counsel. Furthermore, the rules of evidence do not apply to immigration proceedings and the government may use secret evidence against noncitizens. The constitutional rights stripping of noncitizens made possible by the plenary power doctrine, makes immigration law immune from many standard constitutional protections. As a result, police action that would otherwise be unconstitutional is considered legal when executed in the immigration context. A prime example is the widespread use of racial profiling to regulate immigration.

Section Three: Using Race to Identify Noncitizens

Current Supreme Court precedent allows for the use of racial profiling in immigration enforcement. Amnesty International defines racial profiling as:

> [T]he targeting of individuals and groups by law enforcement officials, even partially, on the basis of race, ethnicity, national origin, or religion, except where there is trustworthy information, relevant to the locality and timeframe, that links persons belonging to one type of the aforementioned groups to an identified criminal incident or scheme.

Based on this definition, the legal use of racial profiling within the immigration context suggests that race *becomes* "trustworthy information" regarding a person's likelihood of being unlawfully present in the country. Current immigration case law demonstrates this correlation.

Under *Brignoni-Ponce*, the Court established the legal use of racial profiling as a tool to enforce immigration laws. Specifically, "Mexican-appearance" in conjunction with other articulable facts was described as creating the reasonable suspicion necessary to stop someone under the Fourth Amendment. In *Brignoni-Ponce*, the Border Patrol had set up a checkpoint in San Clemente, California. One evening, while the checkpoint was closed due to bad weather, Border Patrol officers observed traffic from their vehicle parked on the side of the highway. They stopped respondent's car, stating that the respondent's Mexican-looking appearance was their only reason for doing so. Although the Court found that Mexican appearance alone is not a sufficient reason for stopping a person, it can be used in conjunction with other factors.

Brignoni-Ponce is a pivotal case because it validated the use of racial stereotypes to define "Mexican appearance" and connected race with the likelihood of illegal conduct. The Court took the government at its word that trained officers can detect "the characteristic appearance" of people who live in Mexico based on "such factors as the mode of dress and haircut." In no way did the Court challenge this allegation. In fact, "mode of dress and haircut" are merely examples of what immigration officers use to detect someone from Mexico. Immigration officials may be explicitly using race and accents as factors, but the Court makes no inquiry into this. By not challenging the government's assertion, the Court effectively allowed the government to decide what it means to "look Mexican."

The Court goes a step further by correlating "Mexican appearance" with the likelihood of being unlawfully present in the United States. In the Court's words, "[t]he likelihood that any given person of Mexican ancestry is an alien is high enough to make Mexican appearance a relevant factor." The Court concluded its opinion by stating the Fourth Amendment requires that when a person is stopped there must be at least "reasonable suspicion" that the person is an "alien." In reaching its holding, the Court allowed the notion of "Mexican appearance" based on racial stereotypes to create suspicion of illegal activity. *Brignoni-Ponce* remains the law and therefore, in the context of immigrant regulation, "looking Mexican" carries a presumption of illegality.

The correlation between race and illegal conduct has been extended to target other ethnic groups in the context of the War on Terror. In *Farag*, the Government cited *Brignoni-Ponce* to allow air transportation officials to consider "Arab appearance" as a relevant factor when stopping air passengers because all of the 9-11 hijackers were "Middle Eastern males." Even though the Court rejected the Government's argument, it did reaffirm and distinguish the use of race in *Brignoni-Ponce* since that case was formally within the context of immigration enforcement.

Even though in *Farag*, the Court rejected "Arab appearance" as a relevant factor when stopping air passengers, the government need only turn to its official national security policy to consider race. Federal national security policy recognizes that racial profiling, in certain contexts, is considered legal:

> In investigating or preventing threats to national security or other catastrophic events (including the performance of duties related to air transportation security), or in enforcing laws protecting the integrity of the Nation's borders, Federal law enforcement officers may not consider race or ethnicity *except to the extent permitted by the Constitution and laws of the United States.*

Based on the precedent set forth in *Brignoni-Ponce*, it is likely that the government may target different ethnicities in its national security efforts until a case comes before the court forbidding specific uses of ethnic appearance, such as "Arab appearance." With the increase of local officials obtaining the ability to conduct immigration enforcement, after *Brignoni-Ponce*, racial profiling will continue to be widely used under the guise of immigration enforcement.

Using racial profiling as a valid immigration enforcement tool allows racial stereotypes to gain more social currency, both within and outside of the immigration context. When immigration law allows race to indicate a valid suspicion of illegal presence, race *becomes* a factor that generally indicates illegal activity. Furthermore, racial profiling of noncitizens inevitably affects citizens of the same race. This means that U.S. citizens who happen [to] be the same race as targeted noncitizens will be subject to the racialized standards of reasonable suspicion. Countless examples of this reality include the deportation of U.S. citizens based on "looking illegal." Additionally, racial profiling techniques used by local law enforcement offi-cials under 287(g) are likely to bleed over into standard law enforcement efforts.

7 Mod. Am. 42, 43–48.

Copyright © (2011) Mod. Am.

Reprinted with permission of Mod. Am. and Lisa Sandoval.

C. Current Approach to Race and Immigration

Lisa Sandoval

Race and Immigration Law: A Troubling Marriage*

Section Four: SB 1070

SB 1070 explicitly states that the policy behind the law is "attrition through enforcement," or exclusion of "unlawful aliens" by making their lives so difficult that they voluntarily choose to leave the country rather than being subject to depor-tation. As the law's author, Arizona Senator Russell Pearce, states "Arizona has made it clear through our policies that illegal immigrants are not welcome, and they are self-deporting from the state." SB 1070 creates new immigration crimes and *man-dates* that law enforcement officials determine the immigration status of a person when reasonable suspicion exists that she is "an alien who is unlawfully present in the United States." In fact, the law allows Arizona citizens to sue officials or agencies they believe are not enforcing immigration law to the full extent permissible under federal law.

In many ways SB 1070 is the modern incarnation of *Ping* because it explicitly attempts to exclude an immigrant community based on the alleged threat that that community poses to U.S. citizens. In the process of excluding, SB 1070, like *Ping,* reifies notions of racial inferiority by using race as an indicator of non-belonging. In *Ping* race was a barrier to assimilation and thus justified excluding the Chinese. Under SB 1070, racial profiling is used to identify potential "illegal immigrants" who "are not welcome" in Arizona. As a result many cities have referred to SB 1070 as the "breathing while brown law." The mandated determination of immigration status based on "reasonable suspicion" is akin to mandated racial profiling of mainly Hispanic immigrants. This reality is confirmed by Arizona's failure to articulate on what grounds *other than race* law enforcement officials will base their reasonable suspicion that a person is unlawfully present. Arizona Congressmen have fumbled as they described factors other than race that create reasonable suspicion of unlaw-ful presence: attire, accent, grooming, and shoes. It appears that SB 1070 attempts to codify *Brignoni-Ponce* and mandate that "Mexican appearance" be used in enforc-ing immigration — despite politicians claiming that race will not serve as a factor.

---

* (footnotes omitted).

However disturbing the law's explicit focus on race, what is more problematic is that the current legal battle is focused on notions of preemption: whether Arizona's law conflicts with federal legal immigration and enforcement. While other legal arguments regarding equal protection have ben advanced to overturn SB 1070, presumption remains the strongest threat to the law. This suggests that the true legal battle is over who gets to do the excluding and racial profiling: the federal government or the states? Recognizing that federal immigration law is nearly if not equally troubling as SB 1070, I focus on the Arizona law given its explicit representation of Johnson's notion of transference and Ngai's theory of alien citizenship. In light of this, the popular support SB 1070 has gained across the nation suggests that immigration law continues to be a powerful vehicle of racial subordination.

Criminalizing Immigrants as Transference

SB 1070 creates new immigrant crimes, further criminalizing the immigrant community. Kevin Johnson advances the theory of transference, which occurs when society transfers its racism towards minority citizens to noncitizens. As Johnson explains, "Immigrant status, combined with race ma[kes] such treatment more socially acceptable, and legally defensible." Johnson traces transference, as it applies in the immigration context, to the psychological theory that feelings toward one group of people are refocused on another. As a result of transference, Johnson believes that a society's treatment of noncitizens reveals its feelings toward citizens of color. Thus, Johnson described differential treatment of citizens and noncitizens as a "magic mirror" that reveals "how dominant society might treat domestic minorities if legal constraints were abrogated." Not only does Johnson's theory help explain why immigration law has historically treated noncitizens as inferior, it also explains how immigration law implicates all citizens of color regardless of citizenship—even though citizenship continues to serve as a tool to exclude noncitizens on the basis of race. SB 1070 is, therefore, a grave warning sign for all citizens of color in Arizona.

Unlike federal law, SB 1070 makes it a state crime for an "unauthorized alien" to apply for a job or to solicit work publically. The latter crime would affect mainly Mexican day laborers who congregate in certain areas of town where people come to solicit work. A related crime includes knowingly transporting a person who is unlawfully present in the country. Many of these new crimes come with mandatory jail times. Additionally, SB 1070 makes not carrying immigration papers a crime. In order to enforce these new criminal laws, SB 1070 allows law enforcement officials to ask for proof of citizenship during a "legal stop, detention, or arrest," which can include questioning people who are victims of crimes themselves or stopped for offenses like traffic violations or loitering. If a lawfully present noncitizen is stopped and does not have proper immigration papers, he or she will be subject to arrest and a fee for $500 for a first time violation. The penalties for not carrying one's papers makes life difficult for all noncitizens, suggesting that all immigrants in Arizona are unwelcome—not just those who are undocumented.

In 2006, Hispanics accounted for 29.1% of Arizona's total population. That figure is approximately twice as high as the Hispanic population in the rest of the

United States, which was 14.8% the same year. The Pew Hispanic Center estimates that in 2006, 6.9% to 7.7% of the State's total population was undocumented. These figures suggest that the percentage of undocumented people in Arizona as of 2006 was not overwhelmingly large. However, these figures also suggest that the increase in Hispanics in Arizona was substantial. Applying Johnson's theory of transference, it appears that Arizona's perception of being "invaded" by "illegals" indicates an underlying fear of a general increase in the Hispanic population as a whole. In fact, the Pew Hispanic Center found that while the native- and foreign-born Hispanic population grew substantially from 2000 to 2006, so did the non-Hispanic population. On a percentage basis, Hispanics have contributed no more to population growth in Arizona than they have to the growth of the U.S. population.

If the Hispanic population grew at a similar rate as the non-Hispanic population, Johnson's transference theory indicates that Arizona's fear of "illegal immigration" is based on the fear of a general increase of the Hispanic population, despite the fact that in 2006, the figure of undocumented people was at most 7.7%. In other words, Arizona's "crackdown" on the "invasion" of Hispanic "illegals" is not only inaccurate, but indicates that fear of an increase in the Hispanic population has been translated into a fear of an increase in noncitizens. As Johnson points out, it is much more socially acceptable to target noncitizens of color than it is to target citizens of color. As a result, Arizona's "crackdown" maintains popular support in the state because society has equated Hispanics with illegal immigration.

Due to an increase in the Hispanic population, even though this increase did not outmatch the growth of the non-Hispanic population, Arizona has transferred its general fear of Hispanics to noncitizens by overcriminalizing immigrants. Samuel Huntington's disapproval of Hispanic immigration is mirrored in SB 1070. This fear and racial animosity results in the nation's toughest immigration law.

Reasonable Suspicion as Mandated Racial Profiling: Recreating the Mexican "Illegal Alien"

Particularly troubling is SB 1070's mandate to determine immigration status based on "reasonable suspicion" that a person is unlawfully present in the United States. This mandate leads to increased racial-profiling. As federal law demonstrates, using Mexican appearance as a factor in determining immigration status is lawful. However, federal law indicates that using race *may* be permitted, whereas SB 1070's requirement that immigration law must be enforced "to the *full extent* that federal law permits" suggest that race *must* be used as a factor. SB 1070 states that race must not be the "sole" factor in determining immigration status, suggesting that it is indeed a central factor.

This increased racial profiling highlights what M. Ngai describes as alien citizenship. Ngai described the alien citizen as "an American citizen by virtue of her birth in the United States but whose citizenship is suspect, if not denied, on account of the racialized identity of her immigrant ancestry." Ngai argues that non-white groups are deemed immutable, "making [their] nationality a kind of racial trait." As a result, non-white groups obtain a permanent foreignness that leads to a nullification of U.S. citizenship. SB 1070's mandated racial profiling creates a similar type of permanent foreignness as Hispanics, regardless of citizenship status, become susceptible to being stopped and asked to prove their legal status by producing their papers. No limit exists on the amount of times a person may be stopped, leading to the possibility that one must constantly prove his belonging. As a result, Hispanics carry a strong presumption of foreignness under SB 1070. As Ngai states, "[r]acism thus creates a problem of misrecognition for the citizen of . . . Latino descent. . . ."

To be clear, Ngai believes that alien citizenship is a form of rights modification that has existed throughout history, specifically exemplified by the territorial removal of one million Mexicans during the Great Depression (more than half of whom were U.S. Citizens) and the internment of 120,000 Japanese Americans during World War II (two-thirds of whom were U.S. Citizens). Ngai traces the creation of Mexican "illegal alien" to the Jim Crow segregation of Mexicans in the southwest who were stripped of belonging. I argue that SB 1070 serves as the rebirth of the Mexican "illegal alien."

Public Reaction to SB 1070

If immigration law is a "helpful gauge for measuring this nation's racial sensibilities" as Kevin Johnson suggests, what does the nation's reaction to SB 1070 indicate? A survey conducted on October 31, 2010 revealed that fifty percent of Arizona voters believe that SB 1070 has positively affected the state's image (this figure is up from forty-one percent In May of 2010). The same survey also revealed that sixty-one percent of the state's voters still favor the new immigration law. In fact, Governor Jan Brewer, who signed SB 1070 into law, easily won reelection in the 2010 mid-term elections.

On a national level, civil rights groups have certainly voiced strong disapproval of SB 1070. Litigation intended to overturn the law has also been somewhat successful. However, since SB 1070 was signed into law on April 23, 2010, twenty-three states have introduced legislation molded on the new law. These "copycat" laws suggest support for SB 1070 by much of the country. In fact, during the 2010 mid-term elections, SB 1070 served as a major platform issue to *gain* political support. As Politico reported, in order to win votes, Republican candidates had to explicitly state their support for the law. Furthermore, the day after the injunction on the law, "59 percent of American voters wanted an Arizona-style law in their state, while only 32 percent did not." States with high Hispanic populations show support for an Arizona-style law above the national average. For instance, sixty-two percent of Texas voters favor a law similar to Arizona's and sixty percent of Colorado voters agree.

The plenary power doctrine set forth in *Ping* has led to federal immigration law that strips noncitizens of crucial constitutional protections. This reality has set the stage for state laws like SB 1070 that represent states' frustrations with federal enforcement. Johnson's notion of transference is evidenced when states like Arizona with large Hispanic populations develop animosity toward their immigrant populations and show frustration over the federal government not taking full advantage of the plenary powers it has over immigration enforcement. While SB 1070 represents the modern incarnation of *Ping*, the history of U.S. immigration law suggests that Arizona's attempt at exclusion based on racial difference should come as no surprise. The type of alien citizenship that exists for many in Arizona Is likely to spread as national support for SB 1070 remains strong and states continue to introduce copycat laws.

Section Five: Recommendations

I recognize that the thesis driving the arguments in my paper is unpleasant: U.S. immigration law uses racial difference as an indicator and this reifies notions of racial inferiority. However, this truth is undeniable in light of the evolution of immigration law from *Ping* to SB 1070. Historically, immigration regulation in the United States has explicitly relied on race and notions of racial inferiority to deny people citizenship status. Under current immigration law, Supreme Court precedent allows for "Mexican appearance" to serve as a factor in determining a person's immigration status. Most recently, national support for SB 1070, a law that in practice mandates racial profiling, represents the nation's support for excluding racially different noncitizens. In the United States, it is far too easy to exercise racism under the guise of immigration enforcement.

7 Mod. Am. 42, 48–51.
Copyright © (2011) Mod. Am.
Reprinted with permission of Mod. Am. and Lisa Sandoval.

In June 2012, the United States Supreme Court ruled in *Arizona v. United States*, 567 U.S. 387 (2012), that the provision in S.B. 1070, requiring immigration status checks during routine law enforcement stops, did not violate the Constitution.

D. Questions and Notes

It is often said that the United States is a "melting pot," made up of many different ingredients, different cultures melded together to, allegorically speaking, form a "soup." What kind of soup is it? Is the variety of culture within our historical background and current composition valued as part of our identity? Do we appreciate and prize those cultural differences enough to recognize them and preserve them, or do we somehow relish in the savor of the soup while simultaneously denying the existence of certain ingredients?

E. Point/Counterpoint

Estimates place up to 12 million illegal immigrants in the United States. A substantial majority of these immigrants are Hispanic. Do you support amnesty and/or a pathway to citizenship or deportation for these individuals?

XXVIII. Race and Politics

A. Introduction

Historically, few minority candidates have been successful in national elective politics, in part, because appeals to white racism have been effective. Americans must acknowledge this history and recognize that, while reduced from the Jim Crow era, racism in politics persists.

B. History of Race and Politics

Leland Ware and David Wilson

*Jim Crow on the "Down Low": Subtle Racial Appeals in Presidential Campaigns**

In the Political Brain, Professor Drew Weston concludes, based on a series of clinical studies, that a decision to support a particular candidate is driven largely by the voter's emotions. Choices are made based on voters' feelings about political parties or their feelings about the candidates and, if they are still undecided, their feelings about the candidates' policy positions. The rationale voters give exit pollsters are often post hoc rationalizations for what was, in reality, a choice driven largely by emotions. An objective evaluation may be a part of the decision-making process, but when reason and feelings conflict, emotions almost always prevail.

Candidates for elective office understand this phenomenon. They have, for decades, exploited voters' emotions by appealing to fears and negative racial stereotypes. Candidates or their surrogates use race neutral "code" words to produce subtle appeals. In television commercials, words are used in conjunction with explicit racial images to convey the racial meaning. Irrespective of the medium used, subtle appeals activate racial resentment. As Tali Mendelberg explains:

> Implicit racial appeals convey the same message as explicit racial appeals, but they replace the racial nouns and adjectives with more oblique references to race. They present an ostensibly race-free conservative position on an issue while incidentally alluding to racial stereotypes or a perceived threat from African Americans. Implicit racial appeals discuss a nonracial matter and avoid a direct reference to black inferiority or to white group interest. They forgo professions of racial antipathy and do not endorse segregation or white prerogatives. They convey a message that may violate the norm of racial equality by submerging it in nonracial content. In an implicit racial appeal, the racial message appears to be so coincidental and peripheral that many of its recipients are not aware that it is there. Coded racial appeals fueled a historic restructuring of party affiliations in the

---

* (footnotes and chapter headings omitted).

South. The Fifteenth Amendment, enacted shortly after the end of the Civil War, granted voting rights to African American males. During the Reconstruction Era that followed, blacks served in many elective offices in the south. In 1877, however, the Hayes-Tilden Compromise, which resolved a contested presidential election, resulted in the withdrawal of federal troops from the South. Within a few years, whites seized control of state legislatures, often using violence and intimidation to achieve their goals. It was in this context that racial segregation was established. The Reconstruction Civil Rights laws were eviscerated by a series of Supreme Court cases decided from 1880–1900, including *Plessy v. Ferguson*, which endorsed racial segregation. By the first decade of the 20th Century, the Fourteenth and Fifteenth Amendments were effectively nullified in the South. African Americans were disenfranchised. When they regained power, white Southerners embraced the Democratic Party creating what became known as the "Solid South." For the next seventy years, the South voted consistently for Democratic candidates who endorsed white supremacy, supported Jim Crow laws, and enforced racial segregation.

The first crack in the Solid South came in 1948, when Harry Truman took a Pro-Civil Rights stance and desegregated the military. Strom Thurmond led a delegation of Southern Democrats who walked out of the convention. Thurmond ran for president that year as a "Dixiecrat." In 1960, President John F. Kennedy's sympathetic stance towards Civil Rights further eroded the Democratic Party's support in the South. In 1964, when Barry Goldwater ran against Lyndon Johnson, he carried the Southern vote based in large measure on his opposition to the Civil Rights Act of 1964 and his support for "states' rights." This took place against the backdrop of "massive resistance," in which efforts to desegregate public schools were actively resisted in the South. "State's rights" were code words for resistance to the federal government's efforts to desegregate schools and Civil Rights laws that protected the rights of African Americans.

It has been said that when President Lyndon Johnson signed the Civil Rights Act of 1964, he put his pen down and told an aide we have lost the South for a generation. As Johnson anticipated, Republican strategists recognized potential for appealing to the resentment of white Southerners who were becoming disenchanted with the Democratic Party. In 1968, Richard Nixon and his advisors devised what became known as the "Southern Strategy." Nixon adopted tactics that contributed to Barry Goldwater's success in the 1964 presidential election, and George Wallace's strength as a third party candidate in 1968. Nixon's code words were "law and order," "states' rights" and "freedom of choice."

Nixon's promise to restore "law and order" appealed to white voters in the South and elsewhere who had been shaken by riots that erupted in several cities during the mid-1960s. Nixon opposed the Fair Housing Act and promised to appoint federal judges who would counter the direction that the Supreme Court had taken Brown v. Board of Education and any subsequent decisions that struck down segregation laws in the South. Nixon also promised "freedom of choice" as an alternative to "forced" busing to desegregate schools. Nixon won Virginia, Tennessee, North Carolina, South Carolina, and Florida. Texas was the only Southern state won by a Democratic nominee. This was the beginning of the Southern realignment in which large numbers of white voters shifted their allegiance from the Democratic Party to the Republic Party. Valentino and Sears attributed this transformation to "symbolic racism," which they defined as a combination of conservatism and racial animosity, rather than explicit racial beliefs.

Ronald Reagan made subtle racial appeals the centerpiece of his campaign strategy. In 1964, three Civil Rights workers, Andrew Goodman, Michael Schwerner, and James Chaney, disappeared in Neshoba County, Mississippi. They were in the State to participate in "Freedom Summer," where thousands of civil rights activists, many of them white college students from the North, descended on Mississippi and other Southern states to try to end the political disenfranchisement of African Americans in the region. Goodman, Chaney, and Schwerner were murdered by local whites who were enraged by their presence. In 1980, Ronald Reagan chose Neshoba County as the first stop for his election campaign. Reagan told the crowd, "I believe in states' rights." The whites In Neshoba County and across the country understood what he was saying. When Reagan used "states' rights," the words had long been a code phrase for resistance to desegregation efforts. Strom Thurmond used the words in 1948; Barry Goldwater used them in 1965; and George Wallace used them in 1968. The symbolism of the location added weight to Reagan's potent message.

In his first inaugural address, Ronald Reagan proclaimed, "government is not the solution to our problem; government is the problem." Reagan attacked the legitimacy of food stamps, stating that working people at grocery check-out counters were outraged when a "strapping young buck" bought T-bone steaks with food stamps. Race was not mentioned, but the connotation was clear. The "strapping young buck" was an undeserving, able-bodied African American who was taking advantage of the system.

Reagan's best known subtle appeal was one he repeated often. It was a story about a Chicago "welfare queen" who drove a Cadillac, had 80 aliases, 30 addresses, 12 Social Security cards, and collected benefits for four, non-existent, deceased husbands, defrauding the government of over $150,000. Race was not mentioned, but the story alluded to the stereotype of a welfare recipient as a dishonest black woman who was cheating the system. This exaggeration played on the stereotypes and resentment held by whites about welfare recipients. Reagan's message also took advantage of the strong association of the black race with poverty.

Lee Atwater, who was a member of the Reagan administration in 1981, described the subtle appeals in Reagan's Southern Strategy in blunt terms:

> You start in 1954 by saying "Nigger, nigger, nigger." By 1968 you can't say "nigger"—that hurts you. Backfires. So you say stuff like forced busing,

states' rights, and all that stuff. You're getting so abstract now that you're talking about cutting taxes, and all these things you're talking about are totally economic things and a by-product of them is [that] blacks get hurt worse than whites. And subconsciously maybe that is part of it. I'm not saying that. But I'm saying that if it is getting that abstract, and that coded, that we are doing away with the racial problem one way or the other. You follow me — because obviously sitting around saying, "We want to cut this" is much more abstract than even the bussing thing and a hell of a lot more abstract than "Nigger, nigger."

In the 1988 campaign, George H.W. Bush presented himself as the heir to Ronald Reagan's legacy. The Bush campaign successfully employed what is perhaps the best known subtle appeal. Willie Horton was convicted of murder and sentenced to life imprisonment. He was granted a weekend leave by the Massachusetts prison furlough program. Horton left Massachusetts and traveled to Maryland where he assaulted a white couple, beating the man and raping the woman. He was eventually recaptured and return[ed] to prison. After Bush's campaign aides discovered the Horton controversy, Bush made repeated references to the Massachusetts furlough program in his campaign speeches.

Later, a commercial was produced by an external organization, Americans for Bush. The commercial began with images of Bush and Dukakis. An announcer stated, "Bush and Dukakis on crime." In the next scene, the commercial switched to a picture of George Bush. The voice over stated, "Bush supports the death penalty for first-degree murderers." The following scene showed a photograph of Dukakis. The narrator stated, "Dukakis not only opposes the death penalty, he allowed first-degree murderers to have weekend passes from prison." The next scene showed a mug shot of Willie Horton. The voice over continued, "One was Willie Horton, who murdered a boy in a robbery, stabbing him nineteen times." Another photo flashed on the screen showing Horton dressed in army fatigues, with a straggly beard and an unkempt Afro. Horton was accompanied by a police officer that was apparently placing him under arrest.

The narrator stated, "Despite a life sentence, Horton received ten weekend passes from prison. Horton fled, kidnapped a young couple, stabbed the man and repeatedly raped his girlfriend." The words "kidnapping" "stabbing" and "raping" appeared on the screen. The final scene showed a photograph of Dukakis. The words "weekend passes" appeared on the screen, and suggested Dukakis' lax stance on crime. Horton's race was never mentioned in the narrative, but his image activated a stereotype of a dangerous black criminal in the minds of white viewers. Dukakis did not challenge the commercials. The racial implications of the ads were not challenged until Jesse Jackson accused the Bush campaign of racism.

Subtle appeals did not end with Willie Horton. At a meeting of Jesse Jackson's Rainbow Coalition in Washington in June of 1992, Bill Clinton, who was then the Democratic nominee for president, criticized the Rainbow Coalition for providing a platform to rap artist Sister Souljah who had been quoted as saying, after the riots in Los Angeles, "If black people kill black people every day, why not have a week and kill white people?" In a press conference, Sister Souljah stated that she had been "used as a vehicle, like Willie Horton and other various black victims of racism."

During the 2000 Presidential campaign, George W. Bush delivered a speech at Bob Jones University, located in Greensville, South Carolina. The school had a reputation for being one of the most conservative religious schools in the United States, and had refused to admit any African American students until 1971. President Ronald Reagan fought to remove the Internal Revenue Services' authority to deny the school's charitable tax exemption, which had been imposed based on the school's ban on interracial dating. Bush's appearance at Bob Jones had the same symbolic appeal to race as Ronald Reagan's speech in Neshoba County, Mississippi. After the racial message was exposed by the press, Bush sent a letter of apology to John O'Connor, Archbishop of New York.

In Harold Ford's 2006 gubernatorial race in Tennessee, a commercial was shown in the final days of the campaign featuring a blonde woman wearing heavy make-up and cheap jewelry. Her shoulders were bare and the rest of her body was not shown. The viewer had to imagine what she was, or was not, wearing. She gushed, explaining that she met Mr. Ford at a Playboy party and, at the end of the ad, she winked and said, "Harold, call me." The image tapped into a deep and longstanding southern taboo; black men lusting after white women. Ford lost the election.

24 St. John's J.L. Comm. 299, 307–314 (2009).
Copyright © (2009) St. John's J. L. Comm.
Reprinted with permission of St. John's J. L. Comm. and
Leland Ware and David Wilson.

C. Current Approach to Race and Politics

F. Michael Higginbotham

Bush and the Black Vote

In a recent speech before the National Urban League, President Bush acknowledged that the Republican Party has a lot of work to do in order to increase Black support. Such an acknowledgement reflects the realization of the simple truth that since 1964, the Republican nominee has never received more than a dismal 15 percent of the Black vote, and in 2000, Bush received only 9 percent. While the Republican Party appears to have made advances with other constituencies, such as women and Latinos, who traditionally have leaned Democratic, success with Black voters seems much more elusive. Bush has challenged Blacks—the Democrats' most loyal constituency—to take another look because in his view, Democrats take them for granted. He concluded his remarks by asking rhetorically, "What has the Democratic Party ever done for Blacks?" While it is a fair question to ask of all parties in this election season, the answer is likely to backfire on the president.

First and foremost, Blacks are just like other Americans. They vote for the party and the candidate they believe will best represent their interests and their perception of the nation's interests. The dubious Republican record and President Bush's own actions indicate an overall indifference and, in some cases, an outright hostility to positions overwhelmingly supported by Blacks.

Despite having Blacks in key cabinet positions, President Bush has proven harmful to Black interests overall. He twice nominated to a federal appeals court Charles Pickering, who formally opposed interracial marriage in the early 1960s, who left the Mississippi Democratic Party to become a Republican when the national Democratic Party tried to integrate the state delegation to the national convention in 1964, and who as a judge drastically reduced the sentence of a man convicted of burning a cross on the lawn of an interracial couple. Bush opposes plans that might increase Black political representation, such as statehood for the District of Columbia. Most Blacks favor affirmative action; Bush opposes it.

In addition, President Bush appears insensitive to Blacks. His first campaign stop in 2000 was a visit to Bob Jones University, a school that continues to restrict interracial dating. Bush was the first presidential candidate to ever refuse an invitation to speak to the National Association for the Advancement of Colored People, the oldest and largest civil rights organization. Furthermore, he failed to publicly condemn Trent Lott, former Republican Senate majority leader who, in December 2002, praised Strom Thurmond's 1948 presidential campaign that was based on preserving racial segregation. Despite Lott's outrageous claim that the nation would have been better off had Thurman won, Bush remained silent.

Bush's vice president shares a similar history. While it is hard for most blacks to imagine how anyone could oppose a national holiday honoring Dr. Martin Luther King, Dick Cheney did just that. He also opposed a congressional resolution encouraging the release of Nelson Mandela, who was serving a life sentence in South Africa for opposing the government's racist practices. Cheney never seemed to care about the connection between Black Americans and the struggle against apartheid. Many Blacks who support today's initiatives to democratize Afghanistan recognize the hypocrisy of past Republican characterizations of Nelson Mandela as a terrorist. The Republican Party has a long record of being on the wrong side of Black issues. Conservative Republicans, who currently make up 75 percent of the party, argued against the 1964 Civil Rights Act prohibiting racial discrimination in employment and public accommodations. Several years later, the party created the "southern strategy" whereby Republicans supported policies that would limit integration in schools in the hope of encouraging White Democrats in the south to switch parties. Blacks recognize the continuation of this strategy in Republican characterizations of the Democratic Party today as representing "special" or "urban" concepts, code words for minority.

Rather than Blacks routinely "riding the donkey," as Al Sharpton coined it, the uncompromising presidential election provides an opportunity to reevaluate their commitment to the Democrat Party.

As a result, John Kerry will have to continue to demonstrate that he can earn the Black vote as other Democratic nominees have. Through their actions, the Republican Party and President Bush have already proven that they cannot.

Washington Afro American A13 (October 30, 2004).
Copyright © (2004) F. Michael Higginbotham.
Reprinted with permission of F. Michael Higginbotham.

F. Michael Higginbotham

The Case of the Missing Post-Racial Election

In 2004, Senator Barack Obama captured the nation's attention. He called for an end to the politics of racial division: "There's not a Black America and White America and Latino America and Asian America; there's the United States of America." As Election Day nears and political differences are magnified, it is important to remind Americans, Democrats and Republicans, of those unifying sentiments.

Soon Americans will determine who will serve as the next president. In the last election, a majority voted for Obama, making him the first minority Commander in Chief. Obama's historic victory caused many to wonder if America had entered a post-racial period where color would be irrelevant. Recent events suggest that America remains far from that imagined utopia.

Our history is filled with race-baiting politics. For example, in 1868, black delegates to the South Carolina Constitutional Convention were called "baboons, monkeys and mules." Forty years later, when President Theodore Roosevelt invited black educator Booker T. Washington to dine with him at the White House, Governor James Vardaman of Mississippi commented: "Probably old lady Roosevelt, during the period of gestation, was frightened by a dog, and the fact may account for the qualities of the male pup that are so prominent in Teddy. I would not do either an injustice, but am disposed to apologize to the dog for mentioning it."

President Obama has been the recipient of similarly offensive treatment. Newt Gingrich questioned his work ethic when he referred to Obama as "the food stamp president," Donald Trump questioned his admission into Harvard University when he referred to Obama as "the affirmative action president," and congressman Doug Lamborn (R-Colo) questioned his veracity when he compared Obama to a tar baby.

These references tap into false stereotypical notions of black inferiority such as Obama wants a free ride just like blacks on welfare; Obama couldn't possibly have earned those degrees based on merit; or Obama is biased against whites. Not even George W. Bush, whose college performance was said to be marginal, was asked to produce transcripts. Yet Obama, the leader of an organization reserved for top students, faced such inquiry.

Moreover, some whites oppose Obama's policies because they imagine those policies are intentionally designed to harm whites. For example, Rush Limbaugh said that Obama's health-care legislation enabled Obama to redistribute wealth from whites to blacks. Limbaugh's reasoning was based on the fact that higher percentages of whites (90 percent) retained health insurance coverage than blacks (81 percent) and Obama's legislation would provide free coverage for those previously uninsured blacks.

Of course, many oppose Obama for political reasons. But when treatment deviates significantly from the normal opposition, such as the request to produce a birth certificate when no previous leader had to present such credentials, it causes thoughtful Americans to ponder whether race is the motivation.

Some of today's rhetoric is eerily reflective of our painful past. Obama has been depicted as a monkey or analogized to an ape. Most disparaging was the e-mail circulated by federal judge Richard Cebull denigrating Obama's mother by comparing blacks to animals in analogizing interracial marriage and sexuality to bestiality. Unfortunately, subtle appeals to racist notions, what I call ghosts of Jim Crow, continue to haunt us.

While much of this language is generated by Republican tea party supporters, Democrats are not immune from such appeals. Last July before a predominantly black audience, Vice-President Biden characterized Republican nominee Mitt Romney's policies as an attempt to "put y'all back in chains" reminding many of slavery.

Romney and Obama have different visions, especially with respect to immigration policy, abortion protections, and gender equality laws. As former Secretary of State Colin Powell, a Republican, did in his recent endorsement of Obama, Americans should examine these positions carefully rejecting appeals to consider either candidates' race.

Polls suggest Obama will receive over one third of the white vote while Romney will receive a slightly smaller percentage of the minority vote. For some the percentages reflect recognition by these voters that a particular candidate's platform, philosophy, or record is more appealing. Yet for others, like the white voter who attended a Romney rally wearing a tee shirt that read "Put the white back in the White House," it may be a simple case of color.

Baltimore Afro American A7 (November 5, 2012). Copyright © (2012) F. Michael Higginbotham. Reprinted with permission of F. Michael Higginbotham.

F. Michael Higginbotham

America's Racial Soul

With the requisite number of delegates needed for victory secured, Donald Trump and Hillary Clinton appear ready to receive their respective party nominations. Make no mistake: When they face each other in the fall of 2016, it will be nothing less than a battle for America's racial soul.

During the primary campaign, Donald Trump was asked by a reporter whether he would disavow the support of former KKK leader David Duke and white supremacist groups in general. Mr. Trump sidestepped the question, saying "I know nothing about David Duke; I know nothing about white supremacists." As criticism to his response mounted, Mr. Trump said he did actually disavow Duke and blamed his earlier noncommittal statement on a "bad earpiece." Because of the equipment malfunction, Mr. Trump said, "I could hardly hear what he's saying."

For American voters, what really matters is not what Mr. Trump could or could not hear during a television interview, but what David Duke heard by listening to Donald Trump. Duke explained that he supported Mr. Trump for president because he believes that Mr. Trump is a leader who will "break-up Jewish dominated lobbies" and "ensure that White Americans are allowed to preserve and promote their heritage and interests."

Why does Duke feel so certain that Mr. Trump shares his hate-filled vision of America? Because so much of Mr. Trump's appeal is based on racial code words and turning back the clock on civil rights progress since World War II.

When Mr. Trump entered the presidential race, he launched his campaign by impugning an entire population. Mexicans coming into the United States, according to Mr. Trump, might include a few good people, but far too many were "rapists" and "criminals." He proposed keeping Muslims from coming to America, at least on a temporary basis. Of course this is unworkable, how would he possibly identify the religious faith of everyone coming into this country? The significance of the proposal is that it deliberately insults a religion of over 15 billion people, much to the delight of the religiously intolerant.

When asked about the problem of the use of excessive force by police against minorities, Mr. Trump responded that "police are absolutely mistreated and misunderstood." Mr. Trump shows frighteningly little concern for minority victims of police brutality. To Mr. Trump, the primary solution is giving "power back to the police, because crime is rampant."

Modern-day candidates like Donald Trump always deny using racial code words. Mr. Trump confidently declares "I have a great relationship with the blacks" and "the Hispanics love me." The best way to tell, however, that a racial dog whistle is being used, is when racists like David Duke come racing over in support . . .

Baltimore Sun A15 (June 9, 2016). Copyright(c)(2016) F. Michael Higginbotham. Reprinted with permission of F. Michael Higginbotham.

D. Questions and Notes

Which do you believe, subtle or blatant appeals to racial bias, are most effective in the political arena today?

Is the current debate over recognition of the Confederate Battle Flag another example of an appeal to subtle racial bias in the political arena?

Part Eight

Appendix

XXIX. Conclusion

Government-mandated segregation lasted until 1954, when the Supreme Court rejected the rationale of *Plessy* and struck down racially segregated public schools in *Brown*. Like *Plessy*, *Brown*'s holding extended beyond schools, leading to the end of such segregation in a variety of institutions such as libraries, parks, businesses, and beaches. *Brown*, however, was not a panacea. The Court ruled segregated schools unconstitutional but declined to impose a direct desegregation mandate. This ill-fated strategy, intended in part to avoid a backlash from whites in the South, instead inspired a campaign of massive resistance that included brutal violence and intimidation tactics. Only when regional violence threatened the stability of the Nation did congress and the executive branch move to force compliance with *Brown*. With political backing, courts, too, became more aggressive, finally issuing creative injunctive relief, such as mandatory busing, to bring about desegregation. Some integration in schools and in housing occurred, but, by the early 1970s, urban whites had already begun their flight to the suburbs where they were insulated from minorities by discriminatory real estate and lending practices.

By the 1980s, political pressures from whites for state autonomy and restriction of federal authority limited the power of federal judges to construct effective deseg-regation orders. Moreover, white flight created racially identifiable communities in once racially mixed districts, resulting in racially identifiable school zones. Federal courts were not permitted to force whites back into urban schools, and local legisla-tors had little incentive to do so, since so many whites supported racial isolation and privilege not only in schools, but also in the workplace and community.

As a result, today, progress towards integrated schools has been lost, and edu-cational segregation serves as both a cause and consequence of race-based hous-ing patterns. In addition, public school financing structures produce disparities between the quality of education offered at suburban and urban schools. Inept educational offerings translate into future losses for minority students in terms of higher education opportunities, job prospects, and wealth accumulation. Moreover, negative racial perceptions of minorities pervade the criminal justice system, while economic and cultural practices cause widespread disparities in healthcare.

This continuing racial divide makes it impossible to achieve, much less maintain, equality. Although government-mandated racial inequality has been abandoned, race discrimination continues because far too many Americans continue to accept notions of white superiority and racial hierarchy that skew discretionary choices in housing, education, criminal justice matters, healthcare services, and other life issues. So-called "race-neutral" laws, procedures, policies, and practices facilitate these racist choices, hindering decades of progress made since *Brown*.

F. Michael Higginbotham

A Request from Heaven to President Obama: Don't Forget the Race Issue

Since the passing of A. Leon Higginbotham, Jr. in 1998, many have wondered what the award winning author, longest serving black federal judge, first black to head a federal regulatory agency, recipient of the Spingarn Medal and the Congressional Medal of Freedom, and author of the famous "Open Letter To Clarence Thomas," would think of the state of race relations today. Appointed to the Federal Trade Commission in 1962, Higginbotham served in several powerful federal positions including Vice-Chair of the National Commission on the Causes and Prevention of Violence, member of the first wiretap surveillance court, and Chief Judge of a United States Court of Appeals. Known as the conscience of the American judiciary on race issues, Higginbotham caused controversy in 1992, when he publicly reminded Justice Clarence Thomas of his predecessor's contributions to racial equality. In the 18 years since this first public letter, much progress has been made, including Higginbotham's former student, Michelle Obama, becoming the first black "First Lady." As a law professor related to Higginbotham, who worked closely with him, I feel compelled to share "his letter" to President Obama after one year in office.

January 20, 2010
Dear President Obama:

Congratulations on completing your first year as president. In these tumultuous times, your job is of vital importance. The unemployment rate is the highest it has been in over twenty-five years. The nation is involved in two military conflicts. The incarceration rate is the highest in the world, and the American people are divided. The country desperately needs a unifying leader, because there is another monumental problem—this one of longstanding stature—that also must be addressed, racial inequality.

No doubt, your inauguration ended an era in American history. When I arrived at Yale Law School as a student in 1949, a black janitor hugged me, with tears in his eyes, exclaiming that he was just so happy to see a black face in the student body. Many years of experience however, taught me that it takes much more than positions and accolades to impact inequality that has persisted for centuries.

Neither your swift rise to the Presidency, nor the presence of any minority in a position of power, marks the end of racism. Black unemployment, incarceration, and poverty rates are twice that of whites. Overt racism, expressly sanctioned by laws, has given way to covert racism, tacitly approved through "colorblind" policies and "race neutral" programs. Inequality is caused and maintained by choices that result in inadequate anti-discrimination laws, inequitable school funding, education deficiencies, housing isolation, economic exploitation, criminal justice stereotyping, and political under representation. If true equality is ever to be achieved, the "hearts and minds" of the American people must change first.

Your 2008 Father's Day speech encouraging black male familial responsibility was inspiring. Without a serious change in how blacks view their own destinies (as being at least to some extent out of their control due to racism), it will be impossible to resolve the race issue. You should also remind whites that white privilege must stop. A failure to acknowledge structural racism, white isolationism and overvaluation, ignores the reality of current race relations.

The debate over affirmative action provides a prime example. Five states, including California and Florida, have forbidden race from being used as a factor in public college or university admissions. Yet, these same states allow a preference for children of alumni even when blacks were excluded from those schools in the past or did not attend in large numbers. Under such circumstances, prohibiting a preference for under-represented blacks, while permitting a preference for children of mostly-white alumni, exacerbates racial disparities, even though on its face it appears race-neutral.

In your 2008 campaign speech from Philadelphia, you called for a new conversation on race. Since then however, with the exception of the profiling incident involving Cambridge, Massachusetts police officer James Crowley and Harvard Professor Henry Louis Gates, and the controversy surrounding inappropriate language about your candidacy by Senator Harry Reid, you have said very little on the subject. I recognize that the economic, crime, and military problems facing the country are enormous. As a black man appointed to several powerful positions in my time, I know, firsthand, the weight of office. But racial inequality, in good times and bad, has plagued America since its founding, and it will not end without new and more vigorous efforts. That is why I feel compelled to encourage you to continue the conversation on race even as you grapple with other problems. I will watch your progress, from my vantage point in Heaven, with pride and hope for your success as the 44th president of the United States.

Sincerely,
A. Leon Higginbotham, Jr. Chief Judge (Retired)
United States Court of Appeals for the Third Circuit

As an American with mixed-racial heritage and a multiracial coalition, President Obama is in a unique position to initiate and lead the race conversation. Americans on Earth and in Heaven anxiously wait.

This "request" articulates the author's best judgment as to what Judge Higginbotham might have felt and written had he been living today.

F. Michael Higginbotham

*Keynote Speech: A Letter From The Original Cause Lawyer**

There are alarmingly wide racial disparities in terms of the socio-economic index. Any category on that index whether it be unemployment levels, income levels, educational attainment, political representation, death rates, poverty rates, any classification you want to choose, you can put a blindfold on and throw a dart at the board—at the socio-economic status categories—and whatever you hit, there will be an alarmingly wide disparity. For unemployment, it's a 2-to-1 gap. It's often said that when white folks catch a cold with respect to employment, minorities get pneumonia. That 2-to-1 gap would seem to affirm that notion. For wealth accumulation, it's a 20-to-1 gap. It sounds almost unbelievable, but it is a 20-to-1 gap for wealth accumulation with white families and with respect to minority families. These disparities are severe and they are getting wider.

There is a whole lot of debate today and discussion about the causes of these disparities. No one disputes that these disparities exist, but there is widespread debate about the cause. Conservative arguments tend to explain the root causes in terms of personal responsibility and tend to rely upon stereotypical notions of minority intellectual, moral, and cultural deficiencies, basically ignoring the misguided laws and legal decisions that not only created these gaps, but also continue to maintain them and help to enlarge them.

Today's racial disparities are rooted in a longstanding paradigm dating back well before the creation of the Constitution in 1789. Discrimination and physical separation of blacks, legally and extra legally, has become not only enmeshed in our social fabric, but has prevented us from eliminating racial disparities. The paradigm is one of false beliefs of white superiority at one end, and black victimization at the other, created by racial hierarchy notions and sustained by physical isolation of the races. Each part of the paradigm is interdependent on the other, and to destroy it, each aspect needs to be eradicated. Addressing only one part of the paradigm will not solve the problem. The causes of disparities have to be dealt with in their totality in order for America to move toward true equality for all.

One thing that we need to recognize is that there is still a problem. The eye cannot see what the mind does not comprehend. Secondly, once we recognize that there is a problem, we need to empower minorities politically, educationally, and economically. There is an American Jobs Act that President Obama and the Obama Administration have been supporting—an American Jobs Act, which will target areas of the country with high unemployment. Not only in terms of job education and job training, but also of job creation in these areas. This is significant. It will have a tremendous impact on reducing the disparities in the unemployment

---

* (footnotes omitted).

arena, and this can be done legislatively in other areas such as education and politics that could also have the same impact on eliminating these disparities. Third and finally, I stood throughout my career as an integrationist. I don't run away from that ever. We need to integrate our society more in terms of housing, in terms of schools. It's something that I fought for most of my life as a Cause Lawyer, and as Solicitor General, and as a Supreme Court Justice. It's something I stood for. I still believe in it, and think that certain things can be done in this society to facilitate integration. And by the way, we need to eliminate racial profiling period. End of discussion. It is un-American. It's ineffective, but more so it is un-American and it needs to end.

This letter articulates the author's best judgment as to what Justice Marshall might have felt and written had he been living today.

A. Leon Higginbotham, Jr.

Book Review: Race, Racism, and American Law

[Can] American Justice, American Liberty, American Civilization, American Law, and American Christianity . . . be made to include and protect alike and forever *all* American citizens in the rights which have been guaranteed to them by the organic and fundamental laws of the land?

Almost a century ago the distinguished abolitionist and statesman Frederick Douglass, born a slave, pondered whether non-whites would be full and equal participants in the American dream and asked the above question. Despite the millions of words espoused by lawyers, by lawyer-politicians, and sometimes even by law professors proclaiming the progress of American law, among many there still persists the nagging doubt whether legally sanctioned racism of the past and its present impact will be eradicated.

While America has made a great deal of progress, we continue to grapple with persistent racial disparities that threaten our country's global stature. The goal of racial equality has not been accomplished. Rates of black poverty and homelessness are twice that of whites. Wealth accumulation for blacks is 1/20th of that of whites. Similar disparities exist for Hispanics. Over the last few years, the gap has only widened. There are numerous causes for this inequality, which can only be addressed if we are willing to talk honestly with one another about the complex intersection of race, history and culture.

Immigration, voting rights and unemployment are just a few of the critical issues at the center of this intersection that must be faced if America is ever to achieve its full potential. Today's partisan gridlock preventing national legislative efforts such as the Dream Act, granting educational opportunities to certain illegal immigrants; an updated Voting Rights Act, restoring federal protection against racial discrimination in state election laws; and the American Jobs Act, providing education and training opportunities in areas of high unemployment to address disparities so troubling to proponents of equality, have allowed the racial divide to grow.

The election of Donald Trump as president in 2016 has made the racial divide worse. On August 12, 2017, violence engulfed the city of Charlottesville, Virginia. Hundreds of white nationalists clashed with counter protesters over the removal of confederate statues throughout the South. By the end of the day, Heather Hier, one of the counter protesters, was dead. Ms. Hier had been run over by a car driven by James Fields, a white supremacist. Nineteen other counter protesters had been seriously wounded before the protesters were dispersed by law enforcement officials.

The protest, labelled "Unite The Right," had been planned months in advance and included groups like the Ku Klux Klan and Neo Nazis. Leaders in attendance included David Duke and Richard Spencer. Slogans chanted by protesters included "Jews will not replace us," "our blood our soil," and "White lives matter."

In commenting on the day's events, President Donald Trump condemned the violent protests but he did not expressly criticize the white nationalist rally or the slogans expressed by any attendees. Instead, President Trump seemed to lay blame equally on white nationalists and counter protesters condemning "hatred bigotry, and violence on many sides." Three days later, after the counter protesters and white supremacists had departed Charlottesville and after widespread and vehement criticism, President Trump reversed his course and condemned the white supremacist groups.

As I listened to President Trump's remarks about Charlottesville, I began to think about America's long journey with white supremacist violence against Americans who sought and embraced racial equality. Make no mistake. This journey indicates a culture clash of the highest order. Democrats and Republicans, liberals and conservatives, blacks and whites, must be willing to enter a dialogue with ideological opponents, negotiate in good faith, compromise when appropriate, and implement effective bi-partisan solutions if America is ever to become post-racial.

While I am disappointed in the fact that post-*Brown* Supreme Court decisions fail to adequately address the widespread racial inequity that continues to exist, I remain convinced that the law can be a powerful weapon in reducing such inequity. As the material contained in this book suggests, how one uses that weapon often depends largely on the values he or she embraces. Accordingly, I encourage all of those present and future decision-makers to consider the values reflected in the following poem written to encourage those involved in the civil rights movement of the 1960s.

Langston Hughes

Dream of Freedom

There is a dream in the land
With its back against the wall
By muddled names and strange
Sometimes the dream is called.
There are those who claim
This dream for theirs alone—
A sin for which, we know,
They must atone. Unless shared in common
Like sunlight and like air,
The dream will die for lack
Of substance anywhere.
The dream knows no frontier or tongue,
The dream no class or race.
The dream cannot be kept secure
In any one locked place.
This dream today embattled,
With its back against the wall—
To save the dream for one
It must be saved for all.

XXX. Documents

A. The Constitution of the United States

We the People of the United States, in Order to form a more perfect Union, establish Justice, insure domestic Tranquility, provide for the common defence, promote the general Welfare, and secure the Blessings of Liberty to ourselves and our Posterity, do ordain and establish this Constitution for the United States of America.

Art. I

Sec. 1. All legislative Powers herein granted shall be vested in a Congress of the United States, which shall consist of a Senate and House of Representatives.

Sec. 2. [1] The House of Representatives shall be composed of Members chosen every second Year by the People of the several States, and the Electors in each State shall have the Qualifications requisite for Electors of the most numerous Branch of the State Legislature.

[2] No Person shall be a Representative who shall not have attained to the Age of twenty five Years, and been seven Years a Citizen of the United States, and who shall not, when elected, be an Inhabitant of that State in which he shall be chosen.

[3] Representatives and direct Taxes shall be apportioned among the several States which may be included within this Union, according to their respective Numbers, which shall be determined by adding to the whole Number of free Persons, including those bound to service for a Term of Years, and excluding Indians not taxed, three fifths of all other Persons. The actual Enumeration shall be made within three Years after the first Meeting of the Congress of the United States, and within every subsequent Term of ten Years, in such Manner as they shall by Law direct. The Number of Representatives shall not exceed one for every thirty Thousand, but each State shall have at Least one Representative; and until such enumeration shall be made, the State of New Hampshire shall be entitled to choose three, Massachusetts eight, Rhode Island and Providence Plantations one, Connecticut five, New York six, New Jersey four, Pennsylvania eight, Delaware one, Maryland six, Virginia ten, North Carolina five, South Carolina five, and Georgia three

[4] When vacancies happen in the Representation from any State, the Executive Authority thereof shall issue Writs of Election to fill such Vacancies.

[5] The House of Representatives shall choose their Speaker and other Officers; and shall have the sole Power of Impeachment.

Sec. 3. [1] The Senate of the United States shall be composed of two Senators from each State, chosen by the Legislature thereof, for six Years; and each Senator shall have one Vote.

[2] Immediately after they shall be assembled in Consequence of the first Election, they shall be divided as equally as may be into three Classes. The Seats of the Senators of the first Class shall be vacated at the Expiration of the second Year, of the second Class at the Expiration of the fourth Year, and of the third Class at the Expiration of the sixth Year, so that one third may be chosen every second Year, and if Vacancies happen by Resignation, or otherwise, during the Recess of the Legislature of any State, the Executive thereof may make temporary appointments until the next Meeting of the Legislature, which shall then fill such Vacancies.

[3] No Person shall be a Senator who shall not have attained to the Age of thirty Years, and been nine Years a Citizens of the United States, and who shall not, when elected, be an Inhabitant of that State for which he shall be chosen.

[4] The Vice President of the United States shall be President of the Senate, but shall have no Vote, unless they be equally divided.

[5] The Senate shall choose their other Officers, and also a President pro tempore, in the Absence of the Vice President, or when he shall exercise the Office of President of the United States.

[6] The Senate shall have the sole Power to try all Impeachments. When sitting for that Purpose, they shall be on Oath or Affirmation. When the President of the

United States is tried, the Chief Justice shall preside: And no Person shall be convicted without the Concurrence of two thirds of the Members present.

[7] Judgment in Cases of Impeachment shall not extend further than to removal from Office, and disqualification to hold and enjoy any Office of honor, Trust, or Profit under the United States: but the Party convicted shall nevertheless be liable and subject to Indictment, Trial, Judgment and Punishment, according to Law.

Sec. 4. [1] The Times, Places and Manner of holding Elections for Senators and Representatives, shall be prescribed in each State by the Legislature thereof; but the Congress may at any time by Law make or alter such Regulations, except as to the Places of choosing Senators.

[2] The Congress shall assemble at least once in every Year, and such Meeting shall be on the first Monday in December, unless they shall by Law appoint a different Day.

Sec. 5. [1] Each House shall be the Judge of the Elections, Returns and Qualifications of its own Members, and a Majority of each shall constitute a Quorum to do Business; but a smaller Number may adjourn from day to day, and may be authorized to compel the Attendance of absent Members, in such Manner, and under such Penalties as each House may provide.

[2] Each House may determine the Rules of its Proceedings, punish its Members for disorderly Behaviour, and, with the Concurrence of two thirds, expel a Member.

[3] Each House shall keep a Journal of its Proceedings, and from time to time publish the same, excepting such Parts as may in their Judgment require Secrecy; and the Yeas and Nays of the Members of either House on any question shall, at the Desire of one fifth of those Present, be entered on the Journal.

[4] Neither House, during the Session of Congress, shall, without the Consent of the other, adjourn for more than three days, nor to any other Place than that in which the two Houses shall be sitting.

Sec. 6. [1] The Senators and Representatives shall receive a Compensation for their Services, to be ascertained by Law, and paid out of the Treasury of the United States. They shall in all Cases, except Treason, Felony and Breach of the Peace, be privileged from Arrest during their Attendance at the Session of their respective Houses, and in going to and returning from the same; and for any Speech or Debate in either House, they shall not be questioned in any other Place.

[2] No Senator or Representative shall, during the Time for which he was elected, be appointed to any civil Office under the Authority of the United States which shall have been created, or the Emoluments whereof shall have been increased during such time; and no Person holding any Office under the United States, shall be a Member of either House during his Continuance in Office.

Sec. 7. [1] All Bills for raising Revenue shall originate in the House of Representatives; but the Senate may propose or concur with Amendments as on other Bills.

[2] Every Bill which shall have passed the House of Representatives and the Senate, shall, before it become a Law, be presented to the President of the United States; If he approve he shall sign it, but if not he shall return it, with his Objections to that House in which it shall have originated, who shall enter the Objections at large on their Journal, and proceed to reconsider it. If after such Reconsideration two thirds of that House shall agree to pass the Bill, it shall be sent, together with the Objections, to the other House, by which it shall likewise be reconsidered, and if approved by two thirds of that House, it shall become a Law. But in all such Cases the Votes of both Houses shall be determined by yeas and Nays, and the Names of the Persons voting for and against the Bill shall be entered on the Journal of each House respectively. If any Bill shall not be returned by the President within ten Days (Sundays excepted) after it shall have been presented to him, the Same shall be a Law, in like Manner as if he had signed it, unless the Congress by their Adjournment prevent its Return, in which Case it shall not be a Law.

[3] Every Order, Resolution, or Vote to which the Concurrence of the Senate and House of Representatives may be necessary (except on a question of Adjournment) shall be presented to the President of the United States; and before the Same shall take Effect, shall be approved by him, or being disapproved by him, shall be repassed by two thirds of the Senate and House of Representatives, according to the Rules and Limitations prescribed in the Case of a Bill.

Sec. 8. [1] The Congress shall have Power To lay and collect Taxes, Duties, Imposts and Excises, to pay the Debts and provide for the common Defence and general Welfare of the United States; but all Duties, Imposts and Excises shall be uniform throughout the United States.

[2] To borrow Money on the credit of the United States;

[3] To regulate Commerce with foreign Nations, and among the several States, and with the Indian Tribes;

[4] To establish an uniform Rule of Naturalization, and uniform Laws on the subject of Bankruptcies throughout the United States;

[5] To coin Money, regulate the Value thereof, and of foreign Coin, and fix the Standard of Weights and Measures;

[6] To provide for the Punishment of counterfeiting the Securities and current Coin of the United States;

[7] To establish Post Offices and post Roads;

[8] To promote the Progress of Science and useful Arts, by securing for limited Times to Authors and Inventors the exclusive Right to their respective Writings and Discoveries;

[9] To constitute Tribunals inferior to the supreme Court;

[10] To define and punish Piracies and Felonies committed on the high Seas, and Offences against the Law of Nations;

[11] To declare War, grant Letters of Marque and Reprisal, and make Rules concerning Captures on Land and Water;

[12] To raise and support Armies, but no Appropriation of Money to that Use shall be for a longer Term than two Years;

[13] To provide and maintain a Navy;

[14] To make Rules for the Government and Regulation of the land and naval Forces;

[15] To provide for calling forth the Militia to execute the Laws of the Union, suppress Insurrections and repel Invasions;

[16] To provide for organizing, arming, and disciplining, the Militia, and for governing such Part of them as may be employed in the Service of the United States, reserving to the States respectively, the Appointment of the Officers, and the Authority of training the Militia according to the discipline prescribed by Congress;

[17] To exercise exclusive Legislation in all Cases whatsoever, over such District (not exceeding ten Miles square) as may, by Cession of particular States, and the Acceptance of Congress, become the Seat of the Government of the United States, and to exercise like Authority over all Places purchased by the Consent of the Legislature of the State in which the Same shall be, for the Erection of Forts, Magazines, Arsenals, dock-Yards, and other needful Buildings;—And

[18] To make all laws which shall be necessary and proper for carrying into Execution the foregoing Powers, and all other Powers vested by this Constitution in the Government of the United States, or in any Department or Officer thereof.

Sec. 9. [1] The Migration or Importation of such Persons as any of the States now existing shall think proper to admit, shall not be prohibited by the Congress prior to the Year one thousand eight hundred and eight, but a Tax or duty may be imposed on such Importation, not exceeding ten dollars for each Person.

[2] The Privilege of the Writ of Habeas Corpus shall not be suspended, unless when in Cases of Rebellion or Invasion the public Safety may require it.

[3] No Bill of Attainder or ex post facto Law shall be passed.

[4] No Capitation, or other direct, Tax shall be laid, unless in Proportion to the Census or Enumeration herein before directed to be taken.

[5] No Tax or Duty shall be laid on Articles exported from any State.

[6] No Preference shall be given by any Regulation of Commerce or Revenue to the Ports of one State over those of another; nor shall Vessels bound to, or from, one State, be obliged to enter, clear, or pay Duties in another.

[7] No Money shall be drawn from the Treasury, but in Consequence of Appropriations made by Law; and a regular statement and Account of the Receipts and Expenditures of all public Money shall be published from time to time.

[8] No Title of Nobility shall be granted by the United States; And no Person holding any office of Profit or Trust under them, shall, without the Consent of the

Congress, accept of any present, Emolument, office, or Title, of any kind whatever, from any King, Prince or foreign State.

Sec. 10. [1] No State shall enter into any Treaty, Alliance, or Confederation; grant Letters of Marque and Reprisal; coin Money; emit Bills of Credit; make any Thing but gold and silver Coin a Tender in Payment of Debts; pass any Bill of Attainder, ex post facto Law; or Law impairing the Obligation of Contracts, or grant any Title of Nobility.

[2] No State shall, without the Consent of the Congress, lay any Imposts or Duties on Imports or Exports, except what may be absolutely necessary for executing it's inspection Laws; and the net Produce of all Duties and Imposts, laid by any State on Imports or Exports, shall be for the Use of the Treasury of the United States; and all such Laws shall be subject to the Revision and Controul of the Congress.

[3] No State shall, without the Consent of Congress, lay any Duty of Tonnage, keep Troops, or Ships of War in time of Peace, enter into any Agreement or Compact with another State, or with a foreign Power, or engage in War, unless actually invaded, or in such imminent Danger as will not admit of delay.

Art. II

Sec. 1. [1] The executive Power shall be vested in a President of the United States of America. He shall hold his Office during the Term of four Years, and together with the Vice President, chosen for the same Term, be elected, as follows.

[2] Each State shall appoint, in such Manner as the Legislature thereof may direct, a Number of Electors, equal to the whole Number of Senators and Representatives to which the State may be entitled in the Congress; but no Senator or Representative, or Person holding an Office of Trust or Profit under the United States, shall be appointed an Elector.

[3] The Electors shall meet in their respective States, and vote by Ballot for two Persons, of whom one at least shall not be an Inhabitant of the same state with themselves. And they shall make a List of all the Persons voted for, and of the Number of Votes for each; which List they shall sign and certify, and transmit sealed to the Seat of the Government of the United States, directed to the President of the Senate. The President of the Senate shall, in the Presence of the Senate and House of Representatives, open all the Certificates, and the Votes shall then be counted. The Person having the greatest Number of Votes shall be the President, if such Number be a Majority of the whole Number of Electors appointed; and if there be more than one who have such Majority, and have an equal Number of Votes, then the House of Representatives shall immediately choose by Ballot one of them for President; and if no person have a Majority, then from the five highest on the List the said House shall in like Manner choose the President. But in choosing the President, the Votes shall be taken by States, the Representation from each State having one Vote; A quorum for this Purpose shall consist of a Member or Members from two thirds of the States, and a Majority of all the States shall be necessary to a Choice. In every Case, after the Choice of the President, the Person having the greatest Number of Votes of

the Electors shall be the Vice President. But if there should remain two or more who have equal Votes, the Senate shall choose from them by Ballot the Vice President.

[4] The Congress may determine the Time of choosing the Electors, and the Day on which they shall give their Votes; which Day shall be the same throughout the United States.

[5] No Person except a natural born Citizen, or a Citizen of the United States, at the time of the Adoption of this Constitution, shall be eligible to the Office of President; neither shall any Person be eligible to the Office who shall not have attained to the Age of thirty five Years, and been fourteen Years a Resident within the United States.

[6] In Case of the Removal of the President from Office, or of his Death, Resignation, or Inability to discharge the Powers and Duties of the said Office, the Same shall devolve on the Vice President, and the Congress may by Law provide for the Case of Removal, Death, Resignation or Inability, both of the President and Vice President, declaring what Officer shall then act as President, and such Officer shall act accordingly, until the Disability be removed, or a President shall be elected.

[7] The President shall, at stated Times, receive for his Services, a Compensation, which shall neither be increased nor diminished during the Period for which he shall have been elected, and he shall not receive within that Period any other Emolument from the United States, or any of them.

[8] Before he enter on the Execution of his Office, he shall take the following Oath or Affirmation:—"I do solemnly swear (or affirm) that I will faithfully execute the Office of President of the United States, and will to the best of my Ability, preserve, protect and defend the Constitution of the United States."

Sec. 2. [1] The President shall be Commander in Chief of the Army and Navy of the United States, and of the Militia of the several States, when called into the actual Service of the United States; he may require the Opinion, in writing, of the principal Officer in each of the executive Departments, upon any Subject relating to the Duties of their respective offices, and he shall have Power to grant Reprieves and Pardons for Offences against the United States, except in Cases of Impeachment.

[2] He shall have Power, by and with the Advice and Consent of the Senate, to make Treaties, provided two thirds of the Senators present concur; and he shall nominate, and by and with the Advice and Consent of the Senate, shall appoint Ambassadors, other public Ministers and Consuls, Judges of the supreme Court, and all other Officers of the United States, whose Appointments are not herein otherwise provided for, and which shall be established by Law; but the Congress may by Law vest the Appointment of such inferior Officers, as they think proper, in the President alone, in the Courts of Law, or in the Heads of Departments.

[3] The President shall have Power to fill up all Vacancies that may happen during the Recess of the Senate, by granting Commissions which shall expire at the End of their next Session.

Sec. 3. He shall from time to time give to the Congress Information of the State of the Union, and recommend to their Consideration such Measures as he shall judge necessary and expedient; he may, on extraordinary Occasions, convene both Houses, or either of them, and in Case of Disagreement between them, with Respect to the Time of Adjournment, he may adjourn them to such Time as he shall think proper; he shall receive Ambassadors and other public Ministers; he shall take Care that the Laws by faithfully executed, and shall Commission all the Officers of the United States.

Sec. 4. The President, Vice President and all civil Officers of the United States, shall be removed from Office on Impeachment for, and Conviction of, Treason, Bribery, or other high Crimes and Misdemeanors.

Art. III

Sec. 1. The judicial Power of the United States, shall be vested in one supreme Court, and in such inferior Courts as the Congress may from time to time ordain and establish. The Judges, both of the supreme and inferior Courts, shall hold their Offices during good Behaviour, and shall, at stated Times, receive for their Services, a Compensation, which shall not be diminished during their Continuance in Office.

Sec. 2. [1] The judicial Power shall extend to all Cases, in Law and Equity, arising under this Constitution, the Laws of the United States, and Treaties made, or which shall be made, under their Authority;—to all Cases affecting Ambassadors, other public Ministers and Consuls;—to all Cases of admiralty and maritime Jurisdiction;—to Controversies to which the United States shall be a Party;—to Controversies between two or more States;—between a State and Citizens of another State;—between Citizens of different States,—between Citizens of the same State claiming Lands under Grants of different States, and between a State, or the Citizens thereof, and foreign States, Citizens or Subjects.

[2] In all Cases affecting Ambassadors, other public Ministers and Consuls, and those in which a State shall be Party, the supreme Court shall have original Jurisdiction. In all the other Cases before mentioned, the supreme Court shall have appellate Jurisdiction, both as to Law and Fact, with such Exceptions, and under such Regulations as the Congress shall make.

[3] The Trial of all Crimes, except in Cases of Impeachment, shall be by Jury; and such Trial shall be held in the State where the said Crimes shall have been committed; but when not committed within any State, the Trial shall be at such Place or Places as the Congress may by Law have directed.

Sec. 3. [1] Treason against the United States, shall consist only in levying War against them, or in adhering to their Enemies, giving them Aid and Comfort. No Person shall be convicted of Treason unless on the Testimony of two Witnesses to the same overt Act, or on Confession in open Court.

[2] The Congress shall have Power to declare the Punishment of Treason, but no Attainder of Treason shall work Corruption of Blood, or Forfeiture except during the Life of the Person attainted.

ART. IV

Sec. 1. Full Faith and Credit shall be given in each State to the Public Acts, Records, and judicial Proceedings of every other State. And the Congress may by general Laws prescribe the Manner in which such Acts, Records and Proceedings shall be proved, and the Effect thereof.

Sec. 2. [1] The Citizens of each State shall be entitled to all Privileges and Immunities of Citizens in the several States.

[2] A Person charged in any State with Treason, Felony, or other Crime, who shall flee from Justice, and be found in another State, shall on Demand of the executive Authority of the State from which he fled. be delivered up, to be removed to the State having Jurisdiction of the Crime.

[3] No Person held to Service or Labour in one State, under the Laws thereof, escaping into another, shall, in Consequence of any Law or Regulation therein, be discharged from such Service or Labour, but shall be delivered up on Claim of the Party to whom such Service or Labour may be due.

Sec. 3. [1] New States may be admitted by the Congress into this Union; but no new State shall be formed or erected within the Jurisdiction of any other State; nor any State be formed by the Junction of two or more States, or Parts of States, without the Consent of the Legislatures of the States concerned as well as of the Congress.

[2] The Congress shall have Power to dispose of and make all needful Rules and Regulations respecting the Territory or other Property belonging to the United States; and nothing in this Constitution shall be so construed as to Prejudice any Claims of the United States, or of any particular State.

Sec. 4. The United States shall guarantee to every State in this Union a Republican Form of Government, and shall protect each of them against Invasion; and on Application of the Legislature, or of the Executive (when the Legislature cannot be convened) against domestic Violence.

ART. V

The Congress, whenever two thirds of both Houses shall deem it necessary, shall propose Amendments to this Constitution, or, on the Application of the Legislatures of two thirds of the several States, shall call a Convention for proposing Amendments, which, in either Case, shall be valid to all Intents and Purposes, as Part of this Constitution, when ratified by the Legislatures of three fourths of the several States, or by Conventions in three fourths thereof, as the one or the other Mode of Ratification may be proposed by the Congress; Provided that no Amendment which may be made prior to the Year One thousand eight hundred and eight shall in any Manner affect the first and fourth Clauses in the Ninth Section of the first Article; and that no State, without its Consent, shall be deprived of its equal Suffrage in the Senate.

Art. VI

[1] All Debts contracted and Engagements entered into, before the Adoption of this Constitution, shall be as valid against the United States under this Constitution, as under the Confederation.

[2] This Constitution, and the Laws of the United States which shall be made in Pursuance thereof; and all Treaties made, or which shall be made, under the Authority of the United States, shall be the supreme Law of the Land; and the Judges in every State shall be bound thereby, any Thing in the Constitution or Laws of any State to the Contrary notwithstanding.

[3] The Senators and Representatives before mentioned, and the Members of the several State Legislatures, and all executive and judicial Officers, both of the United States and of the several States, shall be bound by Oath or Affirmation, to support this Constitution; but no religious Test shall ever be required as a Qualification to any office or public Trust under the United States.

Art. VII

The Ratification of the Conventions of nine States, shall be sufficient for the Establishment of this Constitution between the States so ratifying the Same.

Done in Convention by the Unanimous Consent of the States present the Seventeenth Day of September in the Year of our Lord one thousand seven hundred and Eighty seven and of the Independence of the United States of America the Twelfth. In witness whereof We have hereunto subscribed our Names.

G. WASHINGTON — President and deputy from Virginia

New Hampshire	John Langdon
Pennsylvania	B. Franklin
	Nicholas Gilman
	Thomas Mifflin
	Rob Morris
Massachusetts	Nathaniel Gorham
	Geo. Clymer
	Rufus King
	Thos. Fitzsimons
	Jaret Ingersoll
Connecticut	Sm. Sam Johnson
	James Wilson
	Roger Sherman
	Gouv Morris

New York	Alexander Hamilton
Delaware	Geo. Read
	Gunning Bedford
New Jersey	Wil. Livingston
	John Dickinson
	David Brearley
	Richard Bassett
	Wm. Paterson
	Jaco. Broom
	Jona. Dayton
Maryland	James McHenry
North Carolina	Wm. Blount
	Dan of St. Thos.
	Rich. Dobbs Spaight
	Danl Carroll
	Hu Williamson
	John Blair
South Carolina	J. Rutledge
Virginia	James Madison, Jr.
	Charles Cotesworth Pinckney
	Charles Pinckney
	Pierce Butler
Georgia	William Few
	Abr. Baldwin

Articles in addition to, and Amendment of the Constitution of the United States of America, proposed by Congress, and ratified by the Legislatures of the several States, pursuant to the fifth Article of the original Constitution.

[The first ten amendments went into effect November 3, 1791.]

AMEND. I

Congress shall make no law respecting an establishment of religion, or prohibiting the free exercise thereof; or abridging the freedom of speech, or of the press; or the right of the people peaceably to assemble, and to petition the government for a redress of grievances.

AMEND. II

A well regulated Militia, being necessary to the security of a free State, the right of the people to keep and bear Arms, shall not be infringed.

AMEND. III

No Soldier shall, in time of peace be quartered in any house, without the consent of the Owner, nor in time of war, but in a manner to be prescribed by law.

AMEND. IV

The right of the people to be secure in their persons, houses, papers, and effects, against unreasonable searches and seizures, shall not be violated, and no Warrants shall issue, but upon probable cause, supported by Oath or affirmation, and particularly describing the place to be searched, and the persons or things to be seized.

AMEND. V

No person shall be held to answer for a capital, or otherwise infamous crime, unless on a presentment or indictment of a Grand jury, except in cases arising in the land or naval forces, or in the Militia, when in actual service in time of War or public danger; nor shall any person be subject for the same offence to be twice put in jeopardy of life or limb; nor shall be compelled in any criminal case to be a witness against himself, nor be deprived of life, liberty, or property, without due process of law; nor shall private property be taken for public use, without just compensation.

AMEND. VI

In all criminal prosecutions, the accused shall enjoy the right to a speedy and public trial, by an impartial jury of the State and district wherein the crime shall have been committed, which district shall have been previously ascertained by law, and to be informed of the nature and cause of the accusation, to be confronted with the witnesses against him; to have compulsory process for obtaining witnesses in his favor, and to have the Assistance of Counsel for his defence.

AMEND. VII

In Suits at common law, where the value in controversy shall exceed twenty dollars, the right of trial by jury shall be preserved, and no fact tried by a jury, shall be otherwise re-examined in any Court of the United States, than according to the rules of the common law.

AMEND. VIII

Excessive bail shall not be required, nor excessive fines imposed, nor cruel and unusual punishments inflicted.

AMEND. IX

The enumeration in the Constitution, of certain rights, shall not be construed to deny or disparage others retained by the people.

AMEND. X

The powers not delegated to the United States by the Constitution, nor prohibited by it to the States, are reserved to the States respectively, or to the people.

AMEND. XI Jan. 8, 1798

The Judicial power of the United States shall not be construed to extend to any suit in law or equity, commenced or prosecuted against one of the United States by Citizens of another State, or by Citizens or Subjects of any Foreign State.

Amend. XII Sept. 25, 1804

The Electors shall meet in their respective states, and vote by ballot for President and Vice-President, one of whom, at least, shall not be an inhabitant of the same state with themselves; they shall name in their ballots the person voted for as President, and in distinct ballots the person voted for as Vice-President, and they shall make distinct lists of all persons voted for as President, and of all persons voted for as Vice-President, and of the number of votes for each, which lists they shall sign and certify, and transmit sealed to the seat of the government of the United States, directed to the President of the Senate;—The President of the Senate shall, in the presence of the Senate and House of Representatives, open all the certificates and the votes shall then be counted;—The person having the greatest number of votes for President, shall be the President, if such number be a majority of the whole number of Electors appointed; and if no person have such majority, then from the persons having the highest numbers not exceeding three on the list of those voted for as President, the House of Representatives shall choose immediately, by ballot, the President. But in choosing the President, the votes shall be taken by states, the representation from each state having one vote; a quorum for this purpose shall consist of a member or members from two-thirds of the states, and a majority of all the states shall be necessary to a choice. And if the House of Representatives shall not choose a President whenever the right of choice shall devolve upon them, before the fourth day of March next following, then the Vice-President shall act as President, as in the case of the death or other constitutional disability of the President.—The person having the greatest number of votes as Vice-President, shall be the Vice-President, if such number be a majority of the whole number of Electors appointed, and if no person have a majority, then from the two highest numbers on the list, the Senate shall choose the Vice-President; a quorum for the purpose shall consist of two-thirds of the whole number of Senators, and a majority of the whole number shall be necessary to a choice. But no person constitutionally ineligible to the office of President shall be eligible to that of Vice-President of the United States.

Amend. XIII Dec. 18, 1865

Sec. 1. Neither slavery nor involuntary servitude, except as a punishment for crime whereof the party shall have been duly convicted, shall exist within the United States, or any place subject to their jurisdiction.

Sec. 2. Congress shall have power to enforce this article by appropriate legislation.

Amend. XIV July 28, 1868

Sec. 1. All persons born or naturalized in the United States, and subject to the jurisdiction thereof, are citizens of the United States and of the State wherein they reside. No State shall make or enforce any law which shall abridge the privileges or immunities of citizens of the United States; nor shall any State deprive any person of life, liberty, or property, without due process of law; nor deny to any person within its jurisdiction the equal protection of the laws.

Sec. 2. Representatives shall be apportioned among the several States according to their respective numbers, counting the whole number of persons in each State, excluding Indians not taxed. But when the right to vote at any election for the choice of electors for President and Vice President of the United States, Representatives in Congress, the Executive and Judicial officers of a State, or the members of the Legislature thereof, is denied to any of the male inhabitants of such State, being twenty-one years of age, and citizens of the United States, or in any way abridged, except for participation in rebellion, or other crime, the basis of representation therein shall be reduced in the proportion which the number of such male citizens shall bear to the whole number of male citizens twenty-one years of age in such State.

Sec. 3. No person shall be a Senator or Representative in Congress, or elector of President and Vice President, or hold any office, civil or military, under the United States, or under any State, who, having previously taken an oath, as a member of Congress, or as an officer of the United States, or as a member of any State legislature, or as an executive or judicial officer of any State, to support the Constitution of the United States, shall have engaged in insurrection or rebellion against the same, or given aid or comfort to the enemies thereof. But Congress may by a vote of two-thirds of each House, remove such disability.

Sec. 4. The validity of the public debt of the United States, authorized by law, including debts incurred for payment of pensions and bounties for services in suppressing insurrection or rebellion, shall not be questioned. But neither the United States nor any State shall assume or pay any debt or obligation incurred in aid of insurrection or rebellion against the United States, or any claim for the loss or emancipation of any slave; but all such debts, obligations and claims shall be held illegal and void.

Sec. 5. The Congress shall have power to enforce, by appropriate legislation, the provisions of this article.

Amend. XV March 30, 1870

Sec. 1. The right of citizens of the United States to vote shall not be denied or abridged by the United States or by any State on account of race. color, or previous condition of servitude.

Sec. 2. The Congress shall have power to enforce this article by appropriate legislation.

Amend. XVI February 25, 1913

The Congress shall have power to lay and collect taxes on incomes, from whatever source derived, without apportionment among the several States and without regard to any census or enumeration.

Amend. XVII May 31, 1913

[1] The Senate of the United States shall be composed of two Senators from each State, elected by the people thereof, for six years; and each Senator shall have one

vote. The electors in each State shall have the qualifications requisite for electors of the most numerous branch of the State legislature.

[2] When vacancies happen in the representation of any State in the Senate, the executive authority of such state shall issue writs of election to fill such vacancies: *Provided*, That the legislature of any State may empower the executive thereof to make temporary appointments until the people fill the vacancies by election as the legislature may direct.

[3] This amendment shall not be so construed as to affect the election or term of any senator chosen before it becomes valid as part of the Constitution.

AMEND. XVIII January 29, 1919

Sec. 1. After one year from the ratification of this article, the manufacture, sale, or transportation of intoxicating liquors within, the importation thereof into, or the exportation thereof from the United States and all territory subject to the jurisdiction thereof for beverage purposes is hereby prohibited.

Sec. 2. The Congress and the several States shall have concurrent power to enforce this article by appropriate legislation.

Sec. 3. This article shall be inoperative unless it shall have been ratified as an amendment to the Constitution by the legislatures of the several States, as provided in the Constitution, within seven years from the date of the submission hereof to the States by Congress.

AMEND. XIX August 26, 1920

[1] The right of citizens of the United States to vote shall not be denied or abridged by the United States or by any States on account of sex.

[2] The Congress shall have power by appropriate legislation to enforce the provisions of this article.

AMEND. XX February 6, 1933

Sec. 1. The terms of the President and Vice-President shall end at noon on the twentieth day of January, and the terms of Senators and Representatives at noon on the third day of January, of the years in which such terms would have ended if this article had not been ratified; and the terms of their successors shall then begin.

Sec. 2. The Congress shall assemble at least once in every year, and such meeting shall begin at noon on the third day of January, unless they shall by law appoint a different day.

Sec. 3. If, at the time fixed for the beginning of the term of the President, the President-elect shall have died, the Vice-President-elect shall become President. If a President shall not have been chosen before the time fixed for the beginning of his term, or if the President-elect shall have failed to qualify, then the Vice-President-elect shall act as President until a President shall have qualified; and the

Congress may by law provide for the case wherein neither a President-elect nor a Vice-President-elect shall have qualified, declaring who shall then act as President, or the manner in which one who is to act shall be selected, and such person shall act accordingly until a President or Vice-President shall have qualified.

Sec. 4. The Congress may by law provide for the case of the death of any of the persons from whom the House of Representatives may choose a President whenever the right of choice shall have devolved upon them, and for the case of the death of any of the persons from whom the Senate may choose a Vice-President whenever the right of choice shall have devolved upon them.

Sec. 5. Sections 1 and 2 shall take effect on the 15th day of October following the ratification of this article.

Sec. 6. This article shall be inoperative unless it shall have been ratified as an amendment to the Constitution by the legislatures of three-fourths of the several States within seven years from the date of its submission.

AMEND. XXI December 5, 1933

Sec. 1. The eighteenth article of amendment to the Constitution of the United States is hereby repealed. . . .

AMEND. XXII February 26, 1951

Sec. 1. No person shall be elected to the office of the President more than twice, and no person who has held the office of President, or acted as President for more than two years of a term to which some other person was elected President shall be elected to the office of the President more than once. But this Article shall not apply to any person holding the office of President when this Article was proposed by the Congress, and shall not prevent any person who may be holding the office of President, or acting as President, during the term within which this Article becomes operative from holding the office of President or acting as President during the remainder of such term.

AMEND. XXIII March 29, 1961

Sec. 1. The District constituting the seat of Government of the United States shall appoint in such manner as the Congress may direct:

A number of electors of President and Vice-President equal to the whole number of Senators and Representatives in Congress to which the District would be entitled if it were a State, but in no event more than the least populous state; they shall be in addition to those appointed by the states, but they shall be considered, for the purposes of the election of President and Vice-President, to be electors appointed by a state; and they shall meet in the District and perform such duties as provided by the twelfth article of amendment.

Sec. 2. The Congress shall have power to enforce this article by appropriate legislation.

AMEND. XXIV January 24, 1964

Sec. 1. The right of citizens of the United States to vote in any primary or other election for President or Vice-President, for electors for President or Vice-President, or for Senator or Representative in Congress, shall not be denied or abridged by the United States or any state by reason of failure to pay any poll tax or other tax.

Sec. 2. The Congress shall have power to enforce this article by appropriate legislation.

AMEND. XXV February 23, 1967

Sec. 1. In case of the removal of the President from office or his death or resignation, the Vice-President shall become President.

Sec. 2. Whenever there is a vacancy in the office of the Vice-President, the President shall nominate a Vice-President who shall take the office upon confirmation by a majority vote of both houses of Congress.

Sec. 3. Whenever the President transmits to the President pro tempore of the Senate and the Speaker of the House of Representatives his written declaration that he is unable to discharge the powers and duties of his office, and until he transmits to them a written declaration to the contrary, such powers and duties shall be discharged by the Vice-President as Acting President.

Sec. 4. Whenever the Vice-President and a majority of either the principal officers of the executive departments, or of such other body as Congress may by law provide, transmit to the President pro tempore of the Senate and the Speaker of the House of Representatives their written declaration that the President is unable to discharge the powers and duties of his office, the Vice-President shall immediately assume the powers and duties of the office as Acting President.

Thereafter, when the President transmits to the President pro tempore of the Senate and the Speaker of the House of Representatives his written declaration that no inability exists, he shall resume the powers and duties of his office unless the Vice-President and a majority of either the principal officers of the executive department, or of such other body as Congress may by law provide, transmit within four days to the President pro tempore of the Senate and the Speaker of the House of Representatives their written declaration that the President is unable to discharge the powers and duties of his office. Thereupon Congress shall decide the issue, assembling within 48 hours for that purpose if not in session. If the Congress, within 21 days after receipt of the latter written declaration, or, if Congress is not in session, within 21 days after congress is required to assemble, determines by two-thirds vote of both houses that the President is unable to discharge the powers and duties of his office, the Vice-President shall continue to discharge the same as Acting President; otherwise, the President shall resume the powers and duties of his office.

AMEND. XXVI July 7, 1971

Sec. 1. The right of citizens of the United States, who are eighteen years of age or older, to vote shall not be denied or abridged by the United States or by any State on account of age.

Sec. 2. The Congress shall have power to enforce this article by appropriate legislation.

AMEND. XXVII May 19, 1992

No law varying the Compensation for the services of the Senators and Representatives shall take effect, unless an election of Representatives shall have intervened.

B. The Earliest Protest against Slavery (February 18, 1688)

This is to the monthly meeting of Germantown Mennonites held at Richard Worrell's:

These are the reasons why we are against the traffic of men-body, as followeth: Is there any that would be done or handled in this manner? viz, to be sold or made a slave for all the time of his life? How fearful and faint-hearted are many at sea, when they see a strange vessel, being afraid it should be a Turk, and they should be taken, and sold for slaves into Turkey. Now, what is *this* better done, than Turks do? Yea, rather it is worse for them, which say they are Christians; for we hear that the most part of such negers are brought hither against their will and consent, and that many of them are stolen. Now, though they are black, we cannot conceive there is more liberty to have them slaves, as it is to have other white ones. There is a saying, that we should do to all men like as we will be done ourselves; making no difference of what generation, descent, or colour they are. And those who steal or rob men, and those who buy or purchase them, are they not all alike? Here is liberty of conscience, which is right and reasonable; here ought to be likewise liberty of the body, except of evil-doers, which is another case. But to bring men hither, or to rob and sell them against their will, we stand against. In Europe there are many oppressed for conscience-sake; and here there are those oppressed which are of a black colour. And we who know that men must not commit adultery—some do commit adultery in others, separating wives from their husbands, and giving them to others; and some sell the children of these poor creatures to other men. Ah! do consider well this thing, you who do it, if you would be done at this manner—and if it is done according to Christianity! You surpass Holland and Germany in this thing. This makes an ill report in all those countries of Europe, where they hear of [it], that the Quakers do here handle men as they handle there the cattle. And for that reason some have no mind or inclination to come hither. And who shall maintain this your cause, or plead for it? Truly, we cannot do so, except you shall inform us better hereof, viz.: that Christians have liberty to practice these things. Pray, what thing in the world can be done worse towards us, than if men should rob or steal us away, and sell us for slaves to strange countries; separating husbands from their wives and children. Being now this is not done in the manner we would be done at; therefore, we contradict, and are against this traffic of men-body. And we who profess that it is not lawful to steal, must, likewise, avoid to purchase such things as are stolen, but rather help to stop this robbing and stealing, if possible. And such men ought to be delivered out of the hands of the robbers, and set free as in Europe. Then is Pennsylvania to have a good report, instead, it hath now a bad one, for this sake, in other countries; Especially whereas the Europeans are desirous to know in what manner *the Quakers* do rule in *their* province; and most of them do look upon us with an envious eye. But if this is done well, what shall we say is done evil?

If once these slaves (which they say are so wicked and stubborn men,) should join themselves — fight for their freedom, and handle their masters and mistresses, as they did handle them before; will these masters and mistresses take the sword at hand and war against these poor slaves, like, as we are able to believe, some will not refuse to do? Or, have these poor negers not as much right to fight for their freedom, as you have to keep them slaves?

Now consider well this thing, if it is good or bad. And in case you find it to be good to handle these blacks in that manner, we desire and require you hereby lovingly, that you may inform us herein, which at this time never was done, viz., that Christians have such a liberty to do so. To the end we shall be satisfied on this point, and satisfy likewise our good friends and acquaintances in our native country, to whom it is a terror, or fearful thing, that men should be handled so in Pennsylvania.

C. Declaration of the Causes and Necessity of Taking Up Arms (July 6, 1775)

Franklin, Jay, Rutledge, Livingston, Johnson, Jefferson and Dickinson were the members of the committee appointed to draw up this declaration. The final draft is the work of Dickinson and Jefferson.

If it was possible for men, who exercise their reason to believe, that the divine Author of our existence intended a part of the human race to hold an absolute property in, and an unbounded power over others, marked out by his infinite goodness and wisdom, as the objects of a legal domination never rightfully resistible, however severe and oppressive, the inhabitants of these colonies might at least require from the parliament of Great Britain some evidence, that this dreadful authority over them, has been granted to that body. But a reverence for our great Creator, principles of humanity, and the dictates of common sense, must convince all those who reflect upon the subject, that government was instituted to promote the welfare of mankind, and ought to be administered for the attainment of that end. The legislature of Great Britain, however, stimulated by an inordinate passion for a power not only unjustifiable, but which they know to be peculiarly reprobated by the very con situation of that kingdom, and desperate of success in any mode of contest, where regard should be had to truth, law, or right, have at length, deserting those, attempted to effect their cruel and impolitic purpose of enslaving these colonies by violence, and have thereby rendered it necessary for us to close with their last appeal from reason to arms. — Yet, however blinded that assembly may be, by their intemperate rage for unlimited domination, so to slight justice and the opinion of mankind, we esteem ourselves, bound by obligations of respect to the rest of the world, to make known the justice of our cause . . .

We have received certain intelligence, that General Carleton, the Governor of Canada, is instigating the people of that province and the Indians to fall upon us; and we have but too much reason to apprehend, that schemes have been formed to excite domestic enemies against us. In brief, a part of these colonies now feel, and all of them are sure of feeling, as far as the vengeance of administration can inflict them, the complicated calamities of fire, sword, and famine. We are reduced to the alternative of choosing an unconditional submission to the tyranny of irritated ministers, or resistance by force. — The latter is our choice. — We have counted the cost of this contest, and find nothing so dreadful as voluntary slavery. — Honour, justice, and humanity, forbid us tamely to surrender that freedom which we received from our gallant ancestors, and which our innocent posterity have a right to receive from us. We cannot endure the infamy and guilt of resigning succeeding generations to that wretchedness which inevitably awaits them, if we basely entail hereditary bondage upon them.

Our cause is just. Our union is perfect. Our internal resources are great, and, if necessary, foreign assistance is undoubtedly attainable. — We gratefully acknowledge, as signal instances of the Divine favour towards us, that his Providence would not permit us to be called into this severe controversy, until we were grown up to our present strength, had been previously exercised in warlike operation, and possessed of the means of defending ourselves. With hearts fortified with these animating reflections, we most solemnly, before God and the world, declare, that, exerting the utmost energy of those powers, which our beneficent Creator hath graciously bestowed upon us, the arms we have been compelled by our enemies to assume, we will, in defiance of every hazard, with unabating firmness and perseverance, employ for the preservation of our liberties; being with one mind resolved to die freemen rather than to live slaves.

Lest this declaration should disquiet the minds of our friends and fellow subjects in any part of the empire, we assure them that we mean not to dissolve that union which has so long and so happily subsisted between us, and which we sincerely wish to see restored. — Necessity has not yet driven us into that desperate measure, or induced us to excite any other nation to war against them. — We have not raised armies with ambitious designs of separating from Great Britain, and establishing independent states. We fight not for glory or for conquest. We exhibit to mankind the remarkable spectacle of a people attacked by unprovoked enemies, without any imputation or even suspicion of offence. They boast of their privileges and civilization, and yet proffer no milder conditions than servitude or death.

In our own native land, in defence of the freedom that is our birth-right, and which we ever enjoyed till the late violation of it — for the protection of our property, acquired solely by the honest industry of our forefathers and ourselves, against violence actually offered, we have taken up arms. We shall lay them down when hostilities shall cease on the part of the aggressors, and all danger of their being renewed shall be removed, and not before.

With an humble confidence in the mercies of the supreme and impartial Judge and Ruler of the Universe, we most devoutly implore his divine goodness to protect us happily through this great conflict, to dispose our adversaries to reconciliation on reasonable terms, and thereby to relieve the empire from the calamities of civil war.

D. The Declaration of Independence (July 4, 1776)

WHEN, in the Course of human events, it becomes necessary for one people to dissolve the political bands which have connected them with another, and to assume among the powers of the earth, the separate and equal station to which the Laws of Nature and of Nature's God entitle them, a decent respect to the opinions of mankind requires that they should declare the causes which impel them to the separation.

We hold these truths to be self evident, that all men are created equal, that they are endowed by their Creator with certain unalienable Rights, that among these are Life, Liberty and the pursuit of happiness. That to secure these rights, Governments are instituted among Men, deriving their just powers from the consent of the governed, That whenever any Form of Government becomes destructive of these ends, it is the Right of the People to alter or to abolish it, and to institute new Government, laying its foundations on such principles and organizing its power in such form, as to them shall seem most likely to effect their Safety and Happiness. Prudence, indeed, will dictate that Governments long established should not be changed for light and transient causes; and accordingly, all experience hath shown, that mankind are more disposed to suffer, while evils are sufferable, than to right themselves by abolishing the forms to which they are accustomed. But when a long train of abuses and usurpations, pursuing invariably the same object evinces a design to reduce them under absolute Despotism, it is their right, it is their duty, to throw off such Government and to provide new Guards for their future security. Such has been the patient sufferance of these Colonies; and such is now the necessity which constrains them to alter their former Systems of Government. The history of the present King of Great Britain is a history of repeated injuries and usurpations, all having in direct object the establishment of an absolute Tyranny over these States. To prove this, let Facts be submitted to a candid world.

He has refused his Assent to Laws, the most wholesome and necessary for the public good.

He has forbidden his Governors to pass Laws of immediate and pressing importance, unless suspended in their operation till his Assent should be obtained, and when so suspended, he has utterly neglected to attend to them.

He has refused to pass other Laws for the accommodation of large districts of people, unless those people would relinquish the right of Representation in the Legislature, a right inestimable to them and formidable to tyrants only.

He has called together legislative bodies at places unusual, uncomfortable, and distant from the depository of their public Records, for the sole purpose of fatiguing them into compliance with his measure.

He has dissolved Representative Houses repeatedly, for opposing with manly firmness his invasions on the rights of the people.

He has refused for a long time, after such dissolutions, to cause others to be elected; whereby the Legislative powers, incapable of Annihilation, have returned to the People at large for their exercise; the state remaining in the meantime exposed to all the dangers of invasion from without and convulsions within.

He has endeavored to prevent the population of these States; for that purpose obstructing the Laws for Naturalization of Foreigners; refusing to pass others to encourage their migrations hither, and raising the conditions of new Appropriations of Lands.

He has obstructed the Administration of Justice, by refusing his Assent to Laws for establishing Judiciary powers.

He has made Judges dependent on his Will alone, for the tenure of their offices, and the amount and payment of their salaries.

He has erected a multitude of New Offices, and sent hither swarms of Officers to harass our people, and eat out their substance.

He has kept among us, in times of peace, Standing Armies, without the Consent of our legislatures.

He has affected to render the Military independent of and superior to the Civil power.

He has combined with others to subject us to a jurisdiction foreign to our constitution and unacknowledged by our laws; giving his Assent to their Acts of pretended Legislation: For quartering large bodies of armed troops among us: For protecting them by a mock Trial from punishment for any Murders which they should commit on the Inhabitants of these States: For cutting off our Trade with all parts of the world: For imposing Taxes on us without our Consent: For depriving us in many cases of the benefits of Trial by Jury: For transporting us beyond Seas to be tried for pretended offenses: For abolishing the free System of English Laws in a neighbouring Province, establishing therein an Arbitrary government, and enlarging its Boundaries so as to render it at once an example and fit instrument for introducing the same absolute rule into these colonies: For taking away our Charters, abolishing our most valuable Laws and altering fundamentally the Forms of our Governments: For suspending our own Legislatures, and declaring themselves invested with power to legislate for us in all cases whatsoever.

He has abdicated Government here by declaring us out of his Protection and waging War against us.

He has plundered our seas, ravaged our Coasts, burnt our towns, and destroyed the lives of our people.

He is at this time transporting large Armies of foreign Mercenaries to complete the works of death, desolation and tyranny, already begun with circumstances of cruelty and perfidy scarcely paralleled in the most barbarous ages, and totally unworthy the Head of a civilized nation.

He has constrained our fellow Citizens taken Captive on the high Seas to bear Arms against their Country, to become the executioners of their friends and Brethren, or to fall themselves by their Hands.

He has excited domestic insurrections amongst us, and has endeavored to bring on the inhabitants of our frontiers, the merciless Indian Savages, whose known rule of warfare is an undistinguished destruction of all ages, sexes and conditions. In every stage of these Oppression We have Petitioned for Redress in the most humble terms. Our repeated Petitions have been answered only by repeated injury. A Prince, whose character is thus marked by every act which may define a Tyrant, is unfit to be the ruler of a free people. Nor have We been wanting in attentions to our British brethren. We have warned them from time to time of attempts by their legislature to extend an unwarrantable jurisdiction over us. We have reminded them of the circumstances of our emigration and settlement here. We have appealed to their native justice and magnanimity, and we have conjured them by the ties of our common kindred to disavow these usurpations, which would inevitably interrupt our connections and correspondence. They too have been deaf to the voice of justice and of consanguinity. We must, therefore, acquiesce in the necessity, which denounces our Separation, and hold them as we hold the rest of mankind, Enemies in War, in Peace Friends.

WE THEREFORE, the REPRESENTATIVES of the UNITED STATES OF AMERICA, IN GENERAL CONGRESS, Assembled, appealing to the Supreme Judge of the world for the rectitude of our intentions, do, in the Name, and by authority of the good People of these colonies, solemnly PUBLISH AND DECLARE, That these United Colonies are, and of Right ought to be FREE AND INDEPENDENT STATES: that they are Absolved from all Allegiance to the British Crown, and that all political connection between them and the State of Great Britain is and ought to be totally dissolved; and that as FREE AND INDEPENDENT STATES, they have full Power to levy War, conclude Peace, contract Alliances, establish Commerce, and to do all other Acts and Things which INDEPENDENT STATES may of right do. And for the support of this Declaration, with a firm reliance on the protection of Divine Providence, we mutually pledge to each other our Lives, our Fortunes, and our sacred Honor.

Charles Thomason   John Hancock
       Secretary   President

(Signed as the President and Secretary of the Continental Congress)

SIGNERS OF THE DECLARATION OF INDEPENDENCE

CONNECTICUT
Samuel Huntington
Roger Sherman
William Williams
Oliver Wolcott

DELAWARE
Thomas McKean (The last signature was affixed in 1781 by Thomas McKean)
George Read
Caesar Rodney

GEORGIA
Lyman Hall
Button Gwinnett
George Walton

MARYLAND
Charles Carroll of Carrollton
Samuel Chase
William Paca
Thomas Stone

MASSACHUSETTS
John Adams
Samuel Adams
Elbridge Gerry
John Hancock
Robert Treat Paine

RHODE ISLAND
William Ellery
Stephen Hopkins

SOUTH CAROLINA
Thomas Heyward, Jr.
Thomas Lynch, Jr.
Arthur Middleton
Edward Rutledge

PENNSYLVANIA
Benjamin Franklin
George Clymer
John Morton
George Ross
James Wilson
Robert Morris
Benjamin Rush
James Smith
George Taylor

NEW HAMPSHIRE
Josiah Bartlett
Matthew Thornton
William Whipple

NEW JERSEY
Abraham Clark
John Hart
Francis Hopkinson
Richard Stockton
John Witherspoon

NEW YORK
William Floyd
Francis Lewis
Philip Livingston
Lewis Morris

NORTH CAROLINA
Joseph Hewes
William Hooper
John Penn

VIRGINIA
Carter Braxton
Benjamin Harrison
Thomas Jefferson
Richard Henry Lee
Francis Lightfoot Lee
Thomas Nelson, Jr.
George Wythe

E. The Articles of Confederation (March 1, 1781)

To ALL TO WHOM these Presents shall come, we the undersigned Delegates of the States affixed to our Names send greeting. Whereas the Delegates of the United States of America in Congress assembled did on the fifteenth day of November in the Year of our Lord One Thousand Seven Hundred and Seventy seven, and in the Second Year of the Independence of America agree to certain articles of Confederation and perpetual Union between the States of New Hampshire, Massachusetts-bay, Rhode Island and Providence Plantations, Connecticut, New York, New Jersey, Pennsylvania, Delaware, Maryland, Virginia, North Carolina, South Carolina and Georgia in the Words following, viz. "Articles of Confederation and perpetual Union between the states of New Hampshire, Massachusetts-bay, Rhode Island and Providence Plantations, Connecticut, New York, New Jersey, Pennsylvania, Delaware, Maryland, Virginia, North Carolina, South Carolina and Georgia.

ART. I. The Stile of this confederacy shall be "The United States of America."

ART. II. Each state retains its sovereignty, freedom and independence, and every Power, Jurisdiction and right, which is not by this confederation expressly delegated to the United States, in Congress assembled.

ART. III. The said states hereby severally enter into a firm league of friendship with each other, for their common defence, the security of their Liberties, and their mutual and general welfare, binding themselves to assist each other, against all force offered to, or attacks made upon them, or any of them, on account of religion, sovereignty, trade, or any other pretence whatever.

ART. IV. The better to secure and perpetuate mutual friendship and intercourse among the people of the different states in this union, the free inhabitants of each of these states, paupers, vagabonds and fugitives from Justice excepted, shall be entitled to all privileges and immunities of free citizens in the several states; and the people of each state shall have free ingress and regress to and from any other state, and shall enjoy therein all the privileges of trade and commerce, subject to the same duties, impositions and restrictions as the inhabitants thereof respectively, provided that such restriction shall not extend so far as to prevent the removal of property imported into any state, to any other state of which the Owner is an inhabitant; provided also that no imposition, duties or restriction shall be laid by any state, on the property of the united states, or either of them.

If any Person guilty of, or charged with treason, felony, or other high misdemeanor in any state, shall flee from Justice, and be found in any of the United States, he shall upon demand of the Governor or executive power, of the state from which he fled, be delivered up and removed to the state having jurisdiction of his offence.

Full faith and credit shall be given in each of these states to the records, acts and judicial proceedings of the courts and magistrates of every other state . . .

AND WHEREAS it hath pleased the Great Governor of the World to incline the hearts of the legislatures we respectively represent in congress, to approve of, and to authorize us to ratify the said articles of confederation and perpetual union. KNOW YE that we the undersigned delegates, by virtue of the power and authority to us given for that purpose, do by these presents, in the name and in behalf of our respective constituents, fully and entirely ratify and confirm each and every of the said articles of confederation and perpetual union, and all and singular the matters and things therein contained: And we do further solemnly plight and engage the faith of our respective constituents, that they shall abide by the determinations of the united states in congress assembled, on all questions, which by the said confederation are submitted to them. And that the articles thereof shall be inviolably observed by the states we respectively represent, and that the union shall be perpetual. In Witness whereof we have hereunto set our hands in Congress. Done at Philadelphia in the state of Pennsylvania the ninth Day of July in the Year of our Lord one Thousand seven Hundred and Seventy-eight, and in the third year of the independence of America.

F. The Northwest Ordinance (July 13, 1787)

*An Ordinance for the government of the Territory of
the United States northwest of the River Ohio.*

. . . *Be it ordained by the authority aforesaid,* That there shall be appointed from time to time by Congress, a governor, whose commission shall continue in force for the term of three years, unless sooner revoked by Congress; he shall reside in the district, and have a freehold estate therein in 1,000 acres of land, while in the exercise of his office . . .

So soon as there shall be five thousand free male inhabitants of full age in the district, upon giving proof thereof to the governor, they shall receive authority, with time and place, to elect representatives from their counties or townships to represent them in the general assembly: *Provided,* That, for every five hundred free male inhabitants, there shall be one representative, and so on progressively with the number of free male inhabitants shall the right of representation increase, until the number of representatives shall amount to twenty-five; after which, the number and proportion of representatives shall be regulated by the legislature: *Provided,* That no person be eligible or qualified to act as a representative unless he shall have been a citizen of one of the United States three years, and be a resident in the district, or unless he shall have resided in the district three years; and, in either case, shall likewise hold in his own right, in fee simple, two hundred acres of land within the same: *Provided, also,* That a freehold in fifty acres of land in the district, having been a citizen of one of the states, and being resident in the district, or the like freehold and two years residence in the district, shall be necessary to qualify a man as an elector of a representative . . .

It is hereby ordained and declared by the authority aforesaid, That the following articles shall be considered as articles of compact between the original States and the people and States in the said territory and forever remain unalterable, unless by common consent, to wit:

Art. 1. No person, demeaning himself in a peaceable and orderly manner, shall ever be molested on account of his mode of worship or religious sentiments, in the said territory.

Art. 2. The inhabitants of the said territory shall always be entitled to the benefits of the writ of *habeas corpus*, and of the trial by jury; of a proportionate representation of the people in the legislature; and of judicial proceedings according to the course of the common law. All persons shall be bailable, unless for capital offenses, where the proof shall be evident or the presumption great. All fines shall be moderate; and no cruel or unusual punishments shall be inflicted. No man shall be deprived of his liberty or property, but by the judgment of his peers or the law of the land; and, should the public exigencies make it necessary, for the common preservation, to take any person's property, or to demand his particular services, full compensation shall be made for the same. And, in the just preservation of rights and property, it is understood and declared, that no law ought ever to be made, or have force in the said territory, that shall, in any manner whatever, interfere with or affect private contracts or engagements, *bona fide*, and without fraud, previously formed.

Art. 3. Religion, morality, and knowledge, being necessary to good government and the happiness of mankind, schools and the means of education shall forever be encouraged. The utmost good faith shall always be observed towards the Indians; their lands and property shall never be taken from them without their consent; and, in their property, rights, and liberty, they shall never be invaded or disturbed, unless in just and lawful wars authorized by Congress; but laws founded in justice and humanity, shall from time to time be made for preventing wrongs being done to them, and for preserving peace and friendship with them . . .

Art. 5. There shall be formed in the said territory, not less than three nor more than five States; and the boundaries of the States, as soon as Virginia shall alter her act of cession, and consent to the same, shall become fixed and established as follows, to wit: The western state in the said territory, shall be bounded by the Mississippi, the Ohio, and Wabash Rivers; a direct line drawn from the Wabash and Post Vincents, due North, to the territorial line between the United States and Canada; and, by the said territorial line, to the Lake of the Woods and Mississippi. The middle State shall be bounded by the said direct line, the Wabash from Post Vincents to the Ohio, by the Ohio, by a direct line, drawn due north from the mouth of the Great Miami, to the said territorial line, and by the said territorial line. The eastern State shall be bounded by the last mentioned direct line, the Ohio, Pennsylvania, and the said territorial line: *Provided, however,* and it is further understood and declared, that the boundaries of these three States shall be subject so far to be altered, that, if Congress shall hereafter find it expedient, they shall have authority to form one or two States in that part of the said territory which lies north of an east and west line drawn through the southerly bend or extreme of lake Michigan. And, whenever any of the said States shall have sixty thousand free inhabitants therein, such State shall be admitted, by its delegates, into the Congress of the United States, on an equal footing with the original states in all respects whatever, and shall be at liberty to form a permanent constitution and State government: *Provided*, the constitution and government so to be formed, shall be republican, and in conformity to the principles contained in these articles; and, so far as it can be consistent with the general interest of the confederacy, such admission shall be allowed at an earlier period, and when there may be a less number of free inhabitants in the State than sixty thousand.

ART. 6. There shall be neither slavery nor involuntary servitude in the said territory, otherwise than in the punishment of crimes whereof the party shall have been duly convicted: *Provided, always,* That any person escaping into the same, from whom labor or service is lawfully claimed in any one of the original States, such fugitive may be lawfully reclaimed and conveyed to the person claiming his or her labor or service as aforesaid.

Be it ordained by the authority aforesaid, That the resolutions of the 23rd of April, 1734, relative to the subject of this ordinance, be, and the same are hereby repealed and declared null and void.

G. The Fugitive Slave Act (1793)

An Act respecting fugitives from justice, and persons escaping from the service of their masters.

SECTION 1. *Be it enacted by the Senate and House of Representatives of the United States of America in Congress assembled,* That whenever the executive authority of any state in the Union, or of either of the territories northwest or south of the river Ohio, shall demand any person as a fugitive from justice, of the executive authority of any such state or territory to which such person shall have fled, and shall moreover produce the copy of an indictment found, or an affidavit made before a magistrate of any state or territory as aforesaid, charging the person so demanded, with having committed treason, felony or other crime, certified as authentic by the governor or chief magistrate of the state or territory from whence the person so charged fled, it shall be the duty of the executive authority of the state or territory to which such person shall have fled, to cause him or her to be arrested and secured, and notice of the arrest to be given to the executive authority making such demand, or to the agent of such authority appointed to receive the fugitive, and to cause the fugitive to be delivered to such agent when he shall appear: But if no such agent shall appear within six months from the time of the arrest, the prisoner may be discharged. And all costs or expenses incurred in the apprehending, securing, and transmitting such fugitive to the state or territory making such demand, shall be paid by such state or territory.

SEC. 2. *And be it further enacted,* That any agent, appointed as aforesaid, who shall receive the fugitive into his custody, shall be empowered to transport him or her to the state or territory from which he or she shall have fled. And if any person or persons shall by force set at liberty, or rescue the fugitive from such agent while transporting, as aforesaid, the person or persons so offending shall, on conviction, be fined not exceeding five hundred dollars, and be imprisoned not exceeding one year.

Sec. 3. *And be it also enacted*, That when a person held to labour in any of the United States, or in either of the territories on the northwest or south of the river Ohio, under the laws thereof, shall escape into any other of the said states or territory, the person to whom such labour or service may be due, his agent or attorney, is hereby empowered to seize or arrest such fugitive from labour, (b) and to take him or her before any judge of the circuit or district courts of the United States, residing or being within the state, or before any magistrate of a county, city or town corporate, wherein such seizure or arrest shall be made, and upon proof to the satisfaction of such judge or magistrate, either by oral testimony or affidavit taken before and certified by a magistrate of any such state or territory, that the person so seized or arrested, doth, under the laws of the state or territory from which he or she fled, owe service or labour to the person claiming him or her, it shall be the duty of such judge or magistrate to give a certificate thereof to such claimant, his agent or attorney, which shall be sufficient warrant for removing the said fugitive from labour, to the state or territory from which he or she fled.

Sec. 4. *And be it further enacted*, That any person who shall knowingly and willingly obstruct or hinder such claimant, his agent or attorney in so seizing or arresting such fugitive from labour, or shall rescue such fugitive from such claimant, his agent or attorney when so arrested pursuant to the authority herein given or declared; or shall harbor or conceal such person after notice that he or she was a fugitive from labour, as aforesaid, shall, for either of the said offences, forfeit and pay the sum of five hundred dollars. Which penalty may be recovered by and for the benefit of such claimant, by action of debt, in any court proper to try the same; saving moreover to the person claiming such labour or service, his right of action for or on account of the said injuries or either of them.

H. The Missouri Compromise (1820)

An Act to authorize the people of the Missouri territory to form a constitution and state government, and for the admission of such state into the Union on an equal footing with the original states, and to prohibit slavery in certain territories.

Be it enacted by the Senate and House of Representatives of the United States of America, in Congress assembled, That the inhabitants of that portion of the Missouri territory included within the boundaries hereinafter designated, be, and they are hereby, authorized to form for themselves a constitution and state government, and to assume such name as they shall deem proper; and the said state, when formed, shall be admitted into the Union, upon an equal footing with the original states, in all respects whatsoever.

Sec. 2. *And be it further enacted*, That the said state shall consist of all the territory included within the following boundaries, to wit: Beginning in the middle of the Mississippi river, on the parallel of thirty-six degrees of north latitude; thence west, along that parallel of latitude, to the St. Francois river; thence up, and following the course of that river, in the middle of the main channel thereof, to the parallel of latitude of thirty-six degrees and thirty minutes; thence west, along the same, to a point where the said parallel is intersected by a meridian line passing through the middle of the mouth of the Kansas river, where the same empties into the Missouri river, thence, from the point aforesaid north, along the said meridian line, to the intersection of the parallel of latitude which passes through the rapids of the river Des Moines, making the said line to correspond with the Indian boundary line; thence east, from the point of intersection last aforesaid, along the said parallel of latitude, to the middle of the channel of the main fork of the said river Des Moines; thence down and along the middle of the main channel of the said river Des Moines, to the mouth of the same, where it empties into the Mississippi river; thence, due east, to the middle of the main channel of the Mississippi river; thence down, and following the course of the Mississippi river, in the middle of the main channel thereof, to the place of beginning: *Provided*, The said state shall ratify the boundaries aforesaid; *And provided also*, That the said state shall have concurrent jurisdiction on the river Mississippi, and every other river bordering on the said state, so far as the said rivers shall form a common boundary to the said state; and any other state or states, now or hereafter to be formed and bounded by the same, such rivers to be common to both; and that the river Mississippi, and the navigable rivers and waters leading into the same, shall be common highways, and for ever free, as well to the inhabitants of the said state as to other citizens of the United States, without any tax, duty, impost, or toll, therefor, imposed by the said state.

Sec. 3. *And be it further enacted*, That all free white male citizens of the United States, who shall have arrived at the age of twenty-one years, and have resided in said territory three months previous to the day of election, and all other persons qualified to vote for representatives to the general assembly of the said territory, shall be qualified to be elected, and they are hereby qualified and authorized to vote, and choose representatives to form a convention, who shall be apportioned amongst the several counties as follows. . . .

Sec. 8. *And be it further enacted*, That in all that territory ceded by France to the United States, under the name of Louisiana, which lies north of thirty-six degrees and thirty minutes north latitude, not included within the limits of the state, contemplated by this act, slavery and involuntary servitude, otherwise than in the punishment of crimes, whereof the parties shall have been duly convicted, shall be, and is hereby, forever prohibited, — *Provided always*, That any person escaping into the same, from whom labour or service is lawfully claimed, in any state or territory of the United States, such fugitive may be lawfully reclaimed and conveyed to the person claiming his or her labour or service as aforesaid.

I. The Fugitive Slave Act (1850)

. . . Sec. 5. That it shall be the duty of all marshals and deputy marshals to obey and execute all warrants and precepts issued under the provisions of this act, when to them directed; and should any marshal or deputy marshal refuse to receive such warrant, or other process, when tendered, or to use all proper means diligently to execute the same, he shall, on conviction thereof, be fined in the sum of one thousand dollars, to the use of such claimant . . . and after arrest of such fugitive, by such marshal or his deputy, or whilst at any time in his custody under the provisions of this act, should such fugitive escape, whether with or without the assent of such marshal or his deputy, such marshal shall be liable, on his official bond, to be prosecuted for the benefit of such claimant, for the full value of the service or labor of said fugitive in the State, Territory, or District whence he escaped: and the better to enable the said commissioners, when thus appointed, to execute their duties faithfully and efficiently, in conformity with the requirements of the Constitution of the United States and of this act, they are hereby authorized and empowered, within their counties respectively, to appoint, . . . any one or more suitable persons, from time to time, to execute all such warrants and other process as may be issued by them in the lawful performance of their respective duties; with authority to such commissioners, or the persons to be appointed by them, to execute process as aforesaid, to summon and call to their aid the bystanders, or *passe comustus* of the proper county, when necessary to ensure a faithful observance of the clause of the Constitution referred to, in conformity with the provisions of this act, and all good citizens are hereby commanded to aid and assist in the prompt and efficient execution of this law, whenever their services may be required, as aforesaid, for that purpose; and said warrants shall run, and be executed by said officers, any where in the State within which they are issued . . .

SEC.8 [I]n all cases where the proceedings are before a commissioner, he shall be entitled to a fee of ten dollars . . . the person or persons authorized to execute the process . . . shall also be entitled to a fee of five dollars each for each person he or they may arrest and take before any such commissioner.

J. The Emancipation Proclamation (January 1, 1863)

Whereas, on the twenty-second day of September, in the year of our Lord one thousand eight hundred and sixty-two, a proclamation was issued by the President of the United States, containing, among other things, the following, to wit:

"That on the first day of January, in the year of our Lord one thousand eight hundred and sixty-three, all persons held as slaves within any state or designated part of a state, the people whereof shall then be in rebellion against the United States, shall be then, thenceforward, and forever, free; and the Executive Government of the United States, including the military and naval authority thereof, will recognize and maintain the freedom of such persons, and will do no act or acts to repress such persons, or any of them, in any efforts they may make for their actual freedom.

"That the Executive will, on the first day of January aforesaid, by proclamation, designate the states and parts of states, if any, in which the people thereof, respectively, shall then be in rebellion against the United States; and the fact that any state, or the people thereof, shall on that day be in good faith represented in the Congress of the United States, by members chosen thereto at elections wherein a majority of the qualified voters of such states shall have participated, shall, in the absence of strong countervailing testimony, be deemed conclusive evidence that such state, and the people thereof, are not then in rebellion against the United States."

Now, therefore, I, Abraham Lincoln, President of the United States, by virtue of the power in me vested as commander-in-chief of the army and navy of the United States, in time of actual armed rebellion against the authority and Government of the United States, and as a fit and necessary war measure for suppressing said rebellion, do, on this first day of January, in the year of our Lord one thousand eight hundred and sixty-three, and in accordance with my purpose so to do, publicly proclaimed for the full period of one hundred days from the day first above mentioned, order and designate as the states and parts of states wherein the people thereof, respectively, are this day in rebellion against the United States, the following, to wit:

Arkansas, Texas, Louisiana, (except the parishes of St. Bernard, Plaquemines, Jefferson, St. John, St. Charles, St. James, Ascension, Assumption, Terre Bonne, Lafourche, St. Mary, St. martin, and Orleans, including the city of New Orleans,) Mississippi, Alabama, Florida, Georgia, South Carolina, North Carolina, and Virginia, (except the forty-eight counties designated as West Virginia, and also the counties of Berkeley, Accomac, Northampton, Elizabeth City, York, Princess Ann, and Norfolk, including the cities of Norfolk and Portsmouth,) and which excepted parts are for the present left precisely as if this proclamation were not issued.

And by virtue of the power and for the purpose aforesaid, I do order and declare that all persons held as slaves within said designated states and parts of states are, and henceforward shall be, free; and that the Executive Government of the United States, including the military and naval authorities thereof, will recognize and maintain the freedom of said persons.

And I hereby enjoin upon the people so declared to be free to abstain from all violence, unless in necessary self-defence; and I recommend to them that, in all cases when allowed, they labor faithfully for reasonable wages.

And I further declare and make known that such persons, of suitable condition, will be received into the armed service of the United States to garrison forts, positions, stations, and other places, and to man vessels of all sorts in said service.

And upon this act, sincerely believed to be an act of justice, warranted by the Constitution upon military necessity, I invoke the considerate judgment of mankind and the gracious favor of Almighty God.

In witness whereof, I have hereunto set my hand and caused the seal of the United States to be affixed.

Done at the city of Washington this first day of January, in the year of our Lord one thousand eight hundred and sixty-three, and of the Independence of the United States of America the eighty-seventh.

ABRAHAM LINCOLN.

K. The Freedmen's Bureau (March 3, 1865)

Be it enacted, That there is hereby established in the War Department, to continue during the present war of rebellion, and for one year thereafter, a bureau of refugees, freedmen, and abandoned lands, to which shall be committed, as hereinafter provided, the supervision and management of all abandoned lands, and the control of all subjects relating to refugees and freedmen from rebel states, or from any district of country within the territory embraced in the operations of the army, under such rules and regulations as may be prescribed by the head of the bureau and approved by the President. The said bureau shall be under the management and control of a commissioner to be appointed by the President, by and with the advice and consent of the Senate. . . .

SEC. 2. That the Secretary of War may direct such issues of provisions, clothing, and fuel, as he may deem needful for the immediate and temporary shelter and supply of destitute and suffering refugees and freedmen and their wives and children, under such rules and regulations as he may direct.

SEC. 3. That the President may, by and with the advice and consent of the Senate, appoint an assistant commissioner for each of the states declared to be in insurrection, not exceeding ten in number, who shall, under the direction of the commissioner, aid in the execution of the provisions of this act; . . . And any military officer may be detailed and assigned to duty under this act without increase of pay or allowances . . .

SEC. 4. That the commissioner, under the direction of the President, shall have authority to set apart, for the use of loyal refugees and freedmen, such tracts of land within the insurrectionary states as shall have been abandoned, or to which the United States shall have acquired title by confiscation or sale, or otherwise, and to every male citizen, whether refugee or freedman, as aforesaid, there shall be assigned not more than forty acres of such land, and the person to whom it was so assigned shall be protected in the use and enjoyment of the land for the term of three years at an annual rent not exceeding six per centum upon the value of such land, as it was appraised by the state authorities in the year eighteen hundred and sixty, for the purpose of taxation, and in case no such appraisal can be found, then the rental shall be based upon the estimated value of the land in said year, to be ascertained in such manner as the commissioner may by regulation prescribe. At the end of said term, or at any time during said term, the occupants of any parcels so assigned may purchase the land and receive such title thereto as the United states can convey, upon paying therefor the value of the land, as ascertained and fixed for the purpose of determining the annual rent aforesaid. . . .

L. Black Code of Mississippi (1865)

1. Civil Rights of Freedmen in Mississippi

SEC. 1. *Be it enacted*, . . . that all freedmen, free negroes, and mulattoes may sue and be sued, implead and be impleaded, in all the courts of law and equity of this State, and may acquire personal property, and chooses in action, by descent or purchase, and may dispose of the same in the same manner and to the same extent that white persons may: *Provided*, That the provisions of this section shall not be so construed as to allow any freedman, free negro, or mulatto to rent or lease any lands or tenements except in incorporated cities or towns, in which places the corporate authorities shall control the same. . . .

SEC. 3. . . . All freedmen, free negroes, or mulattoes who do now and have heretofore lived and cohabited together as husband and wife shall be taken and held in law as legally married, and the issue shall be taken and held as legitimate for all purposes; that it shall not be lawful for any freedman, free negro, or mulatto to intermarry with any white person; nor for any white person to intermarry with any freedman, free negro, or mulatto; and any person who shall so intermarry, shall be deemed guilty of felony, and on conviction thereof shall be confined in the State penitentiary for life; and those shall be deemed freedmen, free negroes, and mulattoes who are of pure negro blood, and those descended from a negro to the third generation, inclusive, though one ancestor in each generation may have been a white person . . .

SEC. 6. . . . All contracts for labor made with freedmen, free negroes, and mulattoes for a longer period than one month shall be in writing, and in duplicate, attested and read to said freedman, free negro, or mulatto by a beat, city or county officer, or two disinterested white persons of the county in which the labor is to be performed, of which each party shall have one; and said contracts shall be taken and held as entire contracts, and if the laborer shall quit the service of the employer before the expiration of his term of service, without good cause, he shall forfeit his wages for that year up to the time of quitting.

SEC. 7. . . . Every civil officer shall, and every person may, arrest and carry back to his or her legal employer any freedman, free negro, or mulatto who shall have quit the service of his or her employer before the expiration of his or her term of service without good cause; and said officer and person shall be entitled to receive for arresting and carrying back every deserting employee aforesaid the sum of five dollars, and ten cents per mile from the place of arrest to the place of delivery; and the same shall be paid by the employer, and held as a set-off for so much against the wages of said deserting employee: *Provided*, that said arrested party, after being so returned, may appeal to the justice of the peace or member of the board of police of the county, who, on notice to the alleged employer, shall try summarily whether said appellant is legally employed by the alleged employer, and has good cause to quit said employer; either party shall have the right of appeal to the county court, pending which the alleged deserter shall be remanded to the alleged employer or otherwise disposed of, as shall be right and just; and the decision of the county court shall be final. . . .

SEC. 9. . . . If any person shall persuade or attempt to persuade, entice, or cause any freedman, free negro, or mulatto to desert from the legal employment of any person before the expiration of his or her term of service, or shall knowingly employ any such deserting freedman, free negro, or mulatto, or shall knowingly give or sell to any such deserting freedman, free negro, or mulatto, any food, raiment, or other thing, he or she shall be guilty of a misdemeanor, and upon conviction, shall be fined not less than twenty-five dollars and not more than two hundred dollars and the costs; and if said fine and costs shall not be immediately paid, the court shall sentence said convict to not exceeding two months' imprisonment in the county jail, and he or she shall moreover be liable to the party injured in damages; *Provided*, if any person shall, or shall attempt to, persuade, entice, or cause any freedman, free negro, or mulatto to desert from any legal employment of any person, with the view to employ said freedman, free negro, or mulatto without the limits of this state, such person, on conviction, shall be fined not less than fifty dollars, and not more than five hundred dollars and costs; and if said fine and costs shall not be immediately paid, the court shall sentence said convict to not exceeding six months imprisonment in the county jail. . . .

2. Mississippi Apprentice Law

SEC. 1. . . . It shall be the duty of all sheriffs, justices of the peace, and other civil officers of the several counties in this State, to report to the probate courts of their respective counties semi-annually, at the January and July terms of said courts, all freedman, free negroes, and mulattoes, under the age of eighteen, in their respective counties, beats or districts, who are orphans, or whose parent or parents have not the means or who refuse to provide for and support said minors; and thereupon it shall be the duty of said probate court to order the clerk of said court to apprentice said minors to some competent and suitable person, on such terms as the court may direct, having a particular care to the interest of said minor: *Provided*, that the former owner of said minors shall have the preference when, in the opinion of the court, he or she shall be a suitable person for that purpose.

SEC. 2. . . . The said court shall be fully satisfied that the person or persons to whom said minor shall be apprenticed shall be a suitable person to have the charge and care of said minor, and fully to protect the interest of said minor. The said court shall require the said master or mistress to execute bond and security, payable to the state of Mississippi, conditioned that he or she shall furnish said minor with sufficient food and clothing; to treat said minor humanely; furnish medical attention in case of sickness; teach, or cause to be taught, him or her to read and write, if under fifteen years old, and will conform to any law that may be hereafter passed for the regulation of the duties and relation of master and apprentice. . . .

SEC. 3. . . . In the management and control of said apprentice, said master or mistress shall have the power to inflict such moderate corporal chastisement as a father or guardian is allowed to inflict on his or her child or ward at common law: *Provided*, that in no case shall cruel or inhuman punishment be inflicted.

Sec. 4. . . . If any apprentice shall leave the employment of his or her master or mistress, without his or her consent, said master or mistress may pursue and recapture said apprentice, and bring him or her before any justice of the peace of the county, whose duty it shall be to remand said apprentice to the service of his or her master or mistress; and in the event of a refusal on the part of said apprentice so to return, then said justice shall commit said apprentice to the jail of said county, on failure to give bond, to the next term of the county court; and it shall be the duty of said court at the first term thereafter to investigate said case, and if the court shall be of opinion that said apprentice left the employment of his or her master or mistress without good cause, to order him or her to be punished, as provided for the punishment of hired freedmen, as may be from time to time provided for by law for desertion, until he or she shall agree to return to the service of his or her master or mistress: . . . if the court shall believe that said apprentice had good cause to quit his said master or mistress, the court shall discharge said apprentice from said indenture, and also enter a judgment against the master or mistress for not more than one hundred dollars, for the use and benefit of said apprentice. . . .

3. Mississippi Vagrant Law

Sec. 2. . . . All freedmen, free negroes and mulattoes in this State, over the age of eighteen years, found on the second Monday in January, 1866, or thereafter, with no lawful employment or business, or found unlawfully assembling themselves together, either in the day or night time, and all white persons so assembling themselves with freedmen, free negroes or mulattoes, or usually associating with freedmen, free negroes or mulattoes, on terms of equality, or living in adultery or fornication with a freed woman, free negro or mulatto, shall be deemed vagrants, and on conviction thereof shall be fined in a sum not exceeding, in the case of a freedman, free negro or mulatto, fifty dollars, and a white man two hundred dollars, and imprisoned at the discretion of the court, the free negro not exceeding ten days, and the white man not exceeding six months. . . .

Sec. 7. . . . If any freedman, free negro, or mulatto shall fail or refuse to pay any tax levied according to the provisions of the sixth section of this act, it shall be *prima facie* evidence of vagrancy, and it shall be the duty of the sheriff to arrest such freedman, free negro, or mulatto or such person refusing or neglecting to pay such tax, and proceed at once to hire for the shortest time such delinquent taxpayer to any one who will pay the said tax, with accruing costs, giving preference to the employer, if there be one. . . .

4. Penal Laws of Mississippi

Sec. 1. *Be it enacted*, . . . that no freedman, free negro or mulatto, not in the military service of the United States government, and not licensed so to do by the board of police of his or her county, shall keep or carry fire-arms of any kind, or any ammunition, dirk or bowie knife, and on conviction thereof in the county court shall be punished by fine, not exceeding ten dollars, and pay the costs of such proceedings, and all such arms or ammunition shall be forfeited to the informer; and it shall be the duty of every civil and military officer to arrest any freedman, free negro, or mulatto found with any such arms or ammunition, and cause him or her to be committed to trial in default of bail.

Sec. 2. . . . Any freedman, free negro, or mulatto committing riots, routs, affrays, trespasses, malicious mischief, cruel treatment to animals, seditious speeches, insulting gestures, language, or acts, or assaults on any person, disturbance of the peace, exercising the function of a minister of the Gospel without a license from some regularly organized church, vending spirituous or intoxicating liquors, or committing any other misdemeanor, the punishment of which is not specifically provided for by law, shall, upon conviction thereof in the county court, be fined not less than ten dollars, and not more than one hundred dollars, and may be imprisoned at the discretion of the court, not exceeding thirty days.

Sec. 3. . . . If any white person shall sell, lend, or give to any freedman, free negro, or mulatto any firearms, dirk or bowie knife, or ammunition, or any spirituous or intoxicating liquors, such person or persons so offending, upon conviction thereof in the county court of his or her county, shall be fined not exceeding fifty dollars, and may be imprisoned, at the discretion of the court, not exceeding thirty days. . . .

Sec. 5. . . . If any freedman, free negro, or mulatto, convicted of any of the misdemeanors provided against in this act, shall fail or refuse for the space of five days, after conviction, to pay the fine and costs imposed, such person shall be hired out by the sheriff or other officer, at public outcry, to any white person who will pay said fine and all costs, and take said convict for the shortest time.

M. Indian Removal Act (May 28, 1830)

Be it enacted by the Senate and House of Representatives of the United States of America, in Congress assembled, That it shall and may be lawful for the President of the United States to cause so much of any territory belonging to the United States, west of the river Mississippi, not included in any state or organized territory, and to which the Indian title has been extinguished, as he may judge necessary, to be divided into a suitable number of districts, for the reception of such tribes or nations of Indians as may choose to exchange the lands where they now reside, and remove there; and to cause each of said districts to be so described by natural or artificial marks, as to be easily distinguished from every other.

Sec. 2. *And be it further enacted*, That it shall and may be lawful for the President to exchange any or all of such districts, so to be laid off and described, with any tribe or nation of Indians now residing within the limits of any of the states or territories, and with which the United States have existing treaties, for the whole or any part or portion of the territory claimed and occupied by such tribe or nation, within the bounds of any one or more of the states or territories, where the land claimed and occupied by the Indians, is owned by the United States, or the United States are bound to the state within which it lies to extinguish the Indian claim thereto.

SEC. 3. *And be it further enacted*, That in the making of any such exchange or exchanges, it shall and may be lawful for the President solemnly to assure the tribe or nation with which the exchange is made, that the United States will forever secure and guaranty to them, and their heirs or successors, the country so exchanged with them; and if they prefer it, that the United States will cause a patent or grant to be made and executed to them for the same: *Provided always*, That such lands shall revert to the United States, if the Indians become extinct, or abandon the same.

SEC. 4. *And be it further enacted*, That if, upon any of the lands now occupied by the Indians, and to be exchanged for, there should be such improvements as add value to the land claimed by any individual or individuals of such tribes or nations, it shall and may be lawful for the President to cause such value to be ascertained by appraisement or otherwise, and to cause such ascertained value to be paid to the person or persons rightfully claiming such improvements. And upon the payment of such valuation, the improvements so valued and paid for, shall pass to the United States, and possession shall not afterwards be permitted to any of the same tribe.

SEC. 5. *And be it further enacted*, That upon the making of any such exchange as is contemplated by this act, it shall and may be lawful for the President to cause such aid and assistance to be furnished to the emigrants as may be necessary and proper to enable them to remove to, and settle in, the country for which they may have exchanged; and also, to give them such aid and assistance as may be necessary for their support and subsistence for the first year after their removal.

SEC. 6. *And be it further enacted*, That it shall and may be lawful for the President to cause such tribe or nation to be protected, at their new residence, against all interruption or disturbance from any other tribe or nation of Indians, or from any other person or persons whatever.

SEC. 7. *And be it further enacted*, That it shall and may be lawful for the President to have the same superintendence and care over any tribe or nation in the country to which they may remove, as contemplated by this act, that he is now authorized to have over them at their present places of residence: *Provided*, That nothing in this act contained shall be construed as authorizing or directing the violation of any existing treaty between the United States and any of the Indian tribes.

SEC. 8. *And be it further enacted*, That for the purpose of giving effect to the provisions of this act, the sum of five hundred thousand dollars is hereby appropriated, to be paid out of any money in the treasury, not otherwise appropriated.

N. Executive Order 8802 (June 25, 1941)

WHEREAS it is the policy of the United States to encourage full participation in the national defense program by all citizens of the United States, regardless of race, creed, color, or national origin, in the firm belief that the democratic way of life within the Nation can be defended successfully only with the help and support of all groups within its borders;

WHEREAS there is evidence that available and needed workers have been barred from employment in industries engaged in defense production solely because of considerations of race, creed, color, or national origin, to the detriment of workers' morale and of national unity:

Now, THEREFORE, by virtue of the authority vested in me by the Constitution and the statutes, and as a prerequisite to the successful conduct of our national defense production effort, I do hereby reaffirm the policy of the United States that there shall be no discrimination in the employment of workers in defense industries or government because of race, creed, color, or national origin, and I do hereby declare that it is the duty of employers and of labor organizations, in furtherance of said policy and of this order, to provide for the full and equitable participation of all workers in defense industries, without discrimination because of race, creed, color, or national origin;

And it is hereby ordered as follows:

1. All departments and agencies of the Government of the United States concerned with vocational and training programs for defense production shall take special measures appropriate to assure that such programs are administered without discrimination because of race, creed, color, or national origin;

2. All contracting agencies of the Government of the United States shall include in all defense contracts hereafter negotiated by them a provision obligating the contractor not to discriminate against any worker because of race, creed, color, or national origin;

3. There is established in the Office of Production Management a Committee on Fair Employment Practice, which shall consist of a chairman and four other members to be appointed by the President. The Chairman and members of the Committee shall serve as such without compensation but shall be entitled to actual and necessary transportation, subsistence and other expenses incidental to performance of their duties. The Committee shall receive and investigate complaints of discrimination in violation of the provisions of this order and shall take appropriate steps to redress grievances which it finds to be valid. The Committee shall also recommend to the several departments and agencies of the Government of the United States and to the president all measures which may be deemed by it necessary or proper to effectuate the provisions of this order.

O. Executive Order 9981 (July 26, 1948)

It is hereby declared to be the policy of the President that there shall be equality of treatment and opportunity for all persons in the armed forces without regard to race color, religion, or national origin. This policy shall be put into effect as rapidly as possible, having due regard to the time required to effectuate any necessary changes without impairing efficiency or morale.

P. Southern Manifesto (March 1956)

The Declaration of Constitutional Principles (known informally as the Southern Manifesto) was written in March 1956, in the United States Congress, in opposition to racial integration of public places. The manifesto was signed by 101 congressmen (99 Southern Democrats and two Republicans) from Alabama, Arkansas, Florida, Georgia, Louisiana, Mississippi, North Carolina, South Carolina, Tennessee, Texas, and Virginia. The document was drafted to counter the landmark Supreme Court decision in *Brown v. Board of Education*, which determined that government required segregation of public schools was unconstitutional.

Q. § 2000a of the Civil Rights Act of 1964 (Public Accommodations)

To combat pervasive segregation in all places of public accommodation [schools, government, parks, as well as private facilities like gas stations, sporting events, pool rooms, taverns, hotels, restaurants, etc.] Act generally outlaws discrimination because of "race, color, religion, or national origin," in any arena affecting interstate commerce. At its core, the Act was calculated to "eliminate the inconvenience, unfairness and humiliation of racial discrimination."

R. § 2000d of Title VI of the Civil Rights Act of 1964 (Federally Assisted Programs)

The Act was designed to root out discrimination in any "program or activity receiving federal financial assistance." The Act was passed pursuant to Congress' spending power, which allows Congress to set conditions on receipt of federal funds, as well as under the Fourteenth and Thirteenth Amendments.

By definition, Title VI reaches a wide range of discriminatory practices [e.g. occurring in recreational facilities, health care programs, political parties, banks, schools, agencies, child care programs], and places the duty on federal officers to enforce its terms. A federal agency may threaten to terminate funding to violating entities, but must first seek voluntary compliance.

S. § 2000e-2 of Title VII of the Civil Rights Act of 1964 (Employment)

It shall be an unlawful employment practice for an employer to fail or refuse to hire or to discharge any individual . . . because of his race.

T. Voting Rights Act of 1965

SEC. 2. No voting qualification or prerequisite to voting, or standard, practice, or procedure shall be imposed or applied by any State or political subdivision to deny or abridge the right of any citizen of the United States to vote on account of race or color.

SEC. 3. (a) Whenever the Attorney General institutes a proceeding under any statute to enforce the guarantees of the Fifteenth Amendment in any State or political subdivision the court shall authorize the appointment of Federal examiners by the United States Civil Service Commission, in accordance with section 6, to serve for such period of time and for such political subdivisions as the court shall determine is appropriate to enforce the guarantees of the Fifteenth Amendment (1) as part of any interlocutory order if the court determines that the appointment of such examiners is necessary to enforce such guarantees or (2) as part of any final judgment if the court finds that violations of the Fifteenth Amendment justifying equitable relief have occurred in such State or subdivision: *Provided,* That the court need not authorize the appointment of examiners if any incidents of denial or abridgement of the right to vote on account of race or color (1) have been few in number and have been promptly and effectively corrected by State or local action, (2) the continuing effect of such incidents has been eliminated, and (3) there is no reasonable probability of their recurrence in the future.

(b) If in a proceeding instituted by the Attorney General under any statute to enforce the guarantees of the Fifteenth Amendment in any state or political subdivision the court finds that a test or device has been used for the purpose or with the effect of denying or abridging the right of any citizen of the United States to vote on account of race or color, it shall suspend the use of tests and devices in such State or political subdivisions as the court shall determine is appropriate and for such period as it deems necessary.

(c) If in any proceeding instituted by the Attorney General under any statute to enforce the guarantees of the Fifteenth Amendment in any state or political subdivision the court finds that violations of the Fifteenth Amendment justifying equitable relief have occurred within the territory of such State or political subdivision, the court, in addition to such relief as it may grant, shall retain jurisdiction for such period as it may deem appropriate and during such period no voting qualification or prerequisite to voting, or standard, practice, or procedure with respect to voting different from that in force or effect at the time the proceeding was commenced shall be enforced unless and until the court finds that such qualification, prerequisite, standard, practice, or procedure does not have the purpose and will not have the effect of denying or abridging the right to vote on account of race or color: *Provided,* That such qualification, prerequisite, standard, practice, or procedure may be enforced if the qualification, prerequisite, standard, practice, or procedure has been submitted by the chief legal officer or other appropriate official of such State or subdivision to the Attorney General and the Attorney General has not interposed an objection within sixty days after such submission, except that neither the court's finding nor the Attorney General's failure to object shall bar a subsequent action to enjoin enforcement of such qualification, prerequisite, standard, practice, or procedure . . .

SEC. 4. When Congress enacted the Voting Rights Act of 1965, it determined that racial discrimination in voting had been more prevalent in certain areas of the country. Section 4(a) of the Act established a formula to identify those areas and to provide for more stringent remedies where appropriate. The first of these targeted remedies was a five-year suspension of "a test or device," such as a literacy test as a prerequisite to register to vote. The second was the requirement for review under Section 5 of any change affecting voting made by a covered area either by the United States District Court for the District of Columbia or by the Attorney General. The third was the ability of the Attorney General to certify that specified jurisdictions also required the appointment of federal examiners. These examiners would prepare and forward lists of persons qualified to vote. The final remedy under the special provisions is the authority of the Attorney General to send federal observers to those jurisdictions that have been certified for federal examiners.

THE FORMULA FOR COVERAGE UNDER SECTION 4 OF THE VOTING RIGHTS ACT

As enacted in 1965, the first element in the formula was whether, on November 1, 1964, the state or a political subdivision of the state maintained a "test or device" restricting the opportunity to register and vote. The Act's definition of a test or device included such requirements as the applicant being able to pass a literacy test, establish that he or she had good moral character, or have another registered voter vouch for his or her qualification.

The second element of the formula would be satisfied if the Director of the Census determined that less than 50 percent of persons of voting age were registered to vote on November 1, 1964, or that less than 50 percent of persons of voting age voted in the presidential election of November 1964. This resulted in the following states becoming, in their entirety, certain "covered jurisdictions": Alabama, Alaska, Georgia, Louisiana, Mississippi, South Carolina, and Virginia. In addition, political subdivisions (usually counties) in four other states (Arizona, Hawaii, Idaho, and North Carolina) were covered. In fully covered states, the state itself and all political subdivisions of the state are subject to the special provisions. In "partially covered" states, the special provisions applied only to the identified counties. Voting changes adopted by or to be implemented in covered political subdivisions, including changes applicable to the state as a whole, are subject to review under section 5.

In 1970, Congress recognized the continuing need for the special provisions of the Act, which were due to expire that year, and renewed them for another five years. It added a second prong to the coverage formula, identical to the original formula except that it referenced November 1968 as the relevant date for the maintenance of a test or device and the levels of voter registration and electoral participation. This addition to the formula resulted in the partial covered states, including Alaska,

Arizona, California, Connecticut, Idaho, Maine, Massachusetts, New Hampshire, and Wyoming. Half of these states (Connecticut, Idaho, Maine, Massachusetts, and Wyoming) filed successful "bailout" lawsuits.

In 1975, the Act's special provisions were extended for another seven years, and were broadened to address voting discrimination against members of "language minority groups," which were defined as persons who are American Indian, Asian American, Alaskan Natives or of Spanish heritage." As before, Congress expanded the coverage formula, based on the presence of tests or devices and levels of voter registration and participation as of November 1972. In addition, the 1965 definition of "test or device" was expanded to include the practice of providing any election information, including ballots, only in English in states or political subdivisions where members of a single language minority constituted more than five percent of the citizens of voting age. This third prong of the coverage formula had the effect of covering Alaska, Arizona, and Texas in their entirety, and parts of California, Florida, Michigan, New York, North Carolina and South Dakota.

In 1982, the coverage formula was extended again, this time for 25 years, but no changes were made to it. In 2006, the coverage formula was again extended for 25 years.

TERMINATING COVERAGE UNDER THE ACT'S SPECIAL PROVISIONS

Section 4 also provides that a jurisdiction may terminate or "bailout" from coverage under the Act's special provisions. Originally enacted in 1965 as a means to remedy any possible over inclusiveness resulting from application of the trigger formula. Congress amended this procedure in 1982 so jurisdictions that meet the statutory standards can obtain relief. The amendment which took effect on August 5, 1984, establishes an "objective" measure to determine whether the jurisdiction is entitled to "bailout".

Before being allowed to "bailout", the jurisdiction must have eliminated those voting procedures and methods of election that inhibit or dilute equal access to the electoral process. It also must demonstrate that it has made constructive efforts to eliminate intimidation and harassment of persons seeking to register and vote and expand opportunities for voter participation, such as opportunities for registration and voting, and to appoint minority officials throughout the jurisdiction and at all levels of the stages of the electoral process. The jurisdiction must also present evidence of minority electoral participation.

U. § 3601 of the Fair Housing Act of 1968 (Housing)

"It is the policy of the United States to provide, within constitutional limitations, for fair housing throughout the United States." The Act further provides that it is unlawful to deny "a dwelling to any person because of race, color, religion, sex, familial status or national origin," or "to discriminate in the terms . . . or in the provision of services or facilities" associated with the sale of real estate.

The purpose of the statute was to promote "open, integrated, residential housing patterns and to prevent the increase of segregation, in ghettoes, of racial groups whose lack of opportunities the Act was designed to combat."

V. Restitution for World War II Internment of Japanese Americans and Aleuts (August 10, 1988)

(a) With regard to individuals of Japanese ancestry

The Congress recognizes that, as described by the Commission on Wartime Relocation and Internment of Civilians, a grave injustice was done to both citizens and permanent resident aliens of Japanese ancestry by the evacuation, relocation, and internment of civilians during World War II. As the Commission documents, these actions were carried out without adequate security reasons and without any acts of espionage or sabotage documented by the Commission, and were motivated largely by racial prejudice, wartime hysteria, and a failure of political leadership. The excluded individuals of Japanese ancestry suffered enormous damages, both material and intangible, and there were incalculable losses in education and job training, all of which resulted in significant human suffering for which appropriate compensation has not been made. For these fundamental violations of the basic civil liberties and constitutional rights of these individuals of Japanese ancestry, the Congress apologizes on behalf of the Nation.

W. Senate Resolution Apologizing for the Enslavement and Racial Segregation of African Americans (June 11, 2009)

MR. HARKIN (for himself, MR. BROWNBACK, MR. LEVIN, MR. DURBIN, MR. KENNEDY, MR. LAUTENBERG, MS. STABENOW, MR. BOND, and MR. COCHRAN) submitted the following concurrent resolution; which was ordered held at the desk.

Concurrent Resolution

Apologizing for the enslavement and racial segregation of African-Americans.

Whereas, during the history of the Nation, the United States has grown into a symbol of democracy and freedom around the world;

Whereas the legacy of African-Americans is interwoven with the very fabric of the democracy and freedom of the United States;

Whereas millions of Africans and their descendants were enslaved in the United States and the 13 American colonies from 1619 through 1865;

Whereas Africans forced into slavery were brutalized, humiliated, dehumanized, and subjected to the indignity of being stripped of their names and heritage;

Whereas many enslaved families were torn apart after family members were sold separately;

Whereas the system of slavery and the visceral racism against people of African descent upon which it depended became enmeshed in the social fabric of the United States;

Whereas slavery was not officially abolished until the ratification of the 13th amendment to the Constitution of the United States in 1865, after the end of the Civil War;

Whereas after emancipation from 246 years of slavery, African-Americans soon saw the fleeting political, social, and economic gains they made during Reconstruction eviscerated by virulent racism, lynchings, disenfranchisement, Black Codes, and racial segregation laws that imposed a rigid system of officially sanctioned racial segregation in virtually all areas of life;

Whereas the system of de jure racial segregation known as 'Jim Crow,' which arose in certain parts of the United States after the Civil War to create separate and unequal societies for Whites and African-Americans, was a direct result of the racism against people of African descent that was engendered by slavery;

Whereas the system of Jim Crow laws officially existed until the 1960s—a century after the official end of slavery in the United States—until Congress took action to end it, but the vestiges of Jim Crow continue to this day;

Whereas African-Americans continue to suffer from the consequences of slavery and Jim Crow laws—long after both systems were formally abolished—through enormous damage and loss, both tangible and intangible, including the loss of human dignity and liberty;

Whereas the story of the enslavement and de jure segregation of African-Americans and the dehumanizing atrocities committed against them should not be purged from or minimized in the telling of the history of the United States;

Whereas those African-Americans who suffered under slavery and Jim Crow laws, and their descendants, exemplify the strength of the human character and provide a model of courage, commitment, and perseverance;

Whereas, on July 8, 2003, during a trip to Goree Island, Senegal, a former slave port, President George W. Bush acknowledged the continuing legacy of slavery in life in the United States and the need to confront that legacy, when he stated that slavery 'was . . . one of the greatest crimes of history. . . . The racial bigotry fed by slavery did not end with slavery or with segregation. And many of the issues that still trouble America have roots in the bitter experience of other times. But however long the journey, our destiny is set: liberty and justice for all';

Whereas President Bill Clinton also acknowledged the deep-seated problems caused by the continuing legacy of racism against African-Americans that began with slavery, when he initiated a national dialogue about race;

Whereas an apology for centuries of brutal dehumanization and injustices cannot erase the past, but confession of the wrongs committed and a formal apology to African-Americans will help bind the wounds of the Nation that are rooted in slavery and can speed racial healing and reconciliation and help the people of the United States understand the past and honor the history of all people of the United States;

Whereas the legislatures of the Commonwealth of Virginia and the States of Alabama, Florida, Maryland, and North Carolina have taken the lead in adopting resolutions officially expressing appropriate remorse for slavery, and other state legislatures are considering similar resolutions; and

Whereas it is important for the people of the United States, who legally recognized slavery through the Constitution and the laws of the United States, to make a formal apology for slavery and for its successor, Jim Crow, so they can move forward and seek reconciliation, justice, and harmony for all people of the United States: Now, therefore, be it

Resolved by the Senate (the House of Representatives concurring), That the sense of the Congress is the following:

(1) APOLOGY FOR THE ENSLAVEMENT AND SEGREGATION OF AFRICAN-AMERICANS—The Congress—

(A) acknowledges the fundamental injustice, cruelty, brutality, and inhumanity of slavery and Jim Crow laws;

(B) apologizes to African-Americans on behalf of the people of the United States, for wrongs committed against them and their ancestors who suffered under slavery and Jim Crow laws; and

(C) expresses its recommitment to the principle that all people are created equal and endowed with inalienable rights to life, liberty, and the pursuit of happiness, and calls on all people of the United States to work toward eliminating racial prejudices, injustices, and discrimination from our society.

(2) DISCLAIMER—Nothing in this resolution—

(A) authorizes or supports any claim against the United States; or

(B) serves as a settlement of any claim against the United States.

XXXI. History Timeline

The Earliest Known Record Dating the Arrival of blacks at an American Colony (1619)

(John Rolfe, Secretary and Recorder of the Virginia Colony noting the arrival by boat and sale to the colony of 20 Africans).

The Earliest Protest Against Slavery (1688)

(Meeting held by Quakers disparaging the institution of slavery and those who participated in it).

The Declaration of the Causes and Necessity of Taking Up Arms (1775)

(Stating grievances, including taxation without representation, by the colonies against Great Britain).

The Declaration of Independence (1776)

(Declaring colonial independence from Great Britain and stating that all men are created equal and are endowed by their creator with certain inalienable rights).

The Revolutionary War (1776–1781)

(A war to secure colonial independence from Great Britain).

The Articles of Confederation (1781–1788)

(A failed attempt at federal authority over the colonies).

The Northwest Ordinance (1789)

(A law for the government of the Territory of the United States northwest of the Ohio River that included a prohibition on slavery).

The Constitution of the United States (1789)

(Delineating the rules governing inhabitants of the United States including several provisions sanctioning the institution of slavery and vesting legislative power to the Congress of the United States, executive power to the President of the United States, and judicial power to the Supreme Court of the United States).

The Fugitive Slave Act (1793)

(A law implementing the return of fugitives from justice and slaves escaping from the service of their owners).

State v. Boon, 11 N.C. 246 (1801)

(Holding that it was not a crime for a white person to kill a slave).

Hudgins v. Wrights, 11 Va. 134 (1806)

(Holding that slavery or freedom depended upon the status of one's mother at the time of birth, and declaring that there was a presumption in the law that if a person looked white, then he was presumed free, and if he looked black, then he was presumed to be a slave).

The Missouri Compromise (1820)

(A law to authorize the people of the Missouri Territory to form a state government and to be admitted into the Union as a slave state on an equal footing with the original states, providing that for each slave state admitted to the Union a corresponding free state must also be admitted).

Johnson v. McIntosh, 21 U.S. 543 (1823)

(Holding that without Congressional authorization, American Indians had no legal authority under the Constitution to convey title of land to private individuals that could be recognized in an American court).

State v. Mann, 13 N.C. 263 (1829)

(Holding that cruel and unreasonable battery on a slave by the hirer is not indictable because of the recognition of full dominance of the owner over the slave except where the exercise of it is forbidden by statute).

The Indian Removal Act (1830)

(A law providing for an exchange of lands with the American Indians residing in any of the states or territories in the East, and for their removal west of the Mississippi River).

The Cherokee Nation v. Georgia, 30 U.S. 1 (1831)

(Holding that American Indians do not constitute a foreign nation entitled to the rights and privileges thereof).

Crandall v. Connecticut, Conn. Rep. 339 (1834)

The issue in this case was whether blacks were citizens under the Constitution.

(The lower court ruled that blacks were not citizens. The appellate court did not reach a decision on the merits but dismissed the case on a technicality).

The United States v. Amistad, 40 U.S. 518 (1841)

The issue in this case was whether captured blacks born in Africa were the property of slave-owners. (Holding that the captured blacks were free due to the Congressional prohibition of the international slave trade).

Prigg v. The Commonwealth of Pennsylvania, 41 U.S. 539 (1842)

(Holding that the Pennsylvania law prohibiting the forcible removal of escaped slaves from the state violated the Fugitive Slave Clause of the Constitution).

The Commonwealth of Virginia v. Jones, 43 Va. (2 Gratt.) 477 (1845)

(Holding that cohabitation of a white man with a slave was not a common law crime but was punishable under the criminal code).

Abolitionist Frederick Douglass publishes his autobiography, *Narrative of the Life of Frederick Douglass, an American Slave* **(1845)**

(Describing slavery and how Douglass escaped to freedom).

The Treaty of Guadalupe Hidalgo (1848)

(The Treaty settled the war between the United States and Mexico by drawing the boundary line between the two countries at the Rio Grande River and providing for the sale of vast portions of land from Mexico to the United States).

Roberts v. The City of Boston, 59 Mass. 198 (1850)

The issue in this case was whether race segregation was reasonable. (Holding that based on tradition, segregation was reasonable and, therefore, lawful).

The Fugitive Slave Act (1850)

(A law—amending the first fugitive slave act making it easier to return fugitive slaves).

Souther v. The Commonwealth of Virginia, 48 Va. 673 (1851)

The issue in this case was whether the slave-owner who fatally beat his slave was liable for murder. (Holding that under certain rare circumstances, a slave-owner could be convicted for murdering his slave).

Harriet Beecher Stowe publishes her novel *Uncle Tom's Cabin; or, Life Among the Lowly* **(1852)**

(Describing slavery and slave life in brutal detail).

People v. Hall, 4 Cal. 399 (1854)

(Holding that the term "black" includes all those not classified as white).

Scott v. Sandford, 60 U.S. 393 (1857)

The issue in this case was whether a person of African descent could be a citizen of the United States. (Holding that Scott was not a citizen within the meaning of the Constitution of the United States, and, therefore, not entitled to sue in its courts).

George v. State, 37 Miss. 316 (1859)

(Holding that it was not a crime to rape a slave woman).

The Civil War (1860–1865)

(A war between Northern and Southern states over the withdrawal of some Southern states from the Union and disagreements over the abolishment of slavery).

The Emancipation Proclamation (1863)

(Executive order by President Abraham Lincoln that those held in slavery in states in rebellion are free, and that the government "will recognize and maintain" their freedom).

The Thirteenth Amendment (1865)

(Prohibiting slavery and involuntary servitude and giving Congress the authority to enforce the prohibitions).

The Freedman's Bureau Act (1865)

(A law to establish financial and social assistance to freed slaves and refugees).

The Black Code of Mississippi (1865)

(Creation of state laws impeding the civil rights of freed slaves in Mississippi).

The Civil Rights Act (1866)

(Declaring that all persons born in the United States including former slaves are citizens; prohibiting racial discrimination in the sale or lease of land, the issuance and enforcement of contracts, the bringing of law suits and presentment of testimony, and all other laws and proceedings for the security of person and property; and, providing that the federal courts would have jurisdiction over all disputes under the Act and could punish any persons in violation).

The Fourteenth Amendment (1868)

(Declaring that all persons born in the United States are citizens, guaranteeing them equal protection of the laws, due process, and privileges and immunities of citizenship, and giving Congress the authority to enforce the provisions).

The Fifteenth Amendment (1870)

(Prohibiting racial discrimination in voting and giving Congress the authority to enforce the prohibition).

The Enforcement Act (1870)

(A re-enactment of the jurisdictional component of the Civil Rights Act of 1866 providing that the federal courts would have jurisdiction over all disputes involving alleged violations of the civil and constitutional rights of African Americans and resident Chinese aliens).

Hiram Rhodes Revels becomes a United States Senator representing Mississippi (1870)

(Becoming the first African American to hold a seat in the Senate).

The Slaughterhouse Cases, 16 Wall. 36 (1873)

(Holding that a Louisiana statute creating one slaughterhouse in the state for all butchers did not violate the Thirteenth or Fourteenth Amendment because of narrow definitions given to the terms contained in the amendments).

The Civil Rights Act (1875)

(Prohibiting racial discrimination in public accommodations).

United States v. Cruikshank, 92 U.S. 542 (1875)

(Holding that the United States did not show that it was the intent of the defendants, by their conspiracy, to injure and murder black members of the Republican Party or to hinder or prevent the enjoyment of any right granted or secured by the Constitution).

Article XIX of the California State Constitution (1879)

(Placing severe hiring restrictions on state corporations that sought to hire resident alien Chinese laborers) (subsequently invalidated by a federal circuit court in 1880).

Strauder v. West Virginia, 100 U.S. 303 (1880)

(Holding that a state law barring African Americans from jury service violated the Equal Protection Clause of the Fourteenth Amendment).

The Civil Rights Cases, 109 U.S. 3 (1883)

The issue in these cases was the constitutionality of exclusionary laws prohibiting Blacks access to public accommodations. (Holding that Congress did not have the authority to prohibit racial discrimination in public accommodations under either the Thirteenth or Fourteenth Amendment).

Elk v. Wilkins, 112 U.S. 94 (1884)

This case involved an action brought by an American Indian residing in Nebraska, against the registrar of one of the wards of the city of Omaha, for refusing to register him as a qualified voter. (Holding that the plaintiff, not being a citizen of the United States under the Fourteenth Amendment of the Constitution because he was an American Indian, has been deprived of no right secured by the Fifteenth Amendment).

Yick Wo v. Hopkins, 118 U.S. 356 (1886)

(Holding that Chinese persons, born outside of the United States and remaining subjects of the Emperor of China, are "subject to the jurisdiction thereof" under the meaning of the Fourteenth Amendment including the protection of the federal government in the same sense as all other aliens residing in the United States).

Ping v. United States, 130 U.S. 581 (1889)

This case involved an appeal of the validity of the act of Congress of October 1, 1888, prohibiting Chinese laborers from entering the United States. (Holding that Congress retained plenary power under the Constitution to exclude aliens and that Congress could exercise such power on any reasonable basis it chose including nationality).

The Geary Act (1892)

(Requiring resident Chinese aliens to have either a certificate of residence issued by the collector of internal revenue or testimony of a white witness).

Ting v. United States, 149 U.S. 698 (1893)

(Holding that the provisions of the Geary Act were within the powers of Congress and did not violate the Constitution).

W.E.B. DuBois completes his doctoral degree at Harvard University (1895)

(Dubois is the first African American to receive a PhD from Harvard; his lifetime of research, writing, advocacy, and teaching explored and documented racism in the twentieth century).

Plessy v. Ferguson, 163 U.S. 537 (1896)

(Creating the "separate but equal" doctrine that permitted states to separate people on the basis of race in railroad cars, and in all social activities and public accommodations. The "separate but equal" doctrine becomes the basis of Jim Crow laws, state and local laws that imposed racial segregation).

United States v. Ark, 169 U.S. 649 (1898)

The issue in this case was whether a child, born in the United States of parents of Chinese descent who were not American citizens, becomes at the time of his or her birth a citizen of the United States. (Holding that such a child is a citizen of the United States within the meaning of the Fourteenth Amendment).

Cumming v. County Board of Education, 175 U.S. 528 (1899)

(Affirming a decision refusing an injunction against a local board of education to prevent maintenance of a high school for white children without also maintaining one for black children).

Berea College v. Commonwealth of Kentucky, 211 U.S. 45 (1908)

(Upholding the validity of a 1904 Kentucky statute that prohibited a private college from teaching white and black pupils in the same classroom).

The California Alien Land Law (1913)

(Placing restrictions on aliens owning land within the state).

World War I (1914–1918)

(Major military confrontation between Germany, Austria, the United States, Great Britain and France. United States military forces were segregated by race).

Buchanan v. Warley, 245 U.S. 60 (1917)

(Striking down racial segregation ordinances in housing as a violation of the Due Process Clause of the Fourteenth Amendment).

Ozawa v. United States, 260 U.S. 178 (1922)

(Holding that Japanese are not considered white for purposes of immigration and naturalization law).

Lum v. Rice, 275 U.S. 78 (1927)

(Holding that the Equal Protection Clause of the Fourteenth Amendment does not prohibit the state from placing Asian Americans and African Americans in the same school under a two-school segregation program where one school is for whites and the other school is for everyone else).

Charles Curtis is elected Vice President of the United States (1928)

(Becoming the first person with American Indian ancestry to hold this position).

Octaviano Larrazolo is elected to the United States Senate representing New Mexico (1928)

(Becoming the first Latino/a member of the Senate).

Gaines v. Canada, 305 U.S. 337 (1938)

(Declaring that the Equal Protection Clause of the Fourteenth Amendment must be satisfied within the confines of a particular state).

The Executive Order 8802 (1941)

(Reaffirming the policy of full participation in the defense program by all persons, regardless of race, creed, color, or national origin, and directing certain action in furtherance of the policy).

World War II (1942–1945)

(Major military confrontation between the Axis Powers, Germany, Italy, and Japan and the Allied Powers, the United States, Britain, France, China, and the Soviet Union. United States military forces were segregated by race).

Korematsu v. United States, 321 U.S. 760 (1944)

(Holding that the Equal Protection Clause of the Fourteenth Amendment did not prevent the government's forcible internment of thousands of Americans of Japanese ancestry).

Morgan v. Commonwealth of Virginia, 328 U.S. 373 (1946)

(Holding that racial segregation on interstate buses and trains violated the Commerce Clause).

Jackie Robinson makes his debut in Major League Baseball (1947)

(Becoming the first African American player in the League since the early 1900s).

The Executive Order 9981 (1948)

(Desegregating the armed forces of the United States and requiring equality of treatment without regard to race).

Shelley v. Kraemer, 334 U.S. 1 (1948)

(Holding that judicial enforcement of racially restrictive covenants violated the Equal Protection Clause of the Fourteenth Amendment).

McLaurin v. Oklahoma State Regents for Higher Education, 339 U.S. 637 (1950)

(Declaring that the Equal Protection Clause of the Fourteenth Amendment requires that, once admitted, a black student must be treated the same as other students including no racial segregation within the institution).

Sweatt v. Painter, 339 U.S. 629 (1950)

(Holding that new, underfunded, graduate schools for blacks violated the Equal Protection Clause of the Fourteenth Amendment and would not be viewed as the constitutional equivalent to the long-established, well-endowed, and highly esteemed schools that had been open to all other races for decades).

Hernandez v. Texas, 347 U.S. 475 (1954)

(Holding that Mexican Americans may be a distinct group under certain circumstances for purposes of applying the Equal Protection Clause of the Fourteenth Amendment).

Brown v. Board of Education (Brown I), 347 U.S. 483 (1954)

(Holding that *de jure* racial segregation in education violated the Equal Protection Clause of the Fourteenth Amendment).

Brown v. Board of Education (Brown II), 349 U.S. 294 (1955)

(Mandating desegregation of previously *de jure* segregated schools).

Dr. Martin Luther King, Jr. leads the Montgomery, Alabama, bus boycott (1955)

(Mass strike opposing racial segregation on public buses).

Declaration of Constitutional Principles (commonly known as the Southern Manifesto) (1956)

(A written public statement signed by 101 Congresspersons *requesting* the reversal of *Brown I* and opposing racial integration in public accommodations and schools).

Dalip Singh Saund is elected to the United States House of Representatives representing a central California district (1957)

(Becoming the first Indian American member of Congress).

Daniel Inouye is elected to the United States House of Representatives representing Hawaii (1959)

(Becoming the first Japanese American member of Congress).

Hiram Fong is elected to the United States Senate representing Hawaii (1959)
(Becoming the first Chinese American member of the Senate).

The Civil Rights Movement (1960–1970)
(Mass protests by blacks, other racial minorities, and whites against continuing racial discrimination and segregation).

A. Leon Higginbotham, Jr. appointed by President John F. Kennedy to the Federal Trade Commission (1962)
(Becoming the first African American appointed to a federal commission).

Dr. Martin Luther King, Jr. delivers his speech, "*I Have a Dream*," on the steps of the Lincoln Memorial at the culmination of the March on Washington, protesting racial oppression (1963)
(The following year, he is awarded the Nobel Peace Prize for working to end racial segregation and discrimination through non-violent means).

Title II of the Civil Rights Act (1964)
(Providing for desegregation in all places of public accommodation).

Title VI of the Civil Rights Act (1964)
(Enacted to prevent discrimination in federally funded activities or programs).

Title VII of the Civil Rights Act (1964)
(Proscribes employment discrimination based on race, color, religion, sex or national origin).

The Voting Rights Act (1965)
(Preventing states from imposing any voting qualifications or prerequisites to voting that would deny the rights of any United States citizens to vote on account of race or color).

***Loving v. Virginia*, 388 U.S. 1 (1966)**
(Holding that a state law barring interracial marriage violated the Equal Protection Clause of the Fourteenth Amendment).

Robert C. Weaver becomes Secretary of Housing and Urban Development, a cabinet position under President Lyndon Johnson (1966)
(Becoming the first African American to serve in a presidential cabinet).

Thurgood Marshall is appointed to the United States Supreme Court (1967)
(Becoming the first African American member of the Court).

Fair Housing Act (1968)
(Providing that it was unlawful to deny housing to anyone based on race, sex, color, religion, familial status or national origin).

Milliken v. Bradley, 418 U.S. 717 (1974)

(Limiting desegregation remedies to intra-district solutions absent a showing of *de jure* segregation between districts or throughout the entire state).

Batson v. Kentucky, 476 U.S. 79 (1986)

(Requiring prosecutors to provide a non-racial explanation for exclusion during jury selection).

Martin Luther King, Jr. Day is celebrated as a national holiday (1986)

(Becoming the first African American recognized with a federal holiday).

McCleskey v. Kemp, 481 U.S. 279 (1987)

The issue in this case was whether a complex statistical study, which indicated a high probability that racial considerations enter into capital sentencing determinations proves that McCleskey's capital sentence is unconstitutional under the Fourteenth Amendment. (Holding that the risk of racial bias posed by this statistical study does not make McCleskey's capital sentence unconstitutional).

Civil Liberties Act — Restitution for World War II Internment of Japanese Americans and Aleuts (1988)

(Providing an apology for the relocation and internment of Japanese Americans during World War II and acknowledging that the internment was primarily motivated by racial prejudice).

Shaw v. Reno, 509 U.S. 630 (1993)

(Holding that the Equal Protection Clause of the Fourteenth Amendment prevents political districts from being drawn based upon racial considerations unless the state has a "compelling government interest").

Adarand Constructors, Inc., v. Pena, 515 U.S. 200 (1995)

(Holding that federal racial classifications for affirmative action programs in business, like those of a state, are subject to the most stringent judicial scrutiny and, therefore, must serve a compelling governmental interest, and must be narrowly tailored to further that interest).

Grutter v. Bollinger, 539 U.S. 982 (2003)

(Holding that the Equal Protection Clause of the Fourteenth Amendment does not prohibit a law school's narrowly tailored use of race in admissions decisions to further a compelling interest in obtaining the educational benefits that flow from a diverse student body).

Parents Involved In Community Schools v. Seattle School District No. 1, 127 S.Ct. 2738 (2007)

(Holding that the Equal Protection Clause of the Fourteenth Amendment prohibited a public primary and secondary school district from using race as the sole factor in a voluntary school-assignment desegregation plan).

Barack Obama is elected President of the United States (2008)

(Becoming the first African American to hold this position).

Ricci v. DeStefano, 129 S.Ct. 2658 (2009)

(Holding that an employer may avoid disparate-impact liability under Title VII of the Civil Rights Act based on the strong basis in evidence, that had the employer not certified the results of an employment evaluation test, the employer would have been subject to disparate treatment liability).

Apology For Slavery Resolution (2009)

(Providing an apology to African Americans from the 111th Congress of the United States, unanimously, for slavery and segregation but not taking a position on any claims for reparations, and indicating that the resolution cannot be used as a basis in claims for reparations).

Sonia Sotomayor is appointed to the United States Supreme Court (2009)

(Becoming the first Latino/a member of the Court).

Shelby County v. Holder, 133 S.Ct. 2612 (2013)

(Holding that section 4 of the Voting Rights Act is unconstitutional because the constraints that the Act placed on specific states, while relevant in the 1960s and 1970s, are outdated by today's standards).

Fisher v. Univ. of Tex., 133 S.Ct. 2411 (2013)

(Holding that while the Equal Protection Clause of the Fourteenth Amendment does allow for the consideration of race in undergraduate admissions, it is only permissible in the absence of judicial deference to a college's or university's claim that race was used in good faith).

Schuette v. Coalition to Defend Affirmative Action, 134 S.Ct. 1623 (2014)

(Holding that a Michigan law, passed by popular vote, barring affirmative action at some state universities and colleges was constitutional and did not violate the Equal Protection Clause of the Fourteenth Amendment).

Texas v. Inclusive Communities Project, 135 S.Ct. 2507 (2015)

(Holding that the Fair Housing Act applies even in cases of "disparate impact" discrimination, when housing policies perpetuate the effects of prior racial discrimination).

Trump v. Hawaii, 138 S.Ct. 2392 (2018)

(Holding that a presidential proclamation that placed entry restrictions on foreign nationals from several predominantly Muslim countries did not violate the Establishment Clause of the First Amendment).

The execution of 38 Sioux Indians by the U.S. authorities at Mankato, Minnesota, Friday, December 26, 1862. (Artist: W. H. Childs. Copyright (1996) The Minnesota Historical Society. Reprinted with permission of the Minnesota Historical Society.)

The picture above depicts the largest mass execution in United States history. Thirty-eight Lakota Sioux warriors were found guilty of "murder and other outrages" by a military commission and ordered executed by President Abraham Lincoln on December 26, 1862, in Mankato, Minnesota.[1]

The causes of the Dakota Conflict were complex. The treaties of 1851 and 1858 eroded the authority of tribal chieftains causing factions among the Sioux.[2] Exorbitant annuity payments left the Sioux dependent upon a corrupt system of Indian agents. Under the treaties, the Sioux could only purchase goods from licensed traders at a 100% to 400% markup.[3] Moreover, the treaties left the Sioux without effective means of seeking relief. Their only option for survival was theft and violence.[4]

Late annuity payments in the summer of 1862 heightened the tension between the Sioux and Minnesotans. In an August 15, 1862 meeting between Sioux and government officials, licensed trader Andrew Myrick, when asked to extend credit to feed the starving Sioux, bluntly stated, "so far as I am concerned, if they are hungry,

---

1. THROUGH DAKOTA EYES: NARRATIVE ACCOUNTS OF THE MINNESOTA INDIAN WAR OF 1862 (G. ANDERSON AND A. WOOLWORTH, EDS. 1988).
2. CHARLES S. BRYANT AND ABEL B. MURCH, A HISTORY OF THE GREAT MASSACRE BY THE SIOUX INDIANS IN MINNESOTA, (2d ed. 1864) 1977.
3. *Id.*
4. *Id.*

let them eat grass."[5] Bloodshed began on August 17, 1862, when four young Dakota Sioux men killed three white men, a white woman, and a fifteen-year-old white girl while hunting for food.[6] In the following days, nearly 250 white Minnesotans were killed and thousands left homeless as townships were burned to the ground.[7] Among the dead was Andrew Myrick, who reportedly was found with his mouth stuffed full of grass.[8]

On August 26, 1862, Governor Alexander Ramsey appointed Colonel Henry Sibley to command 1,400 soldiers to quell the Sioux uprising.[9] Colonel Sibley's troopers took 1,250 Sioux prisoners. On September 28, 1862, Colonel Sibley, without clear authority to do so, appointed a five-member military commission to "try summarily" Sioux and mixed-bloods for "murder and other outrages" committed against Americans.[10] These hearings were conducted expeditiously without due process considerations. Ultimately, 393 cases were heard in seven days, resulting in the conviction of 323 Sioux and sentencing 303 of those convicted to death.[11] President Lincoln, in response to a meeting with Henry Whipple, the Episcopal Bishop of Minnesota, expressed concern about the convictions, yet recognized that a stay of execution would only subject all 303 condemned men to mob justice.[12] As a result of this recognition, President Lincoln isolated 39 condemned Sioux, and in a handwritten note ordered their executions. To convince Governor Ramsey to agree to his plan, President Lincoln promised to remove every American Indian from the state and provide Minnesota with $2,000,000 in federal funds.[13]

---

5. THROUGH DAKOTA EYES: NARRATIVE ACCOUNTS OF THE MINNESOTA INDIAN WAR OF 1862 (G. ANDERSON AND A. WOOLWORTH, EDS. 1988).

6. MARION P. SATTERLEE, A DETAILED ACCOUNT OF THE MASSACRE BY THE DAKOTA INDIANS OF MINNESOTA IN 1862 (1923).

7. *Id.*

8. THROUGH DAKOTA EYES: NARRATIVE ACCOUNTS OF THE MINNESOTA INDIAN WAR OF 1862 (G. ANDERSON AND A. WOOLWORTH, EDS. 1988).

9. WILLIAM WATTS FOLWELL, A HISTORY OF MINNESOTA, 109–264 (1926).

10. *Id.*

11. *Id.*

12. STEPHEN B. OATES, WITH MALICE TOWARDS NONE, THE LIFE OF ABRAHAM LINCOLN, 367, 368 (Harper Perennial 1994) (1977).

13. *Id.*

Index

A

Abolition, 12, 42, 67, 68, 77, 79, 117,
140, 150, 167, 172, 176, 182, 196, 205,
210, 245, 335, 339, 461
Abolitionists, 67, 78, 79, 81, 100, 118,
123, 130, 132, 135–137, 140, 167, 173,
175, 176, 186, 196, 369, 404
    Educating free blacks, 81
    Germantown Mennonites, 748
Act of 1819, 118, 121, 623
Act to Preserve Racial Integrity, 46,
468
Adams, John, 69, 70, 76, 116–118, 330,
753
Adams, John Quincy, 76, 116–118
Addams, Jane, 365
Adultery, 48, 467 (*see also* Interracial
Sex)
Affirmative action, 36, 62, 63, 65, 66,
184, 189, 192, 194, 195, 280, 459,
496, 497, 501, 505–508, 513, 515,
525, 527, 537, 538, 540, 541, 546–
548, 559–563, 565, 566, 598, 641,
643, 646, 647, 668–672, 674, 675,
678–680, 682, 684, 687, 688, 697,
698, 701, 725, 726, 730, 777, 778
    Compelling government interest,
    505, 508, 516, 522, 526, 529, 536,
    540, 541, 668, 687, 777
    Narrowly tailored, 498, 499, 501,
    504, 508, 510, 511, 513, 516, 517,
    519–522, 525, 527, 530, 533, 536–
    538, 543–545, 547, 565, 566, 569,
    602, 604, 643, 668, 777, 778
    Strict-scrutiny, 562, 564, 565

African ancestry, 27, 29, 44, 46, 47, 53,
63, 65, 768
Aiyetoro, Adjoa, 193
Alamo, 374
Alito, Samuel, 679, 687
All deliberate speed, 471, 476, 493
Allan, Lewis, 219
Allensworth, Allen, 237
Allensworth, California, 237
Allotment Act, 300, 312, 317
Amazing Grace, 432, 433
American Civil Liberties Union, 281,
386, 561, 689
American Missionary Association, 183,
370, 404
American racism, 3, 32, 58, 60, 177,
180, 186, 236, 237, 362, 460, 471, 598,
641, 645, 650, 653, 658, 673, 732, 733,
774
    African Americans (*see* specific
    topic)
    American Indians (*see* American
    Indian, Indians, Native
    American)
    Chinese (*see* Chinese)
    Japanese (*see* Japanese)
    Mexican (*see* Latinos/as)
American Veterans Committee, 474
Antimiscegenation, 45, 199, 452, 464,
470, 471
Articles of Confederation, 68, 70, 77,
87, 88, 115, 122, 152, 153, 156, 163,
754, 771
    Delegates of the United States, 71,
    754, 756

Firm League of Friendship, 754
Full faith and credit, 754
Aryan, 258, 266, 437
Asian Americans, 62, 64, 189, 255, 276, 280, 289, 312, 330, 500, 707, 775
Associated Charities, 366
Atchison, Topeka, & Santa Fe Railway Co, 363
Aubert, Vilhelm, 9

B
Bailout
Bailyn, Bernard, 172
Baldus study, 584–590, 595, 597
Banishment, 49, 279
Banneker, Benjamin, 110, 176
Barnett, Ross, 477
Bell, Derrick, 57, 177, 180, 186, 187, 191, 236, 237, 461, 462, 641, 645, 658
Benton, Thomas Hart, 116
Berea College, 356, 359, 362, 363, 367–369, 382, 385, 402, 411, 416, 425, 456, 775
Biden, Joe, 694
Bill of Rights, 68, 102, 103, 105, 111, 171, 190, 194, 197, 210, 215, 225, 237, 241, 244, 318, 360, 368, 425, 437, 467, 567, 622, 655
Biracial, 61, 429
Birth of a Nation, 372–374
Bittker, Boris, 190
Black, Hugo, 45, 432, 663, 664, 667
Black Codes, 182, 186, 196–198, 200, 222, 223, 335, 769
Black power, 216, 217, 405, 418, 477, 478, 599, 660, 666, 676, 730
Blackmun, Harry, 560, 652, 664, 670
Blair Bill, 342
Blair, Francis P., 199
Blassingame, John, 13, 664
Blow, Peter, 141, 165
Blow, Taylor, 165
Bok, Curtis, 652

Booth, John Wilkes, 229
Bradley, Bill, 684
Bradley, Joseph, 221, 254, 368, 559
Branch, Taylor, 477
Brandeis, Louis, 422, 651
Brazil, 13, 27, 78, 171
Brennan, William, 652, 664
Brewer, David, 363–366
Brooks, David, 538
Brown, John, 138, 173, 174, 229, 370, 430
Buchanan, James, 167
Bureau of Indian Affairs, 317, 640
Burger, Warren, 70, 73
Bush, George H. W., 649, 678, 691, 723
Bush, George W., 649, 678, 679, 691, 723, 724, 726, 769

C
Cabranes, Jose, 689
Calabresi, Guido, 652
Calhoun, John C., 116
Campbell, John, 165, 212
Capital punishment, 585–590, 594, 595, 639, 708 (*see also* Criminal Justice System)
    Baldus Study, 584–590, 595, 597
    David Baldus, 584
    Reliance on race, 594
    Risk of racial bias, 590, 777
Carlisle Indian School, 300
Carpetbaggers, 253, 373
Carter, Robert L., 445, 453, 463, 473
Caste, 26, 48, 50, 51, 53, 55–57, 63, 66, 79, 84, 90, 100, 101, 190, 210, 217, 266, 350, 429, 471, 506, 560
Census, 41, 58, 59, 61–63, 65, 66, 69, 78, 111, 139, 268, 280, 328, 428, 590, 599, 610, 616, 625, 651, 713, 737, 745
Chaney, James, 683, 697, 722
Cherokees, 216, 299, 306–312, 316, 321, 327, 328, 330, 772 (*see also* Native Americans)

Chinese, 53, 54, 64, 65, 206, 255–259, 272, 273, 275–280, 345, 347, 352, 365, 368, 400, 414–419, 423, 424, 433, 456, 469, 471, 477, 586, 590, 710–713, 716, 774
  Assimilation, 280
  Exclusion Act, 272, 710, 711
  Fourteenth Amendment, 276–278, 280, 711, 712
  Laborers, 272, 273, 275, 276, 711, 714, 717, 774
  Naturalization, 710, 712, 713
  Penal code, 279
  Segregation, 283, 414–419, 775
Christian, 17, 18, 160, 168, 313, 316, 318, 361, 478, 479, 661
Churchill, Ward, 62
Cinque, 118, 119, 122
Citizenship, 4, 16, 56, 64, 65, 86–88, 145–147, 152–155, 159, 163–167, 170–172, 181–334, 337–339, 345, 349, 353, 370, 371, 377, 384, 424, 436, 457, 469, 471, 515, 596, 710–713, 717–720, 773
  African Americans, 64, 65, 80, 81, 105, 110, 184–194, 198–200, 367–371, 376, 423, 424
  Aliens, 56, 86, 88, 90, 153, 164, 774
  Assimilation, 64, 267, 280, 285, 294, 295, 306, 312, 317, 712, 713, 716
  Chinese, 64, 65, 272, 273, 275–280, 774
  Native Americans, 28, 39, 40, 42–46, 51, 62, 64, 65, 73, 105, 186, 257, 258, 312, 328, 330, 772
Civil Liberties Act, 289, 777
Civil Rights, 9, 37, 46, 59–62, 79, 84, 89, 90, 98, 151, 171, 177, 178, 181, 185, 190, 194, 197–201, 207, 209–211, 213–216, 223–225, 229, 237, 238, 240, 241, 244, 248–251, 253, 255, 280, 281, 289, 295, 319, 323, 336, 337, 340, 345, 348–354, 356, 364, 367–369, 371, 374, 376, 383–385, 389, 397, 398, 401, 405, 412, 425–429, 434, 438, 450, 452, 456, 459, 460, 462, 467, 470, 471, 477, 478, 495–497, 507, 510, 552, 559–561, 563, 567, 574, 578, 587, 600, 608, 610, 620, 629, 630, 638, 641–643, 645, 649, 651, 652, 654, 656–662, 664, 669, 672, 675, 677–679, 681, 683, 689, 697, 719, 721, 722, 725, 761, 766, 768, 773, 774, 776–778
Civil Rights Act of 1866, 181, 198, 200, 201, 213, 248, 323, 467, 773
Civil Rights Act of 1871, 216, 224
Civil Rights Act of 1875, 216, 238, 240, 405, 412, 774
Civil Rights Act of 1964, 470, 497, 510, 563, 574, 578, 587, 629, 630, 638, 642, 654, 721, 722, 725, 766, 776, 777
Civil War, 16, 38, 39, 42, 45, 52, 64, 73, 102, 115, 121, 122, 137, 139, 140, 170, 174, 181, 185, 186, 189, 191, 193, 196, 199, 201, 209, 213, 215, 222, 223, 233, 237, 251, 254, 256, 258, 269, 304, 314, 316, 341–343, 351, 357, 362, 364, 369, 376, 403–405, 422, 428, 507, 576, 588, 591, 610, 623, 642, 721, 750, 768, 769, 773, 777
Cleveland, Grover, 434
Clinton, Bill, 691, 723, 769
Cochran, Johnnie, 695, 696
Colonization, 26, 117, 118, 175, 176, 317
Compromise of 1850, 116, 133, 165
Compromise on slavery, 78, 79, 116, 134
Concerned Alumni of Princeton, 683, 688
Confederacy, 16, 102, 181, 195, 197, 216, 217, 219, 225, 251, 252, 424, 671, 754, 756
Congress, 16, 56, 68, 69, 73, 77, 84, 87, 89, 90, 113–118, 122–125, 128–135, 139, 144–146, 152–154, 156–160, 163–165, 167, 170, 172–174, 176, 178, 181, 182, 184, 185, 187, 190–193,

195–201, 204–209, 212–214, 216, 217,
223, 224, 226–228, 230, 234–236,
239–251, 254–261, 263, 264, 266–
273, 275–278, 281–283, 289, 290,
292, 297, 299, 300, 306–308, 310–
313, 316, 318, 321–324, 326, 328, 336,
337, 346, 348, 364, 372, 378, 385,
387, 388, 390, 393, 394, 412, 413, 419,
445, 451, 455, 467, 470, 501–503, 506,
507, 559, 564, 574, 576, 589, 599, 604,
608–612, 614–625, 627, 631–633,
638, 643, 654, 659, 672, 711–713, 729,
734–742, 744–748, 752–757, 759, 764,
766, 768–771, 773, 774, 776, 778

Congressional Black Caucus, 184, 192

Congressional Medal of Freedom, 730

Connecticut, 77, 78, 81, 83, 86–88, 91,
94, 95, 119, 150, 151, 210, 364, 370,
628, 634, 657, 734, 742, 753, 754, 772

Conservative, 229, 364, 445, 540, 562,
649, 654, 656, 659, 660, 666–670,
672–674, 678–680, 682, 684, 686–
689, 697, 706, 721, 724, 725, 732

Constitution, 56, 67–91, 98, 101, 102,
105, 113–117, 122–136, 144–168,
170–173, 179, 181, 185, 186, 197, 199,
201, 203, 204, 206–209, 211, 213, 215,
217, 223, 230, 233–236, 241, 245–
248, 250, 253, 255, 257, 258, 262, 270,
271, 273–278, 288, 293, 305–311,
316, 317, 319–322, 325–327, 335–340,
344, 346–354, 357, 359–363, 366,
368, 379, 381–384, 387, 390, 391, 394,
396, 400, 406, 408, 409, 412, 413,
415–418, 420, 421, 423, 424, 429,
439–441, 443, 444, 451, 453, 454,
458, 479, 482, 484, 486–488, 490,
493, 495, 497–499, 502–505, 508,
513, 525, 529, 530, 533, 534, 536, 537,
539, 547–550, 554–558, 560, 563,
568, 570, 572, 573, 580, 584, 586–
589, 595, 596, 599, 601, 603, 604, 609,
613, 614, 617, 618, 620, 622–624, 632,
633, 642, 644, 652–655, 659, 662,
663, 670–672, 675, 680, 681, 688,

711, 714, 716, 720, 732, 734, 737–743,
745, 746, 752, 756–760, 765, 768, 769,
771–774

Amendments, 73, 79, 95, 123, 199–
203, 205–209, 211, 212, 215, 224,
235, 237, 244–246, 251, 253, 255,
259, 263, 297, 320, 322, 335–337,
339, 349–351, 353, 354, 357, 364,
394, 422–424, 428, 452, 455, 467,
504, 537, 575, 577, 584, 603, 607,
611, 619–624, 642, 655, 721, 736,
741, 742, 766, 774

Civil War Amendments, 73, 199,
215, 357, 428, 623

Commerce Clause, 113, 115, 308,
316, 385, 391, 393, 394, 775

Fifteenth Amendment, 181, 199,
206, 208, 223, 224, 237, 245, 271,
272, 325, 349, 354, 557, 586, 607,
609, 610, 617, 620, 623, 626, 721,
767, 773, 774

Fourteenth Amendment, 38, 181,
197, 198, 200–202, 204, 205, 207,
208, 210, 212–216, 223–225, 236,
237, 239, 240, 242–245, 248, 249,
252–255, 257, 276–278, 280, 319,
320, 322–327, 336, 337, 339, 340,
344, 345, 347–350, 353, 354, 356,
357, 363, 364, 368, 369, 379, 381–
385, 391, 396–402, 405, 407–409,
412–414, 418–421, 423–426, 439,
443, 446–448, 450–452, 454, 455,
458, 463, 464, 466–468, 473, 475,
490, 491, 495–499, 501, 502, 507,
508, 510, 512, 520, 521, 525, 528,
532, 533, 541, 543, 548, 558, 559,
572, 573, 577, 585, 602, 604, 607,
626, 628, 629, 632, 638, 641, 643,
652, 654, 668, 671, 675, 684, 711,
712, 773–778

Thirteenth Amendment, 181, 196,
198, 200, 204, 205, 208, 210, 212,
214, 222, 242–245, 248, 249, 253,
278, 322, 344, 345, 349, 370, 496,
773, 774

Constitutional Convention, 67, 69, 70, 72, 75–77, 80, 113, 125, 216, 217, 252, 262, 270, 613, 726
  Commercial interests, 72
  Delegates, 68–72, 75, 77, 114, 163, 216, 252, 726
  Enumerated powers, 114, 128, 157, 158, 201
  Fugitive Slave Clause, 70, 78, 122, 125, 131, 135, 246, 772
  Preamble, 67, 73, 82, 92, 148, 150, 175, 255
  Racist provisions, 68
  Ratification, 72, 125
  Slave Trade Clause, 69, 77, 78
  Territory Clause, 115, 135, 152
  Three-Fifths Clause, 69
Continental Congress, 68, 753
Conyers, John, 185, 189, 190, 193, 194
Cornyn, John, 682, 689
Courtney, Samuel, 341
Covenant, 67, 79, 395–397, 399–402
Crandall, Prudence, 81, 91, 94, 151, 657, 664
Creole, 159, 176, 229
Criminal liability, 14
Criminal justice system, 187, 420, 580, 581, 583, 588–594, 682, 683, 696, 697, 709, 729 (see also Capital Punishment)
  Discretion, 585, 588–595
  Jury selection, 338, 575–577, 579–582, 586, 593, 777
  White victims, 571, 585, 708
Critical race theory, 4, 643
Crowley, James, 693, 710, 731
Cuffe, Paul, 80
Curtis, Benjamin, 165

D
Danforth, John, 650, 652
Darden, Christopher, 696
Dartmouth, 80, 165, 262, 265, 368

Davis, Jefferson, 116
Davis, John W., 453
Davis, Jordan, 708
Davis, William, 214, 404
Dawes Act, 300
Death penalty, 50, 571, 583–594, 640, 680, 708, 723 (see also Capital punishment)
Declaration of Independence, 80, 86, 110, 147–149, 156, 172, 176, 235, 652, 656, 671, 750, 753, 771
Degler, Carl, 171
Delgado, Richard, 460
Democrat, 185, 190, 193, 212, 213, 253, 373, 423, 649, 686, 691, 725
Desdunes, Rodolphe, 342, 343
Detroit, 190, 192, 376, 477, 479, 482–491, 493–495
Dewey, Thomas, 459
Dilworth, Richardson, 652
Discrimination, 30, 31, 37, 38, 53, 57, 60, 65, 81, 95, 100, 102, 165, 167, 170, 171, 177, 178, 184, 186, 187, 189–192, 209, 210, 213, 214, 224, 245, 246, 249, 251, 254–257, 259, 271, 272, 282, 284, 286, 288, 295–298, 312, 335–340, 345–347, 350, 354–356, 362, 374, 376, 384, 386, 390, 399, 408, 409, 416, 418, 420, 421, 423, 424, 428, 435–437, 441–444, 452, 455, 457–459, 461, 462, 466–468, 470, 474, 475, 480–482, 485, 489, 496, 498, 501–508, 510, 511, 513, 514, 521, 522, 526, 527, 529, 531, 532, 536, 538, 540, 543, 550–552, 556, 557, 560, 561, 565, 566, 569, 571–575, 577–582, 586, 588–593, 596–598, 602, 606, 607, 609–611, 613, 615–632, 634, 635, 637–646, 651, 653, 654, 657, 662–664, 668–672, 674, 679–683, 686–688, 725, 729, 732, 733, 765, 766, 770, 773, 774, 776, 777
  Housing, 34, 37, 38, 62, 181, 187, 295, 328, 329, 372, 376–378, 385,

394, 395, 401, 402, 420, 463, 478, 480, 481, 485, 495, 496, 501, 506, 507, 528, 530, 535, 550, 551, 554, 571, 578, 579, 586, 588, 602, 639, 651, 656, 661, 662, 664, 690, 722, 729, 730, 732, 767, 768, 775, 777

Public accommodations, 80, 201, 238, 239, 242–245, 250, 345, 364, 382, 427, 438, 470, 507, 559, 639, 659, 675, 725, 766, 774

Transportation, 53, 166, 182, 230, 252, 291, 341, 363, 382, 385, 387, 389–391, 402, 419, 453, 454, 456, 476, 484, 485, 489–491, 493, 500, 517, 562, 642, 643, 715, 745, 766

Dixon, Thomas, 372

Douglas, William, 651, 668

Douglass, Frederick, 26, 106, 174, 228, 377, 657, 664, 732, 772

Due process, 38, 124, 125, 131, 136, 158, 171, 200, 204, 215, 235, 236, 239, 244, 284, 288, 336, 337, 340, 345, 348, 349, 354, 364, 369, 381–385, 398, 401, 408, 451, 455, 458, 463, 464, 500, 548, 575, 608, 743, 744, 773, 775, 780

Duke, David

Dunbar, Paul Lawrence, 19

E

Eisenhower, Dwight, 459

Electoral College, 69, 254

Ely, John, 646

Emancipation, 18, 42, 51, 57, 78, 83, 103, 111, 125, 161, 175, 176, 181, 186, 191, 204, 428, 459, 655, 657, 745, 759, 769, 773

Deed of, 42, 161

Proclamation 78, 181, 186, 191, 195, 196, 204, 205, 323, 459, 655, 759, 760, 773

Emerson, John, 141, 166

Equal protection, 31, 38, 73, 80, 95, 121, 200, 201, 204, 208, 239, 242,

244, 245, 255, 256, 284, 335–340, 345, 348, 349, 356, 364, 385, 396, 398–401, 406–410, 413, 414, 418–424, 433, 439, 441–444, 446–448, 450–452, 454, 455, 457, 458, 463–468, 470, 473, 480, 481, 491, 495–506, 508, 511–513, 521, 522, 525–528, 530, 531, 533, 534, 537, 540, 541, 543–545, 548, 550, 552–554, 556, 559–562, 565–567, 570–573, 576, 577, 579–581, 585, 586, 588, 589, 592, 593, 596, 597, 601, 603–607, 625, 628, 629, 632, 633, 638, 639, 641, 643–646, 658, 668, 671, 672, 675, 680, 684–687, 717, 744, 773–778

Equitable principles, 475, 487, 492

Ethiopian, 50

Evers, Medgar, 626, 683, 697

Executive order 9066, 282

F

Fair Housing Act, 722, 767, 777

Faubus, Orval, 477

Federal Bureau of Investigation, 287, 478

Fields, Cleo, 672

Fifteenth Amendment, 181, 199, 206, 208, 223, 224, 237, 245, 271, 272, 325, 349, 354, 557, 586, 607, 609, 610, 617, 620, 623, 626, 721, 767, 773, 774

Foner, Eric, 140

Foner, Philip, 73, 657

Forman, James, 479

Forten, James, 81

Forty acres and a mule, 191

Founding Fathers, 37, 68, 73–75, 78, 79, 166, 167, 567

Fourteenth Amendment, 38, 181, 197, 198, 200–202, 204, 205, 207, 208, 210, 212–216, 223–225, 236, 237, 239, 240, 242–245, 248, 249, 252–255, 257, 276–278, 280, 319, 320, 322–327, 336, 337, 339, 340, 344, 345, 347–350, 353, 354, 356, 357, 363, 364, 368, 369,

379, 381–385, 391, 396–402, 405,
407–409, 412–414, 418–421, 423–
426, 439, 443, 446–448, 450–452,
454, 455, 458, 463, 464, 466–468,
473, 475, 490, 491, 495–499, 501,
502, 507, 508, 510, 512, 520, 521, 525,
528, 532, 533, 541, 543, 548, 558, 559,
572, 573, 577, 585, 602, 604, 607, 626,
628, 629, 632, 638, 641, 643, 652,
654, 668, 671, 675, 684, 711, 712,
773–778

Frankfurter, Felix, 426, 471, 561, 568, 652

Franklin, John Hope, 136, 175, 182, 186, 187, 195, 372, 394, 403, 412, 478, 657, 664

Free blacks, 8, 41, 44, 46, 51, 57, 67, 75, 77, 79–81, 84, 85, 94, 100–102, 106, 113, 117, 131, 135, 136, 140, 141, 165–167, 169, 170, 173, 174, 193, 255, 311, 428, 496, 581, 591, 599, 671, 704, 726, 772

Freedmen's Bureau, 181–184, 195, 197, 220, 403, 404, 467, 760
  Abandoned lands, 182, 760
  Relief, 182, 183

Freedom suits, 44, 53, 102, 106
  Burden of proof, 44, 102

Frist, Bill, 684

Fugitive Slave Act, 125, 130, 131, 139, 166, 247, 756, 758, 771, 772

G

Gandhi, Mohandas, 113

Garfield, James, 198

Garrison, William Lloyd, 67, 79, 81, 124, 132, 175, 664

Garvey, Marcus, 174

Gassama, Ibrahim, 191

Gates, Henry Louis, 135, 693, 710, 731

General Court of Virginia, 463

Gender discrimination, 506, 508, 561, 591, 670, 671

Georgia, 46, 64, 69, 70, 75, 76, 222–225, 252, 258, 304, 306, 310–312, 315, 316, 321, 327, 377, 382, 387, 388, 392, 403, 404, 406–409, 413, 414, 437, 465, 470, 508, 563–565, 571, 578, 579, 581, 583–593, 595–597, 610–612, 620, 625, 652, 653, 656–658, 663, 671, 673, 678, 734, 742, 753, 754, 760, 772

Ginsburg, Ruth, 525, 560, 561

Goodell, William, 3

Goodman, Andrew, 683, 697, 722

Grant, Ulysses S., 199, 221

Great Depression, 296, 713, 719

H

Habeas corpus, 105, 130, 205, 208, 224, 272, 367, 584, 737, 755

Hampton Institute, 183, 370

Harlan, James, 427–429, 431, 432

Harlan, John Marshall, 364, 371, 412, 425–429, 431, 432, 651, 653
  Black brother, 352, 427

Harlan, Robert, 427–432

Harvard, 71, 168, 169, 188, 189, 191, 213, 355, 435, 444, 460, 462, 510, 517–519, 568, 570, 576, 650, 653, 666, 668, 669, 693, 694, 726, 731, 774

Hastie, William Henry, 656, 657, 664

Hayden, Tom, 194

Hayes, Rutherford, 253, 254, 378, 412, 422

Hemings, Sally, 110, 111

Henderson, Wade, 192

Henry, Patrick, 38, 70, 74

Higginbotham, A. Leon, 3, 38, 47, 68, 75, 106, 109–111, 168, 177, 185, 186, 353, 362, 377, 378, 401, 434, 444, 468, 606, 608, 650, 655, 664, 665, 673, 676, 687, 695, 701, 730–732, 776

Higginbotham, Moses, 653

Hill, Anita, 649, 676–679

Holmes, Oliver Wendell, 4, 358, 366, 582, 651

Holocaust, 186, 192, 194

Homestead Act, 191

House of Burgesses, 40, 47

Housing, 34, 37, 38, 62, 181, 187, 295, 328, 329, 372, 376–378, 385, 394, 395, 401, 402, 420, 463, 478, 480, 481, 485, 495, 496, 501, 506, 507, 528, 530, 535, 550, 551, 554, 571, 578, 579, 586, 588, 602, 639, 651, 656, 661, 662, 664, 690, 722, 729, 730, 732, 767, 768, 775, 777

   American Law Institute's Restatement of Property, 401

   Desegregation, 776–778

   Migration, 401

   Racially restrictive covenants, 401, 402, 480, 662, 776

Houston, Charles Hamilton, 401, 438, 650, 656, 657, 664, 668

Howard, Oliver Otis, 183

Howard Law School, 402, 493, 639

Howard University, 28, 183, 402, 437–439, 496, 651, 668

Hushpuppies, 169

I

Immigration, 46, 64, 79, 256–259, 264, 267, 268, 272, 275, 283, 290, 293, 295–298, 424, 710–712, 714–720, 727, 733, 775

   Naturalization laws, 158, 256–259, 261, 278, 320, 736, 751

Indentured servants, 73

Indians, 38, 40, 42–45, 53–56, 62, 71, 81, 83, 84, 87, 88, 102–105, 145, 153, 200, 255, 261, 262, 269, 271, 289, 298–308, 310–332, 400, 465, 564, 590, 640, 734, 744, 749, 756, 764, 765, 779, 780 (see also Native American)

Indian Removal Act, 306, 318, 764, 772

Indian Reorganization Act, 312

Industrialization, 376, 461

Inferior, 12, 32, 39, 40, 44, 50, 51, 56, 57, 84, 90, 110, 141, 147, 149, 151, 152, 156, 166, 167, 290, 311, 313, 314, 327, 337, 339, 342, 348, 351, 371, 374, 429, 434, 453, 454, 457, 470, 479, 552, 596, 647, 671, 674, 676, 678, 717, 737, 739

Institution of slavery, 38, 57, 58, 68, 74, 76, 102, 112, 114, 122, 123, 125, 130, 132, 133, 135, 139, 140, 160, 166, 169, 176, 185, 186, 188, 190, 193, 204, 246, 248, 249, 349, 353, 433, 771

Integration, 33, 38, 252, 285, 436, 477, 479, 484, 523, 528, 530, 533–538, 548, 552, 557, 565, 725, 729, 732

International slave trade, 69, 70, 75, 77, 78, 112, 118, 122, 168, 169, 433, 772

Interracial marriage, 30, 38, 49, 171, 199, 371, 464–466, 468–471, 662, 725, 726, 777 (see also Miscegenation)

   Prohibitions, 38, 465, 466

   Racial Integrity Act of 1924, 46, 466, 468, 662

Interracial sex, 38–40, 43, 47, 48, 53, 58, 362, 429, 463, 468–471 (see also Interracial marriage)

Interstate Commerce Act, 385, 386, 766

Irish, 39, 256, 257, 277

J

Jackson, Andrew, 164, 168, 299, 311, 312, 683, 697

Jackson, Jesse, 188, 192, 723

Jackson, Jimmie Lee, 683, 697

Japanese, 65, 186, 192, 194, 260, 263, 264, 268, 280–289, 365, 400, 452, 463, 590, 713, 719, 768, 775, 777

   Camps, 192, 280, 283, 452

   Civil Liberties Act (1988), 289, 777

   Curfews, 280

   Incarceration, 280, 288

   Relocation, 280, 283, 452, 768, 777

Jay, John, 330

Jefferson, Thomas, 38, 69, 70, 74, 76, 95, 110, 111, 314, 753

Jews, 71, 191, 192, 229, 400, 590, 700

Jim Crow, 3, 37, 38, 63, 64, 177, 190, 252, 341–343, 354, 364, 371, 378, 424, 450, 481, 496, 571, 626, 627, 645, 653, 708, 719–721, 726, 769, 770, 775

Johnson, Andrew, 16, 187, 191, 193, 196, 198, 221, 222, 230

Johnson, Samuel, 76, 677

Johnston, James Hugo, 45

Jordan, Winthrop, 42, 44, 48

Judiciary Act of 1925, 422

Jury selection, 338, 575–577, 579–582, 586, 593, 681, 682, 777
    Exclusion, 575, 576, 578, 580, 582
    Peremptory challenges, 577, 579–581, 593, 594

Justice, administration of, 330, 338, 350, 571, 577, 580, 582, 593, 693, 708, 751
    Racial disparity, 573, 585, 590, 596, 629, 637, 685
    Sentencing, 582–590, 592–596, 708, 709, 777 (see also Capital punishment)

K

Kansas, 100, 133, 134, 173, 238, 268, 321, 323, 324, 328, 364–366, 387, 388, 440, 453, 456, 457, 474, 475, 658, 758

Kansas-Nebraska Act, 115, 134, 135, 166

Kellogg, William Pitt, 221, 227

Kennedy, Anthony, 525, 539, 560

Kennedy, John, 178, 478, 721, 776

Kerner Commission, 385

King, Coretta Scott, 192, 611, 621

King, Martin Luther Jr., 37, 174, 459, 478, 669, 776, 777

King, Rodney, 701, 702, 709

Korematsu, Fred, 64, 280, 281

Ku Klux Klan, 199, 201, 221, 223, 224, 233, 341, 342, 372, 373, 376, 432

L

Latinos/as, 255, 270–272, 289, 291, 297, 330, 640, 724

Lee, Robert E., 174

Legally white, 39, 42, 44–48, 64, 111, 416, 599

Lewis, Timothy, 682

Liberal, 33, 75, 78, 156, 191, 217, 224, 225, 227, 340, 365, 366, 419, 459, 527, 542, 639, 641–643, 647, 649, 667, 674, 678, 680, 684, 686, 687, 690

Lincoln, Abraham, 78, 167, 181, 186, 198, 378, 759, 760, 773, 779, 780

Lincoln University, 439, 440, 442, 443

Litwack, Leon, 73, 657

Liuzzo, Viola Gregg, 683, 697

Logan, Rayford, 378

M

MacArthur, Douglas, 434

Madison, James, 71, 72, 74, 76, 77, 110, 160, 167, 742

Mandela, Nelson, 174, 725

Manifest destiny, 316, 317

Marbury, William, 330

Marshall, John, 21, 164, 168, 221, 305, 315, 329, 330, 364, 371, 412, 425–429, 431, 432, 453, 651–653

Marshall, Thurgood, 73, 385, 394, 395, 434, 438, 448, 451, 453, 458, 460, 473, 505, 561, 626, 639, 649, 651, 652, 654, 656, 660, 662, 664–667, 669, 670, 672–674, 678, 680, 682, 777

Martin, Trayvon, 703–705, 708

Maryland, 38, 61, 70–72, 76, 87, 115, 116, 126, 127, 131, 149, 155, 161, 164, 166, 169, 171, 183, 205, 221, 235, 386, 437–440, 442, 465, 474, 475, 586, 599, 618, 623, 657, 658, 723, 734, 742, 753, 754, 769

Mason, George, 71, 76

Massachusetts, 21, 62, 69, 70, 78, 80, 83–85, 87, 95, 96, 98, 100, 101, 111, 114, 150, 165, 168, 171, 176, 186, 187, 224, 252, 304, 343, 346, 355, 357, 360, 404, 419, 470, 533, 576, 581, 588, 713, 723, 731, 734, 742, 753

McCain, John, 689

McClellan, John, 423

McKee, Theodore, 681

McReynolds, James, 445, 650, 668

Mexican Americans, 289, 291, 292, 294–296, 420, 669, 672, 719, 776

Mexicans, 64, 189, 256, 269–271, 289–297, 374, 400, 421, 719

Michigan, 51, 123, 162, 185, 193, 211, 228, 355, 399, 401, 477, 482–484, 486, 488–491, 493, 494, 508–510, 522, 525, 527, 529, 538, 542, 548–550, 554–560, 563–569, 611, 670, 756, 778

Miscegenation, 42, 51, 452, 464–471
    Adultery, 48, 467
    Cohabitation, 464, 470
    Fornication, 467
    Punishment, 38,464,467
    Race of participants, 466, 467
    Racial Integrity Act of 1924, 46, 466, 468, 662
    Rape, 39
    Voluntary, 38, 49, 464–466, 468–471 (see also Interracial marriage)

Mississippi, 75, 115, 123, 138, 139, 141, 161, 182, 225, 226, 250, 302, 346, 367, 368, 371, 388, 390, 392, 405, 415, 416, 419, 437, 465, 470, 477, 546, 562, 581, 608, 610, 611, 615, 616, 620, 625, 670, 671, 673, 722, 724–726, 756, 758, 760–764, 772, 773
    Black code of, 243, 591, 761, 773
    Contracts for labor, 761
    Freedmen, Negroes or mulattoes, 761, 763

Mississippi Apprentice Law, 762, 763

Mississippi Vagrant Law, 763

Penal Laws of Mississippi, 763

Missouri Compromise, 123, 124, 130, 133, 134, 140, 141, 144, 162, 164–166, 757, 772

Mitchell, Arthur, 385

Mixed-race, 39, 40, 43–46, 48, 52, 61, 63, 64, 96, 229, 271, 707 (see also Mulatto)

Monroe, James, 74, 117

Monticello, 111

Moors, 43, 103, 104

Morgan, Irene, 394

Morgan, J.P., 71

Morgan, John Tyler, 342

Morris, Robert, 71, 95, 664, 753

Mulatto, 38, 40–42, 44–50, 53, 54, 56, 57, 79, 105, 110, 126, 150, 171, 342, 427, 429, 432, 470, 761–764
    Bastards, 48–50
    Decision to classify with blacks, 50
    Free, 40–42, 44, 46, 47, 49–51, 53, 56, 57
    Incompetent to testify, 46, 47
    Naturalized, 56
    Octoroons, 429
    Quadroons, 44, 429
    Statutory definition of, 38, 40, 45–47
    White/mulatto boundary, 40, 44

Multiracial, 37, 58, 61, 64, 253, 373, 603, 731

Muslim

Mustee, 46

Myrdal, Gunnar, 190, 470, 471, 592, 664

N

NAACP, 64, 192, 256, 374, 375, 377, 394, 401, 402, 435–437, 439, 443,

451, 452, 461, 477, 552, 626, 639, 656–658, 660, 662 (*see also* National Association for the Advancement of Colored People)
Treaties, 298–300, 306, 307, 310–312, 314–316, 321, 323
Tribal affiliation, 327
Western territories, 306
National Association for the Advancement of Colored People, 64, 192, 256, 374, 375, 377, 394, 401, 402, 435–437, 439, 443, 451, 452, 461, 477, 552, 626, 639, 656–658, 660, 662 (*see also* NAACP)
National Bar Association, 654, 665, 666, 673–675
National Conference of Black Lawyers, 193
Native American, 42, 44–46, 60–65, 258, 263, 328, 330–333, 518, 523, 524, 639, 640
    Citizenship, 64, 65, 318–334
    Discrimination, 298, 312
    Enslavement, 42, 43
    Fifteenth Amendment, 325
    Foreign nation, 307, 309, 311, 327
    Fourteenth Amendment, 319, 320, 322–327
    Genocide, 298, 313–316, 332, 333
    Indian Removal Act, 306, 318, 764, 772
    Inferiority, 299, 305, 311, 313, 315
    Isolation, 298
    Pocahontas exception, 45, 468
    Property rights, 303, 305, 306, 315, 327
    Relocation, 298, 312, 313
    Reserved lands, 316, 327
    Sovereignty, 298–334
    Taxation, 321, 324–327
New Deal, 296, 445
New England, 29, 68, 78, 90, 140, 160, 165, 170, 369, 393, 432
New Jersey, 78, 87, 136, 138, 165, 391, 398, 478, 684, 687, 688, 734, 742, 753, 754
New York, 15, 64, 71, 78, 82–85, 87, 88, 100, 106, 112, 136, 138, 139, 165, 176, 177, 189, 190, 199, 216, 224, 228, 232, 235, 238, 253, 259, 268, 307, 321, 328, 331, 342, 348, 373, 374, 376, 385, 387, 395, 404, 434, 435, 448, 453, 467, 488, 538, 579, 582, 590, 611, 661, 666, 667, 690, 691, 708, 724, 734, 742, 753, 754
Norris, Austin, 652
North Carolina, 4, 5, 8–11, 13, 15–18, 20, 26, 29, 69, 75, 85, 87, 110, 137, 165, 170, 175, 182, 225, 342, 387, 392, 437, 463, 465, 469–471, 474, 475, 477, 594, 599, 600, 603–605, 610, 611, 722, 734, 742, 753, 754, 760, 769
Northwest Ordinance, 114, 115, 122, 123, 144, 755, 771

O
Obama, Barack, 37, 688, 690, 726, 778
Obama, Michelle, 730
O'Connor, Sandra Day, 525, 559, 562, 565, 568, 679, 680
Ogletree, Charles, 189, 666, 673, 693
Ohio, 134, 137–139, 166, 175, 176, 184, 216, 229, 235, 335, 339, 346–348, 367, 387, 389, 391, 418, 427, 431, 459, 467, 551, 587, 589, 594, 707, 755–757, 771

P
Parks, Rosa, 394, 611, 621, 669
Pearl Harbor, 280, 287, 288
Pocahontas, 45, 299, 465, 468
Police powers, 135, 235, 347, 356, 362, 371, 381, 383, 385
Political apartheid, 602, 606
Poll taxes, 272, 415, 557, 608, 626
Polk, James, 269
Pound, Roscoe, 21

Powell, Lewis, 561, 563, 568, 652, 664, 669

Prince Edward County, 453, 454, 477, 492

Princeton University, 21, 71, 364, 688

Prosser, Gabriel, 106

Public education, 95, 216, 403, 409, 411, 413, 418, 426, 427, 437, 442, 444, 453, 455–458, 462, 474, 475, 483, 484, 486, 491, 508, 514–516, 521, 535, 538, 540, 548, 554, 557, 561, 564, 639, 671, 682, 729

   Equity power, 475, 487, 538

   Optional attendance zones, 493

R

Race-conscious remedies, 598, 628, 697

   De jure segregation, 495, 526, 540

Racial discrimination, 30, 31, 38, 53, 65, 81, 95, 177, 178, 186, 187, 213, 254, 256, 257, 259, 271, 272, 284, 286, 288, 296, 312, 335, 354, 355, 362, 374, 384, 436, 437, 452, 459, 462, 466–468, 470, 474, 475, 481, 485, 502, 504–506, 526, 532, 540, 551, 556, 565, 566, 571–573, 579, 582, 588, 589, 592, 593, 596, 597, 602, 606, 609, 615, 616, 619, 622–626, 629, 630, 632, 638–646, 651, 654, 662, 664, 671, 672, 679, 682, 683, 687, 725, 729, 732, 733, 766, 770, 773, 774, 776

   Benign, 497, 503–506, 513, 531, 532, 543, 546, 601, 641, 644, 669, 671

Racial Integrity Act of 1924, 46, 466, 468, 662

Randolph, A. Philip, 178, 436, 657, 664

Randolph, John, 111

Ransom, Leon, 385, 394

Rape, 39, 75, 106, 108, 298, 584, 591–593, 709, 773

Raspberry, William, 667

Reagan, Ronald, 32, 73, 80, 654, 659, 682, 722–724

Reconstruction, 4, 37, 140, 181–335, 340, 343, 364, 369, 370, 372–374, 385, 394, 404, 413, 423, 424, 452, 507, 559, 599, 604, 647, 712, 721, 769

   Amendments, 199–203, 205–209, 211, 212, 215, 224, 235, 237, 244–246, 251, 253, 255, 259, 263, 297, 320, 322

   Radical reconstruction, 198–200, 223, 226, 373, 374

   Reconstruction Act, 181, 197–199, 201, 216, 223, 257, 268, 712

   Stages of, 198

Reparations, 184–195, 217, 289, 313, 479, 778

   Apology,184, 289, 778

   Civil Liberties Act (1988), 289, 777

   Forty acres and a mule, 191

Republican party, 134, 140, 182, 186, 187, 196, 221, 222, 225, 227, 230, 231, 253, 254, 355, 374, 403–405, 412, 431, 722, 724, 725, 727, 774

Restrictive covenant, 395, 396, 401, 402

Rolfe, John, 45, 465

Rooney, Andy, 683, 697

Roosevelt, Franklin, 178, 436, 445, 657

Roosevelt, Theodore, 422, 434, 445, 660, 726

Ruffin, Thomas, 9, 15, 17–22

   Biography, 15

   Pardon, 16, 17

Ruffin, Sterling, 17, 18, 20

S

Sanjek, Roger, 26, 57

Scalia, Antonin, 525, 674

School desegregation, 402, 425, 438, 444, 462, 476, 478–480, 483, 484, 486–490, 492, 493, 528, 536, 537, 729, 778

Schwerner, Michael, 683, 697, 722

Scott, Dred, 76, 117, 131, 141–145, 156, 158, 163–167, 170, 181, 258, 289, 351, 423, 444, 470, 596, 668, 675, 710–712

Segregation in education, 437, 457, 473, 481, 565, 776 (*see also* School desegregation)

Segregation in housing, 295, 377, 385, 401, 402, 463, 485, 495, 535, 639, 664, 729, 768, 775

Segregation in public facilities, 457, 641, 766

Separate but equal doctrine, 95, 100, 101, 178, 335, 354–356, 395, 402, 422, 426, 434, 437, 438, 443, 444, 450–452, 454, 456, 459, 473, 495, 653, 675, 774, 775 (*see also* Jim Crow)

Sessions, Jeff, 689

Seymour, Horatio, 199

Sheridan, Philip, 222

Sioux, 323, 328, 329, 779, 780

Skousen, W. Cleon, 74

Slave, 3, 5–7, 9–15, 17–20, 22–26, 39–44, 48, 49, 53, 57, 58, 65, 68–72, 74–78, 80, 81, 83, 94, 102, 104–119, 121, 122, 125–142, 144, 148–151, 153–155, 157–162, 165–174, 176, 186, 188, 189, 191, 194–196, 205, 206, 225, 228–230, 243, 244, 246–248, 289, 313, 336, 337, 340, 343, 427–429, 432, 433, 459, 469, 496, 508, 591, 592, 607, 653, 655, 671, 709, 732, 745, 748, 756, 758, 769, 771–773

  Assault and battery, 5, 9, 11, 24

  Catchers, 130, 135

  Slave auction, 112

  Slave revolts, 114, 169

  Slave status, 40–44, 49, 53, 57, 65, 107, 131, 135, 162, 166, 167, 171, 427, 771

  Slave Trade Clause, 77, 113–115 (*see also* Fugitive Slave Act)

Slavery, 4, 6–9, 11–14, 17–19, 21–25, 37–42, 47–49, 51–53, 57, 58, 63, 64, 66–182, 184–196, 198–200, 204–206, 210, 213, 214, 222, 242–246, 248, 249, 251, 255, 262, 278, 289, 313, 314, 322, 326, 335, 336, 344, 345, 349, 353, 354, 374, 383, 394, 405, 422, 428, 431–433, 461, 463, 465, 469, 478, 479, 496, 505, 507, 583, 591, 607, 641, 657, 660, 664, 673, 676, 709, 727, 744, 748, 750, 756–758, 768–773, 778

  Abolition of, 12, 42, 67, 68, 77, 79, 117, 140, 150, 167, 172, 176, 182, 196, 205, 210, 245, 335, 339, 461

Sotomayor, Sonia, 560, 690

Southern Manifesto, 659

Spingarn medal, 730

Stanford, 30, 33, 78, 562, 598, 650, 655

Stereotypes, 52, 110, 330, 332, 333, 515, 516, 523, 543, 553, 554, 602, 603, 605, 606, 705, 715, 716, 721, 722

Stevens, John Paul, 525, 564, 652, 664

Stevens, Thaddeus, 187, 191, 197

Stigma, 64, 171, 556, 562, 646, 652

Storey, Moorfield, 377

Story, Joseph, 167, 168, 651

Strange Fruit, 219

Stuart, Charles, 683

Sumner, Charles, 95, 187, 196, 224, 252, 258, 346, 412, 657, 664

Supreme Court, 4, 10, 11, 15, 21, 22, 51, 52, 62, 65, 71, 75, 76, 81, 83, 88, 91, 94–96, 98, 100, 101, 106, 111, 113, 115–117, 122, 124, 126, 127, 129–131, 134–136, 141–143, 151, 159, 161–166, 168, 173, 179, 181, 183, 187, 201, 202, 207, 209–213, 220, 221, 223, 233, 236–238, 254, 255, 257, 258, 263, 268, 271, 276, 288, 307, 311–313, 317, 328, 335, 339, 340, 342, 343, 346, 354–358, 362–369, 371, 372, 377, 378, 382–386, 392, 394–396, 401, 402, 405–408, 410–414, 416–419,

422, 425–428, 430–432, 437–439,
442–444, 448, 450, 452, 454,
458–466, 468–471, 473, 476, 477,
479, 484, 491–493, 495–497, 505,
507, 508, 525, 533, 540, 547, 550,
554, 559–564, 567, 571, 574–576,
597, 607, 626–628, 638–641, 643,
644, 649–691, 698, 706, 711, 713,
714, 719–722, 729, 732, 737, 739,
740, 771, 777

T

Taft, William, 422

Taney, Roger, 116, 164, 166, 168, 169,
181, 470

Tappan, Arthur, 81

Thirteenth Amendment, 181, 196, 198,
200, 204, 205, 208, 210, 212, 214,
222, 242–245, 248, 249, 253, 278,
322, 344, 345, 349, 370, 496, 773, 774

Thomas, Clarence, 525, 649, 650, 652,
654, 660, 663, 665–671, 673, 675–
679, 730

Three-Fifths Clause, 69

Thurmond, Strom, 73, 659, 721, 722,
725

Tilden, Samuel, 253

Tillman, Benjamin, 434, 660

Title VI, 497, 498, 510, 521, 563, 564,
574, 575, 654, 766, 776

Title VII, 50, 211, 578–580, 587,
628–634, 636–639, 657, 777, 778

Tonto, 328, 329

Tourgee, Albion, 199, 342, 343

TransAfrica, 189, 191

Trumbull, Lyman, 198

Trump, Donald, 342–344, 348, 874–
876, 882, 939

Truth, Sojourner, 174, 664, 676

Tubman, Harriet, 106, 136, 138, 139,
664

Tucker, St. George, 111

Turks, 103, 104, 748

Turner, Nat, 106, 175, 176

Tuskegee Airmen, 435

U

Unitary school systems, 483, 487
    Disestablishment of dual system,
    491
        Unitary and dual systems, 487,
        489
Underground Railroad, 136–140, 228

V

Van Buren, Martin, 118

Vassar College, 365

Virginia, 17, 19, 38–48, 70–72, 74, 76,
85, 89, 95, 100, 102–104, 106, 107,
109, 111, 115, 116, 138, 140, 161, 174,
186, 187, 225, 229, 240, 248, 250,
255, 258, 279, 322, 329, 335, 336,
338–340, 346, 350, 366, 378, 385,
386, 388, 389, 391–394, 398, 399,
401, 403, 416, 437, 452–456, 463–
471, 474, 475, 486, 492, 512, 544,
576, 586, 590, 602, 610, 611, 624,
652, 661–663, 709, 722, 734, 741,
742, 753, 754, 756, 760, 769,
772, 774, 775, 777
    Anti-miscegenation law, 45, 465
Virginia Bill of Rights, 102
Voting rights, 51, 80, 214, 223, 271,
272, 367, 600, 602, 604, 605, 607–
612, 614–624, 626, 627, 642, 651,
656, 672, 679, 684–686, 721, 733,
767, 777, 778
    Democratic party, 223, 229, 253,
    608, 721, 722, 724, 725
    Gerrymandering, 481, 557, 603,
    604, 621, 684
    Majority-minority districts, 603
    Polarized voting, 605, 607, 622
    Poll tax, 424, 747
    Racial bloc voting, 603, 605
    Reapportionment, 600–604, 607

Redistricting, 600–602, 604, 625, 627, 640, 672, 684, 685, 698

White primary, 96, 100, 201, 255, 377, 403, 407, 660

Voting Rights Act (1965), 272, 600, 608–610, 616, 617, 619, 621, 622, 672, 684, 767, 777

W

Waite, Morrison, 221

Wallace, George, 477, 492, 673, 722

Warmoth, Henry Clay, 221, 227

Warren, Earl, 451, 459, 460, 493, 652, 664

Washington, Booker T., 341, 370, 405, 410, 411, 425, 434, 660, 726

Washington, D.C., 115, 363, 366, 372, 385, 395, 438, 445, 611, 612, 614, 645, 651, 657, 668

    Abolitionist petitions, 116

    Slavery legalized, 115

Washington, George, 38, 72, 74, 110, 136, 281, 330, 697

Wells, H.G., 423

West, Cornel, 695

White supremacy, 51, 57, 58, 169, 198, 352, 369, 466, 468, 721

Wilson, Woodrow, 372, 374, 377, 378

Wisconsin, 141, 334, 370, 388

Woods, Tiger, 64

Woodward, C. Vann, 363, 369, 496

World War II, 65, 140, 184, 192, 194, 258, 288, 369, 435, 437, 450, 452, 460, 461, 690, 713, 719, 768, 775, 777

Wounded Knee, 314

Wythe, George, 71, 111, 753

Y

Yale, 53, 71, 81, 89, 179, 180, 188, 190, 355, 364–366, 404, 419, 422, 504, 622, 652, 653, 658, 664, 666, 675, 678, 687, 690, 730

Z

Zimmerman, George, 703, 706, 708